CW01020926

EDUCATIONAL PSYCHOLOGY

FOR **LEARNING** AND **TEACHING**

6TH EDITION

**SUE DUCHESNE
ANNE McMAUGH**

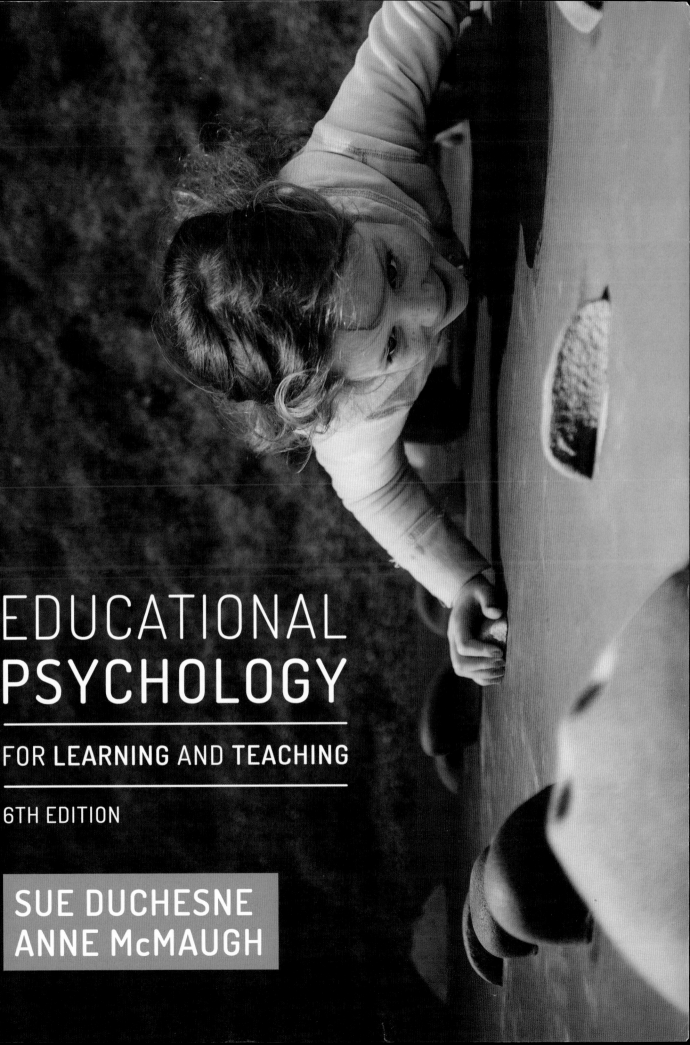

EDUCATIONAL PSYCHOLOGY

FOR **LEARNING** AND **TEACHING**

6TH EDITION

SUE DUCHESNE
ANNE McMAUGH

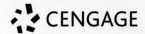

Educational Psychology for Learning and Teaching
6th Edition
Sue Duchesne
Anne McMaugh

Head of content management: Dorothy Chiu
Senior content manager: Fiona Hammond
Content developer: James Cole
Project editor: Raymond Williams
Project designer: Linda Davidson
Cover designer: Jenki
Text designer: Jenki
Editor: Diane Fowler
Proofreader: James Anderson
Indexer: Julie King
Permissions/Photo researcher: Wendy Duncan
Cover: Getty Images/Peter Lourenco
Cenveo Publisher Services

Any URLs contained in this publication were checked for currency during the production process. Note, however, that the publisher cannot vouch for the ongoing currency of URLs.

5th edition published 2016

Acknowledgements
Module openers: Shutterstock.com/Kamira; Shutterstock.com/Syda Productions; Shutterstock.com/Africa Studio; Shutterstock.com/Joana Lopes
Contents: Shutterstock.com/Poprotskiy Alexey
Icons: made by Nice and Serious, Vectors Market, Gregor Cresnar, Freepik from www.flaticon.com

© 2019 Cengage Learning Australia Pty Limited

Copyright Notice
This Work is copyright. No part of this Work may be reproduced, stored in a retrieval system, or transmitted in any form or by any means without prior written permission of the Publisher. Except as permitted under the Copyright Act 1968, for example any fair dealing for the purposes of private study, research, criticism or review, subject to certain limitations. These limitations include: Restricting the copying to a maximum of one chapter or 10% of this book, whichever is greater; providing an appropriate notice and warning with the copies of the Work disseminated; taking all reasonable steps to limit access to these copies to people authorised to receive these copies; ensuring you hold the appropriate Licences issued by the Copyright Agency Limited ("CAL"), supply a remuneration notice to CAL and pay any required fees. For details of CAL licences and remuneration notices please contact CAL at Level 11, 66 Goulburn Street, Sydney NSW 2000, Tel: (02) 9394 7600, Fax: (02) 9394 7601
Email: info@copyright.com.au
Website: www.copyright.com.au

For product information and technology assistance,
in Australia call **1300 790 853**;
in New Zealand call **0800 449 725**

For permission to use material from this text or product, please email
aust.permissions@cengage.com

National Library of Australia Cataloguing-in-Publication Data
ISBN: 9780170410823
A catalogue record for this book is available from the National Library of Australia

Cengage Learning Australia
Level 7, 80 Dorcas Street
South Melbourne, Victoria Australia 3205

Cengage Learning New Zealand
Unit 4B Rosedale Office Park
331 Rosedale Road, Albany, North Shore 0632, NZ

For learning solutions, visit **cengage.com.au**

Printed in Singapore by 1010 Printing Group Limited
1 2 3 4 5 6 7 23 22 21 20 19

CONTENTS IN BRIEF

CONTENTS

MODULE IV EDUCATIONAL PSYCHOLOGY IN CONTEMPORARY CLASSROOMS 520

CHAPTER 12 INFORMATION AND COMMUNICATION TECHNOLOGY (ICT) IN LEARNING AND TEACHING 522

CHAPTER 13 ASSESSMENT AND REPORTING 570

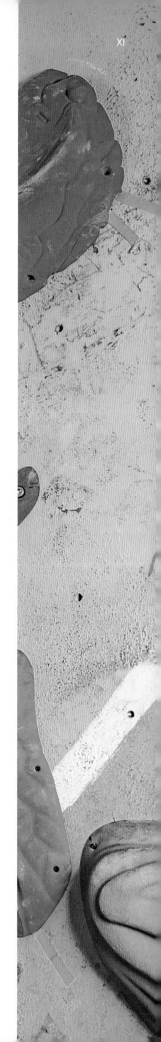

ABOUT THE AUTHORS

Dr Sue Duchesne coordinates the teacher education programs at the University of Wollongong's Bega Campus. Sue has teaching experience in primary and secondary schools, as well as in the tertiary sector. She currently lectures in educational psychology, child development and pedagogy. Her research interests include engagement in language classrooms, the roles of peers in language learning, and teacher education, with a particular interest in pre-service teacher development.

———————

Dr Anne McMaugh is a Senior Lecturer in the Department of Educational Studies at Macquarie University. Anne teaches in child development, educational psychology, inclusive education and pedagogy, with a focus on childhood social development. Her research interests encompass child and adolescent education and development, with a special interest in the developmental and educational experiences of children with disability and chronic health conditions. Anne has teaching experience in primary and secondary schools, as well as in the tertiary sector, and has conducted research in school, hospital and community education settings.

ACKNOWLEDGEMENTS

This book is the result of the combined efforts, energies and encouragement of many of our colleagues, students, friends and family. We thank the team at Cengage Learning Australia who have supported us in the development of this sixth edition. Ann Crabb, Fiona Hammond, James Cole, and Raymond Williams have all been involved in our discussions about text design, photographs and text support materials.

Our colleagues and students in teacher education at the University of Wollongong and at Macquarie University have contributed to our understanding of the field and have continual input into our thinking about educational psychology and how it can be taught.

We have consulted various classroom teacher colleagues, whose practical classroom experience has made an important contribution to our text. In particular, we would like to thank the following teachers who have provided ideas and content for the text and its supplements:

- Chrisanthi McManus, Mumbulla School for Steiner Education
- Gabbie Stroud
- Tracey Hughes-Butters, Lumen Christi Catholic College
- Ann-Louise Clark, Sapphire Coast Anglican College
- Alyson Whiteoak, Jervis Bay Public School
- Ursula Brown
- Anne Warburton
- Cheryl Russell.

Our thanks go to the children who have contributed ideas, images and content to the text: Natalie, Jake, Jesse, Etienne, Odette, Katie, Kirsty, Jed, Tully, Nicole, Hannah, Hannah, Kai, Henry and Pete. A special thank you to our families who have provided constant support, good humour and encouragement along the way.

Sue Duchesne

Anne McMaugh

Cengage Learning and the authors would like to thank the following reviewers for their incisive and helpful feedback:

- Kymberley Barbary – La Trobe University
- Daniela Falecki – Western Sydney University
- Ange Fitzgerald – Monash University
- Martin Hall – Charles Sturt University
- Gayle Jenkins – Deakin University
- Sean Kearney – Notre Dame University
- Caroline Mansfield – Murdoch University
- Loraine McKay – Griffith University
- Penelope Watson –The University of Auckland
- Anna Whitehead – Auckland University of Technology
- Joseph Zajda – Australian Catholic University.

The publishers would like gratefully to credit or acknowledge the following sources.

- Anna Whitehead, Auckland University of Technology
- Anne Tietzel, University of the Sunshine Coast
- Cedric Greive, Avondale College
- Christine Rubie-Davies, University of Auckland
- Craig Deed, La Trobe University

- Danielle Tracey, University of Western Sydney
- Katie O'Brien, Australian Catholic University
- Karen Swabey, University of Tasmania
- Madeleine Laming, Australian Catholic University
- Maxine Cooper, University of Ballarat
- Sue Sharp, Edith Cowan University.

Every attempt has been made to trace and acknowledge copyright holders. Where the attempt has been unsuccessful, the publishers welcome information that would redress the situation.

Guide to the text

As you read this text you will find a number of features in every chapter to enhance your study of Educational Psychology and help you understand how the theory is applied in the real world.

MODULE OPENING FEATURES

Chapters are grouped into four colour-coded modules that cover a particular set of theories or issues.

1 Module concept maps and **2 core questions** introduce each of the chapters within the part and give an overview of how the chapters in the module relate to each other.

The **Putting it together** sections at the end of modules encourage a holistic view of children, of learning and of teaching by highlighting links across groups of chapters, complementing the connections given at the end of each chapter.

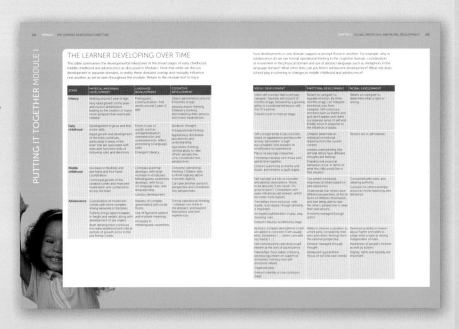

CHAPTER OPENING FEATURES

1 Visualise how each chapter is organised and how key topics are connected by exploring the chapter opening **Concept maps**.

2 A list of **Key questions** gives you a broad outline of what the chapter will cover. After reading the chapter, return to this list to check your understanding of each topic.

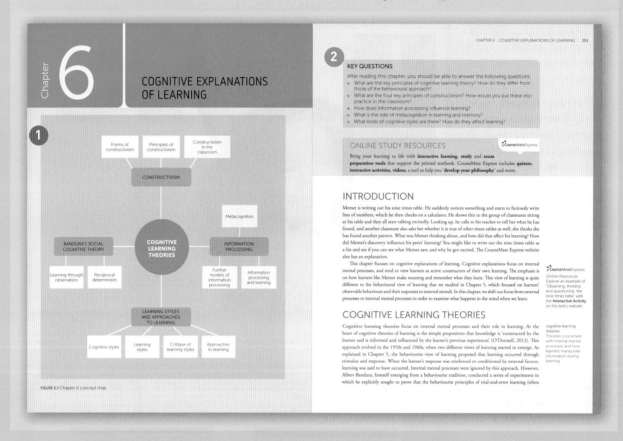

CHAPTER 6   COGNITIVE EXPLANATIONS OF LEARNING   253

Chapter 6

COGNITIVE EXPLANATIONS OF LEARNING

KEY QUESTIONS

After reading this chapter, you should be able to answer the following questions:
- What are the key principles of cognitive learning theory? How do they differ from those of the behavioural approach?
- What are the four key principles of constructivism? How would you put these into practice in the classroom?
- How does information processing influence learning?
- What is the role of metacognition in learning and memory?
- What kinds of cognitive styles are there? How do they affect learning?

ONLINE STUDY RESOURCES

Bring your learning to life with **interactive learning**, **study** and **exam preparation tools** that support the printed textbook. CourseMate Express includes **quizzes**, **interactive activities**, **videos**, a tool to help you '**develop your philosophy**' and more.

INTRODUCTION

Memet is writing out his nine times table. He suddenly notices something and starts to furiously write lists of numbers, which he then checks on a calculator. He shows this to the group of classmates sitting at his table and they all start talking excitedly. Looking up, he calls to his teacher to tell her what he has found, and another classmate also asks her whether it is true of other times tables as well; she thinks she has found another pattern. What was Memet thinking about, and how did that affect his learning? How did Memet's discovery influence his peers' learning? You might like to write out the nine times table as a list and see if you can see what Memet saw, and why he got excited. The CourseMate Express website also has an explanation.

This chapter focuses on cognitive explanations of learning. Cognitive explanations focus on internal mental processes, and tend to view learners as active constructors of their own learning. The emphasis is on how learners like Memet make meaning and remember what they learn. This view of learning is quite different to the behavioural view of learning that we studied in Chapter 5, which focused on learners' observable behaviours and their responses to external stimuli. In this chapter, we shift our focus from external processes to internal mental processes in order to examine what happens in the mind when we learn.

COGNITIVE LEARNING THEORIES

Cognitive learning theories focus on internal mental processes and their role in learning. At the heart of cognitive theories of learning is the simple proposition that knowledge is 'constructed by the learner and is informed and influenced by the learner's previous experiences' (O'Donnell, 2012). This approach evolved in the 1950s and 1960s, when two different views of learning started to emerge. As explained in Chapter 5, the behaviourist view of learning proposed that learning occurred through stimulus and response. When the learner's response was reinforced or conditioned by external factors, learning was said to have occurred. Internal mental processes were ignored by this approach. However, Albert Bandura, himself emerging from a behaviourist tradition, conducted a series of experiments in which he explicitly sought to prove that the behaviourist principles of trial-and-error learning (often

CourseMateExpress
Online Resources
Explore an example of 'Observing, thinking and questioning: the nine times table' with the **Interactive Activity** on this text's website

cognitive learning theories
Theories concerned with internal mental processes and how learners manipulate information during learning

FIGURE 6.1 Chapter 6 concept map

FEATURES WITHIN CHAPTERS

RESEARCH LINKS

Examine important and current research in teaching and learning in specific studies highlighted in the **Research Links** boxes.

BOX 1.3 RESEARCH LINKS
ACTION RESEARCH
Carlyn Sproston (2008) conducted an action research study in her Year 8 English classroom to investigate how involving students in negotiating their learning affected their motivation.
In the first cycle, students were asked about their perceptions of their English class through questionnaires and journal entries. They saw it as 'static and boring'. In particular, they didn't like the amount of writing and inactivity in the class. They then had a class meeting at which students' views were discussed and suggestions shared about what might make it more interesting.
The action that followed this was to start a unit on children's stories, which involved students analysing these stories and then writing their own. They visited a local primary school to read

CASE STUDIES

Case studies help you see how theories have been applied within Australian and New Zealand classroom settings.

BOX 2.9 CASE STUDY
BEGINNING TO READ
As with other aspects of development, there are multiple pathways to reading. These case studies provide examples of four children's stories of reading development.
Case study A
Anna loves to read, picking up books whenever she can. Her mother reports that Anna used to 'read' to the family dog, telling stories from her picture

Case study C
Josie also likes to look at books, but she enjoys them best when they are being read to her. Her teacher reports that she didn't understand the connection between the letters on the page and the words read out loud until it was clearly explained to her. The phonics program in her class is helping Josie to make this connection, and to be able to

IMPLICATIONS FOR EDUCATORS

Consider the implications of theory on classroom practitioners with learning and teaching examples in the **Implications for Educators** boxes

BOX 1.2 IMPLICATIONS FOR EDUCATORS
GUIDELINES FOR COLLECTING DATA THROUGH INTERVIEWS
At the start of an interview, you need to establish rapport with the interviewee. Your aim is to give them the opportunity to tell you a little more about themselves.
- Step 1: Commence by telling participants there are no right or wrong answers.
- Step 2: As a way of making participants feel comfortable, ask them to tell you or write down a list of ways in which they learned or taught that day (or the day before). This will prompt them to think about the learning activities they engage in and how they feel about them.
- Step 3: Ask participants to elaborate and explain why they have given their answers. Remember to always ask participants to tell you why!

CLASSROOM LINKS

Connect theory to practice via examples of research or applications of theory in classroom settings in the **Classroom Links** boxes

BOX 3.5 CLASSROOM LINKS
HOW CAN STUDENTS BE SUPPORTED TOWARDS MORE ADVANCED THINKING?
One of the key challenges to Piaget's theory also provides suggestions for supporting the development of children's thinking. When the tasks are presented in different ways, children at various ages have been shown to be able to think in ways that Piaget's theory would suggest is not possible or consistent with their stage of thinking. Miller (2011) suggested that these studies may reveal the beginnings of more complex concepts in young children's thinking. They challenge Piaget's notion of structurally distinct stages of thinking.
Performance factors that challenged Piaget's description of the competence of children of

ABOUT

About... boxes profile leading contemporary and historical psychologists and their theories.

BOX 7.1 ABOUT ABRAHAM MASLOW
Abraham Maslow (1908–70) was born on 1 April 1908 in New York, the eldest of seven children. He remembered his childhood as being very unhappy (Boeree, 2000a), describing himself as 'extremely shy, nervous, depressed, lonely and self-reflecting' up to the age of 20 (De Carvalho, 1991, p. 19). Unhappy at home and isolated at school, he spent many hours in the library (De Carvalho, 1991).
As a student, Maslow did well. He spent a brief period studying law in New York, as advised by his father, but this did not interest him. He then married and enrolled in psychology at the University of Wisconsin. At this time, he was interested in the work of John Watson and the behaviourists (see Chapter 5), and his early research was concerned with emotional and social relationships in dogs and apes. Later, Maslow worked with Harry Harlow (Harlow & Zimmerman, 1959), known for his

THINK ABOUT

Think about... panels encourage you to reflect critically on important concepts and your beliefs about the processes of learning and teaching as you progress through each chapter.

THINK ABOUT
- Have you ever experienced the 'undermining effect'?
- Why do you think the brain responds differently after rewards have been given for previously interesting or engaging activities?
- Why do you think rewards enhanced memory performance only for 'boring' materials?

ICONS

Throughout the book you'll find **CourseMate Express** icons that direct you to additional online materials. These include **videos**, **interactive activities** and materials to help you **Go further** and deepen your understanding of particular topics. The icons also suggest opportunities for you to **Develop your philosophy** of learning by the interactive tool on this text's website.

CourseMateExpress

Online Resources
Try the **Interactive Activity** about storytelling on this text's CourseMate Express website.

END-OF-CHAPTER FEATURES

At the end of each chapter you will find several Study tools to help you to review key concepts and extend your learning.

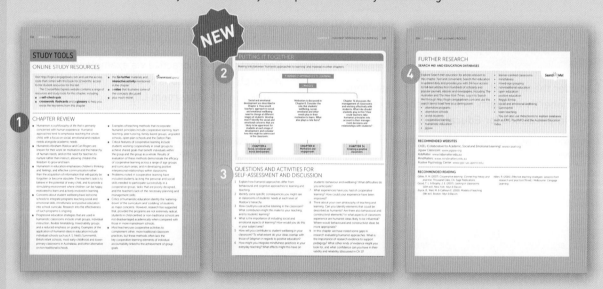

1 **Chapter review** sections summarise the key concepts and issues.

2 The **NEW** visual **Putting it together** section illustrates the ways that material in the chapter is related to other chapters.

3 **Questions and activities for self-assessment and discussion** assist you to revise key topics and consolidate your learning.

4 You'll find suggestions for **further research**, including Search Me! Education and education databases, key websites to visit, recommended readings and references to help you find more information.

Guide to the online resources

FOR THE INSTRUCTOR

Cengage is pleased to provide you with a selection of resources that will help you prepare your lectures and assessments. These teaching tools are accessible via cengage.com.au/instructors for Australia or cengage.co.nz/instructors for New Zealand.

COURSEMATE EXPRESS

CourseMate Express is your one-stop shop for learning tools and activities that help students succeed. As they read and study the chapters, students can access videos, interactive activities, and extension material. Students can review with flashcards, as well as check their understanding of the chapter with interactive quizzing. CourseMate Express also features the Engagement Tracker, a first-of-its-kind tool that monitors student engagement in the content. Ask your Learning Consultant for more details.

MINDTAP

MindTap is an interactive, customisable and complete online course solution. MindTap integrates authoritative text book pedagogy with customisable student 'learning paths', an innovative 'app' model of instructional utilities, LMS interoperability, and the power of social media to create a personal learning experience for today's mobile students.

To prescribe MindTap for your students, please contact your Learning Consultant.

INSTRUCTOR'S MANUAL

The Instructor's Manual includes:

• Chapter overview and key topics • Student activities • Research ideas • Additional cases
• Additional video discussion questions • Useful websites, and more.

VIDEOS

This series of online **Instructor videos** provides relevant and engaging visual teaching demonstrations for instructors to illustrate in class the concepts covered in Educational Psychology. These visual resources are available to instructors prescribing the text.

TEST BANK

This bank of questions has been developed in conjunction with the text for creating quizzes, tests and exams for your students. Deliver these through your LMS and in your classroom.

POWERPOINT™ PRESENTATIONS

Use the chapter-by-chapter **PowerPoint** slides to enhance your lecture presentations and handouts by reinforcing the key principles of your subject.

ARTWORK FROM THE TEXT

Add the digital files of graphs, tables, pictures and flow charts into your course management system, use them in student handouts, or copy them into your lecture presentations.

FOR THE STUDENT

New copies of this text come with an access code that gives you a
12-month subscription to the **CourseMate Express** website and Search Me! education.
Visit http://login.cengagebrain.com and log in using the access code card.

COURSEMATE EXPRESS FOR EDUCATIONAL PSYCHOLOGY

Access your CourseMate Express website, which includes
a suite of interactive resources designed to support your learning, revision and further research.

Includes:
- Videos
- Interactive learning objects
- Glossary and Flashcards
- Revision quizzes
- The Develop your Philosophy Tool
- And more!

SEARCH ME! EDUCATION

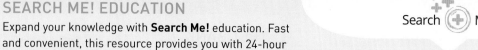

Expand your knowledge with **Search Me!** education. Fast
and convenient, this resource provides you with 24-hour
access to relevant full-text articles from hundreds of scholarly and popular journals and newspapers, including
The Australian and *The New York Times*. Search Me! education allows you to explore topics further and quickly
find current references.

MINDTAP

A new approach to highly personalised online learning,
MindTap is designed to match your learning style
and provides you with an engaging interface to interact with the course content, multimedia resources as
well as your peers, lecturers and tutors. In the **MindTap Reader**, you can make notes, highlight text and
even find a definition directly from the page.

To purchase your MindTap experience for Educational Psychology, please contact your instructor.

EDUCATIONAL PSYCHOLOGY FOR LEARNING AND TEACHING

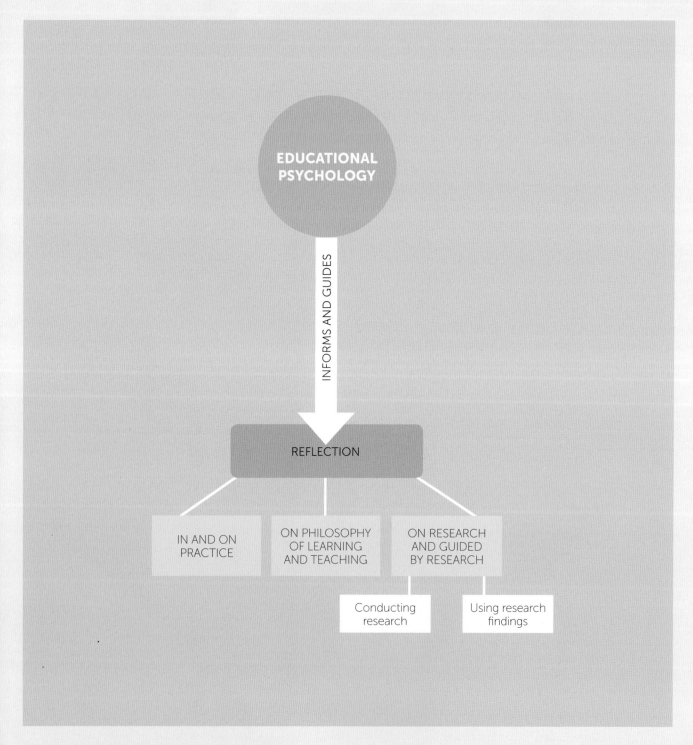

FIGURE 1.1 Chapter 1 concept map

KEY QUESTIONS

After reading this chapter, you should be able to answer the following questions:
- What is the purpose of educational psychology?
- How can educational psychology contribute to my development as a teacher?
- What is the role of reflection in teaching, and which tools will help?
- What role does research play in reflection and teaching?
- How can I use these reflective tools in quality ways to enhance my teaching?

ONLINE STUDY RESOURCES

 CourseMateExpress

Bring your learning to life with **interactive learning**, **study** and **exam preparation tools** that support the printed textbook. CourseMate Express includes **quizzes**, **interactive activities**, **videos**, a tool to help you '**develop your philosophy**' and more.

INTRODUCTION

For many students using this book, the field of educational psychology – or 'ed. psych.', as you may soon call it – will represent uncharted waters. You may have chosen this area because you have always been interested in psychology, or perhaps you are studying to be a teacher and educational psychology is a compulsory subject. We hope that, whatever your reason for using this text, it will help you to develop your understanding and thinking about learning and teaching.

In this chapter, we explore the broad topic of educational psychology, and why it is of use to teachers.

WHAT IS EDUCATIONAL PSYCHOLOGY?

Some students ask: 'Why not just simplify and call it *psychology*?' The reason is that **educational psychology** is a discipline in its own right, and connects the disciplines of education and psychology (Walberg & Haertel, 1992). It involves not only scientific research on the various dimensions of learning and teaching, but also the investigation of ways to apply psychological principles to educational contexts with the aim of enhancing learning and teaching quality.

One of the things students enjoy most about this subject is that, by studying theories of learning and development, they learn a lot about their own development and what influences their learning. A number of the effective teaching practices you experienced at school could be traced back to some element of educational psychology. As you read this book, you will begin to understand your own learning processes and how to improve them. You will also be challenged to think about ways in which teaching could be improved to cater for student differences and particular student needs.

educational psychology
A branch of psychology concerned with studying how people learn and the implications for teaching

WHO STUDIES EDUCATIONAL PSYCHOLOGY?

The discipline of educational psychology can be applied in many contexts. You may have taken up this book because you plan to be a teacher, and must study educational psychology as a foundation unit. Other readers may be psychology students who are interested in working with children or adolescents, whether in professional practice or as a counsellor in a school setting. Others may be preparing to be educational psychologists: qualified psychologists who specialise in applying their expertise in educational contexts, and who work in schools or other institutional settings (for example, university, government or corporate settings) where education takes place. Still others may be reading this text to better understand their own learning and the education process.

We recognise that the majority of this book's readers will be planning a teaching or related career. For this reason, our examples focus on early childhood, school-aged children and youth.

WHY STUDY ALL THOSE THEORIES?

It is true that when you first start studying educational psychology, you are introduced to many theories. Some educational psychology students have been heard to say: 'Ed. psych. is just a lot of theory … I came to uni to learn how to teach kids!' Our advice to you is to not lose heart and to remember that theories have an important purpose.

You will discover that theories form the foundation for understanding many critical issues that face learners and educators in the 21st century. Throughout this book, and particularly in the first half, we link theory to practice and encourage you to do the same. You will find that theories help us answer questions such as: What are the best ways of studying? How can I improve motivation – both mine and others'? Why do some young people give up on themselves, and what can I do about it? How can technology be used to enhance learning? Is education redundant in the information age?

Educational psychology and the theories of development and learning covered in this text will:

- help you understand your own development and factors that have contributed to it
- provide strategies to enhance the quality of your learning and motivation
- guide your understanding of how learners learn and how educators can become more effective in their teaching practice
- contribute to your personal philosophy of learning and teaching.

CHANGES IN THE EDUCATION LANDSCAPE

In the past few years, Australia has experienced major changes in policy and curriculum relating to schools and teaching, with the introduction of the Early Years Learning Framework (EYLF) in 2009, the *Australian professional standards for teachers* in 2011 and the Australian Curriculum in 2012. New Zealand also underwent changes to its assessment framework in 2011, and an expansion of Ka Hikitia, the Māori education strategy, into a third phase in 2018. You will find references to all of these documents in this edition of the text. Here, we consider how your study of educational psychology using this text might contribute to your development of knowledge towards the relevant teacher standards.

Educational psychology will contribute towards a number of elements of your professional knowledge, professional practice and professional engagement. Table 1.1 provides an overview.

TABLE 1.1 Teaching standards and this text

CHAPTER	ELEMENTS FROM THE *AUSTRALIAN PROFESSIONAL STANDARDS FOR TEACHERS*	ELEMENTS FROM THE *GRADUATING TEACHER STANDARDS: AOTEAROA NEW ZEALAND*
	1 Know students and how they learn	2 Know about learners and how they learn
Module I: Chapters 2, 3 and 4	1.1 Physical, social and intellectual development and characteristics of students Demonstrate knowledge and understanding of physical, social and intellectual development and characteristics of students and how these may affect learning	2a Have knowledge of a range of relevant theories and research about pedagogy, human development and learning >>

CHAPTER	ELEMENTS FROM THE *AUSTRALIAN PROFESSIONAL STANDARDS FOR TEACHERS*	ELEMENTS FROM THE *GRADUATING TEACHER STANDARDS: AOTEAROA NEW ZEALAND*
Module II: Chapters 5, 6 and 7	1.2 *Understand how students learn* Demonstrate knowledge and understanding of research into how students learn and the implications for teaching	2a *Have knowledge of a range of relevant theories and research about pedagogy, human development and learning*
Module IV: Chapter 13		2b *Have knowledge of a range of relevant theories, principles and purposes of assessment and evaluation*
Module II: Chapter 6		2c *Know how to develop metacognitive strategies of diverse learners*
		3 *Understand how contextual factors influence teaching and learning*
Module III: Chapter 11	1.3 *Students with diverse linguistic, cultural, religious and socioeconomic backgrounds* Demonstrate knowledge of teaching strategies that are responsive to the learning strengths and needs of students from diverse linguistic, cultural, religious and socioeconomic backgrounds 1.4 *Strategies for teaching Aboriginal and Torres Strait Islander students* Demonstrate broad knowledge and understanding of the impact of culture, cultural identity and linguistic background on the education of students from Aboriginal and Torres Strait Islander backgrounds	3a *Have an understanding of the complex influences that personal. social and cultural factors may have on teachers and learners* 3c *Have an understanding of education within the bicultural, multicultural, social, political, economic and historical contexts of Aotearoa New Zealand*
Module III: Chapters 9 and 10	1.5 *Differentiate teaching to meet the specific learning needs of students across the full range of abilities* Demonstrate knowledge and understanding of strategies for differentiating teaching to meet the specific learning needs of students across the full range of abilities	
Module III: Chapter 10	1.6 *Strategies to support full participation of students with disability* Demonstrate broad knowledge and understanding of legislative requirements and teaching strategies that support participation and learning of students with disability	
	2 *Know the content and how to teach it*	
Module I: Chapter 2	2.5 *Literacy and numeracy strategies* Know and understand literacy and numeracy teaching strategies and their application in teaching areas	
Module IV: Chapter 12	2.6 *Information and communication technology (ICT)* Implement teaching strategies for using ICT to expand curriculum learning opportunities for students	
	3 *Plan for and implement effective teaching and learning*	
Module II: Chapters 5, 6 and 7	3.2 *Plan, structure and sequence learning programs* Plan lesson sequences using knowledge of student learning, content and effective teaching strategies 3.3 *Use teaching strategies* Include a range of teaching strategies	

CHAPTER	ELEMENTS FROM THE *AUSTRALIAN PROFESSIONAL STANDARDS FOR TEACHERS*	ELEMENTS FROM THE *GRADUATING TEACHER STANDARDS: AOTEAROA NEW ZEALAND*
Module IV: Chapter 12	*3.4 Select and use resources* Demonstrate knowledge of a range of resources, including ICT, that engage students in their learning	
	4 Create and maintain supportive and safe learning environments	**4 Use professional knowledge to plan for a safe, high quality teaching and learning environment**
Module II: Chapters 5, 6 and 7		*4a Use and sequence a range of learning experiences to influence and promote learner achievement*
Module III: Chapters 8, 9, 10 and 11	*4.1 Support student participation* Identify strategies to support inclusive student participation and engagement in classroom activities	
Module IV: Chapter 14	*4.2 Manage classroom activities* Demonstrate the capacity to organise classroom activities and provide clear directions *4.3 Manage challenging behaviour* Demonstrate knowledge of practical approaches to manage challenging behaviour *4.4 Maintain student safety* Describe strategies that support students' wellbeing and safety working within school and/or system, curriculum and legislative requirements	*4f Demonstrate commitment to and strategies for promoting and nurturing the physical and emotional safety of learners*
Module IV: Chapter 12	*4.5 Use ICT (information and communications technology) safely, responsibly and ethically* Demonstrate an understanding of the relevant issues and the strategies available to support the safe, responsible and ethical use of ICT in learning and teaching	
	5 Assess, provide feedback and report on student learning	**5 Use evidence to promote learning**
Module IV: Chapter 13	*5.1 Assess student learning* Demonstrate an understanding of assessment strategies, including informal and formal, diagnostic, formative and summative approaches to assess student learning *5.2 Provide feedback to students on their learning* Demonstrate an understanding of the purpose of providing timely and appropriate feedback to students about their learning *5.3 Make consistent and comparable judgements* Demonstrate an understanding of assessment moderation and its application to support consistent and comparable judgements of student learning *5.4 Interpret student data* Demonstrate the capacity to interpret student assessment data to evaluate student learning and modify teaching practice *5.5 Report on student achievement* Demonstrate an understanding of a range of strategies for reporting to students and parents/carers and the purpose of keeping accurate and reliable records of student achievement	*5b Gather, analyse and use assessment information to improve learning and inform planning* *5c Know how to communicate assessment information appropriately to learners, their parents/caregivers and staff*

>>

CHAPTER	ELEMENTS FROM THE *AUSTRALIAN PROFESSIONAL STANDARDS FOR TEACHERS*	ELEMENTS FROM THE *GRADUATING TEACHER STANDARDS: AOTEAROA NEW ZEALAND*
		6 *Develop positive relationships with learners and the members of learning communities*
Module III: Chapter 11		6a *Recognise how differing values and beliefs may impact on learners and their learning*
		6d *Promote a learning culture which engages diverse learners effectively*
	6 *Engage in professional learning*	7 *Are committed members of the profession*
Chapter 1	6.4 *Apply professional learning and improve student learning* Demonstrate an understanding of the rationale for continued professional learning and the implications for improved student learning	7d *Are able to articulate and justify an emerging personal, professional philosophy of teaching and learning*

Sources: © Education Services Australia (ESA) (2015). ESA is the legal entity for the Standing Council on School Education and Early Childhood (SCSEEC). The Australian Professional Standards for Teachers were developed by the Australian Institute for Teaching and School Leadership (AITSL). This extract has been used with permission from ESA and AITSL; Copyright © 2015 by New Zealand Teachers Council. Used by permission.

INTRODUCING REFLECTIVE TEACHING

THINK ABOUT

- What makes an effective teacher, in your experience?

Students sometimes enter teacher education courses with the aim of discovering 'the best way to teach'. Researchers in educational psychology have also looked at what makes an effective teacher. In one international study, Clarke, Keitel and Shimizu (2006) researched the practices of competent teachers in 16 different countries, including Australia, and found that many different approaches were used. They also discovered that effective teachers drew on a variety of teaching and learning strategies. In line with their conclusions, we argue in this book that there is no one best way to teach, but rather that effective teaching is linked to making effective choices for yourself as a teacher, and about your subject matter and for your students. These may involve choices about curriculum content, learning and teaching strategies, methods of assessment and reporting, how to motivate students, catering for individual difference and classroom management. How do teachers evaluate whether their choices were good ones? Educational psychology can help.

Teaching can be described as a complex problem-solving activity. As such, research on effective problem solving and effective learning is applicable to teaching. In Chapter 6 you will see that effective learners are reflective about their learning, and have knowledge of themselves, the task they are undertaking and strategies they can implement. Planning, monitoring and evaluating are metacognitive (thinking about thinking) strategies employed by effective learners. In the same way, reflective teachers draw on metacognitive knowledge of self, task and strategies as they plan, monitor and evaluate their teaching.

TEACHING AS A REFLECTIVE PRACTICE AND PROCESS

Reflection has been described as important to quality teaching practice for some time. Dewey (1933) described reflection as a type of problem solving, and argued that reflection involves teachers in the important work of connecting their beliefs and knowledge to current actions and situations, potentially leading to the reframing of those ideas and beliefs, and more effective action. Schön (1983, 1987) coined the term 'reflective practice', focusing on the ways in which people think about their experiences and formulate responses as they happen ('thinking on your feet', which he called 'thinking in action'), as well as afterwards ('thinking on action'). In teaching, reflective practice occurs at all stages of the teaching process (see Figure 1.2).

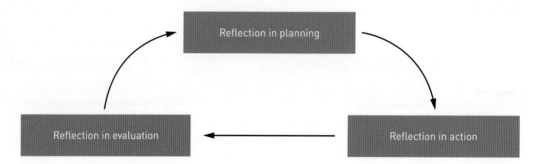

FIGURE 1.2 The cyclical nature of the reflective teaching process

Levels of reflection

A number of researchers have developed typologies of reflection on teaching, distinguishing between several levels of reflection (for example, Lane, McMaster, Adnum & Cavanagh, 2014; Nelson & Sadler, 2013; Thorsen & DeVore, 2013). Collin, Karsenti and Komis (2013) caution that levels of reflection should not be used to distinguish between reflection that is 'good' or 'bad', as what is most useful may depend on the circumstance. Table 1.2 combines aspects from a number of the typologies to summarise the levels in broad terms.

TABLE 1.2 Levels of reflection

LEVEL	EXPLANATION	EXAMPLE
1 *Description*	At the most basic level, there is a *description* of what happened in the situation and its context (in Dewey's terms, this is not yet reflection)	'The students were working in groups to solve an addition problem. Not all of the students participated in the groups, with some sitting back and letting others do all the talking.'
2 *Evaluation*	The next level adds some *evaluation* to the description	'In group work there's a range of participation. I need to make note of who does and doesn't participate, and think of how to involve them all in the learning.'
3 *Analysis*	At a higher level, teachers *analyse* what happened in the situation	'I think in these group tasks some are silent but still thinking, one or two are dominating the thinking and talking, while others are being lazy and letting the rest of the group do the thinking. My setting up of group tasks will need to include strategies to ensure that all need to think, and that all can be heard.'
4 *Integration and reframing*	The highest level of reflection *integrates* the three previous tasks of description, evaluation and analysis, makes plans for proposed actions, and involves some kind of *reframing* of ideas with reference to theory	'Group work helps some students to learn, while others do more learning in individual tasks. There may be a way of combining the two so that both sets of students are catered for in the one activity, but perhaps using a mix of individual, pair and group tasks would be best – both for optimum learning, and for inclusivity.'

This chapter outlines four main tools to help you become a more reflective practitioner, all of which draw on educational psychology. These are:

1   reflecting on your teaching practice
2   developing your personal philosophy of learning and teaching
3   using existing research to inform your practice
4   conducting research of your own.

REFLECTING ON YOUR TEACHING PRACTICE

Critical reflection involves analysing your own and others' thoughts and beliefs. It involves thinking about why people – yourself and others – behave in certain ways. When you reflect critically, you analyse and question existing knowledge and assumptions.

Reflection is a constant process, linked to practice. It can be supported by a range of activities, including reflective journals and portfolios, observation, and consulting with colleagues such as mentors or critical friends.

critical reflection
Analysing what we are thinking and learning by questioning assumptions, perspectives and values related to our thoughts or to new information

KEEPING A REFLECTIVE JOURNAL AND PORTFOLIO

A reflective journal is written as a record of your experience with the purpose of examining and evaluating it. Portfolios extend this idea with the collection of work samples, lesson plans, worksheets and other artefacts of your teaching, accompanied by reflective commentary on the collection. Some prompts for reflection might be research reports, other professional reading, or discussions with colleagues.

Here are some questions to guide your reflection on your teaching:

1   What are my goals for this class/this lesson?
2   How does what I do reflect those goals?
3   What are students responding well to?
4   What is not working? What are students responding poorly to?
5   What is frustrating me or the students?
6   Are my goals being met? Why or why not?
7   What does research and my professional reading tell me about what is happening or what should be happening in this class?
8   What have I seen or heard about in other classes that might be helpful?
9   What other goals do I need to focus on?
10 What new strategies do I need to explore?

These questions focus reflection on students' learning:

1   What learning is happening in the lesson? By whom?
2   What evidence of it is visible?
3   What did the teacher, the student, the task or others do for the learning to eventuate?
4   What is blocking learning for another student or students?
5   At what points in the lesson did most learning happen?
6   When in the lesson did I see the least learning?
7   What could be changed to maximise learning in this class?

Box 1.1 gives an example of one teacher's reflective journal.

CourseMateExpress

Online Resources
Go Further: Find a copy of these questions to download in CourseMate Express

BOX 1.1 CASE STUDY

ANNE'S REFLECTIVE JOURNAL

Anne was teaching a Year 8 French class. The following is from her Term 1 journal:

I want to use immersion but it is too overwhelming for some students – they just give up. There is a wide range of abilities, with some students able to translate the cartoon with ease, and others with no idea of the basics (pronouns!). It's difficult for them to do exercises with minimal vocab, and for some, little understanding of how the language works. I think group work would allow the better students to move ahead while the beginners learn the basics. Will have to work on my classroom management skills for this to work. Spoke to [another teacher] about what she does with her German class. She has set formal grammar exercises for a small group of difficult ones who were way behind the rest of the class and very disruptive. Not sure how motivating this would be, but she says they are powering through them, and like the structure, and the idea that they can do it. Success is everything. Should look up the research on using immersion in Australia. I'm sure other teachers must have encountered this. Meanwhile for next lesson: set up activities with a series of exercises, stems on board, and some direct instruction. Small groups with cards in English (advanced students) or French (beginners) to complete the stems.

Je veux … or je ne veux pas …	Je peux … or je ne peux pas …
Money for the show	Visit grandma
Buy clothes/a skateboard	Play at a friend's house
Do the washing up	Go to a movie
Go to Europe for the holiday	Stay at home

ACTIVITIES

Keep a journal of your ideas about teaching at present, and compare them with those you have at the end of your training, when you start teaching full-time, and several years hence.

USING MENTORS, CRITICAL FRIENDS AND COLLEAGUES

mentor
An expert practitioner inducting a novice into their profession

Mentors, critical friends and colleagues play quite different roles in relation to your reflection and development as a teacher. Mentors are expert practitioners who take on a responsibility to share their skills and experience with a novice to help them to develop professional expertise. Helping novices to reflect on their practice is the central aim of mentoring; this can be supplemented by pointing them in the right direction to seek help, modelling practice, and working collaboratively to solve problems and answer mutual questions (Education Council New Zealand, 2017). Mentor programs may be formal or informal, but mentors do more than simply providing tips for teaching, or collegial support. Rather, they provide support for reflection on teaching.

Many universities and education departments in Australia and New Zealand make use of mentors in teacher education and beginning teacher induction programs, and mentors are also seen at other levels of professional development, such as school leadership.

As well as expertise, there are a number of characteristics you may want to consider when choosing who you will approach to request a mentor relationship. You will need to think about someone who communicates well with you, is reflective, whom you trust, and who has expertise (in mentoring, as well as in teaching), and a degree of match with your philosophy of learning and teaching. You are entering into a relationship that will involve demands on their time, and you will need to consider that as well. Is the person likely to have the time to listen to and talk with you, to come and watch you teach, and to reflect on your concerns? In your conversations about your teaching, are you mainly listening to them give advice? Do you feel that they listen to you, and help you to think about your practice?

Critical friends and colleagues can also provide emotional and professional support for your teaching. Consider how you can work with them to deepen reflection on your teaching as well, through team teaching and professional conversations focused on observations of one another's classes. Colleagues provide an important source of assistance and input for reflection, as is discussed further below in the section on observation.

OBSERVATION

It can be helpful to observe your own class with fresh eyes, as well as observing others teaching. Aids to observation may include video and audio. Of course, you must gain the consent of your students to record them in this way, and make clear to them the purpose of the recording. McFadden, Ellis, Anwar and Roehrig (2014) reviewed a number of studies showing that observing and annotating videos facilitated reflection and increased depth of thinking, particularly when the process involved interaction with others.

Observing and reflecting together with a mentor or colleagues can deepen reflection in – and on – teaching (Camburn & Han, 2017). Professional learning communities can participate in this process together by observing, describing and analysing – but importantly, not evaluating – one another's teaching, in 'instructional rounds' (Elmore, 2007). An example in NSW applied the NSW Quality Teaching Framework in 'Quality teaching rounds', and was found to improve teacher quality and morale (Gore et al., 2017).

Additionally, you may choose to focus on certain behaviours you or your students are exhibiting. In this case, an anecdotal record or checklist may be useful. An anecdotal record is a simple description of an activity or event, giving information on the setting of the activity, the individuals involved, what was said or done and by whom, and the length of time involved. Such information is useful for analysing what is happening in a problematic situation, and for describing and defining specific behaviours. An example of an observation record sheet is given in **Figure 1.5** (see page 17).

CourseMateExpress

Online Resources
Watch a **video** of a
pre-service teacher
reflecting on how
she used some of the
reflection activities
during professional
experience

REFLECTING ON YOUR PERSONAL PHILOSOPHY OF LEARNING AND TEACHING

Studying educational psychology provides an ideal opportunity to develop the ability to reflect critically, and in so doing to develop a personal philosophy of learning and teaching. A philosophy is like a personal mission statement: it guides your choices, behaviours, thoughts and feelings. Whether you plan to teach in classrooms, work as a school counsellor, support your own children's learning or simply be a responsible and informed member of society, your personal philosophy will be central to what you believe, how you think and behave, and how you relate to others.

All of us have experience as learners, and possibly as teachers as well. As such, we come to the learning–teaching process with implicit theories, and preferences regarding learning and teaching. It can be helpful to examine that implicit knowledge, and to become aware of its origins. As you study units in education, and gain further experience, your philosophy may well change. We hope, for example, that studying educational psychology will give you new insights into the learner, the learning–teaching process and some of the choices available to you as a teacher. With further teaching experiences, and deepening knowledge, your philosophy of learning and teaching is likely to continue to evolve. One way your implicit theories and assumptions might be revealed, for example, is when your actions as a teacher do not align with your philosophy; how you think you *should* be as a teacher. Developing a personal philosophy helps you to be aware of your beliefs, how they are related to your knowledge and experience, and the ways in which they can have an impact upon your learning and teaching. As a teacher, your philosophy should be informed by relevant theory and research in educational psychology. It will help you to set goals, make choices and evaluate your progress.

Here are some questions that might help you to start thinking about your personal philosophy of learning and teaching:

- What does teaching involve?
- What (and who) has an impact upon learning?
- What is the role of the teacher?
- What makes an effective teacher?
- What is the role of the learner?
- What is learning?
- What makes an effective learner?

Having drafted your philosophy of learning and teaching, the next step is to consider how you will enact it in practice; what will these principles look like in the classroom? The 'putting it together' sections in Module II of this text (pp. 248, 295 and 333) provide some examples of how answers to these questions link with what teachers do, and the choices they make.

On the CourseMate Express website, you will find 'Develop your philosophy', which provides a space for you to consider your philosophy of learning and teaching related to each module of this text.

CourseMateExpress

Online Resources
Take a moment to consider your personal philosophy. You may wish to use the **Develop your philosophy** tool on this text's CourseMate Express website

USING RESEARCH AS A REFLECTIVE TEACHER

Research in educational psychology can assist the reflective teacher in several ways. First, it can be a source of new strategies or ideas for teaching. In studying this text, you may identify some ideas and strategies of which you were previously unaware. Second, research can help teachers to evaluate a number of choices in order to select the most appropriate one for their circumstance.

Research in educational psychology can also help teachers to make sense of their experiences by comparing them with others' findings and with theory.

John Hattie (1999, 2003, 2009) has conducted a number of meta-analyses, combining the results of thousands of studies to compare the effects of various factors on student achievement. He reported that student factors account for about 50 per cent of variance in achievement, while teachers accounted for about 30 per cent, and home, peers, schools and school principals each accounted for between 5 per cent and 10 per cent of achievement variance (see Figure 1.3). Hattie (2009) argued that beyond student ability, what teachers do in classrooms makes the greatest contribution to student learning, so it is important to think about how we evaluate what we do.

Hattie's research showed that almost all teacher interventions made some difference to student learning. This is in part because of the process of reflection the teachers go through in preparing, conducting and evaluating the program. This is a strong argument for research as a tool for reflection. Hattie argued that because the average effect size was 0.4, we should look for effects above this figure to identify truly effective interventions. His results are summarised in Table 1.3. You can explore many of the influences in the chapters of this book, as indicated in the table.

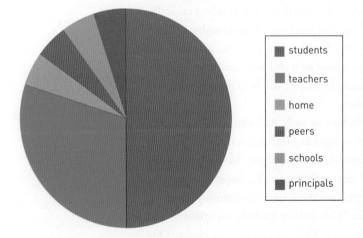

- students
- teachers
- home
- peers
- schools
- principals

FIGURE 1.3 Percentage of achievement variance according to Hattie's research

TABLE 1.3 What makes a difference to students' achievement? Comparison of effect sizes

BIGGEST EFFECTS	EFFECT SIZE	CHAPTER	SMALLEST OR NEGATIVE EFFECTS	EFFECT SIZE	CHAPTER
Piagetian programs	1.28	3	Programmed instruction	0.24	5
Classroom behaviour	0.80	14	Finances	0.23	11
Comprehensive interventions for learning disability	0.77	10	Class size	0.21	
Reciprocal teaching	0.74	3	Web-based learning	0.18	12
Feedback	0.73	13	Problem-based learning	0.15	6
Metacognitive strategies	0.69	6	Ability grouping	0.12	9, 10
Prior achievement	0.67	9	Gender	0.12	11
Creativity programs	0.65	9	Open versus traditional	0.01	7
Cooperative learning	0.59	6, 7	Summer vacation	−0.09	
Study skills	0.59	6	Retention	−0.16	10
Direct instruction	0.59	5	Television	−0.18	
Socioeconomic status	0.57	11	Mobility (changing schools)	−0.34	11
Quality of teaching	0.44	6, 7, 8			

Source: Adapted from Hattie, J. A. C., *Visible learning: A synthesis of over 800 meta-analyses relating to achievement.* Published by Taylor & Francis Group, © 2009.

READING AND EVALUATING RESEARCH

There is an enormous well of research in educational psychology from which to draw. Judging what is useful is an important skill for teachers to develop, as you will encounter numerous new approaches, theories and strategies in your practice. Hattie's rough guide of looking for effect sizes larger than 0.4 is one way to judge research studies showing an effect from a particular intervention. Other questions you might ask include:

- What evidence supports the theory, strategy or finding? Has it been researched? Is the research valid and reliable? Are the claims fully or only partially supported by the evidence? What other explanations of the research outcomes are there?
- Does it fit with other research in the area?
- Is it well supported by educational theory?
- What other views are there? Throughout this book, you will find presentations of different views on particular topics. By reviewing the research, you can make judgements about which view is best supported by the evidence, and perhaps identify what research still needs to be conducted.
- Where has the work been published? Is it only on the Internet? A vast amount of information on the Internet is very mixed in terms of quality and reliability. Research published in journals that have fellow academics review the articles submitted has been through a rigorous process before publication. Your university librarian can help you to locate appropriate journals for your area of interest.

CONDUCTING RESEARCH AS A REFLECTIVE TEACHER

Conducting your own research in educational psychology can give you an insight into the research process, as well as giving you direct answers to your own questions, thus deepening reflection. It also helps teachers to integrate their experience with theory and previous research. In order for research to be helpful, and to ensure it meets its purposes, it needs to be carefully designed and conducted. In this section we discuss some of the questions, options and principles to be considered in conducting research.

THE RESEARCH PROCESS

The research process involves asking questions that are themselves informed by prior research and theory, and then seeking answers to those questions through the collection and analysis of some kind of data. The conclusions drawn by the researcher about the meaning of the data are tested by reference to previous research and theory, and by presentation of the results for others to evaluate.

Figure 1.4 summarises the research process. Note that although this has been presented in a step-wise fashion, in reality, researchers may take a different path; for example, reframing a new research question after collecting interesting data, returning to design a second study linked to the first, or changing the research question if the original one proves unworkable to test.

CourseMateExpress

Online Resources
Explore an example of a research report with the **Interactive Activity** on this text's website.

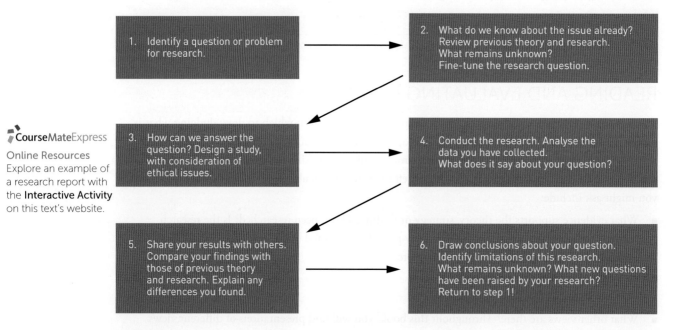

FIGURE 1.4 The research process

RESEARCH METHODS

In learning and teaching, there are a number of research methods that can be useful for helping teachers to reflect on their practice. These include, for example, experimental approaches, interviews and observations. You will see examples of these and other research methods in research projects that are described throughout this book.

Experiment

An experiment is a particular research technique involving the manipulation of one or more **independent variables** so that you can observe the result in a **dependent variable**. Experiments generally test a hypothesis about the effect of one variable on another.

For example, Jen, a primary teacher, has been introduced to an online application (app) to support her Year 3 students' learning of fractions. Although the students love using the class tablets for educational games, she isn't sure whether this app would be as helpful for their learning as the hands-on activities she currently uses. Jen decides to design an experiment to determine the relative effectiveness of the two strategies.

In this situation, the dependent variable would be students' score on a fractions test following a week of using the activity. The independent variable would be the learning activity (use of the app, or participation in a hands-on activity). Students would be assigned to two conditions: one in which they used the fractions app, and another in which they did a hands-on activity relating to fractions. In order to be sure that it was the learning activity that was creating any difference found, Jen would need to be careful to match the type of activity in the two conditions, ensuring that they are both addressing the same content and level of learning about fractions. She would also need to ensure that the two groups of students were equivalent in ability level. For this reason, sometimes students were not randomly assigned to experimental groups, but matched, with equal numbers of high-achieving and low-achieving students in each group.

Quasi-experimental designs compare outcomes (dependent variables) in two groups that already exist, such as two classrooms. There is less control, and therefore less certainty about the result, but this method is more realistic, and so results are more likely to 'fit' the real world of the classroom.

Interviews and focus groups

Interviews and focus groups directly ask participants for their views, or experiences. They are thus high in **validity** (are likely to tell you what the participants think). However, you may not be sure that the participant would give you the same answer if you asked them at a different time, or in a different way – **reliability** may be compromised.

An interview might be used, for example, to discover students' attitudes towards a particular teaching approach (such as use of the fractions app, compared with hands-on activities). If the students were interviewed following a lesson in which they received some negative feedback on a task, however, their response might be different than if interviewed following another lesson.

Some guidelines for collecting data through interviews are included in Box 1.2. Interviews are generally held with individuals, but can also be held in focus groups that combine groups of people with common experiences or attributes. An ideal size for a focus group is 4–6, as this allows all members opportunity to speak. Focus groups can be helpful in generating discussion, as participants spark one another's ideas. Care needs to be taken, however, that one or two members do not dominate the discussion, or skew it in a particular direction.

independent variable
The variable that is controlled or manipulated in an experiment, to determine its effect

dependent variable
The variable that is measured in an experiment, to determine whether the independent variable had any effect

validity
The extent to which a test or measurement device measures what it purports to measure

reliability
The extent to which a test or measurement device obtains the same result when used on successive occasions

BOX 1.2 IMPLICATIONS FOR EDUCATORS

GUIDELINES FOR COLLECTING DATA THROUGH INTERVIEWS

At the start of an interview, you need to establish rapport with the interviewee. Your aim is to give them the opportunity to tell you a little more about themselves.

- Step 1: Commence by telling participants there are no right or wrong answers.
- Step 2: As a way of making participants feel comfortable, ask them to tell you or write down a list of ways in which they learned or taught that day (or the day before). This will prompt them to think about the learning activities they engage in and how they feel about them.
- Step 3: Ask participants to elaborate and explain why they have given their answers. Remember to always ask participants to tell you why!
- Step 4: Now you can introduce the topic that you want to talk about in the interview.

Ideas for eliciting information

In order to promote discussion during the interview, you might ask participants to write down their ideas and let them think about them first, before they elaborate and tell you more. You can refer to each point on this list in turn as you progress through the interview.

Some interviewers also encourage participants (of all ages) to draw pictures or some form of visual representation, and then get them to comment on these in response to questions. You may wish to experiment with this technique.

It may be helpful to use information from the literature to help develop your questions.

Using background reading to develop questions

Do plenty of background reading so that you can ask appropriate questions. If necessary, tailor your reading and literature review to suit the subjects of your study. In other words, if you select an adolescent student, your literature review might look at research on adolescents.

Conducting interviews

Making sure you are well prepared is essential to conducting a successful interview. Devise a list of questions beforehand so you are familiar with them, and during the interview remember to adapt them, depending on the age of the interviewee. The set of questions does not have to be identical for each interviewee, but you should cover the same material so that you can compare and contrast answers.

Before you start the interview, take some time to get to know your interviewees (if necessary) and make sure they feel comfortable. Let them know that the purpose of the interview is to find out their views and opinions, and assure them there are no right or wrong answers. Also, make it clear that they are under no obligation to answer any question.

It is important to avoid any distractions during the interview. To this end, it is a good idea to record the interview (you will need to get ethics permission for this). Not only will this ensure you are able to focus completely on the interview, but it will be vital in preparing your transcript. Make sure your equipment is set up and ready to go so you don't need to attend to it during the interview.

Finally, try not to talk too much, and encourage the interviewees to talk. You may need to think of some prompts; for example, 'Can you tell me more about ...?', or 'Can you explain that a little more?'

Keeping track of the interview

Some interviewers electronically record interviews, while others rely on written notes containing key points and quotes from participants. A transcript is usually included as an appendix.

In verbatim transcripts, do not include 'ums' and 'aahs', but note any breaks or extended pauses in the interview. Body language or gestures may be noted in brackets if appropriate.

Ensure that your transcript does not contain the name/s of any schools, students or teachers. When interviewees mention names, you may include the first names only or make up pseudonyms. It is vital to maintain confidentiality throughout the report.

Questionnaires

Questionnaires allow participants to report their own attitudes, beliefs, perceptions and ideas, without the researcher needing to be present. This means that larger numbers of participants can be surveyed than with interviews. However, care needs to be taken in the construction of the questionnaire to ensure that questions are clear and easy to understand, yet do not lead the participants' answers. Questions can be open-ended (requiring a written response) or closed (typically requiring respondents to choose a particular response from a list of options), and questionnaires may be analysed qualitatively or quantitatively. As with interviews, the design of questions in questionnaires is guided by the broader research question. Figure 1.5 gives some examples of types of questions that can be used.

---

1 What is your favourite way of learning about fractions? Why?

**2 In the questions below, circle the response that is closest to your view.
When learning about fractions:**

I learn best with hands-on activities	Strongly disagree	Disagree	Agree	Strongly agree
I learn best with online activities	Strongly disagree	Disagree	Agree	Strongly agree
I learn best with a worksheet	Strongly disagree	Disagree	Agree	Strongly agree
I learn best with the teacher explaining to me	Strongly disagree	Disagree	Agree	Strongly agree

3 Put the activities in order of your preferred way of learning about fractions, by numbering them from 1 to 4:

☐ Hands-on activities   ☐ Worksheets
☐ Online activities   ☐ Teacher explaining

FIGURE 1.5 Questionnaire items can be open-ended, and qualitatively analysed as in the first question, or closed, and quantitatively analysed as in the second and third questions. Which do you think will give you more accurate information about students' views?

Observation

Observation was discussed above as a strategy for reflective teaching. It can also be a research tool. When observing in this context, it is useful to have a clear operationalisation of the variables you want to observe: What will they look like? How could they be measured? This is particularly important for abstract constructs such as 'student engagement', for example. It is also helpful to have a systematic way of collecting the data. For example, information can be organised in the form of a checklist, with data organised in segments of time, or by student behaviour, with the observational categories listed in the left-hand column and time units or student names listed across the top.

An example is given in Figure 1.6. Observation can also be broader, noting elements of the context, activities and participants (teacher, learners) in the situation. Anecdotal records are a useful tool with which to collect information both about the broader situation and specific events. In either case, observation will be guided by particular research questions such as 'What is contributing to the observed outcome?' or 'How is this initiative affecting students' learning?'

The observation record sheet in Figure 1.6 has as its focus student engagement in a lesson. It could be used to research student engagement in respect to particular lesson activities, timing in a lesson, and/ or relationships in learning. Having more than one observer, and comparing their records, can act as a check of the reliability of the data.

Class:		Lesson:					Date:		Time:	

Record number of students engaged in each activity at time intervals of five minutes in a 50-minute block. Write the main activity of each phase of the lesson that corresponds to the time period being observed.

	Time									
	1	2	3	4	5	6	7	8	9	10
Lesson activity:										
On task – independent										
On task – with peer										
On task – with teacher										
Off task – independent										
Off task – with peer										
Off task – with teacher										

FIGURE 1.6 Observation record sheet

Document analysis

Documents surround us, and can help to provide a picture of the context in which we teach and students learn. Authored documents can also reveal our, and our students' thinking. Examples of documents that could be analysed include syllabus, policy or school documents, student work samples, and posts to online websites or social media. Themes may be identified in the document that are linked to the research question. For example, if a teacher–researcher was interested in her students' concerns about the environment, she might analyse student work samples to identify particular environment-related themes in their writing. Documents should be de-identified, so that individuals' and schools' names are not discernible.

Case study

Case studies look in depth at a particular situation, group or person. They typically combine a number of methods, such as interview, observation, questionnaire, and document analysis (described above), to compose a total picture of the case. This combination of methods allows the researcher to 'triangulate' the data: to ensure that a consistent and accurate picture of the case is being drawn. Cases are carefully chosen as an example of a broader group, to allow for the findings to be meaningful beyond the specific case.

Researchers are careful to choose the appropriate method to answer their research questions and that fit the purpose of their research. Table 1.4 links various methods to relevant questions and purposes you might have as a classroom teacher-researcher.

TABLE 1.4 Research methods are determined by research purpose and research question

RESEARCH PURPOSE	EXAMPLE QUESTION	RELEVANT METHODS
Evaluation	How effective is collaborative learning for students' learning of science concepts?	**Experiment.** In the classroom, you may wish to conduct an experiment to observe the result of a particular teaching strategy. In general, this requires two groups: one that received the treatment (were taught by the strategy) and another control group that did not. Use of a control group allows the researcher to test whether any effect found was a result of the treatment or whether it would have occurred anyway.
Description	What patterns exist in students' answering of questions in this class?	**Observation.** When observing for research, it is useful to have a systematic way of collecting the data. For example, information can be organised in the form of a checklist, with data organised in segments of time, or by student behaviour, with the observational categories listed in the left-hand column and time units or student names listed across the top. An example is given in **Figure 1.6**.
	What changes are evident in students' self-concept during their transition to secondary school?	**Case study.** In-depth, detailed study of an individual, situation or context. It will typically use a number of sources of data, including interview and observation, for example.
	What are students' attitudes towards NAPLAN?	**Questionnaire.** This allows the researcher to gain responses from a larger number of participants, and to examine the data statistically, allowing correlations and comparisons to be made across groups. Questionnaires need to be carefully designed to maximise clarity, and to ensure validity and reliability of the data collected.
Explanation	How does students' day-to-day experience on social media influence them in their peer interactions at school?	**Interview.** Interviews are useful for gaining insights into the views or thinking strategies of students, parents and teachers. For example, your students' feedback on your teaching (and their learning experiences) can provide powerful information to prompt your reflection. However, if you are the interviewer, they may simply tell you what they think will please you. Some guidelines for collecting data through interviews are included in **Box 1.2**.
	How does *x* influence *y*?	**Experiment.** An experiment is a particular research technique involving the manipulation of one or more variables so that you can observe the result. An experiment may test a hypothesis about a relationship between two variables.
Exploration	When are my students most engaged in learning? What classroom factors influence this?	**Observation.** Observation can also be broader than the checklist described above, noting elements of the context, activities and participants (teacher, learners) in the situation. Anecdotal records are a useful tool with which to collect information both about the broader situation and specific events. In either case, observation will be guided by particular research questions such as 'What is contributing to the observed outcome?' or 'How is this initiative affecting students' learning?'
		Interviews and focus groups. Note that interview data can also answer this exploration question. Using a combination of methods can strengthen the reliability of findings (reliability is discussed below).
	What kinds of errors are typical in students' free writing?	**Content or text analysis.** The text of a document is analysed in systematic ways.
Prediction	Is group work more effective with particular groups of students? (more capable/ less capable/ mixed)	**Experiment.** Experiments can be used to test predictions or hypotheses. Care needs to be taken to set up treatment and control groups to ensure that explanations other than the one being tested can be excluded.

(Source: Draws from information in Jackson, 2006)

QUALITY CONSIDERATIONS IN RESEARCH

If it's worth doing, it's worth doing well! In particular, researchers need to ensure that the information they collect can be trusted and will answer the questions, and that the conclusions they draw from it are reasonable, based on the information collected. The two key interrelated aspects of quality to consider in designing research are reliability and validity.

Reliability

The principle of reliability ensures that any findings would be found on another occasion under the same conditions. It avoids 'one-off' results, and seeks to limit researcher bias. As a teacher, it is particularly important to protect against bias that might influence the results of your research. You can do this by using others to compare and confirm judgements made, and by collecting data from a range of sources or instruments.

Validity

This asks whether the research findings relate to what is claimed. For example, students' results on a reading test might be used to evaluate the effectiveness of a teaching strategy, but in fact students may have encountered other teaching strategies as well as the one under investigation, or the results may simply reflect students' reading ability rather than the effect of teaching. Validity can be strengthened by using established measures of the specific topic being researched, and by using a control group and randomly assigning participants to either group.

ACTION RESEARCH

action research
Professionals evaluating their own practice with the goal of improving it

Action research is a particular type of research that can utilise any of the research methods described above. It is not confined to educational contexts but is undertaken by professionals across many spheres. It is defined simply as professionals investigating their own practice with the goal of improving it. It is therefore closely related to reflective teaching. The process of conducting action research involves the four steps of reflection, planning, action and reflection:

1   *Reflection.* Identify the issue you are concerned about. Develop some questions concerning this issue. Learn more about the issue by reading and consulting colleagues.
2   *Planning.* Develop a strategy.
3   *Action.* Take action – implement your strategy. Share the results with your students and colleagues. Action research is a collaborative process. Evaluate the evidence about the outcomes of your strategy.
4   *Reflection.* Revise your plans based on your evaluation. This restarts the cycle. An example of action research conducted by a teacher is given in Box 1.3.

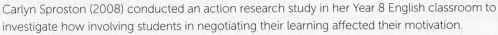

BOX 1.3 RESEARCH LINKS

ACTION RESEARCH

Carlyn Sproston (2008) conducted an action research study in her Year 8 English classroom to investigate how involving students in negotiating their learning affected their motivation.

In the first cycle, students were asked about their perceptions of their English class through questionnaires and journal entries. They saw it as 'static and boring'. In particular, they didn't like the amount of writing and inactivity in the class. They then had a class meeting at which students' views were discussed and suggestions shared about what might make it more interesting.

The action that followed this was to start a unit on children's stories, which involved students analysing these stories and then writing their own. They visited a local primary school to read their stories to the children, and showed excitement and engagement in the activity. Students' journal entries at the end of the unit showed that they had enjoyed the narrative writing, particularly because it was a 'real' task. Carlyn's own reflection on the first cycle includes:

> As I reflected on the first cycle, I re-read some of the student journal entries. It seemed to me that the majority of the students had no idea of what to write; they just wrote what I asked for. When asked for their opinions about the activities, they wrote a word or a phrase and seemed to have no idea of how to evaluate their own work. However, when I interviewed students they were able to give me some opinions about the work, and what they thought about their own learning.

This led to a second cycle of action, in which Carlyn decided to build in some strategies to help students to evaluate their own work. Students developed informative pieces to present to the class. They had choice in their topic and the mode of presentation. They were given five guiding questions to support their evaluation of their work. Once again, the action was evaluated through students' journal entries and interviews, as well as Carlyn's own reflections. The students' evaluation was much more detailed. Another finding was that some students had found having a broad choice difficult, so that while ability to choose was motivating, they needed some boundaries within which to do this.

In the third cycle – a unit on school with students' work to be presented as a speech – Carlyn referred to work by Boomer (1992) and Reid (1992) on negotiated learning. Students were given the choice of topic, task, who they worked with and the audience, with the broader topic of school as the boundary. Students' journal entries indicated a real change from the attitudes to English they had expressed at the beginning of the year. They identified 'having a choice in learning activities; being involved and having a voice in the class; positive relationships with teacher and peers; variety and activity in their classes; collaboration and teamwork; having a real or authentic audience for their work; being committed to their work and to their class community; and having fun' as important elements that resulted from the negotiation of their learning.

Carlyn's final evaluation of the process concluded that there was greater motivation and commitment to learning from her students as a result of their involvement in the decision-making process.

Source: Sproston, C. (2008). When students negotiate: An action research case study of a year 8 English class in a secondary college in Victoria, Australia. Educational Action Research, 2(16), 187–208.

ACTIVITIES

1   Identify the steps in the action research cycle in this study.
2   Read the original article that relates the study in detail.
3   How is action research different from the reflection that teachers do in the course of their work?
4   Design your own action research study for a class you are involved in (it could be a school or a university class). You will need to negotiate this with everyone involved – teachers and students.

STRENGTHS AND LIMITATIONS OF RESEARCH METHODS

When selecting a research method to help you to answer a particular question, it is also important to recognise the strengths and limitations of each method. Below in Table 1.5 we summarise this for each of the research methods we have introduced in this chapter.

A number of books are available describing methods of educational research in depth (for example, Johnson & Christensen, 2017).

TABLE 1.5 Summary of research methods

RESEARCH METHOD	STRENGTHS	LIMITATIONS
Experiment	Control of variables means that conclusions can confidently be drawn about what has affected the result.	As variables are controlled in an experiment, validity is compromised: it may not reflect the true (messy) world of an actual classroom.
Interview	Provides rich and deep data: in-depth insight into participants' views.	Interviewer, and interview questions can bias the responses. This can be minimised by careful construction of the interview schedule, and training of the interviewer.
Focus group	Interaction between participants can result in greater reflection, and richer responses, as participants' thinking is sparked by others' responses.	Interaction between participants can result in bias, for example if one student dominates the group, and others respond to please him or her.
Questionnaires	Allows for sampling of large numbers of people. Can provide quantitative data that can be analysed statistically.	Requires reasonable level of literacy, which may limit its usefulness with young children. Relies on self-report of information, which may be influenced by participant's bias, level of self-awareness, and/or social desirability.
Observation	Data is collected in real time, and authentic context. Contextual information can be gathered to provide a richer picture of the situation	Potential bias from observer. This can be minimised by having more than one observer, and reporting inter-rater reliability. An observer (or camera or microphone) being present may influence the result; people may not behave as they would normally.
Document analysis	Authentic data that has been produced for a purpose other than the research.	There is the potential for researcher bias in what is picked out of the data for analysis, as well as how it is interpreted. Having clear guidelines for doing this can improve reliability in this respect.
Case study	Focus on one or a few cases allows for deeper data analysis, and consideration of complexities involved. Multiple data sources can be triangulated to strengthen reliability of conclusions drawn.	Limited generalisability. Cases need to be carefully selected to ensure they are representative of the relevant group or situation.

ETHICAL CONSIDERATIONS IN CONDUCTING RESEARCH

When conducting research with humans or animals, a number of ethical guidelines must be followed. In Australia, these have been set down by the Australian Psychological Society (APS) and other bodies such as the National Health and Medical Research Council (NHMRC). Also, universities in Australia and New Zealand have ethics committees that check that research studies fulfil the appropriate guidelines.

Some of the issues to consider include:

■ *Informed consent*. You must provide a description of the research, its purpose and what participation would involve. Parents' consent must be obtained when conducting research with children.

- *Anonymity and confidentiality.* You should take every step to ensure that you maintain confidentiality. This means that you should not include participants' names or other identifying characteristics in any report you make of the results. You should also keep any records of the research in a secure place, to ensure privacy.
- *Voluntary participation.* Participants must be informed that their participation is voluntary, and that they can stop the interview or withdraw from the study at any time. This includes the right to withdraw their permission for you to use their data. Participation should be entirely voluntary. Participants must not be pressured or coerced into participating in the research.
- *Sharing of results.* Your participants should be given a copy of any report of results and have it explained to them.

THINK ABOUT

- How can you ensure that your own students' consent to participating in your research is informed and voluntary?

REPORTING RESEARCH

Having conducted your research, analysed the data and reflected on the findings, it is important to report your results to others – for example, to the students who participated in the research, to your colleagues, and to the wider community. This can be done in a presentation or in writing. You may also have opportunity to share findings with the wider professional or academic communities through a peer reviewed journal. In reporting research, it is important to maintain the confidentiality of those who participated, as discussed in the ethical considerations section above. Details must be given about the research methods used, the research sample and method of analysis of the data, so that readers (or hearers) know the basis for any conclusions drawn. A guide to writing a research report is provided on the CourseMate Express site.

CourseMateExpress

Online Resources
Go further: See guidelines for writing a research report in Education on this text's website

CONCLUDING COMMENTS

As you study educational psychology, we hope that you will develop your skills of reflection and critical inquiry, and that it will be helpful in broadening your understanding of learning and teaching. The material we cover in this book will be most meaningful to you if you see connections between theories and issues in the real world – and, in particular, links to your own learning and teaching experiences. The book contains four modules. The first two modules introduce you to theories of development and learning, which we encourage you to think about in relation to your own development and learning processes so as to understand practical applications. The third module is about individual differences that affect learning and teaching. The final module draws on these theories as the basis for discussing issues related to the learning–teaching process.

As you start reading, prepare to learn many new terms – especially in the first half of the book. Students often become discouraged because they forget what they have read and feel overwhelmed. The key is to deal with small chunks of new information at a time. Talk with fellow students and with your lecturer or tutors about the most effective ways to learn and revise this material. Return to the questions at the start of each chapter to check your understanding. Usually, as students become more familiar with educational psychology and with discussing its application in the classroom or other contexts, they start to see connections. At the end of each module, a summary table makes links between or compares key content in each chapter. Take some time to review the relevant table as you finish a chapter, to help you connect ideas as you go, and to build your own philosophy of learning and teaching, guided by research.

STUDY TOOLS

ONLINE STUDY RESOURCES

Visit http://login.cengagebrain.com and use the access code that comes with this book for 12 months' access to the student resources for this text.

The CourseMate Express website contains a range of resources and study tools for this chapter, including:

- a **self-check quiz**

- **crosswords**, **flashcards** and a **glossary** to help you revise the key terms from this chapter
- the **Go further** materials and **interactive activity** mentioned in the chapter.

CourseMateExpress

CHAPTER REVIEW

- Educational psychology is the application of psychological principles to the study of learning and teaching.
- Studying educational psychology can contribute to your understanding of yourself as a learner and teacher, as well as of your students, and to your understanding of the learning and teaching processes themselves.
- Effective teaching is linked to making effective choices, and educational psychology can help to guide teachers in both making and evaluating their choices.
- Educational psychology informs and deepens reflection on teaching practice.
- Tools for critical reflection include reflective journals, portfolios, mentors and observation.
- Developing a personal philosophy of learning and teaching can guide choices; provide insights into your

own behaviours, thoughts and feelings; and reveal implicit knowledge and theories you bring to your practice.

- Using existing research can inform practice, provide new ideas for teaching, evaluate choices and make sense of experiences.
- Conducting research involves asking questions, and seeking answers to those questions. Methods include experiment, interview, questionnaire, observation, document analysis and case study.
- Research quality is determined by validity and reliability, as well as ethical considerations such as confidentiality, informed consent and voluntary participation.
- Action research links reflection on teaching to research. It involves a cycle of reflection, planning and action.

PUTTING IT TOGETHER

Making links between 'educational psychology for learning and teaching' and material in other chapters

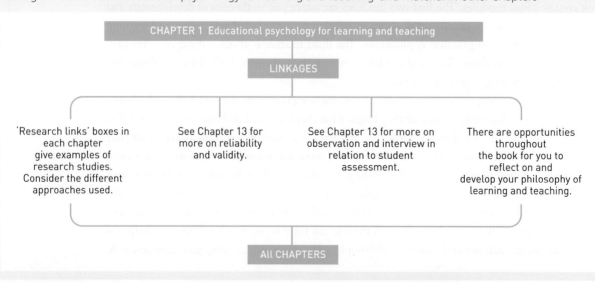

CHAPTER 1 Educational psychology for learning and teaching

LINKAGES

'Research links' boxes in each chapter give examples of research studies. Consider the different approaches used.

See Chapter 13 for more on reliability and validity.

See Chapter 13 for more on observation and interview in relation to student assessment.

There are opportunities throughout the book for you to reflect on and develop your philosophy of learning and teaching.

All CHAPTERS

QUESTIONS AND ACTIVITIES FOR SELF-ASSESSMENT AND DISCUSSION

1   List some ways in which educational psychology can guide teacher reflection.
2   Identify strategies teachers can employ to reflect on their teaching, and students' learning.
3   Name some research methods teachers can use in their work. What benefits could this have for students' learning, and for your teaching?
4   What makes for quality research? What issues should be considered?
5   Reflect on your past experience (if any) as a participant in a research study.
    a   How were you informed of the purposes of the research and your role in it?
    b   How was your voluntary consent obtained?

FURTHER RESEARCH

SEARCH ME! AND EDUCATION DATABASES

Explore Search Me! education for articles relevant to this chapter. Fast and convenient, Search Me! education is updated daily and provides you with 24-hour access to full-text articles from hundreds of scholarly and popular journals, ebooks and newspapers, including *The Australian* and *The New York Times*. Log in to Search Me! through http://login.cengagebrain.com and use the search terms listed here as a starting point:

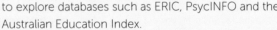

- action research AND teaching
- mentoring AND teaching
- reflective practice AND teaching.
  You can also use these terms

to explore databases such as ERIC, PsycINFO and the Australian Education Index.

RECOMMENDED WEBSITES

Australian Institute for Teaching and School Leadership: www.aitsl.edu.au/australian-professional-standards-for-teachers. This website also has illustrations of practice in each of the various standards.
New Zealand Teachers Council: https://educationcouncil.org.nz/content/graduating-teacher-standards

RECOMMENDED READING

Johnson, R.B. & Christensen, L. (2017). *Educational research: Quantitative, qualitative and mixed approaches*. 6th Edition. Thousand Oaks, California: Sage Publications.

Larrivee, B. (2000) Transforming teaching practice: Becoming the critically reflective teacher. *Reflective Practice: International and Multidisciplinary Perspectives*, 1(3), 293–307.
Stringer, E. T. (2014). *Action research*. Thousand Oaks, CA: Sage.

REFERENCES

Boomer, G. (1992). Curriculum composing and evaluating: An invitation to action research. In G. Boomer, L. Lester, C. Onore & J. Cook (Eds), *Negotiating the curriculum: Educating for the 21st century* (pp. 33–47). London: The Falmer Press.

Camburn, E.M. & Han, S.W. (2017). Teachers' professional learning experiences and their engagement in reflective practice: a replication study. *School Effectiveness and School Improvement, 28*(4), 527–554.

Clarke, D., Keitel, C. & Shimizu, Y. (2006). (Eds), *Mathematics classrooms in twelve countries: The insider's perspective.* Rotterdam, Netherlands: Sense Publishers.

Collin, S., Karsenti, T. & Komis, V. (2013). Reflective practice in initial teacher training: Critiques and perspectives. *Reflective Practice: International and Multidisciplinary Perspectives, 14*(1), 104–17.

Dewey, J. (1933). *How we think: A restatement of the relation of reflective thinking to the educative process.* Boston: Heath & Co.

Education Council, New Zealand (2017). *Code of Professional Responsibility and Standards for the Teaching Profession.*

Elmore, R. F. (2007). Professional networks and school improvement. *School Administrator, 64*(4), 20–25.

Gore, J.M., Lloyd, A., Smith, M., Bowe, J., Ellis, H., & Lubans, D. (2017). Effects of professional development on quality of teaching: Results from a randomised controlled trial of Quality Teaching Rounds. *Teaching and Teacher Education, 68*, 99–113.

Hattie, J. (1999). *Influences on student learning.* Inaugural professorial address, University of Auckland, June.

Hattie, J. (2003). *Teachers make a difference: What is the research evidence?* Background paper to invited address presented at the 2003 ACER Research Conference, Melbourne. Retrieved from www.acer.edu.au/documents/ Hattie_TeachersMakeADifference.pdf

Hattie, J. (2009). *Visible learning: A synthesis of over 800 meta-analyses relating to achievement.* London: Routledge.

Jackson, S. (2006). *Research methods and statistics: a critical thinking approach.* 2e. Belton, California: Thomson Wadsworth.

Johnson, R.B. & Christensen, L. (2017). *Educational research: Quantitative, qualitative and mixed approaches.* 6th Edn. Thousand Oaks, California: Sage Publications.

Lane, R., McMaster, H., Adnum, J. & Cavanagh, M. (2014). Quality reflective practice in teacher education: A journey towards shared understanding. *Reflective Practice: International and Multidisciplinary Perspectives, 15*(4), 481–94.

McFadden, J., Ellis, J., Anwar, T. & Roehrig, G. (2014). Beginning science teachers' use of a digital video annotation tool to promote reflective practices. *Journal of Science Education and Technology, 23*(3), 458–70.

Nelson, F. L. & Sadler, T. (2013). A third space for reflection by teacher educators: A heuristic for understanding orientations to and components of reflection. *Reflective Practice: International and Multidisciplinary Perspectives, 14*(1), 43–57.

Reid, J. (1992). Negotiating education. In G. Boomer, L. Lester, C. Onore & J. Cook (Eds), *Negotiating the curriculum: Educating for the 21st century,* (pp. 101–17). London: The Falmer Press.

Schön, D. (1983). *The reflective practitioner: How professionals think in action.* New York: Basic Books.

Schön, D. (1987). *Educating reflective practitioners.* San Francisco: Jossey Bass.

Sproston, C. (2008). When students negotiate: An action research case study of a year 8 English class in a secondary college in Victoria, Australia. *Educational Action Research, 2*(16), 187–208.

Thorsen, C. A. & DeVore, S. (2013). Analyzing reflection on/for action: A new approach. *Reflective Practice: International and Multidisciplinary Perspectives, 14*(1), 88–103.

Walberg, H. J. & Haertel, G. D. (1992). Educational psychology's first century. *Journal of Educational Psychology, 84*(1), 6–19.

1

THE LEARNER DEVELOPING OVER TIME

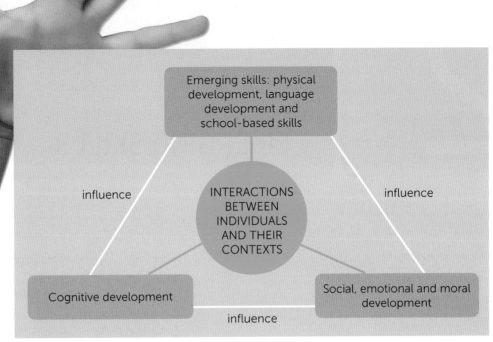

FIGURE MI Module I concept map

Core question: How can theories of development enhance the understanding of learning and teaching?

Human development occurs in many areas: physical, cognitive, social, emotional and moral, to name a few. None of these aspects of development occurs in isolation. To understand the learner as a whole person, you need to see the interconnections between the different facets of development and the ways in which these contribute to the emergence of a complex but integrated individual.

Although genetic influences on development are significant, social and cultural factors (that we sometimes refer to as 'the environment') work with them to shape the individual as he or she develops. The actions of the individual themselves also play an important role in development, both influencing their environment, and determining developmental outcomes at each point in time that will provide a basis for future development.

These two principles – of relations between developmental domains, and the interaction of person and context in development – result in the considerable variation we see across individuals in their development, with multiple pathways to a common result (of acquiring language, for example), as well as multiple outcomes from a common event (such as experience of adversity, for example). You will see both of these examples in Chapter 2, and are encouraged to look for further examples in the following chapters.

The three chapters in this module highlight the learner's complex and multidimensional nature. In Chapter 2 we explore the physical and linguistic dimensions of development, including brain development, and how these relate to learners who are developing the basic skills of literacy and numeracy. Chapter 3 focuses on the learner's mind and the ways in which thinking and reasoning develop over time. Chapter 4 examines what makes the learner unique – the self – and how thinking about the self and others develops as cognitive processing abilities become more complex. We also examine the relationship between cognitive, social and emotional development, the capacity for moral reasoning and the development of values and beliefs.

Recognising how developments in one dimension support and contribute to developments in other areas helps teachers consider all aspects of their students' lives in order to design appropriate learning and teaching experiences. In each chapter of this module, we encourage you to consider how the principles of development are at work, and how teachers can draw on these principles, adapting their teaching to cater for the varying developmental needs of students.

EMERGING SKILLS

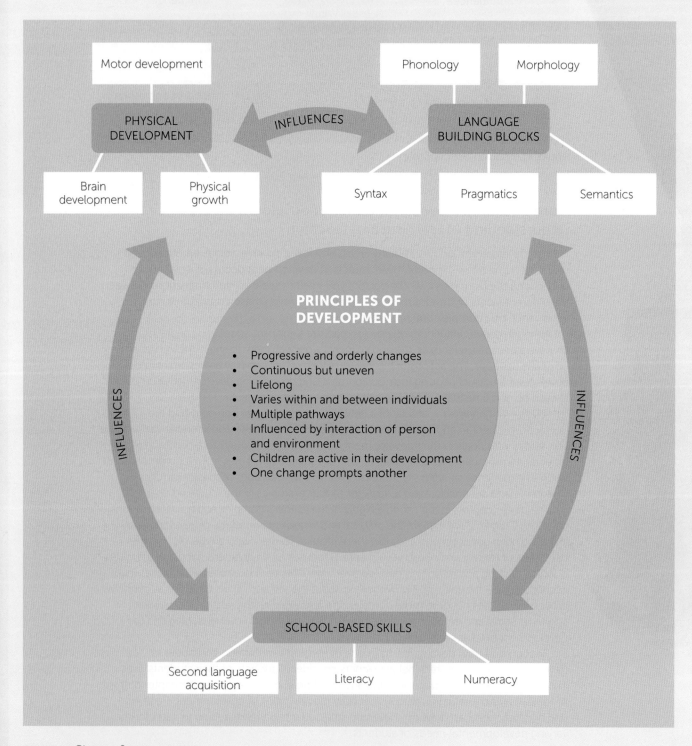

FIGURE 2.1 Chapter 2 concept map

KEY QUESTIONS

After reading this chapter, you should be able to answer the following questions:

■ What are some milestones of physical development from early childhood to adolescence?

■ How are physical development, language development and school skills connected? Give examples of the relationships between them.

■ How do developments in the brain over time explain the broad patterns of development seen in physical, language and school skills?

■ Broadly describe the course of language acquisition. What influences it?

■ How does the teaching of literacy and mathematics build on earlier developments?

■ What are some key principles of development? Give examples of how these are evident in research on the development of children's body, motor skills, brain, language and/or school skills.

ONLINE STUDY RESOURCES

Bring your learning to life with **interactive learning**, **study** and **exam preparation tools** that support the printed textbook. CourseMate Express includes **quizzes**, **interactive activities**, **videos**, a tool to help you '**develop your philosophy**' and more.

INTRODUCTION

Students starting at Sparrow High School are all individuals. They look different – are different heights, for example – and Kate has started puberty while Rosie won't show signs of this for two full years. They come from different cultural and socioeconomic backgrounds. They also have different interests, different friends and varied family backgrounds. Steph finds school easy, Sam finds it more difficult and Cody is not interested at all; Tara is interested and involved in sport, Ben in music and Jason in computer games. Where might these differences have originated? How will they influence their progression through high school?

Development is embedded in the biology and psychology of the individual, as well as in the sociocultural contexts within which they live. Relational developmental systems theories (Lerner, 2015; Mascolo & Fischer, 2015)

FIGURE 2.2 Development is influenced by complex interactions between person and environment. What factors might have interacted in the development of these children?

recognise the interactions between multiple genetic, biological, psychological, family and contextual factors in development. As we look at physical and language development in this chapter, look out for these relations between the systems of the person and of their environment. You may also see their influence on the school-based skills of literacy and numeracy.

PHYSICAL DEVELOPMENT OVER TIME

As we explore development in this chapter and throughout Module I, we look at four phases of the child's life: 'infancy' (the first two years), 'early childhood' (from three years old until seven years), 'middle childhood' (from seven years old to adolescence) and 'adolescence' (about 12 years old to adulthood). Development does not stop at adolescence, of course, but continues throughout the lifespan. This text focuses mainly on the school years: early and middle childhood, and adolescence.

PHYSICAL DEVELOPMENT IN INFANCY

Physical development sometimes seems to happen without our noticing. Yet the physical developments of childhood – changes in growth, in motor skills, and in the structure of the body and the brain – accompany, are influenced by, and form an important basis for developments in cognition (thinking) and emotion.

Consider a newborn baby. Right now she has no control over her movements, yet within 18 months she will be walking, in another year running, and soon after jumping and throwing and kicking balls. In the first two years, children develop physically at a faster rate than at any other time in their lives. Although we do not describe infants' physical development here in any detail, it forms an important basis for children's development – not just physical, but also social, emotional and cognitive – in later years.

Physical development, cognition and emotion

Infants' exploration of their worlds has far-reaching consequences for their development across domains, and motor skills facilitate that exploration. An infant's shift from staying in one place to independent mobility has consequences parents rapidly become aware of; suddenly the whole house seems to need to be rearranged to keep the baby safe … and to keep the household items safe from his reach! This shift in physical development also has consequences for the child, with increased opportunities to explore the environment through crawling, as well as the physical work of crawling, which is itself linked to improvements in visual perception, wariness of heights, spatial search strategies and brain development (Anderson et al., 2013). Developmental scientists refer to these kinds of far-reaching consequences across time and across domains that are set off by achievement of a particular milestone, as **developmental cascades** (Adolph & Robinson, 2015). Another example is given by Bornstein, Hahn & Suwalsky (2013) who were able to show links from motor and exploratory skills at 5 months to adolescent achievement at 14 through vocabulary and intelligence at 4 and 10 years, and academic achievement at 10.

What about infants who are unable to crawl because of disabilities? Or infants from cultures in which children are discouraged from crawling because of environmental dangers? There may be some effects on other domains of development. For example, it appears that there is a delay in spatial search for infants whose crawling is delayed (Campos et al., 2000). However, lack of crawling may only delay its development, not prevent it entirely. In addition, crawling is not invariably linked to spatial search, so it can be said that crawling is neither necessary nor sufficient for this cognitive ability to develop. This relates to another principle of development: there are more likely to be multiple pathways to development, rather than a common one for all individuals.

developmental cascades
Far-reaching consequences for learning and development that are instigated by a particular developmental achievement

With walking comes another developmental cascade, as the child's line of sight moves forward and upward, rather than being directed largely at the floor and lower walls when crawling (Kretch, Franchak & Adolph, 2014). Language development is affected as the child interacts with their environment in new ways, prompting parents to respond by talking about their environment, thus building vocabulary. Walking infants are also reported by parents to be more independent, which relates to their socioemotional development (Walle & Campos, 2014). Emotional development is affected too, as infants become frustrated by parents blocking their goals, or experience joy at attaining them (Adolph & Robinson, 2015) – see Figure 2.3. The child's activity of crawling, and later of walking, is an important force in their development.

The close relationship between physical, cognitive, social and emotional development is one that persists throughout childhood and adolescence. As you read this chapter, try to look for more connections between the development of one skill and others. There are other connections, too, with later development building on what has gone before. In infancy, children are already developing the physical, cognitive and emotional bases for the skills they will use at school.

FIGURE 2.3 How might children's new achievement of walking affect their social, cognitive, emotional and physical development?

THINK ABOUT

■ Consider other times when a child's activity might prompt development in a number of domains. What does this reveal about the forces that shape development? And how domains of development are interrelated?

PHYSICAL DEVELOPMENT IN EARLY CHILDHOOD

Although the rate of physical growth slows in early and middle childhood, age brings further increases in children's size, strength and coordination. This development of children's muscle strength, plus improved balance and coordination, along with a lower centre of gravity, brain maturation and children's activity itself, all support the development of children's motor skills (Adolph & Berger, 2010) (see Figure 2.4).

Motor-skill development in early childhood

Gross motor skills are those skills involving large muscle groups and often whole-body movements such as rolling, jumping, clapping, throwing and running. **Fine motor skills** are skills involving smaller muscle movements, usually of the hands and

FIGURE 2.4 A shift in the centre of gravity, together with increased strength, balance, coordination and flexibility, contribute to improvements in running skill that occur with age.

gross motor skills
Movement skills using
large muscle groups

fine motor skills
Movement skills using
small muscle groups

CourseMateExpress

Online resources
Watch **videos** of
children of different
ages running on this
text's website.

fingers, and include grasping and manipulating pencils or scissors. As children's development progresses and their control becomes increasingly refined, they move from requiring large pieces of paper on which to work, and large implements with which to write, to being able to write with a variety of pens and pencils between ruled lines on a page.

Acquisition of motor skills is one of the main developmental tasks of early childhood, and for this reason most preschool and early-school programs in Australia and New Zealand attach great importance to it. Climbing over obstacle courses; rolling, throwing and catching balls; and running, jumping, hopping and skipping all help to develop gross motor skills. Likewise, using dough, clay, crayons and paint, and activities that involve crumpling, cutting or tearing paper, all contribute to fine motor-skill development (see Figure 2.5).

Source: Matthew Duchesne. © Milk and Honey Photography, 2010.

FIGURE 2.5 Children's activities in early childhood help to develop gross and fine motor skills. What skills are being developed here?

Motor-skill development is also controlled by neurological growth. As the speed and efficiency of information processing improves (see later in this chapter and in Chapter 3), this enables children to intentionally control and combine movements (Adolph & Berger, 2010).

Parents contribute to motor-skill development at home through undertaking everyday activities with children, such as going to the park for a swing, drawing and doing puzzles. In some communities, motor skills are developed through community or traditional activities, as well as in formal preschool contexts. In the Torres Strait region of Australia, for example, Indigenous children's motor skills are developed through involvement in community dances from the time they can walk. The dances are taught more formally at school, which refines these skills (J. Davis, personal communication, 2001). Likewise, Māori communities in New Zealand develop *te reo kori* (the language of movement) within *ngā mahi a r-ēhia* – Māori recreational and leisure activities such as *poi*, *rakau* and *whai* (New Zealand Ministry of Education, 2007).

Children's spontaneous activity also contributes to their motor-skill development. The seemingly constant movement of preschoolers has a purpose in developing their gross motor skills, strength, coordination and sense of balance. Children also benefit from such activity in other ways, since (as we have seen) motor and cognitive development are related. The contribution of motor activity to cognition continues beyond the early years, influencing later academic skills such as reading and calculation. Box 2.1 describes further the relationship between physical activity and cognition.

BOX 2.1 RESEARCH LINKS

EXERCISE AND COGNITION

Best (2010) reviewed the research literature examining links between aerobic exercise and children's goal-directed cognition or executive function (see Chapter 3 for a description of the development of this aspect of cognition). He reported that single bouts of exercise and also more extended exercise programs had been shown to increase children's cognitive skills related to executive function. These skills include inhibition (the ability to selectively attend to a stimulus, ignoring others), shifting (the ability to shift between cognitive tasks) and creativity. Davis et al., (2011), working with overweight children, found that aerobic exercise also improved their achievement in mathematics, even when the children received no specific instruction in mathematics.

Best suggested several explanations for the links. Exercise is often cognitively demanding – we are using executive function, for example, when working with a team, or judging where to move to in order to intercept a ball in soccer. The cognitive skills that are developed through physical activity are then available for purely cognitive tasks. Coordination of motor movements that develops in middle childhood also involves executive function, and may be a contributor to brain development in the particular areas of the brain involved in executive function (addressed later in this chapter). Chemicals released in the brain during exercise also contribute to cognition; thus, exercise shows benefits for cognition in the short and long term.

The strength of the relationship between physical exercise and cognition underscores the importance of physical activity as a part of the school day. This may happen through structured lessons as well as in school break times. Parrish and colleagues (2009, 2012) have explored factors in primary school environments that influence children's physical activity levels in the playground. They found that longer break times, access to non-fixed equipment, ball play, and environmental aspects such as unshaded areas, painted targets and soft play surfaces all contributed to increases in children's physical activity.

ACTIVITIES

1 What place should physical activity have in the school curriculum? Develop a recommendation for a school to maximise children's physical activity during the school day.
2 How would you encourage students who are reluctant to be physically active at break times?

PHYSICAL DEVELOPMENT IN MIDDLE CHILDHOOD

Continued increases in size, strength, flexibility and coordination during the school years enable children to master the skills involved in sports. However, rather than learning entirely new skills – as occurs in early childhood – the task now is to refine and recombine existing skills to suit new challenges. Consider as an example the running, turning and kicking involved in playing soccer; or the running, throwing and catching required in netball. The jumping and chasing games and ball throwing and kicking done in early childhood are precursors of the advanced skills that are combined in specialised ways to play each sport. Younger children may be able to jump, hop, run, turn and throw a ball in isolation, but being able to combine these skills is a new achievement of the middle-childhood years. The ability to coordinate motor skills, such as in eye–hand and foot–hand coordination, is a significant development of middle childhood.

Motor-skill development in middle childhood

Children's playground games such as hopscotch, skipping, elastics, chasing, handball and jacks all contribute to the development of motor skills during the middle-childhood period (see Figure 2.6).

Swimming, riding bikes and scooters, and similar activities enjoyed by children in their leisure hours are also important. In addition to contributing to motor-skill development, links have been made between physical activity and *social outcomes*, such as the learning of social skills and reduced isolation; *emotional outcomes*, such as reduced depression, anxiety and stress, and increases in self-esteem and confidence; and *cognitive outcomes*, such as concentration, memory and learning (Commonwealth of Australia, Department of Health and Ageing, 2005). Two reviews of research found a positive relationship between physical activity and academic achievement (Singh et al., 2012) and academic skills and behaviours such as attention, memory and on-task behaviour (Centers for Disease Control and Prevention, 2010). Links have also been found between exercise and neuroplasticity, explained later in this chapter (Hötting & Röder, 2013).

FIGURE 2.6 Children's physical activity contributes to cognitive, social and emotional development.

Questions about the impact of screen-based leisure time on motor development

One of the concerns expressed about the amount of time children spend watching television or playing computer games is the time that these activities take away from more active pursuits. For example, the Australian Bureau of Statistics reported in 2012 that Australian children spent more of their leisure time watching television (including movies and DVDs) than in any other recreational activity. Adolph and Berger (2010) stated that sedentary activity is more likely to account for overweight and obesity rates than will overeating. However, research suggests that the relationship is not simple; De Jong et al., (2013) found that reduced sleep is more likely to account for relations between screen time and overweight than is reduction of physical activity. Melkevik et al. (2010) found that spending large amounts of time in screen-based sedentary behaviour was not necessarily linked to lower levels of physical activity; this depended on gender (with boys more likely to engage in screen-based pursuits *and* physical activity than girls) and on region, with differences across the 69 countries sampled in their study. Issues of technology use are discussed further in Chapter 12, but the findings presented above are a reminder that simple explanations should be viewed with caution. There are likely to be multiple environmental and personal factors that contribute to development in any domain, alongside developments in social, emotional and cognitive domains that influence motor development.

Declines in physical activity are attributed to other environmental factors as well as competition of screen time. The Australian Sports Commission (2004) reported screen time as a major competitor with physical activity for children's time, but also attributed the decline in physical activity to factors such as concerns for children's safety, modern street design, less play space, smaller home blocks, longer working hours of parents and a general disintegration of neighbourhood social networks, all of which restrict opportunities for free play.

The importance of physical education

Physical education forms an important part of school curricula in Australia and New Zealand, with the New Zealand Ministry of Education (2004) setting a priority on physical activity in the *National education goals*, and introducing the Play.sport project in 2016 to support schools and families to improve the quality of young people's experience in physical activity and sport through professional development and support for teachers, and sharing of sporting facilities. The Australian Government recommends at least one hour a day of moderate to vigorous physical activity for children and young people (Commonwealth of Australia, Department of Health, 2014). In addition, the Australian Sports Commission in 2015 initiated Sporting Schools, a program designed to engage sporting organisations across Australia, with a view to increasing children's participation in sport by delivering activities before, during and after school hours. The program is offered to Primary and Junior Secondary classes.

CourseMateExpress

Online resources
Go further: View the Physical Activity Guidelines via the link on this text's website.

PHYSICAL DEVELOPMENT IN ADOLESCENCE

During adolescence, physical growth resumes the rapid pace of growth in infancy. The hands, feet and legs are the first to increase in size, which sometimes results in a 'coltish' look and in clumsiness. The trunk of the body lengthens last, bringing adolescents to adult body proportions (Berk, 2012). These developments are accompanied by significant muscle growth, although this is greater in boys than in girls, for whom there is a 40 per cent increase in body fat. These sex differences result in the different body shapes of adulthood, with men generally leaner and more muscular than women.

Sex differences in adolescent development

Often, the terms **adolescence** and **puberty** are used synonymously, but they are not the same thing. The period of adolescence is usually associated with the teen years (ages 13 to 19) but may be defined as the period between childhood and adulthood. Thus, in Western societies, adolescence can stretch from 11 to 21 years and is typically defined in terms of age and social circumstances. Puberty, however, is defined by physical changes, specifically the physical and biological changes associated with sexual maturity. Puberty generally occurs during adolescence but may start some years earlier than the age of 13, particularly in girls in industrial societies. Puberty tends to be completed within four years; adolescence, however, may last from six to 10 years and tends to be longer in industrial societies, where young people are often engaged in education for long periods before they are truly independent of their parents (Cote & Allahar, 1996).

adolescence
The period between childhood and adulthood

puberty
The biological changes associated with sexual maturity

In girls, puberty is signalled by rapid increases in height and weight, which trigger the onset of 'menarche', or first menstruation. This is accompanied by other physical changes that are related to reproduction, including breast development (which precedes menarche), and the enlargement of the uterus and the appearance of pubic hair (which usually follow menarche).

In boys, sexual maturity starts with changes to the testes and scrotum, followed by the appearance of pubic hair and then growth of the penis. Increases in height generally occur later in boys' developmental patterns than in those of girls, which explains why girls may be taller than boys in the early years of high school. 'Semenarche' (or first ejaculation) commonly follows the height spurt in boys, just as menarche does in girls. Other changes associated with the later stages of puberty for boys include the growth of facial and body hair, and the deepening of the voice as the larynx lengthens. This can initially cause boys some embarrassment as the voice 'breaks', with sudden changes in pitch.

Connections among physical, cognitive and socioemotional development in adolescence

The dramatic physical changes of puberty are accompanied by social, cognitive and emotional changes. One of the most significant results of physical changes is a concern with body image. A feeling of 'not fitting' the new, taller body with its bigger hands and feet may bring self-consciousness for boys, while girls may become dissatisfied with their increased weight and body fat that do not match the 'ideal' body image promoted in the media. Recent studies, however, show that comparison with peers has a greater role than the media (Carey, Donaghue & Broderick, 2014), which may suggest social media's role in the process.

Body image issues and eating disorders in adolescence

Australian and New Zealand studies of body image and dieting behaviour have shown that dieting and dissatisfaction with body image are widespread, and are greater among girls than boys. The New Zealand Ministry of Health (2012) reported on a 2007 youth survey that showed just 36 per cent of girls and 44 per cent of boys were happy or very happy about their weight, while 48 per cent of these young people were trying to lose weight and 14 per cent were trying to gain weight. There were variations across different ethnic groups, with more Māori, Pasifika and Asian youth positive about their weight compared with European young people in the study. There were gender differences, too, with more girls reporting they were trying to lose weight and more boys trying to gain weight. In Mission Australia National Youth Survey's annual reports over the 9 years from 2009 to 2017, body image is listed among the top three concerns for young people (aged 15–19) surveyed, which has ongoing implications in relation to mental as well as physical health (Butterfly Foundation, 2017).

In some children, this widespread pattern develops into eating disorders such as compulsive eating disorder, anorexia and bulimia. If teachers or parents suspect a child of having an eating disorder, it is important that they consult an expert, as these illnesses are complex, difficult to treat and have potentially severe outcomes.

Puberty and coping with developmental change

The timing of puberty appears to affect how adolescents cope with developmental changes, as well as with others' reactions to these changes. Adolescents who mature 'on time' fare best. Early maturing girls are at greater risk for social anxiety, depression, substance use and deviant behaviour (Ge & Natsuaki, 2009), while boys can experience depression, anxiety and problematic behaviour from either early or late maturing (Negriff & Susman, 2011). A number of explanations have been given for these effects, including the possibility that with early maturation, girls may seek peers similar to themselves, exposing them to older peers and risky behaviours before they are emotionally ready to evaluate the risks (Stattin, Kerr & Skoog, 2011). Stattin, Kerr and Skoog reported that the context (such as school) can moderate this exposure to older peers.

In Australia, early maturing boys *and* girls demonstrated more negative emotional states, poorer peer relationships, and more school-related issues compared to their peers. However these differences disappeared with age, as peers started puberty, indicating that it is the experience of feeling out of step with the peer group that is problematic for early maturing adolescents (Warren & Yu, 2015). The link between physical and emotional development here is evident but complex: there is considerable scope for individual difference in outcomes depending on context, level of support and personality factors.

In this section we have looked at variation within groups of boys or girls. In the next section, we consider variations in physical development among groups. Box 2.2 summarises the developmental trends we have discussed, and links them to contributions made by brain and body development and children's behaviour. It then gives some suggestions for ways in which the teacher or parents can contribute to development at each stage.

BOX 2.2 IMPLICATIONS FOR EDUCATORS

CONTRIBUTING TO MOTOR DEVELOPMENT

	MOTOR DEVELOPMENTS	CONTRIBUTIONS OF BODY, BRAIN AND BEHAVIOUR	WHAT TEACHERS AND PARENTS CAN DO
Infancy 	Sitting independently Crawling Walking	*Body:* Changes in body proportion contribute to balance, stability and increased strength; greater muscle-to-fat ratio in legs and stronger back and hip muscles allow weight bearing. *Brain:* Increases in processing speed and efficiency allow infants to combine movements, and to control them. *Behaviour:* Exploration is both a motivation for and a consequence of greater mobility; practice contributes to strength, balance and visual–motor learning.	Encourage exploration, which motivates crawling, walking and reaching behaviour. Child-rearing routines influence motor development by providing opportunities to practise, by strengthening muscles and stability, and by facilitating visual–motor learning.
Early childhood	Fine motor skills Gross motor skills	*Body:* Longer arms and legs and greater muscle control contribute to smoother, more coordinated movement. *Brain:* Myelination leads to improved coordination of various regions of the brain, which is necessary for motor control. *Behaviour:* Constant activity contributes to skill and muscle development.	Provide opportunities for practising fine motor skills, such as manipulating pencils and scissors, zips, laces and buttons, and for use of gross motor skills, such as climbing, running, jumping, throwing and kicking balls.
Middle childhood	Combining skills Refinement of gross and fine motor skills	*Body:* There are increases in strength, agility and balance with continued growth in height and muscle mass. *Brain:* Development of executive function contributes to coordination of motor movements. *Behaviour:* Activity levels remain high; organised games played at school contribute to coordination and movement problem solving; common school activities such as handwriting practise fine motor skills.	Encourage physical activity, including team games. Fundamental movement skills can be explicitly taught to improve children's enjoyment of and skill in games.

>>

	MOTOR DEVELOPMENTS	CONTRIBUTIONS OF BODY, BRAIN AND BEHAVIOUR	WHAT TEACHERS AND PARENTS CAN DO
Adolescence	Increased strength and coordination of both fine and gross motor skills	*Body:* There is increased height and muscle mass, particularly in boys. *Brain:* Further development of executive function contributes to coordination and control of behaviour. *Behaviour:* Individual differences in motor skill are strengthened by young people's choices about involvement in physical activity.	Encourage involvement in physical activity, including vigorous intensity activities. Break up time spent sitting.

Sources: Adapted from Adolph and Berger (2010); Kopp (2011); McDevitt and Ormrod (2010)
Image sources: 1: © Spass/Shutterstock.com, 2: © Temych/Shutterstock.com, 3: Christopher Futcher/Getty Images, 4: Dotshock/Shutterstock

VARIATIONS IN PHYSICAL DEVELOPMENT

Individual differences in the rate of physical development and the timing of major milestones such as puberty occur between males and females, and across different social and cultural groups (see **Figure 2.7**). These differences attest to the combination of environmental and inherited factors involved in development.

Environmental influences

A number of areas of physical (and as you will see in later chapters, cognitive, social and emotional) development are influenced by environmental

Source: wavebreakmedia/Shutterstock

FIGURE 2.7 The timing of puberty varies from individual to individual.

factors. Some of these are associated with a child's development in the womb; for example, pregnant mothers' consumption of alcohol and tobacco (as well as less widely available drugs) is associated with abnormal physical and brain development (Berk, 2012). Other influences may be felt later in the child's life; for example, high levels of family conflict are associated with earlier onset of menarche (Manuck et al., 2011), while Whittle et al. (2014) reported from a longitudinal study that warm and supportive parenting influenced the development of adolescent brain structures that are associated with positive emotional and behavioural outcomes. Environment is a significant force throughout the course of development. We discuss some examples of areas of physical development in which the effect of environment is visible in this section.

Differences in the timing of puberty

Adolescent girls in industrial societies tend to experience menarche earlier than those living in countries with widespread poverty. As the onset of menarche is associated with increases in body fat, nutritional factors are likely to be responsible for this difference. In industrial societies, and in some developing nations, the age for menarche onset has declined steadily over the past century or more, probably as a result of improvements in nutrition and general health, although increased experience of stress is also likely to play a role (Bellis, Downing & Ashton, 2006).

How do we define early onset of puberty? Typically, girls commence puberty between 10–11 years, and boys between 11–12 years, with the range for healthy children extending two years either side of these averages (i.e. 8–13 years for girls, and 9–14 years for boys) (Mensah et al., 2013). In Australia, drawing on data from the Longitudinal Study of Australian Children (LSAC), one study found that experiencing puberty early (at 8 or 9 years) was uncommon, with relatively few children (4 per cent of boys, and 14 per cent of girls) showing any signs of puberty at this age. Most children (80 per cent of boys, and 96 per cent of girls) had shown some signs of puberty by 14 years (Warren & Yu, 2015). Warren & Yu also found that mothers' and fathers' age of puberty was correlated with children's timing of puberty, indicating that both genes and environment are likely to be involved in pubertal timing. Another study, also drawing on the LSAC data, found that socioeconomic disadvantage played a significant role in pubertal timing, with boys from low socioeconomic backgrounds four times more likely, and girls from these backgrounds twice as likely to experience puberty early (Sun, Mensah, Azzopardi, Patton & Wake, 2017).

Piekarski et al. (2017) suggested that the shift in the timing of puberty is of concern, as the onset of puberty may coincide with the closing of a stage of greater brain plasticity in childhood that is important for learning of key skills such as reading, writing and language. Shortening this period will also have effects, then, on learning; and given that earlier age of onset of menarche (and to some degree, also semenarche) is greater in lower socioeconomic groups, this may contribute to educational disadvantage.

Differences in growth rates

Differences in growth rates and eventual height also have been observed among people from different countries (Evelyth & Tanner, 1990). There may be genetic factors involved in these differences, but it is likely they are also related to diet and to health issues such as the prevalence of disease in particular countries. People from countries with widespread poverty tend to be smaller on average than those from industrialised nations such as Australia and New Zealand, although there is also variation within populations.

Development of children with physical disabilities

Some physical conditions, such as cerebral palsy, spina bifida, Down syndrome and muscular dystrophy, result in a different developmental path, and the acquisition of motor skills may be challenging for some students with specific physical disabilities. Nonetheless, you should not assume that a child with a physical disability also has an intellectual disability, nor that they do not need to develop their physical or motor skills. Supporting students with physical disabilities to participate in the classroom may involve making adjustments to the way in which you teach, the physical environment, equipment and tasks. For example, a student in a wheelchair may be able to participate in a long-jump exercise by using their arms to propel the chair forward, a parallel task to the spring another child must make using their legs. Chapter 10 deals in detail with the inclusion of children with special needs.

Sex and gender differences

You have probably heard it said that girls mature faster than boys. Physically, this tends to be true, with girls reaching some milestones several weeks ahead of their male counterparts during infancy, and the gap widening through childhood so that girls may reach the end of puberty as much as two years ahead of boys (Tanner, 1990). Boys are generally taller and heavier than girls throughout childhood, with the exception of a brief time in early puberty (around 11 years old) when girls go through the pubertal growth spurt about two years ahead of boys.

Differences such as this, which have a strong biological basis, are generally referred to as sex differences. Other differences between boys and girls have a mixture of biological and social origins. The term 'gender difference' is generally used to refer to these kinds of differences. As it is often difficult to determine whether a difference we observe has a biological or social origin, in this book, we tend to use the term 'gender difference'. Chapter 11 discusses gender differences in more detail.

CourseMateExpress

Online resources
Go further: See
resources for
developing children's
fundamental
movement skills.

CourseMateExpress

Online resources
Watch a **video** of an
adolescent girl talking
about why her friends
go to the gym.

Gender differences in motor-skill development are increasingly evident from early childhood through to adolescence. In early-childhood tests of motor ability, girls perform better at locomotor skills and stability such as are used in balance tasks, while boys have better manipulative skills such as are used in hitting and ball skills (Iivonen & Saakslahti, 2014). This difference persists through childhood, with boys proving more proficient at object-control skills and girls at locomotor skills in grades 4 and 5 in one Australian study. One study also found that children proficient at object control were more likely to be involved in physical activity as adolescents (Barnett et al., 2009). This finding is consistent with trends reviewed by Iivonen and Saakslahti. Later, boys tend to be better at sports that involve force and power, while girls are more skilled in fine motor tasks and activities that require agility (Malina, 1998). These differences are partly a result of boys' greater muscle mass and heart and lung capacity, but can also be attributed to the societal roles apportioned to males and females. Boys tend to be encouraged to play ball sports, while girls are steered towards dance and gymnastics. While a five-year-old boy might be given a football or basketball as a gift, a girl is more likely to receive (and to ask for) a skipping rope. In addition, boys tend to be admired by peers for sporting prowess, something that tends to be far less important to girls and that is probably related to the relative significance placed by the media and society on men's versus women's sport.

Gender differences in physical activity and exercise involvement are more widespread than this, however. The 2007 Australian National Children's Nutrition and Physical Activity Survey (Australian Government, 2008) found that girls spent less time than boys in vigorous physical activity, though this mainly related to the amount of time spent playing sport (see Figure 2.8), and a 2016 report of an Australian longitudinal study (the LOOK study) found similar gender differences in children's activity patterns (Telford, Telford, Olive, Cochrane & Davey, 2016). Given the links between physical activity and

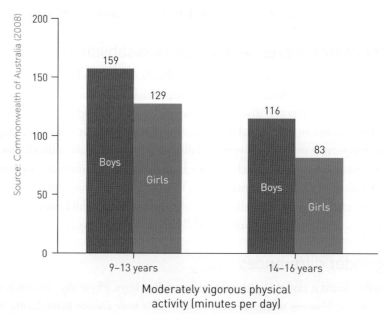

Participation in sport is the main source of the difference.

FIGURE 2.8 Comparing boys' and girls' physical activity.

learning discussed earlier, as well as the demonstrated relationship between physical exercise and the risk of disease, these differences are of widespread concern, and schools have sought to address students' physical activity levels. However, Telford et al. (2013) reported from the LOOK longitudinal study that physical activity levels in Primary school aged children tended to build up during the week, when children are at school, and then drop over the weekend. Percentages of children meeting international guidelines for physical activity on Sundays were just 21 per cent for boys and 18 per cent for girls, these figures dropping to 16 per cent of boys and 10 per cent of girls engaged in the recommended levels of moderately vigorous physical activity. This suggests that parents and community also need to be involved in supporting physical activity. Iivonen and Saakslahti (2014) and Barnett et al. (2009) – cited above – argued that developing girls' object-control skills in early and middle childhood is an important part of the solution.

The effects of environment on physical development, as well as connections observed between physical development and developments in cognition and emotion suggest that opportunities for a range of physical activities should form part of schooling. Box 2.3 summarises some of the principles schools can consider in supporting students' physical development.

BOX 2.3 IMPLICATIONS FOR EDUCATORS

PHYSICAL DEVELOPMENT IN SCHOOLS

- Motor-skill development is an important part of the curriculum in preschool education in Australia and New Zealand, and health and physical education is a Learning Area in the Educational Goals for Young Australians (MCEETYA, 2008) and in the New Zealand Curriculum (New Zealand Ministry of Education, 2007).
- The New Zealand Curriculum adopts the Māori philosophy of health and wellbeing, or *Hauora*, which recognises the interconnection of *taha tinana* (physical wellbeing) with *taha hinengaro* (mental and emotional wellbeing), *taha whanao* (social wellbeing) and *taha wairua* (spiritual wellbeing).
- Physical exercise can contribute to academic learning through motivation as well as cognitive skills such as attention and memory.
- Children with physical disabilities may take a different developmental path, but they still require opportunities to participate in physical activity at school. Adjustments can be made to tasks, equipment and the environment to enable them to participate alongside their peers.
- Involvement in physical activity on weekends, and support of parents and community for this is also important.

BRAIN DEVELOPMENT

One dimension of physical development that is particularly important in the learning and teaching processes is brain development. The brain directs the course of overall development and responds to environmental stimuli to promote its own growth. In this section we consider how the brain's physical structures develop, and how this development is related to visible changes in thinking and behaviour.

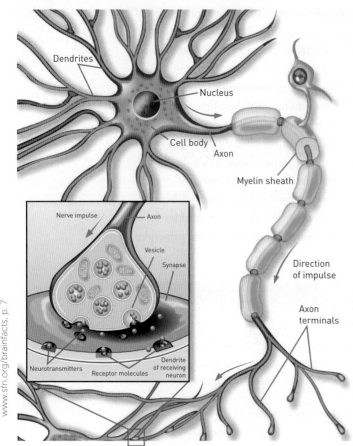

Source: *Brain facts: A primer on the brain and nervous system*, © 2008 Society for Neuroscience, www.sfn.org/brainfacts, p. 7

FIGURE 2.9 The neuron receives messages through its dendrites and passes them along its axons and across the synapse to other cells.

neuron
A nerve cell

axon
The long 'arm' of a neuron that carries messages to other cells by means of electrical impulses

dendrites
Branch-like protrusions from a neuron that receive messages from other cells

synapse
The gap between the axon and dendrites of two neurons

neurotransmitter
A chemical substance that carries messages across the synapse between neurons

THE BRAIN'S PHYSICAL STRUCTURES

The development of the brain begins soon after conception. **Neurons** or nerve cells develop and are responsible for storing and transmitting messages throughout the brain system. As the embryo grows, neuron proliferation results in between 100 and 200 billion neurons at birth; most of the neurons it will need to grow and develop.

Information is transmitted between neurons via a long arm-like projection known as an **axon**. When a neuron is activated or 'fired', an electrical impulse travels along the axon and crosses a gap or **synapse** between it and the adjacent neuron, by means of a chemical **neurotransmitter**. The synapse thus forms a junction between neurons. The branch-like **dendrites** of the neighbouring neuron receive the message (see Figure 2.9).

Over time, neurons develop in size and complexity, growing axon branches and dendrites that connect to other cells. More synapses are formed as thousands of neurons connect to each other, organised into networks that interact with other networks. A process of **myelination** also occurs, in which the axon is insulated in a fatty sheath that improves the speed of transmission across the neural networks by up to 100 times.

The developing brain produces many more neurons and synapses than are eventually used or needed. During the first two years, an estimated million or more synapses are formed every second (Center on the Developing Child, 2016). Some neurons die off naturally, and unused or unnecessary synapses are pruned. The adult brain contains only about half the number of neurons generated during the developmental phase. It is believed that this pruning enables faster and more efficient communication between the remaining cells, and allows new connections to develop.

The process of the brain changing and adapting itself is known as **brain plasticity**. This is a relatively new concept; it was once thought that 'hard wiring' occurred relatively early in life. Although there seem to be 'optimal' periods of brain development, such as in early childhood, the brain retains its capacity for change throughout life.

Different forms of brain plasticity enable the brain to develop or recover certain functions. Developmental processes such as synapse pruning are one form. Learning can also be considered as a form of plasticity, as our neural networks alter to accommodate new information or skills. Changes such as a change in eyesight or a traumatic brain injury may lead to another form of plasticity (Vanderbilt Kennedy Center, 2012). Brain plasticity has been observed in adults who have had a major neurological injury such as a stroke, and then recovered some function by remapping the brain through activation of the motor cortex (Johansson, 2011). However, with increasingly established patterns of connection and specialisation of the brain during development, plasticity requires increasing effort with age (Center on the Developing Child, 2016).

INTERNAL STRUCTURES OF THE BRAIN

The brain is made up of both internal and external structures. It is generally the 'grey matter' of the external structures that we are most familiar with in images of the brain; however, the internal structures of the brain are just as important.

The internal structures of the brain are complex systems that control and activate some of the most basic functions of human life (see Figure 2.10). The hindbrain section, also known as the brain stem, contains structures such as the pons and the medulla, which control and regulate our breathing and heart rate; it also contains the cerebellum, which helps us control our movements as well as thinking processes that require careful timing and coordination. The centre of the brain also acts as a relay station to other parts of the brain. In the midbrain area are very small structures that take in sensory information (sight, hearing, smell, taste, touch) and relay this information to other parts of the brain. Higher in the central part of the brain is an area known as the limbic system, which is critical in the regulation and control of automatic drives and responses in the body, as well as emotional responses and memory. In this system, the hypothalamus helps relay information coming from the autonomic nervous system of the body, which helps regulate automatic and unconscious processes such as our sleep patterns, hunger, the activation of the pituitary gland and stress responses such as our classic 'flight or fight' response to stress. The hippocampus is believed to be very important in the memory of recent events we have experienced by helping us organise the 'what', 'where' and 'when' of these episodic memories (Society for Neuroscience, 2008). The amygdala is associated with emotional memories and learning, and is particularly associated with our fear responses. Many of these internal structures are linked and connected to the outer regions of the brain.

myelination
The process by which axons are insulated with a sheath of fatty cells, which improves the speed and efficiency of message transmission

brain plasticity
The capacity of the brain to change and develop new neural connections throughout the lifespan

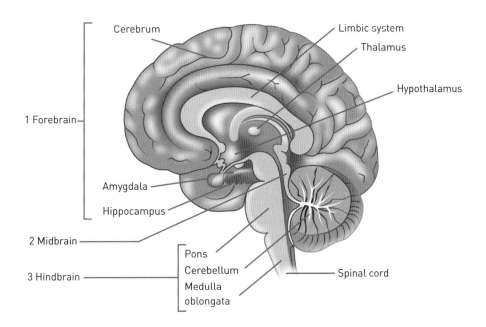

Source: *Brain facts: A primer on the brain and nervous system*, © 2008 Society for Neuroscience, www.sfn.org/brainfacts, p. 5

FIGURE 2.10 The internal brain structures

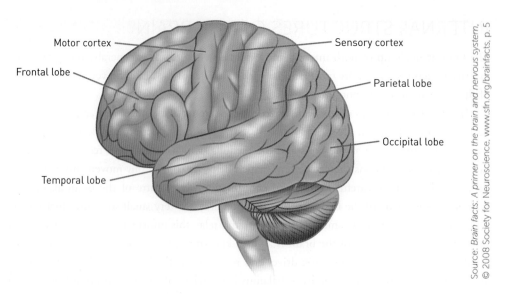

Source: *Brain facts: A primer on the brain and nervous system,* © 2008 Society for Neuroscience, www.sfn.org/brainfacts, p. 5

FIGURE 2.11 The cerebral cortex. Particular functions are localised in specific areas of the cortex; most skills involve the coordination of messages from a number of areas.

The cerebral cortex

cerebral cortex
The outer layer of the brain, which is responsible for human intelligence

The **cerebral cortex** is the largest and last area of the brain to complete development and is considered the most important contributor to children's cognitive functioning (see Figure 2.11). The cerebral cortex is made up of two hemispheres that are linked by an internal brain structure known as the corpus callosum. In this way the inner structures of the brain can communicate with the outer structures of the cerebral cortex.

The left and right brain, and lateralisation

lateralisation
The specialisation of functions in the two hemispheres of the cerebral cortex

Different regions or lobes of the cerebral cortex are associated with specific bodily functions and abilities; for example, the motor cortex is associated with physical movement, and the visual cortex is associated with vision. One of the most important specialisations of the brain is known as **lateralisation,** in which the two hemispheres of the brain specialise in different functions. For example, the right side of the brain controls the left side of the body and the left side of the brain controls the right side of the body. The right hemisphere also processes visual–spatial information, non-speech-related sounds such as music, and recognition of faces and facial expressions. The left region of the brain is associated with the processing of spoken language and some logical thought processes. However, the lateralisation of the brain is strongly supported by *connectedness* between the parts of the brain. Not all processes function independently in one side or other of the brain; emotion, for example, is processed by the whole brain. The internal structures of the brain are critical for relaying emotional signals to the outer regions of the brain where, broadly speaking, the right side processes negative emotions and the left side positive emotions. Language is also processed in both hemispheres of the brain. It was once thought that all language abilities resided in the left brain, but it is now understood that recognition of spoken words and sounds occurs in both sides of the brain, and it is speech production that is strongly controlled in the left part of the brain. Damage in one of two critical areas in the left part of the brain, known as Broca's area and Wernicke's area, can produce specific deficits in speech output (Society for Neuroscience, 2008).

The degree to which our brains are specialised in these ways varies between individuals; for example, lateralisation is believed to be influenced by genetics or family similarities – it may be less strong in females than males, while left-handed people may also have less lateralisation than right-handed people. Studies of the brains of mathematicians show use of centres from both sides of the brain when solving problems and doing simple arithmetic (Dehaene, Molko, Cohen & Wilson, 2004). In fact, most activities involve coordination of messages from both sides of the brain (see Box 2.4).

BOX 2.4 IMPLICATIONS FOR EDUCATORS

THINKING CRITICALLY ABOUT BRAIN RESEARCH AND THE CLASSROOM

Research into brain development has been prolific over the past two decades, but applying this new understanding of how the brain works to classrooms is still in its infancy. Teachers around the world report that they are being bombarded by requests to join 'brain-based learning' workshops or attend seminars on 'brain-based teaching'. Although we are learning more about the structure of the brain, how this relates to its function in learning and teaching is still being examined and is very difficult to research. A number of research centres worldwide have begun to investigate the applications of brain research to education.

Goswami (2004) reviewed links between neuroscience and education, and suggested some areas for useful application, such as in understanding reading acquisition and dyslexia, or in training children with autism to understand emotion. However, be cautious of recommendations that are billed as being 'brain-based' (Fischer, 2004). Sometimes this label is used to describe educational applications that are based on educational psychology generally (for example, Caine & Caine, 1991), but others have claimed direct applications of neurological research to learning and teaching strategies that are not supported by research evidence. These are sometimes called 'neuromyths' (OECD, 2007) and some examples are included below, with relevant research evidence.

Examples of neuromyths

NEUROMYTH	RESEARCH EVIDENCE
Some educators have used brain lateralisation to explain children's academic strengths and weaknesses, describing students as being 'left-brained' or 'right-brained' (for example, McCarthy & McCarthy, 2005). Others have used this as a basis for programs that seek to tap into the skills of one or other side of the brain (for example, Edwards, 1981).	Bruer (1999) warned against such simplistic applications of brain-lateralisation research, pointing out that most skills involve the coordination of messages from both sides of the brain. Healthy brains rely on the two hemispheres working together for most tasks.
There are sometimes suggestions that males and females learn differently, based on differences in the structure of male and female brains.	Fine (2010, 2013) drew on neuroscience research to show that there are in fact few reliable differences between male and female brains (differences within each group are larger than differences between them), and that those differences that do exist are not relevant to learning or education. Chapter 11 discusses gender differences in more detail.
Because of the idea of 'critical periods' of brain growth and the concept of synapse proliferation, some programs targeted at teachers have suggested special teaching interventions that promote 'neuroplasticity'.	In fact, any teaching intervention or life experience that leads to a change in behaviour and knowledge will be 'remapped' in the brain – neuroplasticity occurs naturally, without the need for costly programs.
Knowledge of the importance of early experience to brain development has sometimes been taken up with 'enrichment' programs that claim to accelerate cognitive development by providing experiences early.	Nagel (2013) spelled out a number of dangers in this approach, including the importance of the in-built developmental timetable of the brain, which supports learning at particular periods when the brain is 'ready' for them; this built-in timetable also ensures that cognitive and emotional development occur in tandem, and support one another.

NEUROMYTH	RESEARCH EVIDENCE
Brain development is rapid in the early years of life, and it is sometimes assumed that the brain (or intelligence, or personality) you have in adulthood is set, with no further changes likely to occur.	There may be sensitive periods during which the development of certain abilities is optimised, but these do not prevent learning from occurring later. For example, London taxi drivers who are particularly good at navigating around the city have been found to have enlarged hippocampi (the area responsible for spatial memory), suggesting they have developed synapses in this area in response to their task (Maguire et al., 2000, as cited in Goswami, 2004).

ACTIVITIES

What 'neuromyths' have you heard of in the classroom? Use the accompanying CourseMate Express link to visit centres for research in the application of neurological research to learning and teaching, and discover some of the evidence-based findings.

CourseMateExpress

Online resources
Go further: Visit centres for research into the brain and learning via the link on this text's website.

How are these processes reflected in the developments observed in children? As we discussed earlier in this chapter, one of the patterns of development is an increase in skill complexity and coordination that relates, in part, to the increase in networks of nerve pathways. In this section we will continue to explore developmental changes that occur in infancy, early childhood, middle childhood and adolescence. We also look at important factors that may influence brain development.

BRAIN DEVELOPMENT IN INFANCY

The infant brain experiences rapid growth and neuron proliferation. All experiences, especially sensory experiences, are important in the growth and development of the infant brain. As mentioned previously, in the first year of a child's life, the brain produces many more synapses than it will need; thus, the infant brain is readied for experience. Synapses that are not used – that is, do not receive stimulation – are pruned, while those that are used through environmental stimulation are strengthened.

One of the most well-known concepts in the development of the infant brain is the notion of a 'sensitive period' or 'critical period' of development. From late in pregnancy to two years of age, brain development occurs at a great pace, and high-quality nutrients and an adequate 'energy supply' are important for the developing brain. However, it is the quality of the life experiences of the infant that are believed to be the foundation stones of a healthy future brain. As such, this critical period of development requires careful attention to factors that influence brain development and growth.

attachment
The strong emotional bond established between infant and caregiver

In this period of life, the warmth and security of relationships with primary care givers, known as the **attachment** relationship (see Box 2.5), is believed to be critical for the development of the social and emotional processing centres of the brain (Center on the Developing Child, 2015). Brain-imaging studies support the idea that brain development in infancy is greatly dependent on positive experiences and interactions with others, particularly primary caregivers. Brain imaging has been used to study the responses of mothers and infants when looking at each other's smiling faces. The brain images show that important social information-processing areas of the brain are activated when a very young infant sees an image of his mother's smile; similarly, the same region of the mother's brain is activated when she sees a smiling image of her child. In this way, critical neural networks are developed in the child's brain, and the attachment relationship between parent and child is strengthened.

The infant brain readily absorbs sensory information but is also active in sorting and understanding this information. This is especially clear in the area of understanding language. The newborn brain not only appears to recognise the native language but shows different brain activation in response to the familiar native language compared with an unfamiliar language (May, Byers-Heinlein, Gervain & Werker, 2011). The infant brain shows discrimination of features of language such as melodic rhythm and stress, and babies as young as four months of age appear to show language-specific neural representations of word forms (Friederici, Friedrich & Christophe, 2007).

The quality of early life experiences is critical to healthy brain development in infancy and early childhood. As explained in the following sections, there is a significant difference between the brain development of an infant raised in a normal, caring environment and that of a child who has early experiences of abuse or neglect (see Figure 2.12).

BRAIN DEVELOPMENT IN EARLY CHILDHOOD

The period of early childhood sees rapid growth and development in areas of the brain that allow the child greater self-control. In particular, a growth spurt in the frontal region of the brain corresponds to the development of executive function skills, such as the ability to follow rules and directions and control impulses. For example, by three years of age most children can complete tasks that require them to follow two rules simultaneously, and by five years of age children can shift their attention from one rule to another to accommodate different situations. Young children can inhibit and control some impulses, allowing them to complete more complex tasks and follow instructions from caregivers, but they still need a lot of practice, positive experience and support from adults to reinforce these new skills in the brain (Center on the Developing Child, 2011). (You will see more on executive function in Chapter 3.)

Stress and executive functioning

This frontal area of the brain, the prefrontal cortex, also develops connections to other parts of the inner brain, including those structures that help us control our response to threat or stress (our 'flight or fight' systems). As such, the growth of executive functioning abilities requires a range of early-childhood experiences that allow executive skills to be tested within a caring and regulated environment.

A number of studies have shown that very dysfunctional (unregulated) and stressful early-life environments lead to a type of toxic stress that actually inhibits executive functioning. As an adult you might recognise such an effect when you have experienced the feeling of not being able to 'think straight' or remember critical actions when you have been faced with extreme stress or anxiety. In such situations the body releases chemicals, such as cortisol (also known as hydrocortisone), in response to the stress; these chemicals activate inner regions of the brain that send us into 'fight or flight' mode, inhibiting clear functioning of the prefrontal cortex. In the developing brain of the child, repeated and prolonged exposure to the chemicals released under stress seems to impair the neuronal 'architecture', leading to less-well-developed executive functioning systems. As an adult, you have the capacity to calm yourself or use your executive function to think of a response, but the young child's brain is still developing this ability (Center on the Developing Child, 2011, p. 7).

The impact of trauma and neglect on the developing brain

The brains of children who have suffered extreme neglect or abuse (physical, emotional or sexual) in early childhood appear to show stunted or reduced growth patterns (see Figure 2.12). The cerebral cortex and limbic areas of the brain appear to be significantly reduced in size (Perry & Pollard, 1997), and subsequent developmental problems in diverse areas of functioning have been noted (Kreppner et al., 2007).

Studies of Romanian orphans have shown that pervasive developmental problems persist for children whose neglect extends beyond the first six months of life. Due to brain plasticity, children whose circumstances improve within the first six months of life show greater brain recovery. The prolonged

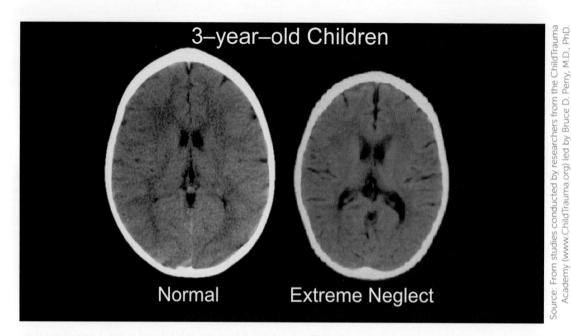

Source: From studies conducted by researchers from the ChildTrauma Academy (www.ChildTrauma.org) led by Bruce D. Perry, M.D., PhD.

FIGURE 2.12 These images illustrate the negative impact of neglect on the developing brain. The CT scans are from three year olds – one healthy, on the left, with an FOC (head circumference) in the 50th percentile, and on the right is a child who experienced total global neglect (including sensory deprivation). The image on the right is from a series of 122 severely neglected children of many ages. In general, the brains of the neglected children were significantly smaller and demonstrated various forms of abnormal development (e.g. cortical under-development and enlarged ventricles).

nature of neglect beyond six months of age seems to be related to psychological deprivation rather than nutritional deprivation. However, these studies have also shown the clear capacity of the human brain to improve and adapt beyond the early childhood years, enabling some improvement in cognitive function to occur into the middle childhood years for children with the greatest level of cognitive impairment at age six (Kreppner et al., 2007).

BRAIN DEVELOPMENT IN MIDDLE CHILDHOOD

The heavy focus in research and the media on the importance of brain development in early life has led to some concern that we may be neglecting or overlooking the fact that the brain continues to grow and develop throughout childhood and into adulthood (Cashmore, 2001). By the end of early childhood, the brain has reached 90 per cent of its adult size, and thus the main type of change seen in middle childhood relates to continued growth of the cerebral cortex, further synapse pruning, and myelination of more extended connections across regions of the brain.

In the middle years of childhood, executive function skills continue to improve as networks and interconnections between parts of the brain grow stronger. These connections, visible as the 'white matter' in neuroimaging studies, show thicker neural connections starting to grow across and between different areas of the brain, hence connecting multiple areas of functioning together. The learning experience of middle childhood is about reinforcing and building upon these new connections. This is clearly visible in the classroom as children become much better at rule-based understanding, thinking about diverse topics and verbally expressing their ideas with greater confidence and clarity.

Although the amount of energy consumed by the brain seems to decline in middle childhood, indicating a slowing down of synapse proliferation, certain areas of the brain show continued energy consumption and activity. In particular, certain structures in the limbic system continue to grow, and these systems aid in the integration of emotional and bodily signals so that bodily awareness of pain or recognition of threats to the body is enhanced (Campbell, 2011). These areas of the limbic system are also implicated in the distress a child feels when experiencing social exclusion in middle childhood. This connection has been established in studies using a virtual game of 'Cyberball' along with brain imaging. During the game, other players deliberately bypass the child participant by throwing the ball to other players, leading to a feeling in the child of mild distress and rejection that can be measured in images of the brain. These studies have shown that the neural experience of the distress of rejection is very similar to that of physical pain and sensation (Crowley, Wu, Molfese & Mayes, 2010). This provides vital evidence that an increase in bullying and social ostracism in the middle childhood years (for more detail, see Chapter 4) corresponds with the emerging capacity of the brain to understand and respond to this 'pain'.

Developmental differences in middle childhood

Middle childhood is also the period in which many developmental differences in functioning between children are observed. Conditions such as attention deficit hyperactivity disorder (ADHD) and other learning problems associated with a lack of focus or ability to 'sit still' are observed by teachers. Some studies have linked the presence of ADHD with delays in the development of certain regions of the central cortex. Although the mechanisms of brain development or difference in ADHD are much debated, some researchers have found that slower maturation of the prefrontal cortex during middle childhood may explain some of the notable differences in executive functioning for children with this condition (Shaw et al., 2007), particularly impulse control, and maintenance and shifting of attention.

Brain development in middle childhood is the expression and refinement of many of the processes started in early childhood. Neural networks are faster and the regions of the cerebral cortex continue to grow, culminating in the final stages of growth in adolescence.

BRAIN DEVELOPMENT IN ADOLESCENCE

The adolescent brain enters a new 'critical period' of development during which two processes appear to underpin the emergence of the adult brain. First, as the grey matter of the cerebral cortex completes development, a process of synapse pruning begins, resulting in an adult brain that is actually *less* dense in grey matter than the childhood brain. This process of pruning is believed to make communication between different regions of the cerebral cortex extremely efficient. A second process also speeds up communication between different areas of the brain. An increase in myelination results in stronger and longer neural connections (or white matter) that extend to different parts of the brain.

One of the most interesting findings of the past decade relates to the final stages of growth of the cerebral cortex, and particularly to the finding that the prefrontal cortex is the final area of the brain to complete growth at some time in the third decade of life, possibly as late as 25 years of age (Hickie & Whitwell, 2009). It is also known that male brains complete this final stage of development slightly later than female brains, probably due to the slightly later onset of puberty in males.

Adolescent brain development and risky behaviours

The continuing maturation of the adolescent brain has been linked to the slow and gradual emergence of frontal-lobe control of behaviour, and has been used as an explanation for impulsive and risky behaviour during adolescence (Romer, 2010). If you reflect upon the importance of the prefrontal cortex for executive functioning, as discussed in earlier sections, you will understand that the slow development of this part of the brain means that even adolescents still have limitations in their thinking and reasoning skills. Could the slow development of the prefrontal cortex make the adolescent particularly prone to impulsive or risky behaviours?

A number of researchers have adopted a 'brain-maturation' explanation of adolescent risk-taking behaviour (Casey, Getz & Galvan, 2008). This explanation proposes that the 'risky' adolescent brain may be caused by different rates of development of two key areas of the brain. First, activation of certain areas of the brain known as the 'reward' circuits occurs relatively early in the adolescent brain. These circuits may encourage the adolescent towards novel and sensation-seeking activities. These activities may be of the kind that provide instant reward or gratification to the individual (for example, driving very fast or sexual activities). Second, the prefrontal cortex of the adolescent brain develops more slowly and is not yet mature enough to help the adolescent handle these risky situations (Romer, 2010). A more mature and adult-like prefrontal cortex is what enables us to step back and carefully assess a situation, engage in forward thinking, and plan or prepare for likely outcomes. Adolescents who engage in sensation-seeking or rewarding behaviours may often say to adults 'Oh, I didn't think of that!' when confronted with the outcome of their behaviour. The brain-maturation perspective suggests that the adolescent is not just making an excuse but has a real problem in connecting sensational activities to risky outcomes.

Another view of risk-taking in adolescence

However, other neurological research has challenged this model of adolescent brain development (Romer, Reyna & Satterthwaite, 2017). Romer et al. identify two types of risk taking in adolescence. One of these is unhealthy, and associated with low impulse control – an indicator of weak executive function. However, this pattern of risk taking (and the negative outcomes that result from it such as drug dependence, fatal car accidents, sexually transmitted disease, and depression and suicide) is limited to a fairly small group of adolescents, and is seen to emerge before adolescence, and to extend into early adulthood for this group (Bjork & Pardini, 2015). In view of our discussion earlier of the role of early-life experiences in shaping and setting up the foundations of a healthy future brain, it is possible that these patterns of behaviour owe their emergence to other factors than an imbalance in the development of regions of the brain in adolescence. For example, early-life exposure to toxic stress has been linked to several negative outcomes in adolescence, including suicide, drug use and development of addictions (Shonkoff et al., 2012). In fact, research suggests that the majority of adolescents show good impulse control from early adolescence (Humphrey & Dumontheil, 2016).

Another pattern of risk taking is based on sensation seeking and is adaptive, enabling adolescents to explore and to learn from experience in important ways that contribute to their development towards adulthood. When this kind of risk taking is paired with good executive function (impulse control), as it is for the majority of adolescents, it is associated with the weighing up of risk and reward, and with learning from experience (Romer et al., 2017). Hence adolescents may explore drug taking or sexual activity within what they judge to be safe limits, but are likely to learn from their experiences, and to benefit from public education campaigns about their dangers. What happens with development in adolescence, then, is the gaining of wisdom; an increasing ability to judge between reasonable and unreasonable risks.

The role of the parent and school when approaching risk

There is clearly a role here for parents and schools to engage in discussions with adolescents around situations of possible risk, whether this be driving, using social media, sexual activity, or drugs and alcohol. Just as with other stages of brain development we have studied, the role of experience

Source: Image courtesy NSW Government

FIGURE 2.13 Campaigns such as this help adolescents to make good judgements about reasonable risk.

and nurturing guidance is likely to be critical for the healthy maturation of the adolescent brain, as it was for the early-childhood brain. Learning to take risks in 'safe' and regulated environments may be one such solution, and graduated licensing schemes are an example of experiential learning that has significantly reduced adolescent crash rates and injuries (Romer, 2010).

The impact of harmful substances on the adolescent brain

The continuing plasticity and growth of the brain into young adulthood also raises significant concerns about protecting the brain from harmful substances for as long as possible. Alcohol and cannabis use during this vital period of brain development are believed to affect parts of the brain that are still developing. Studies of the cognitive function of teenage drinkers show deficiencies in executive functions such as memory, attention, future planning and abstract reasoning (Hickie & Whitwell, 2009), while cannabis users show similar difficulties with executive function tasks, and these difficulties remain even after abstinence of four weeks (Meruelo, Castro & Cota, 2017). Reduced brain volume in a number of areas that results from heavy drinking or regular cannabis use is likely to contribute to these deficiencies (Meruelo et al., 2017). Memory deficits in teenage drinkers are likely to be associated with a shrunken or underdeveloped hippocampus; the hippocampus is very important in the formation of memories. Executive functioning skills may be generally impaired because the prefrontal cortex region is also shrunken and reduced in size. Impulsive or risky patterns of longer-term behaviour may be established because of damage to these regions of the growing brain (Hickie & Whitwell, 2009). Further damage to the brain is likely to result when adolescents injure themselves as a result of drinking or other impulsive behaviours. Due to the 'critical period' of brain development, the adolescent brain is especially vulnerable to injuries that tend to result in much more severe damage to brain architecture and a lesser chance of a full recovery than might have occurred earlier in life (Hickie & Whitwell, 2009).

Despite these serious concerns about risky or impulsive behaviours during adolescence, it is important to remember that the adolescent brain is indeed developing and making significant advances that are very important for learning in the classroom and life in general. Executive function skills in shifting and maintaining attention improve. Memory skills improve, and the adolescent has a greater capacity to hold something in mind while they do another task or try to solve another part of the problem; for example, the adolescent who is learning to drive learns to be flexible in shifting attention from the primary task of driving to observing road signs. Social reasoning and perceiving emotional signals and cues also improves, leading to the deepening and greater intensity of adolescent friendships and other relationships (see more on social development in Chapter 4). It is also important to remember that many adolescents achieve incredible feats of deep intellectual thought (such as students who accelerate into university at young ages) and great displays of empathy and community awareness (such as adolescents who volunteer in their communities and abroad), and some show considerable self-control even while undertaking extremely risky pastimes.

THINK ABOUT

- What changes in behaviour would you see in the classroom from early childhood to adolescence as a result of brain development?
- What activities or supports could you offer as a teacher during each of the stages?

ADVERSITY, RISK AND RESILIENCE IN DEVELOPMENT

Some children experience adversity which can significantly affect development through stress, or through poor responsiveness from key family members as a result of their circumstances. As we have seen, stress can have significant effects on brain development, and just as we saw in physical development, and will

FIGURE 2.14 Parents' interactions with infants play a vital role in developing essential skills that support resilience as well as social, emotional, cognitive and language skills.

see again when we discuss language development, the responsiveness of a parent or carer to the child is a vital input in the child's developing brain (see Figure 2.14). This responsiveness influences a multiplicity of domains: social, emotional, and cognitive as well as neurological (Center on the Developing Child, 2016). Family stress can influence parents' ability to respond to their children, and hence influences the child's development in multiple ways.

When vulnerable children show healthy adjustment despite these risks, we call it **resilience**. It is important to note that resilience is not a character trait. Rather, resilience is the outcome of a process that is influenced by the complex interaction of characteristics of the family, the community, and the

BOX 2.5 RESEARCH LINKS
ATTACHMENT AND DEVELOPMENT

Attachment illustrates the important role of relationships in human development, as well as how individual characteristics and environment interact in the process of development. This close emotional bond between infant and caregiver is influenced by the interaction of parents' sensitivity and responsiveness with children's temperament and dispositions. Proposed by Bowlby (1969, 1973) as an evolutionary mechanism by which survival is ensured through children staying close to their parents, and those parents nurturing and protecting them, it is evident in infants using parents as a safe haven and a secure base from which to explore the world. Bowlby's theory proposed that attachment arises from parents' interactions with their infant over time (and particularly in the first two years of life), and that the quality of attachment influences personality in later life (Sroufe, 2005).

Mary Ainsworth and colleagues (1970, 1978) developed a means of evaluating the quality of attachment between an infant and his/her parent, called the Strange Situation, in which a one-year-old infant is observed in a series of three-minute combinations with their parent, a stranger, parent and stranger, and alone. Children's behaviour is recorded in terms of seeking and maintaining proximity and contact with the caregiver, exploratory and search behaviours, and displays of emotion. Ainsworth and her colleagues were able to identify three patterns of attachment: secure, avoidant, and resistant (Ainsworth & Bell, 1970), with a fourth pattern, of disorganised attachment, identified later (Main & Solomon, 1990).

1   *Securely attached* infants actively explored the environment while their mother was there, even moving out of her sight, but became distressed and stopped exploring when she left. They were readily comforted on her return to the room. These children were friendly to the stranger in the room when the mother was there, but avoided her once the mother had left. Approximately 70 per cent of infants showed secure attachment.
2   *Resistant* infants were clingy when the mother was in the room, and reluctant to explore. They became extremely distressed when the mother left, showing fear of the stranger, and were not easily comforted on the mother's return, even pushing her away. Fifteen per cent of infants were characterised as resistant.
3   *Avoidant* infants did not show distress when the mother left, and little interest on her return to the room. They were not concerned by the stranger's presence, whether or not

>>

individual over the lifespan (Luthar, Crossman & Small, 2015). It can therefore change over time with varying experiences and conditions, be different for different situations, and will vary for different children.

resilience
Positive adjustment despite the experience of significant risk or adversity

Family contributors to resilience

The foundations for resilience are established early. Responsive and supportive parenting helps to build brain networks in infancy that support resilience later in life. This can be as simple as a parent playing peekaboo with their child, or looking and smiling in response to the infant's looks and smiles (Center on the Developing Child, 2016). Having at least one close and supportive parent also protects children from the effects of a wide range of stressful and adverse events (Masten, 2011), and quality care from alternate caregivers can equally provide this protection (Luthar, Crossman & Small, 2015).

For this reason, a child having secure attachment to their caregivers is protective in adversity (see Box 2.5). These relationships also provide a developmental context for important skills that themselves support children to show resilience despite risk, such as self-regulation and executive function (Center on the Developing Child, 2015). Self-regulation and executive function are discussed in chapters 3 and 4. Other

the mother was in the room, and when distressed, were comforted equally by the mother or the stranger. Fifteen per cent of children showed avoidant attachment.

4 *Disorganised attachment* is characterised by fearful, disjointed and difficult to explain responses of infants upon being reunited with their mother. It is seen in children who have been mistreated, or who come from high-risk environments (Ainsworth et al., 1978/2015).

The *Minnesota Longitudinal Study of Risk and Adaptation* commenced in Minnesota, USA in 1975, to follow parents and their children from three months before birth until the current day. Researchers have looked at family factors such as attachment, as well as individual factors in multiple domains of development across a range of contexts. Here we look at their findings on attachment (Sroufe, 2005; Sroufe, Egeland, Carlson & Collins, 2005; Sroufe, Coffino & Carlson, 2010). Go to the study's website to see more about this study: http://www.cehd.umn.edu/icd/research/parent-child/

Through their data, the research team observed that patterns of attachment in infancy predicted children's later self-regulation, curiosity and successful interaction with peers at preschool; friendship and competence at primary school; and identity, intimacy and self-reflection in adolescence (Sroufe, 2005). However, the links between attachment and these later skills are probabilities rather than inevitabilities; attachment was proposed to form a foundation on which later experiences could build further developmental skills.

Numerous factors following the initial two years can build on, or move away from the initial start made in the infant–parent relationship, with parents and others (peers and siblings, for example) providing multiple developmental supports, and context also playing a role. The researchers concluded, in line with Bowlby's theory, that the child's total developmental history influenced outcomes, rather than attachment alone, and that all periods of development are vitally important (Sroufe, 2005). As they were looking at the families at multiple points over time, the researchers were also able to see shifts and changes in circumstance and how these influenced development. For example, some children who had displayed insecure attachment (either avoidant or resistant) in infancy did not experience negative effects in childhood, after changes in family circumstance (reduction of stress) and greater support, while quality romantic relationships in adulthood were transformative for others who had experienced avoidant attachment early (Sroufe, Coffino & Carlson, 2010). The study also identified ways in which effects of early attachment patterns were still observable following changes in circumstance, and this has contributed to the work on risk and resilience.

We will see more on the role of attachment in development in Chapter 4.

aspects of parenting that are protective in adolescence include the combination of high levels of warmth and demandingness or control, and monitoring and granting of autonomy (Luthar, Crossman & Small, 2015).

Community contributors to resilience

Community bodies such as schools and childcare centres can protect against adversity by supporting and working with families, and by encouraging teachers to develop supportive relationships with children (Luthar, Crossman & Small, 2015). Schools can also provide stability, safety, and routine in an uncertain world (Masten & Narayan, 2012). Children's peers can offer acceptance and friendship, and provide both a developmental context for building of key skills, and protection from some of the effects of adversity – although friends can also teach maladaptive skills and attitudes, such as aggression or substance abuse (Lansford, Criss, Pettit, Dodge & Bates, 2003; Rose, Carlson & Waller, 2007). Some neighbourhood characteristics can reduce risk for children; these include a sense of belonging, cohesion and participation in community groups (Luthar, Crossman & Small, 2015).

Individual contributors to resilience

Biological, genetic, psychological and neurological elements interact with one another in complex ways to support resilience in individuals. Individual differences occur in genetic sensitivity to environmental inputs, so that two individuals may have varying biochemical responses to a stressful event. Sensitive children may respond strongly both to stressful events, *and* to interventions (Boyce & Ellis, 2005), indicating the importance of the interaction between individual and environmental factors. Brain chemicals are influenced by early life experience of stress, and can then influence later stress responses. Cognitive skills such as executive function and self-regulation help children to respond to adverse situations, to generate solutions to problems and to plan. So too do a sense of mastery, self-efficacy, humour, and religious or cultural practices that support hope and optimism. Emotional intelligence (see Chapter 9) is also important to adaptive coping, enabling children to recognise, manage and reason about their own and others' emotions (Luthar, Crossman & Small, 2015). Community and family factors interact with these individual factors in creating the means for resilience; interaction with parents is vital for the development of self-regulation, for example. (Center on the Developing Child, 2015).

LANGUAGE DEVELOPMENT

Language expresses our intentions and desires, allows us to frame and express our thoughts, helps us to achieve our goals, and is fundamental to our relations with others. It is central to our cognition and social interaction, but its development is also influenced by cognitive, social and emotional development. Unlike physical development, language development does not occur without social interaction or the child's interaction with the environment. Language develops in context, and with a particular set of purposes.

LANGUAGE BUILDING BLOCKS

In describing the process of language acquisition, linguists have divided language into a series of five 'systems':

phonology
The sound system of language

- **Phonology** refers to the sound systems of a language. Awareness of the influence of the combination of sounds in a word on their production, such as 'cc' making a single hard 'c' sound when followed by 'o', as in 'occupy', but a double, hard and then soft sound when followed by 'e', as in 'accept' is an example of phonological knowledge. For the majority of us, our knowledge of phonology, and indeed, of all the systems, is implicit, and how children learn the rules without any explicit teaching of them is one of the questions explored by developmental linguists.

- The **semantics** of a language are the relationships between words and their meanings; for example, you know what the words 'cat' and 'dog' refer to because of your semantic knowledge.
- **Morphology** describes the way in which words are made up according to tense, gender, number and so on; for example, the difference between the forms write, writes, wrote and writing are aspects of morphology.
- **Syntax** refers to the grammatical systems that combine words into phrases and sentences. For example, in English, we order phrases by subject, then verb, then object, which enables you to understand 'the cat ate the mouse' as a logical statement, and 'the mouse ate the cat' as unlikely.
- **Pragmatics** is concerned with the appropriate use of language in social settings; for example, 'Give me some cake now' is syntactically correct, but it is an impolite way to phrase a request in English. Knowing how to achieve your aims using language and how to express yourself appropriately are part of your pragmatic knowledge of language.

Linguists tend to describe the five systems as separate, but of course they interact and work together to form the larger language system. As children learn language, they don't build it up system by system. Rather, as Tomasello (2006) argued, children acquire 'speech forms' or chunks of speech that have a particular purpose, and extract elements such as words from these larger chunks.

Children develop the key features of language in the first three to four years of life. Knowing the early processes of language development can help us understand later developments in literacy and second-language learning.

LANGUAGE DEVELOPMENT DURING INFANCY

In the first days after birth there are signs that language is developing. Infants' early cries use sound to communicate emotion, and infants discriminate between speech and other sounds, and between their mother's and others' voices (Sachs, 2001). They also learn the rules of taking turns in conversations in these first months, with 'visual conversations' observable in exchanges of eye contact between mothers and their babies. These early 'conversations' affect the rate of language development – a clue that social interaction is an important influence in language acquisition – and are complemented by verbal turn-taking conversations at about three months. Games such as peekaboo also contribute.

Sounds and gestures

The sounds made by infants progress from cooing (mainly vowels) at about two months, to babbling (strings of consonants and vowels such as 'dadadada') about two months later. By about seven months, the babbling starts to sound more like language, and by the end of the first year, when the first words appear, they have the intonation and other sound patterns of the child's native tongue.

Gestures are the other pre-linguistic element that emerges at about the end of the first year, accompanying the emergence of language and significantly contributing to language development (see Figure 2.15). A number of studies have linked young children's use of gestures to growth of vocabulary and the shift to two-word utterances (for example, Blake, Vitale, Osborne & Olshansky, 2005; Özcaliskan & Goldin-Meadow, 2005).

FIGURE 2.15 Infants' gestures contribute to their language development and extend their communicative competence at this early stage of development.

Source: Westend61/Getty Images

semantics
The system of meanings associated with language

morphology
The combination of units of meaning in words; for example, listen + ed = past tense of 'listen'

syntax
The grammatical system that orders the construction of sentences

pragmatics
Rules for the appropriate use of language in social contexts

The use of gesture reflects the fact that children comprehend language long before they produce it, and this priority of comprehension over production continues throughout the course of language acquisition. The production of language forms appears closely linked to developments in cognition.

First words and vocabulary development

The first words tend to be limited in number, simple in pronunciation, and refer to familiar, concrete objects or important people – 'mum', 'dog', 'juice'. These words are used like phrases. In English, first words tend to be nouns, with verbs appearing later as they are more difficult to make sense of. The first verbs tend to refer to simple, frequent actions. Other languages show a different order of acquisition (Levey, 2014). Tomasello (2006) identified the typical purposes of 'holophrases' (words used like phrases) across many languages. Just as in infants' pre-linguistic gestures or utterances, they are generally statements or requests, asking for or describing a person or thing; more of something ('more', 'again'); movement of objects ('up', 'in', 'open'); actions of people ('eat', 'kick'); and comments on the locations of objects and people ('here', 'outside'). Added to these are simple questions ('What's that?') and social formulae ('thank you', 'bye bye').

Towards the end of the second year, the child's vocabulary increases rapidly to about 50 words, and words start to be combined to produce **telegraphic speech** of two words – usually to ask for more ('more milk'), to say no ('no bath') or to notice the presence or absence of something ('all gone'). With time, the range of meanings expressed broadens, although children in the two-word stage are still constrained to talking about the here and now. Aspects such as tense, gender and number appear as the length of children's utterances grows.

telegraphic speech
Communication using
two-word sentences,
leaving out smaller
words

Links to cognitive and emotional development

There are links in this early development to cognitive and emotional development (Perszyk & Waxman, 2018). The spurt in vocabulary that occurs at the end of the second year has been associated with a number of changes in the nature of children's thought (Bloom, 1998).We have already noted that children first learn words referring to people or objects that are important to them. Infants' early words are also usually related to their actions: they first learn the names of objects that move ('car', 'ball') and words relating to actions themselves ('up', 'gone', 'more'). With the development of object permanence (see Chapter 3), terms such as 'all gone' appear, and with early understanding of causality terms such as 'oh dear' and 'uh oh' are heard. One explanation of the link between cognition and this aspect of language is that children's vocabulary is acquired around the particular cognitive problems they are solving (Gopnick & Meltzoff, 1997). Tomasello (2011) argues that children use their cognitive and social-cognitive abilities to acquire language. Language also contributes to cognitive development; words help with concept formation (Lupyan & Thompson-Schill, 2012; Perszyk & Waxman, 2018) and cognitive flexibility (McWhinney, 2010).

LANGUAGE DEVELOPMENT DURING EARLY CHILDHOOD

Between two and three years of age, children start to speak in three-word sentences, and with the word order of their native language (in English, subject–verb–object) (Maratsos, 1998). Grammar also develops, with categories such as nouns, pronouns and verbs appearing in sentences as adults would use them. Thus, preschoolers' speech begins to more closely resemble that of adults.

Language, errors and problem solving

The kinds of errors children make as they acquire language reveal the process of problem solving in which they are engaged. Very young children 'underextend' and 'overextend' meanings of words as they work to define the limits of a category; that is, they may use the word 'dog' to refer to all animals (an example of **overextension**) or to refer only to their own dog (an example of **underextension**). They may also develop their own expressions for words they do not know by combining words. For example, Jake, who is four years and seven months old, said:

> You can't touch his head because there's a hole and you might hurt his thinking thing.

while Eloise, who is two years and four months old, said:

> Don't fall me down [drop me].

Over-regularisation of grammatical forms occurs at the preschool stage as children recognise a particular rule and attempt to apply it. Initially, they tend to ignore irregular forms and apply the rule universally; for example:

> I goed to the zoo with Nana and we seed a baby giraffe.

and

> He did it well-ly, Mummy.

It is a measure of children's understanding of the language system that such over-regularisations are limited to the appropriate part of speech (verbs, in 'I goed … we seed') and tense (the past, in this case). Some of these kinds of errors are also made by learners in the process of acquiring a second language, and by children learning to spell.

Grammar, finding patterns and forming categories

The emergence of grammar has been linked to children's ability to find patterns and form categories (Tomasello, 2005, 2011). As children begin to form more complex sentences by joining phrases together, another sequence is evident that appears to parallel cognitive development. The first joining word is 'and', followed by 'then' or 'when' and 'because' or 'so'. Children learn in a similar way about concepts: first that things can be grouped together ('and'), then that they can be sequenced ('then'), and finally that relationships may be causal ('because') (Bloom, 1998). Bloom reminds us that the same sequence is seen in children's storytelling and understanding of stories.

The pragmatics of children's language also develop throughout the periods of infancy and early childhood, as children's use of language moves from simple expressions of emotion to a realisation that language can be used to direct and control others. Children as young as two years old adjust what they say to take account of the listener (Dunn & Kendrick, 1982), although they do this imperfectly until their awareness of others' points of view (perspective-taking ability) improves.

LANGUAGE DEVELOPMENT DURING MIDDLE CHILDHOOD

Although most of children's language development is complete by the time they enter school, there are some further developments in middle childhood. There is a greater use and understanding of abstract words and constructions through middle childhood and adolescence, and children's use of correct grammar improves as a result (McDevitt & Ormrod, 2013). Children's vocabulary increases from 50 words at 18 months old, to about 10 000 words in the first year of school, to 20 000 words by Year 3, and to 40 000 words as the child enters adolescence (Anglin, 1993). Reading contributes to this increase in vocabulary, as do direct instruction and increased opportunities to converse with adults about a range of topics, as happens at school. A more complex grammar develops in order to deal with the increasing number of words used, and there is a close relationship between vocabulary size and grammatical complexity (Bates & Goodman, 1999).

---

overextension
Inappropriate use of a word for a class of things rather than for one particular thing

underextension
Inappropriate use of a word for one thing rather than for a class of things

over-regularisation
Application of a grammatical rule, ignoring its exceptions

CourseMateExpress
Online resources
Explore an example of children's storytelling with the **Interactive Activity** on this text's website.

Metalinguistic awareness

metalinguistic
awareness
Awareness of and
understandings about
language

These changes are accompanied by a greater awareness of language itself, which we refer to as **metalinguistic awareness**. Children's awareness progresses from appropriate use of phonology, morphology, syntax, semantics and pragmatics to specific knowledge of the rules being followed and the ability to express these rules. Such awareness is particularly important as children learn literacy skills. It may be that the school context itself focuses children's attention on the nature of language (Gombert, 1992). Bloom (1998) suggested that children's language develops around and in response to the meanings and intentions of the child's activity. In the early years, the first words tend to refer to the important people, events and objects in the child's world. Then, as the child's context changes from home to school, the activities on which the child focuses attention also change. Quite a bit of time is spent in classrooms talking with children about what language does and how it works. The meanings talked about are often to do with language itself, which helps children to develop their cognitive understanding of language.

Children's language play reveals a developing metalinguistic awareness. Early play with language tends to focus on phonological (sound-related) features. For example, this is from Harry (four years old):

> Hello Jacob wacob
>
> Jacob wacob cacob macob

This kind of play with the sounds of language contributes to later developments in reading. It can be supported with nursery rhymes and stories that make use of repetition and rhyme (Bryant, Bradley, McClean & Crossland, 1989).

Developing semantics and syntax

As children become more aware of other features of language, they move from being concerned with purely phonological features to an interest in playing with semantics and syntax. For example, Jack (aged six) said of his baby brother:

> Harry will be good at basketball when he grows up, because he dribbles a lot.

Jacob (aged five) said this when he learnt his cousin's name:

> I'm not going to call him Henry. I'm going to call him Chickenry.

This shift is displayed through an interest in riddles when children are about six to eight years old. Once again, there is a link between the ability to understand riddles and reading ability (Ely & McCabe, 1994). The metalinguistic skills involved in interpreting riddles are the same as those involved in making sense of a text.

In late middle childhood and adolescence, with increasing awareness of the rules for language use, children can become pedantic about what is said and how (and delight in picking up their teachers or parents on errors!); for example:

> 'Can you take the garbage out?'
>
> 'Yes I can … Oh, do you want me to? I thought you were just asking if I was strong enough. Ha, ha!'

LANGUAGE DEVELOPMENT DURING ADOLESCENCE

Adolescents have greater opportunities to acquire specific language forms and practices through participation in contexts outside home and school (for example, in workplaces or interest groups), and may shape their language to fit a variety of contexts (Smith Gabig, 2014). In addition, they spend considerable time in school navigating the academic language used in classrooms, with its particular rules.

By the final year of schooling, adolescents may have a vocabulary of up to 50 000 words (Stahl & Nagy, 2006). Increases in vocabulary during adolescence include the wider use of a variety of forms such as connectives ('although', 'however', 'nonetheless') and more complex words using prefixes and suffixes (for example, 'hope' may be expanded through the use of 'hopefulness', 'hopeless' or 'unhopeful'). There are also further developments in syntax, with mastery of complex forms such as passive ('It was taken by him' rather than 'He took it') and nested clauses ('The man who was riding the elephant's camera'), and use of more cohesive devices such as pronouns and conjunctions (Smith Gabig, 2014). Wider reading and exposure to subject-specific texts contribute both to vocabulary and to syntax development. Correct use of subtle distinctions in word use – as in the use of 'can' and 'want' in the garbage example given above – are probably learnt through formal instruction (Smith Gabig, 2014).

Development of abstract thinking

Development of abstract thinking in adolescence is reflected in language. The ability to compare what is said with the underlying reality allows adolescents to go beyond the literal. This ability shows itself in increased use and understanding of figurative speech, sarcasm and multiple meanings (McDevitt & Ormrod, 2013). Such developments are also related to further increases in metalinguistic awareness, with some students enjoying debating, arguing for the sake of arguing, and using language to think through ideas.

Nippold (2009) argued that more complex thinking, as well as the need to give information through exposition, prompts the use of more complex language in middle childhood and adolescence to communicate the new ideas and information students are thinking about. This parallels the link described earlier between younger children's language development and their cognition.

ADULTS' ROLE IN LANGUAGE ACQUISITION

There are a number of ways in which those around the child influence his or her language acquisition, through the things they say, responses to the child, and even interactions that might not involve language.

Joint attention

When parents and children both focus on an object or activity in **joint attention** sessions, language learning is more rapid when parents do not interrupt or change the focus but instead talk about the object of the child's attention (Carpenter, Nagell & Tomasello, 1998). In these interactions, adults are supporting children's language development by labelling their environment for them. Tomasello (2005) suggested that children's ability to follow and direct attention underpins language development, as the purpose of language lies in responding to and manipulating others' thinking.

Rogoff (1990) showed that children play an important, active role in such situations, directing much of their interaction with adults and initiating conversations or joint attention sessions. By being in charge, children can direct the focus to an issue of concern to them, keeping learning at an appropriate level. Implicit in this is the assumption that children attend to their environment selectively, learning from the experiences they are interested in and can make sense of.

joint attention
When carer and child together attend to a stimulus, such as when reading books or playing peekaboo games

THINK ABOUT

■ How might we let individual children control the focus and pace of their learning in the school context?

Child-directed speech

child-directed speech
A type of speech
directed to young
children and
characterised by high
pitch, short and well-
spaced sentences,
simple vocabulary and
exaggerated intonation

Adults worldwide adjust their language when talking to children, producing a special register of speech termed 'motherese' or **child-directed speech**. This type of speech tends to be higher in pitch than other speech, simple in grammar and vocabulary, and characterised by exaggerated expression and enunciation of words. It appears to help children separate the flow of speech into words, and to attend to the key words in a communication (Snow, 1995). Even children adjust their speech in this way when talking to babies. Infants show a preference for child-directed speech compared with other adult talk (Cooper & Aslin, 1994), and its use in the first year is positively related to infants' language comprehension at 18 months (Murray, Johnson & Peters, 1990).

The content of child-directed speech is also important in children's language development. Cameron-Faulkner, Lieven and Tomasello (2003) found that there was a limited number of phrases with which mothers in their study initiated utterances to their two- and three-year-old children. In fact, there were 17 phrases that initiated 45 per cent of utterances. They included units such as 'what', 'that', 'it' and 'you'. The children used the same initiating phrases in their own speech. The researchers concluded that the often-repeated phrases help the children to reduce the variety of the great number of utterances they hear (5000–7000 per day) and seek to comprehend and to use themselves.

Adults' speech and gestures directed to infants help them to make connections between words and their meanings (Zammit & Schafer, 2011). Children influence the words they hear as mothers interact with them around objects in which they show an interest. Mothers also tailor their language to children's ability level (Ucelli & Pan, 2013).

Expansion and recasting

expansion
Parents' tendency to
respond to young
children's utterances
by restating them in a
more elaborate form

recasting
Parents' tendency to
respond to children's
utterances by restating
them in the correct
grammatical form

As well as simplifying what they say, parents may amplify what the child says, repeating the child's statement with an **expansion**, and **recasting** errors in grammar. For example, the child's phrase 'Daddy work' may be responded to with 'Yes, Daddy's gone to work in his car, hasn't he?', expanding the information by adding 'in his car', and recasting the phrase into correct grammar: 'Daddy's gone to work'. Children repeat adults' recasts, but the contribution that expansions and recasts make to children's language acquisition is a matter of debate (Nicholas, Lightbown & Spada, 2001).

Language input

As we have seen, direct instruction at school and the language of school contribute to growth in children's vocabulary, use of correct forms and metalinguistic awareness. It has been estimated that children are exposed to an average of 3000 new words in every school year (Smith Gabig, 2014). This contributes not just to vocabulary but also to knowledge of morphology – how words are put together – that in its turn contributes to further language skills.

It is also clear that the amount of language in the home affects the rate at which children acquire vocabulary. This is one explanation for differences in language detected between people of various social classes. In a landmark study, Hart and Risley (1995) found significant differences in the amount of language directed at children in different socioeconomic groups. Particularly affected were children of families in situations of poverty: these children had a third of the interaction and experience with language of children in families from higher socioeconomic strata. The acquisition rate also links to later achievements. In the same study, Hart and Risley found a positive correlation between children's language experience before three years of age, and verbal intelligence scores at ages nine to 10. Socioeconomic status is not the only factor at work here. Pan, Rowe, Singer and Snow (2005) found variation within low-income families, with observed variation in the growth of young children's vocabularies positively linked to maternal language and literacy skills, and negatively linked to maternal depression.

In Chapter 11 we explore the contribution of socioeconomic factors to individual differences in more depth, including the variability observed within and among different social and ethnic groups.

Later studies have suggested that children also learn from overheard speech, particularly when they are being talked about, or when others are talking about something they are interested in (Floor & Akhtar, 2006). However, a 2013 study found that in naturalistic settings, overheard speech from multiple others in the household (such as siblings, aunts, uncles or grandparents) did not contribute to children's vocabulary, although the researchers pointed out that it is likely that overheard speech contributes to other aspects of language, and/or that in other cultures it may play a greater role (Shneidman, Arroyo, Levine & Goldin-Meadow, 2013).

Bryant (2013) identified a number of strategies parents use to 'socialise' language in their children, contributing to their communicative competence. These include prompts, modelling, reinforcement, evaluation and other forms of input. Activities engaged in at home that prompt language also play a role. Rodriguez et al. (2009) found that three-year-old children's vocabulary was predicted by a combination of the frequency of their participation in literacy activities, the quality of the mother's engagement, and the availability of age-appropriate learning materials in the home.

THINK ABOUT

■ How could you contribute to children's language development at school?

THE ROLE OF PEERS IN LANGUAGE ACQUISITION

Adults (parents and others) are not the only ones who influence children's development of language. Throughout this chapter, we have seen a number of ways in which children's activity contributes to their development, and language acquisition is no exception. Siblings and peers also play an important role.

Language play

Play is a particular kind of activity that is especially important to language learning. Children's play with language contributes to their metalinguistic awareness, as they play with sounds or with meanings.

In fantasy play, children negotiate meaning with one another, and must experiment and revise what they say in order to clearly communicate their ideas for the imaginary situation (Smith Gabig, 2014). Vygotsky (1977) described play as a supportive context for the development of children's thinking; for more on Vygotsky's view of the role of play in cognitive development, see Chapter 3. It also clearly supports their language development.

Peer interaction

The importance of friendship and peer relations to children makes this a motivating context in which language is shaped to achieve acceptance and maintain friendships. In peer interactions, children develop and practise language skills in coordinating play, resolving conflict, and negotiating with and persuading others (Smith Gabig, 2014). The role of peers in second-language acquisition (discussed later in this chapter) is also important (Philp, Adams & Iwashita, 2013). For example, children acquire and practise new language forms in the context of interactions with peers (as seen in Figure 2.16), and may adopt the language forms of their peers to appear more like them (Philp & Duchesne, 2008). Language both contributes to and is influenced by the social development of the child. We explore social development in greater detail in Chapter 4.

Source: Gladskikh Tatiana/Shutterstock

FIGURE 2.16 Children's interaction with peers during play contributes to their language development, with new requirements for using particular forms, opportunities to practise, and motivation for communicating effectively.

INDIVIDUAL DIFFERENCES IN PATHWAYS TO DEVELOPMENT

As we have seen, children's communication skills are developed through interactions with multiple others: parents, siblings, teachers, peers and others, each of these working differently to provide different kinds of interaction, feedback and input, depending on who is being conversed with, and in what context. Opportunities for language learning vary for different children, and for different families (Goldfield, Snow & Willenberg, 2013). The child's own interest and motivation play a role as well, influencing what they attend to (Bryant, 2013), with the result that there are individual differences in pathways to language development as well as in the language that develops.

In the section that follows, we discuss how children's prior experiences in language and other areas contribute to their understanding and to their learning in school. Being aware of the interests and activities for which children use language, including playing with language itself, can help us as teachers to make learning relevant for students.

Box 2.6 describes some implications for educators of the principles of language acquisition discussed in this section of the chapter.

BOX 2.6 IMPLICATIONS FOR EDUCATORS

LANGUAGE DEVELOPMENT AND THE CLASSROOM

Some of the principles drawn from how children learn language suggest initiatives that teachers can implement in classrooms to contribute to language development:

- Interaction contributes to language development: give students opportunities to interact with a wide range of partners on a range of topics.
- Develop vocabulary through talking with students and encouraging reading about a variety of topics.
- Allow children to direct the focus of interaction.
- Explicitly teach students how to use irregular forms. They may not hear them used consistently in everyday speech.
- Build students' awareness of language by talking about how language works, and by drawing attention to specific language features in relation to content areas.
- Contribute to metalinguistic awareness with the use of riddles, rhymes, jokes and metaphors in middle childhood – but ensure that all students understand them. Remember that there are individual differences in the rate of development.
- Similarly, explore proverbs and multiple meanings in adolescence, allowing students both to find layers of meaning in texts and to construct their own.
- You will see more examples of ways in which language contributes to learning in the section on the school-based skills of literacy and numeracy below.

SCHOOL-BASED SKILLS

Children do not arrive at school without knowledge or skills. Physical and language skills developed in infancy and early childhood form an important basis for the skills that are the focus of schooling. In this section, we discuss three sets of skills that are central to the work of schools: additional-language learning – for many children an essential skill necessary to access education – and the skills of literacy and numeracy. In each case, children's knowledge develops from very early in life and is built upon by formal teaching in schools. Each of these skills, too, is needed for learning across the curriculum throughout schooling and, indeed, life.

ADDITIONAL-LANGUAGE ACQUISITION

We described the process of first-language acquisition earlier, but for many children in Australia and New Zealand, English is not their first but their second, or maybe even third or fourth language. Some children grow up with several languages. Others must acquire an additional language when their families migrate to a new country, or when they start school if their families do not speak Standard Australian English. The term 'learners of **EAL/D**' (English as an additional language or dialect) has replaced the older ESL (English as a second language) term, recognising the range of language backgrounds these learners of English may have. For these children, acquiring an additional language is an essential skill for success at school. Snow and Kang (2006) have drawn several conclusions from research on children's learning of an additional language, in this context:

EAL/D
English as an additional language or dialect (replaces ESL or English as a second language); applied to acquisition or learning of English

- Acquiring an additional language in childhood can be intimidating and difficult, lead to temporary emotional problems, and take several years.
- The first language is at some risk of loss or decline under the influence of the additional language.
- A child's continued development of the first language is more likely if the parents are bilingual and/or highly educated in the first language.
- Higher status languages and languages associated with schooling and literacy are in general less subject to attrition than lower status languages.
- First language literacy skills can be a support to additional-language acquisition.
- Learning to read an additional language is easier if one is already literate in a first language.
- Literacy skills contribute to higher levels of oral proficiency in both a first and an additional language.
- Older children typically learn an additional language faster than younger children, perhaps because of their better developed literacy skills, but also likely because of more efficient brain networks.
- Transfer of literacy skills can support additional language literacy but may not occur automatically across even closely related languages (Snow & Kang, 2006, pp. 78–9).

Comparing first- and additional-language acquisition

There are some similarities between the ways in which first- and additional-language learners use language, which seem to be related to the nature of the language-learning process. There are also important differences arising from the contexts in which people learn first and second languages. The focus in this discussion is on learning EAL/D, something that confronts non-English-speaking migrants in Australia and New Zealand and some Indigenous children in Australia. Foreign-language learning (for example, speakers of Standard Australian or New Zealand English who learn French or Vietnamese in classrooms in Australia or New Zealand) is a different although related process.

Similarities between first- and second-language acquisition include an early dependence on routine phrases such as those in telegraphic speech. Young children may use phrases such as 'all gone' for all situations where an absence of something is indicated, later recognising that these phrases can be combined with other language units to make phrases such as 'all gone milk', or separated to make phrases such as 'Mummy gone'. Additional-language learners at early stages similarly depend on remembered language chunks – formulaic phrases that have not been separated into their component parts, and that cannot therefore be applied flexibly or adapted and expanded upon. Such use of formulaic phrases is an important support in the learning of a second language. Some common examples are the questions 'Where is it post office?', 'How are you your father?' and 'Who is she this man?' The constraint at this early stage may be one of memory, since when confronted with a large, unfamiliar system, people commonly start with a small sample of language and build from there. The overgeneralisation of grammatical rules is another feature of both first- and second-language acquisition. The problem-solving nature of the language-development task is evident here.

BOX 2.7 CLASSROOM LINKS

STAGES OF ADDITIONAL-LANGUAGE ACQUISITION IN THE CLASSROOM

There will be considerable variation in learners' progress in English as an additional language or dialect, depending on their age, experience and context, but five broad stages of development have been identified. Goldstein (2014) summarised the features of these stages of additional-language acquisition. As you read through this below, consider how you could support students' language learning at each stage, if they were in your classroom.

Stage 1: Preproduction

As in first-language acquisition, learners' receptive language advances further than their expressive language in the early stages of language learning. There may be a silent period of up to six months during this stage, and/or a period when students converse with peers but not with adults in the new language. This should be seen as a natural aspect of the early stage of second-language acquisition. Students respond to simple commands and can understand up to 500 words.

Stage 2: Early production

The focus on receptive language continues. Approximately 3–6 months after being introduced to the new language, students understand yes/no and what/when/why questions, and generally use one- to three-word phrases and formulaic expressions such as 'How-are-you?'. They understand and use up to 1000 words.

Stage 3: Speech emergence

Six months to two years after being introduced to the language, learners' comprehension improves, and their vocabulary expands to allow them to talk in simple sentences. Some grammatical errors are shown in their speech and writing as they start to use more complex grammar. Vocabulary increases to about 3000 words.

Stage 4: Intermediate fluency

Approximately three years on, comprehension improves still further, and learners show competent skills in face-to-face conversations. They can express their thoughts and opinions using complex constructions, and show few grammatical errors. Vocabulary continues to increase, to approximately 6000 words.

Stage 5: Advanced language proficiency

Five to seven years after being introduced to the language, students' grammar and vocabulary are similar to those of a native speaker. They can use the specialised vocabulary of particular subject areas and can participate in classroom activities at their grade level.

ACTIVITIES

1   Identify the supports that learners would need in the mainstream classroom at each of the stages. See Box 2.8 for further ideas relating to particular age groups.
2   One of the first things students learn is to ask to go to the toilet. Consider other practical needs, and particular language that students may need to participate in your subject area.

Differences between learning a first and additional language

There are some important differences between learning a first and an additional language, however (remembering that we are not discussing bilingualism at this point, but the learning of an additional language at school). In particular, while the learning of a first language can be assumed for the majority of children, such assumptions cannot be made about the learning of an additional language. Children learning an additional language bring with them understandings about language and the way it operates that can both assist and hinder them in their learning of the new language. Nicholas and Lightbown (2008) point out that learning an additional language is a different process that has implications for teachers in their support of second-language learners alongside native-language learners in the classroom (see **Box 2.8**). They also caution that the age of the child makes a difference: under seven years of age, there appears to be a different process than for children over seven, due in part to the rapid development of understandings about language that are occurring at this earlier stage, apparently without instruction, and in part to the importance of literacy from the age of seven onwards.

BOX 2.8 IMPLICATIONS FOR EDUCATORS

SUPPORTING ADDITIONAL LANGUAGE LEARNERS

Nicholas and Lightbown (2008) pointed out that the process of learning a second language differs for children of different ages. Following are some suggestions from the literature for supporting additional-language learners in early childhood, middle childhood and adolescence.

Early childhood

- Young children (under seven) draw on features of their first language, such as word order, to help them to meet the challenges of producing a second language.
- There may be extended periods (months, or even a year such as in one case) of silence during which students understand but do not produce the second language. This may be strategic, with children focusing on learning from input before they attempt to produce it.
- Children may 'code-switch' – use a mixture of first and second language – and need to learn when this is appropriate, and when they might not be understood.
- Language play is an important feature of young children's use of first language and, through it, additional-language learners can learn and explore the features of the new language. For example, teachers can use language play to explore difficult features such as pronunciation through tongue twisters and rhymes. Children can also attain an identity as a peer in the classroom through language play and mimicry (Philp & Duchesne, 2008). Lightbown and Spada (2013) point out that it is important, however, for children to move on to adult forms.

- For young children, the focus should be on language associated with activities, actions and simple thinking operations, with language presented and used in context.

Middle childhood

- Children need not only to learn the additional language, but to learn through it as well, so that they can develop skills in using the language for academic purposes.
- An additional language can be taught in the context of, and through, all curriculum areas, not just in English classes.

Adolescence

- Older children may learn from decontextualised language, and from language associated with more complex thinking.
- Students apply their knowledge of their first language and may rely on translating to a greater degree than younger learners. They need also to develop knowledge of the additional language and how it works, so that they can draw on this knowledge independently of the first.
- Identity can be particularly important for students in adolescence, and language is part of identity. Consider how to support additional-language learners to construct identities as full members of the class group.
- Opportunities to interact informally with native speakers are important both to provide input and to allow the practice of output. Encouraging positive relationships between native and non-native peers in the classroom can thus be valuable.

Sources: Nicholas and Lightbown (2008); Ellis (2005); Gibbons (2002); Muñoz (2007).

The 'difficulty' of learning an additional language

Why is it that learning our first language sometimes seems effortless and automatic, while learning an additional language can be a long and difficult process? The contextual features of second-language acquisition make it a more difficult task than learning a first language. In first-language acquisition, children tend to be supported by their parents, with intense one-to-one interaction focused on the child's level and the activities the child is engaged in. Additional-language acquisition rarely occurs with this level of intense support. In addition, as we have seen, the child's emotional, social and cognitive development is progressing in tandem with language development, supporting and being supported by it. When additional-language acquisition happens later, this match does not occur, and the child has often quite complex thoughts, ideas and emotions to express in the new language. There are emotional and motivational differences, too. As we saw earlier, first-language acquisition is an intrinsically motivating task for the child due to caregivers being involved in the process. There are many rewards for success – and even for failure – when parents respond to the child's requests and attend closely to clarify meaning. Additional-language learning can be frustrating and anxiety-producing, particularly for a newly arrived non-English speaker in an Australian or New Zealand school. When additional-language acquisition occurs in the school context, there is also the double demand of learning about other curriculum areas through the additional language (Nicholas & Lightbown, 2008).

THINK ABOUT

- How might the school context be shaped to support additional-language acquisition?

Bilingualism and learning English as an additional language or dialect in schools

A review of bilingual education programs worldwide found that schools that are organised to support children's first language result in cognitive, social and educational advantages for their bilingual students. Programs that teach English at the expense of the first language, by contrast, produce negative cognitive, social and educational outcomes for these students. For bilingual students, the most effective programs are bilingual, particularly if these aim to maintain and build up the first language. Less effective are integrated EAL/D programs, then EAL/D withdrawal programs, with English-only programs the least effective (May, Hill & Tiakiwai, 2004). This may be because strength of the first language supports the learning of another with considerable knowledge about language and the way it works already in place (Lightbown & Spada, 2013). Children for whom English is an additional language tend to learn English and other subjects more effectively when their first-language skills are strong (Cummins, 1979; Thomas & Collier, 1999). The majority of programs in Australian and New Zealand schools involve EAL/D withdrawal or integrated EAL/D, although there are some schools with bilingual programs supporting Aboriginal languages and *te reo* Māori, as described in Chapter 11.

EAL/D learners may be of any age, with differing levels of cognitive development and skill in their first language. In addition, they may differ in their experience of English prior to starting school. Thus, effective evaluation and teaching programs are marked by flexibility. Rather than being guided by a specific developmental path, teachers focus on students' needs.

EAL/D programs in Australian schools vary across states, but are currently of two types: intensive English programs for newly arrived migrants, and support programs in mainstream schools. The latter may be within classes, where specialist and general classroom teachers support the development of English while studying the curriculum; or in withdrawal situations where English may be the sole focus (Cox, 2015). For The Australian Curriculum assumes teachers will provide for EAL/D learners within each curriculum area, and has produced a resource to support this integration (ACARA, 2014). migrants in New Zealand, there are intensive English classes, with some immersion in mainstream English classrooms, to ready these students for mainstream classes once the intensive class ends. Curriculum materials are available to support teachers in teaching students English as an Additional Language or Dialect (New Zealand Ministry of Education, 2017).

Immersion and bilingual programs in *te reo* Māori are also run in New Zealand schools, at levels ranging from whole-school immersion to bilingual units within schools. These were introduced in the 1980s following concerns that the language was diminishing in use (May, Hill & Tiakiwai, 2006). In a review of these programs, May, Hill and Tiakiwai urged that students need to be taught a language (such as English or *te reo* Māori), and to be taught in that language, so that they develop *academic* English or *te reo* Māori.

LITERACY DEVELOPMENT

Traditionally, **literacy** has been conceptualised in terms of the written language skills of reading and writing, but as our society becomes more technological, the written word is used in increasingly wider contexts. More recent approaches to literacy have also recognised the close relationship that reading and writing have with listening, speaking and viewing.

The Australian Curriculum identifies literacy as a general capability underpinning learning. It states, 'Literacy involves students in listening to, reading, viewing, speaking, writing and creating oral, print, visual and digital texts, and using and modifying language for different purposes in a range of contexts' (ACARA, 2012). The New Zealand literacy and numeracy strategy is even broader than this. It defines literacy as 'the ability to use and understand those language forms required by society and valued by individuals and communities' (New Zealand Ministry of Education, 2002). How does this add to our understanding of literacy?

Have you ever noticed how your use of English changes depending on where you are and who you are with? You may be more casual with your family, and more formal when you need to give a presentation to a group; teenagers often speak in particular ways with their peer group (Gee, Allen & Clinton, 2001). Similarly, your handwriting, grammar and even spelling probably differ when writing lecture notes, and when writing a letter to a friend, an essay, an email message or a text message. We use different forms of English in different contexts, and we need to adapt our language to the use we are making of it. Similarly, along with a variety of texts, there is a wide range of ways in which we interact with texts. The way you read a website is different from the way you read a book, which is different again from how you read a shopping list, or watch a television program. **Multiliteracies** is the term that has been used to refer to this variety in types of language we need to master to be literate in our society (Cope & Kalantzis, 2000; Zammit & Downes, 2002).

> **literacy**
> Engaging with various kinds of texts, and using and modifying language for use in a variety of contexts

> **multiliteracies**
> The variety of types of language we need to master to be literate in our society

---

THINK ABOUT

■ How can we broaden the range of literacies taught in the classroom?

Learning to be literate: emergent literacy

Reading and writing print are two key literacy skills. We have seen a number of features and practices in language development that later contribute to literacy development. Although children commonly learn to read and write once they are at school, many precursors of these skills are developed in the preschool years.

Early awareness of literacy has been termed **emergent literacy** (Clay, 1991). This includes understandings about conventions of print, such as the left–right, top–bottom ordering of print on a page in English, and the knowledge that letters represent sounds and are combined to form words separated by spaces. It also includes attitudes about the purposes and value of reading and writing.

> **emergent literacy**
> Understandings about and attitudes towards reading and writing, which are the precursors of acquiring those skills

Activities that promote emergent literacy

Activities such as looking at books, reading environmental print such as street signs or the title of a favourite television show, and simple rhymes and songs all contribute to reading, as does writing. Similarly, writing is developed through reading and activities such as drawing and telling stories, as well as adult-supported writing such as writing a letter, a birthday 'wish list' or a story dictated by the child. A child's home environment is an important contributor to emergent literacy, in terms of both direct and indirect literacy support from parents. For instance, a relationship has been demonstrated between children's reading ability and such features of the home environment as length of family meal times (Anderson, Wilson & Fielding, 1988), number of books in the home, library membership and the amount that parents (and particularly fathers) read (Share et al., 1983), as well as more direct activities such as parents or other family members reading books with the child (Raikes et al., 2006). This is by no means an exhaustive list. There are many different literacy practices in families, including direct activities to teach literacy and all the informal ways in which reading and writing occur. Literacy also builds on language development, so language activities such as talking and listening are themselves important preliteracy activities. Diehl (2014) explained that good oral language supports literacy, while literacy activities themselves contribute to oral language development. This reciprocal relationship continues throughout development, as we will see, and Kang (2006) observed that children use emerging literacy skills alongside and in similar ways to other developing skills: in play, to communicate, as part of everyday routines, and as problems to solve.

Recognising differences in literacy skills and experiences

Teachers need to recognise the literacy skills and experiences that students bring from home, which may differ from those of the school, and to work with these. The closer the match between the literacy practices of home and school, the better chance there is of good literacy outcomes at school (Comber et al., 2005). There can be a mismatch between home and school literacy practices. Some projects aim to add to the home literacy experiences of children to improve the match (for example, Niklas, Cohrssen & Tayler, 2016). Others have suggested that teachers should acknowledge the knowledge and skills their students do have, so that students can make use of what they know to develop their literacy (Comber et al., 2005). McNaughton (2002) has identified rich literacy resources in families in low socioeconomic areas in New Zealand, which he suggested could be harnessed for their literacy learning in schools. Families would benefit from a combination of these approaches, both providing a bridge from family to school practices, and building up and broadening home literacy.

Literacy development throughout the school years

We sometimes think of literacy as something learnt in the early years of schooling, and those years are certainly important, but literacy learning also continues beyond Year 2. Consider the literacy skills students need for researching topics in upper primary school, or for preparing essays during secondary school, or the further learning you have done about how to read and write academic texts since starting university. The purpose of reading and writing changes, as well as the types of texts. Chall (1996) described a shift in reading development from 'learning to read' in the early years to 'reading to learn' in the later years of schooling. These skills need to be taught as carefully and explicitly as those in the early years. They also rest on those early literacy and language skills – another example of development building on what has gone before. For this reason, some students in upper primary and secondary schools may need to consolidate basic skills in reading ('learn to read') before they can effectively 'read to learn'.

Learning to read and write

There are many possible paths to literacy (Clay, 1998). Different children learn to read and write by different means (see Box 2.9). Here, we describe the development of skills used in reading and writing, focusing particularly on the aspect of literacy that is described as 'code breaking' (Freebody & Luke, 1999) or 'decoding'. Some other skills are described under the heading 'Teaching literacy in schools'.

Reading and writing are complex skills that involve the coordination of a number of individual skills. For expert readers, reading tends to be automatic, but for children the process is demanding and a little like solving a puzzle in code. Readers must simultaneously recognise the pattern of marks on the page as letters, decode individual letters as sounds, group strings of letters together to form new sounds, and check the word formed against their vocabulary – and that is just to read one word! As readers continue the process with subsequent words in a sentence, they must keep each word in their working memory so as to combine it with the other words in a meaningful way, and attend to punctuation to obtain clues about intonation and stress. It is little wonder that comprehension is often set aside as children tackle the complexities of decoding. The information-processing approach (see Chapter 3) describes reading as an information-processing problem that makes demands on working memory. The individual skills must become automatic in order for working memory to operate efficiently, or reading performance will be affected (Perfetti, Yang & Schmalhofer, 2008).

BOX 2.9 CASE STUDY

BEGINNING TO READ

As with other aspects of development, there are multiple pathways to reading. These case studies provide examples of four children's stories of reading development.

Case study A

Anna loves to read, picking up books whenever she can. Her mother reports that Anna used to 'read' to the family dog, telling stories from her picture books, from about three years old. Anna's teacher reports that she is moving quickly through the school readers, picking up new words by sight and making sense of what she reads even when the words are difficult for her to sound out. Anna writes long sentences in her 'journal' (a scrapbook students spend time writing and/or drawing in each day), and many words are written with standard spelling, though she hasn't 'learnt' them formally.

Case study B

Fred participates in all the literacy activities in his kindergarten class. At home, his mother was reading *The Lion, the Witch and the Wardrobe* to the children in the evenings. At an exciting point in the adventure, the readings were interrupted for a few nights. To her surprise, Fred picked up the book and finished it himself. He was able to read well beyond his years before anybody had noticed, seemingly learning to read overnight.

Case study C

Josie also likes to look at books, but she enjoys them best when they are being read to her. Her teacher reports that she didn't understand the connection between the letters on the page and the words read out loud until it was clearly explained to her. The phonics program in her class is helping Josie to make this connection, and to be able to sound out words herself. Josie is also learning to read a bank of words by sight, to help her reading to become more automatic. Josie's journal entries are usually pictures, but she is starting to write sentences as well, inventing spelling by joining sounds together that she hears in the words. Occasionally, she copies words from word banks around the room.

Case study D

David is mystified by some of the reading activities at school. He doesn't yet hear individual sounds in words, so is not ready for the school's phonics program. A teacher aide works with David to develop his phonemic awareness. In his journal, he writes in scribbles, copying the children around him by making marks on the page, though he doesn't yet connect those marks to the specific shapes of letters.

ACTIVITIES
1   How does the reading development of these four children differ?
2   What would you do, if you were the teacher, to support each child's reading development?

Beyond learning to read

Once reading becomes more automatic, attention is increasingly focused on a variety of purposes, so that rather than 'learning to read', children start to 'read to learn' at around nine years old (Chall, 1996). In primary school, children progress from reading aloud to silent reading, and show increases in 'sight vocabulary' (the number of words they can recognise automatically) that affect fluency. The purpose of reading expands from reading simple stories to reading to obtain new information. At school, students don't just read, but also use reading as a tool for study. Going into adolescence, there are further increases in fluency and in the ability to read complex, unfamiliar and abstract texts. The range of materials and viewpoints further expands. This builds on learners' ability to go beyond the literal meaning and consider multiple viewpoints, and to draw inferences from a text with the development of abstract reasoning (see Chapter 3). By the end of school, many students define the purpose of reading for themselves, and are able to integrate their own viewpoint with that of the writer. Decoding skill is automatic and efficient, allowing for these broader functions of reading (Ely, 2005). Similarly, in writing, children progress from focusing on form to using writing as a tool. For example, Jacob enjoyed playing 'cafés' with his family, taking down each person's order on a notepad. To begin with, when Jacob was four years old, the orders were a series of scribbles on the page. Later, Jacob progressed to writing strings of letters and numbers. By the time he was six years old, his letters approximated the sounds they are meant to make, and others could read what he had written.

With further formal instruction at school, children's spelling and punctuation become more standard. There is a wide age range in children's development of these skills: in the same kindergarten class there may be one child still writing in unrecognisable scribbles, while another is writing elaborate stories.

In parallel with developments in their reading, children in middle childhood start to use writing as a learning tool to help make sense of information or events (Daiute & Griffin, 1993). Instruction becomes focused on writing for different purposes (genres) as children become more proficient and their understanding of other perspectives improves.

In adolescence, writing shows more complex syntax, better planning and editing, and an increasing depth of topic. The earlier focus on the mechanics of the writing process is replaced in these older learners by the ability to phrase things in their own words and to adapt their writing for a variety of purposes and audiences (McDevitt & Ormrod, 2013).

Teaching literacy in schools

Teachers make an important contribution to students' literacy throughout the school years (Comber et al., 2005).

There are many developmental pathways to literacy, and there is no 'best' way to teach literacy. There are, however, a number of elements that are essential to include in a literacy program. For example, Lonigan (2015) argued that in order for readers to make meaning from the texts they read, they need both word decoding and language comprehension skills. If either is missing or weak, reading will suffer. Different aspects of literacy development require different inputs, with phonemic awareness and letter knowledge vital for decoding, while vocabulary and grammar skills contribute to reading comprehension (Adams, 2011; Lonigan, 2015). Reading practice contributes to the automatic, high-speed retrieval that is vital for reading skill, and exposure to print is fundamental to reading development (Snowling & Gobel, 2011). Indeed, the best way to ensure that all students have the skills they need across a range of contexts is to combine a number of approaches. You may have heard of approaches to literacy teaching such as the phonics, whole language, genre, functional or critical literacy approaches. Combining a number of such approaches in a balanced program appears to create the best outcome for the greatest number of students (Deakin University, 2005). Box 2.10 gives an example of such a combined approach. In keeping with this, in a study of Australian Year 1-to-Year 4 teachers associated with the Longitudinal Study of Australian Children, the majority of teachers indicated equal emphasis on 'phonetics and decoding' and 'reading and comprehending whole texts', although there was a shift towards 'reading and comprehending whole texts' in Years 3 and 4 (Vassallo, Daraganova, Zhenyu Zhang & Homel, 2016).

CourseMateExpress

Online resources
Go further: See samples of Jacob's writing on this text's CourseMate Express website.

CourseMateExpress

Online resources
Go further: Explore the value of teaching skills and context in reading.

BOX 2.10 CLASSROOM LINKS

A BALANCED APPROACH TO TEACHING READING

Center (2005) recommended a balanced approach to the teaching of reading, balancing the systematic teaching of phonics with teaching children to make meaning from texts. These skills need to be combined so that children have the skills both to decode the text and to make meaning from the sounds and words they decode. In the first year, she suggests that teachers:

- read a variety of texts daily with the children to develop listening comprehension, vocabulary, knowledge and enjoyment of the reading process
- read texts interactively, including predicting, discussing and retelling the story
- use Big Books (large-format texts) to develop print awareness
- explain to children how learning individual sounds will help them to read all the books they encounter
- introduce each sound over the year, helping children to identify them in words, and to write them
- give children 'decodable texts' (that is, readers with simple text using the sounds the children can recognise)
- have other books available for children to read and have read to them
- develop phonemic awareness through activities such as thinking of words starting with a sound, blending sounds together to form words, and pulling words apart orally to separate phonemes
- encourage children to write in response to literature and to put in practice their phonological knowledge and skills
- teach spelling systematically to support children's reading and writing skills
- start to teach syntactic awareness
- include plenty of oral language activities, particularly for students of language backgrounds other than English.

Source: Adapted from Center, Y. (2005) 'Beginning Reading', a balanced approach to literacy instruction during the first three years of school. Sydney: Allen and Unwin.

ACTIVITIES

1   Interview a teacher about their approach to teaching reading, and think about the skills that are being developed.

Luke and Freebody (1999) developed a model of the resources that literate people draw on to make meaning from and in texts. The resources are interdependent, so although there are four families of resources, each of these is necessary for literacy, but is not sufficient on its own. The resources reflect the four practices of literate people as code breakers, participants, users of texts and analysts of texts:

- *Code breakers* combine knowledge of graphophonic cues, spelling and grammar with other cues to meaning, such as pictures and context, to decode or create a text. A number of studies have shown the importance of explicit, systematic teaching of phonics to reading fluency and comprehension. Lonigan (2015) reviewed the research literature on teaching reading, and identified the importance of phonics taught 'first and fast', with evidence supporting the explicit teaching of code-breaking skills early on, and for children with difficulties in reading. Diehl (2014) listed phonemic awareness, phonics, reading fluency, vocabulary and text comprehension as supportive of literacy skills in the primary school years.
- *Participants* apply their knowledge of culture and society to make meanings in texts. Research has shown that the teaching of skills needs to occur in meaningful contexts, as reading is a purposeful activity (Comber et al., 2005).

- *Users of texts* are able to recognise and use different genres of text for different purposes. The functional approach (Gibbons, 2014) teaches about what texts do, and how different text types are structured and defined. Students' attempts to write for particular purposes are supported by modelling and guided practice.

- *Analysts of texts* read between the lines to judge the point of view of the writer, and to write for particular purposes themselves. Critical literacy is particularly important in the later years of schooling, as students select between a number of resources, judge the appropriateness and validity of what they read, and write for particular audiences. This skill is highlighted when searching for information on the Internet, for example.

Teachers can contribute a range of practices within each resource family to each student's repertoire. As different students will use different practices in different contexts, having a range of practices available within each resource family is important. In a classroom reading lesson, you might see students learning to associate letters with their sounds and to blend sounds, predicting what will come next, taking part in a shared reading activity in which they talk about a book and what it is about, sequencing text, reading alone, reading aloud to someone else, rewriting a story to put it into a different context, exploring the structure of a fairytale, writing a response to a story they have read, using the computer to find out what others have thought of the story, and talking together about the story and what they liked or disliked about it. In another classroom, students might be looking at a different kind of text on a website, reading pictures and icons to navigate through the site, judging the truthfulness and relevance of what they have read, linking to other sites, talking together about what they want to find out and where and how they might find it, and discussing why different sites give conflicting 'facts' and how to determine which is correct.

NUMERACY DEVELOPMENT

numeracy
The ability to use mathematics effectively and with confidence in a range of contexts

Numeracy is often used as a partner term to literacy. The New Zealand Ministry of Education (2009a) uses the following definition: 'To be numerate is to have the ability and inclination to use mathematics effectively – at home, at work and in the community'. The Australian Curriculum (ACARA, 2012) states that 'numeracy involves students in recognising and understanding the role of mathematics in the world and having the dispositions and capacities to use mathematical knowledge and skills purposefully'. It involves mathematics, but goes beyond the mathematics classroom to be involved in all curriculum areas. Numeracy is identified as a general capability addressed across the Australian Curriculum. It is conceived as having six elements: estimating and calculating with whole numbers; recognising and using patterns and relationships; using fractions, decimals, percentages, ratios and rates; using spatial reasoning; interpreting statistical information; and using measurement (ACARA, 2012).

Knowledge of number starts to develop shortly after birth, as we discuss below, and is argued to be an inherent part of our experience of the world. It goes further than what is taught in school, with early number knowledge influencing not just later mathematical achievement, but also cognitive development as well as being linked to socioeconomic outcomes in later life (Ritchie & Bates, 2013; Siegler & Braithwaite, 2017).

Just as literacy is thought to be intrinsic to everyday functioning in our society, numeracy is also recognised as a key skill for learning and life. In 2008, the Australian Government set goals for literacy and numeracy that included: 'All young Australians become successful learners: have the essential skills in literacy and numeracy … as a foundation for success in all learning areas' (MCEETYA, 2008). New Zealand's *National education goals* similarly state: 'Priority should be given to the development of high levels of competence (knowledge and skills) in literacy and numeracy' (New Zealand Ministry of Education, 2004).

Bryant and Nuñes (2011) identify three main contributors to children's mathematical knowledge and understanding: their development of logical thinking (see Chapter 3 for more on this), meaningful experiences with quantity and number, and teaching of conventional systems such as counting. We will see examples of each of these contributors as we look at the development of numeracy throughout childhood and adolescence.

Emergent numeracy

As with language, awareness of mathematical principles seems to be biologically determined. Research with infants shows that they are aware of quantity from the first days after birth, recognising changes in numbers of small sets of objects (Antell & Keating, 1983). By the time they are two years old, children also show expectations that adding something will increase an amount, and that taking something away will decrease it (Sophian & Adams, 1987).

These early understandings are built upon by the developing child's experiences in the physical and social world. Look around you: almost unconsciously, you may notice that the level of tea in your cup is lower than it was earlier, that there is less text on this page than on the last, that the hands on the clock have moved from four towards five. We operate in and are surrounded by a world of quantities, measurements and spaces. Children's daily experiences habituate them to think about mathematical constructs. Stacking blocks and fitting cups inside one another help understandings about seriation to develop; playdough and sand and water play all help to develop understandings about quantity, and helping pour and mix in real or pretend cooking, or comparing the size of dessert portions to ensure the ice-cream is divided 'fairly', contribute to understandings about measurement. In addition, activities and the games parents play with young children help them to learn the number names, as well as ideas about quantity, size and shape. Rhymes such as 'one, two, buckle my shoe' are examples, as is the common game of walking or jumping up and down steps, counting as you go (see Figure 2.17). In an Australian longitudinal study that followed children from preschool into the first two years of Primary school, Reid & Andrews (2016) identified a range of understandings of early number among the preschool children in their study. They suggested a variety of activities parents and early childhood teachers can undertake with children to support their learning about number.

Source: Getty Images/Westend61

As children get older, these everyday activities change, but can still contribute: games with dice and cards help children to 'subitise' numbers – immediately recognise the number of items in a group – while setting the table for dinner develops an understanding of one-to-one correspondence. Still later, working out probability while playing a card game or watching a television game show, estimating costs for a mobile phone, comparing prices for items bought in the supermarket, and translating recipes from imperial to metric measurement, or adjusting quantities in a recipe for a larger or smaller number of people, continue to draw on and develop mathematical understandings.

As we have seen with other fields of development we have explored in this chapter, children's mathematical knowledge progressively builds on earlier developments. For example, Siegler & Braithwaite (2017) have established that knowledge of the size of numbers is foundational for arithmetic and other mathematics achievements in Primary and Secondary school. Similarly, knowledge of counting provides

FIGURE 2.17 Children's informal activities and games help them to learn about numbers.

a foundation for understanding addition, addition knowledge supports understanding of subtraction, addition and subtraction are the basis for understanding of multiplication, and multiplication knowledge supports learning about division (Siegler & Braithwaite, 2017).

Learning to be numerate

There are parallels to literacy development in numeracy development. A number of these are discussed here.

The role of language

Numeracy also builds on children's language development. LeFevre et al. (2010) showed that foundation skills in language (phonological awareness) predicted early mathematics performance, while Austin, Blevins-Knabe and Lokteff (2013) found a relationship between the language skills of letter awareness, letter sounds and name writing, and scores in early mathematics ability. Purpura & Napoli (2015) suggested that this relationship between language and numeracy is indirect rather than direct; language skills support informal numeracy, which supports the development of number knowledge. Ginsburg, Klein and Starkey (1998) pointed out that students without a vocabulary for mathematics have the most difficulty in understanding numeracy. Developing a vocabulary to describe numbers, shapes and measurements, and to explain how a mathematical problem might be solved, forms an important part of early numeracy activities in preschool and school. Children start with informal ways of describing mathematics, gradually developing more formal and specialised mathematical language as they move through primary and secondary school. Language is central to developing an understanding of mathematics (Anthony & Walshaw, 2007). Children are encouraged to talk about their strategies to explain how they arrived at an answer, and to describe their observations in mathematics classrooms (Bobis, Mulligan & Lowrie, 2013). This can involve oral and written language, as well as pictures and symbols. It helps children to make sense of their ideas and to learn to communicate their understandings, as well as to develop the important belief that mathematics is something that is not just transmitted (taught) by a teacher, but can be discovered, constructed and elaborated by each person. It can also help teachers to assess students' understandings. In Figure 2.18, a child describes his strategies in solving two maths problems, which enables the teacher to see his thought process and to guide him.

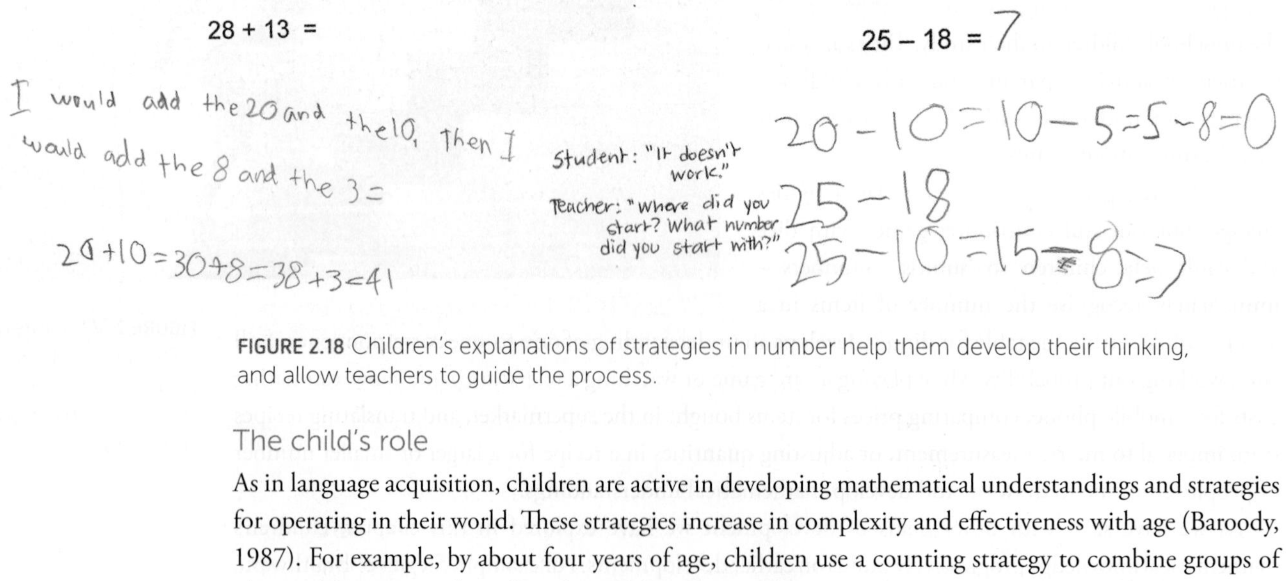

FIGURE 2.18 Children's explanations of strategies in number help them develop their thinking, and allow teachers to guide the process.

The child's role

As in language acquisition, children are active in developing mathematical understandings and strategies for operating in their world. These strategies increase in complexity and effectiveness with age (Baroody, 1987). For example, by about four years of age, children use a counting strategy to combine groups of objects: 'one, two … three, four (2 + 2)' (Ginsburg, Klein & Starkey, 1998). Such strategies for addition and subtraction appear spontaneously before the child starts school. These strategies are later extended by combining counting and the use of memorised number facts ('one and one is two … three, four, five (1 + 1 + 3)'), then by more sophisticated strategies such as recombining or restructuring numbers to simplify a problem ('nine and one are 10 and six are 16 (9 + 7)'). Children (and adults) typically draw on multiple strategies when solving number problems. With age, their strategies not only become more sophisticated, as we saw above, but they are able to choose increasingly more efficient strategies, improving in accuracy and speed (Siegler & Braithwaite, 2017). Children are able to apply strategies first with concrete objects they can see, then with invisible objects ('doing it in your head'). You may see why this is so in the description of Piaget's theory in Chapter 3. There is evidence that these strategies are constructed by the child, as well as being taught formally in school (de Corte & Verschaffel, 2006), and informally at home (Nunes & Bryant, 2015). Both the child's own activity and the experiences parents and teachers engage in with them are important to their development.

Just as children's errors in language show their developing understanding, the errors children (and adults) make in number are testimony to their own role in constructing their strategies and knowledge about mathematics (see Figure 2.19 for an example). Helping students to become aware of their strategies, by asking them to explain and justify how they solved a problem, along with sharing and comparing strategies with other students, contributes to their ability to evaluate and improve their learning. Table 2.1 gives a developmental framework for numeracy that identifies how strategies change with development. Such knowledge can help teachers to identify the counting strategies students are currently employing, and to help students to develop more advanced strategies.

Numeracy involves more than just number sense: the development of children's understanding of space, shapes and measurement has also been described, and has connections to art, science, engineering and making sense of the visual world around us (Bobis, Mulligan & Lowrie, 2009).

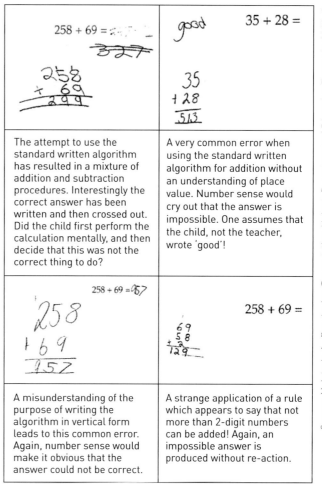

Source: McIntosh, A., *Developing Computation*. Hobart: Department of Education Tasmania, 2005. © Commonwealth of Australia reproduced by permission.

FIGURE 2.19
Common student errors when using algorithms without understanding.

Numeracy in the classroom

Children's exposure at school to more formal systems, with written rules and procedures, parallels learning to read and write, and the formal systems of language. The informal mathematics developed before school provides children with an important base on which to build new understandings. As with reading and writing, the challenge for teachers is to help children connect their informal understandings with new ways of thinking about and representing mathematics. One way in which teachers do this is with the use of concrete materials.

Children are faced at school with the task of learning formal systems for representing numbers: for example, that twenty-four is written as '24' and not as it is said ('20-4'). Children also learn formal ways of carrying out operations with number, such as in algorithms for addition and subtraction, or the procedure for long division or for multiplying numbers with more than two digits. Recent approaches to the teaching of numeracy in Australia and New Zealand focus on building connections between students' understandings and formal ways of doing things. They do this by developing students' understanding of mathematics using concrete materials such as fingers, blocks and counters, then encouraging the students to develop mental operations ('doing it in your head') and exploring strategies for operating with numbers, before using formal written approaches such as algorithms (for example, see McIntosh, 2005; New Zealand Ministry of Education, 2005). McIntosh points out that common student errors with algorithms result from their use of them as a formula, without understanding (see Figure 2.19). He suggests that when students develop their own written strategies for addition and subtraction, the connections with meaning are less likely to be lost. Sharing strategies for solving problems helps students to articulate their thinking, as well as recognise other ways of approaching a task.

Parents and others sometimes express a concern about when number facts will be learnt under this approach. There is still a place for the learning of number facts (addition and multiplication tables), but this follows work with numbers so that those facts are meaningful rather than simply a rhyme learnt by rote. Just as with reading, being able to retrieve the facts automatically frees up short-term memory for processing other aspects of a problem. As you can see in Table 2.1, it also allows students to recombine those facts to solve more complex problems. Box 2.11 outlines principles of effective mathematics teaching that have been identified from research.

TABLE 2.1 The number framework

Stage 0: Emergent	The student is unable to consistently count a given number of objects because they lack knowledge of counting sequences and/or one-to-one correspondence.
Stage 1: One-to-one counting	The student is able to count a set of objects or form sets of objects, but cannot solve problems that involve joining or separating sets.
Stage 2: Counting from one on materials	The student is able to count a set of objects or form sets of objects to solve simple addition and subtraction problems. The student solves problems by counting all the objects.
Stage 3: Counting from one by imaging	The student is able to visualise sets of objects to solve simple addition and subtraction problems. The student solves problems by counting all the objects.
Stage 4: Advanced counting	The student uses counting on or counting back to solve simple addition or subtraction tasks.
Stage 5: Early additive part–whole	The student uses a limited range of mental strategies to estimate answers and solve addition or subtraction problems. These strategies involve deriving the answer from known basic facts (for example, doubles, fives, making 10).
Stage 6: Advanced additive/early multiplicative part–whole	The student can estimate answers and solve addition and subtraction tasks involving whole numbers mentally by choosing appropriately from a broad range of advanced mental strategies (for example, place value partitioning, rounding and compensating, or reversibility). The student uses a combination of known facts and a limited range of mental strategies to derive answers to multiplication and division problems (for example, doubling, rounding or reversibility).
Stage 7: Advanced multiplicative part–whole	The student is able to choose appropriately from a broad range of mental strategies to estimate answers and solve multiplication and division problems. These strategies involve partitioning one or more of the factors (for example, place value partitioning, rounding and compensating, or reversibility).
Stage 8: Advanced proportional part–whole	The student can estimate answers and solve problems involving the multiplication and division of fractions and decimals using mental strategies. These strategies involve recognising the effect of number size on the answer and converting decimals to fractions where appropriate. These students have strongly developed number sense and algebraic thinking.

Source: 'The Number Framework'. Copyright © 2005 by New Zealand Ministry of Education. Used by permission.

BOX 2.11 CLASSROOM LINKS

EFFECTIVE PEDAGOGY IN MATHEMATICS

Anthony and Walshaw (2009) identified from research the following principles for effective mathematics teaching. They emphasised that the principles are interrelated, working together to engage learners in mathematics learning. They sit within wider family, school, community and education system practices.

- *An ethic of care:* With a focus on mathematical goals, effective teachers encourage model sharing and evaluation of ideas, which allows students to develop confidence in themselves as learners and mathematicians, and to take personal responsibility for their learning.
- *Arranging for learning:* Students are given opportunities to work independently, as well as in pairs or small groups and as a whole class, as they make sense of mathematical ideas. Each of these modes offers different benefits for learning.
- *Building on students' thinking:* Effective teachers start with students' current knowledge, interests and abilities and use them as a platform to develop further understanding. Real tasks can help to expose students' thinking, and to extend it. Misconceptions are viewed as steps on the way to full understanding, and are used to develop further opportunities for learning. Starting with students' current level of understanding enables effective teachers to adjust teaching to provide an appropriate level of challenge for each student.
- *Worthwhile mathematical tasks:* Tasks are selected that require students to use mathematical concepts and to think in mathematical ways. The same task may provide opportunities for practice, while also presenting a challenge and provoking thought.
- *Making connections:* Making meaningful links between different mathematical ideas contributes to conceptual knowledge. Being able to represent concepts in multiple ways similarly helps with flexible thinking and conceptual development. Effective teachers also help students to connect mathematics to their life experiences, and new knowledge to existing knowledge.
- *Assessment for learning:* Effective teachers use a variety of strategies to assess students' understanding. They make use of this information to guide instruction, give feedback that informs students about how they can improve, and encourage students to evaluate their own work. (See Chapter 13 for more on assessment for learning.)
- *Mathematical communication:* Effective teachers encourage students to explain their strategies and justify solutions. They model and explicitly teach students how to do this, and set up situations in which students take opposing viewpoints and defend their ideas to help them to develop the appropriate communication skills.
- *Mathematical language:* Mathematical terms are taught explicitly and modelled, with links made to home language and to everyday concepts.
- *Tools and representations:* A range of tools and representations link to mathematics; some examples are the number system, graphs and charts, number lines, formulae, concrete materials, student-made pictorials and ICT tools (see Chapter 12). Careful selection of tools supports students' visualisation, mathematical reasoning and conceptual understanding.
- *Teacher knowledge:* Teachers' knowledge of mathematics helps them to judge students' level of understanding and where to take them next, what they need to teach and how to teach it, and to connect concepts and ideas in multiple, complex ways. They can anticipate likely misconceptions and respond to them in ways that move students' understanding forwards.

Source: Adapted from Anthony and Walshaw (2009).

CourseMateExpress

Online resources
Go further: See a case study of the principles outlined in **Box 2.11** put into action to improve mathematics achievement for diverse learners.

Box 2.12 looks at the classroom implications of skills development. Vygotsky's work, described in Chapter 3, may help you think about how to assess children's abilities and how to take account of these in your own teaching. Chapter 13, which deals with assessment, contains further strategies that might be helpful.

BOX 2.12 IMPLICATIONS FOR EDUCATORS

DEVELOPING CHILDREN'S SKILLS FOR SCHOOL

1   Supporting EAL/D learners is important to their success, not only in English, but also across the curriculum.

2   Encouraging children to think and talk about new concepts in their native language can help them acquire the concepts and learn to express those concepts in English.

3   Involving parents in the classroom and encouraging them to talk to children in their own language can help facilitate the process of acquiring and expressing concepts in English.

4   Students bring important skills and knowledge to their learning, as well as attitudes about particular subjects or skills and about learning itself.

5   Recognising students' past experiences is important for accurately matching teaching to students' abilities and experiences.

6   Current approaches to teaching language, literacy and numeracy take account of what the student already knows, in order to build new knowledge. (Examples of this in numeracy are the Mathematics K–10 Continuum of key ideas developed in NSW (NSW Department of Education and Communities, 2014), and the Numeracy Project in New Zealand (Ministry of Education, 2005), which aim to help teachers match teaching to students' number strategies.)

7   Language is vital to the development of competence in additional language, literacy and numeracy.

8   There are connections between literacy, numeracy and other curriculum areas, which mean that these skills should be directly addressed in teaching, irrespective of the curriculum area.

9   Literacy, numeracy and additional-language competency are required, and continue to develop, throughout schooling.

PRINCIPLES OF DEVELOPMENT

In this chapter, we have examined the acquisition of a number of different skills in the domains of physical development, language, literacy and numeracy. Despite the range of domains and skills, some principles of development can be deduced that also apply across the cognitive and socioemotional domains discussed in chapters 3 and 4. The principles are as follows:

Development involves a series of progressive and orderly changes leading to maturity

Development involves change of a particular type, and is generally orderly (we learn to crawl first, then to walk, then to run). It is also directional: the changes, at least in childhood and adolescence, tend to lead towards more complex, effective ('mature') behaviour. This trend towards complexity and more organisation is seen in all aspects of development, and reflects brain development.

Development is continuous but uneven

One of the enduring debates in theories of development is about whether we describe it as continuous or discontinuous (see Box 2.13). Different areas of the body and brain develop at different times, as do different functions. In addition, there are cascade events in human development that create opportunities for significant shifts across multiple domains. These include independent locomotion (crawling and walking), language acquisition, and puberty. Arguably, there are also cultural cascade events that similarly create opportunities for developmental shifts across domains. Starting school is an example in Western cultures.

Development is a lifelong process

Although we develop at different rates in different areas, we can be said to be developing throughout the lifespan. Commonly, children's development is described as occurring in a number of stages: infancy (0–2 years), early childhood (3–7 years), middle childhood (8–11 years) and adolescence (12–20 years). You will recognise the age ranges associated with these stages in the descriptions of Piaget's theory in Chapter 3, and in Erikson's theory in Chapter 4.

A number of researchers have noted the shifts that occur in children at about two to three years old, seven to eight years old and 11–12 years old – not only in cognitive development, but also in the social and personal areas. Growth spurts have also been observed in the brain at these ages. The shifts can be attributed to changes in both maturation and environment. Although there are physiological changes that occur in all cultures, the precise age at which the shifts occur varies due to environmental factors such as diet or cultural practices.

Development can vary from one individual to another, as well as within each individual

The most obvious developmental variations occur between males and females, with girls tending to lead boys in physical development. Other group variations can be observed among different ethnic groups. There are many other sources of variability too, including variations within individuals, with development in different domains, and sometimes within a single domain, proceeding at different rates. The discussion of brain development in adolescence is an example of this. The chapters in Module III of this book examine a number of these sources of difference in detail. In general, while genes play a role, the variability in development can be explained by looking at the multiple and complex interactions between forces affecting that development.

There are multiple pathways of development

These variations may be in timing, but they may also be in the pathways of development: the particular pattern of factors that contribute to development may vary as a result of contextual and individual factors. We have seen this in motor, language and literacy development.

Development results from both maturation and learning

This position represents the nature–nurture debate discussed in Chapter 9, and in Box 2.13. As we have seen, both innate and environmental forces combine to influence development across the physical and language domains. Other chapters in this module similarly illustrate the influence of a mixture of innate and environmental forces in development.

BOX 2.13 IMPLICATIONS FOR EDUCATORS

THINKING CRITICALLY ABOUT DEVELOPMENT

There are some long standing debates that have distinguished many of the theoretical approaches to development that you will encounter in this module. Current relational systems theories of development recognise the complex interaction between the biological and psychological systems of the individual, and the sociocultural contexts within which they develop (Overton & Molenaar, 2015; Mascolo & Fischer, 2015). This has implications for how we view these debates, and in particular, suggests that at different time points, for different processes, and for different individuals, the processes, patterns and influences on development will vary. Implications of this for educators are suggested below.

1   *Is development continuous or discontinuous?* Does it progress as an abrupt series of changes, like ascending a staircase, or in small increments, like going up an escalator? Both may be true. Continuous theories propose that children's behaviour and skills are less complex versions of what adults can do. With development, they gain more knowledge and practice, which contributes to gradual improvements in these skills and abilities. Discontinuous theories hold that there are qualitative differences between the ways in which children and adults think about and operate in the world, and that with development, children's thinking and behaviour undergoes radical, relatively sudden changes from one stage to the next. Evidence for both patterns of development can be found, depending on the scale at which the research is focused. When working with children, educators need to both understand and start from the child's current level of thinking and acting, and have in mind the more advanced skill or understanding to which they are guiding them.

2   *Are the course and processes of development general or specific?* Can we describe the same set of developmental processes for all people and for all domains, or do we need a separate picture of development for different skills, and for different contexts (perhaps for different people, or for people at different times in their lives)? Some theories seek to distil the basic processes of development that occur across all people, while others investigate the effects of different contexts on development. Some emphasise general processes across domains, while others propose that each area of development has its own process, particular to it. The study of development involves the challenging task of both finding order and patterns across individuals, and explaining variations in development (Mascolo & Fischer, 2015). Teachers also typically work with groups, and need to look for both the common processes and needs they can address for the whole group, and the individual differences that they must cater for.

3   *Is development mainly influenced by innate or environmental factors?* You may have heard of this is 'the nature–nurture debate'. However, current evidence suggests that both innate *and* environmental factors are important, and interact in development. For example, genes may be expressed in different ways in response to different environmental conditions; and a particular genetic pattern may lead one person to respond to an environmental condition in a different way from another. The work on children's responses to stress, discussed earlier in this chapter, is an example of this. There is evidence of both sets of influences in all aspects of development, irrespective of domain. For educators, this suggests that we can expect children or young people to respond differently to the experiences they encounter, and can understand their responses in terms of a combination of genetic and environmental influences.

4   *Is development fixed or changeable?* The nature–nurture debate also gave rise to another debate, between views of development as fixed or stable from birth or early experience, and views of development as changeable over time. We have seen evidence in this chapter of the importance of experiences in infancy, in particular for brain development. However, we have also seen evidence of plasticity of brain development throughout life. The work on attachment in **Box 2.5** is another example of both enduring and changeable elements

>>

in development for different individuals. While early experience undoubtedly plays a role in later development, there is potential for change through later experience and contextual effects. This highlights the important role that educators play in the development of the children they teach, through the experiences, relationships and contexts they shape throughout early childhood care and primary and secondary schooling.

ACTIVITIES

1 Consider an example of development from your own experience or the experience of someone you know. What evidence of the interaction of nature and environment can you discern in this example? What influences on development are evident, and how have they interacted with one another?

2 Trace back through the chapter to collect examples of development as continuous and discontinuous, general and specific, fixed and changeable. This is something you might look for in the other chapters in this module as well. Go to the personal philosophy section of the student companion website and fill in your views after reviewing this evidence.

3 Think about how your growing understanding of these issues might influence your teaching practice.

Development occurs in context and is influenced by environment

Examples are the environmental influences on language development in the social interactions children hear and are involved in, and the importance of parent–infant interactions for brain development in infancy. In terms of physical development, family and community activities and the formal activities of school contribute to children's motor skills.

Children are active in development

Far from being something that simply 'happens' to children, development grows out of children's activity. For example, crawling produces changes in brain structure that support physical, perceptual and cognitive changes. Children actively try to make sense of language and of mathematics. These attempts may result in errors, but they are testimony to the important role children play in their own development in all domains. Children's activity also shapes their environment; for instance, as parents respond to their children, children respond to their peers, and teachers respond to individual students in their classes. Figure 2.20 gives an example.

Development is cumulative

One change provides a basis for further change. In this chapter we have seen a number of examples of the close interaction between different dimensions of development. As one area develops, it changes the kinds of activities children engage in and their relationships with those around them, providing new opportunities for development in it and in other areas. One example is adolescents' capacity for

FIGURE 2.20 Children's activity contributes to their development, and shapes their environment. How is these children's play changing the social environment they are interacting in, and adding to their development?

Shutterstock.com/Robert Kneschke

abstract thinking, which changes the way in which they deal with their emotions. This in turn affects their friendships and influences their thoughts and behaviours.

Box 2.14 looks at a number of the implications for educators of considering the developmental principles.

CourseMateExpress

Online resources
Take a moment
to consider your
philosophy of learning
and teaching. You
may wish to use
the **Develop your
philosophy** tool on the
textbook's CourseMate
Express website.

BOX 2.14 IMPLICATIONS FOR EDUCATORS

CONSIDERING DEVELOPMENT IN THE CLASSROOM

- Because development is orderly and progressive, teaching must be tailored to children's developmental levels (that is, there is no point teaching calculus to preschoolers, or basketball to babies). This involves teachers being aware of the course of development across a number of domains. This chapter and others in Module I should help you develop such knowledge.
- Stages in development coincide with stages of schooling, in that middle childhood roughly coincides with the primary years, and adolescence with secondary schooling. Recognising developmental shifts that occur with age, some states and territories in Australia further break these broad groupings into stages of two years each. The aim is that teachers plan learning and teaching strategies to match each student's developmental stage, and that students develop skills appropriate to their developmental level.
- Developmental variations are important for teachers to consider. One explanation of gender differences in literacy outcomes is the relatively slower development of language in boys. It has been suggested that boys should receive a different kind of literacy instruction to cater for this developmental difference (Rowe & Rowe, 2002). Chapter 11 explores this and other gender issues in greater depth.
- Because development occurs in context, what happens around children influences their development. It is important for teachers to consider not just what is taught, but how it is taught. Other environments children are involved in also influence their development through the experiences and knowledge provided. Teachers therefore need to know about children's home environments in order to effectively consider children's needs. Chapter 11 explores this issue in relation to culture and poverty.
- That children are active in development suggests that students should be mentally and physically active in their learning, too. For example, learners can be encouraged to make sense of how new and old experiences and knowledge fit together.
- Students make sense of their experiences. We can encourage this process in schooling by asking students to develop their own approaches to tasks before introducing them to standard methods. It is also important to check on students' understandings of new material. What sense are they making of these new experiences?
- Development is cumulative, so it is important when teaching skills to build up from what students can do first, and towards the final goal. Identifying a number of steps or component skills in a complex task can help in this process. Task analysis, described in Chapter 5, is one approach to this strategy. Designing tasks that draw on skills from a number of areas can help students consolidate earlier achievements, as well as integrate, coordinate and apply their skills.

CONCLUDING COMMENTS

Development is influenced by the complex interaction of genetics, environment and the activity of individuals themselves. Effective teaching therefore recognises each of the possible influences on a student's development. This chapter has explored these influences on physical and language development, and on the development of some school-based skills. In Chapter 3, we look at some theories of cognitive development.

STUDY TOOLS

ONLINE STUDY RESOURCES

Visit http://login.cengagebrain.com and use the access code that comes with this book for 12 months' access to the student resources for this text.

The CourseMate Express website contains a range of resources and study tools for this chapter, including:

- a **self-check quiz**

- **crosswords**, **flashcards** and a **glossary** to help you revise the key terms from this chapter
- the **Go further** materials and **interactive activity** mentioned in the chapter.

CourseMateExpress

CHAPTER REVIEW

- There are connections between physical, cognitive, language, social and emotional development throughout the lifespan.
- Maturation, parents, the community and school, the physical environment and the child's own activity all contribute to motor-skill development.
- The development of fine and gross motor skills is important in early childhood, while middle childhood sees increased coordination and the combining of motor skills.
- Puberty is the major physical development in adolescence, presenting challenges to adolescents' self-image and family relationships. Individual differences in the timing of puberty affect adolescents' ability to adapt successfully to these changes.
- There are group differences in development due to environmental factors such as nutrition, and sociocultural factors such as gender-typed activity.
- Brain development also shows complementary influences from genetics, environment and the child's activity. Each of these things affects the others in the child's development.
- Developmental increases in complexity and coordination of thoughts, feelings and behaviours are associated with structural neurological changes such as increases in neuronal size and complexity, as well as myelination, which improves the efficiency of message transmission.

- The course of first-language acquisition is remarkably consistent across cultural and language groups. It shows children's active involvement in their acquisition of language.
- Adults make important contributions to language development, which continue into a child's school years.
- The school-based skills associated with second-language learning, literacy and numeracy all build upon early developments in physical, motor and language skills, as well as the cognitive, social and emotional developments discussed in Chapters 3 and 4.
- Children's active involvement in making sense of their world shows itself in their understandings about language and number from the first days after birth. In schools, we build upon these early understandings and so need to be aware of and recognise them.
- Development is a series of progressive and orderly changes leading to maturity, which shows both consistency across humanity and also individual difference. Development is lifelong, with each change providing a basis for future changes.
- Development also occurs in context, with elements of the individual and the environment interacting to produce the results we see. It is influenced by both the individual's maturation and their learning from interactions with the environment.

PUTTING IT TOGETHER

Making links between 'emerging skills' and material in other chapters

CHAPTER 2 Emerging skills

LINKAGES

Principles of development introduced in this chapter are also evident in cognitive, social, emotional and moral development, discussed in chapters 3 and 4.

Consider how physical, brain and language development contribute to, and are influenced by, cognitive, social and emotional development.

CHAPTER 3
Cognitive development

CHAPTER 4
Social, emotional and moral development

QUESTIONS AND ACTIVITIES FOR SELF-ASSESSMENT AND DISCUSSION

1 What are some influences on development? Describe this in relation to the development of a particular skill such as reading, learning to play the clarinet or playing basketball.

2 Explain motor development in terms of contributions of brain, body and behaviour.

3 What variation in physical development exists between groups, and how can individuals' development be supported in schools?

4 Why does the number of neurons decrease with age after infancy? What role does learning play in this process?

5 What factors contribute to resilience for children at risk of poor developmental outcomes? Draw a diagram of the factors and their interaction.

6 How do adults contribute to language development? How can you apply this to the roles of teachers and parents in students' language learning in schools?

7 How are the development of literacy and numeracy both similar and different?

8 What aspects of physical, brain and language development support learning in school?

9 Describe how meaningful experiences, logical development, language and formal teaching contribute to the development of mathematical understanding. What implications does this have for you as a teacher of numeracy?

10 What are the four key debates in development research? Explain how the elements work together rather than in opposition to one another in development.

11 Identify an event that triggers a developmental cascade, the opportunities it presents for development, and the consequences for development in other domains.

12 Provide examples of how children's activity contributes to their development, and of the contribution the environment makes. How do these things interact?

FURTHER RESEARCH

SEARCH ME! AND EDUCATION DATABASES

Explore Search Me! education for articles relevant to this chapter. Fast and convenient, Search Me! education is updated daily and provides you with 24-hour access to full-text articles from hundreds of scholarly and popular journals, ebooks and newspapers, including *The Australian* and *The New York Times*. Log in to Search Me! through http://login.cengagebrain.com and use the search terms listed here as a starting point:

- brain development
- EAL/D
- language development
- literacy
- motor skills
- numeracy
- physical development
- second-language acquisition
- risk and resilience.

Adding terms such as 'early childhood', 'middle childhood' and 'adolescence' will limit the results to the age group you are interested in.

You can also use these terms to explore databases such as ERIC, PsycINFO and the Australian Education Index.

RECOMMENDED WEBSITES

Visit the website of your local department of education to look at their approach to teaching physical education, EAL/D, literacy and numeracy:

Australia: http://education.gov.au

New Zealand: http://www.education.govt.nz

Australian Capital Territory: www.det.act.gov.au

New South Wales: www.schools.nsw.edu.au

Northern Territory: www.education.nt.gov.au

Queensland: http://education.qld.gov.au

South Australia: www.decd.sa.gov.au

Tasmania: www.education.tas.gov.au

Victoria: www.education.vic.gov.au

Western Australia: www.education.wa.edu.au

Centres of neurological research relating to education:

Centre for Educational Neuroscience (UK): www.educationalneuroscience.org.uk

Science of Learning Centre (AUS): http://qbi.uq.edu.au/science-of-learning-centre

RECOMMENDED READING

Berk, L. E. (2013). *Child development* (9th ed.). Boston: Allyn & Bacon.

Berko Gleason, J. & Ratner, B. (Eds) (2017). *The development of language* (9th ed.). Needham Heights, MA: Allyn & Bacon.

Levey, S. (2014). *Introduction to language development*. San Diego: Plural Publishing.

Lightfoot, C., Cole, M. & Cole, S. R. (2018). *The development of children* (8th ed.). New York: Worth.

McDevitt, T. M. & Ormrod, J. E. (2016). *Child development and education* (6th ed.). Saddle River, NJ: Pearson.

REFERENCES

Adams, M. (2011). Advancing our students' language and literacy: The challenge of complex texts. *American Educator, 53,* 3–11.

Adolph, K. E. & Berger, S. E. (2010). Physical and motor development. In M. H. Bornstein & M. E. Lamb (Eds), *Developmental science: An advanced textbook,* (6th ed.). Hillsdale, NJ: Lawrence Erlbaum Associates.

Adolph, K. E., Robinson, S. R. (2015). Motor development. In Liben, L., Muller, U. (Eds.), *Handbook of child psychology and developmental science Vol. 2 Cognitive Processes,* (7th edn). pp. 114–157. New York, NY: Wiley.

Ainsworth, M.D.S., & Bell, S.M. (1970). Attachment, exploration, and separation: Illustrated by the behavior of one-year-olds in a strange situation. *Child Development, 41,* 49–67.

Ainsworth, M.D.S., Blehar, M.C., Waters, E. & Wall, S. (1978). *Patterns of attachment: A psychological study of the strange situation.* Hillsdale, NJ: Erlbaum.

Anderson, D. I., Campos, J. J., Witherington, D. C., Dahl, A., Rivera, M., He, M., Uchiyama, I. & Barbu-Roth, M. (2013). The role of locomotion in psychological development. *Frontiers in Psychology, 4*(440), 1–17.

Anderson, R., Wilson, P. & Fielding, L. (1988). Growth in reading and how children spend their time outside of school. *Reading Research Quarterly, 23,* 285–303.

Anglin, J. M. (1993). Vocabulary development: A morphological analysis. *Monographs of the Society for Research in Child Development, 58*(10, Serial No. 238), 1–165.

Antell, S. & Keating, D. (1983). Perception of numerical invariance in neonates. *Child Development, 54,* 595–701.

Anthony, G. & Walshaw, M. (2007). *Effective pedagogy in Mathematics/Pangarau: Best evidence synthesis iteration [BES].* Wellington: Ministry of Education.

Anthony, G. & Walshaw, M. (2009). Effective pedagogy in mathematics. *Educational Practices Series, 19.* Belley, Fr: International Bureau of Education.

Austin, A. M. B., Blevins-Knabe, B. & Lokteff, M. (2013). Early mathematics and phonological awareness in two child care settings. *Early Child Development and Care, 183*(9), 1197–214.

Australian Curriculum, Assessment and Reporting Authority. (2012). *The Australian Curriculum: Numeracy background.* Retrieved from www.australiancurriculum. edu.au/generalcapabilities/numeracy/introduction/background

Australian Government. (2008). *Australian national children's nutrition and physical activity survey.* Retrieved from www.health.gov.au/internet/main/publishing.nsf/Content/8F4516D5FAC0700ACA257BF0001E0109/$File/childrens-nut-phys-survey.pdf

Australian Sports Commission. (2004). *Children's sport: An overview. A research report by the University of South Australia.* Canberra:

Australian Sports Commission. (2011). *Active after school communities: Facts and figures.* Retrieved from www.ausport.gov.au/participating/aasc.

Barnett, L. M., van Beurden, E., Morgan, P. J., Brooks, L. O. & Beard, J. R. (2009). Childhood motor skill proficiency as a predictor of adolescent physical activity. *Journal of Adolescent Health, 44*(3), 252–9.

Baroody, A. J. (1987). *Children's mathematical thinking.* New York: Teachers College Press.

Bates, E. & Goodman, J. (1999). On the emergence of grammar from the lexicon. In B. MacWhinney (Ed.), *The emergence of language.* Mahwah, NJ: Erlbaum.

Bellis, M., Downing, J. & Ashton, J. (2006). Adults at 12? Trends in puberty and their public health consequences. *Journal of Epidemiology and Community Health, 60*(11), 910–911.

Berk, L. (2012). *Child development* (9th ed.). Boston: Allyn & Bacon.

Best, J. R. (2010). Effects of physical activity on children's executive function: Contributions of experimental research on aerobic exercise. *Developmental Review, 30,* 331–51.

Bjork, J.M. & Pardini, D.A. (2015). Who are those risk-taking adolescents? Individual differences in developmental neuroimaging research. *Developments in Cognitive Neuroscience, 11,* 56–64.

Blake, J., Vitale, G., Osborne, P. & Olshansky, E. (2005). A cross-cultural comparison of communicative gestures in human infants during the transition to language. *Gesture, 5,* 201–17.

Bloom, L. (1998). Language acquisition in its developmental context. In D. Kuhn & R. S. Siegler (Eds), *Handbook of child psychology, Vol. 2: Cognition, perception, and language* (5th ed., pp. 309–70). New York: J. Wiley.

Bobis, J., Mulligan, J. & Lowrie, T. (2009). *Mathematics for children* (2nd ed.). Melbourne: Pearson Education Australia.

Bobis, J., Mulligan, J. & Lowrie, T. (2013). *Mathematics for children: Challenging children to think mathematically* (4th ed.). Sydney: Pearson Education.

Bornstein, M.H., Hahn, C.S. & Suwalsky, J.T.D. (2013). Physically developed and exploratory young infants contribute to their own long-term academic achievement. *Psychological Science, 24,* 1906–1917.

Bowlby, J. (1969), *Attachment and loss, Vol. 1: Attachment.* New York: Basic Books.

Bowlby, J. (1973). *Attachment and loss, Vol. 2: Separation.* New York: Basic Books.

Boyce, W.T., & Ellis, B.J. (2005). Biological sensitivity to context: I. An evolutionary-developmental theory of the origins and functions of stress reactivity. *Development and Psychopathology, 17*(2), 271–301.

Bruer, J. T. (1999). In search of ... brain-based education. *Phi Delta Kappan, 80*(9), 648–54.

Bryant, J. B. (2013). Language in social contexts: Development of communicative competence. In J. B. Gleason & N. B. Ratner (Eds), *The development of language* (8th ed., pp. 163–89). Boston: Allyn & Bacon.

Bryant, P. E., Bradley, L., McClean, M. & Crossland, J. (1989). Nursery rhymes, phonological skills, and reading. *Journal of Child Language, 16,* 407–28.

Bryant, P. E. & Nuñes, T. (2011). Children's understanding of mathematics. In U. Goswami (Ed.), *The Wiley-Blackwell handbook of childhood cognitive development* (2nd ed., pp. 549–73). Oxford: Blackwell.

Caine, R. N. & Caine, G. (1991). *Making connections: Teaching and the human brain.* Alexandria, VA: ASCD.

Cameron-Faulkner, T., Lieven, E. & Tomasello, M. (2003). A construction-based analysis of child directed speech. *Cognitive Science, 27,* 843–73.

Campbell, B. C. (2011). Adrenarche and middle childhood, *Human Nature, 22,* 327–49.

Campos, J. J., Anderson, D. I., Barbu-Roth, M. A., Hubbard, E. M., Hertenstein, M. J. & Witherington, D. (2000). Travel broadens the mind. *Infancy, 1*(2), 149–219.

Carey, R. N., Donaghue, N. & Broderick, P. (2014). Body image concern among Australian adolescent girls: The role of body comparisons with models and peers. *Body Image, 11*(1), 81–4.

Carpenter, M., Nagell, K. & Tomasello, M. (1998). Social cognition, joint attention, and communicative competence from 9 to 15 months of age. *Monographs of the Society for Research in Child Development, 63*(4, Serial No. 255).

Casey, B.J., Getz, S., Galvan, A., (2008). The adolescent brain. *Developmental Review, 28*(1), 62–77.

Cashmore, J. (2001). Early experience and brain development. *National Child Protection Clearinghouse Newsletter, 9,* 6–9.

Center, Y. (2005). *Beginning reading: A balanced approach to literacy instruction during the first three years at school.* Sydney: Allen & Unwin.

Center on the Developing Child at Harvard University. (2011). *Building the brain's 'air traffic control' system: How early experiences shape the development of executive function, Working Paper No. 11.* Retrieved from http://developingchild.harvard.edu/index.php/resources/reports_and_working_papers/working_papers/wp11/

Center on the Developing Child at Harvard University (2015). *Supportive relationships and active skill-building strengthen the foundations of resilience: Working paper no. 13.* Retrieved from http://www.developingchild.harvard.edu.

Center on the Developing Child at Harvard University (2016a). *8 Things to Remember about Child Development*. Retrieved from https://developingchild.harvard.edu/resources/8-things-remember-child-development/

Center on the Developing Child at Harvard University (2016b). *From Best Practices to Breakthrough Impacts: A Science-Based Approach to Building a More Promising Future for Young Children and Families*. http://www.developingchild.harvard.edu

Centers for Disease Control and Prevention. (2010). *The association between school based physical activity, including physical education, and academic performance*. Atlanta, GA: U.S. Department of Health and Human Services.

Chall, J. (1996). *Stages of reading development*. Orlando, FL: Harcourt Brace.

Clay, M. M (1991). *Becoming literate: The construction of inner control*. Birkenhead, NZ: Heinemann Education.

Clay, M. M. (1998). *By different paths to common outcomes*. York: Stenhouse.

Comber, B., Cormack, P., Nixon, H., Grant, P., Nichols, S. & Shore, S. (2005). *Submission to the National Inquiry into the teaching of literacy. Submission no. 316*. Centre for studies in literacy, policy, and learning cultures, University of South Australia. Retrieved from www.dest.gov.au/nitl/submission_index.htm

Commonwealth of Australia. (2008). *National Numeracy Review*. Canberra: Council of Australian Governments.

Commonwealth of Australia, Department of Health. (2011a). Australia's physical activity and sedentary behaviour guidelines for children (5–12 years). Retrieved from www.health.gov.au/internet/main/publishing.nsf/content/health-pubhlth-strateg-phys-actguidelines#apa512

Commonwealth of Australia, Department of Health. (2011b). Australia's physical activity and sedentary behaviour guidelines for young people (13–17 years). Retrieved from www.health.gov.au/internet/main/publishing.nsf/content/health-pubhlthstrateg-phys-act-guidelines#apa512

Commonwealth of Australia, Department of Health and Ageing. (2005). *Discussion paper for the development of recommendations for children's and youths' participation in health enhancing physical activity*. Canberra: Commonwealth of Australia.

Cooper, R. P. & Aslin, R. N. (1994). Developmental differences in infant attention to the spectral properties of infant-directed speech. *Child Development, 65*, 1663–77.

Cope, B. & Kalantzis, M. (Eds). (2000). *Multiliteracies: Literacy learning and the design of social futures*. London: Routledge.

Cote, J. E. & Allahar, A. L. (1996). *Generation on hold: Coming of age in the late twentieth century*. New York: New York University Press.

Cox, R. (2015). Contextualising multilingualism in Australia today. *English in Australia, 50*(1), 13–20.

Crowley, M. J., Wu, J., Molfese, P. J. & Mayes, L. (2010). Social exclusion in middle childhood: Rejection events, slow-wave neural activity, and ostracism distress. *Social Neuroscience, 5*, 483–95.

Cummins, J. (1979). Cognitive/academic language proficiency, linguistic interdependence, the optimal age question, and some other matters. *Working Papers in Bilingualism, 9*, 1–43.

Daiute, C. & Dalton, B. (1993). Collaboration between children learning to write: Can novices be masters? *Cognitive Instruction, 10*, 281–333.

Davis, C. L., Tomporowski P. D., McDowell, J. E., Austin, B. P., Miller, P. H., Yanasak, N. E., Allison, J. D. & Naglieri, J. A. (2011). Exercise improves executive function and achievement and alters brain activation in overweight children: A randomized, controlled trial. *Health Psychology, 30*(1), 91–8.

Davis, J. (2001). Personal communication.

Deakin University. (2005). *Submission to the National Inquiry into the Teaching of Literacy. Faculty of Education Deakin University. Submission No. 306*. Retrieved from www.dest.gov.au/nitl/submissions/301-320.htm

De Corte, E. & Verschaffel, L. (2006). Mathematical thinking and learning. In K. A. Renninger & I. E. Sigel (Series Eds), R. M. Lerner & W. Damon (Eds), *Handbook of child psychology, Vol. 4: Child psychology in practice* (6th ed., pp. 103–52). Hoboken, NJ: John Wiley & Sons.

De Jong, E., Visscher, T., HiraSing, R., Heymans, M., Seidell, J., & Renders, C. (2013). Association between TV viewing, computer use and overweight, determinants and competing activities of screen time in 4- to 13-year-old children. *International Journal of Obesity, 37*(1), 47–53.

Dehaene, S., Molko, N., Cohen, L. & Wilson, A. J. (2004). Arithmetic and the brain. *Current Opinion in Neurobiology, 14*(2), 218–24.

Diehl, S. F. (2014). The development of literacy skills. In S. Levey, *Introduction to language development* (pp. 247–70). San Diego: Plural Publishing.

Dunn, J. & Kendrick, C. (1982). *Siblings: Love, envy and understanding*. Cambridge, MA: Harvard University Press.

Edwards, B. (1981). *Drawing on the right side of the brain*. London: Souvenir.

Ellis, R. (2005). *Instructed second language acquisition. A literature review. Report to the Ministry of Education*. Wellington: New Zealand Ministry of Education.

Ely, R. (2005). Language and literacy in the school years. In J. B. Gleason (Ed.), *The development of language* (6th ed, pp. 395–443). Boston: Pearson.

Ely, R. & McCabe, A. (1994). The language play of kindergarten children. *First Language, 14*, 19–35.

Evelyth, P. B. & Tanner, J. M. (1990). *Worldwide variation in human growth* (2nd ed.). Cambridge: Cambridge University Press.

Fine, C. (2010). *Delusions of gender: How our minds, society and neurosexism create difference*. Melbourne: WW Norton.

Fine, C. (2013). Debunking the pseudoscience behind 'boy brains' and 'girl brains'. *ACER Research Conference Proceedings*. Retrieved from http://research.acer.edu.au/research_conference/RC2013/

Fischer, K. (2004). The myths and promises of the learning brain. *Ed. Magazine*, Spring. Retrieved from www.gse.harvard.edu/news/features/fischer12012004.html

Floor, P. & Akhtar, N. (2006). Can 18-month-old infants learn words by listening in on conversations? *Infancy, 9*, 327–39.

Freebody, P. & Luke, A. (1999). A map of possible practices: Further notes on the four resources model. *Practically Primary, 4*(2), 5–8.

Friederici, A. D., Friedrich, M. & Christophe, A. (2007). Brain responses in 4-month-old infants are already language specific. *Current Biology, 17*, 1208–11.

Ge, X. & Natsuaki, M. N. (2009). In search of explanations for early pubertal timing effects on developmental psychopathology. *Current Directions in Psychological Science, 18*, 327–31.

Gee, J. P., Allen, A-R. & Clinton, K. (2001). Language, class and identity: Teenagers fashioning themselves through language. *Linguistics and Education, 12*, 175–94.

Gibbons, P. (2002). *Scaffolding language, scaffolding learning: Teaching second language learners in the mainstream classroom*. Portsmouth, NH: Heinemann.

Gibbons, P. (2014). *Scaffolding language, scaffolding learning* (2nd ed.). New York: Heinemann.

Ginsburg, H. P., Klein, A. & Starkey, P. (1998). The development of children's mathematical thinking: Connecting research with practice. In I. E. Siegel & K. A. Renninger (Eds), *Handbook of child psychology, Vol. 2: Cognition, perception and language* (5th ed., pp. 401–76). New York: Wiley.

Goldfield, B. A., Snow, C. E. & Willenberg, I. A. (2013). Variation in language development: Implications for research and theory. In J. Berko-Gleason & N. B. Ratner (Eds), *The development of language* (8th ed.). New York: Allyn & Bacon.

Goldstein, B. A. (2014). Factors associated with delivering speech and language services to bilinguals. In S. Levey (Ed.), *Introduction to language development*. San Diego: Plural Publishing.

Gombert, J. E. (1992). *Metalinguistic development*. Hemel Hempstead, Harvester Wheatsheaf.

Gopnick, A. & Meltzoff, A. N. (1997). *Words, thoughts and theories*. Cambridge, MA: MIT Press.

Goswami, U. (2004). Neuroscience and education. *British Journal of Educational Psychology*, *74*(1), 1–14.

Hart, B. & Risley, T. R. (1995). *Meaningful differences in the everyday experience of young American children*. Baltimore, MD: Paul H. Brookes.

Hickie, I. B. & Whitwell, B. G. (2009). *Alcohol and the teenage brain: Safest to keep them apart*, BMRI Monograph 2009-2. Sydney: Brain & Mind Research Institute.

Hötting, K. & Röder, B. (2013). Beneficial effects of physical exercise on neuroplasticity and cognition. *Neuroscience & Biobehavioral Reviews*, *37*(9), 2243–57.

Humphrey, G. & Dumontheil, I. (2016). Development of Risk-Taking, Perspective-Taking, and Inhibitory Control During Adolescence. *Developments in Neuropsychology*, *41*(1–2), 59–76.

Iivonen, S. & Saakslahti, A. K. (2014). Preschool children's fundamental motor skills: A review of significant determinants. *Early Child Development and Care*, *184*(7), 1107–26.

Johansson, B. B. (2011). Current trends in stroke rehabilitation: A review with focus on brain plasticity. *Acta Neurologica Scandinavica*, *123*(3), 147–59.

Kopp, C. B. (2011). Development in the early years: Socialisation, motor development, and consciousness. *Annual Review of Psychology*, *62*, 165–87.

Kreppner, J. M., Rutter, M., Beckett, C., Castle, J., Colvert, E, Groothues, C., Hawkins, A., O'Connor, T. G., Stevens, S. & Sonuga-Barke, E. J. S. (2007). Normality and impairment following profound early institutional deprivation: A longitudinal follow-up into early adolescence, *Developmental Psychology*, *43*(4), 931–46.

Kretch, K. S., Franchak, J. M. & Adolph, K. E. (2014). Crawling and walking infants see the world differently. *Child Development*, *85*(4), 1503–18.

Lansford, J. E., Criss, M. M., Pettit, G. S., Dodge, K. A., & Bates, J. E. (2003). Friendship quality, peer group affiliation, and peer antisocial behavior as moderators of the link between negative parenting and adolescent externalizing behavior. *Journal of Research on Adolescence*, *13*, 161–184.

LeFevre, J. A., Fast, L., Skwarchuk, S. L., Smith-Chant, B. L., Bisanz, J., Kamawar, D. & Pener-Wilger, M. (2010). Pathways to mathematics: Longitudinal predictors of performance. *Child Development*, *81*, 1753–67.

Lerner, R. M. (2015). Preface. In R. M. Lerner (Ed.) *Handbook of Child Psychology and Developmental Science*. 7th Ed. Wiley.

Levey, S. (2014). *Introduction to language development*. San Diego: Plural Publishing.

Lightbown, P. & Spada, N. (2008). *How languages are learned* (3rd ed.). New York: Oxford University Press.

Lightbown, P. & Spada, N. (2013). *How languages are learned* (4th ed.). New York: Oxford University Press.

Lonigan, C.J. (2015). Literacy Development. In R.M. Lerner (Series Ed.) Handbook of Child Psychology and Developmental Science, Vol. 1. Theory and Method. Wiley.

Luke, A. & Freebody, P. (1999). A map of possible practices: Further notes on the four resources model. *Practically Primary*, *4*(2), 5–8.

Lupyan, G. & Thompson-Schill, S. L. (2012). The evocative power of words: Activation of concepts by verbal and nonverbal means. *Journal of Experimental Psychology: General*, *141*(1), 170–86.

Luthar, S.S., Crossman, E.J. & Small, P.J. (2015). Resilience and Adversity. In *Handbook of Child Psychology and Developmental Science*, *1*. https://doi.org/10.1002/9781118963418.childpsy307

Maguire, E.A., Gadian, D.G., Johnsrude, I.S., Good, C.D., Ashburner, J., Richard S. J., Frackowiak, R.S.J. & Frith, C.D. (2000). Navigation-related structural change in the hippocampi of taxi drivers. *Proceedings of the National Academy of Sciences USA*, *97*(8): 4398–4403.

Main, M., & Solomon, J. (1990). Procedures for identifying infants as disorganized/disoriented during the Ainsworth Strange Situation. In M. T. Greenberg, D. Cicchetti & E. M. Cummings (Eds.), *The John D. and Catherine T. MacArthur Foundation series on mental health and development. Attachment in the preschool years: Theory, research, and intervention* (pp. 121-160). Chicago, IL: University of Chicago Press.

Malina, R. M. (1998). Motor development and performance. In S. J. Ulijaszek, F. E. Johnston & M. A. Preece (Eds), *The Cambridge encyclopedia of human growth and development* (pp. 247–50). Cambridge, UK: Cambridge University Press.

Manuck, S. B., Craig, A. E., Flory, J. D., Halder, I. & Ferrell, R. E. (2011). Reported early family environment covaries with menarcheal age as a function of polymorphic variation in estrogen receptor. *Development and Psychopathology*, *23*(1), 69–83.

Maratsos, M. (1998). The acquisition of grammar. In W. Damon, D. Kuhn & R. S. Siegler (Eds) *Handbook of child psychology, Vol. 2: Cognition, perception, and language* (5th ed., pp. 421–66). New York: Wiley.

Mascolo, M.F. & Fischer, K.W. (2015). Dynamic development of thinking, feeling, and acting. In Lerner, R. & Overton, W. (eds), *Handbook of Child Development and Developmental Science, Volume 1, Theory and Method*. (pp. 113–161). New York: John Wiley.

Masten, A.S. (2011). Resilience in children threatened by extreme adversity: Frameworks for research, practice, and translational synergy. *Development and Psychopathology*, *23*, 493–506.

Masten, A. S. & Narayan, A. J. (2012). Child development in the context of disaster, war and terrorism: Pathways of risk and resilience. *Annual Review of Psychology*, *63*, 227–57.

May, L., Byers-Heinlein, K., Gervain, J. & Werker, J. F. (2011). Language and the newborn brain: Does prenatal language experience shape the neonate neural response to speech? *Frontiers in Psychology*, *2*, 222. Retrieved from www.ncbi.nlm.nih.gov/pmc/articles/PMC3177294

May, S., Hill, R. & Tiakiwai, S. (2004). *Bilingual/immersion education: Indicators of Good Practice*. Final report to the Ministry of Education. New Zealand Ministry of Education. Retrieved from educationcounts. edcentre.govt.nz/publications/downloads/bilingual-education.pdf

May, S., Hill, R. & Tiakiwai, S. (2006). *Bilingual Education in Aotearoa/New Zealand*. New Zealand Ministry of Education. Retrieved from www.educationcounts.govt.nz/publications/schooling/5075

McCarthy, B. & McCarthy, D. (2005). *Teaching around the 4MAT cycle: Designing instruction for diverse learners with diverse learning styles*. Thousand Oaks, CA: Corwin Press.

McDevitt, T. M. & Ormrod, J. E. (2010). *Child development and education* (4th edn.). Upper Saddle River, NJ: Pearson Education.

McDevitt, T. M. & Ormrod, J. E. (2013). *Child development and education* (5th ed.). Upper Saddle River, NJ: Pearson.

McIntosh, A. (2005). *Developing computation*. Hobart: Department of Education Tasmania. Retrieved from www.dest.gov.au/NR/rdonlyres/488C3231-4AD4-469F-8686-7031E51221C6/4581/tas_developing_computation_booklet.pdf

McNaughton, S. (2002). *A meeting of minds*. Wellington: Learning Media.

Melkevik, O., Torsheim, T., Iannotti, R.J. & Wold, B. (2010). Is spending time in screen-based sedentary behaviors associated with less physical activity: A cross national investigation. *International Journal of Behavioral Nutrition and Physical Activity*, *7*(46), 1–10.

Mensah, F. K., Bayer, J. K., Wake, M., Carlin, J. B., Allen, N. B & Patton, G. C. (2013). Early puberty and childhood social and behavioral adjustment. *Journal of Adolescent Health*, *53*(1), 118–124.

Meruelo, A.D., Castro, N., Cota, C.I. & Tapert, S.F. (2017). Cannabis and alcohol use, and the developing brain. *Behavioural Brain Research*, *325*(Pt A), 44-50.

Ministerial Council on Education, Employment, Training and Youth Affairs. (2008). *Melbourne declaration on educational goals for young Australians*. Canberra: Curriculum Corporation.

Muñoz, C. (2007). Age-related differences and second language learning practice. In R. DeKeyser (Ed.), *Practice in a second language: Perspectives from applied linguistics and cognitive psychology* (pp. 229–55). Cambridge, UK: Cambridge University Press.

Murray, A. D., Johnson, J. & Peters, J. (1990). Fine tuning of utterance length to preverbal infants: Effects on later language development. *Journal of Child Language, 17*, 511–25.

Nagel, M. C. (2013). *The brain, early development and learning*. Paper presented at the ACER Research Conference, Melbourne, August. Retrieved from http://research.acer.edu.au/cgi/viewcontent.cgi?article=1163&context=research_conference

Negriff, S. & Susman, E. J. (2011). Pubertal timing, depression, and externalizing problems: A framework, review, and examination of gender differences. *Journal of Research on Adolescence, 21*(3), 717–46.

New South Wales Department of Education and Communities. (2014). Mathematics K-10 continuum of key ideas. Retrieved from www.curriculumsupport.education.nsw.gov.au/primary/mathematics/k6/continuum

New Zealand Ministry of Education. (1994). *English in the New Zealand curriculum*. Wellington: Ministry of Education.

New Zealand Ministry of Education. (2002). *NCAE letter to parents: Last update: 27 Aug 2002*. Retrieved from www.minedu.govt.nz

New Zealand Ministry of Education. (2004). *The national education goals*. Wellington: Ministry of Education. Retrieved from www.minedu.govt.nz/NZEducation/EducationPolicies/Schools/PolicyAndStrategy/PlanningReportingRelevantLegislationNEGSAndNAGS/TheNationalEducationGoalsNEGs.aspx

New Zealand Ministry of Education. (2005). *The Number Framework*. Wellington: Ministry of Education.

New Zealand Ministry of Education. (2007). *The New Zealand curriculum. For English medium teaching and learning in Years 1–13*. Wellington: Ministry of Education.

New Zealand Ministry of Education. (2009). *The New Zealand Curriculum: Mathematics standards for years 1–8*. Wellington: Ministry of Education.

New Zealand Ministry of Health. (2012). *Food and nutrition guidelines for healthy children and young people (aged 2–18 years): A background paper*. Wellington: Ministry of Health.

Nicholas, H. & Lightbown, P. M. (2008). Defining child second language acquisition, defining roles for L2 instruction. In J. Philp, R. Oliver & A. Mackey (Eds), *Second language acquisition and the younger learner* (pp. 27–51). Amsterdam: John Benjamins.

Nicholas, H., Lightbown, P. & Spada, N. (2001). Recasts as feedback to language learners. *Language Learning, 51*(4), 719–58.

Niklas, F., Cohrssen, C. & Tayler, C. (2016). Parents supporting learning: a non-intensive intervention supporting literacy and numeracy in the home learning environment. International. *Journal of Early Years Education, 24*(2), 121–142.

Nippold, M. A. (2009). School-age children talk about chess: Does knowledge drive syntactic complexity? *Journal of Speech, Language, and Hearing Research, 52*, 856–71.

Nunes, T. & Bryant, P. (2015). The Development of Mathematical Reasoning. *Handbook of Child Psychology and Developmental Science, 1*. https://doi.org/10.1002/9781118963418.childpsy217

Organization for Economic Cooperation and Development. (2007). *Understanding the brain: The birth of a learning science*. Paris: OECD.

Overton, W. F. & Molenaar, P. C. (2015). Concepts, theory, and method in Developmental Science: A view of the issues. In W. F. Overton & P. C. M. Molenaar (Eds.). *Handbook of child psychology and developmental science, Theory and Method. Volume 1* (7th edn) (pp. 2–8) Hoboken, NJ: Wiley.

Özcaliskan, S. & Goldin-Meadow, S. (2005). Gesture is at the cutting edge of language development. *Cognition, 96*, B101–B113.

Pan, B. A., Rowe, M. L., Singer, J. D. & Snow, C. E. (2005). Maternal correlates of growth in toddler vocabulary production in low-income families. *Child Development, 76*(4), 763–82.

Parrish, A., Russell, K., Yeatman, H. & Iverson, D. (2009). What factors influence children's activity? *British Journal of School Nursing, 4*(1), 6–11.

Parrish, A., Yeatman, H., Iverson, D. & Russell, K. (2012). Using interviews and peer pairs to better understand how school environments affect young children's playground physical activity levels: A qualitative study. *Health Education Research, 27*(2), 269–80.

Perfetti, C., Yang, C.-L. & Schmalhofer, F. (2008). Comprehension skill and word-to-text integration process. *Applied Cognitive Psychology, 22*(3), 303–18.

Perry, B. D. (2002), Childhood experience and the expression of genetic potential: What childhood neglect tells us about nature and nurture. *Brain and Mind, 3*, 79–100.

Perry, B. D. & Pollard, D. (1997). *Altered brain development following global neglect in early childhood*. Society for Neuroscience: Proceedings from Annual Meeting, New Orleans. Retrieved from www.juconicomparte.org/recursos/Altered_brain_development_ruu6.pdf

Perszyk, D.R. & Waxman, S.R. (2018). Linking language and cognition in infancy. *Annual Review of Psychology, 69*, 232–250.

Philp, J., Adams, R. & Iwashita, N. (2013). *Peer interaction and second language learning*. New York: Taylor & Francis.

Philp, J. & Duchesne, S. (2008). When the gate opens: The interaction between social and linguistic goals in child second language development. In J. Philp, R. Oliver & A. Mackey (Eds), *Second language acquisition and the younger learner: Child's play?* Amsterdam: John Benjamins.

Piekarski, D.J., Johnson, C., Boivin, J.R., Thomas, A.W., Lin, W.C., Delevich, K., Galarce, E. & Wilbrechta, L. (2017). Does puberty mark a transition in sensitive periods for plasticity in the associative neocortex? *Brain Research*, 1654(Pt B): 123–144.

Purpura, D. & Napoli, A. (2015). Early numeracy and literacy: Untangling the relation between specific components. *Mathematical Thinking and Learning: An International Journal, 17*(2–3), 197–218.

Raikes, H., Pan, B. A., Luze, G., Tamis-LeMonda, C. S., Brooks-Gunn, J., Constantine, J., Tarullo, L. B., Raikes, H. A. & Rodriguez, E. T. (2006). Mother-child bookreading in low income families: Correlates and outcomes during the first three years of life. *Child Development, 77*(4), 924–53.

Reid, K. & Andrews, N. (2016). Fostering Understanding of Early Numeracy Development. Longitudinal Literacy and Numeracy Study: Transitions from Preschool to School. Camberwell, Vic: ACER Accessed 25/9/17 http://research.acer.edu.au/cgi/viewcontent.cgi?article=1028&context=monitoring_learning

Ritchie S.J. & Bates T.C. (2013). Enduring links from childhood mathematics and reading achievement to adult socioeconomic status. *Psychological Science, 24*(7): 1301–8

Rodriguez, E. T., Tamis-LeMonda, C. S., Spellmann, M. E., Pan, B. A., Raikes, H., Lugo-Gil, J. (2009). The formative role of home literacy experiences across the first three years of life in children from low-income families. *Journal of Applied Developmental Psychology, 30*, 677–94.

Rogoff, B. (1990). *Apprenticeship in thinking: Cognitive development in social context*. New York: Oxford University Press.

Romer, D. (2010). Adolescent risk taking, impulsivity, and brain development: Implications for prevention. *Developmental Psychobiology, 52*(3), 263–76.

Romer, D., Reyna, V.F. & Satterthwaite, T.D. (2017). Beyond stereotypes of adolescent risk taking: Placing the adolescent brain in developmental context. *Developmental cognitive neuroscience, 27*, 19–34.

Rose, A.J., Carlson, W. & Waller, E.M. (2007). Prospective associations of co-rumination with friendship and emotional adjustment: considering the socioemotional trade-offs of co-rumination. *Developmental Psychology, 43*(4), 1019 –1031.

Rowe, K. J. & Rowe, K. S. (2002). *What matters most: Evidence-based findings of key factors affecting the educational experiences and outcomes for girls and boys throughout their primary and secondary schooling*. Supplementary submission to House of Representatives Standing Committee on Education and Training: Inquiry into the Education of Boys. Melbourne: Australian Council of Educational Research.

Sachs, J. (2001). Communication development in infancy. In J. Berko-Gleason (Ed.), *The development of language* (pp. 39–61). New York: Allyn & Bacon.

Share, D. L., Jorm, A. F., Maclean, R., Matthews, R. & Waterman, B. (1983). Early reading achievement, oral language ability, and a child's home background. *Australian Psychologist, 18*(1), 75–87.

Shaw, P., Eckstrand, K., Sharp, W., Blumenthal, J., Lerch, J. P., Greenstein, D., Clasen, L., Evans, A., Giedd, J. & Rapoport, J. L. (2007). Attention-deficit/hyperactivity disorder is characterized by a delay in cortical maturation. *Proceedings of the National Academy of Sciences of the USA, 104*(49), 19 649–54.

Shneidman, L., Arroyo, M., Levine, S. & Goldin-Meadow, S. (2013). What counts as effective input for word learning? *Journal of Child Language, 40*, 672–86.

Shonkoff, J.P., Garner, A.S., Siegel, B.S., Dobbins, M.I., Earls, M.F., Garner, A.S., McGuinn, L., Pascoe, J. & Wood, D.L. (2012). The Lifelong effects of early childhood adversity and toxic stress. *Pediatrics, 129*(1), 232–46.

Siegler, R.S. & Braithwaite, D.W. (2017). Numerical development. *Annual Review of Psychology, 68*, 187–213

Singh, A., Uijtdewilligen, L., Twisk, J. W. R., van Mechelen, W. & Chinapaw M. J. M. (2012). Physical activity and performance at school: A systematic review of the literature including a methodological quality assessment. *Archives of Pediatrics and Adolescent Medicine, 166*(1), 49–55.

Smith Gabig, C. (2014). Language development in middle to late childhood and adolescence. In S. Levey (Ed.), *Introduction to language development* (pp. 211–46). San Diego: Plural Publishing.

Snow, C. E. (1995). Issues in the study of input: Fine-tuning, universality, individual and developmental differences, and necessary causes. In P. Fletcher & B. McWhinney (Eds), *Handbook of child language*. Oxford: Blackwell.

Snow, C. E. & Kang, J. Y. (2006). Becoming bilingual, biliterate, and bicultural. In A. Renninger & I. Sigel (Eds), *Handbook of child psychology, Vol 4: Child psychology in practice* (pp. 75–102). Hoboken, NJ: John Wiley & Sons.

Snowling, M. J. & Gobel, S. M. (2011). Reading development and dyslexia. In U. Goswami (Ed.), *The Wiley-Blackwell handbook of childhood cognitive development* (2nd ed.). Oxford: Blackwell.

Society for Neuroscience. (2008). *Brain facts: A primer on the brain and nervous system*. Washington, DC: Society for Neuroscience.

Sophian, C. & Adams, N. (1987). Infants' understanding of numerical transformations. *British Journal of Developmental Psychology, 5*, 257–64.

Sroufe, L.A. (2005). Attachment and development: A prospective, longitudinal study from birth to adulthood. *Attachment & Human Development, 7*(4), 349–367.

Sroufe, L. A., Coffino, B., & Carlson, E. A. (2010). Conceptualizing the role of early experience: Lessons from the Minnesota Longitudinal Study. *Developmental Review, 30*(1), 36–51.

Sroufe, L.A., Egeland, B., Carlson, E.A. & Collins, W.A. (2005). *The Development of the Person: The Minnesota study of risk and adaptation from birth to adulthood*. New York: Guilford Press.

Stahl, S. A. & Nagy, W. E. (2006). *Teaching word meanings*. Mahwah, NJ: Lawrence Erlbaum.

Stattin, H., Kerr, M. & Skoog, T. (2011). Early pubertal timing and girls' problem behavior: Integrating two hypotheses. *Journal of Youth Adolescence, 40*, 1271–87.

Sun, Y., Mensah, F.K., Azzopardi, P., Patton, G.C. & Wake, M. (2017). Childhood Social Disadvantage and Pubertal Timing: A National Birth Cohort from Australia. *Pediatrics, 139*(6) [e20164099].

Tanner, J. M. (1990). *Foetus into man* (2nd ed.). Cambridge, MA: Harvard University Press.

Thomas, W. P. & Collier, V. P. (1999). Evaluation that informs school reform of programs for language minority students. Paper presented at the American Education Research Association Conference, Montreal.

Tomasello, M. (2005). *Constructing a language: A usage-based theory of language acquisition*. Cambridge, MA: Harvard University Press.

Tomasello, M. (2006). Acquiring linguistic constructions. In D. Kuhn & R. Siegler (Eds), *Handbook of child psychology, Vol. 2: Cognition, perception, and language* (6th ed., pp. 225–98). New York: Wiley.

Tomasello, M. (2011). Language development. In U. Goswami (Ed.), *The Wiley-Blackwell handbook of childhood cognitive development* (2nd ed.). Oxford: Blackwell.

Uccelli, P. & Pan, B. A. (2013). Semantic development. In J. Berko-Gleason & N. B. Ratner (Eds), *The development of language*. Boston: Allyn and Bacon.

Vanderbilt Kennedy Center. (2012). *Brain development and plasticity*. Retrieved from http://kc.vanderbilt.edu/site/topics/98/brain-development-and-plasticity.aspx

Vassallo, S., Daraganova, G., Zhenyu Zhang, G. & Homel, J. (2016). 'Teaching practices in Australian primary schools'. *Longitudinal Study of Australian Children Annual Statistical Report 2016*, Chapter 7. Australian Institute of Family Studies.

Vygotsky, L. S. (1977). Play and its role in the mental development of the child. In M. Cole (Ed.), *Soviet developmental psychology* (pp. 76–99). White Plains, NY: M. E. Sharpe. (Original work published 1933/1966.)

Walle, E. A. & Campos, J. J. (2014). Infant language development is related to the acquisition of walking. *Developmental Psychology, 50*(2), 336–48.

Warren, D. & Yu, M. (2015). Pubertal status and emotional, scool and social functioning. *LSAC Annual Statistical Report 2015*, Chapter 6. Australian Institute of Family Studies.

Whittle, S., Simmons, J. G., Dennison, M., Vijayakumar, N., Schwartz, O. S., Yap, M. B. H., Sheeber, L. & Allen, N. B. (2014). Positive parenting predicts the development of adolescent neural reward circuitry: A longitudinal study. *Developmental Cognitive Neuroscience, 8*, 7–17.

Zammit, M. & Schafer, G. (2011). Maternal label and gesture use affects acquisition of specific object names. *Journal of Child Language, 38*(1), 201–21.

Zammitt, K. & Downes, T. (2002). New learning environments and the multiliterate individual: A framework for educators. *Australian Journal of Language and Literacy, 25*(2), 24–38.

COGNITIVE DEVELOPMENT

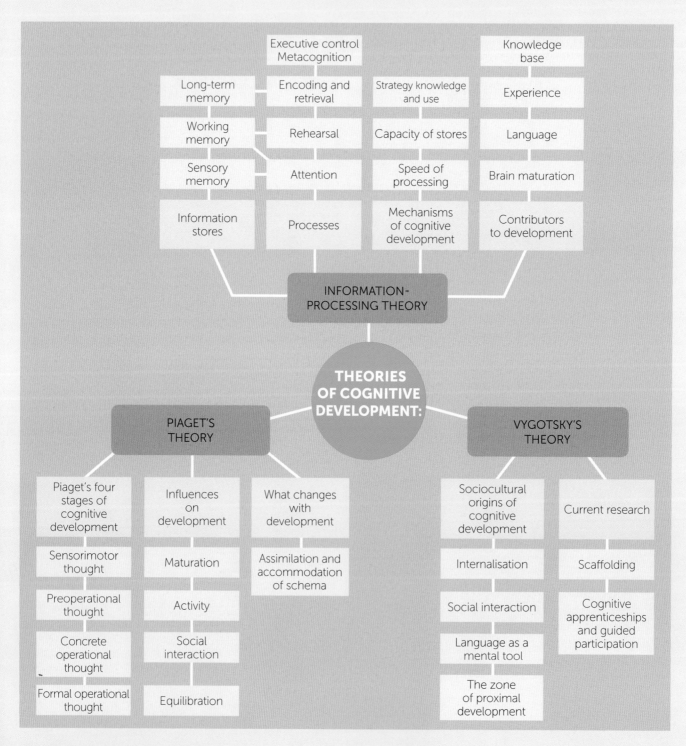

FIGURE 3.1 Chapter 3 concept map

KEY QUESTIONS

After reading this chapter, you should be able to answer the following questions:

- What are the four factors that, according to Piaget, contribute to the development of thinking from infancy to adulthood?
- What are the key developmental milestones in Piaget's sensorimotor, preoperational, concrete-operations and formal-operations stages of cognitive development?
- What are some issues educators need to consider when working with those in the sensorimotor, preoperational, concrete-operations and formal-operations stages?
- What roles do social and cultural influences play in Vygotsky's ideas about children's cognitive development?
- What changes in children's processing of information with development, and how can these developments explain changes in reasoning such as Piaget and Vygotsky observed?
- What mechanisms influence cognitive development according to information-processing theories? What additional mechanisms could be involved?

ONLINE STUDY RESOURCES

CourseMateExpress

Bring your learning to life with **interactive learning**, **study** and **exam preparation tools** that support the printed textbook. CourseMate Express Includes **quizzes**, **interactive activities**, **videos**, a tool to help you '**develop your philosophy**' and more.

INTRODUCTION

A family is bushwalking. Jack (13) has taken charge of the map, to see if he can work out an easier way to get through the pass ahead of them. Charlotte (10) is drawing her own map of the path they are taking in her head. When they pause for a break, she will whip out her pencils and paper and record the trail, and their journey along it. Mia (4) is walking in step with the song she's singing with her Mum, who is thinking about how enjoyable it is to have this time all together. Will (7) is collecting rocks, and has noticed that those higher up the path are rougher than the ones he found by the stream earlier. His Dad is wondering at what point he will be given the task of carrying Will's rocks back home. Each member of the family is thinking about different things, and interacting with different elements of the environment around them. How are their different thoughts and responses to the environment a reflection of their cognitive development? How are

Source: Alamy Stock Photo/P&F Photography

FIGURE 3.2 Cognitive development results from individuals' actions in response to experiences in their environment. See if you can map the experiences, actions and cognitions (thoughts) that are occurring here.

these thoughts and this activity themselves contributing to that development? These questions are typical of those developmental psychologists might ask about cognitive development.

cognition
The mental processes involved in perceiving, attending to, understanding and recalling information

Cognitive development is concerned with our ability to think, to reason, to understand and to remember the world around us. It involves mental processes that are associated with taking in, organising and making sense of information – processes that include perceiving, attending to, understanding and recalling information. These mental functions are part of what is referred to as **cognition**. In this chapter, we look in some detail at the work of two of the most important and influential theorists in this area: Jean Piaget and Lev Semanovich Vygotsky. We then consider some more recent work in information processing that offers a different perspective on some of the observations Piaget and Vygotsky made about children's cognitive development. Yet cognitive development theory and research does not stop with information processing theory. We conclude the chapter by looking at recent directions in thinking about cognitive development.

PIAGET'S THEORY OF COGNITIVE DEVELOPMENT

A nine-month-old infant sits in a highchair. She drops her cup and observes it fall. Her mother picks it up and replaces it. The infant drops it again, and her sister picks it up for her. She will continue to drop the cup as many times as there is someone there to retrieve it. Her four-year-old sister is playing with playdough, cutting it into many pieces with a wooden popstick. As she works, she talks: 'Cut cut cut. Dinner!' Ten-year-old Kyle is working on his homework. He is developing his own system for classifying organisms, and hesitates over whether to put flying insects with birds that fly, or with things with six legs. 'And where do I put emus?' he thinks. 'Are they land animals, because they don't fly, or birds, because they have feathers and lay eggs?' Stephanie, 17, is also doing homework. As part of a debate for History on whether the Allied occupation of Japan at the end of the Second World War was a positive thing, she is thinking about what Japan and the rest of the world might be like if this had not happened.

What are the factors that influence cognitive development, and how do the changes we observe come about? The theorist Jean Piaget (see **Box 3.1**) sought to identify universal processes of cognitive development. Working from observing his own children, he focused not just on what children know, but also on how they represent and interact with the world, and how they organise that knowledge. He saw children as little scientists, acting on the world, reflecting on their experiences and testing hypotheses. The nine-month-old infant described above is not just dropping a cup; she is observing and learning about gravity (when I let go of something it falls), cause and effect (when I drop something it is picked up), and her relationships with others (I can influence their behaviour by dropping my cup). Kyle is reflecting on his experiences and knowledge of the physical world to organise and reorganise his thinking. Stephanie is using her knowledge of the world to hypothesise about an imaginary event.

Piaget was interested in what changes as children's thinking develops, and in what influences these changes. He described a broad picture of cognitive development, as well as the processes of change.

Piaget was one of the first theorists to attempt to comprehensively describe the process of cognitive development in children. Aspects of his work have been disputed over the years, but his ideas remain influential. For example, the principle that children are active in development, described at the end of the last chapter, originated with Piaget. Subsequent theories of cognitive development have had to address many of the issues Piaget initially raised. In particular, his method of questioning children about how they make sense of their experiences – probing to understand their errors and then following up with further questions – is one of his most significant contributions.

CourseMateExpress

Online Resources
Watch a **video** showing children of different ages reasoning about what happens to the sun at night. What influences the changes in thinking we observe with age?

BOX 3.1 ABOUT JEAN PIAGET

Jean Piaget (1896–1980) was born in Neuchâtel, Switzerland to well-educated, professional parents (Brainerd, 1996). His childhood was not happy – his mother had mental health problems, and this led Piaget, like his father, to spend his time in scientific study rather than pursuing more conventional leisure activities. It also stimulated an interest in psychology.

Piaget showed early promise of intellectual ability. At the age of seven he began to study molluscs, carrying out very detailed observations in the lakes around Neuchâtel. By 10 years old he had published his first scientific article, and at 14 years old he was offered a curator's position at the Geneva Museum of Natural History but was too young to take it up (Wadsworth, 1996). At the age of 18, he gained a Bachelor's degree from the University of Neuchâtel, then a PhD, and by the age of 21 had published 25 scholarly papers.

As well as his study of science, Piaget was also interested in philosophy and in the origins and nature of human knowledge. His dual involvement in the biological sciences and philosophy was highly influential in his later work on children's intellectual development.

Piaget's interest in how people acquire knowledge led him in 1919 to study psychology at the Sorbonne in Paris. While there, he worked in the laboratory of Alfred Binet, who was interested in measuring intelligence (see Chapter 9). Piaget assisted in standardising a French version of a reasoning test. His task was to identify norms for the average French child and compare them with those for an English child. This was a rather dull, mechanical task, and Piaget's interest was captured by the wrong answers that children gave to items on the test. Using interview techniques he had learned at the Sorbonne, Piaget asked the children to explain their answers, and found their explanations of errors were much more interesting than explanations of correct answers. During these interviews, Piaget noted that six-year-olds, eight-year-olds and 13-year-olds made different types of errors. He also noticed that children of roughly the same age not only got the same items wrong, but also made the same kinds of errors. He became convinced that children think in ways that are qualitatively different from the ways in which adults think.

FIGURE 3.3 Piaget observed children and questioned them about the way they solved problems. His work changed the way we think about cognitive development.

Source: Getty Images/Patrick Grehan

Piaget held chairs of psychology, sociology and related areas at universities in Switzerland between 1925 and 1964, and he was director of the International Centre for Genetic Epistemology in Geneva from 1955 until 1980. He continued to publish scholarly works until just before his death in 1980 at the age of 84. His enormous productivity over a 60-year period is one of the reasons his ideas have been so influential.

In reviewing some of the main questions that interested Piaget, and in looking at the implications of his ideas for educators, it is important to be aware that Piaget's language can be confusing. The meaning of some of the words he used is different from that in common usage, such as his use of 'conservation', 'assimilation', 'accommodation' and 'egocentrism' (defined later in this chapter). This can be attributed in part to Piaget's background as a biologist, and to his use of biological terms to explain cognitive development.

WHAT INFLUENCES DEVELOPMENT?

As discussed in Chapter 2, the changes that occur in development have both biological and environmental origins. Changes in cognitive skills such as perceiving, understanding, remembering, problem solving and reasoning are influenced by the child's experiences, both with objects and events in the physical world and through social interaction with peers, family, teachers and others. They are also influenced by their genetic or biological make-up, which determines the mental structures that shape and constrain thinking at different stages. These factors interact with one another. Piaget suggested that there are four main factors that work together to influence the development of children's thinking over the years from early childhood to adulthood: maturation, activity, social interaction and equilibration.

Maturation

The first factor ('maturation') is innate or biological in origin. Considerable research into the development of the brain supports Piaget's notion that the brain's maturation provides children with the means to reason in more advanced ways (Fischer, 2008), and of the interaction between this maturation and children's activity and experience. We saw some of this interaction in Chapter 2, when children's activity leads to the strengthening of neural networks and the pruning of inefficient pathways.

Activity and social interaction

The second factor ('activity') and the third factor (**social interaction**, sometimes called **social transmission**) are associated with the physical and social world in which children develop. According to Piaget's perspective, children actively exploring their world are acting as 'miniature scientists', learning by experimenting through physical and mental activity. A number of theorists, following Piaget, have taken up this notion of children as little scientists (Gopnic & Meltzoff, 1997; Wellman & Gelman, 1998). Rather than passively receiving knowledge passed on from parents or teachers, the child actively constructs knowledge. Piaget described himself as a constructivist, and was in fact one of the fathers of **constructivism**, with its emphasis on students constructing understanding through direct experience (see Chapter 6 for more on this approach to learning). The constant processes of exploration, testing hypotheses, adapting of schemas and reorganisation of knowledge are central to this process of construction.

Social interaction is particularly important when children are interacting with their peers; that is, those who think in similar ways and who have had similar experiences, but who have a slightly different perspective that challenges children's thinking and stimulates cognitive development. The resulting **sociocognitive conflict** (that is, the conflict within the child as they try to fit together others' views that differ from their own) is one of the key processes in development. Two aspects of peer relations facilitate this process. First, peers are more willing to challenge one another's ideas than they are the views of an adult. Second, children are particularly motivated to resolve the differences as they form part of their relationships – whether it is a matter of being right, of maintaining a friendship, or of keeping the interaction going (Philp & Duchesne, 2008).

Equilibration

The fourth factor (**equilibration**) is concerned with the way in which children respond to conflicts and inconsistencies between what they already know and what they experience in daily life. The concept of equilibration – according to Piaget, probably the most important influence driving cognitive development – can be traced to Piaget's background as a scientist. Just as organisms adapt to the physical environment, Piaget argued that humans make mental **adaptations** in order to ensure that new experiences fit with what they know.

social interaction (social transmission)
The interactions with others (parents, peers, teachers and so on) that contribute to children's learning experiences

constructivism
An explanation of learning that views it as a self-regulated process that builds on learners' existing knowledge, and in which learners are active participants

sociocognitive conflict
Conflict within the child's thinking resulting from social interaction

equilibration
Achieving cognitive balance between what is familiar and known, and what is new or unfamiliar, through the processes of assimilation and accommodation

adaptation
The process of adjusting to new situations and experiences through the modification of existing schemas (assimilation) or the creation of new schemas (accommodation)

Assimilation and accommodation

Just as our physical body has to be in balance for us to function properly, Piaget claimed we also need to have cognitive or mental balance. When we encounter objects or events that are unfamiliar, our cognitive balance is upset. We become confused and uncertain about how to think or act. Equilibration is the process of seeking to restore the balance between what is familiar and known – the child's existing cognitive system – and new information or the external world (Siegler, 1998). Balance is regained through the processes of assimilation and accommodation. Piaget used the biological terms 'assimilation' and 'accommodation' to identify the two processes involved in adaptation. **Assimilation** refers to the adjustment of an existing schema to fit a new experience. In **accommodation**, new information is used to establish a new model or schema. Some examples are given below.

An infant is in his cot, reaching and grasping for what is in reach, and bringing it to his mouth to explore it. He reaches through the bars of the cot for a bright rattle on the table close by. He tries a few times to pull it towards him, but the bars of the cot are in the way, and he gets frustrated. Then he happens to turn his arm, and the rattle is able to pass through the bars of the cot. When he then reaches for a cloth book and a bear, the infant uses the schemes he already knows, making minor changes to allow for the position, size and shape of the objects. This is assimilation. When this scheme does not work, he experiences **disequilibrium**, or cognitive discomfort. His new scheme of turning his arm represents accommodation. In time, he will practise the new scheme and it will become part of assimilation. The two operate in tandem.

Building knowledge of the world through experience

This does not just happen with infants. Piaget argued that it is a constant process in thinking. Children (and adults) are constantly using experience to build on their knowledge of the world, and reorganising that knowledge. Experience leads to changes in thinking as we fit new knowledge (assimilate it) into existing schemas, and add new schemas to allow for (accommodate) the new knowledge. Think about the following scenarios.

Three-year-old Gina uses the word 'bird' to refer to something flying in the air. It is one of the words most children learn fairly early. One day Gina sees a dragonfly and hesitates because it is different from other things she has seen flying in the air. It looks like a leaf. It also looks like a bird flying through the air. However, although the dragonfly is different in a number of ways from a bird, it is closer to 'bird' than to any of Gina's other schemas for flying things. So the dragonfly is fitted into the 'bird' schema, which gradually becomes more effective for detecting 'birdness' (WJF, personal communication, October 2001). The account of Gina looking at a dragonfly and deciding it is a 'bird' is an example of seeing something new and adjusting an existing schema to include it. It is an example of assimilation.

Aaron's word for anything that has four legs and walks around is 'dog'. One day he sees a horse. Although a horse has four legs, it is quite different from a dog. The horse does not quite fit Aaron's existing schema for 'dog', and he feels confused. Rather than just saying 'dog', he asks 'Dog?' with rising intonation, looking at his father. Recognising Aaron's uncertainty, his father says, 'No, not dog, horse'. For the child, accepting this

FIGURE 3.4 Children's experiences expose them to new information that can challenge their existing understandings of the world. How did Piaget explain this as contributing to cognitive development?

Source: microgen/iStockphoto

assimilation
Adjusting an existing mental model or schema to fit a new experience

accommodation
Using fresh information to form a new mental model or schema

disequilibrium
Cognitive imbalance resulting from inconsistency between what is known and expected, and something strange and unexpected

new information involves creating a new schema for 'horse'. This is an example of accommodation: new information is used to establish a new model or schema. Aaron now has two schemas for four-legged animals: if the animal is not too big, it is 'dog'; if it is very big, it is 'horse'. This works well until Aaron goes to the zoo and encounters another four-legged animal such as an elephant or a giraffe, neither of which fits easily into the 'dog' or 'horse' schemas. Perhaps Aaron's father will help his son create more 'four-legged animal' schemas during their next visit to the zoo.

The process of adaptation, involving either assimilation or accommodation, occurs regularly in daily life, and with great frequency in the lives of young children. Another mental process – 'organisation' – is also underway, although we are not conscious of it happening. As new ideas and information are identified and processed mentally, we organise this material in terms of existing schemas, or create new schemas. This organisational process is essential so that we can store and later retrieve information.

CHANGES IN ORGANISATION OF THINKING WITH DEVELOPMENT

Piaget argued that across the age range, *how* we think remains basically the same. We all eat, sleep and breathe in the same way at every age. So, too, the act of thinking remains the same for everyone, across all age groups. What changes, particularly during childhood and adolescence, is the way in which we *organise* our thoughts into what Piaget called 'schemas' (or schemes).

Above, in the example with Aaron, we introduced the idea of a **schema**. A schema is an abstract concept or mental image – a cluster of ideas about a particular object or experience – that is used to organise existing knowledge and make sense of new experiences. The idea of a schema as an organised collection of thoughts or ideas associated with a particular topic or experience is a useful device for thinking about how children accumulate information about specific aspects of their experience. It can be helpful in understanding their behaviour and in guiding our responses to them.

How do children modify the schemas they have developed? Under what circumstances does such modification occur? As we saw above, the need for modification arises when children experience disequilibrium; that is, when an inconsistency arises between what is known and expected, and something strange, unexpected and new. This is where the process of adaptation takes place. The mental processes of adaptation and organisation described here continue throughout the lifespan, but they are most obvious in childhood because change occurs most rapidly during this period. This is why examples of these processes are largely taken from the childhood years, although these phenomena are also common in adults.

schema
A mental image or cluster of related ideas used to organise existing knowledge and to make sense of new experiences

THINK ABOUT

- Think of your first few weeks of university. Did you have to develop new schemas in order to adapt to your new context?
- Can you identify examples of adaptation, assimilation and accommodation in your thinking in the past six months?

readiness
Having the prior experiences and knowledge needed for learning

closeness of the match
The distance between what is already known and new learning

There is one proviso – particularly relevant to education – that needs to be made when thinking about the organisational process involved in assimilation and accommodation. When we attend to new material (such as an unfamiliar insect or a mathematics formula) and the process of adaptation is about to be triggered, the concepts of **readiness** and **closeness of the match** become relevant. In teaching anything to a child, the new material must be close enough to what is already known by the child in order for a link to be made between old and new. If such a link is made, the process of either assimilation or accommodation can begin. The term 'readiness' is used to describe a child who has the prior knowledge or experiences needed to make a link between the known and the unknown. The phrase 'closeness of the match' (sometimes called 'goodness of fit') refers to the relative distance, in terms of the child's experience and understanding, between what is already known and new information. Neo-Piagetians such as Pascual-Leone (1970) have suggested that there are also aspects of mental capacity such as working memory, discussed later in this chapter, that are involved in readiness. Children need both particular levels of understanding and specific mental capacities to think at higher levels. These concepts have important implications for those working with children. It is important to determine the child's current understanding, and to consider their readiness for learning a particular concept. Piaget's theory directs us to the child as an important participant in learning.

PIAGET'S COGNITIVE STAGES

Piaget believed that rather than being continuous, children's cognitive development is discontinuous, proceeding sequentially through a series of distinct 'stages' from birth to adulthood, with thinking at one stage building on the one before, and being qualitatively different from it (see Figure 3.5). A stage-based concept of development can be likened to climbing stairs: each step (or stage) in the hierarchical sequence of development involves the progression to a more advanced level of functioning, which is followed by a period of consolidation before an individual proceeds to the next step. Piaget believed that the stages he identified had two very important properties: first, they are *universal* (that is, they apply to everyone); second, they are *invariant* (that is, unchanging), meaning that the order in which children

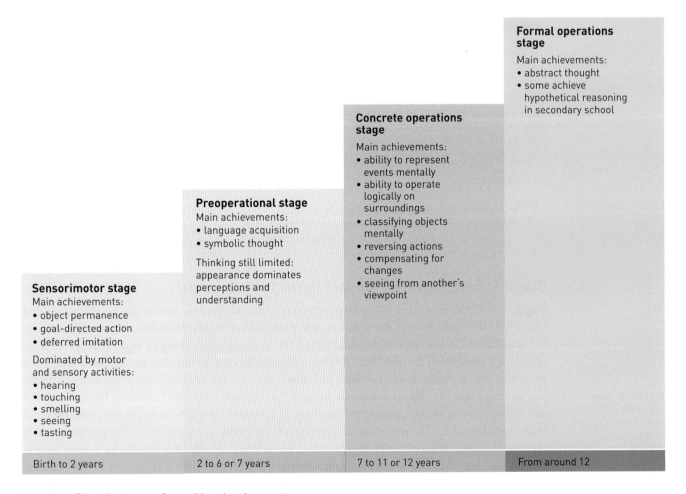

FIGURE 3.5 Piaget's stages of cognitive development.

pass through the stages cannot be varied. Children must progress through them in sequence, beginning with the sensorimotor stage, although some may never reach the final stage of formal operations.

For each of his stages of cognitive development, Piaget identified what he called 'developmental milestones' – key achievements that have to be attained by a child at each cognitive level. A number of developmental milestones have been identified for each of Piaget's four stages, and selected examples from each level are shown in Table 3.1.

TABLE 3.1 Main developmental milestones at each cognitive stage

COGNITIVE STAGE	DEVELOPMENTAL MILESTONES	DEVELOPMENTAL MILESTONES IN ACTION
Sensorimotor	*Object permanence* Knowing that something continues to exist even when it is out of sight	• Looking for a lost ball
	Goal-directed or intentional action Actions that are produced consciously for the purpose of achieving a desired end	• Hitting a musical toy to elicit a sound
	Deferred imitation Repeating an action observed on a previous occasion	• Making a sweeping action with a broom after watching someone sweep the floor
Preoperational	*Symbolic thought and language* Using gestures, signs, sounds and words to represent and convey meaning	• Pointing to something of interest • Waving goodbye • Saying 'brm' while pushing a toy car • Asking for 'mo' (more)
Concrete operations	*Conservation* Understanding that objects or quantities remain the same despite changes in physical appearance	• Understanding that the amount of juice remains the same whether it is in a tall, thin glass or a short, fat glass (see Box 3.2)
Formal operations	*Abstract thought and propositional reasoning* Attaining the capacity to think abstractly; that is, using propositional and hypothetical–deductive reasoning	• Solving logical problems such as 'If Jo is taller than Sue and shorter than Eve, who is the tallest?' • Hypothesising about future or distant events

Stage 1: Sensorimotor period (birth to two years)

Piaget termed the first stage of development 'sensorimotor' because infants act on the world and understand the world through those actions, and particularly through their senses and through motion. We saw this in the examples of the child in the cot, grasping and seeking to explore things with his mouth, and the child in the high chair, dropping the cup. Schemas at this stage are organised patterns of behaviour. When you compare a newborn with a two-year-old, you become aware of the enormity of the changes that occur over the **sensorimotor stage** of development. Newborn infants are basically helpless and will not survive without assistance. They have no language, very little mobility and primitive social skills (see Chapter 2). The sensorimotor stage usually lasts only two years, but is the period in which the most dramatic developmental changes occur. From being capable of only reflexive actions such as sucking and grasping, infants begin to gain voluntary control over their actions, and steadily develop new strategies and schemes for exploring and interacting with objects and people. They learn to imitate the actions of others and, in the latter months of the sensorimotor period, engage in simple forms of

sensorimotor stage
The earliest of Piaget's developmental stages, characterised by object permanence, intentional or goal-directed behaviour and deferred imitation

pretend play. Three of the developmental milestones achieved during this period – object permanence, the beginning of goal-directed or intentional action, and deferred imitation – are of particular interest.

Until they reach about four months of age, infants do not fully understand that concrete objects have a permanent existence (Lutz & Sternberg, 1999). However, by approximately eight months (see, for example, Baillargeon, 1991, 2008; Mareschall, 2000; Moore & Meltzoff, 2008; Spelke, Breinlinger, Macomber & Jacobson, 1992) they have attained **object permanence**; that is, if a toy drops out of sight, babies will look for it, even if they cannot reach out to search for it. Research that measured infants' awareness of object permanence by the length of time they look at a stimulus, and their heart rate or brain wave activity, indicates that babies have some awareness of object permanence from as young as two and a half months, although its mastery is not completed until about 14 months (Cohen & Cashon, 2006). Complete mastery of object permanence appears to depend on development of the frontal lobes in the brain's cerebral cortex (Bell, 1998) as well as experience.

From about six months of age, infants become capable of **goal-directed or intentional action**, meaning that they begin to use their own actions and vocalisations to influence the actions of others in order to achieve a desired goal, such as attention, comfort or food (see, for example, Tomasello & Carpenter, 2007).

Deferred imitation refers to children's ability to reproduce actions they have seen and remembered, such as when, towards the end of the sensorimotor stage, children begin to copy actions, speech sounds and facial expressions they have seen previously. Although Piaget studied deferred imitation by observing his children, and didn't theorise it as occurring until late in the stage, laboratory research has shown babies to show deferred imitation of facial expressions from as early as six weeks after birth (Meltzoff & Moore, 1994). As with object permanence, there is further development of this ability throughout the sensorimotor stage as memory capacity improves.

Piaget's Stage 1 in education

For those working with infants and toddlers in the age range from birth to about two years of age, the skills likely to be of most interest include imitation (immediate or deferred), social interaction and play (appropriate use of objects) (Bochner & Jones, 2003). Most children acquire these skills as a natural outcome of their daily experiences, although children who have an intellectual disability or who are at risk of delay in some aspect of their development may need extra help. Successful progression through Stage 1 is evident in children's play and in the emergence of age-appropriate language and communication skills that facilitate progress to the next stage.

Stage 2: Preoperational period (two years to six or seven years)

Carlie is sorting her toys and her mother is talking to her about what she has done.

Mother: 'What are these ones in this pile?'

Carlie: 'They're blue.'

Mother: (pointing to a blue car that is set apart) 'What about this one?'

Carlie: 'That's a big one.'

Carlie is sorting without a 'logical' system. Piaget used the word **operations** to refer to actions that are performed in the mind and governed by rules and logic (Singer & Revenson, 1996). He argued that the young child's thinking at the **preoperational stage** precedes the ability to perform actions mentally rather than just physically, and to think logically.

object permanence
Piagetian term used to refer to children's understanding that objects continue to exist even when they are out of sight

goal-directed or intentional action
A sequence of acts produced intentionally to achieve a desired outcome

deferred imitation
Actions copied from models no longer present, the actions having previously been observed and remembered

operations
Actions that are governed by rules and logic, and are performed mentally rather than physically

preoperational stage
Piaget's second stage, in which a child is not yet able to 'operate' or carry out logical physical actions mentally, but is reliant on manipulating real materials

symbolic thought
The ability to represent objects and events mentally

Symbolic thought is a critical milestone for the preoperational stage, seen in the acquisition of language, and also in children's play. As we saw in Chapter 2, over the period from about two years of age to the first years of formal schooling, some astonishing changes occur in communication and language skills. This acquisition of language permits children to refer to objects that are not present, and to interact with their environment in much broader ways.

The emergence of symbolic (or representational) thought is probably most evident in children's play over the preoperational period. At the simplest level, a toddler learns to pretend that Teddy is drinking from a cup or having a bath. Stones become cakes and a broom is a horse. Language also accompanies this play, and Piaget argued that it directs the child's action and thinking. Play is very important at this stage. It is a platform for developing a child's understanding of symbols and the ways in which symbols can be used to represent objects and events. Later, games are played that involve role-taking (Mummy and Daddy, the doctor, Batman, a princess), and imaginary friends appear. Types of play and their development are discussed in Chapter 4.

During this period, children begin to create their own stories and to draw representational pictures (see Figure 3.6). Earlier, in the sensorimotor stage, children draw largely random scribbles; but gradually they begin to attempt to draw realistically. These developments are dependent on the emergence of representation or the use of symbols.

three years

six years

four years

eight years

FIGURE 3.6 Jesse drew these four drawings at age three, four, six and eight. At the sensorimotor stage, children's drawings are largely scribbles. As they develop symbolic thought, they begin to represent familiar objects and people in increasingly realistic ways.

While there are major achievements in thinking in this stage, Piaget identified limitations too. Here, Piaget identified three related issues: egocentrism; centration, or a tendency to be perception-bound; and animism.

Egocentrism

egocentrism
An individual's belief that everyone sees the world in exactly the same way as that individual

Egocentrism, or the tendency for children to think and talk about things from their own immediate perspective, is most evident in children's use of language. For example, a child may talk to a stranger about familiar people or events and be surprised that the stranger does not share the child's knowledge of those people and events. You may be familiar with this when talking to young children on the phone: they are likely to nod for 'yes' and to point to someone in the room with them, not accounting for the fact that you cannot see what they see. Piaget used a task known as the 'three-mountains problem' to explore children's egocentrism. This involved showing children a model of three mountains: one snow-capped, the second with a red cross and the third with a small house on top. The children were then shown some photographs of the mountains from different perspectives and were asked to choose one that represented what a doll sitting at the opposite side of the table would see. Most four-year-olds did not realise that theirs was not the only possible view of the model. They could not imagine what another person, looking from a different angle, would see. They could only describe what another person might see in terms of what they themselves saw. Their thinking was egocentric.

Researchers following Piaget have challenged Piaget's findings and conclusions about children's egocentrism, and the three-mountains task in particular. Piaget's conclusions have been questioned because of the difficulties presented by the three-mountains task, with its unfamiliar context, use of photographs and abstract nature. In alternative tasks, Borke (1975), Hughes (in Donaldson, 1978) and Newcombe and Huttenlocher (1992) have found that children as young as three years old are aware of others' different viewpoints, when the task is presented to them in a familiar context. This has been one of the key challenges to Piaget's theory: when children's tasks are placed within a familiar context, and they are given a purpose they can understand, they show more advanced thinking than Piaget described.

THINK ABOUT

- What does this suggest about how to support children in classrooms? Think about the kinds of support you could provide to help children to think in more sophisticated ways. See **Box 3.4** for some ideas.

Centration

Centration refers to children's inability to focus on more than one or two conspicuous aspects of a situation, and their tendency not to notice other, less dominant features. A characteristic of children at the preoperational stage is that they are 'perception-bound', meaning that they attend to the physical appearance of objects and situations, and that they believe what they see. If one object looks taller than another, they will say that the taller object is the bigger of the two. If one object looks wider, they will say that object is bigger (see **Box 3.2**).

centration
Concentrating attention on one aspect of a stimulus while ignoring other features

Animism

Katie (aged three) touched an electric fence and got a shock. 'Ow, it bit me – bad fence!' was her reaction. This exemplifies another characteristic of preoperational children, that of **animism**, or the tendency to think of inanimate objects as being alive and capable of thinking and feeling like humans (Flavell, 2004; Piaget, 1929). Later work has extended this to describe magical thinking in children at this stage: for example, young children may believe that the Easter bunny scatters chocolate eggs for them to find, or that the moon is watching over them (Subbotsky, 2010). Some argue that the animism Piaget observed in children's thinking at the preoperational stage is learned, rather than being characteristic of this developmental stage. Adults often talk in animistic ways to children, and children's books and cartoons often include animism and magical thinking (for example, the stories of Peter Rabbit, or Walt Disney cartoons). Understanding the distinction between animate or living things and inanimate objects is a fundamental task in cognitive development (Rakison, 2005; Rakison & Poulin-Dubois, 2001).

animism
The tendency to attribute human characteristics to inanimate objects

Piaget's Stage 2 in education

Those caring for children in Piaget's preoperational stage must give them opportunities to explore their physical world during play and problem-solving activities. It is through such activities that children's existing concepts are challenged and modified, or new concepts formed. 'Hands-on' experiences are needed that involve the many different types of materials generally available in early-childhood settings such as preschools, and child care centres. The Early Years Learning Framework for Australia (DEEWR, 2009) spells this out in detail. For most children, the need for access to 'hands-on' activities continues beyond preschool years.

BOX 3.2 RESEARCH LINKS

EXAMPLES OF PIAGET'S CONSERVATION TASKS

The following conservation tasks are examples of those used by Piaget in his studies of children's thinking. Notice that the materials used in each task are presented in two ways. The first presentation represents the way the task is initially given to children; that is, the first question that is asked and the way the materials are initially set out in front of the child. The second presentation shows the way Piaget changed or rearranged the materials before he asked the second question.

1   Number

> First presentation: 'Are there the same number of Smilies in each row, or does one row have more than the other?'

> Second presentation (transformation): 'Now are there the same number of Smilies in each row, or does one row have more?'

2   Substance (mass)

> First presentation: 'Is there the same amount of dough in each ball, or does one ball have more than the other?'

> Second presentation (transformation): 'Now does each ball have the same amount of dough, or does one have more?'

CourseMateExpress

Online Resources
Explore more examples
of conservation tasks
with the **Interactive
Activity** on this text's
website

ACTIVITIES

Present one of the tasks shown above to children in the four to 12-plus age range. Try to find at least three children, one from each of the 4–5 years, 8–9 years and 12-years-plus age groups. You should use real materials, not the diagrams shown here. Remember to ask the children to explain their answers to your questions.

1   Record your conversation with each child while doing the tasks.

2   Compare the responses of the younger and older children.

3   Can you identify which children have achieved conservation in the area covered by the task you used (for example, conservation of number, or substance)?

4   Were the results what you expected in terms of the age and developmental level of the children? If not, can you explain any anomalies?

More activities like this can be found on the CourseMate Express website.

For teachers, the egocentric and perception-bound characteristics of the preoperational child are the most relevant. Children at this stage have difficulty understanding others' thinking. Researchers since Piaget have investigated this in terms of the development of children's 'Theory of mind'; see, for example, Wellman (2011). While from late infancy children are aware of others' thinking, their ability to understand how this thinking differs from their own continues to develop through early childhood. Some assistance could be given to help children to understand that others see the world differently. Opportunities to talk both with peers and with adults about activities they are engaged in extend their understanding and language skills. For older children, introduction to early reading and number skills will contribute to this process. (These topics were introduced in Chapter 2.)

Stage 3: Concrete-operations period (seven years to 11 or 12 years)

The developmental milestones for the child at the **concrete-operations stage** are many, but there is one that is particularly significant: **conservation**, or the child's understanding that certain characteristics (such as length or volume) of an object do not change when the object's physical appearance changes. There are a number of logical principles involved in conservation at the concrete-operations stage, but in this chapter we focus on the following five principles: identity, reversibility, compensation, seriation and classification. These can readily be demonstrated in Piaget's conservation tasks (see Box 3.2).

Three of the conservation principles – identity, reversibility and compensation – underlie successful performance of the conservation tasks. All three principles are linked to the very first property of matter children have to understand: that is, object permanence. Children must learn that things have a relatively permanent 'identity' or existence. We saw the beginnings of this understanding emerge in the preoperational period, when children understand that things (and people) continue to exist even when out of sight. In conservation, this is extended to properties such as volume and number. A quantity of water is still the same even though its height changes when you pour it into a flat saucer or into a tall glass. A quantity of playdough is still the same whether you have it in one lump or break it up into 100 little pieces and spread the pieces over a larger space. Children also learn that any changes made to objects and materials can be reversed and the materials changed back into their original form; that is, the water can be poured back into the glass and the little bits of playdough rolled back into one big lump. This is **reversibility**.

Compensation

Similarly, children learn that changes in any one part of a closed system or situation will lead to **compensation**, or complementary changes in another part. For example, in the water example above, the width of the water in one glass is compensated by the height of the water in a thinner glass. These principles appear in children's explanations for their answers in the conservation tasks. They are acquired very slowly. Piaget argued that young children tend to focus on just one dimension of a situation – usually the most obvious one – which contributes to this limitation in thinking about compensation. An explanation of this tendency to focus on one dimension at a time is young children's limitations in the ability to control attention, which depends on development of the prefrontal cortex (Galotti, 2011).

Seriation

Seriation is concerned with the ability to order objects according to a dimension such as length or thickness. A child's game of nesting boxes (as seen in Figure 3.7) is a good example of seriation: each box must be fitted into the next by size so that at the end of the game, all the boxes disappear inside the largest one. Seriation is important to concepts such as measurement.

concrete-operations stage
Piaget's third stage, in which a child is able to mentally manipulate and think logically about objects that are present

conservation
The ability to see that certain characteristics (size, height, length, amount) of an object do not change with changes in the object's physical appearance

reversibility
The ability to mentally reverse thought, such as adding back something that has been taken away or remoulding something to its original shape

compensation
The ability to see that an increase in one dimension (such as height) is compensated for by a decrease in another dimension (such as width)

seriation
The ability to mentally arrange objects or elements in terms of a dimension such as length, weight or volume

CourseMateExpress

Online Resources
Explore development of logical operations with the **Interactive Activity**

Source: Alamy Stock Photo/Glasshouse Images

FIGURE 3.7 The ability to use a logical system to group objects is an important milestone of cognitive development in the first years of school.

classification
The ability to mentally group objects in terms of similar characteristics; for example, pansies, daffodils and roses are all 'flowers'

class inclusion
Understanding that a number of small collections can be combined in different ways to form a larger collection

Classification

Classification occurs when objects are grouped together according to a criterion such as shape, colour, function or size. It includes, for example, the knowledge that dogs, cows and donkeys are all 'animals', and that pencils, computers and words are all 'tools for communication'. Seriation and classification are among the most important achievements of the concrete-operations stage. They develop late in this period and indicate that the child has developed 'logical operations', or the ability to apply logical reasoning to a problem-solving task.

Class inclusion

One of the key aspects of classification is **class inclusion**, or the understanding that a number of small collections can be combined in different ways to form a larger collection. This is sometimes called 'multiple classification', such as occurs when a preoperational child recognises that something can be a flower *and* it can be a rose. 'Simultaneous multiple classification' occurs at the concrete-operations stage and is demonstrated when a five- or six-year-old looks at his mother quizzically and asks, 'Mummy, when you are at school being a teacher, are you still my mummy?' (WJF, personal communication, October 2001). You can try this yourself. Ask a five-year-old 'How many boys are coming to your party?' The child might answer 'Eight'. Now ask the child 'How many girls?' and the reply might be 'Two'. 'Are there more boys or more girls?' 'More boys.' 'Will there be more boys or more children at your party?' The child is likely to reply 'More boys'. This last response is not related to the child not knowing what 'children' means, because if you ask the child a separate question, 'What are children?', the answer will be 'Children are boys and girls'. The problem is that the child is focused on only one dimension (in this case, the larger group 'boys') and does not understand that there can be subgroups (that is, 'boys and girls') that can be combined into a bigger, single class (in this instance 'children').

At the concrete-operations stage, children may seem to use words such as 'some' and 'all' appropriately, but their understanding of these terms is not yet fully consistent with adult usage. Once children realise that objects can be classified in terms of more than one dimension (that is, the children can solve a class-inclusion problem), they seem amazed if you ask questions such as 'Are there more boys or more children?' and can then respond very quickly to the question. Consider how much of our education system depends on this type of understanding: you can see why these cognitive skills are so important and why children need to master them.

The main limitation in children's thinking at the concrete-operations stage of development is that their understanding of mental operations is restricted to concrete situations. They are concerned with the present and are not yet able to think hypothetically, in the abstract. However, their thinking is no longer dominated by what they see: they can now carry out tasks that require logical or mathematical reasoning; for instance, arranging objects in terms of a dimension such as length or weight (seriation), grouping objects in terms of similar features such as shape or colour (classification), or predicting if various weights placed at different points on each side of a balance beam will tip the balance or keep it horizontal (proportion).

Piaget's Stage 3 in education

The main limitation of children's thinking at the concrete-operations stage is their inability to think in abstractions, so one of their main needs is for teaching to be carried out in contexts that provide plenty of concrete experiences. Opportunities should be provided for students to experiment with materials, to test ideas and to begin to think logically about the problems they encounter. Students' current ways of thinking should be challenged, forcing them to extend and expand their existing knowledge as a basis for later learning. This is congruent with the constructivist principles of learning discussed more fully in Chapter 6.

BOX 3.3 RESEARCH LINKS

THINKING CRITICALLY ABOUT CLASSIFICATION

To assess children's understanding of classification, Piaget used squares and circles of different sizes (large and small) and colours (red and blue). The interviewer presents the squares and circles and asks the child to sort them into groups that are alike. When the child has finished, the interviewer asks: 'Tell me why you sorted the objects into these groups. What shall we call this group? ... And this one?' They then ask: 'Can you think of another way to sort them?' Finally, taking one of the groups (and using the child's labels), the interviewer asks: 'These are all squares; some are red and some are blue. Are there more red squares or more squares?'

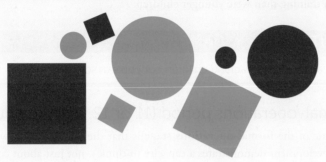

- *Level 1:* At age four to five, children tend to mix the basis of their classification: they may put blue and red circles together (both circles), add a white square to a white circle (both white) and then put a grey square with a white square (both squares).
- *Level 2:* At about age seven, children may sort logically but have trouble with the last question. They do not understand the logical relationship between a class (squares) and a subclass (red squares). If the red squares dominate the group of squares, Piaget argued, then the child has trouble focusing away from what they see.
- *Level 3:* Children typically demonstrate an understanding of class inclusion at about eight years of age. They will answer correctly that there are more squares (and may think you are foolish for asking).

Some researchers have questioned whether the difficulty young children have with this task is a logical reasoning problem or an attention problem: difficulty inhibiting a competing schema for sorting the shapes (Houdé, 2000). In the transition between levels 1 and 2, children may sort logically using one schema (for example, colour) but have difficulty shifting to another schema for sorting when asked to think of another way to sort the shapes (Brooks, Hanauer, Padowska & Rosman, 2003). Thus, the difficulty is one of controlling attention rather than of logical reasoning, as Piaget proposed. The CourseMate Express site includes details of some of the research work investigating this link.

ACTIVITIES

Try the classification task with children aged four, seven and 10 years or older. Document and report your findings.

1 Do you get the same results with both younger and older children? If not, can you explain why?
2 Do you think the difference is a result of understanding the task, ability to reason logically, or attention? Go to the CourseMate Express site to see some of the research on this issue.

For educators, the most important aspect of the concrete-operations stage is concerned with its upper limits and with students' transition to the next stage of formal operations. At this point, students are no longer dependent on concrete experiences to solve their problems, and can begin to think hypothetically. One of the tasks to be addressed by teachers and others working with students at this level is to provide experiences that will promote or stimulate more advanced ways of thinking. Piaget (1972) argued that educational experiences emphasising symbolic thought can promote the emergence of higher-order thinking skills such as formal and abstract thought.

The question of the benefits of directly teaching or training children to solve the Piagetian tasks was widely researched in the 1970s and 1980s. Miller (2011) reviewed this research and found that in many of these studies, researchers were able to teach Piagetian concepts. Strategies included explaining a concept, teaching the underlying thinking required for a task, creating cognitive conflict (through questioning, or exposure to peers' ways of thinking about the task), directing children's attention, and verbalising the rule involved. In line with Piaget's statements about readiness, older children were more able to benefit from training than were younger children.

THINK ABOUT

■ How could you apply this to teaching children concepts at school?

Stage 4: Formal-operations period (11 or 12 years to adulthood)

formal-operations stage
Piaget's fourth stage, in which the individual is now able to think abstractly and logically, to form hypotheses and to solve problems systematically

The key characteristic of the **formal-operations stage** is that the young person who has reached this level of cognitive development demonstrates a capacity to think – not just about concrete realities, but also about abstract possibilities or 'an infinite number of imaginable realities' (Siegler, 1998, p. 43). One task Piaget devised to demonstrate this was 'the third eye'. He asked children where they would put a third eye if it were possible to have one, and to explain their thinking (Piaget, 1970). Children at the concrete-operational stage tend to put the eye on their forehead, in a similar position to their existing eyes, whereas by the formal-operational stage, they are more inventive, putting it at the back of their head, in their hand or on a foot (see Figure 3.8), and to imagine other uses for their eye.

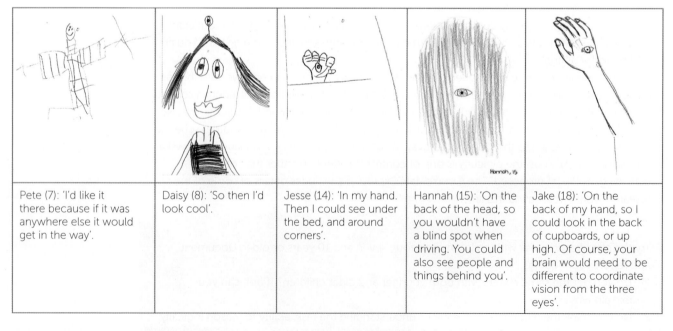

| Pete (7): 'I'd like it there because if it was anywhere else it would get in the way'. | Daisy (8): 'So then I'd look cool'. | Jesse (14): 'In my hand. Then I could see under the bed, and around corners'. | Hannah (15): 'On the back of the head, so you wouldn't have a blind spot when driving. You could also see people and things behind you'. | Jake (18): 'On the back of my hand, so I could look in the back of cupboards, or up high. Of course, your brain would need to be different to coordinate vision from the three eyes'. |

FIGURE 3.8 If you had a third eye, where on your body would you want it to be put? Why?

Piaget saw 'thinking about one's own thought' as the key element of cognitive development in the formal-operational stage. Kuhn and Franklin (2006) likewise provide evidence to suggest that in adolescence, what develops is an 'executive function' that gives control over thinking and monitoring of thought processes, which makes thinking and learning more effective – we discuss this executive function later in this chapter, and again in Chapter 6, in the section on metacognition. The main developmental task for the formal-operations stage is attainment of the capacity for abstract thought, and for propositional and hypothetical reasoning.

Adolescents are able to reason logically, speculate and hypothesise far more readily than concrete-operational children, who are more dependent on what they see, hear and experience. Adolescents no longer need a reference to real-life situations in order to do a task. Ideas can be formulated, tried out mentally, and later tested in real-life situations. Reasoning is now **deductive reasoning**, meaning that rules or general principles are used to form hypotheses about possible solutions to specific problems, with these hypotheses then being tested to see if the predictions are true. This can be contrasted with **inductive reasoning**, or the ability to induce general principles or rules from knowledge of specific examples, then apply the rules to predict new instances (see the discussion of discovery learning in Chapter 6). Ideas about infinity, humanity, democracy or compassion can now be conceptualised. The key developmental milestones to be achieved in the period of formal-operational thinking are therefore:

- 'propositional thinking', or reasoning about the logic of statements such as:

  Edith is fairer than Susan. Edith is darker than Lily. Who is the darkest?

  and

  A is greater than B and B is greater than C. Is A greater than C or less than C?

- 'hypothetico-deductive reasoning', or the ability to form hypotheses and argue from them.

Not surprisingly, in view of his background in science, Piaget used mathematical and scientific-type tasks that involved propositional and hypothetico-deductive thinking in the studies he conducted into formal-operational thinking (Inhelder & Piaget, 1958).

Examples of the scientific-type tasks Piaget used with older children include a problem that involves probability (see Box 3.4), and one that involves a pendulum. In the pendulum problem, students are asked to identify the variables that influence the rate of oscillation in a pendulum's swing. Is it the attached weight, the height from which the weight is released, the length of the string, the amount of pressure exerted to set the pendulum swinging, or some other factor that affects the oscillation rate? Children at the concrete-operations stage usually consider all possible factors at the same time and 'have great difficulty in excluding the weight factor' (Piaget & Inhelder, 1969, p. 148). Older children who have reached the formal stage in thinking are able to separate the factors and establish that the rate of the pendulum's swing reflects the length of the string and is unaffected by other factors. (Wadsworth, 2004). There is a version of this and other formal operations tasks that you can try on the CourseMate Express website.

deductive reasoning
Using rules or general principles to find general solutions to specific problems

inductive reasoning
Inducing general rules or principles from observation of specific examples

CourseMateExpress

Online Resources
Try some formal operations tasks yourself with the **Interactive Activity** on this text's website

BOX 3.4 RESEARCH LINKS

AN EXAMPLE OF PIAGET'S FORMAL-OPERATIONS TASKS

Probability

In a study of the development of formal thinking in adolescents, Flieller (1999) used a problem described by Piaget and his colleague Barbel Inhelder (see, for example, Inhelder and Piaget, 1958) to assess children's understanding of probability. To understand probability, or the likelihood or chance of something occurring, children must understand the concepts of chance

>>

and proportion (Wadsworth, 1996, p. 121). They need to be able to consider the ways in which the particular elements of a situation can be combined, and they also need to be able to calculate proportions. Children generally do not understand probability before they have reached formal operations, so this test is best given to adolescents and children in the late primary years.

Small coloured discs or tokens are used in this task. Some of the tokens are marked with a large black 'X' and others are unmarked. For each item in the test, the student is shown two sets of tokens, each set including some tokens marked with an 'X' and some unmarked tokens. The sets of tokens are presented in sequences that represent the Piagetian stages.

FIGURE 3.9 Students' reasoning about probability reveals an ability to consider how elements can be combined in various ways, and to calculate proportions.

Source: Matthew DJchesne, © Milk and Honey Photography, 2010

The student is shown two sets of tokens (for example, 1/4 – one X token and three unmarked tokens in a group of four – and 2/4 – two X tokens and two unmarked tokens in a group of four) and asked: 'If I take one token from each of these sets, from which of the sets will I be more likely to take a token with an X on it, at the first try and without first looking?' Encourage the student to explain the answer that is given.

At the preoperational stage, children's predictions are usually based on a guess or some other factor such as their favourite number. Concrete-operational children will use a reasoning strategy inconsistently. By the time they reach formal operations, children understand the concept of probability and this will be evident in their predictions (Wadsworth, 1996).

Source: Adapted from Flieller, A., 'Comparison of the development of formal thought in adolescent cohorts aged 10 to 15 years (1967–1996 and 1972–1993)', *Developmental Psychology*, 35(34), 1999, 1048–58. Copyright © 1999 by the American Psychological Association. Reproduced by permission.

PIAGETIAN STAGE	ITEMS*	SCORING
Concrete operations	1/4 and 2/4; 3/5 and 3/7; 1/3 and 1/2; and 2/4 and 3/7	Stage reached if more than two items correct
Transition to formal operations	1/2 and 2/4	Correct answer required for this stage
Formal operations (level a)	2/6 and 1/3; 3/9 and 2/6	One correct answer required for this stage
Formal operations (level b)	2/6 and 3/8	Correct answer required

*Note: the numerator represents the number of tokens with 'X' and the denominator is the total number of tokens in each set the student is shown.

ACTIVITIES

Try this task with students in the 13–15 years age range.

1   Keep a record of what the students do and any explanations they give.
2   Do the students solve the problems in the way you expected?
3   Can you explain any unexpected outcomes?
4   Score your results using the categories listed above and compare them with those reported by Flieller for the probability component of his test results (Flieller, 1999, p. 1054).

Solving problems such as those of the probability task or the pendulum task – which involve considering two or more variables – requires the ability to be systematic, to form hypotheses and to make deductions from findings. Many adults find such tasks exceedingly difficult. Even Piaget (1974) conceded that most people only reach a formal-operational level of thinking in the area of their greatest expertise. For many people it is much easier, or less challenging in a cognitive sense, to function at a concrete-operations level. Interestingly, it has been suggested that Piaget's formal-operations stage may not be the final stage of cognitive development. According to this view, adult thinking – when compared with the thinking of children and adolescents – is characterised by greater flexibility, and sensitivity to ambiguity and the impact of social, political and moral influences (Basseches, 1984; Labouvie-Vief, 1980). Most current research has challenged the notion of formal operations as a stage, given that younger children show some deductive and inductive reasoning, and many adults fail to use formal thinking on unfamiliar tasks (Kuhn & Franklin, 2006). View the CourseMate Express site for a review of some of this research.

CourseMateExpress

Online Resources
Go further: Is formal thinking a 'stage'? Read about research on deductive and inductive reasoning on this text's website

Piaget's Stage 4 in education

Teachers need to provide opportunities for more advanced students to be challenged cognitively, so that students can be encouraged to find creative solutions to unusual problems that can later be tested in real-life contexts. Students can be grouped into teams to work on problems, with each team including students who think at both the concrete- and the formal-operational levels. This would allow the more advanced thinkers to challenge and stimulate the thinking of the less advanced students. Implementing the best plans would provide the 'formal' thinkers with opportunities to test their ideas in real-life situations, while also giving the more 'concrete' thinkers the opportunity to operationalise or work out their ideas in practical ways.

Piaget argued that the hallmark of formal operations was the ability to 'operate on operations' – or metacognition (Flavell, 1979). Numerous studies have demonstrated that metacognition can be taught (Pennequin, Sorel & Mainguy, 2010) and that metacognitive knowledge and skill is related to academic achievement, to reasoning (Kuhn, 2000) and to intelligence (Sternberg, 1985; see Chapter 9). Metacognition is discussed later in this chapter, and its relation to learning in Chapter 6.

Opportunities for challenging students' thinking at both the concrete and formal levels can be identified in most teaching situations. For example, the plot in one of Shakespeare's plays can be studied in terms of a sequence of events that follows logically from beginning to end. At the same time, attention can be directed to the more abstract themes that underlie the action: compassion, jealousy, pride, desire. Hypothetical situations can be identified from the plot, and a sequence of events identified as being possible if alternative actions had been taken or different motives followed. Here, the main focus is to encourage and provide opportunities for students to begin to think abstractly about possibilities, divergent solutions and so on. These thinking patterns are most likely to be achieved in areas of activity in which students are 'experts'. Teachers at the secondary level who want to stimulate more advanced patterns of thinking in their students can begin by capturing students' interest and creating enthusiasm for the curriculum area in which they are working. Teachers cannot assume that all high school students are able to reason hypothetically, as would be expected if they had attained formal operations. Many will still reason at the level of concrete operations.

Some studies suggest that children in primary classrooms are able to reason hypothetically (Metz, 1995). Furthermore, Piaget's contention that children develop cognitively as a consequence of their interaction with the environment, as well as from maturation, suggests that providing these experiences for primary students is important to developing their thinking skills. Metz (1997) argued that teachers should not avoid hypothetico-deductive tasks in primary school programs.

BOX 3.5 CLASSROOM LINKS

HOW CAN STUDENTS BE SUPPORTED TOWARDS MORE ADVANCED THINKING?

One of the key challenges to Piaget's theory also provides suggestions for supporting the development of children's thinking. When the tasks are presented in different ways, children at various ages have been shown to be able to think in ways that Piaget's theory would suggest is not possible or consistent with their stage of thinking. Miller (2011) suggested that these studies may reveal the beginnings of more complex concepts in young children's thinking. They challenge Piaget's notion of structurally distinct stages of thinking.

Performance factors that challenged Piaget's description of the competence of children of various ages include the following list.

■ *Task complexity* – presenting tasks with simpler demands led to earlier demonstration of competence (for example, having fewer places for infants to search in the object permanence studies) (Wellman, Cross & Bartsch, 1987).

■ *Task familiarity* – designing tasks with scenarios that were familiar to children (using a character from *Sesame Street* (Borke, 1975) or a policeman/person hiding scenario (Hughes & Donaldson, 1979). In the three mountains task, preoperational children were able to take the perspective of another).

■ *The role of experience or expertise* – studies by Chi (1978) with chess champions showed that they used formal thinking in reasoning about chess – an area of expertise – and concrete thinking in other areas.

What do these studies suggest to teachers wanting to support children's thinking?

1   When children are being introduced to a concept, and when they are having difficulty with a concept, reduce the complexity of tasks or activities. For example, one-to-one counting is acquired earlier with small groups of items than counting with larger groups (Gelman & Gallistel, 1978). Similarly, children can be challenged or extended by increasing the complexity of a task.

2   Present new concepts in a familiar context, with familiar examples. Use familiar ideas when students are required to reason in complex ways.

3   Develop and strengthen students' content knowledge before requiring them to manipulate or reason about this knowledge. For example, Marzano and Simms (2014) suggested a questioning sequence in which students are prompted to build knowledge and understanding before they are asked questions that require them to analyse and evaluate.

4   Teach concepts in order. If students are having difficulty with a concept, go back to the foundational understandings that underpin it.

STRENGTHS OF PIAGET'S IDEAS

Piaget taught us to listen to children and to appreciate the intelligence they bring to the task of attempting to make sense of their world. Piaget was interested in how children think and how they come to understand concepts such as time, space, movement and self. The types of tasks and the procedures he used to collect data stimulated new ways of thinking about children's cognitive development. Probably Piaget's most important contributions to the study of child development concern the way in which we think about children and the methods we use to study them (Feldman, 2013; Miller, 2011). Piaget's focus on analysing the errors children make when they solve problems was also significant (see, for example, Gelman and Gallistel's 1978 work on children's understanding of number concepts).

Piaget viewed children's cognitive development as a gradual process of change, with new mental schemas emerging from pre-existing structures. This view has resulted in a general recognition by educators that it is the *stage* of development a child has reached that is important – not the age. Some curricula in Australia and New Zealand have taken up this notion. The term 'developmentally appropriate education' is sometimes used to refer to this idea. The 'stage not age' concept, or the idea of matching instructional strategies to children's current level of understanding, means that teachers need to be aware of their students' level of reasoning, and plan accordingly. For example, younger students who still need concrete experiences in their learning need real objects, diagrams and the written word, not just verbal instruction. At the secondary level, teachers cannot assume that students are thinking hypothetically; adolescents may need considerable assistance not only to begin to reason at this level, but also to reason at this level consistently. Indeed, many studies (see Moshman, 2004, for a review) have found that only a minority of adolescents show advanced formal-operational thinking.

One aspect of Piaget's theory that has not been challenged is the idea that children actively create their own learning and that direct experience is essential for such learning to occur. Constructivism, discovery learning, inquiry-based learning, cooperative learning and other related approaches (see Chapters 6 and 7) are extensions of this principle. Piaget's theory also reminds us that children's thinking is not the same as that of adults. It is both different and less efficient. Teachers need to be aware of the process of thinking, not just the outcome. It is not just a question of children getting a problem right or wrong, but how they do the task, the types of errors they make and the processes they use to reach an answer that are important for teachers to assess their understanding.

LIMITATIONS TO PIAGET'S IDEAS

Anyone who strives to develop a grand theory is likely to be criticised, and this is true of Piaget. The length of time that elapsed between his first publications in the area of children's cognitive development (in the 1920s) and his last (in 1981), the amount of data he collected and the very large number of his major publications make such criticism inevitable (Lourenco & Machado, 1996). There was remarkable coherence in Piaget's work over these six decades (Brainerd, 1996), but there was also variability as his ideas and research methods changed direction and new interpretations and emphases emerged (Beilin, 1992). However, much of the criticism that has been levelled at Piaget's theory has stimulated further research that, in turn, has expanded our understanding of how cognitive development occurs. In this sense, criticism can be seen to have had a positive effect on the field of educational psychology as a whole.

Ages and stages

One of the first criticisms often made of Piaget's theory concerns his ideas about the timing of children's attainment of developmental milestones within the different stages. For example, studies have shown that he overestimated what the average 12-year-old could do and underestimated what the preoperational child could do. In particular, researchers have pointed out instances in young children's behaviour of taking others' perspectives into account (such as when they use baby talk to talk to younger children, or turn a picture around to show someone else), and the ability to show higher levels of reasoning when tasks are simplified or put into a familiar context. Children also show evidence of deductive reasoning earlier than Piaget proposed, with gradual improvements over time towards formal reasoning (Kuhn & Franklin, 2006).

Piaget himself commented that the ages at which different stages are attained are highly variable, and depend on the child's experiences and social environment (Piaget, 1972). The important issue here is the *sequence* of changes that occurs in the way children think, rather than the ages at which such changes occur. Research generally supports this sequence of changes, although researchers take issue with the notion of stage-like development, as proposed by Piaget.

Stage concept

Doubts have been raised about Piaget's notion of stages. Evidence such as that we have discussed from studies showing partial understanding of formal operations (such as deductive reasoning) earlier in childhood, and an ability to take others' perspectives in early childhood, suggests development is not a matter of the absence and then the sudden presence of skills, as Piaget described, but a gradual acquisition of these abilities. Other studies showing that children can be trained to successfully respond in the Piagetian tasks (for example, Beilin, 1978; Siegler & Svetina, 2006) also challenge the notion of stages, as such training builds on basic understandings children have developed.

Questions have also been raised about whether stages are general, applying across domains, or particular to specific content domains, such as number, spatial awareness or social understanding. Neo-Piagetians such as Case (1992, 1998) and Fischer (Fischer & Rose, 1996) described development within a domain as proceeding in a stage-like manner; but rather than a single staircase, Case described development as multiple staircases that link together. Fischer and Bidell (2006) described a net of pathways to competence in a domain, with multiple skills and understandings contributing to competence. Their theory is not as neat as Piaget's, but the picture of development gained from research is not neat either. The theory accounts for the variability that is observed within and between children in development, which is discussed later in this chapter.

Current models of development describe it as dynamic and influenced by interactions between characteristics and actions of people and environments, that shift in various contexts (Mascolo & Fischer, 2015). We discussed this view in Chapter 2. This contrasts with the fixed notion of stages that Piaget described, and with his focus solely on the cognitive domain, as we will see below.

Absence of skills

A further criticism concerns the very negative view of development that Piaget presented, particularly in relation to the thinking of young children, who are described in terms of what they *cannot* do, rather than what they can do. For example, Piaget saw the preoperational child as incapable of thinking logically and lacking any understanding of seriation, conservation, reversibility and so on. His focus was on a transition from the absence to the presence of a particular type of understanding (with hypothetico-deductive reasoning as the pinnacle), rather than on the quite remarkable cognitive capacity that the preoperational child has already achieved. In Piaget's defence, it is claimed he did not see children at the sensorimotor or preoperational stage as lacking specific abilities, but rather as being capable of certain types of understanding that are gradually transformed over time into new schemas or cognitive structures (Smith, 1993). It may be more useful, as Piaget did in one work (1951), to describe children's thinking in terms of tendencies rather than abilities; that is, his theory describes what children usually do, rather than what they are capable of in ideal conditions. Interestingly, his description of adults' thinking appears to take the opposite approach: describing what thinking adults are capable of, rather than the ways in which they usually think.

Role of social context

Some critics of Piaget's theory claim that Piaget's explanation of cognitive development pays insufficient attention to the role of others or to the child's social environment. However, you might recall that social interaction, as seen in Figure 3.10, is one of the contributors to development Piaget identified. He was particularly interested in peer interaction as a means for children to expand their ideas, to overcome conflicts (disequilibrium), and to achieve shared solutions (equilibrium) that are more mature than individual efforts (Brown, Metz & Campione, 1996). The place of peer interaction is particularly evident in Piaget's work on moral development (see Chapter 4). However, while it had obvious implications for education, the theory had no significant role for educators. Within a

Piagetian-based curriculum, the role of the teacher is primarily concerned with assessing the level of children's thinking and providing appropriate experiences rather than teaching students directly. By describing children as 'solitary scientists', Piaget places them at the centre of their development, and interactions with others are one of several environmental influences that might prompt development in the child's thinking. Piaget focused on the child's role, and did not explore the corrective feedback and explicit teaching that occurs not just in schools

FIGURE 3.10 Social interaction is an important contributor to cognitive development.

but at home, and which is a large part of children's experience of the world. Vygotsky's theory, described later in this chapter, describes a different role for adults and peers in development.

Additional factors in development

Other limitations often attributed to Piaget's model, particularly by theorists interested in information processing and motivation (see Chapters 6 and 8), are that it does not sufficiently take into account memory, motivation and emotion (that is, feelings or 'affect'). Feldman (2013) pointed out that Piaget was not writing a theory of psychology (or education) but of knowledge, and so it should not be surprising that he did not focus on these factors. In fact, Piaget perceived memory as part of the process whereby children create schemas to represent aspects of their experience, such as with the concept of a 'dog', and then reactivate these schemas when retrieving (remembering) information during their next encounter with a dog. Motivation is seen as an element in the process of disequilibrium, in that the experience of cognitive conflict motivates children to strive to resolve their uncertainty and to regain equilibrium. Cognitive development occurs as an outcome of this process. Emotions contribute to development by influencing the selection of what is attended to. Children are most likely to become involved in an activity if their interest (and emotion) is roused. Work on emotion (discussed in Chapter 4) and motivation (discussed in Chapter 8) attributes more complex roles in development to these factors than Piaget described.

Individual differences

Criticisms of Piaget have also included claims that he paid insufficient attention to individual differences among children; for example, differences in gender or cultural background, or the presence of a disability. Piaget did not report any differences in the ways in which males and females develop intellectually, for example (Sutherland, 1992; Wadsworth, 2004). His aim was to identify the universal processes of cognitive development. Differences in the ages at which children reached each stage might occur depending on children's experience, but the processes and structure of development would not vary.

Many cross-cultural studies have tested the universality of the theory and, when adjustments are made for language, context and content of test items, have found that the same structure of development exists, although rates of development appeared to vary in some studies (see, for example, Dasen, 1973, 1977; Goodnow, 1962). Studies showing that years of formal, Western-style schooling affect the age at which children attain concrete operations and formal operations as measured by standard Piagetian tasks can be explained by the familiarity children in schools have with the testing situation, which can be overcome with fairly brief training in the testing and by adjusting task content to more closely reflect the child's culture (Lightfoot, Cole & Cole, 2009). At the same time, participation in related activities as part of everyday experience contributes to developments in cognition, just as Piaget's theory described. McDevitt and Ormrod (2010) described a village of potters in Mexico whose children reach conservation much earlier than would be expected in Piaget's theory, because of their experiences with clay and water. A number of studies have suggested that formal schooling is necessary for the development of formal-operational thinking, because the experiences offered in formal schooling demand abstract reasoning (Segall, Dasen, Berry & Poortinga, 1999).

In fact, Piaget's studies have been successfully replicated in many different contexts involving children with a range of disabling conditions and from a variety of cultural backgrounds. He appears to have been successful in identifying the universals he sought, at least in the sequence of cognitive development.

Variability

Cultural context aside, considerable variation within, as well as between, children has been noted in research (Siegler, 2007). This challenges Piaget's claims that development happens in the same way for all children, and that development reflects structural changes leading to qualitatively different forms of reasoning. Children (and adults) do not reason at a consistent level at any point in time – their reasoning may vary, depending on context, experience and knowledge of the topic – and Siegler (2007) reported that children use different strategies on similar problems they are presented with close together in time.

Box 3.6 contains some issues relevant to classroom applications of Piaget's ideas, as well as some suggestions for classroom activities derived from Piaget's theory of cognitive development in **Table 3.2**.

BOX 3.6 IMPLICATIONS FOR EDUCATORS

APPLYING PIAGET'S IDEAS IN THE CLASSROOM

Some of the issues relevant to classroom instruction that are highlighted by Piaget's theory (see also **Table 3.2**) include the need for teachers to:

- listen to children and observe what they do, in play and in other activities
- take into account the critical factors that influence children's cognitive development, including maturation or biologically based changes associated with growth, which may result in individual differences in development
- give children time to explore their world and to work things out, recognising children's role as 'miniature scientists' and the learning that results from their physical and mental activity
- consider children's interaction with adults and other children, providing opportunities for them to discuss their thinking and to debate viewpoints
- ensure that children maintain equilibration or cognitive balance between new experiences and what is already known, challenging their thinking by providing opportunities for them to find links between the unfamiliar and existing knowledge, which may involve creating new schemas or adjusting existing ones
- ensure that information given to children is close enough to their current level of understanding so that linkages can be made between the old and the new.

TABLE 3.2 Summary of Piaget's ideas

STAGE	CLASSROOM ACTIVITY	EXAMPLES OF ACTIVITIES
Sensorimotor (birth–2 years)	Turn-taking; imitation of actions and sounds; appropriate play	• Play peekaboo; roll a ball or toy car back and forth; build a tower of three blocks and knock it over while saying 'uh-oh', with the child to do the same • Sit beside the child in front of a mirror, imitate actions (smile, poke out tongue, touch nose); sing songs such as 'Everybody do this' and 'Old MacDonald had a farm'; look at books together, naming objects and making appropriate sounds ('cow, duck, dog' or 'moo, quack, woof-woof') • Provide a variety of materials for play; model appropriate behaviour
Preoperational (2 years to 6 or 7 years)	Hands-on experiences that allow child to 'construct' own knowledge; group activities involving peers; variety of activities to encourage symbol development and language (early literacy and numeracy)	• Provide practical experiences with a variety of concrete materials (sand, water, blocks; see free-play areas in early-childhood programs) • Keep in mind children's egocentrism; encourage activities that increase awareness of others' points of view, such as 'pretend' (imaginary) games; play turn-taking games such as lotto and board games • Sing nursery rhymes; play word games (I spy); read alphabet books; play rhyming and counting games; do sorting, matching, pattern-making and counting activities in play and during daily routines
Concrete operations (7 years to 11 or 12 years)	Concrete experiences to allow for experimentation, for testing ideas and for beginning to think logically; situations that challenge existing ideas, create disequilibrium and expand vocabulary; opportunities to explore new areas, expand experience and develop a wider knowledge base; work in groups	• Provide concrete resources to support learning • Provide opportunities for problem solving and logical thinking using a variety of materials • Encourage students to discuss problems, share ideas, identify possible solutions, plan alternatives, implement plans and revise, finding solutions as needed (for example, work out how to better organise the space in the classroom so that they don't keep bumping into each other) • Encourage group work, with students challenging each other's ideas; give a range of experiences to expand knowledge base and vocabulary
Formal operations (12 years to adulthood)	Think hypothetico-deductively; understand and appreciate irony, satire, fantasy and paradox	• Provide opportunities for students to extend their knowledge and ideas, challenge current assumptions, express their ideas in written forms through a variety of different genres (including poetry and prose) and express their ideas orally by engaging in discussions and debates on hypothetical and theoretical topics

VYGOTSKY'S SOCIOCULTURAL THEORY

Lev Semanovich Vygotsky (see Box 3.7) was a contemporary of Piaget's for a short period, from when Piaget began publishing in 1920 to Vygotsky's death in 1934. Pass (2007) reports that Piaget and Vygotsky communicated and exchanged ideas for about five years, and suggests that they may each have adjusted their theories as a result. In Vygotsky's first collection of writings (*Thought and language*, 1934), he criticised some aspects of Piaget's theory, such as Piaget's concept of egocentrism and, in particular, egocentric language.

In many ways there was significant overlap between Piaget's and Vygotsky's work. For example, like Piaget, Vygotsky's early interest in psychological research arose from a request to replicate Binet's intelligence test in Russia (Shayer, 2003). There were also major differences in their ideas, which reflected, in part, the differences in their social and cultural backgrounds. For example, Piaget focused on the individual, but, by contrast and largely as a result of the social and political system operating in the Soviet Union at that time, Vygotsky's concern was with learning and development occurring within a sociohistorical and sociocultural context: This orientation was an outcome of the particular society, period of history and culture in which he worked. Vygotsky argued very strongly that the child and the environment interact to mould cognition in culturally appropriate ways. This view is evident in the themes that distinguish Vygotsky's ideas, including the sociocultural and sociohistorical origins of cognitive development, language as a mental tool, the role of private speech and the zone of proximal development.

BOX 3.7 ABOUT LEV SEMANOVICH VYGOTSKY

Lev Semanovich Vygotsky (1896–1934) was born into an intellectual Russian-Jewish family that lived within the restricted territory (the Pale) in the southern Byelorussian town of Gomel, close to the Ukrainian border (Dixon-Krauss, 1996). His father was a bank manager and his mother was a teacher. Lev was the second-born of eight children.

Intellectually gifted and with an extraordinary memory, Vygotsky was educated at home and, at the secondary level, at the local gymnasium (a European secondary school that prepares students for university). Vygotsky won a place at the University of Moscow in 1913, and received a degree in law, with a specialisation in literature, in 1917. He was widely read in literature, poetry and the arts (Miller, 1993).

Vygotsky returned to Byelorussia after his graduation and taught a range of subjects to adults and children, including language and literature, logic and psychology, and art history and theatre (Dixon-Krauss, 1996, p. 2). He became interested in children with learning difficulties and intellectual disabilities, and established several clinics that conducted research into the problems of such children. He

FIGURE 3.11 Vygotsky emphasised the social nature of children's learning and the contribution of social interaction to this process.

was particularly interested in devising ways in which to assess children's intellectual abilities and to evaluate the efficacy of intervention strategies (Wertsch, 1985).

In 1924, Vygotsky was invited to join the Institute of Psychology in Moscow. He moved there with his family and began a collaboration with two other Russian psychologists, Alexander Luria (1902–77) and Alexei Leontiev (1903–79). Together, they developed a 'cultural-historical' or 'sociohistorical' view of human development that emphasised cognitive activities such as thinking, memory and reasoning (Miller, 1993). The three worked together until Vygotsky's death in 1934, the year his most popular book, *Thought and language*, was published in Russia.

From the early 1930s, the Communist Party increasingly controlled the intellectual life of Soviet academics, and Vygotsky's work was banned from 1936 to 1956 (Miller, 1993; Palmer, 2001). By the 1960s, when Piaget's theory was becoming more widely known in the West, interest in Vygotsky's work and access to his writings outside Russia began to increase. An English translation of *Thought and language* was published in 1962, and the first of six volumes of Vygotsky's collected writings appeared 15 years later (Miller, 1993).

Source: Ria Novosti/Science Photo Library

SOCIOCULTURAL ORIGINS OF COGNITIVE DEVELOPMENT

While Piaget was interested in describing what was universal in children's cognitive development, Vygotsky was interested in differences, and particularly in how those differences arose from the social, historical and cultural context in which children grow.

Vygotsky's ideas about the way in which our social, cultural and historical background and experiences shape cognition are demonstrated in descriptions of children's behaviour in early infancy (see, for example, Bruner, 1975; Kaye, 1982; Lock, 1978). According to Vygotsky, infants are born with an inherited capacity for specific patterns of action. They have also had prenatal experiences. But from the time of birth, their task is to acquire a sequence of skills and competencies that are uniquely human, with language being probably the most important of these skills. This acquisition, or learning, is achieved through social interaction. As carers interact with infants, they unconsciously structure the baby's experiences in ways that reflect the carers' own social, cultural and historical background.

In this way, the child develops not just as an individual, but as a member of a particular society and culture. The role of adults in development is to help to *socialise* the child (see Chapter 11) – to develop his or her thinking in ways particular to the culture and society in which they live.

Vygotsky described humans' mental abilities as:

- 'lower mental functions' (meaning inherited, involuntary capacities such as vision, hearing and taste) that are controlled by external objects and events
- 'higher mental functions' (meaning those developed through social interaction, including logical and abstract thinking, and language) that operate internally (that is, 'in the head') and are used to control lower mental functions, to think and to solve problems concerning external objects and events.

In reviewing Vygotsky's ideas about adults' role in structuring infant cognitive development, Lock, Service, Brito and Chandler (1989) highlight his notion that the developmental process is primarily concerned with the infant gaining control over lower mental functions, such as hearing and vision, that are present at birth. A child has to learn which of the many stimuli in the environment are considered (by carers) to be important and should be attended to. For example, Dad points to Mum getting into the car and says 'Wave goodbye to Mum', but the baby finds Dad's eyes much more interesting to look at and to touch. Dad turns the baby's head towards Mum, points and says 'Look!' Vygotsky argued that children learn to control lower mental functions and begin to acquire higher-level functions through such interactive experiences.

In their 'peekaboo' study, Bruner and Sherwood (1975) gave a fine example of the emergence of early communicative behaviour in mother–infant pairs. They cited data from observation of one mother–infant pair who were seen, over a period of time, to play peekaboo 22 times, the first time when the baby was 10 months of age, and the last when the baby was aged 15 months. The game always began with face-to-face contact between mother and child, and sometimes included a vocalisation by the mother to attract the child's attention. The mother initiated almost all of the episodes observed (19 out of 22), her face being hidden almost as often as the child's face was hidden. In the few instances in which the game was initiated by the child, the child's face was hidden, not the mother's face. Peekaboo (shown in Figure 3.12) is a good example of the 'social-structuring' process described by Vygotsky. Here, the helpless newborn is gradually transformed, through recurring interactive experiences with familiar partners, from passive respondent to active participant, with increasing control of cognitive functions. The skills learned have been internalised. Note that in thinking about these exchanges, Vygotsky recognised that what is passed from adult to child includes aspects of current and past experience, knowledge, attitudes, and the beliefs and values of the child's social group, as represented by the carer. This explains the use of both 'sociocultural' and 'sociohistorical' to refer to Vygotsky's model.

Source: Larry Williams/Corbis

Source: Shutterstock.com/c12

FIGURE 3.12 Interactions between parents and children help children to take on cultural knowledge, such as these children are learning about communication.

INTERNALISATION

internalisation
The transformation of external processes into internal processes that guide action and thought

One of the key concepts that distinguished Vygotsky's theory of cognitive development from that of Piaget is the notion of **internalisation**. This is the notion that individuals internalise the ideas and processes they observe and participate in during social interaction as new ways of thinking. Their thinking is gradually transformed through interaction. Like Piaget, Vygotsky described individuals as active agents in their development. While Piaget focused on the individual as the agent and constructor of their own cognitive development, Vygotsky saw development as arising out of social interaction (in which the child is a participant) and, from there, being internalised by the individual. Vygotsky expressed it in this way: 'The true direction of the development of thinking is not from the individual to the social, but from the social to individual' (Vygotsky, 1986, p. 36). Consider how this might work in the classroom, when a teacher is discussing the causes of the First World War with her students. In the course of the discussion, the students put forward theories, while the teacher extends their thinking about the topic with questions and evidence from her knowledge of history. She responds to students' ideas, corrects misconceptions, and asks questions to prompt them to think in new ways about history. Students also draw on and respond to one another's ideas. As a result of the discussion, students *internalise* these new ways of thinking, and may apply them to other topics.

SOCIAL INTERACTION

Vygotsky argued very strongly that it is in interaction with others that we learn how to think. The teacher's mediation of the students' learning in the above example is not merely a passing of knowledge from expert to novice, nor is it simply construction by the student of new ideas about history. It is a co-construction, made by both the teacher and the student together as they interact. Thus, for Vygotsky, the individual is active in development, but so are others; their development arises from social interactions. He argued that this is particularly important when thinking about the development of higher mental functions:

> Every function in the child's cultural development appears twice: first, on the social level and, later, on the individual level; first, between people (interpsychological) and then inside the child (intrapsychological). This applies equally to voluntary attention, to logical memory and to the formation of concepts. All the higher functions originate as actual relations between human individuals.

Source: Vygotsky (1978, p. 57).

A study that explored this issue (Wertsch, McNamee, McLane & Budwig, 1980, p. 1219) looked at how individual mothers interacted with their three-year-old when the child was presented with a simple shape-puzzle. The researchers found that mothers structured the task, giving assistance rather than just letting the child do it randomly. A mother would direct attention to a relevant piece, pointing to a wheel piece and asking: 'What is happening here?' Similar results are reported in studies of children teaching other children to play a board game that they had earlier constructed with another child (LeBlanc & Bearison, 2004). In the board game example, the (teacher) child begins by demonstrating and stating the rules and goal of the game while the (learner) child indicates that the instructions are understood by affirming or restating the information given, as in this example involving two six-year-old boys:

T (teacher): One (small game piece in the shape of a robot) goes here (in the centre of the board). Then you put this (a second small robot) here (also in the centre).

L (learner): So this (robot) is one player and that's (robot) the other?

T: Yeah.

L: So you have to spin this (spinner)?

T: No, you don't. That's not the way you do it.

L: OK.

T: You use these (dice).

Reprinted from LeBlanc, G. & Bearison, D. J. (2004). Copyright 2004, with permission from Elsevier.

Later, the learner may contribute to the development of the game by suggesting new rules that enhance the complexity of the game, as in the following exchange between 10-year-olds:

L: What happens when it (the spinner) lands on the black (the line dividing the different coloured spaces on the spinner)?

T: We don't have to worry about that. It doesn't happen.

L: But it could, right?

T: Yeah, I guess it could.

L: Then what do you do?

T: Spin again.

L: But black is the colour on the board (the outer edge of the board). Maybe we could use it?

T: Yeah, we could say that you have to land on the black and then you have to stay there until the other person goes around the board once.

L: Yeah, that's good.

T: OK. We'll play it like that.

Reprinted from LeBlanc, G. & Bearison, D. J. (2004). Copyright 2004, with permission from Elsevier.

FIGURE 3.13 In Vygotsky's view, adults and older or more knowledgeable children play important roles in the development of children's thinking. What are some of the contributions one child might be making while helping another child play a game?

In the section on scaffolding we discuss this role of experts in helping children to achieve new or difficult tasks further.

Gelman (2009) looked at how the individual and others work together to construct knowledge. As we've seen in these examples, and as Vygotsky argued, it is neither a matter of the child constructing understanding without any input from others; nor of children passively receiving input from others in their environment. Rather, children are active in processing the information they receive from others, and language is a key element in that process.

LANGUAGE AS A MENTAL TOOL

Vygotsky argued that each culture has a set of artefacts – physical and mental tools – through which the culture is expressed and passed on. Just as technological tools are used to shape the environment, mental tools shape thinking, and are part of the process of construction of ideas. These mental tools are particular to each culture, and shape individuals' thinking in the ways of the culture. The mental tools passed from adults and peers to children during social interaction include language, as well as 'various systems for counting; mnemonic techniques; algebraic symbol systems; works of art; writing; schemes, diagrams, maps, and mechanical drawings; all sorts of conventional signs, and so on' (Vygotsky, 1981, p. 137, cited by Daniels, 2011).

If Vygotsky had lived into the 21st century, he no doubt would have included phones, computers and other electronic devices on his list of mental tools. Computers exemplify the way in which a mental tool can shape thinking (see Chapter 12). Miller (1993) used the invention of (and access to) paper to illustrate changes in the mental tools needed by children growing up in earlier centuries, or in more primitive societies with oral rather than written traditions. A similar example can be found in the impact of maps and other technologies on navigation at sea. The southern continents of Australia and New Zealand were located by navigators such as Captain James Cook using primitive charts, a compass, a sextant and a chronometer. By contrast, the island of Tahiti had earlier been located by people from the Hawaiian Islands travelling in large canoes, their navigators reading the waves, stars and the flight of birds, and using charts made of sticks and knotted twine (Lewis, 1972). In the 21st century, these earlier methods appear very primitive. Navigators now work with computers and satellite technology to plan their routes. Imagine how diverse the mental maps of the Pacific Ocean would be for these different groups of navigators. These examples illustrate Vygotsky's claim that the mental tools acquired by individuals are the products of their social, cultural and historical backgrounds. One of the responsibilities of adults, including parents and teachers, is therefore to give children the mental tools or cognitive strategies they will need to function effectively and independently within their own cultural and social environment.

Private speech and self-talk

For Vygotsky, language is the most important mental tool. Initially, it has a social function, providing a means for interacting with others. However, as children's language skills increase, it begins to serve an intellectual function, as a tool for problem solving and self-regulation. The change is reflected in a shift from reliance on external devices for solving problems (for example, counting on fingers, or tying a knot in a handkerchief to remember something) to speech that is 'internalised' (that is, 'in the head'), or **private speech**. With very young children, self-instructional language – egocentric speech, in Piaget's terms – is often spoken out loud. Piaget thought this **self-talk** was just a primitive way of using language, since it drops out as children develop. But Vygotsky thought such language was actually helping children to think. He gave an account of a child of five-and-a-half years who talked to himself as he was drawing a picture of a tram. While drawing a wheel on the tram, the child pressed too hard on the pencil and the lead broke. When the child tried to finish the wheel by pressing hard on the paper, there was no mark on the paper apart from the indentation made by the blunt pencil. When this happened, the child said 'Broken'.

private speech
Speech used to guide own thinking and actions; it can be both internal (silent) and external (audible)

self-talk
Private speech uttered aloud

He then put the pencil down, picked up a paint brush and began to draw a tram that had broken down after an accident and was being repaired. He continued to talk to himself about the broken tram as he worked on the drawing.

Vygotsky noted that the pencil breaking, the child's awareness of his difficulty in drawing with a broken pencil, and his utterance ('Broken') represented a turning point in the activity. The drawing changed from a picture of a tram to a picture of a tram being repaired. In this situation, the self-talk was clearly a part of the child's thinking and not simply something that accompanied that thinking (Vygotsky, 1987, p. 70, cited by Newman & Holzman, 1993, p. 116).

Vygotsky used tasks with increasing levels of difficulty to explore the use of self-talk, finding that as thinking became more sophisticated, this type of speech ceased or the children became silent. Box 3.8 describes research on the role of private speech in regulating attention. Attention is addressed further later in this chapter.

BOX 3.8 RESEARCH LINKS

STUDIES OF PRIVATE SPEECH IN YOUNG CHILDREN

Vygotsky (1978, 1986) proposed that private speech is used to communicate both with others and with ourselves, and that it is a tool for thinking, particularly for logical thought, self-monitoring and self-direction.

Vygotsky found that private speech increases when tasks become more difficult. Research since has likewise found that private speech helps children with motor control and task performance (Fernyhough & Fradley, 2005), and that children who use private speech tend to have greater levels of attention and involvement (Winsler, Naglieri & Manfra, 2006). The answer to the question 'How much should teachers in early childhood settings allow children to talk to themselves in classrooms?' seems clear, but should they *encourage* children to do this?

Winsler, Manfra and Diaz (2007) examined this in a preschool setting with children with and without behavioural difficulties, and found that both groups of children talked aloud when asked to, and that their performance on motor sequencing and counting tasks was improved when they were asked to talk to themselves while working. (Indeed, some children were not able to stop talking when asked to complete a task in silence.)

Corkum, Humphries, Mullane and Theriault (2007) compared the private speech of children with and without ADHD, and found that those with ADHD produced more external private speech, irrespective of language ability. Some of this was relevant to the task and some was not. The authors suggest that private speech is an important way in which these children compensate for their difficulties in attention.

The implications of the studies are that external (verbalised) private speech may be relied on by children with behavioural difficulties to control their behaviour and thinking, particularly when undertaking difficult tasks. When this self-talk is relevant to the task, it should be encouraged, as it may help with self-regulation.

ACTIVITIES

1. Sit quietly near a four- or five-year-old who is engaged in a practical activity such as drawing or painting, building in a sandpit, or playing with blocks and farm animals. Pretend to be reading a book or to be involved in some similar activity. Look and listen for any self-talk. Keep a note of what the child says and does.
2. Think about what is happening as the child talks. Is the language simply an accompaniment to the activity, or is it more closely involved in the child's thought processes? What is the social context?

Vygotsky suggested that private speech has an intellectual function, being an important tool for structuring intellectual activity. Children often model (or replicate) the process of moving from external language to inner speech when they learn to read. In the early stages, printed symbols are recognised and sounded aloud, initially in a social context such as a classroom, or with the help of a tutor. As word-recognition skills increase, the reader becomes more confident and the need for social support diminishes. Reading aloud is replaced by 'mumble reading', which contributes to fluency (Frandsen, 2011), and then by silent reading. The shift from dependence on external and social processes to internalised (or purely mental) functioning has been achieved. Reading has become a tool for use in intellectual activities.

THINK ABOUT

- Consider your own behaviour when you are faced with a challenging task.
- Under what circumstances does your own private speech become 'self-talk'?
- What is the function of such speech?

ZONE OF PROXIMAL DEVELOPMENT

zone of proximal development (ZPD) The distance between children's current level of competence on a task and the level they can achieve with support or guidance

In thinking about the social context in which children learn, Vygotsky identified what he called the **zone of proximal development (ZPD)**, or the distance between what children can do by themselves and what they can do with the help of others.

This is illustrated in the following example (also see **Figure 2.18**). A student was given an addition and a subtraction problem to solve. He was able to solve the addition problem independently. When solving the subtraction problem, however, he had difficulty. The teacher gave him a hint, asking 'What number did you start with?' to help him restart at the correct point. Following this assistance from the teacher, the child was able to successfully solve the problem. This task was in his zone of proximal development – something he was unable to do on his own, but capable of carrying out with the teacher's assistance. Importantly, the teacher did not tell the student how to solve the problem, but gave him the amount of assistance he required to solve it himself. The child was still active in learning. In time, with further practice of this type, this problem will also be something the child can achieve independently, and the teacher will move him on to more difficult problems.

Vygotsky argued that teaching should be focused on the zone of proximal development, and that assessment should aim not to determine what children can do independently (what they have already learnt to do), but to find out what the child can do with assistance – what is in their zone of proximal development. This is so that teaching can be directed at the optimum level for each child, to lead their development forward. This example also shows the role of the teacher in Vygotsky's theory, which is to assist children to develop understandings and to regulate their own learning, rather than to tell or demonstrate to them what they are required to know.

Think about this. If you give a series of tasks to two children and they perform at the level of the average eight-year-old, most people would say the children were performing at the same level. This represents their unassisted level, or what they can do by themselves. Now, imagine a situation in which you give both children the same amount of assistance to do the task. You might give a series of hints or prompts, or structure the task to make it easier – such as setting out the materials in the order in which they should be used, or simplifying the instructions. After getting this help, one child performs like a 12-year-old and the other like a nine-year-old. Given this outcome, can you claim that the two children are at the same level? Vygotsky argued that what differs between the two children is their zone of proximal development. One child is able to benefit much more from your assistance than the other. The one who progresses further is in some way more advanced in relation to the required area of knowledge than the other child. This difference between what children can do by themselves and what they can do with the help of others is very important, and gives educators and other experts a significant role in assisting learners to progress (Rasku-Puttonen, Etelapelto, Arvaja & Hakkinen, 2003; Warwick & Maloch, 2003).

THINK ABOUT

- Do you learn best alone or with others – studying by yourself or with the help of experts?
- Consider something you have learned recently. To what degree did your learning result from direct instruction, from discussion, from assistance, and from your own thinking?

Pretend play as a zone of proximal development

Vygotsky described pretend or make-believe play as a zone of proximal development in which the activity supports children as they try out the roles and skills of adults, and learn to take on cultural modes of behaving. When Natalie (aged two years) picked up a toy phone and said 'Hello. Oh, OK. Goodbye', she was practising the telephone-answering behaviour she would use when older.

Consider a child 'playing schools'. While engaged in this play with others, he will learn about and practise how to coordinate his actions and wishes with others in the game, regulate his emotion and behaviour to fit the game, and explore how adult and child talk is different, as well as what happens at school. In taking the role of another person, his perspective-taking ability will also develop. The play context allows children to act in roles beyond their current situation, and to develop the skills these roles will require – a zone of proximal development.

There are other ways in which Vygotsky described pretend play as contributing to development, too: in substituting real for imagined things (a broom for a horse, a bowl for a bath), he argued that children learn to separate ideas from the objects they represent, and to recognise that ideas and words can be used to guide action. Additionally, Vygotsky suggested that pretend play helps children to understand social roles and ways of behaving, and to behave in accordance with them. Both Piaget and Vygotsky asserted the importance of play to children's learning, as have other influential educationalists such as Rousseau and Montessori. The Australian Early Years Learning Framework describes play as 'a context for learning through which children organise and make sense of their social worlds, as they actively engage with people, objects and representations' (DEEWR, 2009, p. 46).

Bodrova and Leong (2005) found that quality play experiences in the preschool years are related to improved memory skills, language development and self-regulation, all skills related to children's academic success at school. Researchers working in information processing claim that play supports development of self-regulation, and metacognition in particular, which are necessary for problem solving and creativity (Whitebread et al., 2009). Other researchers have also linked children's involvement in pretend play with cognitive skills such as attention, memory, logical reasoning, language, emotional understanding, metacognition, impulse control and perspective-taking (see Berk, 2009, for a review of this research).

BUILDING ON VYGOTSKY'S IDEAS

Vygotsky's theory was developed in the 1920s, and a number of psychologists have since built on and developed the theory and its applications to education.

Bruner's notion of scaffolding

Revisit the examples given above of the teacher helping the child with his mathematics task, and the child teaching his friend how to play a game. Jerome Bruner talked about this particular type of support given by adults (and expert peers) as **scaffolding**, using the metaphor of a scaffold that supports a building during construction, but is later removed (Wood, Bruner & Ross, 1976). This is the support provided to learners to enable a task to be done successfully and more independently by adjusting the assistance to fit the learner's current level of performance, by breaking the task into small parts, directing the learner's attention, giving both general and specific strategies to solve the problem, and providing lessons in 'how' to learn. However, there is also a gradual ongoing exchange of knowledge between teacher and learner, as suggestions made by the learner for modifying the rules are considered. Vygotsky described this as *learning through teaching* (LeBlanc & Bearison, 2004, p. 513). Collaboration with another, particularly in a naturalistic context such as a board game, leads to an exchange of roles of teacher and learner, and cognitive growth in both participants. What is happening here? Who does the problem solving? To begin with, one child (the teacher) knows how the game is played and the other child is learning. But as the learner becomes more confident, they gradually co-construct new rules for the game. This is an example of what Vygotsky meant when he said that thinking can be a social activity. It is quite different from Piaget's ideas about the child as 'solitary scientist', or even the role he gave to social interaction in development. It also suggests a more active role for educators and teachers. Scaffolding is more than a matter of teachers guiding a child through an activity; the social interaction and co-construction of knowledge are important features.

Educational terms associated with this type of learning are 'active learning', 'assisted learning', 'reciprocal teaching', 'assisted discovery' and 'collaborative cognition'.

The metaphor of the scaffold also extends to the temporary nature of the support; it is given only until the student is able to perform the task independently. This is one of the features that distinguishes scaffolding from other types of teacher support. The student is assisted to become an independent learner, at increasing levels of cognitive complexity. Bruner (1986) argued that it is through scaffolding that a child's zone of proximal development moves forward.

scaffolding
The support provided to learners to enable a task to be done successfully and more independently by adjusting the assistance to fit the learner's current level of performance

THINK ABOUT

- Can you describe examples of scaffolding in your own experience, both as learner and teacher? Think about times when you may have worked with someone else on a task at which you were still a novice.

Rogoff's notions of cognitive apprenticeships and guided participation

cognitive apprenticeships
Relationships within communities, in which children learn adult ways of thinking, through both explicit teaching and more indirect observation and listening to adult talk

Barbara Rogoff (1993, 2003) examined children's learning through their participation in communities, both in and out of school. From her observation of communities in a number of cultures, she argued that various cultures have differing ways of apprenticing children into the ways of learning, thinking and acting in that culture. Thus, children are involved in **cognitive apprenticeships** through the activities of their cultural group. These apprenticeships operate on distinct levels: they may involve children being taught directly, being involved in conversations and activities alongside adults, or being involved as observers – observing and listening to adults as they engage in adult activities. Different cultural groups may place more emphasis on one of these levels than another. In Western societies, we tend to separate adults and children into distinct settings and activities, and to emphasise explicit teaching.

Rogoff et al. (2003) described how, in cultures in which children are involved in community activities alongside adults, observation and listening are emphasised as ways of learning.

Rogoff's notion of **guided participation** has been taken up as a way of developing similar apprenticeships in the Western school context. In some communities, as children are involved in activities with adults in their community, they may at first observe, then be supported to take part in a limited way, before moving towards full, adult-like participation in the activity. An example is given in Figure 3.14.

Consider how this might work at school. A class of Year 7 students observe and listen to their Science teacher explaining how to use a microscope by using the interactive whiteboard to demonstrate each step. They are then given a sheet of instructions to work through to guide their use of the equipment for a very specific task. The teacher also moves around the room to help students who are having difficulty, and to remind them of key points such as the order in which to insert the slide and adjust the eyepiece and focus. With continued guided practice of this type, by the following year, the students are confident in preparing slides and using the microscope to view them. Another example is the 'modelled, guided and independent' activities in teaching literacy (discussed further in Chapter 6). The balance of explicit modelling, guided participation and independent practice will depend on the individual student's needs, and their point in development. Language is an important part of this process: it makes the teacher's thinking explicit to the learner, and the student's thinking explicit to the teacher. It is also part of the collaborative learning that takes place in the course of social interaction.

Source: Shutterstock.com/Farik gallery

FIGURE 3.14 What other examples of guided participation can you think of?

guided participation Support provided to enable students to participate in expert activities in increasingly expert ways

Building on Vygotsky's ideas about how children learn

Extending Vygotsky's ideas about the link between mental tools being passed from adults to children over time during shared activities, Wells (2000, pp. 7–8) suggested that:

- *classrooms are a type of collaborative community* – they involve not just a collection of individuals, but a collaborative group participating in shared activity
- *purposeful and meaningful learning activities involve the whole person* – they are not restricted to a set of isolated skills and separate items of information
- *all activities are unique in terms of participants, place and time* – although there may be shared features, each activity has its own history, which affects the way in which the activity unfolds
- *curriculum is a means and not an end in itself* – therefore, the aim of education should be to engage students in activities that are personally and socially productive, with knowledge and skills identified in the curriculum seen as items in a 'cultural toolkit' that are needed to engage in meaningful activities
- *outcomes of learning activities cannot be known or prescribed in advance* – goals may be identified prior to an activity, but the way in which the activity is implemented depends on the actual situation, including the participants, the available resources and the problems encountered
- *activities must allow for originality and diversity* – for both individuals and the group as a whole, problem solving requires novel solutions, otherwise current activities are endlessly recycled with no possibility of development for either individuals or the community.

An application of the theory: reciprocal teaching

reciprocal teaching
A teaching approach in which a teacher guides a group of students to ask questions that guide learning

Reciprocal teaching was pioneered by Annemarie Sullivan Palincsar (1982) and her colleague Ann Brown (Palincsar & Brown, 1984, 1989; Palincsar, Brown & Campione, 1993) to assist learners with reading comprehension. It has since been adapted for a range of contexts and cultures (see, for example, Roh, 1997; Taylor and Cox, 1997). Reciprocal teaching combines teacher intervention and student-directed learning (Palincsar, 1998). It adopts the Vygotskian principles of scaffolding, social interaction, and the use of language to direct thinking through collaborative learning (see Chapter 6), in that peers assist each other but learning takes place under the guidance of an expert – usually the teacher – who helps the group to understand the content matter and with group-thinking processes (Rogoff, 1998). Cole (1996) found that reciprocal teaching encouraged student interaction and improved their engagement with learning by enhancing their opportunities to make meaning of their learning in a social context.

Reciprocal teaching involves four strategies – 'predicting', 'questioning', 'summarising' and 'clarifying' – with the aim of helping readers to construct the meaning of a text and to monitor their comprehension of it (see Box 3.9). Teachers explicitly model each of the four strategies, with the intention of increasing students' responsibility for their own strategy use by asking them to take turns leading the discussion of the text (Palincsar, 1998). As students lead discussions, teachers provide support as they practise predicting what will happen next or practise clarifying the meaning of a text portion.

BOX 3.9 RESEARCH LINKS

RECIPROCAL TEACHING

Findings from several studies of primary and secondary school students confirm the positive effects of reciprocal teaching on reading comprehension. Palincsar (1986, 1987) and associates (see Brown & Palincsar, 1989; Palincsar & Brown, 1987; Palincsar & Herrenkohl, 1999) experimented with reciprocal teaching in several ways, such as:

1   whole-group instruction
2   small-group instruction
3   one-to-one tutorials
4   small-group sessions led by peers.

Reading comprehension improved in each situation.

Reciprocal teaching has been particularly effective in improving the reading comprehension skills of students with learning disabilities (Klingner & Vaughn, 1996; Lederer, 2000; Little & Richards, 2000). Often, reciprocal teaching is combined with other approaches, as discussed in Chapter 6. For example, Koutselini and Hadjiyianni (1999) reported on the success of an intervention program designed to help Year 3 students become conscious of their own deficiencies in reading comprehension, and to assist them to develop metacognitive strategies and improve their reading comprehension. The program combined reciprocal teaching and cooperative learning with the explicit teaching of metacognitive strategies.

Wilson's (1994) research, involving children from years 4 and 5 in a middle-sized rural school in Australia, found that reciprocal teaching was a major contributor to building students' confidence in their abilities as problem solvers.

Rosenshine and Meister (1994) reviewed 16 studies on reciprocal teaching and additional related studies, and found that students who had been engaged in reciprocal teaching achieved significantly higher reading-comprehension scores than students who had not.

Similar findings were reported in a New Zealand study of Year 8 adolescents who had reading comprehension deficits (Westera & Moore, 1995). Greenway (2002) found that reciprocal teaching enhanced the autonomy and self-regulation of a group of Year 6 students who followed the teacher's example and gradually adopted the teacher's role and style of questioning (as used in the reciprocal teaching method) as they became more confident in their learning (see also King & Johnson, 1999).

A similar approach has been used to teach writing, where the four strategies of reciprocal teaching were used to help seven- to nine-year-olds develop their story-writing skills. Peer collaboration combined with teacher guidance resulted in forms of writing that were more mature than writing children had produced when working alone (Daiute & Dalton, 1993). Box 3.10 further discusses results from research into reciprocal teaching.

STRENGTHS OF VYGOTSKY'S THEORY

One of the most influential of Vygotsky's ideas is that cognitive development is essentially a social process. Ways of thinking and acting are first acquired through social interaction and then gradually internalised, or processed silently in the mind, so that learning proceeds from the 'outside in' (Lutz & Sternberg, 1999, p. 292). Vygotsky's focus on the social nature of children's learning, and the extent to which social experiences structure the way children think – and in particular the meaning they attribute to language concepts – is one of the most influential of his ideas for psychology and education (Duveen, 1997; Wells, 2000).

Vygotsky's work underpins much of the group work and interactivity that is characteristic of learning spaces in the 21st century (see Chapter 7). Thus, it may be said that one of the key strengths of his approach to cognitive development is its wide-ranging applicability to learning and teaching, particularly in classrooms with a diverse social and cultural mix (Winsler, 2003). These advantages are highlighted in Chapters 6 and 7, in which we discuss the practical applications of Vygotsky's ideas.

Limitations of Vygotsky's theory

As with Piaget, criticisms of Vygotsky's ideas are frequently associated with the vagueness or the very general terms in which the ideas are expressed (Miller, 1993). This can lead to problems when practitioners attempt to apply them. Some of the problems associated with Vygotsky's concept of the zone of proximal development concern the vagueness of the concepts involved. For example, is the width of a child's zone the same across all areas of learning? Does it vary at different times of the day, or with different levels of motivation in the child or the partner in a tutoring situation? Is it generally stable? Is it wider if a child is unfamiliar with a particular curriculum area or tutor, and narrower if the child has already received some help or is familiar with the tutor? Is there always a gap between what a child can do alone and what can be done with assistance? Concern has also been raised about the risk that excessive teacher support – such as ensuring that children understand key concepts before introducing a topic – may act as a barrier to spontaneous discovery and independent learning (Myhill & Warren, 2005), and to children's development of self-regulation skills (de Corte & Verschaffel, 2006). Commenting on the concept of the zone of proximal development, Bryant (1990) suggested there is no direct evidence to prove that children's *cognitive skills* develop as a result of help from a parent or tutor, although research has shown that cooperative and collaborative learning approaches were effective in mathematics, particularly with students with special education needs (Baker, Gersten & Lee, 2002; Kunsch, Jitendra & Sood, 2007). However, the concept of the zone of proximal development has been further developed by theorists (see Daniels, 2011, for a review).

There has also been doubt expressed about the relevance of Vygotsky's ideas – developed in 1920s and 1930s Soviet Russia in the context of Marxist–Leninist ideology – to Western education systems in the 21st century (Lambert & Clyde, 2000). Another criticism concerns Vygotsky's failure to acknowledge the role of developmental influences, such as physical maturation.

Rogoff (1993) has commented on an overemphasis on the role of language in intellectual development in Vygotsky's theory. In cross-cultural studies, she has shown that in many societies, observation and participation in activities alongside adults are the primary means of learning, rather than language. Eickelkamp (2008) describes the practice of sand storytelling, or *milpatjunanyi*, among girls in Ernabella in central Australia, which she argues is less about the transmission of knowledge from adults to children than about the individual's role in shaping development and culture. The activity itself contributes to understandings about the world – the act of drawing in the sand is not just a thinking tool, shaping thought through the images used, but it also shapes understandings about individuals' relationship to the earth.

You will notice that this critique of Vygotsky's work is much briefer than that of Piaget's work. One reason for this is that Vygotsky's views of cognitive development were not developed as extensively as Piaget's stage theory. Nevertheless, Vygotsky's ideas offer a very useful, socially oriented perspective on cognitive development (see Box 3.10) that complements Piaget's individualistic model, and has inspired subsequent research work. Constructivist approaches to learning, such as discovery learning, inquiry learning and cooperative learning, discussed in Chapter 6, build on Piaget's and Vygotsky's ideas about how children's thinking develops.

BOX 3.10 IMPLICATIONS FOR EDUCATORS

APPLYING VYGOTSKY'S IDEAS IN THE CLASSROOM

In interpreting Vygotsky's ideas for classroom application, teachers need to do the following:

- In assessment, take account of what children can do independently and also what they can do with assistance or social support. This is sometimes referred to as 'dynamic assessment' (see Chapter 13).
- Centre instruction at the point between what the child can do without support and what can be achieved with assistance from an adult, a more advanced peer or even an interactive computer program (see Chapter 12).
- Start with the learner. Focus on the learner's potential, rather than on a set of predetermined outcomes (Daniels, 2011).
- Ensure active participation of the learner; for example, in collaborative activity.
- Remember that learning and teaching can occur at the same time when children working in pairs or groups interact to share knowledge and solve problems cooperatively. This is sometimes called 'collaborative cognition'.
- Recognise that Vygotsky's approach potentially assists all learners, including children experiencing problems resulting from learning difficulties or intellectual disabilities, given that much of Vygotsky's work was in the area of 'defectology or mental abnormality' (Lambert & Clyde, 2000, p. 26) (see Chapter 10).
- Structure tasks by breaking them into manageable parts, repeating instructions, limiting the number of components presented at one time or providing appropriate resources (Rogoff, 1990). This is sometimes called 'guided participation'.
- Transfer control of learning to the learner (Daniels, 2011). There may be shifting back and forth between the teacher taking the lead in instruction and the learner being given more control, but the goal should be for the learner to have control of the learning as it develops.
- Allow opportunities for children to engage in play, particularly pretend play in the preschool years, recognising its support for development as children practise and explore roles.
- Provide opportunities for students to see complete or expert models of tasks that lead them towards more expert practice (Cairney, 1995).
- Allow for social negotiation of learning and teaching. Think of the classroom as a community of learners, of whom the teacher is one (Rogoff, 1994). This opens possibilities for co-construction of knowledge.

LINKING PIAGET AND VYGOTSKY

Shayer (1997, 1999, 2003; Shayer & Adhami, 2007, 2010) provides information on the outcomes of a series of large-scale research projects in which the ideas of both Piaget and Vygotsky were used in primary and secondary school programs; for example, CASE and CAME (Adey, Robertson & Venville, 2001; Adhami, Johnson & Shayer, 2002). Shayer (1999) described how the CASE program was used to promote formal-operational thinking in 12- to 14-year-olds in the area of science. The aim of this study was to ensure that students reached formal operations during secondary school, as this is the level of cognitive functioning that is a prerequisite for success in Science, Mathematics and other areas of the curriculum at the major examinations held at the end of Year 9. To achieve this goal, Piagetian-type activities were devised and implemented using a Vygotskian framework that included a combination of discussion and individual work. Shayer (2003, p. 484) described this process as combining Piaget's ideas about cognitive development with Vygotsky's concern with classroom management and the social processes that underlie learning. The results of the studies reported by Shayer and colleagues suggest that the programs are successful in increasing the achievement level of the students involved – not only in the target curriculum areas, but also more generally (see Shayer & Adey, 2002; Shayer & Adhami, 2010).

A further significant application of Vygotskian theory is the recognition of the role that social interaction plays in promoting cognitive development. Social interaction may occur in various forms in the classroom. Using group work and encouraging children to learn from each other in pairs within larger groups is one application of Vygotsky's and Piaget's theories. Social interaction in productive, carefully organised groups can promote cognitive development, while group work allows students to use language as a tool for learning and for scaffolding the learning of others. It also allows students to experience 'cognitive apprenticeship' (Roth & Bowen, 1995), a related application of group work that recognises the value of social interaction in the use of 'experts' to scaffold novices' learning in the classroom. In the early years, this process occurs at home, where parents and family members – the 'experts' – communicate with and scaffold the infant's or novice's cognitive development in the course of everyday interaction. In the school context, this can continue when parents, community helpers and older students are invited into the classroom to assist teachers and to work with individuals or small groups to develop skills such as reading. In a multicultural classroom, it is particularly helpful if these 'expert' assistants represent a range of multicultural backgrounds, as this helps to recognise and validate the contribution of individuals from a range of cultures within the sociocultural context. Chapters 6 and 7 of this book expand on the use of group work in teaching and learning.

CourseMateExpress

Online Resources
Go further: Explore a case study of a mathematics lesson using Piagetian and Vygotskian principles on this text's website

INFORMATION-PROCESSING APPROACHES TO COGNITIVE DEVELOPMENT

While Piaget and Vygotsky described development in terms of global changes in children's thinking, another group of theorists has explained cognitive development in terms of changes in children's ability to process information. Information-processing approaches are not associated with any one theorist, but describe an approach taken by many psychologists who have examined the particular mechanisms, strategies and structures by which we process information. In doing so, they have also uncovered developmental changes in cognition, which variously explain, challenge and go beyond a number of the observations about children's cognitive development made by Piaget and Vygotsky.

encoding
Process of storing information in the long-term memory

retrieval
Process of bringing information stored in long-term memory back to be manipulated in working memory

multistore model
Depicts how information is processed and stored in memory

Early models of information processing used the computer as an analogy of the human brain, and one research approach has been to develop computer models to simulate thinking. Of course, when you consider how complex factors such as emotion, social interaction, motivation and creativity influence thinking, you may conclude that the human brain is in fact more unlike than it is like a computer; however, this approach has yielded important information about how thinking works. Much of the language of information processing continues to use terms borrowed from the computer metaphor, such as processing, **encoding**, storage and **retrieval**.

THINK ABOUT

■   Consider ways in which your thought process works like – and unlike – a computer. You might like to make two lists, and add to them as you read through this section.

There are many models of information processing. One of the most widely used is the **multistore model**, built on a computer analogy first described by Atkinson and Shiffrin (1968) and progressively developed since by a range of theorists (for example, Baddeley & Hitch, 1974). Figure 3.15 gives a representation of the model. Note that there are various *stores* of information, and *processes* by which we act on the information to move it from one store to the next.

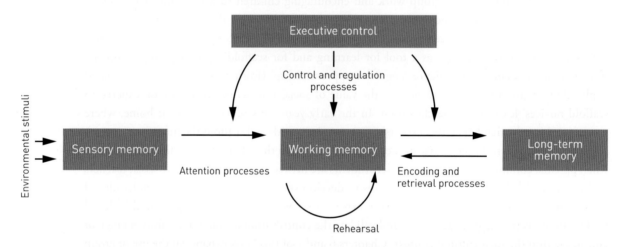

FIGURE 3.15 The multistore model identifies a number of stores of information and processes that move information between these stores.

INFORMATION STORES AND PROCESSES

CourseMateExpress

Online Resources
Explore the Multistore model in action with the **Interactive Activity** for Chapter 6 on this text's website

Shani comes to class with her friends, who are chattering with her about the party they all attended on the weekend. On the wall are posters displaying some of their work and lists of vocabulary. Already in the classroom are groups of other students, some talking, some unpacking bags, and the teacher, who is setting up the computer for the interactive whiteboard. Shani notices the boy she is keen on, and sees that he is also watching her. Gradually the class becomes quiet – the teacher has signalled that it is time for class to start. Shani shifts her attention to the teacher, and what she is saying, ignoring the students who are still finishing their chat behind her. As the teacher introduces the lesson, Shani recalls the work that was done on this the previous week, and opens her book to add to her notes. Suddenly, she realises she forgot to get her pen out of her bag. There is a sudden laugh behind her as someone makes a joke. Everyone turns to look, then shifts back to the teacher as she puts up on the whiteboard a concept map for the topic and asks them to fill in what they currently know. At first Shani struggles to remember anything much, but gradually she finds the ideas coming more easily as the map is filled in.

What is happening here? There are a number of fundamental thinking processes:

- *Sensation* (sights, sounds, smells, tastes, touch) that surrounds Shani's experience of the class, and *perception*, which happens as Shani recognises and makes sense of these things. Some, but not all of these, are attended to – she perceives the posters on the way in, but pays no *attention* to them; she sees and recognises other students in the room, but attends to the boy she is interested in (maybe there's another boy who is also looking at Shani whom she does not notice). Shani directs her attention in a purposeful way to the teacher when required, *screening out the distractors* in the room.

- When the lesson starts, Shani *recalls* information that she has stored from the last lesson and starts to *work with* that information by *organising* it into the concept map. While doing this, she is also *storing* it for future use.

- In later lessons, she may use this information to *reason* about an essay question or *solve a problem* in an assignment. These are the more complex cognitive processes that rest on the basic ones.

Each of these fundamental processes is present in infancy, and improves with development. According to information-processing theorists, development involves improvements both in the capacity of the stores and in the efficiency of the processes. A number of information-processing theorists argue that the cognitive differences Piaget observed between children at different stages of development are actually due to differences in these basic processes (for example, Case, 1992; Demetriou, Christou, Spanoudis & Platsidou, 2002; Halford, 1993).

Later in this chapter, we summarise the factors associated with information processing that influence cognitive development (see Box 3.11). We will return to this model in Chapter 6, when we consider its implications for learning. In this chapter, our focus is on children's development of the various components in the information-processing system.

Sensory memory

We take in information from the environment through our senses (**sensation**) and make sense of it (**perception**) almost automatically. Sensory facilities are largely developed in infancy, with the visual cortex, for example, fully developed by the time the child is in preschool (Kellman & Arteberry, 2006). Some aspects of perception continue to improve into the early school years, as a result of learning and experience – in particular the ability to discriminate between sounds, and to segment syllables and words: the phonemic awareness that is foundational for reading and writing. Learning to read also involves visual discrimination between letters that are similar, such as b and d, p and q. This is a matter of perceptual learning rather than development (Galotti, 2011; Gibson & Gibson, 1955) – hence the importance of early language experiences to literacy learning and development, as noted in Chapter 2.

According to the multistore model, information taken in through the senses and perceived is held in a store within the **sensory memory**, with separate stores for information from each sense. However, the sensory memory has a very limited capacity – at most two or three seconds for auditory, and less than a second for visual information, after which the information is lost (Schneider & Bjorklund, 1998). In order for the information we take in to be retained and made use of, it must be attended to.

Attention

The number and range of stimuli that constantly bombard us exceed the amount we can process, and as we cannot process everything, we must be selective. At the same time, many actions are complex, and we need to plan (give attention to) what actions to take in particular order. The central process associated with this stage is **attention**. When we focus on certain information with the aim of remembering it, we are said to be 'paying attention'. If we attend to information, it moves to the next storage box, the working memory, for further processing. If we do not pay attention, the information decays and disappears.

sensation
Information taken in from the environment through the five senses

perception
Allocation of meaning to an experienced sensation

sensory memory
Stores new information, which enters via the sensory register through the five senses, for between one and three seconds

attention
Allocation of resources to process information

Children's ability to control their attention improves with age; its several components are:

- *sustained attention*: also called 'attention span'
- *selective attention*: ability to focus on relevant details – and screen out or inhibit distractors
- *adaptive attention*: ability to shift focus of attention when required.

In infancy, children attend to novel and eye-catching stimuli, but have difficulty sustaining this attention. By the age of two to three years, children are less attracted to novel things and exhibit sustained attention, particularly during play (see Figure 3.16). In early childhood, children start to show regulation of their attention, with intentional, goal-directed behaviour – although they are still easily distracted. You may have noticed this with preschoolers who appear totally focused on a particular game or task, sometimes for quite lengthy periods. Adults contribute to this ability by keeping children's attention on an activity or stimulus with interaction, questions and comments. This role of social, emotional, and contextual factors influencing attention is an important revision to the original information processing theories that has emerged in research over the past decade (Ristin & Enns, 2015). You will see further examples of this interaction between social, emotional and cognitive domains as we look at each of the processes.

Source: Shutterstock.com/Goran Bogicevic

FIGURE 3.16 Social and emotional processes influence cognitive processes such as attention.

CourseMateExpress

Online Resources
Go further: Try your own capacity for inhibition with the Stroop test on this text's website

In middle childhood, this capacity for sustained attention is paired with an increase in selective attention: the ability to attend to relevant stimuli and ignore distractions. These distractions can be internal as well as external stimuli. The ability to inhibit irrelevant thoughts and responses to stimuli is also important in children's social and emotional development, as we will see in Chapter 4.

School experience is likely to play a role here; teachers employ multiple strategies to sustain students' attention, and also require their students to gradually take responsibility for this. This ability increases from six to 10 years, and continues to improve into adulthood. During this stage, children also show the ability of adaptive attention, flexibly adapting their attention to the demands of particular tasks.

In adolescence, self-regulation of attention is facilitated by development of the executive function (see below) as students employ strategies to control and direct their own attention in increasingly more efficient and sophisticated ways.

Working memory

Information that is taken in through the sensory register, and attended to, may be operated on in the **working memory**. This is sometimes referred to as short-term memory, with emphasis on its storage function. The term 'working memory' acknowledges the manipulation of information that is vital to all thinking, and that is proposed to take place within this store. A further function of working memory proposed by Baddeley (1986, 2012; Baddeley & Hitch, 1974) is the executive control of processes such as attention, and strategies such as elaboration and organisation, which organise, monitor and regulate thinking.

working memory
A working space for short-term storage and manipulation of small amounts of information; contains your conscious thought

Working memory has limited capacity and duration. It contains only that information being processed at a current point in time. So once we stop processing the information, it will disappear – either to be lost or stored in long-term memory. To maintain information in the working memory, we need to rehearse it. (Think of someone giving you their phone number – you will say it over in your head as you search for a pen to write it down, thus keeping it in your working memory.) Otherwise this information decays rapidly, as with the sensory memory, within 18–20 seconds according to Peterson and Peterson (1959).

When measured as the number of random items remembered just after they have been presented, adults have been shown to have a working-memory capacity of seven plus or minus two items (Miller, 1956), although these limits are smaller in children: six items at age nine to 10, and four items at age four to five (Schneider & Pressley, 1997). Speed of processing is one factor in these differences, with younger children taking longer to repeat the words, so that duration of working memory interacts with capacity (Case, Kurland & Goldberg, 1982). Another factor is knowledge. One way in which we increase the number of items in working memory is through chunking; for example, when learning to spell a new word such as 'metacognition', you may view some parts of it as chunks – 'meta', 'cogni', 'tion' – so that rather than having to hold and order 13 separate letters in your working memory, you need process only three chunks. Children have less knowledge with which to do this, so their working memories operate less efficiently than those of adults.

THINK ABOUT

- Consider the implications of this for the material you present to children of different ages. You may need fewer and simpler items for younger children, while older children can process increasingly more complex information. Observe classrooms at different stages to see this in action.

What happens when the information is too complex or there is too much to be processed? Try this yourself. Have someone read the following list of 20 words to you, with about five seconds between them, then write down as many as you can remember. How many did you recall? At what point in the list did you think to yourself 'There are too many words here'?

dolphin	castle	vineyard	bedroom	suitcase	spectacles	snow
cheese	table	teeth	violin	detective	forest	train
weed	candle	stove	paintbrush	fire	boat	

Improvements in the capacity of the working-memory store contribute to children's ability to coordinate a number of ideas. For example, think back to the coordination of perspectives that Piaget observed emerging in the concrete-operations period. Case (1996) explained this developmental difference in terms of differences in working-memory capacity. In adolescence, greater working-memory capacity allows students to weigh up a number of factors when making decisions. Working-memory capacity has also been related to children's achievement at school (Alloway, Gathercole, Willis & Adams, 2004) and the acquisition of vocabulary (Baddeley, Gathercole & Papagno, 1998).

There are also qualitative improvements in working memory with age prior to the age of six; for example, younger children may not automatically integrate phonological and visual information, but will show a preference for visual processing (Fry & Hale, 2000). Baddeley (2012) proposed that these are held in different stores in the working memory, so it may be that their integration occurs after the child starts school, when further improvements in working memory are all about speed and capacity. Halford and Andrews (2004) argued that it is not only the number of items remembered that is important, but also the relationships between them, and have shown that the capacity to represent increasingly complex relations improves with age.

One contributor to improvements in working memory with age is automaticity: as particular processes become automatic, they free up space in working memory for other thinking. So, for example, as you read this paragraph you do not need to take up working memory for the process of reading itself, but can allocate this precious resource to thinking about the ideas being presented. This is one reason why time is spent in primary schools (and in homework) developing fluent reading, or automatic retrieval of number facts. Case (1998) has argued that automaticity is the basis for the development of children's thinking from one Piagetian stage to the next through the freeing up of working memory for more complex tasks as schemas are automatised.

Central executive

central executive
In Baddeley's theory of working memory, it controls what working memory attends to, and how it interacts with long-term memory

Baddeley (1986, 2012) proposed that as well as storing and processing information, the working memory contains a **central executive**, which controls that processing. Consider for example, a mathematics problem in which you must count backwards orally by threes from 231, stopping when you reach the closest number to 199. At the same time, you are attending to the number you are currently counting back from, identifying the number three less from it (perhaps by drawing on your long term memory of number facts, or simply of number sequences), and maintaining memory of the task, with the number that is your goal in this exercise (199). The central executive allows you to maintain your attention on the relevant activity, and draw from long term memory, while keeping the goal in mind. This central executive is also called by other researchers executive control, central attention and executive attention, depending on their focus (Vandierendonck, 2016).

In Baddeley's model, such a system plays a critical role in controlling attention for single and multiple stimuli, shifting between tasks, retrieving information from the sensory and long-term memory stores, and generally moving information back and forth between the working memory and the long-term memory. In particular, the central executive may help us inhibit or suppress attention from distracting stimuli, and may help us process more than two types of information simultaneously. Thus, in this theory, processes such as attention and use of strategies for encoding and retrieval of information from long-term memory are all controlled within the central executive of the working memory. Other theorists have proposed a different mechanism: the **executive functions**, which regulate cognition (not just working memory as the central executive is proposed to do), and include working memory among other functions that also influence regulation in the social and emotional domains. While there is some overlap with Baddeley's model, there are also important differences. We discuss the development of executive functions in detail below.

executive functions
These control the processing of information. Key executive functions include inhibitory control, working memory and cognitive flexibility

Long-term memory

long-term memory
A permanent storage facility for information

The **long-term memory** store contains information that we are not currently thinking about. Unlike the other stores, long-term memory is believed to have unlimited capacity and duration. Information stored in long-term memory must be retrieved from here back into the working memory in order to be manipulated (thought about). Hence the key processes associated with long-term memory are *encoding* and *retrieval*. These processes involve particular strategies, and it is strategy use that explains developmental differences in memory at this level.

Rehearsal strategy

rehearsal
Repeating items as a memory strategy

We introduced the strategy of **rehearsal** above, when thinking about the typical approach to keeping a phone number in your working memory. You may also have used it in learning the list of words above. Before about the age of seven, children are unlikely to use strategies to remember a list of items. It is thought that their awareness of their thinking (metacognition) is weak, and they are unrealistic about their ability to remember the items. At about this age, they may start to rehearse, but inefficiently.

For example, they may repeat each word separately ('dolphin, dolphin, dolphin') whereas you may have rehearsed the words in a list ('dolphin, castle, vineyard').

Organisation strategy

In learning the list of words, you may perhaps have grouped them in particular ways. This is called **organisation**. Organising information helps to provide cues that facilitate their retrieval, thus improving memory. Children spontaneously use organisation strategies from about eight years, and may at first do this inefficiently – simply pairing items together rather than using larger categories (Galotti, 2011).

Elaboration strategy

You might also have linked the words in a story to help you remember them. **Elaboration** is another strategy that provides cues for retrieving information from long-term memory. For example, if your story involved items in the rooms of a castle, visualising these areas would have helped you to remember the words by providing cues for your memory. One example of a simple organiser is shown in Figure 3.17. This strategy tends not to be used by children until approximately 12 years (Galotti, 2011). Elaboration and organisation are not just useful for learning lists of words. They also help us to remember more complex information, as, for example, when you add new information to something you already know (elaboration), make connections between ideas, or organise your knowledge in a concept map (organisation). Children's increasing use of these strategies with age contributes to improvements in memory abilities.

If taught these strategies, young children will use them, but they do not tend to spontaneously apply them themselves, or generalise the use of a strategy to a later task.

Planning and using strategies

With development, children's knowledge of strategies improves, and they become more skilled in planning and using strategies. As they start to use a strategy, children may use it imperfectly or with indifferent results, and may fall back on more familiar strategies. Gradually, however, they are likely to use it more regularly, become more skilled in its use, and see the value of the strategy. Older children may use a combination of strategies effectively to improve memory. (See Schneider and Bjorklund, 2003, for a detailed review of the research on memory strategy use.)

Siegler (2006) has developed a theory to describe the pattern of gradual acquisition of strategies called the **overlapping waves model**. He observed that children (and adults) have a wide range of strategies that they employ during any period of time, rather than just one, as described by Piaget. For example, Alibali (1999, cited in Siegler, 2006) found that children in years 3 and 4 used six incorrect and four correct strategies when solving a particular set of mathematical problems – maintaining some strategies, generating new strategies and abandoning old ones during the course of the session. The pattern is similar to what is seen in children's use of memory strategies such as rehearsal, organisation and elaboration described above.

Although Piaget described a linear transition from less efficient to more efficient strategies in thinking, Siegler has observed that, on the same problem, people may go backwards and forwards in the sophistication of strategies they choose from a wide repertoire. Over time, however, the set of strategies they choose from becomes more efficient. Furthermore, Siegler found that this process is adaptive: high initial variation in strategy use predicted later learning on a task (Siegler, 2006).

organisation
Process associated with storage and retrieval of information in long-term memory

elaboration
Process of linking new information with what is stored in long-term memory

overlapping waves model
Siegler's model of strategy use, which states that people have a set of strategies they choose from, and that over time, less efficient strategies are replaced with more efficient ones

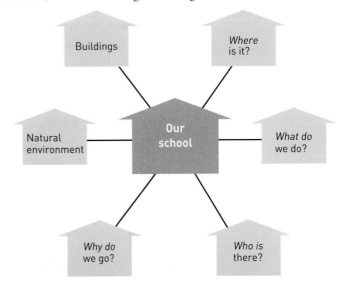

FIGURE 3.17 Younger students may not spontaneously use strategies of organisation and elaboration, but teachers can encourage this through use of graphic organisers.

Executive functions

executive functions
These control
the processing of
information. Key
executive functions
include inhibitory
control, working
memory and cognitive
flexibility

As well as individual processes that can operate automatically, theorists have identified effortful processes that control these. (We identified this as 'executive control' in Figure 3.15). **Executive functions** are proposed to operate in a 'top-down' manner on other processes during goal-directed activity, and are important processes of self-regulation in cognitive, social and emotional domains (McClelland, Geldhof, Cameron & Wanless, 2015). In cognition, they allow us to ignore distractions, to focus on and use information, to switch between tasks or ideas, and to problem solve. Core components of executive function include inhibition of impulses, which includes the ability to selectively attend to a stimulus, screening out distractors; working memory; and cognitive flexibility. These support one another, and in turn support the next level of higher order executive functions: planning, reasoning and problem solving (Diamond, 2013; Serpell & Esposito, 2016). Hence, the developments described above for attention, working memory and long-term memory processes reflect developments in executive function.

Development of executive functions

Executive functions develop in connection with structural and functional changes in the pre-frontal cortex of the brain (see Chapter 2). However, while the pre-frontal cortex does not complete development until early adulthood, young children show the beginnings of executive functions in infancy; it is the efficiency of these processes that increases with further brain development. The relationship is not simple, moreover; there are different patterns of development for each of the executive functions, and evidence that activities such as self-directed play, involvement in structured physical activity, mindfulness exercises, and even starting school strengthen and support development of executive functions (Serpell & Esposito, 2016; Muller & Kerns, 2015). Language is another important influence on development of executive function, helping children to regulate their thinking, in line with Vygotsky's theory as discussed in Box 3.8 (Muller & Kerns, 2015).

An activity called 'Head-Toes-Knees-Shoulders' (Ponitz, McClelland, Matthews & Morrison, 2009) in which children do the opposite of what the experimenter directs (for example, touch their toes when instructed to touch their head) can be used to measure the executive functions of inhibitory control, as well as working memory and cognitive flexibility. Figure 3.18 illustrates this activity.

INHIBITORY CONTROL

Inhibitory control appears at around three years, with children showing ability to inhibit responses between three and four years. This capacity develops further throughout childhood and adolescence, with responses increasing in accuracy with age. Neurological measures indicate increased efficiency of use of brain networks in these tasks with development (Best & Miller, 2011). Best and Miller suggested that brain maturation contributes to development, along with improvements in metacognition (see below), the ability to use rules and to cope with complexity of tasks. Inhibitory control supports the developments in attention that were described above.

Source: Getty Images/ Highwaystarz-Photography

FIGURE 3.18 Playing games like 'Simon Says' can help children to develop executive function.

WORKING MEMORY

The development of *working memory* as related to executive function is closely related to inhibitory control and to cognitive flexibility, involving ability to selectively attend to information held in the working memory, and to switch attention between pieces of information. As discussed above, what changes with development is the number of things that can be held in consciousness and manipulated at one time. In the Head-Toes-Knees-Shoulders task described above, younger (4–5-year-old) children are able to succeed at this task for two instructions (heads and toes) while older (5–6-year-old) children can succeed for four (heads, toes, knees and shoulders) (Ponitz et al., 2009). In accordance with this, Best & Miller (2010) reported in their review that working memory improves from preschool through childhood and adolescence, with older children being able to master more complex tasks, involving multiple items. Brain activity associated with working memory becomes more localised with development.

COGNITIVE FLEXIBILITY

Cognitive flexibility develops later than inhibitory control and working memory, and depends on these capacities (Diamond, 2013). It involves the ability to take different perspectives, or to take a different approach to a problem. In this way, creativity (discussed in detail in Chapter 9) draws on cognitive flexibility. Typically, tasks measuring cognitive flexibility ask children to sort objects by one characteristic, such as colour, and then by another, such as shape. Think back to Piaget's work on this, discussed in Box 3.3. By 4.5–5 years, the majority of children are able to switch sorting dimensions, and by 7–9 years, they can do this in ways that are more resourceful and better organised, adopting a strategy for their responses to a set of similar tasks, rather than reacting to each one separately; and slowing down with age to improve accuracy (Diamond, 2013).

Executive functions at school

Executive functions are essential to both academic and social-emotional school readiness (Center on the Developing Child, 2011; Mann, Hund, Hesson-McInnis & Roman, 2016), linking to learning of literacy and mathematics skills at school (Diamond, 2013), as well as to social and emotional understanding (Mann, Hund, Hesson-McInnis & Roman, 2016). The importance of executive functions extends beyond the beginning years of school however, their influence being demonstrated throughout schooling (Best, Miller & Aguileri, 2011). They also link to self-regulation of emotion and social skills, important to school success (McClelland, 2015).

Importantly, executive functions can be supported and strengthened throughout childhood and adolescence (Serpell & Esposito, 2016). Parenting plays an important role here, although other experiences such as involvement in team sports and other structured physical activities (including games like 'Simon Says', shown in Figure 3.18); learning of a musical instrument; sociodramatic play; computer-based training of specific executive function skills; and mindfulness training (see Chapter 7) have been demonstrated to affect executive function (Muller & Kerns, 2015). Serpell & Esposito argued that many of these activities can be built into school programs.

Metacognition

Another important aspect of cognition related to executive function is **metacognition** – or our capacity to think about our own thinking. Perhaps you just read that sentence, and wondered to yourself what it meant. You may even have read it over again slowly, to help to make sense of it. These are both examples of metacognition, as you monitor and reflect on your understanding, and put strategies in place to improve it. Metacognition was considered a key process in the theories of Piaget and Vygotsky, although the term itself was first used by Flavell in the 1970s (see Flavell, 1979). Metacognition is theorised to have several components: metacognitive awareness; metacognitive knowledge, which includes knowledge of self, of tasks and of strategies; and metacognitive strategy use, which is the implementation of strategies that enable the regulation of thought through planning, monitoring and evaluation. Chapter 6 reviews these concepts in further detail. Developments in metacognition are important contributors to the executive functions described above, and also influence learning in general as well as literacy and numeracy learning in particular (see chapter 2 for more on the development of these skills).

Children have been shown to have awareness of thinking from quite young – three-year-olds have awareness of thinking as separate from action, for example (Flavell, Green & Flavell, 1995), although they tend to see this as a passive rather than active thing.

metacognition
Higher-order thinking which involves knowledge of and control over our own cognitive processes

As we saw with memory strategies above, young children tend to overestimate their ability to remember, and so tend not to use strategies even if they know of them – their metacognitive knowledge is weak. In middle childhood, and with schooling, children become more aware of the need to use strategies, as well as gaining knowledge of a wider range of strategies, and becoming more adept at applying them. These developments relate to the metacognitive knowledge and metacognitive strategy dimensions of metacognition. It is in adolescence and early adulthood that metacognition reaches maturity, with abilities to plan, monitor, evaluate and self-regulate thinking advancing during this stage (Kuhn, 2006). Maturation of the cerebral cortex during adolescence is likely to contribute to these developments (see Chapter 2 for details of brain development).

MECHANISMS OF COGNITIVE DEVELOPMENT ACCORDING TO INFORMATION-PROCESSING RESEARCH

- *Speed of processing.* Whether measured by response time or task completion, the processing of information gets faster from early childhood through to mid-adolescence (Demetriou, Christou, Spanoudis & Platsidou, 2002). Why should faster processing make a difference to problem solving or memory? One theory proposes that faster speed leads to greater operating space, more efficient connections, and the ability to inhibit irrelevant stimuli or responses (Case, 1992).

- *Capacity of stores.* The working memory, in particular, increases in capacity throughout childhood, allowing more information to be held and manipulated at one time. This contributes to more complex thinking in late childhood and adolescence.

- *Strategy knowledge and use.* Linked with increased working-memory capacity is children's increasingly efficient use of strategies to optimise working-memory space, through chunking and rehearsal. With age, children also employ more strategies to encode and retrieve information linking long-term and working memory more efficiently.

Contributors to development

- *Neurological maturation.* In the preceding section, we have seen numerous examples of cognitive capacities that improve with developments in the cerebral cortex. In particular, speed of processing increases with myelination, which, as you may recall from Chapter 2, is the insulation of the axon that greatly speeds transmission of messages between neurons. Neurological maturation is not simply a matter of growth, however. One of the developments observed in adolescence is a reduction in grey matter as inefficient connections are pruned (Casey, Giedd & Thomas, 2000; see Chapter 2). If we consider the pattern of memory-strategy use with development, we can see one example of a more efficient neural network that replaces less efficient connections with age.

- *Language.* Language provides children with conceptual categories that help them to organise information and make linkages between ideas, and with a means of regulating their thinking, as Vygotsky proposed.

- *Experience.* As we gain experience in particular skills, these skills become automatic, freeing space in working memory for other thinking. We gave examples of this for children learning to read or use mathematics. Learning to write, spell, drive or use particular software on a computer are other examples. Experience also contributes by strengthening particular neural connections, and weakening and eventually leading to the pruning of other, less used, less efficient connections. As we saw in Chapter 2, the particular experiences children engage in are important in shaping their thinking.

- *Knowledge base*. Older children and adults have greater knowledge than younger children, and this knowledge base allows them to remember, elaborate and organise new knowledge more readily. Chi (1978) demonstrated this with child chess experts, who were better than adults without chess expertise at remembering chessboard arrangements. On a test of memory of numbers, however, the adults showed better memory than the children. Schneider and Bjorklund (1992) showed that child soccer experts used strategies of organisation to aid memory, while non-experts did not use such strategies – which suggests that knowledge base is a factor in strategy use.

These contributors to information-processing development work together in a complex and dynamic system. For example, working-memory capacity may not be sufficient on its own; knowledge and experience are also important. Maturation may provide the upper limits for children's development, but their learning experiences, particularly at school, are crucial for potentials provided by maturation to be realised. Learning experiences also contribute to maturation by strengthening neural networks and determining which connections might be pruned through infrequent use.

Strengths of information-processing theory

Using the computer as a metaphor for the human mind, the classical views of information processing help us understand the complexity of cognitive processing and the many stages and processes involved in storing and recalling information. This approach facilitates close study and analysis of cognitive processes, and details the processes involved in the developments Piaget observed, such as categorisation.

Limitations of information-processing theory

The detailed focus on individual processes makes it difficult to build this into an overarching picture of cognitive development such as that of Piaget. Researchers such as Case have attempted to address this by combining the two approaches.

Studies within the information processing theoretical model tend to be laboratory based, isolating particular processes, which helps in understanding how the processes work, but limits our understanding of the complexity that is the reality of children's lives. For example, how might emotion or interaction with adults and peers influence children's attention, memory, or strategy use in processing of information? More recent work has moved beyond the traditional paradigm, finding complex processes at work in everyday life, as discussed below.

Finally, information processing describes one part of the picture of cognition, but not the whole picture. Demetriou, Christou, Spanoudis and Platsidou (2002) examined relations between processing abilities and higher-order reasoning in children aged eight to 14, and found that information processing is necessary, but not sufficient, for higher-order reasoning to develop. They proposed that there are other cognitive structures above and operating upon the information-processing system. We must also recognise the roles of learning experiences, both in contributing to brain development and strategy use, and in providing the context for the application of information processing.

MOVING BEYOND TRADITIONAL INFORMATION PROCESSING MODELS

Still focusing on the key processes of perception, attention, memory and reasoning, recent research has looked at how adults and children choose what to prioritise (are agents in their development – see Chapter 2), and how social, emotional and motivational factors influence those choices. For example, Kensinger, Choi, Murray and Rajaram (2016) found that memories for emotional events were more likely to be remembered faithfully than for neutral events, and were more likely to resist distortion by social interactions around that event.

Tyng, Amin, Saad & Malik (2017) reported influences of emotion on a wide range of cognitive processes, including perception, attention, reasoning, learning and problem solving as well as memory. For examples of social influences, think back to our discussion of parent–infant interactions in Chapter 2. Ristic & Enns (2015) pointed to such social interactions as examples of ways the social and cognitive domains are interconnected; they are essential to infants' developing understanding of the world, directing what they should pay attention to and how they should interpret it. They also reported findings from studies showing that social–emotional content takes priority for attention.

THINK ABOUT

- How do social and emotional factors influence your processing of information?
- How could you use social and emotional processes to support your learners' attention, memory and learning?

Source: Shutterstock.com/Red Pepper

FIGURE 3.19 Parent-infant interactions illustrate the importance of social influences in processes such as attention.

Psychological models have traditionally viewed cognition as a 'cool' system separate from 'hot' emotions (Ristic & Enns, 2015; Tyng et al., 2017), but more recent work has challenged this view, showing how emotion and cognition are integrated into one complex system (e.g. Okon-Singer, Hendler, Pessoa & Shackman, 2015). As individuals' personal characteristics (including their emotions and motivations) interact with aspects of their social and physical environments, cognitive processes are put into play, and in their turn influence ongoing development.

Traditional models of information processing are 'bottom up' theories, in that they have a stimulus at the starting point of information processing, as is visible in Figure 3.15. 'Top-down' models start from the learner's prior experience and conceptions, arguing that these shape processing of information. The current models of theorists such as Ristic and Enns, and Okon-Singer et al. look at the interaction of these processes, operating in multiple directions, and influenced by factors operating at multiple levels. Marshall (2015) argued that current neuroscience shows cognition as 'embodied' in action and experience – it is no longer thought of as something that happens separate from other domains; instead brain, body and behaviour interact together with the sociocultural environment.

BOX 3.11 IMPLICATIONS FOR EDUCATORS

APPLYING IDEAS FROM INFORMATION-PROCESSING RESEARCH ON COGNITIVE DEVELOPMENT IN THE CLASSROOM

- **Attention:** Make explicit what students need to attend to, and make this easy for them by reducing distractors. Rather than putting the whole day's (or lesson's) activities up on the board, reveal only one topic or activity at a time.
- **Working memory limitations:** If your students can only hold between two and five chunks of information in their working memory at a time, limit what you give them to work with to the essentials. For young children, direct them to do each step in turn. For older children, have steps written down so students don't have to use working memory to remember them. Allow students to use other strategies – visual prompts, drawing or writing – to include extra material if this is necessary. See also the section on cognitive load theory in Chapter 6.
- **The value of drill and practice:** Skills, such as automatic retrieval of number facts or spelling and fluent reading, that come with practice are important to free up space in working memory for other thinking.
- **Scaffolding organisation and elaboration of material:** Although students may not spontaneously use organisation and elaboration strategies in their learning, they can still be helped to remember information by the teacher:
  > making connections between ideas
  > linking new knowledge to what students already know
  > organising information using visual maps (see **Figure 3.16**)
  > encouraging elaboration of concepts through discussion and student-created notes.
- **The importance of the knowledge base and experience:** We saw that knowledge base influences strategy use. Providing multiple experiences with a concept, and exploring it from various angles, will help students to remember, to have deeper understanding, and to engage with the concept in more sophisticated ways.
- **The impact of social, emotional and contextual factors on information processing.** Information processing does not occur in isolation. Motivation, past experiences, social relationships and emotions surrounding the current situation all influence processing of information. Activating these things can support students in processing new information, and knowledge of what is operating on their processing is vital for teachers to consider.

    In Chapter 6 we look in detail at the implications of information-processing research for learning.

CONCLUDING COMMENTS

As we have seen in this chapter, Piaget, Vygotsky and information-processing theorists have asked similar questions about the origins of children's cognitive development, and the reasons they think and behave in the ways that they do. Although their focus has been different and they have not agreed on all aspects, there has been considerable overlap in their ideas. Each tradition has had profound influence on teachers' ideas about learning and instruction, particularly by highlighting the need for teachers to start by observing the child and their current level of understanding and working from there, and to recognise the contribution to the learning process of factors within the learner's social and physical environment.

CourseMateExpress

Online Resources
Take a moment
to consider your
philosophy of learning
and teaching. You
may wish to use
the **Develop your
philosophy** tool on the
textbook's CourseMate
Express website

STUDY TOOLS

ONLINE STUDY RESOURCES

Visit http://login.cengagebrain.com and use the access code that comes with this book for 12 months' access to the student resources for this text.

The CourseMate Express website contains a range of resources and study tools for this chapter, including:

- a **self-check quiz**

CourseMateExpress

- **crosswords**, **flashcards** and a **glossary** to help you revise the key terms from this chapter
- the **Go further** materials and **interactive activity** mentioned in the chapter.

CHAPTER REVIEW

- Cognitive development is concerned with how our capacity to think, reason and remember develops over time.
- Two of the most influential theorists in the area of cognitive development are Piaget and Vygotsky. Piaget viewed the child as a 'little scientist', whereas Vygotsky saw cognitive development as occurring within a social context that is framed by the child's social, cultural and historical background.
- Piaget identified four universal and invariant stages of cognitive development: the sensorimotor stage (birth to two years), the preoperational stage (approximately two years to six or seven years), the concrete-operations stage (approximately seven years to 11 or 12 years), and the formal-operations stage (approximately 11 or 12 years to adulthood).
- Piaget also identified four factors that together influence the development of children's thinking from early childhood to adulthood: maturation, activity, social interaction and equilibration.
- The strengths of Piaget's ideas concern his focus on children's thinking, the questions he raised and the research methods he pioneered in this field of study.
- Doubts have been raised about Piaget's notion of stages, particularly in terms of his failure to take into account the impact of contextual factors on children's performance of his tasks.
- Vygotsky was interested in the way in which our social, cultural and historical background shapes our thinking. He argued that infants and children interact from birth with carers, who scaffold the child's experiences in ways that reflect the carer's own background.
- Vygotsky saw language as a mental tool that can be used to control intellectual activity. Initially its function

is social, but it is gradually internalised as inner or private speech and used for self-regulation.

- Vygotsky identified the zone of proximal development as the distance between what a child can do alone, without help, and what the child can do with assistance from a more experienced partner. He argued that teaching should be aimed at this zone – at what is just beyond the student's current capacity.
- Vygotsky's theory has been extended to further consider the roles of adults in a child's cognitive development. Scaffolding, cognitive apprenticeships, collaborative learning and guided participation are all concepts that have been applied to education contexts out of this work.
- Information-processing theorists study the mechanisms, strategies and structures by which we process information. They argue that cognitive development results from changes in these aspects of information processing.
- The multistore model proposes a number of stores of information: the sensory memory, working memory and long-term memory; and processes that move information between the stores: attention, rehearsal, encoding and retrieval. An executive control operating within working memory allocates resources and coordinates movement of information between stores. Each of these stores and processes shows increases in capacity and efficiency with age.
- Executive functions of inhibitory control, working memory, and cognitive flexibility control processing of information and support thinking. They develop throughout childhood and adolescence, and can be supported through activities at school.
- Information-processing research identifies speed of processing, capacity of stores, and strategy knowledge

and use as key mechanisms in cognitive development. Contributing to these mechanisms are neurological maturation, language, experience and the knowledge base. All of these factors work together and mutually contribute to one another.

- Information-processing research has enabled close analysis of the various processes involved in cognition, and their development. It has helped to explain many of the observations Piaget and Vygotsky made about children's cognitive development. At the same time,

the information-processing approach is lacking in an overall framework, in its ability to explain the complexity of thinking in real-life situations, and is limited to one part of cognition.

- Recent systems theories of development view cognitive development as just one part of a complex system, with language, social, emotional and cognitive development all interacting and mutually influencing each other.

PUTTING IT TOGETHER

Making links between 'cognitive development' and material in other chapters.

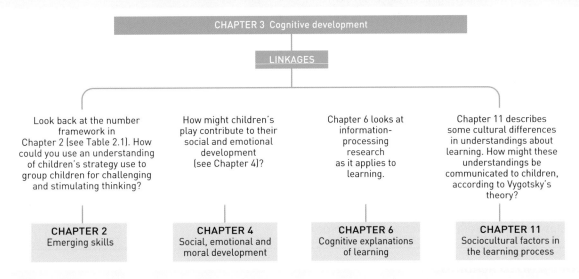

CHAPTER 3 Cognitive development

LINKAGES

Look back at the number framework in Chapter 2 (see Table 2.1). How could you use an understanding of children's strategy use to group children for challenging and stimulating thinking?

CHAPTER 2
Emerging skills

How might children's play contribute to their social and emotional development (see Chapter 4)?

CHAPTER 4
Social, emotional and moral development

Chapter 6 looks at information-processing research as it applies to learning.

CHAPTER 6
Cognitive explanations of learning

Chapter 11 describes some cultural differences in understandings about learning. How might these understandings be communicated to children, according to Vygotsky's theory?

CHAPTER 11
Sociocultural factors in the learning process

QUESTIONS AND ACTIVITIES FOR SELF-ASSESSMENT AND DISCUSSION

1 Define Piaget's concept of 'schema' and give an example of how a schema develops.

2 According to Piaget, what are the four main factors that influence development?

3 How has Piaget's work been taken forward? What new insights into cognitive development have been gained by recent research?

4 Compare and contrast the ideas of Piaget and Vygotsky concerning the role of social interaction in children's development.

5 How does the notion of the zone of proximal development help to explain the process of cognitive development?

6 What did Vygotsky refer to as 'mental tools'? How do they work to shape thinking?

7 Explain how teachers and students learn together in a Vygotskian approach. What is the role of the teacher? What is the role of the learner?

8 How can the ideas of Piaget and Vygotsky be applied to teaching, learning and assessment?

9 Draw the multistore model and describe the way you processed the information you have been learning about in this chapter through its components.

10 Explain how children in kindergarten, Year 6 and Year 10 would go about learning how to spell a new word. How could you best help the child at each stage?

11 Create a visual representation of the factors influencing cognitive development of information processing. How might this help you to remember the ideas?

12 To your drawing from 9 or 11, add factors from social and emotional domains, and from the environment.

FURTHER RESEARCH

SEARCH ME! AND EDUCATION DATABASES

Explore Search Me! education for articles relevant to this chapter. Fast and convenient, Search Me! education is updated daily and provides you with 24-hour access to full-text articles from hundreds of scholarly and popular journals, ebooks and newspapers, including *The Australian* and *The New York Times*. Log in to Search Me! through http://login.cengagebrain.com and use the search terms listed here as a starting point:

- attention
- deductive reasoning
- encoding
- executive function
- inductive reasoning
- information processing
- long-term memory
- memory development
- Piaget
- private speech
- rehearsal
- retrieval
- scaffolding
- Vygotsky
- working memory
- zone of proximal development.

Search Me!

You can also use these terms to explore databases such as ERIC, PsycINFO and the Australian Education Index.

RECOMMENDED WEBSITES

Jean Piaget Society: www.piaget.org

Lev Vygotsky archive: www.marxists.org/archive/vygotsky

Educational Psychology Interactive – the information processing approach:
www.edpsycinteractive.org/topics/cognition/infoproc.html

RECOMMENDED READING

Daniels, H. (Ed.). (2005). *An introduction to Vygotsky*. New York: Routledge.

Galotti, K. M. (2016). *Cognitive development, infancy through adolescence*. 2nd Edition. Thousand Oaks, CA: Sage.

Palmer, J. A. (Ed.). (2001). *Fifty modern thinkers: From Piaget to the present*. London: Routledge. (Available as print or electronic resource.)

Wadsworth, B. J. (2004). *Piaget's theory of cognitive and affective development* (5th ed.). White Plains, NY: Longman.

REFERENCES

Adey, P., Robertson, A. & Venville, G. (2001). *Let's think!* Windsor: NFER-Nelson.

Adhami, M., Johnson, D. C. & Shayer, M. (2002). *Primary CAME thinking maths teachers' guide*. Beam Education, London.

Alloway, T. P., Gathercole, S. E., Willis, C. & Adams, A. M. (2004). A structural analysis of working memory and related cognitive skills in early childhood. *Journal of Experimental Child Psychology, 87*, 85–106.

Atkinson, R. C. & Shiffrin, R. M. (1968). Human memory: A proposed system and its control processes. In K. W. Spence & J. T. Spence (Eds), *The psychology of learning and motivation* (Vol. 2, pp. 89–195). London: Academic Press.

Baddeley, A. D. (1986). *Working memory*. Oxford: Oxford University Press.

Baddeley, A. D. (2012). Working memory: Theories, models, and controversies. *Annual Review of Psychology, 63*, 1–29.

Baddeley, A. D., Gathercole, S. E. & Papagno, C. (1998). The phonological loop as a language learning device. *Psychological Review, 105*(1), 158–73.

Baddeley A. D. & Hitch G. J. (1974). Working memory. In G. A. Bower (Ed.), *The psychology of learning and motivation: Advances in research and theory* (pp. 47–89). New York: Academic.

Baillargeon, R. (1991). Object permanence in young infants: Further evidence. *Child Development, 62*, 1227–46.

Baillargeon, R. (2008). Innate ideas revisited. For a principle of persistence in infants' physical reasoning. *Perspectives on Psychological Science, 3*(1), 2–13.

Baker, S., Gersten, R. & Lee, D. S. (2002). A synthesis of empirical research on teaching mathematics to low-achieving students. *Elementary School Journal, 103*, 51–73.

Basseches, M. (1984). *Dialectical thinking and adult development.* Norwood, NJ: Ablex.

Beilin, H. (1978). Inducing conservation through training. In G. Steiner (Ed.), *Psychology of the 20th century, Vol. 7: Piaget and beyond* (pp. 260–89). Zurich: Kindler.

Beilin, H. (1992). Piagetian theory. In R. Vasta (Ed.), *Six theories of child development: Revised formulations and current issues* (pp. 85–131). London: Jessica Kingsley.

Bell, M. A. (1998). Frontal lobe function during infancy: Implications for the development of cognition and attention. In J. E. Richards (Ed.). *Cognitive neuroscience of attention: A developmental perspective,* pp. 287–31. Mahwah, NJ: Erlbaum.

Berk, L. (2009). *Child development* (8th ed.). Boston: Pearson Education.

Best, J. R. & Miller, P. H. (2010). A developmental perspective on executive function. *Child Development, 81*(6), 1641–1660.

Bochner, S. & Jones, J. (2003). *Child language development: Learning to talk* (2nd ed.). London: Whurr.

Bodrova, E. & Leong, D. J. (1996). *Tools of the mind: The Vygotskian approach to early childhood education.* Englewood Cliffs, NJ: Merrill.

Bodrova, E. & Leong, D. J. (2005). Uniquely preschool: What research tells us about the ways young children learn. *Educational Leadership, 63*(1), 44–7.

Borke, H. (1975). Piaget's mountains revisited: Changes in the egocentric landscape. *Developmental Psychology, 11*, 240–3.

Brainerd, C. J. (1996). Piaget: A centennial celebration. *Psychological Science, 7*, 191–5.

Brooks, P. J., Hanauer, J. B., Padowska, B. & Rosman, H. (2003). The role of selective attention in preschoolers' rule use in a novel dimensional card sort. *Cognitive Development, 18*, 195–215.

Brown, A. L., Metz, K. E. & Campione, J. C. (1996). Social interaction and individual understanding in a community of learners: The influence of Piaget and Vygotsky. In A. Tryphon & J. Voneche (Eds), *Piaget–Vygotsky: The social genesis of thought* (pp. 145–70). London: Psychology Press.

Brown, A. L. & Palincsar, A. S. (1989). Guided, cooperative learning and individual knowledge acquisition. In L. B. Resnick (Ed.), *Knowing, learning, and instruction: Essays in honor of Robert Glaser* (pp. 393–451). Hillsdale, NJ: Erlbaum.

Bruner, J. S. (1975). The ontogenesis of speech acts. *Journal of Child Language, 2*, 1–19.

Bruner, J. S. & Sherwood, V. (1975). Peekaboo and the learning of rule structures. In J. S. Bruner, A. Jolly & K. Sylva (Eds), *Play –its role in development and evolution* (pp. 277–85). Harmondsworth, Middlesex: Penguin.

Bryant, P. E. (1990). Empirical evidence for causes in development. In G. Butterworth & P. Bryant (Eds), *Causes of development: Interdisciplinary perspectives* (pp. 33–45). Hemel Hempstead, Herts: Harvester Wheatsheaf.

Cairney, T. H. (1995). *Pathways to literacy.* London: Cassell.

Case, R. (1992). *The mind's staircase: Exploring the conceptual underpinnings of children's thought and knowledge.* Hillsdale, NJ: Erlbaum.

Case, R. (1996). Introduction: Reconceptualizing the nature of children's conceptual structures and their development in middle childhood. In R. Case & Y. Okamoto, The role of central conceptual structures in the development of children's thought. *Monographs of the Society for Research in Child Development* (pp. 1–26), *246*(6).

Case, R. (1998). The development of conceptual structures. In W. Damon (Series Ed.) & D. Kuhn & R. S. Siegler (Vol. Eds), *Handbook of child psychology, Vol. 2: Cognition, perception, and language* (5th ed., pp. 745–64). New York: John Wiley & Sons.

Case, R. D., Kurland, D. M. & Goldberg, J. (1982). Operational efficiency and the growth of short-term memory span. *Journal of Experimental Child Psychology, 33*, 386–404.

Casey, B. J., Giedd, J. N. & Thomas, K. M. (2000). Structural and functional brain development and its relation to cognitive development. *Biological Psychology, 54*, 241–57.

Center on the Developing Child at Harvard University. (2011). Building the brain's 'air traffic control' system: How early experiences shape the development of executive function, Working Paper No. 11. Retrieved from http://developingchild. harvard.edu/index.php/resources/reports_ and_working_papers/working_papers/ wp11/

Chi, M. T. H (1978). Knowledge structure and memory development. In R. Siegler (Ed.), *Children's thinking: What develops?* (pp. 73–96). Hillsdale, NJ: Erlbaum.

Cohen, L. B. & Cashon, C. H. (2006). Infant cognition. In W. Damon & R. M. Lerner (Series Eds) & D. Kuhn & R. S. Siegler (Vol. Eds), *Handbook of child psychology, Vol. 2: Cognition, perception, and language* (6th ed., pp. 214–51). New York: Wiley.

Cole, K. A. (1996). Structuring academic engagement in classrooms. *Dissertation Abstracts International Section A: Humanities and Social Sciences, 56*(10-A), 3885.

Commonwealth of Australia, Department of Education, Employment and Workplace Relations. (2009). *Belonging, being and becoming: The early years learning framework for Australia.* Canberra: DEEWR.

Corkum, P., Humphries, K., Mullane J. C. & Theriault F. (2007). Private speech in children with ADHD and their typically developing peers during problem-solving and inhibition tasks. *Contemporary Educational Psychology, 33*(1), 97–115.

Daiute, C. & Dalton, B. (1993). Collaboration between children learning to write: Can novices be masters? *Cognitive Instruction, 10*, 281–333.

Daniels, H. (Ed.). (2005). *An introduction to Vygotsky.* New York: Routledge.

Daniels, H. (2011). Vygotsky and psychology. In U. Goswami (Ed.), *Childhood cognitive development* (2nd ed., pp. 673–97). Chichester: Wiley-Blackwell.

Dasen, P. R. (1973). Piagetian research in central Australia. In G. E. Kearney, P. R. deLacy & G. R. Davidson (Eds), *The psychology of Aboriginal Australia.* Sydney: Wiley.

De Corte, E. & Verschaffel, L. (2006). Mathematical thinking and learning. In K. A. Renninger & I. E. Sigel (Series Eds), R. M. Lerner & W. Damon (Eds), *Handbook of child psychology, Vol. 4: Child psychology in practice* (6th ed., pp. 103–52). Hoboken, NJ: John Wiley & Sons.

DEEWR (2009). See Commonwealth of Australia, Department of Education, Employment and Workplace Relations (2009).

Demetriou, A., Christou, C., Spanoudis, G. & Platsidou, M. (2002). The development of mental processing: Efficiency, working memory, and thinking. *Monographs of the Society of Research in Child Development, 67*, Serial Number 268.

Dixon-Krauss, L. (1996). Vygotsky's sociohistorical perspective on learning and its application to western literacy instruction. In L. Dixon-Krauss (Ed.), *Vygotsky in the classroom: Mediated literacy instruction and assessment* (pp. 7–24). White Plains, NY: Longman.

Donaldson, M. (1978). *Children's minds.* Glasgow: Fontana.

Duveen, G. (1997). Psychological development as a social process. In L. Smith, J. Dockrell & P. Tomlinson (Eds), *Piaget, Vygotsky and beyond: Future issues for developmental psychology* (pp. 67–90). Kidlington, Oxford: Routledge.

Eickelkamp, U. (2008). Play, imagination and early experience: Sand storytelling and continuity of being among Anangu Pitjantjatjara girls. In G. G. Robinson, U. Eickelkamp, J. Goodnow & I. Katz (Eds), *Contexts of child development* (pp. 138–52). Darwin: Charles Darwin University Press.

Feldman, D. H. (2013). Cognitive development in childhood: A contemporary perspective. In R. M. Lerner, M. A. Easterbrooks & J. Mistry (Eds), *Handbook of psychology, Volume 6: Developmental psychology* (2nd ed., pp. 289–316). Hoboken, NJ: John Wiley & Sons.

Fernyhough, C. & Fradley, E. (2005). Private speech on an executive task: Relations with task difficulty and task performance. *Cognitive Development 20*(1), 103–20.

Fischer, K. W. (2008). Dynamic cycles of cognitive and brain development: Measuring growth in mind, brain, and education. In A. M. Battro, K. W. Fischer & P. Lena (Eds), *The educated brain* (pp. 127–50). Cambridge, UK: Cambridge University Press.

Fischer, K. W. & Bidell, T. R. (2006). Dynamic development of action and thought. In R. M. Lerner & W. Damon, (Eds), *Handbook of child psychology, Vol 1: Theoretical models of human development* (6th ed., pp. 313–99). Hoboken, NJ: John Wiley & Sons.

Fischer, K. W. & Rose, S. P. (1996). Dynamic growth cycles of brain and cognitive development. In R. Thatcher, G. R. Lyon, J. Rumsey & N. Krasnegor (Eds), *Developmental neuroimaging: Mapping the development of brain and behavior* (pp. 263–79). New York: Academic Press.

Flavell, J. H. (1979). Metacognition and cognitive monitoring: A new area of cognitive-developmental inquiry. *American Psychologist, 34*, 906–11.

Flavell, J. H. (2004). Theory-of-mind development. *Merrill-Palmer Quarterly, 50*(3), 274–90.

Flavell, J. H., Green, F. L. & Flavell, E. R (1995). Young children's knowledge about thinking. *Monographs of the Society for Research in Child Development, 60*(1), Serial No. 243.

Flieller, A. (1999). Comparison of the development of formal thought in adolescent cohorts aged 10 to 15 years (1967–1996 and 1972–1993). *Developmental Psychology, 35*(34), 1048–58.

Frandsen, B. (2011). *Slaying the dragons: 21st century literacy.* Bloomington, IN: Author House.

Fry, A. F. & Hale S. (2000). Relationships among processing speed, working memory, and fluid intelligence in children. *Biological Psychology, 54*, 1–34.

Galotti, K. M. (2016). *Cognitive development: Infancy through adolescence.* 2e. Thousand Oaks, CA: Sage.

Gelman, R. & Gallistel, C. R. (1978). *The child's understanding of number.* Cambridge, MA: Harvard University Press.

Gibson, J. J. & Gibson, E. (1955). Perceptual learning: Differentiation or enrichment? *Psychological Review, 62*, 32–41.

Goodnow, J. J. (1962). A test of milieu differences with some of Piaget's tasks. *Psychological Monographs, 76*(555).

Gopnick, A. & Meltzoff, A. N. (1997). *Words, thoughts and theories.* Cambridge, MA: MIT Press.

Greenway, C. (2002). The process, pitfalls and benefits of implementing a reciprocal teaching intervention to improve the reading comprehension of a group of year 6 pupils. *Educational Psychology in Practice, 18*(2), 113–37.

Halford, G. S. (1993). *Children's understanding: The development of mental models.* Hillsdale, NJ: Erlbaum.

Halford, G. S. & Andrews, G. (2004). The development of deductive reasoning: How important is complexity? *Thinking & Reasoning, 10*(2), 113–21.

Houdé, O. (2000). Inhibition and cognitive development: Object, number, categorization, and reasoning. *Cognitive Development, 15*, 63–73.

Hughes, M. & Donaldson, M. (1979). The use of hiding games for studying the coordination of perspectives. *Educational Review, 31*, 133–40.

Inhelder, B. & Piaget, J. (1958). *The growth of logical thinking from childhood to adolescence: An essay on the construction of formal operational structures* (Trans. A. Parsons & S. Milgram). London: Routledge and Kegan Paul.

Kaye, K. (1982). Organism, apprentice, and person. In E.Z. Tronick (Ed.), *Social interchange in infancy: Affect, cognition and communication* (pp. 183–96). Baltimore, MD: University Park Press.

Kellman, P. J. & Arterberry, M. E. (2006). Infant visual perception. In W. Damon, R. M. Lerner & N. Eisenberg (Eds), *Handbook of child psychology, Vol. 3: Social, emotional, and personality development* (pp. 109–60). Hoboken, NJ: John Wiley & Sons.

King, C. M. & Johnson, L. (1999). Constructing meaning via reciprocal teaching. *Reading Research and Instruction, 38*(3), 169–86.

Klingner, J. K. & Vaughn, S. (1996). Reciprocal teaching of reading comprehension strategies for students with learning disabilities who use English as a second language. *The Elementary School Journal, 96*(2), 275–94.

Koutselini, M. & Hadjiyianni, I. (1999). Intervention in metacognition and learning: A case study in the elementary school. *Curriculum and Teaching, 14*(2), 75–94.

Kuhn, D. (2000). Metacognitive development. *Current Directions in Psychological Science, 9*(5), 178–81.

Kuhn, D. (2006). Metacognitive development. In Karen L. Freiberg (Ed.), *Annual editions: Human development* (34th ed.). Dubuque, IA: McGraw-Hill.

Kuhn, D. & Franklin, S. (2006). The second decade: What develops (and how). In W. Damon & R. Lerner (Series Eds), D. Kuhn & R. Siegler (Vol. Eds), *Handbook of child psychology, Vol. 2: Cognition, perception, and language* (6th ed., pp. 953–93). Hoboken, NJ: Wiley.

Kunsch, C. A., Jitendra, A. K. & Sood, S. (2007). The effects of peer-mediated mathematics instruction for students with disabilities: A review of the literature. *Learning Disabilities Research & Practice, 22*(1), 1–12.

Labouvie-Vief, G. (1980). Beyond formal operations: Uses and limits of pure logic in life-span development. *Human Development, 23*, 141–61.

Lambert, B. & Clyde, M. (2000). *Rethinking early childhood theory and practice.* Katoomba, NSW: Social Science Press.

LeBlanc, G. & Bearison, D. J. (2004). Teaching and learning as a bi-directional activity: Investigating dyadic interactions between child teachers and child learners. *Cognitive Development, 19*(4), 499–515. Published by Elsevier.

Lederer, J. M. (2000). Reciprocal teaching of social studies in inclusive elementary classrooms. *Journal of Learning Disabilities, 33*(1), 91–107.

Lewis, D. H. (1972). *We, the navigators: The ancient art of landfinding in the Pacific.* Canberra: ANU Press.

Lightfoot, C., Cole, M. & Cole, S. (2009). *The development of children* (6th ed.). New York: Worth.

Little, Q. & Richards, D. R. T. (2000). Teaching learners – learners teaching: Using reciprocal teaching to improve comprehension strategies in challenged readers. *Reading Improvement, 37*(4), 190–4.

Lock, A. J. (Ed.). (1978). *Action, gesture and symbol: The emergence of language.* London: Academic Press.

Lock, A. J., Service, V., Brito, A. & Chandler, P. (1989). The social structuring of infant cognition. In A. Slater & G. Bremner (Eds), *Infant development* (pp. 243–71). Hove, UK: Erlbaum.

Lourenco, O. & Machado, A. (1996). In defense of Piaget's theory: A reply to 10 common criticisms. *Psychological Review, 103*, 143–64.

Lutz, D. J. & Sternberg, R. J. (1999). Cognitive development. In M. H. Bornstein & M. E. Lamb (Eds), *Developmental psychology: An advanced textbook* (pp. 275–311). Mahwah, NJ: Erlbaum.

Mareschall, D. (2000). Object knowledge in infancy: Current controversies and approaches. *Trends in Cognitive Sciences, 4*, 408–16.

Marzano, R. J. & Simms, J. A. (2014). *Questioning sequences in the classroom.* Bloomington, IN: Marzano Research Laboratory.

McDevitt, T. M. & Ormrod, J. E. (2010). *Child development and education* (4th edn.). Upper Saddle River, NJ: Pearson Education.

Meltzoff, A. N. & Moore, M. K. (1994). Imitation, memory, and the representation of persons. *Infant Behavior & Development, 17*, 83–99.

Metz, K. E. (1995). Reassessment of developmental constraints on children's science instruction. *Review of Educational Research, 65*, 93–127.

Metz, K. E. (1997). On the complex relation between cognitive developmental research and children's science curricula. *Review of Educational Research, 67*(1), 151–63.

Miller, G. A. (1956). The magical number seven, plus or minus two: Some limits on our capacity for processing information. *The Psychological Review, 63*, 81–97.

Miller, P. (1993). *Theories of developmental psychology* (3rd ed.). New York: W. H. Freeman.

Miller, P. H. (2011). Piaget's theory: Past, present, and future. In U. Goswami (Ed.), *The Wiley-Blackwell handbook of childhood cognitive development* (2nd ed.), pp. 649–72. Oxford: Blackwell.

Moore, M. K. & Meltzoff, A. N. (2008). Factors affecting infants' manual search from occluded objects and the genesis of object permanence. *Infant Behaviour and Development, 31*(2), 168–80.

Moshman, D. (2004). *Adolescent psychological development: Rationality, morality, and identity* (2nd ed.). Mahwah, NJ: Erlbaum.

Müller, U. & Kerns, K. (2015). The development of executive function. In L. S. Liben, U. Müller, & R. M. Lerner (Eds.), *Handbook of child psychology and developmental science: Cognitive processes* (pp. 571–623). Hoboken, NJ, US: John Wiley & Sons Inc.

Myhill, D. & Warren, P. (2005). Scaffolds or straitjackets? Critical moments in classroom discourse. *Education Review, 57*(1), 55–69.

Newcombe, N. S. & Huttenlocher, J. (1992). Children's early ability to solve perspective taking problems. *Developmental Psychology, 28*(4), 635–43.

Newman, F. & Holzman, L. (1993). *Lev Vygotsky: Revolutionary scientist*. Abingdon, UK: Routledge.

Okon-Singer, H., Hendler, T., Pessoa, L. & Shackman, A.J. (2015). The neurobiology of emotion–cognition interactions: fundamental questions and strategies for future research. *Frontiers of Human Neuroscience, 9*(58). doi: 10.3389/fnhum

Palincsar, A. S. (1982). Improving the reading comprehension of junior high school students through the reciprocal teaching of comprehension-monitoring strategies. Unpublished Doctoral Dissertation, University of Illinois at Urbana-Champaign.

Palincsar, A. S. (1986). The role of dialogue in providing scaffolded instruction. *Educational Psychologist, 21*, 73–98.

Palincsar, A. S. (1987). Collaborating for collaborative learning of text comprehension. Paper presented at the Annual Meeting of the American Educational Research Association, Washington, DC.

Palincsar, A. S. (1998). Social constructivist perspectives on teaching and learning. *Annual Review of Psychology, 49*, 345–75.

Palincsar, A. S. & Brown, A. L. (1984). Reciprocal teaching of comprehension-fostering and comprehension-monitoring activities. *Cognitive Instruction, 1*, 117–75.

Palincsar, A. S. & Brown, A. L. (1987). Enhancing instructional time through attention to metacognition. *Journal of Learning Disabilities, 20*(2), 66–75.

Palincsar, A. S. & Brown, A. L. (1989). Classroom dialogues to promote self-regulated comprehension. In J. Brophy (Ed.), *Advances in research on teaching* (pp. 35–72). Greenwich: JAI.

Palincsar, A. S. & Herrenkohl, L. R. (1999). Designing collaborative contexts: Lessons from three research programs. In A. M. O'Donnell & A. King (Eds), *Cognitive perspectives on peer learning: The Rutgers invitational symposium on education series* (pp. 151–77). Mahwah, NJ: Lawrence Erlbaum Associates.

Palincsar, A. S., Brown, A. L. & Campione, J. C. (1993). First grade dialogues for knowledge acquisition and use. In E. A. Forman, N. Minnick & C. A. Stone (Eds), *Contexts for learning: Sociocultural dynamics in children's development* (pp. 43–57). New York: Oxford University Press.

Palmer, J. A. (Ed.) (2001). *Fifty modern thinkers: From Piaget to the present*. London: Routledge.

Pascual-Leone, J. (1970). A mathematical model for the transition rule in Piaget's developmental stages. *Acta Psychologica, 32*, 301–45.

Pass, S. (2007). When constructivists Jean Piaget and Lev Vygotsky were pedagogical collaborators: A viewpoint from a study of their communications. *Journal of Constructivist Psychology, 3*(20), 277–82.

Pennequin, V., Sorel, O. & Mainguy, M. (2010). Metacognition, executive functions and aging: The effect of training in the use of metacognitive skills to solve mathematical word problems. *Journal of Adult Development, 17*(3), 168–76.

Peterson, L. R. & Peterson, M. J. (1959). Short-term retention of individual verbal items. *Journal of Experimental Psychology, 58*, 193–8.

Philp, J. & Duchesne, S. (2008). When the gate opens: The interaction between social and linguistic goals in child second language development. In J. Philp, R. Oliver & A. Mackey (Eds), *Second language acquisition and the younger learner: Child's play?* Amsterdam: John Benjamins.

Piaget, J. (1929). *The child's conception of the world* (J. & A. Tomlinson, Trans.). New York: Harcourt, Brace & World.

Piaget, J. (1951). *Psychology of intelligence*. London: Routledge and Kegan Paul.

Piaget, J. (1970). *Science of education and the psychology of the child*. New York: Orion Press.

Piaget, J. (1972). Intellectual evolution from adolescence to adulthood. *Human Development, 15*, 1–12.

Piaget, J. (1974). *Understanding causality* (D. Miles & M. Miles, Trans.). New York: Norton.

Piaget, J. & Inhelder, B. (1969). *The psychology of the child* (H. Weaver, Trans.). London: Routledge & Kegan Paul.

Ponitz, C. C., McClelland, M. M., Matthews, J. S. & Morrison, F. J. (2009). A structured observation of behavioral regulation and its contributions to kindergarten outcomes. *Developmental Psychology, 45*, 605–619. doi: 10.1037/a0015365

Rakison, D. H. (2005). Developing knowledge of objects' motion properties in infancy. *Cognition, 96*(3), 183–214.

Rakison, D. H. & Poulin-Dubois, D. (2001). *Psychological Bulletin, 127*(2), 209–28.

Rasku-Puttonen, H., Etelapelto, A., Arvaja, M. & Hakkinen, P. (2003). Is successful scaffolding an illusion? Shifting patterns of responsibility and control in teacher–student interaction during a long-term learning project. *Instructional Science, 31*(6), 377–93.

Rogoff, B. (1990). *Apprenticeship in thinking: Cognitive development in social context*. New York: Oxford University Press.

Rogoff, B. (1993). Children's guided participation and participatory appropriation in sociocultural activity. In R. H. Wozniak & K. W. Fischer (Eds), *Development in context: Acting and thinking in specific environments* (pp. 121–53). Hillsdale, NJ: Lawrence Erlbaum Associates.

Rogoff, B. (1994). Developing understandings of the idea of communities of learners. *Mind, Culture, and Activity, 1*(4), 209–29.

Rogoff, B. (1998). Cognition as a collaborative process. In W. Damon (Series Ed.) & D. Kuhn & R. S. Siegler (Vol. Eds), *Handbook of child psychology, Vol. 2: Cognition, perception, and language* (5th ed., pp. 679–744). New York: John Wiley and Sons.

Rogoff, B., (2003). *The cultural nature of human development*. Oxford: Oxford University Press.

Roh, K. (1997). An understanding of higher order thinking in social studies: A naturalistic case study of a Korean middle school classroom. *Dissertation Abstracts International. Section A: Humanities and Social Sciences, 58*(6–A), 2060.

Rosenshine, B. & Meister, C. (1994). Reciprocal teaching: A review of the research. *Review of Educational Research, 64*(4), 479–530.

Roth, W-M. & Bowen, G. M. (1995). Knowing and interacting: A study of culture, practices and resources in a Grade 8 open-inquiry science classroom guided by a cognitive apprenticeship metaphor. *Cognition and Instruction, 13*, 73–128.

Schneider, W. & Bjorklund, D. F. (1992). Expertise, aptitude, and strategic remembering. *Child Development, 63*, 461–73.

Schneider, W. & Bjorklund, D. F. (1998). Memory. In W. Damon (Series Ed.), D. Kuhn & R. S. Siegler (Vol. Eds), *Handbook of child psychology, Vol. 2: Cognition, perception, and language* (5th ed., pp. 467–552). New York: John Wiley and Sons.

Schneider, W. & Bjorklund, D. F. (2003). Memory and knowledge development. In J. Valsiner & K. Connolly (Eds), *Handbook of Developmental Psychology* (pp. 370–403). London: Sage.

Schneider, W. & Pressley, M. (1997). *Memory development between 2 and 20.* Hillsdale, NJ: Erlbaum.

Segall, M. H., Dasen, P. R., Berry, J. W. & Poortinga, Y. H. (1999). *Human behavior in global perspective: An introduction to cross-cultural psychology* (2nd rev. ed.). Boston: Allyn & Bacon.

Shayer, M. (1997). Piaget and Vygotsky: A necessary marriage for effective educational intervention. In L. Smith, J. Dockrell & P. Tomlinson (Eds), *Piaget, Vygotsky and beyond: Future issues for developmental psychology and education* (pp. 36–59). London: Routledge.

Shayer, M. (1999). Cognitive acceleration through science education II: Its effects and scope. *International Journal of Science Education, 21*(8), 883–902.

Shayer, M. (2003). Not just Piaget, and certainly not Vygotsky as *alternative* to Piaget. *Learning and Instruction, 13,* 465–85.

Shayer, M. & Adey, P. S. (Eds). (2002). *Learning intelligence: Cognitive acceleration across the curriculum from 5 to 15 years.* Milton Keynes, UK: Open University Press.

Shayer, M. & Adhami, M. (2007). Fostering cognitive development through the context of mathematics: Results of the CAME Project. *Educational Studies in Mathematics, 64*(3), 265–91.

Shayer, M. & Adhami, M. (2010). Realising the cognitive potential of children 5 to 7 with a mathematics focus: Post-test and long-term effects of a two-year intervention. *British Journal of Educational Psychology, 80,* 363–9.

Siegler, R. S. (1998). *Children's thinking* (3rd ed.). Upper Saddle River, NJ: Prentice Hall.

Siegler, R. S. (2006). Microgenetic studies of learning. In W. Damon & R. Lerner (Series Eds), D. Kuhn & R. Siegler (Vol. Eds), *Handbook of Child Psychology, Vol. 2: Cognition, Perception, and Language* (6th ed., pp. 464–510). Hoboken, NJ: Wiley.

Siegler, R. S. (2007). Cognitive variability. *Developmental Science, 10,* 104–9.

Siegler, R. S. & Svetina, M. (2006). What leads children to adopt new strategies? A microgenetic/cross sectional study of class inclusion. *Child Development, 77,* 997–1015.

Singer, D. G. & Revenson, T. A. (1996). *A Piaget primer: How a child thinks* (Rev. ed.). New York: Plume.

Smith, L. (1993). *Necessary knowledge: Piagetian perspectives on constructivism.* Hove, UK: Lawrence Erlbaum.

Spelke, E. S., Breinlinger, K., Macomber, J. & Jacobson, K. (1992). Origins of knowledge. *Psychological Review, 99,* 605–32.

Sternberg, R. J. (1985). *Beyond IQ: A triarchic theory of intelligence.* New York: Cambridge University Press.

Subbotsky, E. (2010). *Magic and the mind: Mechanisms, functions, and development of magical thinking and behavior.* New York: Oxford University Press.

Sutherland, P. (1992). *Cognitive development today: Piaget and his critics.* London: Paul Chapman.

Taylor, J. & Cox, B. D. (1997). Microgenetic analysis of group-based solution of complex two-step mathematical word problems by fourth-graders. *Journal of the Learning Sciences, 6*(2), 183–226.

Tomasello, M. & Carpenter, M. (2007). Shared intentionality. *Developmental Science, 10*(1), 121–5.

Tyng, C. M., Amin, H. U., Saad, M. N. M. & Malik, A. S. (2017). The Influences of Emotion on Learning and Memory. *Frontiers in Psychology, 8,* 1454.

Vandierendonck, A. (2016). A working memory system with distributed executive control. *Perspectives on Psychological Science, 11*(1), 74–100.

Vygotsky, L. S. (1978). *Mind in society: The development of higher psychological processes.* Cambridge, MA: Harvard University Press.

Vygotsky, L. S. (1981). The genesis of higher mental functions. In Wertsch, J. V. (Ed. and Trans.), *The concept of activity in Soviet psychology.* Armonk, NY: M. E. Sharpe.

Vygotsky, L. S. (1986). *Thought and language.* (A. Kozulin, trans.). Cambridge, MA: MIT Press. (Original work published 1934.)

Wadsworth, B. J. (1996). *Piaget's theory of cognitive and affective development.* White Plains, NY: Longman.

Wadsworth, B. J. (2004). *Piaget's theory of cognitive and affective development: Foundations of constructivism* (5th ed.). Boston: Pearson.

Warwick, P. & Maloch, B. (2003). Scaffolding speech and writing in the primary classroom: A consideration of work with literature and science pupil groups in the USA and UK. *Reading, Literacy and Language, 37*(2), 54–63.

Wellman, H. M. (2011). Developing a theory of mind. In U. Goswami (Ed.), *The Blackwell handbook of childhood cognitive development* (2nd ed., pp. 258–84). Oxford: Blackwell.

Wellman, H. M., Cross, D. & Bartsch, K. (1987). Infant search and object permanence: A metaanalysis of the A-not-B error. *Monographs of the Society for Research in Child Development, 51,* 1–51.

Wellman, H. M. & Gelman, S. A. (1998). Knowledge acquisition in functional domains. In W. Damon (Series Ed.), D. Kuhn and R. S. Siegler (Vol. Eds), *Handbook of child psychology, Vol. 2: Cognition, perception, and language* (5th edn., pp. 523–73). New York: Wiley.

Wells, G. (2000). *Dialogic inquiry in education: Building on the legacy of Vygotsky.* Ontario Institute for Studies in Education, University of Toronto. Retrieved from www.oise.utoronto.ca/oise/Home/index.html

Wertsch, J. V. (1985). *Vygotsky and the social formation of mind.* Cambridge, MA: Harvard University Press.

Wertsch, J. V., McNamee, G. D., McLane, J. B. & Budwig, N. A. (1980). The adult–child dyad as a problem-solving system. *Child Development, 51,* 1215–21.

Westera, J. & Moore, D. W. (1995). Reciprocal teaching of reading comprehension in a New Zealand high school. *Psychology in Schools, 32*(3), 225–32.

Whitebread, D., Coltman, P., Pasternak, D. P., Sangster, C., Grau, V., Bingham, S., Almeqdad, Q. & Demetriou, D. (2009). The development of two observational tools for assessing metacognition and self-regulated learning in young children. *Metacognition and Learning, 4*(1), 63–85.

Wilson, F. J. (1994). The use of analogical reasoning as a problem solving strategy. Unpublished Masters thesis. Queensland University of Technology.

Winsler, A. (2003). Introduction to the special issue: Vygotskian perspectives in early childhood education. *Early Education and Development, 14*(3), 253–70.

Winsler, A., Manfra, L. & Diaz, R. M. (2007). Should I let them talk?: Private speech and task performance among preschool children with and without behavior problems. *Early Childhood Research Quarterly, 22*(2), 215–31.

Winsler, A., Naglieri, J. A. & Manfra, L. (2006). Children's search strategies and accompanying verbal and motor strategic behavior: Developmental trends and relations with task performance among children age 5 to 17. *Cognitive Development, 21,* 232–48.

Wood, D., Bruner, J. S. & Ross, G. (1976). The role of tutoring in problem-solving. *Journal of Child Psychology and Psychiatry, 17,* 89–100.

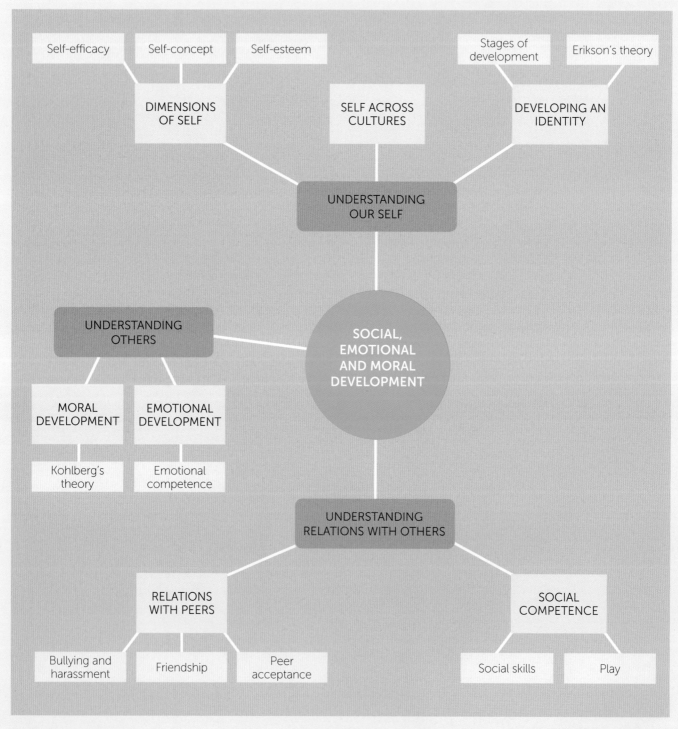

Chapter 4

SOCIAL, EMOTIONAL AND MORAL DEVELOPMENT

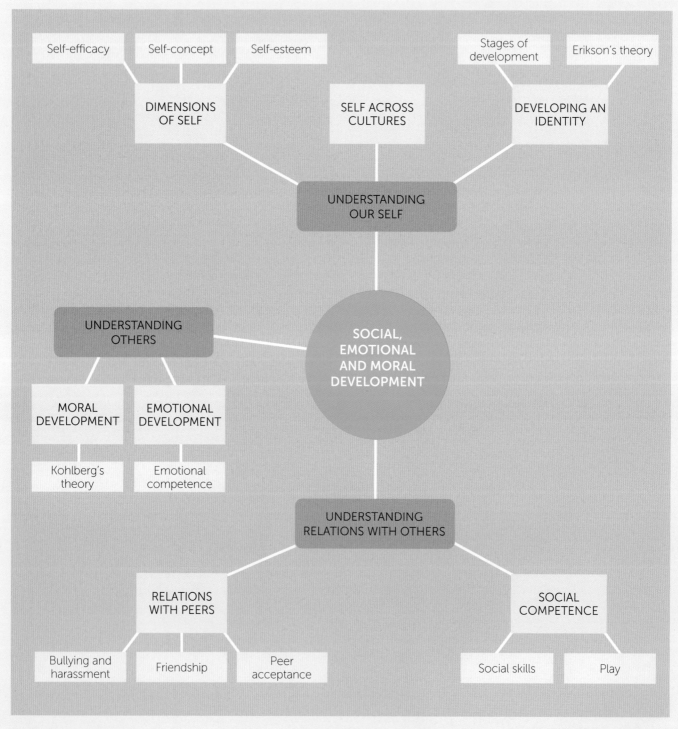

FIGURE 4.1 Chapter 4 concept map

KEY QUESTIONS

After reading this chapter, you should be able to answer the following questions:

- What is the difference between self-esteem, self-concept and self-efficacy?
- What are the self and identity challenges faced by school-aged children?
- What is the teacher's role in fostering a healthy sense of self?
- How do we develop a sense of right and wrong?
- How is emotional competence related to understanding others?
- How do peer acceptance and friendship contribute to development?

ONLINE STUDY RESOURCES

Bring your learning to life with **interactive learning**, **study** and **exam preparation tools** that support the printed textbook. CourseMate Express includes **quizzes**, **interactive activities**, **videos**, a tool to help you '**develop your philosophy**' and more.

INTRODUCTION

Taylah is four years old and her brother Jake is 12 years old. It is only fairly recently that Taylah has started to talk about herself using terms like '*I'm a big girl now. I've got a brother and a sister. My favourite colour is green.*' Jake, meanwhile, has been bragging about himself for a while: '*I'm a pretty good skater; so are my mates. We muck around a bit but I try not to do bad stuff, like Jonno; he found 10 bucks in his mum's car and didn't tell his mum. He bought us drinks at the skate park. But I don't do stuff like that. I'm OK at school work but much better at sports.*' Their older sister Sarah is 15 and seems to understand herself very well: '*I'm 15 years old and my friends say I'm a pretty nice person and they are all really nice people too. You know, very caring, and we like volunteering and helping out. We all do OK at school too, like we are in the top classes. My best subjects are Maths and Science, but I'm only average at English. My friends always get better marks than me. That's embarrassing! But I try to be pretty cool about it, not make a big deal of it. I like relaxing and hanging out with my friends, they are great and we understand each other; we all like the same kind of things.*'

As Taylah, Jake and Sarah have grown up, their understanding of self, notions of right and wrong, and their relationships with other people have developed and become more sophisticated. How does development explain why Taylah's self-description is so different to Sarah's? What developmental factors influence Jake's sense of right and wrong when he is hanging out with his friends? Why is Sarah able to describe her emotions so well, while Jake and Taylah didn't mention these things? This chapter presents an introduction to three major areas in the study of personal development. First, it focuses on the connections between our concepts of self and the development of a sense of self-identity. Next, it focuses on the gradual development of emotional, moral and social understanding. Finally, this chapter explores the formation of relationships with other people, looking closely at peer relationships, and interactions between the self and others in contexts such as classrooms.

UNDERSTANDING OUR SELF

As we can see in the cases above, our sense of self is very closely related to our cognitive development (see Chapter 3). Taylah talks about herself in very 'concrete' and tangible ways, while Jake's self-report is more detailed. Increasingly, our self-understanding is also related to relationships with others, and like

Jake and Sarah, we often compare ourselves to friends or classmates as we grow up. As our emotional understanding develops, we become much better at using emotional labels to describe ourselves or other people, as shown in Sarah's story. Each young person is saying 'This is who I am!' and this sense of **self** differentiates each person as a unique individual and separates us from one another. It lies at the core of who we are.

self
Who we are, what makes us unique and who we believe ourselves to be

DIMENSIONS OF THE DEVELOPING SELF

According to Susan Harter (2012, p. 1), one of the most prominent researchers in the area, 'the construction of the self is inevitable … our species has been designed to actively create *theories* about our world, including the construction of a theory of self in order to make meaning of our experiences'. Over time, notions of the 'self' have changed and today the word 'self' is most commonly attached to other words, such as 'self-concept', 'self-esteem', 'self-control' and 'self-help'. As early as 1890, one of the earliest researchers in this field, William James (1890, as cited in Harter, 2012), stated that individuals form *multiple Me-selves* that describe the multiple roles individuals need to perform in society. Today, it is a common view that the self is not a single entity; rather, we are made up of many 'selves' and dimensions (Barrett, 2000; Fogel, 1995). These self dimensions develop and become more complex over time as we mature and interact with our environment.

Self-concept

self-concept
A collection of information, ideas, attitudes and beliefs we have about ourselves

Social comparison
Evaluation of our self that is based on comparing our abilities to others or social standards

Self-concept refers to the collection of knowledge, ideas, attitudes and beliefs we have about ourselves. It is formed through interaction with our environment and the people in it. Self-concept is particularly influenced by feedback and evaluation from significant others, such as teachers, peers and parents (Marsh, 1990). As shown in Figure 4.2, it is also influenced by **social comparison**, such as comparing performance or grades with those of classmates. Self-concept is a cognitive appraisal and has no concrete or observable features as seen in areas of physical development, but it plays an important part in understanding ourselves.

For many years it has been accepted that self-concept is multidimensional and differentiated (Marsh, Xu & Martin, 2012). This is evident when we look at Sarah's self-report. Sarah clearly has a *multidimensional* view of her self-concept in academic domains such as Maths, Science and English. However, her self-concept is also *differentiated* in that she can distinguish between these areas and reports a high, or very positive sense of herself in Maths and Science but does not feel so sure of her ability in English; her self-concept in this subject appears to be lower. Sarah

FIGURE 4.2 Social comparison plays a significant role in learners' academic self-concept.

Source: Matthew Duchesne, © Milk and Honey Photography, 2010.

also seems to have a positive self-concept about her relationships with other friends and if we probed further she might have another level of self-concept for her relationships with the wider peer group. Self-concept can be measured and distinguished in different areas of academic and social abilities (Marsh et al., 2012). See the Go Further link to learn how researchers measure self-concept.

This theory of a multidimensional self-concept has been well studied in the area of academic self-concept. 'Academic self-concept' is derived from views of personal achievements in specific curriculum areas such as Maths and Reading. Further study has confirmed that as we develop as learners, self-concept perceptions become more defined and specific across academic areas such as Economics, Foreign Languages and the Arts (Marsh, Byrne & Shavelson, 1988; Vispoel, 1995; see also Byrne & Gavin, 1996).

One of the most enduring questions in educational psychology research has concerned the link between academic self-concept and academic performance. In particular researchers have been interested in a 'Which came first: the chicken or the egg?' type of question: Does academic self-concept influence our academic performance or does our academic performance influence our academic self-concept? Some of the most important findings illustrate a reciprocal link between our academic self-concept and academic achievement. For example, Marsh and Yeung (1998) found that the level of an adolescent's self-concept can predict their later performance in school *and* the level of self-concept can be affected by prior academic performance. Researchers have now suggested that in the case of academic self-concept in particular a *reciprocated effects model* explains the relations between academic self-concept and academic performance. This means that academic self-concept can influence academic performance but knowledge of our academic performance can also influence our academic self-concept (Marsh & Craven, 2006; Marsh et al., 2012) suggesting that the relationship between academic self-concept and achievement is a reciprocal one.

THINK ABOUT

- What are the implications of the reciprocal effects model for classroom practice?
- For example, when would the teachers focus on enhancing a child's academic self-concept and when would it be appropriate to enhance their skills to improve their performance?

Another very important research finding concerns the way in which adolescents develop their academic self-concept. One type of research has examined the theory that students develop their academic self-concept in two ways: first, through social comparison to external sources of information, such as peers; and second, by comparison to internal sources of information, such as their ability in one subject versus another (Marsh, 1986). This idea of social comparison to external sources has been used to examine the effects of different types of academic streaming on student self-concept.

In schools where academic streaming occurs (that is, where students are grouped in separate classes according to their abilities), social comparison plays a significant role in students' perceptions of their academic abilities. This occurs because students tend to make comparisons with others in upward or downward directions. For example, if Sarah compares herself to her peers who perform better than her in English, this type of upward comparison to students better than herself can result in feelings of inferiority and a low self-concept. In contrast, comparing oneself to someone of lower ability (a downward comparison) is somewhat protective of the self-concept and does not lead to lower self-views. This was demonstrated in studies such as that by Burleson, Leach and Harrington (2005), which tested the role of social comparison on artistic self-concepts of adolescents moving to a selective art school. By measuring those with whom the students were comparing themselves, the researchers were able to determine if they were making upwards or downwards comparisons. Consistent with self-concept theory, those students

CourseMateExpress

Online resources
Go further: View the
material on measuring
self-concept on this
text's website

who made upwards comparisons suffered a reduced artistic self-concept. Such effects seem to occur when high-ability students attend academically selective schools and are faced with a larger pool of highly competent peers with whom they compare themselves. This paradoxical situation is known as the 'big-fish-little-pond effect' (see **Box 4.1**), in which their self-concept may actually decline once they are no longer the biggest and 'brightest' fish in the school pond (see **Figure 4.3**).

BOX 4.1 RESEARCH LINKS

BIG-FISH-LITTLE-POND-EFFECT

Research consistently demonstrates that students in high-ability and academically selective classes have lower academic self-concepts than same-ability students who are educated in average-ability or non-selective environments (Marsh et al., 2008). Researchers have also found similar effects for academically disadvantaged students in comprehensive classrooms (Marsh et al., 2012). This effect is known as the 'big-fish-little-pond effect' (BFLPE). As students move from relative success in one school or classroom where they are like big fish dominating a little pond, to a school or classroom where the competition and pressure to succeed are increased, academic self-concept tends to suffer and self-esteem declines. Once this effect has been established it can increase and even be maintained for several years after the student graduates from high school (Marsh et al., 2007).

Figure 4.3 demonstrates the relationships between an individual's ability, their academic self-concept and the average ability of the class or school in which they are learning. A student's individual ability is positively related to academic self-concept. However, when the average ability of the class or school is high, it exerts a negative influence on academic self-concept. In fact, the strongest BFLPE effects have been found *within* classrooms, meaning that students are mostly comparing themselves to students within their own classes (Marsh et al., 2014). The BFLPE is also evident across cultures. Using data from the Program for International Student Assessment (PISA) database, Seaton, Marsh and Craven (2009) demonstrated that the BFLPE is universal, being apparent across a large sample of students from 38 countries. Moreover, Marsh et al. (2014) found that such effects are true for both high-ability *and* weaker students.

CourseMateExpress

Online resources
Go further: Read the
case study about the
big-fish-little-pond
effect on this text's
website

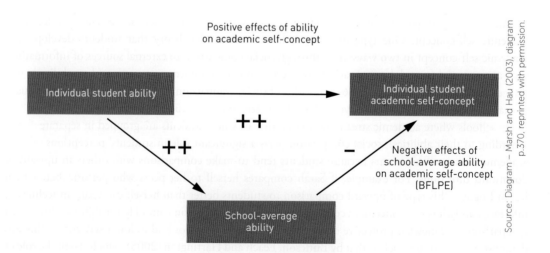

FIGURE 4.3 The big-fish-little-pond effect (BFLPE): theoretical predictions.

Self-esteem

Self-esteem and self-concept appear to be closely related concepts, with many researchers using the terms interchangeably, which can cause confusion (Byrne, 2002). Theoretically, self-concept and self-esteem are different ways of evaluating the self. In self-concept evaluations, it is believed that we are making a cognitive (thoughtful) judgement about our competence in different domains that are relevant in our lives (for example, 'I am good at Maths, but not so good at English'). Self-esteem, on the other hand, is believed to reflect a higher-order cognitive evaluation of our self that describes our integrated sense of our worth as a person. It is *not* believed to be a simple summary of our differentiated self-concept but rather a higher-order integration of many different aspects and views of the self (Harter, 2012). Harter's research appears to show that this global sense of self is revealed when we develop the verbal ability to make global statements about our sense of self (Harter, 2006). This is seen in measurement of the global sense of self with somewhat abstract higher-order questions such as 'I feel that I am a worthwhile person'. It is harder for younger children to articulate the less concrete and rather more abstract sense of person-hood or 'worthwhileness' that the global self-esteem is thought to reveal.

The distinction between self-esteem and the differentiated self-concept becomes apparent when we look at their association with specific and differentiated domains of our life. For example, the differentiated academic self-concept is highly correlated with academic achievement in those domains. The global sense of self is less correlated with academic achievement (Marsh et al., 2012). On the other hand, self-esteem does seem to be strongly associated with particular self-concept evaluations such as our physical self-concept.

Self-esteem seems to be associated with many critical areas of our life that contribute to our wellbeing, and may also reflect certain cultural factors in our lives. For example, self-esteem is consistently and strongly correlated with our sense of physical appearance, often measured as our physical self-concept. Various studies by Harter (2012) have found that perceptions of physical appearance are a stronger predictor of global self-esteem than other forms of self-perception for young children right through to adult populations. For example, in studies of gifted children and children with learning disabilities it was predicted that academic self-concept would most strongly predict their self-esteem. Similarly, in a study of children with conduct (behavioural) disorders, it was thought that their behavioural self-perceptions would most strongly predict their global self-esteem. In each of these studies it was found not to be the case. Rather, the perceived physical appearance of each group of children was the strongest correlate with their global self-esteem (Harter, 2012).

self-esteem
The level of satisfaction and pride that individuals have in the self

---

THINK ABOUT

■ How could we explain the strong association between our sense of physical appearance and global self-esteem? Think about the range of reasons why this might be the case.
■ Are there any cultural factors that might explain why our self-esteem is so linked to our perception of our physical appearance?

Many studies have shown that self-esteem plays an important role in our lives and is associated with our overall wellbeing in many ways (Orth & Robins, 2014). For example, research indicates a connection between low self-esteem, depression and drug abuse (Sowislo & Orth, 2013) , depression and suicide (Bos et al., 2010), eating disorders (Gila, Castro, Gomez & Toro, 2005), and crime and violence (Ackard & Neumark-Sztainer, 2002).

Studies across the lifespan from ages 16 to 97 have shown that self-esteem is associated with lifetime trajectories of wellbeing including affect and depression; the effects vary, however, and are not consistent for all lifetime indicators (Orth, Robins & Widaman, 2012). For example, Wheeler (2010) found that although high self-esteem predicted lower substance abuse by early adolescent females, it did not predict substance abuse by boys; nor did high self-esteem among the same girls influence their decision to engage in early sexual activity one year later. Unlike these longitudinal studies, many of the research studies are correlational, and we must take care not to assume causation in any of the links between self-esteem and the other variables measured. This is a general rule that should be applied to all studies based on correlational evidence.

Self-efficacy

self-efficacy
An individual's sense of being able to manage a task effectively and successfully in a particular domain

human agency
The capacity of a person to act on and shape their world

A third dimension of self relates to an individual's belief about their ability to perform tasks successfully. This is known as **self-efficacy**, which is a highly specific cognitive judgement of our ability, and closely reflects our belief that we can accomplish actions and tasks effectively. For this reason it is also known as our 'can do' judgement of self. Perceptions of self-efficacy influence how we feel, think and act (Bandura, 1997). Of all the self-constructs, self-efficacy is the most specific form of self-judgement. This means that we may have high self-efficacy for writing creative stories, for example, but low self-efficacy for writing argumentative essays. Self-efficacy is based on Albert Bandura's social cognitive theory of **human agency**, which is a belief that people can intentionally influence, control and direct their actions to make things happen (Bandura, 2001). It is through this sense of agency that our self-efficacy emerges.

When Albert Bandura first proposed this concept of human agency in 1977, it represented a significant shift from the behaviourist philosophy of the time. As discussed in Chapter 5, behaviourist approaches posited that humans had little or no influence over their own behaviour and instead learnt to respond to external forces. In contrast to these behaviourist philosophies, Bandura proposed that human behaviour was shaped by a combination of internal and external factors. He believed that human beings had the capacity to observe and learn from their social environment, internalising and forming cognitive beliefs about their experiences in the social world. This theory gradually became known as *social-cognitive theory*, reflecting the combined influences of social (external) and cognitive (internal) processes. These social and cognitive processes are reflected in four factors that are believed to build and shape our sense of efficacy (Bandura, 1997):

1   *Enactive mastery experience:* This refers to the valuable experience we gain from performing tasks successfully. A sense of success and mastery provides us with an 'I can do it!' attitude towards future tasks. Failing a task undermines this sense and does not build self-efficacy. For example, 15-year-old Sarah doesn't feel positive about her ability in English. Her Year 9 English classes are focusing heavily on essay writing and argumentative prose and Sarah has not achieved a high grade in these tasks; and thus she has not experienced mastery in English classes this year.

2   *Vicarious experience:* This refers to the experience we gain when we see others perform a task successfully. These modelling effects are strongest when the model is someone we can relate to, such as a peer. Seeing someone else complete a task successfully leads to an 'If they can do it, so can I' sense of belief (Pajares, 2002). Ten-year-old Jake has a strong perception of his skating ability and his skating skills have been enhanced by watching his peers master certain skating tricks. He thinks 'If they can do that trick, I can give it a try too'. The vicarious experience of seeing his peers perform a new trick successfully has a very powerful influence on his self-efficacy for trying the same tricks.

3   *Social persuasion:* This refers to the social and verbal feedback we get from other people. This feedback has a powerful persuasive force. If teachers are hoping to use persuasion, they must do it carefully and realistically within the bounds of the person's capability. Negative feedback undermines efficacy. Young children like Taylah are particularly susceptible to verbal persuasion from adults or older peers. Taylah's phrase 'I'm a big girl now' probably reflects adult forms of praise or persuasion when they are encouraging more 'grown-up' behaviours from Taylah as she gets ready to start school. As children get older, however, verbal persuasion such as praise needs to be more specific and closely related to the skill or task the child is trying to master. Self-efficacy develops when the verbal persuasion tells the

child they can be successful or were successful at a specific task, and especially when this is followed by or associated with a successful mastery experience.

4   *Our physiological and affective state:* Feelings caused by anxiety and stress (such as butterflies in the stomach or a depressed mood) provide us with important information about our sense of efficacy. Strong feelings and reactions act as a cue to warn us about our feelings of success or failure on a task. Sarah tells her mum that she feels sick on the morning of her English exam, but she seems relaxed on the morning of her Maths exam. Sarah's negative experiences with English have become associated with a physiological feeling in her stomach, further influencing her self-efficacy as she walks into the English exam.

Addressing teenagers' self-efficacy requires close attention to the sources of self-efficacy. Extensive research has demonstrated that self-efficacy can be enhanced with structured interventions to improve a wide range of life outcomes such as health, physical activity, smoking cessation, parenting and, of course, learning. Such interventions, whether they be in health or educational settings, provide opportunity for mastery experiences, effective models and positive verbal persuasion, and reduce the stress or anxiety the person may feel while trying the new tasks. These strategies are demonstrated in Box 4.2, which explains how teachers might intervene to increase the writing self-efficacy of students like Sarah, who finds essay writing difficult in her Year 9 English classroom.

BOX 4.2 CLASSROOM LINKS

INTERVENTIONS TO ENHANCE WRITING SELF-EFFICACY

For teenagers such as Sarah, the changing nature of the school curriculum can place additional demands on their sense of efficacy as the tasks became more demanding. Sarah's teachers realised that it was not only Sarah who appeared to be experiencing a decline in interest and engagement in English classes in the middle years of high school. They identified a number of students who appeared to be experiencing similar problems. An analysis of recent essays submitted by students revealed two common writing problems: some students appeared to have a weak understanding of essay-writing strategy, and others seemed to have good strategies but few skills in revising, proofreading or monitoring their own writing. The teachers decided to hold small-group workshops during their English classes where they targeted the development of these skills using specific self-regulation strategies, and through which they hoped to increase the writing self-efficacy of their students.

In the first group, the teachers employed a writing strategy intervention where they modelled and explained the steps of essay writing. At each step they carefully explained how valuable the step was by linking it to the argument in the essay. Students practised the strategy and took turns explaining to each other the steps they had used to build their argument. They were trained to give words of encouragement to their peers by pointing out the actual steps the peer had employed correctly and how these had improved their argument. Students also set personal achievement goals (a form of self-regulation) where they practised each step in an assigned essay writing task and evaluated the learning outcome, keeping a record of their progress against their essay-writing goals.

In the next group, teachers modelled writing revision strategies and employed peer modelling, where students shared their own writing examples during the tasks. Students were specifically taught how to reduce long or repetitive sentences into smaller, more succinct sentences by reducing redundant phrases and practising transitions between ideas and paragraphs. The teacher helped students understand the revision strategy by showing examples of her own writing and self-correcting, removing the redundancies and repetition and using transitional phrases to link ideas. Students then examined their own writing with the help of

>>

a peer and practised correcting their sentences using the steps that had been modelled. The teacher gave lots of positive feedback and specifically commented on how the steps taken had improved the sentences or flow of the paragraph as the students were practising. Finally, the students were set process goals and asked to record the number of steps practised correctly to arrive at improved sentences and paragraphs.

In both groups of learners, the teachers found that students improved. Sarah was a little bit ambivalent at first but said to her friend, 'Finally, it's like someone has given me a recipe for writing an essay! I know what an argument is now and I can do it step by step!' Learners in the revision group continued to use the revision strategies, and some kept working with their peers to review each other's work and correct sentences using the steps they had been shown. Both groups' sense of writing self-efficacy had improved.

Identifying the effective components of self-efficacy interventions

There are several examples of effective practices in these simple classroom interventions:

- *Enhancing self-regulation* – Each strategy is based on the principles of self-regulated learning by allowing opportunities to practise by the self, opportunities to set goals, and opportunities to self-regulate and employ the strategy by the self.
- *Mastery modelling* – Students have the chance to see a model effectively applying a self-correction strategy. This is much more effective for these students than simply viewing a model completing the skills effectively in the first place.
- *Peer modelling* – It can be useful to expose students to multiple models and multiple sources of persuasive feedback, both by seeing peers perform the strategy and also receiving feedback from peers. Students are likely to feel efficacious if they realise peers can do it too.
- *Feedback* – Positive and constructive feedback is an important source of verbal persuasion. It provides reassurance, and immediate correction avoids failure experiences. It is important that interventions monitor student performance, applying feedback and correcting skills as practice occurs.
- *Differentiated environments* – By placing students in small groups, teachers are able to address specific self-regulation goals and closely monitor each student. This differentiation may reduce anxiety and avoids potential boredom or distractions in students who may not need certain types of skill development.

Source: Adapted from evidence in Schunk and Zimmerman (2007).

---

self-regulation
A metacognitive activity that involves planning, directing and evaluating one's cognitive processes

Both self-efficacy and self-concept show similar levels of association with academic achievement. For example, the reciprocal effects model has also been demonstrated for academic performance and academic self-efficacy (Usher, 2015). Self-efficacy is particularly associated with **self-regulation** – a key factor associated with academic success. Self-regulated learning behaviours such as goal setting and self-monitoring of learning are associated with higher levels of self-efficacy (Zimmerman & Cleary, 2006). Individuals with a strong sense of self-efficacy for self-regulation are also able to manage their time well, organise themselves effectively and have lower levels of anxiety (Usher, 2015). Self-efficacy theory proposes that feeling efficacious promotes a sense of agency and control. Hence high-efficacy learners generally have a greater sense of control over their work and may even select more difficult tasks if given the choice. In contrast, learners with low self-efficacy often feel powerless and incompetent.

The sense of enablement that comes with high perceived self-efficacy is particularly important to adolescents who find themselves managing major biological, educational and social-role changes concurrently (Pajares & Urdan, 2006). In the school context, adolescents experience major environmental changes as they move from primary school to the high school environment. They experience new social arrangements, as they may have six or seven different classes with a different peer group in each. During this period, young adolescents may experience some loss of personal control, become less confident in their self, and experience lower levels of self-efficacy (Bandura, 1997; Eccles & Wigfield, 1995; Jacobs et al., 2002).

DEVELOPMENT OF OUR SENSE OF SELF

Our sense of self across the various self-constructs develops gradually and changes over time. Many of these changes are influenced by other processes of development, including the development of more sophisticated cognitive skills (such as abstract thinking) and improvement in our memory and language skills – quite simply, we become better at reflecting upon and describing ourselves in greater detail as we get older. As we grow older, we also acquire more life experience, information about our self greatly expands, and the number of categories of self-concept and self-efficacy beliefs also expands. As summarised in Table 4.1, in early childhood, children's self-descriptions are very much concerned with concrete and observable characteristics of the self. These self-descriptions are usually very positive, sometimes unrealistically so, as illustrated in the following account of exceptional feats of strength and bravery from a three-year-old: 'I can run real fast … I can kick a soccer ball real far … I can climb to the top of the jungle gym, I'm not scared! I'm never scared! … I'm really strong. I can lift this chair, watch me!' (Harter, 2012, p. 29).

As children move into middle childhood, they start developing categories of information about the self and can describe some strengths and weaknesses. They also start making comparisons to their younger self – recognising how much they have changed or improved. By later childhood, older children develop a firmer sense of stable characteristics and use a wider range of descriptive terms about the self, such as 'popular', 'smart', 'dumb' or 'nice' (Harter, 2012). When older children are using these terms, they also seem to understand that a person can be 'smart' or 'dumb' in different school subjects, or may be popular with their friends but still pretty shy when meeting new people.

TABLE 4.1 Development of sense of self over time

DEVELOPMENTAL STAGE	SELF STATEMENT	CHARACTERISTICS OF THE STATEMENT
Infancy	No language-based statements	Gradually comes to recognise self in mirror Attachment to caregivers forms a basis for a model of self
Early childhood	'I am a boy. I like soccer.'	Concrete self-perception based on appearance, observable characteristics and favoured activities
Middle childhood	'I watch my brother do it first, then I know I can do it!'	Descriptions become more elaborate, specific competencies noted, social comparison becomes an important source of self-perceptions
Adolescence	'I'm fairly shy with new people but I'm pretty "out there" with my friends!'	Interpersonal characteristics such as emotions, personality or other traits; differentiates ability and efficacy in different social contexts

FIGURE 4.4 Rejection by peers contributes to low sense of self

In adolescence, self-descriptions reveal stronger links with the social context of the individual, and show great sensitivity to social comparison and feedback from significant others, particularly peers. In contrast to the self-descriptions of younger children, adolescents are likely to use many more abstract terms to make higher-order generalisations about their self, such as 'I'm pretty intelligent' or 'Sometimes I'm simply an airhead' (Harter, 2012, p. 75). The sense of self grows in adolescence to acknowledge the multiple roles that a person may take on in different contexts, and the expanded range of skills and tasks to which the adolescent is exposed. Harter (2012) has also illustrated that adolescents' social self-understanding expands to include a clear distinction between the sense of self with friends versus the general peer group, and in later adolescence includes a romantic sense of self.

The social context appears to be particularly relevant during adolescence. The point of transition to high school has been identified as a vulnerable point when many adolescents report a decline in self-esteem and academic self-concepts (Eccles et al., 1989). Eccles and colleagues proposed that the changed environmental (and social) context of high school prompts such a decline. For example, researchers comparing 6th- to 9th-grade students found a successive decline in science self-efficacy from Grade 6 to Grade 9. The most significant decline occurred in Grade 9 when these students transitioned from middle school to high school (Lofgran, Smith & Whiting, 2015). However, other research has shown that self-esteem gradually grows and increases from age 14 through to adulthood (Erol & Orth, 2011).

There is also some evidence of gender differences in self-perceptions that are not easily summarised, as the research findings vary depending on domains of ability assessed. For example, studies often show that female students' self-perceptions for Science or Maths are consistently lower than male students' beliefs. This was demonstrated by Lofgran et al. (2015), in their study of science self-efficacy. However, research by Erol and Orth (2011) found that the self-esteem trajectories of male and female adolescents did not differ over time. Nevertheless, the most consistently significant gender differences across age groups are in the areas of physical appearance and physical ability, with girls reporting significantly worse body image than boys (Davidson & McCabe, 2006), and boys regularly expressing more positive views of their physical abilities than girls (Hau et al., 2005). These gender differences may be explained by the different sources of social persuasion or feedback or vicarious effects of

Source: Matthew Duchesne. © Milk and Honey Photography. 2010.

modelling and social comparison that may be experienced by both girls in boys in classrooms, family environments and the media.

Box 4.3 discusses programs and strategies that relate to building and enhancing self-concept, self-efficacy and self-esteem in the classroom.

BOX 4.3 IMPLICATIONS FOR EDUCATORS

BUILDING SELF-CONCEPT, SELF-EFFICACY AND SELF-ESTEEM

Enhancing learners' self-perceptions is central to teaching and preparing students for life beyond school. Many helpful programs have been developed to help teachers and young people, such as Kiwi Can in New Zealand (see www.dinglefoundation.org.nz/kiwican) and the Resiliency Resource Centre (http://resilienceresearch.org). KidsMatter (www.kidsmatter.edu.au) and MindMatters (www.mindmatters.edu.au) are particular resources for primary and secondary school teachers, with many strategies to use in the classroom. A common theme in these programs is valuing individuals for who they are and what they bring to the learning context. Suggested strategies include the following:

- Look for ways in which to monitor your students' self-perceptions, particularly when these are negative and may interfere with their learning, peer relationships and general wellbeing. This may involve looking for signs of self-deprecating statements, beliefs that they will fail tasks, and withdrawal or avoidance of tasks or playground situations.
- Build learner resilience by developing their strengths and enhancing their capacity to successfully adapt to stressful or changing circumstances.
- Teach self-regulatory strategies for goal setting, self-monitoring and self-correction. Help learners to see that they can succeed if they use strategies and a step-by-step approach to learning.
- Celebrate students' achievements but de-emphasise unhealthy comparisons and competition – all learners need to understand their personal strengths and see their work celebrated.
- Maintain a healthy sense of the learner's strengths and a sense of how they can improve upon areas of weakness. Look for opportunities to encourage and build strengths while working on areas in need of development.
- Provide 'can do' opportunities for all students to gain mastery and to experience success – self-efficacy depends on it.
- Look at the experience and achievements of the learner beyond the classroom, including their involvement in sport and community activities, as a way of fostering a positive area of self-perception.
- Examine the values you are promoting when you give feedback or pass judgement on students' work, bearing in mind that self-esteem is grounded on what the learner values.
- Value differences, whether they be of ethnicity, race, language, ability, gender, sexual orientation or appearance.
- Encourage peer-support programs and 'buddy programs' in which older students team up with younger students to offer them support. These focus on developing communication skills, self-confidence and self-esteem, and can help students resist peer-group pressure that may be harmful to them.

THINK ABOUT

- How will you identify students with low self-perceptions in your classroom?
- What practical strategies will you use to enhance student self-concept and build their self-efficacy in your teaching?

DEVELOPING AN IDENTITY

identity
An internal
self-structure in which
we organise our
beliefs, abilities, needs
and self-perceptions

Another 'self'-related concept is the notion of **identity**. While psychology has held a long interest in self-perceptions, another field of psychology has studied the concept of identity to explain the deeply personal quest to find out 'who we are'. Influenced by the earlier work of Sigmund Freud (1856–1939), psychologists began to adopt a **psychoanalytic approach** to explaining the personality, development and competence of individuals. Although psychoanalytic approaches have declined in influence, the notion of a 'search for identity' continues to play a central role in everyday language about the process of growing up, particularly during adolescence.

psychoanalytic approach
A theoretical stance
proposing that
personality develops
when children move
through a series of
stages that present
conflicts that have to
be resolved

ERIKSON'S THEORY OF IDENTITY DEVELOPMENT

Erik Erikson (1902–94) was a prominent identity theorist who studied the interrelationship between psychological development and the way individuals interact socially and with their environment. He argued that psychological and social facets of development occur concurrently and are interdependent. Erikson viewed development as occurring in stages, with development in each stage dependent on development in previous stages. According to this theory, the stages of development are invariant and build progressively on one another, yet they are qualitatively different.

Theory overview

psychosocial
development
Psychological
development in a
social context

Erikson proposed that we move through a series of eight **psychosocial development** stages in which our identity and sense of worth may be developed or crushed, depending on how we resolve issues and interact with others along the way. Each stage is characterised by a **psychosocial crisis**, or 'turning point' (see Table 4.2). During these turning points, we experience a temporary state of conflict and disequilibrium that must be resolved before we may move to the next stage of psychosocial development.

psychosocial crisis
A 'turning point', where
individuals experience
a temporary state
of conflict and
disequilibrium

According to Erikson, individuals face a choice between two ways of coping with these crises. One way is to resolve crises in a positive way, which leads to healthy personality development. The alternative is to resolve crises in a negative way, which leads to difficulties and problems in later stages if issues are unresolved. As individuals resolve crises they develop psychosocial strength, which in turn helps them move to the next stage. Erikson believed that those who fail to resolve particular conflicts may continue to struggle with these conflicts later in life. He saw the tension between negative and positive polarities as necessary for healthy psychosocial development. The ways in which individuals interact with others help to determine how each crisis will be managed.

Stages of identity development in the school years

Erikson's theory is very significant because it represents a lifespan view of development from birth to death. Table 4.2 identifies the characteristics of each stage of development. In each stage, the child's or adult's relationship with significant others is clearly implicated in how they resolve the psychosocial crisis.

The focus of this section is identity development in the school years addressed by Erikson's Stage 3 (ages four to six years) and Stages 4 and 5 (middle childhood and adolescence). Each of these stages presents implications for the relationships between teachers and their students.

The preschool and kindergarten years

The early years of preschool or school are described in Stage 3 as 'initiative versus guilt'. Young children may attempt to show initiative by trying adult activities such as cleaning house or attempting simple chores, and using toys that are just like Mum and Dad's 'big tools'. You might remember trying to show initiative in the kitchen by trying to make toast but burning it instead. If children are punished for such

TABLE 4.2 Erikson's stages of psychosocial development

STAGE (AGE)	PSYCHOSOCIAL CRISES	CHARACTERISTICS
1 Infancy (0–1 year)	Basic trust vs basic mistrust	Warm and responsive care leads to trust, while infants who are treated harshly or not comforted develop mistrust.
2 Early childhood (2–3 years)	Autonomy vs shame and doubt	Children desire autonomy and want to test new skills and abilities. Reasonable free choice can assist in development of autonomy. Discouragement can lead to shame and doubt.
3 Play age (4–6 years)	Initiative vs guilt	'Initiative' is a sense of independence and responsibility fostered when children are praised for new initiatives. Guilt emerges if adults exercise too much control and punish children for their actions.
4 School age (7–12 years)	Industry vs inferiority	Children develop a sense of 'industry' through school work and working with others. Inferiority develops when negative experiences and failure lead to self-doubt and incompetence. Teachers play a role in reinforcing a sense of competence.
5 Adolescence (13–18 years)	Identity vs role confusion	Adolescents search for a definition of their self and their place in society. Confusion arises when they remain uncertain about their place and future role in life. Peer groups and adult role models provide important feedback about identity.
6 Young adulthood (the 20s)	Intimacy vs isolation	Young adults try to achieve intimate ties to others, but isolation arises if they cannot form such ties and lasting relationships.
7 Adulthood (late 20s to late 50s)	Generativity vs stagnation/ self-absorption	'Generativity' refers to the act of giving to the next generation of people through child rearing, work or caring for other people. 'Stagnation' arises when we become 'self-absorbed' and do not take on a productive role in society.
8 Old age (60s and beyond)	Ego integrity vs despair	At about the age of retirement, individuals reflect on life and come to a sense of 'ego integrity', but despair is felt by those who are dissatisfied and fear dying.

Source: Adapted from Erikson, E. H. (1982). *The life cycle completed: A review*, pp. 32–3. © 1982, published by Rikan Enterprises

mistakes and made to feel guilty for being 'naughty', Erikson suggests that guilt and self-doubt arise in the young child. However, if children are praised or supported for taking initiative, they learn to try new things and test boundaries without feeling anxious or guilty. Erikson suggests that the central task of this stage of life is to build independence and autonomy without feeling too much guilt or shame.

Crises or 'turning points' emerge because children of this age are also starting to understand a range of more complex emotions, such as guilt and shame. Children may start to feel guilty when they misbehave or have ideas they believe to be wrong or unacceptable in the eyes of parents or significant others. A parent or carer may also promote feelings of guilt through punishing misbehaviour. Once again, Erikson argued for a balanced approach. The crisis or turning point must be managed to ensure children grow up with a healthy sense of responsibility. Encouraging children to take the initiative and to think for themselves, while considering the consequences of their actions, helps to promote a healthy personality in preparation for the next stage of psychosocial development.

The primary school years

Stage 4 spans the ages of approximately seven to 12 years. During Stage 4, most children are at school and industriously engaged in activities related to acquiring basic skills and the social and cultural tools that enable them to participate in society. The dominant task for children at this stage is to appreciate the value of industry and productive activities while avoiding an excessive sense of inferiority. Erikson understood that healthy or normative development must be understood within the context of each culture. In indigenous societies, for example, children may be educated within the wider family group – learning to track animals, find food or make utensils (Crain, 2000) – while in Western cultures, children typically attend school and learn basic literacy and numeracy skills.

FIGURE 4.5 Teacher feedback contributes to students' sense of industry or inferiority.

Children need to experience feelings of success, whether at home or in a wider learning environment, whether academically or socially (see Figure 4.5). If they experience repeated failure, they are likely to develop a sense of inferiority or incompetence. Additional sources of inferiority mentioned by Erikson include racism, sexism and other forms of discrimination. Teachers play a particularly important role (Erikson, 1959), as they can encourage skills and a sense of competence among learners.

Crises or turning points occur in this stage because children are seeking a balance between industry and inferiority, but the conflicts of earlier stages do not disappear. For example, young children starting school must develop trust in teachers and a sense of autonomy in their new school environment in order to develop as successful learners. Although each stage of the theory builds on the conflicts resolved in previous stages, people may revisit the conflicts of earlier stages when they encounter new social situations and contexts.

The high school years

Stage 5 describes the period of adolescence, beginning with puberty and ending at about 18 or 20 years of age. The primary task during adolescence is to develop an identity, which lays the foundation for adulthood. Although the identity-forming process is lifelong, it is most intense during adolescence (see also Erikson, 1997). Identity means knowing who you are and how you fit into the larger society. Think about all the roles you played as an adolescent: a son or daughter, a good mathematics student, a naughty student, a popular person, and many more. How did you balance all these roles? Were you satisfied with your identity or did you long to be someone else? This is all part of resolving the identity-versus-role-confusion conflict.

'Role confusion' may result when adolescents have difficulty deciding which roles to play in life, and may stem from uncertainty about their place in the world. The idea that adolescents are confronted by role confusion has led to the populist use of the phrase 'identity crisis' for this stage of life. The term 'crisis' should be used with caution, however. Some people have the perception that adolescence is, by definition, a tumultuous period characterised by rebellion, and that it is traumatic for parents, teachers and teenagers alike. You may know of some adolescents who fit this stereotype, but many adolescents pass through adolescence with little difficulty (Bandura, 1997). As a result of this stereotype, some researchers have set out to challenge these negative ideas about adolescent development. The Positive Youth Development (PYD) perspective (Eccles & Gootman, 2002; Roth & Brooks-Gunn, 2003) emphasises the strengths of positive development during adolescence by focusing on the 'Five Cs': competence, confidence, character, connection and caring (Lerner et al., 2012).

Erikson's use of the word 'crisis' was meant to reflect the fact that the stages of development reflect the interaction of the individual with the demands of their social context. As we discussed in the previous section on the development of self-perceptions, some personal and societal factors pose new challenges for adolescents. In particular, the onset of puberty means accommodating a new sense of the physical self as the body and physical appearance start to change (see Chapter 2), and the formation of sexual identity as interest in more intimate relationships develops. For some students, the development of sexual identity presents a real challenge, particularly those with gay or lesbian identities who may experience serious harassment and ostracism from their peers (Berlan et al., 2007;

Source: Getty Images/damircudic

FIGURE 4.6 What issues of identity might these students face over the next few years? What approaches could they take to dealing with identity?

Ford, 2004). Homophobic sentiments are a common form of sexual harassment in the middle years of high school, suggesting that sexual identity and related themes are frequent features of school bullying (Espelage, Basile, De La Rue & Hamburger, 2015).

Social, political and economic influences may also have an impact on adolescents' identity development. Harris (2006) documents a challenging social context for youth development in Australia and New Zealand. She suggests that young people growing up in each of these countries have experienced the positive features of an era that pays greater attention to basic human rights and freedoms, including antidiscrimination legislation and equal employment opportunity. These factors may present young people with many more freedoms than their parents' generation. At the same time, this freedom may be contradicted by economic or labour market forces that may mean 'freedoms' are curtailed in other ways, such as longer periods of mandatory school education, later entry to the workforce, and longer periods living at home. Teachers can play an important role in this stage of identity development, as teenagers look for appropriate role models and a trusting environment in which to discuss and share ideas during uncertain or changing periods of their life (see Box 4.4).

Identity status in adolescence

The period of adolescence has captured the attention of many researchers who have extended Erikson's seminal work, including Marcia (1980, 1993, 2002), who expanded on adolescent identity development. Marcia was interested in the developmental process by which adolescents *committed* to an identity, and the extent of this commitment (Kroger & Marcia, 2011). He developed an interview

identity achievement
Occurs when adolescents explore several identity roles, but resolve conflicts and feel comfortable with who they are and who they hope to be

identity foreclosure
Describes adolescents who typically form their identity by adopting the occupational and ideological goals of significant others, often their parents

identity diffusion
Occurs when young people have little direction, their life and career goals are unclear, and they do not know who they are or who they want to be

moratorium
Refers to the state of adolescents who postpone making a definitive commitment to a single identity or set of values

measure of this commitment and proposed four identity statuses – **identity achievement, identity foreclosure, identity diffusion** and **moratorium** – which describe the ways in which adolescents attempt to resolve the conflict of identity versus role-confusion. These four statuses are outlined in Table 4.3.

Marcia believed that the central task of adolescence is about recognising the need to develop an identity in preparation for adult life, and that true identity achievement occurs when the adolescent has made a commitment to an identity pathway. However, the avoidance of any commitment can cause role confusion, and not exploring different roles or pathways can prematurely shut off or 'foreclose' on a sense of identity. The process of committing to an identity has been linked to self-esteem, anxiety and a range of other factors. Adolescents in the status of identity achievement, for example, generally have the highest self-esteem (Ryeng, Kroger & Martinussen, 2013). In contrast, those in moratorium generally have higher anxiety scores (Lillevoll, Kroger & Martinussen, 2013). Subsequent research has confirmed Marcia's classification of identity (Meeus, 2011) but has also refined ideas about how identity develops. Rather than viewing identity as a series of stages or steps, researchers tend to view identity formation as a continuous process of moving between commitment, exploration of those commitments and then reconsideration of those commitments (Meeus, van de Schoot, Keijsers & Branje, 2011).

TABLE 4.3 Marcia's four identity statuses

IDENTITY STATUS	DESCRIBES YOUNG PEOPLE WHO:
Identity achievement	• May have explored several identity roles, but have resolved the conflicts and generally feel comfortable with who they are and who they hope to be • Pursue self-chosen occupations or studies and ideological goals
Identity foreclosure	• Avoid the dilemma of role confusion by adopting the occupational and ideological goals of significant others such as parents, but also of religious cults, militaristic organisations or groups divorced from mainstream society • May follow in the footsteps of others without working through identity issues for themselves
Identity diffusion	• Have no direction for the future • Are unclear about their goals and do not know what occupation to pursue • Have not made any decision about their identity and may feel confused and frustrated
Moratorium	• Postpone a definitive commitment to a single identity or set of values • Choose to take time out between childhood and adulthood before making a commitment about who they want to be • Experiment with different roles in areas such as gender, occupation and family

Source: Adapted from Marcia (1980, p. 161).

THINK ABOUT

Think about the sense of identity in each of Erikson's and Marcia's stages.

■ Can you remember passing through any of these stages?

■ Why are teenagers in a state of 'moratorium' likely to experience higher anxiety?

■ What are some of the ways in which a teacher can support the formation of positive self-identity?

Strengths and limitations of Erikson's theory

Erikson's theory has much to offer the classroom teacher, but the theory's benefits and utility should always be interpreted in light of its possible limitations.

A stage theory

Erikson's stage approach is helpful because it provides a framework for interpreting psychosocial development across the lifespan. However, stage theories have limitations (see Chapter 3). For example, Erikson describes a single central conflict in each psychosocial stage, whereas in reality, individuals confront many conflicts that may not be restricted to particular stages. Questions have also been raised about the universal applicability of the order of stages and the relevance of this theory's lock-step approach to development. For this reason, some theorists prefer the terms 'phases' or 'transitions' rather than 'stages'.

The role of society and culture

A useful aspect of Erikson's theory is his emphasis on the role of social relationships in development. This is especially important for classroom teachers, as they need to understand their students' development in social and cultural contexts. However, Erikson's theory is primarily Western in orientation, and many argue that his stages do not apply across cultures and across historical contexts. For example, Barrett (2000) questions whether Stage 2 (autonomy versus shame and doubt) holds true for collectivistic cultures (see the next section, 'The self across cultures') in which autonomy and independence are not valued as highly as they are in individualistic cultures. Erikson and other researchers have argued that the general stage pattern and characteristic psychosocial crises do hold across cultures (Wang & Viney, 1996), although social and cultural factors play a significant role in shaping identity (see, for example, Comunian & Gielen, 2000).

Biological determinism

A controversial aspect of Erikson's work is his assumption (in agreement with Freud) that personality differences between the sexes are biologically based. Erikson believed that we are genetically programmed to proceed through stages of development, and that our biological make-up interacts with social and cultural factors to contribute to development. Some theorists have challenged this view, seeing it as deterministic and problematic.

Gender differences

Critics of Erikson's theory say the theory is more applicable to males than to females. Gilligan (1982) argued that Erikson's focus on autonomy, independence and industry is more characteristic of males than of females, who tend to consider themselves in terms of relationships rather than in terms of separateness and individuality.

In balance, Erikson's theory offers several important insights into the interrelationships between physical, psychological and emotional development in a social context, and has inspired ongoing research, particularly in the area of identity development. Erikson's work has many practical implications for classroom teachers.

The table in Box 4.4 gives guidelines and examples for activities with students in stages 3 to 5.

BOX 4.4 IMPLICATIONS FOR EDUCATORS

Erikson's theory of psychosocial development has several implications for classroom practitioners. **Table 4.4** below presents guidelines and sample activities for classroom application.

TABLE 4.4 Erikson's psychosocial stages in the classroom

STAGE	GUIDELINES FOR TEACHERS	EXAMPLES OF ACTIVITIES FOR EACH STAGE
Stage 3: Initiative vs guilt (preschool and early primary years)	Foster initiative and creativity; encourage responsibility; balance punishment for wrongdoing with encouragement of individuality	• Encourage students to make decisions about a group project or about how a game will be played • Allocate free-choice time where learners select their activity • Be flexible and listen to students' ideas. If they suggest inappropriate or dangerous activities, discuss ways of reworking their suggestions in acceptable ways rather than discouraging and ignoring them
Stage 4: Industry vs inferiority (primary school years)	Value hard work and industry; encourage individuals to do their best no matter what their ability; some competition is healthy, but discourage excessive competition, which may lead to feelings of inferiority and low self-worth	• Set tasks to match students' ability levels, being aware of each learner's abilities and trying to develop activities accordingly • Provide choices to allow for different interests and abilities • Help students to set learning goals for themselves to encourage a sense of achievement • Be patient when students make mistakes. Avoid public humiliation. When students feel they are not keeping up with their peers, they will want to give up, so develop individual learning programs and encourage students to work at their own pace • Acknowledge successes outside the classroom in sport or other endeavours
Stage 5: Identity vs role confusion (high school years)	Provide opportunities to explore and discuss different identities and viewpoints; be aware that adolescents will experiment with different roles; be observant regarding potential risk-taking and harmful behaviours; encourage open communication with parents, teachers, peers and significant others; be supportive, especially during students' times of uncertainty	• Invite guest speakers to discuss relevant life issues such as safe driving. Provide role models, such as sportspeople, who discuss the value of healthy life choices • Provide a forum for students to discuss problems and share ideas. This should be done in a safe classroom environment. Adolescents appreciate the opportunity to express themselves in writing; they may also use online technologies or some other medium • Acknowledge students' interests: learn a bit about their sports, magazines or music, and provide for this in assignments – for example, one assignment topic could be based on a hobby or sports magazine of their choice (which you have approved!)

THE SELF ACROSS CULTURES

As Erikson acknowledged, the self should be understood in light of our relationships with others and our environment, recognising that cultural contexts bring unique perspectives to the question of self or identity. Culture plays a critical role in determining how we view ourselves, how we relate to others and what we value. Until the late 20th century, most of the documented theories of self came from Western researchers, but research indicates that views of self differ across cultures (see, for example, Purdie et al., 2000; Wang, 2004). One way of explaining these differences is to categorise cultures into 'individualistic' and 'collectivistic' cultures, and to contrast them (although conclusions that arise from such a generalised approach should be treated cautiously).

In **individualistic cultures** the focus is on the individual self, which is thought of as autonomous and unique. The successful pursuit of individual goals is most highly regarded in such cultures. Western societies such as those of the United States of America and Australia are typically classified as individualistic societies. On the other hand, **collectivistic cultures** tend to be group-centred, viewing individuals in terms of their relationships with others in a cohesive community group.

In collectivistic cultures, focusing on individual goals may seem rude or even be a cause for embarrassment or shame (Shweder & Haidt, 2000), as individuals are typically defined in terms of their roles, responsibilities and relationships within their community. Although the multidimensional nature of self-concept holds true for both Indigenous and non-Indigenous Australians (Purdie & McCrindle, 2004), it has been suggested that some Indigenous Australian youth may also base their identity on factors such as kinship group, sense of communal history, language, traditional practices and place (Purdie et al., 2000) (see Figure 4.7).

Similarly, Heine (2001) argues that in many East Asian cultures, the sense of self is bound up in knowing one's relationships and obligations to others; in this sense, the self is based on interdependence between the self and others. One shortcoming of categorising cultures as either 'individualistic' or 'collectivist' is that escalating globalisation means that boundaries between the views and values of different cultures are increasingly blurred (see, for example, Cha, 1994). For example, New Zealand combines the typically individualistic cultures of Western societies with the collectivist values of the Māori cultures. Similarly, in Australia, Western individualistic cultural values exist beside collectivist values such as those of Australian Indigenous cultures or Confucian-heritage cultures. These cultural groups influence one another as they interact.

Another limitation of the individualist–collectivist dichotomy is that cultures comprise complex social and cultural subgroups. Nevertheless, the individualist–collectivist categorisation provides general principles that may help you to better understand the young people you work with.

> **individualistic culture** Focuses on the self as an autonomous individual; successful pursuit of individual goals is valued

> **collectivistic culture** Typically group-centred, viewing individuals in terms of their relationships, roles and responsibilities in the community

FIGURE 4.7 A sense of belonging to a cultural group stems from communal activities, shared values and common goals.

Source: © David Hancock/Alamy.

UNDERSTANDING OTHERS

So far, we have learnt that the development of self-understanding is a complex process influenced by many factors, including those of a social and cultural nature. We now consider the interaction between self-understanding and our understanding of other people. In this section, moral development is explored along with emotional development, specifically our ability to understand other people because of these developmental processes.

MORAL DEVELOPMENT

morality
The fundamental questions of right and wrong, justice, fairness and basic human rights

As children's sense of self develops, they encounter situations that extend and challenge their thinking about what is 'moral'. **Morality** is concerned with fundamental questions of right and wrong, justice, fairness and basic human rights. Cultural values and norms have a strong bearing on how individuals think and act, so notions of 'morality' are mediated by sociocultural factors (Miller & Bland, 2013). The study of moral development in educational psychology is particularly interested in how young people develop or learn a sense of right and wrong, and how they learn to reason about challenging social or moral issues.

Moral development as socialisation

Like other dimensions of development, moral development progresses gradually. There are several views about how this occurs. One approach argues that children develop morals as a result of gradual immersion and socialisation into the adult world (Leman, 2001). This view adopts the principles of social learning theory (see Chapter 5). Social learning theorists such as Bandura (1977, 2001) contend that we learn to behave in moral or immoral ways primarily by observing others, particularly parents, caregivers and significant others such as teachers and peers. The view that moral development is moulded by society's values has been supported by theorists who claimed that the quality of children's relationships with their parents greatly influences moral development (for example, Durkheim, 1925/1961; Freud, 1930/1963). Clearly, this view is limited by the fact that people do not always conform to social values and sometimes they deliberately violate cultural norms of behaviour, but these behaviours are not necessarily immoral. For example, people may choose to stand up against something they see as unjust, even though that practice or belief is rooted in social values.

FIGURE 4.8 We learn to behave morally, in part, by observing parents and significant others

Moral development as moral reasoning

An alternative to the socialisation approach is the argument that children actively construct their own ways of understanding the world, including what is right and wrong, good and bad. This seems to be evident in Jake's comments about his friend Jonno's behaviour at the start of this chapter. Cognitive–developmental approaches emphasise moral reasoning rather than moral behaviour alone, yet they do not rule out the impact of social context. Moral reasoning involves analytical thinking about why we respect and follow 'moral rules' (Piaget, 1932). A moral rule is a generally accepted rule about human behaviour within a particular society. For example, 'You should not steal' is a moral rule in most Western communities (Langford, 1995), and Jake appears to be developing a reasoned moral stance on this issue.

Piaget and moral reasoning

moral dilemma
A moral problem requiring individual judgements and moral reasoning

Piaget proposed that cognitive development is connected to the individual's ability to reason morally. To test his theory, Piaget developed carefully constructed stories, or a **moral dilemma**, about issues such as clumsiness, stealing and lying that are relevant to the lives of children and adolescents. The stories were designed to provoke a judgement about the level of guilt or naughtiness of the young people in the story. Piaget's findings led him to describe two types of moral reasoning, which are closely aligned with cognitive development: heteronomous morality and autonomous morality.

Source: Matthew Duchesne, © Milk and Honey Photography, 2010.

Heteronomous morality is typical of younger children (aged four to 10 years). It focuses on following rules unswervingly and obeying authority figures such as parents, whose moral authority is supreme. Children who reason about moral issues using heteronomous morality do not consider the motives or intentions behind actions. Heteronomous morality is most typical of children; the ages given are only a guide, as some adults are thought to operate at this level of moral reasoning.

The ability to reason about moral issues at a deeper level is known as **autonomous morality**, and is characterised by a capacity for appreciating the perspectives of others and the motives behind words and actions. The development of autonomous morality parallels the development of formal operations and abstract thought, which typically occurs at approximately 10 or 11 years old and continues through to adulthood. Jake seems to be right on the cusp of developing an autonomous sense of morality.

Piaget's theory was broadly correct about the change in moral reasoning over time, but, as illustrated by Kohlberg's expansion of the theory, the development of children's moral reasoning is more extensive than that envisaged in Piaget's two stages. In particular, young children are not quite as limited in moral understanding as the heteronomous stage would suggest.

heteronomous morality
Moral decisions based on the rules of authority figures such as parents

autonomous morality
Moral reasoning that appreciates the perspectives of others and the motives behind their words and actions

KOHLBERG'S THEORY OF MORAL DEVELOPMENT

Like Piaget, Kohlberg believed that the development of moral reasoning was closely linked to cognitive development, and used a moral dilemma to explore this. The 'Heinz dilemma' (Box 4.6), which formed the basis of much of Kohlberg's research, was presented to research participants; their answers provided insight into their moral reasoning. From this, he proposed a six-stage sequence of moral development within three broad levels (see Table 4.5). Moving from one stage to the next requires a combination of cognitive development and socialisation. As we interact with others, learn to appreciate differing viewpoints and have our own views challenged, our mental processes are stimulated and we develop new ways of interpreting the world and making moral judgements.

BOX 4.5 ABOUT LAWRENCE KOHLBERG

Lawrence Kohlberg (1927–87) grew up in New York and attended Andover Academy, an academically demanding private school in Massachusetts. In 1948, Kohlberg enrolled at the University of Chicago, where he completed graduate work in psychology. He soon became interested in Piaget's work and began interviewing children and adolescents on moral issues. Kohlberg taught at the University of Chicago from 1962 to 1968 and at Harvard University from 1968 until his death in 1987.

Kohlberg was an unassuming man. When he taught, he frequently went to class dressed in a flannel shirt and baggy pants – as though he had thought it was his day off. In the first days of the university year, students did not always know what to make of him, but they soon realised they were in the presence of a true scholar – a man who had thought long and deeply about critical issues in philosophy and psychology. Unfortunately, Kohlberg suffered from a tropical disease that caused him intense pain at the age of 59, he walked into a river and drowned; it is believed he may have ended his own life.

Source: Getty Images/Lee Lockwood/Time & Life Pictures.

FIGURE 4.9 Lawrence Kohlberg.

Source: Adapted from Crain, William, *Theories of development: Concepts & applications*, 4e, © 2000, pp. 147–8. Adapted by permission of Pearson Education, Inc., Upper Saddle River, NJ.

THE STAGES IN KOHLBERG'S THEORY

preconventional morality
Morality is seen as a set of rules handed down by adults

conventional morality
Being a good member of society and helping those close to you is a priority

postconventional morality
Individuals move beyond the conventional rules of their community to focus more broadly on what is best for society at large, and on ways of promoting justice in society

In Level I (**preconventional morality**), children do not yet see themselves as members of society, and understand morality as a set of rules handed down by adults. As children move from Stage 1 to Stage 2, they begin to see that there may be different views on a single issue. However, they are still self-focused and reason in terms of what will benefit them. In Level II (**conventional morality**), older children and adolescents start to see themselves as conventional members of society. In Stage 3, being a good person and helping those close to you, such as family and friends, is a priority. As the individual moves to Stage 4, the reasons for behaving morally revolve around obeying society's laws in order to maintain law and order.

In Level III (**postconventional morality**), the focus is on what is best for society and on ways of promoting justice. While in Level II the smooth functioning of society is paramount, in Level III people begin to ask 'How can we improve society?' and 'What is just and fair for all?' In Stage 5, for example, individuals may argue that it is appropriate to break some laws if this means protecting the rights of all. At this highest stage it is possible to suggest a range of responses to the Heinz dilemma (see Box 4.6): it is right to steal the drug because the right to life is a value above all else; it was wrong to steal the drug because others may need it too; stealing it prevents everyone from benefiting from the drug. However, due to difficulties with scoring responses at this stage, Kohlberg eventually labelled it a 'theoretical' stage and collapsed stages 5 and 6 in his later analyses (Colby, Kohlberg & Kauffman, 1987).

TABLE 4.5 Kohlberg's stage theory

LEVEL I: PRECONVENTIONAL MORALITY	
Stage 1 Heteronomous morality	• Avoidance of breaking rules for fear of punishment • Obedience for obedience's sake
Stage 2 Individualism, instrumental purpose and exchange	• Acting in accordance with individual interests – fairness is an equal exchange based upon motivations of self-interest
LEVEL II: CONVENTIONAL MORALITY	
Stage 3 Mutual interpersonal expectations, relationships and interpersonal conformity	• Living up to what is expected of you • Mutual relations of trust and respect should be maintained provided they conform to your expected social role
Stage 4 Social system and conscience	• Rules are to be upheld except when they conflict with other social duties • Right is contributing to society and fulfilling social duties
LEVEL III: POSTCONVENTIONAL MORALITY	
Stage 5 Social contract or utility and individual rights	• Awareness of the social contract between individuals, but also of the different moral perspectives of others • Some individual rights, however, transcend the different perspectives of others and therefore should be upheld
Stage 6 Universal ethical principles	• Following self-chosen ethical principles • When such principles conflict with existing moral standards, these principles should be upheld regardless of majority opinion

Source: Adapted from Weiten, W. (2001). *Psychology: Themes and variations* (with InfoTrac), 5th edn, p. 455, Figure 11.16, Reprinted with permission of Wadsworth, a division of Cengage Learning.

CourseMateExpress

Online resources
Explore an example of moral development stages with the
Interactive Activity

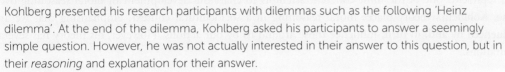

KOHLBERG AND THE HEINZ DILEMMA

Kohlberg presented his research participants with dilemmas such as the following 'Heinz dilemma'. At the end of the dilemma, Kohlberg asked his participants to answer a seemingly simple question. However, he was not actually interested in their answer to this question, but in their *reasoning* and explanation for their answer.

In Europe, a woman was near death from a particular kind of cancer. There was one drug that doctors thought might save her – a form of radium that a pharmacist in the same town had recently discovered. The drug was expensive to produce, but the pharmacist was charging 10 times the cost of production – it cost him $200 to make a small dose of the radium and he charged $2000 per dose. The sick woman's husband, Heinz, went to everyone he knew to borrow the money, but he could only raise about $1000. He told the pharmacist that his wife was dying and asked him to sell the drug cheaper or let him pay later. But the pharmacist said: 'No, I discovered the drug and I'm going to make money from it.' Heinz became desperate and broke into the pharmacy to steal the drug for his wife.

Should Heinz have done that? Why or why not?

Source: Adapted from Kohlberg (1963, p. 19).

NEO-KOHLBERGIANS

Some theorists have rejected Kohlberg's view of morality, but neo-Kohlbergians contend that his theory is still valid, although some elements require modification. Recognising the limitations of a stage theory, Rest (1979, 1986) built on Kohlberg's work and proposed the Four-component Model for describing moral behaviour. Rest initially presented moral understanding as one of four interactive psychological processes, and later added a fifth process known as moral character:

- *moral judgement* – being able to judge the ethics of possible responses; to weigh up and judge the merits of different arguments and positions
- *moral sensitivity* – being sensitive to the emotions and interpretations of others
- *moral motivation* – the goals and drives of our moral decisions and behaviours; can we put others' needs or perspectives before our own?
- *moral action* – once a moral decision has been made, implementing the decision with sensitivity; being able to communicate the decision to others and express reasons for actions
- *moral character* – having strength in your convictions; being courageous and persisting despite obstacles (Bebeau, Rest & Narvaez, 1999; Rest, 1986).

Rest emphasised that moral judgement is a process of deciding what is a moral thing to do in a moral dilemma. According to Rest and other neo-Kohlbergians, moral judgements reflect a person's underlying organisation of thought about matters of right and wrong. Rest and colleagues (Rest, 1986; Rest & Narvaez, 1994) developed an instrument – the Defining Issues Test (DIT) – that highlights the role of moral judgement in moral development (see also Rest, Thomas & Edwards, 1997). Neo-Kohlbergians like Rest have responded to the limitations of Kohlberg's theory by examining the role of factors such as age and education trends, cross-cultural issues and educational interventions in moral development.

CourseMateExpress

Online resources
Go further: Read more about the Defining Issues Test on this text's website

STRENGTHS AND LIMITATIONS OF KOHLBERG'S THEORY

Kohlberg's theory provides a comprehensive guide for understanding how moral reasoning progresses, and represents one of the most coherent attempts to chart the development of moral reasoning over time. Kohlberg's theory places moral reasoning in a sociocultural context, emphasising that we are influenced by and, in turn, influence those around us by our actions. However, his theory has several limitations.

Moral reasoning versus moral behaviour

An important assumption of cognitive approaches is the belief that our reasoning or understanding is a driving force for our behaviour. Indeed, higher levels of moral reasoning are related to positive interactions with others (Schonert-Reichl, 1999; Walker, Hennig & Krettenhauer, 2000). However, there are many examples in everyday life in which people's capability to reason morally is not necessarily associated with their behaviour. Take the example of damage to someone else's property, such as a scratch or dent in your car the last time you parked in a public car park. Did the perpetrator leave a note to explain the damage, or offer compensation? Perhaps they didn't. Most adults would probably believe it is wrong to damage someone else's property, but many adults may not uphold this behaviour themselves, such as in the example given above. As we will see below, some people have questioned the role of stages in defining the level of moral reasoning, with some evidence that people slip between stages as the circumstances dictate.

Problems with stages

We have learnt (see Chapter 3) that stage theories can be problematic, and a number of criticisms have been levelled at Kohlberg's theory in this regard. First, it must be stated that a wide range of longitudinal research shows that people *do* generally progress through the stages in the predicted sequence (for example, Colby et al., 1983; Rest, 1986). However, the stages are not self-contained: children may be predominantly in one stage, but may reason at a different stage depending on the situation. There is some evidence that real-life moral dilemmas result in slightly lower levels of reasoning, perhaps because the circumstances or the personal stakes are higher. For example, moral reasoning is lower in dilemmas that indicate the person may be punished or negatively affected in some way (Sobesky, 1983). Do you think this may explain the way adults resolve the 'car park dilemma' when owning up (or not!) to damaging someone else's property? Could their fear of 'punishment', or of having to pay for the damage, affect their level of moral reasoning?

Cultural considerations

Another problem associated with the stage-based theory is the assumption that the stages are universal or applicable to all people. Kohlberg (1987) argued that his theory holds true across cultures, based on research in such countries as India, Taiwan, Kenya, Japan and Israel. These findings were supported by other researchers at the time (for example, Power, Higgins & Kohlberg, 1989; Snarey, 1985), many of whom were Kohlberg's contemporaries (see contradictory evidence below).

Recent research has considered in greater depth the elements of cultural difference in the way people reason and develop morally. This research has found that cultural variations do exist, and Kohlberg's theory has been criticised for failing to take account of the importance of cultural differences, social conventions and contexts on the development of moral reasoning (Miller & Bersoff, 1992). Nucci (2001) argues strongly that moral reasoning is connected to the social conventions and the sociocultural contexts in which individuals live. There is some evidence, for example, that people holding predominantly individualistic cultural values (such as those dominant in Australia and in the United Kingdom) interpret moral questions differently from people in typically collectivistic cultures (such as those of Japan and India) (Markus & Kitayama, 1991). The concern with any generalisation about moral reasoning in any culture is that these cultures are far from homogeneous, and the effects of increasing globalisation will no doubt spur further research in this area.

Gender roles

An important limitation of Kohlberg's initial research was the fact that it was conducted exclusively with males aged 10 to 16 years who came from middle- and lower-class families in Chicago. Moreover, Kohlberg's moral dilemmas are predominantly male-oriented, such as Heinz's dilemma (see Box 4.6). One of Kohlberg's own PhD students, Carol Gilligan, raised concerns about the gender bias in Kohlberg's research (Gilligan, 1982). Gilligan argued that girls reason in a different way (probably because they are socialised into the female gender role) and their moral reasoning is centred around an 'ethic of care' and concern for others. This level of reasoning is reflected at stages 3 and 4 of Kohlberg's model, which is seen as a lesser level of moral reasoning. However, later studies have shown that both males and females reason in similar ways about the Kohlbergian dilemmas (Jadack, Hyde, Moore & Keller, 1995; Walker, 1995), with some notable differences for females in certain areas, as will be discussed below (Garmon, Bassinger, Gregg & Gibbs, 1996).

Despite these limitations, Kohlberg's theory has inspired ongoing research and debate in the field of moral development. Later research on moral development is an example of this.

THINK ABOUT

- Kohlberg argued for a connection between emotional development and moral reasoning. Can you explain some ways that emotion may be linked to moral reasoning?
- Should principles such as 'always tell the truth' or 'never cheat' be taught as absolute principles (that is, as being always the case), or as qualified principles (that is, as being sometimes the case)? Can you think of examples or contexts that might run counter to absolutist moral positions such as these? (Adapted from Leming, 2000.)

FURTHER PERSPECTIVES ON MORAL DEVELOPMENT AND VALUES

There are ongoing debates about what is of value in moral terms, whether there is a universal core set of values that binds individuals across cultures, and whether or not educators play a role in moral development. We cannot examine all these questions here, but we encourage you to consider them carefully for yourself and in your class discussions.

Several other theories have been proposed, including Gilligan's ideas of female moral development.

GILLIGAN'S THEORY OF FEMININE MORAL REASONING

As outlined above, Gilligan (1982) raised significant concerns about Kohlberg's theory of moral development, noting that the primarily male orientation of Kohlberg's theory centres on concerns about justice, rules and rights as reasons for acting morally. Her research on women's morality found that women considered interpersonal relationships, connections between people, compassion and care for others as important reasons for behaving morally. Gilligan contended that, because males and females reason differently about moral dilemmas, females tend to score lower than males on Kohlberg's scoring system.

Gilligan's views have been challenged (Crain, 2000; Walker, 1984; see also Evans, Forney & Guido-DiBrito, 1998), but there is general acceptance that there are two different moral orientations: one focusing on justice and one motivated by care and compassion. Although studies show that the care orientation tends to be more apparent among women and girls (Garmon, Bassinger, Gregg & Gibbs, 1996), another approach is to realise that both the justice and the care-and-compassion orientations may exist in females and males. For example, Vikan, Camino and Biaggio (2005) found no relationship between gender and an ethic-of-care orientation. Gilligan (1982) herself acknowledged that, as people progress in their moral development, the two orientations become more closely connected and integrated in both sexes (see also Walker, DeVries & Trevethan, 1987).

EISENBERG'S THEORY OF PROSOCIAL MORAL REASONING

Prosocial moral reasoning is concerned with social dilemmas in which our thinking is in conflict with another person's needs, in situations where laws or rules don't apply (Carlo, 2006). Examples of prosocial reasoning include the development of beliefs about helping others, showing empathy and concern or resolving conflicts. Like Kohlberg, Nancy Eisenberg (1986, 1989) also adopted a stage-based theory to explain prosocial moral reasoning. As with other stage-based theories we have studied (for example, Piaget and Kohlberg), Eisenberg's model shows children moving through more egocentric or 'hedonistic' stages, to having a greater concern for others, and incorporation of more abstract views of dignity, rights and equality (Eisenberg, 1982). However, Eisenberg believed that people could move across stages depending on the context and demands of the situation, although her research has found that higher levels of reasoning are associated with age-based advances in thinking. A number of researchers have found strong links between high levels of prosocial moral reasoning and prosocial behaviour (Carlo, 2006). Emotional capacities, such as the ability to have empathy and sympathy, are also linked to prosocial behaviours that, in turn, are linked to the ability to inhibit aggression or antisocial behaviours, and to show greater community awareness and greater sensitivity to intergroup processes (Eisenberg, Eggum & Di Giunta, 2010).

There are also some suggestions that confirm Gilligan's thoughts about the care-and-concern orientation of girls and women. Longitudinal research has found some gender differences in prosocial moral reasoning (Eisenberg, Hofer, Sulik & Liew, 2014), leading the authors to conclude that women tended to use more sophisticated prosocial reasoning than men during the course of the study. Prosocial reasoning is also considered very important in the emotional development of children, as we will see later in this chapter.

BANDURA'S THEORY OF MORAL AGENCY AND DISENGAGEMENT

Employing his social-cognitive theory, Bandura strongly believes that moral agency is the linking concept between moral behaviour and moral reasoning (Bandura, 2002). Moral agency describes the use of self-regulatory processes to mediate the link between moral reasoning and moral behaviour. In this view, people are capable of monitoring their conduct and the situations in which certain behaviours occur, they are capable of self-assessing or evaluating their response against their own moral standards, and they may moderate their behaviour through feelings of guilt or acknowledging that their behaviour is wrong. Bandura is particularly interested in why people choose to ignore known moral standards and engage in moral behaviours that don't match these standards. He called this moral disengagement. This theory proposes that humans self-activate or self-regulate the application of these moral standards and, most critically, are also capable of deactivating or disengaging from these same moral standards. Bandura termed these 'psychological manoeuvres' in which a person could disengage these standards from reprehensible or inhumane conduct (Bandura, 2002, p. 102). Obvious examples of such reprehensible or inhumane conduct might be seen in catastrophic acts of human genocide, torture or other acts that run so counter to typical moral standards.

More recently, the theory of moral disengagement has been employed to examine a range of other puzzling inhumane acts such as engagement in political or religious extremism (Lieber, Efreom-Lieber & Rate, 2010), organisational unethical behaviour or corruption (Moore et al., 2012) and cyberbullying (Bussey, Fitzpatrick & Raman, 2014). Moral disengagement is emerging as a novel way to view the disjuncture between moral reasoning and moral behaviour.

CourseMateExpress

Online resources
Watch a **video**
interview with Albert
Bandura that discusses
moral disengagement

MORAL DEVELOPMENT IN EDUCATION

One of the other questions raised by the study of moral development concerns the role of school education in teaching students about moral behaviour. In recent years, a range of terms have been used – including 'values education' and 'character education' – to express this debate. Haydon (2004) argues that, just as we have responsibility for the quality of the physical environment in which we live, so we should collectively attend to the quality of the ethical environment by integrating values into education. However, he acknowledges that teachers might be understandably cautious of exactly what their role should be in promoting this notion of values and ethics. Haydon suggests that the notion of ethics and values in education need not be seen as very different from what teachers are already doing in their classrooms, in so far as they are concerned with maintaining a suitable ethical environment for their students. However, Haydon cautions that there may be greater concern about values education approaches that suggest a one-dimensional view, which might be promoted to all schools through a common program. Rather, schools are quite pluralistic environments, in which a range of different viewpoints could be considered healthier (Haydon, 2004).

In the past decade, Australia has strongly promoted values education at a curriculum level. For example, New South Wales has trialled a secular ethics curriculum for students in years 5 and 6, resulting in positive engagement from students and increased use of ethical principles in their responses to ethical problems (NSW Department of Education and Training, 2010). Core values are acknowledged in multiple curriculum frameworks around Australia and in New Zealand. For instance, in New Zealand, Māori values, including spirituality, are integrated into the national curriculum for secular schools. A study of Māori teachers (Fraser, 2004) highlighted their shared view that moral decisions often reflect spiritual beliefs and practices. Fraser argues that schooling has a moral obligation to reflect indigenous values if understanding, respect and cultural identity are to be maintained and fostered.

Webster (2007) and Noddings (2002) have also raised concerns about the promotion of generalised approaches to values and character education, identifying some practices as potentially 'indoctrinatory' and stifling students' ability to raise questions or debate the values being promoted. For example, Webster suggests that rather than children being expected to conform to a single, 'universal' set of values, it may be more relevant to foster the capacity of students to think critically and evaluate values.

THINK ABOUT

- What are your views about moral values in education? Do you agree that ethical or spiritual values should form part of the school curriculum?
- What kinds of values do you remember learning about at school? How will these affect your own teaching?

As an educator, it is impossible for you to stay out of the debate about moral and values education; as suggested by Haydon (2004), values and ethics are already promoted in the outcomes and aims we expect our students to develop. Philosopher Nel Noddings has implored educators to return to an overall ethic of caring in schools and classrooms, and the development of a shared vision of care and concern for others (Bergman, 2004). She has suggested that teachers have a role to play in modelling and demonstrating an ethos of care and respect by upholding these values in relationships with their students (Noddings, 1990). Indeed, research indicates that a classroom characterised by predictability, trust, emotional warmth and reciprocal respect is conducive to the development of the moral self (Arsenio & Lover, 1995). Some strategies to guide your practice are outlined in Box 4.7.

BOX 4.7 IMPLICATIONS FOR EDUCATORS

STRATEGIES FOR FOSTERING MORAL DEVELOPMENT AND VALUES

- Develop an attitude of respect for children and young people. This respect is expressed in your classroom organisation and management, in activities, and in your interactions with learners.
- Make time to learn about your students' interests, feelings, values and ideas.
- Expose learners to different viewpoints. Encourage class discussions about current news items.
- When discussing sensitive moral issues, let students know ahead of time what is appropriate behaviour. For example, all voices will be heard unless they are deliberately offensive and contravene basic human rights.
- Social experiences stimulate mental processes and help to promote development. Consider excursions or guest speakers to encourage social interactions and exposure to different viewpoints.
- Debates challenge students' positions on topics and further stimulate mental processes.
- Role-playing opportunities help learners imagine what it would be like to be someone else.
- Develop cases, problems or scenarios that involve values that students can discuss.
- Provide opportunities for students to discover how various cultural groups reason about moral issues.
- Every subject – even disciplines such as mathematics – offers opportunities for helping students develop their skill in moral reasoning.

Source: Adapted from Crain, William, *Theories of Development: Concepts & Applications*, 4e, © 2000, pp. 147–8. Adapted by permission of Pearson Education, Inc., Upper Saddle River, NJ.

EMOTIONAL DEVELOPMENT

You may have noticed that each of the topics we have discussed so far contains some references to the emotional states of or consequences for people when they are engaging with developmental tasks such as self-perception, identity or moral reasoning. Increasingly, educational psychologists and researchers acknowledge that emotions are central to learning and teaching, and that an understanding of their role in the learner's experience is essential (Pekrun & Stephens, 2012)). Emotional development plays a central role in our capacity to understand ourselves and others.

An **emotion** is a mental or physiological state associated with a wide variety of feelings, thoughts and behaviours. We usually experience emotions as a type of mental state that is closely connected to our actions and sense of wellbeing. It is well accepted that humans are born with a biological capacity for experiencing a range of **basic emotions**, and that emotions are also shaped by interaction with the social environment, including cultural and social forces (Fischer, Wang, Kennedy & Cheng, 1998; Menon, 2000; Panksepp, 2004). Recent theories of emotional development can be organised around functionalist and social constructivist perspectives.

The **functionalist perspective** maintains that emotion is a central force that directs, shapes and organises our behaviour (see Barrett & Campos, 1987; Fischer, Wang, Kennedy & Cheng, 1998; Lazarus, 1991). This perspective includes the study of emotion in relation to cognitive processing; in other words, emotion helps us make meaning of our world in ways that cold, hard, rational thinking cannot (Dalgleish & Bramham, 1999). Emotions such as fear can redirect our thinking to work out safer solutions to a problem; a certain level of anxiety can sometimes direct us to focus on a task, but just a little too much anxiety can tip us over the edge into poor cognitive processing (see Chapter 8).

Functionalist perspectives also examine the role of emotion in shaping our social behaviour. For example, our ability to interpret and understand emotional expressions plays a critical role in our survival. By the time infants are three months of age, they and their mothers have developed a complex array of signals to convey and respond to emotion, including the ability to convey 'stranger danger' and fear, along with warmth and security (Boccia & Campos, 1989) (see Figure 4.10). Another critical area of research in the functionalist approach concerns the interaction between emotion and health. For example, states of psychological stress can depress the body's immune system, leading to ill health and development of the common cold virus (Cohen, Tyrell & Smith, 1991). Emotional deprivation in the mother–child relationship has been associated with the child's failure to thrive and develop at an expected rate (Iwaniec, 2006).

The **social constructivist perspective** is largely reflected in the work of Carolyn Saarni and colleagues. This perspective incorporates elements of the functionalist perspective but also emphasises the role of the context in shaping our interpretation of situations. In this view, emotion allows an individual to maintain or change a relationship with their environment on a matter of importance to that person (Saarni, Mumme & Campos, 1998). Both the functionalist and social constructivist perspectives suggest that emotions also have strong ties to our social functioning and ability to cope with our world. Saarni (1999) describes this ability as **emotional competence**. Saarni's view of emotional competence incorporates both the functionalist and social constructivist approaches, and has great relevance to understanding the role of emotion in the lives of children and young people. Table 4.6 outlines the key skills of emotional competence described by Saarni (1999).

emotion
A mental or physiological state associated with thoughts, feelings and behaviours

basic emotions
The emotions that babies are born with, such as happiness, sadness, anger and fear

functionalist perspective
An approach that views emotions as shaping and organising thoughts and behaviours

social constructivist perspective
An approach that emphasises the role of the social context in shaping the development of emotional understanding

emotional competence
The skills needed to negotiate the demands of the immediate social context

Source: Matthew Duchesne, © Milk and Honey Photography, 2010.

FIGURE 4.10 This young child's emotions are clearly conveyed to his parents through facial expressions, body language and crying.

Emotional competencies and their development

The development of emotional competence is closely connected to our relationships with other people. For example, the earliest relationship in the child's life is characterised by attachment to a primary caregiver. As described in Chapter 2, this attachment relationship is critical for the development of social and emotional processing regions of the brain. It is within this earliest relationship that the foundations of emotional competence are formed. The following section explores several features of emotional development that hold important implications for learning and relationships with others.

Each of the emotional competencies presented in Table 4.6 are interdependent; this means that skill or ability in one area is dependent on the development of skill in another area. The first of Saarni's (1999) emotional competencies requires *awareness of our emotional state*. The ability to be aware of one's emotional state is also referred to as the development of **self-conscious emotions** (Lewis, 1993b; Saarni, Mumme & Campos, 1998). Self-conscious emotions vary with age. They first appear between 18 and 24 months, when babies are capable of experiencing pride, shame and embarrassment. By about three years of age, children are able to experience emotions of envy and guilt (Lewis, 1993a; Sroufe, 2000). In the early years, these emotions are evoked primarily through adults' influence, such as when adults' praise for a job well done evokes pride in a child. Alternatively, parents or caregivers punish children for lying, making them feel shame and guilt for being deceitful (Zahn-Waxler & Robinson, 1995). Later in life, as a sense of self develops, external agents are no longer necessary in order to arouse these emotions. We usually feel proud of our accomplishments or ashamed of our weaknesses.

These are known as 'higher-order' emotions because they require higher-order cognitive processing such as metacognitive awareness (see Chapter 2) and because they depend on our capacity to reflect on our self. Self-conscious emotions are associated with our core values, such as the valuing of good academic results, or the valuing of others' opinions of our honesty or trustworthiness (Turner, Husman & Schallert, 2002). To experience self-conscious emotions, we require an awareness of our self and of the ways in which that self might be harmed or enhanced. Higher-order emotions develop with adults' encouragement. For example, we experience the emotion of pride when we feel positive about ourselves for doing a good job. Thus, if a teacher praises a student for doing well on a test, the student feels proud of his achievement. Conversely, that student may feel shame if he fails a test and his parents are disappointed or even angry. The student's sense of self is harmed and he feels negative about himself for his failure.

Being aware of our emotional state is a necessary precursor to our ability to *discern the emotions of others*. This form of emotional understanding is a cornerstone of our ability to understand and get along with others. Emotional understanding expands rapidly in early childhood when children take cues from the facial expressions of parents or caregivers to interpret situations. Relying on the emotional signals and cues of others is called **social referencing**, as infants look to caregivers and other adults for clues about their social world.

self-conscious emotions
Higher-order emotions (such as pride and shame) that require advanced cognitive processes and a capacity to understand how the self might be harmed or enhanced

social referencing
Taking cues from another person's emotional reaction to interpret a situation

TABLE 4.6 Skills of emotional competence

SKILL	UNDERSTANDING REQUIRED
1 Awareness of our emotional state	It is possible to experience more than one emotion at a time; awareness that we might not be entirely conscious of our feelings
2 Ability to discern the emotions of other people	Ability to read situational and expressive cues, such as facial expressions, that hold a clear emotional meaning
3 Ability to use the vocabulary of emotion	Our culture and subcultures have a common language to describe emotion, and cultural scripts (schemes) that link emotion with social roles
4 Capacity to be empathic and sympathetic	To be involved in others' experiences by showing care and concern
5 Understanding that inner emotional feelings need not match outward emotional expressions	It is possible for the self and others to hide emotional feelings; awareness that our emotional expression can affect other people and ability to alter our presentation if necessary
6 Ability to cope with unpleasant and distressing emotions	To use self-regulation skills to soften or lessen the effect of our emotional states
7 Awareness that relationships are partly defined by immediate and honest emotional expressions	There is an expectation in mature, close relationships of the mutual sharing of genuine emotions
8 Emotional self-efficacy	To feel confident and satisfied with our emotional state; capable of achieving a balance in our emotional state

Source: Adapted from Saarni (2000), pp. 77–8.

It seems that the easiest facial expressions to interpret are positive ones, such as happiness, whereas negative emotions such as fear, anger or sadness are more difficult for children to interpret (Fabes, Eisenberg, Nyman & Michealieu, 1991; Gross & Bailiff, 1991). Older children are more able to incorporate additional information to help them make sense of the emotions of others. For example, they have a greater capacity to infer or predict a person's likely emotional response based on knowledge of that person's previous response in a similar situation. Younger children tend to rely on current contextual information to judge a person's likely emotional response (Gnepp, 1989; Gnepp & Gould, 1985). This difference appears to be attributable to the abstract and higher-order thinking skill associated with being able to infer or predict an outcome by transferring information from one time point to another.

The skill of discerning emotions has important implications for children's relationships with peers. Children who are very good at discerning emotions are better accepted by their peers (Cassidy, Parke, Butkovsky & Braungart, 1992; Walden & Knieps, 1996). In contrast, children who are rejected by their peers sometimes misinterpret or misread the social cues conveyed in the emotional responses of those peers (Crick & Dodge, 1994). This is discussed in more detail in the next section of this chapter, in which we examine the development of relationships between children.

One of the most important emotional skills that connects us to others is the *capacity for empathy and sympathy*. Empathy is the ability to detect others' emotions, take their perspective and understand how they might be feeling, while sympathy is the capacity to feel for others (Saarni, Mumme & Campos, 1998; Zahn-Waxler & Radke-Yarrow, 1990). The ability to respond to the feelings of others with empathy and sympathy begins early in life. Zahn-Waxler, Radke-Yarrow, Wagner and Chapman (1992) investigated empathy in children from the ages of one to two years. At one year of age, children tried to pat, hug or touch a person showing distress; by 18 to 20 months of age, children added other gestures such as trying to give the distressed person a blanket and verbalising their concern: 'Are you OK?'; and by two years of age, children expressed even more empathy in shows of concern and a willingness to offer help.

As children move through the school years, the capacity for perspective taking assists the development of empathy. **Perspective taking** is the ability to imagine oneself in another's position. Empathy and perspective-taking skills promote **prosocial behaviour**, which is an enduring tendency to think about the wellbeing and rights of others, to feel concern and empathy, and to voluntarily behave in ways that benefit others (Bierhoff, 2002; Eisenberg, Eggum & Di Giunta, 2010; Penner & Finkelstein, 1998). Selman (1976) believed that the core task of perspective taking was the child's ability to coordinate multiple points of view, but the child must also be *willing* to engage with another person's point of view (Selman & Shultz, 1990). Selman's research strategy is explained in Box 4.8.

perspective taking
The ability to imagine the self in another's position and to understand others' feelings

prosocial behaviour
Positive social behaviours, such as helpfulness, intended to benefit others

Selman's five-stage model and perspective-taking ability

Selman's five-stage model of perspective-taking skills illustrated development from preschool to adulthood. It shows that the capacity to understand others' feelings is facilitated by the ability to think abstractly (see Box 4.8 and Table 4.7).

Although children begin to show empathy quite early in life, Selman's research suggests that it is not until late childhood or early adolescence that children develop more sophisticated perspective-taking skills. Young children tend to be more egocentric and have difficulty incorporating the viewpoints of others, while adolescents can move beyond individual concerns to consider the perspectives of a wider range of people. They become more concerned with whole groups of people and with larger issues such as poverty in the Third World, or the greenhouse effect and its impact on world population.

BOX 4.8 RESEARCH LINKS

SELMAN'S PERSPECTIVE-TAKING STAGES

Robert Selman interviewed young people and asked them to respond to stories that presented a social dilemma. The following is an extract from a story known as 'Holly's dilemma'. After reading the story, children respond to the questions.

Holly is an eight-year-old girl who likes to climb trees. She is the best tree climber in the neighbourhood. One day she falls off a branch and her father becomes upset and asks her not to climb trees any more. Holly promises not to. Later, Holly meets up with her friend Sean, who is upset because his kitten is stuck up a tree. Something has to be done straight away or the kitten may fall. Holly is the only one who can climb trees well enough to reach the kitten, but she remembers her promise to her father.

- Should Holly climb the tree?
- Does Sean understand why Holly can't climb the tree?
- If Holly climbs the tree, what would her father think?
- Should Holly be punished if she climbs the tree?

Selman used the children's responses to come up with a five-stage model of perspective-taking ability (see Table 4.7). Before you look at this model, try the first activity listed below.

Source: Adapted from Selman and Byrne (1974).

ACTIVITIES

1   Take a moment to write down your thoughts about whether or not Holly should climb the tree, and whether or not she should be punished if she does.

2   As you read the next section, return to your answers and reflect on the multiple perspectives you included in coming up with your response.

3   Try this activity with a child much younger than yourself. How do their answers differ from your own? Can you identify their stage of perspective taking?

TABLE 4.7 Stages of perspective-taking ability

STAGE	APPROXIMATE AGE (YEARS)	DESCRIPTION	CHILD RESPONSE
Level 0 Undifferentiated	3–6	Limited understanding that the self and others can have different thoughts and feelings	Holly should climb the tree; her father will be happy because he also likes kittens.
Level 1 Social-informational	4–9	Understanding that people have different perspectives because they have different information	Holly's father will be angry if he sees Holly in a tree, but he doesn't know about the kitten. He will be OK if he sees that the kitten is stuck.
Level 2 Self-reflective	7–12	The ability to 'step into another person's shoes' and reflect on their own stance through the other person's eyes	Holly won't be punished because her father will understand why she climbed the tree and wanted to save the kitten.
Level 3 Third party	10–15	The ability to 'step outside' a two-person situation and imagine how another person (the third party) might view the situation	Holly should not be punished because although she knows she shouldn't climb trees, she also knows she should save the kitten. If she can get her father to see this, then she won't be punished.
Level 4 Societal	14 to adulthood	Understanding that the third-party perspective can be influenced by wider societal values	Holly should not be punished because the humane treatment of animals justifies her breaking her promise. Her father also appreciates this value.

Finally, one of the overarching emotional competencies that tie together the effective performance of other emotional skills is our capacity to *cope with our emotions*, also known as **emotional self-regulation**. Regulation of emotion allows children to cope with their emotions by being able to exercise control over them. Good emotional regulation is also related to prosocial moral reasoning (Eisenberg, 1992; Eisenberg & Fabes, 1998), probably because the ability to control and direct emotions helps us to control and direct our thinking more generally. School poses many challenges to children's abilities to control their emotion, such as when they experience the disappointment of failing a test or not being selected for a team. The belief that we can control our emotions and handle stressful situations is associated with our capacity to cope with stressful life events (Frydenberg & Lewis, 2002). Adolescents recognise that positive emotions such as maintaining hope and happiness are an important part of coping (Andrews, Ainley & Frydenberg, 2004). It is not surprising, then, that the capacity for emotional regulation is associated with the process of developing resilience in the face of adversity. (Masten & Coatsworth, 1998). These important aspects of self-regulation are further explored in several other chapters throughout this book. In the following section, we consider the development of our understanding of relations with others.

emotional self-regulation
Awareness of and ability to control or alter our emotional state as necessary

THINK ABOUT

- Self-understanding is said to be connected to our ability to understand other people (empathy). Can you explain this connection from your own experience?
- What should we teach children about controlling their emotions? Can you identify any cultural 'scripts' or schemes that shape our views of when and how we should regulate our emotional behaviour?

UNDERSTANDING RELATIONS WITH OTHERS

social development
The development of skills and understanding necessary for forming relationships and participating in the social context

The developing sense of self, and awareness of the thoughts and feelings of others, unfolds in parallel with our understanding of relationships with other people and between other people. In this section, we broadly consider the **social development** of the child, including the development of social competence, peer relationships and the complex issue of bullying. Unlike other areas we have studied, there is no single theory of development that attempts to explain this domain, simply because the area of social development is far too complex. Rather, a number of theorists have developed a broad range of ideas and knowledge about how we develop in the social world.

THE DEVELOPMENT OF SOCIAL COMPETENCE

Social competence is a complex term that is made up of many different nuances describing the social, emotional and cognitive skills necessary for everyday life (Welsh & Bierman, 1998). Most theorists agree that social competence cannot be defined by any single skill or ability, but rather is made up of multiple integrated factors, including the development of specific social skills, our standing and acceptance by others, the relationships we develop, and the functional outcomes we experience (Cavell, 1990; Rose-Krasnor, 1997).

Social skills

Social skills are the highly specific behaviours that must be taught, learnt and performed in order to carry out any social task, such as answering the telephone, greeting a friend, or saying please and thank you (Gresham, Sugai & Horner, 2001). The list of social skills required for everyday interactions is enormous, and many different attempts have been made to categorise and present lists of these skills (see Chapter 7 for further discussion). Caldarella and Merrell (1997) gathered together these various ideas of social skills and classified them into five broad areas, described in Table 4.8.

TABLE 4.8 A list of social skills

SKILL	DESCRIPTION
Peer relations	Complimenting others, offering help, inviting peers to play
Self-management	Controlling our temper, following rules, reaching a compromise in conflicts
Academic	Completing assigned work, listening to teacher directions, producing work of an appropriate standard
Compliance	Following directions, following rules, using free time appropriately
Assertion	Initiating conversations, acknowledging compliments, asking to join in play

The development of social skills varies with age and experience, and it is safe to say that these skills apply across the years of schooling in one form or another. For example, in the early years of school, academic skills might include listening to teacher directions, sitting quietly in a group or raising a hand before answering a question. As we progress through school, students learn other academic skills, such as completing independent homework tasks, managing a timetable, or working in a group effectively. The academic features of these social skills are further discussed in Chapters 7 and 14. In the following sections, you will see how social skills feature in children's play and peer interactions.

Social-skills training is commonly used as an approach to correct perceived deficiencies in children's social behaviours. Psychologists, and sometimes teachers, will measure a student's social skills by rating the child's ability in different types of social skills on a scale. These sorts of tests help diagnose a social skills problem and allow psychologists and teachers to work out a suitable plan for the child. Approaches to social skills training are widely used with learners with emotional and behavioural difficulties, intellectual disabilities, ADHD and many other conditions. It is beyond the scope of this chapter to explain and identify all the different approaches and strategies that have been used, and this information is readily available in other sources. KidsMatter (https://www.kidsmatter.edu.au/) is an Australian portal that provides a helpful evaluation of a number of social and emotional learning programs that are commonly targeted at children and young people. Teachers should feel confident to ask about the effectiveness of any programs that are to be implemented at their school. For example, we would expect to see a substantial body of published and peer-reviewed research evidence to support any interventions with children and young people. Response Ability (www.responseability.org) is another Australian organisation devoted to promoting teacher understanding of the mental health and wellbeing of their students. A free resource called *Social and emotional wellbeing: A teacher's guide* is available on their website. This guide will help you identify when children's behaviours or social-skills problems seem to suggest competing mental health problems (see also Chapter 10). It is comforting to note that the most effective social-skills interventions are likely to be those that occur in natural contexts, such as the classroom, or even through the 'teachable moments' that arise in play situations, which we will address next.

CourseMateExpress

Online resources
Go further: View the KidsMatter and Response Ability websites on this text's website

Play and development

For younger children, play is a context in which to explore their world with freedom, express a sense of their self, and is often fondly remembered as a time of fun. However, Lifter and Bloom (1998) have argued for a view of play that acknowledges play is for fun *and* for learning. According to this view, play serves an important interpretive function in which children learn about their world and extend their cognitive development. Such a view of play is reflected in other philosophies, including Vygotsky's (1978) view that play serves an adaptive purpose that stimulates cognitive growth, and Montessori's (1967) view that play is 'child's work', in the sense that through play children are acquiring new knowledge (Lifter, 2002).

Play has captured the interest of researchers for many years, and some have attempted to classify or describe stages of play development. Like other researchers of the time, Parten (1932) identified the emergence of different types of play as children grew older, and proposed a stage-based theory of play development. Howes and Matheson (1992) later refined this model of play and concluded that different forms of play do emerge in an order (described in Table 4.9), but that children are not bound to a strict developmental sequence in which one form of play replaces the other. Young children may be able to engage in cooperative play at younger ages than previously thought (Hughes, 2010), and as they grow older, children may continue to use multiple forms of play, including solitary activities.

TABLE 4.9 Types of play

TYPES OF PLAY	EXAMPLES
Solitary play: children play alone	Playing with blocks, water and sand, puzzles, computer and video games for one person, dolls and models (cars and planes). Children do not necessarily show an interest in or awareness of other children playing around them.
Parallel play: children play beside but not with other children	Bouncing a ball, playing with blocks or a doll in close proximity to other children, but not engaging with them. Children start to show more interest in the child playing beside them, but may not engage with the other child.
Cooperative play: children play in pairs or in groups	Playing soccer, hide and seek, building a tree house. Children recognise the advantages of playing with peers.
Pretend or imaginary play	Children assume roles or play with imaginary objects or people.
Solitary pretend play: imaginary play alone	Feeding dolls or teddy bears; pushing toy trains around a track while saying 'chuff chuff'.
Sociodramatic or cooperative pretend play: imaginary play	Assuming different roles such as 'mummies and daddies', 'teachers and students'; playing dress-ups, housekeeping; assuming fantasy roles and identities.

Over the years, researchers have used many terms to describe different types of play, including rough-and-tumble play (such as wrestling and mock fighting), constructive play (making things for fun), formal games (games and sports with designated rules) and pretend play (portraying imaginary roles) (Gray, 1991). Play and play-based interventions are believed to be critical for healthy brain development, particularly the development of 'executive function' discussed in chapters 2 and 3. The Australian Early Years Learning Framework adopts play-based learning as 'the best vehicle for young children's learning providing the most appropriate stimulus for brain development' (DEEWR, 2012). In the early childhood years, play forms a link and bond between children and caregivers, developing attachment and critical emotional understanding in concepts of reciprocity in gestures, smiling or turn taking (for more on emotional development, see the next section). As we learnt in Chapter 2, the critical period of brain development in infancy and early childhood is facilitated by positive experiences. Play allows children to explore the world, building neural pathways between new sensations and emotional feelings, forming rules and symbolic understanding as they work out how things 'work'. Pretend or imaginary play and child-initiated play are particularly linked to the development of self-regulation and symbolic representation, a major early cognitive development milestone (Bodrova & Leong, 2010).

Sophisticated play and developing social skills

As children develop through the primary years, and their cognitive and motor skills develop (see chapters 2 and 3), their play becomes increasingly sophisticated. Everyday games that children play such as 'Simon says …' or waiting one's turn in a game help develop those parts of the brain that help us control our impulses; as children gain in cognitive skills and develop interests in card games and board games, their working memory is called upon to remember rules and scores.

Vital social skills such as sharing and negotiation are also practised in the context of play. Play may enhance students' physical development in the sense that rough-and-tumble play allows children to test their physical strength and agility (Pellegrini & Smith, 1998). Organised forms of play, such as sport and physical activities, may be particularly important during the adolescent years, allowing a break from intellectual activities (Bjorklund & Brown, 1998) and providing a buffer from stress (Brown & Siegel, 1988). As children grow older, peers are present in almost all forms of play and free time. These peers play a critical role in helping children develop in all dimensions, but observation and supervision is important to ensure physical behaviours are mutual and enjoyed by all 'players', as indicated by reciprocated gestures and smiles.

DEVELOPING RELATIONSHIPS WITH PEERS

Think about your own peer experiences over time. Do you remember your best friends at school? Why were some children able to make friends more easily than others? Why were some children rejected and disliked? Why were some more aggressive than others? The stories of Jake and Sarah clearly indicate that relationships with peers are very important in the lives of children. This section will explain why peer relationships are a critical part of our lives from early childhood.

Source: © Pavel L Photo and Video/Shutterstock

FIGURE 4.11 Card games such as Snap, Memory or other matching games assist in the development of cognitive and social skills.

Social interaction with peers forms a significant part of our lives from an early age. There are three main ways in which we engage socially with our peers as we develop and mature over time. These types of peer exchange are categorised according to the depth of interaction and relationship we have with our peers, and have been called **interactions**, **relationships** and **groups** (Rubin, Bukowski & Parker, 1998). Table 4.10 outlines the characteristics of these peer exchanges.

interaction
A first-order (or superficial) social exchange between two or more individuals, with little emotional commitment

relationship
An exchange between two or more people, resulting from several interactions and taking on emotional significance

group
An exchange involving several interacting individuals who have formed a relationship and who have some degree of reciprocal influence over one another

TABLE 4.10 Characteristics of peer exchanges

TYPE OF PEER EXCHANGE	CHARACTERISTICS
Interaction	• Social exchange between two or more individuals
Relationship	• A series of significant interactions between two individuals
	• Involves stronger emotions, more frequent contact than interactions (Hinde, 1995)
	• Predominant emotions in relationships are affection, love, attachment and enmity
	• Requires a shared culture in terms of accepted patterns of communication and appropriate behaviour
	• Friendship is a relationship that is mutually agreed to and reciprocated (Wentzel & Battle, 2001)
Group	• Groups tend to be:
	> formed spontaneously, though they may be established formally, as in a class group at school
	> cohesive, in that there is unity among members, who usually have common interests and reciprocal influence over one another
	> hierarchical, in that there is often a leader or subgroup of leaders
	> homogeneous in one or more observable characteristics such as sex, race, attitudes to school, clothing and socioeconomic status
	> characterised by distinctive group norms or patterns of behaviours and attitudes that distinguish group members from others.

Source: Adapted from Rubin, Bukowski and Parker (1998, pp. 633–44).

Peer acceptance

peer acceptance
The likeability and acceptance of a person by their peer group

One of the most important advances in our understanding of peer relationships has been in understanding the role of peer acceptance in children's lives. **Peer acceptance** is a specific term that refers to the extent to which a child is liked or accepted by other members of the peer group (Asher, Parker & Walker, 1996). It can be influenced by group norms and preferences, as highlighted in the table above, and has important implications for the development and wellbeing of the child.

The extent to which a child is liked or accepted by the peer group has important implications for their wellbeing and adjustment. To describe these outcomes, it is important to distinguish between children who are accepted and those who are not. To do this, researchers have used a special form of assessment known as **sociometric assessment** (see Box 4.9). This form of assessment allows researchers to identify different types of peer acceptance, including the categories of 'popular', 'rejected', 'neglected' and 'controversial' peer status. Each of these classifications has been associated with specific characteristics that may reflect the reasons why, and the outcomes of, peer acceptance and rejection (see Table 4.11).

sociometric assessment
The measurement of social networks and connections between people by assessing people's ratings of one another

As shown in Table 4.11, the peer status groups differ on a number of dimensions, and research is continuing to find out more about these differences. In some cases, the differences seem to be of little consequence. For example, children classified as 'neglected' are not so much disliked by peers as simply not noticed by peers – they receive few positive or negative nominations. Their prosocial skills are rated as 'low' only because they do little to project themselves in a sociable manner; there may be nothing wrong with their other skills. For example, it is a positive sign that their academic skills are quite strong (Wentzel & Asher, 1995). In contrast, children classified as 'rejected' experience many more adjustment difficulties.

Peer rejection

The reality of the peer ratings shows that children who are rejected by their peers have almost no-one in their classroom who likes them. Aggressive behaviours may explain the rejection of some students, but some rejected children are quite withdrawn from the peer group, exacerbating their vulnerability to peer hostilities (Rubin, Bowker, McDonald & Menzer, 2013). However, other correlates of peer rejection mean that some children are simply disliked through no fault of their own (Hymel, Wagner & Butler, 1990). These non-behavioural reasons for peer rejection include:

- *physical appearance* – children hold different behavioural expectations of 'attractive' and 'unattractive' peers leading then to favour attractive peers over less attractive peers
- *obesity, illness and physical disability* – these conditions are associated with lower play preferences and sometimes elicit less sympathy from peers
- *group and cultural norms* – children show a preference for peers who are similar to them; they may be influenced by home and family belief systems to prefer some children over others.

BOX 4.9 RESEARCH LINKS

SOCIOMETRIC ASSESSMENT

Sociometric assessments have been used and refined for a number of years in the fields of sociology and developmental psychology (Asher & Dodge, 1986; Coie, Dodge & Copotelli, 1982; Moreno, 1951). The aim of these assessments is to provide a measure of a person's social standing or acceptance in a group of peers. In the field of developmental psychology, sociometric assessments usually ask each child in a classroom group to rate how much they like each peer on a scale ranging from 'like very much' to 'do not like at all'. Sometimes children are simply asked to list the names of their 'most liked' peers and their 'least liked' peers. Researchers can use these ratings to add up how many times a child is rated as 'most liked' or 'least liked' by their peers. These scores are used to determine the categories of 'popular', 'rejected', 'neglected' and 'controversial' peer status. Researchers have been very interested in the question of why some children are more accepted than others, and have searched for answers by examining the social skills and behaviours of children in different status categories (see **Table 4.11**).

While some of the skills and behaviours are quite well documented, it is important to note that many of these studies are correlational in nature and neither suggest causation nor that these associations always occur. An important example of this applies to the behaviour of aggression. Not all rejected children are aggressive, in the same manner it is known that not all 'popular' children always play nicely. Children who are *perceived* to be popular (but not sociometrically popular) are also reported by peers to be aggressive or stuck up (Parkhurst & Hopmeyer, 1998). Perceived-popular children are known to be different to sociometrically popular children and may in fact use aggression and manipulation as a means to maintain social dominance or group standing (Cilleson & Rose, 2005). It is important to distinguish between the types of measurement and definitions of rejection and popularity when reading studies in this field.

TABLE 4.11 Characteristics of sociometrically defined peer status groups

STATUS	POSITIVE NOMINATIONS	NEGATIVE NOMINATIONS	AGGRESSION	PROSOCIAL SKILLS	ACADEMIC SKILLS
Popular	High	None (or few)	Low	High	Positive
Rejected	None (or few)	High	High*	Low	Poor*
Neglected	Few	Few	Low	Low	Positive
Controversial	High	High	High	High	Poor

* Note: Not all rejected children are aggressive. Researchers distinguish between children known as 'aggressive-rejected' and a smaller subset of rejected children known as 'passive-rejected', who do not display aggressive behaviours and may not show poor academic skills.

Source: Adapted from Newcomb, Bukowski and Pattee (1993); Parker and Asher (1987); Wentzel (1991); Wentzel and Asher (1995).

ACTIVITIES

1 Reflect on some of your answers to the questions posed at the beginning of this section. Can you remember children who were probably classified as 'popular' or 'rejected'?
2 Do you agree that these students reflected the characteristics described above?
3 Sociometric assessments often raise ethical concerns and are not approved for use in many classrooms. What ethical concerns do you think might arise from asking children to participate in this form of assessment?

BOX 4.10 CLASSROOM LINKS

REDUCING PEER REJECTION IN THE CLASSROOM

Researchers Mikami, Boucher and Humphreys (2005) tested an intervention to reduce rejection in middle school students (children in years 6–8). Rather than using traditional social-skills training of the individual rejected child (a common intervention strategy), the researchers targeted the *whole* classroom climate. Why? They argue that classroom climates, including teacher behaviour, can foster a view that 'not everyone is equal in this classroom'. This can arise from ability hierarchies in classrooms where student achievement or differences are on view. It can also arise from classroom norms for aggressive behaviour which can reflect the teacher's beliefs. For example, if a teacher does not prevent peer rejection it can become a classroom norm. An alternative approach is to break down these 'normative' or reputational beliefs about other children by fostering a socially accepting classroom with greater social acceptance and cooperation. This was the basis for the classroom intervention employed in their study.

Method

Teachers and students in 24 year 6–8 classrooms participated in the study (N = approximately 624 students). Teachers formed heterogeneous groups of 4–5 students in each classroom, combining students of different ethnicities, social classes and friendship groups. They avoided putting close friends and sworn enemies together. A control group of students also completed regular classroom activities. Students completed self-report measures of peer acceptance, the proportion of students in their class whom they liked or disliked, and the proportion of peers who treated them with respect at school.

Intervention strategy

The student groups participated in non-academic collaborative games such as solving riddles, or building towers from spaghetti and marshmallows, for 45 minutes per week. They also completed cooperative learning tasks in regular classroom time to integrate the intervention into normal classroom life. These activities lasted for eight consecutive weeks. Teachers also held regular meetings to communicate and share ideas about encouraging respect and cooperation in classroom activities.

Findings

Before the intervention, students reported neutral or only slightly positive feelings about their peer relationships, and only 39 per cent of students felt that all or most peers respected them. Afterwards, the students in the intervention scored higher on the scale of peer relationships, suggesting an increase in positive feelings about their peer relations – 60 per cent of students reported that all or most peers respected them. In contrast, the control group of students had a slight decline in their perception of peer relationships during the same period. There was a statistically significant difference between the intervention and control groups.

Conclusions

The classroom intervention changed feelings of acceptance, with more children feeling accepted. The researchers also observed one child with a history of extreme rejection by peers being included in team bonding activities.

Source: Adapted from Mikami, Boucher and Humphreys (2005).

THINK ABOUT

- Regarding the above box, why do you think the researchers used heterogeneous groups?
- What was the importance of the *non-academic* collaborative games?
- What should teachers in these classrooms do to follow up or maintain these results?

Consequences of rejection

The consequences of peer rejection can be seen in a number of emotional and psychological domains. One of these is the emotional and psychological state referred to as **loneliness**. Loneliness is a cognitive and affective mental state arising from a loss of or threat to our social connections (Rotenberg, 1999). It is a *feeling* state, in that people with loneliness report a feeling of being lost or disconnected, and a sense of inadequate social relationships. Children who experience poor peer relations report high feelings of loneliness. While it is true that rejected children who are aggressive report higher levels of loneliness compared with average accepted children, those who are more withdrawn or submissive in their rejection experience higher levels of loneliness (Boivin, Poulin & Vitaro, 1994). Children who also experience victimisation, such as being picked on and teased, have some of the highest levels of loneliness (Kochenderfer & Ladd, 1996). Although many of us may report a feeling of loneliness from time to time, the emotional and psychological consequences of persistent and prolonged loneliness are very serious, and include depression, alcoholism and suicide among adults (Rotenberg, 1999). Children as young as those attending kindergarten can reliably report a sense of loneliness, and it is clear that they, too, experience the cognitive and affective feelings that are reported by older children and adults (Cassidy & Asher, 1992; Ladd, Kochenderfer & Coleman, 1996). If peer rejection remains stable or persistent over time, loneliness steadily increases, posing a clear risk to the health and wellbeing of these young people. Box 4.10 details a classroom intervention strategy that has been demonstrated to prevent and lessen feelings of rejection in school students.

loneliness
A cognitive and affective state of feeling disconnected and lacking in supportive relationships

Rejection and aggression

Further adjustment difficulties are associated with children who are rejected and also have aggressive tendencies. There is evidence that many of these children do not understand their social world in quite the same way as typically developing children. This understanding of the social world is referred to as **social cognition**. Social–cognitive deficits are apparent in the way in which these children process information about social events (Crick & Dodge, 1994). This means that children may make incorrect judgements about peers due to the way they interpret or process social information such as facial expressions and emotional signals. They may have internal cognitive scripts or schemes that lead them to react with hostility. They may also believe that aggression is the only viable response and may also believe they are more likely to be effective if they use aggression (Rubin, Bowker, McDonald & Menzer, 2013). For example, if accidentally bumped in the lunch line at school, these children are much more likely to make an incorrect assumption that a peer deliberately bumped them. This assumption is known as a hostile attribution bias, in which hostile intent is assumed in an ambiguous situation. As a consequence, the aggressive rejected child typically responds with aggression, which in turn further alienates the child or makes peers react with aggression.

social cognition
A cognitive capacity to think about and process social information

Rejection and long-term adjustment difficulties

One of the most serious consequences of poor peer relationships is the risk of long-term adjustment difficulties. Longitudinal studies have found that a history of peer rejection and a lack of supportive friendships is associated with a risk of poor school performance, early school drop out, antisocial behaviour, criminality and poor relationships in adulthood (Bagwell, Schmidt, Newcomb & Bukowski, 2001; Parker & Asher, 1987; Parker, Rubin, Price & DeRosier, 1995). Classroom interventions such as described in Box 4.10 can be useful but sometimes more intensive social skills interventions can be used to assist children with specific skills such as problem-solving strategies and anger management. However, Mikami, Boucher and Humphreys (2005) suggest that classroom factors can exacerbate or create 'normative' cultures of rejection, and it is these system-level factors that should be addressed first.

Friendship

friendship
A close relationship
between two people
who mutually agree on
the importance of this
relationship

dyadic
Characterised by two
elements, or two
people, as in the case
of friendship

The most positive form of peer relationship experienced by children is **friendship**. Friendship is a **dyadic** relationship that exists between two people who mutually agree that the relationship is unique and very special (Asher, Parker & Walker, 1996). Unlike sociometric forms of peer acceptance, friendship is not defined according to the views of the whole group of students. Rather, in assessing the presence of friendship in a child's life, only one basic criterion must be met – the friendship must be reciprocated. A friendship is said to be reciprocated when two children nominate each other as a best friend. This seemingly simple bond is distinguished from peer acceptance by the high-quality peer interaction and unique benefits of friendship. Friendship serves a very specific developmental function in our lives, and is usually associated with a range of highly positive academic and social outcomes for students (Bukowski, 2001) (see Table 4.12).

Friendship is regarded by developmental researchers as a unique developmental context (Newcomb, Bukowski & Bagwell, 1999). It is distinguished from other peer relationships by the unique emotional and psychological benefits of the relationship. Friendship is particularly characterised by a higher level of intimacy and a sense of reliability and loyalty (Erdley, Nangle, Newman & Carpenter, 2001). Intimacy is a term used to describe a particular form of trust and self-disclosure where people feel safe to share secrets and personal aspects of themselves. High-quality children's friendships are particularly known for their high expectations of absolute trust and loyalty.

Friendships and prosocial behaviours

Those children who have friends also tend to display prosocial behaviour more frequently than their classmates without friends (Wentzel & Caldwell, 1997). In a unique study, Wentzel and Erdley (1993) asked children in grades 6 and 7 to supply 'Advice for Making Friends'. Children provided lists of things you should do to make friends and things you should not do. Among the things children *should do* were being honest and trustworthy, telling the truth and keeping promises. These prosocial skills support the intimacy of friendships. Children also listed other expected prosocial behaviours, including being funny, giving social support, and being caring, kind and considerate. Proximity was also important to the children in that they suggested that friends should sit together, do activities together and be in the same group (see Figure 4.12).

TABLE 4.12 The features and benefits of friendship

FEATURE	BENEFIT
Friendship and the self	A powerful source of self-esteem, as friends regard each other with equal respect and provide the trust to share each other's thoughts and feelings
Friendship as a buffer	A powerful protector against stress, negative family environments, and bullying and harassment
Friendship and learning	The trust and security of friendships allow exploration of ideas in a context of friendly exchanges, challenge of ideas and problem solving.
Friendship as development	Friends contribute to each other's development (in positive and negative ways) by bringing unique histories and expectations, including the will to do better in school or engage in troublesome behaviours.

Although some of these behaviours might also occur among peers, the familiarity within friendship means that these behaviours occur with greater frequency and at much higher quality. As such, peer acceptance and friendship should not be confused. For example, although being popular with peers is associated with lower levels of loneliness, friendship is a more powerful force in directly supporting the mental health and emotional wellbeing of young people (Nangle et al., 2003). Friendships make a unique contribution to protecting children from stress, literally buffering them and reducing the stress hormone, cortisol, in the face of negative experiences (Adams, Santo & Bukowski, 2011). Similarly, a variety of studies have shown that the presence of friendship appears to moderate the relationship between harsh parenting and home environments, with befriended children having fewer negative outcomes (Schwartz, Dodge, Pettit & Bates, 2000). Importantly, children with even one best friend are less likely to be bullied and feel less distressed when victimised (Hodges & Perry, 1999; Hodges, Boivin, Vitaro & Bukowski, 1999).

FIGURE 4.12 Closeness and intimacy between friends plays an important role in development.

Source: © Thomas Cockrem/Alamy.

Development of friendships

A number of researchers have suggested that children's friendships do not arrive at a point of intimacy and sophistication immediately, but rather these qualities develop over time. For example, several early researchers like Damon (1983), Selman (1981) and Bigelow and La Gaipa (1975) conducted interviews with children or asked children to write stories about friendship. Each of these researchers concluded that children's concepts of friendships become increasingly sophisticated with age. William Damon (1977, 1983) proposed and found evidence for three developmental levels of friendship that commence with a relatively concrete understanding of a friend as a 'handy playmate'. These stages become more sophisticated as children grow up:

- Level 1: Friendship as a 'handy playmate' (4–7 years)
- Level 2: Friendship as mutual trust and assistance (8–10 years)
- Level 3: Friendship as intimacy and loyalty (11–15 years +).

Across these studies, descriptions of friends by young children are related to the tangible and practical qualities of the relationships (Level 1 friendship). Damon described this friendship as a 'handy playmate' and Selman as 'momentary friendships'. These relationships are governed by the proximity and availability of friends, such as being nearby or in the same preschool class. While both researchers neglected to investigate the perceptions of friendship of very young children, this does not mean that friendships are less important to very young children or their parents (Yu, Ostrosky & Fowler, 2011). Young children are capable of reporting friendships, and these relationships are characterised by qualities such as coordinated play and warm, affectionate interactions (MacGuire & Dunn, 1997). By middle childhood, the perspectives of self and others become more coordinated, and Selman described greater cooperation between friends at this age. However, he described these relationships as 'fair weather' friendships, indicating that a fair degree of self-interest still prevailed and the friendships could break down easily if agreement or cooperation was not achieved. By adolescence, Damon's stages show a more abstract notion of friendship, characterised by intimacy (such as the sharing of emotions) and loyalty.

CourseMateExpress

Online resources
Watch a **video** showing children discussing their understanding of 'what makes someone a good friend'

Regardless of child age or gender, friendships are important. One of the most important functions of a friendship is its protective quality. This is particularly salient in the case of bullying and victimisation, which we will now examine as a particularly problematic developmental context.

BOX 4.11 IMPLICATIONS FOR EDUCATORS

STRATEGIES FOR DEVELOPING AN AWARENESS OF PEER INTERACTIONS

- Be observant and aware of children or adolescents who have no friends or who are rejected by peers.
- Look for the reasons behind poor behaviour or inattention in class. Rejected children may be more likely to experience behavioural problems, display aggression and attentional difficulties, and may report higher levels of substance abuse and more delinquent offences than their more popular or average peers.
- Seek help and advice if you become concerned about the psychological or emotional wellbeing of any student. Poor peer relationships are associated with wider mental health and adjustment problems such as loneliness, depression and withdrawal.
- Look for opportunities to develop and practise social skills in everyday classroom and playground activities. Natural contexts provide powerful contexts for the development of children's relationship skills.

THINK ABOUT

- Can you distinguish between the benefits of peer acceptance and friendship?
- What role do you think peer acceptance and friendship play in the classroom?
- Why is it important for teachers to be aware of social relationships between students?

BULLYING AND HARASSMENT

bullying
Repeated verbal and/or non-verbal aggression by individuals or groups and directed towards particular victims who find it difficult to defend themselves

If friendship represents the most positive form of peer relationship in childhood, then bullying represents the most negative. **Bullying** is an abuse of power that takes the form of ongoing or repeated aggression involving a wide range of behaviours by individuals or groups, and is directed towards particular victims who find it difficult to defend themselves (Eisenberg, 1998; Olweus, 1999; Smith, Cowie, Olafsson & Liefooghe, 2002).

Bullying can take place in any situation that involves a power relationship. It is a particular problem in hierarchically organised institutions such as schools, but also in work environments such as offices, factories and the armed services. Bullying can occur in any school environment, regardless of the socioeconomic status of the school community. As discussed in Chapter 14, the ethos of the school culture may contribute to bullying in some schools. Chapter 14 provides an extended discussion of how to manage and respond to bullying and harassment in schools.

The problem of bullying in schools is not a recent phenomenon and has been reported in diverse regions of the globe over several decades, including the United States (Espelage & Swearer, 2003), Scandinavia (Olweus, 1978) and elsewhere in Europe (Smith & Morita, 1999), Japan (Morita, 1996) and New Zealand (Lind & Maxwell, 1996; Sullivan, 1999). It is now well recognised as an international problem for teachers and students in schools.

The types of behaviours classified as bullying are diverse and include direct and indirect forms of aggression such as physical assaults, verbal abuse, emotional and psychological abuse (such as implied threats, blackmail, anonymous messages), relational aggression (deliberate social exclusion, spreading rumours, asking other students to hurt the person) and 'cyberbullying': a term used to describe bullying by electronic media such as text messaging, posting videos online and sending or circulating malicious emails (Crick et al., 2001; Kowalski & Limber, 2007; Rigby, 2007). The most common forms of bullying reported by Australian children are teasing, hurtful rumours or lies being told about the child (Cross et al., 2009; McGrath & Noble, 2006). A relatively high number of children report being bullied in covert ways (16 per cent), such as spreading rumours, blackmail, threats or any behaviours teachers cannot see. Estimates of cyberbullying or online bullying vary dramatically. The largest study of Australian children and young people ($N = 20\,832$) aged 8 to 14 years found fewer than 7–10 per cent reported experiencing cyberbullying (Cross et al., 2009). However, estimates are likely to vary among certain age groups, with higher estimated rates of cyberbullying in high schools (IRIS Research, 2014).

Defining bullying

We must take care, however, not to describe any single occurrence of any of these behaviours as bullying. From time to time, all students have disagreements, sometimes serious ones. Acts of violence or aggression may also occur. The term 'bullying', however, is reserved for the particularly harmful behaviour that is characterised by:

- persistent and repeated attacks against a target child …
- over an extended period of time (not just a one-off incident or temporary disagreement) …
- where there is an imbalance of power between the bully and the target child.

For this reason, it has also been defined as 'systematic abuse of power' (Rigby, 2002, cited by Smith, 2004, p. 98).

There is a concern that the overuse or misuse of the word 'bullying' might detract from the seriousness with which people understand it. It is also a concern if acts of violence or harassment are simply dismissed as bullying, when in fact these can represent serious acts of aggression, sexual harassment or racial harassment, and may be serious criminal or antisocial behaviours that cannot be responded to in the same manner as bullying. Another concern is the risk associated with mislabelling a child a 'bully'. In the current climate, there is a lot of concern about bullying in schools, and both bullies and victims can be stigmatised by labels (McGrath & Stanley, 2006).

It is also a 'myth' that bullying involves just a 'bully' and a 'victim'. Rather, Swearer, Espelage and Napolitano (2009) suggest that these behaviours fall on a bully–victim continuum; some students fall into classic bully or victim roles, but other students are classified as 'bully/victims' who engage in bullying behaviour but are also victims. This continuum also includes bystanders who may contribute to a larger group mentality that reinforces bullying behaviours by supporting the aggressors, or doing nothing to intervene and stop them. In other words, bullying is not so much a dyadic problem (between a bully and a victim) as it is a group phenomenon. Studies have identified children taking various roles in bullying, including being ringleaders (who organise and initiate bullying incidents), followers (those who join in once the bullying begins), reinforcers (who passively watch and laugh or otherwise encourage the bullies), bystanders (those who dislike the bullying but are afraid to challenge it) and defenders (who help the victim, get help or try to stop the bullies) (Olweus, 2000). These roles are not stable over time and children may move between these roles at different times (Swearer et al., 2009).

THINK ABOUT

- What kinds of bullying behaviours do you recall from your school experiences? Can you recall the effects of 'bystanders' or other peers on bullying?
- What are your views about the bully–victim continuum? Do you agree that children might fall into several types of bully, victim or bystander roles over time?
- How might this influence the way in which schools should address bullying?

Developmental trends in bullying behaviours

As many as one in four (27 per cent) Australian school children report being bullied every few weeks or more, with the highest rates of bullying reported by Year 5 students (32 per cent) and Year 8 students (29 per cent). Less than one in 10 (9 per cent) Australian children admit to being frequent bullies, with boys reporting the higher rate of 11 per cent and girls 7 per cent (Cross et al., 2009). Both Australia and New Zealand have been shocked by reports that students in both countries report higher rates of bullying than other countries in the OECD (PISA, 2015). While New Zealand students reported the highest rate of exposure to bullying, with 26 per cent of students reporting any type of bullying, Australian students placed number 5 in the world with 24 per cent of students reporting an experience of any type of bullying.

Gender, age and bullying

Gender and age are strongly associated with reported incidents of bullying. It is important to be aware that aggressive behaviour emerges at a very young age and, increasingly, such behaviours are viewed as bullying even in very young children. Tremblay (2008) has identified that children reach the peak of their physical aggression in the preschool years, and that aggression steadily declines after this time and throughout adolescence. Although physical aggression tends to decline from early childhood onwards, the incidence of indirect forms of aggression, such as making a nasty comment behind someone's back (also known as **relational aggression**), increases from four to seven years of age (Tremblay, 2008). Recent Australian research has shown that early childhood teachers identify high levels of relationally aggressive behaviours in 20 per cent of three- to five-year-old children, and this behaviour peaks in the four-to-five-years age range (Swit & McMaugh, 2011).

relational aggression
A form of harm that intentionally seeks to damage a person's social relationships or reputation

The role of gender in bullying behaviours seems to be clear, but also ambiguous. It is very clear from numerous studies, across many countries and age groups, that boys are more physically aggressive than girls (Juvonen & Graham, 2014), and are involved more often than girls in bullying incidents, both as aggressors and victims (Smith & Morita, 1999). However, although it is common to assume that girls must be more involved in indirect or relational (social) forms of aggression, the evidence for this is much more equivocal. Some studies have found that girls are more likely to use and experience indirect or psychological forms of aggression (Björkqvist, Lagerspetz & Kaukiaöinen, 1992; Björkqvist & Osterman, 1999; Owens & McMullin, 1995), and that girls are more likely to use relational bullying (for example, Crick & Grotpeter, 1995). However, other studies report only weak or inconsistent links to gender (Swearer, 2008). In fact, Swearer, Turner, Givens and Pollack (2008) have shown that boys also experience group exclusion and relational aggression, and it is just as detrimental for these boys as it is for girls.

Two large meta-analyses confirm that although girls use more relational rather than physical forms of aggression, there is no difference between boys' and girls' *likelihood* of using relationally aggressive or exclusionary tactics (Juvonen & Graham, 2014). Archer and Coyne (2005) go so far as to suggest that by the middle years of high school, physical forms of aggression become less socially acceptable and are likely replaced by relational forms of aggression for both boys and girls. Australian studies support these conclusions. Hayward and Fletcher (2003) found no gender differences in relationally aggressive behaviours in adolescent populations. Swit and McMaugh (2011) found no gender differences in early childhood populations. Some researchers have suggested that where gender differences are observed, it may reflect biased reporting in teacher or parent observations, because there is a stereotyped expectation that girls should be more involved in such behaviours (Ostrov, Crick & Keating, 2005).

Explanations for bullying

There are various ideas about why bullying occurs and why it appears to decline over time, including a desire for social dominance, inflated self-views and social cognitive biases (Juvonen & Graham, 2014). There is clear evidence that some bullies have a cold and calculating desire to prove their social dominance and desire admiration from peers (Juvonen & Graham, 2014; Salmivalli, Kaukiainen & Voeten, 2005). As such, some forms of bullying and aggression are associated with a desire to maintain status or gain a prominent position in the social group.

Some theories have suggested that the child's attitude and beliefs about aggression contribute to bullying behaviours. As suggested earlier in this chapter, there is quite strong evidence to suggest that aggressive children do have social cognitive biases that make them more prone to view peers with aggressive intent (Crick & Dodge, 1994). They may also receive positive social feedback from peers who laugh at or encourage bullying behaviours (Salmivalli, Lappalainen & Lagerspetz, 1998; Salmivalli, 2010). This social feedback may further reinforce maladaptive aggressive schemes or scripts.

In a similar view, it has also been suggested that bullies may be low in particular social–cognitive skills such as empathy. In some ways, it makes sense to suggest that bullies may be low in empathy, because surely it would be difficult to bully a person if one could understand how the victim was feeling. However, as argued by Espelage and Swearer (2003), much bullying behaviour is deliberately planned with the express intention of hurting others or, in the case of relational bullying, with the intention of destroying the child's social relationships. These planned behaviours suggest that children who bully may have sufficient social understanding to recognise the impact of their behaviour. Sutton, Smith and Swettenham (1999) also reject the social-skills-deficit model and suggest instead that bullies may have quite a sophisticated understanding of others' thoughts and feelings, but that they misuse this understanding to their own advantage, often in manipulative and harmful ways.

Many studies have in fact shown that bullies can hold inflated self-views (Cunningham, Cunningham, Ratcliffe & Vaillancourt, 2010; Johnson & Lewis, 1999). Those seeking power or social dominance tend to feel powerful and effective, and those with maladaptive hostile schemes feel buoyed when aggression works. Juvonen and Graham (2014) have noted that peer-reported bullies have less depression, anxiety or loneliness than typically adjusted children.

Today, views about the development of bullying are not limited to theories of aggression or social–cognitive beliefs. Rather, it is widely acknowledged that a range of factors contribute to bullying, including the social environment in which children develop these negative relationships (Rigby, 2007). As discussed in Chapter 14, school culture has been implicated in the development of attitudes towards bullying, while our understanding of peer acceptance and rejection indicates that wider peer cultures may lead to the victimisation of some children more than others.

Developmental effects of bullying

In understanding the effects of bullying, it is clear that bullying is harmful. Research illustrates that the consequences of being victimised are extensive. Zubrick et al. (1997) found that students who are bullied are more likely to have poor academic performance, high rates of absenteeism, low self-esteem, depression, anxiety, insecurity and significant mental health problems, when compared with students who are not bullied (see also Forero, McLellan, Rissel & Bauman, 1999; Perry, Perry & Kennedy, 1992; Rigby, 1994; Slee, 1995a, 1995b). Nishina, Juvonen and Witkow (2005) found that persistent victims were more depressed, anxious and lonely. Research has also found a link between bullying and physical health. Children classified as victims and aggressors had more visits to school health nurses and more frequent health complaints, including illness, injury and somatic complaints (Vernberg, Nelson, Fonargy & Twemlow, 2011). However, it is important to note that not all children react to victimisation in the same way. Some students report that they do not feel particularly worried by bullying, but their worry increases the more they are victimised (Rigby & Slee, 1999). Boys in this study were more likely to report that bullying made them angry, while girls reported that it tended to make them sad.

Victimisation

Victimisation may happen because children are simply caught in the wrong place at the wrong time or are 'easy targets', and it is important not to draw quick conclusions about why children are victimised. In particular, children who are less preferred by the peer group for non-behavioural reasons such as physical appearance, obesity, disability or sexual orientation are much more likely to be bullied (Juvonen & Graham, 2014). It is clear that peers can choose almost any characteristic to target a child and thus victimisation occurs to a wide range of children.

At a very generalised level, research has identified that victims of bullying tend to be rejected and isolated from their peer groups, and have poor-quality friendships, low numbers of friends and low peer acceptance (possibly as a result of reciprocal interactions between peer-acceptance variables and being bullied), together with low physical strength, low school enjoyment and poor social skills (Card, 2003; Olweus, 1993). However, it is also becoming increasingly clear that such personal characteristics do not necessarily *cause* bullying, but instead there may be a *reciprocal* or cyclical interaction between internal factors (such as depression and anxiety) and victimisation. For example, a large meta-analysis has compared the evidence for such problems acting as either an antecedent or a consequence of victimisation. The results show that evidence is strong for both pathways – internal problems are just as likely to arise from victimisation as to exist before victimisation in some children (see Juvonen & Graham, 2014).

Friendship, social skills and bullying

It is clear that children who are befriended are much less likely to experience bullying, and classroom encouragement of acceptance and tolerance reduces rejection (for example, Mikami, Boucher & Humphreys, 2005). As such, these social factors provide us with a good indication of elements that protect victims and reduce the likelihood of victimisation occurring. Although social-skills deficits may not explain why children are bullies or victimised, it seems that the 'victims' of bullying may be more or less protected by the range of social skills they can employ to respond to bullying. For example, conflict-resolution skills seem to be important in the child's ability to manage bullying.

In Chapter 14 we will continue to explore strategies for addressing bullying in schools, many of which focus on enhancing conflict-resolution skills and accepting personal responsibility for one's actions. While it is clear that bullying is a well-recognised international problem, it is also clear that many students remain reticent to tell their teachers or parents about bullying incidents. Some students have little faith in any positive outcome from teacher actions (Bauman & Del Rio, 2006).

CONCLUDING COMMENTS

This chapter has illustrated important connections between how young people develop an understanding of their self, an understanding of others, and an understanding of relationships with other people. Like other dimensions of development, the skills gained through self-understanding and moral and emotional development remain with children and adolescents throughout adulthood. To ensure healthy development in these areas, young people need to be supported as they come to terms with who they are, how they fit into their sociocultural context, and how to deal with complex social and moral issues. Young people also need to be active agents rather than passive listeners when grappling with moral issues and social dilemmas. These dilemmas present themselves in everyday contexts, not least in those of peer relationships and bullying. The challenge for educators is to provide opportunities for learners to become independent thinkers who are self-aware, critically reflective and conscious of their role in the broader social and cultural contexts in which they live.

CourseMateExpress

Online resources
Go further: More about the impact of bullying on victims can be found on this text's CourseMate Express website

STUDY TOOLS

ONLINE STUDY RESOURCES

Visit http://login.cengagebrain.com and use the access code that comes with this book for 12 months' access to the student resources for this text.

The CourseMate Express website contains a range of resources and study tools for this chapter, including:

- a **self-check quiz**

- **crosswords**, **flashcards** and a **glossary** to help you revise the key terms from this chapter
- the **Go further** materials and **interactive activity** mentioned in the chapter.

CourseMateExpress

CHAPTER REVIEW

- Self-concept, self-esteem and self-efficacy are internal beliefs about who we are, characteristics that make us unique and our ability or competencies in different areas.
- Erikson's theory of identity proposes that our sense of self develops over time and is connected to cognitive development.
- Moral development explains how we reason and make ethical choices and decisions in our lives, and is also related to our cognitive development.
- Kohlberg used a moral dilemma (the Heinz dilemma) to posit a complex six-stage sequence of moral development taking place within three broad levels.

- Emotional development refers to our ability to function and understand our social world. We develop an increasing range of emotional competencies over time.
- Social development refers to our gradual understanding of and ability to maintain relationships with others.
- Positive peer experiences are central to self- and other understanding, and are protective factors in children's lives. These include peer acceptance and friendships.
- Negative peer experiences may bring about low self-perception and mental health and social problems. These include loneliness, peer rejection and bullying.

PUTTING IT TOGETHER

Making links between 'social, emotional and moral development' and material in other chapters

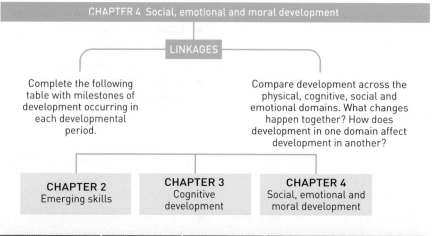

QUESTIONS AND ACTIVITIES FOR SELF-ASSESSMENT AND DISCUSSION

1   Define and explain the concept of a multidimensional self-concept.

2   What is self-efficacy? Comment on the role of self-efficacy in learning.

3   Outline Erikson's concept of a 'crisis' in the development of identity.

4   Define 'emotion' and explain the concept of emotional competence.

5   Identify links between self and emotional and social development in peer experiences.

6   Explain the importance of peer acceptance and friendship in the lives of children and adolescents.

FURTHER RESEARCH

SEARCH ME! AND EDUCATION DATABASES

Explore Search Me! education for articles relevant to this chapter. Fast and convenient, Search Me! education is updated daily and provides you with 24-hour access to full-text articles from hundreds of scholarly and popular journals, ebooks and newspapers, including *The Australian* and *The New York Times*. Log in to Search Me! through http://login.cengagebrain.com and use the search terms listed here as a starting point:

- bullying
- emotional competence
- emotional development
- friendship
- identity development
- moral development AND children
- self-concept
- self-efficacy
- self-esteem
- social development.

You can also use these terms to explore databases such as ERIC, PsycINFO and the Australian Education Index.

Search Me!

RECOMMENDED WEBSITES

Resilience and bullying support for children: www.dinglefoundation.org.nz/kiwican

Resiliency Resource Centre: http://resilienceresearch.org

Response Ability: www.responseability.org

KidsMatter: www.kidsmatter.edu.au

Bullying information for teachers: www.bullyingnoway.com.au

Mental health and student wellbeing: www.mindmatters.edu.au

Mental health information for educators: www.responseability.org

RECOMMENDED READING

Bandura, A. (2011). Social cognitive theory. In P. A. M. van Lange, A. W. Kruglanski & E. T. Higgins (Eds). *Handbook of social psychological theories* (pp. 349–73). London: Sage.

Durlak, J.A. et al. (eds.). (2015). *Handbook of Social and Emotional Learning: Research and Practice*. New York: Guilford Press.

Eisenberg, N. (Ed.) (1998). *Handbook of child psychology: Vol. 3: Social, emotional and personality development* (5th ed.). New York: Wiley.

Erikson, E. H. (1997). *The life cycle completed: Extended version*. New York: WW Norton & Co.

Jimerson, S.R., Swearer, S.M. & Espelage, D.L. (eds.). (2010). *Handbook of bullying in schools: An international perspective*. New York, NY: Routledge/Taylor & Francis Group.

Killen, M. & Smetana, J.G. (eds.). (2014) *Handbook of Moral Development*, 2nd Edition (pp. 23–45). New York: Psychology Press.

Kohlberg, L. (1984). *Essays in moral development. Volume II: The psychology of moral development*. San Francisco: Harper & Row.

Nucci, L. & Narvaez, D. (2008). *Handbook on moral and character education*. Oxford, UK: Routledge.

Purdie, N., Tripcony, P., Boulton-Lewis, G., Fanshawe, J. & Gunstone, A. (2000). *Positive self-identity for Indigenous students and its relationship to school outcomes*. Canberra: Commonwealth of Australia.

Rubin, K.H., Bukowski, W.M. & Laursen, B. (2008). *Handbook of peer interactions, relationships, and groups*. New York: Guilford Press.

White, R. & Wyn, J. (2011). *Youth and society: Exploring the social dynamics of youth experience*. Sydney: Oxford University Press.

REFERENCES

Ackard, D. M. & Neumark-Sztainer, D. (2002). Date violence and date rape among adolescents: Associations with disordered eating behaviors and psychological health. *Child Abuse and Neglect, 26*(5), 455–73.

Adams, R. E., Santo, J. B. & Bukowski, W. M. (2011). The presence of a best friend buffers the effects of negative experiences. *Developmental Psychology, 47*(6), 1786–91. Retrieved from http://dx.doi.org/10.1037/a0025401

Adler, P. A. & Adler, P. (1995). Dynamics of inclusion and exclusion in preadolescent cliques. *Social Psychology Quarterly, 58*, 145–62.

Andrews, M., Ainley, M. & Frydenberg, E. (2004). *Adolescent engagement with problem-solving tasks: The role of coping style, self-efficacy and emotions.* Paper presented at the Australian Association for Research in Education, Melbourne, 29 November–2 December 2004.

Archer, J. & Coyne, S. M. (2005). An integrated review of indirect, relational, and social aggression. *Personality and Social Psychology Review, 9*, 312–30.

Arsenio, W. & Lover, A. (1995). Children's conceptions of sociomoral affect: Happy victimizers, mixed emotions, and other expectancies. In M. Killen & D. Hart (Eds), *Morality in everyday life: Developmental perspectives. Cambridge studies in social and emotional development* (pp. 87–128). New York: Cambridge University Press.

Asher, S. R. & Dodge, K. A. (1986). Identifying children who are rejected by their peers. *Developmental Psychology, 22*(4), 444–9.

Asher, S. R., Parker, J. G. & Walker, D. L. (1996). Distinguishing friendship from acceptance: Implications for intervention and assessment. In W. M. Bukowski, A. F. Newcomb & W. W. Hartup (Eds), *The company they keep: Friendship in childhood and adolescence* (pp. 366–405). New York: Cambridge University Press.

Bagwell, C. L., Schmidt, M. E., Newcomb, A. F. & Bukowski, W. M. (2001). Friendship and peer rejection as predictors of adult adjustment. In D. W. Nangle & C. A. Erdley (Eds), *New directions for child and adolescent development: Issue 91. The role of friendship in psychological adjustment* (pp. 25–50). San Francisco: Jossey-Bass.

Bandura, A. (1977). *Social learning theory.* Oxford: Prentice Hall.

Bandura, A. (1994). Self-efficacy. In V. S. Ramachaudran (Ed.), *Encyclopedia of human behavior* (Vol. 4, pp. 71–81). New York: Academic Press.

Bandura, A. (1997). *Self-efficacy: The exercise of control.* New York: W. H. Freeman.

Bandura, A. (2001). Social cognitive theory: An agentic perspective. *Annual Review of Psychology, 52*, 1–26.

Bandura, A. (2002). Selective moral disengagement in the exercise of moral agency. *Journal of Moral Education, 31*, 101–19.

Barrett, K. C. (2000). The development of the self-in-relationships. In R. Mills & S. Duck (Eds), *The developmental psychology of personal relationships* (pp. 91–107). Chichester: Wiley.

Barrett, K. C. & Campos, J. J. (1987). Perspectives on emotional development II: A functionalist approach to emotions. In J. D. Osofsky (Ed.), *Handbook of infant development* (2nd edn, pp. 555–578). New York: Wiley.

Bauman, S. & Del Rio, A. (2006). Preservice teachers' responses to bullying scenarios: Comparing physical, verbal, and relational bullying. *Journal of Educational Psychology, 98*(1), 219–31.

Baumeister, R. F., Campbell, J. D., Krueger, J. I. & Vohs, K. D. (2003). Does high self-esteem cause better performance, interpersonal success, happiness, or healthier lifestyles? *Psychological Science in the Public Interest, 4*, 1–44.

Bebeau, M. J., Rest, J. & Narvaez, D. (1999). Moving beyond the promise: A perspective for research in moral education. *Educational Researcher, 28*(4), 18–26.

Bellini, S. & Akullian, J. (2007). A meta-analysis of video modelling and video self-modelling interventions for children and adolescents with Autism Spectrum Disorders. *Journal of Exceptional Children, 73*(3), 224–264.

Bergman, R. (2004). Caring for the ethical ideal: Nel Noddings on moral education. *Journal of Moral Education, 33*(2), 149–62.

Berlan, E. D., Corliss, H. L., Field, A. E., Goodman, E. & Bryn Austin, S. (2007). Sexual orientation and bullying in adolescents. *Journal of Adolescent Health, 40*(2), S28.

Bierhoff, H. W. (2002). *Prosocial behavior.* Florence, KY: Psychology Press.

Bigelow, B. J. & LaGaipa, J. J. (1975). Children's written descriptions of friendship: A multidimensional analysis. *Developmental Psychology, 11*, 857–8.

Bjorklund, D. F. & Brown, R. (1998). Physical play and cognitive development: Integrating activity, cognition, and education. *Child Development, 69*, 604–6.

Björkqvist, K., Lagerspetz, K. M. J. & Kaukiainen, A. (1992). Do girls manipulate and boys fight? Developmental trends regarding direct and indirect aggression. *Aggressive Behaviour, 18*, 117–27.

Björkqvist, K. & Osterman, K. (1999). Finland. In P. K. Smith, Y. Morita, J. Junger-Tas, D. Olweus, R. Catalano & P. T. Slee (Eds), *The nature of school bullying: A cross-national perspective* (pp. 56–67). London: Routledge.

Boccia, M. & Campos, J. J. (1989). Maternal emotional signals, social referencing, and infants' reactions to strangers. In N. Eisenberg (Ed.), *Empathy and related emotional responses: New directions for child development* (pp. 25–49). San Francisco: Jossey-Bass.

Bodrova, E. & Leong, D. J. (2010). Curriculum and play in early child development. In R. E. Tremblay, M. Boivin & R. DeV. Peters (Eds), *Encyclopedia on Early Childhood Development* [online]. Montreal, Quebec: Centre of Excellence for Early Childhood Development and Strategic Knowledge Cluster on Early Child Development.

Boivin, M., Poulin, F. & Vitaro, F. (1994). Depressed mood and peer rejection in childhood. *Development and Psychopathology, 6*, 483–98.

Bos, A., Huijding, J., Muris, P., Vogel, L. & Biesheuvel, J. (2010). Global, contingent, and implicit self-esteem and psychopathological symptoms in adolescents. *Personality and Individual Differences, 48*, 311–16.

Brophy, J. (1988). Research linking teacher behavior to student achievement: Potential implications for instruction of Chapter I students. *Educational Psychologist, 23*, 235–312.

Brown, J. D. & Siegel, J. M. (1988). Exercise as a buffer of life stress: A prospective study of adolescent health. *Health Psychology, 7*, 341–53.

Buckley, M., Storino, M. & Saarni, C. (2003). Promoting emotional competence in children and adolescents: Implications for school psychologists. *School Psychology Quarterly, 18*, 177–91.

Bukowski, W. M. (2001). Friendship and the worlds of childhood. In D. Nangle & C. Erdley (Eds), *The role of friendship in psychological adjustment: New directions for child and adolescent development, 91*, 93–106. San Francisco: Jossey-Bass.

Burks, V. S., Dodge, K. A. & Price, J. M. (1995). Models of internalizing outcomes of early rejection. *Development & Psychopathology. Special issue: Developmental Processes in Peer Relations and Psychopathology, 7*(4), 683–95.

Burleson, K. P., Leach, C. W. & Harrington, D. (2005). Upward social comparison and selfconcept: Inspiration and inferiority among art students in an advanced program. *British Journal of Social Psychology, 44*, 109–23.

Bussey, K., Fitzpatrick, S. & Raman, A. (2014). The Role of Moral Disengagement and Self-Efficacy in Cyberbullying, *Journal of School Violence, 14*(1), 30–46.

Byrne, B. M. (2002). Validating the measurement and structure of self-concept: Snapshots of past, present, and future research. *American Psychologist, 57*(11), 897–909.

Byrne, B. M. & Gavin, D. A. (1996). The Shavelson model revisited: Testing for the structure of academic self-concept across pre-, early, and late adolescents. *Journal of Educational Psychology, 88*, 215–28.

Caldarella, P. & Merrell, K. (1997). Common dimensions of social skills of children and adolescents: A taxonomy of positive behaviors. *School Psychology Review, 26*, 264–78.

Card, N. A. (2003). Victims of peer aggression: A meta-analytic review. Presented at Society for Research in Child Development biennial meeting, Tampa, Florida, April.

Carlo, G. (2006). Care-based and altruistically based morality. In M. Killen & J. G. Smetana (Eds), *Handbook of moral development* (pp. 551–79). Mahwah, NJ: Erlbaum.

Cassidy, J. & Asher, S. (1992). Loneliness and peer relations in young children. *Child Development, 63*(2), 350–65.

Cassidy, J., Parke, R. D., Butkovsky, L. & Braungart, J. M. (1992). Family–peer connections: The roles of emotional expressiveness within the family and children's understanding of emotions. *Child Development, 63*, 603–18.

Cavell, T. (1990). Social adjustment, social performance, and social skills: A tri-component model of social competence. *Journal of Clinical Child Psychology, 19*, 111–22.

Cha, J. H. (1994). Aspects of individualism and collectivism in Korea. In U. Kim, H. C. Triandis, C. Kagitcibasi, S. Choi & G. Yoon (Eds), *Individualism and collectivism: Theory, methods, and applications* (pp. 157–74). Thousand Oaks, CA: Sage.

Cillessen, A. H. N. & Rose, A. J. (2005). Understanding popularity in the peer system. *Current Directions in Psychological Science, 14*, 102–5.

Cohen, S., Tyrrell, D. A. J. & Smith, A. P. (1991). Psychological stress in humans and susceptibility to the common cold. *New England Journal of Medicine, 325*, 606–12.

Coie, J. D., Dodge, K. & Copotelli, H. (1982). Dimensions and types of social status: A cross-age perspective. *Developmental Psychology, 18*, 557–71.

Colby, A., Kohlberg, L. & Kauffman, K. (1987). Theoretical introduction to the measurement of moral judgment. In A. Colby & L. Kohlberg (Eds), *The measurement of moral judgment* (Vol. 1). Cambridge, UK: Cambridge University Press.

Colby, A., Kohlberg, L., Gibbs., J., Lieberman, M., Fischer, K. & Saltzstein, H. D. (1983). A longitudinal study of moral judgment, *Monographs of the Society for Research in Child Development, 48*(1/2), 1–124.

Commonwealth of Australia, Department of Education, Employment and Workplace Relations. (2012). *Early years learning framework.* Canberra: DEEWR. Retrieved from www.deewr.gov.au/EarlyChildhood/Policy_Agenda/Quality/Pages/EarlyYearsLearningFramework.aspx.

Comunian, A. L. & Gielen, U. P. (Eds). (2000). *International perspectives on human development.* Lengerich, Germany: Pabst Science Publishers.

Crain, W. (2000). *Theories of development: Concepts and applications* (4th ed.). Upper Saddle River, NJ: Prentice Hall.

Crick, N. R. & Dodge, K. A. (1994). A review and reformulation of social information-processing mechanisms in children's social adjustment. *Psychological Bulletin, 115*, 74–101.

Crick, N. R. & Grotpeter, J. K. (1995). Relational aggression, gender, and social-psychological adjustment. *Child Development, 66*, 710–22.

Crick, N. R., Nelson, D. A., Morales, J. R., Cullerton-Sen, C., Casas, J. F. & Hickman, S. E. (2001). Relational victimisation in childhood and adolescence: I hurt you through the grapevine. In J. Juvonen, A. Nishina & S. Graham (Eds), *Peer harassment in school: The plight of the vulnerable and victimized* (pp. 196–214). New York: Guilford.

Cross, D., Shaw, T., Hearn, L., Epstein, M., Monks, H., Lester, L. & Thomas, L. (2009). *Australian Covert Bullying Prevalence Study (ACBPS).* Perth: Child Health Promotion Research Centre, Edith Cowan University.

Cunningham, C. E., Cunningham, L. J., Ratcliffe, J. & Vaillancourt, T. (2010). A qualitative analysis of the bullying prevention and intervention recommendations of students in grades 5 to 8. *Journal of School Violence, 9*, 321–38.

Curriculum Council. (1998). *Western Australian curriculum framework.* Retrieved from www.curriculum.wa.edu.au/internet/years_K10/Curriculum_Framework

Dalgleish, T. & Bramham, J. (1999). The cognitive perspective on emotion. In D. Levinson, J. J. Ponzetti, Jr. & P. F. Jorgensen (Eds), *Encyclopedia of Human Emotions* (pp. 118–21). New York: Macmillan.

Damon, W. (1977). *The social world of the child.* San Francisco: Jossey Bass.

Damon, W. (1983). *Social and personality development.* New York: W. W. Norton.

Davidson, T. E. & McCabe, M. P. (2006). Adolescent body image and psychosocial functioning. *Journal of Social Psychology, 146*, 15–30.

DEEWR (2012). See Commonwealth of Australia. Department of Education, Employment and Workplace Relations.

Durkheim, E. (1925/1961). *Moral education: A study in the theory and application of the sociology of education.* (Foreword P. Fauconnet; trans. E. K. Wilson & H. Schnurer; edited with a new introduction E. K. Wilson.) New York: Free Press of Glencoe.

Eccles, J. S. & Gootman, J. A. (Eds). (2002). *Community programs to promote youth development.* Washington, DC: National Academy Press.

Eccles, J. S. & Midgley, C. (1989). Stage/environment fit: Developmentally appropriate classrooms for young adolescents. In R. Ames & C. Ames (Eds), *Research on motivation and education: Goals and cognitions* (Vol. 3, pp. 139–86). New York: Academic Press.

Eccles, J. S. & Wigfield, A. (1995). In the mind of the actor: The structure of adolescents' achievement task values and expectancy-related beliefs. *Personality & Social Psychology Bulletin, 21*(3), 215–25.

Eisenberg, N. (1982). The development of reasoning regarding prosocial behavior. In N. Eisenberg (Ed.), *The development of prosocial behavior* (pp. 219–49). New York: Academic Press.

Eisenberg, N. (1986). *Altruistic emotion, cognition and behavior.* Hillsdale, NJ: Lawrence Erlbaum.

Eisenberg, N. (1989). Empathy and related emotional responses. *New Directions in Child Development, 44.* San Francisco: Jossey Bass.

Eisenberg, N. (1992). *The caring child.* Cambridge, MA: Harvard University Press.

Eisenberg, N. (1998). Introduction. In N. Eisenberg (Ed.), *Handbook of child psychology, Vol. 3: Social, emotional, and personality development* (5th ed., pp. 1–24). New York: Wiley.

Eisenberg, N., Eggum, N. D. & Di Giunta, L. (2010). Empathy-related responding: Associations with prosocial behavior, aggression, and intergroup relations. *Social Issues Policy Review, 4*(1), 143–80.

Eisenberg, N. & Fabes, R. A. (1998). Prosocial development. In N. Eisenberg (Ed.), *Handbook of child psychology, Vol. 3: Social, emotional, and personality development* (5th ed., pp. 701–78). New York: Wiley.

Eisenberg, N., Hofer, C., Sulik, M. J., & Liew, J. (2014). The development of prosocial moral reasoning and a prosocial orientation in young adulthood: Concurrent and longitudinal correlates. *Developmental Psychology, 50*(1), 58–70. http://dx.doi.org/10.1037/a0032990

Erdley, C. A., Nangle, D., Newman, J. & Carpenter, E. (2001). Children's friendship experiences and psychological adjustment: Theory and research. In D. Nangle & C. A. Erdley (Eds), *The role of friendship in psychological adjustment* (pp. 5–24). San Francisco: Jossey-Bass.

Erikson, E. H. (1959). *Identity and the life cycle: Selected papers.* Oxford: International Universities Press.

Erikson, E. H. (1982). *The life cycle completed: A review* pp. 32–3. © 1982, published by Rikan Enterprises

Erikson, E. H. (1997). *The life cycle completed: Extended version.* New York: WW Norton.

Erol, R. Y. & Orth, U. (2011). Self-esteem development from age 14 to 30 years: A longitudinal study. *Journal of Personality and Social Psychology, 101*, 607–19.

Espelage, D. L. & Swearer, S. M. (2003). Research on school bullying and victimization: What have we learned and where do we go from here? *School Psychology Review, 32*(3), 365–83.

Espelage, D. L. & Swearer, S. M. (2009). Contributions of three social theories to understanding bullying perpetration and victimization among school-aged youth. In M. J. Harris (Ed.), *Bullying, rejection, and peer victimization: A social cognitive neuroscience perspective* (pp. 151–70). New York: Springer.

Espelage D. L., Basile K. C., De La Rue, L. & Hamburger, M. E. (2015). Longitudinal associations among bully, homophobic teasing, and sexual violence perpetration among middle school students. *Journal of Interpersonal Violence, 30*(14): 2541–2561.

Evans, N. J., Forney, D. S. & Guido-DiBrito, F. (1998). *Student development in college: Theory, research, and practice.* San Francisco: Jossey-Bass.

Fabes, R. A., Eisenberg, N., Nyman, M. & Michealieu, Q. (1991). Young children's appraisals of others' spontaneous emotional reactions. *Developmental Psychology, 27*, 858–66.

Finke, L. & Williams, J. (1999). Alcohol and drug use of inter-city versus rural school age children. *Journal of Drug Education, 29*(3), 279–91.

Fischer, K. W., Wang, L., Kennedy, B. & Cheng, C-L. (1998). Culture and biology in emotional development. In D. Sharma & K. W. Fischer (Eds), *Socioemotional development across cultures* (No. 81, pp. 21–44). San Francisco: Jossey-Bass.

Flook, L., Repetti, R. L. & Ullman, J. B. (2005). Classroom social experiences as predictors of academic performance. *Developmental Psychology, 41*(2), 319–27.

Fogel, A. (1995). Relational narratives of the prelinguistic self. In P. Rochat (Ed.), *The self in infancy: Theory and research* (pp. 117–39). Amsterdam: Elsevier North Holland.

Ford, T. (2004). Queering education from the ground up: Challenges and opportunities for educators. *Canadian Online Journal of Queer Studies in Education, 1*(1). Retrieved from http://jqstudies.library. utoronto.ca/index.php/jqstudies/article/ view/3273/1404

Forero, R., McLellan, L., Rissel, C. & Bauman, A. (1999). Bullying behaviour and psychosocial health among school students in New South Wales, Australia: A cross-sectional survey. *British Medical Journal, 319*(206), 344–8.

Fraser, D. (2004). Secular schools, spirituality and Māori values. *Journal of Moral Education, 33*(1), 87–95.

Freud, S. (1930/1963). *Civilisation and its discontents* (Ed. J. Strachey, Trans. J. Riviere). London: Hogarth Press and the Institute of Psycho-Analysis.

Frydenberg, E. & Lewis, R. (2002). Adolescent well-being: Building young people's resources. In E. Frydenberg (Ed.), *Beyond coping: Meeting goals, visions, and challenges* (pp. 175–94). New York: Oxford University Press.

Garmon, L. C., Bassinger, K. S., Gregg, V. R. & Gibbs, J. C. (1996). Gender differences in stage and expression of moral judgment. *Merrill-Palmer Quarterly, 42*, 418–37.

Gila, A., Castro, J., Gomez, M. J. & Toro, J. (2005). Social and body self-esteem in adolescents with eating disorders. *International Journal of Psychology and Psychological Therapy, 1*, 63–71.

Gilligan, C. (1982). *In a different voice.* Cambridge, MA: Harvard University Press.

Gnepp, J. (1989). Children's use of personal information to understand other people's feelings. In C. Saarni & P. L. Harris (Eds), *Children's understanding of emotion.* New York: Cambridge University Press.

Gnepp, J. & Gould, M. E. (1985). The development of personalized inferences: Understanding other people's emotional reactions in light of their prior experiences. *Child Development, 56*, 1455–64.

Gray, P. (1991). *Psychology* (2nd ed.). New York: Worth.

Gresham, F. M., Sugai, G. & Horner, R. H. (2001). Interpreting outcomes of social skills training for students with high-incidence disabilities. *Exceptional Children, 67*(3), 331–44. Published by Sage Publications.

Gross, A. L. & Bailif, B. (1991). Children's understanding of emotion from facial expressions and situations: A review. *Developmental Review, 11*, 368–98.

Harris, A. (2006). Critical perspectives on child and youth participation in Australia and New Zealand/Aotearoa, *Children, Youth, and Environments, 16*(2), 220–30.

Harter, S. (2006). Developmental and individual difference perspectives on self-esteem. In D. K. Mroczek & T. D. Little (Eds), *Handbook of personality development* (pp. 311–34). Mahwah, NJ: Erlbaum.

Harter, S. (2012). *The construction of the self: Developmental and sociocultural foundations.* New York: Guilford Press.

Hau, K. T., Sung, R. Y. T., Marsh, H. W., Yu, C. W. & Lau, P. W. C. (2005). Factorial structure and comparison between obese and non-obese children's physical self-concept. In H. W. Marsh, R. G. Craven & D. M. McInerney (Eds), *Advances in self-research* (Vol. 2, pp. 257–78). Greenwich, CT: Information Age Publishing.

Hay, I. (1997). Investigating the influence of achievement on self-concept using an intra-class design and a comparison of the PASS SDQ-1 self-concept tests. *British Journal of Educational Psychology, 67*, 311–21.

Haydon, G. (2004). Values education: Sustaining the ethical environment. *Journal of Moral Education, 33*(2), 115–29.

Hayward, S. M. & Fletcher, J. (2003). Relational aggression in an Australian sample: Gender and age differences. *Australian Journal of Psychology, 55*(3), 129–34.

Hinde, R. A. (1995). A suggested structure for a science of relationships. *Personal Relationships, 2*, 1–15.

Hodges, E. V. E., Boivin, M., Vitaro, F. & Bukowski, W. M. (1999). The power of friendship: Protection against an escalating cycle of peer victimisation. *Developmental Psychology, 35*, 94–101.

Hodges, E. V. E. & Perry, D. G. (1999). Personal and interpersonal antecedents and consequences of victimization by peers. *Journal of Personality and Social Psychology, 76*, 677–85.

Howes, C. & Matheson, C. C. (1992). Sequences in the development of competent play with peers: Social and social pretend play. *Developmental Psychology, 28*, 961–74.

Hughes, F. P. (2010). *Children, play, and development* (4th ed.). Thousand Oaks, CA: Sage.

Hymel, S., Wagner, E. & Butler, L. J. (1990). Reputational bias: View from the peer group. In S. R. Asher & J. D. Coie (Eds), *Peer rejection in childhood* (pp. 156–88). Cambridge, UK: Cambridge University Press.

Irving, L. M., Wall, M., Neumark-Sztainer, D. & Story, M. (2002). Steroid use among adolescents: Findings from Project EAT. *Journal of Adolescent Health, 30*(4, Suppl.), 243–52.

Iwaniec, D. (2006). *The emotionally abused and neglected child.* New York: Wiley.

Jacobs, J. E., Lanza, S., Osgood, D. W., Eccles, J. S. & Wigfield, A. (2002). Changes in children's self-competence and values: Gender and domain differences across grades one through twelve. *Child Development, 73*(2), 509–27.

Jadack, R. A., Hyde, J. S., Moore, C. F. & Keller, M. L. (1995). Moral reasoning about sexually transmitted diseases. *Child Development, 66*, 167–77.

Jaffe, S. & Hyde, J. S. (2000). Gender differences in moral orientation: A meta-analysis. *Psychological Bulletin, 126*, 703–26.

James, W. (1890). *The principles of psychology.* New York: Henry Holt.

Jensen, E. & Browne, R. (2008). Our kids in worst class of bullies. *Sydney Morning Herald*, 14 December.

Johnson, D. & Lewis, G. (1999). Do you like what you see? Self-perceptions of adolescent bullies. *British Educational Research Journal, 25*(5), 665–77.

Juvonen, J. & Graham, S. (2014). Bullying in schools: The power of bullies and the plight of victims. *Annual Review of Psychology, 65*, 159–85.

Juvonen, J., Graham, S. & Schuster, M. A. (2003). Bullying among young adolescents: The strong, the weak, and the troubled. *Pediatrics, 112*, 1231–7.

Klassen, R. (2002). Writing in early adolescence: A review of the role of self-efficacy beliefs. *Educational Psychology Review, 14*(2), 173–203.

Kochenderfer, B. J. & Ladd, G. W. (1996). Peer victimisation: Cause or consequence of school maladjustment. *Child Development, 67*, 1305–17.

Kohlberg, L. (1963). The development of children's orientations toward a moral order. I. Sequence in the development of moral thought. *Human Development, 6*, 11–33. Published by Karger Medical and Scientific Publishers.

Kohlberg, L. (1987). The development of moral judgment and moral action. In L. Kohlberg, *Child psychology and childhood education: A cognitive-developmental view* (pp. 259–328). New York: Longman.

Kowalski, R. M. & Limber, S. P. (2007). Cyber bullying among middle school students. *Journal of Adolescent Health, 41*(Suppl.), S22–S30.

Kroger, J. & Marcia, J. E. (2011) The identity statuses: Origins, meanings, and interpretations. In S. J. Schwartz, K. Luycky & V. Vignoles. (Eds), *Handbook of identity theory and research* (pp. 31–54). New York: Springer Science+Business Media.

Ladd, G. W., Kochenderfer, B. J. & Coleman, C. C. (1996). Friendship quality as a predictor of young children's early school adjustment. *Child Development, 67*(3), 1103–18.

Lane, A. M., Jones, L. & Stevens, M. J. (2002). Coping with failure: The effects of self-esteem and coping on changes in self efficacy. *Journal of Sport Behavior, 25*(4), 331–45.

Langford, P. E. (1995). *Approaches to the development of moral reasoning.* Hove, UK: Lawrence Erlbaum Associates.

Lazarus, R. S. (1991). *Emotion and adaptation.* New York: Oxford University Press.

Leary, M. R., Schreindorfer, L. S. & Haupt, A. L. (1995). The role of low self-esteem in emotional and behavioral problems: Why is low self-esteem dysfunctional? *Journal of Social and Clinical Psychology, 14*(3), 297–314.

Leman, P. J. (2001). The development of moral reasoning. In C. Fraser & B. Burchell (Eds), *Introducing social psychology* (pp. 195–215). Cambridge, UK: Polity Press.

Leming, J. S. (2000). Tell me a story: An evaluation of a literature-based character education programme. *Journal of Moral Education, 29*(4), 413–27.

Lerner, R. M., Lerner, J. V., Phelps, E. et al. (2012). *Waves of the future: The first eight years of the 4-H study of positive youth development.* Retrieved from http://ase.tufts.edu/iaryd/documents/4HStudyWavesOfFuture.pdf

Leslie, M. B., Stein, J. A. & Rotheram-Borus, M. J. (2002). Sex-specific predictors of suicidality among runaway youth. *Journal of Community Psychology, 31*(1), 27–40.

Lewis, M. (1993a). The emergence of human emotions. In M. Lewis & J. M. Haviland (Eds), *The handbook of emotion* (pp. 223–46). New York: Guilford Press.

Lewis, M. (1993b). Self-conscious emotions: Embarrassment, pride, shame, and guilt. In M. Lewis & J. M. Haviland (Eds), *The handbook of emotion* (pp. 563–73). New York: Guilford Press.

Lieber, S., Efreom-Lieber, Y. & Rate, C. (2010). Moral disengagement: Exploring support mechanisms for violent extremism among young Egyptian males. Proceedings of the 1st Australian Counter Terrorism Conference.

Lifter, K. (2002). Developmental play assessment and teaching. In J. K. Luiselli, D. C. Russo, W. P. Christian & S. M. Wilczynski (Eds), *Effective practices for children with autism: Educational and behavioral*

support interventions that work (pp. 299–324). New York: Oxford University Press.

Lifter, K. & Bloom, L. (1998). Intentionality and the role of play in the transition to language. In A. M. Wetherby, S. R. Warren & R. Reichle (Eds), *Transitions in prelinguistic communication: Preintentional and presymbolic to symbolic* (pp. 161–95). Baltimore, MD: Paul H. Brookes.

Lillevoll, K. R., Kroger, J. & Martinussen, M. (2013). Identity status and anxiety: A metaanalysis. *Identity: An International Journal of Theory and Research, 13*(3), 214–27.

Lind, J. & Maxwell, G. (1996). *Children's experiences of violence at school.* Wellington: Office of the Commissioner for Children.

Lofgran, B., Smith, L. & Whiting, E. (2015). Science Self-Efficacy and School Transitions: Elementary School to Middle School, Middle School to High School. *School Science and Mathematics, 115*(7), 366–376.

Marcia, J. E. (1980). Identity in adolescence. In J. Adelson (Ed.), *Handbook of adolescent psychology* (5th ed., pp. 159–87). New York: John Wiley & Sons, Inc.

Marcia, J. E. (1993). *Ego identity: A handbook for psychosocial research.* New York: Springer-Verlag.

Marcia, J. E. (2002). Adolescence, identity, and the Bernardone family. *Identity: An International Journal of Theory and Research, 2*(3), 199–209.

Markus, H. R. & Kitayama, S. (1991). Culture and the self: Implications for cognition, emotion, and maturation. *Psychological Review, 98*, 224–53.

Marsh, H. W. (1986). Verbal and math self-concepts: An internal/external frame of reference model. *American Educational Research Journal, 23*, 129–49.

Marsh, H. W. (1990). *Self-description questionnaire, II.* San Antonio, TX: The Psychological Corporation.

Marsh, H. W. (1992). Content specificity of relations between academic achievement and academic self-concept. *Journal of Educational Psychology, 84*, 35–42.

Marsh, H. W., Byrne, B. M. & Shavelson, R. J. (1988). A multi-faceted academic selfconcept: Its hierarchical structure and its relation to academic achievement. *Journal of Educational Psychology, 80*, 366–80.

Marsh, H. W. & Craven, R. (2006). Reciprocal effects of self-concept and performance from a multidimensional perspective: Beyond seductive pleasure and unidimensional perspectives. *Perspectives on Psychological Science, 1*(2), 133–63.

Marsh, H. W., Kong, C-K. & Hau, K-T. (2000). Longitudinal multilevel models of the big-fish-little-pond effect on academic self-concept: Counterbalancing contrast and reflected-glory effects in Hong Kong schools. *Journal of Personality and Social Psychology, 78*(2), 337–49.

Marsh, H. W., Kuyper, H., Morin, A. J. S., Parker, P. D. & Seaton, M. (2014). Big-fish-little-pond social comparison and local dominance effects: Integrating new statistical models, methodology, design, theory and substantive implications. *Learning and Instruction, 33*, 50.

Marsh, H. W., Seaton, M., Trautwein, U., Lüdtke, O., Hau, K. T. et al. (2008). The big-fish-little-pond-effect stands up to critical scrutiny: Implications for theory, methodology, and future research. *Educational Psychology Review, 20*(3), 319–50.

Marsh, H. W., Trautwein, U., Ludtke, O., Baumert, J. & Köller, O. (2007). Big-fish-little-pond effect: Persistent negative effects of selective high schools on self-concept after graduation. *American Educational Research Journal, 44*, 631–69.

Marsh, H. W. & Yeung, A.-S. (1998). Longitudinal structural equation models of academic self-concept and achievement: Gender differences in the development of math and English constructs. *American Educational Research Journal, 35*, 705–38.

Martin, M. O., Mullis, I. V. S. & Foy, P. (with Olson, J. F., Erberber, E., Preuschoff, C. & Galia, J.). (2008). *TIMSS 2007 international science report: Findings from IEA's Trends in International Mathematics and Science Study at the fourth and eighth grades.* Chestnut Hill, MA: TIMSS & PIRLS International Study Center, Boston College.

Masten, A. S. & Coatsworth, J. D. (1998). The development of competence in favorable and unfavorable environments. *American Psychologist, 53*(2), 205–20.

McGrath, H. & Stanley, M. (2006). A safe school (anti-bullying) template for schools. In H. McGrath & T. Noble (Eds), *Bullying Solutions: Evidence based approaches to bullying in Australian Schools* (pp. 229–78). Sydney: Pearson Education.

MacGuire, M. C. & Dunn, J. (1997). Friendships in Early Childhood, and Social Understanding. *International Journal of Behavioral Development, 21*(4). http://journals.sagepub.com/doi/abs/10.1080/0165 02597384613

Meeus, W. (2011). The study of adolescent identity formation 2000–2010: A review of longitudinal research. *Journal of Research on Adolescence, 21*, 75–94. doi: 10.1111/j.1532-7795.2010.00716.x

Meeus, W., van de Schoot, R., Keijsers, L. & Branje, S. (2011). Identity statuses as developmental trajectories: A five-wave longitudinal study in early-to-middle and middle-to-late adolescents, *Journal of Youth and Adolescence.* doi:10.1007/s10964-011-9730-y

Menon, U. (2000). Analyzing emotions as culturally constructed scripts. *Culture and Psychology, 6*(1), 40–50.

Mikami, A. Y., Boucher, M. A. & Humphreys, K. (2005). Prevention of peer rejection through a classroom-level intervention in middle school. *Journal of Primary*

Prevention, 26, 5–23. Published by Springer.

Miller, J. G. & Bersoff, D. M. (1992). Culture and moral judgment: How are conflicts between justice and interpersonal responsibilities resolved? *Journal of Personality and Social Psychology, 62*(4), 541–54.

Montessori, M., (1967), *The absorbent mind*. New York: Dell Publishing.

Moore, C., Detert, J. R., Treviño, L. K., Baker, V. L. & Mayer, D. M. (2012). Why employees do bad things: Moral disengagement and unethical organizational behavior. *Personnel Psychology, 65*, 1–48.

Moreno, J. L. (1951). *Sociometry, experimental method and the science of society: An approach to a new political orientation*. Ambler, PA: Beacon House, Inc./Horsham Foundation.

Morita, Y. (1996). Bullying as a contemporary behaviour problem in the context of increased 'societal privatization' in Japan. *Prospects: Quarterly Review of Comparative Education, 26*, 311–29.

Nangle, D., Erdley, C., Newman, J., Mason, C. & Carpenter, E. (2003). Popularity, friendship quantity and friendship quality: Interactive influences on children's loneliness and depression. *Journal of Clinical Child and Adolescent Psychology, 32*(4), 546–55.

New Zealand Ministry of Education. (2001). *Briefing for the incoming Minister of Education 1999*. Retrieved from www.minedu.govt.nz/

Newcomb, A. F., Bukowski, W. M. & Bagwell, C. L. (1999). *Knowing the sounds: Friendship as a developmental context –Relationships as developmental contexts*. Mahwah, NJ: Lawrence Erlbaum Associates Publishers.

Newcomb, A. F., Bukowski, W. M. & Pattee, L. (1993). Children's peer relations: A metaanalytic review of popular, rejected, neglected, controversial and average sociometric status. *Psychological Bulletin, 113*, 99–128. American Psychological Association.

Nishina, A., Juvonen, J. & Witkow, M. R. (2005). Sticks and stones may break my bones but names will make me feel sick: The consequences of peer harassment. *Journal of Clinical Child and Adolescent Psychology, 34*, 37–48.

Noddings, N. (1990). Constructivism in mathematics education. *Journal for Research in Mathematics Education, Monograph, 4*, 7–18.

Noddings, N. (2002). *Educating moral people: A caring alternative to character education*. New York: Teachers College Press.

NSW Board of Studies. (2000). *Geography syllabus: NSW stages 4 and 5 geography syllabus*. Retrieved from www.boardofstudies.nsw.edu.au

NSW Department of Education and Training. (2010). *Ethics course trial: Final report*. Retrieved from www.det.nsw.edu.au/detresources/Ethics_Evaluation_Final_Report_11112010_HQssrhmwpK.pdf

Nucci, L. P. (2001). *Education in the moral domain*. Cambridge, UK: Cambridge University Press.

Olweus, D. (1978). *Aggression in schools: Bullies and whipping boys*. Washington, DC: Wiley.

Olweus, D. (1993). *Bullying in schools: What we know we can do*. Oxford, UK: Blackwell.

Olweus, D. (1999). Sweden. In P. K. Smith, Y. Morita, J. Junger-Tas, D. Olweus, R. Catalano & P. Slee. (Eds), *The nature of school bullying: A cross-national perspective* (pp. 7–27). New York: Routledge.

Olweus, D. (2000). Peer harassment: A critical analysis and some important issues. In J. Juvonen & S. Graham (Eds), *Peer harassment in school: The plight of the vulnerable and victimised* (pp. 3–20). London: Guilford Press.

Organisation for Economic Cooperation and Development. (2017). *PISA 2015 Results (Volume III): Students' Well-Being*, PISA, OECD Publishing, Paris. http://dx.doi.org/10.1787/9789264273856-en. ISBN (print) 978-92-64-27381-8

Orth, U., & Robins, R. (2014). The Development of Self-Esteem. *Current Directions in Psychological Science, 23*(5), 381–387.

Orth, U., Robins, R., Widaman, K., & King, Laura. (2012). Life-Span Development of Self-Esteem and Its Effects on Important Life Outcomes. *Journal of Personality and Social Psychology, 102*(6), 1271–1288.

Ostrov, J. M., Crick, N. R. & Keating, C. F. (2005). Gender biased perceptions of preschoolers' behavior: How much is aggression and prosocial behavior in the eye of the beholder? *Sex Roles: A Journal of Research, 52*, 393–8.

Owens, L., Daly, A. & Slee, P. (2005). Sex and age differences in victimisation and conflict resolution among adolescents in a South Australian school. *Aggressive Behaviour, 31*(1), 1–12.

Owens, L. & McMullin, C. E. (1995). Gender differences in aggression in children and adolescents in South Australian schools. *International Journal of Adolescence and Youth, 6*, 21–35.

Pajares, F. (1997). Current directions in self-efficacy research. In M. Maehr & P. R. Pintrich (Eds), *Advances in motivation and achievement* (Vol. 10, pp. 1–49). Greenwich, CT: JAI Press.

Pajares, F. (2002). *Overview of social cognitive theory and of self-efficacy*. Retrieved from www.emory.edu/EDUCATION/mfp/eff.html

Pajares, F. & Schunk, D. H. (2001). Self-beliefs and school success: Self-efficacy, self-concept, and school achievement. In R. J. Riding & S. G. Rayner (Eds), *Self perception: International perspectives on individual differences* (Vol. 2, pp. 239–65). Westport, CT: Ablex Publishing.

Pajares, F. & Urdan, T. (Eds). (2006). *Adolescent self-efficacy: Adolescence and Education series* (Vol. 5). Greenwich, CT: Information Age Publishing.

Panksepp, J. (2004). Emotions as natural kinds within the mammalian brain. In M. Lewis & J. M. Haviland-Jones, *Handbook of emotions*. New York: Guildford Press.

Parker, J. G. & Asher, S. R. (1987). Peer relations and later personal adjustment: Are low accepted children at risk? *Psychological Bulletin, 102*, 357–89. American Psychological Association.

Parker, J. G., Rubin, K. H., Price, J. M. & DeRosier, M. E. (1995). Peer relationships, child development and adjustment: A developmental psychopathology perspective. In D. Cicchetti & D. J. Cohen (Eds), *Developmental Psychopathology Volume 2: Risk, Disorder, and Adaptation* (pp. 96–161). Toronto, ON: Wiley–Interscience Publication.

Parkhurst, J. T. & Hopmeyer, A. (1998). Sociometric popularity and peer-perceived popularity: Two distinct dimensions of peer status. *Journal of Early Adolescence, 18*, 125–44.

Parten, M. (1932). Social participation among preschool children. *Journal of Abnormal and Social Psychology, 27*, 242–69.

Pekrun, R. & Stephen, E.J. (2012) Academic Emotions. In *APA Educational Psychology Handbook: Vol. 2. Individual Differences and Cultural and Contextual Factors*, K. R. Harris, S. Graham, and T. Urdan (Editors-in-Chief) Copyright © 2012 by the American Psychological Association. All rights reserved.

Pellegrini, A. D. & Smith, P. K. (1998). Physical activity and play: The nature and function of a neglected aspect of play. *Child Development, 69*, 577–98.

Penner, L. A. & Finkelstein, M. A. (1998). Dispositional and structural determinants of volunteerism. *Journal of Personality and Social Psychology, 49*, 237–47.

Perry, D. G., Perry, L. C. & Kennedy, E. (1992). Conflict and the development of antisocial behavior. In C. U. Shanz & W. W. Hartup (Eds), *Conflict in child and adolescent development* (pp. 301–29). New York: Cambridge University Press.

Piaget, J. (1932). *The moral judgement of the child* (M. Gabain Trans.). London: Kegan Paul, Trench, Trubner & Co.

Power, C., Higgins, A. & Kohlberg, L. (1989). *Lawrence Kohlberg's approach to moral education*. New York: Columbia University Press.

Purdie, N. & McCrindle, A. (2004). Measurement of self-concept among Indigenous and non-Indigenous Australian students. *Australian Journal of Psychology, 56*(1), 50–62.

Purdie, N., Tripcony, P., Boulton-Lewis, G., Fanshawe, J. & Gunstone, A. (2000). *Positive self-identity for Indigenous students and its relationship to school outcomes*. Canberra: Commonwealth of Australia.

Raab, V. C. (2001). Multiple risk factors in adolescent suicide: A meta-analysis of the published research. *Dissertation Abstracts*

International Section B: The Sciences and Engineering, 61(12-B), 6719.

Response Ability. (2013). Social and Emotional Wellbeing: A Teacher's Guide. http://www.responseability.org/__data/assets/pdf_file/0009/4878/Social-and-Emotional-Wellbeing-A-Teachers-Guide.pdf

Rest, J. R. (1979). *Development in judging moral issues.* Minneapolis, MI: University of Minnesota Press.

Rest, J. R. (1986). *Moral development: Advances in research and theory.* New York: Praeger.

Rest, J. R. & Narvaez, D. (Eds). (1994). *Moral development in the professions: Psychology and applied ethics.* Hillsdale, NJ: Lawrence Erlbaum.

Rest, J. R., Thomas, J. & Edwards, L. (1997). Designing and validating a measure of moral judgment: Stage preference and stage consistency approaches. *Journal of Educational Psychology, 89*(1), 5–28.

Rigby, K. (1994). Family influence, peer relations and health effects among school children. In K. Oxenberry, K. Rigby & P. T. Slee (Eds), *Children's peer relations. Conference proceedings* (pp. 294–304). Adelaide: The Institute of Social Research, University of South Australia.

Rigby, K. (2002). *New perspectives on bullying.* London: Jessica Kingsley.

Rigby, K. (2007). *Bullying in schools and what to do about it.* Melbourne: ACER.

Rigby, K. & Slee, P. T. (1999). Australia. In P. K. Smith, Y. Morita, J. Junger-Tas, D. Olweus, R. Catalano & P. T. Slee (Eds), *The nature of school bullying: A cross-national perspective* (pp. 324–55). London: Routledge.

Rose-Krasnor, L. (1997). The nature of social competence: A theoretical review. *Social Development, 6*, 111–35.

Rotenberg, K. J. (1999). Childhood and adolescent loneliness: An introduction. In K. J. Rotenberg & H. Shelley (Eds), *Loneliness in childhood and adolescence* (pp. 3–8). Cambridge, UK: Cambridge University Press.

Roth, J. L. & Brooks-Gunn, J. (2003). What exactly is a youth development program? Answers from research and practice. *Applied Developmental Science, 7*, 94–111.

Rubin, K. H., Booth, C., Rose-Krasnor, L. & Mills, R. S. L. (1995). Social relationships and social skills: A conceptual and empirical analysis. In S. Shulman (Ed.), *Close relationships and socioemotional development. Human development* (Vol. 7, pp. 63–94). Westport, CT: Ablex Publishing.

Rubin, K. H., Bowker, J. C., McDonald, K. L. & Menzer, M. (2013). Peer relationships in childhood. In P. Zelazo (Ed.), *Oxford handbook of developmental psychology, Vol 2: Self and other* (pp. 242–75). Oxford, UK: Elsevier.

Rubin, K. H., Bukowski, W. M. & Parker, J. G. (1998). Peer interactions, relationships, and groups. In N. Eisenberg (Ed.), *Handbook of child psychology, Vol. 3: Social, emotional and personality development* (5th ed.,

pp. 619–700). New York: John Wiley & Sons, Inc.

Rubin, K. H., Fein, G. G. & Vandenberg, B. (1983). Play. In E. M. Hetherington (Ed.), *Handbook of child psychology, Vol. 4: Socialization, personality, and social development* (4th ed., pp. 693–744). New York: Wiley .

Ryeng, M. S., Kroger, J. & Martinussen, M. (2013). Identity status and self-esteem: A meta-analysis. *Identity: An International Journal of Theory and Research, 13*(3), 201–13.

Saarni, C. (1999). *The development of emotional competence.* New York: Guilford Press.

Saarni, C. (2000). Emotional competence. A developmental perspective. In R. Bar-On & J. D. A. Parker (Eds) *The handbook of emotional intelligence* (pp. 68–91). San Francisco: Jossey-Bass Publishers.

Saarni, C., Mumme, D. L. & Campos, J. J. (1998). Emotional development: Action, communication, and understanding. In N. Eisenberg (Ed.), *Handbook of child psychology*, Vol. 3: Social, emotional, and personality development (5th ed., pp. 237–309). New York: Wiley.

Salmivalli, C. (2010). Bullying and the peer group: A review. *Aggression and Violent Behavior, 15*, 112–20.

Salmivalli, C., Kaukiainen, A. & Voeten, M. (2005). Anti-bullying intervention: Implementation and outcome. *British Journal of Educational Psychology, 75*(3), 465–87.

Salmivalli, C., Lappalainen, M. & Lagerspetz, K. (1998). Stability and change of behavior in connection with bullying in schools: A two-year follow-up. *Aggressive Behavior, 24*, 205–18.

Schonert-Reichl, K. A. (1999). Relations of peer acceptance, friendship adjustment, and social behavior to moral reasoning during early adolescence. *The Journal of Early Adolescence, 19*(2), 249–279.

Schutz, P. A. & Lanehart, S. L. (2002). Introduction: Emotions in education. *Educational Psychologist, 37*(2), 67–8.

Schwartz, D., Dodge, K. A., Pettit, G. S. & Bates, J. E. (2000). Friendship as a moderating factor in the pathway between early harsh home environment and later victimisation in the peer group. *Developmental Psychology, 36*, 646–62.

Schwartz, D., Gorman, A. H., Nakamoto, J. & Tobin, R. L. (2005). Victimization in the peer group and children's academic functioning. *Journal of Educational Psychology, 97*(3), 425–35.

Schwarzer, R. & Fuchs, R. (1995). Changing risk behaviours and adopting healthy behaviours: The role of self-efficacy beliefs. In A. Bandura (Ed.), *Self-efficacy in changing societies* (pp. 259–88). Cambridge, UK: Cambridge University Press.

Seaton, M., Marsh, H. W. & Craven, R. G. (2009). Earning its place as a pan-human

theory: Universality of the big-fish-little-pond effect across 41 culturally and economically diverse countries. *Journal of Educational Psychology, 101*(2), 403.

Selman, R. L. (1976). Social-cognitive understanding: A guide to educational and clinical practice. In T. Lickona (Ed.), *Moral development and behavior: Theory, research, and social issues* (pp. 299–316). New York: Holt, Rinehart & Winston.

Selman, R. L. (1981). The child as friendship philosopher. In S. R. Asher & J. M. Gottman (Eds), *The development of children's friendships* (pp. 242–72). Cambridge, UK: Cambridge University Press.

Selman, R. L. & Byrne, D. F. (1974). A structural-developmental analysis of levels of role taking in middle childhood. *Child Development, 45*, 803–6. Published by John Wiley & Sons, Inc.

Selman, R. L. & Schultz, L. (1990). *Making a friend in youth.* Chicago: University of Chicago Press.

Shweder, R. A. & Haidt, J. (2000). The cultural psychology of the emotions: Ancient and new. In M. Lewis & J. Haviland (Eds), *Handbook of emotions* (2nd ed., pp. 397–414). New York: Guilford.

Schunk, D. H., & Zimmerman, B. J. (2007). Influencing children's self-efficacy and self-regulation of reading and writing through modeling. *Reading and Writing Quarterly, 23*, 7–25.

Slee, R. (1995a). *Changing theories and practices of discipline.* London: Falmer Press.

Slee, R. (1995b). Educating for all: Arguing principles or pretending agreement? *Australian Disability Review, 2*, 3–19.

Smith, P. K. (2004). Bullying: Recent developments. *Child and Adolescent Health, 9*(3), 98–103.

Smith, P. K. & Morita, Y. (1999). Introduction. In P. K. Smith, Y. Morita, J. Junger-Tas, D. Olweus, R. F. Catalano & P. T. Slee (Eds), *The nature of school bullying: A cross-national perspective* (pp. 1–4). London: Routledge.

Smith, P. K., Cowie, H., Olafsson, R. F. & Liefooghe, A. P. D. (2002). Definitions of bullying: A comparison of terms used, and age and gender differences, in a fourteen-country international comparison. *Child Development, 73*(4), 1119–33.

Smokowski, P. R., Fraser, M. W., Day, S. H., Galinsky, M. J. & Bacallao, M. L. (2004). School-based skills training to prevent aggressive behavior and peer rejection in childhood: Evaluating the Making Choices program. *The Journal of Primary Prevention, 25*(2), 233–51.

Snarey, J. (1985). Cross-cultural universality of social-moral development: A critical review of Kohlbergian research. *Psychological Bulletin, 97*(2), 202–32.

Sobesky, W. E. (1983). The effects of situational factors on moral judgements. *Child Development, 54*, 575–84.

Sowislo, Julia Friederike, & Orth, Ulrich. (2013). Does Low Self-Esteem Predict Depression and Anxiety? A Meta-Analysis of Longitudinal Studies. *Psychological Bulletin, 139*(1), 213–240.

Sroufe, A. L. (2000). Early relationships and the development of children. *Infant Mental Health Journal, 21*(1–2), 67–74.

Sullivan, K. (1999). Aotearoa/New Zealand. In P. K. Smith, Y. Morita, J. Junger-Tas, D. Olweus, R. Catalano & P. Slee (Eds), *The nature of bullying: A cross-national perspective* (pp. 340–55). London: Routledge.

Sutton, J., Smith, P. K. & Swettenham, J. (1999). Bullying and 'theory of mind': A critique of the 'social skills deficit' view of anti-social behaviour. *Social Development, 8*, 117–27.

Swearer, S. M. (2008). Relational aggression: Not just a female issue. *Journal of School Psychology, 46*(6), 611–16.

Swearer, S. M., Turner, R. K., Givens, J. E. & Pollack, W. S. (2008). 'You're so gay!': Do different forms of bullying matter for adolescent males? *School Psychology Review, 37*, 160–73.

Swit, C. & McMaugh, A. (2011). Relational aggression in preschoolers: Can theory of mind development explain such complex forms of social manipulation? *Proceedings of the Annual Conference of the Australian Association for Research in Education*, Hobart, 27 November – 1 December. Retrieved from www.aare.edu.au/11pap/papers_pdf/aarefinal00298.pdf

Tremblay, R. E. (2008). Development of physical aggression from early childhood to adulthood (Rev. ed.). In R. E. Tremblay, R. G. Barr, R. DeV. Peters & M. Boivin (Eds), *Encyclopedia on early childhood development* [online]. Montreal, Quebec: Centre of Excellence for Early Childhood Development. Retrieved from www.child-encyclopedia.com/documents/TremblayANGxp_rev.pdf

Turner, J. E., Husman, J. & Schallert, D. L. (2002). The importance of students' goals in their emotional experience of academic failure: Investigating the precursors and consequences of shame. *Educational Psychologist, 37*(2), 79–89.

Usher, E.L. (2015). Personal Capability Beliefs. In L. Corno and E.L. Anderman (Eds.) *Handbook of Educational Psychology*, (pp. 146–159). New York; Routledge.

Vernberg, E. M., Nelson, T. D., Fonagy, P. & Twemlow, S. W. (2011). Victimization, aggression, and visits to the school nurse for somatic complaints, illnesses, and physical injuries. *Pediatrics, 127*(5), 842–8.

Vikan, A., Camino, C. & Biaggio, A. (2005). Note on a cross-cultural test of Gilligan's ethic of care. *Journal of Moral Education, 34*(1), 107–11.

Vispoel, W. P. (1995). Self-concepts in the arts: An extension of the Shavelson model. *Journal of Educational Psychology, 87*, 134–45.

Vygotsky, L. S. (1978). *Mind in society: The development of higher psychological processes.* Cambridge, MA: Harvard University Press.

Walker, L. J. (1995). Sexism in Kohlberg's moral psychology? In W. Kurtines & J. Gewirtz (Eds.), *Moral development: An introduction* (pp. 83–107). Boston: Allyn & Bacon.

Walker, L. J. (1984). Sex differences in the development of moral reasoning: A critical review. *Child Development, 55*, 677–91.

Walker, L. J., de Vries, B. & Trevethan, S. D. (1987). Moral stages and moral orientations in real-life and hypothetical dilemmas. *Child Development, 58*, 842–58.

Walker, L. J., Hennig, K. H. & Krettenauer, T. (2000). Parent and peer contexts for children's moral reasoning development. *Child Development, 71*, 1033–48.

Wang, Q. (2004). The emergence of cultural self-constructs: Autobiographical memory and self-description in European American and Chinese children. *Developmental Psychology, 40*(1), 3–15.

Wang, W. & Viney, L. L. (1996). A cross-cultural comparison of Eriksonian psychosocial development: Chinese and Australian children. *School Psychology International, 17*(1), 33–48.

Webster, S. (2007). Does the Australian National Framework for Values Education stifle an education for world peace? Retrieved from www.education.monash.edu/research/conferences/moral-education/docs/webster-moral-education-paper2007.pdf

Weiten, W. (2001). *Psychology: Themes and variations (with InfoTrac)*, 5th edn. Wadsworth.

Welsh, J. A. & Bierman, K. L. (1998): *Social competence. Gale encyclopedia of childhood and adolescence.* Farmington Hills, MI: Gale Research.

Wentzel, K. R. (1991). Social competence at school: Relations between social responsibility and academic achievement. *Review of Educational Research, 61*, 1–24. Sage Publications.

Wentzel, K. R. & Asher, S. R. (1995). The academic lives of neglected, rejected, popular, and controversial children. *Child Development, 66*(3), 754–63. John Wiley & Sons, Inc.

Wentzel, K. R. & Battle, A. (2001). Social relationships and school adjustment. In T. Urdan & F. Pajares (Eds), *Adolescence and education* (pp. 93–118). Greenwich, CT: Information Age Publishing.

Wentzel, K. R. & Caldwell, K. (1997). Friendships, peer acceptance, and group membership: Relations to academic achievement in middle school. *Child Development, 68*, 1198– 1209.

Wentzel, K. R. & Erdley, C. A. (1993). Strategies for making friends: Relations to social behavior and peer acceptance in early adolescence. *Developmental Psychology, 29*, 819–26.

Wheeler, S. B. (2010). Effects of self-esteem and academic performance on adolescent decision-making: An examination of early sexual intercourse and illegal substance use. *Journal of Adolescent Health, 47*, 582–90.

Whitney, I. & Smith, P. K. (1993). A survey of the nature and extent of bullying in junior/middle and secondary schools. *Educational Research, 35*, 3–25.

Witt, S. D. (2000). The influence of peers on children's socialisation to gender roles. *Early Child Development and Care, 162*, 1–7.

Yu, S. Y., Ostrosky, M. M. & Fowler, S. A. (2011). Children's friendship development: A comparative study. *Early Childhood Research and Practice, 13*(1), 1–16.

Zahn-Waxler, C. & Radke-Yarrow, M. (1990). The origins of empathic concern. *Motivation and Emotion, 14*, 107–30.

Zahn-Waxler, C. & Robinson, J. (1995). Empathy and guilt: Early origins of feelings of responsibility. In J. P. Tangney & K. W. Fischer (Eds), *Self-conscious emotions* (pp. 143–73). New York: Guilford.

Zahn-Waxler, C., Radke-Yarrow, M., Wagner, E. & Chapman, M. (1992). Development of concern for others. *Developmental Psychology, 28*(1), 126–36.

Zimmerman, B. J., & Cleary, T. J. (2006). Adolescents' development of personal agency. In F. Pajares & T. Urdan (Eds), *Adolescence and education, Vol. 5: Self-efficacy beliefs of adolescents* (pp. 45–69). Greenwich, CT: Information Age.

Zubrick, S. R., Siburn, S. R., Gurrin, L., Teoh, H., Shepherd, C., Carlton, J. & Laurence, D. (1997). *Western Australian Child Health Survey: Education, health and competence.* Perth: Australian Bureau of Statistics and the TVW Telethon Institute for Child Health Research.

THE LEARNER DEVELOPING OVER TIME

This table summarises the developmental milestones in the broad stages of early childhood, middle childhood and adolescence as discussed in Module I. Note that while we discuss development in separate domains, in reality these domains overlap and mutually influence one another, as we've seen throughout the module. Return to the module text to trace

STAGE	PHYSICAL AND BRAIN DEVELOPMENT	LANGUAGE DEVELOPMENT	COGNITIVE DEVELOPMENT
Infancy	Walking around 1 year of age. Very rapid growth of the brain and neuron proliferation, leading to the creation of many more synapses than eventually needed.	Prelinguistic communication. First words around 1 year of age.	Object permanence around 9 months of age. Sensory-motor thinking. Children's thinking dominated by their sensory and motor experiences.
Early childhood	Development of gross and fine motor skills. Rapid growth and development of the brain continues, particularly in areas of the brain that are associated with executive functions skills of following rules and directions.	Errors in use of vocab, such as overgeneralisation, overextension and underextension, reflect processing of language rules. Emergent literacy.	Symbolic thought. Preoperational thinking. Appearance dominates perceptions and understanding. Egocentric thinking. Limited ability to take others' perspective, or to coordinate two perspectives.
Middle childhood	Increases in flexibility and eye-hand and foot-hand coordination. Continued growth of the cerebral cortex and improved myelination and connections across the brain.	Complex grammar develops, with large increase in vocabulary. Metalinguistic awareness develops, with focus on language rules, and language play. Literacy development.	Concrete operational thinking. Children able to think logically about concrete objects. Can take another person's perspective and coordinate two perspectives.
Adolescence	Coordination of movement comes with more complex linking networks in the brain. Puberty brings rapid increases in height and weight, along with development of sex organs. Brain development continues into early adulthood and critical periods of growth occur in the pre-frontal cortex.	Mastery of complex grammatical and vocab forms. Use of figurative speech and multiple meanings. Increases in metalinguistic awareness.	Formal operational thinking – children can think in the abstract, and beyond themselves and their experiences.

how developments in one domain support or prompt those in another. For example, why in adolescence do we see formal operational thinking in the cognitive domain, coordination of movement in the physical domain and use of abstract language such as metaphors in the language domain? What other links can you find in adolescent development? What role does school play in ushering in changes in middle childhood and adolescence?

SOCIAL DEVELOPMENT	EMOTIONAL DEVELOPMENT	MORAL DEVELOPMENT
Infant self-concept tied to primary caregiver. Separate self around 15 months of age, followed by a growing ability to coordinate behaviour with that of a partner. Erikson's trust vs mistrust stage.	Reliant on caregiver to regulate emotion. By three months of age, can interpret emotional cues from caregiver. Self-conscious emotions such as shame and guilt don't appear until there is a separate sense of self and initially occur in response to the influence of adults.	Reliant on caregiver to determine what is right or wrong.
Self-concept tends to be concrete, based on appearance and favourite activity. Self-esteem is high but unrealistic (and resistant to modification by experience). Play is increasingly interactive. Friendships develop with those who spend time together. Erikson's autonomy vs shame and doubt, and initiative vs guilt stages.	Children determine an individual's emotional response from the current context. Limited understanding that self and others have different thoughts and feelings. Empathy and prosocial behaviour occur, in terms of what the child would like in that situation.	Tend to act in self-interest.
Self-concept is a mix of concrete and abstract descriptions. Tends to be absolute ('I am clever. I'm good at sport'). Comparison with peers influences self-esteem, which becomes more realistic. Friendships more exclusive, with loyalty, trust valued, though similarity is important. Increased sophistication in play; play involving rules. Erikson's industry vs inferiority stage.	Can predict emotional responses of others based on past experience. Understands that others have different perspectives, at first in terms of different information, and later being able to take the other's perspective to view their own actions. Emotions managed through action.	Concerned with rules, and obeying authority. Concern for others prompts prosocial moral reasoning and behaviour.
Abstract, complex descriptions of self are added to concrete ('I am *usually* kind; *Sometimes* I ...; when I am *with my friends* I ...'). Self-consciousness and drop in self-esteem at the start of adolescence. Friendships more stable, enduring, decreasingly reliant on superficial similarities. Intimacy and self-disclosure valued. Organised play. Erikson's identity vs role confusion stage.	Ability to observe a situation as a third party, considering their own and others' feelings from this external perspective. Emotion managed through thought. Adolescent egocentrism (focus on self and own needs).	Developing ability to reason about higher principles to judge what is right or wrong independent of rules. Awareness of people's motives as well as actions. Dignity, rights and equality are important.

Module

II

THE LEARNING PROCESS

MODULE CONTENTS

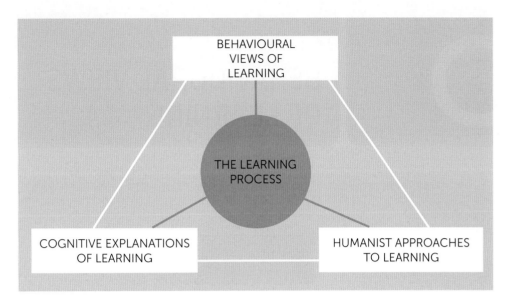

FIGURE MII Module II concept map

Core question: How can theories of learning enhance the understanding of learning and teaching?

As children develop, they learn. Changes that come about through learning can relate to such things as knowledge, skills, beliefs, attitudes, habits and feelings. Such changes are enduring. They can result from instruction or be an unintended outcome of experience.

This module focuses on ways of understanding the learning process. It explores different theoretical explanations of how we learn, and the implications these explanations have for teachers in how they view their role, relate to learners, arrange their classrooms, deliver content and assess students' work.

Chapter 5 presents behavioural explanations of learning, which are concerned with learners' observable behaviours, and where the quality and extent of learning is measured by what learners can show or do to demonstrate what they have learnt. Chapter 6 explores cognitive and constructivist explanations of learning, which draw attention to the learner as an active participant in learning and as a constructor of meaning, and which view learning as a collaborative partnership in which social interaction is particularly important. Chapter 7 discusses humanist approaches to learning, which draw attention to personal, social and qualitative aspects, and which are concerned with the whole learner and with developing learners' full human potential.

Each chapter of this module encourages you to consider different theories of learning and what these can teach you about the roles of the learner and the teacher in the classroom and in learning. Teachers often enhance their effectiveness by being eclectic – that is, by using elements of different theories to achieve the best possible results for their students. You may wish to keep this in mind as you study this module and consider your developing philosophy of learning and teaching.

5

BEHAVIOURAL VIEWS OF LEARNING

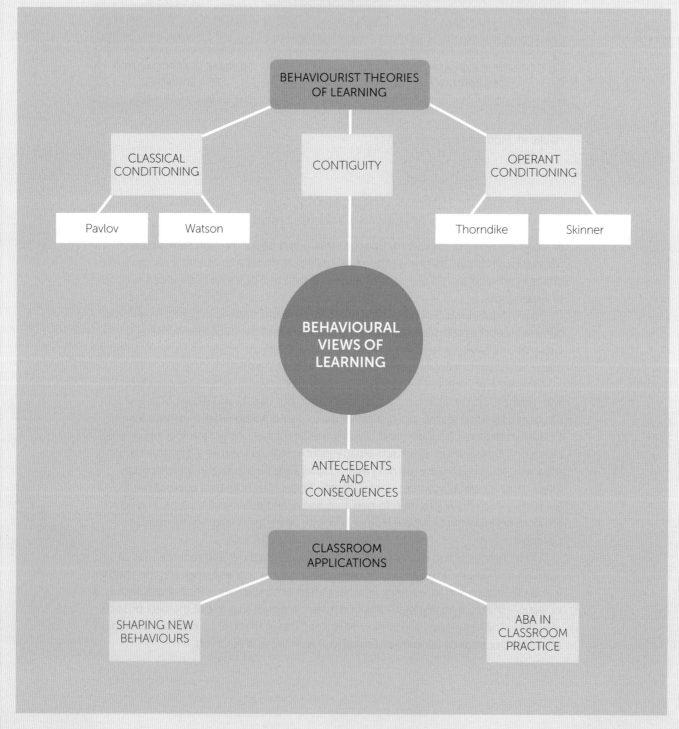

FIGURE 5.1 Chapter 5 concept map

KEY QUESTIONS

After reading this chapter, you should be able to answer the following questions:

- What is the behaviourist definition of learning? How does this differ from a cognitive explanation of learning?
- What are the main characteristics that distinguish classical conditioning from operant conditioning?
- Can you describe the principles of positive and negative reinforcement and give an example of their use in everyday life?
- How can a teacher apply the principles of antecedent–behaviour–consequence (A–B–C) to understand and manage behaviour?

ONLINE STUDY RESOURCES

 CourseMateExpress

Bring your learning to life with **interactive learning**, **study** and **exam preparation tools** that support the printed textbook. CourseMate Express includes **quizzes**, **interactive activities**, **videos**, a tool to help you 'develop your philosophy' and more.

INTRODUCTION

Tom and Sam have been working on the same assessment tasks in class but gain different marks. Sam is rewarded for his assignment with an extra sticker on the achievement chart that is displayed behind the teacher's desk. Tom did reasonably well on the task considering his learning difficulty, but he did not receive any sticker or special comment from the teacher. The teacher in this classroom also takes stickers off the chart for misbehaviour and Tom has lost quite a few stickers. Sam feels pretty pleased with himself and talks about how long his line of stickers is. Tom feels pretty ambivalent and couldn't really care less about the stickers. He never gets any anyway!

Teachers can reward students with stickers or points for academic achievement or good deeds, but teachers can also punish students (sometimes with the removal of stickers or privileges). Students respond to these reward or punishment systems in different ways. No doubt some learn the warm feeling of pride as a result of their reward, and some might try to avoid the actions that lead to the unpleasant feeling of punishment, but what type of learning is occurring for these students? Does it teach students in this class anything about improving the quality of their assignments? Do students learn to change their behaviours? Some students such as Tom simply avoid trying or avoid getting caught. How might students like Tom and Sam respond to future classroom experiences if they are constantly rewarded or punished in these ways?

BEHAVIOURAL EXPLANATIONS OF LEARNING

The strategy of rewarding students for good **behaviour** or removing something from them for misbehaviour is a classic behavioural approach to managing student behaviour, but also for the encouragement of learning. Essentially, **behaviourism** views learning as a 'cause and effect' mechanism, in which external factors lead to a response. Over time, behaviourists believe this response becomes a learnt behaviour. For example, when Sam was rewarded for success in the classroom, behaviourists would say that this increases the likelihood that the behaviours leading to this success will be repeated, and they refer to this as **learning**. In this behaviourist approach, learning is said to occur when observable and

behaviour
Actions that are observable and measurable

behaviourism
Explanations of learning concerned with the effect of external events on behaviour

learning
Permanent or relatively permanent changes in individuals that result from instruction or experience

permanent (or relatively permanent) changes in behaviour result from the influence of external factors such as instruction and experience.

Behavioural approaches stand in contrast to the work of the cognitive theorists you read about in Chapter 3 and the approaches that will be described in Chapter 6. The main difference between these theories is the behaviourists' concern with measurable and observable changes in behaviour. They are much less concerned with unseen factors such as the cognition, emotions or personal belief systems of learners (Arthur-Kelly, Lyons, Butterfield & Gordon, 2006). In contrast to theories of cognitive development that you read about in Chapter 3, learning and behaviour are *not* believed to be the outcome of maturation, or cognitive development (for example, Piaget's theory), or any other processes internal to the person. Rather, behaviourism is concerned with the effect of external events, such as reward or punishment, on behaviour.

Some aspects of behavioural principles and their application in specific situations are controversial, and this view of 'learning' has become strongly critiqued over time. These principles result from a strong history of research and experimentation (often with animals) which we explore first in this chapter. Many features of the behavioural approaches to learning that have resulted from this research do provide educators with very powerful tools to use as part of instruction. These approaches are explored in the second part of this chapter, along with a considered discussion of the careful and ethical use of behavioural strategies in the classroom setting.

CONTIGUITY

As explained above, the 'cause and effect' mechanism of learning is a basic principle of behaviourist theory. Cause and effect occurs because people associate or make a connection between a certain event and the outcome they experience. The behaviourists referred to these associations as **contiguity**, and to the cause as a **stimulus (S)** (something that affects the senses) and effect as a **response (R)** (a reaction to a stimulus). At the most basic level, this stimulus–response mechanism occurs through our senses, such as our sense of smell. For example, do you associate the smell of salt in the air with the ocean? If you have learnt this association, the smell of salty air might trigger thoughts of summer holidays at the beach. Similarly, learning to recite the alphabet or to count to 10 involves building associations: saying 'a, b, c, d' or '1, 2, 3' triggers even quite young children to recite the next letters or numbers in these sequences. Contiguity assumes that whenever two events or sensations occur at the same time, and frequently enough, then an association will develop – meaning that in the future, only one of the events or sensations is needed for the other to also be remembered.

Contiguity is a simple theoretical principle that can be used to help learners develop associations between specific stimuli (objects, events, sensations) that often occur at about the same time or that are closely paired in terms of similarity and contrast. Examples include learning the alphabet and learning to associate concepts such as 'hot–cold', 'good–bad' and 'big–little'. Instances of applied contiguity in learning include the use of drill and practice or rhyme to teach simple facts such as the spelling of irregular words (for example, '*i* before *e* except after *c*') or number facts (for example, '5 × 5 = 25'). The principles of contiguity are also used to help children to remember the details of their name, address and telephone number.

Tabula rasa

The principle of contiguity can be traced back to the Greek philosopher Aristotle (384–322 BCE). He described the mind of an infant as a blank slate, or what the English philosopher John Locke (1632–1704) called a *tabula rasa* (Latin for 'scraped tablet'): 'I imagine the minds of children are as easily turned, this way or that way, as water itself' (cited by Gay, 1964, p. 20). According to this 'associationist'

contiguity
The association of two events that are always closely paired, or that repeatedly occur at about the same time

stimulus (S)
An environmental condition or event that activates the senses

response (R)
An observable reaction to a known (or unknown) stimulus

view of learning, the newborn baby knows nothing but has the potential to learn from experience as a result of an innate ability to perceive sensations and to build associations among them. Particular sensations are remembered if they are associated in memory as a result of contiguity (that is, they occur in the same time and place), similarity (they are alike) or contrast (they are dissimilar, or opposites). However, although associationism's principles of contiguity can be used to explain simple learning that involves stimulus–response (S–R) linkages, most learning cannot be adequately understood in such terms, and more complex explanations are needed. These behaviourist explanations gradually emerged, over time, as a result of more systematic study of the learning process in children and animals.

CourseMateExpress

Online Resources
Go further: Read about Locke's concept of tabula rasa on this text's website

CLASSICAL CONDITIONING

One of the most important contributions to our understanding of stimulus-response processes in learning was made by the Russian physiologist Ivan Petrovich Pavlov (see Box 5.1). His work identified a process known as **classical conditioning**, discovered during his study of digestion and the production of saliva in dogs. This section also introduces the work of John B. Watson who conducted experiments with children and infants. As you will learn, each of these approaches has certain strengths and limitations that we review at the end of this section.

classical conditioning
The association of an automatic response with a new stimulus

BOX 5.1 ABOUT IVAN PETROVICH PAVLOV

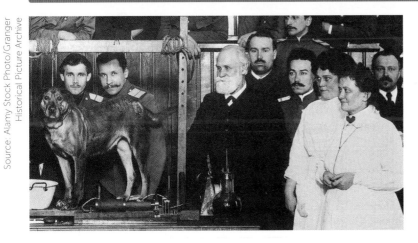

Source: Alamy Stock Photo/Granger Historical Picture Archive

FIGURE 5.2 Pavlov (at right) contributed to our understanding of classical conditioning through his studies of salivation and digestion in dogs.

Ivan Petrovich Pavlov (1849–1936) was born in Ryazan, a rural village in central Russia. His father was the village priest and the family hoped the boy would follow his father into the priesthood. Pavlov attended the church school, and later the seminary in Ryazan. However, after reading translations of the scientific work of Charles Darwin and others, he left the seminary and enrolled at the University of St Petersburg, where he studied chemistry and physiology, gaining a doctorate in 1879. In 1883, he completed medical studies at the Imperial Medical Academy. His early research was concerned with the physiology of the heart and the nervous system (Nobel e-Museum, 2003).

Pavlov is best known for his studies of the digestive system in dogs, exploring as he did the relationship between salivation and digestion. As a result of his research into the relationship between the brain and the body's physiological processes, he identified a set of basic principles concerning the brain's role in relation to the overall functioning of the organism. Pavlov was awarded the Nobel Prize for Physiology and Medicine in 1904.

PAVLOV'S APPROACH

Pavlov (1928) was attempting to study dogs' salivation and digestion when he encountered an unexpected development in his laboratory. Pavlov's laboratory studies were concerned with the relationship between salivation and the digestive process. Salivation triggers digestion in the stomach, and if salivation does not occur, then digestion does not begin. Pavlov argued that salivation is not innate, but rather is a 'conditioned' (or learnt) response (as opposed to an innate or involuntary response like blinking) that originates in the brain's cerebral cortex and that is governed by the central nervous system (Nobel e-Museum, 2003).

This research employed Pavlov's surgical skills, which he used to create permanent openings in the body of the animal that could be used to directly observe processes such as digestion (Nobel e-Museum, 2003). For the purposes of Pavlov's study of digestion, a small operation was performed on the outside of the dog's cheek to alter the flow of saliva to an opening (or fistula). A glass funnel was attached to the opening to collect the flowing saliva and the dog was taught to stand quietly on a table while loosely harnessed (see Figure 5.3). Pavlov noticed that the dog began to salivate when it was about to be fed, before it had seen or smelt the food. He then discovered something unexpected had occurred in his experimental protocol. The dog also began to salivate whenever the laboratory assistant who regularly fed the dog came into the room. The dog began to salivate as though it had been given food. Intrigued by this unexpected development, Pavlov changed the focus of his study from digestion to the process by which a dog salivated at the sight or sound of the person who fed him, rather than solely at the sight or smell of food (Hilgard & Marquis, 1961).

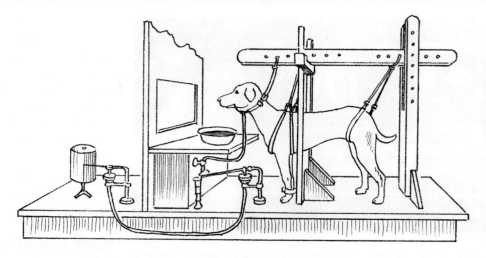

Source: © Yerkes and Morgulis (1909), reproduced in Hilgard and Marquis (1961, Figure 3.1).

FIGURE 5.3 Pavlov's arrangement for the study of salivary conditioning.

Pavlov devised a study to examine the way in which the dog learnt to salivate at a sound rather than at food. He applied the following procedures, and used the following terms to describe the stimulus-response process.

Neutral stimulus and unconditioned response

First, a tuning fork was sounded for seven to eight seconds before a small amount of food was moved close to the dog's mouth. At this stage, the sound of the tuning fork was a **neutral stimulus (NS)** – that is, a stimulus that does not excite or provoke activity – and the dog did not respond to it. There was no salivation. However, the dog salivated copiously while eating the food, the food being an **unconditioned stimulus (US)** or natural, unlearnt, primary stimulus that elicited the uncontrollable response of salivation in the dog. In this case, the dog's salivating was an automatic or **unconditioned response (UR)**; that is, no prior training or **conditioning** was needed to elicit salivation from the dog in response to food.

neutral stimulus (NS)
An event or happening that has no effect on an organism

unconditioned stimulus (US)
An object, event or happening in the physical environment that causes spontaneous activity in an organism

unconditioned response (UR)
An action triggered spontaneously by a stimulus

conditioning
The establishment of a new association between a stimulus and a response

Conditioned stimulus and conditioned response

Pavlov then sounded the tuning fork just *before* food was presented to the dog. His aim was to train or 'condition' the dog to salivate to the sound of the tuning fork. Initially, salivation occurred after the tuning fork had been sounded for 18 seconds, but on later tests, salivation occurred within just one to two seconds. The previously neutral sound of the tuning fork had become a **conditioned stimulus (CS)**. The dog now salivated, or gave a learnt or **conditioned response (CR)**, to the sound of the tuning fork (see Figure 5.4).

Discrimination, generalisation and extinction

Subsequently, Pavlov taught the dog to respond to one specific tone from the tuning fork while ignoring other tones. This taught the dog stimulus **discrimination** by learning to only respond to one specific sound. Pavlov was then able to 'generalise' the learnt responses by teaching the dog to respond to a range of different sounds, not just a single tone of the tuning fork. Finally, he 'extinguished' the learnt behaviour after he repeatedly presented the conditioned stimulus (the sound of the tuning fork) *without* producing the food. Here, the learnt or conditioned response (salivation) gradually disappeared as the association between the two events (sound and food) weakened and disappeared.

FIGURE 5.4 Steps in conditioning a dog to salivate at the sound of a bell.

Pavlov's influence

Pavlov's research into classical conditioning had a tremendous impact on ideas about learning. In particular, his use of precise observation and measurement, derived from his work as a physiologist, established an invaluable framework for future research into human learning and behaviour. His work attracted the interest of American psychologists, who adopted Pavlov's terminology as well as his research strategy (Hilgard & Marquis, 1961).

WATSON AND BEHAVIOURISM

Pavlov's behavioural principles were developed further by John B. Watson (1878–1958), an American psychologist who introduced the term 'behaviourism' into US psychology. Like Pavlov, Watson worked with animals. He believed that behaviour could be explained not in terms of instincts and other inherited mental characteristics, but rather in terms of S–R associations and, in particular, conditioned reflexes and responses. He argued that it was not necessary to study thoughts, feelings, intentions or meanings – which was common practice at the time – in order to understand behaviour.

According to Watson's view of early development (1913, 1919, 1925), infants are born with innate reflexes and emotional reactions such as fear, love and anger. As they develop, other S–R associations are formed. In this way, the newborn infant's limited range of innate responses is gradually extended and expanded as a result of experience.

Little Albert and the rat

Watson is best known for an experiment in which he and Rosalie Rayner used Pavlov's classical conditioning principles to induce fear in 'Little Albert', who was a healthy infant about nine months old (Watson & Rayner, 1920).

conditioned stimulus (CS)
A previously neutral stimulus that elicits a conditioned response after pairing with an unconditioned stimulus

conditioned response (CR)
A response evoked by a conditioned stimulus

discrimination
Learning that it is appropriate to respond to some stimuli but not to others

CourseMateExpress
Online Resources
Go further: Read about unconditioned responses in early behavioural research on this text's website

When first shown a white rat, Albert reached out to touch it. At this stage, the rat was a neutral stimulus (NS), but as Albert again tried to touch it, Watson and Rayner made a loud sound (US) behind Albert's head by striking a hammer on a steel bar. As expected, Albert began to cry (UR). After a number of trials in which the loud sound was made each time Albert reached out to touch the rat, even just the appearance of the rat (CS) caused poor Albert to cry (CR). He had been conditioned (or had learnt) to fear the rat. Subsequently, Albert's fear extended or 'generalised' spontaneously to objects that resembled the rat, such as a white rabbit, cotton wool and a Father Christmas mask.

A few years later, classical conditioning was used to extinguish fear in a young boy called Peter, who was fearful of white rabbits (Jones, 1924). In this study, Peter was seated in a highchair and given food he liked. While he was eating, someone brought a white rabbit in a small cage as close as possible to Peter without distracting him. This process was repeated, with the white rabbit (CS) always presented at the same time as Peter's favourite food (US), until Peter's fear response (CR) decreased.

It is not known if Little Albert's conditioned fears decreased or remained with him for some time after the experiment. Albert left the experiment after a short period of time so there is some chance his conditioned fear may have remained.

STRENGTHS AND LIMITATIONS OF CLASSICAL CONDITIONING

All research and theory in educational psychology can be subject to critique and further refinement in later years. This can help us identify the strengths and limitations of any given approach. This is particularly relevant in the case of behaviourism and behaviourist views of learning.

Strengths

Pavlov's studies of classical conditioning had an impact on research methodology, both in terms of the value placed on precise observation and measurement, and the use of a number of experiments to explore one topic with great precision.

At a more practical level, therapists and others often use classical conditioning principles to reduce fearful or irrational behaviour in children and adults. Many irrational fears and phobias are formed as a result of the pairing of neutral stimuli with stimuli that trigger an involuntary response such as anxiety or panic. For example, throwing a child who cannot swim into deep water on the assumption that this will make the child learn to swim is likely to result in the child developing a fear of water. Therapists often use procedures derived from classical conditioning to help us overcome such problems (Alberto & Troutman, 2013).

Limitations

Classical conditioning is largely limited to explaining those behaviours associated with automatic responses or reflex actions such as fear, sweating when anxious, or salivating like Pavlov's dog. Not all behaviours are like these automated responses, however. Rather, some actions and responses are initiated or controlled by the person, or the person has conscious intent that is not under the direct or immediate control of an external stimulus. It is not possible to trigger such actions in the way Pavlov triggered salivation in his dog.

Sometimes it is difficult to find responses that can provide a starting point for instruction, such as when a child is mute at the time when speech should be emerging. As a result, formal instructional procedures based on classical conditioning principles are not often used, although classical conditioning can come about inadvertently, and many irrational fears and phobias, as well as negative or inhibiting responses to daily experiences, are formed in this way.

Quite apart from these inherent limitations, experimentation with children such as that done with Little Albert would not be possible today. The ethical notion of 'harm' in research is concerned with any practices that might cause unnecessary levels of physical harm or psychological and emotional distress to a research participant. It is very unlikely that such research would be allowed today, or even considered necessary. Albert would need serious behavioural treatment for his learnt fear response to be extinguished, and one would hope that the treatment would be successful.

The implications of classical conditioning for teaching practice are explored in Box 5.2.

BOX 5.2 IMPLICATIONS FOR EDUCATORS

CLASSICAL CONDITIONING IN CLASSROOMS

Instances of classical conditioning in classrooms and in daily life are easy to find. It involves a previously neutral stimulus leading to a conditioned or learnt response. For example, the common fear of dentists can easily be explained in terms of Watson and Rayner's 1920 study with Little Albert. Going to the dentist was once an unconditioned stimulus but now produces a conditioned anxious or fearful response. For some people, even the strong smell of disinfectants or fluoride toothpastes can trigger these memories of visits to the dentist. Instances of classical conditioning in schools and classrooms includes for example, feelings of embarrassment or anxiety that can be associated with classes taught by teachers who use shaming or ridicule to make students conform.

Children's natural or existing behaviours can be used to train a response to certain stimuli. For example, the tendency of children to stop and look when they hear a loud or unusual sound is exploited in order to teach students to respond immediately to the sound of a school bell or teacher using a whistle or clap of the hands. Teachers could also use their knowledge of classical conditioning to deliberately create a positive classroom feeling around events that cause anxiety, such as tests or delivering a presentation.

THINK ABOUT

- Do you feel nervous or uncertain about any areas of learning? For example, does spelling or long division create butterflies in your stomach?
- Can you think about any experiences from school that you associate with these tasks that might explain your negative feelings?
- If a child felt anxious about attempting these tasks at school, could the teacher use classical conditioning to change this response?

OPERANT CONDITIONING

Answers to some of the problems identified in the use of classical conditioning (such as the need to find an automatic response as a starting point for instruction) were provided by the discovery of 'operant conditioning', which is concerned not with unintentional or automatic responses to environmental stimuli, but with behaviour that is conscious, intentional or voluntary.

A toddler will look for a toy in a play box out of curiosity or boredom, a dog will sniff around a tree to find out if other dogs have passed by recently, and a kookaburra will swoop down to catch a lizard because of hunger. All of these behaviours are initially spontaneous, initiated by the child or animal,

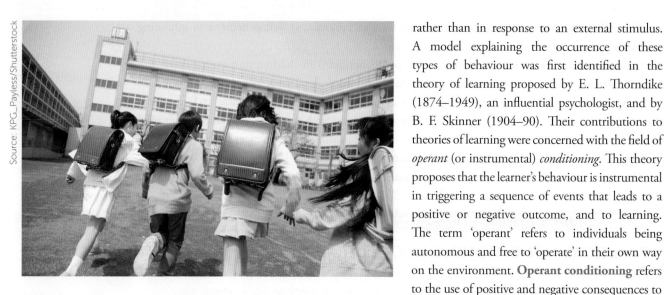

Source: KPG_Payless/Shutterstock

FIGURE 5.5 School students are trained to respond to the sound of a school bell ringing.

rather than in response to an external stimulus. A model explaining the occurrence of these types of behaviour was first identified in the theory of learning proposed by E. L. Thorndike (1874–1949), an influential psychologist, and by B. F. Skinner (1904–90). Their contributions to theories of learning were concerned with the field of *operant* (or instrumental) *conditioning*. This theory proposes that the learner's behaviour is instrumental in triggering a sequence of events that leads to a positive or negative outcome, and to learning. The term 'operant' refers to individuals being autonomous and free to 'operate' in their own way on the environment. **Operant conditioning** refers to the use of positive and negative consequences to strengthen or weaken behaviour.

operant conditioning
The use of positive and negative consequences to strengthen or weaken voluntary behaviour

associationism
An explanation of learning as the formation of connections between stimuli and responses

THORNDIKE, TRIAL-AND-ERROR LEARNING AND THE LAW OF EFFECT

Thorndike's (1911, 1931) main contribution to the development of behaviourism was his work on the effect of rewards on behaviour. His explanation of learning as involving the formation (or 'stamping in') of associations or connections between stimulus and response came to be known as **associationism**.

Cats and the puzzle box

In a series of now-famous studies, Thorndike (1911) trained cats to escape from a 'puzzle box' to obtain food. The box used in the studies had vertical slats so that once the cat was in the box, it could see but not reach food that had been placed outside (see Figure 5.6). To open the door of the box and reach the food, the cat had to perform an action such as pressing a latch or pulling a cord. If a hungry cat was put into a puzzle box, it became very active – clawing, scratching and moving around the box in its eagerness to get to the food. During this random activity, the cat could accidentally trigger the door to open and was immediately rewarded with the food. If the cat was put into the box again, it would again begin to claw, scratch and push, but this time its movements would be concentrated in the area from where the latch had previously been released. After more trials, during which the cat would direct its activity towards the latch mechanism, other actions would gradually drop out as the correct act was learnt or 'stamped in'. By this stage, the cat would perform the correct action as soon as it was put into the box.

Source: Thorndike (1909), reproduced in Hilgard and Marquis (1961).

FIGURE 5.6 The cat has to find a way to escape from the puzzle box in order to reach the food.

Thorndike described this process as trial, error and accidental success (Thorndike, 1898), and called the cat's actions **trial-and-error learning**. He explained the processes involved in terms of the **law of effect**; that is, responses that have a satisfying outcome (such as when the cat reached the food) are likely to strengthen and be repeated, whereas those that are followed by discomfort or annoyance are likely to weaken or not be repeated. Over time, the terms 'satisfaction' and 'annoyance' were replaced by words such as 'reward', 'reinforcement' and 'punishment'. Thorndike also expressed his belief that the connections between actions and new outcomes are strengthened the more often they are repeated, which is known as the **law of exercise**.

Thorndike showed that the trial-and-error actions resulting in the delivery of a reward need not be associated just with mechanical acts such as stepping on a latch or nudging a lever. For example, he taught a cat to lick itself in order to get food. The key factor is that the action results in receipt of the reward. An everyday example of the law of effect is a dog putting out a paw to 'shake hands'. This trick has been taught through the law of effect, by giving the dog a reward such as food or a pat every time it carries out the action. If the trick is practised often, the law of exercise is also being applied. Can you think of other everyday examples of this type of learning?

SKINNER AND OPERANT CONDITIONING

From the 1930s and, more particularly, from the 1950s to the 1970s, Skinner (1938, 1948, 1957, 1968, 1971) was, and remains, the most famous name in the field of operant conditioning, and has been a major influence in the fields of education and psychology. His main interest was in the relationship between behaviour and its consequences.

Skinner acknowledged the principles of classical conditioning demonstrated by Pavlov and Watson. However, he argued that these principles were incomplete and did not account for the much larger number of behaviours that individuals initiate spontaneously. He called these self-initiated behaviours **operants** because they involved actions that are produced or emitted voluntarily by the individual as an operator in the environment. Operant behaviours were contrasted with **respondents**, these being elicited or reflex reactions produced when an individual responds (often involuntarily) to recognised stimuli in the environment. Skinner believed that many of these voluntary responses could be conditioned and reinforced.

The early research of Skinner (see Box 5.3) was mainly concerned with white rats. Skinner devised an ingenious method for studying these rats. A rat would be placed in a cage-like box. The box could be opened with a device, such as a lever, that the rat could operate to obtain food. Later, having observed some pigeons flying, and noting their excellent vision and ability to manoeuvre, Skinner began to use pigeons in his studies, again placing them in boxes that were totally under his control (see Figure 5.8). These boxes became known as 'Skinner boxes'. As described in Box 5.3, Skinner even created a special box or crib for his own daughter. The crib had a controlled and comfortable environment that suited the cold climate and allowed for the 'safe' depositing of the child, freeing the mother from constant observation of the child. This led to significant criticism of his attempts to apply his 'Skinner boxes' to humans, but rumours that Skinner 'raised his daughter in a Skinner box' are not accurate reports of his intentions in designing a warm crib for his daughter.

Skinner's experimentation with animals was extensive and led to a strong belief that his results were applicable to all animal species (including humans), and to an insistence that learning could only be demonstrated when observable change occurred after reinforcement. Skinner's experiments certainly supported this view. He successfully trained pigeons (mainly) to perform various 'antics' such as playing the piano, dancing together and even redirecting guided missiles, simply by repeatedly reinforcing their

trial-and-error learning
An explanation of learning that states that when an individual is placed in a problem-solving situation, the correct response will be learnt through being reinforced

law of effect
Responses that have a satisfying outcome are likely to be strengthened and repeated

law of exercise
Connections between actions and new consequences are strengthened the more they are repeated

operants
Voluntary actions, usually goal-directed

respondents
Elicited or reflex reactions to a specific stimulus

CourseMateExpress
Online Resources
Go further: See more about trial-and-error learning in the classroom on this text's website

BOX 5.3 ABOUT B. F. SKINNER

Burrhus Frederick Skinner (1904–90) was born in Susquehanna, a small Pennsylvanian railroad town close to the New York state border. The family lived in a comfortable two-storey wooden house with a yard that was 'strewn with debris, the garden overgrown' (Bjork, 1993, p. 3), a paradise for an enterprising boy with a vivid imagination and an interest in construction. From an early age, Skinner enjoyed making gadgets from junk lying around the yard. For example, after frequent scolding by his mother for forgetting to hang up his pyjamas, Skinner built a device involving a hook, nails and a string that led to the bedroom door with a sign 'Hang up your pyjamas'. When the pyjamas were on the hook, the sign lifted out of sight. When they were off the hook, the sign came down as a reminder to put them away (Bjork, 1993, p. 13).

FIGURE 5.7 Skinner's work on the principles of operant conditioning and the relationship between behaviour and its consequences had a major impact on learning and teaching in classrooms.

At school and at college, Skinner was interested in literature and biology, and considered becoming a poet and novelist. However, he became interested in psychology after reading books by Pavlov and Watson. He enrolled at the psychology department at Harvard University, gaining a PhD in psychology in 1931. In 1948, he returned to Harvard to work in the psychology department, remaining professionally active until his death in 1990 (Skinner Foundation, 2002).

Skinner is remembered for three specific initiatives: one involving pigeons he attempted to train as navigator-bombardiers during the Second World War; a thermostatically controlled, enclosed 'baby box' he designed for his second daughter, and which he tried to commercialise without success; and 'teaching machines' that gave immediate feedback and reduced the time wasted by students who worked more quickly than their peers.

---

reinforcement
Increasing or strengthening the likelihood of a behaviour recurring through use of contingent feedback

responses (see **Figure 5.8**). Skinner had successfully shown that a pattern of action very quickly emerges in response to the feedback, or **reinforcement**, received. As we will read in the next section, this view of reinforcement was rapidly transferred to the human learning and classroom contexts.

STRENGTHS OF OPERANT CONDITIONING

As shown in the next section, the work of Skinner in particular has had an enormous influence on classroom practices. As stated by Alberto and Troutman (2013), few people in Skinner's era could possibly have imagined the amount of research and application his studies would generate. The ultimate strengths (and limitations) of the operant conditioning approaches are reviewed at the end of the next section, where we examine the school- and classroom-based applications of these principles. In particular, some of Skinner's principles first tested with animals have emerged as concepts that could be applied to humans, such as the importance of reinforcement.

LIMITATIONS OF OPERANT CONDITIONING

A main and enduring criticism of behaviourism in general, and of Skinner's principles in particular, is a concern for the dehumanisation of the human condition. This refers to a concern that deliberate attempts to modify another person's behaviour with extrinsic factors might undermine or deny the

Source: National Library of Medicine.

human their own personal agency or free will. A further concern about behaviourism relates to the denial of the role of cognition or innate human dispositions in influencing learning.

Specifically, some of Skinner's principles have been soundly critiqued and have not stood up to rigorous testing. For example, Tolman and Honzik (1930) provided a challenge to Skinner's belief that cognition had to be discounted as a factor

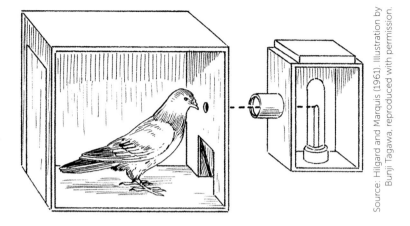

Source: Hilgard and Marquis (1961). Illustration by Bunji Tagawa, reproduced with permission.

FIGURE 5.8 A typical Skinner experiment. The pecking of a key by a pigeon in the 'Skinner box' is reinforced by a flashing light.

in learning because it could not be observed, and to his belief in the fundamental role of reinforcement in conditioning learning. Their research with rats showed an idea of 'latent' learning that did *not* occur as a result of reinforcement – rather, rats wandering in mazes by themselves seemed to form a 'cognitive map' of the maze just as successfully as those rats who were reinforced for learning to get out of the maze. This view of a cognitive map extends the earlier idea of cognitive schemes that you were introduced to in Chapter 3, and later research showed that humans certainly do form mental representations of their world. Other researchers challenged Skinner's view that his results would be maintained across all species. Although this was certainly true for many species, including humans, some research with other animals such as raccoons showed that these animals had such strong, instinctual and innate behaviours that they could not be as effectively conditioned as Skinner proposed (for example, Breland & Breland, 1961). Cognitive approaches to learning have also adopted rigorous scientific methods and have proposed that other factors also influence learning, such as the unique cognitive processes of the individual, motivational factors or unique and innate personal characteristics, as are explored in other chapters in this text.

CLASSROOM APPLICATIONS OF BEHAVIOURIST VIEWS

The application of the principles of operant conditioning to instructional contexts has been quite extensive and well researched but has also led to debate and controversy (Arthur-Kelly, Lyons, Butterfield & Gordon, 2006). In this section, we explore the basic principles of behaviourist research that have been applied to foster learning as well as to manage student behaviour.

One particular application of the principles of operant conditioning can be found in **applied behaviour analysis (ABA)**. This refers to the use of behavioural learning principles to change behaviour in settings such as classrooms and play areas (Alberto & Troutman, 2013; Schloss & Smith, 1998). The primary focus is on behaviour that is observable (for example, academic, communicative, social, motor, vocational and self-help behaviour) and quantifiable. The goal is to change behaviour that is socially important (not trivial) (Baer, Wolf & Risley, 1968). For this reason, one of the most common applications of behaviour analysis is to the management of challenging behaviours often associated with severe and disabling conditions such as autism

applied behaviour analysis (ABA)
The use of behavioural principles to change behaviour

spectrum disorders, where repetitive behaviours can be difficult to treat. Applied behaviour analysis is characterised by:

- careful observation and identification of the target behaviours; initial periods of observation and assessment are necessary to pinpoint the precise nature of the problem
- clearly stated objectives for the targeted behavioural change, taking account of the data gathered in the observation and assessment period
- a carefully sequenced instructional plan that directly addresses the target behaviours; the teaching program is then tailored to the student's specific learning needs
- a reward system for the learner that is developed by carefully structuring a reinforcement schedule
- continual monitoring of progress, measurement of change and adjustment to the program if necessary.

Applied behaviour analysis methods are precise and complex and require specific training in the method before application in the classroom. Therefore, in this section we explore basic principles and elements of this approach, including classroom applications of monitoring and observing children's behaviour, and use of consequences that increase desired behaviours and decrease undesirable behaviours. Further training in the method would be required before attempting to apply an applied behaviour analysis approach in any learning condition.

ANTECEDENTS AND CONSEQUENCES OF BEHAVIOUR

One of the most enduring legacies of the behaviourist emphasis on observable behaviour has been in the observation and analysis of behaviour, with a particular concern for the causes and consequences arising from behaviour. In accordance with behaviourist theory, 'behaviour' is defined as the actions or activities of a living organism that are observable and measurable. Such activities do not occur in isolation but are part of an ongoing string of actions, reactions, responses and initiations. For example, if we return to the example of Tom and Sam, from the introduction to this chapter, we could take a moment to step into their classroom and observe any of their actions or behaviours. If we observed very carefully, we might notice that Tom and Sam's behaviours are embedded in a complex array of ongoing events. Their actions or behaviour may involve other people (their teacher, their peers) or the classroom setting (desk, chair, books, pencils). These may also involve all of the child's previous experiences that we may not be able to observe (Sam had a good breakfast at home, Tom was picked on during the trip to school on the bus, or Tom missed out on a sticker on the achievement chart). In addition, these events may involve internal processes such as expectations and emotions but we may not be able to observe these internal processes; instead, the behaviourist observer would concentrate on outward emotional displays or gestures. For example, does Sam work more diligently after being rewarded with the sticker? Will you see Tom being bullied by the same people in the classroom? It is impossible to isolate a single behaviour or action of Sam and Tom from all the events and influences that have preceded it and that will follow it. So, for any single action (such as a rat pressing a lever or Tom throwing his work in the bin), it is important to take account of what precedes this action ('antecedents') and what follows it ('consequences').

Behaviourists believe that all voluntary (intentional) behaviour is controlled by antecedents and consequences. Both types of information are important in understanding the actions of humans and other animals. In ABA, the connection between these factors is represented by the symbolic **antecedent–behaviour–consequence (A–B–C)**. A–B–C has become an analytical strategy used by teachers to specify the exact nature of problem behaviour and any contextual factors that may be contributing to its occurrence. Reflecting the behaviourists' emphasis on careful observation and 'scientific' recording, the analysis involves the teacher or other observer recording the behaviour of a particular 'target' child in terms of the events that immediately precede the behaviour and that follow it.

CourseMateExpress

Online Resources
Go further: Learn about the key steps of applied behaviour analysis on this text's website

antecedent–behaviour–consequence (A–B–C) Behaviour represented as an ongoing chain of activity involving events that immediately precede the behaviour and that follow it

When a child makes a rude sign to another child, who reacts by hitting and spitting, it is the initial actions of the child making the sign that trigger the behaviour of the other child. The **antecedents** of behaviour, or the conditions that precede particular actions, contribute to the action's occurrence. **Consequences** are conditions or events that immediately follow actions and that can *increase* the likelihood of a specific behaviour recurring. Consequences can also *decrease* the likelihood of recurrence, such as when you rebuke a child for walking on a clean floor with muddy feet. Sometimes a consequence has no effect on the behaviour it follows – that is, it is neutral in its impact on the behaviour – such as when a child ignores a reprimand. (See Table 5.1 in Box 5.4 for an example of an A–B–C record of a disruptive classroom situation.)

antecedent
An event that precedes a behaviour

consequence
An event that follows a behaviour

APPLYING THE A–B–C METHOD

The teacher is concerned and rather annoyed that Tom seems to be frequently involved in minor classroom arguments and fights. To find the antecedents of his involvement in a fight, and to achieve planned instructional outcomes, his teacher needs to watch what is happening before these fights erupt (see Box 5.4). The teacher also needs to understand the effect of the consequences that immediately follow these disturbances. This will help the teacher to learn how to decrease undesirable behaviour (in Tom's case, arguing or fighting with peers) and increase the rate of occurrence of more appropriate activity. Obviously, it is impossible to predict when a fight or argument may occur, therefore the A–B–C method may require multiple observations at different times to capture examples of the target behaviour. The information that Tom's teacher needs from observation of the boy's disruptive classroom behaviour includes:

- *antecedents* – When and where does the disruption occur? What happens immediately before? What is the child doing? Who is with the child?
- *behaviour* – What does the child do, when does the child do it and what is usually happening when the behaviour occurs? (Describe the behaviour in precise terms so that another person can reliably observe and record its occurrence.)
- *consequences* – What happens immediately following the behaviour? What is the function of the behaviour and what are the outcomes (positive and negative) for the child?

Having identified the behaviour, its antecedents and consequences, the teacher then collects **baseline** data (information collected on at least three occasions to identify the existing level of a behaviour as a basis for measuring changes in behaviour after intervention). Baseline data can describe behaviour in terms of *rate* (frequency of occurrence), *duration* (how long the behaviour lasts) and *latency* (length of time delay between antecedent event and occurrence of behaviour). A management program is then planned and implemented. This will involve consideration of:

baseline
Level of a specific behaviour prior to intervention

- *antecedents* – What should be changed in the classroom environment? (For example, a curriculum that is more interesting and at the child's developmental level; consistent application of classroom rules that include consequences for both appropriate and inappropriate behaviour)
- *behaviour* – What behaviours can the child learn that replace the problem behaviour?
- *consequences* – What can be done to block the reinforcing consequences of the problem behaviour and encourage (or reinforce) appropriate behaviour?

Other factors that Tom's teacher needs to consider include events that occur in the classroom, on the way to school or in some other setting, and that are linked to the problem behaviour. These might include Tom's learning difficulty, his previous reactions to the achievement chart, or bullying or harassment on the school bus. A management program can include better communication with Tom and his parents and help in managing situations in the classroom or playground that might contribute to his problems at school, responding to his learning difficulties and attending to any other problems he may be experiencing (see more about behaviourist approaches to classroom-management strategies in Chapter 14).

BOX 5.4 CLASSROOM LINKS

AN A–B–C SITUATION

Tom's classroom teacher has prepared a recording sheet to monitor his behaviour. The teacher wants to pinpoint specific behaviours in Tom that need to be changed, as well as any classroom events that may be contributing to the problem. A teacher's assistant has observed Tom and made the following recordings on the recording sheet:

TABLE 5.1 The number framework

TIME	ANTECEDENTS	BEHAVIOUR (TARGET CHILD)	CONSEQUENCES
9.16	1 *Teacher:* 'Get out your workbooks and get ready to write answers to these problems'.	Tom (T) did not listen to teacher. Continued to talk to child next to him	Teacher repeated the instruction to T
	2	T walked over to pencil sharpener, bumped another child's desk – all the books fell to the ground	Child hit T
	3 *Child hit T*	T hit child back and swore at him	Teacher: 'Stop that, Tom! Or you'll have to leave the room.'
	4	T and child continued to fight	Other child now crying
	5 *Teacher:* 'Tom, I said stop it immediately. Go to your own desk.'	T went to pencil sharpener	Teacher: 'I'm nearly ready to start now. Just waiting for Tom.'
9.20	6	T sharpened three pencils	Teacher: 'Hurry up, T.'
	7	T returned to desk, tried to find workbook	
9.22	8 *Teacher:* 'Are you ready?'	T: 'No, I can't find my book.'	

Source: Adapted from Martin (1987, p. 164).

ACTIVITIES

1   Can you identify the precise nature of the inappropriate actions that annoyed Tom's teacher, and the A–B–Cs associated with these actions?
2   What changes could Tom's teacher make to reduce Tom's inappropriate actions?
3   What appropriate behaviour could be encouraged? How might this be done?

UNDERSTANDING CONSEQUENCES

Consequences are anything that follows a behaviour that serves either to reinforce the behaviour or to stop or decrease it. In the case of the A–B–C chart, the consequences were the events that followed Tom's behaviours. Some of these consequences occurred spontaneously, such as the other child's reaction to Tom that reinforced Tom's aggressive response and led to more fighting. Similarly, you may remember a child from your school classroom who was a 'class clown' and whose behaviour was probably reinforced when peers laughed at him or her. While these consequences and reinforcements occur naturally in everyday contexts, behaviourists were specifically interested in manipulating and employing deliberate consequences to reinforce or shape behaviour.

Documentaries made on the topic of behaviourism often include short segments from Skinner's studies with rats and pigeons (see, for example, Zimbardo, 1987). Typically, such segments show a rat turning a wheel or pressing a bar, or a pigeon pecking a disc or pulling a string in order to receive a reward of food pellets. The behaviour of these animals was deliberately manipulated by the use of the food pellet **reinforcer** (or reward), that ensured the actions would be repeated. However, in some studies, an **aversive** (undesirable consequence) such as a loud noise was given, and these had the effect of reducing or eliminating the target actions. In thinking about operant conditioning, a distinction needs to be made between these two types of consequences: *reinforcers* which act to strengthen a behaviour or increase the likelihood of its being repeated, and *aversives*, which have the opposite effect in that they weaken a behaviour or reduce the likelihood of it recurring.

reinforcer
Any event that strengthens the behaviour it follows

aversive
A contingently applied stimulus that the recipient finds undesirable and which reduces the behaviour it follows

Reinforcement

A student studies hard for a test and gets a good mark. A swimmer wins a race and receives a cheer from the watching crowd. A game player successfully completes a level on a computer game and receives bonus points and access to the next level. The student, the swimmer and the gamer have been 'reinforced' for their efforts, and this will (in theory) motivate them to try harder next time or continue playing the game. A reinforcer is any consequence that has the effect of maintaining a specific behaviour, or increasing the rate at which the behaviour occurs and the probability that it will occur again. Whether it be a spontaneous reinforcer such as a cheer from a crowd, or a deliberate reinforcer such as the awarding of bonus points in a game, the main point is that reinforcement maintains or increases the behaviour that it follows. It also needs to have **contingency**, meaning that it is given *immediately after* the particular identified *behaviour occurs*, such as good marks on a test or the fastest time in a race. Reinforcement should occur *immediately* and be clearly linked to the target behaviour, since any delay or uncertainty may result in the wrong behaviour being reinforced (see Alberto & Troutman, 2013).

contingency
Reinforcement that is only given when the target behaviour is produced

When a specific behaviour, such as finishing a page of sums or completing a level in a game, is immediately followed by the delivery of a desirable consequence, such as a smile from the teacher, an achievement sticker or bonus points, then **positive reinforcement** has occurred. Reinforcement has the effect of *increasing* the frequency of the behaviour it follows, and most reinforcement delivered by teachers (and computer games) is positive, in that it involves contingent presentation of a rewarding object or activity immediately following the target behaviour. Examples of common reinforcers that usually have a positive effect on behaviour include praise, showing happiness or delight, and monetary rewards.

positive reinforcement
Increasing the likelihood of a behaviour occurring by contingent presentation of a reward immediately following it

In some situations, the frequency of target behaviour is increased by the contingent removal or withdrawal of an aversive (negative) consequence. Take, for example, the statement: 'If you finish piano practice you will not have to take out the garbage'; or, in a computer game, a barrier is removed if you achieve a certain state or meet certain conditions. Here, the individual is rewarded for desirable behaviour by being allowed to escape from an unwanted experience or progress with a task. This process is called **negative reinforcement**.

Although teachers mainly use positive reinforcement, in some situations, negative reinforcement may be appropriate. For example, a teacher might allow students who finish their work on time to escape the task of cleaning up the classroom after a messy art activity.

negative reinforcement
Increasing the likelihood of a behaviour being repeated by contingently removing an aversive object or activity

Selecting reinforcers

Not all reinforcers mean the same thing to all people. What one person finds reinforcing may be quite off-putting to another person. A warm smile or a thumbs-up sign may be positively reinforcing for many

CourseMateExpress

Online Resources
Watch a **video**
entitled 'An ABA
practitioner discusses
reinforcement'

children. However, physical gestures or touch, such as a pat on the back, may not be acceptable for some cultural groups and may be negatively reinforcing for those who do not want to be touched. It is important to remember that objects and actions usually considered to be positive or negative reinforcers may not function in the expected way for particular individuals. So when designing a program that includes positive and negative reinforcers, it is essential to check that the reinforcers used have the required effect on the person for whom they are selected. In the CourseMate Express website you can view a video of an applied behaviour practitioner who discusses the role of individual child reinforcers in her program. As she explains, it is possible to select reinforcements that are suitable for each child, rather than assuming, for example, that all children are reinforced by an achievement sticker chart.

Source: Matthew Duchesne, © Milk and Honey Photography, 2010.

FIGURE 5.9 What strategy could the teacher use to reinforce the students taking part in this activity? Think of examples for both those who have worked well and those who were not so engaged in the lesson. Could the teacher use A–B–C observations to help diagnose any problems in the group setting?

Primary and secondary reinforcers

The reinforcers used to reward behaviour can be of two types: primary and secondary. **Primary reinforcers** include naturally occurring or 'unconditioned' (unlearnt) stimuli that are innately rewarding for the individual. They are usually associated with the satisfaction of basic needs; for example, food, drink and a comfortable environment are classed as primary reinforcers. Typically, primary reinforcers might include small, edible items such as lollies or preferred food items. However, primary reinforcers are not overly effective in interventions because they reach a **satiation** point very rapidly. This means that primary reinforcers lose their effectiveness quite quickly and hence any intervention that depends on such forms of reinforcement may be very limited in effectiveness (Sturmey, 2008). While these types of reinforcers can be very effective in establishing new behaviours rapidly, especially when training animals, it is not advisable to use primary reinforcers such as food in classrooms for obvious health and safety reasons.

primary reinforcer
An unconditioned (unlearnt) stimulus that is innately rewarding

satiation
The point at which a stimulus that originally functioned as a reinforcer no longer functions as a reinforcer

secondary reinforcer
A conditioned (learnt) stimulus that functions as a reward

Secondary reinforcers are 'conditioned' or learnt rewards, such as a smile, praise, good grades and applause. In classroom interventions, secondary reinforcers can be preferred activities or games that the child enjoys. In order to be learnt, secondary reinforcers must apply the principles of contiguity and contingency very carefully. The reinforcer must be contiguous or close in timing with the behaviour to be reinforced. An association or contingency between the stimulus and the behaviour must also be learnt, with frequent pairing of the two. Computer games such as Candy Crush exploit the principles of reinforcement very well with reward points, sounds and visual imagery often used to signal the reward.

The Premack principle

Premack principle (Grandma's rule)
Any behaviour that is enjoyed and that occurs often can be used to reinforce behaviours that are not enjoyed and that do not occur often

Everyone will be familiar with 'Grandma's rule'; for example, 'First eat your vegetables and then you can have your dessert'. In Grandma's terms, this means 'Do what I want and then you can do what you want'. Based upon the research of psychologist Professor David Premack (1965), the key principle here is that activities individuals enjoy, and do often, can be used contingently as positive reinforcers for activities that do not occur often and that are less enjoyable. In other words, things that individuals enjoy doing can be used to reinforce the completion of a less enjoyable activity. Otherwise known as the **Premack principle**, Grandma's rule is a very useful strategy for increasing the performance frequency of undesirable, dull or difficult tasks. We may apply this principle to ourselves as adults when we use little 'bribes' to force ourselves to study even when we find it boring: 'I can watch an episode of my favourite TV show when I finish studying this chapter'.

REINFORCEMENT SCHEDULES

One of the decisions that must be made when planning a behavioural program concerns the selection of a **reinforcement schedule** (see Table 5.2). For example, when you first introduce a new task for a student to acquire, it may be appropriate to reinforce the target behaviour every time it occurs. However, extensive behavioural research in the field of operant conditioning has shown that specific schedules of reinforcement are very important to the learning process and can determine the rate at which people learn. It seems that different types of learning and different learning situations require different schedules of reinforcement; research has demonstrated the effects of different schedules.

reinforcement schedule
The frequency with which reinforcement is delivered

TABLE 5.2 Types of reinforcement schedule

TYPE OF REINFORCEMENT SCHEDULE	COMMENT	EXAMPLES
Fixed ratio or a set number of behaviours to occur before reinforcement is given	In the early stages of establishing a new behaviour or learning something new, it may be necessary to reward every correct action, with the rate of reinforcement being gradually reduced as the behaviour becomes established.	• 'John will get a smiley stamp every time he puts up his hand to answer a question.' • 'Mary must get five sums correct before she can play on the mat.'
Fixed interval or reinforcement after a set period of time	This type of reinforcement schedule leads to short bursts of activity just before the expected reinforcement takes place.	• 'Awards for a tidy room will be given at the beginning of each week.'
Variable ratio or an unpredictable number of behaviours to occur before reinforcement is given	This type of reinforcement is associated with high rates of the target behaviour.	• A lottery or a poker machine where the player has no idea when the next payout will occur. • Random checks by the teacher on students' work.
Variable interval or an unpredictable time interval between reinforcements	As with variable-ratio reinforcement, variable-interval reinforcement leads to a high rate of appropriate behaviour. This behaviour is also resistant to extinction.	• Random checks of drivers' licences. • Random correction of homework assignments.

Continuous reinforcement

When you are working with very young children, continuous reinforcement is useful, particularly in the early stages of teaching a new skill. The problem with continuous reinforcement is satiation, when the reinforcer being used loses its appeal as a motivator. For this reason, alternative schedules, or different reinforcers, need to be used in order to maintain the momentum of learning.

Intermittent reinforcement

Once a new behaviour has been established, it is usually appropriate to systematically reduce the rate at which rewards are given, using a schedule that involves 'intermittent reinforcement'. Some, but not all, correct responses are now reinforced. This is useful when an individual is at risk of satiation, or is losing interest in a particular reward, such as food. It is also useful in maintaining a behaviour and ensuring that learning has actually occurred independent of the reinforcer.

Source: Alamy Stock Photo/PhotoAlto

ratio schedules
When a reward is given in a predetermined ratio to the number of responses

interval schedules
When a reward is given after a set period of time

extinction
Reduction and cessation of a response following the withdrawal of reinforcement

Intermittent reinforcement can take two forms. **Ratio schedules** refer to when a reward is given in a predetermined ratio to the number of responses. The ratio used can be 'fixed' (preset), such as with a reward for every fourth response; or 'variable' (changeable), such as with a reward for correct responses at an average rate of one in four. **Interval schedules** refer to when a reward is delivered after a predetermined period of time, such as every 60 seconds. Interval schedules can also be fixed or variable. In thinking about the relative effectiveness of these different ways of giving reinforcement, it is useful to remember the power of poker machines, with their variable-interval reinforcement schedule, in holding the attention of some punters. As anyone who has observed the actions of a person who is addicted to gambling will know, a variable reinforcement schedule has a very powerful effect on the behaviour that it reinforces. Such behaviour is very difficult to extinguish.

EXTINCTION AND PUNISHMENT

Classroom applications of operant conditioning principles and ABA are also concerned with modifying and decreasing less desirable behaviours. However, too often, teachers seek to decrease unwanted behaviours by punishing the student (Alberto & Troutman, 2013). Operant conditioning also offers a means to change behaviour through the use of extinction and differential reinforcement schedules, with punishment as a last resort.

FIGURE 5.10 Providing no attention to a child, via planned ignoring, allows a teacher or parent to avoid positively or negatively reinforcing the behaviour.

Extinction

Extinction refers to the gradual weakening and elimination of a behaviour when the reinforcer (either positive or negative) is removed. A classic example of extinction employed in everyday classrooms is the use of planned ignoring of undesirable behaviours. This is usually done by ignoring a behaviour that the teacher would normally and inadvertently reinforce by responding to it. Common classroom behaviours such as talking out of turn or being off-task often earn a teacher or peer response that inadvertently reinforces the student. For example, earning the attention of the teacher or status among peers can be a reinforcer for some students, although unintended by the teacher. Planned ignoring, as seen in Figure 5.10, removes any form of reinforcement, positive or negative, for such behaviours.

However, the use of planned ignoring as a single extinction strategy can be difficult to carry out in real-life classroom situations. This is because the problematic behaviour usually goes through a period of increasing or getting worse before it is extinguished. This temporary increase in unwanted behaviour can lead teachers to believe that planned ignoring is not effective and can also create classroom-management problems.

To resolve this problem, extinction almost always occurs as a part of wider program of reinforcement in the classroom using a simple reinforcement schedule known as differential reinforcement (Landrum & Kauffman, 2006). At a very simple level, this involves applying a reinforcer for a desired response and withholding reinforcement when desirable responses are not forthcoming. As such, in the application of planned ignoring, the teacher would have to be sure to show positive reinforcing responses to students 'doing the right thing' while also ignoring off-task or calling-out behaviours. As with all rules of contingency, it would be especially important to immediately reinforce positive behaviours as soon as they are noticed. This is also known as the 'fair pair rule', in which the teacher strives to ensure that at the same time as they apply a punishment to reduce a behaviour, they seek out another behaviour that can be rewarded and increased. This is otherwise known as the teacherly skill of 'catching them while they are being good'. Further applications of differential reinforcement in the case of severe undesirable behaviours associated with disabling conditions are explained in Alberto and Troutman (2013).

Punishment

As with the term 'reinforcement', most people have some idea of what the word 'punishment' means. However, this word also needs to be understood within the context of behavioural theory. **Punishment** functions as an unpleasant or negative experience that individuals will strive to avoid or remove. The most important aspect of this definition concerns the effect of punishment on the likely recurrence of the behaviour that it follows. The main effect of punishment is to weaken (and eventually eliminate) a behaviour by presenting an aversive object or event immediately after the behaviour occurs. Punishment involves establishing a contingency that has the effect of decreasing the likelihood of a target behaviour recurring. Consequences that have the effect of reducing the occurrence of a behaviour or eliminating it altogether are referred to as 'punishers'. However, as will be discussed, punishment as a teaching strategy has been strongly criticised and is largely seen as ineffective. Skinner himself wrote about the use of punishment, believing that while positive reinforcement changed behaviour with lasting results, punishment might only change or reduce a behaviour superficially without actually teaching the individual any skills to avoid the behaviour or action that is undesirable (Skinner, 1965).

punishment
Weakening or reducing behaviour through contingent use of aversive objects or events

Forms of punishment

Like reinforcement, punishment can take the form of giving something, in this case an unpleasant or aversive stimulus, such as a reprimand or a ticket for exceeding the speed limit. Alternatively, punishment can also involve taking away something pleasant, such as when points are lost in a contest or privileges are withdrawn (for example, the loss of a driving licence if a person is caught speeding repeatedly). Punishers also parallel reinforcers, in that they are either primary (that is, unconditioned – unlearnt or innate) or secondary (that is, conditioned – learnt). The feel of a very hot kettle to a child who touches it could be classed as an unconditioned punishment, in that the heat of the kettle acts as a punisher to the child even if the child has never before touched something hot. The child does not need to have had a prior experience of touching a hot kettle in order to experience the sensation of touching one as unpleasant or painful. The effect of the experience is that the child learns (is conditioned) to avoid touching hot kettles – and hopefully other hot objects – in the future.

Aversive modes of punishment

As mentioned, the use of punishment in which the student is presented with an aversive stimulus is strongly criticised. Punishments, as explained above, are based on the idea that a contingent application of an aversive stimuli will decrease the unwanted behaviour. Aversive stimuli range from very harsh stimuli that could cause pain or discomfort, such as a smack or use of corporal punishment, to milder but still discomforting stimuli such as verbal scolding, reprimanding or yelling at the student (Landrum & Kauffman, 2006). Historically, aversives have been used in the treatment of persons with disabilities for whom it was believed that no other measures would be effective or 'get through' to the person's limited understanding. This type of use of strong aversives, such as corporal punishment, is now abolished or strongly discouraged in many regions of the world, including schools in Australia and especially in the treatment of persons with disabilities. Today, the use of aversives is generally considered only as a last resort in responding to severe behaviour problems that have failed to respond to all other treatment options, and which could be potentially dangerous or debilitating to the person.

Apart from the dehumanising impact of aversive modes of punishment, there are strong reasons why aversive punishments are no longer advocated in many systems of schooling today (Landrum & Kauffman, 2006):

- These punishments do not reduce the unwanted behaviour in the long term. Short-term and instantaneous effects may be observable, but the behaviour the aversive was applied to does not generally decrease.

- Aversive punishments generally do not include any teaching strategy that allows the child or student to learn a more appropriate behaviour.

- Strong aversives or signs of aggression (such as yelling) can provoke retaliation from the student, and may inadvertently 'teach' the student to conceal behaviours or not to perform them when the teacher is looking.

Modifying unwanted behaviour with response cost punishment

response cost
Removal of privileges or something pleasant as a punishment

token economy
Behavioural system using tokens to reward desirable behaviour

contingency contract
Students sign a contract to indicate that they understand and agree with an intervention plan

If a teacher is seeking to change unwanted behaviours they may choose to use a type of punishment that involves **response cost**, or the removal of privileges. In this sort of punishment, some type of previous reinforcement or earned reward is removed. Other examples include the withdrawal of some earned free time if the student misbehaves in class or fails to complete work. The removal of points or stickers from reward charts, as described in the example at the beginning of this chapter, is a typical example of a response-cost punishment. This is viewed as a more preferable approach when punishment is deemed necessary (Landrum & Kauffman, 2006). Response cost is often used in association with a **token economy** where students can earn points or tokens, such as stickers, as rewards for good behaviour and a **contingency contract** where students sign a contract to indicate that they understand and agree with an intervention. In Box 5.5, we review an example of a classroom intervention that combines several principles of reinforcement and punishment.

Concerns about reinforcement, punishment and token economies

Although the behavioural change techniques discussed here are supported by considerable research, it is important to consider some general concerns that have been raised about the use of reinforcement, punishment and token economies. A chief concern relates to the idea that the use of tokens and reinforcement weakens the intrinsic desire of the child to learn, and increases dependency on an outside agent to foster learning (read more about the use of token reinforcement and motivation in Chapter 8). However, behaviourists strongly refute such claims that intrinsic desire to learn is decreased by the use of reinforcers or rewards (see Alberto & Troutman, 2013). As you will see in Chapters 6, 7 and 8, there are other views about how learning occurs and motivation develops. As noted above, punishment and aversive treatments also raise a concern that they may not change the actual behaviour, and may lead to resentment, hostility or worse behaviours (Burden, 1995; Lewis, Romi, Xing & Katz, 2005). These concepts are discussed further in Chapter 14 when we examine punishment in relation to classroom management. It is therefore very important for teachers to distinguish between the behaviourist's meaning of negative reinforcement and punishment.

BOX 5.5 RESEARCH LINKS

AN INTERVENTION TO CHANGE BEHAVIOUR

Researchers designed an intervention to reduce the disruptive classroom behaviour of two eight-year-old girls in a regular Year 2 classroom. The intervention involved a number of principles that illustrate behaviourist theory and approaches to learning.

First, baseline data about the girls' behaviours was collected in a series of classroom observations. Next, the teacher was trained to deliver precision requests for compliant behaviour (e.g. 'Please sit down in your chair Anne') followed by a five-second delay to wait for compliance before repeating the request (e.g. 'Anne, you *need* to sit down in your chair now.') Students were praised when they complied.

The intervention was explained to the Year 2 students who agreed to participate in the intervention and signed contingency-contracts in which they agreed to comply with the following class rules:

- Do what the teacher asks.
- Raise your hand when you wish to speak.
- Do not make noises during class.
- Remain in your seat during class.
- Look only at the teacher or your work during class.

If students followed these rules during a class they were rewarded with a token, and three tokens could be redeemed for a 'mystery motivator' (for example, an arts-and-craft kit or a class lunch on the school premises).

If students did not follow the rules and did not respond after five seconds of receiving a repeated request, the student lost an opportunity to win a token. The intervention was conducted for two weeks and then was withdrawn for a period of two weeks. After this break the intervention was reinstated but this time, the token rewards and mystery motivator were removed from the intervention. The intervention was effective in reducing the disruptive behaviour of the two eight-year-old girls. Their behaviour improved during the intervention trials and worsened when the intervention was stopped for two weeks. Teachers also rated the intervention as very satisfactory to implement and relatively unobtrusive to use in the classroom.

Source: Adapted from De Martini-Skully et al., 2000.

ACTIVITIES

1 Can you identify the elements of behavioural theories or approaches employed in this intervention?
2 Why did the researchers stop the intervention for a period of two weeks?
3 How do you think the 'mystery motivator' worked in this intervention? What effect on students might this have had?

*Source: Adapted from Ellis (2005)

CourseMateExpress

Online Resources
Go Further: Read about using a mystery motivator in a high school classroom

Distinguishing between negative reinforcement and punishment

People are generally familiar with the word 'reinforcement' and understand its meaning when it is used in a positive way. However, there is usually much more confusion about the meaning of the concept of 'negative reinforcement' and how to distinguish it from punishment. It is important to remember the theoretical distinction: negative reinforcement *increases* usually desirable behaviour while punishment *decreases* usually unwanted behaviour. It is incorrect for a teacher to claim that he or she used negative reinforcement to stop a behaviour. Table 5.3 gives some examples of positive and negative reinforcement, and punishment being used to increase or decrease behaviour.

TABLE 5.3 Types of reinforcement and punishment

ACTION	AIM	
	Reinforcement (that is, to increase behaviour)	**Punishment** (that is, to decrease behaviour)
Give something	Positive reinforcement; for example, 'You've finished all your class work, now you can have some computer time!'	Punishment; for example, 'You haven't stopped talking all class, so I'm giving you one demerit point.'
Take something away	Negative reinforcement; for example, 'If you finish your homework, you don't have to wash the dishes.'	Punishment; for example, 'You haven't finished what I asked you to do, so you can't play football this week.'

THINK ABOUT

- A group of teacher education students have prepared a slide presentation for their classmates on the topic of 'Reinforcement'. On the first slide they define positive and negative reinforcement with the following two dot points:

    Reinforcement

    - An example of positive reinforcement is when the teacher gives a prize for the best essay.
    - An example of negative reinforcement is when a student walks into class late and the teacher sends them to the school office, saying they can't come into the classroom.

1   Can you identify the error in the students' presentation above?
2   Can you identify any problems in the assumptions the students might have made in their choice of 'reinforcers'?

TEACHING NEW BEHAVIOURS

The applications of behaviourism in the classroom discussed so far include techniques that apply many of the principles learnt in laboratory research. Early behaviourists such as Pavlov and Watson, in their studies of dogs salivating and infants being scared by white rats, were concerned with controlling or conditioning actions and innate or involuntary responses to stimuli. Later behaviourists – such as Thorndike with his trial-and-error studies of cats escaping from boxes, and Skinner in his work with rats and pigeons spontaneously acting to obtain food – focused on behaviours that were already in animals' repertoires and that were exhibited with high frequency. But what about teaching a completely new skill to an individual – a skill that involves the individual producing totally unfamiliar actions? If you have to wait until an action is produced spontaneously, new learning may never occur. When teaching a new behaviour involving actions that are unfamiliar to a student, the techniques known as 'shaping', 'chaining', 'cueing', 'prompting', 'modelling' and 'task analysis' are tools for helping the student learn.

SHAPING, CHAINING, CUEING, PROMPTING AND MODELLING NEW BEHAVIOURS

shaping
Reinforcement of gradual approximations of the target behaviour

Shaping involves the reinforcement of gradual actions or behaviours that approximate or are similar to the desired or target behaviour. To shape a new behaviour, you look for an instance of a behaviour that approximates, or has features in common with, the behaviour you want to teach. Over time, you can selectively reinforce the actions that approximate your goal so that these gradually take the form of the final target behaviour. When a mother responds to a baby's 'm–m–m' by saying 'Mum' and smiling, she is shaping what she sees as the baby's first attempts to communicate with the 'm' sound. Similarly, when trying to teach a child to dive into a swimming pool, you can begin by getting the child to roll into the water from a sitting position at the edge of the pool. Then you begin to selectively reinforce those parts of the rolling action that form the first step in learning to dive, such as tucking the head between outstretched arms and gradually moving to a standing position before eventually 'diving' into the water. Over time and with practice, the child will learn to dive into the swimming pool.

Chaining occurs when a 'chain' of behaviours is created, with each behaviour in the chain functioning both as a reinforcer for the preceding act and as a stimulus for the next. Actions in the chain can be taught in any sequence; for example, beginning in the middle of the chain and working backwards to the beginning of the task ('backward chaining'), or working forwards to the completion of the task ('forward chaining').

Cueing, prompting and modelling are additional forms of stimulus that increase the likelihood of a target response occurring. **Cueing** occurs when a specific stimulus is used as a 'cue' to elicit a desired response. For example, when asking a child to recall a word in a poem, the teacher can provide a cue by saying the preceding line of the poem. **Prompting** occurs when an additional stimulus (or hint) is used to assist the child in discriminating the relevant features of the stimulus; for example, a teacher can prompt the child's recall of a word by saying 'It is an a–' (with mouth wide open and shaped to say 'a' for 'apple') so as to help the child remember the correct word. **Modelling** is a form of prompting that involves demonstrating a desired response for a learner to imitate. For example, a teacher can model the word 'apple' while touching the picture of an apple and encouraging the child to imitate the model. As discussed in Chapter 4, modelling is also an important technique for demonstrating more complex behaviours such as social skills. Cues, prompts and models are removed through **fading**, or the gradual removal of prompts as the learner becomes more able to complete the task without help. In social skills training, for example, it is hoped that the child can learn to exhibit appropriate social behaviours without the need for cueing or prompting.

TASK ANALYSIS

In order to teach a new skill, a teacher must have a clear understanding of all of the steps or sequences involved in that skill. **Task analysis** entails breaking a task down into a sequence of more manageable steps, and can be used to help students acquire a new skill. When linked together, the steps form a sequence that becomes a more complex behaviour. For example, the task of learning to write your own name involves the following steps: holding a pencil correctly, using a pencil to make a mark on paper, drawing shapes of characters similar to a model, drawing character shapes without a model, and writing characters of the correct shape and size to form a word.

Scope-and-sequence charts associated with curriculum areas (such as early literacy and numeracy) are examples of task analysis drawn from the educational field. Steps in a sequence, such as that for the attainment of early numeracy, can be used in the initial stages of instruction to assess what students know and do not know (see the discussion of diagnostic assessment in Chapter 13). Each of the steps can be broken down further – or task-analysed – to make a set of more manageable steps for students who are having difficulty learning tasks at a particular level.

---

chaining
When one action functions both as a reinforcer for the previous action and as a stimulus for the next

cueing
Using a specific stimulus to elicit a desired response

prompting
Providing an additional stimulus to elicit a desired response

modelling
A form of prompting that involves demonstrating a desired response for someone to imitate

fading
The gradual removal of prompts or reinforcers

task analysis
Breaking a task into a series of manageable steps to assist learning

CourseMateExpress
Online Resources
Explore an example of a task analysis activity with the **Interactive Activity** on this text's website

MAINTENANCE AND GENERALISATION OF BEHAVIOUR

Once a skill has been learnt, issues such as 'maintenance' and 'generalisation' need to be considered to ensure that what has been learnt is not forgotten, and that newly acquired skills are used outside the context in which they were taught. As discussed in Chapter 4, social-skills training programs, many of which are based on behavioural training methods, can be very useful but may often suffer from problems of maintenance and generalisation of the new social skills.

When teaching an individual a new skill or behaviour, one of the teacher's most important goals is to ensure that learning outcomes are maintained, or continue, long after instruction has ceased. With much new learning, **maintenance** is assured after instruction stops because the newly learnt skill is incorporated into a more complex set of skills that are in regular use. Examples of skills that are incorporated in this way are the subskills that contribute to early reading or numeracy, such as learning to identify the letters in your name and learning to count to 10. However, skills or behaviours that are not embedded into more complex hierarchies may extinguish over time if reinforcement is withdrawn. For example, learning how to make a bird using origami will be forgotten if this new skill is not practised for a long while. Intermittent 'maintenance checks' are sometimes included in a unit of instruction as a way of ensuring that the skills learnt in the unit are durable and not lost through lack of practice and attention.

Generalisation refers to the process whereby individuals learn to respond to stimuli that are similar to but not the same as those that triggered the original response. For example, a newly acquired skill or behaviour learnt in one context and with one teacher has been generalised if it is reproduced in another setting and with different people. However, a fundamental criticism of behavioural approaches concerns the failure of researchers to demonstrate that treatment effects generalise to other settings. As noted by Landrum and Kauffman (2006), teachers can have success in fostering behavioural change in one classroom setting, 'but there is no guarantee that effects will generalise across time (maintenance), or to other settings or responses' (p. 59). In designing an instructional program based on behaviourist principles, provision must be made to ensure that both maintenance and generalisation occur. Such provision may involve checks of previously mastered material to ensure that skills have been maintained, and allowing for newly acquired behaviours to be practised in (that is, generalised to) different settings and with different people, and ensuring skills can be maintained after prompts or reinforcements have been faded.

maintenance
The continued performance of a learnt action after instruction has ceased

generalisation
Learning to respond to stimuli that are similar to but not the same as those that previously triggered a response

APPLIED BEHAVIOUR ANALYSIS IN SCHOOL AND CLASSROOM PRACTICE

The principles of operant conditioning have found wide application in the specific use of ABA and in general everyday classroom practice. Most recent reports on the use of ABA principles describe interventions involving small numbers of children with challenging behavior, intellectual disability, autism spectrum disorder or ADHD (see, for example, Coelho et al., 2015; Durand et al., 2013. Implementation of a program based on ABA principles is intensive for the student, families and teachers, involving one-to-one instruction with continual monitoring of progress coupled with the need to adapt existing materials or prepare new resources (such as practice exercises and worksheets or probes for checking on progress) to accommodate the specific difficulties (including pace of change and areas of difficulty) encountered by individual students at each point in a learning sequence.

Although there are many reports attesting to the effectiveness of ABA, it is important to also acknowledge the concerns about this instructional approach. As shown in the following examples, there are positive and negative reports, often concerning the strength or quality of the research evidence, or the perspective of 'learning' itself.

Teaching approaches based on ABA principles include direct instruction, precision teaching and mastery learning.

Direct instruction

Direct instruction is a teaching method that is based on explicit teaching and testing of skills considered essential for mastery in a subject area. Learning objectives are clearly defined and carefully sequenced, with the teacher actively controlling each lesson in a highly organised and formal manner. The teacher follows a highly scripted routine and focuses on the sequential development of specific skills. There is opportunity for plenty of practice (often described as 'drill and practice') and frequent use of positive reinforcement, There is considerable evidence that supports the effectiveness of direct instruction for teaching specific types of skills (Martens, Daly, Begeney & VanDerHeyden, 2011). As shown in Chapter 1, direct instruction does have a moderate positive effect size, which also suggests the effectiveness of these interventions (Hattie, 2009). However, there is also debate about whether teacher-led and controlled instruction is always necessary or sufficient (see Box 6.1).

Precision teaching

This is a data-based method of instruction involving direct daily observation, measurement and assessment of learning. Each learning task is broken down into a set of manageable steps (e.g. task-analysed), and a set number of examples of the task that has just been taught (referred to as 'probes') is used during daily instruction to check learning at each step. Learning is precisely recorded on specialised charts at set intervals (for example, number of correct responses per minute). This supports the teacher to visualise a student's progress. Precision teaching has been shown to be particularly effective in teaching academic skills (Fuchs & Fuchs, 1986). Nonetheless, a consistent criticism of this approach has been that it lacks rigorous research and evaluation of its effectiveness, despite being in use for several decades (Winzer & Mazurek, 2000; Martens et al., 2011).

Mastery learning

This is a method of instruction that aims to allow all learners, to reach 'mastery' or a predetermined level in an instructional sequence before moving on to the next learning task. Research on the effectiveness of this method varies from strongly positive to cautious. For example, Stallings and Stipek (1986) wrote that the method was overly narrow, focusing on a small range of educational outcomes with rigid, 'mechanistic' instruction. Slavin (1987) was less than positive, stating that although the students performed well on the educators' self-designed achievement tests, they did not necessarily perform better on standardised tests of achievement.

Positive Behaviour Support (PBS)

Positive Behaviour Support (PBS) emerged from ethical concerns about the application of behavioural approaches and particularly the use of aversive methods to manage behaviour of people with disabilities (Hieneman, 2015). PBS, and the school-based application known as School-wide Positive Behaviour Support (SWPBS), were developed with the goal of maintaining the principles of Applied Behaviour Analysis (ABA) while also using approaches that were more positive and acceptable to the community (De Nobile, Lyons, & Arthur-Kelley, 2017; Hieneman, 2015; Sugai et al., 2000).

CourseMateExpress

Online Resources
Watch a **video** of a secondary school teacher discussing a behavioural approach to classroom management in her school

Positive Behaviour Support (PBS)
A behaviourist intervention designed to improve student behaviour

De Nobile et al., (2017) describe four key features of PBS approaches.

1   These approaches are informed by scientific approaches including behavioural sciences, developmental sciences and understanding of social and environmental factors that contribute to behaviour.

2   They focus on the use of specific and targeted interventions to change behaviour that are based on solid data collection and evidence from the school environment. ABA principles such as explicit and direct instruction, and the use of positive reinforcement are applied (see Box 5.6).

3   The interventions must be committed to positive, holistic lifestyle changes for the targeted individuals or students including better academic, emotional and social outcomes. Humiliating and physically punitive strategies must not be used.

4   A system-wide approach must be used. In school, for example, all staff and community must be supportive and involved, including the leadership team, teachers, parents and any other stakeholders.

BOX 5.6 CLASSROOM LINKS

A THREE-TIER APPROACH TO SUPPORTING BEHAVIOUR

The teaching and intervention pyramid presents a three-tier approach to support behaviour. This concept originated in health prevention models. The approach describes a need for primary, secondary, and tertiary levels of prevention and intervention in order to address all support needs.

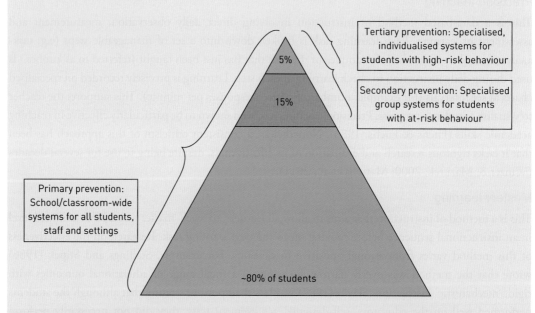

FIGURE 5.11 The three-tiered intervention pyramid

Source: Adapted from Sugai, G. & Horner, R.R. (2006) A promising approach for expanding and sustaining school-wide positive behavior support, *School Psychology Review*, 35 (2) 245–259.

Tier 1 – primary tier

At Tier 1, the *primary* prevention level of support, behaviour support is *universal* or applies to all students in the school community. It is estimated that around 80 per cent of students can be adequately supported with interventions at this level. This would include school-wide identification of expected behaviours; school-wide teaching, modelling, practice and

>>

Generally, there is extensive research supporting the effectiveness of School-wide PBS. For example, this method of addressing positive behaviour across the school has been applied to bullying and aggressive behaviour with positive results (Dunlap et al., 2010). The research is also self-critical including close analysis of school data to identify cases of inequitable disparities in office referrals (for poor behaviour) for students with disabilities and certain racial groups (McIntosh, Ellwood, McCall & Girvan, 2017).

When considering behavioural approaches to learning and intervention Alberto and Troutman (2013) caution there is a strong need for teachers to consider the ethical grounds of any teaching or behavioural support intervention, before embarking on the intervention. This includes school-wide intervention programs such as PBS. The consent of children and their carers to participate in behavioural change programs is essential. Alberto and Troutman (2013) also caution strongly against the overly simplistic use of these behavioural techniques. It is too easy for a teacher to use reinforcement inappropriately (such as token rewards and sticker charts), and as a result cheapen and weaken the

reinforcement of those behaviours, and school-wide data collection to monitor success of those interventions. At Sam and Tom's school they decide to implement a school-wide bullying prevention program that teaches positive bystander behaviour; this is an example of a primary tier of behaviour support.

Tier 2 – Secondary tier

Tier 2 is known as the *secondary* tier of behaviour support. This is targeted at a smaller number of students who may need a more intensive level of support. This could be for a small group of students like Tom who might be taught some coping strategies for how to deal with bullies on the school bus; it might also include a counselling or behaviour-monitoring approach for a group of bullies (see more in Chapters 4 and 14 about approaches to bullying).

Tier 3 – Tertiary tier

At Tier 3, the *tertiary* tier, a much smaller proportion of students may need a more individualised and highly targeted approach to supporting their behaviour. These approaches would holistically consider the systems surrounding the child. Tom, for example, may not have responded well to the Tier 2 intervention, and his aggressive responses may be increasing; similarly the bullies may also become more covert and aggressive. At this level an individualised behaviour support plan will usually be developed and the student may be referred for counselling and will receive an individualised intervention. Punitive strategies like school suspension are always avoided and alternative strategies are used to support the student within the school in a positive environment.

In PBS models all students continue to receive the Tier 1 universal supports, regardless of what level they are at. School participation is maintained and continues as usual in the most normative and positive environment possible. Constant data collection informs the school about whether the strategies are working and all interventions are evidence-based and implemented with high fidelity.

Source: Adapted from Sugai, G. & Horner, R.R. (2006) A promising approach for expanding and sustaining school-wide positive behavior support, *School Psychology Review*, 35(2) 245–259.

ACTIVITIES
1 Can you think of other examples of common primary or secondary interventions used in schools today?
2 What sort of data would the school need to collect to assess if bullying prevention interventions at each of the levels above had actually worked?

effectiveness of reinforcement. Similarly, the effectiveness of programs like PBS can be undermined if schools simplistically choose only to apply behaviour monitoring procedures (e.g. merit and demerit systems) rather than a holistic, systematic model of support. Chapter 14 contains a more extensive discussion of ethical and philosophical concerns about classroom management and behavioural approaches.

In summary, the main features of operant conditioning and ABA, as it is used in classrooms, include:

- observing and identifying behaviours that we seek to change using procedures such as A–B–C observational recordings
- developing and implementing an intervention plan using reinforcement strategies to increase or decrease behaviours
- monitoring and measuring the results of interventions and teaching programs.

Source: Shutterstock.com/antoniodiaz

FIGURE 5.12 A typical use of behavioural approaches may include teaching specific skills with individualised reinforcement strategies.

STRENGTHS OF BEHAVIOURAL APPROACHES TO LEARNING

The main strengths of behavioural approaches to learning are that they provide educators with effective strategies that can be used quite easily to teach new skills and behaviours quickly and efficiently (see Figure 5.12), particularly to young children and to students with intellectual disabilities and behaviour problems. Such strategies are especially useful for teaching action sequences that need to be performed at an automatic level, such as tying shoelaces, cleaning teeth or even the mechanical aspects of driving a car. These methods are also effective for managing the many forms of undesirable behaviour, often minor in nature, that disrupt most classrooms at some time during the day. Teachers using behavioural methods to manage such behaviour can respond to student disruptions quickly, consistently and without emotional involvement.

LIMITATIONS OF BEHAVIOURAL APPROACHES TO LEARNING

A major criticism of behavioural approaches is that they neglect the contribution of cognition, or cognitive skills, to the learning process. This is particularly relevant for more complex forms of behaviour, such as problem solving, for which other approaches may be more appropriate (see Chapters 6, 7 and 8). Additional problems that have been identified include concerns about the impact of long-term dependence on extrinsic rather than intrinsic forms of reinforcement (see Kohn, 1993), and ethical issues concerning the use of some types of punishment and aversive techniques (see Alberto & Troutman, 2013; Schloss & Smith, 1998).

CONCLUDING COMMENTS

This chapter has presented a complex and sometimes challenging perspective of 'learning' that is based on the belief that external factors rather than internal processes lead to learning. Although there have been some criticisms of behavioural theories and the methods of teaching derived from them, behavioural approaches have found widespread use in classrooms today. This is probably because techniques of reinforcement are relatively easy to use, are effective in teaching new skills and behaviours quickly, and can be implemented with a variety of learners in a range of contexts. The basic principles of ABA can be learnt through courses for teachers, parents and others who work with children and adults. Indeed, behavioural principles are used in everyday settings by people who may be unaware of the underlying learning principles. Tom and Sam were no doubt 'shaped' and influenced by their teacher's instructional strategies, but even this fictional example highlights some of the cautions and sensitivities needed when using what may seem to be everyday systems of rewards or token economies in our classrooms. Unfortunately, the injudicious use of reinforcement and aversive punishments has also found its way into contemporary classrooms. As with other approaches to learning and teaching, when correctly implemented, behavioural methods provide a powerful pedagogical tool for educators, but this tool must be used responsibly.

CourseMateExpress

Online Resources
Take a moment
to consider your
personal philosophy.
You may wish to use
the **Develop your
Philosophy** tool on this
text's website

STUDY TOOLS

ONLINE STUDY RESOURCES

Visit http://login.cengagebrain.com and use the access code that comes with this book for 12 months' access to the student resources for this text.

The CourseMate Express website contains a range of resources and study tools for this chapter, including:

- a **self-check quiz**

 **CourseMate**Express

- **crosswords**, **flashcards** and a **glossary** to help you revise the key terms from this chapter
- the **Go further** materials and **interactive activity** mentioned in the chapter.

CHAPTER REVIEW

- Behavioural explanations of learning focus on learners' behaviour, observable actions or activity.
- Contiguity, or a close association in meaning or time between two events or sensations, can lead to learning so that the occurrence of one event triggers recall of the associated event.
- Classical conditioning (Pavlov) is concerned with learning that is produced when involuntary or automatic responses are triggered by specific stimuli in the environment.

- Operant conditioning is concerned with actions that an organism initiates, and includes trial-and-error learning, the law of effect and the law of practice (Thorndike), and the learning that occurs when behaviours are rewarded or reinforced (Skinner).
- Applied behaviour analysis (ABA) refers to the application of behavioural principles in the classroom, with clear specification of the target behaviour and goals, development and implementation of an intervention plan, and monitoring of results with changes implemented as required.

PUTTING IT TOGETHER

Making links between 'behavioural views of learning' and material in other chapters

CHAPTER 5 Behavioural views of learning

LINKAGES

How would you integrate knowledge of child development with knowledge of behavioural views of learning? Is development irrelevant under this approach? (See Chapters 2, 3 and 4.)

Consider how behavioural and cognitive views of learning differ. Can both be used in the classroom? (See Chapter 6.)

| **CHAPTER 2**
Emerging skills | **CHAPTER 3**
Cognitive development | **CHAPTER 4**
Social, emotional and moral development | **CHAPTER 6**
Cognitive explanations of learning |

QUESTIONS AND ACTIVITIES FOR SELF-ASSESSMENT AND DISCUSSION

1 Describe two behaviours that change over time and that can be called examples of learning. Describe two other behaviours that also change over time but that are not examples of learning.
2 Can you think of any fears or anxieties you have learnt as a result of unplanned classical conditioning?
3 Give an example from your own experience of learning that occurs as a result of operant conditioning.

4 Explain the different aims of the primary, secondary and tertiary levels of the intervention and prevention pyramid.
5 Think about your personal philosophy of teaching. Does it contain elements that you would describe as a 'behaviourist' philosophy? If so, what are the ethical implications that arise from these philosophical principles?

FURTHER RESEARCH

SEARCH ME! AND EDUCATION DATABASES

Explore Search Me! education for articles relevant to this chapter. Fast and convenient, Search Me! education is updated daily and provides you with 24-hour access to full-text articles from hundreds of scholarly and popular journals, ebooks and newspapers, including *The Australian* and *The New York Times*. Log in to Search Me! through http://login.cengagebrain.com and use the search terms listed here as a starting point:

• applied behaviour analysis
• behaviorism OR behaviourism
• classical conditioning
• contingency contract
• direct instruction
• mastery learning
• operant conditioning
• precision teaching
• reinforcement
• task analysis
• token economy.

You can also use these terms to explore databases such as ERIC, PsycINFO and the Australian Education Index.

Search Me!

RECOMMENDED WEBSITES

Association for Behavior Analysis International: www.abainternational.org
Council for Children with Behavioral Disorders: www.ccbd.net
Positive Behavioral Support: www.pbis.org
Positive behaviour for learning: http://pb4l.tki.org.nz/

RECOMMENDED READING

Alberto, P. A. & Troutman, A. C. (2013). *Applied behavior analysis for teachers* (6th ed.). Upper Saddle River, NJ: Prentice-Hall International.
W. Fisher, C. C. Piazza & H. S. Roane (Eds). (2011) *Handbook of Applied Behavior Analysis*. New York: The Guilford Press.

Sailor, W., Dunlap, G., Sugai, G., Horner, R. (Eds.) (2009) *Handbook of Positive Behavior Support*, Springer, US.

REFERENCES

Alberto, P. A. & Troutman, A. C. (2013). *Applied behavior analysis for teachers* (6th ed.). Upper Saddle River, NJ: Prentice-Hall International.

Arthur-Kelly, M., Lyons, G., Butterfield, N. & Gordon, C. (2006). *Classroom management: Creating positive learning environments* (2nd ed.). Melbourne: Thomson Learning.

Baer, D. M., Wolf, M. M. & Risley, T. R. (1968). Some current dimensions of applied behaviour analysis. *Journal of Applied Behaviour Analysis, 1*, 91–7.

Bjork, D. W. (1993). *B. F. Skinner: A life.* New York: Basic Books.

Breland, K. & Breland, M. (1961). The misbehavior of organisms. *American Psychologist, 16*, 681–4.

Burden, P. R. (1995). *Classroom management and discipline.* White Plains, NY: Longman.

Coelho, L. F., Barbosa, D. L. F., Rizzutti, S., Muszkat, M., Bueno, O. F. A., Miranda, M. C. (2015). Use of Cognitive Behavioral Therapy and Token Economy to Alleviate Dysfunctional Behavior in Children with Attention-Deficit Hyperactivity Disorder. *Frontiers in Psychiatry, 6*, 167.

De Martini-Scully, D., Bray, M. A. & Kehle, T. J. (2000). A packaged intervention to reduce disruptive behaviors in general education students. *Psychology in the Schools, 37*, 149–56.

De Nobile, J., Lyons, G. & Arthur-Kelly, M. (2017). *Positive Learning Environments: Creating and Maintaining Productive Classrooms.* Cengage Learning Australia.

Dunlap, G., Carr, E., Horner, R., Koegel, R., Sailor, W., Clarke, S., . . . Fox, L. (2010). A Descriptive, Multiyear Examination of Positive Behavior Support. *Behavioral Disorders, 35*(4), 259-279. Retrieved from http://www.jstor.org/stable/43153511

Durand, V. M., Hieneman, M., Clarke, S., Wang, M., Rinaldi, M. (2013). Positive family intervention for severe challenging behavior I: a multi-site randomized clinical trial. *Journal of Positive Behavior Interventions, 15*:133–143. doi: 10.1177/1098300712458324

Fuchs, L. & Fuchs, D. (1986). Effects of systematic formative evaluation: A meta-analysis. *Exceptional Children, 53*, 199–208.

Gay, P. (1964). *John Locke on education.* New York: Teachers College, Columbia University.

Hieneman, M. (2015). Positive Behavior Support for Individuals with *Behavior Challenges. Behavior analysis in practice, 8*(1), 101–108.

Hilgard, E. R. & Marquis, D. G. (1961). *Conditioning and learning* (2nd ed.). New York: Appleton-Century-Crofts.

Jones, M. C. (1924). The elimination of children's fears. *Journal of Experimental Psychology, 7*, 383–90.

Kohn, A. (1993). Choices for children: Why and how to let students decide. *Phi Delta Kappan, 75*, 8–21.

Landrum, T. J. & Kauffman, J. M. (2006). Behavioral approaches to classroom management. In C. M. Evertson & C. S. Weinstein (Eds), *Handbook of classroom management: Research, practice, and contemporary issues* (pp. 7–71). Mahwah, NJ: Lawrence Erlbaum.

Lewis, R., Romi. S., Xing, Q. & Katz, Y. (2005). A comparison of teachers' classroom discipline in Australia, China and Israel. *Teaching and Teacher Education, 21* (2005), 729–41.

Martens, B. K., Daly, E.J., Begeny, J. C. & VanDerHeyden, A. (2011). Behavioral Approaches to Education. In W. W. Fisher, C. C. Piazza & H. S. Roane (Eds). *Handbook of Applied Behavior Analysis.* New York: The Guilford Press.

Martin, M. (1987). Managing inappropriate behaviour in the classroom. In J. Ward, S. Bochner, Y. Center, L. Outhred & M. Pieterse (Eds), *Educating children with special needs in regular classrooms: An Australian perspective.* Sydney: Special Education Centre, Macquarie University.

McIntosh, K., Ellwood, K., McCall, L. & Girvan, E. J. (2017). Using Discipline Data to Enhance Equity in School Discipline. *Intervention in School and Clinic. 53*(3), 146–152.

Nobel e-Museum (2003). *Ivan Pavlov – Biography.* Retrieved from www.nobel.se/medicine/laureates/1904/pavlov-bio.html

Pavlov, I. (1928). *Lectures on conditioned reflexes* (W. Gantt, Trans). New York: International Universities Press.

Premack, D. (1965). Reinforcement theory. In D. Levine (Ed.), *Nebraska Symposium on Motivation* (Vol. 13, pp. 123–80). Lincoln, NE: University of Nebraska.

Schloss, P. J. & Smith, M. A. (1998). *Applied behavior analysis in the classroom* (2nd ed.). Boston, MA: Allyn & Bacon.

Skinner, B. F. (1938). *The behavior of organisms: An experimental analysis.* New York: Appleton-Century.

Skinner, B. F. (1948). *Walden two.* New York: Macmillan.

Skinner, B. F. (1957). *Verbal behavior.* New York: Appleton-Century-Crofts.

Skinner, B. F. (1965) Review lecture: The technology of teaching. *Proceedings of the Royal Society of London. Series B, Biological Sciences, 162*(989), 427–43.

Skinner, B. F. (1968). *The technology of teaching.* New York: Appleton-Century-Crofts.

Skinner, B. F. (1971). *Beyond freedom and dignity.* New York: Knopf.

Skinner Foundation (2002). *B. F. Skinner Foundation: Brief biography of B. F. Skinner.* Retrieved from www.bfskinner.org/BFSkinner/Home.html

Slavin, R. E. (1987). Mastery learning reconsidered. *Review of Educational Research, 57*(2), 175–214.

Stallings, J. A. & Stipek, D. (1986). Research on early childhood and elementary school teaching programs. In M. C. Wittrock (Ed.), *Handbook of research on teaching* (3rd ed., pp. 727–53). New York: Macmillan.

Sturmey, P. (2008). *Behavioural case formulation and intervention: A functional analytic approach.* Chichester, UK: John Wiley and Sons Ltd.

Sugai, G., Horner, R. H., Dunlap, G., Hieneman, M., Lewis, T. J., Nelson, C. M., ... OSEP Center on Positive Behavioral Interventions (2000). Applying Positive Behavior Support and Functional Behavioral Assessment in Schools. *Journal of Positive Behavior Interventions, 2*(3), 131–143.

Sugai, G. & Horner, R. R. (2006) A promising approach for expanding and sustaining school-wide positive behavior support, *School Psychology Review, 35*(2) 245-259.

Thorndike, E. L. (1898). Animal Intelligence: An Experimental Study of the Associative Processes in Animals (Psychological Review, Monograph Supplements, No. 8). New York: Macmillan

Thorndike, E. L. (1909). Animal intelligence. An experimental study of the associative process in animals. *The American Journal of Psychology, 10*(1), pp. 149–150. Published by University of Illinois Press.

Thorndike, E. L. (1911). *Animal intelligence.* New York: Macmillan.

Thorndike, E. L. (1931). *Human learning.* New York: Appleton-Century-Crofts.

Tolman, E. C. & Honzik, C. H. (1930). Introduction and removal of reward, and maze performance in rats. *University of California Publications in Psychology, 4*, 257–75.

Watson, J. B. (1913). Psychology as the behaviorist views it. *Psychological Review, 20*, 158–77.

Watson, J. B. (1919). *Psychology from the standpoint of a behaviorist.* Philadelphia: Lippincott.

Watson, J. B. (1925). *Behaviorism.* New York: Norton.

Watson, J. B. & Rayner, R. (1920). Conditioned emotional reactions. *Journal of Experimental Psychology, 3*, 1–14.

Winzer, M. A. & Mazurek, K. (2000). Multicultural special education for increasingly diverse societies. In K. Mazurek & M. A. Winzer (Eds), *Special education in the 21st century.* Washington, DC: Gallaudet University Press.

Yerkes, R. M. & Morgulis, S. (1909). The method of Pavlov in animal psychology. *Psychological Bulletin, 6*(8), 257–73.

Zimbardo, P. (Host). (1987). *Discovering psychology: Learning (Part 8).* Boston: W6BH, in association with the American Psychological Association.

6

COGNITIVE EXPLANATIONS OF LEARNING

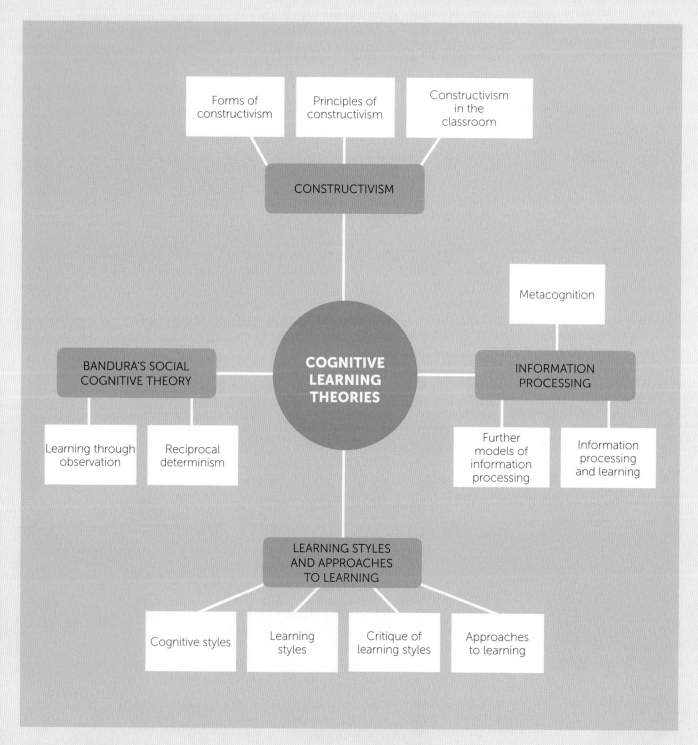

FIGURE 6.1 Chapter 6 concept map

KEY QUESTIONS

After reading this chapter, you should be able to answer the following questions:

- What are the key principles of cognitive learning theory? How do they differ from those of the behavioural approach?
- What are the four key principles of constructivism? How would you put these into practice in the classroom?
- How does information processing influence learning?
- What is the role of metacognition in learning and memory?
- What kinds of cognitive styles are there? How do they affect learning?

ONLINE STUDY RESOURCES

CourseMateExpress

Bring your learning to life with **interactive learning**, **study** and **exam preparation tools** that support the printed textbook. CourseMate Express includes **quizzes**, **interactive activities**, **videos**, a tool to help you '**develop your philosophy**' and more.

INTRODUCTION

Memet is writing out his nine times table. He suddenly notices something and starts to furiously write lists of numbers, which he then checks on a calculator. He shows this to the group of classmates sitting at his table and they all start talking excitedly. Looking up, he calls to his teacher to tell her what he has found, and another classmate also asks her whether it is true of other times tables as well; she thinks she has found another pattern. What was Memet thinking about, and how did that affect his learning? How did Memet's discovery influence his peers' learning? You might like to write out the nine times table as a list and see if you can see what Memet saw, and why he got excited. The CourseMate Express website also has an explanation.

This chapter focuses on cognitive explanations of learning. Cognitive explanations focus on internal mental processes, and tend to view learners as active constructors of their own learning. The emphasis is on how learners like Memet make meaning and remember what they learn. This view of learning is quite different to the behavioural view of learning that we studied in Chapter 5, which focused on learners' observable behaviours and their responses to external stimuli. In this chapter, we shift our focus from external processes to internal mental processes in order to examine what happens in the mind when we learn.

CourseMateExpress

Online Resources
Explore an example of 'Observing, thinking and questioning: the nine times table' with the **Interactive Activity** on this text's website

COGNITIVE LEARNING THEORIES

Cognitive learning theories focus on internal mental processes and their role in learning. At the heart of cognitive theories of learning is the simple proposition that knowledge is 'constructed by the learner and is informed and influenced by the learner's previous experiences' (O'Donnell, 2012). This approach evolved in the 1950s and 1960s, when two different views of learning started to emerge. As explained in Chapter 5, the behaviourist view of learning proposed that learning occurred through stimulus and response. When the learner's response was reinforced or conditioned by external factors, learning was said to have occurred. Internal mental processes were ignored by this approach. However, Albert Bandura, himself emerging from a behaviourist tradition, conducted a series of experiments in which he explicitly sought to prove that the behaviourist principles of trial-and-error learning (often

cognitive learning theories
Theories concerned with internal mental processes and how learners manipulate information during learning

with the use of external reinforcement) were not the only or necessary conditions of learning. Bandura demonstrated that children could learn vicariously simply by observing and modelling the actions of others. Importantly, Bandura demonstrated that children could in fact choose to follow these behaviours and regulate their own behaviours in accordance with what they had learned. This finding introduced a critical cognitive element in the study of human behaviour. Bandura's theories rapidly developed and have become one of the most influential social cognitive theories of learning today.

In the same era, another group of psychologists and researchers developed a cognitive view of learning that was (like Bandura's) based on the idea that humans have greater control over their own learning and could process information in meaningful ways. Broadly, this view of learning came to be called constructivism, but actually reflected several different schools of thought about how learning occurred. Some were particularly interested in how individuals constructed their own knowledge and how these cognitive structures changed and developed. Others likened the act of building these cognitive structures to a series of mental computations through which we process information. For example, the now common view is that we take in information through our senses, and then encode it, store it in memory and later retrieve it for use. This view of learning can be considered the dominant cognitive view of learning today, with a rapidly expanding body of research.

This chapter looks at three main explanations of learning from the cognitive perspective: the constructivist approach, which includes both individualistic views of learning and also the role of social interaction in shaping learning; the information-processing explanation of how we learn, which focuses on mental processing of information; and the social cognitive explanation of learning, which helps explain the role of the individual operating within their social context to influence learning and behaviour. Finally, this chapter also explores the somewhat confusing and rather diverse body of theories that propose cognitive or learning styles, in an attempt to explain the different ways individuals might approach learning.

CONSTRUCTIVISM

Like all cognitive approaches, constructivism is fundamentally underpinned by the idea that meaning is constructed by the learner. Constructivists believe that that the learner is both mentally and physically active in the construction of knowledge, and therefore capable of self-regulating the learning process. Constructivists also hold a developmental perspective of learning, arguing that young children learn by developing increasingly complex cognitive structures, or schemas, and that they add new information to progressively build these schema (Byrnes, 1996; Yager & Lutz, 1994). Some forms of constructivism also propose that the sociocultural context in which knowledge construction occurs provides the thinker with invaluable resources, support and direction (O'Donnell, 2012). In particular, an important part of the constructivist philosophy is that learning is supported by social interaction with peers and adults as the learner develops. As learners interact with their environment, they link new information from current experiences to previous knowledge, and so construct new understandings and knowledge.

FORMS OF CONSTRUCTIVISM

Constructivism takes several forms that indicate slightly different emphases on the process by which learning occurs and knowledge is constructed. Two of these forms are 'psychological constructivism' and 'social constructivism' (Palincsar, 1998; Phillips, 2000). Although they share a focus on individuals constructing their own learning, each has a different emphasis: one on the individual, the other on the social context (see Figure 6.2).

psychological constructivism
Focuses on individual learners and how they construct their own knowledge, beliefs and identity

Psychological constructivism is concerned with individual learners and how they construct their knowledge, beliefs and identity during the learning process. Piaget's theory of cognitive development, with its emphasis on the individual's progression through a series of stages, forms the foundation for

Source: Shutterstock.com/Monkey Business Images

FIGURE 6.2 Do students mainly construct understandings on their own, or as a result of their interactions with others?

psychological constructivism. Like Piaget, psychological (or individual) constructivists acknowledge the importance of the social environment, but see the role of the individual learner in constructing the learning environment as central. In this view, Memet's individual construction of the nine times table would be viewed in terms of his own unique formation of knowledge, and the reshaping of his scheme of numbers that recognises patterns in numbers. The role of the teacher or adult in supporting this development would also be considered in terms of strategies that might build on and prompt Memet's schematic development.

Social constructivism draws heavily on Vygotsky's belief that social processes are integral to learning. This approach rejects the view that the locus of knowledge lies solely within the individual. Rather, the social constructivist view is that social interaction shapes cognitive development and is an essential component of the learning process (Cobb & Yackel, 1996; Prawat, 1996). As seen in Memet's classroom, students are seated in groups and hence knowledge construction is easily shared among individuals at Memet's table. Social constructivists would be very interested in how peer-to-peer learning appears to extend the knowledge of peers at Memet's table and is also reciprocated. They would also be interested in the role of the teacher in structuring the learning environment to support and enable this form of learning through social interaction.

> social constructivism
> Emphasises the role of social and cultural factors in shaping learning

The merits of distinguishing between psychological and social constructivism and the various ways of applying it are open to debate (see, for example, Phillips, 1997). As in Memet's classroom, it is possible to analyse and describe the learning through a combination of these theoretical perspectives.

KEY PRINCIPLES OF CONSTRUCTIVISM

Collectively, constructivist theories encourage educators to recognise the value of the knowledge and experience that students bring to learning, and to provide experiences that help students build on their current knowledge of the world, whether as individuals or in social groups (O'Donnell, 2012).

The following principles may help to guide your reading and practice in this area:

- Learners are *active participants* in their learning. 'Learning by doing' is central to constructivism in practice (Howe & Berv, 2000).
- Learners are *self-regulated*. They construct and monitor their own learning, and metacognition plays an important role in facilitating this self-regulation.
- *Social interaction* is necessary for effective learning. Both Piaget and Vygotsky acknowledged the role of social interaction with peers and significant others (such as parents and teachers) in cognitive development.

Constructivism encourages individuals to make sense of information for themselves (Bruner, 1990). This means that knowledge may be relative and may differ for each learner. (See Matthews, 2000, for a discussion of this issue in the context of mathematics and science education.) And just as individuals construct their own meaning within a social and cultural context, knowledge and understanding may differ across learners and contexts.

CONSTRUCTIVISM IN THE CLASSROOM CONTEXT

The constructivist principles already outlined have many implications for classroom practice, and resulting strategies tend to fall into one of three broad categories, in that they:

- attend to learner-centred experiences and processes
- provide opportunities for learners to work together
- assist novice learners to develop expertise.

This section looks in detail at these three categories of constructivist learning, which, although discussed separately, clearly overlap and share a common focus on the learner. We also explore concepts such as Bloom's taxonomy of learning, which are often related to constructivist ideas.

Attend to learner-centred experiences and processes

Because constructivists believe that learners bring their own knowledge and experiences to the learning context, this is also the theoretical basis of learner-centred approaches. Learner-centred approaches acknowledge that learner experiences may involve many unique learning opportunities or interests that lead to the development of specific knowledge or skills. Therefore, teachers must spend time understanding students' current constructions, and checking what understandings they have constructed from their learning experiences. There is no guarantee that learners will receive knowledge just as teachers have delivered it – it may well be reconstructed by their prior experiences and understandings (Gillies, 2007). Assessment is therefore an important skill for constructivist teachers (see Chapter 13 for more on this topic). Because of constructivism's focus on the value of students' background experiences and prior learning, the teacher can also motivate students through acknowledging their interests, or simply acknowledging the child's desire to explore their own environment. 'Discovery learning' and 'inquiry learning' are two learner-centred practices that reflect constructivist approaches to learning.

Discovery learning

Bruner (1966) argued that if students discover the connections between their learning in a meaningful context, they will be able to make sense of, and remember and apply, what they have learnt. He called this **discovery learning**. In fact 'discovery learning' also occurs quite naturally when children pull a toy apart 'to see how it works', and show a natural tendency to explore the environment; these experiences seem to form an important part of many childhood developmental experiences. In the classroom, the learner might manipulate materials or ideas in the learning environment and discover connections among them. This approach proposes that by being active participants in the problem solving, learners are more likely to remember what they have learnt. It is also often assumed that learners will have increased motivation to continue learning, and will be able to apply their learning to solve new problems in new learning contexts.

In practice however, discovery learning can be approached in very different ways. 'Open' discovery learning approaches allow students a lot of independent or unguided exploration of materials or concepts. Learners are allowed time to explore and have freedom in how to shape their responses or conclusions. On the other hand, in the approach known as 'guided' discovery learning, the learner

CourseMateExpress

Online Resources
Explore an example
of the constructivist
teaching-learning cycle
with the **Interactive
Activity** on this text's
website

discovery learning
The learner actively
manipulates materials
or ideas in the learning
environment and
discovers connections
between them

practises problem solving with the accompaniment of teacher directions for each step, and with closer monitoring by the teacher. This approach provides students with a framework for learning, and at the same time allows students a sense of autonomy within the guidelines provided by the teacher.

Each method has its advantages and limitations. However, guided discovery is more commonly used in classrooms because open discovery learning has been criticised as being less effective than more directed approaches (Mayer, 2004). Box 6.1 describes a debate that occurred between researchers comparing discovery learning with more direct or teacher-led instruction approaches.

Inquiry and problem-based learning

Inquiry learning and **problem-based learning (PBL)** are separate but related approaches in which learners ask questions and find solutions to problems for themselves. Inquiry learning is often applied in science disciplines, while PBL emerged from medical-education contexts (Hmelo-Silver, Duncan & Chinn, 2007). Both approaches are similar in that they focus on relevant, practical and authentic problems; both place a heavy emphasis on collaboration with others; and both place a heavy emphasis on the cognitive activity involved in sense making (Hmelo-Silver, Duncan & Chinn, 2007). They differ slightly, however, on the basis of the inquiry or problem-solving activities. Hmelo-Silver, Duncan and Chinn claim that due to the medical or scientific inquiry bases of the two approaches, they differ slightly in the learning processes emphasised. Inquiry learning, for example, emphasises scientific processes of posing questions, gathering and analysing data, and coming to evidence-based conclusions. PBL may often use text-based sources of information about the data and a self-directed learning process; it emphasises hypothetical–deductive reasoning skills as might be required for medical-education students studying the diagnosis of disease, for example.

The role of the teacher in these approaches is to both provide knowledge and content, while carefully scaffolding the most difficult or complex learning and skills. Both approaches encourage students to frame questions, think in new ways about them, and organise their thinking in effective ways. Like the debate discussed in Box 6.1, there is also a longstanding debate between proponents of these approaches and direct instruction. Kirschner, Sweller and Clark (2006) published a paper called 'Why minimal guidance during instruction does not work', which extensively criticised constructivist approaches as offering minimal guidance for learning and claimed that such learning could be more effectively achieved through direct instruction. Hmelo-Silver, Duncan and Chinn (2007) responded by stating that Kirschner and colleagues had made a serious error in mixing up all constructivist approaches under the label of 'minimal guidance'. In fact, they argued that inquiry learning and PBL approaches are not 'minimally guided' approaches but employ a number of instructional approaches, including direct instruction of knowledge as well as carefully scaffolded and guided instruction when students need support. Kuhn (2007) (see also Box 6.1) and Schmidt, Loyens, van Gog and Paas (2007) also replied, pointing out that many of the direct-instruction pedagogical approaches advocated by Kirschner and colleagues only applied to certain types of learning problems, often non-complex in nature, and often focused on the individuals learning

Source: Matthew Duchesne, © Milk and Honey Photography, 2010.

FIGURE 6.3 Bruner argued that when students discover and actively engage in problem solving, they are more likely to remember what they have learnt.

CourseMateExpress

Online resources Elements of the constructivist approach can be identified in a **video** of a primary teacher describing her teaching approach

inquiry learning Students learn content and discipline-specific thinking and practical skills by collaboratively investigating and solving a problem

problem-based learning (PBL) Students learn content, strategies and learning skills through collaboratively solving problems

these skills rather than on people working together to solve problems. The debate continues, but it is clear that learner-centred approaches address constructivist principles in different ways, with a broad body of evidence offering support for such approaches.

BOX 6.1 RESEARCH LINKS

THINKING CRITICALLY ABOUT THE ROLE OF ADULTS AND CHILDREN IN LEARNING

One of the approaches to learning and teaching that has emerged from Piaget's theory is 'discovery learning', in which children are given materials and activities that invite them to explore their environment and discover properties and principles. A different approach involves direct instruction, in which the teacher instructs students about what they need to know, what to do and how to do it. (See Chapter 5 for a fuller description of these approaches.)

Klahr and Nigam (2004) investigated whether direct instruction or discovery learning was more effective in helping children learn about the control of variables in scientific work. They found that Year 4 children who received instruction showed superior use of control of variables in their design of experiments. Others have similarly argued that direct instruction is a more effective teaching/learning strategy than discovery learning (for example, Kirschner, Sweller & Clark, 2006).

However, Dean and Kuhn (2007) challenged Klahr and Nigam's findings, showing that over a longer period of nearly six months, the differences between direct instruction and discovery learning were not as clear. Although the children who received direct instruction showed superior performance immediately afterwards, this was not sustained unless there was regular practice. Also, direct instruction was not essential for the learning to occur: practice with a range of problems on its own produced the same effect.

Direct instruction may appear to be a quick teaching strategy with measurable learning outcomes, but Dean and Kuhn's study suggests that, particularly for understandings that take time to acquire, it needs to be paired with practice and experience. There is a longstanding debate between the proponents of constructivism and direct instruction.

ACTIVITIES

1   Which topics or learning goals might be suited to direct instruction or discovery learning?
2   Observe a classroom session in which children are learning a concept (for example, in a Mathematics or Science class). What role does the teacher play in this learning? What role do the students play?
3   Consider your own experiences. Do you recall a concept or knowledge that you explicitly gained from 'discovery' learning or a concept for which you required very 'direct' instruction to learn?

Provide opportunities for learners to work together

Constructivist approaches have included both an emphasis on individual cognitive processes and shared cognitive processes when learners work together to solve problems. Social constructivist approaches in particular emphasise the idea that knowledge is constructed from the continual interaction between the individual and his or her environment (O'Donnell, 2012). This includes the critical importance of peers or the community as a source of learning and knowledge construction, and the term 'community of learners' arises from these approaches. Therefore, in many constructivist classrooms, group work features prominently, as students are encouraged to discuss ideas and learn from one another. By working together in a social context, the learner not only brings their personal knowledge or understanding but is also influenced and shaped by that environment. The learning process is reciprocal among members of a group or community and knowledge is often described as co-constructed (Green & Gredler, 2002; O'Donnell, 2012).

There are several ways of enabling students to work together. These include **cooperative learning**, **collaborative learning** and peer-assisted learning, and are also demonstrated in the inquiry learning and PBL approaches discussed previously. Because of the student-focused nature of these strategies, they also illustrate key principles of the humanist perspective of learning (see Chapter 7). For this reason, cooperative learning is outlined in more detail in the next chapter. In this section, we focus on the social constructivist explanations for learning in this way.

Vygotskian and sociocultural theorists (also known as social constructivists; see Chapter 3) propose that cognitive benefits arise from the co-construction and negotiation of meaning that occurs in social interaction. Group members elaborate on and provide feedback for one another's ideas, building a joint understanding that is greater than what they could have produced individually. Scaffolding is critical in this form of instruction. The teacher may be the scaffold, through careful instructional design, that leads groups from the known to the unknown, with teacher support at each step. Good software design or online learning activities can also facilitate this by carefully scaffolding the instructional tasks (see Box 6.2). However, in accordance with Vygotskian theorists, sociocultural theorists also prize the development of peer-to-peer scaffolding. When more competent students work with less competent peers, they can also lead the zone of proximal development forward through scaffolding by modelling of language or thinking strategies. The teacher's role, however, is neither absent nor merely observational. As has been pointed out previously, teachers must guide peer interaction and ensure that foundational knowledge and skills are present, and may even use direct instruction where necessary.

cooperative learning
Students working together to gain rewards for themselves and their group

collaborative learning
Students learning together, drawing on one another's knowledge and skills

BOX 6.2 CASE STUDY

ONLINE COLLABORATIVE LEARNING

In a senior Biology class, students were developing models of DNA for an assignment. The teacher had noticed that many students used Facebook for informal discussion of school work, and decided to build on this for online collaborative learning.

The school's Learning Management System was used to post readings and resources, such as examples of past students' work. It also contained a discussion space that students were encouraged to use to collaborate on assignments while developing their ideas. Students' plans and work were posted on the site, with a space for review comments. Students were asked to use the task outcomes and marking guide to direct their feedback to fellow students. Both the teacher and the students used this public space to comment on student work, and to discuss one another's feedback.

The teacher felt that her involvement was important to guide discussion and feedback towards the learning outcomes and requirements of the task. She found that there was a need to keep the learning outcomes at the front, to ensure quality of collaboration. (Initially, there was a tendency for general 'Great job!'-style statements.)

As a result of the project, students reported stronger understanding of the task requirements and a broader understanding of the topic. They also reported that they were starting to understand the standards and how these related to their work. Students enjoyed being encouraged to work together and share work, and felt they were able to produce quality individual work, benefiting from the input of their peers.

See Chapter 12 for more on using ICT in learning and teaching.

Peer-assisted learning

peer-assisted learning
Encourages social
interaction, as peers
help each other to
learn

peer tutoring
Students are paired in
roles of tutor or learner
and follow specified
learning strategies

Peer-assisted learning (PAL) is another form of student-centred learning that encourages social interaction and gives learners opportunities to construct their learning and support their peers in doing the same. PAL programs are quite widespread and used in many disciplines in higher education including medical education (Ross & Stenfors-Hayes, 2017). You may have noticed that your university or college uses some form of peer-assisted learning program. These programs have also been incorporated in formal interventions in which rigorously designed programs employ peers as agents of learning and support. For example, a long-term reading program known as PALS (Fuchs & Fuchs, 1998) is a class-wide **peer tutoring** program in which pairs of students take turns being the 'coach' or 'reader'. Teachers are carefully trained in specific reading strategies, and then teachers train students in specific learning strategies that they can employ in the coaching and reading sessions. Each pair earns points for good coaching or reading. These types of peer-assisted learning programs are carefully designed and evaluated in intervention studies; for example, Fuchs and colleagues have found that this intervention has evidence-based benefits for students from kindergarten (Fuchs et al., 2002) through to high school (Fuchs, Fuchs & Kazdan, 1999).

Assist learners to develop expertise

A primary aim of constructivism is to help novices develop expertise in a particular area of knowledge so that they may become more independent, autonomous and self-regulated learners. The 'cognitive apprenticeship' concept introduced in Chapter 3 provides a useful metaphor for the way in which a young learner or novice is guided by an expert.

Cognitive apprenticeships (Rogoff, 1990) are a form of social constructivism and describe a process in which the 'apprentice' (or novice) learner is guided by an expert who provides scaffolding, modelling and practice (see Chapter 3). Eventually the novice will be able to perform tasks and work through problems autonomously and achieve expertise. This approach is very much like the traditional notion of a master craftsperson working with an apprentice who learns by following the more expert model, tries to emulate their practices, and is coached and guided by the expert along the way. During this process, the apprentice or 'novice' also becomes immersed in the 'community of practice' that shapes and perhaps defines the nature of the craftsperson's work (Lave & Wenger, 1991). For example, the apprentice would learn what techniques were acceptable in the discipline of their craft, what tools should be used, and what language or words are used to describe things in the discipline. They would learn the social rules of the community, and the roles and places of different people in that community.

This same notion of apprenticeship is employed by Vygotskian sociocultural theorists (see Chapter 3) to describe the 'cognitive apprenticeship' (O'Donnell, 2012). The teacher as 'expert' would also 'model' the cognitive activities in such a way that students can observe the thinking processes of the teacher, or the working process of the teacher as a problem is solved. Peers are also important in this community of learners because they too can 'think aloud', thereby modelling their thinking process to other students and also articulating the language of the learning discipline. The teacher (or more expert adult or peer) gives guidance and assistance in joint problem-solving activities, and is responsive to the novice learner's current level of understanding.

Reciprocal teaching

'Reciprocal teaching', a method of teaching reading comprehension developed by Palincsar and Brown, and based on Vygotsky's work (refer to Chapter 3), is an example of cognitive apprenticeship commonly used in classrooms. As described in Chapter 3, this teacher-guided strategy involves students working in collaborative teams and practising the reading strategies of predicting, questioning, summarising and clarifying. The teacher models these disciplinary practices and then students must emulate these strategies in their collaborative groups.

Skilful questioning and self-questioning are important in reciprocal teaching (see Chapter 3) and in other constructivist approaches (Henson, 1996). Constructivist educators pose thought-provoking questions to stimulate thinking, reflecting and problem solving. Bloom's taxonomy, as revised by Anderson and Krathwohl (2001), can help to frame those questions, and assist educators in considering the level of thinking required by the questions they ask (see Box 6.3). Reflection is central to constructivist learning and teaching (Tobin, 2000). Students need to be encouraged to reflect on their construction of knowledge. Teachers, too, need to reflect on their practice and their own construction of knowledge, and the learning context. Constructivist questioning and self-questioning help promote both reflective learning and teaching.

Apprenticeship occurs in many practical everyday contexts, such as in families where children learn to feed or dress themselves, sometimes with direct guidance from parents, but also by observing and emulating the behaviours of brothers and sisters. However, research shows it can also be applied in classroom contexts with learners of all ages. For example, if you are studying to become a teacher, an experienced teacher may be guiding your apprenticeship as you gain skills and knowledge in their classroom. In any case, the social constructivists have offered us detailed insights into how communities pass on expert knowledge, and how novice or younger members of communities learn from the relatively natural processes of 'apprenticeship'. Adapting these ideas to the classroom is possible, and a range of interventions, such as reciprocal teaching, demonstrate this.

CourseMateExpress

Online Resources
Go further: Read about 'Promoting higher order thinking through constructivist-style questioning' on this text's website

BOX 6.3 CLASSROOM LINKS

BLOOM'S TAXONOMY AND QUESTIONING TECHNIQUES

Bloom (1956) described a hierarchy of learning objectives (known as a 'taxonomy') ranging from knowing and understanding content to more sophisticated ways of evaluating and analysing material. Bloom's taxonomy of learning was originally developed to assist university educators in describing educational objectives for advanced learners (Booker, 2007). However, it has been appropriated by school educators to assist in describing levels of thinking to students, and encouraging learners to extend and develop their thinking skills. It is just as important for learners to be able to analyse their own learning as it is for them to analyse the information they are reading or learning about.

One approach to scaffolding students' learning and providing cognitive apprenticeships in your teaching is to encourage learners to think and analyse in progressively more complex ways. Bloom's taxonomy of educational objectives was revised by Anderson and Krathwohl (2001) – summarised in Table 6.1 – and is widely used as a planning tool by educators. The taxonomy reflects foundational levels of thinking required to first remember and understand concepts, and moves to progressively more complex or higher-order thinking processes. The sequence of cognitive processes is not intended to devalue the initial cognitive processes but rather emphasises the progression in knowledge and understanding as one moves through the cognitive processes.

Caution is advised, however, in applying this taxonomy as a teaching approach in and of itself. It was not designed for this purpose. Cognitive processes are relevant to task requirements and some disciplines place more emphasis on certain processes and forms of knowledge. Teachers must take care not to overemphasise only the higher-order thinking levels of such taxonomies, as in most disciplines students must still develop foundational levels of knowledge as described at the start of the taxonomy.

>>

TABLE 6.1 Anderson–Krathwohl's revision of Bloom's taxonomy and example tasks or activities

| ANDERSON AND KRATHWOHL'S REVISED TAXONOMY | |
COGNITIVE PROCESS DIMENSION	SKILL DESCRIPTIONS
Remembering	Make a time line of events: Can you describe what happened when …?
Understanding	Retell the story in your own words: What do you think will happen next?
Applying	Draw a diagram to show how it works: What would happen if you tried this?
Analysing	Design an interview or survey for the story characters to find out what really happened: What were some of the motives behind …?
Evaluating	Write a half-year report to evaluate a procedure: What changes would you recommend …?
Creating	Create an alternative procedure assuming your changes were put in place: Design a marketing poster or video to promote the changes.

Source: Adapted from Killen (2007).

THINKING CRITICALLY ABOUT CONSTRUCTIVIST APPROACHES

Constructivism has wide support, both from teachers and from research (for example, De Corte & Verschaffel, 2006), but it has also attracted criticism. For example, Rowe (2007; also see Dinham & Rowe, 2008) argued strongly that although constructivism is a well-established theory of learning, it is not a theory of teaching. As we have seen above, several theorists have argued against approaches that leave students to discover or construct knowledge on their own, with minimal instruction, guidance or intervention from the teacher. However as we have demonstrated in this chapter, there are many forms of constructivism that involve teachers in the learning process at every point – scaffolding learning, providing cognitive apprenticeships, asking questions to extend students' thinking, and helping to link new learning to students' existing knowledge.

FIGURE 6.4 Peers can be involved in cognitive apprenticeship through peer-teaching programs.

One way in which constructivism has been effectively integrated into teaching approaches has been through the phases of 'modelled, guided and independent' practices that are common in reading programs (for example, in the NSW K–6 English syllabus). The teacher models a reading or writing practice (explicit teaching phase), then guides students as they transform the new knowledge and make it their own, perhaps through group work, independent activity or work with the teacher (the constructivist phase), after which they engage in independent practice and demonstrate their knowledge (assessment and reflection phase). The focus is on teaching that leads to students constructing learning (Hattie, 2009). Return to the table of Hattie's (2009) research in the introduction to this book (see Table 1.2). In it, you will note that both reciprocal teaching (a constructivist approach that involves the teacher) and direct instruction (an approach associated with behaviourism) have been shown to have strong effects on student learning.

STRENGTHS OF THE CONSTRUCTIVIST APPROACH

Constructivism has many benefits for student learning. Constructivism acknowledges that learners are 'constructors' of meaning, actively seeking to discover and learn. In constructivist classrooms, students are encouraged to participate in their learning, rather than being passive recipients of information transmitted by the teacher. Constructivism also attaches importance to students' prior learning and the background knowledge they bring to the learning environment. In a constructivist approach, as in effective teaching, teachers work with student knowledge to make links between what students know and what they need to learn (Anthony & Walshaw, 2007).

Students' social and cultural heritage plays an important part in learning and is valued in the constructivist approach. Social networks are seen as important in constructivist learning environments, with value attached to dialogues and interactions among students and between students and teachers. There is also scope for parent and community-member involvement as 'experts' who can support students in cognitive apprenticeships. These are just some of the many benefits the constructivist approach offers learners and teachers.

LIMITATIONS OF THE CONSTRUCTIVIST APPROACH

Constructivism has its limitations, however. One limiting factor is that allowing students to construct their own learning takes a lot of time and may be complicated to set up (Bevevino, Dengel & Adams, 1999). Teachers need to ensure that they provide sufficient scaffolding and support structures to facilitate constructivist learning. If students have questions, they need to feel safe enough to ask them. It may take time to develop a safe and supportive learning environment so that this can happen.

There are also many potential disadvantages to group work (Killen, 2007; Tiberius, 1990). It takes time to set up the groups. Teachers need to equip students with the necessary group-work skills in order for those students to be able to manage their work and their relationships within the groups. Teachers may also need to monitor the groups closely, depending on the task and the students involved.

Discovery learning, too, has limitations. It may work well for self-motivated students, but it can be very frustrating for those who do not feel confident or have not had sufficient experience at discovering information for themselves. The uncertainty of this type of learning environment, in which the teacher does not supply the 'answers', may frustrate and discourage some learners. The discovery process can also be time-consuming, as students may venture down thinking pathways that teachers have neither anticipated nor planned for. Brown and Rose (1995) found that the teachers they surveyed were knowledgeable about constructivist principles, yet did not adopt the approach widely in their teaching. The reasons given were that they lacked sufficient time and often did not feel confident about managing discovery learning along with all the other curriculum demands.

Box 6.4 presents a summary of the constructivist approaches that have been discussed throughout this section, as well as some related strategies for classroom use.

THINK ABOUT

- Do you see yourself as a constructivist educator in the making? Why or why not? Discuss your views with your tutorial or study group.

BOX 6.4 IMPLICATIONS FOR EDUCATORS

CONSTRUCTIVIST APPROACHES IN THE CLASSROOM

Constructivist approaches focus on learners actively engaging with making meaning for themselves, supported by peers, teachers, parents and community members. Such approaches place value on the background knowledge and experiences that learners bring to the learning environment.

Table 6.2 summarises the main constructivist approaches to learning, and offers some constructivist strategies for classroom use.

TABLE 6.2 Constructivist approaches and classroom strategies

TEACHING AIM	CONSTRUCTIVIST APPROACH	STRATEGY
1 Encourage learner-centred experiences and activities	**Discovery learning:** The learner works with materials and ideas, discovering connections between them; uses active problem solving **Inquiry learning:** The learner poses questions, researches possible answers and solutions; uses active problem solving	• Facilitate discovery by developing task-appropriate resources, activities and classroom organisation • Provide opportunities for students to develop problem-solving skills • Encourage students' active involvement in learning • Promote students' confidence in their ability to learn and discover new concepts by creating a safe, supportive learning environment • Ask questions to prompt and extend students' thinking, and to expose and correct any weaknesses in their understanding
2 Provide opportunities for students to work together	**Cooperative learning:** Group work, with the teacher managing and organising activities; cooperation required for group rewards **Collaborative learning:** Group work, with greater student autonomy and less teacher involvement **Peer-assisted learning:** Peers teach one another; may be same age or cross-age partnerships	• Develop and implement guidelines for group and pair work • Carefully train students in the skills required to work in groups • Negotiate activities and assessments to encourage student involvement • Arrange the classroom to promote group interaction • Regularly monitor student skills, interactions and achievements • Capitalise on learner strengths and abilities by establishing peer-assisted learning experiences
3 Assist novice learners to develop expertise	**Cognitive apprenticeships:** Experts guide novice apprentice learners with the aim of developing learners' autonomy and expertise **Reciprocal teaching:** Combines collaborative learning with expert guidance and modelling to achieve progressively greater learner autonomy and understanding	• Encourage learner–teacher interaction as a learning partnership • Make time for dialogue – listen and respond to student questions and comments • Draw on the expertise of parents and community members or more able students to develop cognitive apprenticeships in your classroom

THE INFORMATION-PROCESSING APPROACH

We saw in Chapter 3 that the **information-processing model** is a way of depicting how mental processes operate. There are several views of information processing that attempt to explain how we think and how the mind works. In all of these views, thinking is portrayed as a highly rational process, and our capacity to remember information lies at the heart of information-processing theories.

Classical viewpoints consider the human mind as a complex machine, resembling the serial processing that takes place in computers. As in a computer, such theorists are concerned with the processes by which the human mind *encodes*, *stores* and *retrieves* information. This viewpoint is clearly depicted in the multistore model of information processing described in Chapter 3, and is based on the original work of Atkinson and Shiffrin (1968). The original model described how information is processed and stored in three compartments of memory: the *sensory memory* (through which we first perceive information), the *short-term memory* or *working memory* (believed to be a more accurate term to describe the capacity to work with information for a very small amount of time), and the *long-term memory* (which stores information permanently). These three compartments of memory do not completely explain how information is processed. Rather, the intervening processes by which information moves from sensory memory to the working memory are vitally important, as are the processes by which we retrieve information from our long-term memory. An **executive control** system is proposed to oversee these processes (Baddeley, 2012). Return to Chapter 3 to revise your understanding of these processes. In this chapter we will focus on their operation in children's learning.

information-processing model
Likens the human mind to a computer that interprets, stores and retrieves information

CourseMateExpress
Online resources
Explore the Multistore model in action with the **Interactive Activity** on this text's website

executive control
Higher-level functions that help with the control of processes and flow of information

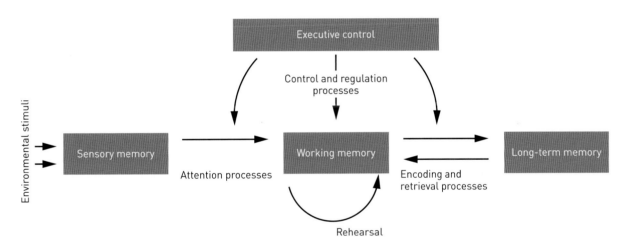

FIGURE 6.5 The multistore model of information processing.

SENSORY MEMORY AND LEARNING

Recall from Chapter 3 that we take in information through our senses and assign meaning to it (perception). Sensory memories extinguish extremely quickly (less than a second for visual information and two to three seconds for auditory information). In that time, we must identify, classify and assign meaning to the new information or it will be gone forever. The role of perception is important here – stimuli that have some meaning to the individual are more likely to be attended to; thus, the two key processes involved at this stage are *recognition* and *attention*. For an example of how sensory memory works, try the activity in Figure 6.6.

Source: © 1998, Dr Graham Cooper, School of Education Studies, The University of New South Wales.

FIGURE 6.6 Look at this image, then quickly shut your eyes and keep them shut for a few seconds. Repeat this several times. What do you notice?

Separate stores for auditory and visual information suggest we can present information in multiple modalities and thereby increase the likelihood of it being attended to (see **Box 6.5**).

Attention and its role in learning

As the sensory memory is extremely limited in capacity and time, attention is a vital process in determining which stimuli are processed in working memory, and encoded into long-term memory.

Sustaining attention over time can be challenging, particularly for young children. Some features – loud noises, bright colours, surprising events – command attention without our deliberate planning. The individual learner also plays a role in controlling their attention through the executive control (described later in this section of the chapter).

Selective attention

We tend to attend to particular features of a situation that have significance for us. Prior knowledge thus directs attention, as do our expectations. (You can try this in the online resources link.) If you expect that what is about to happen in a room is a lecture, you will tend to ignore much of the sensory information you take in (the colour of the seats, and noise coming from outside, for example). If, on the other hand, you are told that this is the room where you will have to sleep for the night, your attention will focus on the arrangement of the space, and the composition of the seats. Learners may fail to attend to the right features of a learning stimulus unless their attention is directed to it; this is one reason why telling students the goal of an activity or lesson at the start can be helpful to their learning. As learners gain more knowledge – develop more complex schemas in memory – their ability to attend to relevant information improves. There is also the possibility that they may focus on one known aspect of what is presented, ignoring other factors. 'Lateral thinking' exercises can help to refocus attention on new facets of a concept or situation that may not have been 'seen' previously.

CourseMateExpress

Online resources
Watch a **video** on selective attention on this text's website

Divided attention

Can we split attention between multiple tasks? You may have tried this by texting on a mobile phone while listening to a conversation. In fact, research suggests that attention generally cannot be shared in this way between unrelated tasks (Shomstein & Yantis, 2004). We appear to do this, for example, when driving and holding a conversation at the same time, but in fact one task is largely automatic – does not require our focused attention – so that the other can receive attention. You will notice this if something happens on the road that requires your attention, such as an accident that requires you to take evasive action. In these situations, you tend to stop talking and listening as you focus on your driving. (This happens with walking and talking as well. If your companion tells you something surprising, you may stop walking to take it in.) The other way in which we can appear to 'multitask' or share attention is by rapid switching of attention from one task to another. Baddeley (2012) has shown that switching leads to a substantial slowing of mental processing, which indicates that this is not conducive to effective learning. In the classroom, then, it is important to ensure that students' attention is not divided between competing stimuli.

WORKING MEMORY AND LEARNING

The next store was originally viewed as a temporary storage place with a limited capacity to store approximately seven items of information at a time for a short period (Miller, 1956), and was termed short-term memory. However, the idea of a working memory (Baddeley & Logie, 1999) reflected a much more active role in processing information, containing the short-term memory store but with added components. Although the capacity of short-term memory was known to be quite limited, storing information for only a few seconds, it became clear that working processes enabled the retention of information through processes of rehearsal and chunking. 'Rehearsal' involves us repeating and practising information to help ourselves remember it. 'Chunking' occurs when we group related pieces of information into a single meaningful unit. You may have used chunking to remember a list of numbers. For example, if your student number is quite long, you may chunk the nine digits as '925–231–378'. Thus, nine pieces of information are reduced to three bundles, which makes the number easier to remember. The rhythm of this grouping may also help you remember the sequence.

Shopping List A		
• vegemite	• nectarines	• toothbrush
• dental floss	• bread	• mangoes
• butter	• soap	• pears

Shopping List B		
pears	bread	toothbrush
mangoes	butter	soap
nectarines	vegemite	dental floss

FIGURE 6.7 An example of chunking is that of a typical shopping list. Which of these identical lists of items would you find easier to remember? In most cases, List B would be easier to remember as the items are chunked in a logical manner.

A different kind of chunking occurs as we develop *schemas* (also referred to as *schemes*) or linked networks of knowledge and ideas (see Chapter 3). Thus, as your understanding of this topic develops, one phrase, 'information processing', might bring up a network of associated ideas from your long-term memory. This frees up your working memory, which no longer has to make sense of each of these individually, but can apply the whole schema to the new task. Schemas play other roles in learning too, linking new knowledge with old and facilitating its encoding in and retrieval from long-term memory.

There are various views about the role of working memory, but generally it is assumed that the more effectively the material is chunked and rehearsed, the more likely it is to be transferred to long-term memory. The limited capacity of working memory means that unrehearsed items will be displaced by new information and quickly forgotten. You could easily test this by reading out several telephone numbers for a friend to remember, with no time between each number to rehearse or chunk the digits. Your friend might try to use their working memory to chunk the first number, but as you keep firing new numbers at them, they may not even have enough time to rehearse and store the first number. The process of attention may help us decide which is the most important information to focus on, and therefore we could ignore (and not remember) subsequent or competing information if we were focused on remembering a specific piece of information. Working-memory processes are quite important, then, in a variety of learning tasks. For example, our working memory would enable us to hold the first part of a sentence in our mind while we were reading the last part of the sentence, hence enabling comprehension of the full sentence, and a range of more complex comprehension tasks (see Engle & Conway, 1998).

Baddeley (2012) has continued to develop the model of working memory, with research suggesting that it processes auditory and visual information separately, through an 'auditory loop' and 'visuo-spatial sketchpad', each with particular links to long-term memory. This has implications for the presentation of information (see Box 6.5).

CourseMateExpress
Online resources
Go further: See an example of information processing in action on this text's website

Cognitive load

Try this problem: *If the problem you solved after you solved the problem you solved before you solved the problem you solved after you solved this one was harder than the problem you solved before you solved the problem you solved after you solved this one, was the problem you solved before you solved this one harder than this one?*

cognitive load
The total demands made on working memory at any one time

Why is this problem so difficult to make sense of? One explanation is that the demands it makes on working memory are too great for its limited capacity – it presents an excessive **cognitive load**. You may have experienced a similar difficulty when trying to listen to a lecture, view a diagram put up by the lecturer, take notes, remember the meaning of new terms that are being used, and make sense of some new and complex information (such as information processing perhaps!).

There are three types of cognitive load that may be experienced. One is the cognitive load presented by the information itself, and its level of complexity or novelty to the learner. This is known as *intrinsic* cognitive load. A second is *extraneous* cognitive load, which is the load imposed by the particular way in which the information has been presented. The third type of load is *germane* cognitive load, which refers to the amount of working memory resources devoted to a task by the learner, and is therefore positive in terms of learning. Increasing the germane load and reducing the intrinsic and extraneous loads are the aim of good instruction, according to cognitive load theory. Implications of this for teaching and learning are to attempt to promote germane load by engaging and motivating the learner (see Chapter 8); reduce intrinsic load by simplifying complex material and building automaticity of skills; and reduce extraneous load by attending to instructional design. Research by cognitive load theorists has focused in particular on the last of these – how careful instructional design can reduce extraneous cognitive load, and therefore maximise the transfer of information into long-term memory (Sweller, Ayres & Kalyuga, 2011). A number of effects have been identified by this research and are described in Box 6.5.

BOX 6.5 CLASSROOM LINKS

COGNITIVE LOAD AND INSTRUCTIONAL DESIGN

John Sweller and colleagues have identified a number of principles for instructional design based on cognitive load theory.

The following effects have been noted in research to show learning benefits. They are theorised to reduce cognitive load and thereby assist learning by facilitating links with long-term memory. The strategies have been shown to be effective in diverse domains including mathematics, science, learning a second language, writing and reading comprehension, among others (see Sweller, Ayres & Kalyuga, 2011, for a detailed review of the research).

Strategies with benefits for novice learners

Goal-free problems:

Novices working on problems that are open-ended, or goal-free, showed better learning outcomes than learners given a specific goal (Sweller, Mawer & Ward, 1983). For example, in the diagram (at right), a goal-specific task would be to ask the students to 'find the length of AB'. A goal-free task, on the other hand, might ask the learner to 'find all the information you can'. This has been shown to reduce cognitive load, as students don't spend time working back and forth between the question and the information given in the diagram.

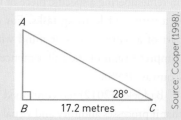

Source: Cooper (1998).

Worked examples:

Studying worked examples of problems proves more effective for learning than solving problems alone. It is most effective to study a worked example, solve a similar problem, study another worked example, solve another similar problem, and so on.

>>

Source: Cooper (1998).

Integrating information to avoid split attention:

When two sets of information need to be considered together, integrating them visually and in time reduces cognitive load and facilitates learning (Ginns, 2006). An example is given in the second diagram.

The modality effect:

Presenting information multimodally can facilitate learning. For example, a diagram accompanied by spoken explanation is more effective than a diagram accompanied by a written explanation. As working memory processes auditory and visual information separately, engaging both of these modalities expands the space available in working memory. The effect applies to two types (visual and auditory) of related information, which are both needed to convey meaning to the learner. Presenting the *same* information in visual and auditory forms (as when text on a PowerPoint slide is read out, for example) inhibits learning, as extra resources are spent processing redundant information.

Some qualifications of these findings should be noted. First, the strategies above only show benefits for novice learners. As students develop expertise in an area of knowledge, strategies such as these will become less effective for learning than other techniques, as they involve processing unnecessary information. In addressing this limitation, Sweller, Ayres and Kalyuga (2011) identified research that showed that imagination (imagining the process of solving a problem, or carrying out a procedure) and self-explanation are helpful strategies that suggest new mental processes to those who already have expertise in an area. Related to this, the strategies only show benefits when intrinsic cognitive load (the complexity of the task) is high. For simple tasks, they would add unnecessary information. It is therefore important to carefully assess students' prior knowledge and understanding when making decisions about instructional design. A third point should be made, which is that these effects have been noted in laboratory research or artificial classroom simulations, with careful control of variables in order to isolate the effects under investigation. In the classroom, however, other factors such as emotion and motivation come into play, interacting with memory and processing of information and potentially altering the outcome.

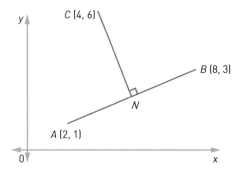

Problem
Find the coordinates of N, and the slope of the line NC, given that N is the midpoint on line AB.

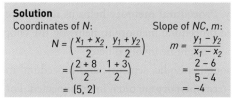

Solution

Coordinates of N:

$$N = \left(\frac{x_1 + x_2}{2}, \frac{y_1 + y_2}{2}\right)$$
$$= \left(\frac{2 + 8}{2}, \frac{1 + 3}{2}\right)$$
$$= (5, 2)$$

Slope of NC, m:

$$m = \frac{y_1 - y_2}{x_1 - x_2}$$
$$= \frac{2 - 6}{5 - 4}$$
$$= -4$$

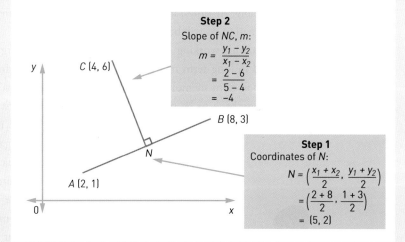

Step 2
Slope of NC, m:
$$m = \frac{y_1 - y_2}{x_1 - x_2}$$
$$= \frac{2 - 6}{5 - 4}$$
$$= -4$$

Step 1
Coordinates of N:
$$N = \left(\frac{x_1 + x_2}{2}, \frac{y_1 + y_2}{2}\right)$$
$$= \left(\frac{2 + 8}{2}, \frac{1 + 3}{2}\right)$$
$$= (5, 2)$$

Source: Examples drawn from Sweller, Ayres and Kalyuga (2011); and Cooper (1998).

LONG-TERM MEMORY AND LEARNING

The third component of the multistore model shown in Figure 6.5 represents an idea of a permanent storage facility for information, known as the long-term memory. As far as anyone can tell, this storage space is unlimited in capacity and storage time. Memories may remain in long-term memory indefinitely, and long-term memories take many forms. Three main types of long-term memory are 'episodic', 'semantic' and 'procedural' (Tulving, 1985).

episodic memory
Memory for life experiences

semantic memory
Memory about information and knowledge in the world around us

procedural memory
Memory about steps or procedures for performing a skill

Episodic memories are the memories we have for life experiences and events that have happened to us personally, such as a school concert in which you played the lead role, or your first kiss. **Semantic memory** is concerned with information and knowledge about the world around us; for example, knowing that computers may crash in an electrical storm if not disconnected from the power source, or that December, January and February are summer months in the Southern Hemisphere. Semantic memories generally lack the specific information about time and place that characterises episodic memories. If you remember something that happened to you while you were eating with chopsticks at your favourite Chinese restaurant last summer, this would be an episodic rather than a semantic memory. **Procedural memory** helps us recall steps or procedures for performing a skill; for example, you need procedural memory to help you use chopsticks for eating. Consider Figure 6.8; which types of memory might be involved here?

Although episodic, semantic and procedural memories differ in content and function, these types of long-term memory are often interconnected. For instance, your semantic memory of chopsticks may be connected to your episodic memory of the first time you tried to eat with them – and perhaps failed miserably! At times, long-term memories may interfere with one another, making it difficult to recall information, as will be discussed later in this chapter.

As with working memory, a range of intervening processes helps us to remember information stored in long-term memory. The two key processes involved are *encoding*, or storing information in the long-term memory store, and *retrieval*, which involves bringing information stored in long-term memory back to be manipulated in working memory. The effectiveness of these processes is the key to the efficiency of our memory. Strategies involved in encoding include rehearsal, elaboration and organisation. Elaboration and organisation involve linking new information to something already stored in the long-term memory. This makes the new material more meaningful because we connect it to something familiar, thus increasing our likelihood of remembering it in the future. Elaboration strategies are positively associated with academic performance, particularly in reading (Sturrock & May, 2002).

Although the original multistore model of Atkinson and Shiffrin (1968) did not include the function of an executive control system, it is now believed that such a system plays a critical role in controlling attention, shifting between tasks, retrieving information, and generally moving information back and forth between the working memory and the long-term memory (Baddeley, 1996, 2012). In particular, the executive control system may help us inhibit or suppress attention

Source: Getty Images/Juice Images Ltd

FIGURE 6.8 The three main types of long-term memory are episodic, procedural and semantic memory. Can you identify which types of memory are being drawn on here as this person thinks about how much paint will be needed to paint a room?

from distracting stimuli, and may help us process more than two types of information simultaneously. We will now consider the role of metacognitive processes in learning; metacognition is also considered to be one process in our executive control system.

METACOGNITION: MANAGING COGNITIVE PROCESSES

So far, both the constructivists and information processing theorists have taught us that cognition describes the mental processes involved in developing schemes, particularly the individual processes of transforming, coding, storing and retrieving information to build and develop these schemes. But how do we know which mental processes to use, and when, how and why? The answer may lie in our capacity for **metacognition**, which literally means 'thinking about thinking', or 'knowledge about knowledge' (Weinert, 1987). It is the capacity to think about our own cognitive processes (Flavell, Miller & Miller, 1993), and refers to our ability to monitor, control and organise our own mental activities. Metacognition can be thought of as a 'higher-order' cognitive process closely linked and implicated in our executive function (Roebers & Feurer, 2016)

As we cannot process all information to the same depth, we need an 'executive' function to oversee the process of encoding, transforming, processing, storing, retrieving and utilising information. This executive function involves both self-monitoring and self-regulation. **Self-monitoring** is a broad monitoring activity that helps us to keep track of our progress in understanding and remembering. Self-regulation, however, is concerned with central executive processes that comprise several specific functions such as planning, directing and evaluating our cognitive behaviour (Nelson & Narens, 1994; Schneider & Bjorklund, 1998). Self-regulated learners regulate their actions, cognitions, beliefs and motivations by selecting their own approach to learning and processing information (Shin, 1998).

When faced with a task, a self-regulated learner will typically:

- analyse the task and interpret task requirements
- set task-specific goals that aid successful task completion
- self-monitor progress and provide 'self-feedback'
- adjust strategies and goals throughout the process
- use self-motivational strategies to ensure task completion.

As shown in Figure 6.9, metacognition functions as an executive control that oversees our capacity to plan, monitor, regulate, question, reflect on and review our cognitive processes.

Metacognitive development

The skills presented above appear to represent fairly complex tasks, perhaps associated with older learners or even professionals in workplaces. This leads to the question: When does metacognition begin to develop? Just as our cognition develops over time, so does our metacognitive skill set. Although it may be assumed that young children are incapable of metacognitive thought, executive control processes and metacognitive monitoring skills can be observed in very young children and become more refined in accuracy, speed and efficiency as children get older (Roebers & Feurer, 2016).

metacognition
Higher-order thinking, which involves knowledge of and control over our own cognitive processes

self-monitoring
A metacognitive activity that involves monitoring how well we are understanding and remembering

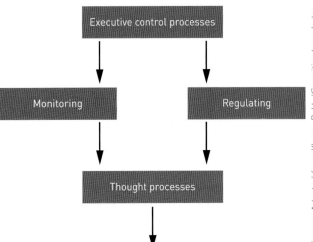

Source: Adapted from Kluwe, R. H. 'Cognitive knowledge and executive control: Metacognition', in D. R. Griffin (Ed.), *Animal Mind – Human Mind*, 1982, pp. 201–24, reproduced with permissions of Springer Science + Business Media.

FIGURE 6.9 Metacognition is like a company executive overseeing (monitoring and regulating) the workers (thought processes) of the company.

Online resources
Go further: Explore
the difference
between cognition and
metacognition on this
text's website

Metacognitive knowledge

Flavell described three forms of metacognitive knowledge: of person, of task and of strategy. These forms of knowledge can also be described as declarative, procedural and conditional forms of knowledge. 'Person knowledge' is often described as declarative knowledge and is the knowledge you have about your own cognition and your understanding of others as cognitive processors. For example, we describe some people as 'reflective' or 'thoughtful', while we describe others as 'good with mathematical problems' or as having a 'bad memory'. These descriptions reflect an awareness of individuals' cognitive characteristics.

'Task knowledge' is the metacognitive knowledge that different tasks require different procedures and different types of skills (Pintrich, 2002). With experience, we learn more about task demands and how we can meet them under different circumstances. For example, we learn that a textbook such as this one is packed with information, and that we need to proceed slowly and carefully in order to process the information effectively. We also hold conditional forms of knowledge that help us understand when to draw on our cognitive forms of knowledge and when to apply specific learning strategies. 'Strategy knowledge' develops over time and there are many types of metacognitive strategies, which can be broadly grouped in three categories: planning, monitoring and evaluating. (Pintrich & DeGroot, 1990; Pintrich & Schunk, 1996; Wittrock, 1991). (See Table 6.3 for some examples of metacognitive strategies.)

TABLE 6.3 Examples of metacognitive strategies

METACOGNITIVE STRATEGY	EXAMPLES OF SELF-QUESTIONS
Planning	• What type of task is this? • What skills and resources do I need? • What are my task goals? • How long will the task take to achieve?
Monitoring	• How are my motivation levels? • How well am I going? • Do I need to change my approach? • Do I need to adapt my task goals?
Evaluating	• How well did I do? • What did I do well? • What did not work too well? • What should I change next time?

Source: Adapted from Pintrich and Schunk (1996); Wittrock (1991).

Strategy knowledge is conditional because it involves knowing which metacognitive strategies to use and when, in order to accomplish a set task. For example, if you want to know whether a book will be useful for your assignment, strategy knowledge would prompt you to skim-read, or check the table of contents, rather than read the book from cover to cover (see Figure 6.10). Strategy knowledge helps learners to be efficient and effective by giving them the means to select the most appropriate metacognitive strategies for their purpose.

Metacognitive experience

We also have 'metacognitive experiences', which include feelings related to particular cognitive activities (Flavell, 1987; Flavell, Miller & Miller, 1993). For example, you may feel anxious when you realise you do not understand something important your lecturer is explaining to the class. This is a metacognitive experience because you are reflecting on how poorly you are processing the information being shared and you are concerned because you do not understand it. Metacognitive experiences are connected to affective processes such as our self-esteem and self-efficacy: if we feel capable of controlling and regulating our cognitive processes, we will feel more positive about ourselves and our abilities (Borkowski, Carr, Rellinger & Pressley, 1990). These experiences can also act as a 'stream of consciousness' (Flavell, 1979) and might be recalled to influence how you cope with future tasks. The interrelationships between the different aspects of metacognition are presented in Figure 6.11, while Box 6.6 presents an example of the role of metacognition in the classroom.

Source: Matthew Duchesne. © Milk and Honey Photography, 2010.

FIGURE 6.10 Metacognitive strategy knowledge involves knowing how to use resources efficiently to solve a problem such as writing an essay.

Metacognitive strategies and learning

As shown in Figure 6.11, Flavell's early work also identified the role of strategies in metacognitive monitoring. Strategies are the ordered or systematic processes we use to direct our cognitive processes and ensure that our goals can be met. These are linked to our metacognitive knowledge and influenced by the nature of tasks as well as influencing task outcomes. Strategies can be either cognitive or metacognitive. A cognitive strategy is a fairly basic rule or process for tasks, such as adding up a list of numbers or remembering the order of operations in a maths task. A metacognitive strategy, however, would be to remind yourself to double-check your addition of three-digit numbers as you often make mistakes when carrying or borrowing digits. Metacognitive strategies essentially allow the learner to monitor their cognitive processes, to double-check their understanding of order of operations or recalculate a list of figures because they often make a known error.

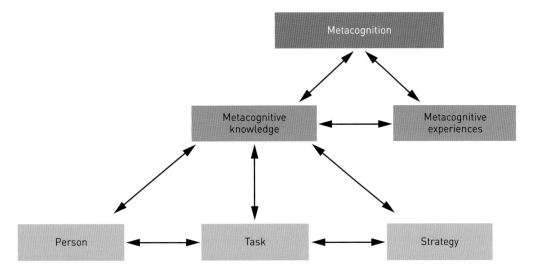

FIGURE 6.11 Dimensions of metacognition

BOX 6.6 CASE STUDY

INFORMATION PROCESSING AND METACOGNITIVE PROCESSES AT WORK

Memet continues to learn about multiplication and is completing a sheet of problems. He focuses on the tasks by completing one at a time, ignoring distractions in the classroom and the building work outside. There is a mix of harder and easier problems and he switches between different strategies for each one. For more complex problems like 12 × _ = 144, he might have to keep the subtotal in mind very briefly, before doing the next part of the calculation to reach the result. Memet also needs to monitor how fast he is working; he only has a limited time and must evaluate his progress. He knows his 12 times tables off by heart, and can simply write an answer for this problem. But what if it was not a times table he remembered, such as 14 × 13 = _? He decides to do all the 'easy' ones first and then concentrate on the harder ones. He can do some of these problems 'in his head' and for some he makes notes on the page. He finishes the sheet and goes back over his answers, checking each solution.

Source: Adapted from Roebers & Feurer, 2016, p. 39.

ACTIVITIES

There are several examples of information processing and metacognition in this scenario.
1   Draw up your own information-processing model for Memet by listing all the different processes and strategies involved at each phase of the model.
2   Can you provide an example of sensory input, attentional processes, working memory or higher-order executive processes?

THINK ABOUT

- Can you recall being taught metacognitive strategies when you were at school? If so, how did you benefit? If not, how did you learn these strategies?
- How do you think your own experience will affect your approach to teaching metacognition?
- Consider the range of subject areas you may teach: Mathematics, Science, Languages, Art and so on. Are there some subject areas in which metacognitive strategies are more important than others? Are they more important for some kinds of tasks?

CourseMateExpress

Online resources
Go further: Learn about teaching metacognitive strategies on this text's website

Research indicates that students benefit from learning about and using metacognitive strategies, with a positive relationship between performance on academic tasks and the level of metacognitive awareness. In a study of 155 Year 5 Mathematics students, Lucangeli, Coi and Bosco (1997) found that poor problem-solvers had lower metacognitive awareness than average or good problem-solvers. The same authors proposed a link between the use of metacognitive strategies and academic performance (see also Carr, Alexander & Folds-Bennett, 1994). Students of lower ability have been found to benefit significantly from direct instruction in metacognitive strategies (Cardelle-Elawar, 1995; Spence, Yore & Williams, 1999). In an Australian study of poor readers in upper primary school, Bruce and Robinson (2001) found that direct instruction in metacognitive word-identification strategies and metacognitive awareness-raising contributed to improved word identification and reading comprehension skills. Studies of students with learning disabilities have also found that metacognitive strategy instruction enhances thinking and social skills (Powell & Makin, 1994; Rosenthal-Malek, 1997). There are even benefits for quite able students. A study of very capable students found that computerised metacognitive strategy instruction proved beneficial in raising performance levels in both reading and writing (Kaniel, Licht & Peled, 2001). Box 6.7 discusses some classroom implications of metacognitive strategies.

BOX 6.7 IMPLICATIONS FOR EDUCATORS

METACOGNITIVE STRATEGIES IN THE CLASSROOM

Research suggests that educators have a significant role to play in raising students' awareness of their own thinking (Paris & Winograd, 1990), and in teaching them how to monitor their strategic behaviour and performance (Borkowski & Muthukrishna, 1992). However, an important first step is for teachers to become more self-aware and develop their own metacognitive skills (Zohar, 1999; Wilson & Bai, 2010). Once you develop these skills, you will be better equipped to model them for your students and to support their learning.

Here are some strategies to use with your students:

- Teach and model metacognitive strategies explicitly (Boekaerts, 1997), particularly in the basic skills of literacy and numeracy (Maqsud, 1997).
- Demonstrate a procedure and encourage students to follow you step-by-step (Wilen & Phillips, 1995), as demonstrated in **Table 6.4** below.
- Journal writing – on paper or online – encourages students to reflect on their learning without worrying about assessment.
- Provide sample questions to encourage self-reflection:
  > What went well in this class today?
  > Did I get distracted? When and why?
  > What will I do next time to keep my attention focused?

This type of reflection encourages students to self-monitor and self-regulate. **Table 6.4** provides an example of how to foster metacognition through modelling.

TABLE 6.4 Modelling essay-writing techniques: strategies for promoting metacognition

INSTRUCTIONS TO USE WHEN MODELLING	COMMENTARY
Students, ask yourselves:	
• What is the essay question asking me to do? • What do I know about this topic? • What else do I need to know? • Where will I go to get information?	• Teachers' aim is to model the self-questioning technique so students can employ this strategy on their own when they have to write an essay.
Spend time planning:	
• Break the task into small steps. • How many paragraphs am I going to write? • What will be the topic of each paragraph?	• Teachers help students believe in their own ability to accomplish a task by breaking it into small, manageable steps. • Teachers demonstrate planning strategies so students learn to implement these for themselves.
During the writing process:	
Stop and go back to your plan to make sure you are on track: • How am I going? • What am I doing well? • What do I need to change or add? • Am I answering the question? • Am I using the appropriate style? • How am I going for time?	• Encourage students to self-monitor throughout the writing task. Students need to become aware of what they are thinking as they write and direct their cognitive resources appropriately.
At the end:	
• How did I go? • Did that plan work? • What might I change next time? • What was successful? • Do I need to proofread the essay and check spelling?	• Promote evaluation and self-reflection. • Encourage students to evaluate their strengths and weaknesses and to set goals for improving their execution of the task next time.

FURTHER MODELS OF INFORMATION PROCESSING

levels-of-processing model
A process-oriented approach that attaches most importance to the type and depth of processing taking place

The classical view of information processing includes many other models and approaches to information processing. The **levels-of-processing model** (Lockhart & Craik, 1990) focuses on the *depth* of information processing and how this affects our ability to recall information. 'Deep processing' means that information is attended to, fully analysed, enriched by association with existing knowledge, and is thus remembered because of the extent of processing that has occurred. 'Shallow processing' occurs when information is not given full attention and is analysed only superficially. It is most likely that information analysed at a surface level will soon be forgotten.

connectionist model
Views the brain as a complex network of interconnected units of information, with information stored in patterns of connectivity

Recent information-processing accounts have tended to focus on how the human brain functions and the role of neural networks in cognitive processing and memory. This focus has led to **connectionist models**, in which information is seen as being stored in multiple locations throughout the brain, forming networks of connections; that is, the brain is depicted as a complex network of interconnected units of information (Ellis & Humphreys, 1999). In Chapter 2, you learnt about brain development and the increasingly complex networks that develop with age (see Figure 2.10). This development of connectivity and complexity in brain networks helps explain why the capacity of a young child's memory is smaller than that of an adult, as we saw in Chapter 3.

Computer-based modelling

As explained by Munakata (2006), many of these views are underscored by an interest in computer-based modelling of the processes that contribute to thinking and behaviour. These computer-based simulations have taught us a great deal about how and why the brain processes information under many different contexts and circumstances. However, computer-based views of the brain, and a dependency on computer simulations of information processing, have also been criticised. These laboratory-based simulations are at once complex as well as overly simple (Munakata, 2006). Computer-based models allow us to process and simulate an infinite array of data, but can models represent the complexity of the child's environment, their social interactions and their individual thought processes? Mayer (2012) distinguishes between these classical views of information processing in which learning is characterised as a set of computer-like sequences, and more constructivist views that are concerned with cognitive processing aimed at sense making. For example, how do individuals actively construct or *orchestrate* those cognitive strategies that help make sense of information?

The constructivist view of information processing is strongly concerned with the various processes or strategies involved in understanding information. In the following section, we will examine instructional applications of information-processing models.

THINK ABOUT

- How well does the multistore model describe the way you have processed information during your reading of the previous one or two pages?
- Are you aware of any types of external stimuli that you tried to avoid storing in your sensory register while you read these pages?
- Did you use any specific processes to enhance your working memory and long-term memory while you read the pages?
- How might the multistore model improve the way you teach your students?

INFORMATION PROCESSING AND LEARNING

How can these views of information processing help the teacher who is trying to ensure that students learn and remember important information? The information-processing model in all its forms helps us to understand how we process and store information cognitively. It also seeks to explain the flipside of remembering – that is, forgetting.

Much of what happens in the learning process relies on students' ability to recall necessary information and put stored knowledge into action quickly. The most common reason for forgetting in the short term is that we fail to pay adequate attention to information that is processed through the sensory register and short-term memory. Another reason for forgetting is that – as mentioned earlier – short-term memory is limited in the number of items it can hold at any given moment, and new information tends to bump old information out of short-term memory store (Engle & Oransky, 1999). Other factors may be a lack of motivation to remember certain information, or a failure to develop adequate memory skills (Guenther, 1998, p. 148). But what about when we forget information we thought we had stored in long-term memory?

Cognitive learning theorists draw on the information-processing model to explain why we forget such information. Sometimes it may feel as if long-term memory 'decays' and disappears over time, but there is little direct support for this explanation (Eysenck & Keane, 2000). A second explanation is the 'interference' approach, which argues that we forget because long-term memories interfere with one another (see Figure 6.5). Old memories interfere with storing new ones, while new memories may make it difficult to retrieve old ones. Thus, forgetting occurs when we cannot access a memory effectively, not because the memory has disappeared. The more information we memorise and the more memories we develop over time, the greater the possibility of interference.

Another explanation for why we forget is 'cue-dependent forgetting' (Tulving, 1974). According to this explanation, we do not lose information: it is held in storage, but we cannot retrieve it because we do not have the right cues. The process of remembering is an interconnected one. Information is recalled, which cues other information that, in turn, cues other information, and so on (Nuthall, 2000). Metacognitive strategies deliberately prompt cueing systems by applying a strategy. For example, a strategy might include a cue for remembering compass points such as the phrase 'Never Eat Sour Watermelons', where the first letter of each word corresponds to a compass point. These letters cue long-term memory for individual compass points, and remind us of the order of the points in a clockwise direction. Thus, one piece of information cues another. Table 6.5 gives some examples of strategies known as mnemonic

TABLE 6.5 Mnemonic devices for the classroom

MNEMONIC DEVICE	EXAMPLE
The 'loci' or 'place' method *Strategy:* Use familiar locations and visual imagery to remember items.	To remember four unrelated items – such as elephant, car, milk and CD – visualise a familiar location such as your home. 'Place' each item in a location around the house and 'pick it up' as you take a mental walk around the house: 'The elephant arrives home by car. First she walks into the kitchen to put the milk away, then she walks into the living room to play her new CD'.
Peg method *Strategy:* Remember sequences of unrelated items in the correct order using familiar peg words (common peg-word sequences are numbers, and letters of the alphabet).	To remember the names of the three largest New Zealand cities in the correct order, use the familiar peg words '1', '2' and '3': *1 is A1 – A is for Auckland* *2 – 2 'l's in Wellington* *3 – 3 'c's in Christchurch*
Rhymes *Strategy:* Use rhyming sounds to assist memory.	'The First Fleet landed in Botany **Bay** on a 1788 January **day**.'
Acronyms *Strategy:* Remember lists of words by chunking or reorganising information to make a word or phrase that is easy to remember.	In an acronym, the first letter of each word in a list forms a key word, name or sentence. For example, in music theory, to remember the notes that occupy the lines on the treble clef (E, G, B, D, F), you may remember that 'Every Good Boy Deserves Fruit', while the acronym 'FACE' represents the notes that occupy the spaces on the treble clef.

devices that help us to remember information by associating new information with meaningful images or contexts. Box 6.8 provides some principles of instruction drawn from cognitive learning theory and research.

BOX 6.8 CLASSROOM LINKS

APPLYING COGNITIVE RESEARCH TO CLASSROOM PRACTICE

In a document for the International Bureau of Education, Rosenshine (2010) identified 10 principles of instruction from research into the brain and learning, cognitive learning theorists' research, and the classroom practices of successful teachers. The 10 principles work together.

1   Begin a lesson with a short review of previous learning. This can strengthen previous learning and help rapid recall of information over the longer term.

2   Present new material in small steps and have students practise after each step. This addresses the limitations of working memory.

3   Asking frequent questions helps the teacher to check for understanding, and allows students to practise new information and connect new material to prior learning.

4   Teacher modelling by thinking aloud, and using worked examples helps reduce cognitive load and guide students' thinking.

5   Guided student practice of new material provides opportunities for elaboration, rehearsal and organisation of information, which facilitates storage and retrieval. Teacher guidance ensures that the information is correct, and reduces cognitive load, easing transfer to long-term memory.

6   Check for student understanding. Students reconstruct what they hear or experience, connecting new information to old, and the schemas they develop can vary in their accuracy. Identifying and correcting misconceptions helps students to learn the material with fewer errors.

7   Obtain a high success rate in students' answers to instructional questions and practice activities. Practising with a high number of errors will reinforce inaccurate concepts in memory – better to reteach the material in a fresh way, until students are practising with at least 80 per cent success.

8   Provide scaffolds as temporary supports for difficult tasks. This may include the teacher thinking aloud, offering prompts or hints, and providing models for doing a task.

9   Provide opportunities for successful independent practice. Practice is necessary to develop fluency and automaticity in performing a skill, freeing up the working memory. It also strengthens neural connections. Successful independent practice should be supported by careful teaching and guided practice.

10 Weekly and monthly review provides ongoing practice to strengthen sound schemas in long-term memory, making long-term memory more accessible for new learning, freeing up working memory, and helping students to organise knowledge by combining old with new. Material that is not frequently reviewed and practised is more easily forgotten.

Source: Adapted from Rosenshine (2010).

ACTIVITIES

1   Watch an experienced teacher and see how these principles are put into practice in the classroom. Compare notes with others and make up a list of strategies.

2   Consider a time when you had difficulty learning or remembering something at school or university. Which of the principles was missing? How could you put the principles to work in your own learning?

STRENGTHS AND LIMITATIONS OF THE INFORMATION-PROCESSING APPROACH

The information-processing account of how we process and remember information is widely accepted in the field of cognitive psychology. There are several models of information processing, each with its own merits and limitations. In contrast to the behaviourist focus on observable behaviours, the information-processing approach attempts to depict the complex mental processes that contribute to learning and remembering.

Strengths

Using the computer as a metaphor for the human mind, the classical views of information processing help us understand the complexity of cognitive processing and the many stages and processes involved in storing and recalling information. This approach facilitates close study and analysis of cognitive processes – something particularly beneficial for educators seeking to understand how best to assist young people to learn and recall important information. The multistore model draws attention to different dimensions of memory (such as sensory, working and long-term memory) and to the value of strategies such as rehearsal and elaboration in enhancing recall. Levels of processing models are advantageous since they distinguish between type and depth of processing and the subsequent effect on quality of memory storage and recall. Connectionist models, which draw upon research into the brain's neural networks, are valuable because they provide insights into the connectedness and interdependence of cognitive processes and stored memories.

Limitations

The information-processing approach is limited in several ways. Some models of information processing (such as the multistore model) suggest that the mind processes information sequentially. This depiction has been criticised as being too idealised and unrepresentative of the complexity and interconnectedness of the brain's neural networks (see Ellis & Humphreys, 1999). The information-processing approach has also been criticised for an over-reliance on the computer as an analogy for how the mind works. The brain is not constructed like a standard computer (Klahr & MacWhinney, 1998): computers are built of hardy electrical components, and individual items can be reliably stored in discrete locations and accessed in predictable ways when needed (Kanerva, 1993). 'Neural hardware', on the other hand, is made out of 'noisy, unstable components', and it is not always possible to guarantee information retrieval (Klahr & MacWhinney, 1998, p. 651). In using computer modelling, most information processing models fail to take account of environmental, genetic and cultural differences in the ways individuals process information. Such models tend to decontextualise information processing, ignoring situational and personal factors (for example, emotional state, time of day and level of ability) that may influence how an individual responds to and processes information.

The models are nevertheless intended as abstract representations that enable researchers to predict behaviour and test hypotheses. Seen in this light, information processing models draw our attention to several important principles of cognitive processing, and are particularly helpful in examining the learning process.

Box 6.9 presents some implications of the information-processing approach for classroom practice.

BOX 6.9 CLASSROOM LINKS

APPLYING INFORMATION PROCESSING IN THE CLASSROOM

The information-processing model draws attention to the complex mental operations involved in processing information. To apply this model in your teaching, you might do the following:

- Teach students to pay attention to important information from the earliest moment of impact in the sensory register.
- Model how to select and pay attention to the most important information.
- Provide opportunities for students to rehearse and repeat information in working memory, to ensure that the information moves into the long-term memory store.
- Activate learners' schemas by revising prior learning that links to new material. This will assist them to make sense of and remember new information by linking it to the old.
- Give learners opportunities to elaborate on information and to link it to existing information so it will be meaningful and easier to recall.
- Encourage students to process information deeply to transform it into meaningful knowledge for different purposes and contexts.
- Teach and model memory skills and metacognitive strategies (see Table 6.5).

BANDURA'S SOCIAL COGNITIVE THEORY

The development of cognitive views of learning was highly dependent on a shift away from the rigid behaviourist views of learning that prevailed in the 1960s. The main criticism of behaviourism was that it neglected the influence of cognition and cognitive skills, such as self-assessment and self-monitoring, on the learning process. It was in this context that Albert Bandura developed his 'social learning theory' (Bandura, 1977). Social learning theory recognised the contribution of personal (mental or psychological) factors to the learning process, providing an explanation of human behaviour in terms of cognitive, behavioural and environmental influences. In his now famous studies of aggression, known as the *Bobo doll* experiments, Bandura demonstrated that children can learn vicariously by observing the behaviour and consequences for others, and this introduced a cognitive component into the traditional behaviourist paradigm.

Learning through observation

Bandura and his colleagues sought to demonstrate that learning could occur vicariously through mere observation of a model performing behaviours. Previously, trial-and-error learning was the main view of learning in the behaviourist tradition. In a series of now famous experiments known as the Bobo doll experiments (see Box 6.10), Bandura and colleagues were able to demonstrate that learning could occur vicariously *without* the use of external consequences (reinforcers), and without the need for repeated trial-and-error learning, contradicting major tenets of behavioural theory (Bandura, 1965).

Bandura had recognised a fundamental flaw in behavioural learning theories: the neglect of the role of individual self-beliefs in the learning process (Simon, 2001). Bandura (1986) combined the notion of individual cognitive processes with external environmental factors to suggest that cognitive processes such as *attention* to the behaviour and *retention* (memory) of the behaviour was necessary for the person to reproduce those behaviours. Both of these behaviours comprise what early behaviourists such as

BOX 6.10 RESEARCH LINKS

BANDURA'S STUDIES OF CHILDREN AND AGGRESSION

Albert Bandura and his team conducted a series of studies that explored the extent to which children's behaviour could be influenced by exposure to adults modelling aggressive behaviour, also known as vicarious learning. Many of the studies involved three groups of children: an experimental group that observed a film of a person acting aggressively, a contrast group that watched an adult behaving in a non-aggressive way, and a control group that did not watch any film.

In one study, the experimental group of children watched an adult directing verbal and physical aggression in relatively novel ways towards an adult-sized inflated plastic Bobo doll that righted itself each time it was hit, while the contrast group watched an adult behave in a subdued and inhibited way towards the same doll (Bandura, Ross & Ross, 1961). The third group saw the aggressive adult, but did not see the doll. Half the children watched an adult model who was the same gender as their own and the other half watched an opposite-gender model. After exposure to the different models, all the children were left alone in a playroom with a few toys that included a Bobo doll. They were then assessed for aggressive and non-aggressive behaviour.

Results showed that the children who had observed an aggressive model showed almost twice as much aggression as did the children in the non-aggressive group. The behaviour of the children in the non-aggressive group was inhibited, like the model they had watched, and they showed less aggression than the children in the third group who had seen the adult behaving aggressively but not the doll. What was so interesting in these findings was the fact that with no reinforcement, children were able to demonstrate very precise imitation (learning) of the model's behaviours; they used the same aggressive strategies, including hitting the doll with a mallet and sitting on the doll, and repeated novel phrases such as 'He just keeps coming back for more!'. This imitation of novel behaviours demonstrated that learning had occurred without the need for trial-and-error learning or reinforcement.

FIGURE 6.12 A Bobo doll is an inflatable self-righting toy that, if knocked down, can stand up again repeatedly.

These findings were replicated using film and cartoon versions of the real-life situations. Bandura (1963) argued that studies in which young children view films that show models of aggression do show that this 'vicarious participation in aggressive activity increases, rather than decreases, aggressive behaviour' (p. 19). Subsequently, his early studies have given rise to a plethora of research studies about the influence of media violence on aggression in children and young people.

Source: Shironosov/iStockphoto

FIGURE 6.13 Self-regulation enables this writer to correct his own writing without needing external reinforcement.

Watson decried as unobservable 'mentalisms', and therefore not measurable or accountable in the learning process. However, Bandura went even further and also maintained that *motivation* was necessary for the learner to reproduce the behaviour. In this he acknowledged that the environment in which the behaviour occurs provides feedback (reinforcement) that probably determines whether the behaviour will be likely to occur again; essentially, Bandura positioned reinforcement not as the cause of learning, but as a motivator for the individual to display what they had learnt (Bandura, 1986; Simon, 2001).

Bandura proposed that human beings were capable of self-regulating (self-motivating) and determining their own behaviour; they did not necessarily need external reinforcement but could self-reinforce to drive their own actions (Bandura, 1978). He used the analogy of writers to illustrate this point. He argued that writing is in fact a self-regulated act guided by our own capacity for self-evaluation and self-perceptions of our own writing. We are capable of setting our own internal standards for our writing, and modifying or changing (regulating) our behaviours to improve or change a piece of writing.

Reciprocal determinism

reciprocal determinism
The interactive, complementary system formed by people and environments

Bandura's research increasingly concentrated on the self-regulatory and cognitive processes such as motivation and self-efficacy beliefs that influence learning (see also Box 6.11). Originally called social learning theory, Bandura (1986) renamed his theory 'social cognitive theory' to highlight an emphasis on social cognitive processes. Social cognitive theory positions learners as having personal agency – they are self-regulating, reflective learners who use forethought, rather than simply responding to the environment (Bandura, 2001). In contrast to behaviourist views, the external environment becomes one of three factors that mutually influence each other; namely, personal, behavioural and external environmental factors. Bandura called this a process of **reciprocal determinism**, in which all three factors act together to explain learning. Bandura based his model on three propositions that explain the deterministic sequence of interactions that shape learning: personal or cognitive factors, behavioural responses or actions, and environmental factors.

- *Personal factors* (also known as cognitive factors) partly determine how external events will be observed and perceived, and whether they will have any lasting effect on the individual. These personal factors include the knowledge we bring to a situation, our beliefs about the situation, how effective we feel in the situation (our self-efficacy), and our emotions. Bandura also included the unique physiological responses of the human body to stress, anxiety or excitement, noting that these biological processes (unique to the individual) send important signals about our likely success or risks in any situation.

- *Behavioural responses* or actions are influenced by cognitive factors because Bandura argued that humans have a unique capacity to alter their own environment by choosing actions and behaviours that will shape or respond to it. These behaviours in turn, affect the wider social environment.

- *Environmental factors* interact with both cognitive factors and behavioural factors. Through their actions, humans can shape and alter their environment, and in turn these environmental conditions can shape future behaviours. All the while, cognitive processes exert an influence and are in turn influenced by responses to the environment and so on (Bandura, 1978).

While this may sound complex, it is an extraordinarily simple proposition that fundamentally shifted views of human behaviour. By proposing that personal (cognitive), behavioural and environmental factors existed in reciprocal determinism, Bandura made a powerful argument that human beings can shape their own environment. They can determine their own behaviours, and they do possess internal mental processes, to control and regulate their own environment. This powerful theory is illustrated in Figure 6.14, which illustrates the reciprocal (bidirectional) links between these factors.

Consider, for example, Memet's classroom (we introduced Memet at the start of this chapter). Memet has his own unique cognitive processes. He seems to have confidence and sufficient self-efficacy to raise his discovery with the teacher.

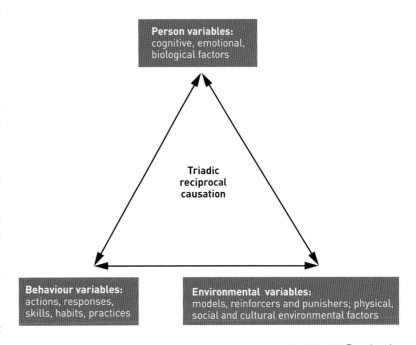

FIGURE 6.14 Bandura's triadic reciprocal causation: behavioural, environmental and personal factors mutually influence one another.

The classroom environment seems to support Memet's open sharing of knowledge, and his own contribution to this environment in turn influences the learning of his peers. In this environment, peers model behaviours to one another and individuals might internalise some of Memet's success and enhance their own maths self-efficacy when they recognise the same pattern in their own times tables. Teacher and peer responses to Memet will likely reinforce his own cognitive processes, and he will go forward to future mathematics classes with confidence and even excitement as he seeks out the next solution or discovery. So, the reciprocal determinism of cognitive, behavioural and environmental conditions continues.

Bandura's work has had an enduring impact on educational psychology in multiple fields. As explained in Chapter 4, self-efficacy has emerged as one of the major constructs that explains how self-perceptions influence learning and other behaviours. Self-efficacy is one of the cognitive beliefs evident in the model of reciprocal determinism. Self-efficacy beliefs can powerfully influence learning behaviours. Low self-efficacy beliefs undermine approaches to learning, while strong self-efficacy beliefs are associated with a willingness to engage with tasks and tackle challenging tasks. As also explained in Chapter 4, the environment is a critical source of information that supports our self-efficacy or undermines it. Vicarious experiences (for example, observing another person trying a new task) can be a powerful source of our self-efficacy. Bandura does not completely neglect the role of external reinforcement in this model of reciprocal determinism. Self-efficacy is also influenced by feedback from significant others such as teachers, and this can be reinforcing. In Chapter 8, we will look further at Bandura's work in considering the influence of his theory on the field of motivation and engagement with learning.

BOX 6.11 ABOUT ALBERT BANDURA

Albert Bandura was born in 1925 in Alberta, Canada. He was one of six children, and his parents were migrants from Poland and the Ukraine who were pioneer farmers. Bandura attended a small school in his town, where Bandura recalled:

> the students had to take charge of their own education. Very often we developed a better grasp of the subjects than the overworked teachers ... The content of most textbooks is perishable, but the tools of self-directedness serve one well over time.
>
> Source: Pajares (2004).

At university, he studied psychology almost by accident, as a filler course, and became enthralled. Later, at the University of Iowa, where he received his Masters and Doctorate degrees, Bandura worked with a team seeking to find (behavioural) learning explanations for Freudian concepts of personality. Bandura became frustrated with trial-and-error learning, and was drawn to explanations of learning based on vicarious experience, modelling and imitation.

Bandura moved to Stanford University, where he started a program of research investigating the determinants and mechanisms of observational learning, starting with the phenomenon of antisocial behaviour in boys from advantaged areas and intact homes. He found that these boys often had parents who modelled aggressive attitudes. The famous Bobo doll experiments followed this work, and showed that observational learning could occur without any reinforcement, which was in conflict with behaviourist views at the time.

In the 1960s, Bandura started to look at self-regulation and self-reward, studies that foreshadowed his later work on personal agency in learning.

Social learning theory was published in 1977, and influenced psychology research through the 1980s. Then, in 1986, Bandura published *Social foundations of thought and action*, which described social cognitive theory and emphasised the agency of the learner, and distinguished his view from other social learning theories.

Work with people who had a snake phobia led to a focus on the power of beliefs in one's own abilities, or self-efficacy, and has had a significant impact in the field of motivation.

Source: Getty Images/Time & Life Pictures, photo by Jon Brenneis/Life Magazine

Bandura has continued to research and publish widely in the fields of self-regulation and self-efficacy.

Source: Adapted from Pajares (2004).

STRENGTHS OF SOCIAL COGNITIVE THEORY

Bandura acknowledged that a broad range of factors – internal (cognitive and personal) and external (environmental or contextual) – influence learning. This broader explanation of learning, with its recognition of the learner's active contribution to behaviour change, is evident in subsequent developments in psychology, including cognitive-behavioural therapies which explicitly recognise the role of the person and their cognition in changing and directing their own behaviour. It has also had a major influence on the study of motivation via the capacity of the human being for self-regulation of behaviour. As with the field of cognitive explanations of learning, motivational explanations of learning increasingly accounted for individual self-regulatory mechanisms in motivation and behaviours (see Chapter 8). Bandura's focus on the place of observation and imitation in learning also meant that his work served to heighten awareness of the possibility of 'calculated manipulation and control of people' (Bandura, 1977, p. 208) through such sources as film and television. Subsequent examination of the media as a source of influence on human behaviour has become a major field of study.

LIMITATIONS OF SOCIAL COGNITIVE THEORY

The conditions under which vicarious learning occurs have been questioned. Why do children imitate some of the behaviours they observe but ignore others? How can educators be sure that desirable behaviours modelled in learning situations have an impact on learners, while undesirable behaviours are ignored and forgotten? Research studies in this field (for example, Bandura, Ross & Ross, 1961) were concerned with children's responses to observed aggression in the period immediately following exposure to a model. How long after this experience would the children remember and imitate what they had seen? What would happen when the children observed models in similar situations behaving differently? Considering the myriad situations that children experience, it is difficult to accept that specific observational experiences will have a long-term impact on viewers. However, the advent of violent, interactive video games has increased concern about a possible link between habitual early exposure to violence in media, and an increase in aggressive behaviour (for example, fighting, arguing and bullying) and a decrease in helping behaviour (Anderson, 2004; Funk, 2005; Gentile, Lynch, Linder & Walsh, 2004; Olson, 2004). Box 6.12 explores some classroom implications of social cognitive theory.

BOX 6.12 IMPLICATIONS FOR EDUCATORS

SOCIAL COGNITIVE THEORY IN THE CLASSROOM

The idea of reciprocal determinism indicates that teachers can adopt a holistic view of the classroom and consider that all aspects of the learning context – individual cognitions, behaviours and the environment itself – have an influence on learning. They can also take account of the place of observation and modelling in the learning process. Teachers can:

- model effective learning behaviours or expectations:
  - > Demonstrate a high self-efficacy by approaching tasks positively, and provide 'think aloud' demonstrations of tasks.
  - > Give feedback that provides a model of self-regulation and self-reinforcement; for example, 'Great proofreading. You used your writing checklist very effectively!'
- create an environment that supports positive behaviour:
  - > Provide self-regulatory checklists for group work.
  - > Encourage peers to be open and sharing of learning discoveries.
  - > Use peers as models of learning and behaviours in providing examples of activities, peer tutoring or collaborative work.
  - > Be aware that watching a teacher reprimand a child, or criticise a child for a wrong answer, can be a powerful disincentive for trying.
- encourage self-regulation and awareness of own learning behaviours:
  - > Task checklists can be used to self-monitor one's own progress.
  - > Reflection strategies such as asking questions about progress – for example, 'How am I going?', 'What did I find confusing on this page?' – can promote self-regulation and awareness of behaviour.
  - > Emphasise skill development and mastery, rather than simply enhancing self-perceptions, by making the skills explicit and the 'can do' elements of the task obvious, providing authentic indicators of success or improvement.

LEARNING STYLES AND APPROACHES TO LEARNING

CourseMateExpress

Online resources
Take a moment
to consider your
philosophy of learning
and teaching. You
may wish to use
the **Develop your
philosophy** tool on
this text's CourseMate
Express website

cognitive style
The way an individual
tends to perceive and
process information

learning style
Learner preferences for
types of learning and
teaching activities

approaches to learning
Learner motivational
approaches to learning

The previous examples of cognitive explanations of learning have attempted to show how learners' cognitive processes influence their learning. We have learnt that individuals process information in unique ways through a range of processes assumed to be common to human beings, including the formation of schemes, the actions of working memory and the long-term storage of information in memory. An alternative viewpoint is offered in the literature concerning cognitive and learning styles, and in another body of literature concerning approaches to learning (Furnham, 2012).

The notion of 'style' (cognitive styles or learning style) refers to the idea that learners have a stable preference for the way in which they process information (Furnham, 2012; Sternberg & Grigorenko, 2001). This idea has gained considerable popularity in recent decades, but is perhaps one of the most controversial areas of educational psychology.

Furnham (2012) outlines two main ways in which styles have been approached; namely, cognitive styles and learning styles. **Cognitive style** refers to the characteristic ways of thinking and perceiving that individuals use to process and remember information (see also Ferrari & Sternberg, 1998; Riding & Rayner, 1998). **Learning style**, on the other hand, tends to be defined in terms of preferred ways of interacting with information, demonstrating learning or acquiring knowledge (Furnham, 2012). **Approaches to learning** is a category of research defined by Furnham (2012) as more reflective of motivational approaches to learning – how and why people approach learning tasks or course selection in the way they do (p. 67). He also describes this body of work as predating the work on cognitive and learning styles and being more coherent than the learning styles literature. First, we examine cognitive and learning style explanations, and then we examine the notion of approaches to learning.

COGNITIVE STYLES

Cognitive style research has developed quite a range of labels identifying various cognitive styles. A review of literature by Messick in 1970 identified 19 cognitive style variables (Furnham, 2012). This list was subsequently reduced in a review of nine cognitive styles by Riding and Rayner (1998), and here we will look closely at just two examples. Each of these cognitive styles reflects a focus on holistic versus analytic thought processes (Furnham, 2012). Quite simply, holistic thinking refers to 'big picture' thinking – thinking about a whole system and how it works, or the patterns and systems of the whole. Analytic thinking tends to refer to a focus on the detail or 'parts' of the system or problem – thinking about the individual elements that make the system work. These concepts are evident in the two cognitive styles described here.

Field dependence–independence

Look at Figure 6.15. What do you see? When shown a picture of this rural landscape containing a cow, a pig, some sheep and a dog, one child might describe the picture in broad terms, as 'in the country'. Another will see the picture in terms of details such as a cow, a pig, some sheep and a dog in a large field, describing it as 'cows and sheep and pigs and a dog in a paddock'. In the first case, the overall scene in the picture dominates the child's perception (field dependence); when describing the picture, the child pays attention to the *overall impression* of the scene rather than the details. On the other hand, the second child's interest is in the *detail* of the picture (field independence), rather than the background scene. The way we perceive the world is an important element of cognitive style.

The terms **field dependence** and **field independence** are used to describe two extreme dimensions of human perception of visual stimuli. The more a learner is able to separate relevant material from its context (or 'field'), the more 'field independent' they are said to be.

The image in Figure 6.15 is known as an 'embedded figures test' and is based on the extensive work of Witkin, Oltman, Raskin and Karp (1971). Research into the impact of field dependence–independence on perception suggests that these are stable traits that affect individual responses in a variety of situations. For example, people who are field-dependent are likely to see problems as a whole and have difficulty separating component parts (Riding & Cheema, 1991). They are typically more intuitive in their perception, and tend to be socially oriented, enjoying situations that allow for interaction and group work (Jonassen & Grabowski, 1993). By contrast, field-independent learners tend to be more analytical and prefer analysing visual stimuli and breaking down problems into component parts. They tend to be more efficient than field-dependent learners in processing information, are better readers, are highly task-oriented, and prefer structured, impersonal situations. Field-dependent learners tend to do better in the humanities, while field-independent learners do better in mathematics and the sciences (Witkin & Goodenough, 1981).

field dependence
A cognitive style related to perceiving items, events or information as an integral part of a broader context (or 'field')

field independence
The tendency to perceive individual items, events or pieces of information analytically, and as distinct from the broader context (or 'field')

FIGURE 6.15 Example of an embedded figures task. Can you find a gargoyle, a key, a hat, five dwarves and a fairy?

In learning contexts, field-dependent learners have been shown to be more likely than their field-independent peers to use rehearsal strategies, repeating information mentally, orally or in writing (Frank & Keene, 1993). Field-independent learners, on the other hand, tend to rely more heavily on elaboration strategies. This is consistent with their greater tendency to be analytical in their approach to learning (Tinajero & Paramo, 1998). Research indicates that field-independent children learn new computer languages more quickly and make fewer errors than do their field-dependent peers (Easton & Watson, 1993; Watson & Brinkley, 1992). In a study of 239 Canadian primary school children (Baillargeon, Pascual-Leone & Roncadin, 1998), field-dependent learners were less efficient in their mental processing and attentional capacity on a set task than were field-independent learners. However, as ever, generalisations should be treated cautiously.

There is some evidence (see, for example, Armstrong, 2000) that the methods of assessment used in educational institutions tend to favour students who are field-independent. Such assessments usually focus on written work involving systematic analysis of information and the development of well-structured, logical arguments. The field-dependent tendency to focus on global aspects may be a problem for tasks that require learners to be more analytical in their approach (Tinajero & Paramo, 1998). Somewhat predictably, studies have demonstrated a positive association between field independence and performance on intelligence tests (Sternberg & Grigorenko, 1997), since the skills measured by most intelligence tests cover the types of learning included in the traditional academic studies in which field-independent people excel (see Chapter 9 for more on intelligence). By contrast, there has been little effort to design tests that are more congruent with the cognitive style of field-dependent learners. Such tests might include elements of dance, art, music, drama, video and film production, and other non-traditional forms of visual and oral presentation.

Impulsivity–reflectivity

impulsivity
Having a cognitive preference for rapid problem solving

reflectivity
Having a cognitive preference for taking time to solve problems and to analyse oneself and the context

Another dimension used to distinguish between learners' cognitive styles is concerned with the speed of their responses to a task, or the degree of 'impulsivity' or 'reflectivity' (also known as 'conceptual tempo') demonstrated in their responses. When presented with a task, some students react very quickly, sometimes without much thought. Others in a similar situation respond more slowly, pausing to consider possibilities. These distinctions, first defined by Kagan (1958, 1966), have been the subject of considerable research. Much of this research has involved the Matching Familiar Figures Test (Kagan, 1966), which consists of a set of pencil and paper tasks and involves selecting, usually from a set of very similar drawings, a drawing that exactly matches a model. Individuals with rapid response times are termed as having **impulsivity** and those who respond more slowly are described as having **reflectivity**.

Source: Matching Familiar Figures Test (MFFT20). Educational Engineering Lab, University of Zurich. Available at: www.project-hortus.net/mfft-framework/groupfiles/webexperimentlist.html

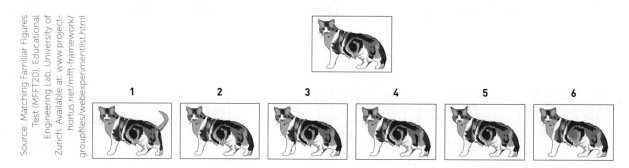

FIGURE 6.16 The speed of response to this kind of task determines impulsivity or reflectivity.

Various studies have reported on the impact of conceptual tempo on children's learning (see, for example, Wagner, Cook & Friedman, 1998). In general, reflective children take longer to complete tasks but are often more accurate than their more impulsive peers (Entwistle, 1991). They are also often better readers (Smith & Caplan, 1988). The value of helping impulsive learners to become more reflective has also been demonstrated. For example, Navarro, Aguilar and Alcalde (1999) reported success in a training program that aimed to help children in Grade 3 solve arithmetic problems by becoming more reflective. Not surprisingly, the intervention program had no impact on the performance of reflective students.

Sociocultural factors and cognitive style

Vygotsky and neo-Vygotskian accounts of cognitive development (see Chapter 3) emphasise the importance of social and cultural factors in cognitive development. It follows, then, that sociocultural factors may have an impact on learners' preferred ways of thinking, processing and remembering. Social structures and processes influence the types of activities we engage in and value, and these activities have a powerful impact on cognitive development (Herbert, 2000; Meadows, 1998). Meadows argues that, as teaching and learning do not occur independently of culture and history, they cannot be studied 'irrespective of the cognitive and affective history of the individual learner' (Meadows, 1998, p. 6).

A study of East Asian learners found them to be holistic and field-dependent in their preferences, compared with Westerners whom the researchers described as more analytic and field-independent in their cognitive styles (Nisbett, Peng, Choi & Norenzayan, 2001). However, more recently, Nisbett and Miyamoto (2005) have concluded that although these differences do exist, they are not as fixed or permanent as previously thought, and they are very much influenced by the surrounding cultural context, and hence malleable or changeable. Biggs (2001), on the other hand, argues that the research focus should not be on cognitive style but on the teaching and assessment methods used and the types of cognitive styles they encourage. He cautions against stereotyping learners from particular cultures, and emphasises the importance of considering cognitive style in a cultural context, just as Nisbett and Miyamoto's research would seem to confirm. This advice is very valuable because it guards against false generalisations. In contrast to the view that there are differences in cognitive styles across cultures, another body of cross-cultural research argues that cognitive style is a universal phenomenon that is not culturally bound (Kubes, 1998; Riding & Al-Sanabani, 1998).

LEARNING STYLES

Learning styles are almost universally acknowledged as being more controversial and problematic than cognitive styles or approaches to learning (for example, Desmedt & Valcke, 2004; Furnham, 2012). Proponents of learning styles also believe the learner develops characteristic preferences over time, but these theorists are concerned with learning modalities, not information processing. These concepts of learning styles have been extensively researched but have also met with significant criticism. In this section, we will briefly review a particularly prominent approach that has gained attention in teaching and popular culture: the idea that learners have modality preferences in terms of visual, auditory or kinaesthetic learning.

This approach is often termed the VAK, VAKT or VARK (visual, auditory, reading, kinaesthetic/tactile) approach to learning styles. Various theories (for example, Dunn & Griggs, 2003; Dunn, Dunn & Price, 1984; Fleming & Mills, 1992) have espoused a view that learners have a preference for receiving information in a visual form (looking at pictures, using diagrams to interpret information), an auditory form (listening, discussing, talking), or a kinaesthetic/tactile form (doing, touching and active interaction with information). These views of learning preference are distinct from, but closely related to, views of learning that emerged from Howard Gardner's (1983, 1993) theory of 'multiple intelligences', in which he described different domains of intelligence, including bodily/kinaesthetic, spatial (which reflects visual abilities), linguistic and many more (see Chapter 9). Both the VAK family of theories and Gardner's theory of intelligence have been popularised as a form of pedagogy in which teachers sought to adapt their teaching to reflect different forms of intelligences, and a belief that learners with strengths in these intelligences would be best served by instructional materials matching that preferred mode of learning. (See Chapter 9 for more on Gardner's theory and its proper application in the classroom.)

Dunn et al. (1995) conducted a meta-analysis of 36 studies based on the 'Dunn and Dunn Learning Style Model', and concluded that learners taught in their preferred learning style have a significant achievement advantage. That is, if a student has a preference for auditory modalities, they should be given learning activities and tasks that support this modality, such as listening rather than reading and so on. However, as discussed below, this view of matching learner preferences to learning activities is also considered very problematic. The range of studies that use this view of learning styles to present different teaching approaches is extensive, and a simple search of an educational database will yield any number of papers in a broad range of domains. The remainder of this section addresses an extensive critique of cognitive and learning styles approaches that is essential for beginning teachers to consider.

CRITIQUE OF COGNITIVE AND LEARNING STYLES APPROACHES

The notion of 'styles' or preferences for learning have been extensively evaluated and critiqued. Many of these reviews and evaluations have concluded that there is very little consistent, quality evidence to support learning style theories. Two reviews are of most relevance here. The first is a review conducted in 2004 by Coffield in the United Kingdom, and the second is a review conducted by Pashler, McDaniel, Rohrer and Bjork for the American Association for Psychological Science (2008). Each review notes significant limitations in this field of study.

An extensive review of 13 models of cognitive and learning styles – including the Dunn, Dunn and Price (1984) learning style model – concluded that there was very little or no evidence to suggest that popular views of learning styles have any place in classroom practice (Coffield, Moseley, Hall & Ecclestone, 2004a, 2004b). In particular, they report that many models have not received adequate, *independent* research, citing a tendency for researchers in this field to make elaborate overstatements of the effectiveness of their own methods, and to hold vested interests in their own models by selling training programs to teachers and practitioners, as well as a serious lack of empirical research by other researchers to support the effectiveness of the models.

The more recent review by Pashler, McDaniel, Rohrer and Bjork (2008) draws a similar conclusion, but is even more specific about the scientific evidence available: specifically, they claim that there are very few, if any, studies that truly meet the rigorous experimental design standards necessary to determine if matching teaching style to learning preference produced better learner outcomes. They also cite a range of recent independent studies that were well-designed experiments, which have found no relationship between learning style and learning ability in the preferred modality, and no benefit for learners who had their learning preferences matched with targeted help in their preference modality.

A particular concern relates to instructional applications of the models that could lead to learners making simplistic or overly generalised assumptions about their abilities, or could lead teachers to stereotype learners in such a way. For example, Coffield, Moseley, Hall and Ecclestone (2004a, 2004b) cite one example of a student who illustrated this point by saying, 'I learned that I was a low auditory, kinaesthetic learner. So there's no point in me reading a book or listening to anyone for more than a few minutes.' This tendency of learning-style models to stereotype or label learners raises a concern that such labels might limit the development of a wider range of skills and abilities. Pashler and colleagues (2008) concluded that attempts to measure or sort people into learning styles in educational institutions is unwise and a wasteful use of resources.

Nonetheless, Coffield and colleagues (2004a) do suggest that some models of cognitive and learning styles offer greater potential than others to assist students. In particular, they identify models that are based on ideas of deep, surface and strategic approaches to learning, as discussed in the next section.

Box 6.13 explores some classroom implications of students' cognitive and learning styles.

> **BOX 6.13 IMPLICATIONS FOR EDUCATORS**
>
> ## COGNITIVE AND LEARNING STYLES IN THE CLASSROOM
>
> - Carefully consider the supporting evidence for any learning intervention before implementing it in the classroom – seek out critical reviews that explore the pros and cons.
> - Recognise the diversity of students in your classes and adapt your teaching by using a variety of teaching methods, resources and assessments:
>   > - Students from some cultural groups may prefer learning in non-competitive, sharing environments; for example, see Charter (1996) on integrating traditional Aboriginal teaching and learning approaches in education.
>   > - It is wise to consider the linguistic differences of students for whom English is not the first language, making use of multimedia and online learning environments to individualise instruction where necessary.
>   > - Expose students to a range of learning approaches and encourage them to experiment with different styles so as to broaden their repertoire of learning skills. This includes using a combination of individual and group work, abstract and concrete examples, and visual and aural learning resources. Provide students with learning strategies that will enable them to cope with situations where their preferred style is not the most appropriate (Riding & Rayner, 1998).

APPROACHES TO LEARNING

Another body of research, a little different but similar to the cognitive styles research, considers how learners approach learning tasks or course selection. This research is distinguished by Furnham (2012) from the cognitive style research above, because it is more concerned with motivational styles.

Deep and surface learning approaches

A number of researchers in the 1970s observed and categorised an interesting tendency of learners when engaging with texts that were about to be examined. Some learners would try to memorise the facts of the text, while others would try to understand and contextualise the big-picture content. These approaches came to be called surface or deep approaches to learning (Furnham, 2012).

Studies of the ways in which children approach a learning task, such as reading text, suggest that from an early age, all learners try to self-regulate and have distinct motives and strategies for learning (Zimmerman, 1998). Students with a 'deep approach' to learning are intrinsically motivated to study, and are interested in satisfying their curiosity about a topic or understanding the meaning of a text. They approach learning tasks using problem-solving strategies (such as questioning, planning and evaluating) to maximise their understanding, as shown in this statement: 'I try to relate what I have learned in one subject to what I already know in other subjects' (Biggs & Moore, 1993, p. 316). Students with a 'surface approach' to learning typically have extrinsic motives and want to avoid failure. They tend to do as little work as possible and use memorisation or rote learning as a key strategy during study, as evidenced in the statement: 'I tend to study only what is set; I usually don't do anything extra' (Biggs & Moore, 1993, p. 316).

Approaches to learning are also related to learner self-concept. In their study of 580 Australian students in years 6 and 7, Burnett and Proctor (2002) found a significant relationship between deep approaches to learning and student self-concept. Deep approaches to learning for both boys and girls showed the highest positive correlations with school self-concept and learning self-concept. Learners with deep approaches to learning perceive their learning environment very differently from those with surface approaches. Campbell et al. (2001) interviewed and surveyed 490 Australian high school students regarding their approaches to learning and their perceptions of teaching and learning in the classroom. Overall, students with deep approaches to learning generally had more sophisticated understanding of the learning opportunities offered to them than did their surface learning peers (see Box 6.14).

BOX 6.14 RESEARCH LINKS

STUDENT APPROACHES TO LEARNING

Students were interviewed about their approaches to learning. The researchers explored the following questions:

1   Do students with differing approaches to learning view the same learning environment differently?
2   Do some learning environments influence students to perceive learning in ways that differ from those more typically generated by their current approaches to learning?

Research method

Four hundred and ninety students from 24 classes at two high schools completed the Learning Process Questionnaire (LPQ) about their approaches to learning (Biggs, 1987a, 1987b). Students were also asked about their perceptions of teaching and learning in the designated class. Ninety-two students and their teachers were interviewed from the 24 classes.

Results

The interview data showed that students with deep approaches repeatedly demonstrated a more sophisticated understanding of the teaching/learning opportunities offered to them than did students with surface approaches.

Students with deep approaches to learning spontaneously mentioned a greater variety of class activities; made links between different learning activities; and had a broader understanding of what they had learnt, of the purposes of learning and of their teacher's objectives. By contrast, students with surface approaches to learning tended to lack understanding of their teacher's efforts to adopt more constructivist teaching and learning strategies, and remained focused on classroom features related to the transmission and reproduction of learning.

Students with deep approaches to learning generally reported taking a more active role in their own learning and using a greater variety of methods, while students with surface approaches tended to focus more narrowly on repetition and reproduction.

Students with deep approaches to learning also tended to have a richer appreciation of what they had learnt, and to relate their learning to broader issues or personal change. Students with surface approaches to learning tended to remain very focused on specific content.

Source: Adapted from Campbell et al. (2001).

ACTIVITIES

1   Search for the article online or in your university library. The full article contains much more detail, with illustrative examples from participants.
2   Discuss the findings with your tutorial group and comment on how you will foster deep learning among learners in your classroom.
3   Consider your own approach to learning. Can you see any benefits in changing or modifying your approach?

In addition to deep and surface approaches, learners may demonstrate an 'achieving approach' to learning (Biggs, 1987a). Learners in this category are typically intrinsically motivated by a desire to do well at school, and adopt study techniques such as efficient use of time and resources to maximise their chances of success, as exemplified in the statement: 'I regularly take notes from suggested readings and put them with my class notes on a topic' (Biggs & Moore, 1993, p. 316). In a review of research on deep and surface approaches to learning, Zhang and Sternberg (2000) concluded that the evidence did not appear to support the existence of Biggs' third category (achieving approach), although there were data to confirm both deep and surface styles.

Critique of approaches to learning theories

Many teachers might seek to encourage a deep rather than surface approach to learning, but students may perceive a need to be pragmatic about their learning, depending on factors such as their workload, number of assignments due or other impinging factors. These issues are closely related to the notion of mastery and performance goals that we will examine in Chapter 8. In this case, some researchers have controversially argued that it might be more strategic for learners to adopt performance or surface goals in some circumstances, especially if courses are structured in a similar way. As such, it seems that learning approaches could be influenced by the environment experienced by learners. It is certainly known that teachers, too, have certain approaches to teaching, and some disciplines might encourage memorisation of facts or rote learning of concepts.

The notion of links between approaches to learning and achievement outcomes could also be complicated by a reported association between approaches to learning and certain personality variables. For example, a tendency towards anxiety in learning has been associated with more surface approaches to learning (Furnham, 2012). Therefore, teachers and researchers trying to understand the connection between approaches and achievement might also need to pay attention to the role of other factors such as personality that could influence learner approaches.

CONCLUDING COMMENTS

Cognitive learning theories attach importance to the cognitive processes that occur as we learn. Different approaches emphasise different aspects of these processes. We began this chapter with a description of the constructivist view of learning which focuses on the construction of schemes or knowledge and understanding in the individual. This theory also focuses on the role of social interaction and sociocultural factors in one's ability to process information. The information-processing account examines how learners acquire and organise information in memory. Inspired by the inner workings of computers, the information-processing approach provides various models of how the mind processes, stores and retrieves information. The social cognitive approach, which links behaviourist and cognitive views, is the most holistic of all theories, integrating personal (or cognitive) processes with consideration of behaviour and environmental processes. Each of these explanations contributes to our understanding of how students learn. Furthermore, such explanations share a focus on the learner and the value of providing learners with opportunities to make meaning of and be active participants in the learning–teaching experience. We examined some concepts and theories often associated with cognitive approaches, such as the notion of cognitive and learning styles, and differing approaches to learning. While there are some overlaps with cognitive learning theories, there are also notable limitations in some of these theories.

STUDY TOOLS

ONLINE STUDY RESOURCES

Visit http://login.cengagebrain.com and use the access code that comes with this book for 12 months' access to the student resources for this text.

The CourseMate Express website contains a range of resources and study tools for this chapter, including:

- a **self-check quiz**
- **crosswords**, **flashcards** and a **glossary** to help you revise the key terms from this chapter
- the **Go further** materials and **interactive activity** mentioned in the chapter.

CHAPTER REVIEW

- Cognitive views of learning focus on internal mental processes, and on learners as active constructors of meaning.
- Constructivist approaches emphasise the role of social interaction and the impact of sociocultural factors on our ability to process information.
- The four key principles of constructivism are:
  > learners are active participants in learning
  > learners are self-regulated
  > social interaction is necessary for effective learning
  > learners' knowledge may be relative, since learners construct their own meaning, which depends on individual factors such as prior knowledge and sociocultural context.
- The information-processing model likens the human mind to a computer, and learning is depicted as the processing of information.
- The multistore model of information processing describes three memory-storage areas in the brain: the sensory memory, the working memory and the long-term memory.
- Metacognition is an executive control process that directs our thinking.
- The levels-of-processing approach distinguishes between deep and shallow information processing. According to this model, depth of processing determines how information is processed and remembered.

- Connectionist models focus on the connectivity between pieces of information that are stored as memories. They depict the brain as a vast computer network, with all of the information interconnected.
- Cognitive learning theory offers several explanations of why we forget. Three reasons for forgetting are that:
  1 memory decays over time
  2 long-term memories interfere with each other and inhibit remembering
  3 we do not always have the necessary cues to retrieve stored information.
- The social cognitive approach refers to reciprocal determinism to explain the interaction between personal (cognitive), behavioural and environmental factors that shape learning.
- Self-regulation is emphasised in social cognitive theory as the individual's control over their learning and behaviour.
- Cognitive styles depict learner differences in the processing of information, and may be understood in terms of field dependence–independence, and impulsivity–reflectivity.
- Learning styles describe learner preference for learning in different ways or through different modalities.
- Significant criticism of learning style approaches suggest they should not be used in classrooms.
- Approaches to learning reflect motivational preferences (for example, deep or surface approaches to learning).

PUTTING IT TOGETHER

Making links between 'cognitive explanations of learning' and material in other chapters

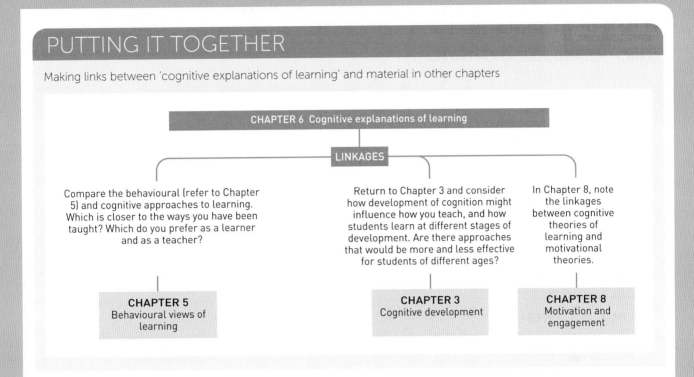

CHAPTER 6 Cognitive explanations of learning

LINKAGES

Compare the behavioural (refer to Chapter 5) and cognitive approaches to learning. Which is closer to the ways you have been taught? Which do you prefer as a learner and as a teacher?

Return to Chapter 3 and consider how development of cognition might influence how you teach, and how students learn at different stages of development. Are there approaches that would be more and less effective for students of different ages?

In Chapter 8, note the linkages between cognitive theories of learning and motivational theories.

CHAPTER 5
Behavioural views of learning

CHAPTER 3
Cognitive development

CHAPTER 8
Motivation and engagement

QUESTIONS AND ACTIVITIES FOR SELF-ASSESSMENT AND DISCUSSION

1   How would a teacher of the constructivist style encourage students to think in more complex ways?

2   Draw a schematic representation of information processing and describe how information is processed according to the multistore model.

3   For each of the processes in information processing (attention, chunking, rehearsal, elaboration and organisation), identify strategies the teacher can employ to support the process and maximise learning.

4   How important is metacognition for learning? Explain how it contributes to the learning process.

5   What are the key features of constructivist theories of learning? How could you use this theory as a learner and as a teacher? What could you do to avoid its limitations?

6   Design a collaborative learning task with the aim of developing students' thinking about a concept. How will you structure the task, the group and your role to maximise the benefits of this approach? Which theories help you to make these decisions?

7   Describe your own cognitive style and approach to learning. To what extent are you a reflective or impulsive, dependent or independent, deep or surface learner? What benefits stem from your particular style? How can you become a more effective learner?

8   Have you ever described yourself as a 'visual' or 'auditory' learner? What new information do you have to guide your thinking about this notion?

FURTHER RESEARCH

SEARCH ME! AND EDUCATION DATABASES

Explore Search Me! education for articles relevant to this chapter. Fast and convenient, Search Me! education is updated daily and provides you with 24-hour access to full-text articles from hundreds of scholarly and popular journals, ebooks and newspapers, including *The Australian* and *The New York Times*. Log in to Search Me! through http://login.cengagebrain.com and use the search terms listed here as a starting point:

- cognitive learning theory
- cognitive style
- constructivism
- discovery learning
- information processing
- learning style
- memory AND children
- memory AND learning
- metacognition
- metacognitive development
- reciprocal teaching

You can also use these terms to explore databases such as ERIC, PsycINFO and the Australian Education Index.

RECOMMENDED WEBSITES

Brain information: http://brainconnection.brainhq.com

The Association for Constructivist Teaching: https://sites.google.com/site/assocforconstructteaching/

Learn about your own learning styles: www.engr.ncsu.edu/learningstyles/ilsweb.html

MindTools memory techniques: www.mindtools.com/memory.html

RECOMMENDED READING

Corno, L.M. & Anderman, E. (2015). *Handbook of educational psychology: Third edition*. Taylor and Francis.

O'Donnell, A. (2012). Constructivism. In K. R. Harris, S. Graham and T. Urdan (Editors-in-Chief). *APA educational psychology handbook: Vol. 1. Theories, constructs, and critical issues* (pp. 61–84). Washington, DC: APA.

Pashler, H., McDaniel, M., Rohrer, D. & Bjork, R. (2008). Learning styles: Concepts and evidence. *Psychological Science in the Public Interest*, 9(3), 105–19.

Ross, M.T., & Stenfors-Hayes, T. (2017) Peer Assisted learning (pp. 345–353). In Dent, J.A., Harden, R.M. & Hunt, D. (eds.) *A practical guide for medical teachers*. Elsevier.

REFERENCES

Anderson, C. A. (2004). An update on the effects of playing violent video games. *Journal of Adolescence, 27*, 113–22.

Anderson, L. W. & Krathwohl, D. R. (Eds) (2001). *A taxonomy for learning, teaching, and assessing: A revision of Bloom's taxonomy of educational objectives.* New York: Longman.

Anthony, G. & Walshaw, M. (2007). *Effective pedagogy in Mathematics/Pangarau: Best evidence synthesis iteration [BES].* Wellington: Ministry of Education.

Armstrong, S. J. (2000). The influence of individual cognitive style on performance in management education. *Educational Psychology, 20*(3), 323–40.

Atkinson, R. C. & Shiffrin, R. M. (1968). Human memory: A proposed system and its control processes. In K. W. Spence & J. T. Spence (Eds), *The psychology of learning and motivation* (Vol. 2, pp. 89–195). London: Academic Press.

Baddeley, A. D. (1996). The concept of working memory. In S. E. Gathercole (Ed.), *Models of short-term memory* (p. 28). Hove: Psychology Press.

Baddeley, A. D. (2012). Working memory: Theories, models, and controversies. *Annual Review of Psychology, 63*, 1–29.

Baddeley, A. D. & Logie, R. H. (1999). Working memory: The multiple component model. In A. Miyake & P. Shah (Eds), *Models of working memory* (pp. 28–61). Cambridge: Cambridge University Press.

Baillargeon, R., Pascual-Leone, J. & Roncadin, C. (1998). Mental-attentional capacity: Does cognitive style make a difference? *Journal of Experimental Child Psychology, 70*, 143–66.

Bandura, A. (1963). The role of imitation in personality. *The Journal of Nursery Education, 18*(3), 207–15.

Bandura, A. (1965). Influence of models' reinforcement contingencies on the acquisition of imitative response. *Journal of Personality and Social Psychology, 1*, 589–95.

Bandura, A. (1977). *Social learning theory.* Oxford: Prentice Hall.

Bandura, A. (1978). The self-system in reciprocal determinism. *American Psychologist, 33*, 344–58.

Bandura, A. (1986). *Social foundations of thought and action: A social cognitive theory.* Englewood Cliffs, NJ: Prentice-Hall.

Bandura, A. (2001). Social cognitive theory: An agentic perspective. *Annual Review of Psychology, 52*, 1–26.

Bandura, A., Ross, D. & Ross, S. (1961). Transmission of aggression through imitation of aggressive models. *Journal of Abnormal and Social Psychology, 63*, 575–82.

Bevevino, M. M., Dengel, J. & Adams, K. (1999). Constructivist theory in the classroom: Internalizing concepts through inquiry learning. *The Clearing House, 72*, 275–78.

Biggs, J. B. (1987a). *Student approaches to learning and studying.* Hawthorn, Vic.: ACER.

Biggs, J. B. (1987b). *The Learning Process Questionnaire: Users manual.* Hawthorn, Vic.: ACER.

Biggs, J. B. (2001). Teaching across cultures. In F. Salili (Ed.), *Student motivation: The culture and context of learning* (pp. 293–308). New York: Kluwer.

Biggs, J. B. & Moore, P. J. (1993). *The process of learning* (3rd ed.). Sydney: Prentice-Hall.

Bloom, B. S. (Ed.). (1956). *Taxonomy of educational objectives: Handbook 1. Cognitive domain.* London: Longmans.

Boekaerts, M. (1997). Self-regulated learning: A new concept enhanced by researchers, policy makers, educators, teachers, and students. *Learning and Instruction, 7*(2), 161–86.

Booker, M. J. (2007). A roof without walls: Benjamin Bloom's taxonomy and the misdirection of American education. *Academic Questions, 20*(4), 347–55.

Borkowski, J. G. & Muthukrishna, N. (1992). Moving metacognition into the classroom: 'Working models' and effective strategy teaching. In M. Pressley, K. R. Harris & J. T. Guthrie (Eds), *Promoting academic competence and literacy in school* (pp. 477–501). San Diego, CA: Academic.

Borkowski, J. G., Carr, M., Rellinger, E. & Pressley, M. (1990). Self-regulated cognition: Interdependence of metacognition, attributions, and self-esteem. In B. F. Jones & L. Idol (Eds), *Dimensions of thinking and cognitive instruction* (pp. 53–92). Hillsdale, NJ: Erlbaum.

Brown, D. F. & Rose, T. D. (1995). Self-reported classroom impact of teachers' theories about learning and obstacles to implementation. *Action in Teacher Education, 17*(1), 20–9.

Bruce, M. & Robinson, G. L. (2001). The clever kid's reading program: Metacognition and reciprocal teaching. Paper presented at the 12th Annual European Conference on Reading, Dublin, Ireland, 1–4 July.

Bruner, J. S. (1966). *Toward a theory of instruction.* Cambridge, MA: The Belknap Press of Harvard University.

Bruner, J. S. (1990). *Acts of meaning.* Cambridge, MA: Harvard University Press.

Burnett, P. C. & Proctor, R. M. (2002). Elementary school students' learner self-concept, academic self-concept and approaches to learning. *Educational Psychology in Practice, 18*(4), 325–33.

Byrnes, J. P. (1996). *Cognitive development and learning in instructional contexts.* Boston: Allyn & Bacon.

Campbell, J., Smith, D., Boulton-Lewis, G., Brownlee, J., Burnett, P. C., Carrington, S. & Purdie, N. (2001). Students' perceptions of teaching and learning: The influence of students' approaches to learning and teachers' approaches to teaching. *Teachers and Teaching: Theory and Practice, 7*(2), 173–87. Published by Taylor & Francis.

Cardelle-Elawar, M. (1995). Effects of metacognitive instruction on low achievers in mathematics problems. *Teaching and Teacher Education, 11*(1), 81–95.

Carr, M., Alexander, J. & Folds-Bennett, T. (1994). Metacognition and mathematics strategy use. *Applied Cognitive Psychology, 8*, 583–95.

Charter, A. (1996). Integrating traditional Aboriginal teaching and learning approaches in post-secondary settings. *Issues in the North, 1.* (ERIC Document Reproduction Service: ED403091.)

Cobb, P. & Yackel, E. (1996). Constructivist, emergent, and sociocultural perspectives in the context of developmental research. *Educational Psychologist, 31*(3–4), 175–90.

Coffield, F. J., Moseley, D. V., Hall, E. & Ecclestone, K. (2004a). *Should we be using learning styles? What research has to say to practice.* Retrieved from www.arasite.org/RMdatabase/Coffield.pdf

Coffield, F. J., Moseley, D. V., Hall, E. & Ecclestone, K. (2004b). *Learning styles and pedagogy in post-16 learning: A systematic and critical review.* Retrieved from www.leerbeleving.nl/wp-content/uploads/2011/09/learning-styles.pdf

Cooper, G. (1998). *Research into cognitive load theory and instructional design,* School of Education Studies, University of New South Wales. Retrieved from http://dwb4.unl.edu/Diss/Cooper/UNSW.htm

Corno, L. M. & Anderman, E. (2015). *Handbook of educational psychology:* Third edition. Taylor and Francis.

Cutting, L. E. & Denckla, M. B. (2003). Attention: Relationships between attention-deficit hyperactivity disorder and learning disabilities. In H. L. Swanson, K. R. Harris & S. Graham (Eds), *Handbook of learning disabilities* (pp. 125–39). New York: Guilford Press.

Davidson, J. E., Deuser, R. & Sternberg, R. J. (1994). The role of metacognition in problem solving. In J. Metcalfe & A. P. Shimamura (Eds), *Metacognition: Knowing about knowing* (pp. 207–26). Cambridge, MA: MIT.

Dean, D. & Kuhn, D. (2007). Direct instruction vs discovery: The long view. *Science Education, 91*(3), 384–97.

De Corte, E. & Verschaffel, L. (2006). Mathematical thinking and learning. In K. A. Renninger & I. E. Sigel (Series Eds), R. M. Lerner & W. Damon (Eds), *Handbook of child psychology, Vol. 4: Child psychology in practice* (6th ed., pp. 103–52). Hoboken, NJ: John Wiley & Sons.

Desmedt, E. & Valcke, M. (2004). Mapping the learning styles 'jungle': An overview of the literature based on citation analysis. *Educational Psychology, 24*(4), 445–64.

Dinham, S. & Rowe, K. (2008). Fantasy, fashion and fact : Middle schools, middle schooling and student achievement. *Teaching and Learning and Leadership.* Melbourne: ACER.

Dunn, R. & Griggs, S. A. (2003). *Synthesis of the Dunn and Dunn learning style model: Who, what, when, where, and so what?* New York: St John's University, Center for the Study of Learning and Teaching Styles.

Dunn, R., Dunn, K. & Price, G. (1984). *Learning style inventory.* Lawrence, KS: Price Systems.

Dunn, R., Griggs, S. A., Olson, J., Gorman, B. & Beasley, M. (1995). A meta-analytic validation of the Dunn and Dunn learning styles model. *Journal of Educational Research, 88*(6), 353–62.

Easton, C. E. & Watson, J. A. (1993). Spatial strategy use during Logo mastery: The impact of cognitive style and development level. *Journal of Computing in Childhood Education, 4,* 77–96.

Ellis, R. & Humphreys, G. W. (Eds). (1999). *Connectionist psychology: A text with readings.* Hove, East Sussex: Psychology Press.

Engle, R. W. & Conway, A. R. A. (1998). Working memory and comprehension. In R. H. Logie & K. J. Gilhooly (Eds), *Working memory and thinking: Current issues in thinking & reasoning* (pp. 67–91). Hove, UK: Psychology Press.

Engle, R. W. & Oransky, N. (1999). Multistore versus dynamic models of temporary storage in memory. In R. J. Sternberg (Ed.), *The nature of cognition* (pp. 515–56). Cambridge, MA: The MIT Press.

Entwistle, N. J. (1991). Cognitive style and learning. In K. Marjoribanks (Ed.), *The foundations of student learning* (pp. 139–46). Oxford, UK: Pergamon.

Eysenck, M. W. & Keane, M. (2000). *Cognitive psychology: A student's handbook* (4th ed.). East Sussex: Psychology Press.

Fang, A. & Cox, B. E. (1999). Emergent metacognition: A study of preschoolers' literate behaviour. *Journal of Research in Childhood Education, 13,* 175–87.

Ferrari, M. & Sternberg, R. J. (1998). The development of mental abilities and styles. In D. Kuhn & R. S. Siegler (Eds), *Handbook of child psychology, Vol. 2: Cognition, perception, and language* (5th ed., pp. 899–946). New York: John Wiley & Sons.

Flavell, J. H. (1979). Metacognition and cognitive monitoring: A new area of cognitive-developmental inquiry. *American Psychologist, 34,* 906–11.

Flavell, J. H. (1987). Speculations about the nature and development of metacognition. In F. Weinert & U. R. Kluwe (Eds), *Metacognition, motivation, and understanding* (pp. 21–9). Hillsdale, NJ: Erlbaum.

Flavell, J. H. (1999). Cognitive development: Children's knowledge about the mind. *Annual Review of Psychology, 50,* 21–45.

Flavell, J. H., Miller, P. H. & Miller, S. A. (1993). *Cognitive development* (3rd ed.). Englewood Cliffs, NJ: Prentice Hall.

Fleming, N. D. & Mills, C. (1992). Not another inventory, rather a catalyst for reflection. *To Improve the Academy, 11,* 137–49.

Frank, B. M. & Keene, D. (1993). The effect of learners' field independence, cognitive strategy instruction, and inherent wordlist organization on free-call memory and strategy use. *Journal of Experimental Education, 62,* 14–25.

Fuchs, D. & Fuchs, L. S. (1998). Researchers and teachers working together to adapt instruction for diverse learners. *Learning Disabilities Research and Practice, 13,* 126–37.

Fuchs, D., Fuchs, L. S., Thompson, A., Al Otaiba, S., Yen, L., Yang, N. & Braun, M. (2002). Exploring the importance of reading programs for kindergartners with disabilities in mainstream classrooms. *Exceptional Children, 68*(3), 295–311.

Fuchs, L. S., Fuchs, D. & Kazdan, S. (1999). Effects of peer-assisted learning strategies on high-school students with serious reading problems. *Remedial and Special Education, 20,* 309–18.

Funk, J. B. (2005). Children's exposure to violent video games and desensitization to violence. *Child & Adolescent Psychiatric Clinics of North America, 14*(3), 387–404.

Furnham, A. (2012). Learning styles and approaches to learning. In K. R. Harris, S. Graham & T. Urdan (Eds-in-Chief), *APA Educational Psychology Handbook: Vol. 2. Individual Differences and Cultural and Contextual Factors* (pp. 59–81). doi:10.1037/13274-003

Gardner, H. (1983). *Frames of mind: The theory of multiple intelligences.* New York: Basic Books.

Gardner, H. (1993). Early giftedness and later achievement. In G. R. Bock & K. Ackrill (Eds), *The origins and development of high ability. Ciba Foundation Symposium 178* (pp. 175–82). Chichester, West Sussex: John Wiley & Sons.

Gentile, D. A., Lynch, P. J., Linder, J. R. & Walsh, D. A. (2004). The effects of violent video game habits on adolescent hostility, aggressive behaviours, and school performance. *Journal of Adolescence, 27*(1), 5–22.

Gillies, R. M. (2007). *Cooperative learning : Integrating theory and practice.* Thousand Oaks, CA: Sage Publications, Inc.

Ginns, P. (2006). Integrating information: A meta-analysis of the spatial contiguity and temporal contiguity effects. *Learning and Instruction, 16,* 511–25.

Green, S. & Gredler, M. (2002). A review and analysis of constructivism for school-based practice. *School Psychology Review, 31*(1), 53.

Guenther, R. K. (1998). *Human cognition.* Upper Saddle River, NJ: Prentice Hall.

Hacker, D. J. (1998). Definitions and empirical foundations. In D. J. Hacker, J. Dunlosky & A. C. Graesser (Eds), *Metacognition in educational theory and practice* (pp. 1–23). Mahwah, NJ: Lawrence Erlbaum Associates.

Hattie, J. (2009). *Visible learning: A synthesis of over 800 meta-analyses relating to achievement.* London: Routledge.

Henson, K. T. (1996). *Methods and strategies for teaching in secondary and middle schools.* White Plains, NY: Longman.

Herbert, S. M. (2000). Motivating male primary underachievers through a technoliteracy curriculum. Unpublished M.Ed. thesis, Victoria University of Technology.

Hmelo-Silver, C. E., Duncan, R. G. & Chinn, C. A. (2007). Scaffolding and achievement in problem-based and inquiry learning: A response to Kirschner, Sweller, and Clark (2006). *Educational Psychologist, 42,* 99–107.

Hogan, D. M. & Tudge, J. R. H. (1999). The implications of Vygotsky's theory for peer learning. In A. M. O'Donnell & A. King (Eds), *Cognitive perspectives on peer learning* (pp. 39–65). Mahwah, NJ: Erlbaum.

Howe, K. & Berv, J. (2000). Constructing constructivism, epistemological and pedagogical. In D. C. Phillips (Ed.), *Constructivism in education: Opinions and second opinions on controversial issues* (pp. 19–40). Chicago: The National Society for the Study of Education.

John-Steiner, V. & Mahn, H. (1996). Sociocultural approaches to learning and development. *Educational Psychology, 31,* 191–206.

Jonassen, D. H. & Grabowski, B. L. (1993). *Handbook of individual differences, learning and instruction.* Hillsdale, NJ: Lawrence Erlbaum Associates.

Kagan, J. (1958). The concept of identification. *Psychological Review, 65,* 296–305.

Kagan, J. (1966). Reflection–impulsivity and reading ability in primary grade children. *Child Development, 36,* 609–28.

Kanerva, P. (1993). Sparse distributed memory and related models. In M. Hassoun (Ed.), *Associative neural memories: Theory and implementation.* New York: Oxford University Press.

Kaniel, S., Licht, P. & Peled, B. (2001). The influence of metacognitive instruction of reading and writing strategies. *Gifted Education International, 15*(1), 45–63.

Killen, R. (2007). *Effective teaching strategies: Lessons from research and practice* (4th ed.). Melbourne: Thomson/Social Science Press.

Kirschner, P. A., Sweller, J. & Clark, R. E. (2006). Why minimal guidance during instruction does not work: An analysis of the failure of constructivist, discovery, problem-based, experiential, and inquiry-based teaching. *Educational Psychologist, 41,* 75–86.

Klahr, D. & MacWhinney, B. (1998). Information processing. In D. Kuhn & R. S. Siegler (Eds), *Handbook of child psychology, Vol. 2: Cognition, perception, and language* (5th ed., pp. 631–78). New York: John Wiley & Sons.

Klahr, D. & Nigam, M. (2004). The equivalence of learning paths in early science instruction: Effects of direct instruction and discovery learning. *Psychological Science, 15*(10), 661–7.

Kluwe, R. H. (1982). Cognitive knowledge and executive control: Metacognition. In D. R. Griffin (Ed.), *Animal mind – human mind* (pp. 201–24). New York: Springer.

Kubes, M. (1998). Adaptors and innovators in Slovakia: Cognitive style and social culture. *European Journal of Personality, 12*(3), 187–98.

Kuhn, D. (2000). Metacognitive development. *Current Directions in Psychological Science, 9*(5), 178–81.

Kuhn, D. (2007). Is direct instruction the answer to the right question? *Educational Psychologist, 42*, 109–13.

Lave, J. & Wenger, E. (1991). *Situated learning: Legitimate peripheral participation*. Cambridge, UK: Cambridge University Press.

Lockhart, R. S. & Craik, F. I. M. (1990). Levels of processing: A retrospective commentary on a framework for memory research. *Canadian Journal of Psychology, 44*, 87–112.

Lucangeli, D., Coi, G. & Bosco, P. (1997). Metacognitive awareness in good and poor math problem solvers. *Learning Disabilities Research and Practice, 12*(4), 209–12.

Maqsud, M. (1997). Effects of metacognitive skills and nonverbal ability on academic achievement of high school pupils. *Educational Psychology, 17*(4), 387–97.

Matthews, M. (2000). Appraising constructivism in science and mathematics education. In D. C. Phillips (Ed.), *Constructivism in education: Opinions and second opinions on controversial issues* (pp. 161–92). Chicago: The National Society for the Study of Education.

Mayer, R. (2004). Should there be a three-strikes rule against pure discovery learning? The case for guided methods of instruction. *American Psychologist, 59*(1), 14–19.

Mayer, R. E. (2003). Memory and information processes. In W. M. Reynolds & G. E. Miller (Eds), *Handbook of psychology: Educational psychology* (Vol. 7, pp. 47–57). New York: John Wiley & Sons.

McLelland, J. L. & Rumelhart, D. E. (1986). A distributed model of human learning and memory. In J. L. McLelland & D. E. Rumelhart (Eds), *Parallel distributed processing: Explorations in the microstructure of cognition* (Vol. 2, pp. 170–215). Cambridge, MA: MIT Press.

Meadows, S. (1998). Children learning to think: Learning from others? Vygotskian theory and educational psychology. *Educational and Child Psychology, 15*(2), 6–13.

Miller, G. A. (1956). The magical number seven, plus or minus two: Some limits on our capacity for processing information. *The Psychological Review, 63*, 81–97.

Munakata, Y. (2006). Information processing approaches to development. In W. Damon & R. M. Lerner (Gen. Eds) & D. Kuhn & R. S. Siegler (Vol. Eds), *Handbook of child psychology, Vol. 2: Cognition, perception, and language* (6th ed., pp. 426–63). New York: Wiley.

Navarro, J. I., Aguilar, M. & Alcalde, C. (1999). Relationship of arithmetic problem solving and reflective–impulsive cognitive styles in third-grade students. *Psychological Reports, 85*(1), 179–86.

Nelson, T. O. & Narens, L. (1994). Why investigate metacognition? In J. Metcalfe & A. P. Shimamura (Eds), *Metacognition: Knowing about knowing*. Cambridge, MA: MIT Press.

Nisbett, R. & Miyamoto, Y. (2005). The influence of culture: Holistic versus analytic perception. *Trends in Cognitive Sciences 9*(10), 467–73.

Nisbett, R. E., Peng, K., Choi, I. & Norenzayan, A. (2001). Culture and systems of thought: Holistic versus analytic cognition. *Psychological Review, 108*(2), 291–310.

Nuthall, G. A. (2000). The role of memory in the acquisition and retention of knowledge in science and social studies units. *Cognition and Instruction, 18*(1), 83–139.

O'Donnell, A. (2012). Constructivism. In K. Harris (Ed.), *APA educational psychology handbook. Vol. 1, Theories, constructs, and critical issues* (1st ed., pp. 61–84). Washington, DC: American Psychological Association.

Olson, C. K. (2004). Media violence research and youth violence data: Why do they conflict? *Academic Psychiatry, 28*(2), 144–50.

Pajares, F. (2004). *Albert Bandura: Biographical sketch*. Retrieved from http://des.emory.edu/mfp/bandurabio.html

Palincsar, A. S. (1998). Social constructivist perspectives on teaching and learning. *Annual Review of Psychology, 49*, 345–75.

Paris, S. G. & Winograd, P. (1990). How metacognition can promote academic learning and instruction. In B. F. Jones & L. Idol (Eds), *Dimensions of thinking and cognitive instruction* (pp. 15–51). Hillsdale, NJ: Erlbaum.

Pashler, H., McDaniel, M., Rohrer, D. & Bjork, R. (2008). Learning styles: Concepts and evidence. *Psychological Science in the Public Interest, 9*(3), 105–19.

Phillips, D. C. (1997). How, why, what, when, and where: Perspectives on constructivism and education. *Issues in Education: Contributions from Educational Psychology, 3*, 151–94.

Phillips, D. C. (2000). An opinionated account of the constructivist landscape. In D. C. Phillips (Ed.), *Constructivism in education: Opinions and second opinions on controversial issues* (pp. 1–16), Chicago, Illinois: National Society for the Study of Education.

Pintrich, P. R. (2002). The role of metacognitive knowledge in learning, teaching, and assessing. *Theory into Practice, 41*(4), 219–25.

Pintrich, P. R. & De Groot, E. (1990). Motivated and self-regulated learning components of academic performance. *Journal of Educational Psychology, 82*, 33–40.

Pintrich, P. R. & Schunk, D. H. (1996). *Motivation in education: Theory, research and applications*. Englewood Cliffs, NJ: Prentice Hall Merrill.

Powell, S. D. & Makin, M. (1994). Enabling pupils with learning difficulties to reflect on their own thinking. *British Educational Research Journal, 20*(5), 20–9.

Prawat, R. (1996). Constructivisms, modern and postmodern. *Educational Psychology, 31*, 215–25.

Riding, R. J. & Al-Sanabani, S. (1998). The effect of cognitive style, age, gender, and structure on the recall of prose passages. *International Journal of Educational Research, 29*, 173–85.

Riding, R. J. & Cheema, I. (1991). Cognitive styles: An overview and integration. *Educational Psychology: An International Journal of Experimental Educational Psychology, 11*(3–4), 193–215.

Riding, R. J. & Rayner, S. G. (1998). *Cognitive style and learning strategies*. London: David Fulton Publishers.

Roebers, C., & Feurer, E. (2016). Linking Executive Functions and Procedural Metacognition *Child Development Perspectives, 10*(1), 39–44.

Rogoff, B. (1990). *Apprenticeship in thinking: Cognitive development in social context*. New York: Oxford University Press.

Rosenshine, B. (2010). Principles of instruction. *Educational Practices Series, 21*. IBE UNESCO. Retrieved from unesdoc.unesco.org/images/0019/001906/190652e.pdf

Rosenthal-Malek, A. L. (1997). Stop and think! Using metacognitive strategies to teach students social skills. *Teaching Exceptional Children, 29*, 29–31.

Ross, M. T. & Stenfors-Hayes, T. (2017). Peer assisted learning (pp. 345–353). In Dent, J.A., Harden, R.M. & Hunt, D. (Eds.) *A practical guide for medical teachers*. Elsevier.

Rowe, K. (2007). *Effective teaching practices*. Australian Policy Online. Retrieved from http://apo.org.au/research/effective-teaching-practices

Schmidt, H. G., Loyens, S. M. M., van Gog, T. & Paas, F. (2007). Problem-based learning is compatible with human cognitive architecture: Commentary on Kirschner, Sweller, and Clark (2006). *Educational Psychologist, 42*, 91–7.

Schneider, W. & Bjorklund, D. F. (1998). Memory. In D. Kuhn & R. S. Siegler (Eds), *Handbook of child psychology, Vol. 2: Cognition, perception, and language* (5th ed., pp. 467–552). New York: John Wiley and Sons.

Shin, M. (1998). Promoting students' self-regulation ability: Guidelines for instructional design. *Educational Technology, 38*(1), 38–44.

Shomstein, S. & Yantis, S. (2004). Control of attention shifts between vision and audition in human cortex. *Journal of Neuroscience, 24*(47), 10 702–6.

Simon, S. D. (2001, rev.). From neo-behaviorism to social constructivism?: The paradigmatic non-evolution of Albert Bandura. Unpublished doctoral thesis, Emory University. Retrieved from www.des.emory.edu/mfp/simon.html

Smith, J. D. & Caplan, J. (1988). Cultural differences in cognitive style development. *Developmental Psychology, 24,* 46–52.

Solomon, J. (2000). The changing perspectives of constructivism: Science wars and children's creativity. In D. C. Phillips (Ed.), *Constructivism in education: Opinions and second opinions on controversial issues* (pp. 283–307). Chicago: The National Society for the Study of Education.

Spence, D. J., Yore, L. D. & Williams, R. L. (1999). The effects of explicit science reading instruction on selected Grade 7 students' metacognition and comprehension of specific science text. *Journal of Elementary Science Education, 11*(2), 15–30.

Sternberg, R. J. & Grigorenko, E. L. (1997). Are cognitive styles still in style? *American Psychologist, 52*(7), 700–12.

Sternberg, R. J. & Grigorenko, E. L. (2001). A capsule history of theory and research on styles. In R. J. Sternberg & L. F. Zhang (Eds), *Perspectives on thinking, learning and cognitive styles* (pp. 1–21). Mahwah, NJ: Lawrence Erlbaum Associates.

Sturrock, F. & May, S. (2002). *Programme for International Student Assessment 2000 (PISA): The New Zealand context.* Wellington: Comparative Education Research Unit, Research Division, New Zealand Ministry of Education.

Sweller, J., Ayres, P. & Kalyuga, S. (2011). *Cognitive load theory, from Explorations in the Learning Sciences, Instructional Systems and Performance Technologies, Vol. 1.* New York: Springer.

Sweller, J., Mawer, R. F. & Ward, M. R. (1983). Development of expertise in mathematical problem solving. *Journal of Experimental Psychology, 112*(4), 639–61.

Tiberius, R. G. (1990). *Small group teaching: A trouble shooting guide.* Toronto: The Ontario Institute for Studies in Education. (ERIC Document ED318690)

Tinajero, C. & Paramo, M. F. (1998). Field dependence–independence and strategic learning. *International Journal of Educational Research, 29,* 251–62.

Tobin, K. (2000). Constructivism in science education: Moving on... In D. C. Phillips (Ed.), *Constructivism in education: Opinions and second opinions on controversial issues* (pp. 227–53). Chicago: The National Society for the Study of Education.

Tulving, E. (1974). Cue-dependent forgetting. *American Scientist, 62,* 74–82.

Tulving, E. (1985). How many memory systems are there? *American Psychologist, 40,* 385–98.

Wagner, D., Cook, G. & Friedman, J. (1998). Staying with their first impulse?: The relationship between impulsivity/reflectivity, field dependence/field independence and answer changes on a multiple-choice exam in a fifth-grade sample. *Journal of Research and Development in Education, 31,* 166–75.

Watson, J. A. & Brinkley, V. M. (1992). Logo mastery and spatial problem-solving by young children: Effects of Logo language training, route strategy training, and learning styles on immediate learning and transfer. *Journal of Educational Computing Research, 8,* 521–40.

Weinert, F. E. (1987). Introduction and overview: Metacognition and motivation as determinants of effective learning and understanding. In F. E. Weinert & R. H. Kluwe (Eds), *Metacognition, motivation, and understanding* (pp. 1–19). Hillsdale, NJ: Lawrence Erlbaum Associates.

Wilen, W. W. & Phillips, J. A. (1995). Teaching critical thinking: A metacognitive approach. *Social Education, 59*(3), 135–8.

Witkin, H. A. & Goodenough, D. R. (1981). *Cognitive styles: Essence and origins.* New York: International Universities Press.

Witkin, H. A., Oltman, P., Raskin E. & Karp, S. (1971). *A manual for the Group Embedded Figures Test.* Palo Alto, CA: Consulting Psychologists Press.

Wittrock, M. C. (1991). Generative teaching of comprehension. *The Elementary School Journal, 92,* 169–84.

Yager, R. E. & Lutz, M. V. (1994). Integrated science: The importance of 'how' versus 'what'. *School Science and Mathematics, 94*(7), 338–45.

Zhang, L. F. & Sternberg, R. J. (2000). Are learning approaches and thinking styles related? A study of two Chinese populations. *Journal of Psychology, 134,* 469–89.

Zimmerman, B. J. (1998). Developing self-fulfilling cycles of academic regulation: An analysis of exemplary instructional models. In D. H. Schunk & B. J. Zimmerman (Eds), *Self-regulated learning: From teaching to self-reflective practice* (pp. 1–19). New York: The Guilford Press.

Zohar, A. (1999). Teachers' metacognitive knowledge and the instruction of higher order thinking. *Teaching and Teacher Education, 15,* 413–29.

HUMANIST APPROACHES TO LEARNING

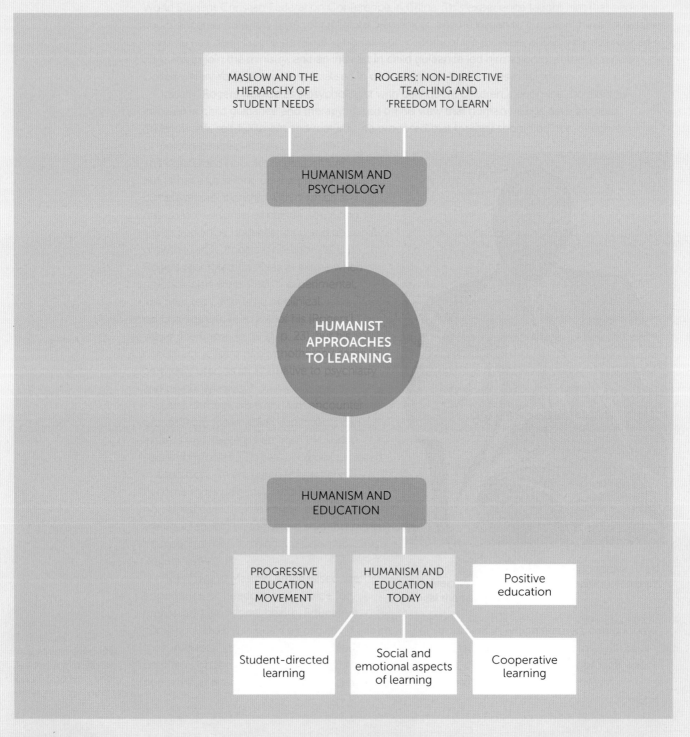

FIGURE 7.1 Chapter 7 concept map

KEY QUESTIONS

After reading this chapter, you should be able to answer the following questions:

- How does Maslow link human needs and learning?
- How have humanist ideas influenced current practices in primary and secondary education?
- How can teachers best support student wellbeing?
- How does social and emotional learning contribute to academic achievement?
- What are the main elements of cooperative learning?
- What elements of humanism do you observe in your own philosophy of teaching and learning, and in the classrooms you have seen?

ONLINE STUDY RESOURCES

Bring your learning to life with **interactive learning**, **study** and **exam preparation tools** that support the printed textbook. CourseMate Express includes **quizzes**, **interactive activities**, **videos**, a tool to help you '**develop your philosophy**' and more.

INTRODUCTION

Sharon comes in to the staffroom looking harassed. 'They're just not going to get to where they need to be by the end of this term!' she exclaims, worried about her Year 11 History class, and their coverage of the syllabus content.

Stephanie asks, 'Is it the content that they're missing, or the skills? Maybe you can build the skills with less content. That's easier to add in later.'

Joanne says, 'They have a lot going on at the moment, maybe for now our concern is to keep them grounded and to minimise stress for them.'

David agrees. '"Where they need to be" is happy and feeling supported. If we can do that, they will do the rest.'

Lee isn't so sure. 'I don't know. There are some real life skills – and values – they could do with, like making choices that benefit others, not just themselves, and being prepared to make sacrifices to get to their goals. Without those, our support on its own won't do much for their learning progress (and neither will our teaching).'

'Well, whose goals are they?' asks David. 'Perhaps they have different goals to the ones we'd like them to have. Maybe they are prepared to sacrifice something – learning History – for their goals of friendship, or feeling competent, or having some control over things in their life.'

'That's all very well,' laments Sharon, 'but meanwhile, I have a syllabus I need to get through by the end of this term, if they're going to be set up for Year 12!'

This chapter is concerned with humanistic approaches to education, which consider the broad needs of students, including not just cognitive but also social and emotional needs. They recognise that, just as we saw for development in Module I, learning is interconnected across the cognitive, physical, social and emotional domains. Links in learning between cognitive (thinking) and affective (feeling) domains are well established (Weissberg & Cascarino, 2013). For example, in Chapter 4, you read about links between self-concept and learning, and in Chapter 8 we examine the links between motivation and learning. This has led to a concern to teach the whole child, and to consider skills such as emotional literacy to be just as fundamental as literacy and numeracy. These concerns are not just the domain of humanist educators, but are shared by many religious schools, which also aim to teach the whole child.

Humanist approaches also tend to emphasise the agency of the learner in directing what and how they learn. The focus in humanist approaches is on the child and his or her needs and wants, rather than on the curriculum content being delivered.

Child-centred views of education can be traced back to the influence of humanistic thinkers such as Jean-Jacques Rousseau, Friedrich Froebel, Johann Pestalozzi, Maria Montessori and, more recently, to the ideas of Abraham Maslow, Carl Rogers and John Dewey. The ideas of Piaget and Vygotsky (discussed in Chapter 3) and Erikson (discussed in Chapter 4) have also been influential.

THINK ABOUT

- What is school education for? What should its main goal be?

WHAT IS HUMANISM?

humanism
An orientation or philosophy that recognises the uniqueness of human beings and the qualities of life that contribute to our humanity

Most dictionaries define the term **humanism** as any system of thought that is predominantly concerned with human experience and reasoning as opposed to the supernatural or divine (see, for example, the *Macquarie Dictionary*). The word 'humanist' is used to describe a general orientation to life or a personal philosophy that recognises the uniqueness of human beings and the qualities of life that contribute to our humanity, in art, literature, music and all aspects of daily living. It upholds the dignity of the human condition and, by extension, of the individual. Humanists believe that individuals have the potential to set goals, solve problems and achieve their own potential (Lamont, 1961). Humanism can be traced back to ancient Greece and thinkers such as Aristotle and Epicurus, who were both interested in everyday life and the real world rather than in religious beliefs and the gods. Humanistic thinking also shows evidence of Chinese and Indian influences through some of the writings of Confucius and Buddha (Brockett, 2000; Misiak & Sexton, 1973).

HUMANISM AND PSYCHOLOGY

Throughout the first half of the 20th century, psychology was strongly influenced by two theoretical approaches: behaviourism, represented by B. F. Skinner (1957) (see Chapter 5), and psychoanalysis, represented by Sigmund Freud (1933). Psychoanalytic explanations of behaviour are derived from Freud's work (Freud lived from 1856 to 1939) and are concerned with psychosexual development and the way in which individuals resolve conflicts between biological drives (or basic needs) such as sexual desires and aggression, and social expectations and values. Humanist psychology began to emerge in the 1950s as a reaction against the 'overscientific' or 'dehumanising' methods of behaviourists, and psychoanalysts' pessimistic obsession with mental illness and disturbance.

self-actualisation
The achievement of one's full potential

The two theorists who contributed most to the development of humanistic ideas in psychology and education in the 20th century were Abraham Maslow and Carl Rogers. Both emphasised the essential goodness of human beings and the need for each individual to achieve **self-actualisation** (or self-fulfilment). Maslow (1969) described humanist psychology, with its focus on the healthy person, as the 'third force' (the other two forces being behaviourism and psychoanalysis). These ideas – particularly Maslow's theory of human motivation and the hierarchy of needs, and Rogers' (1951) model of client-centred therapy and the concept of 'freedom to learn' – have continued to influence professional practice in both psychology and education.

MASLOW AND THE HIERARCHY OF HUMAN NEEDS

The most basic of human needs are physiological, such as a newborn infant's need for food and warmth. Later, infants begin to need safety, social contact and love. During childhood and adolescence, needs extend to include esteem (from the self and others), and finally, in maturity, there is the need for self-actualisation or the achievement of one's full potential. Maslow's early interest in human beings' basic needs arose from his work as a psychotherapist helping people who were psychologically disturbed (see Box 7.1). Through this work, Maslow came to believe that human activity is motivated by an urge to satisfy a set of basic needs and growth needs.

BOX 7.1 ABOUT ABRAHAM MASLOW

Abraham Maslow (1908–70) was born on 1 April 1908 in New York, the eldest of seven children. He remembered his childhood as being very unhappy (Boeree, 2000a), describing himself as 'extremely shy, nervous, depressed, lonely and self-reflecting' up to the age of 20 (De Carvalho, 1991, p. 19). Unhappy at home and isolated at school, he spent many hours in the library (De Carvalho, 1991).

As a student, Maslow did well. He spent a brief period studying law in New York, as advised by his father, but this did not interest him. He then married and enrolled in psychology at the University of Wisconsin. At this time, he was interested in the work of John Watson and the behaviourists (see Chapter 5), and his early research was concerned with emotional and social relationships in dogs and apes. Later, Maslow worked with Harry Harlow (Harlow & Zimmerman, 1959), known for his studies of attachment behaviour in infant rhesus monkeys.

Maslow returned to New York, where he worked in the area of social psychology with E. L. Thorndike (see Chapter 5) at Columbia University. He came to know a number of German psychologists who had escaped to the USA during the Second World War and, through them, developed an interest in mental health and the potential of human beings. He took notes about successful individuals and the way they behaved, finding it significantly different from the behaviour of mentally 'ill' people – his main focus of attention at the time. Maslow argued that human beings were essentially good, but if their basic needs were frustrated or denied, this inner nature could be suppressed, leading to undesirable or bad reactions. He proposed that these needs could be viewed in terms of a hierarchy or pyramid. The base of the pyramid consisted of the most basic human survival needs (see Figure 7.3), with the need for self-actualisation at the apex. Maslow saw motivation as a means for the satisfaction of basic needs.

Maslow had a successful career in psychology. He taught at Brooklyn College, was chair of the Psychology Department at Brandeis University, and in 1968 was president of the American Psychological Association. He died in 1970.

FIGURE 7.2 Maslow believed that humans are essentially good, but that this inner goodness can be suppressed if their basic human needs are denied.

Source: Alamy Stock Photo/Granger Historical Picture Archive

ACTIVITIES

1 How might the events of Maslow's life have shaped his ideas about human needs?
2 How have the events of your life shaped your thinking about learning and teaching?

Lower-level or 'deficit' needs, such as the need for food, safety, love and respect

growth needs
Higher-level or 'being' needs, such as the need for self-actualisation

Maslow (1968, pp. 199–200; Maslow & Lowery, 1998) described humans' **basic needs** and **growth needs** originally in terms of five ascending levels, later extending these to eight (see Figure 7.3) by differentiating the growth needs (Huitt, 2011):

1 *Food, shelter, clothes.* Sometimes referred to as 'physiological needs'; these are the most urgent basic elements needed for survival.
2 *Safety, protection, security.* Once basic physiological needs are satisfied, we seek a sense of security and stability.
3 *Belongingness, love.* Feelings of affection such as those found in a family, a community, a clan, a gang, a friendship.
4 *Respect, esteem, approval, dignity, self-respect.* These involve two sets of needs:
   a. *respect from others,* including status, public recognition and acclaim, even fame and, in some instances, dominance
   b. *self-respect and feelings about the self,* including a sense of competence, self-confidence, independence and freedom.
5 *Cognitive needs.* These include knowledge, understanding and exploration.

Source: Adapted from Lefrancois (2000); Huitt (2011).

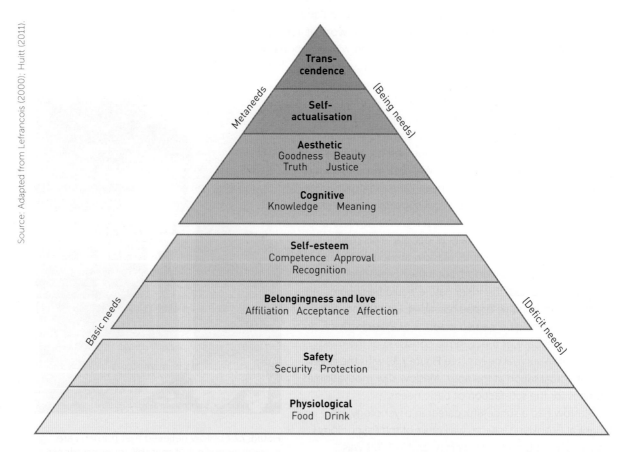

FIGURE 7.3 Maslow's hierarchy of human needs

6   *Aesthetic needs.* These include symmetry, order and beauty.

7   *Self-actualisation.* This means freedom for the fullest development of one's talents and capacities, or the achievement of one's full potential.

8   *Transcendence.* Moving beyond the self, this describes the need to help others find self-fulfilment and achieve their full potential.

Maslow referred to levels 1 to 4 in the hierarchy as **deficit needs (D-needs)** and levels 5 to 8 as representing growth or **being needs (B-needs)**. He believed that only a small percentage of individuals – less than 1 per cent of adults (Maslow, 1968, p. 204) – truly reached the seventh and eighth levels of development, identifying historical figures such as Mahatma Gandhi, Albert Einstein, Abraham Lincoln and Eleanor Roosevelt as examples of people who reached this level.

According to Maslow, children whose basic material needs are satisfied (see Figure 7.4), and who are assured of safety, love and a sense of belonging, are able to cope with some frustration and disappointment, provided these are not overwhelming. Such challenges strengthen the individual and lead to healthy self-esteem that is based not only on the approval of others, but also on a realistic view of the self, an awareness of personal success, and an intrinsic motivation towards achievement and growth.

deficit needs (D-needs)
Basic needs that motivate individuals to action in order to reduce or eliminate the need

being needs (B-needs)
Growth needs that motivate individuals to achieve personal fulfilment and self-actualisation

Source: © JoseGirarte/iStockphoto.

FIGURE 7.4 Maslow's hierarchy of needs reminds us of the importance of considering children's basic needs before their academic needs. These children can focus on learning because their basic needs of safety, shelter, food, love and respect have been met.

Box 7.2 discusses the implications of applying Maslow's ideas in the classroom.

BOX 7.2 IMPLICATIONS FOR EDUCATORS

APPLYING MASLOW'S IDEAS IN THE CLASSROOM

The implications of Maslow's ideas for education mainly concern the place of basic needs and motivation in the learning process. For example:

- Children's basic physiological needs must be met before they can be motivated to learn. School breakfast programs for children who are from economically disadvantaged homes are based on Maslow's human needs model. School health and dental programs have similar origins.
- Strategies that are designed to enhance children's self-esteem and develop positive feelings in children about their own competence and effectiveness (see Chapter 4) reflect Maslow's ideas about the importance of motivation and wellbeing in learning and achievement.
- Children should be provided with opportunities to develop their understanding and appreciation of affective aspects of human achievement as exemplified in music, art, poetry and literature, since for many individuals these provide a means of achieving self-fulfilment.

Strengths and limitations of Maslow's theory

Strengths

Maslow's ideas about human needs and self-actualisation have had a continuing impact on education: the 'needs' hierarchy is mentioned in most educational psychology textbooks. Since Maslow's work, several theorists have expanded and added ideas about the human need for autonomy and self-fulfilment. Ryan and Deci (2000a; Deci & Ryan, 2006) in particular have applied these concepts to education and motivation, as we will see in Chapter 8. Positive psychology also takes up Maslow's ideas of wisdom, meaning and happiness. Their application in Seligman's 'positive education' principles is discussed later in this chapter.

Also significant is the focus on students' needs in a learning situation, rather than those of the teacher or curriculum. Attention is on children's basic needs for food, safety and belonging; on the affective or emotional aspects of their development (feeling, interest, attitudes and values); and on motivation rather than academic achievement.

Limitations

One of the main criticisms of Maslow's work concerns the hierarchical nature of his human-needs model. Critics have argued that the sequence of Maslow's human needs does not always apply, as in the example of the hero who 'may sacrifice his life for honour' (Patterson, 1973, p. 67). In this case, the hero's need for self-actualisation is stronger than his more basic need for safety. Other criticisms of Maslow's work concern the vagueness of terms such as 'self-actualisation', and the uncertainty about measuring its achievement. (For example, when can it be said to have been achieved, and under what conditions?) Although widely accepted, the theory has not been empirically tested, partly because of the difficulty in measuring the concepts (Wahba & Bridwell, 1976).

THINK ABOUT

- Reflect on Maslow's hierarchy of needs as it applies in your life. Can you identify with each of the needs? Which have priority? Are there any that don't apply to you?
- What role do you think Maslow's hierarchy of needs has in a 21st-century classroom?

ROGERS: NON-DIRECTIVE TEACHING AND 'FREEDOM TO LEARN'

Carl Rogers is another key figure associated with humanist approaches. Principally working in the field of psychotherapy, Rogers also wrote about education, both in *Client-centred therapy* (1951) and in *Freedom to learn* (1969, 1983; Rogers & Freiberg, 1994), advocating a person-centred approach to education. Rogers' view was that people had within themselves the ability to solve their problems and heal themselves, and that the therapist's role was to release them to do that. In education, he urged that the teacher's role was to free and assist students to explore their intrinsic interests and enthusiasms, rather than to force them to learn a curriculum determined by others. Rogers argued that real learning can occur only to the degree that problems are real and significant to the learner.

Rogers believed that therapists and others could help people to begin to heal themselves by developing supportive, non-directive relationships with them. Similarly, he argued that teaching must be grounded in such relationships. Teachers' attitudes to students were essential to developing such relationships, and there were three core conditions if learning was to be facilitated:

FIGURE 7.5 Actively listening to a child talk about her worries involves attending carefully to what the child says, then giving calm, brief and accurate feedback.

1 Teachers had to be real or genuine in their relationships with students.
2 Teachers had to prize the learner, accepting them for who they were, and trusting their ability to learn and develop. He termed this 'unconditional positive regard'.
3 Teachers had to have empathic understanding of their students – an ability to see the world through their students' eyes, without judging them (Rogers, 1983; Zimring, 1994).

Active listening

Rogers acknowledged that developing and enacting these attitudes is by no means easy. One vital skill therapists (and teachers) had to develop was to become active listeners (see Box 7.4). For Rogers and other humanists, **active listening**, sometimes called 'reflective listening' (Arthur-Kelly, Lyons, Butterfield & Gordon, 2006; Porter, 2007), involves more than simply hearing individuals describe their difficulties. It involves attending purposefully to the meaning and intention of what is said, then paraphrasing or reflecting back both content and emotion as a way of demonstrating that the message has been received and understood. This response strategy encourages the individual to continue talking. It is also an opportunity to release any tensions or emotions, and to clarify aspects of the communication that might have been misunderstood. Active listening helps teachers to build more effective relationships with their students.

active listening Attending purposefully to the meaning and intention of what another person is saying

BOX 7.3 ABOUT CARL ROGERS

Carl Rogers (1902–87) was born in Chicago, the fourth of six children, into a well-to-do and very religious family that emphasised the value of hard work. When he was about 12 years old, the family moved to the country so the children could escape the temptations of the city. Rogers became interested in agriculture, choosing to study in this area when he left school, but he soon changed to history as preparation for later entry into the ministry.

After graduating from the University of Wisconsin-Madison, Rogers married and moved to New York to enter the very liberal Union Theological Seminary. During this time, he attended a World Student Christian Federation Conference in China. This experience taught him that people could sincerely hold very divergent religious viewpoints, and he began to question the strict religious views he had been taught, developing his own philosophy of life (Boeree, 2000b). He abandoned his plans to join the ministry, and an interest in child guidance led him to enrol at the Teachers College, New York, where he specialised in clinical and educational psychology.

Initially, Rogers worked as a psychologist with delinquent children, becoming increasingly involved in child guidance and therapy. Based on his view that human beings have an inner drive towards self-fulfilment and maturity, he proposed that therapy should be non-directive, or 'person-centred' (Rogers, 1939, 1942), and concerned not with finding a 'cure' but rather with setting up a supportive climate and relationship within which a disturbed or disordered person could find self-acceptance, understanding and personal growth (Carl R. Rogers Collection, 2003). Rogers promoted his ideas at a time when psychologists were 'heavily experimental, "rat-oriented", distrustful of clinical psychology and sceptical of his [Rogers'] views' (De Carvalho, 1991, p. 23), but his non-directive form of psychotherapy came to be widely used as an alternative to psychiatry and psychoanalysis.

Later, through his work with encounter groups – groups in which participants can express their feelings free from the usual social constraints – Rogers became interested in education. He encouraged teachers to become more personal, innovative and non-directive in their teaching, arguing that their goal should be to nurture students rather than control their learning (De Carvalho, 1991; Rogers, 1969).

Both he and Maslow emphasised the importance of freedom and choice for mental and emotional health. Education

Source: Getty Images/The LIFE Picture Collection/Michael Rougier

FIGURE 7.6 Rogers believed that a supportive, non-directive relationship helps individuals begin to heal themselves.

contributed to these goals by providing a nurturing environment in which learners could follow their interests. This could not be achieved through traditional educational programs, with their emphasis on the delivery of a fixed curriculum. A new, **non-directive teaching** approach was needed that would free students to develop their talents through self-directed activity.

non-directive teaching
Teaching in which the teacher is a facilitator, guiding students and nurturing their learning

BOX 7.4 CASE STUDY

THE CLASS FORUM

The idea of conducting a class forum in which all participants – teacher, aides and students alike – have equal say may strike some teachers as too challenging for primary school-aged children, or even as a practice which could, potentially, undermine the teacher's authority in the classroom. One teacher, however, who works in a small, rural school in NSW, believes her weekly classroom forum is a cohesive practice that promotes ownership of classroom behaviour and culture, and provides an opportunity for students to cultivate higher-order thinking and communication skills.

At these forums, participants have the chance to discuss their respective school and classroom experiences. They may choose to air concerns about problems or acknowledge positive developments. At the outset of each forum, the teacher reminds participants that they must raise their hands to speak. Although the teacher plays the role of forum facilitator, at no point do the teacher's comments or tone of voice serve to position her as an authority figure in the forum. The teacher also starts each forum with a reminder of active listening principles, and stresses that responses to comments should be respectful, not dismissive or critical. Consequently, each forum is a free-flowing exchange of ideas during which students offer their opinions without fear of being corrected or ridiculed.

On one occasion, a student expressed his frustration about the frequency of reprimands he experienced in the classroom. The teacher modelled active listening by paraphrasing his comments to show that she had genuinely heard and understood him, and by indicating that she appreciated his feeling of frustration. Significantly, and as a result of the teacher's skilful facilitation of the forum, what was then discussed was not the specific content of the boy's actions and why they warranted reprimands, but what he might be doing to bring about this situation; for example, other students suggested that perhaps he needed to listen more carefully to the teacher's instructions. The upshot of this discussion was that the student concerned was encouraged by his fellow forum participants to reflect on his own behaviour, and that the teacher gained an insight into how frequent reprimands were making this student feel about being in the classroom.

At another forum, a student commented that the incidence of disruptive behaviour in the classroom had decreased and that the class was achieving more as a result. In this way, the weekly forum gave students the chance to acknowledge and celebrate their achievements as a group.

The success of these forums is due largely to the teacher's facilitation skills. By modelling active listening; relating personally with students by using nicknames, eye contact and humour; and by judiciously and efficiently steering the discussion away from attempted disruptions and focusing on positive contributions, this teacher uses the weekly forum to consolidate an inclusive and democratic classroom culture.

Source: Anne Warburton

CourseMateExpress

Online Resources
Go further: Try active listening for yourself on this text's website

ACTIVITIES

1 How does this description of a teacher's practice reflect a humanist approach?
2 What challenges might there be in running class forums such as this? How do they relate to the challenges to Rogers' ideas and to humanist approaches presented in this chapter?

Strengths of Rogers' educational ideas

The strength of Rogers' ideas is in his emphasis on the value of each individual, on the importance of teachers having a positive view of children, and on the need for teachers to actively listen to children. Also significant is his concern that teachers create in their classrooms a climate of trust to support and enhance children's social, emotional and cognitive development. In a meta-analysis, Cornelius-White (2007) found a number of aspects of Rogers' learner-centred approach to have benefits for students' cognitive behaviour and emotional outcomes. Variables of positive relationships, non-directivity, empathy, warmth, and encouragement of thinking and learning all showed above-average correlations (compared with more traditional approaches) with variables such as participation, critical thinking, satisfaction, mathematics achievement, self-esteem, verbal achievement and positive motivation.

Limitations of Rogers' educational ideas

The main limitation of Rogers' ideas is that he presented no guidelines to help teachers who lack the personal or professional skills needed to implement a non-directive program. There are also few suggestions for helping students who lack motivation and are underachieving, or for coping with disruptive behaviour. In addition, the procedures Rogers described may not be appropriate for students who lack the language or cognitive skills needed to negotiate effective classroom arrangements (Kohn, 1996; Porter, 2000).

Box 7.5 discusses the implications of applying Rogers' ideas in the classroom.

BOX 7.5 IMPLICATIONS FOR EDUCATORS

APPLYING ROGERS' IDEAS IN THE CLASSROOM

The major impact of humanist psychology on educational practice has been felt through the work of Rogers (1969, 1983; Rogers & Freiberg, 1994) and his belief that positive human relationships provide children with a context within which they are free to grow. He criticised the traditional approach to education, with its:

> prescribed curriculum, similar assignments for all students, lecturing as almost the only mode of instruction, standard tests by which all students are externally evaluated, and instructor-chosen grades as the measure of learning.
>
> Source: Rogers (1983, p. 21).

Rogers argued that:

- teachers should be non-directive, focusing on their role as a facilitator, guiding students, nurturing their learning and developing student–teacher partnerships, rather than being primarily concerned with subject matter and instructional objectives
- the key to effective education lies not in the curriculum, but in the development of a positive and supportive relationship between learner and teacher
- teachers should treat students with genuineness, empathy and 'unconditional positive regard' – their acceptance is not conditional on students' ability, behaviour or ideas
- the role of the non-directive teacher is to nurture the learner as a person, rather than to instruct
- rather than talking, the teacher needs to listen actively or reflectively
- the key to achieving effective education is in the quality of the relationship between the learner and teacher.

THE PROGRESSIVE EDUCATION MOVEMENT

In the first half of the 20th century, when educators emphasised subject mastery in the context of a traditional classroom, humanists such as John Dewey (1859–1952) began to advocate 'experience-based', 'child-oriented' or **progressive education** that was based on a commitment to democratic ideals. The different forms of progressive education that developed in response to these ideas – usually referred to as 'child-centred' education in Britain, 'open education' in the USA (Darling, 1990, p. 43) and 'progressive education' in Australia (Barcan, 1980) – involved classrooms that provided a warm, caring climate, and that built on children's interests and experiences. Greater emphasis was placed on children's

progressive education
A child-centred approach to education based on a commitment to democratic ideals

thinking, feelings and effective communication than on their acquisition of knowledge 'that may soon be obsolete or forgotten' (Walberg, 1986, p. 226). Students were encouraged to develop personal values and a clear sense of self. The teacher's task was to provide a stimulating environment in which children would be actively involved in the learning process. Strategies included using small groups, individual instruction, flexible timetabling, mixed-ability groups and a reduced emphasis on grading. School would be fun and students would be motivated to learn.

Characteristics of progressive education

The most important characteristics of progressive education reflect the humanist concern with the unique characteristics of each child, and a belief in the capacity of each individual to realise their full potential. Darling (1994) identified some of the critical features of child-centred approaches to learning:

- Development in childhood is seen as a natural progression; children are not miniature adults.
- Children are naturally active. Education involves them in mental (creative) and physical activity.
- Children are respected for their individual talents and needs. Different needs are recognised, diversity is valued and conformity is avoided.
- The curriculum is determined in terms of each child's needs and interests. The classroom atmosphere is relaxed and children are responsible for their own learning; they are 'free to learn'.

Descriptions of humanist education, or what came to be called progressive education, can be found in Dennison (1969), Kohl (1968, 1969), Neill (1968), and in the accounts of those who attempted to establish such schools in the 1970s (see, for example, Conroy, 1980). With the growth of concerns about standards of schooling in the 1980s, the progressive movement lost favour, but humanist principles continued to be implemented in schools. The curricula in most early childhood programs and primary classrooms in Australasia follow humanist principles, including the use of cooperative group work, individual contracts and child-centred teaching. They have been built on constructivist models of learning and teaching (see Chapter 6), but in addition to the cognitive focus there is a concern for children's social and emotional wellbeing. In recent times, there has been a resurgence of interest in humanist aspects of education.

THINK ABOUT

- What difficulties can you see in trying to implement the principles of progressive education in mainstream classrooms?
- What are the potential benefits of progressive education principles?

SOME EXAMPLES OF HUMANIST MODELS IN SCHOOLS IN AUSTRALIA AND NEW ZEALAND

Humanist principles are evident in classroom programs that are described as 'open' or 'open-space' (Bennett, Andreae, Hegarty & Wade, 1980; Doyle, 1986; Sharples, 1990). Also exemplifying these principles is the **Reggio Emilia** approach to early education, which was developed in the northern Italian city of Reggio Emilia and which uses a constructivist project-based approach with a particular focus on children expressing their ideas in many different language modes (such as drawing, sculpture, dramatic play, writing and so on) (Edwards, Gandini & Forman, 1998; New, 2003; Turner & Krechevsky, 2003). Examples of non-traditional or alternative schools in Australia include 'Preshil', the Margaret Lyttle Memorial School in Melbourne; and the Brisbane Independent School. In New Zealand, alternative schools include Tamariki School, and Unlimited Paenga Tawhiti School, a government

Reggio Emilia
A system of education for the early childhood years, with a particular focus on children expressing their ideas in many different language modes

Source: Getty Images/Fat Camera

FIGURE 7.7 Most early years classrooms embody humanist principles with child-centred approaches that develop the whole child.

CourseMateExpress

Online Resources
Watch a **video** of a teacher talking about her approach to humanist education on this text's website

school in Christchurch. Schools based on the educational philosophy of Rudolf Steiner (1865–1925), who was an Austrian-born philosopher and educationalist concerned with the physical, spiritual and mental aspects of children's development, and Maria Montessori (1870–1952), who was an Italian physician and educator who believed in nurturing children's natural love of learning, can be described as humanistic in orientation (Lange & Sletten, 2002).

The Dalton Plan was first implemented in the USA in 1920 and continues to be used in a number of Australian schools; for example, in Ascham in Sydney and the secondary program at the Perth Montessori School. It is based on an individualised, child-centred approach to learning that seeks to introduce the features of a democratic community within the framework of a progressive school. Within the Dalton Plan, each curriculum area is divided into a set of monthly contracts and daily assignments. Students are free to plan their own work timetables, although they are also responsible for finishing one assignment before they begin another. Group work is encouraged (Edwards, 1991; Semel, 1992).

Home schooling, an alternative form of education provided by parents for their children at home, is also based on a humanistic desire for an education that is sensitive to children's unique talents and needs (Rivero, 2002; Romanowski, 2001). 'Unschooling' (Holt, 1977) goes a step further, allowing children to direct their learning, and to learn through activities they choose, with their parents and others as facilitators.

Many middle-school programs in Australia are also based on humanist principles, with the aim of engaging young adolescents in schooling by focusing on students' needs and giving them direction over what and how they learn (Dinham & Rowe, 2008).

Examples of teaching strategies that share common elements with humanist ideas, and that have been widely used and evaluated, include 'cooperative learning', 'problem-based learning', 'peer tutoring', 'team teaching', 'family-based groups', 'ungraded schools' and 'open-plan schools'. Many of these approaches, such as cooperative learning (described in detail later in this chapter) and peer tutoring, are also the domain of cognitive learning theory (described in Chapter 6).

The Queensland School Reform Longitudinal Study (Queensland Department of Education, 2001), which examined effective teaching practices in schools, identified connectedness, a supportive classroom environment and the recognition of difference, together with intellectual quality, as 'productive pedagogies' observed in classrooms (see Box 7.6). It recognised that effective teaching–learning practices consider and involve the whole child in learning. Other States in Australia (see, for example, NSW Department of Education and Training, 2003) have developed similar models of pedagogy to Queensland's.

BOX 7.6 RESEARCH LINKS

PRODUCTIVE PEDAGOGIES: THE QUEENSLAND SCHOOL REFORM LONGITUDINAL STUDY

From 1998 to 2000, 975 classroom lessons were observed in 24 Queensland schools, in an effort to identify classroom practices that resulted in social and academic benefits for *all* students. Teachers were rated as 'high', 'average' or 'low' in the 'productive pedagogies' of intellectual quality, connectedness, supportive classroom environment and recognition of difference. The study found the following differences between high- and low-scoring teachers.

HIGH SCORING TEACHERS	LOW SCORING TEACHERS
• acknowledged that they could not force students to learn	• expressed the belief that students were responsible for their own learning
• considered themselves responsible for providing opportunities for student learning	• held that factors totally outside the teacher's control largely 'determine' student outcomes
• viewed all learners as capable of improving	• aimed instruction at the 'middle level' of the class
• spoke of themselves as facilitators of learning	
• saw it as their task to set up environments where students could explore, and where there was some openness about what students would produce	• assumed that some students would learn, while others would not – it was up to the student
	• saw themselves as explainers of information
• focused more on the development of skills and concepts than on the transmission of content	• complained of lack of time to get through the curriculum
• were more prepared to 'subvert the curriculum' to create spaces for learning activities that they valued	• appeared to have a strong focus on content, rather than on skills or concepts
• problematised assessment practices more often than the low-scoring group	• did not as readily discuss assessment limitations
• tended to have high levels of extracurricular involvement	• seemed largely in the dark about the pedagogical work of their colleagues
• engaged in professional conversations with colleagues about their teaching	• were more guarded than their high-scoring colleagues about their own work
• were willing to talk about their failings and about changes they had made to their teaching.	• reported a greater sense of feeling under surveillance in conducting their work.

ACTIVITIES

1 To what extent does this study reflect a humanist approach to teaching and learning?

2 The 'productive pedagogies' framework has been challenged by a number of teachers and researchers (Mills & Goos, 2007). What do you consider to be 'productive pedagogies'? Are they characteristics of teaching that contribute to positive social and academic outcomes? Test your beliefs against the research literature. Can you find evidence to support them?

3 See www.education.qld.gov.au for more on the study, and on the productive pedagogies.

THINK ABOUT

■ How do you plan to balance in the classroom the goal of teaching content with the goal of meeting students' personal needs?

■ Can you think of situations when these two goals might be in conflict? (See the case study in **Box 13.12**.)

CHALLENGES TO HUMANIST APPROACHES

People who advocate teacher-dominated approaches to instruction criticise humanist models of education on the grounds that these lack the structure needed to ensure that the desired learning outcomes are achieved. The structures referred to here can include a formal course of study, clearly stated teaching objectives or learning outcomes, procedures for regular progress assessment, and defined instructional methods and materials (see Brady & Kennedy, 2012). This view is in conflict with that promoted by humanists, who are more concerned with children's personal and emotional development within a caring and supportive environment than with ensuring that set topics are covered and that students achieve prescribed learning goals. Choosing between these differing positions is a dilemma that must be resolved by parents and anyone planning to become a teacher. The increasing demand for schools to be more accountable in terms of learning outcomes achieved by students can be seen as a reaction against the influence of humanist principles on school practices. Calls for schools (particularly those concerned with the middle years of schooling) to more closely reflect and respond to the needs and interests of students in turn represent a reaction against traditional approaches, and a return to humanist approaches (Hunter, 2007).

More-traditional educators who are critical of the progressive education movement argue that it is simply a fad that leads to 'watering-down the traditional curriculum and coddling students' (Richards & Combs, 1993, p. 256). However, a synthesis of research on open (or progressive) education reported by Walberg (1986) concluded that, provided the programs were not extremely radical, students in open-education programs were not academically disadvantaged when compared with other students. Moreover, they did substantially better on educational goals that were highly valued by educators, parents and students, such as cooperation, critical thinking, self-reliance and constructive attitudes. The more effective programs did not stress multi-age grouping, open space and team teaching, but did emphasise 'the role of the child in learning, use of diagnostic rather than norm-referenced evaluation, individualised instruction, and manipulative materials' (Walberg, 1986, p. 226) (see also Chapter 14).

CourseMateExpress

Online Resources
Consider your own views on how learning is best supported, using the **Develop Your Philosophy** tool on this text's website

HUMANISM AND EDUCATION TODAY

In keeping with their concern to educate the whole child, humanist educators have championed content in fields beyond the traditional curriculum areas covered by the Australian or New Zealand curricula. For example, citizenship and democracy (Freire, 1972, 1995; Giroux, 1983), morals, values and ethics (Veugelers, 2010), philosophy (Topping & Trickey, 2004), and spirituality (Palmer, 1983; Kessler, 2005) – noting that for humanists, 'spirituality' refers to the human spirit responding to experiences in the here and now – have been argued to be important subjects for schools to explore with students, not just in occasional lessons but on a regular basis. Some of these fields have been taken up within the national curriculum documents; in Australia, for example, in the general capability of ethical understanding, and in the Civics and citizenship curriculum (ACARA, 2012).

The content of curriculum is not the only influence of humanism in education today however; pedagogical approaches have also been shaped by humanism. Indeed, the humanist educators cited

FIGURE 7.8 Dialogue and student direction are important aspects of humanist approaches to learning.

above would argue that the content on its own does not reflect a humanist approach. The involvement of students in dialogue, in autonomously directing their learning, and in bringing their own concerns and thoughts to these topics is vital. Three main influences of humanism on pedagogy in schools can be observed:

■ Students are allowed to direct the goals and means of their learning.
■ The whole child is considered, particularly by focusing on the social and emotional aspects of learning.
■ The emphasis is on the relational aspects of learning, including dialogue and the use of cooperative group work.

STUDENT-DIRECTED LEARNING

Instructional models derived from or strongly influenced by humanistic principles give greater primacy to the student's role in the learning process. In contrast to the behavioural models discussed in Chapter 5, where the teacher is seen as controlling all aspects of instruction, the teacher's role in a humanist classroom is more indirect.

The humanist teacher is expected to be open and honest with students as a way of setting up an authentic humanist relationship with them. Such teachers are responsible for planning what happens in the classroom, and for providing an array of intellectual activities that will develop creativity and critical-thinking skills. They should strive to value students' ideas, culture and language, and nurture students' emerging sense of identity and self-esteem. The humanist teacher's role is to facilitate learning, although humanist teachers have no direct control over how and what students learn, which is instead controlled by students.

In the humanist teaching situation, the teacher needs to ensure that students are motivated to learn (see Chapter 8). This is where one of the main characteristics of humanistic approaches to teaching becomes evident. Humanist teachers take advantage of children's natural activity, curiosity and interest in learning, ensuring that students are not 'turned off' by negative experiences at school or by a mismatch between what students want to learn and what teachers want them to learn (Darling, 1990). Students are encouraged to use their inner resources in order to become fully functioning individuals (Rogers, 1969). While Maslow and Rogers contributed to the emergence of a humanistic view of education, the ideas of philosophers such as John Dewey (1916, 1937) and the movement that is referred to as 'progressive education' are also relevant.

EDUCATION FOR SOCIAL AND EMOTIONAL WELLBEING

Concerns about the rate of mental health problems such as anxiety and depression experienced by children and young people have contributed to increasing focus on student resilience and wellbeing. The depression- and anxiety-focused organisation beyondblue reported in 2014 that 26.4 per cent of young Australians had experienced a mental health disorder in the previous 12 months. In the same year, stress was reported as the principal concern of young people aged 16–19 in a Mission Australia Youth Survey (Fildes et al., 2014). These issues also have consequences for student learning. For example, Suldo, Thalji and Ferron (2011) found in a longitudinal study that wellbeing predicted academic achievement a year later. A number of strategies have been employed to address this need.

Pekrun (2014) stressed the importance of teachers recognising students' emotions, given the strong effects they have on learning. As well as attending to students' emotions, teachers can teach students skills to understand and regulate their own emotions. Drawing initially on work such as Maslow's theory suggesting the influence of social and emotional needs on learning, teachers are encouraged to develop students' social and emotional skills as 'basic skills' alongside academic skills, to 'educate the whole child' (Elias, 2003, 2006).

Elias (2003, 2006) identified 10 principles for developing academic and also social and emotional skills in schools:

1   Learning requires caring. Caring relationships and warm, yet challenging classroom environments are important for effective and lasting academic learning, and social and emotional learning.

2   Teach everyday life skills explicitly at every grade level. These include the five key social and emotional competencies identified by the Collaborative for Academic, Social and Emotional Learning (CASEL): self-awareness, self-management, social awareness, relationship skills and responsible decision making.

3   Link social and emotional instruction to other school services such as anti-bullying, drug-education and conflict-resolution programs, and support services for students experiencing difficulty.

4   Use goal setting and problem solving to focus instruction, and to provide direction and motivation for learning.

5   Vary instructional strategies to cater for the preferences and styles of all learners.

6   Build empathy by promoting community service, thereby fostering the generalisation of social and emotional skills.

7   Involve parents in partnerships with the school to maximise students' academic learning, and their social and emotional learning.

8   Develop social and emotional skills gradually and systematically, building on the existing strengths and needs of the school setting, and integrating social and emotional learning with academic learning.

9   Prepare and support staff with ongoing professional development.

10 Evaluate efforts to promote social and emotional learning through ongoing monitoring of the program, assessment of outcomes, and feedback from teachers, learners and parents.

Advocates of social and emotional learning programs cite the changes they can make to students' behaviour and attitudes to school, and through them, to students' academic achievement. A meta-analysis of school-based social and emotional learning programs found benefits for students' social and emotional skills, attitudes, behaviour and academic achievement (Durlak et al., 2011). Sklad et al. (2012) confirmed these outcomes and found additional benefits for mental health from such programs.

Positive education

positive education
Applies the principles of positive psychology to education

Positive education applies the principles of positive psychology, developed by Martin Seligman among others, to classroom contexts. The approach is termed 'positive' as it focuses on individuals' strengths rather than their weaknesses, on positive experiences rather than problems, and on what is working well rather than what is not working (Noble & McGrath, 2008). While Seligman (Seligman & Csikszentmihalyi, 2000) described positive psychology as improving on and being more scientific than humanistic psychology, positive education shares a number of the elements of humanistic approaches to education. Seligman et al. (2009; see also Seligman, 2011) proposed five pillars of wellbeing: positive emotion, engagement, relationships, meaning and accomplishment. In positive education, teachers teach these skills to students both explicitly and implicitly. Box 7.7 describes a framework of practices schools can employ to put the pillars into action.

Source: Alamy Stock Photo/Cathyrose Melloan

FIGURE 7.9 Student wellbeing can be addressed by teaching social and emotional learning, with benefits for students' relationships, behaviour, learning and mental health.

BOX 7.7 IMPLICATIONS FOR EDUCATORS

THE POSITIVE EDUCATIONAL PRACTICES FRAMEWORK

Noble and McGrath (2008) suggested that schools can become places that promote wellbeing by teaching essential skills related to the five pillars identified by Seligman.

Foundation One: Social and emotional competency

This includes teaching of values and skills: *prosocial values* of, for example, respect, cooperation, tolerance and compassion; *resilience skills* including optimistic thinking, seeking assistance and using humour appropriately; *social skills* such as sharing resources, cooperating, disagreeing respectfully, negotiation and conflict management; *emotional literacy skills* that enable students to understand and manage their own emotions and those of others; and *personal achievement skills*, which include recognising one's own strengths and weaknesses, thinking about one's own thinking (or metacognition; see Chapter 6), goal setting, planning and persistence.

Foundation Two: Positive emotions

Rather than focusing on managing negative emotions or attitudes, schools are encouraged to create and nurture positive emotions in students such as:

- *feelings of belonging*, by using cooperative learning approaches, and communicating to students that they are cared for through buddy programs and peer tutoring
- *feelings of safety*, by discouraging put-downs and having an effective positive behaviour management plan (see Chapter 14)
- *feelings of satisfaction, affirmation and pride*, by celebrating success
- *feelings of excitement and enjoyment*, using games for learning and fun
- *feelings of optimism about school success*, by explicitly teaching optimistic thinking, focusing students' attention on positives, and encouraging attributions of effort rather than ability (see Chapter 8).

Foundation Three: Positive relationships

This includes both *positive peer relationships*, which can be encouraged through cooperative learning (discussed later in this chapter), class meetings (see **Box 7.4**), cross-age house systems and peer-support programs, and *positive teacher–student relationships* that teachers can develop by being interested in their students, effective classroom-management programs (see Chapter 14), having more sustained time with students, and being available for students outside class time.

Foundation Four: Engagement through strengths

Teachers identify each student's learning and character strengths, and provide opportunities for them to use and further develop strengths and to work on weaknesses.

Foundation Five: A sense of meaning and purpose

The curriculum should have relevance to students' lived experience. Approaches such as service learning, in which students engage in curriculum learning through service projects, provide a sense of purpose, particularly when students are involved in decision making. Such projects can be arranged within the school as well as outside, as, for example, when one class designs and produces a learning resource for a younger class, or when a group of students travels overseas to work with a disadvantaged community.

Source: Adapted from Noble and McGrath (2008).

ACTIVITIES

1   Think about how these skills might affect students' learning in schools. Investigate the research literature that supports their role in learning.
2   Consider a school you are familiar with. To what degree are these skills taught and encouraged? What could the school do to further develop a culture promoting student wellbeing?

More than 100 schools in Australia were members of the Positive Education Schools Association in Australia in 2017. King's College in Auckland also employs a positive education approach. It is notable that, on the Positive Education Schools Association website (www.pesa.edu.au), the majority of schools adopting this approach are non-government schools in privileged areas, although an increasing number of government schools are members.

THINK ABOUT

■ Refer to the productive pedagogies identified in **Box 7.6**. How do they compare with the pillars of positive education detailed in **Box 7.7**?

Positive education is a more recent movement than social and emotional learning programs, and the research evidence has not yet built up to evaluate this approach (Martin, 2016). Several longitudinal studies of the effectiveness of positive education programs in Australian schools are in train, and it will be interesting to see the results of these programs for student wellbeing and learning. Kristjánsson (2012) evaluated the positive education movement in respect to educational psychology. He identified difficulties with some of the underpinning theory in positive psychology, in particular the clarity of the definition of happiness (equated with wellbeing), and cautioned that some aspects of positive education, such as working first on building signature strengths, and the 'broaden and build' approach that asks students to pretend or imagine positive emotions, require a theoretical and research basis to support them. Other elements, such as teaching social and emotional skills, and mindfulness, draw on approaches described in this chapter.

Mindfulness

Mindfulness is drawn from Buddhist practices of meditation, and is a practice that has been applied in clinical therapy as well as in schools. It involves an open, non-judgemental focus on one's experience in the current situation through meditation, breathing and/or yoga. While mindfulness training was originally developed with adults, it has been adapted to work with pre-school, primary and secondary students. Mindfulness activities for children can include placing a stuffed toy on their belly, and asking the child to rock it to sleep with their breathing, to focus attention on breath, and using a hula hoop to 'scan' and focus on different parts of their body one by one. Activities have also been developed for adolescents, for example asking them to imagine riding their emotions as if they were a surfer on a wave (Lyons & DeLange, 2016).

Executive functions were introduced in Chapter 3, where we discussed their importance for academic success at school. Lyons & DeLange (2016) reviewed work linking mindfulness training and the executive functions of attention, working memory and inhibitory control. While more research is needed with children, initial indications are that mindfulness training can improve these functions, as well as regulation of emotions (discussed in Chapter 4), which is also demonstrated to link to academic achievement.

Broderick & Metz (2016) examined the usefulness of mindfulness training for supporting resilience in the face of potential stresses in adolescence, through emotion regulation. (Resilience is discussed in Chapter 2 and Chapter 11.) In studies of a mindfulness program (Learning to BREATHE) implemented in a number of secondary schools, they found that mindfulness training in the classroom program improved students' symptoms of depression, anxiety, psychosomatic illness, social connectedness and perceived stress, and resulted in improved emotion regulation. Zoogman, Goldberg, Howy & Miller (2015) conducted a meta-analysis of studies of mindfulness interventions with young people (6–21

CourseMateExpress

Online Resources
Go further: Explore one school's approach to Positive Education via the link on this text's website

mindfulness
A series of practices supporting deliberate focus on current experience, while suspending judgement

years) and found that it showed small but significant effects, with larger effects on psychological symptoms such as anxiety, depression and substance abuse. They suggested from their review of the literature that one of the reasons for mindfulness's influence on these symptoms is its use of decentring, emotion regulation, focused attention, and disruption of rumination (repeatedly going over a past negative experience) that is related to worrying.

In schools, mindfulness may be one means used to train students to regulate their emotions and attention, and has been successfully applied for students with ADHD, as well as those experiencing stress, depression and anxiety, as we have seen above (Zenner, Herrnleben-Kurz & Walach, 2014). Zenner and colleagues undertook a meta-analysis of school-based mindfulness programs and found a wide range of programs in practice. Overall, mindfulness interventions were found to influence cognitive performance in attention and learning, resilience and stress, but the authors cautioned that more research is needed to further examine these findings. Cresswell (2017) reviewed randomised controlled trials of mindfulness interventions, and reported that classroom interventions can reduce stress and aggressive behaviour, and improve cognitive performance in students. An Australian randomised controlled trial of a mindfulness program in schools in Victoria is described in Box 7.8.

BOX 7.8 RESEARCH LINKS

SMILING MIND: MINDFULNESS MEDITATION IN AUSTRALIAN SCHOOLS

The Smiling Mind education program aims to support mindfulness meditation in classrooms, through lesson plans designed for years 1–12. Recordings accessed via a website lead the class through a meditation exercise. Students or parents can also access the exercises at home via the website or a free app. Examples of exercises include focusing on breathing, body scans in which people successively focus on each different part of their body, mirroring movement, and exploring the experience of sounds or tastes or everyday activities such as walking. At the end of each session, teachers are encouraged to facilitate a debriefing session, when students can explore and share their experience, thoughts and feelings relating to the exercise, and access support. A 'take home activity' that can be practised at home is linked to each exercise.

The program can be freely accessed via an app and website, so it is available to students whether or not their school is implementing the program, and to the whole school community.

A study of the program conducted in 2015 by Deakin University and Insight SRC, and published on the Smiling Mind website, examined use of the program in 12 primary and secondary schools in Victoria. It found benefits for both teachers and students who participated in Smiling Mind. Compared with control groups at the same schools, students who participated at least three times a week over eight weeks reported improved sleep quality, ability to cope with student misbehaviour, feeling safe at school, and lower classroom disruption and experience of bullying. Those students who reported lower levels of wellbeing at the start of the program also showed improvements in levels of psychological distress, positive wellbeing, ability to manage emotions, concentration, and behaviour. The study authors concluded that mindfulness directly affected students' engagement in learning and positive wellbeing. Support of concentration and management of emotions in turn influenced quality of sleep and reduction in negative wellbeing.

Teachers who participated in the program (using the exercises themselves at least three times a week over five weeks) also benefited, reporting improved sleep quality, less psychological distress and tension, less difficulty concentrating, and improved ability to describe and accept their emotions.

Find the Smiling Mind program, and a link to the research study at https://www.smilingmind.com.au/our-programs/mindfulness-in-the-classroom/.

COOPERATIVE LEARNING

In Chapter 6 we discussed the centrality of cooperative learning in the constructivist classroom. Along with constructivist theorists, humanists value the importance of student-centred classrooms that emphasise student interaction as a way of encouraging learners to make learning meaningful. Glasser (see Chapter 14) believed that cooperative learning was critical in enabling students to gain a sense of belonging and exercise control over their own learning, especially by working with and helping others.

There are many ways in which classrooms may be organised to facilitate student learning (see Chapter 14). Some approaches encourage individualistic and competitive work habits, while others encourage cooperation among students who learn from one another in groups. The way in which you organise your classroom will depend on a number of factors, including your level of expertise and familiarity with the group, what and how you would like the students to learn, and your philosophy of learning and teaching (Palinscar & Herrenkohl, 2005). Johnson and Johnson (2014) identified three ways in which teachers can organise their lessons and classrooms. Each of these approaches achieves different outcomes, as listed below:

1   Students may work *competitively* to do better than their peers on norm-referenced tests (see Chapter 13). Those who know they have a chance of success are highly motivated to work as fast and as accurately as they can, while the rest of the class loses interest.

2   Students may work *individually*, at their own speed, to achieve personal goals on criterion-referenced tests. Students are encouraged to focus on their own learning, to ignore others and to see their own achievements as unrelated to the progress of others.

3   Students may work *cooperatively* in small groups to achieve shared goals that benefit the student and other members of the group. Group members develop an interdependence and a pride in one another's achievements, and recognise that group goals will only be reached if everyone collaborates on each task.

Cooperative learning, the most humanistic of these three alternatives, refers to learning situations in which small groups of students are encouraged and motivated to cooperate and help each other learn in order to gain contingent rewards. Success is dependent on all working together to achieve a common goal. There is a shared-incentive system, with students' work evaluated in terms of personal and group outcomes.

Cooperative groups can operate formally, with students working on a set task or parts of a task during regular class periods (such as the Friday mathematics class), or over a brief or an extended period of time (for example, for three weeks in Term 1 or across the school year). Groups can also be informal, created as appropriate in a lesson to fulfil an immediate need, such as when students are asked to turn to their neighbours and spend five minutes clarifying their ideas about a particular topic. Johnson and Johnson (2014) pointed out two other ways cooperative learning occurs: in 'base groups', in which students support one another over an extended period; and in 'constructive controversy', in which students may take or hold different points of view, and work to come to an agreed position. Before working cooperatively, students need to be taught specific social skills to ensure that the group achieves its particular goals. Required skills include communication, conflict management and decision making, along with group trust-building exercises (Johnson and Johnson, 2014).

Two critical features of cooperative learning concern task structure and the use of contingent rewards. Students can work on a task cooperatively as a group, or individual students may undertake separate components of a common task. Rewards can be contingent on the group's successful completion of a task, or on the average achievement of the group's individual members. Slavin (2014) reviewed research on cooperative learning approaches, finding that group rewards based on individual marks are important to student achievement in cooperative learning. Some form of cooperative activity occurs in all types of group learning, but the use of a system of rewards that are contingent on group performance or on the sum of individual performances within the group is unique to cooperative learning. Slavin's (2014) review of research noted above found that the second of these reward systems is the more effective and that, in fact, cooperative activity without rewards has fewer results for student learning. Teachers often encourage students to share their ideas with others when they are working on a task, arguing that this is a form of cooperative learning (see Model 1 in Box 7.9). However, this type of arrangement does not use contingent rewards and so does not satisfy the criteria for cooperative learning. Models 2 and 3 in Box 7.9, which involve students working individually on elements for a joint outcome (Model 2) and working together for a joint outcome (Model 3), are examples of cooperative learning in practice.

BOX 7.9 CLASSROOM LINKS

ALTERNATIVE MODELS OF GROUP LEARNING

Model 1: Working individually on identical tasks for individual products

This appears to be a group of students working independently on a task. However, the students may share ideas and contribute to others' interest and motivation if the teacher builds such elements into the task. Otherwise, the students are simply working individually, since the task does not demand cooperation.

Model 2: Working individually on 'jigsaw' elements for a joint outcome

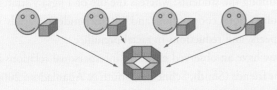

Each student works on one element of the task and parts are eventually fitted together, as in a jigsaw. No student can leave their part of the task incomplete and not jeopardise the group's task completion. With the jigsaw method of working, cooperation is built into the task, together with individual accountability.

Model 3: Working jointly on one task for a joint outcome

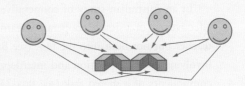

Here, students work cooperatively, as there is only one task. The contribution of each student is important for task completion.

Source: Adapted from Cowie, Smith, Boulton and Laver (1994, pp. 96–8).

Slavin (2014) described four major theories that have been proposed to explain the effects of cooperative learning on student learning achievement, and to provide guidance for cooperative learning design. All four theoretical perspectives on cooperative learning have empirical support. Slavin argued that rather than competing, the four theories can be integrated into a broader model that takes in all four dimensions. These are *motivational* theories, which emphasise the importance of group goals and individual accountability that motivate students to learn the set material and work towards a common outcome; *social cohesiveness* theories, which emphasise students' commitment to the group as the key motivating factor, and hence stress the importance of team building and social skill development; *developmental* theories that draw on Vygotsky's and Piaget's theories (described in detail in Chapter 3), which argued that children's cognition develops through interaction with their peers; and *cognitive elaboration* theories, which emphasise the importance of elaboration – as happens when students explain a concept to someone else, or argue for a particular point of view – to the building of links in long-term memory (this draws on information-processing theory, also described in Chapter 3).

Gillies (2014) focused on the ways that student and teacher talk contributes to both development and learning in cooperative learning, drawing on a number of studies. She concluded that students benefit from listening to one another's ideas, questioning, exploring challenging concepts, sharing strategies and thinking, and, as they explain their own thinking, develop metacognition (see Chapter 6 for more on this)

Johnson and Johnson (2014) identified a number of 21st-century issues that cooperative learning can help to prepare students for, by developing conflict-resolution and relationship skills, and attitudes of tolerance and respect: increasing global interdependence; greater numbers of democracies worldwide; the need for creative entrepreneurs; and the importance of interpersonal relationships, whether these are face-to-face or online.

THINK ABOUT

- Has cooperative learning featured in your educational experiences? If so, what did you like or dislike about it? What skills did you develop?

The impact of cooperative learning on prejudice

Sharan (1980, 1990) presented evidence to confirm claims that cooperative learning not only enhances children's academic progress, but also has a positive impact on interpersonal relationships in classrooms with students from different ethnic backgrounds; see also Duran (1994) and Box 7.10. The approach has also been found to be effective in enhancing the social acceptance of students with disabilities (see, for example, Jacques, Wilton & Townsend, 1998). Walker and Crogan (1998) confirmed these findings, though they also demonstrated the importance of the type of cooperative learning model used in a classroom (see Box 7.9) and the need for training in appropriate social skills as a prerequisite for success.

In an Australian study of cooperative learning, Walker and Crogan (1998) compared the relative effectiveness of a simple cooperative learning environment, in which cooperation is encouraged by the teacher but not built into the task (see Box 7.9, Model 1), and **jigsaw**, a type of cooperative learning involving both cooperation and interdependence, in which each group member works individually on components of a shared task (see Box 7.9, Model 2). They reported that introducing tasks involving simple cooperation in the classroom can exacerbate existing ethnic tensions and **prejudice** (that is, a preconceived, uninformed opinion or feeling) among the students; whereas the use of a jigsaw strategy (Aronson, 2012a; Hedeen, 2003), which involves both cooperation and interdependence, leads to improved academic performance and liking of peers, and reductions in racial prejudice.

Cooperative-learning strategies such as jigsaw have an observed effect on interpersonal relations in classrooms, including finding more and different friends (Smith, Schneider, Smith & Ananiadou, 2004, p. 579). This is consistent with Gordon Allport's (1954) identification of the basic conditions needed to overcome prejudice, which are that:

- contact is direct and involves students from different ethnic (or disability, religious or socioeconomic) groups
- students are equal in status
- contact is concerned with common interests and goals.

Jigsaw learning strategies in context

Aronson (2012b) described how the jigsaw cooperative learning strategy was developed in 1971 in Austin, Texas, following the desegregation of public schools in the USA. At that time, residential areas in Austin were racially segregated, so students were 'bussed' to desegregated schools outside their own area. For the first time, students from White, African American and Hispanic backgrounds came together in

jigsaw
A form of cooperative learning in which each group member works individually on components of the one task

prejudice
A preconceived, uninformed opinion or feeling

desegregated classrooms. However, 'long-standing suspicion, fear and hostility' among students towards those from different ethnic backgrounds (Aronson, 2012b, p. 1) led to an explosive situation, with increasing levels of antagonism and aggression. Aronson and a team of graduate students were asked to help defuse growing classroom tension.

Observation of teaching procedures in the desegregated classrooms showed that the use of traditional individualistic and competitive teaching methods exacerbated student anger. Research had demonstrated that simply bringing groups of children into contact with other groups only heightened any conflicts that already existed between the groups (Sherif, 1967). However, there was also evidence that such contact could be positive when an activity was introduced that involved sharing, particularly where positive interdependence and cooperation was involved (Allport, 1954; Brown & Turner, 1981; Sherif, 1967). Aronson concluded that the climate in the desegregated classrooms needed to be changed from individualistic and competitive to group-focused and cooperative. It was on the basis of this decision that Aronson and his colleagues devised the jigsaw strategy, a cooperative learning technique that required students to work *cooperatively* and *interdependently* to complete a set task.

Working with Grade 5 teachers, the jigsaw strategy was developed around a unit concerned with biographies of famous Americans. Students were divided into groups of five or six, mixed in terms of gender and ethnicity. Biographies to be used in the jigsaw lesson were then 'jig-sawed' (Abrami et al., 1995, p. 143) or divided into five or six segments (for example, family history, childhood and adolescence, early employment, middle age, final years and major contribution). Each student in a group was allocated one segment of the biography, with instructions not to let others in the group have access to that segment. After reading their own segment several times, each student left their own group to join others who had been given the same segment in a temporary 'expert' group. The task of the expert group was to identify the main points in their segment and practise ways of presenting this material to their own group. Once this process was completed (about 10–15 minutes), students returned to their jigsaw groups to teach what they had learnt to the others in the group. In this way, each member of a jigsaw group became an expert in one part of the learning task and was instructed in the remaining parts by the other experts in the group. At the end of the learning period, students were tested individually on their knowledge of the topic as a whole. A case study reported by Aronson (2005) is presented in Box 7.10.

The effectiveness of cooperative learning

Many forms of cooperative learning have been described in the literature (see, for example, Cowie and Rudduck, 1990; Dunne and Bennett, 1990). Examples of cooperative learning in practice can be found in programs such as Group Investigation (Sharan & Sharan, 1992); Learning Together (Johnson & Johnson, 1999); Student Team Learning, which includes Student Teams and Achievement Divisions (STAD) (Slavin, 1994) and Teams–Games–Tournaments (TGT) (De Vries & Slavin, 1978); and Jigsaw (Aronson, Blaney, Stephen, Sikes & Snapp, 1978; Slavin, 1994).

Summarising the results of studies of the efficacy of cooperative learning, Good and Brophy (2008, pp. 200–1) concluded the following:

- Cooperative learning methods can realistically be implemented in many classroom situations and are likely to have positive effects. They do not replace whole-class instruction, however, but are best used as an adjunct to it, with teachers providing instruction of key content.
- Positive effects result from the use of group rewards rather than the cooperative nature of the activities. Cooperation should be emphasised over competition.
- Students need to be supported for cooperative learning, with explicit teaching of required skills such as listening, or dealing with disagreement, and careful choice of tasks and activities suitable for cooperative work.

BOX 7.10 CASE STUDY

A COOPERATIVE-LEARNING EXPERIENCE FOR A STUDENT FROM A MINORITY ETHNIC BACKGROUND

Carlos, a Grade 5 Hispanic student attending a recently desegregated school, was shy, insecure and spoke English as a second language with a slight accent. His previous school was a poorly resourced, substandard school that catered for local Hispanic students, but he now went by bus to a well-resourced school in a middle-class part of town, attended by a mix of White, African-American and Hispanic students.

Participating in the small jigsaw group was initially very confronting for Carlos, particularly when he had to speak in front of his group to give them information on his segment of the biography of Eleanor Roosevelt. The other students in his group ridiculed Carlos for his stammering, blushing and poor English. Hearing comments such as 'You're stupid', 'You don't know what you're doing' and 'You can't even speak English' (Aronson, 2005, p. 2), a graduate student working with Aronson reminded the group that they needed to learn what Carlos knew about Eleanor Roosevelt's life because the test would be in 15 minutes. The students quickly realised that they needed to listen to Carlos so that they could do well on the test. By the end of the first week, the rest of the group had begun to help Carlos to communicate better, asking relevant questions and encouraging him to articulate more clearly the information they needed to be given. Carlos gradually became more confident and began to see the others in his group as friendly and helpful. His communication skills increased and the other students realised that the boy was not stupid. All began to like the others in their group. Their stereotypes about other ethnic groups began to change. They enjoyed school more and absenteeism decreased.

The jigsaw lessons amounted to only three or four hours each week, so students in the jigsaw classrooms spent most of the time in a competitive classroom environment. After eight weeks, when tested objectively on levels of prejudice and ethnic stereotyping, there was evidence that even a small amount of time spent in a jigsaw group resulted in students expressing less prejudice and negative stereotyping, and higher levels of self-confidence. Compared with their peers in traditional classes, the jigsaw students had learnt to cooperate within a group, to empathise with others ('put themselves into another person's shoes') and to tolerate poor performance in both themselves and others. In addition, academic achievement improved, with less successful (or African American and Hispanic) students in jigsaw classes scoring significantly higher on objective tests than similar students in traditional classes, while good (or White) students, who had been encouraged to see themselves as 'teachers' within the jigsaw group, performed at much the same level as similar students in traditional settings.

Source: Adapted from Aronson, E. (2005). 'Jigsaw classroom: History', from http://jigsaw.org/history/, reproduced by permission of Dr Elliot Aronson.

ACTIVITIES

1   How do you explain the impact of cooperative group work on Carlos? Which aspects of the jigsaw technique are crucial for achieving these changes?

2   How might academically gifted students respond to jigsaw classes? What about students with learning difficulties?

3   For teachers, what are likely to be the positive and negative aspects of using a jigsaw technique?

4   If you were Carlos' teacher, would you recommend that a cooperative approach be continued in the next school year? Why? Why not?

5   What other strategies could be used to help address the difficulties experienced by students like Carlos in ethnically diverse classroom settings? (You may find some ideas for this in Chapter 11.)

For subjects such as mathematics, when practice of skills is important, the effects are greatest when there are group rewards, and when students are accountable not only for their own mastery of the task but also for their teammates' mastery. In subjects such as social sciences, in which analysis, synthesis and evaluation are key, cooperative learning methods that emphasise constructive controversy, group discussion, and assigned roles and responsibilities may be more effective.

Although there is considerable evidence of the effectiveness of cooperative methods for enhancing student achievement and learning (Johnson & Johnson, 2014), there is also evidence that students and teachers can experience problems when cooperative learning strategies are introduced into a classroom (Gillies, 2007). Gillies (2008) demonstrated that structured cooperation (that is, groups that are structured in terms of size and composition, type of task, behavioural expectations, individual and group responsibilities, and teacher's role) was more likely to result in positive social and emotional outcomes than unstructured group work.

Applying cooperative learning in teaching

Gillies (2007) identified the following responsibilities for teachers when establishing cooperative learning.

- *Structure groups to ensure positive interdependence, interaction, individual accountability, interpersonal and small-group skills (see* Box 7.10*), and group evaluation of the process.* Interdependence ensures that members are working towards group rather than individual goals. Teaching interpersonal skills is vital for the success of cooperative learning, and should be an ongoing focus. Some training in effective communication (communicating ideas, listening, trying to understand another's point of view and constructively giving feedback), as well as in sharing, taking turns, resolving conflicts, democratic decision making and learning to accept, support and trust others in the group, will be needed prior to the commencement of a cooperative activity, when interpersonal problems arise that students are unable to resolve, and as an ongoing program of development (see Cowie & Berdondini, 2001; Gillies, 2007; Goodwin, 1999). Giving group members the responsibility to evaluate their group skills and outcomes promotes responsibility for the group process as well as the product they produce.

- *Consider the size, ability and gender composition of groups. Group size can have an impact on the success of a cooperative learning program.* Groups need to be small enough to facilitate interaction and interdependence. Fuchs et al. (2000) reported that students working in pairs achieve superior levels of collaboration and higher performance scores than students working in small groups, but the level of cognitive functioning (an outcome of cognitive conflict; see Chapter 3) is higher in the small groups.

  Research by Lou et al. (1996) found that group composition makes a difference: low-ability children tend to learn more in mixed-ability groups, where they receive tutoring from others; medium-ability children learn more in same-ability groups, where they tend to be more active; and high-ability children learn equally well in either setting (although others have found that gifted children benefit from being with gifted peers; see Chapter 9 for a fuller discussion of this issue). In terms of gender, research cited by Gillies (2007) is mixed about whether same-sex or mixed-sex groups are more effective, with a balance between numbers of males and females and group dynamics influencing the outcomes.

- *Set tasks that encourage students to interact.* Examples of this are open-ended and discovery-learning tasks in which students interact over content, planning and decision making.

- *Ensure that all students can participate in the task.* This may mean making adjustments to allow the equal participation of students with learning difficulties, limited social or emotional skills, disabilities, language backgrounds other than English, and varied cultural backgrounds. Examples of adjustments include more tightly structured groups or tasks, consideration of particular combinations of students (avoiding combinations that are likely to have problems working together, for example), time limits on group work, assistive materials or technologies, and use of personal aides to support individuals.

- *Have clear expectations for students' task-related and interpersonal behaviours.* See Box 7.11 for an example of how group behaviours can be discussed with students.
- *Give students individual and group responsibilities.* The task itself should be carefully structured, with the final goals clearly stated and, in the case of the jigsaw strategy, the task and any resources designed so that they can be broken into roughly equivalent parts. Each student should be given a task and the responsibility to complete it within a set time frame and share the information with the group. Students can also be given particular roles (for example, the 'chairman', who ensures everyone gets a turn and that the group stays on track; the 'reporter', who compiles the group's efforts to report to the class; the 'researcher', who locates resources for the group to use). Individual accountability is important to avoid one student doing all the work, or the opposite (and sometimes simultaneous) problem of 'social loafing' – one student relying on the efforts of

BOX 7.11 IMPLICATIONS FOR EDUCATORS

TEACHING INTERPERSONAL AND SMALL-GROUP SKILLS

One way to help students understand what skills are needed in groups and to monitor their own skills is to have them draw up a chart like the following, describing what each skill would look and sound like. The chart could then be displayed to remind students of good interpersonal skills, and for students to refer to when evaluating their group skills.

SKILL	LOOKS LIKE ...	SOUNDS LIKE ...
Listening	Maintain eye contact; nodding, smiling, interested expression	• Mmm, I see, ah ... • So what you're saying is ... • I know what you mean.
Stating ideas clearly	Face group and talk to all; use open gestures; lean forward	• I think ... • What if we ...?
Accepting responsibility	Face group and talk to all	• Use 'I' statements.
Constructive criticism	Open gestures	• That's a good idea. Have you thought about ...?
Taking turns	Facing the group; watching what others do	• It's your turn. • I've had a go. • Have you finished?
Sharing tasks	Pass materials; allocate jobs	• What are you doing? • Do you need ...?
Understanding others	Look interested; make eye contact	• Do you mean ...? • Are you saying ...? • Can you explain what you mean by ...?
Clarifying differences	Eye contact	• I'm not sure I understand. • So what you're saying is ...

Sources: Gillies (2007); Johnson, Johnson and Holubec (1998).

the others. Students need to learn how to get help from other group members (such as by asking questions or watching what others do), how to pace what they do to fit with others in the group, and the particular strengths (and weaknesses) of each group member.

■ *Teach students to monitor their group's progress in terms of their own skills and the effectiveness of the group as a whole.* Students should be encouraged to reflect on their learning, as they would in other circumstances, and on the group processes. This can be done through questionnaires, periodic conferences with the teacher, or journals. Teachers also have a responsibility to monitor the effectiveness of each group, and to intervene where necessary to ensure groups are productive, receive the help they need to complete the task, and that necessary skills are learnt as they are required.

The following are some other issues that may need to be considered when cooperative methods are implemented:

■ *Rivalry among groups, and misbehaviour.* This can disrupt the function of groups. Changing group membership at the end of a unit of work, or after regular periods of time, can help to reduce this effect, but difficulties may still be experienced in classes with a small number of disruptive, difficult, unpopular or non-cooperative students (Cowie, Smith, Boulton & Laver, 1994). Teachers need to have clear expectations concerning the behaviours required for successful classroom functioning, and need to use a group-based positive reward system and appropriate classroom-management techniques (Kagan, 1992; Slavin, 1994). Training in conflict-resolution techniques may be helpful (see Chapter 14).

■ *Arrangement of furniture in the classroom.* Furniture arrangement can influence the success of cooperative learning. The teacher needs to have easy access to each group and there should be space for students to move around as required (see Chapter 14).

■ *Teacher commitment and classroom-management skills.* Teachers implementing cooperative strategies need to be committed to using cooperative learning methods, but they also need reasonably high-level classroom-management skills and/or training before the new methods are implemented. It is also important that, where necessary, there is provision for an aide, a volunteer parent or a student tutor to provide additional assistance to individuals and groups. This is particularly important when there are disruptive students in the class (Cowie, Smith, Boulton & Laver, 1994). Participation in a teaching team or teachers' learning community (Calderon & Slavin, 1999) and ongoing support from colleagues, administrators and students have been shown to have a positive influence on the long-term use of cooperative learning strategies (Ishler, Johnson & Johnson, 1998).

■ *Cooperative learning strategies should complement rather than replace existing classroom practices.* Team-based methods can be used for following up learning after whole-class instruction, and for the practical application of new material. However, cooperative learning strategies should not replace whole-class instruction by the teacher where new subject matter is being introduced, or when the learning tasks are not suited to cooperative activity (such as in routine computation practice).

FIGURE 7.10 Interpersonal skills are a key factor in well-functioning cooperative groups.

Source: Getty Images/Thomas Barwick

Evidence on teachers' use of cooperative methods suggests that many regularly use some form of cooperative activity in their classrooms (see, for example, Antil, Jenkins, Wayne & Vadesy, 1998). In most primary classrooms, students spend much of the day learning in supportive groups sitting at a table with other students, rather than in individual activities at a single desk or listening to whole-class 'teacher talk'. However, few of the teachers Antil and colleagues (1998) surveyed used a recognised form of cooperative learning, primarily because they did not link individual accountability to group goals. Interestingly, the increasing availability of computers in classrooms may contribute to greater use of cooperative learning strategies, as computers have been demonstrated to provide an effective platform for cooperative learning activities among students of varying ages and ability levels (McDonald & Ingvarson, 1997; Sussman, 1998; see also Chapter 12).

STRENGTHS AND LIMITATIONS OF HUMANISM IN THE CLASSROOM

Since the development of humanist learning methods in the mid-1970s, considerable evidence has accumulated about its effectiveness. The results are generally positive, although some problems have been reported, particularly in regard to implementation.

STRENGTHS

Richards and Combs (1993, pp. 266–7) summarised the impact of ideas promoted by humanist psychologists and educators such as Maslow, Rogers and Dewey as:

- recognition of each human being's uniqueness, and support for individualised instruction
- recognition of the importance of a positive self-concept and self-esteem in the objectives of education (see Chapter 4)
- reduction in dependence on whole-class methods of instruction, coupled with more widespread use of small-group and cooperative strategies, an increased emphasis on the teacher's role as facilitator and helper rather than as director and manager, and increased efforts to include students in decision making in schools
- attempts to make schools pleasant and caring places, with warm or positive relationships between teachers and students
- widespread provision of school-based guidance and counselling services.

LIMITATIONS

Much of the criticism directed at humanistic education has resulted from the humanist focus on affective aspects of development, rather than on more objective and quantifiable aspects of learning. Because of the qualitative nature of the outcomes of humanistic teaching models, relatively little research has been reported on their effectiveness. Most accounts of humanistic classrooms have tended to be subjective descriptions of program implementation. Quantitative evaluations have tended to indicate a risk of poor progress in basic skills such as reading and writing within humanistic programs, since attention is focused on affective rather than academic outcomes. A further source of difficulty in evaluating humanistic approaches to learning is that teachers often lack the knowledge and skills needed to implement humanistic ideas (Antil, Jenkins, Wayne & Vadesy, 1998; Rich, 1992). In addition, school systems may be unsympathetic to such instructional models, particularly when comparisons can be made between schools on the basis of widespread basic skills testing (see Chapter 13).

Box 7.12 details the implications of humanism in the classroom.

BOX 7.12 IMPLICATIONS FOR EDUCATORS

HUMANISM IN THE CLASSROOM

The key elements of humanism, or progressive education, in classroom practice include:

- an emphasis on *experience-based instruction* – or 'learning by doing' – building on students' interests and experiences, and involving them in mental and physical activity (see Chapters 3 and 6)
- concern with *students' thinking, feelings and communication skills*, together with respect for their needs and talents
- encouragement for students to develop *personal values and self-awareness* (see Chapter 4)
- provision of a *stimulating environment* to actively involve students in learning, giving them 'freedom to learn'
- provision of *progressive education* as exemplified in the programs of A. S. Neill, Rudolf Steiner, Maria Montessori, the Reggio Emilia early-childhood education model, and non-traditional or alternative schools
- application of *individualised, child-centred teaching strategies*, as used in the Dalton Plan and in the different forms of cooperative learning.

Key elements of cooperative approaches to learning include:

- *positive interdependence,* in which students are linked to others in their group in such a way that if one fails, all fail (none can succeed unless the whole group succeeds), and where tasks and resources are shared and each group member is responsible for completing a task and for ensuring that others in the group complete their tasks
- *face-to-face facilitative interaction*, in which students aid group success by listening to and helping one another, by sharing information and resources, by resolving differences, by giving feedback, and by encouraging and motivating one another to participate fully and to achieve shared goals (Gillies & Ashman, 2000)
- *individual accountability and personal responsibility*, in which the assessment results of each student's work are reported to both the student and the group as a whole – 'students learn together and then perform alone' (Johnson, Johnson & Holubec, 1994, p. 31) – with each member of the group contributing a 'fair share' to the task
- *interpersonal and small-group skills*, in which students learn academic subject matter and small-group social skills in order to function effectively within a team – getting to know the others in their group, learning to trust them, communicating clearly with them, supporting them and resolving conflicts successfully; training may need to be given to ensure that students have these skills
- *group review (processing)*, in which students reflect on how effectively their groups have operated, giving positive feedback about actions that are helpful and those that are not helpful. Research cited by Johnson, Johnson and Holubec (1994, p. 34) indicates that group review of activities is most effective (that is, it contributes to higher levels of student achievement) when teacher and students all participate in the review process.

CONCLUDING COMMENTS

The humanists' most important contribution to the debate about effective education has been to heighten our awareness of teaching as an art to be undertaken by caring individuals committed to helping their students to succeed in the difficult process of growing up. Education is not just a mechanical process. Although highly structured teaching methods and related technologies are very important in the learning process, the humanity of teachers and others who contribute to children's learning should also be recognised.

STUDY TOOLS

ONLINE STUDY RESOURCES

Visit http://login.cengagebrain.com and use the access code that comes with this book for 12 months' access to the student resources for this text.

The CourseMate Express website contains a range of resources and study tools for this chapter, including:

- a **self-check quiz**
- **crosswords**, **flashcards** and a **glossary** to help you revise the key terms from this chapter

- the **Go further** materials and **interactive activity** mentioned in the chapter
- a **video** that illustrates some of the concepts discussed
- plus much more!

 CourseMateExpress

CHAPTER REVIEW

- Humanism is a philosophy of life that is primarily concerned with human experience. Humanist approaches tend to emphasise teaching the whole child, with a focus on social, emotional and creative needs alongside academic needs.

- Humanists Abraham Maslow and Carl Rogers are known for their work on motivation and the hierarchy of human needs, and on the need for teachers to nurture rather than instruct, allowing children the freedom to grow and learn.

- Humanism in education emphasises children's thinking and feelings, and effective communication rather than the acquisition of information that will quickly be forgotten or become obsolete. The teacher's task is to believe in the potential of every child, and to provide a stimulating environment where children can be happy, motivated to learn and actively involved in learning.

- Concerns about student wellbeing have led some schools to integrate programs teaching social and emotional skills, mindfulness and positive education into school curricula. Research into the effectiveness of such programs is ongoing.

- Progressive education strategies that are used in humanistic classrooms include small groups, individual instruction, flexible timetabling, mixed-ability groups and a reduced emphasis on grading. Examples of the application of humanist ideas in education include individual schools such as A. S. Neill's Summerhill, British infant schools, most early-childhood and lower-primary classrooms in Australasia, and other alternative or non-traditional schools.

- Examples of teaching methods that incorporate humanist principles include cooperative learning, team teaching, peer-tutoring, family-based groups, ungraded schools, open-plan schools and the Dalton Plan.

- Critical features of cooperative learning include students working cooperatively in small groups to achieve shared goals that benefit individuals within the group and the group as a whole. Results of evaluation of these methods demonstrate the efficacy of cooperative learning across a range of age groups and curriculum areas, and in developing positive interpersonal relationships within classrooms.

- Problems noted in cooperative learning have included students lacking the personal and social skills needed to participate successfully in a cooperative group, tasks that are poorly designed, and the teacher's lack of the necessary planning and management skills.

- Critics of humanistic education identify the 'watering-down' of the curriculum and 'coddling' of students as major concerns. However, research has suggested that, provided the programs are not extremely radical, students in child-centred or non-traditional schools are not disadvantaged academically when compared with those in more mainstream schools.

- Most teachers use cooperative activities to complement other, more traditional classroom practices, but these methods often lack the key cooperative-learning elements of individual accountability linked to the achievement of group goals.

PUTTING IT TOGETHER

Making links between 'humanist approaches to learning' and material in other chapters

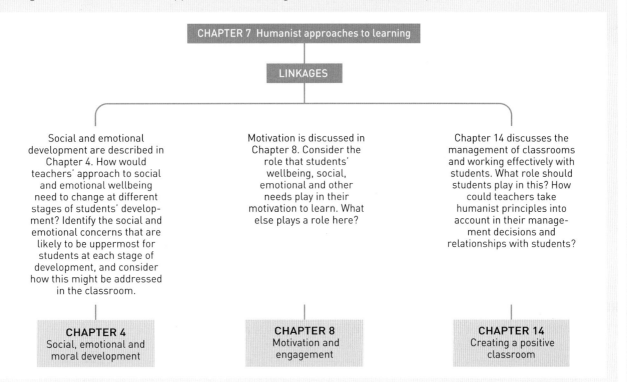

CHAPTER 7 Humanist approaches to learning

LINKAGES

Social and emotional development are described in Chapter 4. How would teachers' approach to social and emotional wellbeing need to change at different stages of students' development? Identify the social and emotional concerns that are likely to be uppermost for students at each stage of development, and consider how this might be addressed in the classroom.

Motivation is discussed in Chapter 8. Consider the role that students' wellbeing, social, emotional and other needs play in their motivation to learn. What else plays a role here?

Chapter 14 discusses the management of classrooms and working effectively with students. What role should students play in this? How could teachers take humanist principles into account in their manage-ment decisions and relationships with students?

CHAPTER 4
Social, emotional and moral development

CHAPTER 8
Motivation and engagement

CHAPTER 14
Creating a positive classroom

QUESTIONS AND ACTIVITIES FOR SELF-ASSESSMENT AND DISCUSSION

1   Explain how humanist approaches differ from behavioural and cognitive approaches to learning and teaching.

2   Identify some specific consequences you might see in classrooms of students' needs at each level of Maslow's hierarchy.

3   How could you use active listening in the classroom? What contribution might this make to your teaching, and to students' learning?

4   What is the importance of including social and emotional aspects of learning? How would you do this in your subject area?

5   How will you contribute to student wellbeing in your classroom? To what extent do your ideas overlap with those of Seligman in regards to positive education?

6   How might you integrate mindfulness practices in your everyday teaching? What effects might this have on students' behaviour and wellbeing? What difficulties do you anticipate?

7   What experiences have you had of cooperative learning? How could your experience have been improved?

8   Think about your own philosophy of teaching and learning. Can you identify elements that could be described as humanist? Are there also behavioural and constructivist elements? In what aspects of classroom experience are humanist ideas likely to be influential? Where would behavioural and constructivist ideas be more appropriate?

9   In this chapter we have noted some gaps in research evaluating humanist approaches. What is the importance of research evidence to support pedagogy? What other kinds of evidence might you look for, and what confidence can you have in their validity and reliability (discussed in Ch 1)?

FURTHER RESEARCH

SEARCH ME! AND EDUCATION DATABASES

Explore Search Me! education for articles relevant to this chapter. Fast and convenient, Search Me! education is updated daily and provides you with 24-hour access to full-text articles from hundreds of scholarly and popular journals, ebooks and newspapers, including *The Australian* and *The New York Times*. Log in to Search Me! through http://login.cengagebrain.com and use the search terms listed here as a starting point:

- alternative programs
- alternative schools
- at-risk students
- cooperative learning
- humanistic education
- jigsaw
- learner-centred classrooms
- mindfulness
- mixed-age grouping
- non-traditional education
- open education
- positive education
- Reggio Emilia
- social and emotional wellbeing
- Summerhill
- team teaching.

You can also use these terms to explore databases such as ERIC, PsycINFO and the Australian Education Index.

Search Me!

RECOMMENDED WEBSITES

CASEL (Collaborative for Academic, Social and Emotional Learning): www.casel.org

Jigsaw Classroom: www.jigsaw.org

KidsMatter: www.kidsmatter.edu.au

MindMatters: www.mindmatters.edu.au

Positive Psychology Center: www.ppc.sas.upenn.edu

RECOMMENDED READING

Gillies, R. M. (2007). *Cooperative learning: Connecting theory and practice*. Thousand Oaks, CA: Sage Publications.

Good, T. L. & Brophy, J. E. (2007). *Looking in classrooms* (10th ed.). New York: Allyn & Bacon.

Joyce, B., Weil, M. & Calhoun E. (2015). *Models of teaching* (9th ed.). Boston: Allyn & Bacon.

Killen, R. (2016). *Effective teaching strategies: Lessons from research and practice* (7th ed.). Melbourne: Cengage Learning.

REFERENCES

Abrami, P. C., Chambers, B., Poulsen, C., De Simone, C., D'Apollonia, S. & Howden, W. (1995). *Classroom connections: Understanding and using cooperative learning.* Toronto: Harcourt Brace.

Allport, G. W. (1954). *The nature of prejudice.* Cambridge, MA: Addison-Wesley.

Antil, L. R., Jenkins, J. R., Wayne, S. K. & Vadesy, P. F. (1998). Cooperative learning: Prevalence, conceptualizations, and the relation between research and practice. *American Educational Research Journal, 35,* 419–54.

Aronson, E. (2005). Jigsaw classroom: History. Retrieved from from http://jigsaw.org/history/

Aronson, E. (2012a). *Jigsaw classroom: Jigsaw in 10 easy steps.* Retrieved from http://jigsaw.org/steps.htm.

Aronson, E. (2012b). *Jigsaw classroom: History of the jigsaw: An account from Professor Aronson.* Retrieved from http://jigsaw.org/history.htm.

Aronson, E., Blaney, N., Stephen, C., Sikes, J. & Snapp, M. (1978). *The jigsaw classroom.* Beverly Hills, CA: Sage.

Arthur-Kelly, M., Lyons, G., Butterfield, N. & Gordon, C. (2006). *Classroom management: Creating positive learning environments* (2nd ed.). Melbourne: Thomson Learning.

Barcan, A. (1980). *A history of Australian education.* Melbourne: Oxford University Press.

Bennett, N., Andreae, J., Hegarty, P. & Wade, B. (1980). *Open plan schools: Teaching, curriculum, design.* Windsor, Berkshire: NFER Publishing.

Boeree, C. G. (2000a). *Abraham Maslow: 1908–1970.* Retrieved from www.ship.edu/~cgboeree/maslow.html

Boeree, C. G. (2000b). *Carl Rogers: 1902–1987.* Retrieved from www.ship.edu/~cgboeree/rogers.html

Brady, L. & Kennedy, K. (2012). *Celebrating student achievement: Assessment and reporting.* French's Forest, NSW: Pearson Education.

Brockett, R. G. (2000). *Humanism as an instructional paradigm.* Retrieved from www-distance.syr.edu/romira1&.html

Brown, R. J. & Turner, J. C. (1981). Interpersonal and intergroup behaviour. In J. C. Turner & H. Giles (Eds), *Intergroup behaviour* (pp. 33–65). Oxford: Blackwell.

Calderon, M. & Slavin, J. (1999). *Theory into Practice, 38,* 66.

Conroy, J. S. (1980). Autonomy vs. authority. In D. Cohen (Ed.) *Alternative education: The Currambena experience.* (pp. 290–304). Sydney: David Cohen.

Cornelius-White, J. H. D. (2007). Learner centered teacher-student relationships are effective: A meta-analysis. *Review of Educational Research, 77*(1), 113–43.

Cowie, H. & Berdondini, L. (2001). Children's reactions to cooperative group work: A strategy for enhancing peer relationships among bullies, victims and bystanders. *Learning and Instruction, 11*(6), 517–30.

Cowie, H. & Rudduck, J. (1990). *Cooperative group work: Transitions and traditions.* London: BP Educational Services.

Cowie, H., Smith, P. K., Boulton, M. & Laver, R. (1994). *Cooperation in the multi-ethnic classroom: The impact of cooperative groups work on social relationships in middle schools.* London: Dave Fulton Publishers.

Darling, J. (1990). Progressivism and individual needs. In N. C. Entwistle (Ed.), *Handbook of educational ideas and practices* (pp. 43–51). London: Routledge.

Darling, J. (1994). *Child-centred education and its critics.* London: Paul Chapman.

De Carvalho, R. J. (1991). *The founders of humanistic psychology.* New York: Praeger.

Deci, E. L. & Ryan, R. M. (Eds) (2006). *The handbook of self-determination research.* Rochester, NY: University of Rochester Press.

Dennison, G. (1969). *The lives of children: The story of the First Street School.* New York: Random House.

De Vries, D. L. & Slavin, R. E. (1978). Teams-games-tournament: Review of ten classroom experiments. *Journal of Research and Development in Education, 12,* 28–39.

Dewey, J. (1916). *Democracy and education.* New York: Macmillan.

Dewey, J. (1937). *Experience and education.* New York: Macmillan.

Dinham, S. & Rowe, K. (2008). Fantasy, fashion and fact : Middle schools, middle schooling and student achievement. *Teaching and Learning and Leadership.* Melbourne: ACER.

Doyle, W. (1986). Classroom organisation and management. In M. C. Wittrock (Ed.), *Handbook of research on teaching* (3rd ed., pp. 392–431). New York: Macmillan.

Dunne, E. & Bennett, N. (1990). *Talking and learning in groups.* London: Methuen.

Duran, R. P. (1994). Cooperative learning for language minority students. In R. A. DeVillar, C. J. Faltis & J. Cummins (Eds), *Cultural diversity in schools: From rhetoric to practice* (pp. 145–59). Buffalo, NY: State University of New York Press.

Durlak, J. A., Weissberg, R. P., Dymnicki, A. B., Taylor, R. D. & Schellinger, K. B. (2011). The impact of enhancing students' social and emotional learning: A meta-analysis of school-based universal interventions. *Child Development, 82*(1), 405–32.

Edwards, C. P., Gandini, L. & Forman, G. E. (Eds) (1998). *The hundred languages of children: The Reggio Emilia approach – advanced reflections* (2nd ed.). Greenwich, CT: Ablex.

Edwards, J. (1991). To teach responsibility, bring back the Dalton Plan. *Phi Delta Kappan, 72,* 398–401.

Elias, M. J. (2003). Academic and social-emotional learning. *Educational Practices Series 11.* International Academy of Education, Bellegarde: SADAG.

Elias, M. J. (2006). The connection between academic and social-emotional learning. In M. J. Elias & H. Arnold (Eds), *The educator's guide to emotional intelligence and academic achievement.* Thousand Oaks, CA: Corwin Press.

Fildes, J., Robbins, A., Cave, L., Perrens, B. & Wearring, A. (2014). *Mission Australia's 2014 youth survey report.* Retrieved from www.missionaustralia.com.au/research-page/young-people-page

Freire, P. (1995). *Pedagogy of Hope. Reliving Pedagogy of the Oppressed,* New York: Continuum.

Fuchs, L. S., Fuchs, D., Kazdan, S. A., Karns, K., Calhoon, M. B., Hamlett, C. L. & Hewlett, S. (2000). Effects of workgroup structure and size on student productivity during collaborative work on complex tasks. *Elementary School Journal, 100,* 183–212.

Gillies, R. M. (2007). *Cooperative learning : Integrating theory and practice.* Thousand Oaks, CA: Sage Publications, Inc.

Gillies, R. M. (2008). The effects of cooperative learning on junior high school students' behaviours, discourse and learning during a science-based learning activity. *School Psychology International, 29*(3), 328–47.

Gillies, R. M. (2014). Developments in cooperative learning: Review of research. *Anales de Psicologia, 30*(3), 792–801.

Gillies, R. M. & Ashman, A. F. (2000). The effects of co-operative learning on students with learning difficulties in the lower elementary school. *Journal of Special Education, 34,* 19–27.

Good, T. L. & Brophy, J. E. (2008). *Looking in classrooms* (10th ed.). Boston: Allyn & Bacon.

Goodwin, M. W. (1999). Cooperative learning and social skills: What skills to teach and how to teach them. *Intervention in School and Clinic, 35,* 29–33.

Hedeen, T. (2003). The reverse jigsaw: A process of cooperative learning and discussion. *Teaching Sociology, 31*(3), 325–32.

Huitt, W. (2011). Motivation to learn: An overview. *Educational Psychology Interactive.* Valdosta, GA: Valdosta State University. Retrieved from www.edpsycinteractive.org/topics/motivation/motivate.html

Hunter, L. (2007). Machinations in the middle. *Australian Educational Researcher, 34*(2), 1–6.

Ishler, A. L., Johnson, R. T. & Johnson, D. W. (1998). Long-term effectiveness of a state-wide staff development program on cooperative teaching. *Teaching and Teacher Education, 14,* 273–81.

Jacques, N., Wilton, K. & Townsend, M. (1998). Cooperative learning and social acceptance of children with mild intellectual disability. *Journal of Intellectual Disability Research, 42,* 29–36.

Johnson, D. W. & Johnson, R. T. (1999). *Learning together and alone: Cooperation, competition and individualization* (5th ed.). Boston, MA: Allyn & Bacon.

Johnson, D. W. & Johnson, R. T. (2014). Cooperative learning in the 21st century. *Anales de Psicologia, 30*(3), 841–51.

Johnson, D. W., Johnson, R. T. & Holubec, E. J. (1994). *The new circles of learning: Cooperation in the classroom and school.* Alexandria, VA: Association for Supervision and Curriculum Development.

Johnson, D. W., Johnson, R. T. & Holubec, E. (1998). *Cooperation in the classroom* (6th ed.). Boston: Allyn and Bacon.

Joyce, B., Weil, M. & Calhoun E. (2008). *Models of teaching* (8th ed.). Boston: Allyn & Bacon.

Kagan, S. (1992). *Cooperative learning: Resources for teachers.* San Juan Capistrano, CA: Resources for Teachers.

Karremans, J. C., Schellekens, M. P. J. & Kappen, G. (2017). Bridging the sciences of mindfulness and romantic relationships: a theoretical model and research agenda. *Personality and Social Psychology Review, 21*(1). doi/abs/10.1177/1088868315615450

Kessler, R. (2005). Nourishing adolescents' spirituality. In J. P. Miller, S. Karsten, D. Denton, D. Orr & I. Colallillo Kates (Eds). *Holistic learning and spirituality in education: Breaking new ground.* Albany: State University of New York Press, 101–107.

Killen, R. (2012). *Effective teaching strategies: Lessons from research and practice* (6th ed.). Melbourne: Cengage Learning.

Kohl, H. R. (1968). *36 children.* London: Victor Gollancz.

Kohl, H. R. (1969). *The open classroom: A practical guide to a new way of teaching.* New York: Random House.

Kohn, A. (1996). *Beyond discipline: From compliance to community.* Alexandria, VA: Association for Supervision and Curriculum Development.

Kristjánsson, K. (2012). Positive psychology and positive education: Old wine in new bottles? *Educational Psychologist, 47*(2), 86–105.

Lamont, C. (1961). *The philosophy of humanism.* London: Vision Press.

Lange, C. M. & Sletten, S. J. (2002). *Alternative education: A brief history and research synthesis.* Alexandria, VA: National Association of State Directors of Special Education.

Lefrancois, G. R. (2000). *Psychology for teaching* (10th ed.). Belmont, CA: Wadsworth.

Lou, Y., Abrami, P., Spence, J., Poulsen, C., Chambers, B. & d'Apollonia, S. (1996). Within-class grouping: A meta-analysis. *Review of Educational Research, 66,* 423–58.

Lyons, K. E. & DeLange, J. (2016). Mindfulness Matters in the Classroom: The Effects of Mindfulness Training on Brain Development and Behavior in Children and Adolescents. In Kimberly A. Schonert-Reichl, and Robert W. Roeser (eds). *Handbook of Mindfulness in Education: Integrating Theory and Research into Practice.* New York: Springer.

Martin, A. J. (2016). Positive Education in Asia and Beyond. *The Asia–Pacific Education Researcher, 25*(3), 493–498.

Maslow, A. (1968). *Towards a psychology of being* (2nd ed.). New York: Van Nostrand Reinhold.

Maslow, A. H. & Lowery, R. (1998), *Toward a psychology of being,* (3rd edn), New York: Wiley & Sons.

McDonald, H. & Ingvarson, L. (1997). Technology: A catalyst for educational change. *Journal of Curriculum Studies, 29*(5), 513–27.

McNellage, A. (2013). At Knox Grammar, the air is positively charged. *Sydney Morning Herald,* 6 April.

Mills, M. & Goos, M. (2007). Productive pedagogies: Working with disciplines and teacher and student voices. Paper presented at the annual conference of the Australian Association for Research in Education, Fremantle, 25–29 November. Retrieved from www.aare.edu.au/07pap/mil07399.pdf

Misiak, H. & Sexton, V. S. (1973). *Phenomenological, existential, and humanistic psychologies: A historical survey.* London: Grune & Stratton.

Neill, A. S. (1968). *Summerhill.* Harmondsworth, Middlesex: Penguin Books.

New, R. S. (2003). Reggio Emilia: New ways to think about schooling. *Educational Leadership, 60*(7), 34–8.

Noble, T. & McGrath, H. (2008). The positive educational practices framework: A tool for facilitating the work of educational psychologists in promoting pupil wellbeing. *Educational & Child Psychology, 25*(2), 119–34. Published by The British Psychological Society.

NSW Department of Education and Training. (2003). *Quality teaching in NSW public schools: Discussion paper.* Retrieved from www.curriculumsupport.education.nsw.gov.au

Palinscar, A. S. & Herrenkohl, L. R. (2005). Designing collaborative learning contexts. *Theory into Practice, 41*(1), 40–6.

Palmer, P. J. (2010). *To know as we are known: Education as a spiritual journey.* San Francisco: Harper Collins.

Patterson, C. H. (1973). *Humanistic education.* Englewood Cliffs, NJ: Prentice Hall.

Pekrun, R. (2014). *Emotions and learning.* Educational Practices Series, 24. Brussels: International Bureau of Education. Retrieved from www.ibe.unesco.org/fileadmin/user_upload/Publications/Educational_Practices/EdPractices_24eng.pdf

Porter, L. (2000). *Behaviour in schools: Theory and practice for teachers.* Buckingham, UK: Open University Press.

Porter, L. (2007). *Student behaviour: Theory and practice for teachers.* St Leonards, NSW: Allen & Unwin.

Queensland Department of Education. (2001). *Queensland school reform longitudinal study.* Brisbane: Queensland Department of Education and the Arts.

Rich, J. M. (1992). *Foundations of education: Perspectives on American education.* New York: Merrill.

Richards, A. C. & Combs, A. (1993). Education and the humanist challenge. In F. J. Wertz (Ed.), *The humanist movement: Recovering the person in psychology* (pp. 256–73). Lake Worth, FL: Gardner Press.

Rivero, L. (2002). Progressive digressions: Home schooling for self-actualization. *Roeper review, 24*(4), 197–202.

Rogers, B. (2003). *Effective supply teaching: Behaviour management, classroom discipline and colleague support.* London: Paul Chapman.

Rogers, C. R. (1939). *The clinical treatment of the problem child.* Boston: Houghton Mifflin.

Rogers, C. R. (1942). *Counseling and psychotherapy: New concepts in practice.* Boston: Houghton Mifflin.

Rogers, C. R. (1951). *Client-centered therapy: Its current practice, implications and theory.* Boston: Houghton Mifflin.

Rogers, C. R. (1969). *Freedom to learn.* Columbus, OH: C.E. Merrill Publishing Co.

Rogers, C. R. (1983). *Freedom to learn for the 80s: A view of what education might become.* Columbus, OH: C.E. Merrill Publishing Co.

Rogers, C. R. & Freiberg, H. J. (1994). *Freedom to learn* (3rd ed.). New York: C.E. Merrill Publishing Co.

Romanowski, M. H. (2001). Common arguments about the strengths and limitations of home schooling. *The Clearing House, 75*(2), 79–83.

Ryan, R. M. & Deci, E. L. (2000a). Self-determination theory and the facilitation of intrinsic motivation, social development, and well-being. *American Psychologist, 55,* 68–78.

Seligman, M. E. P. (2011). *Flourish: A visionary new understanding of happiness and well-being.* New York: Free Press.

Seligman, M. E. P., Ernst, R. M., Gillham, J., Reivich, K. & Linkins, M. (2009). Positive education: Positive psychology and classroom interventions. *Oxford Review of Education, 35*(3), 293–311.

Seligman, M. E. P., & Csikszentmihalyi, M. (2000), Positive psychology: An introduction, *American Psychologist, 55*(1), 5–14.

Semel, S. (1992). *The Dalton School: Transformation of a progressive school.* American University Studies (Series XIV, Vol. 34). New York: Peter Lang.

Sharan, S. (1980). Cooperative learning in small groups: Recent methods and effects on achievement, attitudes and ethnic relations. *Review of Educational Research, 50,* 241–71.

Sharan, S. (1990). Cooperative learning and helping behaviour in the multi-ethnic classroom. In H. C. Foot, M. J. Morgan & R. H. Shute (Eds), *Children helping children* (pp. 151–76). Chichester, West Sussex: John Wiley and Sons.

Sharan, Y. & Sharan, S. (1992). *Extending cooperative learning through group investigation.* New York: Teachers College Press.

Sharples, D. (1990). Teaching styles and strategies in the open-plan primary school. In N. C. Entwisle (Ed.), *Hand-book of educational ideas and practices* (pp. 785–93). London: Routledge.

Sherif, M. (1967). *Group conflict and co-operation.* London: Routledge and Kegan Paul.

Sibinga, E. M. S., Webb, L., Ghazarian, S. R. & Ellen, J. M. (2016). School-based mindfulness instruction: an RCT. *Pediatrics* 137(1), 1–8.

Sin, N. L. & Lyubomirsky, S. (2009). Enhancing well-being and alleviating depressive symptoms with positive psychology interventions: a practice-friendly meta-analysis. *Journal of Clinical Psychology* 65(5), 467–87. doi: 10.1002/jclp.20593

Sklad, M., Diekstra, R., de Ritter, M., Ben, J. & Gravelstein, C. (2012). Effectiveness of school-based social, emotional, and behavioural programs: Do they enhance students' development in the area of skill, behavior, and adjustment? *Psychology in the Schools, 49*(9), 892–909.

Slavin, R. E. (1994). *A practical guide to cooperative learning.* Boston: Allyn & Bacon.

Slavin, R. E. (2014). Cooperative learning and academic achievement: Why does groupwork work? *Anales de Psicologia, 30*(3), 785–91.

Smith, J. D., Schneider, B. H., Smith, P. K. & Ananiadou, K. (2004). The effectiveness of whole-school antibullying programs: A synthesis of evaluation research. *School Psychology Review, 33*(4), 547–60.

Suldo, S. M., Thalji, A. & Ferron, J. (2011). Longitudinal academic outcomes predicted by early adolescents' subjective well-being, psychopathology, and mental health status yielded from a dual factor model. *Journal of Positive Psychology, 6,* 17–30.

Sussman, E. B. (1998). Cooperative learning: A review of factors that increase the effectiveness of cooperative computer-based instruction. *Journal of Educational Computing Research, 18,* 303–22.

Tang, Y-Y., Hölzel, B. K. & Posner, M. I. (2015). The neuroscience of mindfulness meditation. *Nature Reviews Neuroscience, 16*(4), 213–25.

Topping, K. J. & Trickey, S. (2004). Philosophy for Children: A systematic review. *Research Papers in Education, 19*(3), 365–380.

Turner, T. & Krechevsky, M. (2003). Who are the teachers? Who are the learners? *Educational Leadership, 60*(7), 40–3.

Wagner, L. & Ruch, W. (2015). Good character at school: positive classroom behavior mediates the link between character strengths and school achievement. *Frontiers of Psychology, 6,* 610.

Wahba, M. A. & Bridwell, L. G. (1976). Maslow Reconsidered: A Review of Research on the Need Hierarchy Theory. *Organizational Behavior and Human Performance, 15,* 212–240.

Walberg, H. J. (1986). Synthesis of research on teaching. In M. C. Wittrock (Ed.), *Handbook of research on teaching* (pp. 214–29). New York: Macmillan.

Walker, I. & Crogan, M. (1998). Academic performance, prejudice and the jigsaw classroom: New pieces to the puzzle. *Journal of Community and Applied Social Psychology, 8,* 381–93.

Weissberg, R. P. & Cascarino, J. (2013). Academic learning + social-emotional learning = national priority. *Phi Delta Kappan, 95*(2), 1–13.

Zenner, C., Herrnleben-Kurz, S. & Walach, H. (2014). Mindfulness-based interventions in schools: A systematic review and meta-analysis. *Frontiers in Psychology, 5*(603), 1–20.

Zimring, F. (1994). Carl Rogers. *Prospects: The quarterly review of comparative education, 24,* 3/4, 411–22. Retrieved from www.ibe.unesco.org/publications/ThinkersPdf/rogerse.pdf

Zoogman, S., Goldberg, S. B., Hoyt, W. T. & Miller, L. (2015). Mindfulness interventions with youth: A meta-analysis. *Mindfulness, 6*(2), 290–302.

THE LEARNING PROCESS

In this module we have provided an overview of three main approaches to learning and teaching. Take some time to consider your own philosophy of learning and teaching. What elements of each approach will you emphasise? The summary table below might help you

	BEHAVIOURAL EXPLANATIONS OF LEARNING	COGNITIVE EXPLANATIONS OF LEARNING	HUMANIST EXPLANATIONS OF LEARNING	
Main focus	Behaviour – learners' actions and activities that are observable and measurable. Learning – permanent changes in behaviour resulting from experience.	Internal mental processes – how learners make information and experience meaningful and remember what they learn; information processing; cognitive style and constructivism.	Human experience – thinking, feelings, communication skills, needs, talents, motivation, self-esteem. Learning – personal and emotional development within a caring and supportive environment.	
Primary goal	Behaviour change or learning – achievement of defined behavioural or learning objectives.	Effective learning – the cognitive processes that underlie learning, and the complexity of these processes.	Satisfying basic needs and self-fulfilment.	
Role of learners	To participate in planned learning tasks to achieve targeted behavioural outcomes.	To construct meaning from experiences; to work collaboratively with teacher and peers; to negotiate activities and assessment; and to be actively involved in the learning process.	To direct and be actively involved in learning.	
Role of teachers	A direct role – to assess current skills of students, identify behavioural objectives, design structured teaching programs that involve systematic control of stimuli and continuous feedback to learners, and to achieve planned outcomes efficiently.	An active role – to provide learner-centred experiences that encourage student engagement in active learning, confidence in their ability to learn, and opportunities for student–teacher interaction within a learning partnership; to model, guide and support independence in learning.	An indirect role – to facilitate learning by providing a stimulating and supportive environment, to actively involve students in learning, to participate alongside students in a learning community.	
Curriculum	Carefully designed to achieve efficient learning through observation and assessment of behaviour to identify instructional objectives, identification, design and implementation of effective instructional programs, including procedures for presenting material, frequent observation and monitoring of progress, correcting student errors, and modification of program as required (the teach–test–teach cycle).	Designed to encourage and facilitate autonomous learning through planned group activities involving same-age and cross-age partnerships, cooperation with parental or community-based experts, capitalising on student strengths and cognitive style, while also encouraging metacognitive self-knowledge; providing a safe, supportive environment arranged to promote effective interaction and cooperation.	Flexible, based on student interests and needs, allowing each student to negotiate a curriculum and pursue their own interests; cooperative learning, active learning, discovery learning, constructivism.	

as you think about your beliefs about the learner's role, your role as a teacher, and some key aspects of your practice.

Before you start, consider the three approaches to learning and teaching you have read about in this module. Which do you prefer as a learner, overall? Which would you prefer as a teacher? Why might this be?

	BEHAVIOURAL EXPLANATIONS OF LEARNING	COGNITIVE EXPLANATIONS OF LEARNING	HUMANIST EXPLANATIONS OF LEARNING
Assessment	Diagnostic, part of the teaching process, a means of monitoring student progress towards identified goals; involving continuous collection of data that are both descriptive and quantifiable.	Provision for individual cognitive styles, with opportunities for students who need recognition of their accomplishments, those who prefer group-based activities and assessments, and reluctant learners who need motivation to become engaged.	Diagnostic rather than formal testing, with students involved in design and implementation of the assessment process.
Most effective uses and target groups	To teach skills, impart information, control behaviour; particularly useful with students who have difficulty in learning as a result of moderate-to-severe intellectual disability or behavioural disturbance.	To understand how information is processed and how the mind works, to provide for individually distinct learning styles, and to help learners to 'construct' knowledge through physical and mental activity in a social context.	To increase motivation, self-esteem, empathy; to decrease discrimination, prejudice and bullying; particularly useful with students who are not interested in school, lack motivation or have low self-esteem.
Motivation strategies	Use of extrinsic contingent reinforcement, leading to development of intrinsic motivation.	Students with a 'deep', 'achieving' or 'discovery' approach to learning are intrinsically motivated to do well and use time and resources efficiently to maximise chances of success. Need to provide appropriate incentives to motivate unenthusiastic learners and participants in cooperative learning groups.	Ensure a match between learners' interests and curriculum, encouraging natural curiosity and interest in learning; providing opportunities for choice (see Chapter 8).
Behaviour-management strategies	An interventionist approach, with use of positive and negative reinforcement and punishment, extinction and time out; cognitive behaviour modification and self-regulation.	Ensure students are actively engaged in learning, motivated to succeed, and have the skills needed to participate successfully in social interaction; encourage self-regulation and intrinsic motivation.	A non-interventionist approach, with encouragement of self-direction and responsibility; give students autonomy and responsibility, help them to understand consequences of behaviour and identify solutions (see Chapter 14).
Strengths	Provides effective strategies for teaching new skills quickly and efficiently; particularly useful for helping students with intellectual and behavioural difficulties.	Highlights the importance of students being actively involved in learning within supportive social groups.	Supports personal aspects of development – needs, feelings, self-esteem, motivation, counselling and guidance services for students; social and emotional wellbeing; and reducing discrimination, prejudice, bullying.
Limitations	Focus is primarily on achieving set goals, with little attention to implicit (that is, not observable) thoughts, interests and feelings. Risk of long-term dependence on extrinsic rather than intrinsic reinforcement.	Time, skills and resources needed to create safe and effective learning environment. Students need appropriate skills to participate effectively in groups. Students lacking motivation may have difficulties learning in this type of program.	Limited guidance for teachers helping learners who lack motivation or are disruptive. Evaluation tends to be qualitative rather than quantitative, focused on affective rather than academic outcomes.

Module

III

INDIVIDUAL DIFFERENCE IN THE INCLUSIVE CLASSROOM

MODULE CONTENTS

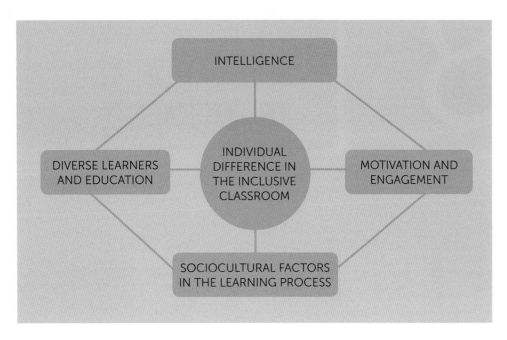

FIGURE MIII Module III concept map

Core question: How does educational psychology help us to understand learner differences?

Each student comes to the learning environment with a different set of experiences, values, interests, needs and abilities. In an inclusive classroom, teachers recognise difference, devise ways to address students' differing needs, and also take into account what each learner brings to the learning process.

School systems and individual teachers also play a significant role in addressing sources of educational disadvantage, and in taking steps to ensure that all learners are catered for and that background factors affecting learning are taken into account. Teachers need to be aware of sources of 'cumulative' disadvantage, and of issues facing students whose cultural backgrounds differ significantly from the dominant culture of the society in which they live.

Chapters 8 and 9 examine motivation, engagement and intelligence – factors intrinsic to all children, which affect school learning and contribute to differences among students. Chapter 10 considers how to include and support students who have diverse learning needs associated with disabilities and learning difficulties. Chapter 11 addresses the complex sociocultural factors that contribute to student difference – factors that are particularly important in understanding equity in education.

Your understanding of and response to the issues discussed in this module should be central to your development as a critically reflective educator and to your developing philosophy of learning and teaching. As you consider sources of student difference, reflect on how teachers might cater for individual differences to maximise the learning of all their students.

Chapter 8

MOTIVATION AND ENGAGEMENT

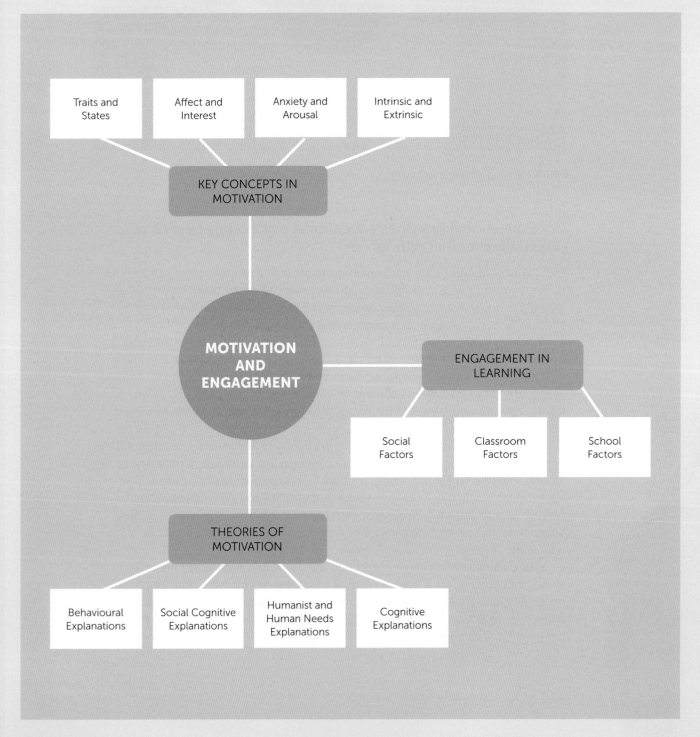

FIGURE 8.1 Chapter 8 concept map

KEY QUESTIONS

After reading this chapter, you should be able to answer the following questions:

- What is motivation and how does it influence behaviour?
- What are some theories of motivation proposed in educational research?
- What is engagement and how does it differ from motivation?
- Can you explain some of the different types of engagement identified by researchers?
- How does engagement influence a student's experience at school?
- Which factors influence or shape engagement in school?

ONLINE STUDY RESOURCES

Bring your learning to life with **interactive learning**, **study** and **exam preparation tools** that support the printed textbook. CourseMate Express includes **quizzes**, **interactive activities**, **videos**, a tool to help you '**develop your philosophy**' and more.

INTRODUCTION

Ben is in his second year of university and his sister Jodie is in the final year of school. Both students are preparing to hand in major assignments, and they discuss their workloads and social plans.

Jodie is quite focused and has a study plan which she discusses on the phone with her friends before agreeing to meet them at a party at a certain time. Ben groans and says, 'Gee, you're so good! I was never that focused at your age. I'm still not. Wouldn't see me giving up a party any day!' Jodie laughs. 'Yeah, but you're a lazybones. How many times have I heard you say "Ps get degrees". Do you think a boss is going to want to see that many passes or fails on your record?'

Feeling insulted, Ben replies, 'Oh, come on, a pass is fine.' Waving his hand at the extra books Jodie has borrowed to complete her history assignment, he says, 'Why learn all that stuff if you don't have to?'

'Well,' says Jodie, 'I learn it because I'm interested. This book has stuff we didn't even talk about in class. It's absolutely scary to look into what the bad guys were thinking of doing!'

Ben rolls his eyes. 'Anyway, I'm off to the footy. Enjoy studying!' he taunts.

Jodie shakes her head and says: 'Honestly, Ben! You've got final exams next week. Anyone would think you didn't want to pass.'

Whether or not Jodie's response actually helped Ben think about his study is unknown, but their conversation highlights a range of interesting processes at work. Jodie and Ben exhibit very different forms of motivation. How do students such as Jodie and Ben develop and maintain their motivation over time? Could students like Ben actively undermine their own performance by starting a task too late or by going to the footy instead of studying? Does it help Jodie to have a strong interest when she is completing her assignments? In this chapter, we will explore these processes and many others by examining the concepts of motivation and engagement in learning.

KEY CONCEPTS IN MOTIVATION

motivation
An internal process that energises, directs and maintains behaviour over time

Motivation can be thought of as an internal process that energises, directs and maintains behaviour over time. Each of these components is important. 'Energising' is what starts you off and gets you going. 'Direction' determines what you do, what choices you make or what interests you pursue, while 'maintenance' ensures that this activity continues over time. The concept of motivation is linked to many other concepts you have studied so far in this book, such as our feelings of self-concept and self-efficacy (Chapter 4), our cognitive ability to focus and maintain our attention (Chapter 6), and our human needs for belonging and security (Chapter 7). Many other factors also contribute to the stimulation of students' interest in learning and their intention to engage in particular activities and achieve various goals.

engagement
The energy that connects and shows our participation in a context or an activity; it consists of behavioural, cognitive and emotional components

Engagement can be described as 'energy in action', reflecting a connection between the person and the activity (Russell, Ainley & Frydenberg, 2005). Engagement at school can be considered to exist in several different contexts including at the level of *school* engagement, *classroom* engagement or engagement with specific *tasks*. We can also be engaged in several different ways. For example, our *behaviour* can show that we are engaged through signs of being on task and following instructions; our *cognitive processes* also show engagement when we are actively thinking about a task and setting goals for ourselves; and our *emotions* can show engagement when we are interested, bored or when we react to teacher feedback (Fredericks, Blumenfeld & Paris, 2004).

The terms 'motivation' and 'engagement' are often used interchangeably, as though they describe the same type of behaviour, but they do not. As described by Russell, Ainley and Frydenberg (2005), a student can be motivated by a task or topic but may be disengaged in the classroom, and this presents a major challenge to educators. In the remainder of this chapter, we will outline major concepts and theories of motivation, followed by an examination of engagement in the school, classroom and task-based contexts.

There are several key concepts or ideas that need to be explained when considering motivation. The first important concept involves asking whether motivation is a 'trait' or a 'state'. This is closely related to another concept, 'anxiety' or 'arousal', which can also be described in terms of a state. Another pair of concepts, 'intrinsic' and 'extrinsic' motivation, is often encountered in discussion of behavioural theories of motivation (see also Chapter 5). Finally, the concepts of 'affect' and 'interest' are relevant to the role of emotions in learning.

TRAITS AND STATES

trait
An enduring characteristic

Traits are stable, lasting dispositions that motivate us to behave in certain ways. They may be innate (for example, instinctive sex and exploratory drives) or learnt (for example, the need for achievement or power in personal relationships). Traits that are learnt become part of an individual's personality and can be displayed across a range of situations. More temporary forms of motivation are described as **states**. These are usually short-term conditions or feelings, although these states can recur and are often innate (such as hunger and thirst). For example, test anxiety (see below) is a learnt response, but it is best described as a state because it is associated with specific, often short-term situations like an exam. Many feelings of motivation are now recognised to be situational or reflective of states in certain situations. This means we cannot generalise about a student's motivation. Simply because they appear less motivated in one classroom does not mean they will hold the same motivational orientation in another classroom.

state
A temporary condition or feeling

ANXIETY AND AROUSAL

Anxiety is a state of **arousal** characterised by heightened alertness and awareness. It is a state described as feelings of tension, uneasiness and apprehension about a particular task or event. The symptoms can vary dramatically in each person or in accordance with a situation, ranging from mild feelings of uncertainty or butterflies in the stomach, to severe sweating, dizziness or fainting. However, it is also a normal response state that enables us to sense danger, escape if we want to, or prepare for a situation. In the context of performance, pianists, dancers, swimmers and golfers say that some anxiety or high arousal is good, provided it does not reach the level where it impedes performance (Hanton & Connaughton, 2002).

Performance on any task is usually best when accompanied by a level of arousal appropriate for the activity, such as high arousal before performing or before taking a test, and lower levels for tasks such as reading for pleasure or watching television. The Yerkes–Dodson law describes a fine balance between a state of arousal and performance (Yerkes & Dodson, 1908). As shown in Figure 8.2, our level of arousal can rise only so high before performance starts to decline. This effect is most evident in **test anxiety** (a fear of performing poorly in tests), which is experienced at some time by as many as 40 per cent of children in the upper primary levels (years 3–6) (Beidel, Turner & Taylor-Ferreira, 1999). Excessive levels of arousal associated with anxiety can lead to poor academic achievement and difficulty adjusting to school (Rodgers & Dunsmuir, 2013).

Increasing levels of anxiety and depression, coupled with a decrease in self-efficacy, have also been observed in students preparing for final examinations such as the Higher School Certificate (Robinson, Alexander & Gradisar, 2009; Smith, 2004). This effect has been explained in terms of Bandura's (1986, 1997) view of motivation, which asserts that anxiety and depression are experienced in situations where the individual has no control over a potentially adverse outcome (Smith, 2004, p. 79). Generalised anxiety often results in poor rates of attendance at school and difficulties in learning. Box 8.1 provides more information about recognising and responding to anxiety in children and school students.

anxiety
Feelings of tension, uneasiness and apprehension

arousal
Alertness and attentiveness

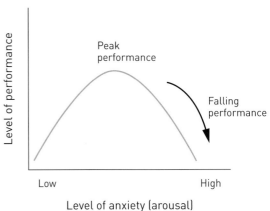

FIGURE 8.2 The Yerkes–Dodson law predicts a falling level of performance when arousal (or anxiety) reaches a certain level.

test anxiety
Fear of performing poorly in tests

INTRINSIC AND EXTRINSIC MOTIVATION

Intrinsic motivation refers to motivation arising from internal factors such as a child's natural feelings of curiosity, excitement, confidence and satisfaction when performing a task. This is the feeling described by Jodie in the opening story, when she explained her discovery of more interesting historical sources. Here, simply undertaking the task is its own reward for Jodie. Intrinsic motivation is the ultimate goal in education at every level. Students who enjoy what they are doing and who learn for the sake of learning are said to be intrinsically motivated (Ryan & Deci, 2000b).

In contrast, **extrinsic motivation** arises from external sources that can influence us to complete a task. For example, as seen in Chapter 5, behaviourists used the ideas of reinforcement to influence a person or animal to complete a task. This has emerged as a powerful (but controversial) means for teachers or parents to stimulate learning by using extrinsic motivators; that is, motivation arising from the use of external rewards or bribes such as food, praise, free time, money or points towards an activity (see the discussion of operant conditioning theory in Chapter 5). These incentives are all external, in that they are separate from the individual and the task. Students who are extrinsically motivated use

intrinsic motivation
Motivation arising from internal sources, such as an individual's feelings of curiosity, excitement and satisfaction

extrinsic motivation
Motivation arising from the use of external rewards such as food or praise

the task as a means to get something they want (such as praise), or as a means of avoiding something unpleasant (such as punishment or a loss of privileges). This raises a concern that 'extrinsic' motivation may be associated with 'surface' rather than 'deep' forms of learning (see Chapter 6).

Evidence suggests that intrinsic motivation decreases across primary and secondary years, while extrinsic motivation remains relatively steady. The decrease in intrinsic motivation is said to result from increasing pessimism among students about their own performance, decreasing relevance of school to their daily lives, and increasing emphasis by teachers and others within the culture of high schools on performance-based achievement (Deemer, 2004; Lepper, Corpus & Iyengar, 2005). As discussed in Chapter 5, there is a serious concern that too much of a focus on external sources of reinforcement (including things such as an emphasis on performance or grades) might lead to a loss of the student's intrinsic motivation (Ryan & Deci, 2000b). However, other evidence also suggests such a decline in intrinsic motivation is not inevitable. Factors such as the student's prior levels of intrinsic motivation can predict later levels of intrinsic motivation, while a cognitively stimulating home environment seems to protect some adolescents from declines in intrinsic motivation (Anderman & Mueller, 2010).

BOX 8.1 CLASSROOM LINKS

HOW DOES ANXIETY AFFECT LEARNERS?

Many children experience anxiety or fearfulness from time to time. Most children learn to cope with normal fears, but teachers and parents should be alert to the following symptoms that may indicate a child or student needs help:

- The child or student feels more anxious than other children of their age or other learners at their level.
- Their anxiety stops them participating in activities at school or in the social context.
- These worries and fears may be out of proportion compared to the actual event in the child's life.
- Their anxiety interferes with or prevents them from doing things other children of their age would normally be able to do.

Anxiety in young people can also manifest itself in physical symptoms such as stomach-aches, headaches, sleeplessness, and stomach upsets like diarrhoea. They can have problems concentrating in the classroom, and become irritable and very tired.

When children and adolescents become more anxious or experience intense feelings of anxiety, they may be diagnosed with an anxiety disorder, for which treatment is available. It is estimated that about 2–9 per cent of Australian children and adolescents have an anxiety disorder.

At school, teachers can look out for the following signs of anxiety in their students:

- Students want their work to be perfect, and are dissatisfied with work to the extent that they may repetitively redo tasks or tear up tasks.
- The student is reluctant to ask for help, due to social anxiety; seeking too much reassurance from teachers can also be a sign of anxiety.
- They have problems joining in with other students – meaning students are fearful – or are reluctant to discuss things in class, go on school camps, or play games and sports.
- There are frequent requests to go to the sick bay, due to stomach upsets and other physical symptoms.
- They have a fear of test situations, meaning children do not perform well in tests; they may also be fearful of performing in front of peers.

>>

How can teachers help?

Early assessment and treatment is important. If a teacher is concerned, they should contact the student's parents and seek advice. Teachers can seek advice from qualified professionals such as the school counsellor or student welfare officer, and they should be prepared to work with other professionals to devise a school-based program.

The following principles can guide your approach to helping children with anxiety disorders:

- Assist children to develop 'helpful' coping skills – reassure them that a problem may not be as bad as they think; help them see situations in another light. Social and emotional learning programs (such as those discussed in chapters 4 and 14) can also be very helpful.
- Teach by example – model positive coping strategies to your students; remain calm and positive when students are anxious, as this gives them confidence and security.
- Avoid taking over – young people with anxiety may be happy to let people take over tasks for them (or get out of doing a task), but if adults take over for them it stops them learning and prevents the development of coping strategies.
- Encourage learners to 'have a go' – having a go and practising a task helps children know that they can cope; use plenty of praise and encouragement for every step they take.

Source: Adapted from KidsMatter (2017).

ACTIVITIES

1 Have you noticed how anxiety affects you as a learner?
2 Have you learnt any 'helpful' coping strategies that you could model for students?
   Test these ideas with your classmates and see if they agree your strategies are helpful.
3 How would anxiety affect a student's motivation and engagement in school?
4 Can you think of some steps you could take to gradually help a child overcome anxiety for a task like public speaking? (See the KidsMatter weblink at the end of this chapter.)

AFFECT AND INTEREST

Although we have quite a good understanding of anxiety and its effect on learning and performance, the role of **affect**, or emotion, has generally been neglected in motivational research (Pekrun & Stephens, 2012). As described in Chapter 4, psychologists use the terms 'affect' or 'affective states' to refer to emotional characteristics. Emotions include both teacher and student appraisals and responses to situations, and can comprise cognitive thoughts as well as physiological states (such as a feeling of butterflies in the stomach, or a rapid heart rate when we are anxious) (Meyer & Turner, 2006). In the last decade, understanding of the importance of emotion in learning has increased (Pekrun & Stephens, 2012). In particular, the emotions that students experience in academic settings are significantly related to their motivation to learn, problem solving, goal setting and self-regulation abilities. These emotional states can also contribute to negative engagement outcomes such as dropping out of school and poor academic performance (Pekrun & Stephens, 2012).

There has also been a renewed focus on the role of **interest** in students' motivation and engagement in the classroom. Interest is both a cognitive and an affective state that has been usefully described by Renninger and Hidi (2011) as a critical motivational variable that guides attention, and is characterised by focused attention and/or engagement with certain objects or events. They even suggest that an interested person may become so absorbed in the object of their interest that they may not even be conscious or aware of this state. Interest has many implications for student engagement in the classroom; this is discussed in the second part of this chapter.

affect
A psychological term used to describe emotional states such as feelings and moods

interest
A cognitive and affective state associated with a heightened state of arousal, leading to increased attention, concentration and persistence

THEORIES OF MOTIVATION

Some students, like Jodie, are highly motivated to learn and seem driven by personal or intrinsic interests while others, particularly adolescents, may feel that school has little relevance to their lives. They become increasingly bored and seem to lose motivation and are generally uninterested in anything that happens in the classroom. Teachers recognise that there is tremendous variation in the level of motivation, energy and interest of students in their classroom.

Early explanations of motivation focused on instincts or innate patterns of activity (traits) (see, for example, James, 1890; McDougall, 1923). However, there were problems with these early theories. Early theories often made no provision for the contribution of other factors – both internal states (such as needs, goals and expectations) and external factors (such as classroom climates or rewards) – to student learning (Pintrich & Schunk, 1996).

Teachers may also explain the differing motivational levels among their students in ways that reflect their own personal philosophy of learning and teaching. Some teachers focus on the place of rewards and punishment in motivating students to learn. Others are more concerned with students' cognitive beliefs such as their expectations of success, or the way in which they attribute failure. (Is it one's own fault or someone else's?) Theories of motivation offer explanations of learner motivation, but each theory highlights a specific process that shapes learner motivation.

BEHAVIOURAL EXPLANATIONS

According to the behaviourist view of learning, reinforcements can be given to increase desirable behaviours (see Chapter 5). When Pavlov taught his dog to salivate to the sound of a bell, he was motivating the dog by associating a pleasant event (eating) with the bell ringing. When children are rewarded with a gold star for doing their sums correctly, they also look forward to the next mathematics lesson, anticipating further rewards. Associations such as these are present whenever students anticipate some form of positive feedback or reward as an outcome of learning. For behaviourists, motivation is simply the product of effective contingent reinforcement, so behaviourists emphasise the use of extrinsic reinforcement to stimulate student behaviours. Reinforcement can take many forms such as praise, a smile, or a reward. Almost all teachers use extrinsic reinforcement in some form to motivate students, although they may not realise they are doing so and may not always use such reinforcement effectively (Brody, 1992).

FIGURE 8.3 Could bored students be motivated by extrinsic rewards?

Using extrinsic reinforcement and motivation

One of the greatest debates of behavioural and cognitive research to emerge over the last century concerns the use of extrinsic reinforcement and rewards to induce learning. In behaviourist laboratory conditions or in specific learning interventions, extrinsic reinforcements and rewards can be used to train a new behaviour or skill. In classroom applications, such reinforcements are frequently used to manage classroom behaviour or increase motivation if the teacher feels the task itself doesn't motivate a student. However, important questions have arisen. Do extrinsic rewards work? Is there a risk that extrinsic forms of motivation might undermine the intrinsic drives of learners? The answer to both questions is a qualified 'Yes' (Reeve, 2006).

Extrinsic forms of motivation, particularly in the form of rewards, seem to 'work', at least on initial appearances, for one very simple reason – they make us feel good! Students (especially young students) get particularly excited when teachers introduce rewards into the classroom or if a reward is offered for the completion of a task. However, there is a major qualification to the assumption that extrinsic rewards or reinforcers lead to a permanent and stable change in a student's learning and motivation; when rewards are no longer offered for a particular target behaviour, the effect of the reward typically declines and the behaviour can return to its former level (Reeve, 2006, p. 649). As such, careful use of reinforcement schedules and the gradual fading of rewards and prompts, as described in Chapter 5, is essential if teachers intend to use extrinsic reinforcers to modify behaviour.

We now return to the question: 'Do extrinsic motivators reduce intrinsic motivation for other learning tasks?' Although at least three decades of research has examined this question, behavioural theorists and motivational theorists tend to disagree about the value of both extrinsic and intrinsic motivation. Generally, researchers opposing the use of extrinsic motivators have found that intrinsic motivation can be undermined by the use of an extrinsic reward (for example, Ryan & Deci, 2000b).

Research on extrinsic reinforcement

These concerns seem to be supported by recent experimental research. A phenomenon known as the **undermining effect** or the 'over-justification effect' has been identified in experiments where participants are asked to complete an interesting activity and are given extrinsic rewards (such as money) in return for certain performance levels. Afterwards, these same participants are allowed to engage in any 'free choice' activity of their choosing. A number of studies have found that those who were rewarded spent significantly less time engaging in the free choice activity. Neuroimaging studies have shown that activity in key areas of the brain had declined, no longer supporting engagement in the task. It seems the reward had in fact reduced intrinsic motivation for the previously interesting activity or materials (Murayama, Matsumoto, Izuma & Matsumoto, 2010). In fact, similar types of studies have shown that extrinsic monetary rewards may enhance memory performance, but only when the materials or questions were boring! (See Murayama & Kuhbandner, 2011.)

undermining effect
The idea that some rewards can undermine intrinsic motivation

THINK ABOUT

- Have you ever experienced the 'undermining effect'?
- Why do you think the brain responds differently after rewards have been given for previously interesting or engaging activities?
- Why do you think rewards enhanced memory performance only for 'boring' materials?

Behaviourists agree that it can be very unwise to use extrinsic rewards in the case of a student who is already motivated to perform at the desirable level, or to use material items or privileges for rewards in the absence of other forms of social approval (Landrum & Kauffman, 2006). Nonetheless, they maintain that judicious and very careful use of extrinsic reinforcers may be helpful when there is a complete absence of intrinsic motivation, and when the student behaviour is very difficult to manage. In fact, recent research looking at different *types* of extrinsic reinforcers tends to suggest that certain extrinsic reinforcers may be useful in fostering motivation if teachers apply them very carefully. Essentially, these researchers have distinguished between different types of extrinsic rewards: verbal rewards, tangible rewards, and expected or unexpected awards.

Verbal rewards

Verbal rewards are things like verbal feedback or praise, also called positive feedback. There are two forms of verbal rewards with different outcomes: *contingent* and *non-contingent* verbal rewards.

Contingent verbal rewards deliver contingent information or feedback that is closely related to the actual performance or task and tend to have a positive effect on motivation; for example, 'You applied that strategy really effectively to solve the problem.' On the other hand, non-contingent verbal feedback statements are often used for managing or controlling behaviour (for example, 'You should try harder'); in these cases the non-contingent and controlling element of the statement undermines the potential for positive motivational effect (Deci, Koestner and Ryan, 2001).

In a research study, Burnett and Mandell (2010) found that teachers are much less likely to use praise or verbal feedback about specific forms of effort and ability (used just 12 per cent of the time) compared with high use of generalised and vague non-contingent praise such as 'Good girl!' (used 77 per cent of the time).

Tangible rewards

Tangible rewards include things such as trinkets or tokens (stickers or food). Early research identified that these undermined intrinsic motivation (for example, Wiersma, 1992); as discussed above in relation to monetary rewards, there is a concern that these type of rewards interfere with *learning processes*, forcing learners to attend to the reward more than to their work, sometimes taking easier task options or cutting corners to gain the reward (Reeve, 2006).

Research has found that tangible rewards *can*, however, support intrinsic motivation if they are closely matched to the desired behaviour (that is, the reward is *contingent*). For example, researchers Marinak and Gambrell (2008) conducted a reading intervention where students were given non-contingent or contingent rewards for good reading. Non-contingent rewards such as trinkets (bracelets, balls or key-chain tokens) were *less effective* in motivating students in comparison to highly contingent rewards such as books, which were more effective as rewards for reading improvement.

Expected rewards

Expected rewards are those offered before a task is completed; for example, 'If you achieve a certain level or grade, you will earn this prize or reward.' Various meta-analyses have identified negative effects.

Deci, Koestner and Ryan (1999) found that expected tangible rewards undermined intrinsic motivation, including interest in the task and free choice (the time spent on tasks after the reward was removed). This is also described in the experimental studies of monetary rewards discussed above.

In contrast, researchers have found that *unexpected* rewards do not demonstrate the same negative effects on motivation (Reeve, 2006). In other words, unexpected rewards could possibly maintain a motivational purpose, but we would have to take care as teachers that these unexpected rewards do not inadvertently become expected by certain students because of their academic prowess or for other reasons.

Source: Getty Images/JGI/Jamie Grill

FIGURE 8.4 Simple tokens, such as star charts and stickers, might interfere with the learning process. Why?

THINK ABOUT

- Many teachers employ gold stars or sticker charts to reward students or encourage motivation. What type of extrinsic reinforcement is being used, and what are the likely consequences for student intrinsic motivation?
- Have you ever received an unexpected reward? Was it motivational?

SOCIAL–COGNITIVE EXPLANATIONS

As discussed in Chapters 4 and 6, Albert Bandura (1977) questioned the behaviourist emphasis on extrinsic sources of motivation, and instead saw motivation as a goal-directed behaviour that is closely linked to feelings of personal effectiveness or self-efficacy. This view of learning suggests that each individual possesses human agency and a capacity for self-regulation that affects their motivation and influences their personal engagement in activities (Bandura, 2001). Bandura's work has informed us that human beings, as agents of their own lives, have the capacity or forethought to organise and direct their lives and motivate themselves. They are also capable of self-regulatory behaviours such as setting goals, monitoring achievements, reflecting on their own behaviour and forming beliefs about their capability to exercise control over events in their lives. This pathway from goals to self-belief is illustrated in Figure 8.5.

FIGURE 8.5 Our capacity to set goals and self-regulate our behaviour (monitor progress) contributes to self-efficacy, motivation and learning.

Goals are one of several motivational processes associated with social–cognitive theories of learning and motivation. Social–cognitive theory, driven by the idea of triadic reciprocal causation (see Chapter 6), proposes that humans are constantly interacting with other environmental factors that also explain and shape their behaviour. Several motivational processes arising from this theory have been identified, as shown in Table 8.1.

Social-cognitive explanations of motivation consider our conscious and regulated cognitive processes, and also propose that these personal cognitive processes interact with and shape our behaviours. However, this theory also acknowledges that our behaviour influences our environment, while the environment, in turn, can influence our cognitive beliefs and behaviours. As we explore other humanist and cognitive views of motivation in this chapter, you will learn that these concepts of self-efficacy, goals, values, outcome expectations and so on appear in several cognitive motivational theories. Furthermore, these cognitive theories also recognise multiple sources of influence on individual motivation.

HUMANIST AND HUMAN NEEDS EXPLANATIONS

Humanist approaches to motivation are interesting not only because they help explain achievement and learning, but also because they consider students' welfare and wellbeing through a concern for basic human needs. Maslow (1954) perceived motivation in terms of a hierarchy of human needs (see Chapter 7) that can also be conceived as 'motives'. According to Maslow's model, once basic

TABLE 8.1 Social–cognitive processes and motivation and learning outcomes

SOCIAL–COGNITIVE PROCESS	MOTIVATION AND LEARNING OUTCOME
Goals	To enhance motivation, goals should be: • specific – a clear, achievable task or outcome identified • proximal – achievable in the near future; longer-term or more distant goals are not as motivating • the right level of difficulty – set against an appropriate standard and not too easy or too hard.
Self-evaluations	Self-evaluations and self-monitoring provide important feedback. Positive self-evaluations are very motivational, while also allowing us to redirect and maintain our attention. Self-evaluations must be realistic and based on relevant criteria.
Self-efficacy	The positive 'can do' sense of self-efficacy arises from mastery experiences (e.g. success on tasks). A poor sense of self-efficacy undermines future performance. Self-efficacy must be based on realistic self-evaluation against important and relevant criteria.
Outcome expectations	People form expectations based on personal experiences and observations of models; for example, 'If I make a study plan like Jodie, I might do better on tests'. Expectations can influence approaches to a task.
Value	The perceived importance or usefulness of the learning task. Learners are agents of their own values and hence motivated by what they value and deem important.
Social comparison	People can set performance standards by comparing themselves with other people; comparisons to people most similar to oneself are most effective for enhancing motivation and supporting a realistic self-efficacy.

Source: Adapted from Schunk (2012).

physiological needs have been satisfied, efforts are directed towards higher-level human needs associated with safety, love and belonging, and eventually self-esteem (see Figure 7.3). Maslow called these deficit needs (or D-needs) and claimed that the challenges arising from them led to healthy self-esteem and motivation for further achievement and self-actualisation. Since, for most people, the highest state of self-actualisation is theoretically never fully attained, motivation to achieve the fullest development of talents and capacities is never satisfied, and continues throughout life.

Needs-based theories of motivation, including Deci and Ryan's (2000) **self-determination theory** of human needs, have been further developed. Self-determination theory is based on the premise that the human being is naturally inclined towards achieving a close integration of their own internal psychological make-up, and between themselves and their social world. In order to achieve this, three basic human needs must be satisfied:

- *competence* – the psychological need to feel effective in interactions; the desire to exercise one's capabilities and master challenges
- *autonomy* – an inner sense of an integrated self and an internal locus of causality; the desire to be determined by our own actions and not the forces of others
- *relatedness* – the psychological need to feel emotionally connected and close to others; to form close bonds and attachments (Reeve, 2006; Ryan & Deci, 2000a).

self-determination theory
People have a basic psychological need for autonomy, a sense of competence and relatedness to other people

These basic needs are believed to underpin our capacity for growth, and are critical for social development and wellbeing (Ryan & Deci, 2000a). If these needs are not met, our capacity for self-motivation and ability to reach our goals may be undermined.

Self-determination theory also has a major interest in extrinsic and intrinsic states of motivation. The main proponents of this theory, Deci and Ryan, are very active in the debate about extrinsic rewards noted previously. In accordance with self-determination theory, extrinsic motivation is not an ideal state for the human being. Rather, a truly self-determined person is said to be intrinsically motivated. This theory proposes that our capacity for self-determination can be viewed on a continuum ranging from a person who experiences amotivation (a complete absence of motivation) to a completely self-determined person who is intrinsically motivated (see Figure 8.6). In contrast, a person who is not fully self-determined is influenced by a range of external factors that can drive and motivate them. A self-determined person is said to be completely autonomous in their self-motivation, needing no external drivers.

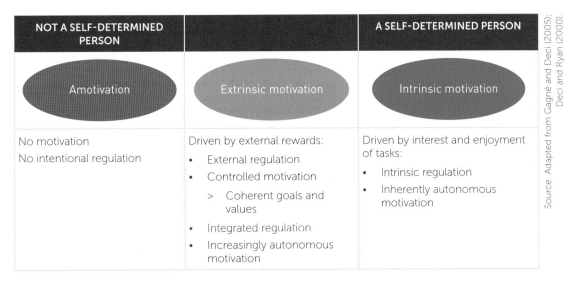

FIGURE 8.6 The self-determination continuum showing motivational approaches, self-regulation and sense of autonomy

Within the classroom setting, teachers can support self-determination and motivation by practising **autonomy-supportive** strategies that enable self-determination and the development of intrinsic motivation (Reeve, 2006). Autonomy-supportive teachers (see Box 8.2) foster an understanding relationship with their students in which they allow students to have personal choices and provide opportunities for decision making. They acknowledge students' feelings and allow for self-direction. In contrast, some teacher behaviours can crush student autonomy, including those that are controlling and offer extrinsic rewards, threats, deadlines and pressures to coerce performance (Ryan & Deci, 2000a).

autonomy-supportive Teacher behaviours that foster students' intrinsic motivational resources

You may be starting to notice that social–cognitive and humanistic approaches to motivation have many similarities, and some of the language or terms used overlap. These theories represent an important shift in motivational research that acknowledged not only cognitive processes that shape and direct behaviour, but many internal processes such as interest, self-regulation and value of the task that also shape student motivation. These ideas are further explored in the following cognitive theories of motivation.

BOX 8.2 CLASSROOM LINKS

AUTONOMY-SUPPORTIVE TEACHING STRATEGIES

Teachers can apply the principles of self-determination theory by using autonomy-supportive teaching strategies outlined in **Table 8.2** (Reeve, 2006). The strategies reflect the philosophy of the theory, while the classroom actions suggest teacher behaviours that can support autonomy and self-determination.

TABLE 8.2 Autonomy-supportive classroom strategies

AUTONOMY-SUPPORTIVE STRATEGY	CLASSROOM ACTIONS
Nurture inner motivational resources	Coordinate instruction with students' preferences or interests; provide a sense of challenge and choice; avoid external regulators.
Use informational, non-controlling language	Messages are informative and flexible, not rigid and controlling; use language to help students control and regulate their own learning, not to be coercive or threatening.
Communicate value, provide rationale	Explain the purpose and rationale of activities and tasks to students, especially when the task appears of little value to students; accept that teachers sometimes ask students to do things that seem to have little purpose.
Acknowledge and accept students' negative affect	Accept that students' negative affect can sometimes be a response to rigid and controlling language. Negative affect may be a genuine reaction to difficult or boring tasks; encourage discussion of affect.
Autonomy-supportive behaviours	• Listening carefully • Create opportunities for students to work in their own ways • Provide opportunities to talk • Arrange learning materials and seating patterns so students are active, not passive • Encourage effort and persistence • Acknowledge signs of mastery and improvement • Offer progress-enabling hints when students are stuck • Be responsive to students' questions and comments • Communicate clear acknowledgement of student perspectives

Source: Adapted from Reeve (2006).

COGNITIVE EXPLANATIONS

Some of the most well-researched theories of motivation have arisen from cognitive explanations of motivation. These theories generally take a constructivist or social constructivist approach – that is, they accept that children are innately active learners – but the focus of this research is often on processes that help explain the link between cognitive processes and achievement or performance in school. Originally, McClelland, Atkinson, Clark and Lowell (1953) used the term 'achievement motivation' to refer to this process. Cognitive processes have since been extensively examined as sources of motivation (or lack of motivation) in schooling. Several of these theories will now be explored.

Achievement motivation theories

John Atkinson (1957) and David McClelland (McClelland, Atkinson, Clark & Lowell, 1953) described the need for achievement, or **achievement motivation**, as a stable personality characteristic that drives some individuals to strive for success. Atkinson explained achievement motivation in terms of the learner's tendency to **approach success** or **avoid failure** in the learning task. The approach-success tendency is associated with students who have a high need for achievement and are motivated to become involved in an activity if they believe they will be successful. These students are moderate risk takers and tend to be attracted to tasks where the chances of success are 50–50, since there is a good chance they will be successful. They like to attempt a task, but not if they know there is a substantial risk of failure. Such students tend to hold mastery goals and are intrinsically motivated to learn.

However, students who have a need to avoid failure, rather than a need to achieve success, will look for tasks that are either very easy and have little risk of failure, or very difficult so that failure is not their fault (Atkinson, 1964). Students who cannot risk failure will avoid an activity when their anxiety about failure is greater than their need for success. The important point here is to recognise that students do not always try to be successful. For some students, and in some situations, the risk of attempting a difficult task can be too great as a result of an overwhelming need to avoid failure (Biggs & Moore, 1993; Galloway, Rogers, Armstrong & Leo, 1998).

Implicit theories of competence and ability

Carol Dweck and colleagues have shown that students may hold implicit theories about the nature of competence, ability or intelligence that can influence their achievement motivation. Two main theories of ability or intelligence have been identified in this research. Students with an **entity theory** of ability believe that intellectual ability is something that is fixed and unchangeable. Students with an **incremental theory** of intelligence believe that intellectual ability is something that can change over time and can be grown and developed (Yeager & Dweck, 2012). These beliefs have also become known as 'mindsets'. In particular, learners holding a **growth mindset** (an incremental view of intelligence) tend to believe that they can achieve success in an activity by trying and persevering. These students hold strong learning goals that tend to reflect mastery goal beliefs (see more on goal theories of motivation later in chapter). In contrast, students holding entity beliefs tend to focus on their capacity to learn as an inherited, biological trait or beyond their control, and hence the notion of effort or trying harder is viewed negatively (Dweck & Molden, 2005). In some cases, students may even believe that putting in effort simply validates their lack of ability in an area.

Research by Dweck and colleagues has shown that mindsets develop very early in life and are shaped by environmental conditions such as sources of feedback from parents or teachers (as seen in Figure 8.7). In particular, the use of praise by parents and teachers is strongly implicated in the type of mindsets formed by young people. Early research identified this 'praise problem' in Grade 5 students. Mueller and Dweck (1998) gave the students 10 questions from a fairly easy non-verbal IQ test (see more about intelligence tests in Chapter 9). They split the students into two groups. One group received *intelligence praise* such as 'Wow, that's a really good score. You must be smart at this.' The other group received *process praise* such as 'Wow, that's a really good score. You must have tried really hard.' They found that those students praised for their intelligence slipped into a fixed mindset more easily. In subsequent trials, students praised for their intelligence avoided challenging task options, and their grades on another easy test actually declined in comparison to the earlier test. In contrast, those praised for process or effort wanted a harder task, showed more persistence, and did well on the next test. More recent research shows these praise effects start early in life. For example, mothers' praise to their one- to three-year-old babies predicted the child's mindset and desire for challenges five years later (Gunderson et al., 2013),

achievement motivation
The need to strive for success

approach success
A stable motivational tendency to strive for success by tackling moderately difficult tasks with a high expectation of success

avoid failure
A stable motivational tendency to avoid tasks because of a fear of failure and an expectancy for failure on tasks

entity theory
A belief that intelligence and ability are fixed traits, and not malleable or easily changed

incremental theory
A belief that intelligence and ability are changeable states that are able to grow and develop

growth mindset
A popular term to describe a state of mind that reflects an incremental theory of intelligence and ability

and mothers' praise to 10-year-olds about their school work was predictive of students who held an entity view of their intelligence.

Fortunately, researchers have also discovered ways to change student mindset beliefs through relatively simple interventions that provide students with information about the brain. One of the aims of these interventions is to improve the academic achievement of learners with entity or fixed mindset beliefs and usually not achieving to their academic potential. In one of the earliest interventions with school students, Blackwell and colleagues (Blackwell et al., 2007) conducted a series of eight workshops with low-achieving Grade 7 students and successfully raised their Maths grades. Mindset interventions are particularly effective for under-achieving students (Paunesku et al., 2015).

The core of most interventions is a brief educational lesson involving reading a scientific article about the brain titled 'You can grow your intelligence' (Blackwell et al., 2017; Paunesku et al., 2015). The article explains basic neuroscience findings; that the brain can grow and get smarter when it is challenged or has to work hard, a bit like a muscle in the body. Students in such interventions also complete writing exercises where they explain the concepts to themselves, such as a time when they did not know something but worked hard and improved. Students may also write a letter explaining the concepts to a future student who may feel 'dumb' and may be struggling with their school work. This technique of telling others about the growth mindset concept is known as '*saying is believing*'. It is also known as a feature of a '*stealth*' intervention. For example, instead of directly telling students about the neuroscience of the brain, the students are instead asked to help develop materials to train and pass on this message to other students (Yeager et al., 2016) (see **Box 8.3**).

Yeager and colleagues suggest that these stealthy interventions may work more effectively because they help students summarise the key messages in their own words and in a way that is more relevant to them. The act of explaining the concept to someone else can also stimulate mental rehearsal of key concepts that may be enacted later and may also be less controlling to the student. It may help them convince themselves of the concepts in order to explain them to another student.

Today the aim of growth mindset interventions is to reduce the delivery time and make interventions scalable to reach many more students quickly and efficiently. Recent studies have adapted materials to online delivery platforms that deliver effective mindset interventions in just two online lessons (e.g. Paunesku et al., 2015). These brief, scalable interventions have been delivered to whole grades of students and have been effective in lifting the marks of low-performing students and improving the attitudes and beliefs of all students (Yeager et al., 2016).

Source: Alamy Stock Photo/Blend Images

FIGURE 8.7 Delivering process praise to student tends to support a growth mindset.

Although interventions may be necessary to change the developed mindsets of vulnerable students, there are also many practical steps parents and teachers can take to develop a positive growth mindset in their children and students. One step is to praise effort and processes – not abilities, intelligence or other fixed traits. By applying praise to the process used, adults can emphasise strategies or skills the child should repeat. This can motivate the child to try these strategies again in the future. Another step is to encourage students to seek challenges, not easy successes. Easy success can confirm for some students that effort is not needed, or they don't have to try hard. Learning from setbacks is a characteristic of growth mindsets and mastery-oriented learners. Importantly, the research findings discussed above also suggest that young people can learn about the brain and simple neuroscience.

BOX 8.3 RESEARCH LINKS

A GROWTH MINDSET INTERVENTION: 'DIRECTLY TELLING' VERSUS 'EXPLAINING TO OTHERS'

Mindset researchers David Yeager and colleagues were interested in the types of lessons and messages conveyed in mindset interventions. One of the things they wanted to test was whether *directly* telling students the research findings about the developing brain was more effective than if students had to explain and tell these research findings to other students (*indirectly* learning the concepts). They compared these different types of interventions in a classic A/B experimental design where condition A is compared to condition B. They tested these research problems among a very large sample of 9th grade students (*N* = 3005).

The research question

Is it more effective to deliver growth mindset information directly or indirectly to students?

Group A: Students read the scientific article about the brain and were *directly* told about the research concepts:

> 'Would you like to be smarter? Being smarter helps teens become the person they want to be in life . . . In this program, we share the research on how people can get smarter.'

Group B: Students *indirectly* learnt about this research concept by explaining it to other students:

> 'Students often do a great job explaining ideas to their peers because they see the world in similar ways. On the following pages, you will read some scientific findings about the human brain. . . . We would like your help to explain this information in more personal ways that students will be able to understand. We'll use what we learn to help us improve the way we talk about these ideas with students in the future.'

The results

The researchers found that directly telling students about the scientific findings (Group A) led to smaller changes in mindsets compared to the 'explaining to others' intervention (Group B). This means that directly telling students about the brain was not quite as good at changing their mindset compared to asking the students to explain the concepts to other students.

The researchers went on to conduct more successful experiments to change the mindsets of students using this 'explaining to others' intervention approach.

Source: Adapted from Yeager et al., 2016.

ACTIVITIES

1 What is the benefit of conducting this type of research about interventions to change a growth mindset?
2 What are the likely implications for the students if they participate in a type B intervention versus a type A intervention?

THINK ABOUT

- It is also known that adults and teachers have mindsets about ability. What types of teacher classroom behaviours might reflect a fixed mindset of the teacher?

Expectancy-value beliefs

Other researchers have also explored motivation through achievement and competence theories. Expectancy-value theory considers learners' expectations of success and the value they give to that success (Eccles, 1983; Wigfield & Eccles, 2000). It is believed that a student's expectation of success on a task interacts with their perceived value of the task, and this, in turn, influences the academic choices they make, the goals they set and ultimately their motivation. Expectancies are shaped by the person's expectation of succeeding or not doing well on a task. Values pertain to the value of the task to each individual. Four key task values have been identified:

1   *intrinsic value* – the personal enjoyment the student receives from doing that task
2   *utility value* – the importance of the activity to a future goal that the student may hold, such as attaining a qualification or advancing towards a career goal
3   *attainment value* – the importance of actually doing well on the task
4   *cost value* – the 'cost' or toll that involvement in the task may take on other physical or emotional resources, such as taking time away from other activities, or causing stress or anxiety.

It seems that the values of tasks are related to the initial drive to approach a task or choice of a task, but it is expectancies that are most strongly linked to motivation. This may be because expectancies are related to our beliefs about ability, as noted by Dweck. Wigfield and colleagues have also found that students' beliefs in their abilities decline across the high school years (Wigfield et al., 2006). Students' intrinsic, attainment and utility values of tasks also decline across the years of schooling. These findings have strong implications for students' engagement in schooling and suggest that teachers must work hard to promote the value of tasks to learners, while also helping them set goals and build appropriate expectancies for success.

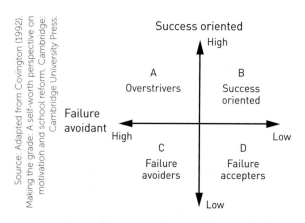

Source: Adapted from Covington (1992). Making the grade: A self-worth perspective on motivation and school reform. Cambridge: Cambridge University Press.

FIGURE 8.8 The overlapping influences of students' needs to avoid failure and strive for success

CourseMateExpress

Online Resources
Go further: Learn about strategies for developing achievement motivation on this text's website

Self-worth theory of motivation

The original theory of achievement motivation was later adapted and integrated with a self-worth theory of motivation (Covington, 1992, 1997). The self-worth motivation theory was proposed by Beery (1975) to account for the role of self-worth in explaining students' need to avoid failure and hence protect their self-worth. Covington combined the approach-success and avoid-failure dimensions with the self-worth theory to explain the behaviours of learners when they are motivated by the need to protect their self-worth. Covington and colleagues proposed that all learners, except the most optimistic and success-oriented, are driven by a need to avoid failure (see Figure 8.8).

As shown in Figure 8.8, most learners are affected by the overlapping influences of a need for success *and* a need to avoid failure. This combination could lead to some students becoming *overstrivers*. Overstrivers work hard to ensure success as a means of avoiding failure. On the other hand, learners can become *failure avoiders*, an approach characterised by learners who are more concerned about avoiding failure than gaining success on a task. These learners might make excuses for poor performances, set themselves low standards, or even avoid studying in order to show that it was their lack of effort rather than lack of ability that led to failure. These learners seek to protect their self-perceptions of ability by avoiding any circumstances that might lead to failure (Covington & Omelich, 1991).

Australian researcher Andrew Martin has extensively studied the implications of students' achievement orientations. In particular, Martin and colleagues have focused on the strategies students employ when they are faced with the dual motives to approach success and avoid failure. One of these strategies is known as **self-handicapping**. These learners place obstacles or create impediments on the pathway to successful performance. These impediments allow the learner to make an excuse for failure in a way that does not deflate their sense of competence (Martin, Marsh & Debus, 2001). Classic self-handicapping strategies include procrastination, reducing effort or avoiding practice for an upcoming task or test (Martin, Marsh & Debus, 2001). These are the types of strategies that Ben suffered from in the opening story of this chapter. Another strategy is known as **defensive pessimism**. Defensive pessimists are thoughtful about the task at hand and their likely performance. They will defensively set lower goals and expectations on tasks that are easy for them to achieve. In this way, defensive pessimism can be protective, 'cushioning the person's failure' by setting safe and low standards against which they will be judged (Martin, Marsh & Debus, 2001, p. 587). Martin integrated many of these concepts into an explanatory framework known as the Student Motivation and Engagement Wheel (see Box 8.4). This conceptualisation of motivation and engagement is unique in that it integrates information from several theories of motivation. These include theories of achievement motivation, self-worth theory and attribution theory, as well as social-cognitive theory and other relevant motivational constructs.

Attribution theories

What happens when students like Jodie and Ben experience success or failure? How do they explain these different outcomes? **Attribution theories** are concerned with the way in which an individual explains success or failure, and how these explanations influence subsequent motivation and behaviour. Learners may attribute success or failure to different causes, depending on their beliefs about who or what 'controls' their success and failure. Jodie might say, 'I didn't do so well on the history essay because I focused on one source too heavily. I'll include more sources next time.' In contrast, if Ben doesn't do so well on his upcoming exams, he might say, 'That lecturer always sets bad exams.' These types of statements about failure experiences highlight three important features of our explanations of success or failure.

- *Internal or external causes:* The factors to which a learner attributes success or failure may be internal or external to the learner. When learners consistently attribute success or failure to internal factors such as their own ability or effort, like Jodie, they are said to have an 'internal' **locus of control**. Those with an 'external' locus of control are more likely to attribute success or failure to external causes such as luck, task difficulty, or perhaps poor teaching, as Ben appears to be suggesting.
- *Stable or unstable causes:* The cause or reason that learners give for success or failure may be stable (such as their aptitude or ability) or unstable (such as their mood at the time of a test). Can you tell if Jodie and Ben's explanations reflect stable or unstable factors?
- *Controllable or uncontrollable causes:* The third element concerns the controllability of the factors influencing performance. This might involve the amount of effort expended on a task (controllable), or the degree of difficulty or quality of the examination questions (uncontrollable) (Weiner, 1992).

self-handicapping
Actions or choices an individual makes to prevent or hinder performance or achievement

defensive pessimism
A defensive or protective cognitive strategy to lower expectations and hence protect the sense of self when faced with negative outcomes

CourseMateExpress

Online Resources
Explore your own motivation and engagement wheel with the **Interactive Activity** on this text's website

attribution theories
Theories concerned with the way in which an individual's explanations of success and failure influence subsequent motivation and behaviour

locus of control
A tendency to attribute success or failure to internal (controllable) or external (uncontrollable) factors

BOX 8.4 RESEARCH LINKS

THE STUDENT MOTIVATION AND ENGAGEMENT WHEEL

Andrew Martin (2003a, 2003b, 2007) created and evaluated a framework of student motivation known as the Student Motivation and Engagement Wheel (see **Figure 8.9**). The wheel describes the role of adaptive and maladaptive factors that support or hinder motivation. Martin's research has investigated whether these motivational effects were associated with stages of schooling, or whether boys and girls were affected differently.

Boosters, guzzlers, and mufflers of school achievement

Adaptive thoughts and behaviours were positively associated with higher achievement on school tests. Martin has referred to these as *boosters* of motivation. For example, positive self-belief and persistence were associated with higher literacy and numeracy scores. Maladaptive behaviours (also called *guzzlers* of motivation) include self-sabotage or self-handicapping behaviours that were associated with the lowest scores on school tests. Feelings of uncertain control, anxiety and failure avoidance tend to *muffle* motivation in some circumstances and generally reduce performance.

Stages of schooling

Senior-school students performed best on measures of adaptive motivation boosters and lower on measures of maladaptive guzzlers. They experienced the highest levels of anxiety, however, which can potentially muffle motivation.

Middle-school students (mainly Year 9 students) scored significantly lower than other year groups on all types of adaptive boosters.

Junior-school students (mainly Year 7 students) scored higher than middle-school students on all

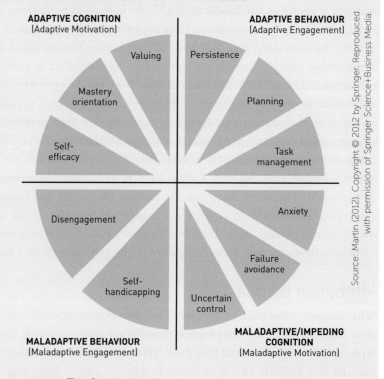

FIGURE 8.9 The Student Motivation and Engagement Wheel

Source: Martin (2012). Copyright © 2012 by Springer. Reproduced with permission of Springer Science+Business Media.

boosters, but scored lower on indicators of control and had higher levels of failure avoidance and self-sabotaging strategies.

Gender effects

Girls reported significantly higher scores than boys in several types of adaptive cognitions, including the value of schooling, their focus on learning, and adaptive behaviours such as persistence, planning, monitoring and study-management skills. Girls reported higher anxiety scores while boys had higher scores of self-sabotage and self-handicapping.

Summary

Martin's motivation and engagement wheel is a useful way of explaining adaptive behaviours to students, and working towards reducing maladaptive sabotaging behaviours and anxiety-provoking situations.

ACTIVITIES

1 Try the motivation and engagement wheel for yourself. Are you higher on 'boosters', 'guzzlers' or 'mufflers'?

2 Why do you think Year 9 students have such low levels of adaptive boosters? (We will look more closely at adolescent engagement in the following section of this chapter.)

3 Can you think of a strategy or lesson plan where teachers could introduce these ideas to students?

The motivational impact of these different attributions is quite important to consider. For example, attributing the causes of our success to stable, internal and controllable factors is likely to be advantageous (e.g. we know what we can control and repeat next time to obtain good outcomes). Similarly, attributing failure to unstable external causes such as bad luck might actually be quite self-protective in some circumstances (e.g. allowing the individual to protect their self-concept). In contrast, attributing failure to stable internal causes or uncontrollable external causes could actually be less adaptive (Chodkiewicz & Boyle, 2014). Why? It may be very limiting if learners believe they lack the ability to do well. This stable, internal attribution may be associated with the tendency to give up easily and avoid learning. It may also be appealing but not very useful to attribute outcomes to good or bad luck. This is an uncontrollable external cause and places no responsibility on the learner to expend effort or take control of their learning.

Perhaps it is not surprising that some attributional styles are considered maladaptive; students with maladaptive attributional styles do not perform as well as their peers and tend to give up easily or be resigned to failing (Chodkiewicz & Boyle, 2014). In contrast, the more adaptive, internally oriented students are more likely than externally oriented students to be viewed positively by their teachers (Schraw & Aplin, 1998).

THINK ABOUT

- Think about tests or assessments you have completed recently and consider the following scenarios. Write down your thoughts and feelings about why you performed in the way you did.
  - < You earned a good grade.
  - < You didn't do as well as you expected.
- Return to the definitions of internal/external, stable/unstable and controllable attributions. Evaluate your responses against each of these criteria.

Attribution and emotion

Research has also shown that attributions can shape subsequent emotions and motivation. For example, Weiner identified an important series of connections between our attributions and emotions that could further influence our future behaviours (see Table 8.3). Emotions such as pride could lead us to repeat the same learning behaviours that led to this positive emotion. If we feel guilty for not studying, and we recognise that this is a behaviour we can control, then this emotion might motivate us to study harder next time.

TABLE 8.3 The link between attributions and emotions

ATTRIBUTION	EMOTION
A learner attributes success to internal attributes such as their own high ability	*Pride*
A learner attributes failure to an internal and controllable cause such as a lack of effort	*Guilt or regret*
A learner attributes failure to internal uncontrollable causes (e.g. low ability)	*Shame, embarrassment*
There are stable causes of failure (e.g. unfair teacher)	*Hopelessness*
There are unstable causes of failure (e.g. bad luck)	*Hope*

Source: Adapted from Weiner (2010).

THINK ABOUT

- Can you think of a situation where you have made any of the attributions and emotions from **Table 8.3**?
- What was the motivational effect of the emotion? Did it motivate you to seek help, for example?

CourseMateExpress

Online Resources
Go Further: Read more about the role of anger in our day to day lives via the link on this text's website

Table 8.3 did not include emotions such as anger. Further research has indicated that a range of negative emotions such as anger can indeed arise from uncontrollable situations where the learner feels a sense of helplessness (for example, Pérez Nieto et al., 2000), or when students or adults are victimised or bullied (for example, Aquino, Douglas & Martinko, 2004). Feelings such as anger may not necessarily be unhelpful to us. These feelings might in fact motivate us to make changes or seek to address the problem that has caused anger. In the Go Further weblink you can read an interesting article in *Psychology Today* that explains why we have begun to rethink the role of anger as an emotion.

Developmental changes in attributional beliefs

There is considerable variation among students in the type of attributions they make. One of these variations is due to the age of the student. For example, there is evidence that younger children do not differentiate between ability and effort; they believe that the harder they try, the better they will do. They believe that working harder will increase their ability: 'Studying harder makes your brain bigger' (Harari & Covington, 1981, cited by Covington, 1998, p. 82). However, the belief that ability can be improved by increased effort gradually changes to recognition that ability and effort are two different things, and a lack of ability can limit the effect of effort on changing one's chances of success (Nichols & Miller, 1983). This developmental trend was confirmed in a recent study in which younger children conflated the meaning of ability and effort, believing that smart students work hard, while older students recognised that ability and effort do not necessarily go hand in hand, with smart students not having to work as hard (Folmer et al., 2008). By the early years of adolescence, students begin to believe that ability is not only distinct from effort, but is also fixed (Covington, 1998).

Attribution retraining

Importantly there is evidence to show that attribution retraining interventions can improve a range of academic emotions, behaviours and achievement outcomes for learners of all ages (Chodkiewicz & Boyle, 2014; Toland & Boyle, 2008). Attribution retraining interventions attempt to modify the student's maladaptive attribution to a more helpful belief pattern. For example, instead of falling into frustration or anxiety, they are taught to retrace their steps to figure out where they went wrong in a problem, to concentrate on the task itself, and to attribute failures to things they can change, rather than stable factors such as a lack of ability (Brophy, 1998). These methods have been used primarily in settings that involve students with special needs, and particularly in situations involving maladaptive learning beliefs.

Toland and Boyle (2008) attempted to modify attributions in a group of primary school aged children, 10–12 years of age with learning difficulties ($N = 21$). They employed a unique cognitive behavioural training approach in which children were taught the link between their thoughts, feelings and actions, and how to reframe their thoughts and feelings using 'I can' statements to replace previous negative statements. These thoughts were then linked to their school work where children were encouraged to attribute success to their own efforts. The researchers assessed children's reading abilities before and after the intervention and found a significant and positive improvement in reading abilities after the intervention and a small but non-significant improvement in spelling ability. On average, about 80 per cent of parents believed they saw positive change in their child, while about 50 per cent of teachers thought they saw a major change; importantly, about 90 per cent of children believed they made a major change.

More recently in a similar intervention approach, Chodkiewicz and Boyle (2016) found that among fifty 10–12 year olds (31 students were in the intervention group and 19 in a control group), students in the attribution retraining group achieved a greater increase in reading scores compared to the control group students. Like the previous Toland and Boyle (2008) students, they did not find significant differences for other learning domains such as spelling, nor did they find any lasting differences for self-concept or attributional style.

This evidence shows that attribution retraining interventions can improve outcomes in some academic domains and can create a sense of optimism in the students. In Box 8.5 we consider other possible ways that teachers could apply learning from these research studies to their classroom practice.

CourseMateExpress

Online Resources
Go Further: Learn more about how children cope with challenge and difficulty; listen to Carol Dweck on 'The power of yet' via the link on this text's website

---

BOX 8.5 IMPLICATIONS FOR LEARNING

CAN TEACHERS INTERVENE TO CHANGE LEARNING COGNITIONS?

So far in this section on cognitive theories of motivation we have learned about two types of interventions to change learner cognitions and improve their motivation. What can teachers learn from these types of interventions?

- *Teacher talk is important:* Teachers should avoid conveying fixed and negative messages about effort and ability in their feedback. This can occur when they use ability praise or make attributions to ability when giving students feedback.
- *Concepts of change:* Teachers can promote a more positive mindset and more adaptive attributions by simply reinforcing and modelling concepts of learning change. Using powerful turnaround phrases like 'Not yet'. When a child says 'I can't do it.' The teacher can use the words 'Not yet' to show that change and development is possible (Dweck, 2014).
- *Modelling mindsets:* Dweck cautions teachers and parents that their own mindsets are reflected in their classroom and parenting practices. Teachers and parents may say they promote a growth mindset but their language and feedback says something different (Dweck, 2015). Check your own attributional style and monitor language and pedagogies to promote success but also learn from failures.

Goal theories of motivation

Goal theories of motivation are also known as achievement goal theories and arose from early theories of achievement motivation. Goal theories are essentially concerned with two overarching goal structures that learners associate with tasks to be performed: mastery and performance. **Mastery goals** are closely related to the concept of intrinsic motivation and are widely viewed as the ultimate achievement goal, and associated with persistence and effort in academic tasks. In addition, students with mastery orientations are more likely to employ deeper thinking strategies associated with self-regulation and metacognition (Coutino, 2007; Elliot, McGregor & Gable, 1999; Vrugt & Oort, 2008). These students are less likely to engage in the self-handicapping strategies discussed earlier in this section, and are more likely to be motivated to move on to advanced studies in the subjects in which they experience a mastery orientation. On the other hand, **performance goals** have typically been viewed as a less desirable approach to achievement. These learners are driven by the extrinsic goals of the task – that is, performing well and earning good grades – and may exhibit the avoidance strategies suggested earlier.

The view that mastery goals are positive and performance goals are negative was challenged, however, by puzzling findings about learners with performance goals. In some research studies, performance goals were found to be quite adaptive, whereas in other studies, performance goals did not lead to positive outcomes (Harackiewicz, Barron & Elliot, 1998). Harackiewicz and colleagues

mastery goal
A personal objective to achieve mastery of a task or skill

performance goal
A personal objective to perform well in an area of achievement

Source: Getty Images/Neustockimages

FIGURE 8.10 Is it better for students with performance-approach goals to show that they 'look smart' or that they can outperform others?

performance-avoid goal
A personal objective to complete academic work in order to avoid appearing incompetent

performance-approach goal
A personal objective to perform well by demonstrating competence over others and outperforming classmates

CourseMateExpress

Online Resources
Watch a **video** showing children of different ages discussing how their teachers motivate and engage them.

identified that performance goals seemed to be advantageous for college (or university) students who were participating in performance-oriented, test-driven environments. They suggested that these students might be more advantaged if they adopted performance orientations that aligned with these performance-driven learning contexts. Subsequently researchers recognised that two different types of performance goal dimensions were at work in student motivation.

These two different performance goals became known as **performance-approach** and **performance-avoid goals**. Performance-approach goals are seen as more adaptive than performance-avoid goals. Learners who adopt an approach goal, like the college students above and in **Figure 8.10**, are motivated by the desire to appear competent to others and show that they can outperform them; hence they strive to achieve good grades. Performance-avoid learners are more concerned with avoiding the appearance of incompetence, and, thus are associated with less adaptive behaviours than learners with approach orientations (Anderman & Wolters, 2006).

However sometimes the research on performance-approach goals has yielded inconsistent results. This may be because researchers have used different concepts and phrases to measure performance-approach goals. For example, some researchers measure a desire to appear competent (e.g. looking smart) whereas others measure a desire to outperform peers (Linnenbrink-Garcia & Patall, 2015). Why is this difference in measurement approaches so important?

This distinction is very important because very different research findings result from each measurement approach. Specifically, when researchers measure the desire to appear competent (e.g. looking smart), the link between performance-approach goals and academic achievement is *negative*. In contrast, when the researchers measure the desire to outperform others, the association with academic achievement is *positive* (Senko et al., 2011). Why is this the case? Senko and colleagues point to examples of research that suggest that performance goals associated with demonstrating competence are associated with higher test anxiety, loss of interest and lower levels of effort and reduced self-efficacy.

A revised 2 x 2 theory of goals

These research findings have led researchers to apply the approach and avoidance goal dimensions to mastery goals (Elliot & McGregor, 2001). This is known as the 2 x 2 framework where both the mastery and performance goals hold approach and avoidance dimensions. Although mastery-approach goals seem intuitively obvious, reflecting a goal to do better and approach tasks positively, a mastery-avoidance approach is somewhat paradoxical in that the person desires mastery but seeks to avoid learning failure or a loss of their skills. As with the performance-avoidance orientation, mastery-avoidance has also been associated with negative outcomes such as anxiety, loss of self-efficacy and weaker academic performance (Senko et al, 2011).

Research on the mastery-avoidance dimension is rather limited in comparison to other achievement goals (Linnenbrink-Garcia & Pattell, 2015; Senko & Freund, 2015) Some evidence is beginning to emerge about the impact of mastery-avoidance goals in a range of areas. For example, Van Yperen,

Elliot and Anseel (2009) found that mastery-avoidance orientations had a negative effect on the capacity of participants to improve their performance. Senko and Freund (2015) compared the effects of mastery-avoidance goals on younger university students compared with older adults. The two groups of adults were presented with a puzzle task and were assigned mastery-approach goals (*try to do better* than their last attempt) or mastery avoidance goals (*try to avoid doing worse* than their last attempt). The researchers found that younger adults struggled to cope under the avoidance goal orientation; they felt more performance pressure, had a reduced interest in the task, and reduced perception of competence. On the other hand, older adults were able to cope more readily with the avoidance goal dimension. The researchers hypothesised that this may be due to their stage of life and work experience where workplace standards encourage striving to avoid loss of something valued; for example, the loss of income.

Today, it is generally accepted that motivational goals can be broken into approach and avoidance dimensions; however, the causes or full implications of mastery-avoidance goals has not been fully explained (Graham & Weiner, 2012). It seems fair to say that many researchers agree that a mastery-approach orientation remains the 'gold-standard' of classroom goal orientations because it leads to a range of positive adaptive learning behaviours. However, it is also pragmatic to suggest that in some circumstance some types of performance-approach orientations may be beneficial to achievement of certain types of academic outcomes. It is also probably realistic to consider that most learners do hold mixed motivational profiles and their goal orientations may differ across subjects and even across their life course.

THINK ABOUT

- Consider your motivational goals. Can you identify with a mastery or performance orientation? Do you have different goals for different subjects or different learning situations?
- Are there good reasons for encouraging mastery goals among school-age learners? What benefit might this have?

SUMMARY OF MOTIVATION THEORIES

The different views of motivation vary considerably depending on the theoretical views and philosophical positions of the researchers. However, there are also many overlaps and commonalities in the theories described here. Many of the theories also make similar recommendations for practice; this has significant implications for classroom practice and requires teachers to think carefully about the approaches they emphasise in their classrooms. Not all of these classroom practices may be feasible or practical in every classroom situation or context (Urdan & Turner, 2005). Table 8.4 summarises the different theoretical approaches to motivation discussed in this section, and Box 8.6 looks at their application in the classroom.

Thus far, this discussion of motivation has largely focused on motivation as an individual state. In the following section of this chapter, we turn to an examination of engagement, which suggests that broader pedagogical and classroom-related factors also shape the motivation and engagement of learners.

STRENGTHS OF MOTIVATION THEORIES

Motivational theories highlight the positive impact of motivation on students' achievement, self-confidence and independence as learners. Such theories also draw attention to the need for educators to recognise the range of student needs, including those associated with physical and personal

TABLE 8.4 Theories of motivation

THEORIES	BEHAVIOURAL	SOCIAL–COGNITIVE	HUMANIST AND HUMAN NEEDS	COGNITIVE
Major theorists	Skinner	Bandura	Maslow Ryan and Deci	Atkinson, Dweck, Weiner and many others
Major focus	Achievement of desired behaviour through external rewards and reinforcement	Learners have agency and capacity for self-regulation, leading to personal standards and a sense of self-efficacy	Satisfying basic needs; achieving self-actualisation and self-determination	Cognitive processes and emotions; achievement needs; beliefs about causes of success and failure; goal setting
Classroom applications	Use of contingent rewards and punishment	Need to ensure students perceive a link between their efforts and success and build self-efficacy through a realistic sense of abilities	Need to be aware of students' needs inside and outside the classroom, and support student autonomy and self-determination	Need for teachers to be aware of beliefs about ability, and to provide accurate/credible feedback
Strengths	Can have positive impact on motivation when initial motivation is absent or tasks are boring	Increases independence and self-confidence, and holistically focuses on personal, behavioural and environmental influences	Identifies human needs that influence behaviour; school programs can address basic needs and teaching approaches can support student autonomy	Focuses on the individual's interpretation of learning situations and on perception of own ability as a cause of learning
Weaknesses	Can encourage surface learning for extrinsic rewards; may reduce intrinsic motivation	May be difficult to change students' negative self-beliefs; interventions may take time to take effect	Concept such as self-actualisation is difficult to define; problems in using autonomy strategies may challenge some teachers' sense of authority	Can be challenging to address internalised cognitive processes; some perspectives disagree on approaches (for example, goal theory)

wellbeing, with students' attributions of personal success and failure, and with students' perception of the links between effort and success. Importantly, recent theories have highlighted the link between motivation and emotion and subsequent influence on learning behaviours. Recognising these different motivational behaviours should provide educators with greater insight into students in their classrooms.

LIMITATIONS OF MOTIVATION THEORIES

Some applications of motivational theories may have a limiting impact on learners. These include the application of external reward systems, which may lead to extrinsic motivation, and a related concern that this form of motivation is associated with surface rather than deep learning approaches. As discussed, an emphasis on performance goals raises similar concerns, leading to disagreement among researchers about whether these types of goals should be encouraged. A further limitation in this body of research concerns a need for further investigation of contradictory or inconsistent results about the type of goals learners adopt. Finally, it is only recently that motivational research has closely considered the role of affect and interest in learning. As discussed in the following section, neglect of these factors in classroom approaches to motivation may be to the detriment of students' motivation and engagement.

CourseMateExpress

Online Resources
Take a moment to consider your personal philosophy. You may wish to use the **Develop your Philosophy** tool on this text's website.

BOX 8.6 IMPLICATIONS FOR EDUCATORS

MOTIVATION IN THE CLASSROOM

Behavioural approaches

To apply behavioural approaches to motivation in classroom settings, teachers need to:

- contingently reinforce students' achievements to ensure that desired behaviour is repeated
- remember that reinforcement to increase desired behaviour motivates further learning of this type
- recognise that student motivation is shaped by previous reinforcing experiences
- understand that concerns have been raised about overuse of external reinforcement that may undermine intrinsic motivation.

Social-cognitive approaches

The social-cognitive approach suggests that teachers need to:

- foster students' goal-directed behaviours and self-efficacy
- ensure that learners experience success, not just failure
- remember that self-evaluation is influenced by personal success and experience on tasks, by observing others' achievements, and by verbal feedback
- recognise that motivation is affected by learners' judgements about their own efficacy.

Humanist and human needs approaches

To apply humanist and needs perspectives in classrooms, teachers need to:

- become more concerned with the wider implications of student welfare, not just with students' education
- be aware that some students are more concerned with feelings of safety, belonging and self-esteem than with the demands of the school curriculum
- understand that students who feel a strong need for group belonging will experience difficulties and lack motivation to learn if a teacher acts in ways that conflict with group mores
- recognise that students with low autonomy will not be motivated to strive for higher levels of achievement (see Chapter 4)
- acknowledge that their own beliefs and values can have a major impact on student motivation
- know that teachers are more likely to be supportive of student motivation where there are clear learning goals, an emphasis on personal and social relationships, and a shared understanding of the student's goals.

Cognitive approaches

Implications of the cognitive view of motivation concern the need for teachers to:

- understand that internal cognitive processes can shape motivation
- accept that students are not always motivated to be successful, and that the risk of attempting to succeed may be overwhelmed by the need to avoid failure
- realise that motivating students by focusing on increasing mastery may develop more high-order learning skills than emphasising performance goals
- be aware that the value of tasks may not be the same for all learners, and might differ from the teacher's perception
- be aware of their own biases and how these might affect the way they attribute success and failure to individual students
- recognise that feedback given to students can have a significant impact on the ways they perceive their ability or form 'mindsets', and the attributions they make about their performance.

ENGAGEMENT IN LEARNING

One of the most challenging situations that teachers face is the paradoxical loss of engagement among otherwise motivated students. How can a student be motivated to do well in school but lose engagement at the same time? Moreover, why does this often occur during adolescence, a time when the school curriculum broadens and offers students greater subject choice?

Engagement is a complex construct that can be described at the level of the individual, school, classroom or task level. Definitions of engagement often focus very narrowly on a few broad behavioural indicators such as school participation, often measured by attendance and absentee rates. Some suggest that the many different explanations of engagement have contributed to a conceptual 'haziness' about what engagement actually is. Reports of engagement at school depend very much on how the researcher has defined engagement, in what context or situation they have measured engagement and exactly what they have measured in their study (Christenson, Reschly & Wylie, 2012). For example, terms such as 'school belonging' and 'connectedness' are also used to describe engagement.

The concept of engagement has been enhanced by an understanding that it is not a unidimensional 'feeling' or state of mind of the individual student. As described at the beginning of this chapter, Fredericks, Blumenfeld and Paris (2004) described engagement as a complex state incorporating features of the student's behaviour, emotion and cognition, as follows:

- *Behavioural engagement* is often quite a visible feature and can be seen in students' attendance, absences or drop-out rates, and also in day-to-day behaviours such as loss of attention, being disruptive or assignment submissions.
- *Emotional engagement* may also be quite visible and clear to teachers in students' expression of negative or positive affect, interest or boredom, and can also encompass much less visible emotions associated with a sense of belonging and connectedness with the school.
- *Cognitive engagement* refers to the investment in learning made by the student and could include willingness to exert effort, self-regulation and motivational goals.

Skinner and Pitzer (2012) offer a multidimensional model of engagement that is particularly useful in thinking about all of these factors and the many contexts of engagement. They show that engagement can exist at many different levels of community institutions, such as families, churches, youth groups and schools. Focusing on schools in particular, they then show that engagement at school can include factors such as sporting involvement, the role of government policies and of course the classroom itself. As you can see in Figure 8.11, this classroom level of engagement includes curriculum and teacher-student relationships, and can be further broken down into engagement with specific learning activities.

WHY IS ENGAGEMENT IMPORTANT?

As shown in Figure 8.11, engagement is a complex multidimensional construct; when it is positive, it is associated with a host of academic, emotional and social learning outcomes. At the level of the school, engagement appears to be particularly significant in the explanation of school dropout and retention rates, and participation in schooling (Christenson et al., 2008). At the level of the classroom, engaged students generally enjoy learning, put in more effort, and seem to persist when faced with challenges (Christenson, Reschly & Wylie, 2012).

It is significant that international studies have identified very large proportions of young people who become increasingly and chronically disengaged throughout schooling. In large national studies in the United States, as many as 66 per cent of high school students report daily boredom in high school classes. Of these students, 81 per cent felt material was not interesting, others wanted more contact and better relationships with teachers, and others felt materials were simply not relevant to life (Shernoff, 2012).

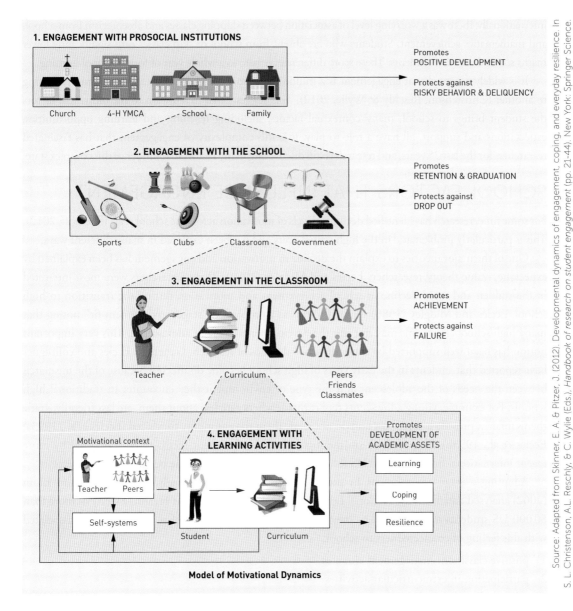

Source: Adapted from Skinner, E. A. & Pitzer, J. (2012). Developmental dynamics of engagement, coping, and everyday resilience. In S. L. Christenson, A.L. Reschly, & C. Wylie (Eds.). *Handbook of research on student engagement* (pp. 21-44). New York: Springer Science.

FIGURE 8.11 A multidimensional view of engagement in different contexts

In Australia it is estimated that as many as 40 per cent of students are not optimally performing or engaged in school (Goss, Sonnermann & Griffiths, 2017). Similarly in New Zealand, as many as one third of all 14-year-olds reported they did not find school engaging and wanted to leave as soon as possible (Gibbs & Poskitt, 2010). In both countries, we know that school participation rates of Māori (New Zealand Ministry of Education, 2009b) and Aboriginal and Torres Strait Islander (Australian Bureau of Statistics, 2011) youth are lower than for non-indigenous youth. Although participation rates are a simplistic behavioural indicator of engagement, it does tell us that engagement may be more problematic for some students than others.

We can paint a broad picture of Australian and New Zealand youth engagement from the international testing program known as the Programme for International Student Assessment (PISA) (OECD, 2013). This data revealed that Australian and New Zealand students do generally feel happy at school (80–83 per cent of students) and feel a sense of belonging at school (78 per cent) at similar levels to the OECD average. Across all countries, students from disadvantaged backgrounds report lower levels of belonging. For all students internationally, there was a worrying level of association between skipping classes and absenteeism from school, and mathematics achievement. Students who are absent from school or skip classes earn significantly lower maths scores than other students. These score differences equate to a whole year of formal school learning.

It is widely accepted that engagement is a multidimensional construct and can vary from one setting to another (Christenson, Reschly & Wylie, 2012). This suggests that in addition to the individual factors the student brings to school, many contextual factors, including teaching and learning opportunities, expectations and support, all have a role to play. It is this complexity of engagement that has fascinated researchers for the last 25 years, and research is still discovering many factors that influence this complex state.

SCHOOL FACTORS THAT INFLUENCE ENGAGEMENT

For some time, research has identified declining levels of motivation across the school years (Shernoff, 2012). This is particularly problematic in the high school years and has been explored in many different ways.

One of the major theories to explain the decline in motivation and engagement has been explained by expectancy-value theory researchers Eccles and Midgley (1989). These researchers were most interested in the sudden and rapid decline in school achievement and motivation during the transition to high school. Eccles and Midgley (1989) referred to this as a problem of 'stage–environment fit', noting that many high school classrooms may not suit the developmental stage of adolescence. This very important notion has been well supported by more than two decades of research. Generally, Eccles and colleagues have reported that students in the early years of high school become disaffected because of the mismatch between the needs of the adolescent and the type of environment they encounter in traditional high schools. For example, young adolescents report that teachers care less about them, are less friendly, grade them unfairly, provide less support and do not allow them the autonomy they need (Eccles et al., 1993a; Eccles et al., 1993b). This research on the high school environment seems to be supported by more recent international findings in the US (Shernoff, 2012), referred to at the beginning of this section.

Adopting a stage–environment fit model (discussed above), McNeely, Nonnemaker and Blum (2002) analysed data from the National Longitudinal Study of Adolescent Health, a study of more than 80 000 US students in grades 7–12. They identified four key features of schools that were associated with this feeling of connectedness to school:

1   positive classroom-management climates
2   participation in extracurricular activities
3   tolerant discipline policies
4   small school sizes.

Schools with positive classroom-management climates were characterised by staff who showed empathy and emphasised student autonomy, allowing student self-management and decision making. These features suggest that schools must support teenagers' need for independence and autonomy.

This also relates to the importance of extracurricular activities for students in these schools. Participation in extracurricular activities is an individual behaviour, but the outcome of this behaviour is linked to school engagement. These students showed higher levels of connectedness to school – they did not skip classes and they earned higher grades.

Importantly, these schools did not employ punitive discipline policies and were more tolerant of student behaviours. The importance of this finding is discussed further in Chapter 14 when we consider classroom-management practices.

Looking closely at data on Australian students from the Longitudinal Study of Australian Youth (LSAY), Gemici and Lu (2014) found little effect of school factors on the engagement of 15-year-olds. They suggested that the greatest impact of school factors may well occur much earlier in the child's life. They found at age 15 some school factors do influence positive engagement, including a positive perception of teacher quality, high academic achievement in the student body, and attendance at school outside large metropolitan areas. However, they also found that individual background factors such as self-concept, intentions to complete Year 12, socioeconomic status, family factors, working for fewer hours, being foreign-born and speaking another language at home outweighed many school factors. They caution, though, that the effect sizes of these factors were so small they are probably not relevant in any practical way. These authors concluded that looking at engagement in 15-year-olds is too late; the 'die has been cast'. They suggest that the factors that influence teenagers' school engagement may have been active *before* the age of 15.

This is a very brief account of school-level factors and engagement. It is important to remember that these findings only relate to the concept of school engagement, and this is not to discount the importance of schools in other aspects of students' lives. For example, we do know, from studies of resilient children and adults who have survived very difficult life circumstances, that school is a very significant protective factor in their lives (Masten & Motti-Stefaniddi, 2009). The connection between these school factors and engagement is not easy to identify or unravel, but is perhaps best summarised by Blum (2005) in discussing the importance of school connectedness:

> 'We need to use what research and experience have taught us to create schools where students feel connected. We want high schoolers who are convinced that the adults with whom they interact care about them as individuals and care about their learning. These schools must establish high standards, challenge all students to reach their potential, and provide the support students need to succeed.'

Blum (2005)

CLASSROOM FACTORS THAT INFLUENCE ENGAGEMENT

Several of the factors identified in the above research relate to classroom factors that support student engagement. Teacher–student relationships largely exist in classroom contexts and, as discussed in Chapter 14, are very important to students' sense of wellbeing and belonging in school. It seems that positive teacher–student relationships are particularly important as students grow older. A recent meta-analysis (Roorda, Koomen, Spilt & Oort, 2011) of studies of engagement showed that the effect of positive teacher–student relationships on engagement was strongest in the secondary school years. In contrast, the effect of negative teacher–student relationships seemed to be higher in primary school grades. It is possible that younger students are more affected by the lack of a close, warm relationship with teachers because they are still dependent on close adult attachments, whereas adolescents have extended close attachments with peers and friends. Overall, positive and negative teacher–student relationships had an effect on students of all age and grades, and had a greater effect on students who were academically at risk because of disadvantaged or minority status in schools. As such, we cannot overlook the importance of teacher relationships with students (both positive and negative) in primary and secondary classrooms. These effects are explored further in Chapter 14, when we examine the role of the teacher in establishing positive classroom climates.

Pedagogy and engagement

It is clear that the links between engagement and achievement are also found in classroom work and pedagogical activities, which are the overarching focus of classroom life. The link between classroom activities and engagement has been explored in a number of ways. Self-determination theorists, for example, believe that engagement is fostered by the development of student autonomy, and this includes giving students more voice and choice in classroom activities (see the autonomy-supportive strategies suggested earlier in this chapter). Goal theorists believe engagement is also closely related to the instructional goals teachers set in classrooms, examined in the next section.

Similarly, researchers who measure engagement by studying the concept of *academically engaged time* consider the amount of measurable time students are actually participating and working on activities as a form of engagement. These studies support many of the conclusions of a range of motivational theories; for example, students spend most engaged time when:

- activities are interesting and viewed as important and relevant
- they are paying attention and on task for most of the period
- they experience a high level of success or accuracy with most of the tasks they complete (Gettinger & Walter, 2012).

There are a number of pedagogical and assessment practices that can be directly or at least theoretically linked to student classroom engagement. The most common approaches discussed in this very wide body of research have been summarised by Goss and Sonnerman as falling into two categories of preventative and responsive practices that promote engagement (see Figure 8.12).

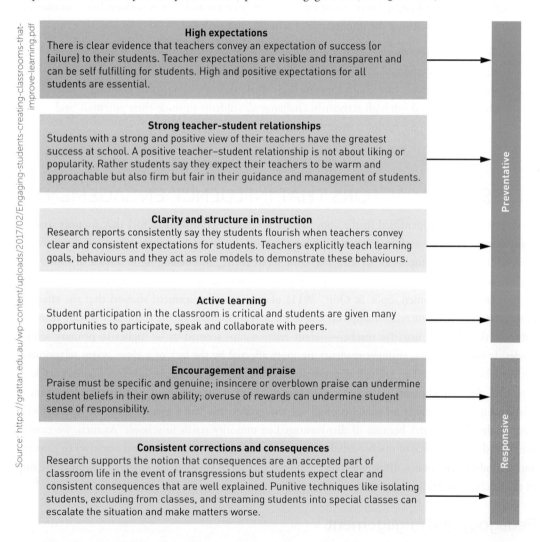

Source: https://grattan.edu.au/wp-content/uploads/2017/02/Engaging-students-creating-classrooms-that-improve-learning.pdf

FIGURE 8.12 Common classroom approaches to support learning and engagement

Some schools have adopted theories of learning and motivation to develop pedagogies of learning that directly foster and support student engagement. Many of the principles advocated in Figure 8.12 are also illustrated in these schools. Box 8.7 illustrates the efforts of one school to create engaging pedagogies that support students in taking risks, and maintain a commitment to learning.

BOX 8.7 CLASSROOM LINKS

PEDAGOGIES OF ENGAGEMENT

The Australian Science and Mathematics School in South Australia is a specialist school that aims to promote and retain student interest in maths and science. The school motto is 'Choose your own adventure'. It has specifically applied the principles of motivation, engagement and interest development to design a curriculum that is student-centred and based on deep learning principles. The following summary explains this pedagogical approach.

Real world curriculum

Guided by principles of inquiry learning (see Chapter 6), students study cutting-edge mathematical and scientific disciplines such as 'nanotechnology' and 'sustainable futures'. Real-world equipment and simulation devices allow students to experience technology in a 'hands on' environment. The school aims to foster deep engagement and sustained careers in maths and science.

Learning studies

All students from years 10–12 complete a learning studies program where they meet with the same teacher in a home group every day. These classes focus on building a sense of belonging and personal control of learning by posing 'fertile questions' such as 'How can I make the ASMS learning environment work for me?'

Personal learning plans

Students take control and responsibility for their learning by developing a personal learning plan. They set personal and academic goals and devise strategies for reaching them.

Inquiry projects

Students can follow an area of individual interest on a specific independent study with support from a mentor teacher. This allows students to work at their own level and differentiates the curriculum for them.

ACTIVITIES

1 Which features of this school environment might contribute to behavioural, emotional and cognitive forms of engagement?
2 Can you link any of these pedagogical strategies to the theories of motivation we discussed in this chapter?
3 Visit the Australian Science and Mathematics School website (www.asms.sa.edu.au). What can you glean about the school's approach to students on this website? Would you want to attend this school?

Classroom goals and engagement

Goal theories of motivation propose that students hold individual goal orientations, which will shape their level of engagement in a task (Anderman & Patrick, 2012). As well, students form their own perceptions of classroom goal structures, through which they construct their own personal beliefs about the meaning and purpose of school or classroom tasks. A mastery orientation suggests that students perceive that learning and understanding is valued and improving is important. On the other hand, a perceived performance–goal orientation in the classroom might include a perception that outperforming others is important. While these are individual student perceptions of the classroom environment, it is known that teachers play an important role in shaping them (Anderman & Patrick, 2012). As asserted by Frydenberg, Ainley and Russell (2005), the type of classroom-achievement goals adopted by the teacher (consciously or unconsciously) shape the motivational goals adopted by students. Classrooms convey messages about the importance of success – they can emphasise performance goals in the form of competition or outperforming other students, and also deeper learning strategies and mastery goals. Turner et al. (2002) found that students' perceptions of mastery goals in their classroom were positively associated with their perceptions of support from their teachers, suggesting that positive feelings about the emotional climate of the classroom went hand in hand with student perceptions of mastery goals in the classroom.

In later research, Patrick, Turner, Meyer and Midgley (2003) compared the climates of different classrooms and were able to identify three distinctive types: those associated with consistently positive climates, those associated with consistently negative climates, and those associated with ambiguous climates that showed a combination of supportive and non-supportive climates. The researchers noted a pattern in the type of climate a teacher set up in the classroom, and observation over time revealed that the level of teacher support demonstrated early in the school year was consistent throughout the school year. Higher levels of avoidant behaviours, disruptive behaviours and cheating were found in both negative and ambiguous classroom climates, showing that consistently positive classroom climates are essential for positive forms of motivation. This early research has been extended to student motivation for physical education, with researchers finding that only climates promoting mastery-approach goals increased students' intrinsic interest in physical education (Wang, Liu, Chatzisarantis & Lim, 2010).

Interest and engagement

Another approach to examining motivation and engagement in the classroom considers the importance of interest in learning. Put quite simply, this approach is based on the premise that 'students will engage with tasks they find interesting, challenging and important' (Russell, Ainley and Frydenberg, 2005). Ainley (2012) goes on to define interest as a *core psychological process energizing and directing* student activities. More specifically, interest researchers acknowledge that interest has complex individual and situational forms and Ainley (2012) asserts that these interact with classroom engagement.

Individual interest is highly specific to each individual and is slow to develop over time because it reflects growing knowledge in a particular area of interest (Ainley, Hidi & Berndorff, 2002; Hidi & Harackiewicz, 2000). Very young children show the development of individual interests and the capacity for surprisingly long periods of sustained attention when they are engaged in these interests. Take, for example, a child who can talk for some time about different types of dinosaurs or different types of ponies, despite the fact that the child has never seen a dinosaur or owned a pony. How does this level of knowledge develop?

Individual interest is a unique process that leads to independent – and persistent – seeking of knowledge and understanding about the particular topic of interest (Renninger, 1992; Renninger & Hidi, 2002). As such, individual interest areas may be a way to spur the development of otherwise 'boring' or quite abstract learning skills, such as the synthesis and analysis of information. This is exactly the type of strategy used in the school outlined in Box 8.7, when students were allowed to use individual interests to conduct research on a topic of their choice. Although this type of interest enables teachers to connect topics of learning with a student's individual interest, it also means that certain features or topics in school classes may capture the attention more than others (Ainley, Hidi & Berndorff, 2002).

Situational interest reflects a psychological state that can be aroused by specific features of the environment or a situation. Early research on interest (Hidi, 1990) identified the specific features of situations that can 'trigger' interest, such as the novelty or ambiguity created when learners first approach a topic. For example, specific features of texts can arouse interest and are associated with increased comprehension and recall (Ainley, Hidi & Berndorff, 2002). Perhaps you can remember such a text that triggered a particularly strong emotion or arousal in you, and thus is still remembered. This notion of a trigger may be particularly important because it suggests a way to develop interest in students who do not have pre-existing individual interests (Ainley, Hidi & Berndorff, 2002).

Hidi and Renninger (2006) suggest a four-phase model to explain the development of interest in the classroom. As shown in Figure 8.13, a number of factors can 'trigger' situational interest and lead to longer-term, sustained individual interest. Research has indicated that situational interest can be generated in three different ways: first, the presentation of course material may grab the students' attention (known as a triggered situational interest); second, the extent to which learning materials are engaging and enjoyable (known as a maintained feeling of situational interest); and third, whether or not the learner viewed the material as valuable and important (known as a maintained value feeling of situational interest) (Linnenbrink-Garcia et al., 2010). This draws teachers' attention to the fact that both contextual factors and internal beliefs contribute to situational interest and its maintenance over time.

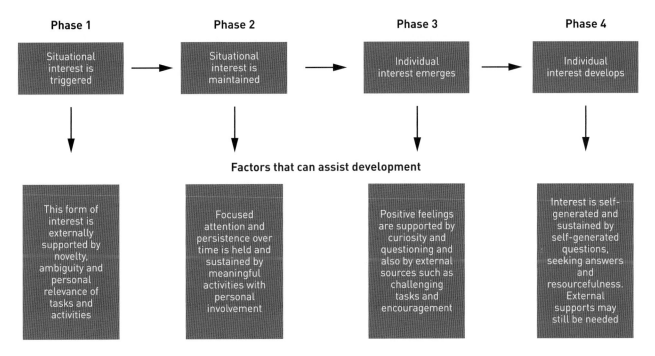

FIGURE 8.13 The development of interest in the classroom. Can you think of an example where your interest might have been 'triggered', leading to sustained individual interest in a topic?

It seems that many features of the classroom context and specific task content play a role in triggering situational interest. This is essential for teachers because not all students will come to school equipped with the background or knowledge to support interest and, of course, not all school topics will reflect the existing individual interests of students. Students may also play a role in triggering and shaping their own interest; for example, Sansone and colleagues (as cited in Ainley, 2006) have noted that university students can find ways to make boring tasks more interesting for themselves by using a range of strategies to focus and direct their attention. While Ben, whom we met at the start of the chapter, seems to have few of these strategies, his younger sister Jodie seems to be able to use her developing research skills to find interesting sources and materials that interest her.

In summary, the classroom context is the place where teachers have the capacity to shape students' motivational experiences and influence engagement by virtue of the lessons and tasks they set for students. For many teachers, this may be a challenging concept because we have our own levels of interest in what we teach, no doubt developed over many years of learning, and it may be hard to understand why students don't share the same interest. The challenge we face is to find ways to engage students in our classrooms, and the concepts of motivation and engagement give us ideas about how to do this. There is, however, an important caution in approaches that attempt to appeal to students with 'fun' or interesting materials. Interest and engagement may be fleeting when the novelty of these new materials or approaches wears off, and Dweck reminds us that learning should not simply be about success but should also challenge. Ultimately, engaging pedagogies should provide meaningful ways to learn that have relevance to students' daily lives and lead to sustained interest and engagement.

SOCIAL FACTORS THAT INFLUENCE ENGAGEMENT

Peers and friends are of immense importance to children and adolescents. As discussed in Chapter 4, these relationships provide critical social and emotional supports. It can be assumed that while positive peer relationships and friendships may motivate and engage students in their schools and classrooms, it must also be assumed that negative peer relationships and behaviours such as bullying and peer rejection would be a barrier to engagement. Juvonen, Espinoza and Knifsend (2012) propose that peer relationships create a sense of belonging at school and this in turn supports school engagement (see Figure 8.14).

FIGURE 8.14 Relationships between peer relationships, belonging and engagement.
Source: Adapted from Juvonen, Espinoza and Knifsend (2012).

In the early discussions and conceptualisation of school engagement, several researchers pointed out that engagement is not just a multidimensional construct; school engagement also exists and is fostered in multiple contexts. In this discussion, Furlong et al. (2003) provide a useful summary of the social context of school engagement by distinguishing research findings in three main domains. We have developed and updated the research in each domain here:

Social–emotional factors

1   As explained in Chapter 4, students' relationships with peers and friends are associated with their adjustment to school and academic performance. Much of this influence comes about because of the affective or emotional climate created by these relationships. For example, a perception of peer support among 5th graders has been associated with affective or emotional engagement in the 6th grade (Estell and Perdue, 2013). Similarly, friendship quality also supported school engagement (Perdue, Manzeske and Estell, 2009). Friends also buffer and support early adolescents against distress during the transition to high school (Wentzel, McNamara, Barry & Caldwell, 2004).

In contrast, Bellmore (2011) found that peer rejection in the 5th grade preceded lower grade-point average scores among children during the transition to high school in the 8th grade. Similarly, a longitudinal study of younger children from kindergarten to Grade 5 found that peer rejection was associated with declining classroom participation and school avoidance (Buhs, Ladd & Herald, 2006). Bullying appears to be particularly damaging to school engagement, with adolescent reports of bullying being associated with lower levels of engagement and a reduction in academic grades across the three years of middle school (Years 6 to 8) (Juvonen, Wang & Espinoza, 2011).

2   Generally, peer relations, whether positive or negative, provide a social–emotional context for school and classroom engagement. Children without friends or satisfactory peer relations may suffer low levels of school engagement because of the distress experienced at school (Furlong et al., 2003). The opposite effect can be seen in good-quality friendships and peer support, with these relationships providing a positive and favourable emotional climate for engagement. As stated in Chapter 4, children's social development requires close attention by teachers at school, not least of all because of these known associations with academic achievement and engagement.

Academic motivation and success

3 The saying that 'birds of a feather flock together' is also true for children's motivational and engagement proclivities. Researcher Thomas Kindermann (1993; 2007) has uniquely mapped the social networks of school students and consistently found that the natural peer groups formed in schools are composed of children with similar motivational orientations, and that even when group memberships change (e.g. a child leaves or joins the group), the group's motivational profile remains the same. Indeed, this form of motivational 'homophily' has been identified in a number of studies related to many engagement constructs including motivation, academic performance and school dropout (Kindermann & Gest, 2009).

4 Wentzel's theory of social motivation suggests that students pursue both social and academic goals that are also valued by their peers and teachers (Wentzel, 2012). Moreover, students' pursuit of social goals is closely related to their pursuit of academic goals (Wentzel, 1989, 1991, 1993). Wentzel, McNamara, Barry and Caldwell (2004) found that adolescents' tendency towards prosocial behavioural goals was influenced by their friends' own tendency, leading to much better motivation and engagement in the early years of high school.

Peer groups and social networks

5 As identified above, children's natural peer groups reflect and influence their motivation and engagement. This process is explicitly acknowledged among students, in that peer groups or 'cliques' come to be identified with certain motivational and engagement profiles: the 'nerds' who value educational achievement and obtain good grades, and the 'homeboys' or 'tough' group who reject academic values and disengage from school (Goto, 1997, as cited in Furlong et al., 2003).

Research on the influence of social context on motivation and engagement contributes further to understanding their complexity. It is not sufficient to focus on any one level of the multilevel model of motivational dynamics proposed by Skinner and Pitzer (2012). Although motivation and engagement in school is typically measured and reported at the level of the individual student, it is also important to consider the antecedent influences of the school, the classroom and social contexts.

It is particularly important to recognise that the social context interacts and often shapes school and classroom engagement. As much as we can shape school and classroom climates and pedagogy, it is also critical to recognise that addressing peer behaviours such as rejection and bullying will also make a significant contribution to the motivation, engagement and academic achievement of our students.

CONCLUDING COMMENTS

Motivation and engagement have been defined in different ways, but each construct represents a critical element in the learning–teaching process. Both have a powerful effect on children's progress at school and on their experiences as adults. Motivation provides the energy, direction and maintenance of behaviours, and is described as an individual-level variable. Engagement reflects various views of this energy in action, and can be viewed as a factor either within the student, or within the wider culture of schools. The educators' task is to motivate learners to realise their potential by engaging them in intellectually challenging learning experiences that involve authentic and meaningful tasks. Educators must also provide support and stimulation to ensure that student engagement is maintained and enhanced, as situational interest may be fleeting. Failure to achieve these goals may reduce the chances of a learner developing a sense of mastery, belonging, and a desire to continue learning beyond the years of schooling.

STUDY TOOLS

ONLINE STUDY RESOURCES

Visit http://login.cengagebrain.com and use the access code that comes with this book for 12 months' access to the student resources for this text.

The CourseMate Express website contains a range of resources and study tools for this chapter, including:

- a **self-check quiz**
- **crosswords**, **flashcards** and a **glossary** to help you revise the key terms from this chapter

- the **Go further** materials and **interactive activity** mentioned in the chapter
- a **video** that illustrates some of the concepts discussed
- plus much more!

CourseMateExpress

CHAPTER REVIEW

- Motivation is an internal process that energises, directs and maintains behaviour over time. It can take the form of a state or trait, and can be stimulated externally or internally.
- Engagement is both an internal process described by behavioural, emotional and cognitive indicators, and one shaped by external processes found in school and classroom climates.
- Poor motivation frequently leads to low achievement at school and, for teachers, problems in classroom management.

- Poor engagement is associated with alienation from school, high rates of students dropping out and, arguably, poor performance in school.
- Motivation and engagement may be enhanced by addressing student behaviours or the features of school, classroom and social climates that influence engagement.
- Certain types of pedagogy, tasks and classroom climates are more facilitative of motivation and engagement than others.

PUTTING IT TOGETHER

Making links between 'motivation and engagement' and material in other chapters

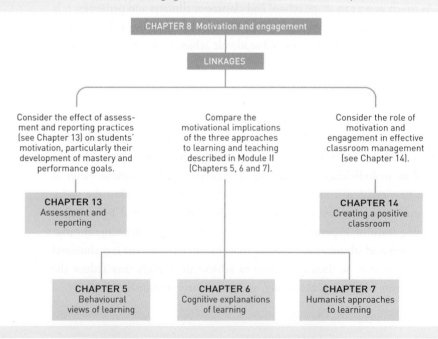

QUESTIONS AND ACTIVITIES FOR SELF-ASSESSMENT AND DISCUSSION

1 What are some of the theories of motivation? Can you give an example of classroom practice that reflects each motivational theory?

2 Explain to someone you know the brain-based concepts that support a 'growth mindset'. How does explaining concepts of a growth mindset benefit the learner?

3 Summarise the debate about the value of mastery versus performance goals.

4 Within your own personal philosophy of teaching, explain your approach to student engagement. How will you respond to students who are less motivated and engaged?

FURTHER RESEARCH

SEARCH ME! AND EDUCATION DATABASES

Explore Search Me! education for articles relevant to this chapter. Fast and convenient, Search Me! education is updated daily and provides you with 24-hour access to full-text articles from hundreds of scholarly and popular journals, ebooks and newspapers, including *The Australian* and *The New York Times*. Log in to Search Me! through http://login.cengagebrain.com and use the search terms listed here as a starting point:

- achievement motivation
- anxiety
- authentic pedagogy
- engagement
- extrinsic motivation
- goal theory
- intrinsic motivation
- mastery goals
- motivation
- performance goals
- school
- school belonging.

Combining these terms with words such as 'schools', 'students', 'learners' or 'adolescents' (as in 'engagement and school') will limit your search to material related to schools and young students.

You can also use these terms to explore databases such as ERIC, PsycINFO and the Australian Education Index.

RECOMMENDED WEBSITES

KidsMatter. Learn more about how anxiety problems and other issues can affect student engagement and wellbeing in school: www.kidsmatter.edu.au/families/mental-health-difficulties/anxiety/anxiety-how-anxiety-problems-affect-children

PERTS-Evidence based education for everyone. Learn more about how researchers developed growth mindset interventions for schools and classrooms https://www.perts.net/

Self-determination theory. Learn more about Ryan and Deci's view of human needs and motivation: www.selfdeterminationtheory.org

RECOMMENDED READING

Christenson, S,.L., Reschly, A.L., & Wylie, C. (2012). *Handbook of Research on Student Engagement*, Springer.

Elliot A. J., Dweck C. S. & Yeager, D. S. (Eds.) (2017). *Handbook of competence and motivation*. 2nd Edn. New York: Guilford Publications.

Goss, P., Sonnemann, J., and Griffiths, K. (2017). Engaging students: creating classrooms that improve learning. Grattan Institute. https://grattan.edu.au/wp-content/uploads/2017/02/Engaging-students-creating-classrooms-that-improve-learning.pdf

Skinner, E. A. & Pitzer, J. (2012). Developmental dynamics of engagement, coping, and everyday resilience. In S. L. Christenson, A. L. Reschly & C. Wylie (eds.), *Handbook of research on student engagement* (pp. 21–44). New York: Springer Science.

Wentzel, K. (2012). Part III Commentary: socio-cultural contexts, social competence, and engagement at school (pp. 479–488). In Christenson S., Reschly A., Wylie C. (eds) *Handbook of Research on Student Engagement*. Boston MA: Springer.

REFERENCES

Ainley, M. (2006). Connecting with learning: Motivation, affect and cognition in interest processes. *Educational Psychology Review, 18*, 391–405.

Ainley, M. (2012). Students' interest and engagement in classroom activities. In S. L. Christenson, A. L. Reschly & C. Wylie (Eds.), *Handbook of research on student engagement*, (pp. 283–302). New York: Springer Science + Business Media.

Ainley, M., Hidi, S. & Berndorff, D. (2002). Interest, learning, and the psychological process that mediate their relationship. *Journal of Educational Psychology, 94*(3), 545–61.

Anderman, E. M. & Mueller, C. E. (2010). Middle school transitions and adolescent development. In J. Meece & J. Eccles (Eds), *Handbook of research on schools, schooling, and human development* (pp. 198–215). Mahwah, NJ: Lawrence Erlbaum Associates.

Anderman, E. M. & Patrick, H. (2012). Achievement goal theory, conceptualization of ability/intelligence, and classroom climate. In S. L. Christenson, A. L. Reschly & C. Wylie (Eds), *The handbook of research on student engagement* (pp. 173–91). New York: Springer Science.

Anderman, E. M. & Wolters, C. A. (2006). Goals, values and affect: Influences on student motivation. In P. A. Alexander & P. H. Winne (Eds), *Handbook of educational psychology* (pp. 369–89). Marwah, NJ: Lawrence Erlbaum Assoc.

Aquino K., Douglas S., Martinko M. J. (2004). Overt anger in response to victimization: Attributional style and organizational norms as moderators. *Occupational Health Psychology, 9*(2), 152–64.

Atkinson, J. W. (1957). Motivational determinants of risk-taking behavior. *Psychological Review, 64*, 359–72.

Atkinson, J. W. (1964). *An introduction to motivation*. Princeton, NJ: Van Nostrand.

Australian Bureau of Statistics. (2011). Australian social trends, June 2011: *Children of the digital revolution*. Cat. no 4102.0. Retrieved from www.abs.gov.au/ausstats/abs@.nsf/Lookup/4102.0Main+Features60Jun+2011

Bandura, A. (1977). *Social learning theory*. Oxford: Prentice Hall.

Bandura, A. (2001). Social cognitive theory: An agentic perspective. *Annual Review of Psychology, 52*, 1–26.

Beery, R. G. (1975). Fear of failure in the student experience. *Personnel and Guidance Journal, 54*, 191–203.

Beidel, D. C., Turner, S. M. & Taylor-Ferreira, J. C. (1999). Teaching study skills and test-taking strategies to elementary school students: The Testbusters program. *Behavior Modification, 23*(4), 630–46.

Bellmore, A. D. (2011). Peer rejection and unpopularity: Predicting GPAs across the transition to middle school. *Journal of Educational Psychology, 103*, 282–95.

Biggs, J. B. & Moore, P. J. (1993). *The process of learning* (3rd ed.). Sydney: Prentice-Hall.

Blackwell, L. A., Trzesniewski, K. H. & Dweck, C. S. (2007). Theories of intelligence and achievement across the junior high school transition: A longitudinal study and an intervention. *Child Development, 78*, 246–63.

Blum, R. (2005). A case for school connectedness. *Educational Leadership, 62*(7), 16–20.

Brody, N. (1992). *Intelligence* (2nd ed.). San Diego: Academic Press.

Brophy, J. (1988). Research linking teacher behavior to student achievement: Potential implications for instruction of Chapter I students. *Educational Psychologist, 23*, 235–312.

Buhs, E. S., Ladd, G. W. & Herald, S. L. (2006). Peer exclusion and victimization: Processes that mediate the relation between peer group rejection and children's classroom engagement and achievement? *Journal of Educational Psychology, 98*, 1–13.

Burnett, P. C. & Mandell, V. (2010). Praise and feedback in the primary classroom: Teachers' and students' perspectives, *Australian Journal of Educational & Developmental Psychology, 10*, 145–54.

Christenson, S. L., Reschly, A. L. & Wylie, C. (Eds). (2012). *The handbook of research on student engagement*. New York: Springer Science.

Christenson, S. L., Reschly, A. L., Appleton, J. J., Berman, S., Spangers, D. & Varro, P. (2008). Best practices in fostering student engagement. In A. Thomas & J. Grimes (Eds), *Best practices in school psychology* (pp. 1099–1120).Washington, DC: National Association of School Psychologists.

Chodkiewicz, A. R., & Boyle, C. (2014). Exploring the contribution of attribution retraining to student perceptions and the learning process. *Educational Psychology in Practice, 30*(1), 78–87. doi: 10.1080/02667363.2014.880048

Chodkiewicz, A.R. & Boyle, C. (2016). Australian students aged 10- to 12-years-old using attribution retraining and cognitive behavioral therapy: A pilot study. *School Psychology International, 37*(5), 519-535. doi10.1177/0143034316667114

Coutino, S. A. (2007). The relationship between goals, metacognition, and academic success. *Educate, 7*(1), 39–47. Retrieved from www.educatejournal.org/index.php/educate/article/view/116/134

Covington, M. V. (1992). *Making the grade: A self-worth perspective on motivation and school reform*. Cambridge: Cambridge University Press.

Covington, M. V. (1997). A motivational analysis of academic life in college. In R. P. Perry & J. C. Smart (Eds), *Effective teaching in higher education: Research and practice*. New York: Agathon Press. Republished from Covington, M. V. (1993). *A motivational analysis of academic life in college. Higher education: Handbook of theory and research*. New York: Agathon Press.

Covington, M. V. (1998). *The will to learn: A guide for motivating young people*. Cambridge: Cambridge University Press.

Covington, M. V. & Omelich, C. L. (1991). Need achievement revisited: Verification of Atkinson's original 2 × 2 model. In C. D. Spielberger., I. G. Sarason., Z. Kulcsar & G.

L. Van Heck (Eds), *Stress and emotion* (Vol. 14.). New York: Hemisphere.

Deci, E. L. & Ryan, R. M. (2000). The 'what' and 'why' of goal pursuits: Human needs and the self-determination of behavior. *Psychological Inquiry, 11,* 227–68. Published by Taylor & Francis.

Deci, E. L., Koestner, R. & Ryan, R. M. (1999). A meta-analytic review of experiments examining the effects of extrinsic rewards on intrinsic motivation. *Psychological Bulletin, 125,* 627–68.

Deci, E. L., Koestner, R. & Ryan, R. M. (2001). Extrinsic rewards and intrinsic motivation in education: Reconsidered once again. *Review of Educational Research 71*(1), 1–27.

Deemer, S. A. (2004). Classroom goal orientation in high school classrooms: Revealing links between teacher beliefs and classroom environments. *Educational Research, 46*(1).

Dowson, M. & McInerney, D. M. (2004). The development and validation of the Goal Orientation and Learning Strategies Survey. *Educational and Psychological Measurement, 64*(2), 290–310.

Dweck, C. S. & Molden, D. C. (2005). Self theories: Their impact on competence motivation and acquisition. In A. Elliot & C. S. Dweck (Eds), *The handbook of competence and motivation.* New York: Guilford.

Dweck, C. (2014). TEDX talk. https://www.youtube.com/watch?v=J-swZaKN2Ic

Dweck, C. (2015). Growth Mindset, Revisited. *Education Week, 35*(5) , 20, 24

Eccles, J. S. (1983). Expectancies, values, and academic behavior. In J. T. Spencer (Ed.), *Achievement and achievement motivation* (pp. 75–146). San Francisco: W. H. Freeman.

Eccles, J. S. & Midgley, C. (1989). Stage/environment fit: Developmentally appropriate classrooms for young adolescents. In R. Ames & C. Ames (Eds), *Research on motivation and education: Goals and cognitions* (Vol. 3, pp. 139–86). New York: Academic Press.

Eccles, J. S., Midgley, C., Wigfield, A., Buchanan, C. M., Reuman, D., Flanagan, C., et al. (1993a). Development during adolescence: The impact of stage-environment fit on adolescents' experiences in schools and families. *American Psychologist, 48*(2), 90–101.

Eccles, J. S., Wigfield, A., Midgley, C., Reuman, D., MacIver, D. & Feldlaufer, H. (1993b). Negative effects of traditional middle schools on students' motivation. *The Elementary School Journal, 93*(5), 553–74.

Elliot, A. J. & McGregor, H. A. (2001). A 2 × 2 achievement goal framework. *Journal of Personality and Social Psychology, 80,* 501–19.

Elliot, A. J., McGregor, H. A. & Gable, S. L. (1999). Achievement goals, study strategies, and exam performance: A mediational analysis. *Journal of Educational Psychology, 76,* 628–44.

Estell, D. B. & Perdue, N. H. (2013). Social support and behavioral and affective school engagement: The effects of peers, parents, and teachers. *Psychology in the Schools, 50*(4), 325–339.

Folmer, A. S., Cole, D. A., Sigal, A. B., Benbow, L. D., Satterwhite, L. F., Swygert, K. E. & Ciesla, J. A. (2008). Age-related changes in children's understanding of effort and ability: Implications for attribution theory and motivation. *Journal of Experimental Child Psychology. 99*(2), 114–34.

Fredericks, J. A., Blumenfeld, P. C. & Paris, A. H. (2004). School engagement: Potential of the concept, state of the evidence. *Review of Educational Research, 74,* 59–109.

Frydenberg, E., Ainley, M. & Russell, V. J. (2005). Student motivation and engagement. *Schooling issues digest,* 2005/2. Australia. Department of Education, Science and Training.

Furlong, M., Whipple, A. D., St Jean, G., Simental, J., Soliz, A. & Punthuna, S. (2003). Multiple contexts of school engagement: Moving toward a unifying framework for educational research and practice. *The California School Psychologist, 8,* 99–113.

Gagné, M. & Deci, E. L. (2005). Self-determination theory and work motivation. *Journal of Organizational Behavior, 26,* 331–62. Published by John Wiley & Sons.

Galloway, D., Rogers, C., Armstrong, D. & Leo, E. (1998). *Motivating the difficult to teach.* London: Longman.

Gemici, S. & Lu, T. (2014). *Do schools influence student engagement in the high school years?* Adelaide: NCVER.

Gettinger, M. & Walter, M. J. (2012). Classroom strategies to enhance academic engaged time. In S. L. Christenson, A. L. Reschly & C. Wylie (Eds), *The handbook of research on student engagement* (pp. 653–74). New York: Springer Science+Business Media.

Gibbs, R., & Poskitt, J. (2010) Student Engagement in the Middle Years of Schooling (Years 7-10): A Literature Review: Report to the Ministry of Education. Ministry of Education New Zealand.

Goss, P., Sonnemann, J., and Griffiths, K. (2017). *Engaging students: creating classrooms that improve learning.* Grattan Institute.

Graham, S. & Weiner, B. (2012). Motivation: Past, present, and future. In K. R. Harris, S. Graham, T. Urdan, C. B. McCormick, G. M. Sinatra & J. Sweller (Eds), *APA educational psychology handbook, Vol. 1: Theories, constructs, and critical issues* (pp. 367–97). Washington, DC: American Psychological Association.

Gunderson, E. A., Gripshover, S. J., Romero, C., Dweck, C. S., Goldin-Meadow, S. & Levine, S. C. (2013). Parent praise to 1–3-year-olds predicts children's motivational frameworks 5 years later. *Child Development, 84*(5), 1526–41.

Hanton, S. & Connaughton, D. (2002). Perceived control of anxiety and its relationship to self-confidence and performance. *Research Quarterly for Exercise and Sport, 73,* 87–97.

Harackiewicz, J. M., Barron, K. E. & Elliot, A. J. (1998). Rethinking achievement goals: When are they adaptive for college students and why? *Educational Psychologist, 33,* 1–21.

Harari, O. & Covington, M. V. (1981). Reactions to achievement behavior from a teacher and student perspective: A developmental analysis. *American Educational Research Journal, 18,* 15–28.

Hidi, S. (1990). Interest and its contribution as a mental resource for learning. *Review of Educational Research, 60*(4), 549–71.

Hidi, S. & Harackiewicz, J. M. (2000). Motivating the academically unmotivated: A critical issue for the 21st century. *Review of Educational Research, 70*(2), 171–9.

Hidi, S. & Renninger, K. A. (2006). The four-phase model of interest development. *Educational Psychologist, 41*(2), 111–27.

James, W. (1890). *The principles of psychology.* New York: Henry Holt.

Juvonen, J., Espinoza, G. & Knifsend, C. (2012). The role of peer relationships in student academic and extracurricular engagement. In S. L. Christenson, A. L. Reschly & C. Wylie (Eds), *Handbook of research on student engagement* (pp. 387–401). New York: Springer Science+Business Media.

Juvonen, J., Wang, Y., & Espinoza, G. (2011). Bullying experiences and compromised academic performance across middle school grade. *Journal of Early Adolescence, 31* , 152–173.

KidsMatter (2017). How to assist children with anxiety problems. © Commonwealth of Australia. Retrieved from www.kidsmatter.edu.au/mental-health-matters/mental-health-difficulties/anxiety

Kindermann, T. A. (1993). Natural peer groups as contexts for individual development: The case of children's motivation at school. *Developmental Psychology, 29,* 970–7.

Kindermann, T. A. (2007). Effects of naturally-existing peer groups on changes in academic engagement in a cohort of sixth graders. *Child Development, 78,* 1186–203.

Kindermann, T. A. & Gest, S. D. (2009). Assessment of the peer group: Identifying social networks in natural settings and measuring their influences. In: Rubin, K. H., Bukowski, W., & Laursen, B. *Handbook of peer interactions, relationships, and groups* (Chapter 6). New York: Guilford.

Landrum, T. J. & Kauffman, J. M. (2006). Behavioral approaches to classroom management. In C. M. Evertson & C. S. Weinstein (Eds), *Handbook of classroom management: Research, practice, and contemporary issues* (pp. 7–71). Mahwah, NJ: Lawrence Erlbaum.

Lepper, M. R., Corpus, J. H. & Iyengar, S. S. (2005). Intrinsic and extrinsic motivational orientations in the classroom: Age differences and academic correlates. *Journal of American Psychology, 97*(2), 184–96.

Linnenbrink-Garcia, L., Durik, A. M., Conley, A. M., Barron, K. E., Tauer, J. M., Karabenick, S. A. & Harackiewicz, J. M. (2010). Measuring situational interest in academic domains. *Educational and Psychological Measurement, 70,* 647–71.

Linnenbrink-Garcia, L & Patall, E.A., (2015) Motivation. In *Handbook of Educational Psychology* (91–103) Routledge. Accessed on: 24 Sep 2017 https://www.routledgehandbooks.com/doi/10.4324/9781315688244.ch7

Marinak, B. & Gambrell, L. (2008). Intrinsic motivation and rewards: What sustains young children's engagement with text? *Literacy Research and Instruction, 47*(1), 9–26.

Martin, A. J. (2003a). *How to motivate your child for school and beyond.* Sydney: Random House/Bantam.

Martin, A. J. (2003b). The Student Motivation Scale: Further testing of an instrument that measures school students' motivation. *Australian Journal of Education, 47,* 88–106.

Martin, A. J. (2007). Examining a multidimensional model of student motivation and engagement using a construct validation approach. *British Journal of Educational Psychology, 77,* 413–40.

Martin, A. J. (2012). Motivation and engagement: Conceptual, operational and empirical clarity. In S. Christenson, A. Reschly & C. Wylie (Eds), *The handbook of research on student engagement* (pp. 303–11). New York: Springer Science.

Martin, A. J., Marsh, H. W. & Debus, R. L. (2001). A quadripolar need achievement representation of self-handicapping and defensive pessimism. *American Educational Research Journal, 38,* 583–610.

Maslow, A. (1954). *Motivation and personality.* New York: Harper.

Masten, A. S. & Motti-Stefanidi, F. (2009). Understanding and promoting resilience in children: Promotive and protective processes in schools. In T. B. Gutkin & C. R. Reynolds (Eds), *Handbook of school psychology* (4th ed., pp. 721–38). Hoboken, NJ: Wiley.

McClelland, D. C., Atkinson, J. W., Clark, R. W. & Lowell, E. L. (1953). *The achievement motive.* New York: Appleton-Century-Crofts.

McDougall, W. (1923). *Outline of psychology* (4th ed.). London: Methuen.

McNeely, C. A., Nonnemaker, J. M. & Blum, R. W. (2002). Promoting School connectedness: Evidence from the National Longitudinal Study of Adolescent Health. *Journal of School Health, 72*(4), 138–46.

Meyer, D. & Turner, J. (2006). Re-conceptualizing emotion and motivation to learn in classroom contexts. *Educational Psychology Review, 18,* 377–90.

Midgley, C., Kaplan, A. & Middleton, M. (2001). Performance-approach goals: Good for what, for whom, under what circumstances, and at what cost? *Journal of Educational Psychology, 93,* 77–86.

Mueller, C. M. & Dweck, C. S. (1998). Praise for intelligence can undermine children's motivation and performance. *Journal of Personality* and *Social Psychology, 75*(1), 33–52.

Murayama, K. & Kuhbandner, C. (2011). Money enhances memory consolidation: But only for boring material. *Cognition, 119*(1), 120–4.

Murayama, K., Matsumoto, M., Izuma, K. & Matsumoto, K. (2010). Neural basis of the undermining effect of extrinsic reward on intrinsic motivation. *Proceedings of the National Academy of Sciences of the United States of America, 107,* 20 911–16. doi: 10.1073/pnas.1013305107

New Zealand Ministry of Education. (2009). *Annual Report of the Ministry of Education 2009.* Retrieved from www.minedu.govt.nz/theMinistry/PublicationsAndResources/AnnualReport/AnnualReportArchive/~/media/MinEdu/Files/TheMinistry/AnnualReport/2009/EducationAnnualReport2009Full.pdf

Nichols, J. G. & Miller, A. T. (1983). The differentiation of effort and ability. *Child Development, 54,* 951–9.

Organization for Economic Cooperation and Development. (2013). *PISA 2012 Results: Ready to Learn: Students' Engagement, Drive and Self-Beliefs* (Volume III), PISA, OECD Publishing. http://dx.doi.org/10.1787/9789264201170-en.

Patrick, H., Turner, J. C., Meyer, D. K. & Midgley, C. (2003). How teachers establish psychological environments during the first days of school: Associations with avoidance in mathematics. *Teachers College Record, 105,* 1521–58.

Paunesku, D., Walton, G. M., Romero, C., Smith, E. N., Yeager, D. S., & Dweck, C. S. (2015). Mind-set interventions are a scalable treatment for academic underachievement. *Psychological Science, 26,* 784–793. http://dx.doi.org/10.1177/0956797615571017

Pekrun, R. & Stephens, E.J. (2012). Academic emotions. In K. R. Harris, S. Graham & T. Urdan (Eds-in-Chief), *APA Educational Psychology Handbook: Vol. 2. Individual Differences and Cultural and Contextual Factors* (pp. 3–31). Washington, DC: American Psychological Association.

Perdue, N. H., Manzeske, D. P. & Estell, D. B. (2009). Early predictors of school engagement: Exploring the role of peer relationships. *Psychology in the Schools, 46,* 1084–1097. doi: 10.1002/pits.20446

Pérez Nieto, M. A., Camuñas, N., Cano-Vindel, A., Miguel-Tobal, J. J. & Iruarrizaga, I.

(2000). Anger and anger coping: A study of attributional styles. *Studia Psychologica, 42,* 289–302.

Pintrich, P. R. (2000). The role of goal orientation in self-regulated learning. In M. Boekaerts, P. R. Pintrich & M. Zeidner (Eds.), *Handbook of Self-Regulation* (pp. 451–501). San Diego, CA: Academic Press.

Pintrich, P. R. & Schunk, D. H. (1996). *Motivation in education: Theory, research and applications.* Englewood Cliffs, NJ: Prentice Hall Merrill.

Pintrich, P. R. & Zeidner, M. (Eds.), *Handbook of Self-Regulation* (pp. 451–501). San Diego, CA: Academic Press.

Reeve, J. (2006). Extrinsic rewards and inner motivation. In C. M. Evertson & C. S. Weinstein (Eds), *Handbook of classroom management: Research, practice, and contemporary issues,* (pp. 645–664). Mahwah, NJ: Lawrence Erlbaum Associates Publishers.

Renninger, K. A. (1992). Individual interest and development: Implications for theory and practice. In K. A. Renninger, S. Hidi & A. Krapp (Eds), *The role of interest in learning and development* (pp. 361–95). Hillsdale, NJ: Erlbaum.

Renninger, K. A. & Hidi, S. (2002). Student interest and achievement: Developmental issues raised by a case study. In A. Wigfield & J. Eccles (Eds), *The development of achievement motivation* (pp. 173–95). San Diego, CA: Academic Press.

Renninger, K. A. & Hidi, S. (2011). Revisiting the conceptualization, measurement, and generation of interest. *Educational Psychologist, 46*(3), 168–84.

Resnick, M. D., Bearman, P. S., Blum, R. W., Bauman, K. E., Harris, K. M., Jones, J., Tabor, J., Beuhring, T., Sieving, R. E., Shew, M., Ireland, M., Bearinger, L. H. & Udry, J. R. (1997). Protecting adolescents from harm: Findings from the National Longitudinal Study On Adolescent Health. *The Journal of the American Medical Association, 278*(10), 823–32.

Robinson, J. A., Alexander, D. J. & Gradisar, M. S. (2009). Preparing for Year 12 examinations: Predictors of psychological distress and sleep. *Australian Journal of Psychology, 61,* 59–68.

Rodgers, A. & Dunsmuir, S. (2013). A controlled evaluation of the 'FRIENDS for Life' Emotional Resiliency Programme on overall anxiety levels, anxiety subtype levels and school adjustment. *Child and Adolescent Mental Health,* doi: 10.1111/camh.12030

Roorda, D. L., Koomen, H. M. Y., Spilt, J. L. & Oort, F. J. (2011). The influence of affective teacher–student relationships on students' school engagement and achievement: A meta-analytic approach. *Review of Educational Research, 81,* 493–529.

Ryan, R. M. & Deci, E. L. (2000a). Self-determination theory and the facilitation of intrinsic motivation, social development, and well-being. *American Psychologist, 55,* 68–78.

Ryan, R. M. & Deci, E. L. (2000b). When rewards compete with nature: The undermining of intrinsic motivation and self-regulation. In C. Sansone & J. M. Harackiewicz (Eds), *Intrinsic and extrinsic motivation: The search for optimal motivation and performance* (pp. 13–54). San Diego, CA: Academic Press.

Schraw, G. & Aplin, B. (1998). Teacher preferences for mastery-oriented students. *Journal of Educational Research, 91,* 215–20.

Schunk, D. H. (2012). Social cognitive theory. In K. R. Harris, S. Graham, T. Urdan, C. B. McCormick, G. M. Sinatra & J. Sweller (Eds), *APA Educational Psychology Handbook, Vol. 1: Theories, constructs, and critical issues* (pp. 101–23). Washington, DC: American Psychological Association.

Senko, C., & Freund, A.M. (2015). Mastery-avoidance achievement goal effects in young versus elderly adults: A laboratory test. *Motivation and Emotion, 39*(4), 477–488. doi:10.1007/s11031-015-9474-1

Senko , C., Hulleman, C.S., & Harackiewicz , J. M. (2011). Achievement Goal Theory at the Crossroads: Old Controversies, Current Challenges, and New Directions, *Educational Psychologist, 46*(1), 26–47, DOI: 10.1080/00461520.2011.538646

Shernoff, D. J. (2012). Engagement and positive youth development: Creating optimal learning environments. In K. R. Harris, S. Graham, T. Urdan, C. B. McCormick, G. M. Sinatra & J. Sweller (Eds), *APA educational psychology handbook, Vol. 1: Theories, constructs, and critical issues* (pp. 195–220). Washington, DC: American Psychological Association.

Skinner, E. A., & Pitzer, J. (2012). Developmental dynamics of engagement, coping, and everyday resilience. In S. L. Christenson, A. L. Reschly, & C. Wylie (Eds.), *Handbook of research on student engagement* (pp. 21-44). New York: Springer Science.

Smith, L. (2004). Changes in student motivation over the final years of high school. *Journal of Educational Enquiry, 5*(2), 64–85.

Toland, J., & Boyle, C. (2008). Applying cognitive behavioural methods to retraining children's attribution for success and failure in learning. *School Psychology International, 29*(3), 286–302.

Turner, J. C., Midgley, C., Meyer, D. K., Gheen, M., Anderman, E. M., Kang, J. & Patrick, H. (2002). The classroom environment and students' reports of avoidance behaviors in mathematics: A multi-method study. *Journal of Educational Psychology, 94,* 88–106.

Urdan, T. & Turner, J. (2005). Competence motivation in the classroom. In A. J. Elliot & C. S. Dweck (Eds), *Handbook of competence and motivation* (pp. 297–317). New York: Guilford Press.

Van Yperen, N. W., Elliot, A. J. & Anseel, F. (2009). The influence of mastery-avoidance goals on performance improvement. *European Journal of Social Psychology, 39,* 932–43.

Veermans, M. & Tapola, A. (2004). Primary school students' motivational profiles in longitudinal settings. *Scandinavian Journal of Educational Research, 48*(4), 373–95. Published by Routledge.

Vrugt, A. & Oort, F. J. (2008). Metacognition, achievement goals, study strategies and academic achievement: pathways to achievement, *Metacognition and Learning, 30,* 123–46.

Wang, C. K. J., Liu, W. C., Chatzisarantis, N. L. D. & Lim, B. S. C. (2010). Influence of perceived motivational climate on achievement goals in physical education: A structural equation mixture modeling analysis. *Journal of Sport and Exercise Psychology, 32,* 324–38.

Weiner, B. (1992). *Human motivation: Metaphors, theories and research.* Newbury Park, CA: Sage.

Weiner, B. (2010). The development of an attribution-based theory of motivation: A history of ideas. *Educational Psychologist, 45*(1), 28–36. DOI: 10.1080/00461520903433596 Published by Routledge.

Wentzel, K. R. (1989). Adolescent classroom goals, standards for performance, and academic achievement: An interactionist perspective. *Journal of Educational Psychology, 81,* 131–42.

Wentzel, K. R. (1991). Social competence at school: Relations between social responsibility and academic achievement. *Review of Educational Research, 61,* 1–24. Sage Publications.

Wentzel, K. R. (1993). Social and academic goals at school: Motivation and achievement in early adolescence. *Journal of Early Adolescence, 13,* 4–20.

Wentzel, K. (2012). Part III Commentary: Socio-Cultural Contexts, Social Competence, and Engagement at School (pp. 479–488). In Christenson S., Reschly A., Wylie C. (eds) *Handbook of Research on Student Engagement.* Boston, MA: Springer.

Wentzel, K. R., McNamara Barry, C. & Caldwell, K. A. (2004). Friendships in middle school: Influences on motivation and school adjustment. *Journal of Educational Psychology, 96*(2), 195–203.

Wiersma, U. J. (1992). The effects of extrinsic rewards in intrinsic motivation: A meta-analysis. *Journal of Occupational and Organizational Psychology, 65,* 101–14.

Wigfield, A. & Eccles, J. S. (2000). Expectancy-value theory of achievement motivation. *Contemporary Educational Psychology, 25,* 68–81.

Wigfield, A., Eccles, J. S., Schiefele, U., Roeser, R. W., Davis-Kean, P. (2006). The development of achievement motivation. In N. Eisenberg (Ed.), *Handbook of child psychology, Vol. 3: Social, emotional, and personality development* (6th ed., pp. 933–1002). New York: Wiley.

Yeager, D. S. & Dweck, C. S. (2012). Mindsets that promote resilience: When students believe that personal characteristics can be developed. *Educational Psychologist, 47,* 1–13.

Yeager, D. S., Romero, C., Paunesku, D., Hulleman, C.S., Schneider, B., Hinojosa, C., Lee, H.Y., O'Brien, J., Flint, K., Roberts, A., Trott, J., Greene, D., Walton, G.M. & Dweck, C.S. (2016). Using design thinking to improve psychological interventions: the case of the growth mindset during the transition to high school. *Journal of Educational Psychology, 108*(3), 374–391.

Yerkes, R. M. & Dodson, J. D. (1908). The relation of strength of stimulus to rapidity of habit-formation. *Journal of Comparative Neurology and Psychology, 18,* 459–82.

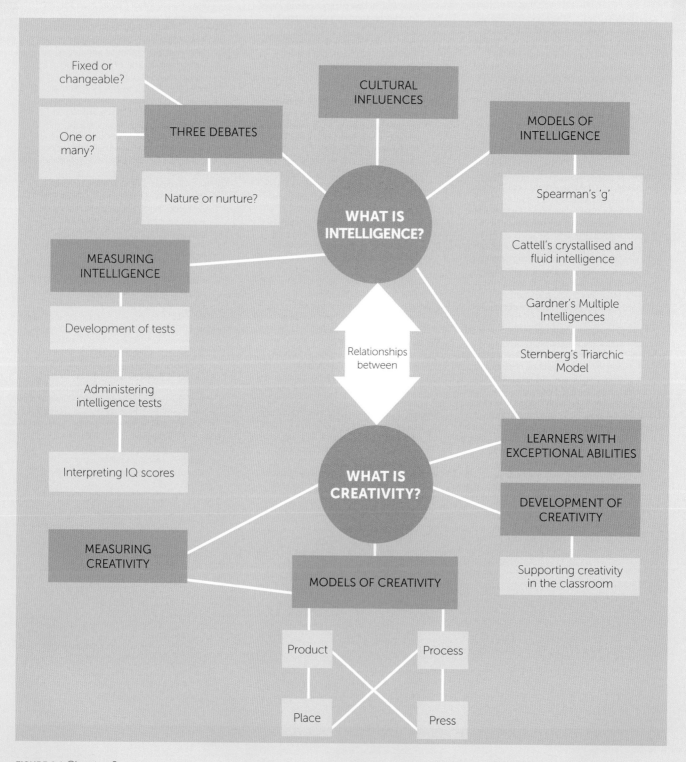

FIGURE 9.1 Chapter 9 concept map

KEY QUESTIONS

After reading this chapter, you should be able to answer the following questions:

- What is intelligence? What characterises intelligent behaviour?
- What are some models of intelligence proposed in scientific studies of intellectual ability?
- What are some ways in which contemporary models of intelligence are applied in classrooms?
- As a teacher, what will your approach to intelligence be?
- What is creativity?
- How can creativity be supported and developed in the classroom?

ONLINE STUDY RESOURCES

Bring your learning to life with **interactive learning**, **study** and **exam preparation tools** that support the printed textbook. CourseMate Express includes **quizzes**, **interactive activities**, **videos**, a tool to help you '**develop your philosophy**' and more.

INTRODUCTION

Four students are working side by side on a design problem. They have been given the task of improving an umbrella. Simon breaks a technical umbrella drawing into its component parts, and suggests they think about each one and how it can be improved. Kumar wants to look at different umbrella designs and take from the best of them to shape their own design. Matt starts with the problems umbrellas have – turning inside out in the wind, dripping on the floor – and thinks about how to solve those. Benji imagines how else he could escape rain and starts to draw a magic shield that would repel the raindrops. Which of these would you class as an intelligent approach? What about creative?

Intelligence and creativity are widely used terms, and both are recognised as important for our schools to support in students. Yet they are each concepts that have been approached in a variety of ways (like the umbrella problem), and that have sparked debate. This chapter explores approaches to intelligence and creativity, and looks at how they can be supported in schools.

CourseMateExpress

Online resources
Explore your own view of intelligence with the **Interactive Activity** on this text's website

WHAT IS INTELLIGENCE?

What is meant when someone is described as 'smart', 'bright', 'clever' or 'intelligent'? It is easy to assume that these terms mean much the same to everyone. But is this so? Think about what is meant by a word such as 'masculine'. Everyone can identify examples of masculinity in daily life, although it can be very difficult for people to pinpoint the specific characteristics that make one person appear 'masculine' and another to lack these qualities. Moreover, perceptions of masculinity differ across social groups and over time. Think of the muscular curves of the famous statue of David in comparison with the image of an Elizabethan fop or a Japanese sumo wrestler (see Figure 9.2). Concepts of intelligence are similar. The term **intelligence** can commonly be taken to mean a general aptitude and capacity for understanding and learning, but different people mean different things when they talk about intelligence, as a result of historical and cultural factors.

In everyday usage, intelligence is usually conceived as a mental ability that is present in individuals in differing amounts: 'Jill is clever; Arnold is a bit dumb'. Words such as 'bright', 'brilliant', 'smart' or 'wise'

intelligence
A general aptitude and capacity for understanding and learning

FIGURE 9.2 Which figure best represents masculinity?

are used to refer to examples of human activity thought to be indicative of high ability or intelligence. For most people, intelligence is valued in terms of 'the more, the better'. Some views of intelligence even seem to imply that it has a physical existence in the human skull. However, few people can give a definition of intelligence, although most can cite examples of intelligent behaviour. More interestingly, as suggested earlier, definitions and examples given differ from individual to individual, from culture to culture, and across time. See Table 9.1 for a comparison of ideas of intelligence across a number of cultures.

TABLE 9.1 Cultural variations in implicit theories of intelligence

WESTERN NOTIONS	JAPANESE NOTIONS	TAIWANESE NOTIONS	KENYAN NOTIONS
• Practical problem solving • Social competence • Verbal ability	• Task efficiency • Positive social competence • Receptive social competence	• General cognition • Interpersonal intelligence • Intrapersonal intelligence • Intellectual self-assertion • Intellectual self-effacement	• Understanding how to handle real-life problems • Initiative • Respect • Knowledge and skills

Source: Compiled from data reported in Sternberg (2007); Azuma and Kashiwagi (1987)

THINK ABOUT

■ Think about what it might mean in a classroom if students and their families have a different concept of intelligence from yours. What would you do?

CULTURAL INFLUENCES ON INTELLIGENCE

The idea of intelligence as mental agility or mental speed is a very Western notion. In some non-Western cultures, speed of thinking and finding solutions to problems are not regarded as particularly important attributes (Biesheuvel, 1969). In such cultures, wisdom can mean the ability to listen, observe, reflect, learn from others, and think through the short- and long-term consequences of an action. Those growing up in communities with such beliefs would be unlikely to give quick, accurate responses to questions in a standard Western intelligence test.

The skills valued by particular societies are likely to represent the skills that are useful in that society (think about this in terms of Vygotsky's sociocultural theory described in Chapter 3). For example, in some Pacific island communities where the skills of navigation (the ability to read the waves, clouds and stars) are regarded as indicative of intelligence, mental agility in a Western sense is irrelevant. Grigorenko et al. (2001) described the concepts of intelligence held by the Luo people living on the shores of Lake Victoria in western Kenya as comprising four attributes: *rieko* or smartness, knowledge, ability, competence and power; *luoro* or social qualities such as respect and care for others, obedience, diligence and readiness to share; *paro* or the thinking involved in problem solving and caring for others; and *winjo* or comprehending and understanding. For Luo children, teachers and parents, the four attributes of intelligence are interrelated and all are used by the Luo people in judging intelligence in others. However, only the concept of *rieko* was associated (positively) with Luo children's scores on a Western test of intelligence and with tests of achievement in English and mathematics. Westerners would base their judgement of the intelligence of Luo children on Western ideas of smartness, knowledge and ability rather than the broader Luo concept that included social qualities and the practical thinking skills needed for success in a Luo community. Grigorenko et al. (2001) concluded that children viewed as intelligent in a Luo community might be judged as 'lacking intelligence' from a Western perspective. Indeed, Luo concepts of intelligence seem to be closer to emerging concepts of practical intelligence (discussed later in this chapter) than to more traditional Western ideas. However, it is likely that, as in other parts of Africa (Booth, 2002), increasing contact with Western ideas and educational practices among the Luo will result in gradual incorporation of Western ideas about intelligence into Luo thinking.

Sternberg (2002, 2003, 2007, 2012) has distinguished between academic intelligence, measured by conventional tests of general mental abilities and academic performance, and 'practical intelligence' or 'successful intelligence', measured in terms of everyday skills as identified by the Luo people. Other examples of culturally based variation in intelligence and intellectual development have been reported in a comparison of mental processing in Greek and Chinese school students, which describes the strength of the Chinese students' performance in visual/spatial tasks (for example, a paper-and-pencil maze test) in comparison with the performance of Greek children (Demetriou et al., 2005). The superior performance of Chinese students is attributed to their experiences when learning the Chinese logographic writing system. Chinese students studying in Australian universities demonstrate well-developed skills in manipulating information, analysing figures, reasoning and memory (fluid intelligence), but appear to demonstrate more limited abilities in critical analysis (integrative thinking and reflective judgement). However, these limitations in performance may simply reflect difficulties in studying within a second language rather than any lack of critical-thinking skills within Chinese culture or differences in perceptions of intelligence (Paton, 2005; Shi, 2004).

In technologically developed societies, intelligence is generally seen as involving high levels of competence in literacy, numeracy and, increasingly, technological skills. Children are expected to acquire such skills from an early age. The paper-and-pencil tasks used in Western-based intelligence tests are typical of the instructions that children encounter at school and at home. However, there are cultural variations within developed societies too. Okagaki and Sternberg (1993) found in the USA that Latino parents placed more emphasis on social competence, while Asian and Anglo parents emphasised cognitive skills. Fletcher and Hattie (2011) suggested that Western societies are experiencing a shift in what is valued as intelligence, from knowledge to problem solving and pattern finding. Clearly, the way we conceptualise an abstract idea such as 'intelligence' is strongly influenced by cultural and social factors.

MODELS OF INTELLIGENCE

There are also disagreements among psychologists as to the concept, structure and origins of intelligence, and these have led to a number of different models of intelligence. Three enduring debates have implications for the relationship of intelligence and education, and influence teachers' practices. They are centred on these questions:

- Is intelligence one thing or many?
- Is intelligence fixed or changeable?
- Is intelligence an innate capacity, or does it derive from a child's experiences in their environment?

ONE THING OR MANY?

intelligence quotient (IQ)
A score on an intelligence test that permits an individual's performance to be compared with the average performance on the test

People often appear to do well on a range of intelligence-test tasks (such as verbal reasoning, abstract and visual reasoning, vocabulary knowledge and sentence comprehension), while others do poorly, and these results would seem to suggest the existence of a general mental capacity, or '*g*'. If intelligence is one overarching capacity, then it could be measured and individuals identified as having varying levels of intelligence. This is the view that is attached to the notion of an **intelligence quotient (IQ)**. It also tends to be the way in which we talk about intelligence – as a singular capacity that people have to varying degrees.

However, closer examination of test results often reveals a consistent pattern in individual responses to different types of items in a test. One person might answer most of the items involving vocabulary, general comprehension, arithmetic and reasoning correctly, but have more difficulty in completing mazes, copying block designs or arranging pictures to tell a story. Another might struggle to get any correct answers on the test, achieving the best scores in digit span (repeating a sequence of digits) and coding (pairing symbols and digits using a key). These different response patterns suggest that intelligence comprises not only a general, overarching mental capacity, but also some specific abilities. The debate continues about whether these specific abilities are connected, or whether they are, in fact, quite separate intelligences.

The debate is not just academic – it has implications for applications of intelligence and intelligence testing in particular. If intelligence is a single thing, it could be measured, and used to identify individuals needing support or enrichment in schools. If it consists of a number of dimensions, these could also be measured to identify an individual's strengths and weaknesses, and support or enrichment could be specifically targeted. Models of intelligence that describe intelligence as multiple things are taken up by teachers to differentiate the curriculum – that is, to provide experiences that are likely to develop and allow students to display a number of intelligences, rather than just one (see the sections on Gardner's theory, and Sternberg's theory).

Spearman and '*g*'

general mental ability (*g*)
Basic intellectual capacity

Charles Spearman (1904, 1927), an English psychologist, was among those who supported the concept of intelligence as comprising a **general mental ability**, or '*g*'. He argued that some people are highly intelligent because they are 'well-endowed with *g*', while others are less intelligent because they are 'low in *g*' (Howe, 1997, p. 27). However, Spearman also observed that there is often considerable variability in how individuals perform on the different types of items used in intelligence tests (such as naming objects, recalling strings of letters and mentally manipulating three-dimensional shapes). One person may be particularly gifted in language-related activities and poor in recalling lists of digits, while another can visualise three-dimensional shapes easily but cannot name objects quickly. Spearman explained these individual variations in terms of **specific mental abilities** (or '*s*') that are overlaid by the general mental ability of the individual. General intelligence, or *g*, reflects the speed and efficiency of the brain's processing or 'mental energy' (Cianciolo & Sternberg, 2004, p. 3), while *s* represents the specific mental abilities tapped by particular tasks.

specific mental abilities (*s*)
A collection of distinct intellectual abilities

Spearman's ideas are sometimes described as a 'two-factor theory of intelligence' – the two factors comprising *g*, or general mental ability, and *s*, or the specific mental abilities tapped by different items in an intelligence test (see **Box 9.7**).

Recent research on the structure of intelligence supports Spearman's notion of *g* (Deary, 2012). It accounts for approximately half of the variance in intelligence tests. Debate continues over the structure of the abilities that make up *g*, and that sit beyond it.

Cattell's crystallised and fluid intelligence

A further view of the concept of intelligence as *g* was proposed by R. B. Cattell (1987), who divided it into two parts: **crystallised intelligence**, involving culturally based, fact-oriented knowledge gained through experience; and **fluid intelligence**, or non-verbal abilities or mental efficiency associated with manipulation of information, seeing complex relationships and solving problems. Crystallised abilities are demonstrated in tests of word knowledge and general information, while fluid abilities, which decline with age, are evident in problem solving, and non-verbal tasks such as digit-symbol substitution and spatial visualisation. The association between fluid abilities and maturation (ageing) explains the common observation that 'as people age they may get wiser but less sharp' (Kay, 2005, p. 10). Carroll (1993) demonstrated that results from intelligence tests support this model of intelligence, with tests of individual abilities falling broadly into the two groups of crystallised or fluid intelligence. These two factors are correlated, suggesting the existence of *g* as an overarching factor. The resulting model has been termed the 'three-stratum model of intelligence', with individual abilities at the first level, crystallised and fluid intelligence at the second level along with memory factors and sensory modalities such as visual or auditory, and *g* at the third; Figure 9.3 illustrates this model. The debate about the structure of intelligence continues, with further models being proposed and tested. (See Hunt, 2011, for a discussion of some of these.)

crystallised intelligence
Culturally based, fact-oriented knowledge gained through experience

fluid intelligence
Non-verbal abilities associated with manipulation of information, seeing complex relationships and solving problems

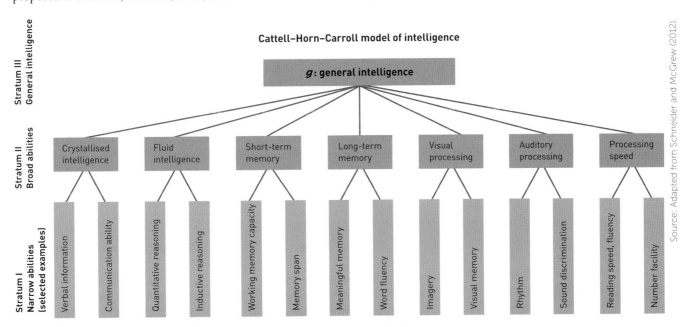

Source: Adapted from Schneider and McGrew (2012).

FIGURE 9.3 Under *g*, at least 16 broad and more than 80 narrow abilities have been identified. A selection of these is shown here.

IS INTELLIGENCE FIXED OR CHANGEABLE?

Do you think of intelligence as something someone has and which cannot be changed, or as something that develops as part of cognition? About 40 per cent of adults believe ability is fixed and unchangeable, and 40 per cent believe it can grow and develop (about 20 per cent of people are unsure or undecided) (Dweck & Molden, 2005). Your answer to this question will influence how you view students in your classroom, and how you view your own teaching. For example, if intelligence is fixed, then what you do as a teacher will need to work around the constraints of the levels of intelligence of your students: you should adapt your teaching to take into account their levels of ability. If intelligence develops, however, then part of your role as a teacher will be to develop intelligence in your students. You might adapt your teaching to fit their current level of intelligence (ability to use and apply knowledge), but you will also be seeking to extend their intelligence so that they can use and apply their knowledge in increasingly sophisticated ways. These views of intelligence also influence students' learning and motivation, as we saw in Chapter 8. Although intelligence has traditionally been viewed as fairly stable

CourseMateExpress

Online resources
Take a moment to consider your philosophy of learning and teaching. You may wish to use the **Develop your philosophy** tool on this text's CourseMate website

from early adolescence, particularly in intelligence testing, Nisbett et al. (2012) identify a number of environmental factors such as schooling that influence it, as we will see later in this chapter.

A number of current theorists, such as Gardner and Sternberg, argue that intelligence is changeable, and that the work of schools should be not just to teach content, but also to develop students' intelligence. These researchers broadened the use of knowledge about intelligence from identifying students with varying levels of intelligence (the psychometric approach) to nurturing intelligence. Intelligence is viewed not so much as something students come to school with, but as something to be developed by the school.

Gardner's theory of multiple intelligences

multiple intelligences (MI)
Eight or more
domains of intellectual
functioning

Howard Gardner's (1983) model of intelligence extended traditional ideas about intelligence to include a wider range of abilities, or **multiple intelligences (MI)**. Gardner dismissed traditional intelligence tests, arguing that they are based on a narrow view of human intelligence that is dominated by Western ideas. He also argued against the notion of *g* and that people with high *g* are equally able across all areas. According to Gardner, intelligence comprises a set of separate intelligences, each of which is specialised for acquiring knowledge and solving problems in different areas of cognitive activity. He identified at least eight domains of intellectual functioning, each of which he argued was quite distinct, in that how we perform in one area is quite separate from how we perform in another. Interestingly, the intelligences identified by Gardner represent distinct areas within our cultural experience, and include language, music, mathematical comprehension and reasoning, spatial awareness, physical movement and social understanding (see Box 9.1).

BOX 9.1 RESEARCH LINKS

GARDNER'S THEORY OF MULTIPLE INTELLIGENCES

Gardner (1983) identified eight distinct domains, or areas, within his model of multiple intelligences.

In 1999, Gardner considered the possibility of two more domains: 'spiritual intelligence' and 'existential intelligence', but cautioned that they did not fulfil sufficient criteria to be counted as full intelligences. Researchers continue to collect data on these and other potential intelligences not yet confirmed.

TABLE 9.2 Gardner's eight domains of intelligence

DOMAIN (AREA) OF INTELLIGENCE	DESCRIPTION OF CONTENT	EXAMPLES OF OCCUPATION	REPRESENTATIVE INDIVIDUALS
Linguistic	Ability to perceive or generate spoken and written language	• poet • lawyer • writer	T. S. Eliot, Judith Wright, Henry Lawson, Patrick White
Musical	Sensitivity to pitch, rhythm and timbre; the ability to create, communicate and understand meaning in sound; the ability to discern sound patterns	• musician • music critic • mechanic	Igor Stravinsky, Percy Grainger, Dame Kiri Te Kanawa, Paul McCartney
Logical-mathematical	Use and appreciation of numerical, causal, abstract or logical relations	• mathematician • scientist • engineer	Albert Einstein, Howard Florey, Douglas Mawson, Frank Macfarlane Burnet, Peter Doherty

>>

Gardner drew on case studies of individuals with highly developed abilities in one area, but weaker abilities in others, as evidence that intelligence can exist variably in different domains (see Box 9.1 for some of the famous people Gardner referred to as intelligent in each domain). He also referred to examples of brain damage from stroke or accident that affect just one domain, but not others, as evidence for separate intelligences. Others have challenged his methods and conclusions (see Box 9.2).

Gardner's ideas remind us that teachers should be aware of students' strengths that could help them to do well in at least one of the intellectual domains. Moreover, teaching programs need to be varied in response to the different strengths of students, rather than expecting them to do everything in the same way. For example, within an English lesson, the personal area can be tapped by asking questions about how a particular character might be feeling or what he or she is thinking at a particular point in the story. Similarly, students' musical talents can be highlighted during the dramatisation of the story. Gardner also reminds teachers to take a broad approach to instruction, rather than focusing exclusively on the academic domain. They also need to remember that exceptional talents are the products not only of natural ability or high levels of intelligence in a particular domain, but also of some type of formal training. Great artists may have outstanding capacities in the spatial domain, but they also need 'formal and informal experiences in the disciplines of the visual arts' (Gardner, Hatch & Torff, 1997, p. 262).

DOMAIN (AREA) OF INTELLIGENCE	DESCRIPTION OF CONTENT	EXAMPLES OF OCCUPATION	REPRESENTATIVE INDIVIDUALS
Spatial	Ability to perceive visual and spatial information, and to transform or modify this information and recreate visual images	• visual artist • draftsperson • navigator	Pablo Picasso, Albert Namatjira, Frida Kahlo, Kay Cottee
Bodily-kinaesthetic	Control of all or parts of one's body to solve problems or create products	• dancer • athlete • hiker	Martha Graham, Vaslaw Nijinsky, Ian Thorpe, Cathy Freeman, Sir Edmund Hillary
Intrapersonal	Capacity to form a mental model of oneself and use the model to make informed decisions about possible actions	• psychoanalyst • psychologist	Sigmund Freud, Melanie Klein, B. F. Skinner
Interpersonal	Capacity to recognise, distinguish between and influence in desired ways others' feelings, beliefs and intentions	• religious leader • politician	Martin Luther King, Nelson Mandela, Mahatma Gandhi
Naturalist	Ability to understand and work effectively in the natural world	• biologist • zoologist • naturalist	Charles Darwin, Jane Goodall, David Attenborough

Source: Adapted from Gardner (1993, 1999); Granott and Gardner (1994, p. 174); McGrath (2005); Torff and Gardner (1999, pp. 143–4).

ACTIVITIES

1   Can you identify a range of intelligences that you possess?
2   How did you identify your intelligences? What indicators did you look for?
3   How would you identify intelligences among the students in your class?
4   Do you notice any cultural bias in the examples of people provided in Gardner's list of intelligences? Can you substitute examples of historic or current figures from within your own country and culture?

BOX 9.2 RESEARCH LINKS

THINKING CRITICALLY ABOUT GARDNER'S THEORY OF INTELLIGENCE

Gardner's theory is an example of an area in which psychologists and educators have different views. This is not to say that either educators or psychologists are necessarily right or wrong, but issues of relevance to psychologists (such as how intelligence is defined, or structured) can be different from those of relevance to educators (such as how we think about and nurture students' abilities).

A number of psychologists working in the area of intelligence have been critical of Gardner's theory, particularly the notion that the intelligences are independent of one another (for example, Brody, 1992; Sternberg, 2003). They argue that his evidence in support of separate intelligences, taken from studies of savants and people with brain damage, does not take into account the changes in the brain that occur as a result of damage, and so are weak indicators. Studies of how the brain works show that in most tasks, we draw on a number of areas at once (see Chapter 2), which is provided as evidence of intelligence as singular rather than multiple. This is something Gardner (1983) also acknowledged – he said that in most tasks, we use a number of intelligences. Others have questioned whether the eight intelligences Gardner describes are all really 'intelligence' (Sattler, 2001). Psychometric studies likewise do not support the theory, showing evidence for a 'g' that links various abilities (Castejon, Perez & Gilar, 2010; Visser, Ashton & Vernon, 2006). Measurement of the intelligences has been difficult to develop, given the broad and sometimes vague description of some of the intelligences (Furnham, 2009). However, Gardner (2006) has stated that he is not interested in measurement of intelligence in the traditional way; that was, in fact, one of the issues his theory contests.

Educators, however, have taken up Gardner's theory, seeing its application to differentiation of the curriculum for their students (for example, McGrath, 2005). It connects with their own experience in classrooms of a wide range of abilities across domains. Its wider view of intelligence also appeals to teachers' desire to see and nurture potential in all children.

Gifted education, discussed later in this chapter, is one area in which educators have applied Gardner's theory, both to identify gifted students who might not be identified by traditional intelligence tests, and to extend the range of ways in which students can develop and display their skills and knowledge. There are also schools and classrooms that have been designed around the eight intelligences. Once again, however, there has been little evidence published of the results of such programs.

ACTIVITIES

1   Think about the evidence that you would require before applying a strategy or theory. Would it be acceptance by the author's peers or by your own peers, the degree to which it fits your own experience, or some other criteria?

2   In Chapter 1, we suggested some tests of evidence. Return to them and decide how they relate to Gardner's theory and its application in classrooms.

Emotional intelligence

Following from Gardner's extended notions of intelligence, a number of writers have argued for the categorisation of a range of abilities as intelligences. These include 'personal intelligence', 'social intelligence' and 'emotional intelligence', as forms of intelligence (Mayer, Caruso, Panter & Salovey, 2012). According to Mayer, Roberts and Barsade (2008, p. 511), **emotional intelligence** is defined as 'an ability to reason about emotions and the capacity to use emotions and emotional knowledge to enhance thought'. It involves the skills of reflectively regulating emotions, understanding emotions, assimilating emotion in thought, and perceiving and expressing emotion.

emotional intelligence
The ability to recognise and understand emotions, and to use emotional information to enhance thought

Daniel Goleman brought the concept of emotional intelligence to popular attention with the publication of a bestselling book, *Emotional intelligence*, in 1995. In it, Goleman argued that emotional intelligence (including such skills as empathy, capacity to delay gratification, impulse control and persistence) is at least as important in guiding behaviour as the cognitive skills tapped by traditional measures of intelligence. Furthermore, Goleman suggested that emotional competence can be taught to children and adults.

In Chapter 4, we examined the development of emotion and its importance to cognition and social interaction. The question is whether these skills constitute 'intelligence' or something else. Research into emotional intelligence has been hampered by the lack of a clear definition of the concept, and by difficulties in its measurement (Mayer, Roberts & Barsade, 2008; Pfeiffer, 2001), but studies have shown emotional intelligence to have positive correlations with verbal and non-verbal intelligence (Kong, 2014; Mayer, Roberts & Barsade, 2008), academic achievement (Barchard, 2003; Fine et al., 2003; Izard et al., 2001; Mayer, Roberts & Barsade, 2008), self-esteem, sociability and life satisfaction (Mayer, Roberts & Barsade, 2008; Mayer, Salovey & Caruso, 2000). The relationship between academic learning and social–emotional intelligence has led to school-based interventions designed to improve school performance by enhancing competencies such as the ability to manage emotions, solve problems and work effectively with others (Payton et al., 2008). There is some evidence that these strategies are effective for improving academic and social skills, and reducing problem behaviours, non-attendance, school alienation and school drop-out rates (Durlak et al., 2011) (see also Chapter 7). Intelligence does not operate independently of emotion, motivation or environment. Whether or not emotions are aspects of intelligence itself, they should be considered as important to the operation of intelligent behaviour. Chapter 4 describes emotional development, and Chapter 8 discusses motivation in detail. Social and emotional learning are discussed in Chapter 7.

STERNBERG'S TRIARCHIC MODEL OF SUCCESSFUL INTELLIGENCE

One of the most prolific writers about intelligence is Robert Sternberg (1985, 1997, 2002, 2003, 2005, 2010) (see **Box 9.3**). Like Gardner, Sternberg rejected the traditional idea of intelligence as a relatively narrow set of abilities closely associated with academic learning. He argued that the concept of *g*, or general mental ability, does not take account of the idea that intelligence is multifaceted and influenced by context. However, whereas Gardner is primarily interested in the *content* of the different intelligences he has identified (for example, linguistic, mathematical, musical and spatial), Sternberg is more interested in the *application* of these intelligences. He has argued that individuals who are more intelligent display their abilities through their ability to learn and process information very rapidly. Such people are also able to respond appropriately in novel situations, and to adapt to the demands of everyday life by modifying their needs and changing their goals when necessary. Sternberg's theory is called the **triarchic model of successful intelligence** because he defined intelligence in terms of successful behaviour and because, in it, he identified three key aspects of intelligent behaviour (Sternberg, 1997, p. 344):

- *Analytic.* The mental aspects of an individual's cognitive activity, as in information-processing skills and metacognition (see Chapter 6). Examples include the critical dissection of ideas by a literary reviewer or mathematician.

- *Creative.* An individual's ability to respond to events in the light of previous experience. This is often evident in responses to unusual or novel situations, or in learning new skills. Examples include the accomplishments of poets, composers or engineers.

- *Practical.* How an individual copes with everyday environments, as in the adaptation of existing skills in response to the demands of particular situations. Examples include the applied skills and expertise of a computer operator, a nurse or a carpenter.

CourseMateExpress

Online resources
Go further: See examples of items from an emotional intelligence test via the link on this text's website

triarchic model of successful intelligence Intelligence defined as thinking (analytic), responding to new experiences (creative) and coping with everyday situations (practical)

BOX 9.3 ABOUT ROBERT STERNBERG

Robert Sternberg (1949–) was born in New Jersey, on the US east coast. He was a bright student who became interested in intelligence and intelligence testing when, as a Grade 6 student, he was forced to retake an intelligence test with students in Grade 5. Sternberg recalled in 1995 that his poor results (due to nerves) on that intelligence test resulted in his teachers having low expectations about what he could achieve at school, which led him to try and please his teachers by meeting those expectations (Plucker, 2005). When he overcame his test anxiety and did well on an intelligence test, teachers' expectations for him increased and he began to do well at school. In Grade 7 he designed the Sternberg Test of Mental Ability for a science project and administered the test to his classmates along with the Stanford–Binet Intelligence Scale, using a copy he had found in the local library.

FIGURE 9.4 Sternberg's ideas about intelligence challenge existing ideas about the relationship between intellectual abilities and learning and teaching.

Later, while at college, Sternberg had summer jobs working at the Educational Testing Service in Princeton, which produced many of the standardised tests used in schools throughout the world. He went to Yale University as an undergraduate and majored in psychology, graduating in 1972 with a BA summa cum laude (the US equivalent to first-class honours), and gaining a PhD at Stanford University in 1975.

Sternberg has been awarded many honours in the field of psychology, including the Distinguished Scientist Award for an Early Career Contribution to Psychology. His major research interests are intelligence, creativity, wisdom, thinking styles, learning and teaching, love and hate. He is Professor of Human Development at Cornell University.

Applying triarchic theory in teaching

Sternberg (1997, p. 359) discussed how the triarchic theory might be applied in curriculum areas such as literature, mathematics, history, biology and art. He suggested that when teaching and evaluating learning, one might emphasise:

- *analytical* abilities – by asking students to compare and contrast, analyse, evaluate, critique, explain why, explain what caused …, or evaluate what is assumed by …
- *creative* abilities – by asking students to create, invent, design, imagine, imagine what you would do if …, show how you would …, suppose that …, say what would happen if …
- *practical* abilities – by asking students to apply, show how you can use …; implement, demonstrate how … .

Application of the successful intelligence theory has been tested with primary- and secondary-aged students, comparing effects of instruction balancing analytical, creative and practical abilities with instruction focused on memory of the content, and instruction based on critical thinking (the analytical abilities listed above) alone. Following teaching of a unit on social studies or science, students in the successful intelligence group did better than those in the other groups on tests of memory for the content, and on performance assessments of analytical, creative and practical learning (Sternberg, Torff & Grigorenko, 1998). In another study, similar results were found for reading comprehension in a number of curriculum areas (Grigorenko, Jarvin & Sternberg, 2002), although a large study that sought to replicate these effects in 223 classrooms with more than 7500 students found effects at near chance level, in which the successful intelligence group did better in some cases, and other groups did better in others (Sternberg et al., 2014).

Sternberg also distinguished between academic intelligence, measured by traditional tests of general or fluid and crystallised intelligence, and successful intelligence (the ability to succeed in life in terms of personal goals and life experiences) or practical intelligence (competence in everyday life as measured by tests of tacit or real-world knowledge and understanding) (Sternberg, 2005, 2014).

Sternberg noted that most instruction and evaluation in schools is concerned with what students know. Teachers tend to focus on instructions: 'Who said …?', 'Summarise …', 'Who did …?', 'What happened?', 'How did it happen?', 'Repeat back' and 'Describe …'. In pointing out the limitations of this type of questioning, Sternberg reminded us that although what you know is important, knowing how to use what you know is even more important (Sternberg, 1997, p. 360).

IS INTELLIGENCE MAINLY INFLUENCED BY NATURE OR NURTURE?

What is the origin of intelligence in humans? Is it a product of genetic inheritance, or is it an outcome of environmental factors such as the way parents talk to infants, the types of toys available in the home, experiences at school or socioeconomic status? Which has primacy: 'nature' or 'nurture'? This question is often referred to as the 'hereditary versus environment' or **nature–nurture debate** (mentioned in Chapter 2). This debate over the relative influence on human development of inherited characteristics (nature) and the role of environmental factors (nurture) has a long history. It has implications for one of the questions discussed previously – whether intelligence is fixed or changeable – and for teachers' practices, as discussed in that section.

'Natural experiments' involving twins living with and apart from their natural families, and families that include both natural and adopted children, have been used to measure the relative influence of genetic and environmental factors on intellectual development. Comparison of the general cognitive abilities of parents and both biological and adopted children living with their own family and apart suggest that the association between parents and their natural children is higher than that between parents and their adopted children. During the early childhood years, the influence of the shared environment is high. However, this environmental influence diminishes as children (adopted children in particular) reach adolescence, perhaps because children have more control over their environment as they mature (Petrill, Pike, Price & Plomin, 2004).

For adopted children, the age at which adoption occurs and the number of years spent in the adoptive home appear to influence general cognitive ability. The influence of environmental factors increases when a child is placed in an adoptive home at an early age and remains with those parents in that home over a number of years (Petrill & Kirby, 2004).

Finding specific genes related to intelligence has proven to be highly complex, with little variance in cognitive ability explained by genetic markers (Nisbett et al., 2012). This probably reflects the contribution of multiple genes to cognitive abilities, the complexity of the construct of intelligence, and the complex relationship between genes and environment in contributing to intelligence.

As we recognise that both nature and nurture contribute to intelligence, it is evident that intelligence is not fixed, but influenced by experience throughout life. Adult scores decrease with ageing, and training in skills such as working memory and executive function can improve scores on intelligence tests (Nisbett et al., 2012).

nature–nurture debate
Controversy over the relative influence that inherent characteristics and environmental factors have on development

The heritability of intelligence

Clearly, 'the true heritability of intelligence in human populations is almost certainly above zero' (Howe, 1997, p. 122). Indeed, there is evidence that in relation to general cognitive ability, the abilities of biological parents and their children are closely linked. Studies of twins, DNA and adoption studies all show the importance of genetics to intelligence (Plomin & Deary, 2015). The degree of association increases steadily from infancy, when the level of similarity is less than 20 per cent, to as much as 80 per cent by late adulthood (Plomin & Deary, 2015). Epigenetic studies examine the interaction of genes and environment, and have shown ways in which environment can influence the expression of genes in intelligence as well as in other areas of human development (Bowes, Grace & Hayes, 2012). Intellectual development is also dependent on a number of non-genetic factors, such as the environmental factors detailed below, and the degree of variance that is explained by heritability or environment varies for individuals from different socioeconomic-status (SES) groups (Nisbett, 2014) and different age groups (Deary, Spinath & Bates, 2006). Nisbett (2014) reported that most variation for people from higher-SES backgrounds is explained by genes, whereas most variation for people from lower-SES backgrounds is explained by environmental factors. He explained that the environments of people from high-SES backgrounds are likely to be supportive of intelligence and to show little variation between one another, so genes explain variance more than environment does. The environments of those from low-SES families, in contrast, may vary from highly supportive to disruptive and chaotic, leaving a stronger role for environment to explain variance in intelligence.

While these findings are about explanations rather than causes, they also highlight the importance of environment to intelligence. There are consistently reported differences in the relative contributions of heredity and environment to intelligence for different age groups, as mentioned above, with the role of environment decreasing and that of heredity increasing with age (Plomin & Deary, 2015; Trzaskowski, Yang, Visscher & Plomin, 2014).

Environmental effects

Source: Getty Images/Westend61.

FIGURE 9.5 School environments can influence intelligence by supporting cognitive challenge, and encouraging students to engage with these challenges

Negative effects on intelligence are easier to find than positive ones (Hunt, 2011). Environmental factors that have been shown to influence intelligence include prolonged malnutrition, alcohol, lead, chronic stress and brain injury. There are also correlations between SES and intelligence, as mentioned above (see also von Stumm & Plomin, 2015), which have multiple environmental explanations, including quality of the home environment, the amount of language in the home, and stress. SES is considered in more detail in Chapter 11.

On the positive side (and as we would hope as educators), schooling affects intelligence (Nisbett et al., 2012). Comparisons of children who attended and did not attend school prior to the Second World War show higher IQ scores for the former group. Children who miss a year of school show a drop in IQ, and children generally experience a drop in IQ over the summer holiday, particularly if their home environments are low in enrichment (Nisbett, 2014). In another study cited by Nisbett et al. (2012), an increase in years of compulsory schooling in Norway produced substantial gains in IQ for the population (Brinch & Galloway, 2011). This prompts the question, 'What are the aspects of schooling that make the most difference to an individual's intelligence?'

Hunt (2011) proposed the challenge hypothesis, which states: 'Intelligence is developed by engaging in cognitively challenging activities. Environments vary in the extent to which they support such challenges, and individuals vary in the extent to which they seek them out' (p. 26). He argued that genetics may constrain the range of intelligence that can develop, and that physical environments can also constrain it through negative effects, such as have been listed above. At the same time, intelligence potential can be realised by interacting with the social environment. The two factors that vary in his hypothesis above – environmental support for cognitive challenges, and individual engagement with challenges – both lie within the influence of educators and, together with the constraining factors, they explain individual differences in intelligence.

THINK ABOUT

- How will you support cognitive challenges in your classroom? How could you encourage learners to engage with these activities?

STRENGTHS AND LIMITATIONS OF MODELS OF INTELLIGENCE

Strengths

One of the main strengths of the different models of intelligence proposed by Spearman, Gardner, Sternberg, and Cattell and Carroll is that they provide us with ways of conceptualising intelligence. The different models also provide guidelines for collecting evidence on intelligence in activities as diverse as reasoning, problem solving, dance, music and art. They draw attention to the need for educators to cater for children's different needs and interests.

Limitations

Limitations of these models include: a lack of empirical research-based evidence to support the specific abilities identified as comprising intelligence; a lack of clarity in the way these abilities are defined; and a lack of agreement about which of the different models of intelligence is the most useful for educators.

Table 9.3 summarises the strengths and limitations of the models of intelligence proposed by Spearman, Gardner, Sternberg, and Cattell and Carroll. Box 9.4 briefly discusses the implications of these models for classroom practice.

TABLE 9.3 Summary of models of intelligence

THEORIST	CONCEPT OF INTELLIGENCE	MEASUREMENT	STRENGTHS	LIMITATIONS
Spearman	General mental ability (*g*) plus specific mental abilities (*s*)	Single intelligence score	Intelligence score a useful predictor of school performance	Doubts that intelligence is a single general mental ability
Cattell, extended by Carroll	General mental ability (*g*) plus secondary abilities (crystallised and fluid intelligence, memory factors, sensory modalities), plus primary abilities measured by individual test items	Battery of test items relating to the various levels	Accounts for variability across individual factors as well as correlations between scores on different tests. Test scores provide a useful profile of an individual's strengths and weaknesses	Has not been successfully replicated in factor analysis studies
Gardner	A set of separate, specialised, multiple intelligences	Individual tests designed to tap a specific intelligence	Helpful in drawing attention to the need to understand and nurture children's special talents	Are Gardner's intelligences just special talents?
Sternberg	A triarchic model of intelligence comprising analytic, creative and practical aspects	Specific tests designed to tap each aspect	Emphasises the practical aspects of intellectual skills and their application in everyday life	Can Sternberg's model be applied successfully to classroom practice?

THINK ABOUT

- Can you think of both inherited traits and everyday experiences within your own background that had an impact on your own intellectual development?
- Of the different models of intelligence covered so far, which is closest to your personal concept of intelligence?
- Can you recall factors in your own life that influenced your ideas about the nature of intelligence?

BOX 9.4 IMPLICATIONS FOR EDUCATORS

MODELS OF INTELLIGENCE IN THE CLASSROOM

The models of intelligence discussed in this chapter visualise intelligence as a complex, multifaceted cluster of abilities associated with every aspect of human activity, not just academic learning. This has major implications for classroom practice, and indicates that:

- school curricula should be broadened to cover the range of activities represented in profiles of student abilities and interests
- teachers should consider matching student abilities to the forms of instruction and assessment used in the classroom, as there is evidence that such matching leads to improvements in student performance (see, for example, Sternberg, 1997; Sternberg, Torff & Grigorenko, 1998)
- teachers need to be aware of each child's particular abilities and ensure that appropriate experiences are provided to promote each child's potential (such experiences can be derived from a particular model of intelligence or from any program that provides a varied curriculum).

MEASURING INTELLIGENCE

Can we measure intelligence? People generally think of intelligence as a score on an IQ test, so if you ask a person what they know about intelligence, they usually tell you something about IQ scores. But what is an 'IQ score'? Such scores are no longer used very much in school systems, but they provide a valuable insight into the history and development of intelligence measurement.

At the beginning of the 20th century, as the principle of universal education became more widely accepted, it became apparent that many children of school age could not cope within the regular school system. There was something 'different' about these children when compared with their peers: intelligence tests seemed to provide a means for identifying and explaining these differences.

THE STANFORD–BINET TEST

The first effective tests of intelligence were devised by Alfred Binet (see Box 9.5) and his colleague Theodore Simon. The tests were designed to measure general mental ability, and were used to screen children in order to identify those who were thought to be capable of benefiting from school education, and those who needed extra help (Brody, 1992) (see also Chapter 10).

Binet and Simon developed a test involving 30 items that tapped (measured) practical knowledge and skills. Test items required children to name objects in pictures, define words, repeat a set of digits, copy a simple shape, tell the time on an analogue clock, and cut a shape from a piece of folded paper and tell what the shape would be when unfolded. The test was standardised (that is, the test's norms, procedures and scoring were established) using 50 children who were judged to be of 'normal' intelligence and 45 people who were judged as having varying degrees of intellectual impairment. In 1916, Lewis Terman at Stanford University adapted and renamed Binet and Simon's test for use in the USA. The revised test came to be known as the Stanford–Binet Intelligence Scale, and it continues to be widely used in the assessment of children (aged from two years) and adults.

The original meaning of intelligence quotient, as developed by psychometricians such as Binet, was 'mental age divided by chronological age multiplied by 100'. If you are 10 years of age, but perform on an intelligence test at the mental age of 12, you have an IQ of 120. This is how the original IQ score was calculated. The procedure is satisfactory when applied to children's scores (although people sometimes make the mistake of assuming that a 10-year-old with an IQ of 120 will behave like a 12-year-old). However, the formula is only applicable when a child's ability to answer questions on an IQ test (that is, their **mental age**) continues to increase steadily with their chronological age. The concept of mental age cannot be used to determine adults' test results because intelligence does not continue to increase during adulthood in the same way it does over the childhood years. A different method of calculating IQ is needed.

mental age
The chronological age that typically corresponds with a particular performance level on an intelligence test

BOX 9.5 ABOUT ALFRED BINET

Alfred Binet (1857–1911) was born in Nice, France, the only child of an artist mother and a physician father. Initially, Binet studied law in Paris, and in 1878 completed his law degree. By this time, he had become interested in following the family tradition of studying medicine, but his interest in psychology increased and he began to read widely in the field, eventually abandoning his medical studies (Imhoff, 2000). One of Binet's first interests in intelligence was 'craniology', which involved measuring the volume of people's skulls as a means of measuring intelligence. After collecting data from several hundred children, he found the differences in skull size were very slight, and the measurements unreliable (Gould, 1981). He subsequently abandoned craniology.

Source: National Library of Medicine.

FIGURE 9.6 Binet's interest in children, and particularly those with intellectual disabilities, led to him devising an intelligence test that became a model for subsequent tests.

By this time, Binet had two daughters (Madeleine and Alice, born in 1885 and 1887) and, like Piaget, he became interested in their development and in the concept of intelligence and its measurement. After studying attention span in his daughters, Binet devised a set of activities to tap the diverse range of 'thinking' abilities that, it was hypothesised, constituted 'intelligence'. The tasks and puzzles Binet created covered everyday reasoning and comprehension problems such as counting coins, pointing to parts of the body and naming items in a picture. Learnt skills, such as reading, were not included. Binet was aware that age was a major determinant of children's capacity to complete tasks, and so included in each set of tasks were examples appropriate for children at different age levels. Children able to complete tasks that could be done by most children of the same chronological age were judged to have 'normal' intelligence. However, children who failed tasks that most children of their chronological age could do, or who completed more tasks than expected for their age, were judged respectively as 'backward' or 'advanced'. From these tests, Binet developed the concept of 'mental age'. The concept continues to be used, and provides a basis for the concept of 'intelligence quotient', or IQ, which was eventually defined as:

$$\frac{\text{mental age}}{\text{chronological age}} \times 100$$

Binet argued that intelligence was not wholly innate, since it was strongly affected by the individual's experiences. In developing a set of tasks to measure intelligence, he tried to devise tasks that would tap common sense, everyday knowledge or practical understanding, rather than knowledge that had been acquired through formal instruction. He was very concerned that his test might be used to rank students in terms of their 'mental worth' (Gould, 1981, p. 152). He did not want the test to be used to label particular children 'dull' or 'stupid', because he feared such labels would become self-fulfilling prophecies. In later years, Binet developed a series of exercises designed to raise the intelligence of children with intellectual disabilities.

WECHSLER'S INTELLIGENCE SCALES

In 1939, David Wechsler proposed the **deviation IQ**, a solution to the problem of calculating adult IQs. He proposed that IQ should be determined in terms of the number of correct items scored on a test (the test score) in relation to the expected average score obtained by people of the same age; that is, 'actual test score divided by expected test score and multiplied by 100'. The deviation IQ measures how far a particular test score is above or below the mean score of the relevant age cohort. It provides a method for rank-ordering individuals in terms of their performance on a test.

To collect the information needed to establish mean scores for different age groups, Wechsler's intelligence tests (such as the Wechsler Adult Intelligence Scale [WAIS], the Wechsler Intelligence Scale for Children, Version V [WISC-V], and the Wechsler Preschool and Primary Scale of Intelligence, Fourth Edition [WPPSI-IV]) were administered to very large samples of adults and children. These samples were selected to represent demographic characteristics such as age, gender and social class. Information derived from the representative group of adults and children (the 'standardisation sample'), such as expected scores for individuals of a certain age and gender, are provided in the test manual and are used by psychologists when interpreting individual scores.

INTERPRETING IQ SCORES

Most intelligence tests are designed to have a mean score of 100, with a 'standard deviation' of approximately 15 or 16 (see Figure 9.7). The **frequency distribution**, or number of times each score occurs, is usually represented as a **bell-shaped curve** (or **normal distribution**). The IQ score of a person gives an indication of that individual's position, in relation to others, on a distribution of IQ scores; that is, where their score is located on the bell-shaped curve.

Notice that across the base of the normal curve in Figure 9.7, the scaling is in terms of 'standard deviation' units. The **standard deviation (SD)** is a measure of how much scores differ, on average, from the mean. For example, on a test with 25 questions, each worth one point, scores from two groups of eight students may have the same mean (10) but one set of scores might be spread out across the range of possible scores (9, 12, 10, 15, 21, 2, 7, 4), while the other set might cluster together (7, 8, 14, 10, 9, 12, 13, 7). The SD (of 6) in scores for students in the first group is much larger than the SD (of 3) in scores for students in the second group, reflecting greater spread or variability in the scores of the first group compared with those of the second. Intelligence tests such as the Stanford–Binet Intelligence Scale have a mean of 100; thus, two-thirds (68 per cent) of scores obtained from the population used to standardise

deviation IQ
An IQ score that compares an individual's performance on a test with the expected average performance of someone in the same age group

frequency distribution
The number of times each score occurs in a range of possible scores

normal distribution (bell-shaped curve)
A representation of test scores, showing their natural tendency to cluster around the middle (mean) of the distribution and taper off at either side

standard deviation (SD)
A measure of how much test scores vary from the mean of the sample

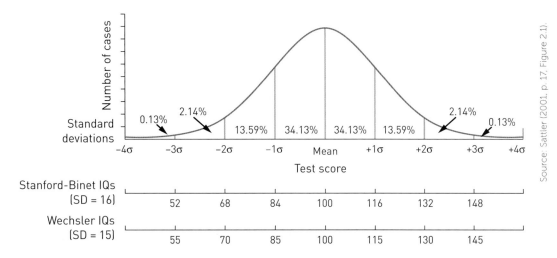

Source: Sattler (2001, p. 17, Figure 2.1).

FIGURE 9.7 The normal curve shows the tendency for most scores to cluster around the middle or mean test score, with smaller numbers of scores at either end of the curve.

the tests fall between one SD below (84) and one SD above (116) that mean. Students with an IQ of 84 on a Stanford–Binet Intelligence Scale have therefore performed better on the test than almost 16 per cent of their age group, whereas those with an IQ of 116 have performed better on the test than more than 84 per cent of their age group. Experience in using IQ test results in schools has shown that this range (that is, one SD below and one SD above the mean) represents roughly the range of scores for children who can progress satisfactorily in the regular school system. The scores of students who are gifted and talented usually fall within the top 2 per cent of the normal distribution curve – that is, these students have an IQ of more than 130 on the Wechsler scale (Braggett, 2002, p. 292) – while the scores of students with mild and moderate-to-severe intellectual disabilities typically have scores falling in the bottom 2 per cent of the curve, in the range below 70 points (Elkins, 2002, p. 80), and these students may require a high level of additional support at school (see Chapter 10).

When IQ test results are used in making decisions about the specialised needs of individual students, care needs to be taken to avoid the impact of factors such as *test bias*, by which particular students are disadvantaged because of age, gender, language or cultural background by factors associated with the content of the test and interpretation of test results. While many psychological tests were normed in the USA, the WISC-IV Australian edition and WPPSI-IV Australian and New Zealand Standardised edition use local norms. An example of an age- and culturally biased test item is cited by Cianciolo and Sternberg (2004, pp. 131–2): 'Harry Potter is to Voldemort as Ronald Reagan is to (a) California; (b) President; (c) John Hinckley; or (d) Reaganomics'. (Voldemort tried to kill Harry Potter and John Hinckley tried to kill Ronald Reagan.) Older people who have not read one of the Harry Potter books and those unfamiliar with American history would probably fail this question.

Another problem arising in the use of intelligence tests over time concerns the steady rise in IQ scores over the 20th century as individuals perform better on the tests over time. Termed 'the Flynn Effect' (Flynn, 1998, 2007; see Box 9.6), these changes in performance became evident when the tests were 're-normed', a process that is usually done every 15 to 20 years when test items are given to large samples and the mean is reset to a score of 100. If performance on the test rises between one norming and the next, the mean of the new revision of the test will be higher than previously, making the test more difficult. This effect is likely to have a significant impact on those who perform very poorly on the test: 'As IQ norms age, fewer students receive MR [mental retardation] services, but when a newly normed test is introduced, the number of students eligible for these services will increase' (Kanaya, Scullin & Ceci, 2003, p. 781). When eligibility for special programs is dependent on IQ test scores, factors such as the Flynn Effect can have a major impact on both individuals (access to programs where access is determined by an IQ score) and governments (the cost of providing programs to more students) (Flynn, 2000; Kanaya, Scullin & Ceci, 2003).

ADMINISTERING INTELLIGENCE TESTS

Tests such as the Stanford–Binet Intelligence Scale and the WAIS, WISC-V and WPPSI-IV are administered individually, in a one-to-one situation, by a trained psychologist. Other tests of intelligence, such as the Draw a Person Test (Goodenough, 1926; Naglieri, 1988) and the Peabody Picture Vocabulary Test, Fifth Edition (PPVT-5), can be administered to children individually or in groups by an experienced teacher or other professional. Individual tests usually include an array of verbal tasks that involve answering questions by giving information or pointing, and performance tasks that involve sorting, matching or arranging blocks, beads or geometric shapes. Group tests are limited to 'paper-and-pencil' tasks. Individual tests are more expensive to administer than group tests, but have higher reliability (that is, the same response is obtained on successive occasions) and validity (that is, the tests measure what they are designed to measure). Group tests are mainly used for screening purposes, to identify exceptionally gifted students or those who may need extra help as a result of intellectual disability. See Chapter 13 for more on tests and assessment procedures.

BOX 9.6 RESEARCH LINKS

THE FLYNN EFFECT: ARE PEOPLE GETTING SMARTER?

Flynn (1987; Nisbett et al., 2012) revealed that widespread intelligence testing in the developed world over the past 100 years demonstrates a cohort effect – scores for each generation (approximately 30 years) are higher than for the last, with gains of about 3 IQ points each decade. In the developing world, nations that are in the process of modernising, such as Kenya, Caribbean nations, South Korea and Argentina, are likewise showing rapid gains in IQ test scores (Flynn, 2012; Meisenberg & Woodley, 2013). Interestingly, gains in a number of Western nations appear to have tailed off and even reversed in some cases over the past decade (Dutton & Lynn, 2013; Flynn, 2013).

Tests of fluid intelligence (problem solving, abstract reasoning) show greater gains than those of crystallised intelligence (cultural knowledge, such as vocabulary and arithmetic). Gignac (2015) found that there were no gains in working memory or short-term memory capacity over 85 years when the Flynn Effect was observed, despite the fact that fluid intelligence and working memory capacity are closely related. This adds to the complexity and puzzle of the Flynn Effect.

What might contribute to these gains in IQ over time?

- *Test taking*. It may be that we are more accustomed to being tested in the modern era, and that this familiarity with the test items, or the kinds of questions they ask, contributes to better scores. This is not supported by the evidence, however, as scores on other kinds of tests (such as assessments of taught knowledge and skills in schools) have remained stable over time (Flynn, 2007). Furthermore, if this were the case, the correlation between IQ score and other factors such as educational achievement or income would have decreased over time, but this has not occurred.
- *Health*. Improvements in health and nutrition have been proposed as one explanation, although the evidence for this is mixed. It would be expected to make a difference to those of low socioeconomic status, and to make less difference in developed nations as time goes on, but this is not consistently the case.
- *Education*. In some countries, gains were greater for the lower half of the population tested. This might suggest that universal education, and increased years of schooling, were factors. However, there are other developed nations where these patterns were not observed, but which have nonetheless had increases in school attendance over the period. Flynn (2007) and Fletcher and Hattie (2011) have suggested that the focus of education has shifted towards scientific reasoning and pattern-finding, which supports the kinds of skills measured in intelligence tests.
- *Modernity*. Flynn (2013) argues that modernity of societies is the ultimate cause of the patterns of results that are seen in the developing world (which is still experiencing modernity, and so seeing gains in IQ scores) and the developed world (which has already achieved the IQ gains from modernity over the last century, so gains have slowed, stopped or reversed). Modernity itself influences IQ largely through a range of environmental forces such as improved diet, education, leisure and parenting practices. Nisbett et al. (2012) propose that more cognitively demanding employment and leisure activities may contribute to the increase.

ACTIVITIES

1   Can you explain the Flynn Effect? How do you account for the various patterns of data?
2   What role does education play in the development of intelligence?

Many older people will remember being given a group intelligence test at school, but younger people are less likely to recall such an experience. Most schools in countries such as Australia and New Zealand phased out IQ testing in the early 1980s. Before that time, children were routinely tested in grades 4 and 6 (ages 9–10 and 11–12 years respectively). Since the 1980s, intelligence tests have generally been used only in special circumstances, such as for entry to a program for gifted students or for the identification of students who need some form of special help in the classroom.

Box 9.7 shows some typical items you might expect to find in an intelligence test.

BOX 9.7 RESEARCH LINKS

TYPICAL ITEMS IN INTELLIGENCE TESTS

Tests of intelligence typically include items tapping a variety of skills:

- *general knowledge* – 'How many days are there in a leap year?'
- *verbal knowledge* (see below) – 'Which picture shows furniture?'

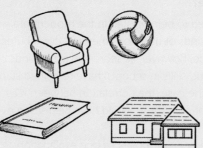

- *logical reasoning* – 'Three sisters were walking downstairs. Jen came downstairs first. The youngest sister followed her. Sue followed Jude. Sue is the middle sister. Who is the oldest?'
- *abstract thinking* (see below) – 'Which of these things does not belong with the others?'

- *number patterns* – 'Which is the next number? 4, 5, 7, 10, …'
- *spatial visualisation* (see below) – 'Which is a rotation of A?'

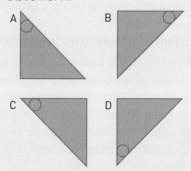

Some tests try to limit 'test bias' by avoiding verbal components in visual and performance items. Items may require the individual to complete a pattern, draw a figure, put a puzzle together or sequence some pictures.

ACTIVITIES

Think about the examples of IQ test items presented above.

1   Can you identify examples of each of the item types that are likely to be subject to test bias, in terms of age, gender, language or cultural background?
2   Give examples of items that are free of bias.

What intelligence tests do not measure

There are a number of skills that influence intelligence and intelligent behaviour, but which are not directly measured by traditional intelligence tests. This was the issue that led Sternberg to develop an alternative model of intelligence, as described above. The first of these abilities is learning. Tests examine current knowledge or skill, but not the ability of participants to develop these over time. In fact, tests are constructed to prevent testees from learning in the process of taking the test – a feature of tests called 'item independence' (Hunt, 2011). Learning is undoubtedly a feature of intelligent people, and one of the outcomes that intelligence scores are designed to predict, but is not directly measured.

The second ability is creativity, which is addressed in greater detail later in this chapter. There are strong correlations between creativity and scores on intelligence tests, and scores on these tests have been shown to predict creative output in life (Lubinski, Benbow, Webb & Bleske-Rechek, 2006), although there are generally no items in intelligence tests that tap creativity itself.

The third set of skills is variously described (Hunt, 2011; Nisbett et al., 2012); the terms used include persistence, impulse control, intellectual engagement, conscientiousness and self-discipline, and are generally linked to motivation. Once again, these skills influence intelligence, but they tend to be excluded from intelligence testing in order to improve the validity and reliability of test results.

THINK ABOUT

- How could you maximise students' thinking abilities for particular tasks, focusing on some of the capacities described here?

Each of these abilities is clearly related to intelligence, but they are difficult to test with the kinds of instruments used for traditional intelligence testing. Alternative methods are required, and these tend not to meet the requirements of psychometric testing. We should also note that, although not directly assessed, each of these skills correlates with scores on traditional tests of intelligence (Hunt, 2011).

STRENGTHS AND LIMITATIONS OF INTELLIGENCE TESTS

Strengths

Intelligence tests are useful for identifying students who may be at risk of problems in learning as a result of impaired intellectual abilities, and for planning appropriate educational programs for such students. Intelligence tests may also be useful for identifying students who are intellectually gifted, particularly those who are underachieving.

Limitations

Limitations to the use of intelligence tests are associated with questions concerning the reliability and validity of scores derived from group tests in particular. Tests may also have limited use as a result of the restricted range of skills measured. There is also a risk that information about an individual student's performance on an intelligence test will lead to expectations about that particular student's future level of achievement, which may have an adverse effect on achievement and self-concept. At a broader level, there is a risk that intelligence tests will have a negative impact on curriculum when children are required to undertake learning tasks that are designed to prepare them for 'taking the test', with the resulting neglect of more interesting and useful activities.

Some issues that need to be considered by educators when using information from intelligence tests are outlined in Box 9.8.

BOX 9.8 IMPLICATIONS FOR EDUCATORS

ISSUES TO CONSIDER WHEN USING INTELLIGENCE TEST SCORES

When considering information derived from intelligence tests, teachers need to be aware of the following:

- Knowledge of students' scores on an intelligence test can lead to unconscious expectations about some students' future progress.
- Scores from intelligence tests are influenced by inherited and environmental factors.
- Data derived from intelligence tests administered individually to children by trained examiners have higher levels of reliability and validity than scores from intelligence tests administered to children in groups.
- Information from intelligence tests can be useful in identifying students who may need extra help or a special program, and also students who are intellectually gifted and talented.
- Teachers need to know how to interpret scores derived from intelligence tests.

LEARNERS WITH EXCEPTIONAL ABILITIES

Josh entered kindergarten with advanced mathematical and reading abilities, at approximately Year 5 level. His teachers were faced with the question of whether to accelerate his studies, or to enrich the kindergarten curriculum for him, so that he could study with same-age peers.

THINK ABOUT

- What would you do if you were Josh's teacher?
- What information would you and his parents require to help you make the decision?

One outcome of the focus on developing effective tools for measuring intelligence has been an interest in individuals who score at the extreme ends of the IQ distribution; that is, those who score very low on an IQ test and those who perform in the very high range. Because of the developmental and learning difficulties experienced by children who are at the very low end of the continuum, considerable attention has been paid to this group, particularly by those working in the field of special-needs education (see Chapter 10). However, interest has also focused on children at the other end of the continuum, whose scores on tests of intelligence and ability are markedly higher than those of their peers. Such children are often labelled as 'gifted', 'talented' or 'creative'. Other terms used include 'high ability', 'genius' and 'prodigy'. However, in some contexts, these children are described as 'underachievers', 'educationally disadvantaged' or having 'special needs' on the grounds that schools fail to provide the programs such children need to ensure that they achieve their full potential (see Moore, Ford & Milner, 2005). Gross (1993, p. 35) claimed that 'the majority of academically gifted students underachieve significantly in the regular classroom and many are seriously de-motivated by the time they have passed through the first few years of elementary school'.

So who are these academically gifted children, and how should they be educated? Box 9.9 offers some case studies.

BOX 9.9 CASE STUDY

CASE STUDIES OF GIFTED STUDENTS

Case study 1

Michael has both endearing and aggravating behaviours in the classroom. He may appear slow and deliberate at times, especially when quick answers are being sought to low-level questions. He sometimes seems to make too much of what was a simple question. He runs on his own time lines, which means there are times when he gets frustrated because he has to put a project down and turn to the next subject. He is usually very systematic and logical, which can make him very uncomfortable when a teacher tries to encourage him to be creative. He is not a willing risk taker and wants structure in many cases when long-term assignments are given. When questions are asked in class, Michael can be annoying at times when he so consistently rewords the question before answering. It is very hard to find enough extra assignments to keep him busy in subjects such as mathematics and science, where generally the class is being taught the facts of that content area. He appears to sop up information as quickly as it can be offered.

Michael scores very highly on almost every aptitude and achievement test, and will usually have very high grades. Yet he may be a serious underachiever because he is not being offered enough content or enough complexity to that content, nor has compacting of his curriculum taken place. Anywhere from three to six years of Michael's school life may be spent without learning a single new idea or concept. The only characteristic that may keep Michael from pure disillusionment with school may be his own perseverance and patience, waiting for the day when school will be 'hard and fun'.

Case study 2

Jamal is a constant hand raiser and totally focused when social studies or history classes are in session. He knows every answer to the teacher's questions in those classes. He has read every children's book and a great many adult books on Australia's participation in the Second World War, in particular. No matter what the subject in social studies, he can find some way to relate it to something he has just read about the war. Jamal probably knows more about that period of history than his teachers do. Jamal gets so excited in discussions, however, that he often forgets to let other children have a chance to answer. He will shout out answers and forget to raise his hand. It is very important to him to let the teacher and his peers know what he knows.

Unfortunately, Jamal does not have the same love or skill for mathematics. His test scores are consistently below grade level and he displays no interest in working hard to improve that area. More than one of his teachers suspects that if there were a way to relate basic maths facts to wartime events, he would learn maths easily. Jamal was not considered for the gifted program at his school, despite the fact that many of the enrichment activities planned involved history. His classroom teacher would not let him be considered because of his poor performance in maths class. Jamal was, of course, highly disappointed.

The major reason Jamal will likely continue to go along with the system in years to come will be his natural love of learning and the cognitive support for his talent area, which he receives at home and from the occasional teacher at school, who will value the very specialised gift Jamal possesses. We can only hope that those teachers don't appear too many years apart as Jamal progresses through school.

Case study 3

Chwee is flamboyant in her dress, really into the vampire look currently, but great to be around. Her excitement when she thinks of an idea is contagious, as is her sense of humour. Her school performance is spotty, to say the least. In classes where the teacher recognises and respects her fine, original mind, she outdoes herself in the quality and quantity of her work. But in classes where 'no exceptions are made', where assignments are rigid and deadlines are enforced, Chwee refuses to produce and does fail. This happens regularly within every subject area in high school. She failed the Rhetoric class, but aced the Creative Writing class. Geometry was a whiz for Chwee, but Maths Analysis represented another low grade for her. One can almost predict in which classes Chwee will do poorly by which teacher she is assigned.

As a result, Chwee's general skill levels are poor and there is some question about whether she will be able to get into university at all. Unlike Jamal, she has no specialised talent area at present, and for her to be able to fully use her high degree of originality, she must become an 'expert' in some area. (That is what some researchers, such as David Feldman and David Perkins, have suggested.) Without that, her creativity will probably never be fully utilised. She may end up being like the creative garbage collector who fashioned unusual junk sculptures that were featured on a television series on creativity several years ago.

There is no doubt that Chwee will be happy in adulthood; she has the natural flexibility to rearrange events for her own comfort. However, it will be a severe loss for our society if Chwee's creativity is not channelled into finding solutions and reformulating the problems that we have been grappling with for years, such as cures for cancer, prevention of ecological destruction, replenishing the ozone layer in the stratosphere, and providing food for the underdeveloped nations of the world.

Source: Vialle and Rogers (2009). Copyright © 2009 by Wilma Vialle. Used by permission.

ACTIVITIES

1   Identify the particular gifts or talents of the three students described here.
2   What difficulties do their particular gifts present for the teacher and for them as students?
3   What strategies might teachers use to identify giftedness and unusual talents or creativity in their students? Are the same strategies appropriate for finding gifted students who are underachieving, or who speak languages other than English?
4   Are you familiar with any special provision that is made for students with unusual or special gifts and talents? How effective are these arrangements for the students involved?

CONCEPTS OF GIFTEDNESS AND TALENT

gifted
Significantly superior potential to achieve in one or more domains

talent
Significantly superior performance in one or more domains

The term 'gifted' has traditionally been used to refer to individuals with high general intellectual ability (Detterman, 1993). More recently, the term has referred to students who demonstrate the potential to achieve at a level that is considerably superior to their age-peers in one or more areas of achievement (intellectual, creative, socioemotional and physical domains), while talent is defined as significantly superior achievement in one or more areas of performance (Gagné, 2003). Appropriate opportunities, application, practice, and teaching and learning all contribute to the translation of a gift (the potential) into a talent (the achievement, which is a realisation of the potential). Other conceptions of giftedness are discussed in Chapter 10.

As we saw earlier in the chapter, high intelligence or ability is partly innate, but it is generally accepted that it is also influenced by external contributing factors, such as a stimulating home background, a supportive school environment, sympathetic teachers, and good role models and mentors, together with hard work, coaching and practice, which interact with personal characteristics such as motivation, confidence, self-esteem, perseverance and personality (Braggett & Bailey, 2005, pp. 365–6; Renzulli, 2013). It is estimated that up to 60 per cent of gifted students underachieve at school (Gross, 1993), often leaving school early. Factors associated with this high level of (often 'invisible') underachievement are both intrapersonal (for example, lack of motivation, low self-esteem, poor health, and learning and language difficulties) and environmental (for example, disadvantaged socioeconomic background, minority cultural group, low teacher expectations and inappropriate or ineffective teaching practices) (Moore, Ford & Milner, 2005; NSW Department of Education and Training, 2004).

Attributes that are frequently (but not universally) present in gifted and talented students include:

- *language and literacy-related skills* – a large, advanced vocabulary for their age; the ability to discuss complex ideas and concepts; enjoyment of reading; and the ability to use two or more languages

- *cognitive and problem-solving skills* – speedy information processing; quick mastery and recall of factual information; the ability to work independently, to be self-critical, and to strive for perfection; an interest and concern for world problems; the ability to apply learning and knowledge from one situation to another; and the ability to grasp relationships and principles, and to draw sound generalisations. Monro (2013) reviewed neurological research revealing that students with high intellectual abilities develop more elaborated and differentiated networks of knowledge, which may explain some of these skills. He argued this allows them to go beyond what is taught to develop new theories, connections and ideas

- *independence and broad interests and activities* – the ability to work independently, to be self-critical and to strive for perfection; an interest and concern for world problems; initiation of their own activities and absorption in them, with little external motivation; wide interests, often in art, music and drama; and the ability to relate well to older students and adults, and enjoy learning from them (NSW Board of Studies, 2001, p. 7).

Renzulli (1978, 2002, 2013), in the three-ring conception of giftedness, described the behaviour of gifted individuals in terms of three interacting sets of traits:

1 *above-average ability* – including both general ability such as memory and word fluency, which remain stable over time, and specific ability or the capacity to apply knowledge and skills to solve problems

2 *high levels of task commitment* – including self-confidence, capacity for high interest level, hard work, determination and setting high standards in a particular area

3 *high levels of creativity* – openness to new experiences, curiosity, willingness to take risks, and fluency, flexibility and originality of thought.

Hence in Renzulli's view, the identification of gifted students must go beyond intelligence test or academic achievement test scores and look also at non-cognitive factors. It will also vary for different situations and tasks, and in different people.

Schools are responsible for identifying gifted students, including those who underachieve as a result of cultural difference, disability and low socioeconomic background, and for providing them with the experiences and resources that will ensure that their potential for outstanding performance is realised.

IDENTIFYING GIFTED AND TALENTED LEARNERS

Intelligence tests, such as those developed by Binet and Wechsler, have traditionally been used to identify children who are gifted: defined as those who are in the top 2 per cent on a distribution of IQ scores (or IQ 130+) for their age group. Indeed, very high general intelligence continues to be seen as one characteristic of gifted children (for example, ACARA, 2012b), and tests of general ability are still used in many school systems to identify such students, alongside other tools (for example, New Zealand Education Review Office, 2008; South Australia Department for Education and Child Development, 2012).

As a result of changes in concepts of intelligence through the increasing level of interest in the multifaceted theories of intelligence proposed by Cattell (1987), Gardner (1983) and Sternberg (1988), there is growing acceptance of much broader concepts of giftedness than simply a high IQ score. For example, it is now generally accepted that a gifted or talented individual can excel in any of a number of different areas of performance. A child may score poorly on a test involving expressive language and, as a result, gain a low IQ score, but at the same time, have exceptional visual or auditory skills not tapped by traditional intelligence tests. Gardner (1997) suggested that children should have the freedom to allow their talents to develop in whatever ways they can.

The Gifted Education Research, Resource and Information Centre of the University of New South Wales (GERRIC) produced a professional development package for teachers in collaboration with the Federal Department of Education, which is available online. The authors of Module 2 in the package, C. Merrick and R. Targett, suggested the following characteristics that teachers can use to identify gifted students. Students may display one or several of these characteristics. As gifted students can vary widely in their abilities, personalities and achievement levels, the identification process is problematic, and this is one reason that the term 'gifted' has been challenged, as discussed in Chapter 10. Further, each characteristic may have positive and negative behaviours associated with it. For example, being highly curious may mean a student asks lots of questions, but it may also mean they could be easily diverted from a task. The characteristics are:

- highly curious
- abstract thinker
- flexible thinker
- clever use of humour
- superior vocabulary
- advanced reading
- fast learner, retention of knowledge
- long attention span
- independent
- high level of responsibility and commitment
- strong feelings and opinions
- strong sense of justice
- original and creative
- high energy level
- immersion learner (Gross, 2005).

The identification of gifted and talented students works best when it can draw on both formal, standardised test results and informal nominations from parents and teachers, based on their own judgements of a student's ability developed from observations and work samples over an extended period of time. In identifying gifted and talented students, it is particularly important to be mindful of gifted students from groups who may have been overlooked in the past. This may include students who are currently underachieving, those from different cultural and/or language backgrounds, those who are 'twice- or multi-exceptional' (that is, who have other identified needs – see Chapter 10), and those from lower socioeconomic backgrounds (New Zealand Ministry of Education, 2012).

CREATIVITY

We sometimes identify creativity with the arts and media, with famous artists such as Brett Whiteley or film director Taika Waititi, and their work is certainly agreed to be creative. Consider these creative endeavours: Josie is designing a solution for keeping possums out of the roof of her house. Janet is working out how to solve a difficult mathematics problem at school. Jo is developing a lesson plan that will challenge her students across a range of ability levels, and engage them with a topic they have been bored by previously. Although early views of creativity tended to focus on select creative individuals (and products), more recent views recognise that we can all be creative in everyday life, and indeed, that creative thinking is essential for solving the problems of the present and the future – on a personal, local and global scale. The Melbourne Declaration on Educational Goals for Young Australians (2008) identified development of all Australians as creative individuals as a core goal, and creative and critical thinking is a competency in the Australian and New Zealand curricula, running across all curriculum areas.

WHAT IS CREATIVITY?

As with intelligence, creativity is difficult to define, and people from different cultures have varying, implicit views of what is creative. Although we would probably all be able to identify people or products we would think of as creative, we might find it more difficult to specify the basis on which we make that judgement (see Figure 9.8).

According to Kaufman & Sternberg (2010), **creativity** refers to novel thinking that leads to the production of innovative and valuable ideas. Most definitions of creativity involve the combined dimensions of novelty, utility and quality. That is, something is judged as creative if it is good, is innovative and is useful for its context. Hence creativity is culturally and contextually determined; what is seen as good, new and useful in one context would not be considered so in another (Lubart, 2010). Creativity, under this definition, is judged by what is produced. Tests of creativity measure people's ability to produce novel and appropriate solutions to various questions, problems or situations (for example, see Torrance, 1988). We discuss measurement of creativity further below.

Sternberg (2012) pointed out that creativity is also a process, or indeed, as he put it, 'habitually respond(ing) to problems in fresh and novel ways' (p. 3). The Australian and New Zealand curricula link to this view in talking about creative *thinking*. In this view, creative thinking may be seen across domains (or subject areas), as well as its results in products within a specific domain (Beghetto & Plucker, 2006).

Stein (1953) and later Csikszentmihalyi (1996) made an important distinction between levels of creativity, calling them 'big C', referring to the work of eminent creative people such as Paul Cézanne or Albert Einstein, that have significantly influenced their domain of art or science, and have endured across time; and 'little c', referring to the creativity we all engage in every day, as exemplified in the introduction to this section. Stein argued that big C tends to focus on creative products, whereas little c looks at creative experiences. Kaufman & Beghetto (2009) extended this further, adding two more categories to differentiate aspects of little c. 'Mini-c' creativity is part of the learning process, and links to the construction of knowledge that Piaget and Vygotsky proposed children are engaged in. 'Pro-c' creativity is that of professional creators who have not yet attained eminent status.

In fact, there are a number of models of creativity, reflecting emphasis on different facets of this complex concept.

creativity
The ability to think in novel ways to produce innovative and valuable ideas

Source: Mathew Duchesne: milk and honey

FIGURE 9.8 Designs for a new creature. Which is most creative? How would you decide?

MODELS OF CREATIVITY

Rhodes (1962) identified four P's of creativity that have distinguished various approaches to the field. Kozbelt, Beghetto & Runco (2010) used these to compare different models. We have already talked about two of the P's above: *product* and *process*. The others are *person* and *place*.

- *Product.* This is the focus of psychometric approaches to creativity; those that seek to measure it. Individuals' responses to a stimulus, or works they produce, may be scored according to various criteria, enabling correlations to be made between creativity scores and other variables. We discuss measurement further below.

- *Process.* Some theories of creativity emphasise the cognitive processes that are involved in creative thinking. Neurological studies of creativity typically take this approach. For example, Cassotti, Agogué, Camarda, Houdé & Borst (2016) identified the prefrontal cortex as involved in both creative thinking and inhibitory control (see Chapter 3 for a discussion of this executive function). In line with work showing interactions between the executive functions of inhibitory control and cognitive flexibility (e.g. Dajani & Uddin, 2015) they argued that inhibitory control supports creativity by allowing people to suppress or inhibit their automatic first response to solving a task, so that they can explore new ideas. Cognitive theories also emphasise process. These might look, for example, at divergent and convergent thinking, both of which are needed to ensure novelty and evaluation of appropriateness (Guilford, 1968), or at the stages of thinking in the creative process (e.g. Runco & Chand, 1995).

- *Person.* Some approaches (such as Simonton, 2008) identify aspects of the person that influence creativity. Sternberg (2012) identified willingness to take risks, perseverance, and self-efficacy as important personality factors, for example, while others have added openness to experience, conscientiousness, self-confidence, nonconformity, and independence, (among others) as personality characteristics related to creativity (Feist, 2010). Amabile & Pillemer (2012) looked at motivation, and identified intrinsic motivation or task-focused motivation as supportive. In some situations, they reported that extrinsic motivation can also be helpful, particularly in encouraging persistence in the face of difficulty, although Amabile's work has shown the need to take care that it does not undermine the intrinsic motivation that is essential to the creative process. (See Chapter 8 for more on motivation.)

- *Place and Press.* 'Press' refers to the press of environments ('places') for an activity. Theories looking at this facet investigate interactions between an individual's characteristics (aspects of person) and the environment in which they operate (see Figure 9.9). Amabile & Pillemer (2012) noted the importance of actions of significant others that influence intrinsic versus extrinsic motivation, for example. Sternberg (2012) recognised that stimulation from people as well as materials was important, and identified the importance of support from adults and peers, as well as from the broader culture, for creativity to flourish. Place is looked at particularly in developmental work on creativity, which has identified the role of child rearing practices such as encouraging exploration, autonomy, questioning and discussion, in children's and adolescents' creativity (Russ & Fiorelli, 2010). We discuss development of creativity in greater detail below.

Source: Getty Images/Monkey Business Images

FIGURE 9.9 Environments can encourage creativity by supporting exploration, curiosity and autonomy. How could you create these conditions in your classroom?

Two additional facets are raised by Kozbelt and coworkers: *persuasion* or the ability of the creative person to persuade others of the value of their novel idea or product; and *potential*, which is particularly seen in developmental theories. A child might have the necessary aspects of *person*, but requires the *press* of environmental factors for their *potential* to be realised (Kokbelt et al., 2010).

Systems theories of creativity look at how the multiple facets of person, process, product and place influence one another. One example is Csikszentmihalyi's (1996, 2006) theory of creativity. Csikszentmihalyi recognised the importance of the social context and culture in which people live, to support and guide an individual's creative effort. He argued that while psychologists have tended to focus on the individual (the person and process), three factors are involved in creativity: person, field and domain. 'Domain' refers to the area in which the person's work is created, each with its own particular cultural rules and practices. Examples are art or music or science. The field contains the social context – the people – who judge creative products. Csikszentmihaly argued that 'Big C' creative works vary the content, rules or practices of their domain in some new way. For this to happen, they must be recognised as valuable by people in the field. Various fields (groups of influential people in various domains) sit within society, that preferences particular problems and solutions, and gives the field its power to make decisions about what is valuable. Similarly, various domains sit within the broader culture, and both influence and are influenced by it.

MEASURING CREATIVITY

Measuring creativity enables us to answer questions about what influences creativity, and to evaluate the effectiveness of interventions that seek to develop it. It has also helped to tease out the relationship between intelligence and creativity (discussed below) (Plucker & Makel, 2010; Silvia, 2015).

The best known measures of creativity are probably tests of the process. These are tests of divergent thinking which ask the participant to come up with multiple responses to a question. This may involve uses for objects, 'How many uses can you find for a brick?'; consequences of improbable situations 'What if the clouds had strings attached to them. How many consequences can you think of?'; or improvements to common objects 'How could you improve a stuffed toy dog?' among many others. They were originally developed by Guilford in the 1950s, and then further by Torrance through the 1960s, who developed the Torrance Tests of Creative Thinking (TTCT) and used criteria of fluency (number of responses), flexibility (number of ideas), originality and elaboration (extension of ideas) to score responses. Torrance continued to develop the tasks through the following decades, later adding other criteria for scoring these tasks, and additional tasks (Torrance, 2008). For example, a series of figural sub-tests was developed, in which people add to an abstract line or shape to develop a picture. This measures a different aspect of divergent thinking to the verbal subtests (Kaufman, 2016).

However, as we saw above in the section on models of creativity, there are other cognitive processes involved in creativity in addition to divergent thinking. Generation of metaphors to describe an experience, musical improvisation, and solutions for impossible problems have been tasks seeking to tap other aspects of creativity. Neurological studies use brain imaging to identify areas of the brain associated with creativity. For example, Kleinbeuker, De Dreu & Crone (2016) linked developments in the frontal cortex with developments in creativity in childhood and adolescence, and Yoruk & Runco, (2014) reported that both hemispheres are involved in creative activity.

Tests focusing on the creative person have been developed from studies of creative people that identified personality characteristics (Simonton, 2016), and aspects of motivation (Amabile, 1985) related to creativity, and sometimes the interactions between the two (Prabhu, Sutton & Sauser, 2008). These characteristics are then included in inventories of creativity traits that people may be asked to respond to in a questionnaire.

Other tests focus on rating of creative products. The Consensual Assessment Technique (Amabile, 1996) asks experts to rate the creativity of a specific product (for example, a story, or a drawing, a drama performance, or a musical composition). An expert is defined as someone with at least 10 years of experience in their field. Interestingly, Baer, Kaufman & Riggs (2009) reported that whether their expertise was in teaching, writing, or creativity research, experts' judgements of the creativity of Year 8 writing tended to agree. By contrast, agreement between experts' and novices' judgements is less likely. Figure 9.8 asked you to rate the creativity of some objects created by children. According to research studies, those of you with expertise (with children, with sculpture, or with creativity research) are unlikely to agree with those who are novices in these areas about the creativity of the pieces (Kaufman, 2016).

More recently, systems theories, recognising the interaction of multiple facets of creativity, have led to other kinds of measures, including measures of creative activity in daily life (Plucker & Makel, 2010). For example, Conner & Silvia (2015) asked people to keep a daily diary of creativity and emotion states, and were able to identify high-activation positive emotions such as feeling enthusiastic as associated with higher levels of creativity, while negative emotional states either had no effect, or suppressed creativity. Personality characteristics such as openness moderated this link, with more open people finding stronger effects of emotional state on their creativity.

See Box 9.10 for some examples of creativity test items.

BOX 9.10 IMPLICATIONS FOR EDUCATORS

MEASURES OF CREATIVITY

Amabile (1996) identified three main types of creativity tests: tests of personality; tests of cognitive behaviour, and biographies or questionnaires about tasks or achievements. Presented here are examples of each of these types of test items.

When measuring creativity, it is recommended that a range of types of assessments are used, as each measures a different aspect.

Tests of creative personality:
Creative personality scale (Gough, 1979)

> 'Please indicate which of the following (30) adjectives best describe yourself.'

Items scored positively include wide interests, original, intelligent, humorous. The scale also includes items that are scored negatively, such as narrow interests, cautious, honest.

Biographies:
Biographical Inventory of Creative Behaviours (Batey & Furnham, 2010)

> Choose from a list of 34 items those you've been actively involved in over the last 12 months: e.g. written a short story, produced your own website, designed and planted a garden, composed a piece of music.

Runco Ideational Behavior Scale (Runco, Plucker & Lim, 2000–2001).

> Rate how often you have the following ideas: 0 = Never; 1 = approximately once a year; 2 = once or twice each month (approximately); 3 = once or twice each week (approximately); 4 = Just about every day, and sometimes more than once each day. e.g. 'Approximately how often do you have ideas for making your work easier? Approximately how often do you have ideas about what you will be doing in the future?'

Tests of cognitive behaviour:
The main tests used are tests of divergent thinking, of which there are many types (Runco, Paek, Alsuwaidi, Abdulla & Al-Jasim, 2016). Responses are generally scored for:

- originality – responses that are not suggested by more than 1 per cent of others
- fluency – the number of responses
- flexibility – the number of different categories of ideas
- elaboration – the number of elements.

>>

1   In three minutes, use the image as a start for a drawing. Try to think of as many different
    pictures as you can, and have fun with this. (The sheet would have a full page of these circles.)

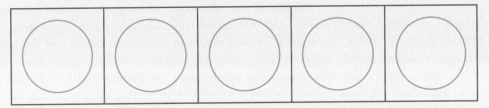

2   'People typically use everyday items for specific purposes. Often there are alternative
    uses for the same objects. For example, a newspaper could be used as a hat or a blanket,
    and many other things. For the following items, list as many alternative uses as you can.
    The more uses you think of, the better. Do not worry about spelling.' (Runco et al., 2016).
    e.g. a comb, a tyre, a brick or a toothbrush

3   'List alternative titles for each movie, play, and book listed below. Spelling does not
    matter and there are no grades for this. Have fun and list as many alternatives as you
    can.' (Runco et al., 2016).
    e.g.   Star Wars: The last Jedi
    Matilda
    Harry Potter and the Philosopher's Stone

4   Realistic problem generation: 'List problems with your friends, peers, schoolmates, or
    spouses (any individual of the same approximate age). These problems might be real, or
    they might be hypothetical and imaginary. Do not limit yourself; the more problems you
    can list, the better. (Do not worry about spelling, and take your time.)' (Runco et al., 2016).

5   'Create a humorous caption for this cartoon:'

ACTIVITIES

1   Consider each of these tests of creativity. Which comes closest to assessing creative
    potential? What are the weaknesses?
2   Are there other elements of creativity that are not addressed here? How would you
    measure them?
3   Is creativity measurable? What issues make it problematic?

DEVELOPMENT OF CREATIVITY

Creativity, like other cognitive skills we looked at in Chapter 3, and social and emotional skills discussed in Chapter 4, develops throughout childhood and adolescence, although the pattern of development is irregular, showing peaks and slumps, and with considerable individual differences evident (Barbot, Lubart & Besançon, 2016). Barbot et al. argued that both the discontinuities and the individual differences can be explained by differences in fit between individuals' resources of motivation, cognition and personality, and the demands of particular creative tasks. Environments play a role here too, in shaping individuals' cognition, motivation and personality, in responding to them, and in the context they provide for each task. Hence, as you may have experienced yourself, people may show high levels of creativity in one task, and quite low levels in another that is perhaps in a different domain, or set in a different situation. Baer (2016) similarly argued that creativity is domain-specific, and that training of creativity needs to also be tied to a particular domain, or even a particular task. We take this idea up further when we consider supporting creativity in the classroom, below. In addition, Barbot et al. pointed out that the various cognitive, personality and motivational resources for creativity each have differing patterns of development, which interact with the demands of each task, resulting in discontinuities in development across tasks and across time.

Nonetheless, brain development is reflected in developments in creativity, suggesting that there are underlying key processes that support creativity (Kleibeuker, De Dreu & Crone (2016). We looked at some of these in the section on models of creativity above. While executive functions supporting creativity such as inhibition control and cognitive flexibility show large changes in early childhood, studies of personality characteristics related to creativity suggest that adolescence and early adulthood are periods in which the greatest change occurs in this domain (Plucker & Merkel, 2010).

Supporting creativity in the classroom

Creative (and critical) thinking is a general capability in the Australian curriculum, and in the New Zealand curriculum, students are encouraged to value 'innovation, inquiry and curiosity, by thinking critically, creatively and reflectively' (New Zealand Ministry of Education, 2007). How can teachers support creativity in their classrooms? Kampylis and Berki (2014) stressed that creative thinking can be supported in all curriculum areas; Baer (2016) went further, arguing that if we want our efforts in supporting creativity to be successful, it must be addressed in each content area, rather than being dealt with in a generic way. Davies et al. (2012) reviewed research on this question from education settings across the range from early childhood to secondary schools, and identified aspects in three main groups: learning environment, learning relationships and pedagogy, as detailed in Box 9.11.

THINK ABOUT

■ What, if any, strategies were used in the schools you attended to encourage and develop creativity? How effective were these strategies?

Gajda, Beghetto & Karwowski (2017) identified classrooms in which there were positive correlations between creativity and academic achievement, and then looked at how teacher and student behaviour differed in these classrooms compared to others without this positive correlation. Teachers in the classrooms with a positive relationship between academic achievement and creativity were more likely to show the caring behaviours of careful listening to questions, delayed assessment of ideas, group work organisation, and authenticity or genuineness. The power of this to support creativity is seen in the student behaviours; students' positive engagement and ideation (generation of ideas) were linked to teachers' caring behaviours. In classrooms that supported creativity, opportunities were provided for students to share, and then further explore their ideas, as shown in Figure 9.10.

BOX 9.11 IMPLICATIONS FOR EDUCATORS

STRATEGIES FOR FOSTERING CREATIVITY IN YOUR CLASSROOM

Kampylis and Berki (2014) summarised characteristics of classrooms that support creative thinking, with considerable overlap with Davies et al.'s (2012) findings. Their paper also contains a number of practical suggestions on how teachers can apply these principles from research.

Learning environment

- Physical environments that have flexible, open spaces
- Consideration of light, colour, sound, air flow and materials as well as furniture arrangement to encourage collaboration (Kampylis & Berki, 2014)
- Taking students outside the classroom to encourage collaboration and ownership of the space; this may be to structured places such as museums and art galleries, as well as informal spaces and outdoor settings

Learning relationships

- Opportunities for collaboration with peers. Collaboration is confirmed in a number of studies as contributing to creativity – Sawyer and DeZutter (2009) describe creativity as arising from distributed (group) learning situations
- Regular teacher–student dialogue about their work
- Mutual respect, and supportive relationships between teachers and students

Pedagogy

- Tasks that are authentic and worthwhile. This element was also identified by Kampylis and Berki (2014), and in the Queensland longitudinal study of productive pedagogies (see **Box 7.6**).
- Novelty in activities, materials and resources stimulates creative thinking. Kampylis and Berki (2014) point out that ICTs, used well (see Chapter 12), provide opportunities for this stimulation, as well as opportunities for other aspects of pedagogy in this list such as collaboration, student direction, play-based learning, flexible time and opportunities to explore and imagine. Of course, these things depend on how ICTs are used.
- Balance of structure and freedom that supports risk taking. Encouraging risk taking and acceptance of mistakes was also identified by Kampylis and Berki (2014) as important to developing creative thinking. They point out that risk taking is essential to the creative process, and that mistakes should be accepted as inevitable along the way.
- Formative assessment practices (see Chapter 13) can foster creativity by shifting the role of assessor to the students themselves and providing regular feedback on how they are progressing.
- Multiple opportunities for students to initiate their own activities and make choices
- Opportunities to explore and imagine, also identified by Beghetto and Kaufman (2014)
- Play-based learning for students in all age groups
- Flexible time: students able to work at own pace, and have time to immerse themselves in an activity
- Teachers model creative thinking
- Beghetto and Kaufman (2014) added to this the importance of teaching students 'creative metacognition' – the ability to recognise when creativity is appropriate and when it is not – as well as teachers explicitly teaching for creative thinking, and encouraging intrinsic motivation.

FIGURE 9.10 Learning environments can support creativity by encouraging collaboration and exploration, and by stimulating ideas.

RELATIONSHIPS BETWEEN INTELLIGENCE AND CREATIVITY

We have seen references to creativity in some of the theories of intelligence reviewed earlier in this chapter. You may recall that Cattell proposed two types of intelligence that sat under *g*: crystallised and fluid intelligence. Fluid intelligence has links to creativity, in reasoning about novel problems (Kim, Cramond & Vantassel-Baska, 2010), while crystallised intelligence may also play a role, providing domain knowledge, and supporting creators in evaluating their work. Sternberg's triarchic theory includes creative intelligence as one of the three dimensions necessary to successful intelligence. Earlier, Guilford (1967) developed a model of human intellect (the Structure of Intellect model) that included both intelligence and creativity. He proposed divergent and convergent operations (which have been related to creativity and intelligence respectively) as separate things. The relationship between creativity and intelligence has been a question through the history of the two constructs.

Kim (2005) conducted a meta-analysis of studies examining the relationship between intelligence and creativity, finding an average correlation of 0.17 (a quite small significant relationship), with a weaker relationship in younger children. As recently as 2008, the agreed position of psychologists was that intelligence and creativity were separate processes (Silvia, 2015). However, in a reminder of the importance of sourcing recent studies, Silvia (2015) identified developments in measurement of creativity in neurological studies and in statistical analysis that have challenged these assumptions. For example, re-analysing previous studies using recent statistical tools showed an increase in the size of correlations between intelligence and creativity. We have already discussed executive functions and their role in creativity. Neurological studies have confirmed links between the executive functions of inhibition control, working memory and cognitive flexibility and divergent thinking (Benedek et al., 2014; Cassotti et al., 2016). Silvia also reviewed studies showing links between fluid intelligence and creative tasks. In addition, Kaufman (2016), reviewing the literature, identified a number of information processing elements (see Chapter 3) that have been linked to creativity via tests of divergent thinking – including retrieval of information from long-term memory, working memory and attention. Taken together, Silvia argues that these studies suggest close links between intelligence and creativity.

Relationships between creativity and academic achievement

Like the relationship between creativity and intelligence, that between creativity and academic achievement has been a question from at least the 1960s (Gajda, Karwowski & Beghetto, 2017). A meta-analysis of studies measuring the relationship reported an overall effect size of 0.22. You might recall from Chapter 1 that Hattie cited 0.4 as the average effect size of factors influencing learning; so although significant, 0.22 is fairly modest by comparison. However, meta-analyses are designed to average out differences across different groups or contexts, and these differences might reveal important information about factors that can influence the relationship.

Beghetto (2016) used the term *creative learning* to refer to the interactions between creativity and learning, which run in both directions. Creativity can influence learning (or achievement) through generation of new ideas, and construction of understanding, as we saw in Piaget's theory in Chapter 3. However, the strength of this relationship varies for different subjects (Beghetto & Baxter, 2012) and

Source: Getty Images/Hero Images

in different classrooms, as we explored with reference to Gajda et al.'s 2017 study (above). Learning can influence creativity through domain knowledge, which has been established as an important influence on creativity, both in the amount of knowledge, and the way that it is used (Beghetto, 2016).

CONCLUDING COMMENTS

Intelligence and creativity have each been conceptualised differently in various cultures, and by different psychologists. The model of intelligence you adopt as a teacher will influence such practices as how you perceive and interact with your students, your approach to and use of testing information, the grouping of students, differentiation of teaching, and procedures for identifying gifted students or students requiring special education assistance. Your model of creativity may influence your approach to questioning, the activities you design, and the ways you organise your classroom around individual or group work. Intelligence provides potential for learning that can be realised if appropriate opportunities are provided within educational programs. Creativity is recognised as a key set of abilities that both influence and are influenced by learning, and that can be supported by teachers' and students' actions. Failure to achieve these goals of intelligence and creativity leaves the whole community poorer.

STUDY TOOLS

ONLINE STUDY RESOURCES

Visit http://login.cengagebrain.com and use the access code that comes with this book for 12 months' access to the student resources for this text.

The CourseMate Express website contains a range of resources and study tools for this chapter, including:

- a **self-check quiz**
- **crosswords**, **flashcards** and a **glossary** to help you revise the key terms from this chapter

- the **Go further** materials and **interactive activity** mentioned in the chapter
- a **video** that illustrates some of the concepts discussed
- plus much more!

CourseMateExpress

CHAPTER REVIEW

- Intelligence is described as a complex, multifaceted cluster of abilities that have a major impact on all aspects of human activity, but particularly on learning at school.
- Early models of intelligence include Spearman's general mental capacity (g) and specific mental abilities (s), and Cattell and Carroll's three-stratum model of intelligence, Gardner's multiple intelligences and Sternberg's triarchic model.
- Teaching programs based on Cattell's, Gardner's and Sternberg's models of intelligence provide a range of academic and non-academic experiences.
- Tests and other assessment procedures designed to measure intelligence need to reflect diverse areas of human experience.
- There is debate about the extent to which intellectual abilities are the product of inherited characteristics or environmental influences; whether intelligence is one thing or many; and the extent to which intelligence can be taught.

- Students with high levels of intelligence have been described as 'gifted', although potential in other areas is also recognised as giftedness. Giftedness is distinguished from 'talent' in which potential is realised, to acknowledge that there are multiple personal and environmental factors that come in between potential and its realisation as achievement.
- Creativity is linked to novelty, utility and quality. As a cognitive process, it has a close relationship with intelligence.
- Models of creativity have focused on Process, Person, Product, and Press, with current systems approaches recognising the interaction of these facets of the construct. Measurement of creativity has also focused on these four Ps.
- Creativity can be supported through learning environments, learning relationships, and pedagogy. It is important to support creativity in each curriculum area, and for specific tasks.

PUTTING IT TOGETHER

Making links between 'intelligence and creativity' and material in other chapters

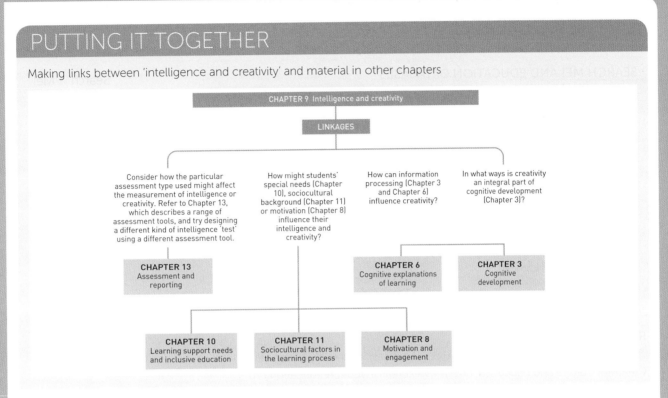

QUESTIONS AND ACTIVITIES FOR SELF-ASSESSMENT AND DISCUSSION

1 List some of the characteristics that are usually included in Western definitions of intelligence. Give examples of characteristics that might be used in a non-Western definition.

2 How would you define an intelligent person? How important is academic intelligence? What about practical intelligence?

3 What are your views on the following debates? Plot your position on the arrows below. Compare your views with those of a friend. Consider how your views on intelligence will influence your teaching and your attitude to students.

Intelligence is a single ability, applied across all tasks	Intelligence is composed of many abilities, and is different for different tasks
←	→

Intelligence is innate, something we are all born with to a particular degree	Intelligence is a function of a person's environment and life experiences
←	→

Intelligence is fixed	Intelligence is changeable
←	→

4 Think of a skilled task you are familiar with (for example, cooking a fruit cake, playing basketball, playing the piano, playing a video game, or negotiating conflict between two children). Identify the particular skills involved in this task. Would you categorise them as intelligences?

5 Present a case for why emotional intelligence should be included as part of the school curriculum. Consider the opposite case.

6 Consider Sternberg's argument that teachers should focus on how students use what they know rather than on knowing content. What was the focus when you were at school? What about at university? How should teachers balance knowledge of content, knowledge of thinking skills, and knowledge of how to apply content and thinking in practical situations?

7 Draw a concept map of the factors contributing to, and resulting from, intelligence.

8 Add creativity to this concept map and consider the interconnections between the various factors and the two concepts.

9 How will you support creative thinking in your classroom? How will you determine whether your efforts are successful?

FURTHER RESEARCH

SEARCH ME! AND EDUCATION DATABASES

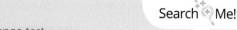

Explore Search Me! education for articles relevant to this chapter. Fast and convenient, Search Me! education is updated daily and provides you with 24-hour access to full-text articles from hundreds of scholarly and popular journals, ebooks and newspapers, including *The Australian* and *The New York Times*. Log in to Search Me! through http://login.cengagebrain.com and use the search terms listed here as a starting point:

- Binet
- creativity
- emotional intelligence
- intelligence

- intelligence test
- multiple intelligences
- nature–nurture
- triarchic model of intelligence.

Combining these terms with words such as 'schools', 'students', 'learners' or 'adolescents' (as in 'engagement and school') will limit your search to material related to schools and young students.

You can also use these terms to explore databases such as ERIC, PsycINFO and the Australian Education Index.

RECOMMENDED WEBSITES

To learn more about approaches to supporting creativity and intelligence in schools, visit the following sites:
Creativity Culture and Education. http://www.creativitycultureeducation.org

RECOMMENDED READING

Amabile, T.M. (1985) Motivation and creativity: effects of motivational orientation on creative writers. *Journal of Personality and Social Psychology 48*(2) 393–399.

Baer, J. Kaufman, J. C. & Riggs, M. (2009). Rater domain interactions in the Consensual Assessment Technique. *International Journal of Creativity and Problem Solving, 19*, 87–92.

Benedek, M., Jauk, E., Sommer, M., Arendasy, M. & Neubauer, A. C. (2014). Intelligence, creativity, and cognitive control: the common and differential involvement of executive functions in intelligence and creativity. *Intelligence, 46*, 73–83.

Csikszentmihalyi, M. (1996). *Creativity: Flow and the psychology of discovery and invention*. New York: Harper Collins.

Davies, D., Jindal-Snape, D., Collier, C., Digby, R., Hay, P. & Howe, A. (2013). Creative learning environments in education: A systematic literature review. *Thinking Skills and Creativity, 8*, 80–91.

Guilford, J. P. (1967). *The nature of human intelligence*. New York: McGraw-Hill.

Guilford, J. P. (1970). Creativity: Retrospect and prospect. *Journal of Creative Behavior, 4*, 149–168.

Hunt, E. (2011). *Human Intelligence*. Cambridge: Cambridge University Press.

Kaufman, J. C. (2016). *Creativity 101*. 2nd edition. New York: Springer Publishing Company.

Kaufman, J. C. & Sternberg, R. J. (2010). Preface. In J. C. Kaufman & R. J Sternberg (Eds) *The Cambridge Handbook of Creativity*. New York: Cambridge University Press.

Lubart, T. (2010). Cross-cultural perspectives on creativity. In J. C. Kaufman & R. J Sternberg (Eds) *The Cambridge Handbook of Creativity*. New York: Cambridge University Press.

Nisbett, R. E., Aronson, J., Blair, C., Dickens, W., Flynn, J., Halpern, D.F. & Turkheimer, E. (2012). Intelligence: New findings and theoretical developments. *American Psychologist, 67*(2), 130–59.

Simonton, D. K. (2016c). Creativity, automaticity, irrationality, fortuity, fantasy, and other contingencies: An eightfold response typology. *Review of General Psychology, 20*, 194–204.

Stein, M. I. (1953). Creativity and culture. *The Journal of Psychology, 36*, 311–322.

The Australian Curriculum. http://australian-curriculum.org/generalcapabilities/critical-and-creative-thinking/
The New Zealand Curriculum. http://nzcurriculum.tki.org.nz/The-New-Zealand-Curriculum#thinking

REFERENCES

Amabile, T.M. (1985) Motivation and creativity: effects of motivational orientation on creative writers. *Journal of Personality and Social Psychology 48*(2) 393–399.

Amabile, T. M., & Pillemer, J. (2012). Perspectives on the social psychology of creativity. *The Journal of Creative Behavior, 46*, 3–15.

Australian Curriculum, Assessment and Reporting Authority. (2012b). *The Australian Curriculum: Numeracy background*. Retrieved from www.australiancurriculum.edu.au/generalcapabilities/numeracy/introduction/background

Azuma, H. & Kashiwagi, K. (1987). Descriptions for an intelligent person: A Japanese study. *Japanese Psychological Research, 29*, 17–26.

Baer, J. Kaufman, J. C. & Riggs, M. (2009). Rater domain interactions in the Consensual Assessment Technique. *International Journal of Creativity and Problem Solving, 19*, 87–92.

Barchard, K. A. (2003). Does emotional intelligence assist in the prediction of academic success? *Educational and Psychological Measurement, 63*, 840–58.

Beghetto, R. A., & Kaufman, J. C. (2007). Toward a broader conception of creativity: A case for 'mini-c' creativity. *Psychology of Aesthetics, Creativity, and the Arts, 1*, 73–79.

Beghetto, R. A. & Kaufman, J. C. (2014). Classroom contexts for creativity. *High Ability Studies, 25*(1), 53–69.

Beghetto, R. A. & Plucker, J. A. (2006). The relationship among schooling, learning, and creativity: 'All roads lead to creativity' or 'You can't get there from here'. In J. C. Kaufman & J. Baer (Eds), *Creativity and reason in cognitive development* (pp. 316–32). Cambridge: Cambridge University Press.

Benedek, M., Jauk, E., Sommer, M., Arendasy, M. & Neubauer, A. C. (2014). Intelligence, creativity, and cognitive control: the common and differential involvement of executive functions in intelligence and creativity. *Intelligence, 46*, 73–83.

Biesheuvel, S. (1969). Psychological tests and their application to non-European peoples. In D. R. Price-Williams (Ed.), *Cross-cultural studies: Selected readings* (pp. 57–75). Harmondsworth: Penguin.

Booth, M. Z. (2002). Swazi concepts of intelligence: The universal versus the local. *Ethos, 30*(4), 376–400.

Bowes, J., Grace, R. & Hayes, A. (2012). The role of context in children's development. In J. Bowes, R. Grace & K. Hodge (Eds), *Children, families and communities: Contexts and consequences* (4th ed., pp. 3–16). South Melbourne: Oxford University Press.

Braggett, E. (2002). Gifted and talented children and their education. In A. Ashman & J. Elkins (Eds), *Educating children with diverse abilities* (pp. 286–348). Sydney: Prentice Hall.

Braggett, E. & Bailey, S. (2005). Gifted and talented children. In A. Ashman & J. Elkins (Eds), *Educating children with diverse abilities* (2nd ed., pp. 361–434). Frenchs Forest, NSW: Pearson.

Brinch, C. N. & Galloway, T. A. (2011). Schooling in adolescence raises IQ scores. *Proceedings of the National Academy of Sciences of the USA*. Retrieved from www.pnas.org/content/early/2011/12/19/1106077109.short

Brody, N. (1992). *Intelligence* (2nd ed.). San Diego: Academic Press.

Carroll, J. B. (1993). *Human cognitive abilities*. Cambridge: Cambridge University Press.

Castejon, J. L., Perez, A. M., & Gilar, R. (2010). Confirmatory factor analysis of Project Spectrum activities: A second-order g factor or multiple intelligences? *Intelligence, 38*, 481–496.

Cattell, R. B. (1987). *Intelligence: Its structure, growth and action*. Amsterdam: North-Holland.

Cianciolo, A. T. & Sternberg, R. J. (2004). *Intelligence: A brief history*. Malden, MA: Blackwell.

Coote, C. (2000). Special needs (gifted) in the mainstream primary classroom. *Gifted, 112*, 25–7.

Csikszentmihalyi, M. (1996). *Creativity: Flow and the psychology of discovery and invention*. New York: Harper Collins.

Davies, D., Jindal-Snape, D., Collier, C., Digby, R., Hay, P. & Howe, A. (2013). Creative learning environments in education: A systematic literature review. *Thinking Skills and Creativity, 8*, 80–91.

Deary, I. J. (2012). Intelligence. *Annual Review of Psychology, 63*, 453–82.

Deary, I. J., Spinath, F. M. & Bates, T. C. (2006). Genetics of intelligence. *European Journal of Human Genetics, 14*, 690–700.

Demetriou, A., Kui, X., Spanoudis, G., Christou, C., Kyriakides, L. & Platsidou, M. (2005). The architecture, dynamics, and development of mental processing: Greek, Chinese, or universal? *Intelligence, 33*(2), 109–41.

Detterman, D. K. (1993). Giftedness and intelligence: One and the same? In G. R. Block & K. Ackrill (Eds), *The origins and development of high ability* (pp. 22–43). Chichester, West Sussex: Wiley.

Durlak, J. A., Weissberg, R. P., Dymnicki, A. B., Taylor, R. D. & Schellinger, K. B. (2011). The impact of enhancing students' social and emotional learning: A meta-analysis of school-based universal interventions. *Child Development, 82*(1), 405–32.

Dutton, E. & Lynn, R. (2013). A negative Flynn effect in Finland: 1997–2009. *Intelligence, 41*(6), 817–20.

Dweck, C. S. & Molden, D. C. (2005). Self theories: Their impact on competence motivation and acquisition. In A. Elliot & C. S. Dweck (Eds), *The handbook of competence and motivation*. New York: Guilford.

Elkins, J. (2002). The school context. In A. Ashman & J. Elkins (Eds), *Educating children with diverse abilities* (pp. 73–113). Frenchs Forest, NSW: Pearson.

Fine, S. E., Izard, C., Mostow, A., Trentacosta, C. J. & Ackerman, B. P. (2003). First grade emotion knowledge as a predictor of fifth grade self-reported internalizing behaviors in children from economically disadvantaged families. *Development and Psychopathology, 15*, 331–42.

Fletcher, R. & Hattie, J. A. (2011). *Intelligence and intelligence testing*. New York: Routledge.

Flynn, J. R. (1987). Massive IQ gains in 14 nations: What IQ tests really measure. *Psychological Bulletin, 101*, 171–91.

Flynn, J. R. (1998). WAIS-III and WISC-III gains in the United States from 1972 to 1995: How to compensate for obsolete norms. *Perceptual and Motor Skills, 86* (3, Pt. 2), 1231–9.

Flynn, J. R. (2000). The hidden history of IQ and special education: Can the problems be solved? *Psychology, Public Policy, and Law, 6*(1), 191–8.

Flynn, J. R. (2007). *What is intelligence? Beyond the Flynn Effect*. Cambridge, UK: Cambridge University Press.

Flynn, J. R. (2012). *Are we getting smarter? Rising IQ in the twenty-first century*. Cambridge, UK: Cambridge University Press.

Flynn, J. R. (2013). The 'Flynn Effect' and Flynn's paradox. *Intelligence, 41*(6), 851–7.

Furnham, A. (2009). The validity of a new, self-report measure of multiple intelligence. *Current Psychology, 28*(4), 225–239.

Gagné, F. (1993). Constructs and models pertaining to exceptional human abilities. In K. A. Heller, F. J. Monks & A. H. Passow (Eds), *International handbook of research and development of giftedness and talent* (1st ed., pp. 69–87). New York: Pergamon.

Gagné, F. (2003). Transforming gifts into talents: The DMGT as a developmental theory. In N. Colangelo & G. A. Davis (Eds), *Handbook of gifted education* (3rd ed., pp. 60–74). Boston: Allyn & Bacon.

Gardner, H. (1983). *Frames of mind: The theory of multiple intelligences*. New York: Basic Books.

Gardner, H. (1997). *Extraordinary minds: Portraits of exceptional individuals and an examination of our extraordinariness*. New York: Basic Books.

Gardner, H. (1999). Are there additional intelligences? The case for naturalistic, spiritual and existential intelligences. In J. Cain (Ed.), *Education: Information and transformation* (pp. 111–32). Englewood Cliffs, NJ: Prentice Hall.

Gardner, H. (2006). On failing to grasp the core of MI theory: A response to Visser et al. *Intelligence, 34*, 503–5.

Gardner, H., Hatch, T. & Torff, B. (1997). A third perspective: The symbol systems approach to intelligence. A novel perspective on the genes and culture controversy. In R. J. Sternberg & E. Grigorenko (Eds), *Intelligence, heredity, and environment* (pp. 243–68). New York: Cambridge University Press.

Gignac, G. E. (2015). The magical numbers 7 and 4 are resistant to the Flynn effect. No evidence for increases in forward or backward recall across 85 years of data, *Intelligence, 48*, 85–95.

Goodenough, F. (1926). *Measurement of intelligence by drawings.* New York: Harcourt, Brace & World.

Gould, S. J. (1981). *The mismeasure of man.* New York: Norton.

Granott, N. & Gardner, H. (1994). When minds meet: Interactions, coincidence, and development in domains of ability. In R. J. Sternberg & R. K. Wagner, *Mind in context: Interactionist perspectives on human intelligence* (pp. 171–201). Cambridge, UK: Cambridge University Press.

Grigorenko, E. L., Wenzel Geissler, P., Prince, R., Okatcha, F., Nokes, C., Kenny, D. A., Bundy, D. A. & Sternberg, R. J. (2001). The organisation of Luo conceptions of intelligence: A study of implicit theories in a Kenyan village. *International Journal of Behavioural Development, 25*(4), 367–78.

Gross, M. (1993). *Exceptionally gifted children.* London: Routledge.

Gross, M. (2005). *The gifted education professional development package.* Sydney: Gifted Education Research, Resource and Information Centre (GERRIC). Retrieved from https://education.arts.unsw.edu.au/about-us/gerric/resources/pd-package/

Guilford, J. P. (1967). *The nature of human intelligence.* New York: McGraw-Hill.

Guilford, J. P. (1970). Creativity: Retrospect and prospect. *Journal of Creative Behavior, 4*, 149–168.

Howe, M. J. A. (1997). *IQ in question: The truth about intelligence.* London: Sage.

Hunt, E. (2011). *Human intelligence.* Cambridge, UK: Cambridge University Press.

Imhoff, T. (2000). *Alfred Binet.* Retrieved from www.muskingum.edu/~psych/psycweb/history/binet.htm

Izard, C. E., Fine, S., Schultz, D., Mostow, A., Ackerman, B. & Youngstrom, E. (2001). Emotion knowledge as a predictor of social behavior and academic competence in children at risk. *Psychological Science, 12*, 18–23.

Jauk, E., Benedek, M., Dunst, B., & Neubauer, A. C. (2013). The relationship between intelligence and creativity: New support for the threshold hypothesis by means of empirical breakpoint detection. *Intelligence, 41*, 212–221.

Kampylis, P. & Berki, H. (2014). *Nurturing creative thinking.* UNESCO International Bureau of Education; Educational Practices Series, 25.

Kanaya, T. Scullin, M. H. & Ceci, S. J. (2003). The Flynn effect and US policies: The impact of rising IQ scores on American society via mental retardation diagnoses. *American Psychologist, 58*(10), 778–90.

Kaufman, J. C. (2016). *Creativity 101.* 2nd edition. New York: Springer Publishing Company.

Kaufman, J. C. & Sternberg, R. J. (2010). Preface. In J. C. Kaufman & R. J Sternberg (Eds) *The Cambridge Handbook of Creativity.* New York: Cambridge University Press.

Kay, J. (2005). Crystallized intelligence versus fluid intelligence. *Psychiatry, 68*(1), 9–13.

Kleibeuker, S. W., De Dreu, C. K. W. & Crone, E. A. (2016). Creativity Development in Adolescence: Insight from behaviour, brain, and training studies. Special Issue, Perspectives on Creativity Development. *New Directions for Child and Adolescent Development, 2016*(1), 73–84.

Kong, D. T. (2014). Mayer-Salovey-Caruso Emotional Intelligence Test (MSCEIT/MEIS) and overall, verbal, and nonverbal intelligence: Meta-analytic evidence and critical contingencies. *Personality and Individual Differences 66*, 171–175.

Lubart, T. (2010). Cross-Cultural Perspectives on Creativity. In J. C. Kaufman & R. J Sternberg (Eds) *The Cambridge Handbook of Creativity.* New York: Cambridge University Press.

Lubinski, D., Benbow, C. P., Webb, R. M. & Bleske-Rechek, A. (2006). Tracking exceptional human capital over two decades. *Psychological Science, 17*, 194–9.

Mayer, J. D., Roberts R. & Barsade, S. G. (2008). Human abilities: Emotional intelligence. *Annual Review of Psychology, 59*, 507–36.

Mayer, J. D., Salovey, P. & Caruso, D. (2000). Selecting a measure of emotional intelligence: The case for ability scales. In R. Bar-On & J. D. A. Parker (Eds), *Handbook of emotional intelligence* (pp. 35–54). San Francisco: Jossey-Bass.

Mayer, J. D., Caruso, D. R., Panter, A. T., & Salovey, P. (2012). The growing significance of hot intelligences. *American Psychologist, 67*, 502–503.

McGrath, H. (2005). Directions in teaching social skills to students with specific EBDs. In P. Clough, P. Garner, J. T. Pardeck & F. K. O. Yuen (Eds), *Handbook of emotional and behavioural difficulties* (pp. 317–52). London: Sage Publications.

Meisenberg, G. & Woodley, M. A. (2013). Are cognitive differences between countries diminishing? Evidence from TIMSS and PISA. *Intelligence, 41*(6), 808–16.

Monro, J. (2013). High ability learning and brain processes: How neuroscience can help us to understand how gifted and talented students learn and the implications for teachers. Paper presented at ACER Research Conference, Melbourne, August.

Moore, J. L., Ford, D. Y. & Milner, H. R. (2005). Underachievement among gifted students of color: Implications for educators. *Theory into Practice, 44*(2), 167–77.

Naglieri, J. A. (1988). *DAP: Draw a person: A quantitative scoring system.* New York: Harcourt Brace Jovanovich.

New Zealand Education Review Office. (2008). *Boys' education: Good practice in secondary schools.* Wellington, NZ: ERO. Retrieved from www.ero.govt.nz/National-Reports/Boys-Education-Good-Practice-in-Secondary-Schools-July-2008

New Zealand Ministry of Education. (2007). *The New Zealand curriculum. For English medium teaching and learning in Years 1–13.* Wellington: Ministry of Education.

New Zealand Ministry of Education. (2012). *Gifted and talented students: Meeting their needs in New Zealand Schools, 2012.* Wellington: Ministry of Education. Retrieved from http://gifted.tki.org.nz/Forschools-and-teachers

Nisbett, R. E. (2014). What teachers need to know about IQ. *Education Digest, 79*, 9.

Nisbett, R. E., Aronson, J., Blair, C., Dickens, W., Flynn, J., Halpern, D. F. & Turkheimer, E. (2012). Intelligence: New findings and theoretical developments. *American Psychologist, 67*(2), 130–59.

Nisbett, R. E. & Miyamoto, Y. (2005). The influence of culture: Holistic versus analytic perception. *Trends in Cognitive Science, 9*, 467–73.

NSW Board of Studies. (2001). *Guidelines for accelerated progression.* Sydney: Board of Studies NSW.

NSW Department of Education and Training. (2004). *Policy and implementation strategies for the education of gifted and talented students. Revised 2004.* Sydney: NSW Department of Education and Training.

Okagaki, L. & Sternberg, R. J. (1993). Parental beliefs and children's school performance. *Child Development, 64*, 36–56.

Paton, M. (2005). Is critical analysis foreign to Chinese students? In E. Manalo & G. Wong-Toi (Eds), *Communication skills in New Zealand education: The international dimension* (pp. 1–11). Auckland: Pearson.

Payton, J., Weissberg, R. P., Durlak, J. A., Dymnicki, A. B., Taylor, R. D., Schellinger, K. B. & Pachan, M. (2008). *The positive impact of social and emotional learning for kindergarten to eighth-grade students: Findings from three scientific reviews.* Chicago, IL: Collaborative for Academic, Social, and Emotional Learning. retrieved from http://casel.org/publications/positive-impact-of-social-and-emotional-learning-for-kindergarten-to-eighth-grade-students-findings-from-three-scientific-reviews

Petrill, S. A. & Kirby, D-D. (2004). The heritability of general cognitive ability: A within-family adoption design. *Intelligence, 32*, 403–9.

Petrill, S. A., Pike, A., Price, T. & Plomin, R. (2004). Chaos in the home and socio-economic status are associated with cognitive development in early childhood: Environmental mediators in a genetic design. *Intelligence, 32*, 445–60.

Plomin, R. & Deary, I. J. (2015). Genetics and intelligence differences: Five special findings. *Molecular Psychiatry, 20*(1), 98–108.

Plucker, J. (2005). *Robert J. Sternberg.* Retrieved from www.Indiana.edu/~intell/sternberg.shtml

Queensland Department of Education and the Arts. (2005). Framework for gifted education. Retrieved from www.education.qld.gov.au

Renzulli, J. S. (1978). What makes giftedness? Reexamining a definition. *Phi Delta Kappan*, *60*, 180–4.

Renzulli, J. S. (2002). Emerging conceptions of giftedness: Building a bridge to the new century. *Exceptionality*, *10*(2), 67–75.

Renzulli, J. S. (2005). Applying gifted education pedagogy to total talent development for all students. *Theory into Practice*, *44*(2), 80–9.

Renzulli, J. S. (2013). What makes giftedness? A four-part theory for the development of creative productive giftedness in young people. In B. J. Irby, J. Beverly, G. Brown, R. Lara-Alecio & S. Jackson (Eds) (2013). *The handbook of educational theories*. (pp. 1119–128). xviii, 1144 pp. Charlotte, NC, US: IAP Information Age Publishing.

Riley, T. L., Bevan-Brown, J., Bicknell, B., Carroll-Lind, J. & Kearney, A. (2004). *The extent, nature and effectiveness of planned approaches in New Zealand schools for providing for gifted and talented students*. Palmerston North: Institute for Professional Development and Educational Research, Massey University.

Sattler, J. M. (2001). *Assessment of children: Cognitive applications* (4th ed.). San Diego: Jerome M. Sattler, Publisher, Inc.

Sawyer, R. K. & DeZutter, S. (2009). Distributed creativity: How collective creations emerge from collaboration. *Psychology of Aesthetics, Creativity, and the Arts*, *3*(2), 81–92.

Schneider, W. J. & McGrew, K. (2012). The Cattell-Horn-Carroll model of intelligence. In D. Flanagan & P. Harrison (Eds), *Contemporary intellectual assessment: Theories, tests, and issues* (3rd ed., pp. 99–144). New York: Guilford. Retrieved from www.iapsych.com/chcv2.pdf

Senate Employment, Workplace Relations, Small Business and Education Reference Committee. (2001). *The education of gifted students*. Retrieved from www.aph.gov.au

Shi, J. (2004). Diligence makes people smart: Chinese perspectives of intelligence. In R. J. Sternberg (Ed.), *International Handbook of Intelligence*, pp. 325–43). New York: Cambridge University Press.

Simonton, D.K. (2016c). Creativity, automaticity, irrationality, fortuity, fantasy, and other contingencies: An eightfold response typology. *Review of General Psychology*, *20*, 194–204.

South Australia Department for Education and Child Development (2012). Gifted and talented children and students policy (updated 2016), DECD.

Spearman, C. E. (1904). 'General intelligence', objectively determined and measured. *American Journal of Psychology*, *15*, 201–93.

Spearman, C. E. (1927). *The abilities of man, their nature and measurement*. London: Macmillan.

Stein, M. I. (1953). Creativity and culture. *The Journal of Psychology*, *36*, 311–322.

Sternberg, R. J. (1985). *Beyond IQ: A triarchic theory of intelligence*. New York: Cambridge University Press.

Sternberg, R. J. (1988). *The triarchic mind: A new theory of human intelligence*. New York: Viking.

Sternberg, R. J. (1997). Educating intelligence: Infusing the triarchic theory into school instruction. In R. J. Sternberg & E. L. Grigorenko (Eds), *Intelligence, heredity and environment* (pp. 343–62). Cambridge, UK: Cambridge University Press.

Sternberg, R. J. (2002). Raising the achievement of all students: Teaching for successful intelligence. *Educational Psychology Review*, *14*(4), 383–93.

Sternberg, R. J. (2003). Our research program validating the triarchic theory of successful intelligence: Reply to Gottfredson. *Intelligence*, *31*(4), 399–413.

Sternberg, R. J. (2005). The theory of successful intelligence. *Interamerican Journal of Psychology*, *39* (2), 189–202.

Sternberg, R. J. (2007). Who are the bright children? The cultural context of being and acting intelligent. *Educational Researcher*, *36*(3), 148–55.

Sternberg, R. J. (2012). The assessment of creativity: An investment-based approach. *Creativity Research Journal*, *24*(1), 3–12.

Sternberg, R. J. (2014). The development of adaptive competence: Why cultural psychology is necessary and not just nice. *Developmental Review 34*, 208–224.

Sternberg, R. J., Torff, B. & Grigorenko, E. L. (1998). Teaching triarchically improves school achievement. *Journal of Educational Psychology*, *90*, 374–84.

Torff, B. & Gardner, H. (1999). The vertical mind: The case for multiple intelligence. In M. Anderson (Ed.), *The development of intelligence* (pp. 139–59). Hove, East Sussex: The Psychology Press.

Torrance, E. P. (1988). The nature of creativity as manifest in its testing. In R. J. Sternberg (Ed.), *The nature of creativity*. Cambridge, UK: Cambridge University Press.

Trzaskowski, M., Yang, J., Visscher, P. M., & Plomin, R. (2014). DNA evidence for strong genetic stability and increasing heritability of intelligence from age 7 to 12. *Molecular Psychiatry*, *19*, 380–384.

VanTassel-Baska, J. (2005). Gifted programs and services: What are the non-negotiables? *Theory into Practice*, *44*(2), 90–7.

Vialle, W. & Rogers, K. (2009). *Educating the gifted learner*. Terrigal: David Barlow Publishing.

Visser, B. A., Ashton, M. C. & Vernon, P. A. (2006). Beyond *g*: Putting multiple intelligences theory to the test. *Intelligence*, *34*(5), 487–502.

Von Stumm, S. & Plomin, R. (2015). Socioeconomic status and the growth of intelligence from infancy through adolescence. *Intelligence*, *48*(1), 30–6.

Western Australia Department of Education. (2015). Gifted and talented: Developing the talents of gifted children. Retrieved from www.det.wa.edu.au/curriculumsupport/giftedandtalented/detcms/portal/

10

LEARNING SUPPORT NEEDS AND INCLUSIVE EDUCATION

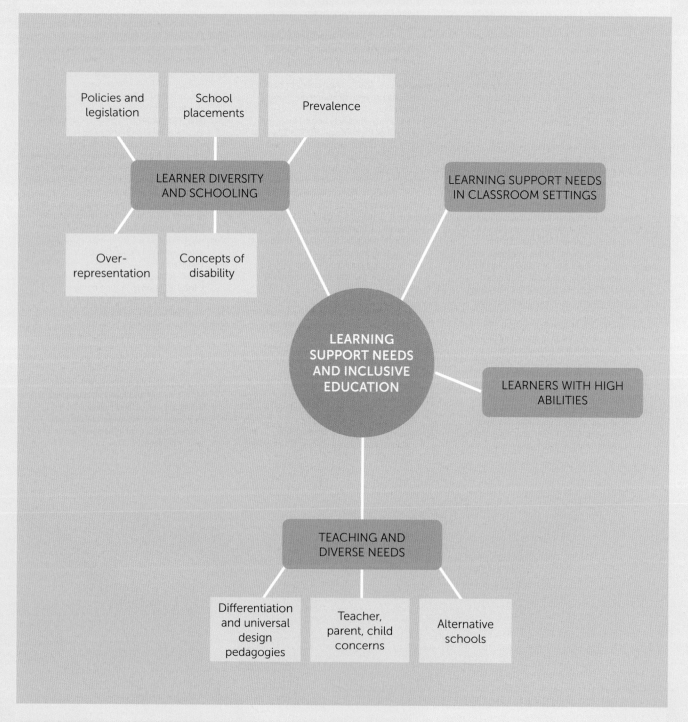

FIGURE 10.1 Chapter 10 concept map

KEY QUESTIONS

After reading this chapter, you should be able to answer the following questions:
- Can you explain the term 'inclusive education'?
- What changes have occurred over time in the language used to refer to disability? Why did these changes occur?
- What standards or policies relate to the provision of education to students with disabilities?
- What are your obligations as an educator under these standards and policies?
- What is meant by a 'non-categorical' approach, and why is this important?
- Which teaching strategies are the most effective for supporting students with a disability in an inclusive class?
- What are the main concerns of teachers about the inclusion of students with a disability in a regular classroom?

ONLINE STUDY RESOURCES

Bring your learning to life with **interactive learning**, **study** and **exam preparation tools** that support the printed textbook. CourseMate Express includes **quizzes**, **interactive activities**, **videos**, a tool to help you '**develop your philosophy**' and more.

INTRODUCTION

Anna is excited and in a rush to get changed into her work clothes for her vocational education placement. Once a week, Anna leaves school after lunch and attends a work-experience placement in a local animal shelter. She loves working with animals and dreams of being a vet or working in a veterinary hospital. She is 16 years old and has a mild intellectual disability, leading to some difficulties with independent problem-solving skills – she can also get a little frustrated and lose her temper if she can't solve problems quickly.

Anna is ready to catch the local bus directly to the animal shelter. Her teacher checks she has her multi-ride bus ticket ready and asks, 'How many rides do you have left on that ticket Anna?' 'Two,' she replies. 'What day do you need to buy a new one?' the teacher asks. The support teacher is encouraging Anna to learn to use public transport and assume more responsibility for everyday life skills, such as making simple plans like working out on which day of the week she needs to buy a new bus ticket.

On arriving at the shelter, the manager greets Anna warmly and reminds her they have a meeting as the first task of the afternoon. Anna heads straight to the staffroom, puts her bag in a locker and collects her schedule from the clipboard on the locker. She has been working with the small animals for the last month, but she knows today is job rotation day and she will be assigned to the large animal area, working with horses and other large animals. The manager is working closely with Anna's support team at the school to help Anna learn to follow simple routines and lists of tasks. They use pictorial diagrams to help her remember how many cups of pellets to feed the horses, and sequence charts with minimal text and clear language can help her remember procedures. Coping with change, following routines and learning to solve simple problems are key goals in Anna's individual education plan. Anna intends to stay at school and has been offered paid weekend shifts at the animal shelter.

Anna is participating in a school-to-work program that marks an important transition in the lives of many young people, but is especially important for young people like Anna. Although students like Anna have similar hopes and dreams as most other students, they may not have the same educational options or ability to go to university and study a course such as veterinary science. Nonetheless, respecting Anna's vocational interests has been of vital importance to her parents and teachers, and they are pleased the animal shelter placement has worked so well.

When Anna approached the middle years of high school, she told her parents and teachers that she wanted to leave school. Like many students with learning difficulties, she had become discouraged and disengaged. In the junior years of high school, she was bullied and picked on by peers when she was withdrawn from the classroom for a special reading program. Her literacy and math skills are still relatively weak. With her teachers' encouragement, Anna decided to stay at school and participate in an integrated work-placement program. She studies modified maths and English units, and her numeracy and literacy skills are still improving. She also plays netball once a week at a local sports club with some of the girls from the school team, and now has a supportive group of friends.

The lives of students like Anna who have any sort of additional learning support needs have changed dramatically in recent decades. Unfortunately, the treatment of persons with disabilities in schooling (and other areas of life) has often been associated with marginalised and discriminatory processes. Today, students like Anna have a wider range of schooling options available to them, and most students with disabilities are now included in regular schools alongside their peers.

This chapter introduces the notion of responding to learners with additional learning support needs in inclusive education classrooms. The concept of disability is explored and the teaching and learning implications associated with a range of learning support needs in school today are introduced. It is important to note that this chapter specifically focuses on learning support needs associated with disability, mental health, chronic health conditions and also learners of high ability (often referred to as 'gifted' learners). Chapter 11 considers other diverse learning support needs associated with a range of sociocultural factors including socioeconomic, ethnicity, race and cultural factors. This chapter is not intended to reflect the curriculum-based pedagogical content of a typical inclusive or special education textbook. Rather, it attempts to dispel myths and erroneous beliefs about learners who need additional support in the classroom. This chapter provides an introduction to the support requirements of learners in regular classrooms, and some key links to educational psychology concepts you have studied in this book.

LEARNER DIVERSITY AND SCHOOLING

normalisation
Giving people with disabilities access to the daily experiences and activities available to those in the community who do not have a disability

Classrooms are heterogeneous. This means they are made up of a diversity of learners. However, this has not always been the case. In the past, learners like Anna, with cognitive learning support needs, may have been automatically excluded from regular schools and placed in special schools or classes. Over several decades, particularly from the 1960s onward, changes in social attitudes such as the principle of **normalisation** began to influence inclusion in regular schools (see Box 10.1). In practice, this process of including all students in regular schools has been gradual and some may argue, incomplete. For example, there is evidence that certain types of learners are still disproportionately excluded from school today. This is explored later in this chapter and further in Chapter 11.

inclusive education
The programs and services provided in most education systems to address the needs of all students in regular schools, regardless of ability or disability

The term 'inclusive education' refers to the programs and services provided to address the needs of any student requiring additional support in their regular neighbourhood school classroom. This term arises from an international movement and acceptance of the view that all students have a right to participate fully in their community (Foreman & Arthur-Kelly, 2014). This includes the right to attend their local school, be accommodated in regular classes, and have their learning support needs addressed. Terms such as 'special education' are also used to refer to the system of programs and services provided for children who require support in school, but this provision does not carry the same inclusive intent of the principles of inclusive education and the term is falling into disuse. In part, this may be because the word 'special' raises philosophical concerns about inclusivity and stigma that may arise with the

special education
The system of programs and services provided in most education systems for children who have difficulties in school for a variety of reasons and who need additional support

term; it may also be associated with the historical use of 'special' schools where children with disabilities were routinely segregated from other students. Fewer of these segregated schools remain in modern educational systems.

BOX 10.1 IMPLICATIONS FOR EDUCATORS

PRINCIPLES OF NORMALISATION

The concept of normalisation was defined by Wolfensberger (1972) and Nirje (1985) who argued that people with disabilities had a right to live 'normal' lives and experience the full range of 'normal' day-to-day activities enjoyed by most people. At this time, many children with disabilities were not eligible to receive a typical education available to other students of their age, and many children and adults with disabilities were housed in institutions for the disabled. The conditions and experiences of many persons in these institutions or segregated schools was harsh and far removed from the typical everyday lives of other children or adults. Hence, the term 'normalisation' was developed to promote the right of people with disabilities to experience the same day-to-day living conditions, rights and 'normative' experiences that any other citizen in a society might expect. During the 1970s, the systematic deinstitutionalisation of people with disabilities began, and in the early 1980s Australian education systems developed the first special-education policies that promoted the mainstreaming of students with disabilities in regular school settings. Over several decades, the principle of normalisation has led to a profound change in views about persons with disabilities.

The principles of inclusive education were first adopted by the United Nations Educational, Scientific and Cultural Organization (UNESCO) in 1994 at the Salamanca World Conference on Special Needs Education, held in Salamanca, Spain. This declaration of support for inclusive education is also known as the Salamanca Declaration and was agreed to by more than 90 countries, including Australia and New Zealand. The statement of inclusion has been restated at successive world conferences and refers to 'all children regardless of their physical, intellectual, social, emotional, linguistic or other conditions', including 'disabled and gifted children, children from remote or nomadic populations, children from linguistic, ethnic or cultural minorities and children from other disadvantaged or marginalised groups' (UNESCO, 1994). This chapter is largely focused on children with learning support needs arising from disability or other conditions that affect learning and participation in school, but we also acknowledge that most of the principles addressed here apply to all learners who may experience educational disadvantage or exclusion.

Australia and New Zealand are also signatories to the United Nations Convention on the Rights of Persons with Disabilities (2006), which makes explicit reference to inclusive education. In this convention, governments from around the world were invited to give priority to:

- make education systems inclusive
- adopt the principle of inclusive education as a matter of policy or law
- establish strategies to plan, monitor and evaluate educational provision for special needs students
- invest in early identification and intervention strategies, and ensure that adequate teacher education programs are available (Elkins, 2005, p. 12).

However, despite these international agreements and the intent of inclusion, there is widespread debate about the extent of inclusion actually experienced by children. This was summed up by Graham and Slee (2007), who noted that 'to include is not necessarily to be inclusive' (p. 278). Misunderstanding of what it means to be 'inclusive' and misappropriation of the term 'inclusion' are just some of the reasons why inclusion may not be practised to the extent requested in international conventions and declarations (Cologon, 2013).

POLICIES AND LEGISLATION

Today in Australia and New Zealand, programs and services for children with additional learning support needs or disabilities are provided in both public and private school systems. Legislative Acts within Australia (*Disability Discrimination Act 1992*) and New Zealand (*Education Act 1989* and *Human Rights Act 1993*) provide a context for allowing people with disabilities to access educational services without discrimination or prejudice. In Australia, the Disability Standards for Education 2005 provides specific standards and guidelines for the provision of education to people with disabilities. These standards provide a legal 'standard' and obligation on the part of the educational provider to ensure that:

- the education provider must take reasonable steps to ensure courses and programs are designed in such a way that a person with a disability can participate in the program on the same basis as a student without a disability and without experiencing discrimination
- the educational provider must consult with the student or an associate of the student (for example, family) about how the disability affects the student's ability to participate in learning experiences
- in light of this information, the educational provider must decide if an adjustment is necessary and, if so, make a reasonable adjustment to ensure the person with a disability can participate in learning on the same basis as a person without a disability (Commonwealth of Australia, Attorney-General's Department, 2005).

This federal Act relates to educational provision in all sectors of education in Australia, including universities, though terms such as 'reasonable adjustment' may be open to interpretation and debate as to what sort of adjustments are considered 'reasonable'. This Act also exists alongside various policies in specific states and territories and, as a result, there are variations in the way special education services are provided across Australia. To learn more about special educational policies in different states and territories, refer to Foreman and Arthur-Kelly (2017).

SCHOOL PLACEMENTS FOR LEARNERS WITH ADDITIONAL SUPPORT NEEDS

In practice, most school systems provide a range of educational services and resources to support the learning needs of students. Following from the principles of normalisaton, the aim is to educate students in what is called the **least restrictive environment (LRE)**, which means a setting that is as close as possible to that experienced by children who do not have disabilities. Today, the term 'least restrictive environment' can be applied to consider which educational services represent the most normative and least restrictive placement for a young person. The LRE can be viewed as a continuum ranging from the least restrictive environment in regular classrooms to the most restrictive environment in segregated special schools or classes. Examples of highly restrictive schools include school suspension centres for excluded students, schools for students with emotional and behavioural conditions who have been excluded from regular schools, and schools located within juvenile justice facilities. In some cases, a particular form of segregation occurs in the case of academically selective high schools. For example, in the state of New South Wales in Australia, where there are higher numbers of selective high schools, only learners with high academic achievement levels may attend these schools.

Students may also experience an environment that is part way along the LRE continuum in a partial form of inclusion, whereby they attend a special classroom or support unit attached to the regular school but have a part-time placement in a regular class. These students may have higher or very specific support needs that can be met in the support unit but may also attend regular school classes as well.

least restrictive environment (LRE)
The setting that is as close as possible to that experienced by children who do not have disabilities

CourseMateExpress

Online Resources
Explore an example of least restrictive environment with the **Interactive Activity** on this text's website

For example, a student with cognitive support needs may attend classes in the support unit that provide highly individualised programming, but the student may also participate in regular classes where fewer adjustments to the curriculum are required, such as visual arts or physical education. Similarly, a child who requires some form of health or medical treatment during the school day may also return to a support unit for such treatments.

Today, in many developed educational regions around the world, students with disabilities are experiencing a higher degree of participation in school than ever before. However, it is important to note that there is considerable variation in the placement and level of inclusion experienced by some students in schools today. As we will explore later in this chapter, certain types of students with conditions leading to emotional or behavioural difficulties are being excluded from regular schools at higher rates than in previous years. Sometimes the school placement of a child might reflect differences in the preferences of students and their families; not all students with specific learning support needs want to attend a regular school, and some may choose to attend a more specialised school, as is seen in the case of academically selective schools for students of high ability.

PREVALENCE OF DISABILITY AND LEARNING SUPPORT NEEDS

The Australian Bureau of Statistics (ABS) routinely collects information about the prevalence of disability in Australia in the Survey of Disability, Ageing and Carers. This type of information is helpful for educational systems as it allows for estimates of the number of students and types of learning support needs that we may encounter in our schools and classrooms. The ABS estimated that in 2012 there were approximately 295 000 children aged 5–17 years with a disability in Australia who were also attending school (ABS, 2014). Boys tended to have a higher prevalence of disability, comprising 61 per cent of the population, compared to girls. Most children with a disability were enrolled in regular school settings (86 per cent) and the remainder attended some type of special school. Regardless of school type, a significant proportion of students with disabilities still experienced significant difficulty at school, with the most common difficulties including learning difficulties (43 per cent) and trouble fitting in socially (35 per cent). As described in Chapter 4, some children with disabilities are vulnerable to peer rejection at school.

OVER-REPRESENTATION AND DISCRIMINATION

In contrast to the discussion of inclusion in school we might also ask questions about why certain types of students are not attending regular mainstream schools and are over-represented in these statistics and special school placements. One of the earliest concerns about the practice of special education raised the possibility that students from certain backgrounds were over-represented in special education classes (generally referring to completely or partially segregated school placements). In a seminal paper, Dunn (1968), a forefather of the **mainstreaming** movement, exposed the over-representation of African-American and other minority children in special education classrooms in the United States. These children were particularly likely to come from poor, inner-city, working-class communities. The social injustice of this over-representation was particularly borne out in what Dunn described as the very poor educational opportunities provided to students in segregated special education classes, and the reduced opportunities for future life experiences of employment and higher education.

Unfortunately, such over-representation and claims of discrimination persist. Similar studies have noted the over-representation of minority youth in special education in Australia. For example, Indigenous youth are significantly more likely to be over-represented in certain forms of special education, particularly schools for students in the identified support categories of emotional disturbance, behaviour

mainstreaming
This term refers to the historical movement (approx. 1960s–1980s) that saw the removal of children with disabilities from institutions and segregated schools and the start of educating these children in regular classrooms

disorder and juvenile detention (Graham, 2010). Indigenous youth are also over-represented in juvenile justice facilities in Australia (Australian Institute of Health and Welfare, 2016). The Australian Human Rights Commission (2008) noted a significant overlap between intellectual disability, mental health concerns and the incarceration of Indigenous youth. Incarcerated Indigenous youth are four to five times more likely than the general population to have an intellectual disability. They also have far higher rates of illiteracy and poorer school outcomes than the general population. In New Zealand, Pasifika and Māori youth are more likely to be 'stood down', suspended or expelled from school, while Māori students have the highest rates of expulsion (New Zealand Ministry of Education, 2016). Some 30 years after Dunn's (1968) original paper, African-American and minority youth in the United States today are still over-represented in school suspension and expulsion rates (Loveless, 2017). The reasons for this over-representation in certain forms of special schooling placements are difficult to assess empirically. Numerous factors such as discrimination, teacher attitudes, teacher quality and curriculum qualities have been suggested to play a role (Graham, 2010). In addition, a pervasive 'deficit' notion of minority students or low expectations for these students may exist, including assumptions about their health and genetic factors such as 'bad genes' passed down through generations (see Graham, 2010, p. 171). As we discussed in Chapter 11 (and will also discuss in Chapter 14), many factors influence the inclusive and positive nature of our school environments and there are many opportunities for teachers to play a role in fostering more inclusive schools.

CONCEPTS OF DISABILITY

Up to this point we have been using the word 'disability' as it is commonly used in everyday language and large surveys like those reported above. Generally, we report broad medical labels or categories of medical conditions grouped under a label like 'intellectual disability' or 'physical disability'. But what is a disability? Is it simply being born with a medical condition? The World Health Organization (WHO) initially developed a classification system that was used internationally to describe health conditions and disabilities using the terms 'disability', 'impairment' and 'handicap'. These terms describe the person and their condition as the source of disability and as the reason for impairment, resulting in handicaps. They do not accurately define or describe disability, or the experience of having a disability, and were discarded when the WHO classification system was extensively revised; it is now referred to as the *International classification of functioning, disability and health* (ICF) (WHO, 2009) (see Box 10.2). The revised ICF system focuses on the interaction between an individual's health condition or disability, and environmental and personal factors that then lead to the experience of disability (see Figure 10.2). The ICF 'combines the major models of disability, recognising the role of environmental factors in the creation of disability and the importance of participation as a desired outcome, as well as the underlying health conditions' (AIHW, 2004, p. 5).

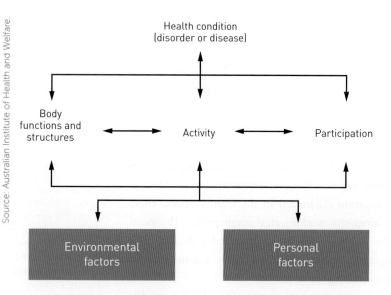

Source: Australian Institute of Health and Welfare.

FIGURE 10.2 Interactions between the health condition, environmental factors and personal factors: components of the ICF.

BOX 10.2 IMPLICATIONS FOR EDUCATORS

HEALTH AND DISABILITY

In the 2001 framework for the ICF, the WHO made a major shift from its earlier 'medicalising' of disability (Pfeiffer, 1998, cited by Foreman & Arthur-Kelly, 2014, p. 26), which focused on the concepts of impairment, disability and handicap and their impact on individuals, to a system concerned with the interaction between the health condition of the person and their environmental and personal circumstances. This new orientation is outlined in the following statement:

> The ICF puts the notions of 'health' and 'disability' in a new light. It acknowledges that every human being can experience a decrement in health and thereby experience some degree of disability. Disability is not something that happens to a minority of humanity. The ICF thus recognises the experience of disability as a universal human experience. It shifts the focus from cause to impact, taking into account the social and environmental aspects of disability. It does not see disability only as a 'medical' or 'biological' dysfunction.

Source: WHO (2009).

THINK ABOUT

- The ICF recognises the role of social and environmental factors in the creation of disability. Can you identify any social or environmental factors in schooling or education that could contribute to disability?
- What do you think the ICF means by declaring that disability is 'a universal human experience'?

Labelling and person-first language

One of the characteristics of all social groups is the tendency to categorise and label people in terms of attributes that seem significant for the group. The WHO, however, made a very deliberate decision to move away from terms such as 'impairment' and 'handicap'. This partly reflects a broader social concern that the tendency to label and identify people according to their disability or condition is stigmatising. Over time, a variety of stigmatising terms have been used to label and identify children with disabilities, such as 'a handicapped child', 'a retarded student', or 'a mentally impaired person'. These terms have been replaced with more neutral terms such as 'intellectual disability', which refers to the condition and not to the person. In some of these cases, the language or label changed because it was often simply wrong and quite derogatory. For example, people who have an intellectual disability are not 'retarded' in intellectual development; although they may have limitations, they still have a capacity to grow and develop intellectually like any other child (see also Box 10.3).

In all cases, it is now considered more acceptable to use **person-first language** by referring to the person first, not their disability or condition; the identification of their disability or condition should only occur if it is relevant and necessary. It is much more acceptable to refer to the person first and separate the person from the characteristics of the condition; for example: 'Anna *has* an intellectual disability', not 'Anna *is* retarded or disabled' – the latter term implies that Anna is defined by the condition of an intellectual disability, rather than acknowledging that she is a person first and foremost who also just happens to have this condition. If there is no particular reason to identify Anna as a student with a disability, it is preferable to simply introduce her as you would any other student: 'This is Anna. She is in Year 10 and training to be an animal care attendant.' Anna's work-experience manager, for example,

person-first language
The practice of referring to the person or individual before you refer to the label of their condition

CourseMateExpress

Online Resources
Go Further: Explore an example of using person-first language with the Interactive activity on this text's website.

never describes Anna as having a disability to her colleagues at the animal shelter. Rather, colleagues who supervise Anna in the workplace know that she needs additional support with the explanation of procedures and they have been trained to address these support needs.

You may notice in textbooks or websites, that there are differences in language referring to disability and learning support needs around the world. For example, until very recently the term 'mentally retarded' was still the official term to describe an intellectual disability in the United States. In 2010, the United States Congress passed 'Rosa's Law' which meant that all references to 'mental retardation' in US laws would change to 'intellectual disability'. Gradual changes in language are now occurring in all public institutions and policy documents across the United States (see United States, 2010). In the UK, the term 'learning disability' may be used to refer to intellectual disability, but in Australia and the USA the terms 'learning disability' and 'learning difficulty' usually refer to people *without* an intellectual disability, but who experience other neurological or information-processing problems. Different terminology can be confusing for people reading textbooks and research papers from different parts of the world. We advise students of teacher education in Australia and New Zealand not to adopt the terms used in international textbooks, such as 'retarded'. Use 'person-first language' at all times, and only refer to the disability or condition if absolutely necessary.

BOX 10.3 CLASSROOM LINKS

LABELLING AND STIGMA

During the last decade of the 20th century, there was considerable debate about the way language had been used to label and identify people, and the need to avoid using expressions that are offensive to some groups in society. In particular, gender-neutral language became preferred, as in the substitution of 'flight attendant' for 'air hostess', and 'actor' for 'actress'. Similarly, the way we identified persons with disability changed from 'a retarded individual' to 'a person with an intellectual disability'. This is known as person-first language.

Why is language important? The words we use influence the way in which we think about people, objects and events. The way we think about those who are different from our perceived norm can be stigmatising and lead to negative evaluations, discrimination and stereotyping of those people (Goffman, 1968). Goffman (1963) described stigma as the means by which a society indicates extreme disapproval for a person and their attributes. He suggested language terms and labels are used to discredit a person or shape an identity that is considered 'spoiled' and not normal. When we react to the person we perceive as 'different' with embarrassment, rejection or overzealous acceptance, we are reacting to the difference rather than to the person as a whole. When thinking about individuals with disabilities, it is important to remember that they are people first, and that any impairment or unusual characteristic is secondary. In fact, we may know very little about the person or the nature of their condition, but the notion of stigma suggests that we form assumptions about the person because of their attributes.

The disadvantages of labelling include:

- a focus on perceived negative aspects of the person with a disability, rather than the strengths or abilities they possess
- an implication that the label defines the person's capabilities
- the likelihood that the label will continue through life, with a significant impact on self-esteem and a self-fulfilling prophecy of failure
- triggering of inappropriate social responses such as pity, teasing and prejudice
- a negative impact not only on the person with a disability, but also on their family and friends (Ashman, 2005, p. 70).

A non-categorical view of disability

The labelling and classification of people with a disability has been commonly based on a medical model, that describes the nature of the medical or health condition very broadly. In some circumstances, understanding the medical aspects of a condition can be very important for teachers; however, doubts about such a classification system began to arise and led to questions being asked about whether such medical classifications should be used for educational purposes. This problem has been particularly acute in systems such as that operating in the USA, where a child's condition must be medically assessed and formally identified as a 'disability' before the child becomes eligible for special needs services. Although there are no legal requirements to assess children in such a way in Australia and New Zealand, there has been a tendency to make assumptions about educational needs based on the medical labels of conditions. However, as you will read in the following sections, while labels might convey some understanding of the nature of a condition, they do not provide adequate information about how each individual will be affected by this condition. Hence, it is necessary to carefully assess each child to determine their educational needs. The focus in non-categorical approaches is on providing a curriculum that is suited to the functional needs of each child (such as help in learning to read or hold a pencil) rather than on a singular program that is erroneously believed to address the needs of any child with a particular condition label.

LEARNING SUPPORT NEEDS IN CLASSROOM SETTINGS

This section considers the educational needs of children in seven areas of prevalent or increasing disability, as identified in surveys such as those described in the previous sections. Although we are describing conditions in this section, we do so for the purposes of explaining condition-related terms, but we also do so with the cautions and caveats outlined in 'A non-categorical view of disability' above. No two individuals in any of these condition groups will have the same learning needs, and their skills and abilities will vary dramatically. We emphasise the range of abilities in each condition, and emphasise approaches in the classroom that make good sense for considering these types of educational needs for any learner who might experience similar difficulties. We are aware that teacher education students may have limited knowledge or life experience of disability, and we are also aware that this can cause confusion and misunderstanding. In some cases, erroneous beliefs may be maintained if some basic information about common disabilities is not provided and myths are not dispelled. We urge all teachers to conduct their own careful research and consultation with parents and other providers, such as paediatricians and psychologists, to gather the most accurate and useful information on a case-by-case basis for individual learners with additional needs in their classrooms.

INTELLECTUAL AND COGNITIVE DIFFERENCES

Conditions that limit cognitive abilities are one of the leading and most prevalent causes of intellectual disability. These conditions include a wide range of congenital or chromosomal disorders, such as Down syndrome, that are present at birth and affect the individual on a lifelong basis. The diagnosis of an intellectual disability is generally based on three key criteria:

1 a significantly below-average level of intelligence, as measured by IQ tests
2 deficiencies in adaptive behaviours such as everyday living skills
3 the manifestation of these symptoms during the developmental periods of a child's life (for example, birth to 18 years of age) (Hudson & Radler, 2005).

Sometimes, a diagnosis might also be made later in a person's life, but in these cases the disability may have been caused by other factors such as a traumatic injury to the brain, drug or alcohol abuse, or other accidents.

There has been a tendency to classify the severity of the condition by the level of IQ into categories of mild, moderate or severe intellectual impairment (a categorical approach). This has often been used in school systems as a proxy assessment for determining placement in regular or 'special classes'. However, the weaknesses of IQ assessments are well known (see Chapter 9) and thus many other measures and tests of adaptive skills are also needed to assess a student's learning support needs. For example, some students may come to school with ability to complete most functional tasks of any child their age, such as holding a pencil or going to the bathroom by themselves. However, some children may have fewer functional skills. This may be because some conditions may be accompanied by other conditions or characteristics such as difficulties with speech and communication, problems with eyesight, fine and gross motor coordination difficulties or difficulty regulating behaviour and emotions. Thorough and wide-ranging assessments of children with such conditions are often made before the child starts school. This is a very sensitive time for parents and caregivers, who may be overwhelmed by unfamiliar psychological, medical and educational assessments. Teachers and practitioners working with children and their families must be especially sensitive and listen carefully to families and children themselves in order to determine the best level of educational support.

FIGURE 10.3 Audrey O'Connor is an actor, dancer, performer and writer who has competed in the Special Olympics and who also has Down syndrome. Audrey was the 2011 face of the Don't DIS my ABILITY campaign.

Source: Don't DIS My Ability campaign, Department of Family and Community Services, NSW, photographer Jamie North, pardalote photography.

Intellectual and developmental disabilities are also some of the most misunderstood conditions and this misunderstanding can lead to labelling and stigma. Erroneous beliefs about intellectual ability have led to assumptions that persons with intellectual disabilities are the equivalent age of a much younger child or cannot learn. These assumptions are untrue. The danger of such 'myths' and assumptions is that they can impose serious limitations on the person with a disability. This is what the WHO was referring to when they stated that disability can arise from the environment. For example, assumptions about the equivalent age of the child can lead to the infantilising or 'babying' of people with intellectual disabilities. In the classroom this can have serious consequences, such as inappropriate work or tasks that include babyish themes or concepts suited to a much younger child (this is also sometimes referred to as 'dumbing down' the curriculum). Similarly, language or talk directed to the child can be overly 'babyish' or directorial. Such teacher treatment of a child is also visible to peers, who may respond to the child in similar ways. Significant advocacy movements, led by people with intellectual disabilities, have attempted to dispel such myths (see Figure 10.3).

Implications

Children with conditions associated with cognitive learning support needs will vary in their individual areas of strengths and support needs. In some cases, certain condition characteristics may mean the child will have problems in organising and sequencing thoughts, in memory or recall of information. Information processing may be slower than for other children, and learning to read may be difficult for some children. Children may also have strengths in specific skills and interests similar to other children their age, such as creative arts, drama and sporting activities. The implications for classroom practice will depend on assessments of each child's specific learning needs; the following are some general strategies for classroom practice that might help any child who needs support with skills like organising and sequencing thoughts to follow instructions, or needs more time to think and solve problems:

- Use direct language with explicit instructions and break tasks down into smaller steps.
  - > As we saw in the case of Anna, instructions can be modified and made more explicit for a range of everyday life skills and vocational tasks.
- Age-appropriate adaptations should always be offered; for example, literacy and reading themes should be the same as for other classmates, but expected outcomes may be adapted.
- Alternative curricula in the senior years, such as the Life Skills curricula (NSW Board of Studies, 2014), offer all students the chance to remain in formal education and attain their school-completion certificates.
- Physical development and gross and fine motor skills should not be neglected. Participation in physical education should consider possible weaknesses of muscle tone, balance or coordination, but lots of practice and experience with motor skills is an essential part of development for all children, as we saw in Chapter 2.

SPECIFIC LEARNING DISABILITIES

The term 'learning disability', was adopted to describe the puzzling case of children who exhibited significant learning or academic difficulties but did not have an intellectual disability or a sensory impairment such as vision or hearing loss (Hannan, 2013). Terms such as 'specific learning disabilities' and 'learning difficulties' have arisen to describe a range of conditions including difficulties in reading and spelling, maths and language processing and comprehension. Diagnostic labels such as 'dyslexia' refer to disorders in the process of learning to read and spell and 'dyscalculia' to disorders relating to maths and numeracy. There are a host of other terms associated with learning disabilities, but many of these terms do not yet have clear or validated diagnostic criteria (Hannan, 2013).

In order for a person to be classified as having such a condition, other possible causes of learning problems must be ruled out. Such causes might include an intellectual disability, vision or hearing impairments, conditions such as depression or anxiety, and environmental causes such as poor teaching or lack of opportunity. Careful assessment must be made of the person's skills in the affected areas, to work out the specific areas of learning that are affected (APS, n.d.). The cause of specific learning disabilities is the subject of much research and many factors, including genetic and environmental factors, that affect neurological development are implicated (Hannan, 2013).

As with other labelled conditions, specific learning disabilities are also widely misunderstood and also subject to a range of untested or non-validated interventions. Sometimes interventions will be offered that do not have scientific validity or have not been rigorously tested and evaluated. Examples include a range of sensory and physical therapies or many food- and diet-based remedies. In contrast, because of intensive research in understanding learning disabilities we now know that there are strong research-based and validated interventions available, including much better understanding of how to intervene in the area of reading disorders, for example (Hannan 2013).

Specific learning disabilities may also be accompanied by other non-academic difficulties, including behavioural or social difficulties, and these can lead to inattention or impulsiveness in the classroom, or difficulties in peer relationships and in making friends (APS, n.d.). As noted, these conditions affect every child very differently, and generalisations about behaviour or social skills should not be made.

Implications

As we have emphasised previously, approaches to learning support needs must address the specific skill areas where difficulties are noted for each individual (this is an example of a non-categorical approach). Therefore it is essential that teachers recognise the widespread heterogeneity and complexity of each individual diagnosis of a specific learning disorder. Collaborate with parents and psychologists to understand reports or diagnostics that will direct specific interventions in the area of concern.

Practise your skills of evaluating and locating evidence to support practices in the classroom. Has the recommended intervention been validated in scientific reports and controlled studies? (See Box 2.4 for some instances of neuromyths and the evidence that counters them.) As with the previous recommendations for practice, consider the impact of any condition on other factors such as fatigue, stress and anxiety, social isolation or peer rejection. It is likely children with specific learning disabilities will also experience co-occurring conditions related to or arising from their condition.

As children move through education, higher cognitive-load tolerance and faster processing is expected. Good teaching practices that 'lighten the load' for learners with specific disabilities include:

- breaking complex instructions into smaller steps and providing worked examples to relieve cognitive load (see Chapter 6)
- providing specific instruction in metacognitive strategies and metacognitive awareness, which has been proven to be effective in this population
- compensating for poor spelling and numeracy skills with ICT applications such as spell checkers and calculators.

ATTENTION DEFICIT HYPERACTIVITY DISORDER (ADHD)

We have included ADHD here as a significant exemplar even though it may also be considered a form of learning disability. This condition is best understood as a syndrome of complex learning and behavioural characteristics that affects each person very differently. Diagnosis is complex and the diagnostic criteria have varied over time, causing confusion and misunderstanding for teachers and parents.

There are three main subtypes within this diagnostic classification: the 'predominantly inattentive' subtype and the 'predominantly hyperactive-impulsive' subtype. Some people have both types in combination. In the 'combined' subtype the person has excessive features of both of the following subtypes:

- The 'predominantly inattentive' subtype characteristics include behaviours such as an inability to focus on details or sustain attention for long periods of time; being easily distracted; being unable to follow a set of instructions or to follow through on tasks; and problems organising actions.
- The 'predominantly hyperactive-impulsive' subtype characteristics include fidgeting, squirming and excessive running and climbing behaviours; being constantly on the go; blurting out or talking constantly; an inability to wait one's turn; and interrupting or intrusive behaviours.

The behaviours in these subtypes must be present before the age of 12 and must be pervasive in that the symptoms are evident in two or more settings of the child's life, such as home life and school (American Psychiatric Association, 2013).

The consequences of deficits in attention and impulse control are very serious for any learner regardless of the specific diagnostic label. Deficits in attention and working memory processes are associated with marked deficiencies in reading and numeracy skills. Deficits in controlling impulses are particularly associated with the appearance of disobedience, and risk taking or 'no limits' in sensation seeking. As we learnt in Chapter 2, working memory and executive-control skills are characteristics of typical brain development and involve the development of neural networks and chemical processes that assist the speed and efficiency of these neural networks. Conditions such as ADHD are widely recognised as neurobiological conditions (see Epstein & Loren, 2013).

Implications

ADHD has been provided here as an exemplar of a syndrome comprised of varying characteristics where a non-categorical view of educational needs is essential. No two children with ADHD will have the same diagnosis, the same learning needs or the same behavioural needs. A wide range of approaches may be needed, including those listed above for specific learning disabilities. Here are some helpful strategies:

- Evidence-based cognitive-behavioural training approaches can assist children to manage behaviour. Interventions such as Stop, Think, Do are one example that can be used universally in the classroom, but will be of particular assistance to any child with impulse control or problem solving difficulties (see Box 14.4).

- All children can benefit from training in simple self-regulation strategies by setting small, manageable goals. Older children may need more support in concepts of time management and self-monitoring their time on- and off-task by using checklists and reminders. There are many ICT apps and tools that are useful in this regard.

- Keeping a firm classroom routine, and giving advance warnings or signals of changes of pace or topic are important for all learners and can be made even more explicit to learners with attentional support needs.

- Allow for rest breaks or periods of cognitive 'down time' – this is helpful for all children, not just those with concentration problems.

- Avoid repeated episodes of 'failing' or 'disciplining' the child; instead work towards learning support strategies that ignore minor symptoms such as fidgeting, and reward and reinforce on-task behaviours.

- Ensure success with doable tasks, combined with precise and constructive verbal feedback early and often during tasks to correct mistakes and avoid the 'failure cycle'.

AUTISM SPECTRUM DISORDERS (ASD)

The term 'autism spectrum disorder' is so named because it includes a wide variety of disorders and effects of these disorders on individuals. The broad term ASD includes three main classes of condition, including autism, sometimes referred to as 'classic autism'; Asperger's syndrome; and pervasive developmental disorder (PDD), sometimes referred to as atypical autism. These disorders appear very early in a child's development and are often referred to as 'developmental disorders', but effects on development vary markedly from one child to another; for example, one child may have very low intelligence as measured on standard IQ tests and another child might have very high intelligence (APS, n.d.). Over the years, the diagnostic criteria have changed; this means that in Australia and internationally it has been very difficult to determine exact incidence or prevalence rates. Suspicion that diagnosis of the disorder has been increasing may be attributed to changes in diagnostic criteria over time (ABS, 2017). Teachers have been advised not to distract themselves with debates about increasing diagnostic rates, but to concentrate instead on the evidence that the learning support needs of children with ASD are very real, as detailed by the mother of a child with autism in the video provided on the website.

CourseMateExpress

Online Resources
Watch a **video** that addresses the inclusive educational experience of a child with autism from a parent's perspective

At a very general level, the APS (n.d.) summarises the key characteristics of ASD into three main areas.

1   *Verbal and non-verbal communication.* Skills involving communicating with others can vary dramatically. Some children may have no or very little speech, while others may have normal and sometimes verbose speech. Some children may appear to talk excessively about an interest, unaware that others are not following; may be blunt and direct in comments to others; or generally have unusual vocal behaviours and topics that can be disruptive or confusing for others. Non-verbal communication skills, such as making eye contact and attending to facial expressions or hand gestures, may be very limited in some children.

2   *Social awareness and interaction.* Some children may have difficulty applying the social 'rules' of behaviour like making eye contact and responding to social cues such as a person saying their name. They might also engage in behaviours that others find socially inappropriate or distressing, such as rejecting touch or cuddles, touching or licking or tasting unusual objects, or verbalising blunt observations about a person. Developing relationships with others may be very challenging, and bullying during the school years is a commonly reported experience. However, it is a myth that persons with autism cannot experience the joy of meaningful social relationships. Many children with autism do enjoy play and social contact with familiar peers, family and relatives.

3   *Activities and interests.* Many young people with ASD do not experience enjoyment of typical childhood games or activities such as ball sports, running or chasing, and may have very specialised interests such as collecting household objects (batteries, string) or objects of certain colours. They may develop strong interest or 'fixations' in usual objects or patterns of arranging objects. Removal or loss of fixated objects can cause enormous distress and they may carry an object constantly. Depending on the level of intelligence or social awareness, the interests of the child can be quite mature or reflective of worldly concerns, but nonetheless the interest level is often excessive and 'fixated', and may lead to excessive talking about the interest or rejection of others to focus on the interest.

Other notable characteristics that have great relevance in the classroom include unusual sensitivities and behaviours. Labels on clothes can be unbearable to some; their sense of smell can be heightened, leading to feelings of nausea or rejection of certain foods; touch can be unwanted; and repetitive and sometimes harmful behaviours such as rocking, head banging or hand flapping may be observed.

There is no known cause or explanation of ASD, although a genetic factor may be involved in some cases – twin studies have shown an increased likelihood of both twins having the condition if one twin is diagnosed. Brain imaging studies have shown some differences in neurological development, particularly in the white matter of the brain that forms vital connections throughout the brain (see Chapter 2) (Just et al., 2012).

The broad spectrum of these behaviours requires very careful assessment and, typically, diagnosis will begin in the preschool years when parents or carers notice unusual behaviours or limited development of speech, for example. All other possible conditions and causes must be eliminated, and families can face years of assessments and testing as this is a lifelong disability with different effects as the person grows up.

Implications

Some basic implications for teaching and learning are outlined here for general consideration.

■   Verbal and non-verbal communication skills may be affected. The student may not make eye contact or look directly at the teacher, so minimise gestures and hand signals.

■   Augmentative or alternative communication systems such as pictorial communication systems have a strong evidence base as an effective way to teach communication skills, and as an ongoing system of communication for children with few verbal skills (see Box 10.4).

- Instructions should be delivered by catching the child's attention first and using direct and positively framed verbal statements or clear and simple pictographs and symbols.

- Abstract, metaphorical or symbolic language may be misunderstood, such as: 'As fast as lightning!'

- Sarcastic, joking or playful language structures commonly used among adolescent peers may not be understood; for example, 'Oh, good one Tom!'

- Social skills instruction may be necessary for everyday social skills, such as saying 'Hello' to someone, using 'I' statements to express needs, using assertive phrases such as 'stop', taking turns or asking to join a game (see Box 10.4 for an example).

- Role plays and activities for which social skills have to be practised can be integrated into everyday classroom activities but may only be suitable for some students with the skills and comfort with such group or peer activities.

- Provide a buddy or support person for playground activities but ensure peers are trained carefully in any alternative communications skills.

- Changes in routine can be very stressful, so prepare for change by providing plenty of advance warning. Use visual aids or photographs to explain a new routine such as a school excursion or new activity; for example, pictographs of a swimming costume and photos of the swimming pool and swimming instructor may be useful to explain a new routine of swimming classes.

- Provide quiet and calm spaces where the child can rest and recover from overwhelming or stressful experiences. Ensure spaces are safe and visible to the teacher at all times.

BOX 10.4 RESEARCH LINKS

INCREASING SOCIAL COMMUNICATION WITH THE PICTURE EXCHANGE COMMUNICATION SYSTEM (PECS)

The Picture Exchange Communication System (PECS) is an augmentative and alternative communication system that allows individuals with severe developmental disabilities to communicate with others (Bondy & Frost, 2001). The method is based on behavioural learning principles of reinforcing verbal behaviours through the mediation and reinforcing acts of a communication partner (Skinner, 1957). PECS is a picture-based system of small cards or pictorial icons that are exchanged between communication partners. A six-step strategy is used to teach this method of communication using the behavioural techniques of reinforcement. In Phase 1, the child is taught to initiate an exchange of a single picture item for a preferred object or item; in Phase 2, the child must locate another nearby adult or peer and initiate and complete the exchange; in Phase 3, the child is taught to recognise the differences in the picture symbols to choose an item they actually want; Phase 4 teaches the child to create sentences with strips of pictures placed together; and in phases 5 and 6, the child learns how to answer simple questions and respond with picture icons (Cannella-Malone, Fant & Tullis, 2010).

The study

Cannella-Malone and colleagues conducted a research intervention to study the effectiveness of a PECS with Peers protocol, which uses PECS to increase social interaction between children with disabilities and their peers.

The participants

Two female students with severe communication delays and developmental disabilities participated in the project. Tulla was 14 years old and did not have a reliable means of communicating with people around her. She was aggressive, could not express her needs

>>

and wants, and did not communicate with peers. London was a six-year-old girl with severe autism. She could use some simple three-word phrases to communicate with adults; she did not communicate with peers, but sometimes observed them. She could be aggressive if interactions with peers did occur.

The method

Each child was supplied with a PECS communication book that holds the PECs pictures on Velcro strips. The participants could create a message with this binder by placing pictures on the Velcro strips. In order to reinforce the training phases, careful reinforcers for each girl were selected on the basis of parent and teacher reports. Behavioural data was recorded by observing each girl, to establish a baseline of behaviours during a small-group activity. The participants were trained in the phases of the intervention as described above, and peers were trained in how to respond to the participant (for example, take the PECS picture and give the participant the requested item). Peers were also reinforced when they responded correctly. As expected, peers quickly learnt to respond appropriately to the PECS greetings and requests.

A social skills intervention was devised in which the girls were taught to use the PECS to interact with peers in small-group activities such as colouring, puzzles and art projects. If a peer had access to a preferred item, the girl was trained to request the item; to teach greetings, the girls were prompted to exchange greetings with peers by selecting the right picture for greeting others, and gradually such prompts were faded away.

Findings

Tulla needed four to five training sessions to reach the desired criterion (of three consecutive sessions with 100 per cent responding) across the phases of the intervention; London needed four to six sessions to reach this desired criterion. During the intervention, significant increases in greetings, responses and requests were found, although greeting behaviours stopped or declined after the

Source: Pyramid Educational Consultants, Inc. (www.pecs. com). All rights reserved. Reproduced with permission.

intervention. Each girl quickly learnt the PECS method and started to integrate this with verbal communication with peers. The girls also started independently using greetings, responses and requests. Teachers and mothers reported that exchanges with peers were more meaningful and appropriate, and more patience was shown by the participants when communicating with peers outside the experimental setting.

Conclusions

Both older and younger students can gain modest benefits in communication with peers by using PECS, and findings suggest that PECS might provide a starting point for further positive communication with peers.

PHYSICAL DISABILITIES AND CHRONIC HEALTH CONDITIONS

Conditions leading to physical disability or limitations on physical mobility include a wide variety of congenital and acquired conditions, and also include many chronic health conditions. Children may be born with physical disabilities, such as spina bifida or cerebral palsy, or may acquire physical restrictions or limitations due to spinal cord injury, or other illnesses such as arthritis, diabetes or cystic fibrosis, to name just a few examples. Some physical disabilities also arise from genetic conditions such as muscular dystrophy.

Cerebral palsy (CP)

The most common cause of physical disability in Australian children is cerebral palsy or CP (Cerebral Palsy Australia, n.d.), a term that describes a wide range of disabling conditions in which messages from the brain to the muscles of the body are distorted, mistimed or sometimes not received at all (Victorian Government, 2012). This breakdown of neurological messaging causes a wide range of symptoms, typically characterised by erratic and uncontrollable body movements. However, these motor-control deficits can also affect all other processes governed by motor control, such as eyesight and the ability to direct and control one's gaze and focus, or speech and the ability to swallow and eat. There are different types of CP known as spastic, athetoid, ataxic and mixed forms. Spastic CP is the most common form and causes 'spasticity' or stiffness and tightness of the muscles; athetoid CP leads to uncontrolled and erratic movements; ataxic CP is the least common and affects balance and coordination, and is characterised by shaky, unsteady tremors. The mixed form can encompass a number of these subtypes. Within each subtype, the degree of physical disability also differs, and can lead to quadriplegia in which all four limbs are affected; paraplegia in which the legs are affected; diplegia in which all four limbs are affected, but the legs more so than the arms; or hemiplegia in which one side of the body is affected (Cerebral Palsy Alliance, n.d.).

Cerebral palsy is detected early in life when parents and caregivers typically become concerned about the muscle tone or movements of their baby and developmental milestones that are not being met. Assessment is a complex range of physical and neurological tests, and sometimes occurs over a long period of time as the child develops and further limitations become evident.

This diverse range of conditions means that every child with CP must be carefully assessed and supported on a case-by-case basis. The impact of the condition can range from extremely mild physical restriction to severe and profound quadriplegia restricting all physical movement. Speech may be very limited for some people. Moderate to severe intellectual disability is known to occur for one in five people, and specific learning disabilities can also be present in many cases. Great caution is needed in making any assumption about a student's intellectual capacity, however, as standard assessments of intelligence cannot be reliably completed with this population due to limitations of speech and motor control. It is recommended that teachers never make assumptions about the child's intellect or learning potential, and instead assume the child can understand what is being said unless it is shown or indicated to be otherwise.

Chronic health conditions

There are also a range of other chronic health conditions that can restrict a child's mobility, involvement in school and general health and wellbeing. Chronic health conditions are those defined by:

- a duration of more than six months
- a pattern of reoccurrence or deterioration
- a poor prognosis
- consequences or sequelae that impact on the person's quality of life (AIHW, 2005).

Chronic health conditions are of interest in education because of the consequences or sequelae that affect the child's life. Obesity is an example of a condition that has sequelae that may lead to the development of other conditions such as diabetes (Type 2) and poorer quality of life due to exercise or movement restrictions. Other child health conditions such as cancer or cystic fibrosis (which affects the lungs) cause frequent or prolonged periods of hospitalisation, meaning the child misses out on school and typical social interactions with peers. Common concerns expressed by children with chronic health conditions include catching up with missed school work, missing out on school life (such as excursions), or feeling they are at risk of not progressing in school. Some also report scrutiny and questions about their condition from peers that can be very personal and discomfiting (McMaugh, 2006).

Generally, it is accepted that children with chronic illnesses and their families are at greater risk of experiencing psychological or emotional difficulties than other children and families (AIHW, 2005). This is thought to be because of multiple factors arising from the chronic stress and burden of illness, including socioeconomic stress, as many parents cannot work or gain full-time employment when caring for a chronically sick child. Siblings also experience stress, and this is well recognised in the health sector with a number of charity and support organisations such as CanTeen addressing the support needs of not only youth with cancer but their siblings as well.

Physical disabilities and health conditions are very broad categories of conditions that lead to different types of heath or physical impairment, mobility restrictions and other impacts on quality of life. These conditions may or may not be associated with other problems, and a high level of participation in schooling can be expected. However, this group of learners requires support and understanding to enable them to access the school environment and to deal with the stigma associated with often visible and obvious chronic health conditions. Bullying and peer abuse related to their chronic condition or disability is widely reported by this group of children, but many can enjoy full participation in school if support is provided (McMaugh, 2011).

Implications

Generally, children with physical disabilities have a high degree of participation in regular school environments. Children with chronic health conditions, however, may miss a larger number of school days compared with other children. Physical adaptations to the school environment have improved access to school for many children with physical or mobility restrictions, but special attention is required to keep a child with a chronic condition on track with school work and meeting educational outcomes.

- Assess mobility and access in all areas of school life, including the built environment and during school excursions and other out-of-school activities. It is discriminatory to plan activities in which children cannot participate due to their disability or health condition (for example, see Box 10.5).
- Many ICT devices and applications or assistive aids can support children who have fine and gross motor limitations for tasks such as writing or maintaining an upright position; e.g. laptop computers, voice recorders and transcribers and posture-supportive seating are simple aids that can enhance the classroom participation of many students.
- Motor-control problems or learning difficulties may mean learners take longer to respond or may have difficulty expressing thoughts in words. These learners may benefit from alternative ways of responding, such as using picture cards or visual symbols (see Box 10.4).
- Posture and body positioning may need to be changed regularly for some students, so activities should be varied between 'sitting and listening' activities and more active tasks.

- Medical needs may need to be addressed in school time, including breaks to take medication, receive physiotherapy, or for changing catheters or checking medical devices.
- Respect the right of the child to privacy at all times. It may be necessary to implement tolerance and diversity training but never use a child as an example or disclose any child's condition without their and their parents' express consent and understanding of possible consequences.
- Adolescence can be an especially sensitive period when heightened concerns about body image and physical appearance are the 'norm' in this age group. Children and teenagers can have mistaken beliefs about illness such as fear of contagion.

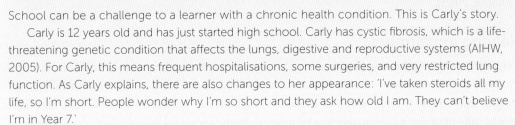

BOX 10.5 CASE STUDY

WHEN CHRONIC ILLNESS GOES TO SCHOOL – CARLY'S STORY

School can be a challenge to a learner with a chronic health condition. This is Carly's story.

Carly is 12 years old and has just started high school. Carly has cystic fibrosis, which is a life-threatening genetic condition that affects the lungs, digestive and reproductive systems (AIHW, 2005). For Carly, this means frequent hospitalisations, some surgeries, and very restricted lung function. As Carly explains, there are also changes to her appearance: 'I've taken steroids all my life, so I'm short. People wonder why I'm so short and they ask how old I am. They can't believe I'm in Year 7.'

Starting high school has been 'interesting' for Carly. She needs to practise some new social skills, such as explaining her condition to peers and keeping her cool when being asked personal questions: 'It was sort of hard introducing myself to people 'cause I always coughed and that, so I had to tell them what was wrong.' Carly is very concerned that her peers are worried about contagion: 'I guess I was worried that they would think they could catch it off me and wouldn't hang around me or anything. So that's why I tell everybody that you can't catch it, because I'm scared that they won't hang around me or talk to me, or something like that.'

Keeping up with school work is also a major concern. Carly hopes to become a writer some day. She misses out on worksheets and homework tasks and often feels as if she is falling behind. Recently she became very upset because she missed out on going on a school excursion: 'The principal has a points system and I didn't get enough points [due to being absent from school] so I didn't get to go on the excursion.' She also finds the physical environment at school very challenging as the sporting fields are a long way from the main school buildings and books are heavy to carry around: 'The bag! The heavy school bag and the walking from every room to the next. And every time we do sport, we're sort of rushed! Run to the change room! Put everything in your bag! It's really hard! Usually I've got a headache by the time I get there from lack of oxygen and go "Ohhhh, I can't do it!".'

Source: McMaugh (2004, 2006, 2011).

ACTIVITIES

1 What are the educational or quality-of-life consequences arising from Carly's condition?
2 Review the Disability Standards for Education (2005). Has Carly experienced any form of discrimination or inappropriate exclusion from school life?
3 Can you think of any reasonable adjustments that could be made to assist Carly in managing the educational restrictions she is experiencing?

SENSORY AND SPEECH DISABILITIES

Sensory and speech disabilities are a very broad range of conditions, and the survey data reported previously included all cases of impairments related to eyes, ears and speech. As such, this broad category includes impairments of vision or hearing, of which there is a diverse range, as well as disorders of speech and communication, which are also diverse in nature. Along with the most common childhood health conditions of asthma and allergies, vision problems are one of the most common long-term health problems of Australian children. However, for the most part, vision problems are relatively mild and treatable, with one in six children requiring glasses or contact lenses to correct vision (AIHW, 2008). Congenital abnormalities of the eye are much less common and instances are steadily decreasing (AIHW, 2008); blindness or severe vision loss is less common, and is estimated to affect approximately four in every 10 000 children (Royal Institute for Deaf and Blind Children, 2012).

Hearing impairment

A significant degree of hearing impairment occurs with much greater frequency in children, with about one in 1000 children born with significant hearing loss (Mehl & Thomson, 1998). A further group of children will acquire hearing loss in childhood through illness, accident or other factors, and require hearing aids to compensate for this loss of hearing. Both vision and hearing loss occur with greater frequency in Indigenous populations, and treatment and access to services may be much less available in remote locations.

In cases of severe vision or hearing loss, compensatory supports are needed. These include braille materials and computers to support reading and writing for students with vision impairments, and sign language, hearing aids or cochlear implants for children with hearing loss. However, the degree of vision and hearing loss can vary widely among those affected, and types of vision loss are diverse. In some cases, learners may require special lighting or larger print and magnifying lenses; those with hearing impairment may use a variety of hearing aids, and sign language must be learnt just like all language. Not all children will necessarily benefit from the same types of assistive devices, and it is a common myth that the cochlear implant will 'cure' children's deafness. This is untrue; such implants are particularly helpful for certain types of hearing loss but not others. In all cases, early intervention is essential to address learning needs such as literacy skills.

Speech and communication disorders

Speech and communication disorders are related to sensory processes such as hearing, but are characterised by a broad range of disorders that include delayed development (usually when accompanied by intellectual or developmental disorders), and problems of expressive and receptive communication. A communication disorder or disability is said to exist when a person has difficulty being understood by others or difficulty in understanding others. Speech Pathology Australia (n.d.) reports that one in seven Australians has such a disability. Communication and speech disabilities can arise from a wide range of causes. Some children may be born with physiological defects of the mouth or palate, such as cleft palate; others may be born with conditions such as cerebral palsy, leading to motor-control problems in the production of speech. Speech and communication disorders also arise from illnesses or traumatic events such as a head injury or stroke, which affect the neurological processes of communication. Some children experience developmental delays or intellectual disability that lead to poor word understanding, reading ability and the ability to express themselves. Others may experience disorders of speech such as stuttering. Many of these conditions lead to problems of expressive communication, so that a person has difficulty expressing their needs and wants. Receptive communication disorders are said to occur when the person does not perceive sound and language in the same way as others. For example, a hearing impairment or loss of hearing can cause a problem in receptive understanding of language, and conditions such as auditory processing disorders mean the person cannot perceive and distinguish sounds in the same way as others.

Communication and speech disorders have a wide range of effects on the developing learner. Literacy skills are clearly most affected, but so is the personal wellbeing of the student. Embarrassment and frustration can occur when the child is teased because of stuttering, or cannot express their needs in class. Confusion and misunderstanding arise when the student cannot follow instructions properly or is always 'out of step' with the class while they try to assess what the teacher has just asked them to do. Auditory processing disorders are said to be one of the leading factors in referrals for behaviour problems in classrooms, with boys more likely to be reported for behavioural concerns arising from auditory processing problems (Rowe & Rowe, 2006).

Implications

The diverse nature of sensory impairments makes it very difficult to state general implications for teaching and learning, but some basic implications are outlined here for general consideration.

- Many students with hearing impairment will use some form of assistive device such as a hearing aid or implant to understand speech; intensive language support and modelling of language is required to gain speaking and listening skills.
- Assistive technologies such as FM (radio) transmitters or SoundField systems may be used in some classrooms, and teachers will require some training in using these devices and systems.
- Students may also use sign language. In Australia sign language is known as Auslan, and is an officially recognised language in Australia. New Zealand Sign Language (NZSL) is an officially recognised language in New Zealand. Both are complex languages with their own vocabulary and grammar, but they can be learnt rapidly by peers in school. In New Zealand, local Māori concepts and terminology are included, which means that sign language can vary from one region to another. Full integration in school and university is possible with trained sign-language interpreters.
- Ensure that background noise is minimised; always face students when talking (don't talk into the whiteboard, for example).
- Support communication for all students by providing visual guides, written translations and subtitles on audiovisual materials.
- Most children with severe vision impairment or blindness will learn how to read by using braille, which is a series of raised dots that represent alphabet, punctuation and numbers. This is a learnt process that requires intensive training.
- Full classroom integration is possible for children with vision impairment with careful planning and attention to acquiring translations of texts and written materials in braille ahead of time. Assistive technologies such as laptop computers and voice recorders also assist learning.
- Some learners with vision impairment may need larger print texts, magnifiers or additional lighting, and hence desk size and positioning in the classroom may need consideration.
- Throughout schooling, children require mobility support and training to learn how to move around the school (this starts in preschool), or to learn how to cross busy roads or catch public transport in the later years of school.

- Positional concepts such as 'in front of' or 'behind' and concepts of textures and shapes are generally acquired through schooling with specific and direct instruction.
- Communication disorders affect all areas of the child's life and care must be taken to be sensitive to the child's feelings, to avoid embarrassing the child when they are slow to follow instructions or respond in class.
- Avoid overuse of 'call and response' strategies in the classroom. These strategies disadvantage a large group of learners with communication disorders and a range of specific learning disabilities. Allow for a range of response or presentation strategies, including time for reflection so students can think and prepare their responses.
- Close liaison with speech therapists and parents will allow teachers to follow the child's progress and allow for the practising of new communication skills in classroom settings.

MENTAL HEALTH CONDITIONS

Psychiatric or mental health conditions are a significant cause of disability among Australian and New Zealand children, but it is extremely difficult to estimate the exact prevalence of such conditions. In some cases, there is a lack of recent data or estimates may be incomplete due to under-reporting in certain sectors of the populations, such as for indigenous youth in each country. In both countries, estimates are based on the inclusion of a number of different conditions, including emotional or behavioural problems, ADHD, anxiety and depressive illnesses. In recent surveys in New Zealand, the prevalence of emotional and behavioural problems has increased to 4.3 per cent in the population of children aged from birth to 14 years (New Zealand Ministry of Health, 2016). In Australia, a study found that 13.9 per cent of children and adolescents aged four to 17 years had experienced a mental health disorder (Lawrence et al., 2015).

Factors and stressors that contribute to mental health conditions

The range of mental health conditions experienced by Australian and New Zealand children is diverse and often co-occurs with other conditions. A range of social and environmental conditions may also contribute. Factors such as poor parent–child attachment, abuse and neglect in the family, experience of bullying or violence at school (see Chapter 4), and the presence of parental mental health disorders are all known risk factors for the emergence of childhood mental health disorders. For example, Pacific Islander youths who were born outside the Pacific or who migrated to Australia or New Zealand have been found to have a higher incidence of depressive and anxious disorders (Foliaki, 2012). Foliaki attributes this to a higher prevalence of maternal postnatal depression, which results in a lack of emotional availability for children as parents struggle with their own mental health difficulties; in turn, Foliaki attributes this to the loss of social support that is normally available to children and families when living in traditional island communities. The stressors of growing up and forming identity in 'a different place' may exacerbate these problems for migrant youths. Similar factors are noted for Australian Indigenous youths, with major stressors and significant stressful life events present for many of the children surveyed. These stressors include family and household stress, experiences of racism, poor physical health of the child and their carers, lack of access to health services, and drug or alcohol use (Andermann & Campbell, 2008).

Major national mental health initiatives in Australia and New Zealand have been specifically designed to assist teachers in responding to these concerns. In New Zealand, the B4 School screening initiative is designed to determine the risk of childhood mental health and wellbeing concerns. In Australia, the KidsMatter initiative is a population-based health initiative designed to support student mental health and wellbeing within the school community.

Implications

Mental health conditions, including dimensions of behavioural problems, can present serious difficulties in every area of a child's life. Classroom learning is affected by both **internalising** and **externalising behaviours**, but teachers are much more likely to respond to externalised behaviours than to attend to signs of internalised behaviours.

- Be alert and help identify when a young person may need additional help or support:
  - > You might see a difference in their behaviours or capacity and skills when compared with peers.
  - > Short-term changes or an isolated incident may not be a problem, but be concerned if behaviours or issues seem severe, persist over time, or if several problems seem to be occurring together (see Commonwealth of Australia, 2010).
- Get a GRIP: understand when you need to seek professional advice and refer young people on to other professionals for help (see Figure 10.4).
- Be aware that internalised signs of mental health problems such as anxiety, withdrawal, overly fearful or stressful responses, unexplained somatic symptoms and illnesses can be easily overlooked by teachers.
- Use caution when identifying and labelling students with mental health concerns; labels such as 'conduct disorder' or 'disturbed' can be very stigmatising. It is important to maintain privacy and confidentiality when dealing with all students who have disabilities or mental health concerns due to such stigma.
- Learning, concentration and attention may all be affected, so apply the strategies discussed above for other conditions as they relate to cognitive learning implications for each child.
- Model and display positive social and emotional health behaviours in your classroom by showing respect for students, solving disputes with students calmly and respectfully, and creating a 'safe space' for discussing troubling issues.
- Update your knowledge regularly and undertake professional development and further training in the social and emotional health and wellbeing of young people.

In summary, this relatively brief introduction to the provision of learning support in regular classrooms is intended to serve as both an information and awareness-raising resource for beginning teachers. It is clear in the brief survey of educational implications that considerable overlap exists in the implications and recommendations for most learners with additional educational needs. Furthermore, it is self-evident that many of the recommendations contribute to effective classroom practice for *all* learners. Hence, this survey of implications and teaching strategies reinforces the importance of non-categorical approaches and the avoidance of generalisations for students with specific diagnoses and labels.

internalising behaviours Inhibited and withdrawn types of behaviours such as loneliness, depression or anxiety

externalising behaviours Acting out behaviours such as displays of aggressiveness, impulsiveness or non-compliance

CourseMateExpress

Online Resources
Go Further: Learn more about what promotes the social and emotional wellbeing of young people

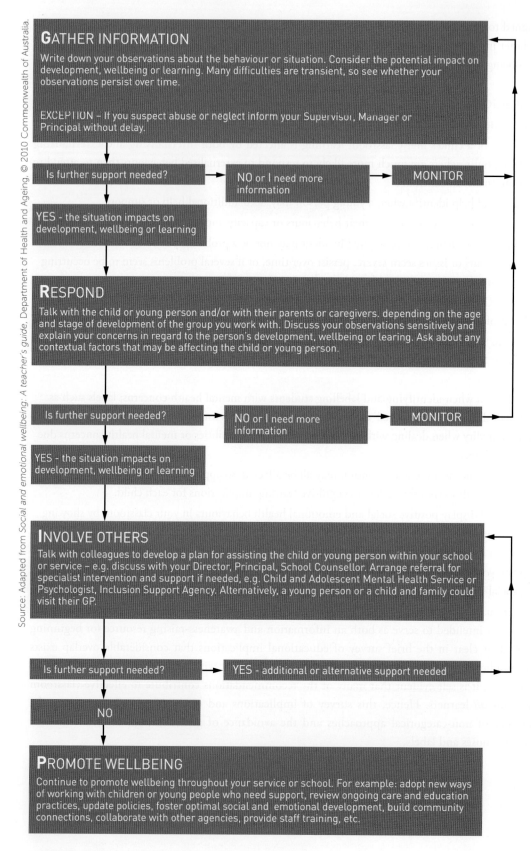

Source: Adapted from Social and emotional wellbeing: A teacher's guide, Department of Health and Ageing, © 2010 Commonwealth of Australia.

GATHER INFORMATION

Write down your observations about the behaviour or situation. Consider the potential impact on development, wellbeing or learning. Many difficulties are transient, so see whether your observations persist over time.

EXCEPTION – If you suspect abuse or neglect inform your Supervisor, Manager or Principal without delay.

Is further support needed? → NO or I need more information → MONITOR

YES - the situation impacts on development, wellbeing or learning

RESPOND

Talk with the child or young person and/or with their parents or caregivers. depending on the age and stage of development of the group you work with. Discuss your observations sensitively and explain your concerns in regard to the person's development, wellbeing or learing. Ask about any contextual factors that may be affecting the child or young person.

Is further support needed? → NO or I need more information → MONITOR

YES - the situation impacts on development, wellbeing or learning

INVOLVE OTHERS

Talk with colleagues to develop a plan for assisting the child or young person within your school or service – e.g. discuss with your Director, Principal, School Counsellor. Arrange referral for specialist intervention and support if needed, e.g. Child and Adolescent Mental Health Service or Psychologist, Inclusion Support Agency. Alternatively, a young person or a child and family could visit their GP.

Is further support needed? → YES - additional or alternative support needed

NO

PROMOTE WELLBEING

Continue to promote wellbeing throughout your service or school. For example: adopt new ways of working with children or young people who need support, review ongoing care and education practices, update policies, foster optimal social and emotional development, build community connections, collaborate with other agencies, provide staff training, etc.

FIGURE 10.4 The GRIP framework. Use this framework when you become concerned about the social and emotional wellbeing of a young person.

LEARNERS WITH HIGH ABILITIES

So far in this chapter we have focused on additional support needs arising from disability or other conditions. There is a further group of learners who are often considered under-served in our classrooms today and these are learners with high abilities or talents in specific areas. These learners are often far advanced compared to peers in one or more areas of academic skills or other abilities. A variety of labels have been applied to these learners including terms such as 'gifted', 'gifted learners', 'gifted and talented learners' and 'exceptional learners' (see Chapter 9). As explained in Chapter 9, high intelligence as measured on IQ tests has often been used to diagnose 'gifted' students. However, today there is a much broader acceptance of a wider definition of higher abilities to include a range of talents and skills.

Both the Australian (ACARA, 2012b) and New Zealand (New Zealand Ministry of Education, 2012) curricula use the term 'gifted and talented' and recognise the needs of high-ability students. In both jurisdictions the terms are defined very broadly to include not just high intellectual ability but skills and talents in other areas as well. In Australia, selective secondary schools and special opportunity classrooms (OCs) in primary schools have been a feature of the provision for students with high demonstrated ability in some States, such as New South Wales, since the 1930s. As explained earlier in this chapter, in New South Wales students qualify to enter such schools on the basis of ability as demonstrated in tests of reading, mathematics, general ability and writing.

Peters, Kaufman, Matthews, McBee, and McCoach (2014) explain that labels such as 'giftedness' can be problematic. They suggest such terms are 'educationally nondescript' and connote some type of endowment and seem to suggest that high academic achievement is a permanent quality. Further, these authors point out that although such labelling may lead to some type of educational programming in special classes or weekly advanced lessons, the idea of offering appropriate challenge to *all* students is overlooked (Peters et al., 2014). Labels may mean that only identified students who meet a certain criteria receive a program or service, but the general principle of offering learning support to any student who shows ability or potential in any area of schooling endeavour may be more inclusive.

Implications

- Terms such as 'gifted and talented' are now common (but controversial) labels for students with advanced abilities; take care to monitor the effects of labelling and maintain the privacy of students and their families; do not disclose diagnostic assessments such as IQ scores.

- Specific forms of educational accommodations such as grade acceleration (allowing students to move faster through the education system) and extension and enrichment activities are recommended to support these students (see **Box 10.6**).

- As suggested by Peters et al. (2014), take care to ensure all students (not just those identified as gifted) are offered appropriate challenges, as this is a key factor in motivation and engagement (see Chapter 8).

- Monitor students' self-concept and the effects of social comparison in selective school and special class placements (see the big-fish-little-pond concept in Chapter 4).

- Exams or tests for special school or class placements can lead to anxiety for some students. See Chapter 4 for more information about anxiety and some appropriate ways to respond.

- Be aware that students identified as gifted and talented are just as susceptible to disability or other conditions as any other child. Teachers must be mindful to monitor and acknowledge high ability in learners who also have other disabilities, particularly those with learning disabilities and conditions like ADHD and autism, who may often be overlooked and not identified.

CourseMateExpress

Online Resources
Watch a **video** on this text's website in which high-ability students talk about their extension science class

acceleration
Allowing students to move faster through the education system

curriculum differentiation
Modification of instruction, materials and assessment procedures to match learner needs

BOX 10.6 CLASSROOM LINKS

ACCELERATION, EXTENSION AND ENRICHMENT

Acceleration, extension and enrichment are forms of educational adjustment and **curriculum differentiation** to enhance students' experiences, knowledge and skills (Van Tassel-Baska, 2005). These provisions involve programs and services at the school and classroom levels, where students are given additional opportunities to learn. This often involves planning and managing their own projects and developing their interests, with the guidance and assistance of teachers. Although the specific strategies listed here are usually applied to the population of high ability learners often labelled 'gifted and talented', it is most inclusive to consider that all learners deserve enrichment and extension at some times in their learning experiences regardless of their diagnostic label.

TABLE 10.1 Strategies for acceleration, extension and enrichment

ACCELERATION STRATEGIES	EXTENSION ACTIVITIES	ENRICHMENT ACTIVITIES
Enables high ability and advanced students to participate in learning based on their own performance level rather than fixed or lock-step grade levels. It may involve grade-level acceleration and content acceleration (curriculum flexibility), for example: • early entry to school or early entry to high school • exemption from knowledge and skills already demonstrated • placement at a higher level for specific content areas (for example, mathematics and physics) • year skipping or placement at higher year level • whole-group acceleration where whole class is given fast-paced learning.	Encourages expansion of knowledge and skills in the regular classroom and can be provided through inquiry-based learning projects, flexible grouping strategies and on-site learning centres using negotiated curriculum contracts, peer tutoring and community mentors, for example: • learning centres where special topics can be explored • challenge centres where advanced problems can be investigated or skills tested • camps and intensive learning opportunities away from the school setting • use of ICT and virtual instruction to bring additional knowledge source into the classroom.	Broadens the range of experiences for all students. It is particularly important for students who experience educational disadvantage as a result of their language, or cultural or socioeconomic background, for example: • excursions • debates and public speaking • clubs or electives • guest speakers and outside experts • use of ICT and digital technologies, particularly for personal projects such as media activities see Chapter 12).

Source: Adapted from VanTassel-Baska (2005, pp. 91–6); Riley et al. (2004, p. 191); Western Australia Department of Education (2015, p. 14).

ACTIVITIES

1   Think about a class that you are familiar with. If you were the teacher in this class, would you try to identify any students with higher and advanced abilities? How would you do this? Give reasons for your answers.

2   How would you provide for the specific needs of the students you identify? Give reasons for your answer.

3   Do you anticipate any difficulties in the implementation of a program specifically for students labelled 'gifted and talented'? How might these difficulties be overcome?

TEACHING AND DIVERSE NEEDS

As you may have noticed in the previous section, many of the implications and recommendations for practice included simple, 'good sense' teaching practices. You may also reflect on the notion of a non-categorical approach and consider this in light of learning that no condition or medical diagnosis described in the previous section has the same learning support implications for every child with that condition. Rather, many conditions involve a syndrome of characteristics which means every child will be affected differently and have different learning support needs. This means that any expectation of a 'recipe book' approach or precise instruction on 'how to teach' to a specific disability is unreasonable. Teachers should be critical and cautious when consulting textbooks or other resources that purport to provide a definitive guide to teaching students with one condition or another.

Rather it is recognised that good teaching practices, positive teacher attitudes and classroom-wide strategies such as curriculum differentiation, in combination with individualised educational programming, can address the support needs of students in the classroom. This brief section is not intended to replace consultation with expert texts in programming and planning for inclusive education. Rather this section provides a brief introduction to the concepts of differentiation and universal design for learning, two prominent terms in learning support today.

DIFFERENTIATION AND UNIVERSAL DESIGN PEDAGOGIES

An international review of best practice and evidence in inclusive education found that most countries practising (or purporting to practise) inclusion employ curriculum modification and individualised education programming of some sort (Forlin et al., 2013). Best practices in Australian classrooms were characterised by use of differentiated and universal design principles alongside use of technologies, planning with the use of individual education programs and an overall focus on quality teaching for all students. As we saw in the case of learners with high ability in the previous section, curriculum differentiation in the form of extension and enrichment activities are particularly recommended.

individual education program (IEP)
A planned program of instruction for an individual student, based on assessed needs, strengths and interests

One approach to the practice of curriculum differentiation occurs at the level of the individual student and may involve the development of an **individual education program (IEP)** for learners who need additional support. An IEP identifies learning objectives for the individual student and the types of support the student will need to address their specific learning needs. For example, Anna has an IEP that sets specific goals for her related to literacy and numeracy, and broader life goals relating to school-to-work transition, and planning and following routines. Anna's English and Maths teachers differentiate her learning tasks by focusing on adapted reading materials and basic skill development in literacy (for example, learning vocabulary) and numeracy (for example, managing money). They try to always relate Anna's tasks to the same themes or topics as the rest of the class and include Anna in all general discussion topics.

These individualised approaches allow teachers to consider very specific and often high-level support needs of the individual child, rather than

FIGURE 10.5 An individual education plan would specify particular learning goals and the type of individual support the student needs to achieve those goals. This may include working with a specialist teacher to learn a specific skill.

Source: © Stephanie Horrocks/iStockphoto.

trying to make the child 'fit into' inappropriate curriculum or learning approaches. They are especially useful for teaching complex skills or arranging for specialist teacher support (see Figure 10.5).

Classroom differentiation

Another approach is to think of differentiation at a whole-classroom level as a routine practice in diverse classrooms. Tomlinson (2014) suggests teachers adopt a mindset that the classroom is a naturally diverse place; this means we need to acknowledge that students come to the classroom in different states of readiness (and that readiness varies for all learners over time and contexts) and different levels of interest, understanding and skills for learning. This can stem from many factors including diagnosed learning support needs, cultural differences or any other personal factors in the student's life.

Specifically, Tomlinson asserts that teachers who regularly and routinely plan for differentiation in their classrooms have attended to data and diagnostic assessment information about their students, alongside personal knowledge of students, and routinely use this information to plan for modifications to their instruction. Tomlinson outlines a model of classroom differentiation at four levels:

1   *Content:* this refers to what the teacher wants their students to learn in a particular sequence of instruction or unit of study. This also includes consideration of the materials or mechanisms that students will use to access this information

2   *Process:* this describes the actual activities the teacher has designed to ensure students employ specific skills to engage with, learn and apply their knowledge and understanding.

3   *Product:* how students can demonstrate what they have learned and also extend and transfer their learning and understanding.

4   *Affect and environment:* refers to condition, climate and affective (or emotional) tone of the classroom. We examined such factors in Chapter 8 when we looked at the notion of motivational goal climates in classrooms, and in Chapter 14 we return to this idea when we examine the creation of a positive classroom environment.

So far in this textbook we have demonstrated examples of interventions and teaching approaches that reflect the dimensions of differentiated instruction outlined here. In Box 4.2 we learned about a classroom intervention to assist Sarah and her peers cope with the higher-level demands of writing tasks in the secondary school classroom. Teachers had combined their knowledge of students' declining interest and engagement with diagnostic information from recent assessment tasks. They subsequently used small learning group instruction to differentiate the instruction in their English classrooms to address students' specific learning support needs. In Box 8.7 we learned of a school that practised engaging pedagogies in the form of inquiry-based project learning. In this school the curriculum was differentiated and enriched for students by supporting and extending their interests in the form of individual learning plans and contracts, and project work to support individual interests.

Universal design for learning

universal design for learning (UDL)
A set of principles for curriculum planning that allows all students an equal opportunity to learn in that curriculum by planning tasks in which all students can participate

In recent years the term **universal design for learning (UDL)** has also been adopted to describe principles of differentiation. As noted in Forlin et al. (2013), universal design approaches are a form of differentiation that occurs at a universal or class-wide level by considering the deliberate creation of lessons that allow all students to participate in the curriculum, and the design of customisable curriculum for all students (van Kraayenoord, 2007, as cited in Forlin et al., 2013). This is very similar to Tomlinson's philosophy of the differentiated classroom described above. Like Tomlinson's approach, UDL approaches have been advocated for the management of learning needs of *all* students in both school and university settings. The UDL approach has a strong basis in the robust application of studies in educational psychology and applying understanding from cognitive neuroscience (see Chapter 2), and is based on the three key principles outlined below. The National Center on Universal Design for Learning in the USA provides numerous empirical and peer-reviewed sources of evidence to support each principle.

1 *Provide multiple means of representation (the 'what' of learning)*. There is no single mode of representation that will meet the needs of all learners, and no definitive idea of the 'best' way to represent knowledge. This principle closely applies a psychological understanding of learner differences in *perception* (for example, learning and sensory disabilities), *linguistic and communicative understanding* (for example, communication disorders, EAL/D backgrounds) and *cognitive understanding* (for example, cognitive disabilities, high-ability learners).

2 *Provide multiple means of action and expression (the 'how' of learning)*. Learners also differ in their ability to navigate the learning environment, and this can range from *physical actions* (for example, learners with cerebral palsy) to *expression and communication* (learners with language or communication barriers who need to express themselves differently) and *executive function* (learners with a range of cognitive and learning disabilities that affect higher-order thinking skills and processing of information). There is no single means of expression and action that is suitable for all learners, and multiple options for action and expression are essential.

3 *Provide multiple means of engagement (the 'why' of learning)*. Learners differ in affect (emotional responses) and reactions to learning, and the curriculum must *recruit learner interest*, have a means of *sustaining effort and persistence*, and develop learners' intrinsic abilities for *self-regulation* of their learning engagement. Some learners will be driven by high intrinsic interest, while others will need external or extrinsic supports from the learning environment; as discussed in Chapter 8, most learners will vary in their engagement and motivation across different subjects and learning environments. As such, no single method of engagement will be optimal for all learners in all contexts, and multiple options for engagement are essential (CAST, 2011).

These elements within the principles of differentiation and UDL reflect the integration of the concepts from educational psychology into holistic curriculum planning for all learners. However, as with any critical reflection on our teaching practices, important questions must be asked about such curricular approaches (McGuire, Scott & Shaw, 2006). For example, is it likely that all instruction can ever be truly universal? The diversity of human needs and differences probably makes it very difficult to avoid the need for unique individual approaches in some circumstances, such as outlined above for the hypothetical student Anna. It is unlikely that any one curricular approach or philosophy of learning will suit every learning context. However, it is important to note that education has made dramatic progress towards inclusion of learners with additional learning support needs in a relatively short space of time, probably because of curricular innovation and careful research. Nonetheless, it is important to recognise that rates of school exclusion and suspension remain high for some students, while disengagement and school dropout are a concern for a significant number of young people. In the next section we look at one approach to addressing the needs of such students.

ALTERNATIVE SCHOOLS

For some students who do not 'fit in' to regular schools, expulsions or suspensions are common and many of these students simply 'drop out' during the secondary years of schooling. Within this discussion of effective instruction, it must be acknowledged that alternative schools are sometimes sought for the education of students who do not 'fit' into the mainstream of educational service provision. In some cases, parents may select alternative school environments for their child, reflecting a view that one type of school does not suit all students. **Alternative schools**, including those described in Chapter 7, may provide a more appropriate educational experience for some students, while McGregor and Mills (2011)

alternative schools
Usually small in size, student-centred and non-traditional, with high staff–student ratio, more individualised instruction, less-structured organisation and a more personal and caring environment

suggest there is much that mainstream schools can learn from these alternative approaches to teaching. For example, alternative schools are usually small in size, student-centred (or more democratic) and non-traditional, with a higher staff–student ratio than other schools (that is, fewer students per staff), more opportunities for individualised instruction, less structured organisation, and a more personal and caring environment.

Terminology in this area of alternative education is varied, with some people using phrases like 'second-chance' education or 're-engagement' programs (te Riele, 2014). Te Riele suggests that terms like 'alternative' or 'second-chance' education might serve to reinforce the idea that these students or schools are on the margins of educational provision. Alternatively, te Riele suggests there are many innovations in pedagogy and curricular approaches, and flexibility in such educational settings.

Three main types of these alternative or flexible education programs have been identified in Australia (te Riele, 2014):

1   those associated with mainstream schools and offering extracurricular activities or electives
2   TAFE or community colleges offering alternative certificates in education for work and training certificates to alternatives for formal school certificates such as tertiary preparation programs
3   separate alternative schools and programs that are registered and accredited schools that operate in their own right; for example, Key College is run by a youth organisation call Youth off the Streets and specifically serves the needs of homeless youth in Sydney.

These Australian programs have been found to be successful in their inclusion of young people who have been marginalised from other school settings, with outcomes including:

- better futures for students (credentials and career pathways)
- successful learning approaches (academic achievement and engagement with learning)
- personal growth of young people (social, emotional and behavioural growth)
- strong links to the community and contribution to the community (te Riele, 2014).

Similarly, in New Zealand it is acknowledged that many young people become alienated from school because of trauma or other factors, and alternative education is often provided by non-school organisations such as churches or private training providers (New Zealand Education Review Office, 2011). The effectiveness of these schools was recently evaluated and varying levels of effectiveness were identified across factors such as engagement of students. Effective schools had strong processes for overseeing the transition of the student between mainstream education and entering and leaving the alternative education setting. Some secondary schools, however, did not closely engage with the transition process and had little connection or contact with the student once they left the mainstream school. Schools that were more engaged in the alternative education process saw more students returning to mainstream education (New Zealand Education Review Office, 2011).

home schooling
The education of children at home by parents or other adults who take primary responsibility for this education

Another form of non-traditional education that involves individualised instruction and a highly personal and caring environment is **home schooling**, or the education of children at home by parents or other adults who take primary responsibility for the education of their child (Barratt-Peacock, 2003; Home Education Australia, 2013). Home schooling gives parents the freedom to choose their own philosophy of education, the content of their child's educational program and the teaching strategies and resources to be used. The decision to educate a child at home often reflects parental dissatisfaction with the practices of schooling for their child and concern that the school cannot meet the needs of their child (Jackson & Allan, 2010; Jolly, Matthews & Nester (2013).

A recent review of home schooling in New South Wales found that there were 3228 students registered for home schooling in the State. However, other estimates suggest there may be more than 10 000 unregistered children in home schooling in Australia. Parents' reasons for home schooling identified in the inquiry included personal philosophy (17 per cent), special learning needs (14 per cent), religious beliefs (5 per cent), and bullying (3 per cent). A large proportion of responders (24.5 per cent) stated some other reason. However, the review noted that about half of the motivations for home schooling included some level of dissatisfaction with mainstream education, including factors such as class sizes, lack of flexibility, and lack of support for children who are gifted, have special learning needs or are subject to social factors such as bullying. The report of one mother summarises some of these factors:

> … he experienced quite severe and prolonged bullying by both children and a couple of teachers. He didn't fit the 'boy mould' expected of him. He wasn't into sport, was quiet and reflective, and preferred the performing arts to cars and rugby. Things came to a head in Year 5 when he would wake up in the morning and make himself throw up into a bucket to prove that he should be allowed to stay home from school for the day … He refused to take food to school and wouldn't eat or drink for fear of having to use the school bathrooms. He came home exhausted each day from having to deal with the physical and psychological bullying he was experiencing … Attempts to approach the school were met with denial and deaf ears.
>
> Source: NSW Legislative Council, Select Committee on Home Schooling (2014, p. 30).
> Published by NSW Legislative Council © 2014.

The body of empirical research evidence on home schooling in Australia is very small, with a larger number of unpublished PhD studies rather than published empirical sources. Nonetheless, of the small number of studies with child evidence included, the reports are generally positive regarding children's experiences of home schooling (Jackson, 2007).

THINK ABOUT

- Can you think of students you have known who would have benefited from attending an alternative school with more personalised programs, smaller class sizes and a structured school environment?
- What options are available for students who are not successful or at risk of dropping out of a traditional, academically oriented school?

CONCLUDING COMMENTS

Today students like Anna can enjoy greater participation in school with the positive support of teachers and peers. The provision of additional learning support to any student should aim to address their specific educational needs in a non-categorical model of practice; this also requires understanding that 'disability' is now defined as a universal human condition arising from social and environmental factors alongside the diagnosed condition. This means that young people cannot be treated as a homogeneous group and that diversity in our classrooms is a natural reflection of human diversity. Curricular strategies such as differentiation offer many solutions to classroom programming for diverse student groups; in Australia this also tends to reflect best educational practice (Forlin et al., 2013). It remains a concern, however, that some young people do not have a positive experience of schooling and are vulnerable to drop out and school exclusion. There is no doubt that this requires further research, reflection and solution seeking on behalf of the whole education community.

STUDY TOOLS

ONLINE STUDY RESOURCES

Visit http://login.cengagebrain.com and use the access code that comes with this book for 12 months' access to the student resources for this text.

The CourseMate Express website contains a range of resources and study tools for this chapter, including:

■ a **self-check quiz**

■ **crosswords**, **flashcards** and a **glossary** to help you revise the key terms from this chapter

■ the **Go further** materials and **interactive activity** mentioned in the chapter

■ a **video** that illustrates some of the concepts discussed

■ plus much more!

 CourseMateExpress

CHAPTER REVIEW

■ Inclusive education is concerned with the provision of programs and services for students with diverse learning needs in regular settings, regardless of the level or type of disability.

■ Educational exclusion is more likely to be experienced by minority and Indigenous youth, and those from poorer socioeconomic backgrounds.

■ The provision of learning support aims to help students who may be at risk of underachieving, and offset any restrictions that may result from the interaction between their personal circumstances and the school environment.

■ A non-categorical approach to learning support seeks to identify solutions to educational needs rather than broad condition labels. Each child may experience very different educational support needs despite having a similar disability or condition label.

PUTTING IT TOGETHER

Making links between 'learning support needs and inclusive education' and material in other chapters

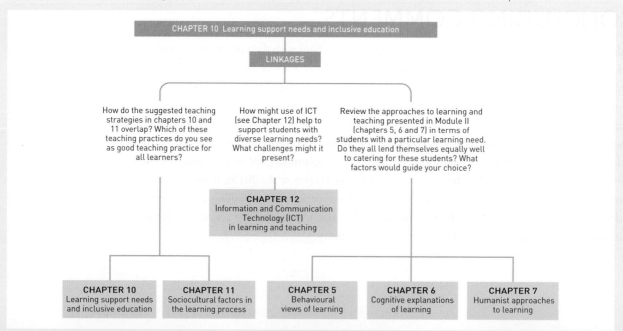

QUESTIONS AND ACTIVITIES FOR SELF-ASSESSMENT AND DISCUSSION

1 Define the terms 'inclusive education', 'normalisation' and 'non-categorical'.

2 Correct the following newspaper headlines to avoid stereotyping and negative attitudes:

   a 'Wheelchair girl fights school'

   b 'Deaf to appeal judgement'

   c 'Angry anorexic attacks authorities'

   d 'Blind twins boycott Olympics'

   e 'Blind school wins appeal'.

3 Which of the following statements reflects a non-categorical philosophy in providing educational services?

   a The program is designed for students with moderate intellectual impairments.

   b The curriculum is suited to the needs of each child.

   c Classroom activities are at the appropriate grade level.

   d The teacher is very sympathetic to the problems experienced by children with disabilities.

4 Do you know what types of programs and services are available in the school district where you live? How do they fit within the inclusion model?

5 Why is the term 'gifted and talented' considered problematic? List the myths and stereotypes associated with this label.

FURTHER RESEARCH

SEARCH ME! AND EDUCATION DATABASES

Explore Search Me! education for articles relevant to this chapter. Fast and convenient, Search Me! education is updated daily and provides you with 24-hour access to full-text articles from hundreds of scholarly and popular journals, ebooks and newspapers, including *The Australian* and *The New York Times*. Log in to Search Me! through http://login.cengagebrain.com and use the search terms listed here as a starting point:

- alternative education
- disability
- home education
- inclusion
- integration
- learning difficulties.

Search Me!

You can also use these terms to explore databases such as ERIC, PsycINFO and the Australian Education Index.

RECOMMENDED WEBSITES

Australian Psychology Society tip sheets: www.psychology.org.au/publications/tip_sheets

Children with Disability, Australia: www.cda.org.au/home

New Zealand Ministry of Education: www.minedu.govt.nz

ResponseAbility: www.responseability.org

KidsMatter: www.kidsmatter.edu.au

MindMatters: www.mindmatters.edu.au

RECOMMENDED READING

Tomlinson, C. A. (2014). The differentiated classroom: Responding to the needs of all learners. Alexandria, Va: Association for Supervision and Curriculum Development.

Foreman, P. & Arthur-Kelly, M. (2017). *Inclusion in action*. Melbourne: Cengage Learning.

Disability and Society
Disability Studies Quarterly
International Journal of Disability, Development and Education
International Journal of Inclusive Education
The Australasian Journal of Special Education

REFERENCES

American Psychiatric Association. (2013). *Diagnostic and Statistical Manual of Mental Disorders*. 5th edition. Washington, DC.: Authoe.

Andermann, J. & Campbell, M. (2008). Indigenous youth reaching their potential: Making the connection between anxiety and school attendance and retention rates. Paper presented at the Australian Association for Research in Education, Coldstream, Victoria. Retrieved from www.aare.edu.au/08pap/ade08382.pdf

Ashman, A. (2005). Opportunities, rights and the individual. In A. Ashman & J. Elkins (Eds), *Educating children with diverse abilities* (2nd ed., pp. 65–95). Frenchs Forest, NSW: Pearson.

Australian Advisory Board on Autism Spectrum Disorders. (2007). *The prevalence of autism in Australia: Can it be established from existing data?* Retrieved from www.autismadvisoryboard.org.au/uploads/pdfs/PrevalenceReport.pdf

Australian Bureau of Statistics. (2009). 'Disability status of children in school', from ABS Survey of Disability, Ageing and Carers. *Profiles of disability, Australia*. Cat. no. 4429.0. Retrieved from www.abs.gov.au/ausstats/abs@.nsf/Lookup/4429.0main+features100302009#

Australian Bureau of Statistics. (2014). *Young people with disability, 2012*. Cat. No. 4427.0.

Australian Bureau of Statistics. (2017). *Disability, Ageing and Carers, Australia: Summary of Findings, 2015*. Cat. No. 4430.0

Australian Human Rights Commission. (2008). *Preventing crime and promoting rights for Indigenous young people with cognitive disabilities and mental health issues*. Sydney: AHRC.

Australian Institute of Health and Welfare. (2004). *Introduction to the International Classification of Functioning, Disability and Health (IDF)*. Canberra: AIHW.

Australian Institute of Health and Welfare. (2005). *Selected chronic diseases among Australia's children*. Bulletin no. 29, cat. no. AUS 62. Canberra: AIHW.

Australian Institute of Health and Welfare. (2008). *Disability in Australia: Trends in prevalence, employment and community living*. Bulletin no. 61, June. Canberra: AIHW.

Australian Institute of Health and Welfare. (2009). *A picture of Australia's children 2009*. Cat. no. PHE 112. Canberra: AIHW.

Australian Institute of Health and Welfare. (2016). *Youth justice in Australia 2014–15*. Bulletin 133. Canberra: AIHW. https://www.indigenousjustice.gov.au/wp-content/uploads/mp/files/resources/files/2016-04-aihw-juv-justice-nat-report.pdf

Australian Psychological Society. (n.d.). *Understanding and managing autism spectrum disorder*. Retrieved from www.psychology.org.au/publications/tip_sheets/autism.

Barratt-Peacock, J. (2003). Australian home education: A model. *Evaluation and Research in Education*, *17*(2&3), 101–11.

Bondy, A. & Frost, L. (2001). The picture exchange communication system. *Behavior Modification*, *25*, 725–44.

Cannella-Malone, H. I., Fant, J. L. & Tullis, C. A. (2010). Using the picture exchange communication system to increase the social communication of two individuals with severe developmental disabilities. *Journal of Physical and Developmental Disabilities*, *22*, 149–63.

CAST (2011). *Universal Design for Learning guidelines version 2.0*. Wakefield, MA: National Center on Universal Design for Learning.

Cerebral Palsy Alliance (n.d.). *What is cerebral palsy?* Retrieved from www.cerebralpalsyaustralia.com/index.php/site/learningcentre/thefacts/whatiscp

Cologon, K. (2013). Inclusion in education: Towards equality for students with disability. *Children with Disability Australia*, 24 October. Retrieved from http://apo.org.au/node/36129

Commonwealth of Australia, Attorney-General's Department. (2005). *Disability standards for education*. Retrieved from www.comlaw.gov.au/Details/F2005L00767

Commonwealth of Australia. (2010). *Social and emotional wellbeing: A teacher's guide*. Retrieved from www.responsibility.org

De Plevitz, L. (2006). Special schooling for Indigenous students: A new form of racial discrimination. *The Australian Journal of Indigenous Education*, *35*, 44–53.

Dunn, L. M. (1968). Special education for the mildly retarded: Is much of it justified? *Exceptional Children*, *35*, 5–22.

Elkins, J. (2005). The school context. In A. Ashman & J. Elkins (Eds), *Educating children with diverse abilities* (2nd ed., pp. 37–64). Frenchs Forest, NSW: Pearson.

Epstein, J. N. & Loren, R. E. A. (2013). Changes in the Definition of ADHD in DSM-5: Subtle but Important. *Neuropsychiatry*, *3*(5), 455–458. http://doi.org/10.2217/npy.13.59

Foliaki, S. (2012, March 28). *Study shows mental health risk for Pacific youths*. [Interview with Pacific Beat, ABC Radio] Retrieved from www.radioaustralia.net.au/international/2012-03-28/studyshows-mental-health-risk-for-pacific-youths/641718

Foreman, P. & Arthur-Kelly, M. (2017). *Inclusion in action*. Melbourne: Cengage Learning.

Forlin, C., Chambers, D., Loreman, T. J., Deppeler, J. M. & Sharma, U. (2013). *Inclusive education for students with disability: A review of the best evidence in relation to theory and practice*. Braddon, ACT: ARACY.

Goffman, E. (1963). *Stigma: Notes on the management of spoiled identity*. Englewood Cliffs, NJ: Prentice-Hall.

Goffman, E. (1968). *Stigma: Notes on the management of spoiled identity*. Harmondsworth, Middlesex: Penguin.

Graham, L. J. & Slee, R. (2007). An illusory interiority: Interrogating the discourse/s of inclusion. *Educational Philosophy and Theory*, *40*(2), 277–93.

Hadderman, M. (2002). Trends and issues: Alternative schools. ERIC document no. ED473003. Eugene, OR: University of Oregon.

Hannan (2013). Learning disorders in children: Recent advances in research and practice. *InPsych*, *35*(6). Available at https://www.psychology.org.au/inpsych/2013/december/hannan/

Home Education Australia (2013). Information on home education in Australia. Retrieved from http://www.hea.edu.au/homeschooling-get-started!/faqs/#15

Hudson, A. & Radler, G. (2005). Psychologists and intellectual disability. *InPsych*, *4*, 10–15.

Hutchins, P. (2007). *ADHD: Comprehensive views and current challenges*. Retrieved from www.cheri.com.au/documents/ComprehensiveViewsandCurrnetChallengesPaulHutchins.pdf

Jackson, G. (2007). Home education transitions with formal schooling: Student perspectives. *Issues in Educational Research*, *17*(1), 62–84.

Jackson, G., & Allan, S. (2010). Fundamental elements in examining a child's right to Education: A study of home education research and regulation in Australia. *International Electronic Journal of Elementary Education*, *2*, 349–364. doi: https://www.iejee.com/index.php/IEJEE/index

Jolly, J. L., Matthews, M. S., & Nester, J. (2013). Homeschooling the gifted: A parent's perspective. *Gifted Child Quarterly*, *57*, 121–134. doi:10.1177/0016986212469999

Just, M. A., Keller, T. A., Malave, V. L., Kana, R. K. & Varma, S. (2012). Autism as a neural systems disorder: A theory of frontal-posterior underconnectivity. *Neuroscience & Biobehavioral Reviews*, *36*(4), 1292–313.

Lawrence, D., Hafekost, J., Johnson, S. E., Saw, S., Buckingham, W. J., Sawyer, M. G., ... Zubrick, S. R. (2015). Key findings from the second Australian Child and Adolescent Survey of Mental Health and Wellbeing. *Australian & New Zealand Journal of Psychiatry*, *50*(9), 876–886. http://dx.doi.org/10.1177/0004867415617836

Lehr, C. A. & Lange, C. M. (2003). Alternative schools serving students with and without disabilities: What are the current issues and challenges? *Preventing School Failure*, *47*(2), 59–65.

McGregor, G. & Mills, M. (2011) Alternative education sites and marginalised young people: 'I wish there were more schools like this one'. *International Journal of Inclusive Education*, *16*(8), 843–862.

McGuire, J., Scott, S. & Shaw, S. (2006). Universal design and its application in educational environments. *Remedial and Special Education, 27*, 166–75.

McMaugh, A. (2004). Social adjustment of children with chronic conditions during the course of school transition: A longitudinal study of social-cognitive and social-ecological factors. Unpublished Doctoral Dissertation. University of Sydney, Australia.

McMaugh, A. (2006). En/countering disablement in school life: Children talk about peer relations and living with illness and disability. Paper presented at the Annual Meeting of the American Educational Research Association, San Francisco, April 7–11.

McMaugh, A. L. (2011). En/countering disablement in school life in Australia: Children talk about peer relations and living with illness and disability. *Disability and Society, 26*(7), 853–66.

Mehl, A. L. & Thomson, V. (1998). Newborn hearing screening: The great omission. *Pediatrics, 101*(1), 1–6.

Miller, C. J., Sanchez, J. & Hynd, G. W. (2005). Neurological correlates of reading disabilities. In L. Swanson, K. R. Harris & S. Graham (Eds), *Handbook of learning disabilities* (pp. 242 55). New York: Guilford Press.

New Zealand Education Review Office (2011). *Alternative Education Schools and Providers*. Wellington; Education Review Office.

New Zealand Education Review Office. (2011). *Secondary schools and alternative education*. Wellington: ERO.

New Zealand Ministry of Education. (2011). *Tataiko: Cultural competencies for teachers of Māori learners*. Wellington: Ministry of Education. Retrieved from www.minedu.govt.nz/~/media/MinEdu/Files/TheMinistry/EducationInitiatives/Tataiako/TataiakoWEB.pdf

New Zealand Ministry of Health. (2012). Food and nutrition guidelines for healthy children and young people (aged 2–18 years): A background paper. Wellington: Ministry of Health.

New Zealand Ministry of Health. (2016). Annual Update of Key Results 2015/16: New Zealand Health Survey. Wellington: Ministry of Health.

Nirje, B. (1985). The basis and logic of the normalization principle. *Australian and New Zealand Journal of Developmental Disabilities, 11*, 65–8.

NSW Board of Studies. (2014). *Stage 6 Life Skills courses: The Higher School Certificate profile of student achievement*. Retrieved from www.boardofstudies.nsw.edu.au/syllabus_hsc/lifeskills_studentprofile.html

NSW Legislative Council, Select Committee on Home Schooling. (2014). *Home Schooling in NSW*. Retrieved from www.parliament.nsw.gov.au/Prod/Parlment/committee.nsf/0/3a5b892ff6c728b6ca257da50019b2d0/$FILE/141203%20 Final%20Report.pdf

Peters, S. J., Kaufman, S. B., Matthews, M. S., McBee, M. T. & McCoach, D. B. (2014). Gifted Ed. Is Crucial, But the Label Isn't, *Education Week, 33*(28), 34, 40.

Reilly, L., Chapman, A. & O'Donoghue, T. (2002). Home schooling of children with disabilities. *QJER, 18*(1), 38–61.

Riley, T. L., Bevan-Brown, J., Bicknell, B., Carroll-Lind, J. & Kearney, A. (2004). *The extent, nature and effectiveness of planned approaches in New Zealand schools for providing for gifted and talented students*. Palmerston North: Institute for Professional Development and Educational Research, Massey University.

Rowe, K. (2003). *Auditory processing: Why many boys are behind the literacy '8-ball' throughout the early and middle-years of schooling*. Invited address presented at the Teaching Boys: Boys to Fine Men Conference Newcastle City Hall, NSW, 27–29 March.

Rowe, K. J. & Rowe, K. S. (2006). *BIG issues in boys' education: Auditory processing capacity, literacy and behaviour*. Retrieved from http://research.acer.edu.au/boys_edu/2

Rowe, K. S., Rowe, K. J. & Pollard, J. (2004). *Literacy, behaviour and auditory processing: Building 'fences' at the top of the 'cliff' in preference to ambulance services at the bottom*. Research conference 2004 proceedings (pp. 34–52). Camberwell, Vic.: ACER. Retrieved from http://research.acer.edu.au/research_ conference_2004/6

Royal Institute for Deaf and Blind Children. (2012). *Facts list: Deafness and blindness*. Retrieved from www.ridbc.org.au/resources/facts_list.asp#blindness

Scheerenberger, R. C. (1987). *A history of mental retardation: A quarter of a century of promise*. Baltimore: Paul H. Brookes.

Skinner, B. F. (1957). *Verbal behaviour*. New York: Appleton-Century-Crofts.

Speech Pathology Australia. (n.d.). *Who has a communication disability?* Retrieved from www.speechpathologyaustralia.org.au/library/1.2_Who_has_a_Communication_Disability.pdf

Tannock, R. (2007). *Pay attention to inattention: Implications for education*. Retrieved from www.cheri.com.au/documents/PayAttentiontoInattentionRosemaryTannock.pdf

Te Riele, K. (2014). *Putting the jigsaw together: Flexible learning programs in Australia. Final report*. Melbourne: The Victoria Institute for Education, Diversity and Lifelong Learning.

Tomlinson, C. (2014). *The differentiated classroom: Responding to the needs of all learners* (2nd edn). Alexandria, VA: ASCD.

Tuohy, P. (2010). *The mental health of New Zealand four-year-olds: Findings from the Strengths and Difficulties Questionnaire*. Retrieved from www.pha.org.nz/documents/Day2-64-mental-health-4-year-olds.pdf

United Nations Educational, Scientific and Cultural Organization. (1994). *The Salamanca statement and framework for action on special needs education*. Retrieved from www.unesco.org/education/pdf/SALAMA_E.PDF

United States. (2010). *Rosa's Law: Report (to accompany S. 2781)*. Washington, D.C.: U.S. G.P.O.

Uniting Care Burnside. (2008). *Early intervention – children and young people 9–14 years in NSW. An additional submission to the Special Commission on Inquiry into Child Protection Services in NSW*. Retrieved from www.lawlink.nsw.gov.au

VanTassel-Baska, J. (2005). Gifted programs and services: What are the non-negotiables? *Theory into Practice, 44*(2), 90–7. Published by Routledge.

Victorian Government. (2012). *Cerebral palsy: Causes and implications*. Retrieved from www.betterhealth.vic.gov.au/bhcv2/bhcarticles.nsf/pages/cerebral_palsy_causes_and_implications?open

Western Australia Department of Education. (2015). Gifted and talented: Developing the talents of gifted children. Retrieved from www.det.wa.edu.au/curriculumsupport/ giftedandtalented/detcms/portal/

Wolfensberger, W. (Ed.). (1972). *The principle of normalization in human services*. Toronto: National Institute on Mental Retardation.

World Health Organization (WHO). (2009). *International Classification of Functioning, Disability and Health (ICF)*. Retrieved from www.who.int/classifications/icf/en

Zubrick, S. R., Silburn, S. R., Lawrence, D., Mitrou, F. G., Dalby, R., Blair, E., Griffin, J., Milroy, H., De Maio, J. A., Cox, A. & Li, J. (2005). The Western Australian Aboriginal Child Health Survey: The social and emotional wellbeing of Aboriginal children and young people. Perth: Curtin University of Technology and Telethon Institute for Child Health Research.

SOCIOCULTURAL FACTORS IN THE LEARNING PROCESS

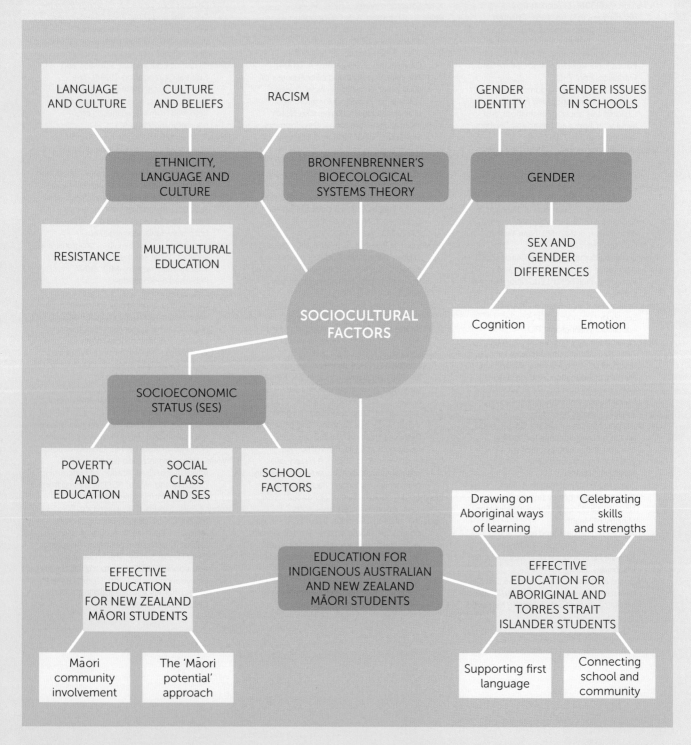

FIGURE 11.1 Chapter 11 concept map

KEY QUESTIONS

After reading this chapter, you should be able to answer the following questions:

■ What are some examples of the interaction of person and environment influencing educational outcomes?
■ Why is it important to consider differences within, as well as among, groups of students?
■ How can poverty influence students' life chances? Give some examples.
■ Why should teachers be aware of gender issues in their classrooms?
■ How can Aboriginal and Torres Strait Islander students in Australia and Māori students in New Zealand be supported in their learning?

ONLINE STUDY RESOURCES

 CourseMateExpress

Bring your learning to life with **interactive learning**, **study** and **exam preparation tools** that support the printed textbook. CourseMate Express includes **quizzes**, **interactive activities**, **videos**, a tool to help you 'develop your philosophy' and more.

INTRODUCTION

A new class of kindergarten pupils is starting school in a rural town. In it are Kari, whose mother is a university lecturer and her father a teacher; Stephan, the son of a local builder, whose brothers are at the school; Jess and Jade, twins whose father is an Aboriginal education worker at the local high school; Sharif, whose parents have asked what extra programs are available for him to continue learning after school; Blaine, who will participate in the school's breakfast program to ensure that he has eaten sufficiently to be able to concentrate; Kirsty, who is silent throughout the first day; and Kade, who never seems to sit still. What experiences do these children bring to the school, and how will all of these children's backgrounds affect their experience at school? What can the teacher do to ensure every child in the kindergarten class has opportunities to learn, and can make use of those opportunities?

Sociocultural factors are those factors that have a basis in society and culture. The previous chapters in this module focused on sources of difference that lie within the individual. In this chapter, we consider some of the social and cultural contexts in which we live, learn and develop, and the ways in which these can contribute to differences among individuals. These factors are particularly important to an understanding of equity and inclusion in education. How can we make sure that the home backgrounds of all students are recognised and supported at school? How can we ensure that all students have access to learning, irrespective of home language, family practices and past experience? We have discussed access for gifted students and students with educational support needs in other chapters in this module.

In an egalitarian society, we expect that everyone should have the same opportunities. Yet, as we will see, some groups do not achieve equal outcomes in terms of achievement and participation in education, which suggests that opportunities are not equally available to all. Where these differences in outcomes have their basis in social or cultural aspects of society, we must ask what role teachers and schools can play in equalising individuals' ability to make use of the educational opportunities available to them.

In considering sociocultural sources of difference, we examine culture, gender, socioeconomic status and issues in education for Aboriginal and Torres Strait Islander students in Australia and Māori

sociocultural factors
Factors contributing to individual difference, which have a basis in society and culture

Source: Fairfax Syndication/Peter Rae.

FIGURE 11.2 What experiences do these children bring to school, and how can the school best cater for their needs?

students in New Zealand. Although this chapter deals with each topic in a separate section, it is important to recognise that the factors interact, and that individuals participate in a number of contexts that they influence and are influenced by. We will see examples of this interaction between factors in the different contexts in this chapter. Because of this complex interaction, which varies from individual to individual, considerable variation exists in the experiences and outcomes of members of any group. Any one variable, such as gender, socioeconomic status or culture, may influence development quite differently in different individuals. Hence developmental psychologists describe development in terms of *probabilities*, rather than certainties (Wachs, 2015).

BRONFENBRENNER'S BIOECOLOGICAL MODEL OF DEVELOPMENT

Urie Bronfenbrenner (1979, 1989, 2005; see also Bronfenbrenner & Morris, 1998, 2006) proposed a theory describing development as a function of the interaction of characteristics of the individual with the various contexts in which the individual exists, and the processes they experience in those contexts over time. While some theories of development you have studied restrict themselves to individuals or, at most, the individual's family context, Bronfenbrenner described a series of contexts that have an impact upon individuals and that, in turn, are influenced by them. The four elements influencing development, according to Bronfenbrenner, are:

1 *person* – the characteristics of the individual, whether these be related to age, as discussed in Module I, dispositions such as motivation (discussed in Chapter 8), abilities (discussed in Chapter 9) or aspects such as gender and culture that interact with context, below.

2 *process* – activities, relationships and practices. Processes are the engines of development, in Bronfenbrenner's theory. They describe the ways individuals interact with people or objects in their immediate environments. Examples in the school context are the relationship between teacher and student; routines for reading and writing that are consistent and ongoing across the term; and students' interaction with social media.

3 *context* – the human and non-human aspects of environments in which individuals are involved, as well as other contexts that affect them. We will see multiple examples of contexts and their effects in this chapter.

4 *time* – stability and instability in individuals' experiences, as well as changes to individuals, processes and contexts over time.

In this chapter, we will focus on the interaction of the 'person' and 'context' dimensions, while recognising that the four elements all interact to influence an individual's development. The person element has been discussed in most previous chapters as we focused on person characteristics such as motivation and intelligence (in this module), or development (in Module I). In this chapter, we will look at some other characteristics of the individual that relate to their membership of certain gender, class or racial groups. In doing this, we consider the processes that different groups experience, and how contexts vary with membership of particular groups.

Bronfenbrenner suggested that the environment can be conceptualised in terms of a series of nested circles, each representing a different contextual system that interacts with features of the individual, and shapes particular processes to impact upon development. An important principle of the theory is that individuals' characteristics and behaviour can affect the environment; while at the same time, that the environment influences each individual's development. Consider a child with ADHD (described in Chapter 10): this disorder is associated with behaviour that can place considerable stress on the parents and teachers who care for the child. This will influence parenting and teaching behaviour, which in turn affects the child. In addition, each system influences the others – for example, what happens between a parent and child in the home (microsystem) influences what happens for parents at work (the exosystem); and what happens in neighbourhoods (mesosystem) influences family relations (microsystem).

Starting from the innermost circle and working outwards (see Figure 11.3), the systems making up the models are the:

1   microsystem
2   mesosystem
3   exosystem
4   macrosystem
5   chronosystem.

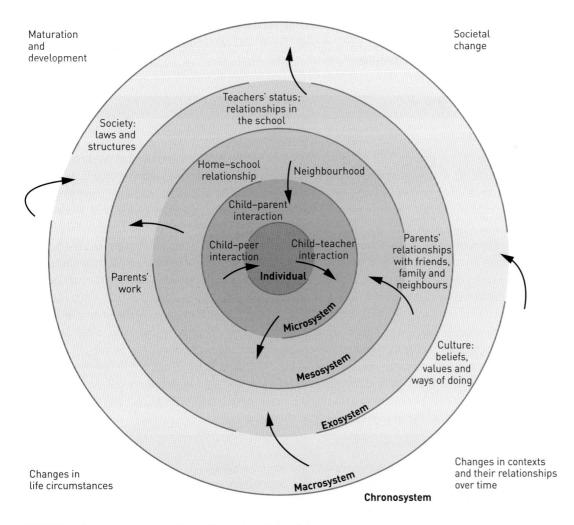

FIGURE 11.3 Bronfenbrenner's bioecological systems theory

Source: Melbourne Declaration on educational goals for young Australians (MCEETYA, 2008). p. 7

microsystem
Interactions and activities in the child's immediate environment

mesosystem
Connections between settings involving the child

exosystem
Settings in which the child is not involved, but which nonetheless influence the child's development

macrosystem
Societal and cultural influences on development

chronosystem
Changes in environments and processes over time that influence development

The **microsystem** describes interactions in the child's immediate environment. Interactions in which the individual is involved (parent–child, child–teacher, and peer or sibling interactions) and those between significant others (such as the quality of marital relationships) can affect and be affected by the individual.

The **mesosystem** involves connections between settings. The relationships between home and school are an important example. Later in this chapter, we argue that home–school and school–community relationships are one key to effectively addressing sociocultural difference.

The **exosystem** describes settings in which the child is not directly involved, but which nonetheless affect that child. Parents' work can affect children in terms of the amount of time and energy it leaves for parenting, and in shaping the goals parents hold for their children (Kohn, 1977). Parents' relationships with friends and family are another example: the support these relationships offer can have an impact on parental efficacy.

The **macrosystem** concerns societal and cultural practices and norms that have an impact on children's development by setting expectations for parent and child behaviour, and by shaping the other settings. Some macrosystem influences are described in the discussion of ethnicity and culture that follows this section.

Finally, the **chronosystem** is the influence of time on each of the settings and interactions in the system. Although the illustration in Figure 11.3 is static, you can think of the effect of the chronosystem as transforming it into a hologram, with the size and shape of the circles shifting with time. As children develop, different settings and systems have differing effects, and impact in different ways.

Box 11.1 describes one student's environment. See if you can identify each of the environmental systems that Bronfenbrenner describes.

BOX 11.1 CASE STUDY

MILLIE

Millie is one of four siblings, and the last to start school. She has watched each of her brothers and her sister go to school and has gone with her mother to readings in each of their classes from the time when she was a baby. At home, Millie's brothers and sister read to her and she has a workbook that she likes to complete while the others are doing their homework. Millie loves it when they stop at the library on the way home for a story.

Millie's mum works at the school as an aide two days a week, when Millie goes to preschool. She knows the teachers well and has shared stories about Millie and her siblings as they have been growing up. Several of the teachers have children the same age, and one will start school with Millie in the new year.

Their dad is no longer around, so the four siblings look after each other in the afternoons while their mother works at a second job at a nursing home. This has helped Millie to become very independent, and has contributed to her eldest brother's highly developed sense of responsibility. Neighbours also keep an eye on the children, and are available if they need help. Millie's mum expects to find things easier when all four children are at school, although in another year's time her eldest will start high school some distance away, and so will be less available to look after the younger ones in the afternoon.

ACTIVITIES
1   What do you think Millie's experience of school will be like?
2   Can you identify microsystem, mesosystem, exosystem, macrosystem and chronosystem influences on Millie's behaviour and approach to school?
3   How has Millie influenced her environment?

Mehan (1979) described how teachers control classroom interaction, so that students' ability to communicate their knowledge appropriately (raising your hand if you want to give the answer; listening and not interrupting when the teacher is instructing) is just as important to academic success as the knowledge itself. Students who do not know the implicit rules of interaction of the classroom, or whose own styles of interaction are not recognised by the teacher, may miss out.

Practices such as assessment and reporting influence students' and society's learning priorities and attitudes. Greenfield and Suzuki (1998) argued that when children are evaluated and rewarded according to individual achievement, we should expect a tendency towards competitiveness to prevail. This tendency might be strengthened by norm-referenced assessment and reporting systems that compare individuals (see Chapter 13).

Teaching resources such as textbooks also contain implicit and explicit messages. A history of Australia or New Zealand that gave a limited place to women and people not of Anglo-Celtic background would relay messages about the relative importance of women and men, and of particular ethnic groups in the society and in society's formation.

INDIVIDUALISM AND COLLECTIVISM

In cultural psychology, the concepts of individualism and collectivism are one way in which different cultural orientations have been described. Cultures that have individualist orientations tend to emphasise individual responsibility and choice, and independence as a goal of development. Valued traits may include creativity, curiosity, assertiveness and self-esteem. Western Anglo cultures tend to have this individualist orientation. Cultures described as collectivist tend to emphasise social relationships and responsibilities, and interdependence as a goal of development. Valued traits may include social responsibility, honesty, respect for elders and loyalty to family. Some Australian Aboriginal and Torres Strait Islander groups, Māori and Polynesian groups, and some Asian groups are described as collectivist. It is important to recognise, however, that cultures are dynamic, and that, particularly in multicultural societies like Australia, there will be variability in the strength of individualist or collectivist orientations from one family to another, and from one individual to another within a family. For example, children may be more collectivist than their teachers, but more individualist than their parents. It appears that formal education contributes to the strengthening of individualism around the world (Greenfield, 2009). At the same time, as we saw in Module II, formal education in Australia and New Zealand has taken on more social pedagogies such as cooperative and collaborative learning, and classrooms being viewed as communities of learners, which illustrates how boundaries between individualist and collectivist cultures are fluid rather than fixed, as is indicated by the dotted line in Table 11.1. Individuals

TABLE 11.1 Contrasting pathways of learning and development

DOMAIN	INDIVIDUALISTIC PATHWAY	COLLECTIVISTIC/SOCIOCENTRIC PATHWAY
Ethnotheory	Independence, individual success	Interdependence, group or family success
Valued intelligence	Cognitive, academic, scientific	Social, relational
Valued knowledge	Physical world, factual knowledge	Social world, narrative knowledge
Models of learning	Independent, active participation, praise	Working in groups, observation, criticism
Communication	Speaking, self-expression	Comprehending, speech that is respectful to authority
Material world	Personal ownership, sharing by choice	Shared use, responsibility to share

Source: Rothstein-Fisch et al. (2010).

may also show varying strength of individual or collective orientation at different times, or in different domains (Greenfield, Suzuki & Rothstein-Fisch, 2006).

Nonetheless, these two concepts can be a helpful way to understand that others may see the world differently, and value things differently. Greenfield, Suzuki and Rothstein-Fisch (2006) highlight some of the misunderstandings and conflicts that can arise in schools when people from individualist and collectivist cultures meet, and the difficulties that this can present for children trying to navigate two different orientations. See Table 11.1 for an overview of the differences. Four possible sites of difference are identified:

1 *Individual achievement.* Emphasising or encouraging individual achievement may be seen as devaluing cooperation and responsibilities to the group. In a study of school conferences (parent–teacher meetings) between immigrant Latino parents and their children's schoolteachers, the parents were uncomfortable when teachers praised a child's individual achievement, but felt more comfortable when this achievement could be related to helping other family members, such as reading to siblings (Greenfield, Quiroz & Raeff, 2000).

2 *Written knowledge.* Learning through written texts is a particularly Western experience. In other societies, knowledge is seen as residing with people, and this is an important connector between people of different generations. To have knowledge based in an object (such as a book) may be seen as disrupting the fabric of society. In addition, differences in the value of writing may require school procedures to be reconsidered. Greenfield, Suzuki and Rothstein-Fisch (2006) give the example of a child asked to pass on a message to the school from his parents. As the message was given orally, it was not accepted by the school, who wanted a signed note from the parents.

3 *Object knowledge.* Western individualist cultures emphasise decontextualised object knowledge, while social relations and social knowledge are valued by collectivist cultures. Thus, children from these cultures may tend to think and talk about objects or events in the context of social interactions, whereas in Western schools we tend to expect students to talk about an object or event in objective ('scientific') terms. Consider how this might influence a science lesson, in which the teacher expects the students to discuss the features and habitat of Australian mammals, while the students discuss what they did when they went out hunting kangaroos with their grandfather. Understanding the basis of such differences may help you to consider how to value the students' orientation, while teaching them other ways of thinking about and representing the world. This approach is discussed further later in the chapter.

4 *Assertiveness.* The Western individualist orientation means that independent thought and assertiveness in opinion are encouraged, and students may be evaluated on this basis – on the quality of questions they ask, and the clarity and independence of their argument, for example. In collectivist cultures, where interdependence is valued, respect for elders is not associated with arguing with or questioning them. Encouraging students to engage with teachers in this way may be seen as encouraging a lack of respect.

In a project called Bridging Cultures, teachers worked on ways to value collectivist values alongside individualist ones. Box 11.2 describes some of the practices they developed in their classrooms.

BOX 11.2 CLASSROOM LINKS

BRIDGING CULTURES: CHANGING CLASSROOM PRACTICES

Teachers in the Bridging Cultures project learnt about individualism and collectivism, and experimented in their own classrooms with ways of valuing both individualist and collectivist goals. Some of the successful innovations included the following.

Using group motivation for mathematics achievement

A star chart marking successful learning of multiplication tables was displayed in the classroom. The children aimed to have the chart filled with stars, and helped each other study for the success of the group. A buddy was allowed to watch a child being tested, to provide support and encouragement, and so that they would know how to help out in a following study session. The buddy would ring a bell if the student was successful, to signal that another star had been added to the chart, and the whole class would stop and applaud.

Support for language development

Several practices are described here. In one case, students shared 'news' with a small group, rather than the traditional practice of one child standing out the front on their own. In another, students did choral reading to provide reading practice while supporting one another.

Making use of narratives

To activate prior knowledge of a topic and build on the importance of personal narrative for some students, stories were shared with a partner before the lesson. In another classroom, a T-chart was drawn, with key phrases from children's stories on the left, and related scientific knowledge on the right.

Classroom management

Children were allowed to sit close on the mat in younger grades, and to touch one another's hair or shoes in a non-disruptive way, as this was understood to be a natural way of behaving for these families.

Family involvement

Recognising that some parents might not feel it appropriate to teach their children at home, children were given the opportunity to discuss homework questions together in small groups, making it easier to complete homework without parental guidance at home. Parent–teacher interviews were held in small groups, one for each cultural group. Parents found this less threatening, and it allowed them to have a group voice. Parents also had an opportunity to meet privately with the teacher if they wanted to after the meeting. Parent volunteers were encouraged by permitting younger siblings to come into the class with them, and experienced parents helped as newer parent helpers watched what they did.

Source: Rothstein-Fisch et al. (2010).

ACTIVITIES

1   Which of these activities could you try in your classroom? What difficulties might arise?
2   These practices were carried out in classrooms with a majority of children of collectivist background. How could you balance the needs of children from individualist and collectivist backgrounds in a class of mixed ethnicity?

OTHER SOURCES OF CULTURAL DIFFERENCE AND MISUNDERSTANDING

Difficulties may arise for students when the beliefs of the home and school differ. As we saw for individualism and collectivism, when an individual's behaviour is interpreted from a cultural perspective that is different from that of the individual in question, misunderstandings and conflict can result. Malcolm, Kessaris and Hunter (2003) described a number of ways in which this can happen for Aboriginal students in mainstream Australian classrooms. In Western Anglo culture, looking people in the eye when you speak to them is a mark of respect, and shows you are attending to them. However, in many other cultures, including some Aboriginal and Asian groups, this would be a mark of disrespect – particularly if shown by a younger person to someone in a position of authority. Without this understanding, teachers might assume that students from cultures that do not favour eye contact are not listening or are not interested. Similarly, teachers who insist on eye contact without explaining that it denotes respect in their culture risk some students and parents assuming that those teachers do not want to be respected.

A second example of culturally based misunderstanding is in students asking questions. For middle-class Anglo groups, asking questions is an important learning strategy, and is also interpreted by teachers as demonstrating curiosity and active engagement with the topic. For other cultures, however, asking questions of a teacher is considered rude, implying doubt about the teacher's willingness to share information. Eades (1993) described this belief–behaviour pattern of Aboriginal people in south-eastern Queensland: unlike in Anglo Australia, knowledge is 'owned' by individuals, and some kinds of knowledge should not be shared with certain groups (such as in mixed company), so questions are inappropriate. Eades explained that in Aboriginal English, hinting or triggering statements may be used rather than direct questions. Silence is also an important feature of Australian Aboriginal interaction. Malcolm, Kessaris and Hunter (2003) add that in some Aboriginal groups, receivers of questions are not obligated to respond – a choice that can be misinterpreted by teachers as defiance or a lack of intelligence. When teachers insist on responses, as in question-and-answer sessions at school, students may feel threatened or embarrassed.

THINK ABOUT

- How might teachers and students misunderstand each other where there are differences in cultural beliefs about questioning?
- How could you, as a teacher, make the value of questioning explicit to your students?

ADDRESSING RACISM AND PREJUDICE

racism
Discrimination based on race or ethnicity

Racism is a form of discrimination based on race or ethnicity. Underlying racism are attitudes of prejudice and cultural stereotypes (that is, assumptions applied to whole groups of people). Because these attitudes reflect beliefs, they influence the way individuals behave and the way they perceive and interpret the actions of others. For this reason, combating racism involves targeting beliefs – or the prejudices underlying racist actions – as much as dealing with the actions themselves.

In schools, racism can be experienced by students and teachers directly, through harassment, abuse and discrimination; or indirectly, such as when the cultural beliefs and practices of students or teachers are not recognised, when others have prejudicial attitudes (such as low expectations) or when cultural stereotypes are promoted. Institutional racism occurs when schools are organised and managed in ways that disadvantage some groups. For Aboriginal people and Torres Strait Islanders in Australia, and Māori in New Zealand, racism is reflected in the poorer educational outcomes these groups experience when compared with others (we discuss this issue in detail later in this chapter).

CourseMateExpress

Online Resources
Go further: Explore teaching resources from Racism No Way! and Kids Together Now via the links on this text's website

Treating Aboriginal, Māori or Torres Strait Islander students – or any other group – identically, as a response to a stereotype of their culture, is a form of racism. Malin (1998) recommended that teachers get to know the community in which they are working, and that they view any student in three ways: as a learner, as a cultural being and as an individual person.

Although committing, inciting or permitting racist acts is illegal in Australia, racism is a daily experience for many school students. Anyone can experience or display racism, but it is more likely to be experienced by some groups than by others. The charity All Together Now, that promotes racial equality through education, reported that while one in five Australians has been a target of verbal racist abuse at some point, approximately half of all culturally and linguistically diverse (**CALD**) people has experienced racism, and three out of four Indigenous Australians experience racism regularly (see www. alltogethernow.org.au).

CALD
Culturally and
linguistically diverse

Racism is destructive to individuals, affecting educational outcomes, emotions, identity and behaviour. It also has far-reaching effects on school climate and school–community relations. Racism works against effective classroom communication, limiting the contributions of some students, and promoting tension and conflict. In addition, racism is an important source of playground violence, both as racist harassment and as a reaction to it.

The website for the Australian educational initiative *Racism. No way!* (2010) identified the following potential consequences for students experiencing racist behaviour: reduced self-esteem and self-confidence, loss of identity; conflict with parents resulting from rejection of their cultural background; development of a 'resistance' culture (discussed later in this chapter); frustration, fear and withdrawal; dropping out; loss of concentration; and non-participation.

Strategies for teaching

Teachers can intervene by taking racist behaviour (such as name calling, teasing and exclusion) seriously rather than by dismissing it as a minor difficulty. Teachers may need to examine their own prejudices or the cultural stereotypes they hold, asking of themselves: 'Are there some groups of which I would have lower expectations than others?', 'Do I treat all students as if they had the same (my) background?' and 'Are my classroom and curriculum built around the ideas and practices I am comfortable with?'

As Figure 11.4 illustrates, culturally sensitive education involves dismantling student prejudice and stereotypes, as well as examining teaching practices, curriculum, resources and schools as institutions. Culturally sensitive education also involves including other cultural viewpoints across the curriculum, such as investigating Aboriginal, Māori, Torres Strait Islander and other non-Anglo views of history alongside Anglo histories, looking at mathematical systems across cultures, and reading literature translated from a number of languages. This conveys to students that cultures other than the dominant culture in the society are valued, and helps students develop an understanding of other cultures – including those of their peers – as a step towards breaking down negative stereotypes.

Promoting equity

On their own, multicultural curriculum programs have not been shown to be particularly effective in reducing prejudice (Pfeifer, Brown & Juvonen, 2007). We also need to consider the make-up of the school population, and practices in the school that contribute. When school practices such as streaming of classes highlight difference, multicultural education alone will not be enough. Classic theories of prejudice (Allport, 1954) have argued that contact between peers of equal status with common goals is necessary to reduce prejudice – one reason cooperative learning programs have been effective (McKown, 2005; see also Chapter 7).

CourseMateExpress

Online Resources
Go Further: View the
Australian Curriculum
guidelines by following
the links from this text's
CourseMate website

Pfeifer, Brown and Juvonen (2007) recommended that programs also take account of the cognitive developmental limitations of young children's thinking, particularly before eight years of age. They argued that lack of conservation skill (ability to discount appearance; see Chapter 3), together with weak ability to classify in multiple ways (and so see people as members of multiple groups), and the egocentric weakness in perspective-taking ability, contribute to the development and expression of racial prejudice in young children: children possessing these skills tend to demonstrate less prejudice. Prejudice in young children is not just due to lack of these skills, but they need to be addressed as part of any solution.

One of the goals of the *Melbourne declaration on educational goals for young Australians* (MCEETYA, 2008) is that Australian schooling promotes equity and excellence, and it includes commitments to:

> provide all students with access to high-quality schooling that is free from discrimination based on gender, language, sexual orientation, pregnancy, culture, ethnicity, religion, health or disability, socioeconomic background or geographic location

> ensure that schools build on local cultural knowledge and experience of Indigenous students as a foundation for learning, and work in partnership with local communities on all aspects of the schooling process, including to promote high expectations for the learning outcomes of Indigenous students

> ensure that schooling contributes to a socially cohesive society that respects and appreciates cultural, social and religious diversity.

Source: *Melbourne declaration on educational goals for young Australians,* 2008. MCEETYA, p. 7

As a result, in the Australian Curriculum, Aboriginal and Torres Strait Islander histories and cultures are taught across the curriculum. Ideally, this would be taught by Indigenous people from the community, increasing opportunities for contact between Indigenous and non-Indigenous Australians.

In addition, intercultural understanding is included as a general capability, and Asia and Australia's engagement with Asia is a cross-curriculum priority in the Australian Curriculum. Figure 11.4 suggests a number of dimensions of effective multicultural education.

CULTURE, ADVANTAGE AND DISADVANTAGE

The beliefs and practices of some cultural groups fit well with our schooling system, while those of other groups do not. In 2016, students of language backgrounds other than English (**LBOTE**) held up to 97 per cent of the places at the top 10 selective schools in Sydney (Ho, 2017), and Ho reported the majority of these students to be of Asian backgrounds such as China, Korea, India and South or South-east Asia. Ho pointed out that the majority of these students are in the top quarter of socio-economic advantage, and so likely to have parents with educational experience and values. However, this success occurs despite considerable barriers to success that have been linked to poorer academic outcomes, such as CALD, difference in culture, and disrupted early education for those who were refugees. Other migrant groups do not show the same results, even though the barriers to success could be said to be similar. This is an example of the complex interconnections between the various contexts of development that were discussed in the section on Bronfenbrenner's theory. In the section on poverty later in this chapter, we discuss risk and resilience, which goes some way to explaining these differences. Another explanation, that of the concept of 'resistance', is set out below.

LBOTE
Language background
other than English

RESISTANCE

Ogbu (1987, 1997, 2003) developed a theory to explain why some minority groups within a particular society succeed educationally, while others do not. Based on groups in the USA, he described different types of minority groups, defining them by the history of their contact with the majority group.

Voluntary minority groups are those such as refugees and other migrants who have chosen to move to a new society in the hope of improving their lives in some way. For such groups, differences can be seen as barriers to be overcome in striving to succeed in the new society. The strategies these groups develop to deal with barriers tend to be adaptive.

    Involuntary minority groups, by contrast, are those such as indigenous peoples or people brought in as slave workers who did not choose to be brought into the society, and whose relationship with the majority has been marked by oppression and/or opposition. For such groups, differences are important markers to be maintained. Educational success in countries such as the USA, Australia and New Zealand may even be seen as 'becoming White', and as rejecting indigenous culture and identity. The case study in Box 11.3 demonstrates one effect of this rejection. These beliefs can be reinforced by schools that communicate low expectations of Indigenous students, either verbally or through their practices (Stronger Smarter Institute, 2014). This is particularly so when the school is strongly tied to non-indigenous culture. Beresford (2012) cited two research reports that described pressure from peers not to succeed as a factor in the attitudes of Aboriginal students to school and achievement patterns. The Stronger Smarter Institute, which seeks to build high-expectations relationships in schools, and the Australian Indigenous Mentoring Experience (AIME) program, which has the motto 'Indigenous equals success', are two programs that seek to shift the mindset that succeeding at school is not possible for Aboriginal people without foregoing their culture. Ka Hikitia, the Māori educational strategy in New Zealand, also seeks to change ideas of Māori students as having a 'deficit' in relation to education ('deficit discourses') that may be communicated through policy or media (Berryman & Eley, 2017). Further strategies for including Aboriginal, Torres Strait Islander and Māori students in school learning are dealt with later in this chapter.

voluntary minority group
A group of people who have at some point chosen to move to a new society in search of a better life

involuntary minority group
A group of people who have at some point been brought into a society against their will

CourseMateExpress

Online Resources
Go further: Investigate the Stronger Smarter, AIME and Ka Hikitia programs through links on Coursemate

BOX 11.3 CASE STUDY

ROSIE'S CHOICE

Rosie, a 10-year-old Aboriginal child, attends a rural district high school (K–10). Both Rosie and her teacher report that she has poor literacy skills and is a quiet student, reluctant to contribute to classroom discussions. Although her teacher relates this reluctance to a lack of ability, Rosie suggests other possibilities when talking about school. There seem to be many barriers to Rosie's success in school, but one that stands out is her view that, to be successful, you have to become like a *wadjella* (white person). Her brother is the only Aboriginal boy in the school to continue through to Year 10 and experience academic success at that level. Rosie views his success as the result of him mixing with Anglo-Australian boys and learning to use 'big words' just like them. She is determined that she will not similarly 'sell out' her family and community for such success.

Source: Haig, Konigsberg and Collard (2005). Reproduced with permission from PETAA – Primary English Teaching Association Australia.

ACTIVITIES

1 How could the school ensure that Rosie does not see education as a choice between her family or community and White culture?

2 Review the Aboriginal and Torres Strait Islander education section later in this chapter to identify some of the strategies that have been successfully used in schools to support Aboriginal students.

MULTICULTURAL EDUCATION

Culture is more than visible aspects such as food or costumes, so multicultural education must go beyond these. Banks and McGee Banks (2015) proposed a model of multicultural education that identified the range of aspects to be considered (see Figure 11.4). Teaching style, implicit beliefs, content, students' attitudes, and the school culture and structure all must be addressed.

Source: *Multicultural Education: Issues and Perspectives* by James A. Banks and Cherry A. McGee Banks. Copyright © 2003 John Wiley & Sons, Inc. Reproduced with permission of John Wiley & Sons Inc.

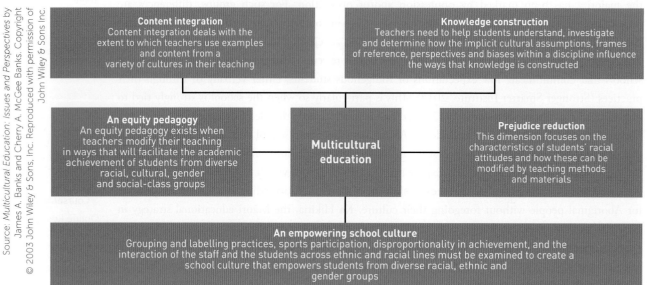

FIGURE 11.4 The dimensions of multicultural education

Box 11.4 gives some strategies for educators to use in multicultural classrooms.

BOX 11.4 IMPLICATIONS FOR EDUCATORS

MULTICULTURAL CLASSROOMS

'Invisible' aspects of culture can be difficult for teachers and students to identify. Teachers must therefore:

- be self-aware of the cultural views they hold, and that are implicit in their teaching
- be aware of the cultural models of the students they teach
- teach cultural differences explicitly, in order to make the invisible visible.

Some common ways of doing things in classrooms might need to be explained to students and/or changed to accommodate their practices. These could include raising your hand to speak, one person talking at a time, looking at the teacher when the teacher is talking, staying in your seat until work is finished, and the use of questions (by teachers to assess learning, and by students to investigate).

Understanding your own culture necessitates reflection and discussion with others.

Understanding the cultures of your students will require interaction with the community, both inside and outside the school. For this to be effective, you will need to be careful to look at the strengths represented by the differences you encounter, rather than regarding another way of doing things as 'wrong' or as a source of difficulty.

Other implications relate to the content of your teaching, such as examining the curriculum and resources to eliminate bias or stereotypes regarding particular groups. Students can be involved in this process so that they are actively involved in detecting and dismantling stereotypes and bias inside and outside the classroom.

GENDER

Look around you. If your education class is typical, there will be many more women than men. Why is it that women tend to choose education in larger numbers than men do? Why are there more women at university than men?

When discussing differences between males and females, we can talk about sex-related differences and gender differences. The use of these terms has been widely debated (Ruble, Martin & Berenbaum, 2006). Traditionally, 'sex' has been used to refer to aspects of masculinity or femininity that have a biological basis, while 'gender' has referred to the cultural aspects of masculinity and femininity. In reality, of course, we are biological *and* cultural beings, so the two sets of factors are difficult to separate. In this text, we use the term **gender** as an inclusive term that encompasses biological and cultural influences, and that recognises the interdependence of biological and cultural sources of difference.

gender
Those aspects of an individual that relate to the individual's sex; they are biologically and culturally determined

GENDER DIFFERENCES

Many of the differences observed between males and females – such as a gendered preference for pink or blue – have a cultural basis, but some appear to be relatively stable and to have a biological component. The physical differences described in Chapter 3 are an obvious example. The trend has been for gender differences in behaviour, emotion and cognition to decrease over time, however, which suggests that environmental factors are also involved (Feingold, 1993). Most of the differences described in this chapter are small, and there are also individual differences within groups of males and females (see Box 11.5).

Gender differences in cognition

Tests of general intelligence do not show differences between males and females in overall test scores, although there are differences in some specific abilities that are components of these tests, and in the variability of the scores (Hunt, 2011). Studies of general knowledge show that males tend to score higher than females, and this difference appears across a number of cultures (Lippa, 2005). Hunt (2011) reported that females tend to be better at verbal thinking and language skills, while males tend to be better at spatial–visual reasoning, although there is considerable overlap. There is more variability in these scores for males than for females, so it should not be assumed that all males are strong in spatial–visual thinking, or all females in language (De Lisi & McGillicuddy-De Lisi, 2002). Hyde (2014) reported that differences in spatial–visual abilities are amenable to change through training, and may be linked to activities such as the higher frequency of boys playing video games, which may train this kind of thinking, although other studies have found a difference as early as infancy (Moore & Johnson, 2008).

Gender differences in emotion

For a combination of biological and sociological reasons, males are more likely to show aggression than are females. A meta-analysis that looked at studies of aggression reported by individuals, peers, teachers and observation research across a number of countries found more aggression reported in boys than in girls. Aggression was highest in youth (18–22 years), decreasing with age (Archer & Mehdikhani, 2004). Girls were slightly higher in indirect or relational aggression – behaviours such as gossiping and exclusion – with the difference strongest during adolescence. Hyde (2014) reported from a review of research that gender differences in aggression show strong contextual effects, and even disappear under some conditions.

Girls are more likely to experience anxiety than boys, although differences are small, and vary with age and context (Chaplin & Aldao, 2013). Contextual effects on emotions like anxiety suggest that schools can play a role in students' experience and expression of emotions, depending both on teachers' relationships with students and pedagogical decisions affecting motivation (see Chapter 8).

A larger difference is found in the incidence of depression, with women more likely to experience this than men, with the difference first appearing in adolescence (Hyde, 2014). Hyde suggests that this gender difference may relate to differences in stress for boys and girls in adolescence, and effects of various life events such as early puberty, peer sexual harassment and body image concerns. This underscores the importance of school programs that support mental wellbeing, with a focus on these issues for girls in particular.

THINK ABOUT

- How might these gender differences show up in students' classroom behaviour?
- How might they be influenced by school factors?

BOX 11.5 RESEARCH LINKS

ARE DIFFERENCES IN BOYS' AND GIRLS' BRAINS THE REASON FOR THE GENDER DIFFERENCES WE FIND IN SCHOOLS?

You may recall from Chapter 2 that one of the neuromyths that persists in education is that boys' and girls' brains are structurally different, and that this is therefore the basis for fundamental differences between boys' and girls' educational outcomes in schools. However, although size and structural differences have been observed in neurological studies (Burgaleta, Head Alvarez-Linera, Martinez, Escorial, Haier & Coom, 2012; Ingalhalikar et al., 2014), many similarities have also been found (Joel et al., 2015). Buckley (2016) reviewed neuroscience research on this question, and reported that insufficient evidence has been found to conclude that there are fundamental differences between male and female brains. The implications of all these findings for students' behaviour have yet to be clearly established.

Just as in other areas of gender difference we have explored, Buckley reports that there is considerable overlap between the sexes, and individual differences tend to be missed when people are put into just two groups.

Source: Adapted from Buckley, S. (2016). Gender and sex differences in student participation, achievement and engagement in mathematics. *Changing Minds: Discussions in Neuroscience, Psychology and Education*, Issue 1 April 201.6
Read the full article at. http://research.acer.edu.au/learning_processes/18

GENDER IDENTITY FORMATION

gender schema theory
A theory proposing that children's schemas or understandings about gender influence the way in which they process information and their choices

How do we form our beliefs about what it is to be male or female? Walk into your local department store. Who is shopping, and what are they buying? What are the predominant colours in the boys' and girls' clothing and toy sections? How are items for men and women advertised? **Gender schema theory** suggests that children form a gender schema (or concept) for their sex from the messages about typical gender preferences and behaviours that are present in their environment. These messages come from people with whom they interact, such as parents, peers and others, as well as from their observations of the environment. As they organise their experiences, children sort objects or actions into 'male' and 'female', and with an awareness of their own sex apply these labels to themselves or to others (see Figure 11.5). Those objects or actions that are classed as being gender-appropriate are more likely to be remembered or persisted with (Liben & Signorella, 1993).

Messages about gender role do not have to be spoken; many are implicit in the ways we do things. Marmion and Lundberg-Love (2004) described a number of these. Parents model gender roles in their own choices and behaviour, by the jobs they are employed in and their leisure activities. They also reinforce gender roles in their children by the kinds of play they encourage, the jobs they assign to boys and girls, and the extent to which independence, assertiveness, compliance and aggression are encouraged or tolerated. The researchers observed parents interacting with their infant children and describing them

FIGURE 11.5 Gender identity is formed through direct and indirect experiences. It is particularly strong and often stereotypic in the preschool years.

in gender-stereotypic ways from as early as 24 hours after birth. Siblings also play a part in gender socialisation. Children have been observed to display more gender-typed behaviour if they have an older sibling of the same sex (Marmion & Lundberg-Love, 2004).

At the same time, and in a reminder that very few characteristics have purely genetic or environmental origins, Hines (2015) reported a range of studies from Japan, the US and Europe that showed effects of androgen (a male hormone) on play preferences. These studies found that girls with a particular condition that resulted in high levels of androgen exposure before birth, were reported by their parents, by themselves and/or by researchers' observations to engage in more male-typical play (preferring to play with cars, trucks and weapons rather than dolls and tea sets, for example; to engage in rough-and-tumble play; and to play with boys).

The formation of gender identity is not without conflict. Gender identity is typically more inflexible among pre-schoolers, who may be heard to say, 'Your dad can't be a nurse, he's a man', or 'He isn't a nurse, he's a doctor'. Peers play important roles in shaping gender identity. Matlin (2004) identified four ways in which peers encourage gender-typed behaviour. They may reject children who behave non-stereotypically, encourage play with peers of the same sex (emphasising the difference with phrases such as 'We're not going to play with the girls, are we?'), show prejudice against children of the other sex ('Ew, boys' germs') and treat boys and girls differently. Witt (2000) suggested that children test out behaviours with peers. If they are teased about them, then they will stop, while behaviours that are rewarded continue. Thus, there is an ongoing shaping of gender-role behaviour throughout childhood. In adolescence, there is an increased rigidity of gender-role stereotypes, with gender intensification (Matlin, 2004). This probably relates to the development of identity formation (see Chapter 4). It can also show itself in 'boundary policing' (Martino & Pallotta-Chiarolli, 2005), where adolescents single out and ridicule any behaviour that does not fit the norm. Box 11.6 is a case study of a student who has experienced this kind of pressure to be 'normal' from his peers.

BOX 11.6 CASE STUDY

BEING 'NORMAL'

I get the occasional snigger, tease 'Faggot, gay, etc.' because I'm real expressive and very in touch with my feminine side. I'm not gay, but I have three sisters, and I can relate and understand them very well. I'm very sensitive too, and at school guys can be like dogs and sniff you out fast. If you stuff up in the sense of wearing the wrong shoes, clothes, friends, you can cop a whole heap of s**t. But the action[s] of those guys are out of fear of not conforming to the pathetic egoistic standards. Being a guy that isn't popular, if you don't fit in, then you're instantly labelled. What you usually find [is] that the way to harass a guy's dignity is to affect his sexuality. Common issues of insults could be 'faggot, gay, homo, sped, etc.' really insulting names. For guys it's also an ego thing. Who's the most heroic, bravest, who can pick up the best chick, who can cop a root or a bit ... first. The peer pressure is pretty strong. You will find that all of the guys are very afraid. You can get the strongest-looking guy, but he's still afraid. Guys think that they have to fit in. I do, sometimes, but I guess I'm realising that it's not worth it, and plus I think, why would I want to be like them. I wish that guys could be more individual because only then, I think the issues mentioned wouldn't occur often (15-year-old male student; CCHS M 2/15).

Source: Martino and Pallotta-Chiarolli (2005).

ACTIVITIES

1. Have you experienced or observed this kind of policing of adolescents' behaviour by their peers? What tactics did they use? What kinds of behaviour were targeted? What impact did it have on the students' behaviour?
2. What role can teachers and schools play in minimising harassment, and broadening ideas of what is 'normal' for boys and girls?

Gender and sexual diversity

As the case study in Box 11.6 implies, students who identify as other than heterosexual can be the targets of such policing, as they challenge ideas of what is normal. As adolescents explore their gender identity, conflicts may also arise for those who are transgender or gender diverse, although some transgender and gender diverse students also report support from their peers as a protective factor in the face of verbal or physical abuse (Jones et al., 2016). Jones and colleagues also found participating in activism for gender and sexual diversity to have positive effects on wellbeing for the transgender and gender diverse young people they surveyed, even when the activism was minimal, as in liking a Facebook post, or signing a petition. Identifying as different to the norm can have effects on self-esteem and other aspects of mental health, involving distress, particularly in a homophobic setting (Willis, 2012). Responses of others are likely to form at least part of the cause of these emotional effects. Jones and colleagues' study found as many as 65 per cent of their respondents had experienced verbal abuse, and 21 per cent had been physically abused as a result of their gender identity. An earlier national study of same sex attracted and gender questioning young Australians found similar rates of abuse were experienced, particularly at school (Hillier et al., 2010). In this study, young people who had been abused were less likely to feel safe at school or elsewhere, and were more likely to have thought about or been involved in self harm and suicide attempts, and to use drugs, compared with those who had not been abused. Loneliness and isolation were also factors in coming to terms with their identity, that were identified by Hillier et al., although the internet went some way to mitigating this, as people reported that they could find information, and like-minded others in a safe and supportive space that offered anonymity (2010). Support of the wellbeing of gender and sexually diverse young people at school is an important implication of these findings.

GENDER ISSUES IN SCHOOLS

Gender difference in schooling has been addressed in Australia, New Zealand and many other western countries since midway through the last century, with first girls' and then boys' underperformance the focus (Hadjar, Krolak-Schwerdt, Priem & Glock, 2014). However, with the emergence of more complex models of development such as Bronfenbrenner's, developmental psychologists increasingly caution that focusing on a single characteristic such as gender as an influence on education can be misleading (Overton & Molenaar, 2015). Instead, gender is recognised as one of several individual factors that interact with aspects of environment in development, resulting in different outcomes for particular groups of girls or boys, in specific areas. For example, Bronfenbrenner & Morris (2006) discuss a study of the effects of the Great Depression; Elder, Van Nguyen & Caspi (1985) found that economic difficulties influenced fathers' behaviour towards their daughters more than towards their sons (with fathers more likely to reject daughters), but also, that attractive daughters were less harshly treated – so gender alone was not the influence.

Sometimes the media picks up on results that compare girls' and boys' results in national or international testing, and it is important to bear in mind the complexities that surround such results. For example, although girls may appear to be doing better than boys at school, this does not appear to translate to better employment opportunities after school (ABS, 2013). With limited employment opportunities for girls, it is not surprising that they should stay at school longer and aspire to higher education. Boys tend to move from education to training and/or employment, whereas this pathway is less available to girls (Teese, 2000). Teese suggested that this pattern is reflected in higher numbers of boys enrolling in TAFE courses, while girls tend to enrol in university programs. Related to this is the pattern of subject choice, which is more likely to translate to employability for boys, but not girls.

Gender differences in mathematics and reading

Gender differences in mathematics performance appear to have been growing smaller over the last two or three decades. Hyde (2014) reviewed meta-analyses of mathematics performance and found the size of the gender difference to be close to zero, while results from the 2015 PISA tests show that it varies from one country to another, with boys performing better than girls in 20 countries (and in most of these cases, the difference was small), girls performing better than boys in four countries, and no difference in 48 countries (OECD, 2016). In Australia there was no significant difference in boys' and girls' mathematical literacy scores, while in New Zealand, there was a small difference in favour of boys (ACER, 2016, Ministry of Education New Zealand, 2016). This data, as well as findings from studies comparing testing or experimental conditions, suggests contextual effects on gender differences in mathematics performance.

In regard to language skills, a study by the Organization for Economic Cooperation and Development (OECD) found that girls' average reading literacy scores in 2015 were significantly higher than boys' in all countries (OECD, 2016). In Australia and New Zealand, there were quite large differences, with girls' reading literacy scores equivalent to being approximately one year of schooling ahead of boys' (ACER, 2017). Once again, these differences refer to averages, and there is considerable overlap in the distributions (see Figure 11.6). Boys and girls are more alike than unlike in both reading and mathematics performance, although what contributes to that performance may vary. In Australian students' 2012 PISA results, for example, mathematics performance was predicted by mathematics self-efficacy (for both boys and girls), mathematics self-concept (for girls only) and mathematics anxiety (for boys only) (Thomson, 2014); these might be factors to consider if we are to address performance differences as well as the drops in performance that were observed in the 2012 and 2015 tests.

Other kinds of gender differences at school

Kessels, Heyder, Latsch & Hannover (2014) argued that the small ability differences between boys and girls in reading or mathematics mask larger effects on subject choices, motivation and engagement that may be influenced by gender identity. For example, they argued that mathematics and science being stereotyped as 'male' subjects may lead girls not to engage in these subjects as they don't see them as fitting their gender identity. In support of this theory, in the 2015 PISA tests, Australian boys were more likely than girls to be interested in and enjoy science, and to have self-efficacy in science. They were also four times more likely than girls to expect to work in a science-related field. This is despite no significant difference being found between boys' and girls' science literacy (ACER, 2017).

Similarly, Kessels et al. suggested that some boys may perceive that showing effort and engagement at school is feminine, and so does not fit with their male gender identity. Lam et al. (2016) reported similar gender differences in secondary school engagement in 12 countries in Asia, Europe and North America, with boys consistently showing lower levels of engagement than girls. A study by King (2016) provided a possible means by which this operates, that relates to Kessels and colleagues' theory. Surveying students in the Philippines, King found that boys were more likely to perceive their friends to have negative attitudes towards school, and that this was related to their own level of disaffection with school, which was greater in boys than in girls.

It is important in all of this to remember that such studies report on mean differences, and so do not reflect the broad differences that exist within groups of boys and girls (see Box 11.7).

BOX 11.7 CLASSROOM LINKS

DIFFERENCES WITHIN AND BETWEEN GROUPS OF BOYS AND GIRLS IN A TYPICAL YEAR 9 CLASS

- George is in the advanced English class.
- Jesse struggles with maths, but likes music.
- Sophie does well in maths, is quiet, and finds it hard to express herself.
- Jon loves English and hates maths and science.
- Joann is very sporty.
- Kevin hates sports and would rather read a book.
- Stacey is in the debating team. She wants to be a lawyer.
- Ben is a computer whiz. He likes maths.
- Simon is good at all sports. He finds it hard to sit still and concentrate on purely academic tasks.
- Fred loves sports, but also does well in school.
- Harry can't wait to leave school.
- Lachlan is the class clown. Relating to his friends is the main thing he likes about going to school.
- Kiani is marking time until she finishes school, keeping a low profile so that she doesn't get called on by the teacher.
- Chloe is keen to participate in class discussions, and is often one of the first to put up her hand.
- Jen also likes class discussions, but usually those between herself and her friends.
- Tim avoids any writing activity.

ACTIVITIES

1 Sort these students into those who are typical and atypical of the descriptions of boys and girls in the text.
2 Can you see a pattern in the boys' or girls' abilities, attitudes or behaviours?
3 If this was your class, what could you do to ensure that you were meeting the needs of all boys and girls?

Understanding differences within and between groups

Figure 11.6 shows the differences between two groups. Differences reported between two groups, such as 'girls achieve more highly in literacy than boys', are typically reporting a difference in the mean or average score. Note in Figure 11.6, however, the size of this difference between means (the black arrow) compared with the difference within each group (the blue and red arrows). The overlap in the two curves also represents the large numbers of boys and girls who are alike on a particular measure.

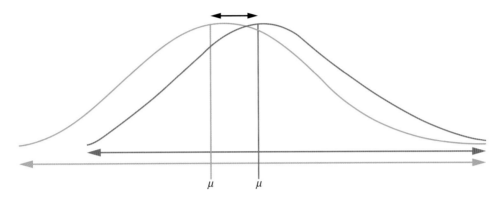

FIGURE 11.6 The difference within each group of boys or girls (the arrows at the base of the diagram) is greater than the difference between the groups' means (the arrow at the top of the diagram). What does this imply for our understanding of individual differences and group differences?

BOX 11.8 CLASSROOM LINKS

PROMOTING BOYS' AND GIRLS' ACHIEVEMENT

Koch (2003) made the following suggestions to ensure inclusive education for boys and girls:

- Use non-sexist, inclusive language.
- Use strategies to ensure you call on male and female students equally.
- Value a range of ways of solving problems and approaching tasks.
- Praise both boys and girls for their achievement (rather than neatness or appearance).
- Coach all students to search for deeper meanings in their answers to questions.
- Use 'wait time' after asking a question, to allow all students a chance to answer.
- Adapt teaching and learning strategies to cater for boys and girls with different preferences, including cooperative learning and technologies.
- Monitor the class to uncover the patterns of dominance in classroom talk. Who is silent and why? Who dominates, and how and why?
- Hold and communicate expectations that both male and female students can accomplish a task or solve a problem.
- Avoid comparisons about the behaviour, achievement and attitudes of boys and girls.
- Encourage emotional expression from boys and girls.
- Ask students whether teachers treat them differently because of their gender.
- Examine the curriculum, texts and other resources you use for bias: Who is included and who is excluded, for example? Does it reflect students' lived experience?
- Examine your practice: Who does it benefit and include, and who does it exclude? (Those girls who struggle using computers? Those boys who struggle with extended writing tasks?)
- Consider how you can best meet the needs of the boys and girls in your classes.

ACTIVITIES

Examine a classroom you are familiar with, using these indicators.

1 What are its strengths and weaknesses as an inclusive classroom?
2 What else could the teacher do?

As well as means, it can be helpful to look at the variability in scores within a particular group. Lippa (2005) reported greater variability in boys' than in girls' scores on measures of mathematical and visual–spatial ability and aggression. As the mean for boys on these measures is higher than that for girls, it suggests (supported by other data) that there are groups of boys who are very aggressive, boys who are very good at maths and boys with very advanced visual–spatial abilities, but that there are corresponding groups of boys who are not at all aggressive, who struggle with mathematics and who have poor visual–spatial abilities. Group generalisations are just that, and we should be aware of individual differences within groups of boys or girls. Box 11.7 shows another way of thinking about individual and group differences.

Box 11.8 gives some strategies for teachers that effectively address the needs of boys and girls.

Effective teaching considers all students, and is flexible so as to cater to students' differing needs. This applies to gender differences as much as to cultural differences. Box 11.9 gives some suggestions for inclusive teaching practices that are relevant to the gender issues discussed in this section.

BOX 11.9 IMPLICATIONS FOR EDUCATORS

GENDER IN THE CLASSROOM

From the findings reviewed in this chapter, it appears that boys and girls can experience gender-related advantages and disadvantages at school. Effective programs consider the needs of boys as well as girls, rather than targeting one group (see **Box 11.8**).

Particular groups of boys and girls appear to be especially vulnerable to gender-based effects; for example, boys in special-education programs, girls who leave school seeking employment, and boys and girls in lower socioeconomic groups. The needs of each of these groups are different from the needs of boys and girls overall.

One key to avoiding gender bias appears to be variety; that is, ensuring that students are offered a mixture of cooperative and competitive approaches to learning, in individual and group work, and a choice of assessment modes and study topics.

Participation is a second component of effective, inclusive teaching, ensuring that all students have a chance to participate in all activities. This may involve structuring activities to ensure that all students have chances to try – and succeed – in a range of tasks.

Being aware of possible gender bias in your teaching and resources can help you limit it by taking active steps to be even-handed in your treatment of boys and girls. Try videoing your class and observing your interactions for gender bias.

SOCIOECONOMIC STATUS (SES)

socioeconomic status (SES)
A measure of social and economic position in society; typically a combination of education, occupation and income

Our education systems in Australia and New Zealand are based on equality of access for all, but there are differences in the educational outcomes of people from different social classes in Australia and New Zealand. The OECD reports a general association between **socioeconomic status (SES)** and educational outcomes in many, but not all OECD countries. Australia and New Zealand are among the countries that show this inequity, with a stronger effect of SES on achievement in both Australia and New Zealand than the OECD average, although this has improved over time (Ministry of Education, 2016). In Australia, the difference between the scores of advantaged and disadvantaged students is equivalent to approximately three years of schooling, and appears at all age levels from the early years through to post school (Lamb, Jackson, Walstab & Huo, 2015). A New Zealand Education Review Office (ERO) report identified a number of schools with lower SES families whose students achieve strong outcomes (ERO, 2014a); refer to Box 11.10 for a summary of the common features of these schools.

An inquiry into schooling in New South Wales (NSW) concerning the outcomes associated with low SES when compared with high SES (Vinson, 2002) found:

- lower levels of literacy, numeracy and comprehension
- lower retention rates
- lower participation rates at university
- higher levels of problematic school behaviour (for example, truancy)
- less likelihood of studying specialised maths and science subjects
- greater likelihood of having difficulties with studies and displaying negative attitudes to school
- less successful school-to-labour market transitions.

In addressing why these differences occur, and what might be done to even them out, a number of explanations have been proposed relating to the nature of the home background, the nature of the school, relationships between home and school, and sociocultural factors. We now explore each of these sets of factors, bearing in mind that it is the *interaction* of these factors that produces the outcomes that are reported in research.

THINK ABOUT

- Think of someone you know who is worse off than you.
- What has contributed to the difference?
- How have your different circumstances affected your opportunities and your attitudes?

SOCIAL CLASS AND SES

Social class is often discussed as consisting of three categories: upper class, middle class and working (or lower) class. It is typically identified by individuals' rating of their own social position on a scale. A related term is socioeconomic status – typically a combined measure of parents' education, occupation and income, though each of these factors contributes separately to children's outcomes (Duncan, Magnuson & Votruba-Drzal, 2015). This recognises that there are economic, social and educational factors affecting parenting, and that parents' situations affect children's outcomes.

Socioeconomic status is not a magical factor that determines educational outcomes any more than do the other factors discussed in this chapter. Differences in achievement are positively correlated with SES because of particular environmental and social factors, experiences, behaviours and beliefs enacted as a result of a family's social and economic situation. Many members of the same social class may share these beliefs and behaviours, but others will not. (Think of your neighbours: they are likely to share your SES, but how many differences can you think of in your belief systems, your experiences, or in the ways you live?) It is important also to note that SES is flexible, not static, and families may move in and out of particular SES groups, and in and out of typical patterns of behaviour and experience associated with their SES.

It is also not inevitable that having low SES will result in poor outcomes. Schools can make a difference. A meta-analysis of studies examining effects of interventions on the reading and mathematics achievement of low SES students identified tutoring, 'feedback and progress monitoring' (providing teachers with feedback about their students' progress) and cooperative learning as interventions that had significant effects (Dietrichson, Bøg, Filges & Jørgensen, 2017). The Comparative Education Research Unit (2004) of the New Zealand Ministry of Education examined data from a large international study of students' achievement to identify those factors that were associated with high achievement in students from low SES backgrounds. They found that there was greater difference among students within each category than between categories. (Do you recognise this pattern from our discussion of gender?) When compared with low achievers, high achievers:

- reported spending more time on homework
- showed more interest and engagement with reading
- indicated strength in competitive and cooperative learning strategies, with more strength in competitive strategies
- were more confident in their own abilities
- reported more availability of educational resources in the home, such as a dictionary, a quiet place to study, a desk for study, textbooks and more calculators
- reported better teacher–student relations (Comparative Education Research Unit, 2004).

Typically, reports of the relationship between SES and education focus on those who are in the lowest groups: those in poverty. Some of the explanations regarding the relationship between poverty and educational outcomes are particular to poverty: poor nutrition or multiple stressors, for example, might be experienced in poor families but are less likely to explain why those in the highest SES bracket do better than those in a middle bracket. Although SES is defined by the three factors of parents' occupation, education and income, poverty tends to be defined by the relationship of income to need, and so focuses on the third indicator (Duncan, Magnuson & Votruba-Drzal, 2015).

It is helpful, however, to understand how poverty affects education, particularly given the numbers of Australians and New Zealanders who are affected by it. Some more-general models of the relationship between SES and education, considering societal and school factors, are discussed later in the chapter.

POVERTY AND EDUCATION

The extent of childhood poverty in Australia and New Zealand is increasing. The Brotherhood of St Laurence reported in 2005 that more than one in 10 Australian children lived in relative poverty – that is, their family had less than 50 per cent of the median income (Scutella & Smyth, 2005) – while the Australian Council of Social Service reported in 2016 (drawing on ABS data) that that figure had risen to 17.4 per cent by 2014. The proportion in New Zealand is even greater, with a figure as high as 27 per cent estimated in the annual child poverty monitor report to the children's commissioner (Duncanson et al., 2017). Particular groups are disproportionately affected, with Aboriginal children in Australia, and Māori and Pasifika children in New Zealand more likely to live in poverty than other ethnic groups (ACOSS, 2016; Duncanson et al., 2017). Poverty is associated with a number of health, cognitive and socioemotional outcomes for children, each of which can affect educational outcomes.

Health factors

In Chapter 2, we saw that children's development can be affected by environmental factors. Poor nutrition, inadequate access to health care and exposure to particular environmental hazards, such as high lead levels, can all have an impact on education, both directly and indirectly. Very poor nutrition affects brain growth, physical growth and protection against disease; and cognitive functions such as long-term memory. Inadequate nutrition can also result in lethargy, which affects motivation. Environmental hazards may include overcrowded, substandard housing and poor air quality. This may result in school absence due to illness, and in a lowering of cognitive functioning (Evans, 2006). Lack of access to health care is an important factor in the high rates of otitis media and associated deafness in Australian Aboriginal children. Similarly, in New Zealand, hearing-loss problems in Māori children are detected later than those in Anglo children, and Māori children have higher rates of hospitalisation for asthma.

Parenting factors

As we saw in Module I, parents are important agents in children's development. Studies of poverty and education reveal links between poverty, low levels of parental education and lower levels of school achievement in children (Bradley & Corwyn, 2002; McLaughlin, Gilfillan & Gordon, 2013; Raffo et al., 2010). Parental education appears to be a strong predictor of student performance.

One explanation of the importance of parents' education is its effect on what parents do with their children at home, and the ways in which they interact with them. Other factors also contribute to parenting practices, such as working arrangements. Box 11.10 describes a research project that compared family life across class groups. The New Zealand reports *Competent children at 12* (Wylie, 2004) and *Competent children at 16* (Wylie & Hogden, 2007) paint a similar picture. Children whose parents (particularly mothers) had higher qualifications tended to have family resources that supported engagement in school, reading comprehension, and mathematics reasoning and understanding skills. These family resources included activities that extend knowledge and communication, as well as analytical skills, parental interest in education, use and enjoyment of reading, and support for children to be assertive. Language experience and use in these homes was linked to development and support of reading and mathematics skills over many years. Wylie suggested that these children were then able to make the most of what school had to offer. Children whose mothers had fewer qualifications did fewer of those activities that contributed to high achievement, and watched more television.

FIGURE 11.7 Childhood experiences help to develop particular selves in children that fit their context. Consider how your experience of childhood has shaped the kinds of choices you make, and the ways it has equipped you to thrive in your context.

Researchers Hart and Risley (1995) illustrated the relationship between SES and parenting behaviour in language when they found that parents from the poorest families in their study used only one-third of the spoken language that other parents in the study used when talking to their children – meaning that the children in the poorest families had more limited parental input when learning language. Parental input is important in children's language development, which is related to cognitive development. Language is also very important to learning and displaying knowledge at school.

Providing cognitively stimulating experiences such as trips to museums, libraries, concerts and the zoo, and learning experiences such as specialist classes in gymnastics or music, is financially within the reach of some parents but not others. Bradley and Corwyn (1999) reported that such experiences provide learning opportunities and motivation for continued learning, while their lack can limit cognitive growth and reduce children's ability to benefit from school.

Parents' experiences of education influence how they interact with their children, their ability to prepare their children for school, and their expectations of and how they view schooling. Polidano, Hanel and Buddelmeyer (2012) found that the educational aspirations of 15-year-olds and their parents were the strongest factor explaining socioeconomic differences in school completion in Australia. If parents' aspirations for their children are low, students are unlikely to extend their participation beyond compulsory schooling, as they are unlikely to perceive this as resulting in any benefit. Parents'

BOX 11.10 RESEARCH LINKS

HOW SCHOOLS WORK WITH SOCIAL CLASS TO SHAPE CULTURE AND SELF

Stephens, Markus and Phillips (2014) described how social class works through much more than access to income and resources to determine life outcomes, also shaping the kinds of selves that people develop, and the behavioural choices they make. They suggested that in different social class contexts, particular 'selves' develop in response to opportunities and constraints, and that these are formed in the key settings of home, school and work. Far from being fixed, they are constantly responding to the varying contexts in which individuals participate, which suggests possibilities to intervene and alter both the cultures and their usefulness in schools. Consistent with modern views of culture (and with Bronfenbrenner's model with which we started this chapter), individuals are not only influenced by, but themselves influence these cultures, which are constantly changing.

Stephens and colleagues drew on a range of research to identify an 'expressive independent' self that developed in response to middle-class contexts, and a 'hard interdependent' self which developed in response to working-class contexts (see Figure 11.8). The expressive independent self involves personal choice, self-expression, power and influence. It suits middle-class contexts, which tend to be relatively safe, predictable and secure, and middle-class jobs, which tend to require independence, decision making, negotiation and creative thinking. The hard interdependent self is described as 'socially responsive and self-protective' (p. 615). It involves considering and responding to others, and sticking up for the self, as well as toughness and resilience. It prepares children for working-class contexts that are characterised by greater constraints, relative instability, unpredictability and risk, and for working-class jobs that tend to require people to follow directions, work in cooperation with others and enforce rules.

Stephens, Markus and Phillips described the cultural selves as socialised in families, schools and workplaces. In families, parents socialise children towards particular selves relating to their class culture, through storytelling, activities and communication styles. In schools, teachers socialise working-class children towards working-class jobs in working-class schools, and middle-class children towards middle-class jobs in middle-class schools. This tends to reproduce the social structure.

At the same time, middle-class selves are institutionalised as 'the best way' in schools and in workplaces – what is needed to succeed in higher education, for example, or in higher-paying jobs. Without realising this, teachers may not recognise that students with working-class selves need help, as they are less likely to ask for it; and they may not identify them as 'good students' as they don't fit the expressive independent style. Difficulties come for working-class students in middle-class schools when they feel that their hard interdependent selves do not fit the school, and that school is 'not for them'. Stephens, Markus and Phillips report that working-class children experience more stress at school, and there is a link between SES and academic performance in the USA (as well as in Australia and New Zealand). Working-class children who grow up in working-class schools may also have restricted avenues available for work.

Stephens, Markus and Phillips argue that this need not necessarily be the way things work. To change it, teachers need to be aware of the class cultures children from different social classes bring to school (and of their own class culture), so that they can support these children, just as is suggested for children from other cultures. They suggest that teachers could support working-class students in middle-class schools by making expectations explicit, and by valuing the hard interdependence that they bring, enabling them to be bicultural, and to draw on multiple skill sets for the varying demands of different contexts.

>>

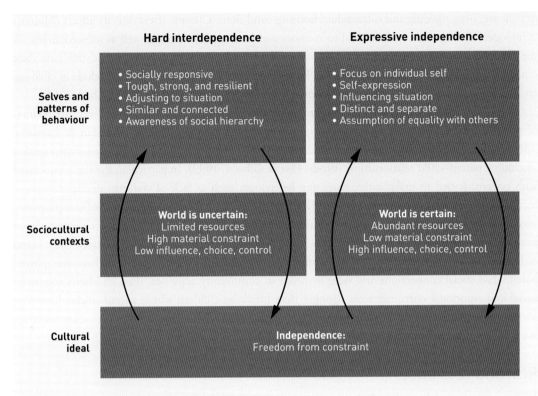

Source: Stephens, N.M., Markus, H.R. & Phillips, L.T. (2014) Social class culture cycles: how three gateway contexts shape selves and fuel inequality. *Annual Review of Psychology*, 65, 611–634. Copyright © 2014 by Annual Reviews. Used with permission.

FIGURE 11.8 US social class culture cycles

ACTIVITIES

1 Stephens, Markus and Phillips' theory is based on the USA. Do you think similar patterns would be found in working-class and middle-class families and schools in Australia or New Zealand? How might they differ?

2 Note as described earlier that SES groupings are not fixed but flexible, and families move in and out of them. Describe how this would influence the situation described by Stephens and colleagues.

3 What activities in school could draw on the strengths of the hard interdependent selves described here? What benefits might they bring for all children?

educational experiences may also affect their view of school itself. Is it seen as a place where their child will be extended and nurtured, or where their child will be misunderstood and mistreated? Most parents value schooling as important, but their experiences influence how effectively they express this value to their children.

Stress factors

One of the major models of the relationship between poverty and education involves the impact of stress on families and children (Boston & Chapple, 2014; Bradley & Corwyn, 2002). Consider some of the likely sources of stress that people living in poverty could encounter: employment uncertainty, lack of financial security, having to move house often, and living in neighbourhoods with high levels of violence, overcrowding and substandard housing conditions. Chronic stress directly affects children's neurological development, and can lead to memory and learning difficulties, as well as reduced ability for the person to cope with stress later in life. However, not all children who experience chronic stress have these outcomes. Sensitive, responsive caregiving can buffer the negative effects, and this may include in childcare and education settings outside the home (National Scientific Council on the Developing Child, 2014).

Stress, uncertainty and low social standing have also been correlated with low self-esteem, feelings of powerlessness and learned helplessness, as well as depression (McLaughlin, Sheridan & Lambert, 2014; McLoyd, 1990). These attitudes, in turn, are linked to poorer-than-average relationship quality (including parent–child relationships) (Brody, Flor & Gibson, 1999). In particular, the stress associated with poverty is tied to maladaptive parenting behaviours such as lack of warmth, unresponsiveness, inconsistency or lack of appropriate control (Raffo et al., 2010). More consistent and positive parenting was linked to better cognitive and social-emotional outcomes in families in which parents were employed as compared with jobless families, in the Longitudinal Study of Australian Children (Baxter, Gray, Hand & Hayes, 2012). The negative results of unemployment are not inevitable, however. When unemployed parents had social connections and were involved in community activities, their children's cognitive, social and emotional outcomes were stronger than for those children whose parents didn't have that social capital. Raffo et al. (2010) also reinforced the value of supportive networks in providing resilience for families and children living in poverty.

Risk and resilience

In interpreting models of the relationship between poverty and educational outcomes, we need to be careful not to generalise negative outcomes to all families in poverty. The notion of risk and resilience was introduced in Chapter 2. The factors just outlined (from the heading 'Poverty and education' onwards) constitute **risk factors** – or factors associated with negative outcomes – that exist for children and families in poverty. They do not inevitably lead to poor outcomes. As we saw with stress factors, there are also factors that engender resilience to such risks, which helps some families and children overcome difficulties such as those described earlier. What provides an individual or a family with resilience can change over time, and exists in balance with risk factors, which can also vary over time.

Garmezy (1993) identified three groups of factors that provide resilience for children at risk through poverty. These align with the individual, family and community factors that were discussed in Chapter 2:

1 *Personality characteristics*. Examples include self-esteem, belief in personal control, mastery motivation (the belief that difficulties can be overcome and that effort leads to success) and persistence, as well as humour, adaptive coping strategies and optimism (for example, remaining optimistic in the face of poverty can make it less likely that negative parenting will result) (Brody et al., 1994).

2 *Family characteristics*. These include cohesion, shared values, patience and the presence of supportive adults. The considerable success of some refugee groups despite their living in poverty has been attributed to such characteristics (Caplan, Whitmore & Choy, 1989).

3 *Availability of external support systems*. Having support from others outside the family can mitigate the effects of poverty by providing access to resources beyond the means of the family, by reducing some causes and consequences of stress, and by providing help to cope with stress as it occurs.

risk factor
A factor associated with negative outcomes

THINK ABOUT

■ How could schools contribute to resilience factors in students considered as being 'at risk'?

Bronfenbrenner's theory at work

You may recall from the start of the chapter that Bronfenbrenner proposed that development occurs through the interaction of characteristics of person, process, context and time. We have seen in this section that the characteristics of the individual child and their environments may help particular children to be resilient to risk factors of poverty, and cause others to have heightened sensitivity to these risks. Poverty potentially influences parenting through the stresses that may arise from the neighbourhood (the mesosystem) and workplace (the exosystem). These in their turn affect the processes the child encounters at home and at school (microsystems), and ultimately shape their development. As the child develops over time, particular factors have greater or lesser impact, with the effect of increases in income, for example, showing a strong impact in early childhood and a lesser impact in adolescence (Duncan, Magnuson & Votruba-Drzal, 2015). The cultures in which the child and family exist (the macrosystem) play a role in influencing both beliefs and behaviours, guiding responses to events and processes encountered by the child at home and at school, as we saw in Box 11.10. Hence simple correlations between socioeconomic status and academic achievement such as are seen in Australia and New Zealand need to be interpreted as outcomes of complex interactions between these various systems, rather than as one thing (SES) influencing the other (academic achievement). This also implies that there are multiple points at which educational disadvantage can be addressed. The OECD (2016a) suggested school-, family- and community-based strategies as well as strategies to support individual students as ways of addressing low performance, for example. In the following section, we focus in on school factors that can influence children's educational outcomes.

SCHOOL FACTORS

Just as children's school outcomes do not arise simply from individual characteristics but also reflect family and environmental factors, so too there are factors in the school and wider society that contribute to these outcomes.

In light of the research reviewed in this chapter, it might be tempting to attribute the lower achievement of children from low SES groups to home background, and even to form lower expectations of those children than of others. But schools also contribute to unequal educational outcomes in important ways, and can also contribute to resilience, as Box 11.11 indicates.

Amount of schooling is related to income, health, cognitive and social outcomes (Vinson, 2007). Children in Australia from disadvantaged groups are less likely to attend preschool than are those of higher SES (Maguire & Hayes, 2014). A review of access to early childhood education in Australia, undertaken by the Australian Institute of Family Studies, found that children from disadvantaged families were indeed more likely to miss out on early childhood education, particularly Indigenous children and those with language backgrounds other than English (Baxter & Hand, 2013). In New Zealand, participation rates are higher overall, but still lower for Māori and Pasifika groups (New Zealand Ministry of Education, 2011a). Worldwide, *quality* preschool experience has been linked to social and academic skills, and better school outcomes (for example, Berlinski, Galiani & Manacorda, 2008; Burchinal et al., 2008).

As well as years of schooling, quality of school experience counts. There are a number of factors based in the school and in its interactions with the family that explain differences in educational outcomes across the broad spectrum of SES groups. Of course, we should recognise that individual schools sit within a society, and that broader forces are also at work. Our focus here, however, is on the difference that individual teachers and schools can make.

CourseMateExpress

Online Resources
Go further: explore how community, family and individual factors interact, contributing to risk and resilience with 'The Resilience Game' - link on this text's website.

Teacher expectations

McLoyd (1998) suggested that teachers tend to perceive the academic ability and behaviour of students from lower socioeconomic backgrounds more negatively than that of students from higher socioeconomic backgrounds. Poor children are likely to receive less positive attention and less reinforcement for academic achievement, which is perhaps in line with teachers' lower expectations of these students.

Home and school difference

Some ways in which a given school may contribute to educational disadvantage are linked to the relationship between school and community. Related to this is the 'closeness of fit' between home and school practices. Although some policymakers have seen this as a problem of the home, others look to the school to accommodate student differences, whether these differences originate from ethnicity, gender, social class or individual characteristics.

Following are some of the key ways in which home and school can interact to contribute to educational disadvantage. You may recognise some recurring themes that run through this chapter. Sources of individual difference are important issues for educators because of the need to consider how these differences impact on, and are impacted by, education. Schools can perpetuate but also act to prevent these outcomes of difference from occurring. In this chapter, you will find a number of examples of schools that have worked effectively with their communities, rather than in opposition to them.

- *Schools advantage children whose home experiences fit the school 'style'* (Comber et al., 2005). Because schools (like the teachers who work within them) tend to be Anglo, middle-class institutions, they tend to favour students who come from such backgrounds. One important example involves the use of language. Language, and particularly decontextualised language (that is, language that discusses something not present in the current context), is central to the work of schools. Studies of the language patterns of different social groups show that the way language is used in schools tends to mirror the language patterns of the middle class (Heath, 1983).
- *Establishing or maintaining a home–school divide.* The values and practices of the school and home may differ. Schools that ignore this difference or denigrate the home values set up a divide between home and school. Eckermann (1994) suggested teaching about differences explicitly, and helping students to judge when one set of values or behaviours applies and when another would be more useful.
- *Differing communication styles of home and school.* Although the language spoken at home and at school superficially may be the same, differences in communication styles used at home and at school can lead to misunderstandings and conflict.
- *Perceptions of and about minority groups.* As described earlier in this chapter, minority groups may see schools as the 'opposition': something to be distrusted at best, and resisted at worst. This is related to societal forces beyond the school, but may be exacerbated by particular practices that reject the minority students' beliefs and behaviours. Negative perceptions may be minimised by involving the community in the school, and the school in the community.

THINK ABOUT

- Can you think of other ways in which differences between home and school could influence students' educational outcomes?

Box 11.11 summarises the findings of a New Zealand report of the practices of schools that achieve high academic outcomes for students from low-SES families.

BOX 11.11 RESEARCH LINKS

TOWARDS EQUITABLE OUTCOMES IN SECONDARY SCHOOLS: GOOD PRACTICE

New Zealand's ERO identified seven schools that enrolled significant numbers of children from families of low SES (decile 1–5 schools), which nonetheless achieved outcomes in attendance and academic achievement that were better than those of similar schools. While the schools were different in many ways, they had the following features in common, which were identified as good practice for achieving success for and engaging every student in the school.

School culture

Schools focused on the students' wellbeing and on building deeply caring relationships.

■ A 'can do' attitude pervaded the schools – schools believed that all students can succeed and that teachers can find ways to help that happen.

■ *Whānau*, parents and community were involved in their teenagers' learning.

■ Responses to problems were solution-focused and restorative practices were used.

Students

■ Students were confident young adults, helped to take responsibility for themselves and their learning.

■ Students were active members of their school community.

Learning

■ Carefully selected and adapted professional learning advanced the schools' strategic plans.

■ School leaders and teachers used extensive, high-quality data to identify students' needs and respond appropriately.

■ Community links extended opportunities for students' learning.

Leadership

■ Senior leaders worked extremely efficiently as a team with high levels of relational trust.

Source: ERO (2014b). 'National reports 2014', published by New Zealand Education Review Office, © 2014.

ACTIVITIES

1   Explore some of the school case studies presented in the ERO report to see how these things worked in practice.

2   Link these practices to the principles presented in this chapter. To what extent do they align? What other principles are represented here? Why would they be important?

THREATENING ENVIRONMENTS

Residents in Australia and New Zealand experience natural disasters such as fires, floods, cyclones and earthquakes on a fairly regular basis, either personally or through media coverage. In addition, refugees may have experienced war or terror before coming to Australia or New Zealand, and further trauma in detention centres. How do these experiences affect children and young people, and how can we support them?

Children may be affected directly as a result of physical dangers, stress, disruption of routine and loss of home, school and community, and indirectly through impacts of parenting quality, economic factors, and 'reading' of parental anxiety in social referencing (Masten & Narayan, 2012). With multiple experiences of trauma, effects increase. Media can contribute to trauma as well, with children re-exposed to the situations they encountered, or exposed to continuing threats. Young children have difficulty realising that repeated broadcasts of an event are not new threats (Masten, Narayan, Silverman & Osofsky, 2015). As we saw in Chapter 2, experience of chronic stress can have long-term effects through children's brain development, on response to stress later in life, on their physical health including the immune system, and on mental health and self-regulation of thoughts and behaviour. Externalising behaviours such as aggression may be seen, particularly if there is aggression in the community, school or family (Boxer et al., 2013).

Children and young people are variously affected, with younger children protected in part by lack of understanding, but vulnerable in not possessing the cognitive and emotional skills to manage emotions and thoughts. Older children and young people are more vulnerable to anxiety through their greater understanding of what is happening, and their ability to imagine further effects, while protected by greater skills in cognitive and emotional regulation.

In a review of the literature, Masten and Narayan (2012) identified the following protective factors. They are proposed to support a sense of safety and connectedness, control and agency, regulation of emotion and behaviour, and optimistic thinking, all of which help individuals to adapt in responding to threats.

■ *Psychological factors.* Intelligence, self-regulation, cognitive flexibility, self-efficacy and a sense of self-confidence are all identified as protective. Teaching these skills as part of disaster readiness might therefore be helpful. Religious beliefs and practices are also helpful in conveying hope, belief and a sense of meaning.

■ *Relationships.* Close and supportive relationships are paramount, particularly attachment relationships with parents. Being close to parents during a terrifying experience is particularly important. Reuniting children with families is thus important when disasters come.

■ *Acculturation.* For refugee children, development of language skills in the new country and a positive bicultural identity were both associated with recovery from traumatic experiences.

■ *Environments in which to play and learn.* Having functional schools or childcare settings, and safe places in which to play are among the keys to restoring normalcy and providing constructive activities, connections to competent adults, peer interaction, respite for parents and a re-establishment of routines.

When a disaster occurs, the following principles of intervention are agreed in the research to be of benefit in promoting resilience: promote a sense of safety, self- and group efficacy, calming, connectedness and hope. Although the care of parents is the key to this, adults such as teachers or childcare providers also have important roles to play in the context of disaster. Masten et al. (2015) reported that for refugee children, the quality of the environment in which children recover from trauma (remembering that environments include families and schools as well as wider communities and societies) is key to the ways that risk and resilience factors operate. The work on risk and resilience discussed in Chapter 2, and earlier in this chapter, is also relevant here.

INCLUSIVE EDUCATION FOR ABORIGINAL AND TORRES STRAIT ISLANDER STUDENTS IN AUSTRALIA, AND MĀORI STUDENTS IN NEW ZEALAND

In this section we focus on two particular groups in Australia and New Zealand, to examine how a number of sociocultural factors work together to influence educational outcomes. Aboriginal and Torres Strait Islander students in Australia, and Māori students in New Zealand are in quite different educational contexts, yet some of the processes they experience, and strategies that have been employed to improve outcomes have commonalities. A focus on students in these groups who have experienced success can both remind us of the variation within groups, and help to identify strategies that can be used in schools to support educational success for all students.

ABORIGINAL AUSTRALIANS AND TORRES STRAIT ISLANDERS: DIVERSITY AND COMMONALITY

Aboriginal people and Torres Strait Islanders are not a homogeneous group. Important differences exist among different peoples and language groups, and among Aboriginal people living in urban, rural and remote locations. Kooris living in inner-city Sydney are no less Aboriginal than Yolngu people living in 'traditional' communities in the Northern Territory, notwithstanding large differences in lifestyle, language and beliefs. In addition, different individuals and communities may have differing experiences of education; for example, Aboriginal people living in remote areas generally have poorer educational outcomes than those living in urban areas. Each State or Territory in Australia has its own education practices and policies regarding Indigenous Australians. For example, the schools in the Torres Strait employ Indigenous teachers and principals in much higher proportions than is the case in many other areas of Australia.

Such diversity in practices and policies across Australia is broadened by individuals or groups moving between States. It is also complicated by individuals moving between urban and rural, and between 'traditional' and 'non-traditional' locations. In one school there may be students from a number of different groups; individuals within any group, too, differ in aspirations, attitudes and values. There are also differences in the aspirations of different communities and their goals for education. Although the majority of Aboriginal and Torres Strait Islander Australians place a high priority on education (DEET, 1989), what they seek from that education may differ. Skills in English literacy and numeracy are important to many, as is maintaining Indigenous culture and language, but the relative importance of these two goals is different for different communities.

Families living in remote communities may place less importance on learning 'White' skills and greater emphasis on the teaching of their own culture. Others might not entrust the teaching of their culture and language to the school, preferring to maintain that function within the community. For still other groups, learning the skills of literacy and numeracy is seen as an essential outcome of schooling, and such groups are concerned that this process might be compromised if too much emphasis is placed on the learning of culture (Nakata, 1995). Once again, listening to the concerns and needs of a particular community is important in ensuring a match between community and school goals.

Notwithstanding the diversity among Aboriginal people and Torres Strait Islanders, there are commonalities among the different peoples in terms of values, ways of relating, and ways of using language (Bourke, Rigby & Burden, 2000). The sociohistorical background of some groups of Indigenous students also has commonalities in terms of status in society and exposure to institutional racism, and the related issues of school attendance, participation and achievement.

WHAT MAKES THE DIFFERENCE TO ABORIGINAL AND TORRES STRAIT ISLANDER STUDENTS' SUCCESS IN SCHOOL?

Many Aboriginal and Torres Strait Islander students do well at school. However, there remain many students who do not succeed (ACARA, 2017). What makes the difference, and how can schools ensure that all students have an opportunity to succeed in school? In a number of reports of successful practice, some common themes emerge.

The National Numeracy Review (Commonwealth of Australia, 2008) identified features of programs that led to improvements in the outcomes of Aboriginal and Torres Strait Islander students. Many of these features are important for other learners as well. The features are:

- valuing by teachers and school communities of the culture, language, skills and strengths that Indigenous students bring to the classroom
- considering cultural ways of learning, both to include students' ways of learning and to teach school ways of learning
- culturally and contextually aligned learning programs, resting on strong community partnerships
- recognising and valuing different pathways to learning
- use of Indigenous educators to help students to bridge school–home differences
- using relevant and meaningful contexts for learning, so that learning can be situated in students' lives
- involvement of first-language speakers in the classroom to help students to think about mathematics in their mother tongue, through scaffolding and elaboration
- high expectations of students and their learning
- stable staffing – linked to the importance of strong relationships teachers build with teachers
- use of strategies to cater for difficulties that affect learning, such as hearing loss, absenteeism and homework not being completed.

A study by DEST (Commonwealth of Australia, 2005) of programs that have been successful in increasing and maintaining the attendance of Aboriginal and Torres Strait Islander students identified the following features of successful programs: developing strong relationships between schools and their Indigenous communities; creating curricula that are practical and relevant to students, and explicitly valuing Indigenous cultures; improving access to schooling; using Indigenous staff to liaise between home and school, and to give students a sense of belonging; helping with transitions from home to school and from school to work; increasing parent involvement in schools; and transporting students to school or preschool. The CourseMate website contains further examples of successful programs for Indigenous students.

In these reports, we can identify the common elements of building partnerships between schools and communities, considering the particular learning strengths and needs of students, the importance of relationships between students and teachers, and support for language, which are all interrelated. These elements are discussed below.

Celebrating skills and strengths

Valuing students' skills and strengths, and the knowledge they bring with them to school, is an important element in engaging them in school learning. Many Indigenous students may be skilled in a number of areas – including spatial, observational and kinaesthetic domains, among others – but as for all students, the presence and depth of skills depend on a student's early experiences. Sarra (2011) described Aboriginal Australians as having ideas of pride, respect, strong sense of family, and multiple ways of connecting to people, Country (the land and sea), and spirituality as well as to knowledge in their identity, and argued that teachers can usefully adopt these approaches with their students. The National Numeracy Review (Commonwealth of Australia, 2008) described the successful highlighting of the strengths of Aboriginal and Torres Strait Islander students in the visualisation of three-dimensional space and subitising (recognising numbers without counting, such as in recognising the pattern of dots on dice as representing particular numbers) to publicly value students and create positive learning environments.

Holding high expectations of students is an important contributor to achievement (Hattie, 2009). The Stronger Smarter Institute (2014) argued that high expectations need to be, not just held, but acted out in educational relationships. This includes relationships with other teachers as well as community, families and students, in which any 'deficit discourse' – ideas that Indigenous students are somehow lacking, unable to achieve at the level of other students, or to blame for low outcomes – should be challenged. This does not mean ignoring difficulties, with 'firm and fair' dialogue described in the Stronger Smarter approach, that also calls for teachers to unpack and become aware of their unspoken assumptions, to engage in challenging conversations, and to create spaces for dialogue. With this framework of trust as a background, it is argued that students can feel confident to be both strong in their culture, and smart in learning, disrupting any 'resistance' beliefs that may have arisen.

Drawing on Aboriginal ways of learning

Numerous authors have described the world views of various Indigenous groups in Australia (for example Harris, 1990; Martin, 2009), and have sought to link these to learning preferences. Others have cautioned against assuming that all Aboriginal people have the same learning style, pointing out that there will be differences in individuals' preferences, as well as across different groups (Groome, 1995). To the extent that they are characteristic of particular cultural groups, ways of learning develop from family and community processes. As these processes vary from one community to another, and from one family to another, and as they intersect with individuals' interests and personalities, so too will individuals' ways of thinking about the world, as well as organising and learning about it.

Partington (2003) pointed out that student learning and retention of knowledge and skills is more likely to be achieved by adapting teaching strategies to the needs of students than by trying to change students' culture and social backgrounds. Box 11.12 gives an example of how one region of NSW has done this, describing pedagogy that fits local ways of knowing and doing. The student companion website contains a description of another Aboriginal pedagogy developed at the Batchelor Institute of Indigenous Tertiary Education in the Northern Territory.

Independence

The child-rearing style of many Australian Aboriginal and Torres Strait Islander communities affords children greater independence and responsibility than that which typically results from Western child-rearing practices. Lohoar, Butera & Kennedy (2014) report that this develops important life skills such as assessing risk, caring for and protecting one another. This means that Aboriginal or Torres Strait Islander students may respond better to adult-education models than to the usual model used in schools, which sees students as dependent on and (in terms of role) subordinate to the teacher.

Source: © Newspix/News Ltd/Tim Carrafa.

FIGURE 11.9 Aboriginal and Torres Strait Islander children in some communities are given greater independence and responsibility than is typically seen with children from other Australian groups.

BOX 11.12 CLASSROOM LINKS

8WAYS

In Western NSW, a research project involving Department of Education and Training staff, James Cook University's School of Indigenous Studies and the Western New South Wales Regional Aboriginal Education Team between 2007 and 2009 developed into an Aboriginal pedagogical model that has been adopted by schools in the region and beyond. They built a wikispace on which the model continued to evolve through ongoing dialogue. The aim is for local Aboriginal values, systems, protocols and processes to be identified by dialogue with the community, and then integrated into mainstream schooling through the pedagogy as it applies to each community. From the wikispace:

> Every place, every People, has its own unique pedagogies. These 8 simple ones are merely a starting point for dialogue. Each school engages in a different way, and produces its own unique frameworks for Aboriginal education through dialogue with the community about local ways of doing things.
>
> Source: http://8ways.wikispaces.com

ACTIVITIES

1   Explore the 8 ways pedagogy through links online. How has it been applied in different contexts?
2   See also Yunkaporta and Kirby (2011) for a discussion of the model by some of those involved in its development.

This independence may also mean that parents take a different role and approach in terms of encouraging children to attend school. For example, they may be reluctant to compel children to attend. Sims, O'Connor and Forrest (2003) suggest that teachers build on the child-caring role often taken by older children by involving these students in peer mentoring.

Interdependence

Lohoar, Butera and Kennedy (2014) identified a number of characteristics of traditional Aboriginal and Torres Strait Islander culture that are protective of children's development, and recommended that these strengths could be drawn on by those working with these communities. In particular, interdependence and community involvement in childrearing are features of the Aboriginal kinship system that could be acknowledged and built on by schools. Western notions of family as parents and their children neglect these wider relationships that contribute to the development and care of Aboriginal children in traditional culture, and in many groups today. Through community ties, Lohoar et al. reported that children are kept safe and receive support, and parents receive support for parenting in practical, social and psychological ways. One parent they interviewed summarised this:

> 'My parents died young, so, I became my brother's mum and dad and I also brought up my own kids as well, but I didn't do that myself, I had my godparents, I had my Uncles and Aunties, so everything I did with them, it was screened before I could even set it out to them. It meant that if anything happened within the families, my Uncle would talk to this Auntie and say, this one needs some help. This person here would be best to talk to them, you know, there's certain people that would know who was best to talk to them and that word would go out. This is just what happened to my family to this day. (Parent, Qld)'

> Source: Lohoar et al. 2014. Strengths of Australian Aboriginal cultural practices in family life and child rearing, CFCA Paper No. 25, p. 5

Cultures that emphasise relationships over tasks (Harris, 1990) lend themselves to collaborative and cooperative learning models (see Chapters 6 and 7 for examples of these approaches). Group work may be favoured over independent tasks, and cooperation over competition, although Ulstrup (1994, cited in Groome, 1995) reported a strong preference for competition held alongside cohesion and cooperative learning preferences. Greenfield and Suzuki (1998) likewise suggested that children from cultures that emphasise relationships tend to be cooperative with groups of which they are members, and competitive with groups of which they are not members.

Box 11.13 outlines the approach of AIME, a strengths-based program that has had success in increasing rates of completion of school and transition to work, university or further education and training for Aboriginal and Torres Strait Islander students in their program, to match or even exceed those of other Australian young people. In a research study of the program, McMahon et al. (2017) identified relationships as a key to its success in engaging students.

BOX 11.13 RESEARCH LINKS

THE AIME PROGRAM

AIME is a program that links Indigenous presenters, university mentors and Aboriginal and Torres Strait Islander students, with the goal of increasing transition to work, university or further education for Aboriginal and Torres Strait Islander students to match the rest of Australia. It has had considerable success in meeting these goals (see figure below).

YEAR 12 ATTAINMENT RATE

- 86.4% NON-INDIGENOUS
- 61.5% INDIGENOUS
- 94.1% AIME YEAR 12 MENTEES

POST-SCHOOL EDUCATION, TRAINING OR EMPLOYMENT

- 73.8% NON-INDIGENOUS
- 42.4% INDIGENOUS
- 73.3% AIME YEAR 12 MENTEES

* These figures are based on the Closing the Gap Prime Minister's Report, 2017

* These figures are based on the Overcoming Indigenous Disadvantage Report, 2016

Source: AIME (2017) The AIME Story. Downloaded from https://aimementoring.com/about/aime

McMahon et al. observed AIME sessions and interviewed students in the program at a number of sites, to determine what elements of the program contributed to the high levels of engagement of students that had been experienced by staff in the program.

Rather than the traditional power relationships of teacher and student that typically exist in schools, at AIME, presenters make themselves vulnerable by sharing personal stories, and trying unfamiliar tasks in 'failure time' sessions. As a result, students reported AIME as being different to school, as they were treated as adults, or as friends, by the presenters. This was despite the fact that presenters ran sessions in similar ways to school lessons, and were careful not to blur the lines of professionalism, with rules about not becoming friends with the students. Instead, McMahon et al. attribute the feeling students had of equality with presenters to the fact that students are trusted by the presenters to hear their personal stories, and to represent AIME in various ways. For example, students may design AIME apparel, write letters on AIME letterhead and messages on AIME business cards, are trained as AIME mentors and encouraged to set up mentoring programs in their own and other schools. Through these activities, high expectations are communicated and reinforce AIME's message that 'Indigenous=success'. Students' stories and ideas are also carefully listened to and explicitly valued by the presenters, which McManhon et al. report as another contributor to the relationships that are developed.

McMahon et al. found that these equal, trust-filled, respectful presenter-mentee relationships, which also include relationships to Country and 'Cosmos' (spirit) through storytelling, were key to the engagement of Secondary students in the program. Drawing on both Western and Indigenous ideas about knowledge, teaching and learning, AIME continues to improve educational outcomes for Aboriginal and Torres Strait Islander students, and in 2017, launched a global campaign to take the AIME model to other Indigenous communities worldwide.

Source: Adapted from McMahon, S., Harwood, V., Bodkin-Andrews, G., O'Shea, S., McKnight, A., Chandler, P. & Priestly, A. (2017). Lessons from the AIME approach to the teaching relationship: valuing biepistemic practice, *Pedagogy, Culture & Society*, 25(1), 43–58. and AIME (2017) The AIME Story. Downloaded from https://aimementoring.com/about/aime

ACTIVITIES

1   Read more about the AIME program at https://aimementoring.com/about/aime
2   How could you adopt some of the principles here in engaging students in your classes?

Supporting first language

Many Aboriginal and Torres Strait Islander students are competent in several languages, and can switch between various languages and dialects when talking in different contexts. This language skill represents a strong understanding of language and how it works, and it can be harnessed in English language and literacy learning.

The majority of Aboriginal and Torres Strait Islander students come to school speaking a language other than **Standard Australian English (SAE)** (Bourke, Rigby & Burden, 2000). They may speak a language completely distinct from English, a 'Creole' (that is, an amalgam of English vocabulary and their own language structure that exists as a new language) or a form of **Aboriginal English**.

It is important to recognise that Aboriginal English is a separate dialect, different in every aspect of language from SAE (Malcolm et al., 1999). Aboriginal English has many different forms across different localities, and 'strong' and 'weak' forms may be used within a community, depending on the context. Although SAE and the Aboriginal English spoken in some areas may be mutually intelligible, Aboriginal English remains an important marker of Aboriginal identity. Like all languages, it bears important aspects of its speakers' culture and world view. Its similarity to SAE may cause difficulties when people – Indigenous and non-Indigenous Australians – fail to recognise its legitimacy and distinction as a separate language. Malcolm et al. (1999) described how students' use of Aboriginal English may not be

Standard Australian English (SAE)
The language of mainstream Australia, and 'standard' in the sense that it does not vary significantly across communities

Aboriginal English
A dialect distinct from Standard Australian English, and having many variants in different Aboriginal communities

accepted. Teachers who are unaware of this issue may correct students' use of Aboriginal English as being incorrect speech or writing, rather than recognising its source and explicitly teaching students about the differences between Aboriginal English and SAE, and when to use SAE and when to use Aboriginal English. The NSW Board of Studies (cited in Malcolm et al., 1999, p. 21) quoted an Aboriginal student as saying: 'Teachers are always correcting what we say or how we say. They say it is bad English. It makes us feel bad.'

Some Aboriginal people may discourage the use of Aboriginal English out of a desire for their children to succeed in the wider society. Another example is given by Malcolm et al. (1999) from earlier research done by Eagleson, Kaldor and Malcolm (1982, p. 237):

> [M]y mother and father, uncles and aunties would constantly tell me not to use Aboriginal English and to speak far more slowly than I did and to speak in standard English … you had to because you went to a white school I would imagine and the whites were the people that you had to sort of mimic and be like.

> Source: Malcolm et al. (1999).

The concern of Aboriginal parents over their children acquiring the literacy and numeracy skills needed for survival and success in Australian society has been reported by Harris (1990). The challenge remains how to provide these skills for Aboriginal and Torres Strait Islander children without degrading or eliminating their own language and culture. One approach to dealing with this challenge has been the development of 'two-ways' (or 'both-ways') schooling, which seeks to teach Western and traditional Aboriginal content and methodology side by side (Harris, 1990).

Researchers at Edith Cowan University in Western Australia developed a program promoting two-way pedagogy, called 'the ABC of Two-way Literacy and Learning'. They suggest that teachers:

- *accept* Aboriginal English at school, recognising, valuing and encouraging its use when appropriate
- *bridge* to SAE, building upon what students know, and teaching explicitly about what they don't know and need to master in SAE
- *cultivate* Aboriginal ways of learning, tapping into the strengths of Aboriginal learning preferences and culture.

A rich cultural heritage

Recognising the richness of Indigenous Australians' cultural heritage involves being aware of contemporary culture as well as that of the past, and recognising different ways of viewing history, time, land and relationships. Students living in traditional communities might have considerable knowledge of the land, of the Dreaming, and of the traditional dance, music and painting particular to their community. Those in urban communities might have a very different cultural heritage. Nonetheless, it is helpful to return to our earlier discussion of culture, remembering that this often involves more than visible characteristics. Students' cultural heritage also influences how they view learning, teachers and fellow students.

Involving the community in the school, and the school in the community

Ideally, Aboriginal and Torres Strait Islander children would be taught by members of their own communities. In practice, Australia has few fully trained Indigenous teachers relative to the size of the Indigenous school population. One way in which this gap has been bridged is by employing Aboriginal and Islander Education Workers (AIEWs), who work alongside non-Indigenous teachers in the classroom. This provides an opportunity for non-Indigenous teachers to gain understanding and insight into issues relevant to their Aboriginal and Torres Strait Islander students. AIEWs often liaise between the school and the community to make the school a welcoming place for Aboriginal and Torres Strait Islander families. An AIEW can also function as an important role model for the children and families involved in the school. Other roles for AIEWs include assisting teachers and students, monitoring students' attendance and behaviour, counselling or advising students, and providing induction for new teachers (HREOC, 2000). In some States, AIEWs are assisted to study to become teachers.

A second way in which schools can consult their Indigenous community is through the local or regional Aboriginal Education Consultative Group (AECG). The role of these groups is to advise schools on educational issues relevant to Aboriginal children in the school. Informal opportunities can also be taken to be involved in the community, and to involve parents and other community members in the school as visitors, teachers or consultants when developing teaching programs.

CourseMateExpress

Online Resources
Watch a **video** in which an Aboriginal teacher offers her approach to involving the Aboriginal community in the school.

Bridging the cultural divide

When ways of learning differ between home and school, two approaches to bridge the divide are to change the school way of learning to match the home way, and to explicitly teach about the differences and support students in developing school ways of learning alongside their home ways. By combining these approaches, teachers can communicate the value of the students' home culture, and help to empower their future learning by giving them access to using school (Western) ways, and an understanding of how they work (see Box 11.14).

For example, some Aboriginal and Torres Strait Islander students have an observational model of learning at home in which they watch a whole task being performed, and avoid shame by waiting until they are confident of success before attempting it themselves. In many situations, observational learning might be of considerable benefit, and can be built into the classroom approach. Not calling on individual students and allowing them to work in small groups can minimise the risk of students feeling shame. Students can also be supported to learn in new ways: to take risks with their learning, and to learn in steps, rather than waiting until they feel confident of succeeding at the whole task before starting (Commonwealth of Australia, 2008).

BOX 11.14 CLASSROOM LINKS

ENHANCING INDIGENOUS AUSTRALIAN STUDENTS' EXPERIENCES

The 'What Works. The Work Program' website was an initiative funded by the Australian government to help teachers to consider how to improve outcomes for Indigenous students. Its checklist prompts teachers to consider how well they are prepared for the task.

Analysing the issues: Some checkpoints for improving the level of student success

This checklist has been found to be a useful way to assess the state of your practice. Check for areas of strength and weakness. If you can answer most of these questions positively, you're doing well.

General

- Have you specifically (and sensitively) investigated the backgrounds, aspirations and needs of your Indigenous students?
- Do you know their families and carers on a friendly basis?
- Are processes in place for liaising and maintaining regular contact with members of local communities?

>>

- Do you have easy access to local data about achievement, retention and attendance of your Indigenous students?
- Do you have specific targets in place for students' success and have you implemented means for their achievement?
- Does each Indigenous student have a Personalised Learning Plan (PLP)?
- Are teachers, students and parents (or carers) all involved in the PLP process?

Acknowledgment, recognition and support of Indigenous cultures

- Are provisions in place for non-Indigenous staff to learn about Indigenous cultures in general and local Indigenous cultures in particular?
- Is there a recognisable Indigenous 'presence' in the school in terms of teaching and employed support staff, guests to the school and other support personnel?
- Does the school recognise and express its respect for the cultures of its Indigenous students?
- Are the ways it does so acceptable to and appreciated by local Indigenous community members?

Developing skills

- Is intensive support available for students whose skills in reading and writing SAE and numeracy are below conventional levels?
- Are procedures in place for testing for hearing or vision impairment and responding to any problems?
- Is regular use made of the life experiences and knowledge of students to make connections with other curriculum content?
- Are Indigenous cultures represented in an accurate and relevant way in the curriculum?
- Are there consistent opportunities available for students to work cooperatively?
- Are learning activities varied (for example, via the use of ICTs)?
- Are learning activities related to students' learning strengths?

Attendance and participation

When regular attendance and consistent participation are problems:

- Do you have an individual 'case management' process in place?
- Are Indigenous peers, mentors or members of staff used to support individual students?
- Have you worked with key members of the local community to discuss possible strategies that might change the situation?

Source: Commonwealth of Australia, Department of Education, Employment and Workplace Relations. (2010). What works. The work program. Initiatives for Indigenous students' success. Canberra: DEEWR. Retrieved from www.whatworks. edu.au © Commonwealth of Australia 2010. Reproduced, communicated and adapted with permission of the Australian Government Department of Education, Employment and Workplace Relations, 2012.

ACTIVITIES

1 Complete the checklist for a school you are familiar with. What are the biggest challenges here?
2 Visit the 'What Works' website at www.whatworks.edu.au to explore these principles further, and to see how some schools are implementing them.
3 Discuss with an Indigenous person their experience of education (or their aspirations for, and experiences of, education for their children). How would the above principles help?

A second example comes from the ways in which language is used. In Western cultures, language is used for learning and teaching as well as social purposes, but in some Aboriginal and Torres Strait Islander groups, learning and teaching do not happen through language, but through observation and participation. Language has a primarily social purpose. The writers of the National Numeracy Review suggest explicitly teaching students to talk about their mathematical thinking for learning purposes, in the context of conversations about the use of language at home and at school.

Although it is helpful to think about learning as a cultural activity, it is worth restating that there is considerable variability within and among Aboriginal groups, as with all groups of children, and that teachers should get to know the learning approaches of the individual children in their classes and the communities where they teach.

Heath issues: otitis media

otitis media
A disease of the middle ear that can affect hearing

One health problem that affects the learning of a great number of Aboriginal Australian students is associated with hearing. **Otitis media** is a disease involving inflammation of the middle ear, and commonly afflicts infants and young children.

Recall from Chapter 2 that language development is foundational to cognitive, social and emotional development. Disruptions in linguistic input in infancy can affect development across a number of domains, and recurrent hearing loss in the school years further affects classroom learning. The NSW Health Department (2000) identified potential effects of otitis media on:

- speech and language development, with up to two years' delay in the development of reading and communication skills in children who have had chronic otitis media in infancy
- auditory processing and listening skills
- the ability to distinguish the soft sounds of speech (affecting phonemic awareness, which is crucial for reading development)
- word identification and comprehension skills
- development of an age-appropriate vocabulary
- short-term auditory memory
- the ability to follow verbal instructions
- reading and maths performance at school
- the ability to pick up contextual cues to meaning
- communication difficulties, leading to behavioural and social problems through frustration and anger
- balance, coordination and motor-skill development.

Many of these effects contribute to learning disabilities, particularly in the early years when learning leans heavily on language. Noise in the classroom can make this process even more difficult. In addition, when children are learning in a second language, difficulties with hearing limit their capacity to learn that language and the curriculum content. When basic skills such as learning to read are affected, further learning in later years is also disrupted. Teachers can assist children who are experiencing difficulties associated with otitis media by supporting learning with non-verbal means of communication, modification of the learning environment, and use of small-group work with peers to assist (Jacobs, Rowlands, Sinclair & Williams, 2011). Box 11.15 describes further strategies that teachers can employ to support students affected by otitis media.

Strategies for enhancing Indigenous students' success

Box 11.14 discusses strategies for enhancing the school experiences of Aboriginal and Torres Strait Islander students. The student companion website describes further results from research about 'what has worked' for schools engaging Aboriginal and Torres Strait Islander students.

BOX 11.15 CLASSROOM LINKS

OTITIS MEDIA IN THE CLASSROOM

Jacobs, Rowlands, Sinclair and Williams (2011) built on a resource developed by the Western Australia Department of Education to develop a website, Do You Hear What I Hear?, to assist teachers in supporting students affected by otitis media. Their suggestions include:

- amplification, used alongside the other support strategies suggested here
- reduction of ambient noise; for example, from air conditioners, furniture scraping on the floor, or classroom chatter at key listening times
- employing teaching strategies to maximise attention and processing of instructions or information delivered verbally: repetition keeping instructions brief, complementary non-verbal means of communication, and ensuring the speaker's face is clearly seen
- developing students' listening skills, as this may have been limited by their experience of conductive hearing loss
- small-group work for activities requiring communication
- peer tutoring and buddy systems.
- Indigenous education workers may also be able to support students with home language and cultural knowledge as well as listening.

Source: Adapted from Jacobs, Rowlands, Sinclair and Williams (2011).

ACTIVITIES

1 Explore the Do You Hear What I Hear? website (www.doyouhear.org.au) for more strategies, resources and information about otitis media.
2 Block your ears with headphones or another device, then attend a lecture in which information is delivered orally. Reflect on your experience. What did you miss out on (both in the explicit information and what went on alongside it, such as peer interaction)? What might have helped you to access the information, and to be socially included?

MĀORI LEARNERS AND NEW ZEALAND'S EDUCATION SYSTEM

Although some of the educational outcomes look similar for indigenous people across the world, the position of Māori people in New Zealand, for instance, is quite different from that of Aboriginal people in Australia, and this difference flows through to the education system. Māori make up 23 per cent of all New Zealand students, and the majority attend mainstream schools (ERO, 2014a). Māori words are used in curriculum documents and are commonly understood.

The New Zealand Ministry of Education is committed to achieving success for Māori students in line with the general population. In 2008, the ministry released Ka Hikitia, a Māori education strategy, which has now been extended into its third phase for implementation between 2018 and 2022. Committed to 'using and acting on evidence of what makes the greatest difference for and with Māori education', and 'increasing *whānau* (extended family) and *iwi* (tribe) authority and involvement in education', the current strategy has five focus areas:

1 Use of Māori language in education, such that all Māori students have access to quality Māori language in all aspects of their education.
2 All Māori children participate in high-quality early education, through increases in quality of provision, and supports to remove barriers and lift participation rates.

3   In primary and secondary education, ensuring all Māori students have strong literacy, numeracy and language skills, and achieve at least NCEA level 2 (Year 12) or its equivalent. The aim is to achieve this by engaging students in quality learning and teaching experiences, ensuring all stakeholders have high expectations for Māori learners, and all collaborate to achieve these outcomes.

4   In tertiary education, ensuring that Māori students succeed at higher levels.

5   Organisational success is needed to support Māori educational success, through leadership, evidence-based practice and effective action.

In addition, Tataiako, a set of cultural competencies, has been developed for teachers and linked to the teaching standards, to guide teachers in ensuring Māori experience success as Māori, and that Māori identity, language and culture are supported. The competencies are:

>   *Wananga:* participating with learners and communities in robust dialogue for the benefit of Māori learners' achievement

>   *Whanaungatanga:* actively engaging in respectful working relationships with Māori learners, parents and *whānau, hapu, iwi* and the Māori community

>   *Manaakitanga:* showing integrity, sincerity and respect towards Māori beliefs, language and culture

>   *Tangata Whenuatanga:* affirming Māori learners as Māori. Providing contexts for learning where the language, identity and culture of Māori learners and their *whānau* is affirmed.

>   *Ako:* taking responsibility for their own learning and that of Māori learners.

Source: New Zealand Ministry of Education (2011b). © Crown 2011.

The approach has had some success in lifting Māori students' educational outcomes, although results such as the PISA reports (OECD, 2016b) show more work needs to be done to achieve equality (Berryman et al., 2016). This is what the third phase of Ka Hikitia seeks to do. While the first phase focused on classroom pedagogy, and the second phase on school leadership, in the third phase a still broader approach is planned that will involve system-wide change, introducing community-led, *iwi* (tribal)-led, and Māori-led models of education. Berryman & Eley (2017) argued that rather than focusing on 'gaps' between outcomes, which results in deficit discourses that accept failure as inevitable for some groups, schools can address 'critical contexts for change', using the Māori concept of '*ako*' as learners and teachers working together to construct new skills, knowledge and understandings, with:

1   culturally responsive and relational practices across the school

2   deliberate professional acts applied with adaptive expertise, and

3   powerful home–school collaborations.

(Berryman & Eley, 2017: 109–110)

The common culture and language shared by Māori communities across New Zealand means the task of developing resources, training teachers in the language and culture, and appropriately shaping the curriculum is less problematic than that faced by education departments in Australia. At the same time, it can mean that Māori students are stereotyped, without consideration for differences between rural and urban, or traditional and non-traditional communities (Bishop & Glynn, 1999).

Source: Alamy/David Hancock

FIGURE 11.10 Māori family and community involvement at all levels of educational planning, implementation and evaluation is a key to Māori engagement and success in education.

Bishop and Glynn (1999) stressed that appropriate approaches to Māori education maximise outcomes, such as participation, by ensuring Māori community involvement in every stage of development, implementation and evaluation. This ensures that Māori aspirations, preferences and practices take central place. Māori-medium preschools (*te kohanga reo*), primary schools (*kura kaupapa Māori*), secondary schools (*wharekura*) and tertiary institutions (*whare waananga* Māori) have been successful not just because education is offered in *te reo* Māori (Māori language), but also because of the links between language and culture described earlier in this chapter. Māori ways of interacting, roles for teachers and students, and learning patterns such as looking, listening, imitating and storytelling are used. Ongoing community involvement ensures that these elements are dynamic, adapt to changes in the aspirations, preferences and practices of the community, and resist stereotyping.

Bishop et al., (2003) interviewed Year 9 Māori students about what promoted their learning, and developed an effective teaching profile. They found that when teachers applied these principles, their students' achievement and attitudes improved. A summary of the profile can be found on the CourseMate website. **Box 11.16** gives further details of the project.

⌐CourseMate Express

Online Resources
Go further: View the Effective Teaching Profile on this text's website

BOX 11.16 CLASSROOM LINKS

TE KOTAHITANGA: IMPROVING THE EDUCATIONAL ACHIEVEMENT OF MĀORI STUDENTS

From 2000 to 2010, Bishop and his colleagues were commissioned by the New Zealand Ministry of Education to investigate how the educational achievement of Māori students could be improved.

In the first phase of this project, years 9 and 10 students were interviewed about what it was like to be Māori in the classroom. They described an absence of respectful, caring relationships with teachers, lack of positive recognition of their culture, and a need to set it aside if they wanted to be 'engaged learners'. Students were also asked what kinds of teacher relations would help them to engage in learning.

Bishop, Berryman, Tiakiwai and Richardson (2003) devised a 'Culturally Responsive Pedagogy of Relations', with the principles for teachers being:

- creating contexts for learning in their classrooms
- sharing power, with interdependent, non-dominating relations between students and teachers
- developing interactive, responsive learning that spirals
- connecting people with a common vision of excellence in educational outcomes and what it looks like.

An Effective Teaching Profile was developed in 2001 to encapsulate what this pedagogy would look like in practice. It rested on the foundation of two key teacher attitudes:

1 Teachers reject explanations of Māori students' achievement levels that place the blame on students' or their families' problems.

2 Teachers commit to accept professional responsibility for students' learning, and to create a change for Māori students' learning.

Bishop and colleagues (2003) theorised that together with these twin attitudes, effective teachers of Māori students would demonstrate daily that they:

- care for their students as culturally located individuals
- have high expectations of students' learning
- manage classrooms to promote student learning
- interact with students in a range of ways involving extended logical dialogue, and help students to interact with others in this way
- use a range of strategies to facilitate learning
- promote, monitor and reflect on learning outcomes that lead to improvements in Māori student achievement, and share that knowledge with their students.   >>

In 2004 and 2005, teachers were involved in an ongoing professional development program to learn about the profile, and be supported in using it with their students. In the third phase of the project, Bishop, Berryman, Cavanagh, Teddy and Clapham (2006) evaluated the effects of the program, and found that 'when Māori students have good relationships with their teachers, they are able to thrive at school'. These relationships were the result of teachers' commitment to building caring and learning relationships with Māori students, teachers' strong belief that Māori students could improve their achievement, and the students' ability to take responsibility for their learning and performance. Students described what it was like to be Māori in these classrooms in terms of good relationships with teachers, being challenged in their learning, and being listened to as individuals. There were also improvements in literacy and numeracy outcomes for the students in the schools involved in the project. Phases 4 and 5 extended the program to further schools, and in 2014, 49 schools were involved. Five of the seven successful schools identified in **Box 11.11** had been involved in this program, and named it as a significant factor in their students' success.

Sources: Adapted from Bishop, Berryman, Tiakiwai and Richardson (2003); Bishop, Berryman and Wearmouth (2014).

ACTIVITIES

1 Read about the current activities of the project and view videos of teacher and school stories at http://tekotahitanga.tki.org.nz.
2 Check the Effective Teaching Profile online and the principles here against your own philosophy of teaching, and against what you have seen in classrooms. What is different? What is similar?
3 What might make the difference for the students you teach?

CourseMateExpress

Online Resources
Take a moment to consider your philosophy of learning and teaching. You may wish to use the **Develop your philosophy** tool on the textbook's CourseMate website

Bishop et al. (2003) found that although teachers were most likely to explain (Māori) students' achievement in terms of student factors and home background, students and principals pointed to classroom interaction and in-class relationships as being the most important. Ka Hikitia, the Māori Education Strategy (New Zealand Ministry of Education, 2008), highlights a shift from 'It's their problem' approaches to a 'Māori potential' approach. This involves a shift in focus, as described in Table 11.2, recognising that: 'all Māori learners have unlimited potential'; 'being Māori is an asset, not a problem'; and 'all Māori are inherently capable of achieving success'. These principles also apply to other groups.

TABLE 11.2 'Māori potential' approach in education

LESS FOCUS ON ...	MORE FOCUS ON ...
Remedying deficit	Realising potential
Problems of dysfunction	Identifying opportunity
Government intervention	Investing in people and local solutions
Targeting deficit	Tailoring education to the learner
Māori as a minority	Indigeneity and distinctiveness
Instructing and informing	Collaborating and co-constructing

Source: 'Māori Potential Approach in education', from Māori Potential Approach. Copyright © 2008 by New Zealand Ministry of Education. Used by permission.

EFFECTIVE TEACHING FOR NEW ZEALAND MĀORI AND ABORIGINAL AND TORRES STRAIT ISLANDER COMMUNITIES

Many of the strategies for effective teaching discussed earlier in this text equally apply to the teaching of indigenous students. However, some specific suggestions have also been put forward in the literature – these are discussed in Box 11.17.

BOX 11.17 IMPLICATIONS FOR EDUCATORS

STRATEGIES FOR ENHANCING MĀORI, ABORIGINAL AND TORRES STRAIT ISLANDER STUDENTS' LEARNING

Some parents may feel wary of school and reluctant to participate, therefore the school has a particular responsibility to bridge the gap by going to parents in formal and informal ways, both to celebrate successes and to resolve difficulties.

Community involvement in the school is invaluable. Support it by inviting parents and elders to be involved in classroom teaching and in educational decision making. If inviting people into the school to teach, let them choose content and methodology. Their choices may help you understand more about community priorities and methods of teaching and learning.

Community involvement in the school needs to be matched by school involvement in the community. Benefits include establishing links between school and community, increasing the school's understanding of the community, and demonstrating the school's commitment to the community. It gives teachers an opportunity to get to know those in the community, their concerns and their goals for education.

- Know your students, and build on their strengths and learning preferences.
- Include Māori, Aboriginal and/or Torres Strait Islander perspectives in mainstream curricula.
- Teach students how to recognise and dismantle stereotypes.
- Consider using cooperative methods (such as 'jigsaw'; see Chapter 7) as a way of reducing racial tension and developing tolerance in students.
- Ensure that the curriculum is relevant to students' needs and interests so as to encourage their participation.
- Have high expectations of all students, and work to help them to meet them.

CONCLUDING COMMENTS

In this chapter, we have examined a number of examples of differences among groups as well as diversity within groups. We have seen examples of factors in students' family, culture, school and teachers that all have an impact on their educational outcomes. Bronfenbrenner's theory, introduced early in the chapter, provided a picture of the complex interaction between individual, contextual, process and time factors that contribute to the differences we see in students' outcomes. It is also worth recalling the finding from Rowe and Rowe's (2002) research that individual teachers make a larger contribution to differences in student outcomes than do SES, ethnicity or gender alone. Effective teachers are aware of, and cater for, student difference and its sociocultural bases. A common element of effective programs that address individual difference is their focus on the *individual* as a learner as well as a member of a group. Successful programs that work with Aboriginal and Torres Strait Islander as well as Māori students (and we would argue, *all* students) focus on relationships.

STUDY TOOLS

ONLINE STUDY RESOURCES

Visit http://login.cengagebrain.com and use the access code that comes with this book for 12 months' access to the student resources for this text.

The CourseMate Express website contains a range of resources and study tools for this chapter, including:
- a **self-check quiz**
- **crosswords**, **flashcards** and a **glossary** to help you revise the key terms from this chapter

- the **Go further** materials and **interactive activity** mentioned in the chapter
- a **video** that illustrates some of the concepts discussed
- plus much more!

 CourseMateExpress

CHAPTER REVIEW

- Bronfenbrenner's bioecological systems theory proposed a number of interconnecting contexts that influence, and are influenced by, the individual in development. This mutual influence contributes to considerable individual difference among members of groups. The contexts range from the immediate interactions within the family outwards to the wider culture.
- Culture is learnt, transmitted and constructed by all of us, and includes the beliefs and behaviours shared by a group and passed on to new members through a constant process of socialisation.
- Cultural differences between groups in society can create misunderstandings and conflict. In the school context, such differences can be sociolinguistic, as well as relating to broader beliefs about learning and understandings of roles. Effective, inclusive teaching involves understanding such cultural differences and teaching about them explicitly.
- Racism is felt directly and indirectly by many students in school. Teachers have a responsibility to deal directly with acts of racism and to target attitudes of prejudice that underlie it.
- Gender differences exist in cognition, emotion and educational achievement, although such differences tend to be small, with larger differences occurring within groups than among them.
- Explanations of gender differences in educational outcomes include a differential focus on employment prospects, biological differences, school structures, and male and female roles in school and society.

- Poverty is associated with poor educational outcomes, as well as a number of other related characteristics, including health, parenting factors and stress. These characteristics constitute risks for poor outcomes, but there are also resilience factors that help individuals to overcome or withstand such difficulties.
- Schools can contribute to educational inequality through teacher expectations, differences between home and school, and the nature of a less-than-satisfactory home–school relationship. Considering children not only as school students but as members of families and communities, and involving those communities in the school, are important strategies in addressing educational inequality.
- Aboriginal and Torres Strait Islander students can bring a number of strengths to school, including independence, interdependence, linguistic competence, a rich cultural heritage and skills across a number of areas.
- In Australia, there is considerable variety in culture, language and goals for education. There are also commonalities in experiences of education across Indigenous groups.
- Māori people in New Zealand share a common language and culture, which has enabled the Ministry of Education to adapt curricula to be more relevant to Māori students.
- Valuing indigenous cultures, support for first language, community involvement in the school, and school involvement in the community are key strategies for improving indigenous students' educational outcomes. Relationships with students are another key.

PUTTING IT TOGETHER

Making links between 'sociocultural factors in the learning process' and material in other chapters

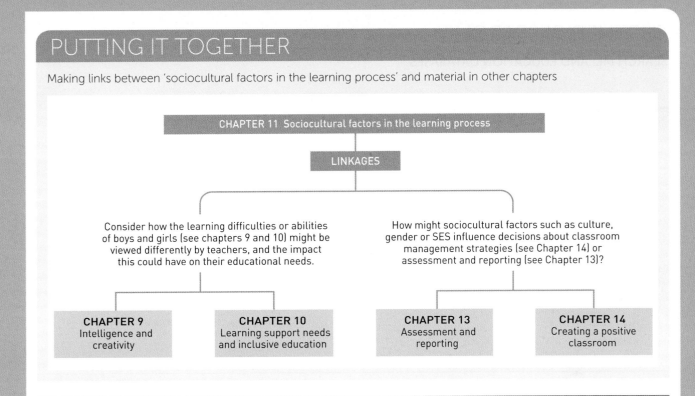

QUESTIONS AND ACTIVITIES FOR SELF-ASSESSMENT AND DISCUSSION

1   How can teachers have an impact on the learning of students from various sociocultural groups?

	POSITIVELY	NEGATIVELY
Boys		
Girls		
Students with language backgrounds other than English		
Students from low-SES backgrounds		
Indigenous students		

2   Describe your own culture:
  a   What are the key beliefs?
  b   How do these key beliefs explain why you behave as you do?
  c   Try to imagine how someone might interpret your behaviour differently.
  d   How would you explain your beliefs and behaviour to others?

3   Develop a pedagogy of education that fits your personal culture. How would you communicate your ideas to students and their parents who were from a cultural background different from your own?

4   Talk to your parents about their experiences of education, and how that might have influenced their parenting and also their goals for your education.

5   Map the influences on boys' and girls' schooling experiences. Discuss how these influences relate to the outcomes for boys and girls that have been reported.

6   Describe some of the strategies that you could employ to ensure that your classroom is inclusive of boys and girls.

7   Give as many examples as you can of differences within groups of people. Do these differences discount the differences reported among groups? Why or why not?

8   What are four key principles of effective practice for Indigenous Australian students? How are they the same and/or different from principles of effective practice for New Zealand Māori students? For other groups?

FURTHER RESEARCH

SEARCH ME! AND EDUCATION DATABASES

Explore Search Me! education for articles relevant to this chapter. Fast and convenient, Search Me! education is updated daily and provides you with 24-hour access to full-text articles from hundreds of scholarly and popular journals, ebooks and newspapers, including *The Australian* and *The New York Times*. Log in to Search Me! through http://login.cengagebrain.com and use the search terms listed here as a starting point:

- Aboriginal
- coeducation
- culture conflict
- gender
- gender bias
- gender difference
- indigenous
- Māori
- multicultural
- poverty
- racism
- risk and resilience
- single sex
- social class
- socioeconomic status.

Try combining these words with 'education' or 'schooling'. Adding 'Australia' or 'New Zealand' to your search terms will limit the results to articles relating to these contexts.

You can also use these terms to explore databases such as ERIC, PsycINFO and the Australian Education Index.

Search Me!

RECOMMENDED WEBSITES

The following government bodies have written or commissioned extensive reports on gender, poverty and indigenous education, and these can be accessed from their websites (also check your local department of education website to look at current policies and support in these areas):

Australian Government Department of Education and Training (formerly DEEWR): http://education.gov.au

Education Council: http://scseec.edu.au

ERO: www.ero.govt.nz

MINEDU: www.minedu.govt.nz

For more information on Aboriginal education, visit:

Australian Indigenous Mentoring Experience: https://aimementoring.com/about/aime

What Works: www.whatworks.edu.au

Dare to lead: www.daretolead.edu.au

Otitis media: www.doyouhear.org.au

Asia Education Foundation support for studies of Asia in Australian schools: www.asiaeducation.edu.au

Racism. No way!: www.racismnoway.com.au

Face the Facts (Human Rights Commission): www.humanrights.gov.au/education/face-facts

RECOMMENDED READING

Banks, J. A. & McGee Banks, C. A. (Eds). (2015). *Multicultural education: Issues and perspectives* (9th ed.). New York: John Wiley & Sons.

Beresford, Q., Partington, G. & Gower, G. (Eds). (2012). *Reform and resistance in Aboriginal education*. Fully revised edition. Crawley: University of Western Australia Publishing.

Grace, R., Hodge, K. & McMahon, C. (2016). *Children, families and communities: Context and consequences* (5th ed.). Melbourne: Oxford University Press.

Raffo, C., Dyson, A., Gunter, H., Hall, D., Jones, L. & Kalambouka, A. (Eds). (2010). *Education and poverty in affluent countries*. New York and London: Routledge.

REFERENCES

ACARA (2017). National Report on Schooling in Australia 2015.

ACER (2017). *PISA 2015: Reporting Australia's Results.* Camberwell, Vic: ACER.

Allport, G. W. (1954). *The nature of prejudice.* Cambridge, MA: Addison-Wesley.

Anderson, D. A. (1994). Lesbian and gay adolescents: Social and developmental considerations. *High School Journal, 77*(1–2), 13–19.

Archer, J. & Mehdikhani, M. (2004). Sex differences in aggression in real world settings: A meta-analytic review. *Review of General Psychology, 8,* 291–322.

Australian Bureau of Statistics. (2013). More women than men in less secure jobs. Media Release 150/2013. 27 August 2013.

Australian Curriculum, Assessment and Reporting Authority, (2014). *National report on schooling in Australia 2012.* Sydney: ACARA.

Bandura, A. (2011). Social cognitive theory. In P. A. M. van Lange, A. W. Kruglanski & E. T. Higgins (Eds) *Handbook of social psychological theories* (pp. 349–73). London: Sage.

Banks, J. A. & McGee Banks, C. A. (Eds). (2012). *Multicultural education: Issues and perspectives* (8th ed.). New York: John Wiley & Sons.

Baxter, J. & Hand, K. (2013). *Access to early childhood education in Australia* (research report no. 24). Melbourne: Australian Institute of Family Studies.

Baxter, J., Gray, M., Hand, K. & Hayes, A. (2012) *Parental joblessness, financial disadvantage and the wellbeing of parents and children.* FaHCSIA Occasional Paper No. 48. Canberra: Department of Families, Housing, Community Services and Indigenous Affairs.

Beresford, Q. (2003). The context of Aboriginal education. In Q. Beresford & G. Partington (Eds), *Reform and resistance in Aboriginal education: The Australian experience* (pp. 10–40). Nedlands, WA: University of Western Australia Press.

Berlinski, S., Galiani, S. & Manacorda, M. (2008). Giving children a better start: Preschool attendance and school-age profiles. *Journal of Public Economics, 92,* 1416–40.

Berryman, M. & Eley, E. (2017). Accelerating success and promoting equity through the Ako: critical contexts for change. *Asian Education Studies, 2*(1), 99–112.

Berryman, M., Eley, E., Ford, T. & Egan, M. (2016). Going beyond the personal will and professional skills to give life to Ka Hikitia. *Journal of Educational Leadership, Policy and Practice, 30*(2), 56–68.

Bishop, R. & Glynn, T. (1999). *Culture counts: Changing power relations in education.* Palmerston North, NZ: Dunmore Press.

Bishop, R., Berryman, M., Cavanagh, T., Teddy, L. & Clapham, S. (2006). *Te Kotahitanga Phase 3 Whakawhanaungatanga: Establishing a culturally responsive pedagogy of relations in mainstream secondary school classrooms.* Wellington: Ministry of Education.

Bishop, R., Berryman, M., Tiakiwai S. & Richardson C. (2003). *Te Kōtahitanga: The experiences of Year 9 and 10 Māori students in mainstream classrooms.* Wellington: Ministry of Education.

Bishop, R., Berryman, M. & Wearmouth, J. (2014). *Te Kotahitanga: Towards effective education reform for indigenous and other minoritised students.* Wellington: New Zealand Council for Educational Research.

Boston, J. (2014). Child poverty in New Zealand: Why it matters and how it can be reduced. *Educational Philosophy and Theory: Incorporating ACCESS, 46*(9), 962–88.

Boston, J. & Chapple, S. (2014). *Child Poverty in New Zealand.* Welllington: Bridget Williams.

Bourke, C. J., Rigby, K. & Burden, J. (2000). *Better practice in school attendance. Improving the school attendance of Indigenous students.* Canberra: Department of Education, Training and Youth Affairs.

Bowes, J., Grace, R. & Hayes, A. (2012). The role of context in children's development. In J. Bowes, R. Grace & K. Hodge (Eds), *Children, families and communities: Contexts and consequences* (4th ed., pp. 3–16). South Melbourne: Oxford University Press.

Boxer, P., Huesmann, L. R., Dubrow, E. F., Landau, S., F., Gvisman, S. D., Shikaki, K., & Ginges, J. (2013). Exposure to violence across the social ecosystem and the development of aggression: A test of ecological theory in the Israeli-Palestinian conflict. *Child Development, 84*(3), 163–177.

Bradley, R. H. & Corwyn, R. F. (1999). Parenting. In C. Tamis-leMonda & L. Balter (Eds), *Child psychology: A handbook of contemporary issues* (pp. 339–62). New York: Psychology Press.

Bradley, R. H. & Corwyn, R. F. (2002). Socioeconomic status and child development. *Annual Review of Psychology, 53,* 371–99.

Brody, G. H., Flor, D. & Gibson, N. M. (1999). Linking maternal efficacy beliefs, developmental goals, parenting practices, and child competence in rural singleparent African-American families. *Child Development, 70,* 1197–208.

Brody, G. H., Stoneman, Z., Flor, D., McCrary, C., Hastings, L. & Conyers, O. (1994). Financial resources, parent psychological functioning, parent co-caregiving, and early adolescent competence in rural twoparent African-American families. *Child Development, 65,* 590–605.

Bronfenbrenner, U. (1979). *The ecology of human development: Experiments by nature and design.* Cambridge, MA: Harvard University Press.

Bronfenbrenner, U. (1989). Ecological systems theory. In R. Vasta (Ed.), *Annals of child development* (Vol. 6, pp. 187–251). Greenwich, CN: JAI Press.

Bronfenbrenner, U. (2005). *Making human beings human: Bioecological perspectives on human development.* Thousand Oaks, CA: Sage.

Bronfenbrenner, U. & Morris, P. A. (1998). The ecology of developmental processes. In R. M. Lerner (Ed.), *Handbook of child psychology, Vol. 1: Theoretical models of human development* (5th ed., pp. 535–84). New York: Wiley.

Bronfenbrenner, U. & Morris, P. (2006). The ecology of developmental processes. In W. Damon & R. Lerner (Eds), *Handbook of child psychology, Vol. 1: Theoretical models of human development* (6th ed., pp. 793–829). New York: Wiley.

Buckley, S. (2016). Gender and sex differences in student participation, achievement and engagement in mathematics. *Changing Minds: Discussions in neuroscience, psychology and education,* Issue 1 April 2016. http://research.acer.edu.au/learning_processes/18

Burchinal, M., Howes, C., Pianta, R., Bryant, D., Early, D., Clifford, R. & Barbarin, O. (2008). Predicting child outcomes at the end of kindergarten from the quality of prekindergarten teacher–child interactions and instruction. *Applied Developmental Sciences, 12*(3), 140–53.

Burgaleta, M., Head, K., Álvarez-Linera, J., Martínez, K., Escorial, S., Haier, R. & Colom, R. (2012). Sex differences in brain volume are related to specific skills, not to general intelligence. *Intelligence, 40*(1), 60–68.

Caplan, N. S., Whitmore, J. K. & Choy, M. H. (1989). *The boat people and achievement in America: A study of family life, hard work, and cultural values.* Ann Arbor, MI: University of Michigan Press.

Chaplin T. M. & Aldao, A. (2013). Gender differences in emotion expression in children: A meta-analytic review. *Psychological Bulletin, 139,* 735–65.

Collins, C., Kenway, J. & McLeod, J. (2000). *Factors influencing the educational performance of males and females in school and their initial destinations after leaving school.* Canberra: Department of Education, Employment, Training and Youth Affairs.

Comber, B., Cormack, P., Nixon, H., Grant, P., Nichols, S. & Shore, S. (2005). *Submission to the National Inquiry into the teaching of literacy. Submission no. 316.* Centre for studies in literacy, policy, and learning cultures, University of South Australia. Retrieved from www.dest.gov.au/nitl/submission_index.htm

Commonwealth of Australia. (2005). *National framework for values education in Australian schools.* Canberra: DEST.

Commonwealth of Australia. (2008). *National Numeracy Review.* Canberra: Council of Australian Governments.

Commonwealth of Australia, Department of Education, Employment and Workplace Relations. (2010). *What works. The work program. Initiatives for Indigenous students' success.* Canberra: DEEWR. Retrieved from www.whatworks.edu.au

Commonwealth of Australia, Department of Education, Science and Training. (2007). *Numeracy across the curriculum.* Canberra: DEST.

Commonwealth of Australia, Department of Education, Training and Youth Affairs. (2000). *The education of boys.* Submission to the House of Representatives Standing Committee on Employment, Education and Workplace Relations. Canberra: DETYA.

Commonwealth of Australia, Department of Employment, Education and Training. (1989). *National Aboriginal and Torres Strait Islander Education Policy: Joint policy statement.* Canberra: AGPS.

Comparative Education Research Unit. (2004). *Focus on low SES students' achievement in reading literacy. Results from PISA 2000.* Wellington: New Zealand Ministry of Education. Retrieved from www.educationcounts.govt.nz/__data/assets/pdf_file/0006/6972/PISA-2000-Focus-onlow-SES-students-achievement-in-readingliteracy.pdf

Conger, R. D. & Donnellan, M. B. (2007). An interactionist perspective on the socioeconomic context of human development. *Annual Review of Psychology, 58,* 175–99.

Connolly, P. (2004). *Boys and schooling in the early years.* London: Routledge Falmer.

Conroy, J. S. (1980). Autonomy vs authority. In D. Cohen (Ed.), *Alternative education: The Currambena experience* (pp. 290–304). Sydney: David Cohen.

De Lisi, R. & McGillicuddy-De Lisi, A. (2002). Sex differences in mathematical abilities and achievement. In A. McGillicuddy-De Lisi & R. De Lisi (Eds), *Biology, society and behavior: The development of sex differences in cognition.* Westport, CT: Ablex.

Deary, I. J., Thorpe, G., Wilson, V., Starr, J. M. & Whalley, L. J. (2003). Population sex differences in IQ at age 11: The Scottish mental survey 1932. *Intelligence, 31,* 533–42.

Duncan, G. J., Magnuson, K. & Votruba-Drzal, E. (2015). Children and socioeconomic status. In R. M. Lerner (Ed.) *Handbook of Child Psychology and Developmental Science,* 7e. John Wiley & Sons.

Duncanson, M., Oben, G., Wicken, A., Morris, S., McGee, M. & Simpson, J. (2017). *Child poverty monitor technical report.* New Zealand Child and Youth Epidemiology Service, University of Otago, Dunedin.

Eades, D. (1993). Aboriginal English. *Primary English Notes (PEN), 93.* Sydney: Primary English Teaching Association.

Eagleson, R. D., Kaldor, S. & Malcolm, I. G. (1982). *English and the Aboriginal child.* Canberra: Curriculum Development Centre.

Eckermann, A-K. (1994). *One classroom, many cultures: Teaching strategies for culturally different children.* St Leonards, NSW: Allen & Unwin.

Eisenberg, N. (1998). Introduction. In N. Eisenberg (Ed.), *Handbook of child psychology, Vol. 3: Social, emotional, and personality development* (5th ed., pp. 1–24). New York: Wiley.

Evans, G. W. (2006). Child development and the physical environment. *Annual Review of Psychology, 57,* 423–51.

Feingold, A. (1993). Cognitive gender differences: A developmental perspective. *Sex Roles, 29,* 91–112.

Garmezy, N. (1993). Children in poverty: Resilience despite risk. *Psychiatry, 56,* 127–36.

Ginsburg, H. P. (1997). *Entering the child's mind: The clinical interview in psychological research and practice.* Cambridge, UK: Cambridge University Press.

Greenfield, P. M. (2009). Linking social change and developmental change: Shifting pathways of human development. *Developmental Psychology, 45,* 401–18.

Greenfield, P. M. & Suzuki, L. K. (1998). Culture and human development: Implications for parenting, education, pediatrics, and mental health. In I. E. Siegel & K. A. Renninger (Eds), *Handbook of child psychology, Vol. 4: Child psychology in practice* (5th ed., pp. 1059–112). New York: Wiley.

Greenfield, P. M., Quiroz, B. & Raeff, C. (2000). Cross-cultural conflict and harmony in the social construction of the child. In S. Harkness, C. Raeff & C. M. Super (Eds), *New directions for child and adolescent development (87).* San Francisco: Jossey-Bass.

Greenfield, P. M., Suzuki, L. K. & Rothstein-Fisch, C. (2006). Culture and human development: Implications for parenting, education, pediatrics, and mental health. In W. Damon (Series Editor) & I. E. Sigel & K. A. Renninger (Vol. Eds), *Handbook of child psychology, Vol. 4: Child psychology in practice* (5th ed., pp. 655–99). New York: Wiley.

Groome, H. (1995). *Working purposefully with Aboriginal students.* Wentworth Falls, NSW: Social Science Press.

Grossman, H. & Grossman, S. H. (1994). *Gender issues in education.* Boston: Allyn & Bacon.

Hadjar, A., Krolak-Schwerdt, S., Priem, K. & Glock, S. (2014). Gender and educational achievement. *Educational Research, 56(2),* 117–125.

Haig, Y., Konigsberg, P. & Collard, G. (2005). *Teaching students who speak Aboriginal English.* PEN 150. Marrickville, NSW: Primary English Teaching Association Australia (PETAA).

Halsey, J. (2017). *Independent review into regional rural and remote education .* Discussion Paper. Canberra: Commonwealth of Australia.

Harris, S. (1990). *Two-way Aboriginal schooling: Education and cultural survival.* Canberra: Aboriginal Studies Press.

Hart, B. & Risley, T. R. (1995). *Meaningful differences in the everyday experience of young American children.* Baltimore, MD: Paul H. Brookes.

Hartung, C. M. & Widiger, T. A. (1998). Gender differences in the diagnosis of mental disorders: Conclusions and controversies of the DSM–IV. *Psychological Bulletin, 123(3),* 260–78.

Hattie, J. (2009). *Visible learning: A synthesis of over 800 meta-analyses relating to achievement.* London: Routledge.

Heath, S. B. (1983). *Ways with words: Language, life, and work in communities and classrooms.* New York: Cambridge University Press.

Hillier, L., Jones, T., Monagle, M., Overton, N., Gahan, L., Blackman, J., & Mitchell, A. (2010). *Writing themselves in 3: the third national study on the sexual health and wellbeing of same sex attracted and gender questioning young people.* Melbourne: Australian Research Centre in Sex Health and Society, La Trobe University.

Ho, C. (2011). 'My School' and others: Segregation and white flight. *Australian Review of Public Affairs*. Retrieved from www.australianreview.net/digest/2011/05/ho.html

Ho, C. (2017): Angry Anglos and aspirational Asians: everyday multiculturalism in the selective school system in Sydney, *Discourse: Studies in the Cultural Politics of Education*, DOI: 10.1080/01596306.2017.1396961

House of Representatives Standing Committee on Education and Training. (2002). Boys: Getting it right. Report on the inquiry into the education of boys. Canberra: Commonwealth of Australia.

Human Rights and Equal Opportunity Commission. (2000). *Rural and remote education inquiry*. Retrieved from www.hreoc.gov.au/human_rights/rural_education

Hunt, E. (2011). *Human intelligence*. Cambridge, UK: Cambridge University Press.

Hyde, J. S. (2014). Gender similarities and differences. *Annual Review of Psychology*, 65, 373–9.

Ingalhalikar, M., Smith, A., Parker, D., Satterthwaite, T. D., Elliott, M. A., Ruparel, K., . . . Verma, R. (2014). Sex differences in the structural connectome of the human brain. *Proceedings of the National Academy of Sciences, 111*(2), 823–828.

Jacobs, A., Rowlands, J. Q. Sinclair, A. & Williams, C. (2011). Do you hear what I hear? Telethon speech and hearing. Published by Telethon Speech & Hearing. Retrieved from www.doyouhear.org.au

Joel, D., Berman, Z., Tavor, I., Wexler, N., Gaber, O., Stein, Y., . . . Margulies, D. S. (2015). Sex beyond the genitalia: The human brain mosaic. *Proceedings of the National Academy of Sciences, 112*(50), 15 468–15 473.

Jones, T., Smith, E., Ward, R., Dixon, J., Hillier, L., & Mitchell, A. (2016). School experiences of transgender and gender diverse students in Australia. *Sex Education: Sexuality, Society and Learning, 16*(2), 156–171. DOI: 10.1080/14681811.2015.1080678.

Kessels, U., Heyder, A., Latsch, M. & Hannover, B (2014). How gender differences in academic engagement relate to students' gender identity, *Educational Research, 56*(2), 220–229.

Kitayama, S. & Uskul, A. K. (2011). Culture, mind, and the brain: Current evidence and future directions. *Annual Review of Psychology, 62*, 419–49.

Koch, J. (2003). Gender issues in the classroom. In W. M. Reynolds and G. E. Miller (Eds), *Handbook of psychology, Vol. 7: Educational psychology* (pp. 259–81). Hoboken, NJ: Wiley.

Kohn, M. L. (1977). *Class and conformity: A study in values, with a reassessment* (2nd ed.). Chicago: University of Chicago Press.

Lam, S-F., Jimerson, S., Shin, H., Cefai, C., Veiga, F.H., Hatzichristou, C., Polychroni, F., Kikas, E., Wong, B.P.H., Stanculescu, E., Basnett, J., Duck, R., Farrell, P., Liu, Y., Negovan, V., Nelson, B., Yang, H. & Zollneritsch, J. (2016). Cultural universality and specificity of student engagement in school: The results of an international study from 12 countries. *British Journal of Educational Psychology, 86*(1), 137–153.

Lamb, S., Jackson, J., Walstab, A. and Huo, S. (2015), *Educational opportunity in Australia 2015: Who succeeds and who misses out*, Centre for International Research on Education Systems, for the Mitchell Institute, Melbourne: Mitchell Institute.

Liben, L. S. & Signorella, M. L. (1993). Gender-schematic processing in children: The role of initial interpretations of stimuli. *Developmental Psychology, 29*, 141–9.

Lippa, R. A. (2005). *Gender, nature and nurture*. Mahwah, NJ: Lawrence Erlbaum Associates.

Lohoar, S., Butera, N. & Kennedy, E. (2014). *Strengths of Australian Aboriginal cultural practices in family life and child rearing*. CFCA Paper No. 25. Melbourne: Australian Institute of Family Studies. Downloaded 6/1/18 from https://aifs.gov.au/cfca/sites/default/files/publication-documents/cfca25.pdf

Maguire, B. & Hayes, A. (2014). 'Access to preschool education in the year before full time school'. *Longitudinal Study of Australian Children Annual Statistical Report 2011*, Chapter 6. Melbourne: Australian Institute of Family Studies.

Malcolm, I., Kessaris, T. & Hunter, J. (2003). Language and the classroom setting. In Q. Beresford & G. Partington (Eds), *Reform and resistance in Aboriginal education*. Crawley, WA: University of Western Australia Press.

Malcolm, I. G., Haig, Y., Konigsberg, P., Rochecouste, J., Collard, G., Hill, A. & Cahill, R. (1999). *Two-way English: Towards more user-friendly education for speakers of Aboriginal English*. Perth: Education Department of Western Australia.

Malin, M. (1998). They listen and they've got respect: Cultural pedagogy. In G. Partington (Ed.), *Perspectives on Aboriginal and Torres Strait Islander education*. Katoomba, NSW: Social Science Press.

Marmion, S. & Lundberg-Love, P. (2004). Learning masculinity and femininity: Gender socialisation from parents and

peers across the life-span. In M. A. Paludi (Ed.), *Praeger guide to the psychology of gender* (pp. 1–26).Westport, CT: Praeger.

Martin, K. L. (2009). Aboriginal worldview, knowledge and relatedness: Re-conceptualising Aboriginal schooling as a teaching-learning and research interface. *Journal of Australian Indigenous Issues, 12*(4), 66–78

Martino, W. & Pallotta-Chiarolli, M. (2003). *So What's a boy? Addressing issues of masculinity and schooling*. Maidenhead, UK: Open University Press.

Martino, W. & Pallotta-Chiarolli, M. (2005). *Being normal is the only way to be: Adolescent perspectives on gender and school*. Sydney: University of New South Wales Press.

Masten, A. S. & Narayan, A. J. (2012). Child development in the context of disaster, war and terrorism: Pathways of risk and resilience. *Annual Review of Psychology, 63*, 227–57.

Masten, A. S., Narayan, A. J., Silverman, W. K & Osofsky, J. D. (2015). Children in war and disaster. In R. M. Lerner (Ed.). *Handbook of Child Psychology and Developmental Science*, 7th Edition. John Wiley & Sons.

Matlin, M. W. (2004). *The psychology of women* (5th ed.). Belmont, CA: Wadsworth.

McKown, C. (2005). Applying ecological theory to advance the science and practice of school-based prejudice reduction interventions. *Educational Psychologist, 40*(3), 177–89.

McLaughlin, K. A., Sheridan, M. & Lambert, H. (2014). Childhood adversity and neural development: Deprivation and threat as distinct dimensions of early experience. *Neuroscience and Behavioral Reviews, 47*, 578–91.

McLaughlin, R., Gilfillan, G. & Gordon, J. (2013). *Deep and persistent disadvantage in Australia*. Productivity Commission Staff Working Paper. Canberra: Productivity Commission.

McLoyd, V. C. (1990). The impact of economic hardship on black families and children: Psychological distress, parenting and socioemotional development. *Child Development, 61*, 311–46.

McLoyd, V. C. (1998). Socioeconomic disadvantage and child development. *American Psychologist, 53*, 185–204.

McLoyd, V. C., Aikens, N. L.& Burton, L. M. (2006). Child poverty, policy and practice. In W. Damon, R. Lerner, A. Renninger & I. Sigel (Eds), *Handbook of child psychology, Vol. 4: Child psychology in practice* (6th ed., pp. 700–75). New York: Wiley.

McMahon, S., Harwood, V., Bodkin-Andrews, G., O'Shea, S., McKnight, A., Chandler, P. &

Priestly, A. (2017). Lessons from the AIME approach to the teaching relationship: valuing biepistemic practice, *Pedagogy, Culture & Society, 25*(1), pp. 43-58.

Mehan, H. (1979). *Learning lessons: Social organization in the classroom.* Cambridge, MA: Harvard University Press.

Milburn, C. (2011). Fears over 'white flight' from selective schools. *Sydney Morning Herald,* 17 October.

Ministerial Council on Education, Employment, Training and Youth Affairs. (2008). *Melbourne declaration on educational goals for young Australians.* MCEETYA, p. 7

Ministry of Education (2016). *PISA 2015: New Zealand Summary Report.* Wellington: Ministry of Education, New Zealand.

Moore, D. S. & Johnson, S. P. (2008). Mental rotation in human infants. *Psychological Science, 19,* 1063–6.

Munns, G., Arthur, L., Downes, T., Gregson, R., Power, A., Sawyer, W., Singh, M., Thistleton-Martin, J. & Steele, F. (2006). *Motivation and engagement of boys: Evidence-based teaching practices.* Canberra: Australian Government.

Munns, G., Arthur, L., Downes, T., Gregson, R., Power, A., Sawyer, W., Singh, M., Thistleton-Martin, J. & Steele, F. (2008). *Motivation and engagement of boys: Evidence-based teaching practices. A report submitted to the Australian Government Department of Education, Science and Training:* Main report. Australian Government quality teacher programme. Retrieved from www.dest.gov.au/NR/rdonlyres/29CFF6D4-7567-4C06-A43CA82079197F1F/13866/FinalReport1.pdf

Nakata, M. (1995). Cutting a better deal for Torres Strait Islanders. *Youth Studies Australia, 14*(4), 29–34.

National Scientific Council on the Developing Child. (2014). *Excessive stress disrupts the architecture of the developing brain: Working Paper 3.* Updated Edition. Retrieved from www.developingchild.harvard.edu

New Zealand Education Review Office. (2008). *Boys' education: Good practice in secondary schools.* Wellington, NZ: ERO. Retrieved from www.ero.govt.nz/National-Reports/Boys-Education-Good-Practice-in-Secondary-Schools-July-2008

New Zealand Education Review Office. (2014a). *Roll by education region and ethnic group, July 2014.* School Roll Summary Reports. Retrieved from www.educationcounts.govt.nz/publications/schooling/2259

New Zealand Education Review Office. (2014b). *Towards equitable outcomes in secondary schools: Good practice.* Retrieved from http://ero.govt.nz/National-Reports/Towardsequitable-outcomes-in-secondary-schools-Good-practice-May-2014.

New Zealand Ministry of Education. (2008). *Ka Hikitia –Managing for success: The Māori education strategy.* Retrieved from www.minedu.govt.nz/theMinistry/PolicyAndStrategy/KaHikitia

New Zealand Ministry of Education. (2011a). *Ministry of Education position paper: Assessment.* Retrieved from www.minedu.govt.nz/theMinistry/PublicationsAndResources/AssessmentPositionPaper.aspx

NSW Health Department. (2000). *NSW Otitis Media strategic plan for Aboriginal children.* Retrieved from www.health.nsw.gov.au

Ogbu, J. U. (1987). Variability in minority school performance: A problem in search of an explanation. *Anthropology and Education Quarterly, 18,* 312–34.

Ogbu, J. U. (1997). Understanding the school performance of urban blacks: Some essential background knowledge. In H. J. Wallberg, O. Reyes & R. P. Weissberg (Eds), *Children and youth: Interdisciplinary perspectives.* Thousand Oaks, CA: Sage.

Ogbu, J. U. (2003). *Black students in an affluent suburb: A study of academic disengagement.* Mahwah, NJ: Lawrence Erlbaum Associates.

Organization for Economic Cooperation and Development. (2014). *Education at a glance 2014: OECD indicators.* Paris: OECD Publishing. Retrieved from www.oecd-ilibrary.org/education/education-at-aglance-2014_eag-2014-en

____ (2016a). *Low-Performing Students: Why They Fall Behind and How to Help Them Succeed.* PISA, OECD.

____ (2016b), *PISA 2015 Results (Volume I): Excellence and Equity in Education,* PISA, OECD Publishing, Paris.

Partington, G. (2003). *Receptivity of teachers to implementing new strategies for literacy teaching.* Paper presented at AARE/NZRE, Auckland 2003. Retrieved from www.aare.edu.au/03pap/par03581.pdf

Pfeifer, J. H., Brown, C. S. & Juvonen, J. (2007). Fifty years since *Brown v. Board of Education*: Lessons learned about the development and reduction of children's prejudice. *Social Policy Report, 21*(2), 3–23.

Polidano, C., Hanel, B. & Buddelmeyer, H. (2012). Explaining the SES School Completion Gap. Melbourne Institute Working Paper Series. Working Paper No. 16/12. University of Melbourne.

Racism. NoWay! (2010). *Recognising racism and its effects in schools.* Retrieved from www.racismnoway.com.au/teaching-resources/school-planning/poster_effects_in_schools.pdf

Raffo, C., Dyson, A., Gunter, H., Hall, D., Jones, L. & Kalambouka, A. (Eds). (2010). *Education and poverty in affluent countries.* New York and London: Routledge.

Rothstein-Fisch, C., Greenfield, P. M., Trumbull, E., Keller, H. & Quiroz, B. (2010). Uncovering the role of culture in learning, development, and education. In D. D. Preiss & R. J. Sternberg (Eds), *Innovations in educational psychology: Perspectives on learning, teaching, and human development* (pp. 269–94). New York: Springer.

Rowe, K. J. & Rowe, K. S. (2002). *What matters most: Evidence-based findings of key factors affecting the educational experiences and outcomes for girls and boys throughout their primary and secondary schooling.* Supplementary submission to House of Representatives Standing Committee on Education and Training: Inquiry into the Education of Boys, May.

Ruble, D. N., Martin, C. L. & Berenbaum, S. A. (2006). Gender development. In N. Eisenberg, W. Damon & R. M. Lerner (Eds), *Handbook of child psychology, Vol. 3: Social, emotional, and personality development* (6th ed., pp. 858–932). New York: Wiley.

Sanelli, M. F. (1999). Identity development of stigmatised adolescents. *Dissertation Abstracts International, 59*(12-A), 4399.

Sarra, C. (2011) *Strong and Smart – Towards a Pedagogy for Emancipation. Education for first peoples.* Routledge: New Studies in Critical Realism and Education.

Scutella, R. & Smyth, P. (2005). *The Brotherhood's social barometer: Monitoring children's chances.* Fitzroy, Vic.: Brotherhood of St Laurence. Retrieved from www.bsl.org.au/pdfs/BSL_social_barom_monitoring_childn_chances.pdf

Sims, M., O'Connor, M. & Forrest, M. (2003). Aboriginal families and the school system. In Q. Beresford & G. Partington (Eds), *Reform and resistance in Aboriginal education.* Crawley, WA: University of Western Australia Press.

Sproston, C. (2008). When students negotiate: An action research case study of a year 8 English class in a secondary college in Victoria, Australia. *Educational Action Research, 2*(16), 187–208, Australian Catholic University.

Stephens, N. M., Markus, H. R. & Phillips, L. T. (2014). Social class culture cycles: How three gateway contexts shape selves and fuel inequality. *Annual Review of Psychology, 65*, 611–34.

Stronger Smarter Institute Limited (2014). *High-Expectations Relationships: a foundation for quality learning environments in all Australian schools*. Stronger Smarter Institute Limited Position Paper. Downloaded 19/12/17 from http://strongersmarter.com.au/wp-content/uploads/2015/01/SSI-HER-Position-Paper-Final-lowres.pdf

Teese, R. (2000). *Academic success and social power: Examinations and inequality*. Carlton, Vic.: Melbourne University Press.

Thomson, S. (2014). *Gender and mathematics: Quality and equity*. Paper presented at ACER Research Conference, Melbourne, August.

Uribe, V. & Harbeck, K. M. (1991). Addressing the needs of lesbian, gay and bisexual youth: The origins of PROJECT 10 and school-based intervention. *Journal of Homosexuality, 22*(3–4), 9–28.

Vinson, T. (2002). *An inquiry into the provision of education in New South Wales*. Retrieved from www.pub-ed-inquiry.org/reports/final_reports

Vinson, T. (2007). *Dropping off the edge: the distribution of disadvantage in Australia*. Jesuit Social Services, Catholic Social Services Australia. Retrieved from www.australiandisadvantage.org.au

Willis, P. (2012). Constructions of lesbian, gay, bisexual and queer identities among young people in contemporary Australia. *Culture, Health & Sexuality, 14*(10), 1213–1227. doi:10.1080/13691058.2012.724087

Witt, S. D. (2000). The influence of peers on children's socialisation to gender roles. *Early Child Development and Care, 162*, 1–7.

Wylie, C. (2004). *Competent children at 12*. Wellington: New Zealand Council for Educational Research.

Wylie, C. & Hogden. E. (2007). *Competent learners at 16*. Wellington: NZCER.

Yunkaporta, T. & Kirby, M. (2011). Yarning up Indigenous pedagogies: A dialogue about eight Aboriginal ways of learning. In R. Bell, G. Milgate & N. Purdie (Eds), *Two way teaching and learning: Toward culturally reflective and relevant education*. Camberwell, Vic.: ACER Press.

Zappalà, G. & Parker, B. (2000). *The Smith Family's Learning for Life program a decade on: Poverty and educational disadvantage*. Research and Advocacy Team Background Paper No. 1.

INDIVIDUAL DIFFERENCE IN THE INCLUSIVE CLASSROOM

Module III has identified key issues contributing to the individual differences you will encounter in classrooms: intelligence, motivation and engagement, additional learning support needs, and sociocultural background. These topics are ones in which you will be challenged to

	MOTIVATION	INTELLIGENCE AND CREATIVITY
Key ideas or topics	Motivation Engagement	Models of intelligence Measuring intelligence Creativity
Main theories and theorists	Behavioural approaches: reinforcement-praise and extrinsic rewards Social cognitive approaches: self-regulation, goal setting, self-efficacy, self-evaluation and social comparison. Human needs approaches: Maslow's hierarchy of human needs and the drive for self-actualisation; Deci and Ryan's self-determination theory and the human need for competence, autonomy and relatedness. Cognitive approaches: Atkinson – achievement motivation; Dweck – implicit beliefs; Weiner – attribution theories; Harackiewicz, Elliot, Martin – goal theories	Models: Spearman – g Thurstone – primary mental abilities Guilford – structure of intellect Gardner – multiple intelligences Sternberg – triarchic theory Emotional intelligence Measurement: Binet, Wechsler Creativity: Sternberg
Catering for these differences in the inclusive classroom	Motivating students: Encourage a sense of mastery, positive goal setting and intrinsic motivators; • avoid overuse of external reinforcement and use contingent rewards that are unexpected; • develop tasks that support student self-determination and autonomy; • use feedback that encourages an incremental rather than fixed view of ability (or a growth mindset); Engaging students: Engagement is multidimensional and can vary from classroom to classroom or subject to subject; • support the cognitive, behavioural and emotional engagement of students with warm teacher-student relationships, firm but supportive and positive classroom discipline, and high expectations of achievement; • give students interesting, important and challenging tasks; • support positive peer relationships.	Intelligence: • Varying classroom activities • Considering each child's abilities and potential • Practical intelligence can be taught • Using measurement wisely to identify students needing special programs, and to plan appropriate help Creativity: • Learning environments that are flexible • Learning relationships that are caring, and provide opportunities for collaboration • Activities that support risk taking, and have a balance of structure and freedom

consider how you will balance the needs, interests and backgrounds of varying learners. As you review the summary table below, consider the research that has been discussed in these chapters, and how you might use it to guide your practice and ensure that all learners' needs are catered for in your classroom.

LEARNING SUPPORT NEEDS	SOCIOCULTURAL FACTORS
Learner diversity Inclusive education Disability Learning support needs Differentiation	Culture Gender Socioeconomic status (SES), poverty Aboriginal and Torres Strait Islander students in Australia Māori students in New Zealand
Inclusive education: educational support provided to allow all students to have their learning needs met within regular school environments.	Bronfenbrenner's bio-social-ecological model of development Explanations of gender difference based on male/female characteristics, culture, and school factors
Acknowledge learner diversity: Inclusive education involves all learners as participants in the classroom community. Learning support needs: no two learners will have the same learning support needs. Consult and use educational assessments to determine learner support needs. Differentiation: Differentiate teaching and learning activities for a range of ability levels. Individual Education Plans (IEPs) may be used for students with high support needs; involve parents and teaching aides; Person-first language: remember the child is a person first; they are not defined by their disability or condition; labels can be stigmatising.	Culture/language: Teach explicitly about cultural and language differences; make explicit the hidden curriculum; be aware of sources of potential cultural misunderstanding; dismantle prejudice and stereotypes Gender: Use a variety of strategies to cater for a range of preferences, avoid comparing boys and girls; communicate high expectations of all SES: Close the gap between home and school by getting to know families, and taking account of students' interests; prior knowledge, and home experience; welcome families into school Indigeneity: Celebrate skills and strengths, highlight potential; connect with community; support first language; draw on Indigenous ways of learning; develop trusting and egalitarian relationships in which learners and teachers can work together in constructing understandings.

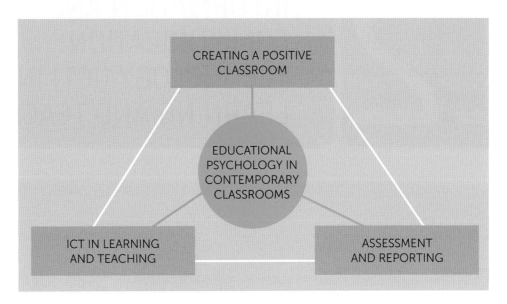

FIGURE MIV Module IV concept map

Core question: How can educational psychology help us address key learning and teaching issues?

Educational psychology plays a central role in equipping educators to deal with the sorts of issues they confront in the learning environment. This final module considers how the theories and principles of educational psychology can help teachers in the 21st century address three significant areas:

■ teaching about, and learning and teaching using information and communication technology (ICT)

■ assessing students' learning, and reporting assessments to others

■ managing the classroom and effectively working with the diverse range of students who comprise a teacher's learning community.

Chapter 12 examines how an understanding of learning theories and the principles of development can guide the successful integration of ICTs into the learning–teaching process, and how ICTs are transforming learning and teaching. Chapter 13 looks at assessment, which lies at the core of effective teaching and which is influenced by teachers' understanding of student development (see Module I), their understanding of how students learn (see Module II) and their understanding of student differences in such areas as ability, motivation and background experiences (see Module III). Chapter 14 deals with creating positive learning environments, and discusses how teachers manage themselves, their students, their resources, their time and their energies in the learning environment. This final chapter presents theories and strategies for classroom implementation.

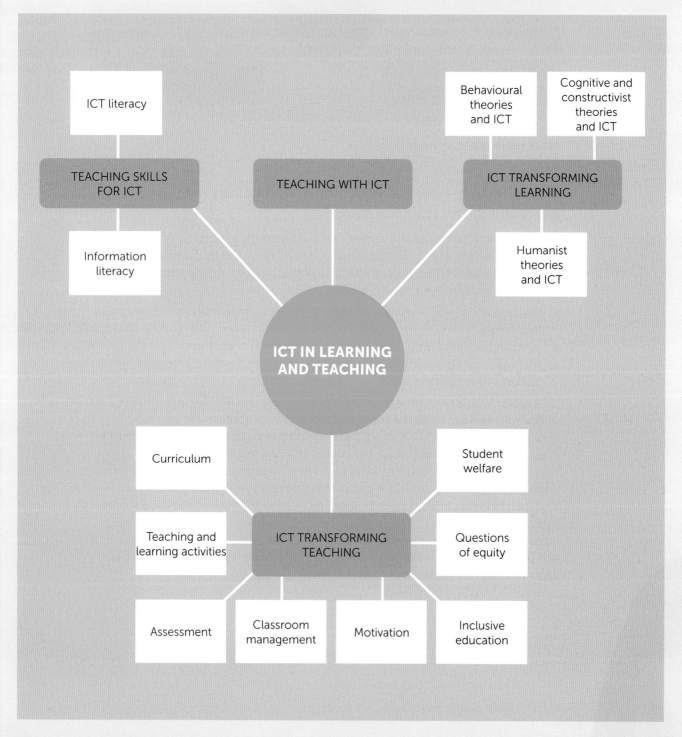

FIGURE 12.1 Chapter 12 concept map

KEY QUESTIONS

After reading this chapter, you should be able to answer the following questions:

- How are ICTs integral to learning and teaching in today's classrooms?
- What are some essential skills for effective use of ICTs by learners?
- How do behavioural, cognitive, constructivist and humanist theories of learning guide the use of ICTs in education?
- How are ICTs transforming learning and teaching in our classrooms?
- How could using ICTs contribute to inequities among learners? Share strategies for addressing these in your teaching.
- What are some potential positive and negative outcomes of the use of ICTs in the learning–teaching process? What could you do to maximise the positive and minimise the negative possibilities?

ONLINE STUDY RESOURCES

 CourseMateExpress

Bring your learning to life with **interactive learning**, **study** and **exam preparation tools** that support the printed textbook. CourseMate Express includes **quizzes**, **interactive activities**, **videos**, a tool to help you '**develop your philosophy**' and more.

INTRODUCTION

Teachers are talking in a staff meeting about recent advances in technology integration at the school and in the curriculum. One teacher is particularly concerned about a media piece she saw on the negative impacts of internet use on students' brains. Another says, 'But I see my students doing amazing things. They have more opportunities, and are motivated to learn because of the technology.' A third teacher comments on the ease with which her students use the technology. 'It's how they think now,' she says. 'We don't really need to teach them to use it; we need them to teach us.' Another objects: 'I'm not so sure. They do seem at ease with it, but they don't all use it well – just look at the cyberbullying we hear about. Or the plagiarism. Doing a research assignment seems to mean "copy and paste from Google" to many of them.'

How might we best respond to these concerns and issues? In this chapter, we present research and theory from educational psychology that can assist us as learners and teachers as we consider the potentials offered by, and issues relating to, ICT in education.

ICT IN LEARNING AND TEACHING

Information and communication technology (ICT) is used in schools throughout Australia and New Zealand for a wide range of educational purposes, including publishing, communicating, instructing, learning, assessing and motivating. It is also widely used outside school, with at least 98 per cent of Australian and New Zealand 15-year-olds reporting use of computers (OECD, 2011). In the 2011 Census, 96 per cent of Australian households with children under 15 reported having access to the internet at home (ABS, 2012). The *Melbourne declaration on educational goals for young Australians* (MCEETYA, 2008) includes the goal that, as successful learners, all young Australians will be 'creative and productive users of technology, especially ICT, as a foundation for success in all learning areas'. As a result, the Australian Curriculum identifies ICT competency as a general capability, one of a series of

information and communication technology (ICT)
Any technology used to access, gather, manipulate and present or communicate information, such as electronic hardware, software and network connectivity

interconnected skills that underpin learning and are integrated throughout the curriculum (ACARA, 2012a). New Zealand's National Curriculum also sees ICT used as a tool for learning, although it is not explicitly included as content to be taught. There is scope for integration of ICT content in developing the competency for using language, symbols and texts in the New Zealand curriculum.

If you are in a teacher education program in Australia or New Zealand, you may also be aware that the *Australian professional standards for teachers* and the *Graduating teacher standards: Aotearoa New Zealand* both include ICT:

> APTS 2.6 Implement teaching strategies for using ICT to expand curriculum learning opportunities for students …

> APTS 3.4 Demonstrate knowledge of a range of resources, including ICT, that engage students in their learning …

> APTS 4.5 Demonstrate an understanding of the relevant issues and the strategies available to support the safe, responsible and ethical use of ICT in learning and teaching.

Source: AITSL (2014).

> Standard 4d Demonstrate proficiency in oral and written language (Māori &/or English), in numeracy and in ICT relevant to their professional role.

Source: New Zealand Teachers Council (2015).

Clearly, ICT is an integral aspect of teaching as well as learning, influencing what we teach, how it is taught and aspects of teaching practice such as engaging students and classroom management.

Box 12.1 describes some ICT applications currently used in e-learning (using technology in classrooms), together with some potential benefits for learning. Rapid development of ICT means these examples are likely to change and expand over time. Keep abreast of new ideas through education pages on social bookmarking sites such as Delicious and Pinterest, or through your local education department.

SHIFTS IN ICT USE IN EDUCATION OVER TIME

ICTs can be thought of as any technology used to access, gather, manipulate and present or communicate information. Under this definition, pencil and paper, books, or chalkboard and chalk can be included as relevant, although the term is usually used to refer to computer hardware, software and connectivity, including mobile devices such as smart phones. Technologies used for education have shifted from mechanical means in previous centuries, to the increasingly complex technologies such as video, overhead projectors, film and television used in the later part of last century. From about 1982, the rapid spread of desktop computers led to a focus on computer technologies, initially primarily used for information gathering and presentation, or drill and practice using teacher-set activities. A more recent shift has come with the widespread use of mobile phones and access to the internet, which has increasingly highlighted the communication aspect of ICT. This more recent approach is sometimes referred to as Web 2.0. Web 3.0 is now being discussed as the next generation of the internet, sometimes referred to as 'the semantic web', involving connective intelligence, in which information from a range of sources will be linked to make searching more sophisticated; it may also generate new data about a learner's preferences, strengths and weaknesses drawn from a range of his or her online activities. The initial use of the internet in classrooms focused on information and resource retrieval, but this has now shifted to the sharing of files, publishing of content (both texts and multimedia files, such as on YouTube), communicating and relating socially online through sites such as Facebook, and collaboration using wiki sites or Google Docs (White, 2008). Some of the

BOX 12.1 CLASSROOM LINKS

HOW MIGHT YOU USE ICT IN YOUR TEACHING?

APPLICATION (AND DEFINITION)	EXAMPLE	POTENTIAL BENEFITS
Interactive whiteboards (IWBs) – typically with software that enables interactive activity	In class discussion, a text is annotated on the IWB. This annotated file is then saved and made available for students. In pairs, students discuss possible answers to a problem. They enter their answer on the IWB and receive feedback via the program.	Benefits depend on teachers' effective use of the software. IWBs can support interactive learning, can be used to demonstrate processes and their outcomes, may provide feedback, are multimodal and can be used for dynamic presentation of information.
Wikis – websites that can be added to and revised by visitors to the site; this 'peer review' of information is the means of keeping it current and accurate	Wikipedia is the most famous wiki. Teachers have also developed wikis with their classes to encourage students to use them not just to gather information, but also to contribute and evaluate knowledge.	Development of critical thinking, and evaluation of information encountered online, when students are involved in developing a wiki site.
Synchronous online platforms – typically allow live video, audio and text interaction, with desktop sharing and an interactive whiteboard space	Centra is used in the Northern Territory and South Australia for distance education, and Elluminate and similar programs are used by many universities.	In distance education, allows easy interaction and file sharing between students, and between students and teachers.
Asynchronous interaction	Email, discussion boards	Broadens student–teacher, student–student and parent–teacher interaction outside class time.
Learning objects – interactive digital files used for learning	The National Digital Learning Resources Network (Australia) has a database of thousands of learning objects that can be accessed by teachers in Australia through Scootle (see links with Activities below). Several of the online resources activities on the student website for this text are learning objects.	Multimodal presentation of material is engaging and allows for processing of the information through multiple mental pathways (see Chapter 6). Interactive aspect allows self-pacing of activity.
File sharing and collaboration sites	Dropbox and Googledrive are two examples of sites that allow sharing of a range of file types. Collaboration can happen both synchronously and asynchronously.	Students can collaborate on files together online. The teacher can also contribute, as a member of a learning community. Individuals' contributions to a work can be tracked.
Learning management systems (LMS)	Moodle is widely used to make content available to students and teachers at home and school, with teachers posting assignments or support files, while students can post their assignments for review or marking, and have discussions with teachers and other students within their course. Your university is likely to use a learning management system for students to access lectures and materials online, and interact with others in your course.	Materials (and support) easily accessed at home as well as school. Parents can see what students are learning. Interaction may support collaborative learning. See the case study in **Box 6.2**.

APPLICATION (AND DEFINITION)	EXAMPLE	POTENTIAL BENEFITS
Videoconferencing and web conferencing	Classes of students are combined across schools to broaden curriculum offerings. Experts may be brought in from a distance to interact with students.	Students in small or remote communities have wider access and global live interaction with other students or experts.
Blogs and vlogs (web logs and video logs)	Students keep a learning journal in blog form, tracking development of their ideas, and integrating work samples or video of performances. Teachers may also post blogs with resources for students.	Teachers can monitor progress of thinking. Students develop reflective skills and receive ongoing feedback from others in their learning community. Parents have ongoing access to how their child's learning is progressing.
SNS – social networking sites	Facebook and Twitter tend to be used socially. Similar private sites can be set up within a learning community using tools such as Ning or Wackwall – enabling students to share video, photographs and comments relating to their learning.	Promotes collaborative learning.
MP3 players and tablets	Many schools have class sets of tablets or MP3 players that are loaded with educational games or applications and used in small groups to encourage students to practise key skills. Students may also use MP3 players to develop podcasts; for example, by recording observations when out in the field. Teachers may use MP3 players to remind students of instructions for an activity.	Students can practise tasks in a different modality. Instructions can be instantly reviewed when required. Data and observations can be easily recorded to take back to class.
Mobile phone apps	'Smart phones' that have an increasing range of internet and other capabilities, such as location services, photography and video or audio recording, make them potentially powerful tools for learning. Their mobility means that they can be used outside the classroom, while their widespread adoption means they can also be used within it.	Learning is integrated with other daily activity. Learning is mobile and accessible – can happen wherever the student is.

ACTIVITIES

1   Which of these have you used in your learning? Which have you seen used?

2   Add more examples and potential benefits by discussing with your peers their experiences.

3   For further examples, explore the technology-related resources at www.scootle.edu.au or technology.tki.org.nz.

shifts in ICT use over time are depicted in Table 12.1. Shifts you may note include changes noted by Knobel and Lankshear (2007) and White (2008); these are:

- from a focus on information to a focus on communication and relationships
- from stand-alone computers to connectivity
- from users as consumers to users as producers of content
- from individual to collaborative practice
- from ICTs as tools of practice to ICTs as transformers of practice.

TABLE 12.1 Shifts in use of ICT tools

PREVIOUS CENTURIES	1970s	1982–1990s WEB 1.0	21ST CENTURY WEB 2.0
Paper, pens	Video, film, television	Word processing, desktop publishing	Webpage creation for sharing of work Creation and online publishing of audio, video and multimedia files
Encyclopaedia searching		WebQuests (searching for information online)	Contributing or editing information in wiki sites such as Wikipedia
Classroom activities		Learning objects (computer-based activities that may be interactive)	Communicating with others around learning through email, SMS, social networking sites
Books		Databases, spreadsheets	Simulations that allow learners to see the results of their actions or choices in real time
Educational games for drill and practice		Educational computer games for drill and practice	Creating environments, identities and pathways within a game Educational games that provide feedback, allow students to self-pace and self-direct learning paths
Chalk boards	Overhead projectors Whiteboards	Learning management systems Asynchronous online interaction such as email	Interactive whiteboards Videoconferencing Synchronous online interaction
		Individual work published	Collaborative work – wikis

THINK ABOUT

- How have you seen or experienced these shifts? What impact might they have had on how you learn? How might they influence how you teach?

THINKING CRITICALLY ABOUT 'DIGITAL NATIVES'

Some commentators have claimed that the arrival and rapid spread of digital technologies towards the end of the 20th century and into the start of the 21st century has fundamentally changed learners to the extent that they are no longer the same type of student whom many teachers have been trained to teach (Prensky, 2001). Prensky coined the term **digital natives** to refer to the generation of learners who have grown up surrounded by new technologies, and have rapidly integrated this technology into their lives on a day-to-day basis. Similarly, Oblinger and Oblinger (2005) referred to the **net generation** as those young people born after 1982 who have grown up in a world in which instant messaging, the internet and constant connectivity are simply expected. The corollary of this is that there is proposed to be a 'digital divide' between these learners and their teachers who are 'digital immigrants', with a challenge for teachers to engage students through use of digital technologies (Prensky, 2001).

Other writers have questioned the notion of the digital native, pointing out the considerable variability that exists between individuals in their access to and use of ICT. Both views may be supported by the results

digital natives
A term used to describe someone who has grown up in the era of digital technologies

net generation
A term used to describe someone who has grown up in the era of internet connectivity

from national and international studies of students' use of ICT, with computer and internet access and usage being high overall in Australia and New Zealand, but also showing variation for different gender and socioeconomic groups in both countries (MCEECDYA, 2010; OECD, 2011). It appears that access and use do not of themselves imply that everyone uses the internet in the same way, or with universal benefit in terms of learning. Consider, as a parallel, a skill such as reading; we have universal access to reading material, and widespread opportunity to read a range of types of texts, yet some reading has better results for our thinking and learning than others. It depends on what we read, and how we engage with a text.

Although studies such as the OECD's PISA report show widespread internet access and activity, writers such as Bennett and Maton (2010) and Kennedy et al. (2008) have demonstrated variation in types of use of the internet between individuals as well as among particular groups. For example, while they could all be said to belong to the net generation, students in early childhood, middle childhood and adolescence show different patterns of use of the internet, as well as variations in level and type of use (ABS, 2011; Grimley & Allan, 2010; Johnson, 2010b; Luckin et al., 2009). Johnson (2010a) reported a range of factors that can influence the use of the internet by children, as well as the ways in which internet use might relate to cognitive development. She found that children access the internet for different purposes and with different results in home, school and community environments, and that there are variations in developmental outcomes through use of different technologies.

Some writers have cautioned that there is a false assumption that familiarity or ease of use are the same as effective use in terms of learning. Patterns of student activity using laptops in classrooms, for example, suggest that students rapidly switch between multiple activities online (Leander, 2007), but this may not support deep engagement with the activities. Work on student online searching shows that students often use poor search strategies, and need to be taught how to search efficiently for information online (Coombes, 2009). Luckin et al. (2009) and Kimber and Wyatt-Smith (2010) similarly found infrequent critical thinking, evaluation or metacognitive reflection in students' online work. Chapter 6 discusses the teaching of these skills to students.

A large study of 2600 students and interviews with more than 100 teachers in the UK showed that teachers and students are rapidly embracing Web 2.0 technologies (BECTA, 2008). Most students (96 per cent) had internet connections at home, and 74 per cent of students had social networking accounts. Teachers employed a range of Web 2.0 applications in their classrooms and believed that these had the following effects on student learning:

- *Increased participation and engagement.* Online discussions and chats were seen to be especially beneficial to quieter students, allowing them the chance to participate without anxiety, and engagement was fostered by allowing students to express themselves in a variety of media, such as video.
- *Discussion outside of school.* Online discussions allowed students to continue learning outside school.
- *Extension of interest.* The availability of online technologies means students can study at any time and extend their areas of interest independently.
- *Sense of ownership.* When students publish and upload their work online, they have a sense of ownership and pay attention to quality.

However, as suggested previously, this report also found that, although students frequently used online technologies, their use of Web 2.0 was 'embryonic' in the sense that they lacked the literacy skills necessary for critical analysis and metacognitive engagement with these new applications. Technical skills were also weak, leading to a lack of knowledge about the full extent of online applications (BECTA, 2008). Subsequent studies report similar findings, suggesting this has not changed with time. For example, a large international study conducted in 2013 found wide variability in the quality of use of ICT by students in Year 8, with some students showing critical and independent skills in using ICT, while many others did not (Fraillon, Ainley, Schulz, Friedman & Gebhardt, 2014).

In summary, we cannot assume that having access to and using technology (even in schools) necessarily means being able to use it to enhance learning (Kennedy et al., 2008). At the same time, Leander (2007) cautioned that there may be a disconnect between students' online activity out of school and in school, with greater communication, focus on relationships, and collaboration evident in out-of-school activity. Certainly these features of Web 2.0 can be taken up by teachers, as we will explore in the section on transforming pedagogy later in this chapter. In the following section, we consider how to support learners to develop the essential skills they need to use ICT effectively for varied purposes, including learning: their **ICT literacy**.

ICT literacy
The capacity for purposeful and effective use of ICTs in one's own setting

ICT LITERACY

The Australian Curriculum identifies ICT literacy as a general capability that underpins learning and work in the digital age. This capability is claimed to have three components: the abilities to use ICT effectively to investigate, communicate and create. It also involves managing and operating ICT, and applying social and ethical protocols and practices when using ICT (ACARA, 2012a). Figure 12.2 shows how these elements interrelate.

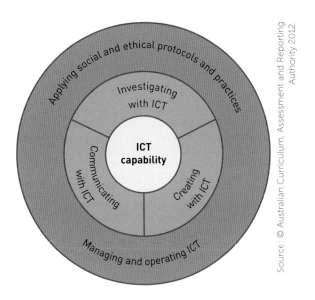

Source: © Australian Curriculum, Assessment and Reporting Authority 2012.

Clearly, ICT literacy is more than simply knowing how to use a computer. For teachers, ICT literacy involves understanding when and how to use the full range of ICTs to support learning, communication and creative processes.

FIGURE 12.2 Elements for ICT capability

Learners need to become ICT literate in order to understand the impact of new technologies on the way we live and learn. This includes awareness of the social and economic impacts of ICTs, and learning how to use ICTs ethically and responsibly. Learners also need to learn how to use ICTs for present and future learning and problem solving. ICTs enable rapid access to vast amounts of information. In order to be ICT literate, students also need to be 'information literate'. Under the National Assessment Program, ICT literacy is assessed in years 6 and 10. Table 12.2 describes the proficiency levels and some data from the 2014 tests.

INFORMATION LITERACY AND ICT LITERACY

Information literacy is the ability to locate, evaluate, manipulate, manage and communicate information to become an independent lifelong learner (Meredyth et al., 1999). Information literacy involves knowledge and skills; it also includes values and attitudes about knowledge and how it is used and shared (Langford, 2000). The concept of information literacy extends beyond computer use, but it is particularly important to be information literate when sifting through all the information that ICTs make available. To be information literate, students need more than technical skills. They also need to apply higher-order cognitive skills of discrimination, interpretation and critical analysis (see Chapter 6). Definitions of ICT literacy typically overlap with this, taking in many of these skills. For example, MCEETYA (2005) defined ICT literacy as "The ability of individuals to use ICT appropriately to access, manage and evaluate information, develop new understandings, and communicate with others in order to participate effectively in society." The difference is the focus in the latter definition on the use of ICT to achieve information literacy purposes.

information literacy
The ability to locate, evaluate and use information; it extends beyond technical skills

TABLE 12.2 Proficiency levels in ICT literacy

LEVEL	PROFICIENCY LEVEL DESCRIPTION	EXAMPLES OF STUDENT ACHIEVEMENT AT THIS LEVEL
6 0% of Y6 0% of Y10	Students working at Level 6 create information products that show evidence of technical proficiency, and careful planning and review. They use software features to organise information and to synthesise and represent data as integrated complete information products. They design information products consistent with the conventions of specific communication modes and audiences, and use available software features to enhance the communicative effect of their work.	• Create an information product in which the flow of information is clear, logical and integrated to make the product unified and complete. • Select appropriate key points and data from available resources and use their own words to include and explicate them in an information product. • Use graphics and text software editing features such as font formats, colour, animations and page transitions, in ways that enhance the structure and communicative purpose of an information product. • Include relevant tables and charts to enhance an information product and support these representations of data with text that clearly explains their purpose and contents.
5 1% of Y6 9% of Y10	Students working at Level 5 evaluate the credibility of information from electronic sources and select the most relevant information to use for a specific communicative purpose. They create information products that show evidence of planning and technical competence. They use software features to reshape and present information graphically consistent with presentation conventions. They design information products that combine different elements and accurately represent their source data. They use available software features to enhance the appearance of their information products.	• Create an information product in which the information flow is clear and logical, and the tone and style are consistent and appropriate to a specified audience. • Select and include information from electronic resources in an information product to suit an explicit communicative purpose. • Use graphics and text software editing features such as font formats, colour and animations consistently within an information product to suit a specified audience. • Create tables and charts that accurately represent data and include them in an information product with text that refers to their contents. • Apply specialised software and file-management functions such as using the history function on a web browser to return to a previously visited page or sorting data in a spreadsheet according to a specified criterion.
4 13% of Y6 43% of Y10	Students working at Level 4 generate well-targeted searches for electronic information sources and select relevant information from within sources to meet a specific purpose. They create information products with simple linear structures and use software commands to edit and reformat information products in ways that demonstrate some consideration of audience and communicative purpose. They recognise situations in which ICT misuse may occur and explain how specific protocols can prevent this.	• Create an information product in which the flow of information is clear and the tone is controlled to suit a specified audience. • Generate searches that target relevant resources and then select relevant sections of these resources to include, with some modification and supporting text, in an information product. • Apply graphics and text software editing features such as font formats, colour and image placement consistently across a simple information product. • Apply infrequently used software and file-management functions such as displaying a specified hidden toolbar in a word processor, or using a single pull-down menu function to save all the attachments of an email to a new location. • Identify security risks associated with internet data and explain the importance of respecting and protecting the intellectual property rights of authors.

>>

LEVEL	PROFICIENCY LEVEL DESCRIPTION	EXAMPLES OF STUDENT ACHIEVEMENT AT THIS LEVEL
Proficient standard for Year 10:		
3 42% of Y6 33% of Y10	Students working at Level 3 generate simple general search questions and select the best information source to meet a specific purpose. They retrieve information from given electronic sources to answer specific, concrete questions. They assemble information in a provided simple linear order to create information products. They use conventionally recognised software commands to edit and reformat information products. They recognise common examples in which ICT misuse may occur and suggest ways of avoiding them.	• Create an information product that follows a prescribed explicit structure. • Select clear, simple, relevant information from given information sources and include it in an information product. • Use graphics and text software editing features to manipulate aspects such as colour, image size and placement in simple information products. • Apply common software and file-management functions such as left aligning selected text, rotating an image, or creating and naming a new file on the desktop. • Recognise the potential for ICT misuse such as plagiarism, computer viruses and deliberate identity concealment, and suggest measures to protect against them.
Proficient standard for Year 6:		
2 31% of Y6 11% of Y10	Students working at Level 2 locate simple, explicit information from within a given electronic source. They add content to and make simple changes to existing information products when instructed. They edit information products to create products that show limited consistency of design and information management. They recognise and identify basic ICT electronic security and health and safety usage issues and practices.	• Locate explicit relevant information or links to information from within a webpage. • Make changes to some presentation elements in an information product. • Apply simple software and file-management functions such as copying and pasting information from one column of a spreadsheet to another column, or adding a webpage to a list of favourites (bookmarks) in a web browser. • Recognise common computer use conventions and practices such as the use of the '.edu' suffix in the URL of a school's website, the need to keep virus-protection software up-to-date, and the need to maintain good posture when using a computer.
1 14% of Y6 4% of Y10	Students working at Level 1 perform basic tasks using computers and software. They implement the most commonly used file-management and software commands when instructed. They recognise the most commonly used ICT terminology and functions.	• Apply graphics manipulation software features such as adding and moving predefined shapes to reproduce the basic attributes of a simple image. • Apply basic file- and computer-management functions such as opening and dragging and dropping files on the desktop. • Apply generic software commands such as the 'save as' and 'paste' functions, or selecting all the text on a page. • Recognise basic computer use conventions such as identifying the main parts of a computer and that the 'shut-down' command is a safe way to turn off a computer.

Source: © 2015 Education Services Australia Limited

THINK ABOUT

■ How could students' levels of proficiency in ICT be developed in your classroom? What would you need to build into learning activities using ICT, for example?

The 2014 ICT assessment framework provides a six-level description of the development of ICT literacy skills across a range of interrelated areas: accessing information, managing information, evaluating, developing new understandings, communicating and using ICT appropriately.

Table 12.2 presents proficiency levels used in the National Assessment Program in Australia for ICT literacy, and the results for the 2014 tests. Levels range from basic tasks at Level 1, and dependence on the teacher to guide information searches, to quite sophisticated, independent skills such as those associated with Level 6. Many readers of this text, as university students, will recognise that they need skills at Level 6 of ICT literacy. Figures in the left column represent the proportion of Year 6 and Year 10 students achieving each level in the 2014 ICT literacy NAP test (ACARA, 2015). These figures represent a significant drop in capacity of students compared to the previous testing period in 2011, with 10 per cent fewer Year 10 students reaching Level 5 (and none reaching Level 6). Note that only 55 per cent of Year 6 students and 52 per cent of Year 10 students met or exceeded the proficient standard for their level. One suggestion for the decline was increased focus on communication rather than information skills with greater use of mobile phones (ACARA, 2015). The 2017 test results will be reported in 2018, and published on the NAPLAN website.

BOX 12.2 IMPLICATIONS FOR EDUCATORS

ICT IN THE CLASSROOM

- *Information technologies are tools to enhance learning and teaching.* Approach ICTs such as computers, interactive whiteboards (IWBs), other devices and their apps as vehicles to promote learning. Do not use them just because they are there. Where appropriate, integrate ICTs into your lessons at the planning stage, and always evaluate their effectiveness for your purposes.
- *Make the most of students' expertise and willingness to experiment with ICTs.* Some students will know more than you do about using computers. Encourage the more capable students to demonstrate their skills and to help you and their peers where appropriate. Monitor how students are using ICTs such as smart phones and the internet. Even if some of these items are banned from use at school, acknowledge student experience and expertise where possible. This will help students to feel valued and will keep you up to date with their ICT interests.
- *Use ICTs' communication capacities.* Use ICTs such as online discussion boards to encourage students to communicate with learners in other countries and from other cultures. Design projects that involve collaborations between students in your classroom and those in rural areas, other cities or other countries. Discuss 'netiquette' (internet etiquette) and sociocultural differences that may emerge from cross-cultural interactions online.
- *Make use of interactivity of ICTs.* Collaborative tools such as wikis and Google Docs support collaborative learning. Whiteboards can be used powerfully to encourage student interaction. Have students work in pairs on individual boards (which can be laminated sheets with whiteboard markers) to solve a problem before trying it on the IWB to receive feedback.
- *Go beyond skills-based computer literacy.* Help students to explore their attitudes, values and judgement-making abilities by developing their information and ICT literacy. Students need time to search and evaluate the internet in meaningful ways. Provide scaffolding to help them do this step by step. Encourage critical thinking and the analysis of information. Give students opportunities to apply their learning by encouraging them to publish their own websites, including digital images and animations.

ICT TRANSFORMING LEARNING

You may recall from Chapter 3 that Vygotsky claimed that cultural tools such as language shape the thinking and behaviour of members of a cultural group. Modern ICTs such as smart phones, tablets, digital cameras, computers and internet connectivity could be said to be cultural tools of this type. How might our thinking patterns be changing as we use these tools? There are several theoretical models in the current literature, and some research evidence to support the notion that there are some changes in thinking that could be attributed to ICT use. As further research is undertaken in this area, we are likely to add to our understanding of this important question.

CHANGING PATTERNS OF COGNITIVE SKILLS?

As discussed above, Vygotsky's theory suggests that we would see changing patterns of cognitive skills with use of the cultural tool. However, Bavelier, Green & Dye (2010) cautioned that 'technology' cannot be regarded as a single thing. Rather, researchers have looked at various types of technology, and people's particular purposes in using it, in seeking answers to this question.

Mills (2014) reviewed literature examining this question in relation to adolescent brain development, and the effects of use of the internet in particular. Citing longitudinal studies of brain images from MRI, she reported that genes have a stronger effect than environmental or behavioural factors such as internet use, at least in the period between middle childhood and adolescence.

Wilmer, Sherman & Chen (2017) reviewed research on smartphone use, and found that there is some evidence for effects of smartphone use on capacity for attention at the time of use; however, long-term effects are less supported by the evidence, with mixed results. There do appear to be effects on memory for events. When smartphones are used, people tend to learn and remember less from the experience. The authors noted that this research, like much of the research on these topics, is in its infancy.

Another hypothesis that has been explored has been the effect of playing video games on particular cognitive skills, and particularly those skills influencing learning, such as perception and attention. For example, Zhang, Green, Lu & Bavelier (2013) explored effects of playing action video games on learning capacity. They found that people who play action video games frequently, learn faster in new tasks than others who don't regularly play such games. Bediou et al. (2018) conducted a meta-analysis of this research, and found an average positive effect of 0.55 in studies examining the cognitive profile of regular action video players. Intervention studies showed a smaller, but still significant effect size of 0.34, suggesting that playing action video games can, indeed, shape cognition, although the authors caution that their findings show that not all games benefit cognition to the same degree.

One of the capacities attributed to digital natives is the ability to multitask (being able to attend to multiple stimuli at once), with Prensky (2001) initially arguing that digital natives might develop this capacity. This does not appear to be the case – in fact, our cognitive architecture allows us to attend to just one stimulus at a time. Although people may learn to switch rapidly between stimuli, studies of learners switching rapidly between tasks show substantial slowing of processing, so this practice is not helpful to learning (Baddeley, 2012). Consistent with this, Cain, Leonard, Gabrielli and Finn (2016) found that adolescents in their study who displayed higher levels of media multitasking, also showed weaker performance in working memory (discussed in chapter 3 as an aspect of executive function that influences cognition and learning), and in academic achievement.

THINK ABOUT

■ Do these research findings align with your experiences in using these technologies? What might explain any differences?

STRENGTHENING OF NEURAL PATHWAYS

In our discussion of neuroplasticity in Chapter 2, we saw that activity strengthens particular neurological pathways or networks, so that tasks that are performed regularly become easier, more fluid and natural. It is likely that this contributes to ease of use and adding on of new ICT skills to existing ones by frequent users of internet applications.

An interesting series of studies examining effects of texting on linguistic abilities such as spelling skills showed that texting was associated with improved spelling skills (Plester, Wood & Joshi, 2009; Wood et al., 2011). Wood et al. (2011) suggest that this may occur by focusing the texters' attention on the visual and orthographic features of words rather than their phonological features, although further research is required to validate the hypothesis.

BUILDING COGNITIVE CAPACITY

Johnson (2010a) found correlations between teacher and parent ratings of cognitive and social development and various internet activities reported by eight- to 12-year-old children. Why might this be? One contributor could be an increase in cognitive capacity. You might recall from previous chapters (see Chapters 2 and 6) that our cognitive capacity expands with development, contributes to intelligence, and is dependent on speed of processing and the size of various memory stores. As mentioned above, in the earlier study, Johnson (2008) found that frequent internet users had significantly better abilities than infrequent users in planning, attention and processing. Johnson noted that the study only showed correlations, not causes, and suggested that there may be a reciprocal relationship between internet use and cognitive capacity – those with greater capacity might seek out this stimulating environment, which, in turn, contributes to increased capacity, and so on. Another study did look at causes: Dye, Green and Bavelier (2009) found that playing action video games increased capacity, leading to faster reaction times without decreasing players' accuracy. It is possible that with practice, automaticity is developed, freeing up working memory.

Johnstone et al. (2012) developed a series of computer games for children with ADHD that were designed to train working memory and control of inhibitions, which are weaknesses related to the condition (see Chapter 10). They found that as well as resulting in improvements in working memory, ignoring distracting stimuli, and sustained attention for the children with ADHD in the study, the program resulted in improvements in behaviour for children with and without ADHD. These findings suggest that playing computer games can indeed build cognitive capacity, although the games in the study were explicitly designed to do this, unlike the majority of computer-based games.

ICT TRANSFORMING PEDAGOGY

CourseMateExpress

Online Resources
Watch a **video** on this
text's website of a
teacher talking about
the role of ICT in
powerful pedagogy

 CourseMateExpress

Online Resources
Explore the TPACK
model and its use in
ICT education with the
Interactive Activity on
this text's website

One of the most important implications of ICT is its potential to transform and change traditional ideas about learning and teaching. Studies of teachers adopting ICT suggest that teachers initially tend to add ICT as another element to traditional classroom practice, carrying out traditional teaching tasks in new ways, and gradually move towards transforming their practice – doing new things in new ways (Betcher & Lee, 2009). One of the shifts shown in Table 12.1 was from ICTs as tools to ICTs as transformers of teaching and learning practices.

As discussed in the section on learning theories and ICTs below, several learning theories have informed and been extended by the integration of ICTs into learning and teaching. ICTs also transform pedagogy by raising new questions or issues for consideration within key facets of teachers' practice: assessment, motivating and engaging students, catering for students' diverse needs, classroom management and student welfare.

Making decisions about how and when this should happen in your classroom will require you to draw on and combine multiple stores of knowledge: theories of learning and teaching and knowledge of classroom practice and your students (pedagogical knowledge), knowledge of your content area (content knowledge), knowledge of how to teach your content area (pedagogical content knowledge), and knowledge of ICT (technological knowledge). Koehler and Mishra (2009) argued that effective use of ICTs in teaching involves the combination of all of these kinds of knowledge, identifying a final kind of knowledge they call TPACK: 'technological pedagogical content knowledge'. They argue that knowledge of how ICT can be used to access and process subject matter, and how ICT can support and enhance learning, are both elements of TPACK. Supporting this, Wood and Ashfield (2008) found that use of IWB technology that resulted in student learning benefits depended on teachers' pedagogical knowledge being employed alongside their technical knowledge of how to use the boards. Figure 12.3 shows Koehler and Mishra's (2009) model of how knowledge of technology and how to use it effectively in teaching interacts with other kinds of knowledge teachers hold.

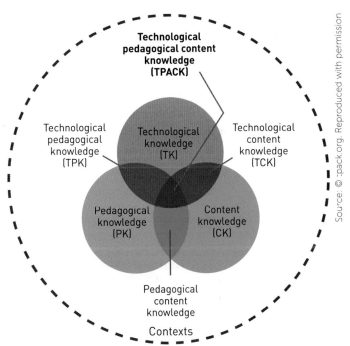

FIGURE 12.3 Technological pedagogical content knowledge

As we discuss in the following sections, it is important that teachers' practices in the use of ICT are guided by careful theoretical principles. Each of the major theories of learning provides some insight into the application of ICT in the classroom.

ICT AND THEORIES OF LEARNING

Clark (1985, 2012) challenged meta-analyses showing the effects of computer-based instruction on achievement, arguing that the gains observed can be attributed to the instructional methods underpinning the applications, rather than to the use of computers themselves. Technology has nonetheless provided new opportunities for the application of learning theories. Hattie's meta-analyses (2009) found that computer use is most effective when a range of teaching strategies is used, and when there are multiple opportunities for learning. Inan, Lowther, Ross and Strahl (2010) found that teachers tended to use more student-centred practices when computers were used as a learning tool, and more teacher-directed practices for drill and practice applications. Module II outlined several theories of learning, which we now revisit as they provide a useful framework for understanding different approaches to ICT use in education.

Behavioural theories and ICT

Behaviourists argue that learning takes place through the association of stimulus and response (see Chapter 5). Learning is defined as mastering subject matter and achieving behavioural objectives. Computers are particularly useful for this purpose. Before the era of personal computers, B. F. Skinner himself supported the use of teaching machines as a way of providing immediate reinforcement to promote learning and to respond to individual learner needs (Skinner, 1968). In the context of ICT, behavioural learning principles can underpin the use of computer software to tutor students. Hattie (2009) reported that tutoring applications are among some of the most effective uses of computers for learning. Using behavioural principles of stimulus–response and reward–punishment, the computer and its software operate as a tutor, teaching the user through **computer-assisted instruction (CAI)**, which is also known as 'computer-based instruction' (CBI) or 'computer-assisted learning' (CAL). (Note that these differ from 'computer-mediated instruction' (CMI, or distributed learning), which is discussed later in this chapter.)

With the computer as tutor, the teaching process is computer-driven, using the following pattern of interaction (see Figure 12.4 for an illustration of this process):

- The computer presents information.
- The user is asked to respond to a question or problem.
- The computer evaluates the user's response using pre-programmed criteria.

computer-assisted instruction (CAI)
A computer and its software are used as a tutor; also known as 'computer-based instruction' (CBI) or 'computer-assisted learning' (CAL)

a Students may choose to test themselves, practise online with immediate feedback or print out an activity sheet.

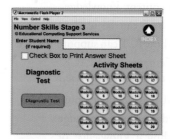

b Activity sheets also have downloadable, printable answers for self-checking.

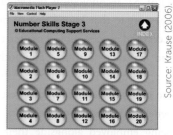

c Students select a module.

Source: Krause (2006).

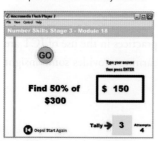

d The problem is set and students enter their response. Instant feedback is provided by pressing the 'Go' button. Notice there is opportunity for feedback for an incorrect response.

e An advantage of the computer as tutor is that students' time on task can be measured, and scores provided instantly.

FIGURE 12.4 Using the computer as a tutor

The computer responds to the user (for example, if the user enters a correct response, the program allows them to move to the next stage – or equivalent – and if responses are inappropriate or incorrect, the computer program may take the user back to repeat an exercise until they are able to provide the correct response). Encouraging and immediate feedback like 'Not quite right, try that once more' helps to maintain learners' motivation and engagement.

A common tutor application is in drill-and-practice activities. Drill-and-practice applications are used widely across a range of curriculum areas. A typical drill-and-practice routine is illustrated in Figure 12.4, in which the student has multiple opportunities to practise a particular problem and provide the correct answer. In some computer programs, students are given additional instruction when they enter incorrect responses; if not, teachers may provide such support.

Drill-and-practice applications are based on the behaviourist principle of mastery learning, which contends that everyone can learn given the right circumstances and sufficient practice (see Chapter 5). The software demonstrated in Figure 12.4 illustrates some of the distinctive capabilities of CAI: the learning is self-paced, the program has an inbuilt stopwatch so that students have direct feedback on their level of accuracy and the time they have taken, and students may go back over problems and repeat them to achieve mastery of the skills. In addition, the computer can be programmed to randomly generate new problems of the same type, so no two students will do the same set of questions, and retesting is meaningful.

Computer games are another example of the computer-as-tutor applications. Their educational value is discussed later in this chapter. Many of your students will have grown up using Sony PlayStation, Xbox or Nintendo Wii. All of these provide examples of competitive play between a user (or users) and the computer, with instant feedback and often an associated high level of interest and motivation. Educational games on online sites such as Studyladder provide a variation on drill and practice, but with a game element that rewards young players who spell simple words, match rhyming words, solve mathematical sums and identify letters or numbers. Such games combine bright colours and animation to motivate and stimulate young learners.

There is some evidence to suggest that, compared with traditional instruction, CAI can enhance achievement when it provides opportunities for extended practice, leading to automaticity of skills (Hattie, 2009; Keengwe & Hussein, 2013). As discussed in Chapter 5, however, such approaches have also been criticised for teaching a narrow range of skills in a highly controlled environment. Crompton, Burke & Gregory (2017) reported in a review of research that 40 per cent of mobile learning activities are designed using behavioural principles. They caution that the focus on acquiring knowledge rather than collaborating and creating knowledge makes limited use of the capacity of mobile technologies for supporting learning.

Source: Getty Images/Gary John Norman

FIGURE 12.5 Computers may be used as tutors or facilitators of learning, to develop automaticity of skills; as intellectual partners, provoking more advanced thinking; to provide authentic learning experiences; and for social interaction around learning.

THINK ABOUT

- Can you see any benefits in using computers for drill-and-practice activities in your teaching area?
- Discuss the following statement with your tutorial or study group: 'Computers enable the teacher to be in the machine. Eventually, computers will replace teachers.'

Cognitive and constructivist theories and ICT

ICTs play a significant role in promoting cognitive and constructivist learning principles in classrooms. Cognitive theorists such as Piaget emphasised active problem solving and meaning-making on the part of the learner. Piaget and Vygotsky (see Chapter 3) pointed out the importance of social interaction in learning. One of the key characteristics of ICTs is interactivity between the computer and the user, between the user and the computer, and between the user and other users in online environments. As illustrated in behaviourist applications, the machine-based view of the computer saw them used for drill-and-practice-type procedures, but ICT may also function as a scaffold that fosters learners' cognitive development in a constructivist manner, and many intelligent tutoring systems (ITS) employ this approach.

De Jong and Pieters (2006) argued that constructivist principles are supported by computer environments that contain cognitive tools or scaffolds to support students' learning. These viewpoints suggest that computers have the capacity to function as 'intellectual partners' to promote critical thinking and higher-order cognitive processing. ICTs provide a range of resources for students to use in problem solving, thinking, reflecting and collaborating with others within physical classrooms and across the globe in virtual learning contexts. As argued by de Jong and Pieters, these computer environments, with their potential for interactivity, are more conducive to active and engaged learning than more traditional teacher-centred approaches. According to its advocates, the constructivist classroom that integrates ICT provides students with a complex laboratory in which to observe, question, practise and validate knowledge.

ICTs can be integrated into constructivist learning environments in a range of ways. According to Hattie's (2009) meta-analyses, effective use of computers includes a number of constructivist principles.

- *The student, rather than the teacher, controls the learning.* This includes control of pacing, time spent achieving mastery, sequence of learning and choice of items.
- *Use of peer learning.* Hattie found that when used in pairs, computers were more effective than when used alone or by larger groups of students. He suggests this is likely to be because of opportunities for exposure to a range of ideas as well as feedback.
- *Optimisation of feedback.* Tasks can be tailored to students' learning needs to ensure they are sufficiently challenging, and feedback that includes explanations and hints can act as scaffolding to support students working within their zone of proximal development.

Simulations and authentic learning

As you will recall from Chapter 6, constructivism examines the ways in which learners make meaning from experience. Rather than viewing learning as the transmission of knowledge, constructivists see it as an internal process of interpretation. Constructivists value 'authentic' or 'situated' learning, in which learners take part in activities that are directly relevant to the application of learning. These authentic tasks enable learners to experience problem solving in real-world contexts. An example of computer technology that encourages students to solve problems in an 'authentic' environment is a computer simulation. **Simulations** are a unique form of tutoring facilitated by computer technology.

simulation
A model of a real system or phenomenon

A computer simulation represents a model of a real system or phenomenon. Simulations make use of **hypermedia**, a system that links pieces of information such as text, graphics, sound and video elements in an online virtual environment. These simulations offer an imaginary environment that is realistic enough to provide meaningful issues and consequences, and allow students to solve problems and interact with the situation. For example, students learning geography may see a computer-simulated volcanic eruption. They may analyse conditions and practise their analytical skills without actually visiting a volcano. Science students may perform a virtual dissection rather than operating on real animals. A stock-market simulation enables students to buy and sell shares and to practise their problem-solving skills without putting real money at risk. Simulations can be beneficial, as they allow users to experience certain phenomena vicariously and with less risk and cost. They offer opportunities for direct experience that students might not have otherwise.

Simulations are particularly useful for addressing controversial issues and challenging learners to consider the perspectives of others. Their strong experiential and interactive focus helps to engage students (Global Education Centre, 2005). For example, the 'Ollie Saves the Planet' online game is a fun children's activity, developed by the Australian Government and industry groups, that introduces players to the concept of sustainability by using simulations to focus on such issues as waste, water, energy, air and biodiversity (see Figure 12.6). Various Australian characters guide players by introducing them to problems, suggesting solutions and providing encouragement along the way.

hypermedia
A system that links pieces of information such as text, sound, visual images, animation and video in electronic environments

Authentic learning experiences

Using email and other forms of social media also facilitates authentic learning. Interacting online provides a medium for written communication that is embedded in an authentic context – that of exchanging ideas and information with peers within the class or elsewhere, including overseas. Email and social media tools such as blogs and discussion boards may be used to encourage students to write for a real audience, such as peers or community members, about topics that affect them. Potential benefits of such authentic learning and assessment experiences supported by computers include an increase in students' motivation for learning as they come to appreciate the relevance of their learning in real-world contexts. In many classes, authentic learning and assessment tasks also encourage collaboration between learners, and they become more active constructors and interpreters of their learning.

Source: © Sustain Ability International Pty Ltd.

FIGURE 12.6 Ollie Saves the Planet – simulation and problem solving online

Gaming and learning

Computer games are an increasingly important part of the lives of many children, and are another kind of authentic learning, that also draws on other aspects of constructivism. James Gee, a prominent theorist in this area, argued that 'video games recruit good learning and that a game's design is inherently connected to designing good learning for players' (Gee, 2008, p. 21). In talking about games, Gee refers to a label familiar to the pre-'net generation' of learners, who commonly referred to them as 'video games', as does Gee. Indeed, for many people, the technology of games commenced many years ago in the form of video games such as Pac-Man, Donkey Kong and Space Invaders, which were played on large video consoles in public game parlours. Then the first home-based game machines arrived; the next generation of learners will be familiar with current forms of these devices – Sony PlayStation, Nintendo Switch and Microsoft Xbox consoles. Internet connectivity is now a feature of the gaming world, enabling virtual interconnections between players, sometimes on a massive scale.

Gee linked the importance of games to modern theories of learning that emphasise experience-based learning and participation in a community of practice, in which the learner forms a social identity based on their interaction with other learners, or, in the case of games, interaction with other gamers. These learning principles emerge from the constructivist and neo-Vygotskian theories of learning (Chapter 6). In citing examples of such games, Gee (2008) referred to a range of games in which the gamers take on the perspective of characters and hence immerse themselves in a situated learning context. Sometimes gamers produce new social identities by creating an 'avatar' – a visual representation of themselves; examples of such games include Half Life and Second Life. Avatars enable the computer user to create new, often anonymous online identities for themselves. Video games also invoke social learning theories in that players situate themselves in another perspective; for example, Civilisation VI and The Sims 4, in which the learner must take on and model the characteristics necessary for the game of survival in another civilisation. Gee suggests that the people designing video games have succeeded in capturing the attention of and engaging learners by applying good theories of learning (Gee, 2007).

Earlier in the chapter, we discussed research showing links between action video games and development of cognitive skills and learning capacity. Games have also been designed (or adapted) to develop skills and knowledge specific to particular curriculum areas, such as Physics (*Physics playground*), Biology (*Crystal island*), Mathematics (*Mathbreakers*), and English (*Mars Generation One: Argubot Academy*). These are called '**serious games**' in the literature, because of their use for specific educational purposes (Jarvin, 2015).

serious games
Digital games that have been either designed or adapted for specific educational purposes

One assumption about the effectiveness of serious games to benefit students' learning has been their motivational aspect. However, in a meta-analysis of the literature, Wouters, van Nimwegen, Oostendorp & van der Spek (2013) found that while serious games were more effective for learning and retaining information than traditional instructional methods, they were not more motivating. It is likely that motivation depends on good game design (just as good pedagogy is required for other activities' motivational and teaching capacity), rather than the simple fact of being presented as a game. The researchers also found that games were most effective when players worked in groups, had multiple training sessions to learn the game, and when there were other pedagogies in addition to the game play.

Despite the potential benefits of using computer games in learning, there remains a concern about the link between computer games and violence. For example, Lam, Cheng and Liu (2013) found that adolescents in their study who had been involved in bullying others online were four times as likely as others to have been exposed to violent online games. Arguments about the links continue in the psychological and medical literature (for example, Ferguson, 2014; Strasburger, Donnerstein & Bushman, 2014). Another concern is that of the apparent dominance of boys and male role models in computer games. As we will discuss in the upcoming section addressing the inclusiveness of ICT, some people question the notion of a 'gender divide' in gaming, while acknowledging a range of other gender-based issues associated with ICT. Table 12.3 outlines a range of implications arising from the use of games in the classroom.

TABLE 12.3 Benefits and issues arising from gaming use in schools

EDUCATIONAL USES AND BENEFITS OF GAMES	ISSUES
• Many students are already familiar with mobile device-based gaming. • Gaming activity can occur with user versus machine on an individual console, or user versus other users on a network, or the internet. • Technology can be used to represent reality – real-life examples that are relevant to the student. • Games can provide an immersive experience. • Well-designed games are able to encourage problem solving and lateral thinking. • Opportunities to develop relationships can arise through games with individuals locally and around the world. • They are able to provide different levels of challenge and thus extended learning opportunities. • They encourage (in fact, demand) active participation in the learning experience. • Games provide opportunities for drill and practice, and can encourage visualisation and experimentation.	• Development of educational games to a level that matches commercial games is expensive and a highly specialised skill. • The gaming element must be supported by sound pedagogy and clearly defined learning outcomes. • Games can be highly competitive and this is not appropriate for some students; some can become obsessed with a game. • Issues related to what kind of device will be used to deliver games, what kind of games will be used, and issues of violence, appropriateness and age level all need to be considered.

Source: Adapted from Millea, J., Green, I. & Putland, G., *Emerging Technologies: A framework for thinking*, ACT Department of Education and Training, 2005, p. 74, released under the National Educational Access Licence for Schools (NEALS).

Collaboration and social interaction

Collaboration among learners is another defining characteristic of constructivist classrooms (see Chapter 6). The internet has strong potential for social interactivity and for supporting collaboration and student-centred learning (Light, 1993; Mercer, 1996). For example, it is possible for virtual communities of learners on the internet to work in small, collaborative groups to achieve a common goal (Dillenbourg & Schneider, 1995). Collaboration can also be encouraged as learners sit around the computer and work on problem solving or interactive activities as a group. Teachers need to be careful when forming such groups, as students may need assistance in maintaining task focus and in sharing responsibilities among group members, as we saw in Chapter 7. In the case of computers, in particular, there may be a tendency for the more competent and confident computer users to dominate. Nevertheless, the heterogeneous grouping of learners around computer-related tasks can assist in creating zones of proximal development (see Chapter 3) and be beneficial for all students.

ICT provides opportunities for students to build shared meaning and to collaborate as they use technology. For example, when students are arranged in groups around computers, they often act as peer coaches for one another, offering advice to those having difficulty with computers or software applications.

ICTs facilitate global collaboration, as the circle of social interaction is enlarged beyond student peers in the classroom to students and experts across the school, the larger community and the world. Through the introduction of a variety of perspectives and increased opportunities to interact with others, learners are challenged to think laterally and to consider other cultural and community perspectives.

Distributed learning

distributed learning (computer-mediated instruction, or CMI)
Teachers, students and learning resources can be in different locations so that learning and teaching occur independently of time and place

One way in which ICTs facilitate collaboration is through **distributed learning (computer-mediated instruction, or CMI)**, which allows teachers, students and learning resources to be in different locations so that teaching and learning can occur independently of time and place. This is particularly useful when learners are in isolated or remote areas, such as in rural Australia or New Zealand. Regular face-to-face interaction with peers and teachers may be impossible, but distributed learning and teaching means that students may learn by means of technology such as web-, video- or audio-conferencing, email and satellite broadcasting.

Distributed learning and teaching has a learner-centred focus and emphasises interaction and communication among learners and teachers. The internet connects teachers and learners to people outside the school environment, thus providing access to expertise not available locally. Web-based videos or photographs provide visual stimuli for learning, hyperlinks expand the information resources available to learners, and online discussion forums and email facilitate collaborative learning activities.

mobile learning (mlearning)
Use of mobile devices for learning at any time or place

Mobile learning (mlearning) has been a particular kind of distributed learning that has gained prominence from the widespread availability and use of mobile devices. Some consequences of mobile learning include:

- schools' adoption of BYOD, or 'bring your own device', to broaden students' access to technology in school
- use of QR codes, which allow students to easily access files or websites by scanning a code
- a blending of boundaries between school and life outside school, with learning happening anywhere and at any time, and learning in school being potentially interrupted by the outside world
- learning content increasingly delivered from outside the school, through websites such as the Kahn Academy (www.kahnacademy.com), or resources to complement classroom learning, such as the Australian Mathematics teacher, Eddie Woo, has done for his students with his 'misterwootube' channel (https://misterwootube.com/).

A meta-analysis of the effects of mobile devices on students' learning found higher achievement as a result of use of mobile devices than traditional teaching across science, mathematics and reading, in Kindergarten to Year 12 classes (Tingir, Cavlazoglu, Caliskan, Koklu & Intepe-Tingir, 2017).

Distributed cognition

distributed cognition
The notion that cognition is shared by individuals who make up communities and who share cultural tools

Related to distributed learning is the concept of **distributed cognition**, which is cognition that is not limited to individuals but is something shared by individuals who form communities, co-construct knowledge and share cultural tools. Technological tools such as computer-mediated communication (CMC) and the internet have fostered the study and understanding of distributed cognition, and have offered opportunities for collaborative learning and shared production of content. Alvarez, Salavati, Nussbaum and Milrad (2013) suggested that this capacity for distributed thinking also links to new media literacies that teachers can assist students to develop (see below).

Information technologies have a significant role to play in enhancing student learning in constructivist classrooms. A WebQuest is an online activity that illustrates many constructivist principles. WebQuests are inquiry activities that present students with a challenging task, provide access to a range of resources (most often accessed through the internet), and scaffold the learning process to promote problem solving and higher-order thinking (Rubin, 2013). WebQuests are an example of online activities that help students to learn and think collaboratively while capitalising on the possibilities of using the internet to facilitate distributed cognition. Students benefit from being linked to a wide variety of web resources, including learners from other cultures and countries, so that they can explore and make sense of the issues involved in each challenge.

HUMANIST LEARNING THEORIES AND ICT

Humanist theories of learning draw attention to the more personal, social and qualitative aspects of learning. They emphasise holistic learning and the development of human potential (see Chapter 7). Some might argue that humanism and technology are incompatible, yet technology provides multiple opportunities for connecting students to others worldwide, for fostering self-understanding, for self-directed learning, and for engendering a greater awareness and appreciation of a student's own culture and those of others. By enabling connectivity and interaction with others from diverse cultures and backgrounds, ICT can play an important role in raising learners' awareness of the interrelationships between themselves and their community, both locally and globally. When educators select and use ICTs with care, such technologies may be used to shape educational experiences that help learners understand themselves better, take responsibility for their learning, and learn to reach beyond their current development to find their full potential. Humanist theories can also direct teachers' attention to particular aspects of students' activity online, such as social presence in online work, and skills for cooperative learning (Cicciarelli, 2007).

STRENGTHS AND LIMITATIONS OF DIFFERENT APPROACHES TO LEARNING WITH ICT

Information technologies can do much to foster learners' construction of meaning and their own learning experiences, whether they are working at their own pace or in collaboration with others. However, if not informed by sound educational principles and theories, computer-based activities can impede learning, waste valuable learning time and become a distraction rather than an asset (Hattie, 2009).

There are obvious limitations to the behavioural approach to learning, as outlined in Chapter 5. These limitations apply equally in the context of ICT use, for since behavioural theory relies almost exclusively on observable behaviour and does not account for individual thought processes, the role of behaviourism in learning is limited to the types of learning that can be easily observed (such as factual recall), rather than less defined learning that involves conceptual change within the learner. Drill and practice and tutoring programs can focus on lower-level thinking skills (Roblyer & Doering, 2013).

Although constructivist classrooms offer much to promote student-centred learning, teaching that is based on constructivist principles is extremely demanding of the teacher, particularly when technology is involved, and requires time and support for the learner. It takes teachers time to locate appropriate resources, plan activities, arrange the classroom so as to promote collaboration, and at the same time ensure quality time on task. Another problem may be that some of the most appealing software websites provide realistic representations of content by using video that may be slow to download. Bandwidth issues and limited computer resources in some schools or remote locations can also work against the creative use of ICT.

Siemens (2005) argued that traditional learning theories are more concerned with the actual process of learning rather than the value of what is being learnt. He argued for a new learning theory for the digital age that reflects what it is to learn in a networked world. Siemens suggested that traditional learning theories do not adequately address questions such as:

- How do we conceive of learning when knowledge is no longer acquired in a linear manner?
- How do learning theories accommodate the fact that technology now performs many of the cognitive operations previously performed by learners (for example, information storage and retrieval)?

As an alternative, Siemens (2005) proposed a learning theory of 'connectivism'. This theory views learning as a process that occurs within nebulous environments that are not entirely under the control of the individual. Learning is focused on connecting specialised information sets that enable us to learn more. The connectivist theory acknowledges that learning may reside in non-human appliances, that it is a process of connecting specialised nodes or information sources, and that nurturing and maintaining connections is required to foster ongoing learning. This is just one example of current attempts to reflect how ICTs are changing the way we learn and interact with information in digital contexts.

Despite the limitations of current learning theories, they work together to add to our understanding of how ICTs contribute to the learning process. Teachers will be more effective in their use of ICTs if they understand these theories and how to apply them effectively.

Using ICTs in classrooms has implications for all aspects of teachers' practice, including curriculum content and how it is taught, classroom management, assessment, motivation and engagement of students, student welfare, ensuring equity of access to education, and supporting students with diverse needs. These topics are each treated in detail in other chapters; here we look at how the use of ICT is transforming teachers' practice relating to each aspect.

TRANSFORMING CURRICULUM

There are two main ways in which ICTs are transforming curriculum: in terms of the content being taught, and in terms of the ways that students learn that content. In this section, we look first at the example of literacy, which has expanded and changed through ICT use in society, and then at the example of mathematics instruction, in which ICT has offered new ways for students to work mathematically and to learn.

New literacies

When did you last 'LOL' (laugh out loud) as you stepped 'AFK' (away from the keyboard) after saying 'B4N' ('Bye for now') to your virtual chat-room friends? And are you feeling ☺ (happy) or ☹ (sad) today? All these words, phrases and symbols are examples of how ICTs and the internet have altered our language. Equally, literacy practices and skills have changed with the incorporation of multimodal texts, hyperlinks, and collaborative production of texts into our society.

Broad notions of literacy are being challenged and changed by new technologies that require multiple forms of literacy to exploit their full potential (Leu, Kinzer, Coiro & Cammack, 2004). This is evident in the way people have redefined standard literacy practices as they have used new technologies to find new ways to communicate and manipulate language as they express their identity in new electronic spaces (Leu, Leu & Coiro, 2004).

Consider, for example, the multimodal texts that are created in a blog incorporating visual, hypertext, video and text components, or a typical Facebook page (see Figure 12.7). Multimodal texts involve the integration of five modes to convey meaning: visual, language, gestural, audio and spatial organisation (Anstey & Bull, 2009). Multimodal texts require new 'grammars' of the various modal elements in these texts. Kimber and Wyatt-Smith (2010) suggested that as students produce these new text types, they need to be supported to create and evaluate quality texts for particular purposes. They proposed that teachers

Source: Reproduced by permission of the Australian Broadcasting Corporation – Library Sales © 2015 ABC.

FIGURE 12.7 Multimodal texts are changing our notions of grammar and the writing process.

use criteria that go beyond print-dominant notions, rather attending to e-proficiency, e-credibility and e-design in discussing and assessing quality of text with their students. Table 12.4 spells out the components of these criteria as described by Kimber and Wyatt-Smith.

TABLE 12.4 Assessment framework for using, creating and sharing knowledge online. Note that while each is presented in its own row, the arrangement is not hierarchical and is considered as a dynamic, mutually informing and overlapping set of learning priorities. Hence, the dotted lines denote both the boundlessness and the opportunity for the coalescence of the several components.

USE EXISTING KNOWLEDGE TEXTS OR MATERIALS	CREATE AND SHARE NEW KNOWLEDGE TEXTS OR MATERIALS
Transmodal facility Ability to work with and across source texts, technology platforms and modes of representation to create a new digital text where critical thinking about content and concepts is balanced with the aesthetics of design.	
e-proficiency	
• Ability to locate and retrieve information in written, visual, auditory and digital modes, using a variety of search engines, databases and strategies • Ability to use a range of software efficiently and fluently • Ability to keep efficient records of source texts for tracking purposes	• Ability to select software and mode of display appropriate for selected audience, the medium and type of content • Ability to exploit the affordances of the software and achieve particular effects in accord with the intended audience/ purposes
e-credibility	
• Ability to establish accuracy, currency, reliability and trustworthiness of sources (sites and authors) • Ability to discern how values and ideologies are operating in source texts and how these work to represent people, cultures, places and eras • Ability to make a discriminating selection of sources, balance viewpoints and find corroborating evidence • Ability to formulate a position on a topic by informed use of a range of source materials • Ability to identify and examine how elements of a text (verbal, visual/auditory channels) work to communicate and 'normalise' a position	• Discriminating choice of material resources for display or communication • Discriminating use of selected sources • To formulate, communicate and defend as appropriate a position, distinguishing it from other possible positions • Ethical/scholarly acknowledgement and use of all sources
e-designing	
• Ability to identify/discern the potential of source material and to select for (a) new applications and (b) appropriate mode/s of display • Ability to utilise sources ethically (for example, with accurate representation and proper acknowledgements) • Ability to be receptive to the contributions of others	• Ability to assemble, compose or design an aesthetic, creative combination/transformation or treatment of existing sources and materials into new, cohesive representations or text (for example, colours, fonts, spatial layout)

Source: Kimber and Wyatt-Smith (2010). Copyright © 2010 by Kay Kimber and Claire Wyatt-Smith. Used by permission.

THINK ABOUT

■ How are these criteria similar to and different from those you would use for a print-based text? How would you help students to develop these skills?

New text formats have also changed the way in which a reader must process and comprehend a text. As Leu et al. (2008) explained, the internet in particular has given rise to new text formats, new reasons for reading, and the need for new reading comprehension skills for information online. For example, hyperlinks in online texts can dramatically change the way a reader navigates or approaches a text. The hyperlinks can allow a reader to choose specific pathways or topics to follow, and hence reading becomes a non-linear process that is quite different from the linear process of following page after page of a standard text. As Leu et al. (2008) pointed out, such changes in texts require new skills and strategies from the reader. The reader must choose the links that are optimal to direct and focus their attention, or work out which links might be distracting and will disrupt their search for specific meaning or knowledge in a text.

new literacies
The skills, strategies and dispositions for using and adapting to rapidly changing ICTs

Teaching **new literacies**, then, involves teaching about these literacies, as well as teaching students how to engage with them and how to produce them. For example, it will involve teaching the information literacy skills we discussed in a previous section that help students to select, read and evaluate information online. It will also involve teaching skills for producing multimodal and collaborative texts alongside traditional print-based texts. Students also need to recognise the purpose for their authoring, with a difference in register between the social blogs they produce out of school, and those they produce for educational purposes in school. Hansford and Adlington (2009) advised that the particular text type chosen for a task should match that task's purpose. They give examples of collaborative online authoring (in a wiki) being used to develop a 'choose your own adventure' text with multiple paths; and a blog being used for a social commentary exercise in geography, with each text type matching a clear educational purpose. They suggest that a blog for educational purposes, for example, needs to have a strong and clear sense of purpose, a well-informed point of view, and quality of presentation.

These new kinds of texts have prompted the need for new tasks associated with them, new approaches to teaching them, and new ways of assessing them. As Knobel and Lankshear (2007) argued, simply transplanting old ways of teaching onto new text types will not work. We now turn to mathematics, where ICTs have opened up new strategies for learning and teaching.

New ways of learning in mathematics

From the 1970s, when handheld calculators first became cheaply available, concerns were expressed about their possible effects on children's abilities to do mental calculation. However, Ellington (2003) demonstrated in a meta-analysis of studies that this is not the case; rather, calculator use was associated with better student attitudes, and operational and problem-solving skills. Goos (2010) proposed that this benefit occurred because calculators provided a means to test hypotheses and speed up calculation, arguing that technology can deepen mathematical learning by focusing students on problem solving and question generation rather than on finding answers. In terms of cognitive load theory (see Chapter 6), calculators could be said to free up working memory by taking over that aspect of a mathematical problem.

CourseMateExpress

Online Resources
Go further: Try a tool for geometry learning via the link on this text's website

Technology can provide several benefits in mathematics learning: as a tool to help students perform mathematical tasks, as a means of visualisation, and as a means of provoking inquiry. Visualisation can be aided by the use of interactive tools; for example, showing how angles change as shapes change, showing relationships between statistics and graphing, and in mathematical modelling. Geiger, Faragher and Goos (2010) described an example of technology acting to support student social interactions around mathematics, with students testing a model using a CAS (computer algebra system) calculator, and being prompted to question their assumptions by the answers they received. Geiger, Faragher and Goos (2010) described the technology in this case as a teaching partner.

CourseMateExpress

Online Resources
Go further: Explore the 'Teaching teachers for the future' and 'Enabling e-learning' websites

The Australian Government has developed a website of resources to help teachers become proficient in their use of ICTs. Termed 'Teaching teachers for the future', it links ICT use to various curriculum areas in the Australian Curriculum. New Zealand also has an e-learning website with resources for teachers. More links are given at the end of this chapter.

TRANSFORMING ASSESSMENT

Information technology has been an invaluable tool for assessment, providing opportunities to assess students formatively in new ways, as well as assisting evaluation and reporting of assessment data. Just as ICT is transforming ways of teaching, it is also contributing to changes in assessment practice.

Computers can be particularly useful for teachers interested in understanding learners' cognitive and thinking processes, since computers can make students' thinking processes visible for teachers in a way that other methods of learning cannot (Tempelaar, Rienties & Giesbers, 2014). For instance, students' choices about how to use a particular computer application can reveal their thinking and problem-solving strategies: word-processing applications facilitate learners' revising and editing on screen, and records of students' internet search strategies are easily reviewed. Teachers can observe students working with computers, monitor their progress, stop and ask about students' goals, and make suggestions for revision or the use of different strategies. A number of programs such as Mathletics and Studyladder keep records of student progress as they complete activities online, which teachers and parents can access to formatively assess students' progress. This provides information about which topics students have mastered, and those they may be having difficulty with.

As technology advances, approaches to assessment become more sophisticated, and able to be integrated into daily learning activities. Shute and colleagues (Shute, 2015; Shute, Leighton, Jang & Chu, 2016) reported on use of 'stealth assessments' that are embedded in games and simulations to assess complex 21st-century skills such as problem solving, creativity and communication, as well as metacognition and other learning skills. For example, they described use of a 'pedagogical agent' designed by Conati (2002) as part of a game, which identified not only the students' errors, but also their affective and physical responses while playing the game (using cues such as furrowing of the brow and heart rate), to determine whether to provide support or not. Thus they argue that stealth assessments can collect information, but also provide instruction when needed, and support engagement.

In Chapter 13, we discuss dynamic assessment, in which teachers assess students' ability to benefit from instruction in order to determine the optimal instruction needed. Computer-based interactive assessments can provide a means for this to happen, by adjusting help according to students' responses, and then pinpointing the specific points at which a student required assistance, and whether they were able to benefit from this. Online assessments that adapt to students' needs to provide questions at their ability level, as revealed by prior responses, are another example of dynamic assessment facilitated by technology.

Another means of tracking student responses is through Temporal Evidence Maps (TEMs) (Zoanetti, 2010), which identify the processes students use in the process of completing a task such as problem solving. These identify errors in students' thinking or strategy use, which can then be addressed by the teacher. Just as teachers may do this by sitting one-on-one with a student 'talking aloud' as they work through the problem, the tracking can be done by a computer without relying on the students' ability to articulate their thinking, or the teacher's time being available to work one-on-one with each student.

Analysis and reporting of assessment results can also be facilitated through ICT. AsTTle (assessment tools for teaching and learning) was developed by the Ministry of Education in New Zealand to provide teachers, parents and students with information about a student's level of achievement in literacy and numeracy in relation to the national standards. Teachers compose tests by selecting items from a pool. The tests are completed and scored online, producing a series of interactive graph reports for individuals and groups, relating student achievement to curriculum levels, objectives and national norms. An example of one of these reports is given in Figure 12.8.

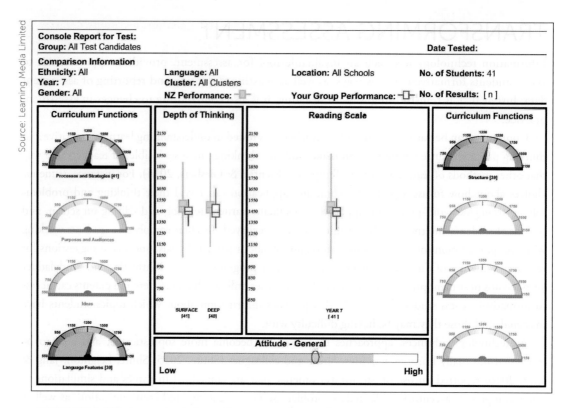

Source: Learning Media Limited

FIGURE 12.8 AsTTle generates information comparing student test results with national norms, curriculum levels and objectives.

Masters (2013) described a number of ways in which ICT can transform assessment practices. He described new technologies as enabling:

- assessment anywhere, on any device, any time
- use of simulations, games and other interactive multimedia applications as environments for assessment
- personalised assessments tailored to students' academic level and need; for example, intelligent systems are able to adjust questions based on the learner's previous responses
- information gathering about learners' thought processes, strategies, misunderstandings and errors, supporting diagnostic assessment
- timely, quality feedback.

Assessment is discussed in further detail in Chapter 13.

TRANSFORMING CLASSROOM MANAGEMENT

Computers can be used as an effective classroom-management tool, both by the opportunities they offer to monitor student engagement in tasks, and to encourage students to collaborate on computer-related tasks. In a review of the literature, Wright (2010) found that e-learning changes the dynamics of classrooms, and noted that teachers' active presence and participation in e-learning is important for its effectiveness. For many teachers using ICT – particularly those new to teaching – integrating computers into the curriculum may present several practical classroom-management challenges. For instance, there are often insufficient computers for individualised use, which means students may need to be grouped around computers. If groups are not effectively arranged, if students are not used to working collaboratively or if they do not have specified roles in their group, they may become distracted as they surf the Web or waste time talking. Time on task may suffer and this may cause undue noise and disruption in the classroom. If students are working online, there may be technical difficulties – such as computers crashing or networks going down – that could mean the planned task cannot be accomplished. In this case, teachers need to have contingency plans and alternative activities organised. Such classroom-management issues can be addressed, but they can also cause frustration and stress for both teachers and learners.

One issue that has arisen as a result of the use of school laptop programs and BYOD policies in schools is the monitoring of student work to ensure that they stay on task (Leander, 2007), and to provide help when students encounter difficulties. One simple response to this is for the teacher to reposition themselves behind the students, so that they can see what is on students' screens. Networked computers can also be monitored from a central computer using software that allows the teacher to view the desktops of individual students, and enter a desktop remotely to provide assistance as the teacher sees the need for it, so that students do not need to stop and ask. (Using this method, teachers can also close down documents or applications that should not be open.)

A further issue is the distraction that computers can pose when the teacher requires the students' attention. In this case, asking students to close their laptop or to turn away from the screen can quickly show compliance, and avoid distractions while students 'just finish what they were working on'. Chapter 14 has more on approaches to classroom management.

TRANSFORMING APPROACHES TO MOTIVATION

In and of themselves, ICT tools such as IWBs, digital cameras and simulation games may initially engage students by offering them new ways to interact and learn in the classroom, although some research suggests that such motivation is limited in duration (Moss et al., 2007). In the end, it will be the ways teachers use the technologies that determine whether and how they motivate and engage students. Careful selection of the appropriate tool and matching to student need are important to ensure ICTs are a learning technology and not simply an entertainment.

Information technologies may contribute to enhanced student motivation (see Figure 12.9), as their use in classrooms has been found to:

- encourage self-regulation and control over learning (McLoughlin & Lee, 2010)
- improve interaction between educators and students in the learning environment
- contribute to self-efficacy through use of digital objects that identify success, give opportunities to 'redo' a task for greater success, allow students to start at simpler levels and work up to more difficult tasks, provide prompts and helps for completing tasks, and allow self-correction (Handley, 2010)

Source: Getty Images/Thomas Barwick

FIGURE 12.9 ICTs may enhance motivation in students, improving their attendance and attitudes towards learning.

- enhance self-efficacy and agency through decision making, controlling the learning environment, social modelling and social persuasion in Web 2.0 applications (Hall & Hall, 2010).

Information technologies are thought to promote student engagement through:

- opportunities for collaboration and co-construction of knowledge in social media applications (Henderson, Snyder & Beale, 2013)
- personalised learning, with ready access to support as it is needed (Wright, 2010)
- action-based discovery learning that is interactive, practical and often experimental (Jukes, 2005; Livingstone & Bober, 2005)
- linking learners rapidly to constantly growing information sources through hyperlinks and hypertext systems (Jukes, 2005)
- tracking learner progress (for self and reporting to others)
- increasing physical involvement and engagement with learning, in that computer users engage by selecting courses of action or search strategies for themselves
- enabling distributed learning and cognition, which may broaden students' experiences and perspectives.

However, as we found with the links between use of technology and learning, links between technology and student engagement are not automatic, but depend on individual learner characteristics as well as the effectiveness of the particular technological application being used and its management (Girard, Ecalle & Magnan, 2013; Gurung & Rutledge, 2014; Nansen et al., 2012).

TRANSFORMING STUDENT WELFARE

Information technologies have introduced new questions for students to consider in relation to identity, as they deal with online identities, create new identities through avatars in gaming, and interact with others exclusively online. They have also introduced new issues of student welfare for schools and teachers to consider, in particular the issue of cyberbullying.

IDENTITY AND PSYCHOSOCIAL DEVELOPMENT

An important part of effective ICT use involves understanding its role in young learners' development in a range of areas. We have seen that computer technologies may be used to enhance learners' cognitive development by providing opportunities to solve problems with the help of scaffolding from the computer. Furthermore, there are opportunities for students to interact with others through computer technology (for example, using email and other forms of social media) or to interact with their peers or teachers as they sit in groups at a computer and work through tasks. ICTs also have the potential to play a role in the personal, social and moral development of learners in the 21st century, depending on the extent of their involvement with the technology. The psychology of the internet is a fast-growing area of study (Riva et al., 2012; Suler, 2006) because of the possibilities of internet communications and the potential for identity experimentation that such communications offer. This branch of psychology is increasingly being referred to as **cyberpsychology**.

Importantly, Mills (2014) reported that social development in adolescence is not harmed by internet activity, with evidence that students who show moderate internet use are also involved in other social activities 'offline', such as sports and clubs (Romer, Bagdasarov & More, 2013). Romer et al. found links between heavy use of the internet, increased depression and withdrawal from sports and clubs, but suggested depression may have been the influencing factor here, rather than internet use.

cyberpsychology
The study of psychology and behaviour associated with the use of ICTs and other technologies

Fullwood & Attrill-Smith (2018) argued that the internet plays a role in people's construction of self, as people explore different selves through avatars and other means online. They suggested that online and offline spaces are intertwined and interact with one another, with behaviour in each space influencing behaviour and perceptions of self in the other. ICTs can also increase people's social connectedness through social media as well as video apps, although the Australian Bureau of Statistics (2015) reported that this is less the case for people in remote and outer regional areas of Australia, either through poor connectivity, or through financial stresses that make accessing the technology difficult. We discuss this below in the section on equity.

MENTAL HEALTH

Increases both in social media use, and in incidence of mental health issues in young people raise questions about whether there is a relationship. Robinson, Bailey & Byrne (2017) summarised research showing both positive and negative effects of social media are possible. Effects seem to depend on the frequency of use, the type of use, and whether there are pre-existing sensitivities to mental health problems.

- *Positive.* For moderate users, social media use contributes to self-esteem, feelings of closeness and connection, and social competence, as well as to empathy (Vossen & Valkenburg, 2016).
- *Negative.* Viewing others' profiles and photographs can give an unrealistic picture of others' lives, and can result in depression, particularly if those profiles and images provoke envy (Duffy, Tandoc & Ferucci, 2015). It appears that actively using social media sites to connect with others is positive, whereas passively viewing others' posts may link to depression. Young people at risk of mental health issues such as self-harm, suicide or eating disorders can be inspired by hearing about others' methods, or may feel that these maladaptive coping mechanisms are normal.

Smartphone-based prevention programs such as *Headspace, smilingmind* (apps with meditation and mindfulness activities), and *Biteback* (a positive psychology program designed by the Black Dog Institute) allow young people to build skills and resilience in mental health and have been shown to reduce depression, anxiety and stress (Spijkerman, Pots & Bohlmeijer, 2016; Manicavasagar et al., 2014).

For people with mental illness, research likewise describes online activity as a 'double-edged sword' with both benefits and risks (Lewis & Seko, 2016). Benefits identified from a review of the literature included social connection or reduction of social isolation; encouragement of recovery; opportunity to disclose feelings and mental health issues; and curbing of harmful impulses. Risks included reinforcement and triggering of harmful impulses; and stigmatisation.

Other benefits of technology for mental health care have been identified by the Black Dog Institute in Australia. They include treatments such as Cognitive Behaviour Therapy that can be delivered online via free apps such as *moodgym*, providing access to those who are unable or unwilling to attend a treatment centre in person. Individuals can also assess their own mental health online, and access help via online apps or helplines.

For teachers, it is important that we are aware of the risks as well as the benefits of technology in relation to mental health, and of possible helpful programs, as we monitor and support the health of the young people we teach.

CYBERBULLYING

The increasing popularity of online interaction and social networking also appears to be linked to the emergence of **cyberbullying**. Cyberbullying is a particular term coined to describe bullying by electronic means or through the use of ICTs such as online technologies (Juvonen & Graham, 2014). It should be noted that this does not imply that ICT *causes* bullying; rather, the new mediums of communication

cyberbullying
The use of ICTs and other electronic devices to bully someone

and interaction merely facilitate different forms of these behaviours. (See Chapters 4 and 14 for more extensive discussions of bullying.)

Cyberbullying differs in some important ways from traditional bullying. Slonje, Smith and Frisen (2013) explained that cyberbullying may not rest with a single perpetrator. The potential of something posted on the internet to 'go viral' means that a single post may be picked up and distributed by others, having a wider audience and impact on the victim than was originally intended. It also tends to have its effect without the perpetrator being present. Slonje and colleagues point out that this has both positive and negative implications. Perpetrators have less opportunity to develop empathy for their victim, with the result that cyberbullying is likely to go on for longer than traditional bullying might, but they also experience less satisfaction, if causing distress is their motivation. Anonymity and the speed and breadth of transmission of messages are other features particular to cyberbullying (Juvonen & Graham, 2014), and are linked to its negative effects for victims, as is discussed below. While bullying in general is reported by up to 94 per cent of students in schools, cyberbullying is less common, reported by around one-third of students (Cassidy, Faucher & Jackson, 2013). Given the effects on students, however, this is still of concern.

Cyberbullying can take many different forms – exclusion, harassment, threats, attacks on reputation, trolling or abuse, and rumours – and its means expand as new technology and applications are developed, with common means currently being texts, calls, images, video clips, internet games, chat rooms, IM messaging and websites. This breadth has complicated research, with different findings in various studies depending on the definition and particular context studied (Cassidy, Faucher & Jackson, 2013).

Tokunaga (2010) found that cyberbullying occurs throughout childhood and extends into adulthood, although it peaks in adolescence, at 13–15 years of age. A New Zealand study of bullying in schools found teachers reported awareness of cyberbullying from the preschool years (Green, Harcourt, Mattioni & Prior, 2013). Relative to traditional bullying, girls are more likely to be involved, both as perpetrators and as victims, although boys are also involved in cyberbullying (Connell, Schell-Busey, Pearce & Negro, 2014). Connell and colleagues found that cyberbullies were likely to have been or to become victims of cyberbullying, and vice versa.

Cyberbullying has also been found to occur in cases where girls in particular might make disclosures in online journals and invite others to comment, leading to criticism and hostility from other respondents (Livingstone, 2008).

Challenges managing cyberbullying

Unfortunately, the medium of cyberspace makes it particularly difficult to manage for the following reasons.

■ *Anonymity*. Being anonymous on the internet can lead to a sense of online self that is separate from real-life identity and responsibilities (Suler, 2004). As with all cases of bullying, the abuse of power is important and can be particularly assisted when the perpetrator remains anonymous. This may lead to a perception that it is 'safe' to bully online (Heirman & Walrave, 2008), as evidenced by one student's comment in a research study: 'I mean, I think it is safer to bully online, because who will find out that you were the bad guy sending the offending email?' (Vandebosch, 2003, as cited in Heirman & Walrave, 2008). The aspect of anonymity also has consequences for the victim, who cannot be sure who it is who is attacking them. Slonje, Smith and Frisen (2013) quote a 13-year-old girl as identifying this as the main aspect: 'Cyberbullying is probably the not knowing and the anonymity about those that bully. Well, that you don't really know what is happening. And you only know that it is someone that is out to get you.'

- *Widespread audience.* Social networking technologies allow for rapid, widespread dissemination to an unknown audience. As in other cases of bullying, online observers and recipients in effect become bystanders to bullying (see chapters 4 and 14). This can foster a heightened sense of insecurity in the victim and is a particularly damaging psychological consequence of cyberbullying (Heirman & Walrave, 2008).

- *24/7 attainability.* The online and distributed nature of cyberbullying means that the victim can never be assured that they are safe or free from bullying, and means that it is harder to monitor or police in school environments (Heirman & Walrave, 2008). It also means that bullying outside the school context can flow into the playground and vice versa.

- *Privacy.* Many online communications between individuals can remain private in that they can escape the supervision of adults. Many victims choose not to discuss this bullying with adults, in some cases because they fear a loss of internet access or removal of their mobile phone. This attachment to electronic connectivity means, in effect, that teenagers risk significant emotional harm because they delay seeking help (Heirman & Walrave, 2008).

- *Lack of social cues.* As discussed in Chapter 4, one of the most important social skills we have is our ability to accurately process social cues, such as facial expressions and emotions. The absence of these cues in online and non-verbal contexts can lead to 'toxic' disinhibition, and in some cases may mean that the perpetrators of this bullying may not realise the effect of their actions on others, as illustrated by these student comments in research studies: 'It's hard to remember that the other person is really seeing it' (Kowalski, Limber & Agatston, 2008, as cited in Heirman & Walrave, 2008), and 'It was a kind of joke to me, but when I saw him at school I realised that I had driven things too far' (Vandebosch, 2003, as cited in Heirman & Walrave, 2008).

These features of cyberbullying suggest that teachers and schools face a challenging task in managing these student behaviours, not least because they often move across the boundary between the school and outside-school lives of students (see Figure 12.10). The psychosocial consequences of bullying are severe (see Chapter 4), and some research suggests that cyberbullying has consequences for both its perpetrators and victims that go beyond those of other types of bullying, including links to depression and thoughts of suicide for adolescents (Bonanno & Hymel, 2013). Not all victims of cyberbullying experience such negative effects, however, with some reporting little or no distress. The type of cyberbullying seems to make a difference, with victims in one study reporting more worry from cyberbullying received on their mobile phones (texts, calls) than the internet (Slonje, Smith & Frisen, 2013). Students have a right to feel safe and protected in their school environment, as we discuss in Chapter 14. Information about cyberbullying, and the strategies teachers and other adults can use to help students, can be found on the Office of the eSafety Commissioner's website (see also Box 12.3).

FIGURE 12.10 How can you ensure that students do not use text messages, email or other forms of technology to hassle or bully other students?

Source: Matthew Duchesne. © Milk and Honey Photography, 2010.

BOX 12.3 CLASSROOM LINKS

HELPING A CHILD WHO IS BEING CYBERBULLIED

One or more of the following signs and changes in behaviour could indicate that a student is being cyberbullied and/or other mental health issues. The signs should be considered in light of the student's usual behaviour.

- decline in social interaction; having less to do with friends
- dislike and avoidance of school, and/or absenteeism
- decline in academic performance
- increased loneliness and/or distress
- increased social exclusion and peer rejection
- sudden changes in friends or groups associated with difficulty focusing on schoolwork and/or sleepiness
- poorer physical health
- negative self-perception
- becoming withdrawn, appearing depressed or anxious, having mood swings, crying for no apparent reason
- having suicidal thoughts – this should be reported to the administration and the parents/carers immediately for appropriate action.

To help a child who is being cyberbullied, organise the following:

1 Ensure the student is safe; arrange support from the school counsellor or a teacher the student trusts. Kids Helpline can offer support outside school.
2 Discuss your concerns with the student and their parents.
3 Monitor the student's peer interaction, particularly at break times.
4 Help them to make connections with other students through established student groups that operate at break times, or by recruiting appropriate students to support them.
5 Put the school's anti-bullying policy into action if any student is being targeted or excluded by particular students.

Students can also be assisted in their response to online bullying:

a Don't respond to any further messages/postings from the bully.
b Block further correspondence from them (block their mobile number or email address, and change privacy settings).
c Talk to others you trust about what is happening (a parent, older brother or sister, teacher, friend).
d Keep evidence of any bullying to assist with tracking down the bully and potentially reporting the matter to the service and police.
e Report any bullying concerns to the administrator of the service used.
f Remember it isn't your fault.
g Don't join in by commenting on or sharing posts that might be hurtful to others.
h Support a friend who is being bullied. Let them know you don't agree with what the bully is saying or doing, and will stand by your friend.

Source: Adapted from Commonwealth of Australia 2015. Information about cyberbullying is available from Australia's Office of the Children's eSafety Commissioner website (formerly the Cybersmart program), http://www.esafety.gov.au. © Commonwealth of Australia. Reproduced with permission.

THINK ABOUT

- Discuss the advantages and disadvantages of the internet as a new psychosocial space that fosters social relationships and allows individuals to play different roles.
- How should schools represent cyberbullying in their school anti-bullying policies? Do schools have a particular responsibility to address this form of bullying?
- Can you think of classroom strategies teachers could use to make students more critical or metacognitive users of online environments? Could this protect students from cyberbullying or other online abuse?

Ethics and safety

The use of ICTs poses several ethical issues for educators. These include the potential for:

- plagiarism – software such as *Turnitin* has been developed to examine digital text and check for similarities between students' work and existing text
- breach of copyright rules through downloading Web resources such as music, videos and graphics
- exposure to obscene or harmful materials (such as pornography) on the Web
- exposure to online interactions that may prove harmful (such as with online stalkers or paedophiles).

The Australian Bureau of Statistics (2011) identified that only 3 per cent of children who used the internet in the past year had experienced some form of safety or security problem. This represented 72 000 children, which is a concern in real terms, although the question combined safety and security concerns and so may overstate the dangers to children. Holmes (2009), Cranmer, Selwyn and Potter (2009) and Dunkels (2008) have all noted that online communication is much less risky than the media tend to portray it, and that it is largely within young people's capacity to manage. The Office of the eSafety Commissioner's site (see the link on this text's website) contains resources for examining issues and strategies with children.

CourseMateExpress

Online Resources
Go further: Find resources on the Office of the Children's eSafety Commissioner's site via the link on this text's website

TRANSFORMING EQUITY ISSUES

ICT has the potential to reinforce differences between economically advantaged and disadvantaged schools and students, and to entrench existing inequities. It costs a great deal to maintain adequate computer equipment and software in schools, and this contributes further to inequities. There are often disparities between students in terms of the types of ICT resources they have, or have access to, at home, as well as the extent to which they use them.

Several other potential sources of disadvantage, such as gender, language background and disability are discussed below.

ACCESS AND USE OF ICT

Lack of access or inequitable access to technology is a significant issue that influences the quality of student learning and learning outcomes. Learners' socioeconomic status and the financial resources of the schools they attend play a significant role in determining access to quality learning resources. This is particularly apparent in the area of ICT, as computer technology can be costly and there are complex access issues related to internet use. In addition, the variable strength of internet connection in various locations in Australia or New Zealand affects people's access to internet resources. The term 'digital divide' was coined to highlight the inequitable distribution of ICT resources and internet access across groups (NTIA, 2000; Smolenski, 2000). Two groups of students are particularly likely to suffer as a result of the digital divide:

1 students in remote rural or poor inner-urban areas where telecommunications are limited and/or expensive, and internet connections are weak
2 students from low-SES homes that lack ICT resources.

In making decisions about how to integrate ICT into the learning process, and to what extent, teachers need to consider factors such as students' access to computer resources at home, and the potential disadvantages that lack of access may cause.

Equitable access to ICTs means that all learners have equal access to ICTs regardless of socioeconomic background, gender, ability level, geographic location, ethnicity or language background. For some students, this may mean providing access to the internet through school. For others, it may involve providing a variety of adaptive devices designed to enable learners with disabilities to take full advantage of the power of technology to enhance personal freedom, or it may involve using a range of innovative resources to extend the more-able students' learning. All learners should have the opportunity to use ICTs for the full range of purposes for which they were designed, including information access and communication through a range of technologies.

ICT has the potential to transform the schooling experiences of children living in rural and remote areas by providing them with access to resources and connections to people and information that they would otherwise not have. Children living on rural properties or attending small or isolated schools have the opportunity to access an expanded range of courses through a combination of ICT and distance education.

Not all children in rural and remote areas benefit from access to new technology and improved communications infrastructures. Excessive distances can make it difficult for students to access necessary ICT resources, and mean that even if they have the hardware and technology, they do not have sufficient internet connectivity to benefit from it. Moreover, the disadvantage brought about by remoteness of location is often compounded by the low SES of some students' families and by limited funding for computers in rural schools. The 2014 national Australian assessment of ICT literacy found lower access to and use of ICT among rural compared with metropolitan and students, and for students of low SES, or Aboriginal and Torres Strait Islander backgrounds (ACARA, 2015).

The Australian Government's Digital Education Revolution (2008–12) sought to address inequities of access by ensuring that all students in years 9–12 had a computer at school, and that all schools had broadband access (DEEWR, 2013). An independent review of the program found that it had achieved most of its objectives, including 1:1 availability of technology, and supportive infrastructure in schools that has led to greater engagement with technology for education. Low-SES schools and their students benefited in particular. Challenges remain for teachers to capitalise on the technology through their teaching practice, to build on the momentum started by the initiative (DEEWR, 2013). Moreover, the results of the National Assessment reported in Table 12.2 suggest there is more to be done to achieve equity of access.

Access alone may not imply equivalence of use of ICT. The 2009 PISA study of access and use of ICT by 15-year-olds in Australia and New Zealand found that socioeconomically advantaged students were more likely to use computers at school than were disadvantaged students. This deepened inequities of use and access the students had at home (OECD, 2011). Further differences were found in gender and ICT use, as described below.

GENDER AND ICT USE

Large-scale studies of computer and internet use have not shown gender differences in Australia or New Zealand (ABS, 2011; MCEECDYA, 2010; OECD, 2011). This is a shift from studies of the 1990s which showed boys used computers at home and in classrooms more than girls did (for example, Scott, 1996). The studies show different patterns of computer use by boys and girls, with girls using the internet more for social communication, while boys are more likely to use it for entertainment (MCEECDYA, 2010); also, girls are more likely than boys to use the internet for educational purposes and social networking, while boys are more likely than girls to use it for online gaming (ABS, 2011). Girls seem to benefit from their computer use more than boys do in terms of academic outcomes, with girls showing higher scores in ICT literacy (ACARA, 2015) and digital reading (OECD, 2012). Johnson (2011) suggested internet use may benefit girls more due to a tendency to focus on accomplishment more than entertainment. And yet, girls are reported to have less positive attitudes towards computers than do boys, and to display less self-confidence in using them (OECD, 2011; ACARA, 2015). One factor that appears to positively affect girls' attitudes is female teachers' use of computers (Meelissen & Drent, 2008).

THINK ABOUT

- Have you seen evidence of a 'digital divide' in your educational experience?
- What strategies will you put in place to minimise disadvantage brought about by ICT use?
- What disadvantages might there be in giving students the option of completing all their assignments on computer? Do you think there is merit in asking that all students submit at least one assignment in handwritten form, rather than in word-processed form?

TRANSFORMING INCLUSIVE EDUCATION

With its potential for addressing the needs of students on an individual basis, ICT can be particularly useful for extending students with high academic abilities, and catering for those with additional learning needs.

Information technologies may be used in unlimited ways to enhance the motivation, intellectual stimulation and achievement of learners of all ages. Some of the benefits of ICT use to engage and stimulate more-capable learners in your class include the fact that ICT can:

- provide opportunities for gifted students to progress at a rate that is appropriate to their individual abilities
- accommodate students' individual learning preferences
- provide opportunities for students to develop and practise higher-level thinking skills
- enable students to communicate with other gifted and talented students around the world
- be used as a powerful and up-to-date information resource when researching any given topic
- provide structured opportunities for individual and small-group investigations of real problems
- provide opportunities to participate in collaborative learning experiences
- enable students to engage in distance learning programs for the exceptionally able (Western Australia Department of Education and Training, 2004).

There are several examples of how ICTs are being used to promote the learning of gifted and talented students in mainstream schools. Online or email mentoring is a very enriching experience, particularly when mentors are experts who are not able to visit the students face-to-face. In this way, experts from around the world can become mentors for gifted students in your class. In particular, this means that geographic isolation can be overcome, while the timing of the mentor–mentee interactions can be more flexible (for example, after working hours as well as during school) (Gross, 2005).

Information technologies are also used in a range of ways to support students with diverse learning needs through the use of technologies to assist learning. In developing online teaching and learning resources, you are now required to apply international standards such as the Web Content Accessibility Guidelines produced by the World Wide Web Consortium (W3C.org) for enhancing accessibility of online materials for all students, including those with disabilities. Computers with assistive devices have the potential to support learners with physical disabilities, including those with cerebral palsy, spinal cord injuries and muscular dystrophy, providing them with learning opportunities that were previously unavailable. Assistive devices include voice-recognition software; translation of musical, science or maths notation into braille; virtual pencils; alternative keyboards and mouses for learners with physical disabilities; and digitised speech devices (Millea, Green & Putland, 2005). In addition, some regular devices such as tablets and smart phones have settings that allow them to be adjusted for particular needs (for example, voice-over and large fonts for vision impairments, autotext for literacy difficulties and assistive touch for motor difficulties).

There is a wide range of possibilities for using ICTs to enhance the learning of students with disabilities. For example, essay questions can be provided as audio files (podcasts) for learners with visual impairments, and podcasts may be transcribed for learners with hearing impairments (Millea, Green & Putland, 2005). Box 12.4 presents a case study of a teacher who used assistive technology to support a student's writing.

STRENGTHS AND LIMITATIONS OF USING ICT IN THE CLASSROOM

As we have seen, ICT is changing schools and classrooms in many ways. It promises a future that is faster, more exciting and better than anything that has gone before. But the mere presence of a computer, tablet or IWB in a classroom does not automatically guarantee improved learning and teaching. Information technology may have many positive benefits for students' learning, providing it is used well, but may also carry disadvantages for learning, when it is not used so well. Research is still continuing to inform teachers of ways to integrate ICTs productively into learning and teaching.

BOX 12.4 CASE STUDY

WORKING WITH CHARLIE: ICT IMPROVING THE WRITING PROCESS FOR A STUDENT WITH LEARNING DIFFICULTIES

Charlie was a reluctant writer. He had difficulty with fine motor coordination, which made handwriting laborious and slow. Although he was in Year 6, his writing skills were still at an early level, with invented spelling and simple sentences. The sample below took him an hour to write. As a result, Charlie disengaged with school. He avoided any writing task, and had behavioural, emotional and self-esteem difficulties. Charlie's teacher noticed, however, that his oral language was well developed. He could tell stories, and pull her in with his descriptions. Clearly his language development was not the problem.

Charlie's teacher decided to try assistive technology to support Charlie in his writing. A predictive writing program reduced the number of key strokes he needed to make in typing, and the computer read back to him what he wrote, so that he could hear the errors that weren't evident to him visually. After two months working with the program, the results were nothing short of amazing. A PowerPoint presentation Charlie developed revealed complex sentences, advanced vocabulary, and considerable pride in his work.

With the help of assistive technology, Charlie was able to produce a text that reflected his understanding, and to see himself as a capable student. His teacher was convinced of the power of technology for learning.

Charlie's writing, without the aid of assistive technology:

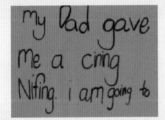
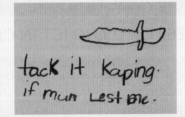

A page of Charlie's PowerPoint presentation on kangaroos:

Where Do They Live?

- Kangaroos live in Australia and New Guinea. Eastern Grey Kangaroos live in Jervis Bay. Kangaroos live in groups or mobs up to one hundred or two hundred. Kangaroos are usually moving during the early morning and late afternoon. They rest during the day under the trees.

Source: Adapted from a lecture by Alyson Whiteoak, 2012. 'Charlie' is a pseudonym.

Strengths of using ICT in the classroom

Information technologies have the potential to enhance learners' academic achievement when effectively integrated into the curriculum. This has been confirmed by research that shows improved overall student achievement in English, mathematics and science in primary schools with good ICT resources (BECTA, 2008; Tingir et al., 2017).

Wright (2010) found that improved learning outcomes from ICTs may occur through:

- facilitating students' motivation and engagement via co-constructive pedagogies, and matching learning activities to students' abilities and needs
- encouraging independent and personalised learning among students, with easy access of supports for their interests and needs
- critical thinking and multiliteracies, which are supported by student-centred pedagogies that allow students to develop deep understanding and metacognition while engaging with multiple texts; Wright argued that technological tools foster socially mediated learning and co-construction, which in turn develop these higher thinking skills
- rapid and flexible access to information, resources and experts; this offers students choice in how and when to work, and they are also able to produce their own texts for real online audiences
- collaboration in wide contexts, which can contribute to motivation as well as enhancing skill development; Wright says that 'in these kinds of contexts, students are learning about, with and through technology'.

BOX 12.5 IMPLICATIONS FOR EDUCATORS

STRATEGIES FOR USING ICT IN CLASSROOMS

- *Decide your aims for the lesson/unit, and select software and online resources accordingly.* Be guided by what you know about how students learn best. If you want to focus on developing students' basic skills, use software that promotes mastery learning. If you want to encourage discovery learning, allow time for students to explore the internet, but provide appropriate scaffolding and guidance to avoid time wasting.
- *Motivate students and develop their interests.* Databases of information available on the internet allow students to examine a multitude of topics to find those of individual interest.
- *Build on students' background knowledge.* As students use computer applications, observe their problem-solving strategies and how they interact with the content. This will give you an indication of what students know. Ask questions about why students have chosen to explore a particular website or use a certain application. This gives opportunities for interaction and for dialogue about students' understandings and knowledge.
- *Encourage different approaches to problem solving on the computer.* Simulations, virtual environments and links to resources that extend well beyond the classroom all expand students' options for learning, and pose problems that engage students' interest, provide complex challenges and give learners opportunities to apply their knowledge.
- *Foster active learning.* When students use technology as a tool or as a means of communicating with others, they take an active role rather than passively receiving information that has been transmitted by a teacher, textbook or television. The student actively makes choices about how to generate, obtain, manipulate or display information.
- *Encourage collaboration.* Technology offers opportunities for student collaboration through social media. Wright (2010) suggested this may help Māori and Pasifika students' motivation and engagement in particular.

>>

- *Support learners as the classroom structure and organisation change.* When technology is used to enhance learning environments, student roles change. Learners often become peer mentors and mentors for their teachers as well. Sometimes this is difficult for teachers and students. Students need help in learning how to function in such roles.
- *Adapt your classroom-management techniques.* Issues such as abuse of expensive equipment and student access to unacceptable material on the internet must be addressed by teachers and schools as they change their practices. Managing group collaboration around computers and encouraging individualised learning using computers all require careful planning.

Limitations of using ICT in the classroom

Despite the many potential positive effects of ICTs on student engagement and learning outcomes, concerns remain about these apparent benefits. Goodwin (2011) noted mixed results about the effect of IWB use on student learning, and that the role of the teacher is central to their level of effectiveness. Teachers' professional development is key to the ongoing effective use of ICTs for learning and teaching, particularly as further research emerges into conditions for learning outcomes to ensue from use of particular ICTs. There are still few longitudinal studies measuring student learning over time and the role of ICTs in promoting learning outcomes.

The need for ICT information and literacy, equity issues, classroom management and student welfare issues discussed earlier in this chapter all highlight ways in which the relationship between ICT use and positive learning outcomes is not a simple one.

THINK ABOUT

- In your experience, have the advantages of ICT use outweighed the disadvantages?
- How do you plan to integrate ICTs into your teaching in light of the benefits and limitations outlined in this chapter?

CONCLUDING COMMENTS

Information technologies are integral to our society and our schools in the 21st century. They offer powerful possibilities for learning and teaching, and are also complex realities that students must navigate as they access knowledge, communicate and create. These technologies are already transforming learning and teaching through the issues they raise – welfare, equity, ethics and management – which teachers and learners must address alongside curriculum and pedagogy. This field is continually growing and evolving, and staying current with the research and its implications for your practice will be important.

CourseMateExpress

Online Resources
Take a moment to consider your personal philosophy. You may wish to use the **Develop Your Philosophy** tool on this text's website

STUDY TOOLS

ONLINE STUDY RESOURCES

COURSEMATE EXPRESS

Visit http://login.cengagebrain.com and use the access code that comes with this book for 12 months' access to the student resources for this text.

The CourseMate Express website contains a range of resources and study tools for this chapter, including:

- a **self-check quiz**
- **crosswords**, **flashcards** and a **glossary** to help you revise the key terms from this chapter
- the **Go further** materials and **interactive activity** mentioned in the chapter.

CHAPTER REVIEW

- Information and communication technology (ICT) encompasses information technology (computer technology) and communications technologies such as videoconferencing and the internet's capacity to facilitate both synchronous (real-time) and asynchronous (virtual time) communication.
- ICT is viewed as a key competence for learning and work. It is integrated throughout the Australian Curriculum and professional teaching standards, and is seen as an important tool for learning in the New Zealand National Curriculum.
- Although some views see the current generation of students as 'digital natives', other work shows considerable variability in use within this group, and the need for explicit instruction in ICT and information literacies.
- Use of ICT may transform learning by strengthening particular neural pathways, and building cognitive capacity in working memory and attention. This will be dependent on the particular technology and how it is used.
- ICTs have the potential to change teaching practices through curriculum, ways of learning and teaching,

assessment, motivation, student welfare concerns and programs for students with diverse needs.
- ICT use may be informed by behavioural learning theories, which see the computer as a tutor and emphasise drill-and-practice activities.
- Cognitive and constructivist theories emphasise the interactive potential of ICTs and their role in scaffolding learning and promoting collaboration.
- From the point of view of humanist learning theory, ICT may be a useful tool for helping learners understand other cultures, for promoting awareness of the self and one's place in a global society, and for promoting tolerance and peace through understanding and communication.
- Use of ICTs in education has the potential to produce benefits which include enhanced motivation, increased student engagement and improved learning outcomes. These need to be balanced by considering limitations such as the potential for inequity, impacts on student welfare, and classroom-management issues.
- Teacher professional development is essential to the effective use of ICTs for learning and teaching.

PUTTING IT TOGETHER

Making links between 'ICT in learning and teaching' and material in other chapters

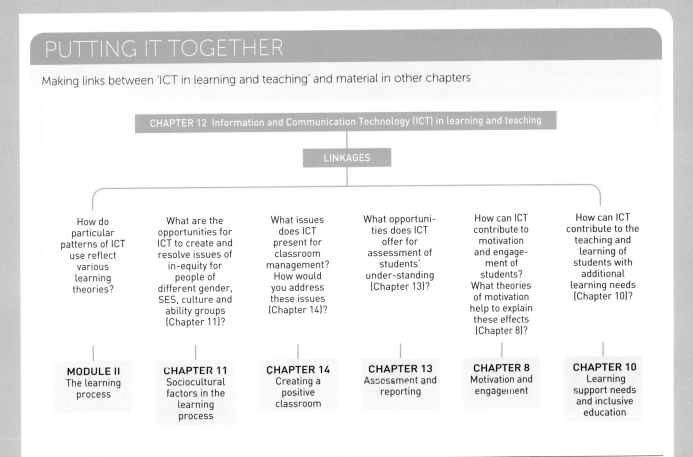

CHAPTER 12 Information and Communication Technology (ICT) in learning and teaching

LINKAGES

How do particular patterns of ICT use reflect various learning theories?	What are the opportunities for ICT to create and resolve issues of in-equity for people of different gender, SES, culture and ability groups (Chapter 11)?	What issues does ICT present for classroom management? How would you address these issues (Chapter 14)?	What opportunities does ICT offer for assessment of students' under-standing (Chapter 13)?	How can ICT contribute to motivation and engage-ment of students? What theories of motivation help to explain these effects (Chapter 8)?	How can ICT contribute to the teaching and learning of students with additional learning needs (Chapter 10)?
MODULE II The learning process	**CHAPTER 11** Sociocultural factors in the learning process	**CHAPTER 14** Creating a positive classroom	**CHAPTER 13** Assessment and reporting	**CHAPTER 8** Motivation and engagement	**CHAPTER 10** Learning support needs and inclusive education

QUESTIONS AND ACTIVITIES FOR SELF-ASSESSMENT AND DISCUSSION

1   List as many examples as you can of ICTs that you use, and that you are aware of being used in schools. How has this changed learning and teaching?

2   Describe the shifts in the use of ICT in schools over time. What is the current emphasis?

3   Explain some considerations in teaching students to use ICTs effectively.

4   How are ICTs transforming learning and teaching in schools? Give some examples.

5   Comment critically on how behavioural, cognitive, constructivist and humanist theories of learning influence the ways in which ICTs are used in education.

6   List ways in which ICTs are contributing to assessment or motivation, and teaching students with diverse needs. Find and evaluate some ICT tools that do this.

7   What new challenges do ICTs present for learners and for teachers? How could learners and teachers be supported in meeting these challenges?

8   How can ICTs support students' mental health? What risks should teachers be mindful of in relation to technology use and mental health?

9   Critically evaluate the benefits and limitations of using ICTs in educational contexts.

FURTHER RESEARCH

SEARCH ME! AND EDUCATION DATABASES

Explore Search Me! education for articles relevant to this chapter. Fast and convenient, Search Me! education is updated daily and provides you with 24-hour access to full-text articles from hundreds of scholarly and popular journals, ebooks and newspapers, including *The Australian* and *The New York Times*. Log in to Search Me! through http://login.cengagebrain.com and use the search terms listed here as a starting point:

- computer-mediated communication
- cyberpsychology
- distributed cognition
- distributed learning
- e-learning
- ICT
- information and communication technology
- information literacy
- information literacy AND school
- information technology AND learning.

You can also use these terms to explore databases such as ERIC, PsycINFO and the Australian Education Index.

Search Me!

RECOMMENDED WEBSITES

Misterwootube: https://misterwootube.com/

Australian Council for Computers in Education: www.acce.edu.au

Cyberpsychology: http://users.rider.edu/~suler/psycyber/decade.html

Office of the eSafety Commissioner: https://esafety.gov.au/education-resources

Edublogs – advice on constructing blogs: http://edublogs.org

ICT school planning – Victorian Department of Education and Training: www.education.vic.gov.au/school/teachers/support/pages/planning.aspx

National Digital Learning Resources Network (NDLRN) – develops digital curriculum resources for Australian and New Zealand schools: www.ndlrn.edu.au

Ministry of Education New Zealand *Te Kete Ipurangi* (TKI): technology.tki.org.nz/

Nesta Future Lab – research on ICTs in education: www.nestafuturelab.org/research/index.htm#p

Web 2.0 information from the Victorian Department of Education and Training: https://fuse.education.vic.gov.au/pages/View.aspx?id=3355664a-b5a9-4f7e-864f-adb18f52a0bb&Source=%252fpages%252fResults.aspx%253fs%253dWeb%252b2.0

RECOMMENDED READING

Bower, M. (2017). *Design of Technology-Enhanced Learning: Integrating Research and Practice*. Bingley, UK: Emerald Publishing.

Coiro, J., Knobel, M., Lankshear, C. & Leu, D. (Eds). (2008). *Handbook of research on new literacies*. Mahwah, NJ: Lawrence Erlbaum.

Howell, J. (2012). *Teaching with ICT: Digital pedagogies for collaboration and creativity*. Melbourne: Oxford.

Roblyer, M. D. & Doering, A. H. (2013). *Integrating educational technology into teaching* (6th ed.). Upper Saddle River, NJ: Pearson.

REFERENCES

ACARA. See Australian Curriculum, Assessment and Reporting Authority

Alvarez, C., Salavati, S., Nussbaum, M. & Milrad, M. (2013). Collboard: Fostering new media literacies in the classroom through collaborative problem solving supported by digital pens and interactive whiteboards. *Computers & Education, 63*, 368–79.

Anstey, M. & Bull, G. (2009). *Using multimodal texts and digital resources in a multiliterate classroom. e:update 004, e:lit:* Primary English Teaching Association, Marrickville.

Australian and New Zealand Institute for Information Literacy. (2004). *Australian and New Zealand information literacy framework.* Retrieved from www.library.unisa.edu.au/learn/infolit/Infolit-2nd-edition.pdf.

Australian Bureau of Statistics. (2011). Australian social trends, June 2011: Children of the digital revolution. Cat. no. 4102.0. Retrieved from www.abs.gov.au/ausstats/abs@.nsf/Lookup/4102.0Main+Features60Jun+2011

Australian Bureau of Statistics. (2012). Year Book Australia, 2012. Cat. no. 1301.0. Retrieved from www.abs.gov.au/ausstats/abs@.nsf/Lookup/by%20Subject/1301.0~2012~Main%20Features~Use%20of%20information%20technology~174

Australian Curriculum, Assessment and Reporting Authority. (2012a). *Information and Communication Technology (ICT) capability.* Retrieved from www.australiancurriculum.edu.au/GeneralCapabilities/Information-and-Communication-Technology-capability/Introduction/Introduction

Australian Curriculum, Assessment and Reporting Authority. (2012b). *The Australian Curriculum: Numeracy background.* Retrieved from www.australiancurriculum.edu.au/generalcapabilities/numeracy/introduction/background

Australian Curriculum, Assessment and Reporting Authority (2015). National Assessment Program–ICT Literacy Years 6 & 10 Report 2014. Sydney: ACARA

Australian Institute for Teaching and School Leadership. (2014). *Australian professional standards for teachers.* Retrieved from www.aitsl.edu.au/australian-professionalstandards-for-teachers/standards/list

Australian School Librarians Association. (2006). *A teacher librarian advocate's guide to building information literate school communities: ASLA Advocacy Kit 2006.* Retrieved from www.asla.org.au/advocacy/advocatesguide.pdf.

Baddeley, A. D. (2012). Working memory: Theories, models, and controversies. *Annual Review of Psychology, 63*, 1–29.

Bavelier, D., Green, C. S. & Dye, M. W. G. (2010). Children, wired – for better and for worse. *Neuron, 67*(5): 692–701.

Bediou, B., Adams, D. M., Mayer, R. E., Tipton, E., Green, C. S. & Bavelier, D. (2018). Meta-analysis of action video game impact on perceptual, attentional and cognitive skills. *Psychological Bulletin, 144*(1), 77–110.

Bennett, S. & Maton, K. (2010). Beyond the 'digital natives' debate: Towards a more nuanced understanding of students' technology experiences. *Journal of Computer Assisted Learning, 26*(5), 321–31.

Betcher, C. & Lee, M. (2009). *The interactive whiteboard revolution: The teacher's guide to IWBs.* Melbourne: ACER Press.

Black Dog Institute. (2017). Integrating technology and mental health care. Accessed 9/2/18 from http://blackdoginstitute.org.au/research/evidence-and-policy/updates-and-insights

Bonanno, R. A. & Hymel, S. (2013). Cyber bullying and internalizing difficulties: Above and beyond the impact of traditional forms of bullying. *Journal of Youth Adolescence, 42*, 685–97.

Bower, M. (2017). *Design of Technology-Enhanced Learning: Integrating Research and Practice.* Bingley, UK:Emerald Publishing

British Educational Communications and Technology Agency. (2008). *Learners' use of Web 2.0 technologies in and out of school in Key Stages 3 and 4: Research Report.* Retrieved from http://dera.ioe.ac.uk/1476/1/becta_2008_web2_learnersuse_report.pdf

Cain, M. S., Leonard, J. A., Gabrieli, J. D. E., and Finn, A. S. (2016). Media multitasking in adolescence. *Psychonomic Bulletin & Review, 23*, 1932–1941.

Cassidy, W., Faucher, C. & Jackson, M. (2013). Cyberbullying among youth: A comprehensive review of current international research and its implications and application to policy and practice. *School Psychology International, 34*(6), 575–612.

Cicciarelli, M. (2007). Behavioral, cognitive, and humanistic theories: Which theories do online instructors utilize? *International Journal of Information and Communication Technology Education, 3*(4), 1–12.

Clark, R. E. (1985). Evidence for confounding in computer-based instruction studies: Analyzing the meta-analyses. *Educational Communications and Technology Journal, 33*(4), 249–62.

Clark, R. E. (2012). Questioning the meta-analyses of computer-based instruction research. In R. E. Clark (Ed.), *Learning from media: Arguments, analysis, and evidence* (2nd ed., pp. 13–35). Charlotte, NC: IAP Information Age Publishing.

Coiro, J., Knobel, M., Lankshear, C. & Leu, D. (Eds). (2008). *Handbook of research on new literacies.* Mahwah, NJ: Lawrence Erlbaum.

Commonwealth of Australia, Department of Education, Employment and Workplace Relations. (2013). *Digital Education Revolution program review.* Canberra: DEEWR. Retrieved from http://docs.education.gov.au/documents/digitaleducation-revolution-program-review

Conati, C. (2002). Probabilistic assessment of user's emotions in educational games. *Applied Artificial Intelligence, 16*, 555–575.

Connell, N. M., Schell-Busey, N. M., Pearce, A. N. & Negro, P. (2014). Badgrlz? Exploring sex differences in cyberbullying behaviors. *Youth Violence and Juvenile Justice, 12*(3), 209–28.

Coombes, B. (2009). Generation Y: Are they really digital natives or more like digital refugees? *Synergy, 7*(1), 31–40.

Cranmer, S., Selwyn, N. & Potter, J. (2009). Exploring primary pupils' experiences and understandings of 'e-safety'. *Education and Information Technologies, 14*(2), 127–42.

Crick, N. R. & Dodge, K. A. (1994). A review and reformulation of social-information processing mechanisms in children's social adjustment. *Psychological Bulletin, 115*, 74–101.

Crompton, H., Burke, D. & Gregory, K. H. (2017). The use of mobile learning in PK–12 education: A systematic review. *Computers and Education, 110*, 51–63.

De Jong, T. & Pieters, J. M. (2006). The design of powerful learning environments. In P. A. Alexander & P. H. Winne (Eds), *Handbook of educational psychology* (2nd ed.). Mahwah, NJ: Lawrence Erlbaum Associates.

Dillenbourg, P. & Schneider, D. (1995). Mediating the mechanisms which make collaborative learning sometimes effective. *International Journal of Educational Telecommunications, 1*(2/3), 131–46.

Dunkels, E. (2008). Children's strategies on the internet. *Critical Studies in Education, 49*(2), 171–84.

Dye, M. G. W., Green, C. S. & Bavelier, D. (2009). The development of attention skills in action video game players. *Neuropsychologia, 47*(8–9), 1780–9.

Education.au (2009). *Collaboration in teaching & learning: Strategic ICT advisory service*. Retrieved from www.educationau.edu.au/jahia/webdav/site/myjahiasite/shared/papers/2009_SICTAS_CTL.pdf

Education Council, New Zealand Teachers and Social Media website: http://www.teachersandsocialmedia.co.nz

Ellington, A. J. (2003). A meta-analysis of the effects of calculators on students' achievement and attitude levels in precollege mathematics classes. *Journal for Research in Mathematics Education, 34*(5), 433–63.

Ferguson, C. J. (2014). Is video game violence bad? *The Psychologist, 27*(5), 324–7.

Fraillon, J., Ainley, J., Schulz, W., Friedman, T. & Gebhardt, E. (2014). Preparing for Life in a Digital Age. The IEA International Computer and Information Literacy Study International Report. International Association for the Evaluation of Educational Achievement (IEA)/ SpringerOpen. Downloaded 29/1/18 from https://research.acer.edu.au/cgi/viewcontent.cgi?article=1009&context=ict_literacy

Fullwood, C. & Attrill-Smith, A. (2018). Special issue on 'Constructing the self online'. *Cyberpsychology, behaviour and social networking, 21*(1), 3–4.

Gee, J. P. (2007). Pleasure, learning, video games, and life: The projective stance. In M. Knobel & C. Lankshear, (Eds), *A new literacies sampler* (pp. 95–113). New York: Peter Lang.

Gee, J. P. (2008). Learning and games. In K. Salen (Ed.), *The ecology of games: Connecting youth, games, and learning* (pp. 21–40). The John D. and Catherine T. MacArthur Foundation Series on Digital Media and Learning. Cambridge, MA: The MIT Press.

Geiger, V., Faragher, R. & Goos, M. (2010). CAS-enabled technologies as 'agents provocateurs' in teaching and learning mathematical modelling in secondary school classrooms. *Mathematics Education Research Journal, 22*(2), 48–68.

Girard, C., Ecalle, J. & Magnan, A. (2013). Serious games as new educational tools: How effective are they? A meta-analysis of recent studies. *Journal of Computer Assisted Learning, 29*(3), 207–19.

Global Education Centre. (2005). *Simulation games*. Retrieved from www.globaleducation.asn.au

Goodwin, K. (2011). Engaging students in literacy learning with interactive whiteboards. *e:update, 17*. Marrickville NSW: Primary English Teaching Association.

Goos, M. (2010). What counts? Technology and mathematics teaching and learning. *Teacher 2010, 215*, 22–5.

Green, V. A., Harcourt, S., Mattioni, L. & Prior, T. (2013). *Bullying in New Zealand schools: A final report*. Victoria University of Wellington. Retrieved from www.victoria.ac.nz/education/pdf/Bullying-in-NZ-Schools.pdf

Grimley, M. & Allan, M. (2010). Towards a preteen typology of digital media. *Australasian Journal of Educational Technology, 26*(5), 571–84.

Gross, M. (2005). *The gifted education professional development package*. Sydney: Gifted Education Research, Resource and Information Centre (GERRIC). Retrieved from https://education.arts.unsw.edu.au/about-us/gerric/resources/pd-package/

Gurung, B. & Rutledge, D. (2014). Digital learners and the overlapping of their personal and educational digital engagement. *Computers & Education, 77*, 91–100.

Hall, R. & Hall, M. (2010). Scoping the pedagogic relationship between self-efficacy and Web 2.0 technologies. *Learning, Media and Technology, 35*(3), 255–73.

Handley, R. (2010). Increasing learning motivation and skills through computer technology for students with behavioural and/or learning difficulties. *Premier's Teacher Scholarship Reports, 7*, 68–76. Sydney: NSW Department of Premier and Cabinet.

Hansford, D. & Adlington, R. (2009). Digital spaces and young people's online authoring: Challenges for teachers. *Australian Journal of Language and Literacy, 32*(1), 55–68.

Hattie, J. (2009). *Visible learning: A synthesis of over 800 meta-analyses relating to achievement*. London: Routledge.

Heirman, W. & Walrave, M. (2008). Assessing concerns and issues about the mediation of technology in cyberbullying: Cyberpsychology. *Journal of Psychosocial Research on Cyberspace, 2*(2), article 1. Retrieved from www.cyberpsychology.eu/view.php?cisloclanku=2008111401

Henderson, M., Snyder, I. & Beale, D. (2013). Social media for collaborative learning: A review of school literature. *Australian Educational Computing, 28*(2), 1–15.

Holmes, J. (2009). Myths and missed opportunities: Young people's not so risky use of online communication. *Information, Communication & Society, 12*(8), 1174–96.

Howell, J. (2012). *Teaching with ICT: Digital pedagogies for collaboration and creativity*. Melbourne: Oxford.

Inan, F. A., Lowther, D. L., Ross, S. M. & Strahl, D. (2010). Pattern of classroom activities during students' use of computers: Relations between instructional strategies and computer applications. *Teaching and Teacher Education, 26*(3), 540–6.

Jarvin, L. (2015). Edutainment, games, and the future of education in a digital world. In E. L.Grigorenko (ed.), The global context for new directions for child and adolescent development. *New Directions for Child and Adolescent Development, 147*, 33–40.

Johnson, G. M. (2008). Cognitive processing differences between frequent and infrequent Internet users. *Computers in Human Behavior, 24*, 2094–106.

Johnson, G. M. (2010a). Internet use and child development: The techno-microsystem. *Australian Journal of Educational & Developmental Psychology, 10*, 32–43.

Johnson, G. M. (2010b). Young children's Internet use at home and school: Patterns and profiles. *Journal of Early Childhood Research, 8*, 282.

Johnson, G. M. (2011). Internet activities and developmental predictors: Gender differences among digital natives. *Journal of Interactive Online Learning, 10*(2), 64–76.

Johnstone, S. J., Roodenrys, S., Blackman, R., Johnston, E., Loveday, K., Mantz, S., Barratt, M. F. (2012). Neurocognitive training for children with and without ADHD. *ADHD Attention Deficit and Hyperactivity Disorders, 4*(1), 11–23.

Jukes, I. (2005). *Understanding digital kids (DKs): Teaching and learning in the new digital landscape*. Retrieved from www.thecommittedsardine.net

Juvonen, J. & Graham, S. (2014). Bullying in schools: The power of bullies and the plight of victims. *Annual Review of Psychology, 65*, 159–85.

Keengwe, J. & Hussein, F. (2013). Computer-assisted instruction: A case study of two charter schools. *International Journal of Information and Communication Technology Education, 9*(1), 70–9.

Kennedy, G. E., Judd, T. S., Churchward, A., Gray, K. & Krause, K. (2008). First year students' experiences with technology: Are they really digital natives? *Australasian Journal of Educational Technology, 24*(1), 108–22.

Kimber, K. & Wyatt-Smith, C. M. (2010). Secondary students' online use and creation of knowledge: Refocusing priority for quality assessment. *Australasian Journal of Educational Technology, 26*(5), 607–25.

Kirriemuir, J. & McFarlane, A. (2004). *Literature review in games and learning*. Bristol: NESTA Futurelab.

Knobel, M. & Lankshear, C. (Eds) (2007). *A new literacies sampler*. New York: Peter Lang.

Koehler, M. J. & Mishra, P. (2009). What is Technological Pedagogical Content

Knowledge (TPACK)? *Contemporary Issues in Technology and Teacher Education, 9*(1), 60–70.

Kowalski, R. M., Limber, S. P. & Agatston, P. W. (2008). *Cyber Bullying: Bullying in the Digital Age.* Malden, MA: Blackwell Publishing.

Krause, R. (2006). *Numeracy support software workshop.* Retrieved from http://ecss.biz/

Lam, L. T., Cheng, Z-H. & Liu, X-M. (2013). Violent online games exposure and cyberbullying/victimization among adolescents. *Cyberpsychology, Behavior, and Social Networking, 16*(3), 159–65.

Langford, L. (2000). Critical literacy: A building block towards information literacy. In L. Hay & J. Henri (Eds), *Enter the millennium: Information services in schools: 1999 online conference proceedings* (pp. 181–7). Wagga Wagga, NSW: Centre for Studies in Teacher Librarianship, Charles Sturt University.

Leander, K. M. (2007). 'You won't be needing your laptops today': Wired bodies in the wireless classroom. In M. Knobel & C. Lankshear (Eds), *A new literacies sampler* (25–48). New York: Peter Lang.

Leu, D. J., Jr., Coiro, J., Castek, J., Hartman, D. K., Henry, L. A. & Reinking, D. (2008). Research on instruction and assessment in the new literacies of online reading comprehension. In C. C. Block, S. R. Parris & P. Afflerbach (Eds), *Comprehension instruction: Research-based best practices* (2nd ed., pp. 321–46). New York: Guilford Press.

Leu, D. J., Jr., Kinzer, C. K., Coiro, J. & Cammack, D. (2004). Toward a theory of new literacies emerging from the Internet and other information and communication technologies. In R. B. Ruddell & N. Unrau (Eds), *Theoretical models and processes of reading* (5th ed., pp. 1568–611). Newark, DE: International Reading Association.

Lewis, S. P. & Seko, Y. (2016). A Double-Edged Sword: A Review of Benefits and Risks of Online Nonsuicidal Self-Injury Activities. *Journal of Clinical Psychology, 72*(3): 249–62.

Light, P. H. (1993). Collaborative learning with computers. In P. Scrimshaw (Ed.), *Language classrooms and computers* (pp. 40–56). London: Routledge.

Livingstone, S. (2008). Taking risky opportunities in youthful content creation: Teenagers' use of social networking sites for intimacy, privacy and self-expression. *New Media and Society, 10*(3), 459–77.

Livingstone, S. & Bober, M. (2005). *UK children go online: Final report of key project findings.* Retrieved from www.lse.

ac.uk/collections/children-go-online/UKCGOfinalReport.pdf

Luckin, R., Clark, W., Graber, R., Logan, K., Mee A. & Oliver, M. (2009). Do Web 2.0 tools really open the door to learning?: Perceptions, practices and profiles of 11–16 year old students. *Learning, Media and Technology, 34*(2), 87–104.

Manicavasagar, V., Horswood, D., Burckhardt, R., Lum, A., Hadzi-Pavlovic, D. & Parker, G. (2014). Feasibility and Effectiveness of a Web-Based Positive Psychology Program for Youth Mental Health: Randomized Controlled Trial. *Journal of Medical Internet Research, 16*(6):e140.

Masters, G. N. (2013). *Reforming educational assessment: Imperatives, principles and challenges.* Melbourne: ACER.

MCEECDYA. See Ministerial Council on Education, Early Childhood Development and Youth Affairs.

MCEETYA. See Ministerial Council on Education, Employment, Training and Youth Affairs.

McLoughlin, C. & Lee, M. J. W. (2010). Personalised and self regulated learning in the Web 2.0 era: International exemplars of innovative pedagogy using social software. *Australasian Journal of Educational Technology, 26*(1), 28–43.

Meelissen, M. R. M. & Drent, M. (2008). Gender differences in computer attitudes: Does the school matter? *Computers in Human Behavior, 24*(3), 969–85.

Mercer, N. (1996). The quality of talk in children's collaborative activity in the classroom. *Learning and Instruction, 6*(4), 346–77.

Meredyth, D., Russell, N., Blackwood, L., Thomas, J. & Wise, P. (1999). *Real time: Computers, change and schooling.* Canberra: Australian Key Centre for Cultural and Media Policy, Commonwealth Department of Education, Training and Youth Affairs.

Millea, J., Green, I. & Putland, G. (2005). *Emerging technologies: A framework for thinking.* Canberra: ACT Department of Education and Training. Retrieved from www.det.act.gov.au/__data/assets/pdf_file/0010/74485/ACT_EmTech_Report_v1_2.pdf

Mills, K. L. (2014). Effects of Internet use on the adolescent brain: despite popular claims, experimental evidence remains scarce. *Trends in Cognitive Sciences 4, 18*(8), 385–387.

Ministerial Council on Education, Early Childhood Development and Youth Affairs. (2010). *National assessment program ICT literacy year 6 and 10 report 2008.* Canberra: Curriculum Corporation.

Ministerial Council on Education, Employment, Training and Youth Affairs (2005). *National*

Assessment Program Information and Communication Technology Literacy 2005 Years 6 and 10. An Assessment Domain for ICT Literacy. Vic: Curriculum Corporation.

Ministerial Council on Education, Employment, Training and Youth Affairs. (2008). *Melbourne declaration on educational goals for young Australians.* Canberra: Curriculum Corporation.

Moss, G., Jewitt, C., Levaãiç, R., Armstrong, V., Cardini A. & Castle, F. (2007). *The interactive whiteboards, pedagogy and pupil performance evaluation: An evaluation of the Schools Whiteboard Expansion (SWE) Project: London Challenge* DfES Research Report 816, London: DfES. Retrieved from www.pgce.soton.ac.uk/ict/NewPGCE/pdfs%20IWBs/The%20interactive%20whiteboard,%20pedagogy%20and%20 pupil%20performance%20evaluation.pdf

Nansen, B., Chakraborty, K., Gibbs, L., Vetere, F. & MacDougall, C. (2012). 'You do the math': Mathletics and the play of online learning. *New Media & Society, 14*(7), 1216–35.

National Telecommunications and Information Administration. (2000). *Falling through the net: Toward digital inclusion.* Washington DC: NTIA. Retrieved from www.ntia.doc.gov/files/ntia/publications/fttn00.pdf

New Zealand Teachers Council. (2015). *Graduating teacher standards: Aotearoa New Zealand.* Retrieved from www.teacherscouncil.govt.nz/sites/default/files/gts-poster.pdf

Oblinger, D. G. & Oblinger, J. L. (2005). Is it age or IT: First steps toward understanding the net generation. In D. G. Oblinger & J. L. Oblinger (Eds), *Educating the net generation* (pp. 2.1–2.20). Retrieved from www.educause.edu/research-and-publications/books/educating-net-generation

Organization for Economic Cooperation and Development. (2011). *PISA 2009 results: Students on line: Digital technologies and performance* (Vol. VI). Retrieved from http://dx.doi.org/10.1787/9789264112995-en

Organization for Economic Cooperation and Development. (2012). *Are girls and boys ready for the Digital Age? PISA in Focus.* Retrieved from www.oecd.org/dataoecd/3/60/49554244.html#education

Pelletier, C. (2005). The uses of literacy in studying computer games: Comparing students' oral and visual representations of games. *English Teaching: Practice and Critique, 4*(1), 40–59.

Plester, B., Wood, C. & Joshi, P. (2009). Exploring the relationship between children's knowledge of text message abbreviations and school literacy outcomes. *British Journal of Developmental Psychology, 27*(1), 145–61.

Prensky, M. (2001). Digital natives, digital immigrants. *On the horizon, 9*(5), 1–6. Retrieved from www.marcprensky.com/writing/Prensky%20-%20Digital%20Natives,%20Digital%20Immigrants%20-%20Part1.pdf

Riva, G., Banos, R., Botella, C., Wiederhold, B. K. & Gaggioli, A. (2012). Positive technology: Using interactive technologies to promote positive functioning. *Cyberpsychology, Behavior, and Social Networking, 15*(2), 69–77.

Robinson, J., Bailey, E. & Byrne, S. (2017). Social media can be bad for youth mental health, but there are ways it can help. *The Conversation*, December 12, 2017.

Roblyer, M. D. & Doering, A. H. (2013). *Integrating educational technology into teaching* (6th ed.). Upper Saddle River, NJ: Pearson.

Romer, D., Bagdasarov, Z. & More, E. (2013). Older Versus Newer Media and the Well-being of United States Youth: Results from a National Longitudinal Panel. *Journal of Adolescent Health, 52*(5), 613–619.

Rubin, J. (2013). Designing WebQuests to support creative problem solving. *Journal of Educational Multimedia and Hypermedia, 22*(2), 185–207.

Scott, V. (1996). Why are girls under represented? Ten years on. *Australian Educational Computing, 11*(1), 16–21.

Shute, V. (2015). *Stealth assessment in video games*. ACER Research Conference, 2015 – Learning assessment: designing the future. Downloaded 28/1/18 from https://research.acer.edu.au/research_conference/RC2015/

Shute, V., Leighton, J.P., Jang, E.E. & Chu, MLeighton, Jang & Chu, 2016. (2016). Advances in the Science of Assessment. *Educational Assessment, 21*, 1, 34–59.

Siemens, G. (2005). *Connectivism: A learning theory for the digital age*. Retrieved from www.itdl.org/Journal/Jan_05/article01.htm

Skinner, B. F. (1968). *The technology of teaching*. New York: Appleton-Century-Crofts.

Slonje, R., Smith, P. K. & Frisen, A. (2013). The nature of cyberbullying, and strategies for prevention. *Computers in Human Behavior, 29*, 26–32.

Smolenski, M. (2000). *The digital divide and American society*. Stamford, CT: Gartner Group. Retrieved from www.gartnerweb.com/public/static/techies/digital_d/national2.html

Sohn, E. (2004). What video games can teach us. *Science News for Kids*, 21 January. Retrieved from www.sciencenewsforkids.org/2004/01/what-video-games-can-teach-us-2/

Spijkerman, M. P. J., Pots, W. T. M. & Bohlmeijer, E. T. (2016). Effectiveness of online mindfulness-based interventions in improving mental health: A review and meta-analysis of randomised controlled trials. *Clinical Psychology Review, 45*, 102–114.

Strasburger, V. C., Donnerstein, E. & Bushman, B. J. (2014). Why is it so hard to believe that media influence children and adolescents? *Pediatrics, 133*(4), 571–3.

Suler, J. (2004). The online disinhibition effect. *CyberPsychology & Behavior, 7*, 321–6.

Suler, J. (2006). *The Psychology of Cyberspace*. http://users.rider.edu/~suler/psycyber/psycyber.html

Tandoc, E. C., Ferucci, P. & Duffy, M. (2015). Facebook use, envy, and depression among college students: Is facebooking depressing? *Computers in Human Behavior, 43*, 139–146.

Tempelaar, D. T., Rienties, B. & Giesbers, B. (2014). In search for the most informative data for feedback generation: Learning analytics in a data-rich context. *Computers in Human Behavior, 47*, 157–167.

Tingir, S., Cavlazoglu, B., Caliskan, O., Koklu, O. & Intepe-Tingir, S. (2017). Effects of mobile devices on K–12 students' achievement: a meta-analysis. *Journal of Computer Assisted Learning, 33*(4), 355–369.

Tokunaga, R. S. (2010). Following you home from school: A critical review and synthesis of research on cyberbullying victimization. *Computers in Human Behavior, 26*, 277–87.

Vossen, G. M. & Valkenburg, M. (2016). Do social media foster or curtail adolescents' empathy? A longitudinal study. *Computers in Human Behavior, 63*, 118–124.

Western Australia Department of Education and Training. (2004). *The education of gifted and talented students in Western Australia*. Retrieved from www.eddept.wa.edu.au/gifttal/provision/provinfo.htm

White, G. (2008). *ICT trends in education*. ACER Digital Learning Research. Retrieved from http://research.acer.edu.au/digital_learning/2

Wilmer, H. H., Sherman., L. E. & Chen, J. M. (2017). Smartphones and cognition: A review of research exploring the links between mobile technology habits and cognitive functioning. *Frontiers in Psychology, 8*, 6015.

Wood, C., Meachem, S., Bowyer, S., Jackson, E., Tarczynski-Bowles, M. L. & Plester, B. (2011). A longitudinal study of children's text messaging and literacy development. *British Journal of Psychology, 102*(3), 431–42.

Wood, R. & Ashfield, J. (2008). The use of the interactive whiteboard for creative teaching and learning in literacy and mathematics: A case study. *British Journal of Educational Technology, 39*(1), 84–96.

Wouters, P., van Nimwegen, C., van Oostendorp, H. & van der Spek, E. D. (2013). A meta-analysis of the cognitive and motivational effects of serious games. *Journal of Educational Psychology, 105*(2), 249–265.

Wright, D. (2010). Orchestrating the instruments: Integrating ICT in the secondary mathematics classroom through handheld technology networks. *Technology, Pedagogy and Education, 19*(2), 277–84.

Zoanetti, N. (2010). Interactive computer based assessment tasks: How problem-solving process data can inform instruction. *Australasian Journal of Educational Technology, 26*(5), 585–606.

Chapter 2

ASSESSMENT AND REPORTING

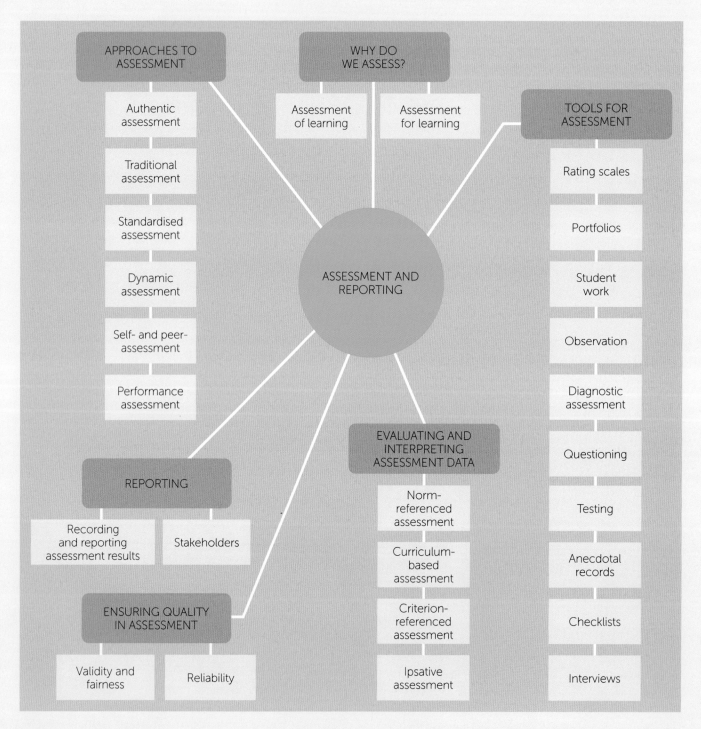

FIGURE 13.1 Chapter 13 concept map

KEY QUESTIONS

After reading this chapter, you should be able to answer the following questions:

- Why do we assess?
- How do teachers, students, parents and governments use assessment information?
- What are some of the main forms of assessment teachers use to shape teaching and learning?
- How can I ensure assessment is effective?
- Who needs to be considered when reporting assessment information, and how will that affect what and how I report?
- What are the features of effective feedback to students?

ONLINE STUDY RESOURCES

 CourseMateExpress

Bring your learning to life with **interactive learning**, **study** and **exam preparation tools** that support the printed textbook. CourseMate Express includes **quizzes**, **interactive activities**, **videos**, a tool to help you '**develop your philosophy**' and more.

INTRODUCTION

Karen is looking through her students' assignments after marking them. She makes some notes to guide her conversations with the students about their work, thinking about what would be useful feedback. She considers what the students have learned from the unit just completed, and flags some who will need follow-up to correct misunderstandings, and others she would like to support with extension work to build on strengths she has identified. Thinking about the unit she is about to start, Karen decides to change her approach, considering what she has learned about her students' needs and her own teaching from the assignments she has marked. She decides to involve the students more in assessment and feedback so they understand what is required, and to set and monitor goals for their learning. Karen also makes notes in her student evaluation book, to share with parents at the end of term, and adds to the class data that she is collecting about student progress, to be shared at a staff meeting.

Assessment in education guides decision making about learning and teaching, whether it is by teachers, students, parents or school systems (Masters, 2013). In this chapter we explore the purposes of assessment and teachers' reporting of the outcomes of assessment to students, parents and others. You may associate assessment with testing, and the reporting of results through marks or grades, but this is just one way in which assessment and reporting happen in schools. The choices teachers make about what and how to assess are influenced by their aims: What will the information gathered be used for? Similarly, reporting methods are influenced by the stakeholders interested in the assessment results, who may be students, teachers, schools, parents, employers or governments.

WHAT IS ASSESSMENT?

When teachers assess students' work, they tend to do several things: they gather some sort of information about what the student knows or can do; they interpret or analyse that information to make sense of what it tells them about the student and their learning; they make judgements about how well the student is achieving, and may record these to share with the student and others; and, generally, they use all of this to form plans for future learning and teaching.

assessment
The purposeful gathering and analysis of information about student learning

Assessment refers to the gathering and analysing of information about student achievement. It is often used as a partner term with 'evaluation'. Assessment can be both qualitative (consisting of descriptions of what students know and can do) and quantitative (students' performance as measured by marks or positions on a scale), and may occur at any time before, during or at the end of a unit of instruction. It can cover a broad range of learning outcomes – cognitive, affective and social – from the simplest to the most complex (Bloom, 1956). See Chapter 6 for more on this topic.

evaluation
The process of making judgements about the quality of something

Evaluation is the process of making judgements about the quality of students' learning and performance. We use the information from assessment to make these judgements, and it is the evaluation that is typically reported to students as feedback, as well as to parents and others.

assessment literacy
Knowledge and skills for collecting, analysing and interpreting assessment data and evidence of learning, and for applying this information

Assessment literacy refers to the knowledge and skills involved in collecting, analysing, and interpreting assessment data and evidence. Heitink, Van der Kleij, Veldkamp, Schildkamp & Kippers (2015) pointed out that assessment literacy also involves teachers' effective use of this information to adapt their instruction, respond to learners' needs, and give effective feedback. You will be building your assessment literacy in this chapter. The concept map in Figure 13.1 might help you to monitor your understanding of the various elements involved.

WHY DO WE ASSESS?

Assessment can have a number of purposes. It can help teachers to:

- find out what students know and can do
- learn about a student's strengths and weaknesses
- evaluate their teaching
- evaluate students' learning
- plan future learning and teaching sessions
- report to others about students' learning and performance
- identify students who need special assistance with learning, and the types of help they need.
  For students, assessment can:
- provide feedback on their performance
- help them to set learning goals
- motivate them
- provide information about how they can improve.
  For schools and schooling systems, assessment can:
- provide information about a group of students
- help them to evaluate their programs
- give information to parents about their child's progress, relative to others
- identify students' progress relative to a particular benchmark
- help with identifying schools and students who need additional help.

assessment for learning
Assessment with the goal of improving learning

assessment of learning
Assessment with the goal of judging what students know and can do at a particular point in time

assessment as learning
Assessment with the goal of helping students to become more conscious of their own thinking and learning processes

Each of these purposes implies a different kind of assessment and reporting practice, and will determine our choice of assessment tool (Masters, 2013). One set of purposes relates to the goal of improving learning. Black and Wiliam (1998) called this **assessment for learning**. It typically happens throughout the learning and teaching process, and can also be called *formative* assessment. They distinguished it from another set of purposes related to accountability, and the summation of students' learning at the end of the year, which they called **assessment of learning**, also referred to as *summative* assessment. Lorna Earl (2003, 2013) added a third set of purposes, related to helping students to take responsibility for their own learning. She called this **assessment as learning**. It is the use of self- and peer assessment to help students to become more conscious of their own thinking and learning processes. It is related to assessment for learning as it ultimately contributes to improvements in students' learning. It is important to realise that the same task may be summative or formative, used as assessment for learning or assessment of learning, or even both at once – it is not the task but the purpose for which it is used that determines what kind of assessment it is (Gardner, 2012). Earl (2013) suggested that teachers' programs contain a balance of the three types of assessment. Your philosophy of learning and teaching, and your approach to curriculum and assessment, will determine how that balance operates in your classroom. In Box 13.1, two contrasting models of assessment are discussed.

BOX 13.1 IMPLICATIONS FOR EDUCATORS

THINKING CRITICALLY ABOUT THE PURPOSES OF ASSESSMENT

Masters (2013) challenged current approaches to assessment, arguing that traditional approaches are based on a model of assessment that is about judging student success, defined by how much students have learnt of what teachers have taught. This model links to our school curriculum, typically organised into units of work. As each unit is taught, it is assessed to determine how well students have learnt (or are learning) the content, or how completely they have achieved the outcomes. Masters argued that this approach does not take into account current understandings of learning, including that all learners have potential for further progress, and that learning should be matched to learner readiness (rather than all learners receiving the same instruction). Motivation is also involved, with students unable to see progress in their learning if they receive the same grade in successive years.

Instead, Masters suggested that assessment should be based on the need to understand where students are in their learning. This would entail drawing on maps of the progression of understanding or skill in a particular learning domain, such as the example in Box 13.3. These maps can be used by teachers to guide teaching, design relevant assessment tasks, develop rubrics for marking and feedback, identify misunderstanding, and provide feedback to a student and information for parents in reports about the progress the student has made over time, and how they can progress further. Masters acknowledged that such a model of assessment has implications for a number of aspects of teachers', schools' and systems' practice. He argued that such changes are necessary and can have considerable benefits.

Advantages of this model of assessment include that:

- teachers have information to guide them in where to target instruction
- teachers and students can monitor students' progress in learning
- students receive feedback on where they are now, where they are going and how to get there, which Hattie and Timperley (2007) identified as effective feedback
- it develops students' metacognitive skills
- it builds students' confidence in themselves as learners
- teachers and students develop a growth mindset, thinking beyond the current task.

ACTIVITIES

1 How might this conception of assessment change teaching practice?
2 What do think assessment should focus on?
3 How can you support your view from theory and research in educational psychology that you have read about in previous chapters?

THINK ABOUT

- What was the balance of assessment for, as and of learning in your school experience? Give examples of each. What will the balance look like in your classroom?

INTRODUCTION TO FORMATIVE AND SUMMATIVE ASSESSMENT

formative assessment
Information gathered while students are learning, to give information about their progress

summative assessment
Information gathered to give information about students' achievements at a particular time

Formative assessment and **summative assessment** are terms widely used in the literature to categorise the two main forms of assessment. Their names refer to the time at which the assessment information is gathered: formative, throughout the teaching–learning process, as learning is *forming*; summative, at a particular point in the process (often the end), in order to *sum up* what students know and can do at that point in time. The change to the terms *assessment for learning* and *assessment of learning* occurred in order to shift attention to the purposes of assessment – to improve learning, or to measure learning at a point in time, respectively. In this chapter, as in other works you may read about assessment in schools, both assessment for learning and formative assessment will be used; and both assessment of learning and summative assessment will likewise be used depending on the context. The distinction is in whether the focus is on timing (formative/summative) or purpose (for/of learning).

ASSESSMENT FOR LEARNING

Assessment is integral to effective teaching practice at every point (Masters, 2011). Masters (2013, p. 6) argued that 'the fundamental purpose of assessment is to establish where learners are in their learning at the time of assessment'. At the start of a unit of work, teachers assess what students already know and can do in order to make plans for what to teach, and to link new material to students' prior learning. They might look for misconceptions students hold that their teaching will need to address, and identify where on a developmental learning path each student sits. As they are teaching the new material, teachers assess students' understanding to ensure that what is being learnt is the same as that being taught. When students are given opportunities to practise, and to demonstrate what they know and can do, assessment of their efforts occurs to determine what additional support or explicit instruction they might need, to give them feedback about their progress, and to plan for what will be taught in the next teaching cycle.

THE PLACE OF ASSESSMENT IN THE TEACHING–LEARNING CYCLE

Assessment *as* learning is a subset of assessment *for* learning, which is related to the process of metacognition discussed in Chapter 6. It is involved in the planning, monitoring and evaluating of their learning that effective learners engage in as they learn (Earl, 2013). Students may be involved in self-assessment in a number of ways while they are learning: deciding what they need help with, or what questions they need answered; considering how they can improve; and reflecting on their learning both during and after the process. Figure 13.2 represents this cycle of teaching and learning, and the place of assessment within it.

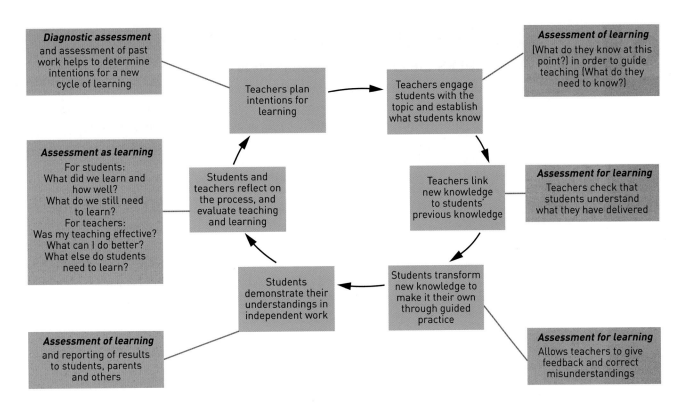

FIGURE 13.2 The place of assessment in the teaching–learning cycle

KEY STRATEGIES IN ASSESSING FOR LEARNING

Drawing on Black and Wiliam's (1998, 1999) original research, Glasson (2009) suggests five strategies that teachers can implement to ensure that assessment is effective for learning. These are:

1   *sharing* with students what you want them to learn, and what will demonstrate that the learning has occurred (the criteria)
2   *strategic questioning* to find out what students know and can do, so that the information can be used to design teaching and learning experiences
3   *effective feedback* based on the learning goals and criteria, which tells students what they have achieved, as well as what and how they can improve – this feedback can come from peers as well as teachers, and avoids comparing students with one another
4   *student self-assessment* that focuses on students taking responsibility for their learning, identifying strengths and weaknesses, awareness of how they learn, setting learning goals, responding to feedback with action, and assessing their work using the success criteria
5   *the formative use of summative assessment* – summative assessments provide information that can be used for learning before, during and after the task (formatively).

These strategies underline how assessment is an integral part of the teaching–learning cycle. Box 13.2 provides some principles to further guide your classroom assessment practice.

BOX 13.2 CLASSROOM LINKS

PRINCIPLES OF QUALITY ASSESSMENT

New Zealand's Ministry of Education published a position paper in 2011 that shaped a system-wide assessment-improvement program for schools, to ensure that every student could reach their full potential. The key principles underpinning this program were as follows:

- *The student is at the centre.* While the curriculum spells out expectations of progress, this will not look the same for all students. Assessment should respond to individual student contexts and characteristics with the aim of helping all students to progress in their learning. This will involve the student in assessing their own learning, as well as ensuring teacher, peer, parent and *whānau* (family/community) interactions have a central focus on the student and their progress.

- *The curriculum underpins assessment.* Assessment practice should be consistent with the New Zealand curriculum, and should support teaching and learning of curriculum content. Success indicators and achievement standards against which student progress is measured are therefore drawn from the curriculum.

- *Building assessment capability is crucial to achieving improvement.* Effective assessment rests on assessment, curriculum and pedagogical knowledge, skills to use that knowledge effectively, and willingness to actively apply knowledge and use skills for the benefit of student learning. People across the whole system need to have appropriate knowledge and skills in assessment, not just teachers.

- *An assessment-capable system is an accountable system.* Whether looking at the performance of individuals or schools, outcomes must be evaluated in light of the context and the progress that is made, rather than being judged on performance alone.

- *A range of evidence drawn from multiple sources potentially enables a more accurate response.* At the system level, this will involve information from classroom, school and sector. At the classroom level, it will involve drawing a full picture of a student's progress by collecting a variety of information from multiple sources such as teacher observation, students' work, parents' view of the child, and peers' judgements. This rich information can then guide judgements, planning, decision making and future practice.

- *Effective assessment is reliant on quality interactions and relationships.* Valuing of the input of all those whose information can contribute to students' learning requires seeking, collecting, interpreting and using that information in sensitive ways. Quality relationships are thus at the centre of this process. Interactions need to be responsive, respectful, reciprocal and learning-focused. This need for collegial, collaborative and cooperative relationships that seek a common goal of improving all students' learning exists at all levels, but particularly at the classroom level.

Source: New Zealand Ministry of Education. (2011a). Ministry of Education position paper: Assessment. Retrieved from www.minedu.govt.nz/theMinistry/PublicationsAndResources/AssessmentPositionPaper.aspx

ACTIVITIES

1 Map out what these principles will look like in assessment practice.
2 Do the principles challenge your ideas about assessment? Which ones, and in what ways?
3 How are the principles similar or different from what you are used to as assessment?
4 Compare these principles with the view of assessment described by Masters in Box 13.1. How are they similar, and how are they different?

ASSESSMENT OF LEARNING

Assessment of learning, or summative assessment, also plays an important role in learning and teaching. It provides information to teachers, students, parents and others about the outcomes of the learning process, and contributes to teachers' accountability. It can be done by an external body as, for example, in final year examinations, or using the National Assessment Program in Literacy and Numeracy (NAPLAN) tests in Australia; or by teachers themselves, such as in New Zealand's Overall Teacher Judgements (OTJ) of student progress and achievement, or when teachers develop assessments at the end of a unit, term or year. Formative assessment information can also be gathered and used for the purpose of assessment of learning (for example, in the use of a portfolio of student work to discuss a student's progress with the parents, or to present to a potential employer). The Assessment Reform Group (2006) worked with teachers in the UK, Australia and the USA to review summative assessment practices. They argued that teachers should be involved in summative assessment, particularly as this limits the role of testing, together with its potential weaknesses (discussed later in this chapter), in summative assessment. When teachers are involved in summative assessment, they need to ensure that their assessment is of a high quality, particularly if the assessment results will have an impact on the future of the students, as in final year results. Aspects of quality assessment are discussed later in the chapter.

APPROACHES TO ASSESSMENT

Schools may choose from a number of different approaches to assessment of students' learning. Each of these approaches aligns with different views of the purpose of schooling, and of the roles of teachers and students. You may find it helpful to return to your philosophy of learning and teaching in the CourseMate website to consider which approach to assessment fits best with your views.

TRADITIONAL ASSESSMENT

Traditional assessment aligns with the purposes associated with 'assessment of learning': accountability and reporting. Traditionally, assessment has focused on testing students as a means of determining 'how much' they have learned, and so has had a focus on measurement and on content rather than on the learning process. Being summative, it has taken a snapshot of students' learning at a particular point in time (usually the end of the year, or the end of a unit of work). Often, students have been assigned marks or grades by which they can be compared with other students ('norm-referenced' assessment). However, there has been a broadening of assessment beyond traditional forms of testing in schools and other educational institutions to include procedures that combine instruction and assessment. These changing assessment procedures are reflected in the increasing use of tests described as 'formative' or 'diagnostic', which contribute to the learning–teaching process, rather than tests described as 'summative' that are concerned with the final outcomes of instruction. Changes in assessment practices are also evident in the way in which test data are interpreted. Comparisons are made with a predetermined outcome in the form of a standard or criterion ('criterion-referenced' assessment) or curriculum objectives ('curriculum-based' assessment), rather than the more traditional procedure of comparing test data with the average performance of other students on the same test ('norm-referenced' assessment).

DYNAMIC ASSESSMENT

The concept of **dynamic assessment** has its origins in Vygotsky's concept of the zone of proximal development (discussed in Chapter 3) and Feuerstein's Learning Potential Assessment Device (Feuerstein, Rand & Hoffman, 1979). It employs *interactive* assessment, as distinguished from *static* assessment, and involves the teacher giving pre-planned hints and prompts, based on the student's current achievement

CourseMateExpress

Online Resources
Take a moment to consider your philosophy of learning and teaching. You may wish to use the **Develop your philosophy** tool on the textbook's CourseMate website

dynamic assessment
A form of interactive assessment that identifies potential for learning and interventions to help achieve this potential

level, to find out the effect of instruction on what an examinee can do, with and without assistance, when given tasks of increasing complexity (Haywood & Lidz, 2007). It is based on the principle that we can learn more about a child's thinking by working with him or her than we could simply by observing the child working unassisted. This allows the teacher to probe the child's reasoning as well as their final answer, and by observing their response to hints and prompts, to understand their thinking processes, rather than simply the product of their thinking. Dynamic assessment has learning as its aim – assessment is never done for its own sake. A key characteristic of dynamic assessment is that both instruction and feedback are incorporated into the testing process, contingent on the examinee's performance and response to any instruction given. Another important feature of dynamic assessment is the active role of the child in the process. Questioning, feedback from the teacher and discussion are encouraged. Both teacher and student work together in the assessment process (Lauchlan & Carrigan, 2013). This can be contrasted with more traditional assessment procedures that provide limited initial guidance, with contingent feedback discouraged on the grounds that it will invalidate the test's standardisation.

Two forms of dynamic assessment have been identified: the sandwich and the cake formats. In the sandwich format, a pre-test is given without assistance and, on the basis of the examinee's responses, contingent instruction is provided, followed by the administration of a second version of the pre-test to measure change after instruction. The cake format does not involve pre- and post-tests, but instead uses a series of items with standardised (a predetermined set of hints) or individualised assistance provided immediately the examinee encounters a problem, with the next item presented once the problem is resolved (Sternberg, 2013).

Dynamic assessment is based on several assumptions:

- Accumulated knowledge is not the best indication of one's ability to acquire new information.
- Everyone functions at less than their full capacity, so everyone can do better.
- The best test of a performance is a sample of that performance, so assessment should involve the use of learning tasks that involve teaching, as this is a characteristic of school learning.
- The ability to function intelligently is masked by obstacles such as ignorance, impulsivity, impoverished vocabulary, cultural differences in learning styles, poor self-concept, and inadequate development of cognitive and metacognitive structures and strategies (Haywood & Lidz, 2007).

Dynamic assessment involves one-to-one testing using clearly specified tasks with more than one level of achievement or degree of complexity, with the teacher expecting success (refusing to accept ignorance as an indicator of inability to do a task) and noting the effect of prompting on the student's performance on the tasks. Special attention is paid to affective or motivational factors that appear to interfere with learning. If the prompts help the student to complete a task, then it is likely that the student will benefit from appropriate instruction.

Some research suggests that dynamic assessment provides more valid results for students from varied social and ethnic backgrounds, closing the gap between middle-class Anglo students and students from other backgrounds that can be observed in traditional assessment; see Sternberg (2013) and Lauchlan and Carrigan (2013) for reviews. Lauchlan and Carrigan (2013) also argued that dynamic assessment allows for emotional and motivational factors to be assessed alongside academic achievement, to give a more rounded picture of the child as a learner.

AUTHENTIC ASSESSMENT

authentic assessment
A mode of assessment that uses tasks similar to those performed in the real world

When the tasks students are given during assessment are concerned with the quality of students' work, are connected to real-life situations, employ a range of tasks rather than just one to get at students' thinking as well as their learning, and position learners as active participants in their learning, they are said to be examples of **authentic assessment** (Brady & Kennedy, 2012). Portfolios, problem-based and performance assessment are sometimes called authentic assessments (Brady & Kennedy, 2012).

In problem-based learning, assessment and feedback are integrated into the task itself – if the problem is solved successfully (the machine works or the patient lives), the students know that their learning has been successful. Authentic assessment uses assessment tasks as learning tasks rather than viewing assessment as the measurement of learning at the end of the learning process. An important element of authentic assessment is the role of the teacher, who should scaffold and support students in their learning as they undertake the task. Authentic assessment is a feature of constructivist classrooms (see Chapter 6), which emphasise the importance of students constructing their own knowledge and meaning within real-world contexts. Authentic assessment tasks may involve integrating knowledge and skills from different areas of the curriculum.

PERFORMANCE ASSESSMENT

In **performance assessment**, students apply what they know, or demonstrate skills in complex tasks. This method is commonly used in curriculum areas in which application of knowledge and skills is important, such as creative arts, foreign languages, physical education, and design and technology. It has also been used in subjects such as English, Science and Mathematics, where students may apply writing skills in writing a persuasive essay, design and conduct an experiment, or solve a problem and explain their reasoning. In each of these instances, students are assessed on their performance of a task, and on specific skills and knowledge that are demonstrated in that context.

performance assessment A mode of assessment that requires a student to engage in a complex task

Performance assessment typically has a greater degree of validity than traditional assessment methods, as it assesses a total, complex activity rather than discrete knowledge or skills. Such assessment tasks require students to use their knowledge and skills in conditions that are similar to those they might encounter in real life (Lane, 2010). In this, performance assessment often overlaps with authentic assessment. Its weakness may be in reliability, as there are multiple factors that might influence the performance of the task on a particular day. Developing portfolios over multiple tasks or performances can assist with this, as can careful construction of marking rubrics. Validity and reliability are discussed further later in this chapter.

In designing performance assessment, teachers need to have a clear set of knowledge and skills that will be assessed in the task, and develop a clear set of criteria for its marking, preferably with a series of levels of expertise described. This improves reliability, and ensures that students know the criteria against which their performance will be assessed. Having examples of expert performances helps to make the standard clear to students and markers. Performance assessment requires careful design and planning. Assessment may be integrated with teaching, as students prepare for, develop and work through tasks. The teacher's role here is that of a coach.

In early childhood settings, performance assessments are linked to observation, and checklists are often used. Here, assessment is more informal, and focused on students' everyday performance of particular skills or knowledge.

Source: Getty Images/golero

FIGURE 13.3 In performance assessment, students are involved in real-world tasks, and may be given wider scope to define what their assessment performance will look like, compared with traditional assessment. What advantages do you see in this approach? How could you apply it in other areas of learning?

Lane (2010) reviewed research on best practice in performance assessment, finding that students' results in performance assessments can be improved by opportunities to work on meaningful real-world tasks during instructional sessions.

Darling-Hammond and Adamson (2010) called for wider use of performance assessment to tap higher-order thinking and performance skills that traditional testing programs find difficult to reach, and identified a number of schooling systems that use performance assessment to assess such complex sets of skills. Examples of large-scale performance assessments include the PISA (Programme for International Student Assessment) tests that compare 15-year-olds across OECD countries, and the International Baccalaureate.

Potential benefits of performance assessment include:

- assessment of learning outcomes
- transfer of skills and knowledge to multiple contexts
- integration and alignment of assessment and teaching
- deeper processing of content through a focus on application of knowledge and skills in a task
- a focus of teachers on teaching essential skills (Darling-Hammond & Adamson, 2010; Lane, 2010).

ASSESSMENT TOOLS

There are many different tools that can be used to gather information for assessment purposes. They vary within the dimensions of formal–informal, direct–indirect and qualitative–quantitative. Masters (2013) argued that the key factor influencing choice of tool or method for assessment should be its ability to provide useful information about the domain being assessed. Research suggests that the best approach is to draw on a range of assessment types to build up a picture of student achievement, rather than relying on a single measure (Masters, 2011; New Zealand Ministry of Education, 2011a). The New Zealand Ministry of Education (2011a) recommends that teachers make overall judgements about student learning and achievement by drawing on three kinds of information source: observation, including observations of behaviour, work samples and student or peer assessments; conversations with students, including interviews, conferences, questions and explanations and discussions; and gathering of results from formal assessment tools such as standardised tests.

OBSERVING STUDENTS

Teachers observe their students for various reasons, which may include, for example, monitoring behaviour, evaluating their own communication effectiveness, and checking students' progress. To provide information that will inform learning and teaching, observation needs to be purposeful and focused on particular indicators of learning or understanding. These indicators may be guided by the learning intention of the lesson, the desired assessment outcomes defined by a syllabus or school system, or by a learning progression or development map (see Box 13.3).

direct observation
Purposeful and focused looking and listening

An example of direct observation is when a teacher scans a classroom, looks purposefully at what students are doing and listens to what they are saying as a reflection of their understanding or skill development, and provides immediate feedback related to the desired learning. **Direct observation** – or purposeful and focused looking and listening – is a most effective form of assessment. It is particularly useful for aspects of learning that the teacher cannot access through products such as essays, written examinations, projects or homework assignments. It is also useful for verifying assessment data collected in other ways (see Box 13.4).

BOX 13.3 CLASSROOM LINKS

LEARNING PROGRESSIONS

In 2018, the Australian government released a report of a review to achieve educational excellence in Australian schools (commonly referred to as Gonski 2.0) and committed to implement its recommendations. In the report, Gonski et al. picked up arguments by Masters (2013) for teachers to use developmental maps, or learning progressions, to pinpoint where students are in their learning, and where to take them next. Gonski et al. recommended that such an approach should replace year-based or stage-based approaches to assessment, reporting and planning, to promote 'growth-focused' thinking. Australia and New Zealand have developed such learning progressions in literacy and numeracy, K-10 (links are at the end of this chapter). Further work in other curriculum areas is planned in Australia.

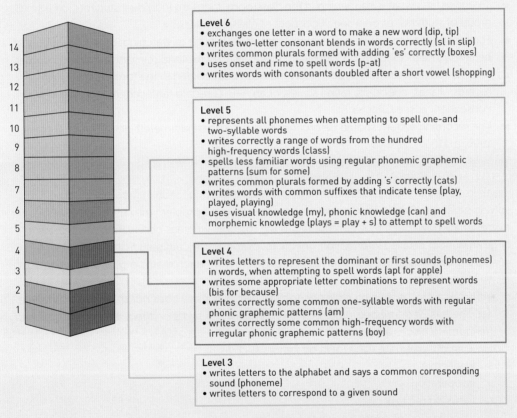

Level 6
- exchanges one letter in a word to make a new word (dip, tip)
- writes two-letter consonant blends in words correctly (sl in slip)
- writes common plurals formed with adding 'es' correctly (boxes)
- uses onset and rime to spell words (p-at)
- writes words with consonants doubled after a short vowel (shopping)

Level 5
- represents all phonemes when attempting to spell one-and two-syllable words
- writes correctly a range of words from the hundred high-frequency words (class)
- spells less familiar words using regular phonemic graphemic patterns (sum for some)
- writes common plurals formed by adding 's' correctly (cats)
- writes words with common suffixes that indicate tense (play, played, playing)
- uses visual knowledge (my), phonic knowledge (can) and morphemic knowledge (plays = play + s) to attempt to spell words

Level 4
- writes letters to represent the dominant or first sounds (phonemes) in words, when attempting to spell words (apl for apple)
- writes some appropriate letter combinations to represent words (bis for because)
- writes correctly some common one-syllable words with regular phonic graphemic patterns (am)
- writes correctly some common high-frequency words with irregular phonic graphemic patterns (boy)

Level 3
- writes letters to the alphabet and says a common corresponding sound (phoneme)
- writes letters to correspond to a given sound

Source: © Commonwealth of Australia 2018. Creative Commons Attribution 4.0 International licence. https://creativecommons.org/licenses/by/4.0/

ACTIVITIES

1. Explore the literacy and numeracy progressions for Australia or New Zealand through the links at the end of this chapter.
2. Such progressions can be used as a basis for observation and review of work samples. View a student's work sample in either writing or mathematics, and use the relevant progression to assess their progress. Where are they now? Where do they need to go next in their learning?

BOX 13.4 CLASSROOM LINKS

USING DIRECT OBSERVATION IN THE CLASSROOM

■ Direct observation is a practical way of collecting information about student behaviour in natural settings, although care needs to be taken to ensure that data collection is not haphazard, unsystematic or subjective.

■ Procedures used to collect data can be quite informal, with the observer simply watching ongoing events and observing more carefully anything that attracts attention.

■ When used as part of an assessment process, observation is usually more structured and purposeful, with behaviour observed more systematically.

■ To use direct observation in a classroom, begin by watching some children and noting anything that seems interesting or unusual.

■ To understand what is happening in the classroom, focus on individual students, on a small group of students, or on a specific aspect of classroom activity.

■ Forster and Masters (1996, p. 9) suggest that 'spotlighting', or watching just a few aspects of behaviour, helps to focus on 'significant events as they relate to relevant learning outcomes'.

■ Information derived from direct observation can be recorded in the form of anecdotal records, diaries, checklists, rating scales, or an A–B–C record (antecedent–behaviour–consequence; see Chapter 5).

■ The recording system should be organised, easy to use and time-efficient (Forster & Masters, 1996, p. 11).

CourseMateExpress

Online Resources
Go further: Find an observational activity to try on this text's website

ACTIVITY

Teachers often have difficulty in knowing how well children function in group problem-solving situations. Simply asking children how they solved a problem may underestimate or overestimate how much they contributed to the solution, whereas observation can provide a large amount of detailed information. Try the following activity, adapted from Siegler (1976):

■ Set a problem-solving task such as the following from nrich.maths.org for a group of 10- to 11-year-olds:

'Amy has a box containing ordinary domino pieces but she does not think it is a complete set. She has 24 dominoes in her box and there are 125 spots on them altogether. Which of her domino pieces are missing?'

Have an observer rate each child on factors such as:
> leadership
> cooperation
> focus on the task
> identification of rules to solve the problem
> originality and relevance of ideas
> willingness to listen to others' ideas.

Collate the information collected on each child and summarise the main findings. Identify which aspects of each student's problem-solving skills could be improved. Suggest ways in which these changes could be achieved.

ANECDOTAL RECORDS

Anecdotal records are objective descriptions of behaviour at a particular time and place, recorded as soon as possible after the behaviour has occurred. Teachers often find it helpful to keep brief notes about any unusual or significant occurrences during the school day, sometimes in a journal or diary. Such notes can be useful in documenting the actions of a particular child whose behaviour is causing concern, as a first step in designing some form of intervention or as a basis for report writing or discussions with parents. Anecdotal records are often used in early-childhood settings and in situations involving children who are having social, emotional or behavioural problems. They can also be helpful to primary and secondary teachers to record learning events for each individual child, and can be drawn upon in reporting to parents, and in developing overall assessment judgements. Similar records can also be kept to document parent or teacher behaviour.

anecdotal record
Objective description of behaviour at a particular time and place, recorded as soon as possible after the behaviour has occurred

CHECKLISTS

A **checklist** comprises a list of descriptions of specific behaviours that can be systematically identified and tallied by observers as they occur ('event sampling') or during a specified period ('time sampling'). Checklists are often used by teachers to collect information about easily observed behaviours such as motor skills ('can hop on one leg for five seconds') or literacy skills ('can find a word in a dictionary'). Checklists are a simple and useful tool for recording observations of a range of behaviours with a number of students.

checklist
A set of descriptions of specific behaviours that an observer records as present or not present

STUDENT WORK

Student work samples are a prolific source of assessment information and come in many forms, from classwork to formal assignments. They can be assessed individually or as a collection, such as in a portfolio (see below). Work samples can be assessed at all stages of their production. Drafts may be self- or peer-assessed, or assessed in a 'conference' with the teacher, to refine a piece of work; finished work may be assessed, commented on by the teacher, and then reworked and resubmitted for further assessment – or left as is. At each point, students' work gives teachers information about their learning progress, and can provide opportunities for further learning.

PORTFOLIOS

A **portfolio** is a collection of samples of a student's work that can be used to assess students' progress over a term or year by comparing, after the fact, work taken from different stages throughout the given period. Portfolios are often used for self-assessment, parent–teacher conferences and parent–teacher–child conferences.

portfolio
A collection of samples of student work used to demonstrate achievement

Portfolios can be built up in different ways. A teacher may say, 'Today's work is for your portfolio.' However, Brady and Kennedy (2012) suggested students be involved from the start in selecting samples of work for inclusion in their portfolio, so that the portfolio is a helpful 'assessment as learning' activity, with students working to improve their work in readiness. Building a portfolio involves the purposeful collection of work samples that reflect a prescribed curriculum standard or criterion, that show evidence of the learner being able to apply knowledge in innovative ways, and that give the learner opportunities to reflect and self-evaluate when selecting work to be included. Brady and Kennedy (2012, p. 64) cite Valencia and Place's (1994) classification of four types of portfolios:

1 the showcase portfolio containing examples of the student's best work
2 the evaluation portfolio that contains samples of marked work
3 the documentation portfolio that has examples of unmarked work
4 the process portfolio that contains examples of ongoing work with student reflection.

Portfolios have become a form of self-assessment, as students negotiate with their teachers about the contents. At the same time, portfolios have been linked to outcomes-based assessment, leading to an increase in teacher understanding of the student and opportunities for negotiation between student and teacher, coupled with enhanced opportunities for student self-assessment. The greatest risk in using the portfolio in student assessment is that it simply becomes a collection of work samples rather than a coherent representation of student achievement over time.

RATING SCALES

rating scale
A procedure for recording the degree to which a specific behaviour or characteristic is present

Rating scales are used to record the degree to which a particular skill has been achieved, or the strength of a particular trait or characteristic in terms of a particular dimension. Rating scales are similar to checklists in that they provide a method for recording the degree to which a specific behaviour or characteristic is present, but they have the added advantage of including a quantitative component in the resulting judgement. Instead of simply recording the occurrence of a specified behaviour (yes/no), a value judgement is also made about the behaviour as the record is compiled ('On a scale of 1 to 10, I would rate John's public speaking skill as 5, Mary's as 3 and Ken's as 9'). Rating scales can take a numerical form, as in the example just cited. They also can be graphic, as in the 'semantic differential' where the judgement is recorded by placing a mark on a point between two opposing descriptors (such as 'simple argument–complex argument' or 'distracted–attentive') to indicate the relative strength of that characteristic in the individual or their performance being assessed (Osgood, Suci & Tannenbaum, 1957).

TESTING

This is likely to be the mode of assessment you are most familiar with from your own schooling. It can take place before, during or after a unit of work. If set before, tests tend to be used to find out what students know and can do, and can be diagnostic in nature (diagnostic tests are discussed later in this chapter). If used during a unit, tests can give students feedback about what they still need to learn and to focus their learning goals. For example, after working through test answers, students can make judgements about their learning using a self-assessment sheet such as the one presented in **Box 13.7**. At the end of a unit, tests tend to be an *assessment of learning*, or summative in nature. This does not have to be the only function of an end-of-unit test, however; teachers can give students feedback from summative tests about how they could improve, to help them to set learning goals for the future (Glasson, 2009). Final-year exams, the NAPLAN tests in Australia or asTTle tests in New Zealand are examples of tests that are assessments of learning. Because the NAPLAN and asTTle test results give information about the kinds of questions the student answered well, and those they had difficulty with, there is also opportunity for these tests to be used to improve learning – as *assessment for learning*.

Source: Getty Images/OJO Images/Chris Ryan

FIGURE 13.4 Testing can have both positive and negative effects on learning. Suggest some ways negative effects can be minimised, and positive ones maximised.

Preparing for tests can have positive benefits for student learning by engaging effective long-term memory strategies

THINK ABOUT

- How could you give feedback on a summative test (perhaps a spelling, Maths, Science or History test) that would improve students' learning?

such as organisation and rehearsal of knowledge, and development of automaticity (Bennett, 2011). Return to chapters 3 and 6 to consider how these strategies work to improve memory and learning. Rohrer and Pashler (2010) report a number of studies demonstrating that the act of taking a test strengthens the representation of the information in memory, and slows forgetting. You can try this yourself by using the review questions at the end of the chapter to help you remember key information about assessment.

Harlen (2005, see also ARG, 2006) warned that overuse of tests, particularly 'high-stakes' tests, can have negative effects. These include demotivation and a drop in self-esteem, particularly in low-achieving students; test anxiety, particularly in girls; a focus on performance goals rather than learning goals; an extrinsic orientation towards grades as status (see Chapter 8 for a discussion of the effect of these orientations); and a tendency for teachers to teach in a transmission style, rather than using more creative and active approaches. High-stakes tests such as final-year examinations can lead to teachers 'teaching to the test' rather than to students' learning needs. Teachers can avoid these negative effects by using varied assessment tools; by ensuring that students are encouraged to monitor their own learning using a variety of sources, not just the tests; and by giving feedback on how to improve their learning – in short, by ensuring that tests are assessments *for* learning as well as *of* learning.

CONVERSATIONS WITH STUDENTS AROUND LEARNING

Talking with students about their learning can have multiple benefits: providing teachers with insight into students' views about what they have learned, and their self-concept; assisting students to take ownership of their own learning, by more clearly understanding where they are now and where they are going; and building a sense of partnership between students and teachers in the learning process.

Interviews

Interviews may be formal or informal, structured or unstructured. A formal or a structured interview using a defined procedure and a prepared set of questions is used in many intelligence tests where the interviewer is given precise instructions about the procedure to be followed. An informal or an unstructured interview has no set procedure or questions, and the interviewer is free to interact with the interviewee in a natural, conversational way. Piaget used an informal interview technique to collect information about the way in which children think about and solve problems (see Chapter 3). Teachers may use structured interviews such as the Schedule for Early Number Assessment (SENA) test in mathematics assessment to determine students' use of strategy, and unstructured interviews or conferences in assessment of writing, which combine an interview with feedback from the teacher. Interviews have been used successfully with children of all ages (think about Piaget's interview technique described in Chapter 3, and the insights it has given us to children's thinking). Numeracy assessment programs such as SENA also use interviews effectively with young children around activities. Interviews with students from cultural backgrounds that have different rules about adult–child verbal interaction may need to be carefully designed to take account of these cultural communication differences.

Discussions with students around learning can reveal to the teacher a student's misconceptions as well as their learning process (Heitink et al., 2016). In these discussions, guiding students to explain the reasons for their answers and their thinking is important for their assessment purpose. Being aware of common misconceptions can assist teachers in pinpointing them as they arise in discussions, as well as in providing helpful feedback. Being able to interpret this information as it arises – 'on the spot' – is important to providing timely feedback and making changes to instruction as they are needed (Heitink et al., 2016).

Questioning

Questions form a large part of classroom practice. Their effectiveness varies, however. Drawing on research, Glasson (2009) identified a number of key aspects of questioning for assessment purposes:

- Be strategic. Identify key questions for your lesson. This involves planning ahead for the questions you will ask to assess students' knowledge and understanding.

- Use a mix of open-ended questions that require higher-order thinking, and closed questions which require a set answer (see the text on Bloom's taxonomy in Box 6.3). Fit the question type to your assessment purpose, but remember that open questions give you a broader picture of students' understanding – closed questions tend to tell you about their knowledge. The type of question may vary depending on the purpose of the assessment and its place in the teaching–learning cycle. For example, the Primary Connections 5E model suggests that teachers use questions to *engage* and elicit prior knowledge, for students to *explore* the phenomenon and *explain* what is happening (in the formative assessment stages), and to *elaborate* (or make connections) and *evaluate*, reflecting on their learning journey and summarising what they know (in the summative stages) (Australian Academy of Science, 2008).

- Leave sufficient 'wait' time before requiring an answer, and before responding to that answer. Most teachers wait only one to two seconds, but it may be better to wait for three to five seconds or more (Rowe, 1986). If seeking a higher order thinking response, waiting even longer can be helpful (Cotton, 2001). This encourages students to think about their response, rather than blurting out their first thought, and allows for greater participation – some students need longer than others to consider their answer. Wait time does not need to be silent – it can be filled by students talking with each other about the answer (as in a 'think–pair–share' strategy), or writing down an answer.

- Use prompts to encourage students to elaborate on a response, or to help the student to clarify their answer.

- Use 'wrong' or faulty answers to develop ideas and probe thinking, within a supportive classroom environment.

- Model positive listening. Allow students to see that you are interested in and listening to their answers by responding with more than a 'Good answer', 'OK' or 'Yes' (especially if it is wrong!).

- Distribute questions around the class. Ensuring that all students have opportunities to answer, to display what they know, is important. This may mean avoiding the age-old tactic of calling on those with raised hands. Another way to do this is with a ball of string that is rolled to a student as the question is asked, and is then rolled back to the teacher – or to another student – as they answer. Another is to move around the room as you ask questions, ensuring that those 'hiding up the back' are also in focus.

- Encourage students to ask questions. Their questions not only help to develop their thinking, they also provide insight into the students' understanding (Glasson, 2009).

Black and Wiliam (2012b) discussed the role of classroom dialogue in formative assessment, emphasising the importance of interactive feedback in questioning sequences. They found that teachers in their project who focused on assessment for learning designed questions and tasks to create 'teachable moments', with an aim to have students do more of the thinking in the class than the teacher. They argue that typical initiation–response–evaluation sequences, such as 'Teacher: "What is four times four?", Student: "16" Teacher: "Right, well done" ' may provide summative information, but they do not encourage learning when teachers' evaluations take centre stage, rather than students' thinking. In the example just given, the student supplied an already known answer, and the teacher's response did not take the student's learning forward. Feedback is discussed further later in this chapter.

FIGURE 13.5 Dialogue between teacher and students can be powerful in assessment for learning. List some of the benefits.

Marzano and Simms (2014) developed a questioning sequence drawing on Bloom's taxonomy, to develop higher-order thinking. They suggested that classroom questioning start with questions that activate student knowledge, then ask students to categorise that knowledge, as a way of developing some claims about the topic. The next set of questions would ask for elaborations, or justifications of claims, while the final set would ask for evidence to support their justifications. This kind of sequence uses questions for learning, but could at the same time be used as formative assessment of students' thinking and understanding at each stage of the process.

STANDARDISED ASSESSMENTS

Assessments are called 'standardised' when they are administered and scored according to a standard set of procedures. They have generally been rigorously designed and pre-tested to ensure that the test is valid and reliable. Because they are given to large numbers of students, a distribution of scores can be reported, along with an individual's score relative to other students in his or her grade. Standardised assessments may be used for diagnostic assessment purposes, for formative assessment purposes, to place students along a learning progression, and for summative assessment.

Increasingly in Australia and New Zealand, and in many other countries, standardised assessment of performance has been introduced to measure student achievement at particular points in schooling, in order to compare the performance of students in different countries and also to identify groups of students who may not be reaching a particular benchmark of performance. Examples are the NAPLAN tests in Australia and asTTle in New Zealand. In the Australian tests, results are reported to parents, usually along a scale, and schools receive an aggregated report of their students' results. In New Zealand, teachers can select items from a test 'battery', to develop tests that will give them information relevant to their teaching goals. Results can be reported to parents and evaluated by teachers to improve their teaching–learning programs. It is important to distinguish between standards (against which students' progress is measured and reported – discussed later in this chapter) and the *standardisation* of testing, which refers to specific types of tests.

BOX 13.5 RESEARCH LINKS

THINKING CRITICALLY ABOUT HIGH-STAKES TESTS

In Australia, the NAPLAN tests were introduced in 2008, through which all students in years 3, 5, 7 and 9 are assessed nationally in reading, writing, language conventions and numeracy. The results of these tests are published school by school on the My School website. They also form the basis of an annual report on Australian schooling (see www.nap.edu.au for the most recent of these reports). The Australian Government argues that the tests make schools accountable for student results, and bring transparency to the education system in Australia, informing parent choice about schooling. Through the testing program, individual students and schools requiring assistance can be identified so that funding can be targeted at those most in need. Schools receive detailed reports that can be used as diagnostic tools – although the lag between the time when students take the test (May) and when the reports are sent to schools and parents (October) limits the usefulness of this data. As the results of the tests are used in the media and by parents to compare schools, and by governments to determine funding of special programs in schools, they may be said to be 'high-stakes tests'. Final year exams may also be termed 'high stakes' as their results determine students' entry into university courses.

Polesel, Dulfer and Turnbull (2012) reviewed the literature on impacts of high-stakes testing on students and families as part of a wider research project that investigated this in Australia. They found that although there is limited data available in Australia thus far, international studies show that such tests negatively influence the wellbeing of children, with a potential to negatively affect students' self-esteem and confidence, and lower teacher expectations. Students have also been found to experience stress, fear, pressure and anxiety from such tests. The quality of students' learning experience was also found to be affected, with narrowing of skills developed, focus by teachers on measurement and reporting rather than learning or the needs of the child, and narrowing of the curriculum. The broader study of NAPLAN testing in Australia interviewed principals, teachers, parents and students across 16 state and independent schools in NSW and Victoria, and found that while there were positive benefits of the testing program, there were also consequences of NAPLAN testing that affected a number of students' mental health and wellbeing, in line with the findings of the earlier literature review (Wyn, Turnbull & Grimshaw, 2014).

Klenowski and Wyatt-Smith (2011) identified the following consequences of the Australian testing program because of the high stakes involved for schools: narrowing of the curriculum as teachers focus on the skills and knowledge assessed in the test at the expense of other skills; stress for students and their teachers; and focus in assessment on measurement rather than learning. Some results for schools have been teachers cheating on the tests, low-achieving students being asked to stay at home on the day of the test, focusing of resources on those students likely to show most change, and teachers coaching students on the test. How then to gather and report evidence of students' achievement of national standards?

New Zealand takes a different approach to the reporting of students' progress, avoiding high-stakes testing in favour of a range of evidence drawn upon to develop an Overall Teacher Judgement (OTJ) (New Zealand Ministry of Education, 2011a). Standardised tests are used in New Zealand, but as they are combined with other forms of assessment, the score on an individual test has less impact – they do not hold such 'high stakes'.

ACTIVITIES

1   Debate the use of national assessment programs such as NAPLAN. What do they offer? What dangers do they pose?

2   How would you develop an assessment program that met both learning and reporting needs?

DIAGNOSTIC ASSESSMENT

'Diagnostic' is generally understood to be a medical term, since doctors diagnose disease. Teachers, however, use **diagnostic assessment** to pinpoint exactly what a student knows and can do, and to identify any gaps or misconceptions in their knowledge in a particular area of learning. It is typically used at the beginning of, or before starting, a unit of work, to guide decisions about instruction for particular students, and may also be used when a student is identified as experiencing difficulty. The SENA test used to gauge students' strategy use in early mathematics is an example of a diagnostic test. Teachers using diagnostic assessment are not just attempting to find out what the students can or cannot do, but why they make particular mistakes. Diagnostic assessment is particularly useful in literacy and numeracy instruction for pinpointing areas of student difficulty (see Box 13.6).

Tests used for diagnostic purposes cover a narrow range of skills and sample these skills in some depth. They often take the form of mastery tests, focusing on the degree to which specific learning outcomes have been achieved or 'mastered'. Understanding the cause of student difficulties is an important first step in helping students overcome them. Mastery tests can also indicate the need for tests of hearing, vision and general health, or alert teachers to problem behaviour and related social- and family-background factors (see Chapters 10 and 11).

> **diagnostic assessment**
> Assessment to determine what a student knows and can do, and why a student might be making particular errors

THINK ABOUT

- What advantages and disadvantages can you identify in each of the information-gathering techniques just discussed?
- Are there any assessment methods listed that you definitely would not use in your classroom? Why?
- Some tools of assessment focus on numerical values and scores for achievement. Are there some forms of learning you cannot measure? How do you deal with this problem in teaching?

CONSIDERING THE ROLE OF STUDENTS IN ASSESSMENT

Students, the learners, are at the centre of what happens in classrooms: the learning–teaching process. Quite separate from their abilities, students' attitudes and behaviours will influence the outcome of any assessment. It is therefore vital to consider and involve students in the assessment process by:

- *informing students.* Students should be informed of when we plan to assess them, as well as how and on what aspects of performance they will be assessed. Teachers should likewise share the results of any assessment with their students
- *motivating and engaging students.* Consider design of assessment tasks to engage students. The role of motivation and engagement in learning is discussed in detail in Chapter 8
- *involving students.* Involving students in designing assessments can help them to set and monitor learning goals. Students can also be involved in assessing their own and their peers' work.

BOX 13.6 CASE STUDY

DIAGNOSING A YEAR 2 STUDENT'S READING PROBLEM

Max was in his third year at school (Year 2) and his mother was worried about his progress in reading. At school, Max was in one of the higher reading groups and his teacher saw no problems, but although an avid listener, Max refused to read on his own at home. Max's father had a history of reading difficulties and this heightened Max's mother's concern about his progress in reading. The teacher thought that the books provided at home did not interest Max, and that his mother should look for reading material that did interest him. Max was able to read all the books in the Year 2 series reading program. Perhaps the mother was overanxious.

The teacher talked to a reading consultant who advised using a diagnostic strategy to assess Max's reading. She suggested that the teacher select a graded Year 2 passage that had no illustrations and that Max had not previously seen. She should then ask Max to read the text, telling him that he would be asked questions about it when he had finished. If he could answer about 75 per cent of the questions correctly, then the suggestion that the books at home did not interest him would be validated. However, if he had problems answering the questions, it was possible that he had a comprehension problem, a fluency problem, a word-recognition problem or a combination of all three.

To eliminate the possibility of a comprehension problem, the teacher read a passage to Max and asked him some questions about it. The boy had no difficulty in answering the questions, though he had earlier refused to read the passage himself and answer queries. Apparently, listening comprehension was not a problem. Next, the teacher timed Max while he read a grade-appropriate passage. His fluency was 30 words per minute (60–90 wpm was accepted as appropriate for early Year 2 students). Poor fluency can result from the inaccurate decoding of words, lack of speed or difficulties in word recognition.

Max's difficulty in word recognition was finally pinpointed when the teacher gave him an appropriate unseen passage to read. This showed that he had difficulty fully sounding out long or unfamiliar content words, though he could easily read common function words. Through repeated readings and contextual assistance, Max had learned to distinguish a number of words based on strategies such as recognition of the first and last letters, but this strategy failed when he encountered novel words in an unfamiliar passage. The teacher confirmed this diagnosis when she presented Max with more complex, less familiar words taken from class readers. Without the help of cues such as context, position in text and illustrations, Max made many errors. It was concluded that Max was still at a partial alphabetic phase in his development of reading skills. His high intelligence, verbal skills and ability to remember whole words without knowing how the graphemes represented individual phonemes had allowed him to progress to Year 2 without his problem being identified.

Max's teacher now needed to use a word-attack skills test to identify his specific difficulties in letter/sound translation, and to then implement a program involving explicit instructions in the letter/sound correspondences that he had failed to learn. These sound/symbol combinations would be practised in connected text. A writing program could also be introduced to help Max begin to attempt to invent the spelling of unfamiliar words. This would provide an opportunity for him to analyse words in order to spell them. It also gave the teacher an opportunity to help him understand that each word could be identified through a unique sequence of letters that distinguished it from other words with similar spelling.

Source: Adapted from Center (2005, pp. 230–4). Used by permission.

ACTIVITIES

1   Identify the sequence of steps Max's teacher followed to diagnose his reading problem.
2   What intervention might Max's teacher introduce to help the boy overcome his problem?
3   Are you familiar with a student who is experiencing difficulty in a specific subject area? Plan a set of steps that can be used to diagnose the exact nature of the problems the student is experiencing.
4   Once you have pinpointed the precise nature of the problem, what will be your next step?

Self-assessment and peer assessment

Encouraging students to assess their own work is a good way of increasing their motivation and of helping them to gain insight into their own learning. Assessing peers' work can help students to clarify what is expected in a task. It also can extend students' learning and develop reflection and self-regulation skills (Earl, 2013).

A review of self-assessment and peer assessment in secondary schools found that these forms of assessment positively affect students' achievement, self-esteem and engagement with learning. Impacts were most positive when teachers were able to discuss learning with students, give effective feedback, and adjust their teaching in response to student feedback (Sebba et al., 2008).

Black and Wiliam (2012a) argued that student self-assessment is essential to the formative assessment process. For teachers, student self-assessment is useful because it provides an additional source of information to supplement more conventional assessment information for instruction planning, and provides an insight into individual students' learning styles. Self-assessment enables students to become aware of their own strengths, weaknesses and needs, allows them to take an active part in the assessment process, builds metacognitive and self-regulation skills, and contributes to improving self-esteem and realistic notions about self-worth. It requires self-efficacy beliefs (see Chapter 8), teaching of thinking skills, and clear goals and success criteria to be made explicit in lessons as well as for assessment tasks (Earl, 2013).

Research has looked at the extent to which students' self- and peer-assessments are accurate (Harris, Brown & Harnett, 2015) finding this can vary, although generally students' assessments of their work correlate positively with other measures (Brown, Andrade & Chen, 2015). Practice, prompts and training can improve the accuracy of peer- and self-assessments, as well as helpfulness of feedback comments (Gan & Hattie, 2014; Nicolaidou, 2013; McDonald, 2009). In a New Zealand study, school students' self- and peer-feedback comments were analysed to find out what kinds of feedback students tended to provide. Students' feedback mostly related to the task (for example, 'good proofreading and writing of words and sentences') and process (for example, 'I need to work on finding information in texts and understanding what I'm reading'). Feedback that mentioned goals ('self-regulation feedback'; for example, 'I think we were really successful today because we worked as a team') was rarely found in self-assessment, and never in peer assessment. The authors suggested that if teachers want to use self- and peer-assessment to support students' self-regulation of their learning, they need to support them with training and practice (Harris, Brown & Harnett, 2015).

Participation in building up a portfolio is a form of self-assessment. This and examples of other forms of self-assessment are presented in Box 13.7.

CourseMateExpress

Online Resources
Go further: Try an example of self-assessment on this text's website

BOX 13.7 CLASSROOM LINKS

SELF-ASSESSMENT

Self-assessment (and peer assessment) by students is an important component of an *outcomes approach* to learning. It ensures that students are aware of instruction goals and that they learn to monitor their own progress towards achieving these goals. Examples of self-assessment formats are listed here.

How do you feel about telling news?

How do you feel about listening to other people's news?

What do you need to remember when telling news?
1 to speek cleley.
2 to not put you're finger in you're mouth.
3 to shaw them you're news

What do you need to remember when listening to news?
1 to not tallk,
2 to lisen,
3 to look at them.

Got it! I found this easy.

I'm on my way but would like you to check that I got it.

I found this hard and would like some help.

>>

STRENGTHS AND LIMITATIONS OF DIFFERENT ASSESSMENT TOOLS

Traditionally, assessment in schools was concerned with giving teachers, students and parents quantitative or norm-referenced information about a given student's performance in particular aspects of the curriculum during the school year. This resulted in the use of assessment strategies that provided a grade or score, as students (and more particularly parents) usually understood this type of information most easily. Interest in more qualitative forms of assessment led to the use of alternative methods for gathering information about student learning, focusing directly on classroom activities and involving observation of a student at work in class, collection of work samples, demonstrations of skill mastery, informal records, checklists, rating scales, interviews and self-assessment.

Study strategies	I use these	I'm working on these	I don't use these.	...because...
Study timetable or schedule			✓	I just do what I feel like
To do list		✓		
Using test or assignment feedback to work out what I need to learn		✓		
Nightly revision of what was covered that day in class		✓		
Practice examples	✓			
Working with a partner to test our knowledge and teach each other	✓			
Drawing concept maps or mind maps		✓		
Thinking aloud	✓			
Flashcards			✓	I dont learn vocab anymore (Italian)
Highlighting or underlining notes and key sections in textbooks	✓			
Writing summaries	✓			
Listing key points	✓			
Taking notes from the textbook	✓			
A reading system like SQ3R (Survey, Question, Read, Recite, Review)			✓	I have never heard of it before

ACTIVITIES

1   The sample self-assessment sheet about telling news above is designed for use in primary school settings. Design a similar self-assessment form that can be used with students in the lower secondary level in a curriculum area of your choice.

2   Have you ever been required to use a self-assessment instrument in a learning context?

If so, how effective was it for you? Try the self-assessment task on the CourseMate website. Do you think tasks like this would help you in your learning?

3   As a teacher, would you include student self-assessment in your own teaching program?

4   As a parent, how would you view the value of this procedure?

The strength of these alternative approaches to assessment lies in their increased validity, in that the process of assessment is more closely tied to the real-life performance of the task or skill being assessed (NSW Department of Education and Training, 2005). Such assessment is directly linked to learning outcomes identified in the syllabus, providing information about student achievement that informs current teaching programs and contributes to the diagnosis of both student strengths and student weaknesses. Teachers can use varied assessment strategies to give students opportunities to demonstrate their learning in different contexts. Alternative assessment strategies are fair, providing all students with opportunities to succeed based on current syllabus outcomes, and students are engaged in the assessment process by actively monitoring their achievement and progress. Through careful planning, teachers can ensure that they have the time and skill required to design and implement such procedures. In addition, it needs to be acknowledged that there is variability in the level of reliability attained from assessments that are based on procedures such as student-performance observation and review of work samples. Such variability needs to be compensated for by using information from multiple rather than single sources.

Assessment involves teachers making choices between assessment types and tools, as well as the timing of assessment, which all relate to the purposes the teacher has for a particular assessment event. Issues that might affect educators' decisions regarding modes of assessment are set out in Box 13.8.

BOX 13.8 IMPLICATIONS FOR EDUCATORS

DECIDING ON ASSESSMENT TOOLS

When deciding on a mode of assessment, teachers need to consider the following:

- The tool should be appropriate for a particular teaching program.
- A range of assessment practices should be used.
- Information should be gathered from a variety of sources, ranging from formal examinations to direct observation of students engaged in an activity.
- The tools of assessment to be used in a unit of instruction should be pre-planned.
- Any resources required for specific assessment procedures should be prepared beforehand. Teachers should endeavour to develop the competencies required to document and interpret assessment results.

ENSURING QUALITY IN ASSESSMENT

In a classroom situation, teachers need to ensure that the procedures they use are reliable, valid and fair (Brady & Kennedy, 2012). This section discusses the concepts of 'reliability' and 'validity', and how these apply to assessment methods and procedures. Teachers also need to ensure that the students are aware of the criteria against which they are being assessed, and the standard of work that is expected.

RELIABILITY

reliability
The extent to which a test or measurement device obtains the same result when used on successive occasions

Those who use test results need to know that such results are not the product of chance. **Reliability** is concerned with the dependability of assessment results. If an assessment is repeated, either by giving a test a second time or by re-marking test protocols, the assessment procedure's reliability is demonstrated if the same results are obtained on both occasions.

Furthermore, for a test or assessment method to be considered reliable, it needs to yield the same results not only if given on separate occasions (also known as 'test-retest reliability'), but also if different people mark or score it ('scorer reliability'); that is, if the same piece of work is given to two independent markers, they should produce much the same result – they should both give an 'A' to the same essay, for instance. Multiple-choice tests, which measure single skills or content identified from a specific program of instruction, are an objective form of assessment that should be 100 per cent reliable because correct answers are invariable and are identified at the time the test is constructed, with items being 'framed' to allow students to select the best option from an array of alternatives. However, forms of assessment that require more subjective judgements (such as essays or portfolios) tend to be affected by examiner judgement, so marks can vary widely. A reliable system for marking an essay or portfolio therefore requires two independent markers, with neither marker being aware of the grade given by the other. The two marks are then averaged to achieve an improved level of scorer reliability.

A single test or assessment task can never measure every aspect of a skill, domain or theoretical construct unless the scope of that skill, domain or construct is very restricted. This means that results from separate tests that measure different aspects or elements of the same skill, domain or construct need to be comparable for such tests to be considered reliable measures. In the same way, results of tests that are of comparable difficulty – whether or not they measure content from the same or different areas – should also be comparable for the tests to be considered reliable measures of that degree of difficulty.

Chance factors can affect test results and compromise the reliability of a test or assessment method. Such factors include those associated with:

- *the student;* fatigue, boredom, lack of motivation and carelessness
- *the test;* ambiguous items, trick questions, poorly worded directions and unfamiliar formats
- *conditions of test-taking and marking;* poor examination conditions, excessive heat or cold, carelessness in marking, disregard or lack of clear standards for scoring, and computational errors.

VALIDITY

A second technical aspect of assessment concerns the notion of **validity**, or truthfulness. A test or assessment procedure's validity relates to its purpose: Does the test or procedure measure what it is designed to measure? If assessment is to give information to teachers and students about what students have learnt, it needs to align with the purposes (the planned outcomes) of that learning, and with the learning and teaching activities the students have experienced. This is an aspect of fairness. (If you haven't been taught about calculus, it would be unfair to have it included in a test of your learning.)

Several kinds of validity are desirable in any test or assessment. **Face validity** is achieved if a test *appears* to measure what it is intended to measure. A test is said to have **content validity** if it can be demonstrably linked to relevant curriculum objectives. **Construct validity** is demonstrated if a test measures the knowledge, attitudes and skills (the 'constructs') that underlie the curriculum objectives.

A valid assessment allows students to demonstrate broad understanding of the curriculum area being assessed, rather than simply recording their performance on a specific set of tasks. In addition, Messick (1995) argued that assessments that are valid may also have unintended consequences, and can have social consequences – a form of validity known as **consequential validity**. He argued that validity goes beyond the test itself to the interpretation of results. Some of the concerns about the effects of high-stakes testing (see Box 13.5) are about consequential validity. It may involve the interpretations made from assessment results (such as ranking schools on the basis of their results).

Validity is a crucial aspect of assessment. In practical terms, if you give a test of number facts, is it only students' knowledge of number facts that influences their performance; or are other factors involved? For example, do the questions require literacy skills for students to understand what is asked? If so, then the test results may measure literacy rather than being a valid test of number skills.

Test bias

When judging an assessment procedure's validity, attention needs to be given to its fairness, or lack of 'test bias'. **Test bias** occurs when an unfair advantage is given to some students; for example, the knowledge or skills required to do well on a test may be found more in particular groups (such as boys, children living in urban areas, or children from a particular religious background) than in others. Lack of bias is established if it can be shown that neither the test content nor the interpretation of its results disadvantages specific groups of students. For example, students with reading problems will be disadvantaged in text-based assessments, but not in assessments where no reading is required.

validity
The extent to which a test or measurement device measures what it purports to measure

face validity
The degree to which a test appears to measure what it is intended to measure

content validity
A measure of the link between a test and relevant curriculum objectives

construct validity
A measure of the link between a test and underlying knowledge, attitudes and skills

consequential validity
Intended and unintended consequences of assessment interpretation and use

test bias
Where particular groups are disadvantaged by factors associated with a test's content and the interpretation of results

Culture-sensitive and culture-fair tests

In developing the first intelligence test, Binet and Simon created items that tapped the practical knowledge of children living in Paris at the end of the 19th century (see Chapter 9). The test was later adapted for use in the USA. Subsequent use of the Stanford–Binet Intelligence Scale and similar tests of intelligence with children from other cultural backgrounds (for example, the children of immigrants who moved to the USA at the beginning of the 20th century) highlighted the inappropriateness of many of the test items for some children. Apart from language differences, the immigrant children often lacked knowledge about objects familiar to American children, such as postage stamps, telephones, pianos or mirrors (Anastasi, 1976). For these children, intelligence tests such as the Stanford–Binet were neither **culture-sensitive** nor **culture-fair tests**. Children from socially disadvantaged or minority-group backgrounds may also experience difficulties with tests that include items requiring unfamiliar, culturally based knowledge.

Mahuika, Berryman and Bishop (2011) argued that culturally responsive assessment must form part of a culturally responsive pedagogy. They cautioned that Māori learners (and, we would add, learners from any other cultural group) are not all the same in culture or learning needs, so cultural sensitivity in assessment will come down to knowing your students, and adapting assessments accordingly, in order to gather meaningful information about where they are in their learning. Cultural sensitivity impacts upon both reliability and validity of assessment. Some assessment strategies that Mahuika and colleagues identified from research as effective for Māori students included formative assessment, particularly when it involved quality academic feedback, and the use of interviews, portfolios and student journals rather than written tests.

It is important to note that each technical aspect of a test or assessment procedure – such as reliability, validity, test bias and cultural bias – needs to be evaluated separately because, for example, a test can be highly reliable but lack validity. The implications for educators that may arise from technical issues in the different modes of assessment are summarised in Box 13.9.

culture-sensitive or culture-fair test
A test that does not require culturally based knowledge

THINK ABOUT

- How will you check to make sure assessment methods are reliable, valid and fair in your classroom?

BOX 13.9 IMPLICATIONS FOR EDUCATORS

TECHNICAL ISSUES IN ASSESSMENT

In using different modes of assessment to monitor student learning, teachers need to be aware of issues associated with reliability and validity:

- Attention needs to be paid to the reliability of an assessment procedure, with provision made to improve reliability if it is judged unacceptable.
- The reliability of an assessment can include factors associated with the examinee, characteristics of the assessment procedure, and the conditions under which the assessment is administered and marked.
- An assessment procedure can be judged to have validity if the consequences of its use are as expected.
- Indications of validity in a test include the absence of test bias and content that is culture-sensitive.

EVALUATION OF ASSESSMENT DATA

Assessment and evaluation are inseparable. When teachers gather information about students' achievements (assess), they also make judgements about (evaluate) what the information tells them about students' learning and their own teaching. Assessment is not just a matter of collecting evidence of learning, but will also involve interpreting that evidence, and using it to adapt instruction (Bennett, 2011). For example, if a student makes an error in an assessment task, the teacher needs to ask how they got to that point, and why they answered as they did. The teacher will make a hypothesis to interpret the evidence they have collected. Both the quality of the evidence collected and the skill in forming hypotheses are important to assessment quality.

Quality assessment, therefore, must involve making quality judgements about the information gathered. It involves three key elements: alignment, or ensuring that judgements relate to what was intended for the learning; consistency of judgement; and transparency of judgement. These correlate with the elements of quality assessment discussed above: validity, reliability and fairness.

So first, *judgements must be aligned* with the aims of learning and assessment.

ALIGNMENT AND THE USE OF STANDARDS

Assessment, learning goals and what is taught (curriculum) need to be aligned to ensure validity and fairness. Alignment of assessment with, and its integration in, classroom teaching ensures that assessment activities are not simply tacked onto the end of a unit of work, but form an integral part of it. Students gain a stronger appreciation of what is required and how it relates to what they have been learning. One approach to this is in curriculum planning, to start with the standards in order to develop clear learning goals. Teachers next spell out what this learning will look like and determine how they will assess whether students have reached the goals. Finally, they plan teaching and learning activities to support students to develop the knowledge and skills needed for the assessment. This is sometimes called 'backwards mapping' or 'backward design' because planning starts rather than ends with assessment (McTighe, 2010). Wyatt-Smith and Bridges (2007) described this approach to alignment undertaken by teachers in Victoria. Another approach to integration, associated with Assessment for Learning, and described by Heitink et al. (2015), is to partner with students in learning and assessment through use of self- and peer-assessment, as discussed above. This has the added benefit of contributing to learners' motivation for learning and their skills and knowledge for self-regulation of learning.

Judgements of assessment performance in Australia must also be aligned with the standards. This both ensures validity of judgements and provides opportunities for learning conversations with students around the quality of their work and their progress (Klenowski & Wyatt-Smith, 2014). Publication of exemplars of student work demonstrating the standards can assist teachers to align their judgements with the standards, and for judgement to be consistent across many teachers (see below).

In a different approach, in 2018 New Zealand's Ministry of Education removed national standards from their requirements for assessment and reporting, encouraging teachers to focus rather on the progress and achievement of each child in relation to the New Zealand Curriculum. The change is intended to support teachers to base learning and teaching decisions on each child's current knowledge, skills and learning needs. Teachers will still assess and report on students' progress and achievement, linking to the curriculum, and drawing on a broad range of assessment approaches to suit the needs of their students and communities (Ministry of Education, 2017, 2018). In Australia, the Gonski review (2018) recommended use of learning progressions rather than stage-based standards for assessment and reporting, which has a similar focus.

THINK ABOUT

- How does each of these approaches support students' learning? Which approach fits best with your philosophy of learning and teaching?

CONSISTENCY THROUGH MODERATION

criteria
The particular indicators that are being assessed to indicate knowledge or understanding

standards
Detailed descriptions of student achievement used to measure progress within a set of sequentially ordered learning outcomes

moderation
The process of teachers comparing and discussing judgements with each other in order to improve consistency of judgement

For reliability of evaluation to exist, the second requirement must be fulfilled: a *consistency of judgement*. For example, two teachers are evaluating their students' work. One gives everyone top marks because she judges that they all 'are striving to do their best, and have done a great job'. The other, however, gives considerably lower marks because she judges that although some have met her expectation for the task, others are still working towards it, and a few have done an outstanding job, beyond what she had expected for the class. The two teachers are using different **criteria** and different **standards** to judge the work. This can lead to confusion for the students and their parents, as they in turn try to evaluate how well the students are progressing with their learning at school. One approach taken by education departments in Australia and New Zealand to improving the consistency of evaluation across different teachers has been to publish exemplars, or samples of students' work for each of the standards. Teachers are encouraged to discuss the samples and standards together to help develop consistent use of the standards for evaluating student work. New Zealand schools moderate OTJs of student progress, with a team of teachers independently judging the range of evidence for a particular student, and then discussing any differences to reach an agreed decision (New Zealand Ministry of Education, 2011a). **Moderation** ensures consistency across teachers, schools, states and time. This moderation of teacher judgement is important in ensuring reliability of assessment. It can also contribute to teachers' practice – as they develop stronger understandings of the standards and what progression through them looks like, they can guide students' progress more effectively (Klenowski & Wyatt-Smith, 2014).

On the CourseMate website, you can try this yourself. Look at the work sample and determine what level it represents, then compare your judgement with that of a peer.

USING RUBRICS TO PROVIDE TRANSPARENCY

Online Resources
Go further: Use standards to judge students' work on this text's website

The third requirement is for *transparency of judgement*. Students should be informed about the purpose, criteria and standards by which they are to be assessed. Informing students about the purpose of assessment allows them to determine the importance of the test for them. The criteria refer to the particular skills and knowledge the teacher is looking for in assessing a performance or piece of work. The standards indicate how well the students have achieved those criteria. One way to do this is with a rubric, an example of which is given below in Table 13.1.

rubric
A tool for marking and giving feedback about student work against particular criteria and standards

When provided with a **rubric** for a task, students know what they have to achieve, and how well they have to achieve it to gain a particular mark or grade. Rubrics are also useful for feedback purposes: students can see how well they performed and what they need to do to improve; although providing improvement feedback together with the rubric maximises its effectiveness. Wollenschlager et al. (2016) compared three ways of providing feedback using a rubric: giving the rubric alone, giving the rubric along with information about the student's task performance, and giving the rubric, information about task performance, and cues on how to improve. They found that the students provided with the improvement information showed higher achievement subsequently, had more positive evaluations of their competence, and were more accurate in evaluating their own performance.

TABLE 13.1 Rubric for a narrative writing task

STANDARDS					
	Limited – please come and see me for some help	Satisfactory – keep working on it!	Good – you have done just what was asked	Excellent – your narrative is even better than expected at this stage	Outstanding – you are working well above expectations!
CRITERIA					
Accuracy of spelling and grammar	Major spelling and grammatical errors. Difficult to read	Some spelling and grammatical errors. Meaning can be followed	Few errors in spelling and/or grammar. Easy to read	Minor errors in spelling or grammar. Easy to read	No errors in spelling or grammar. Pleasant to read
Appropriate use of the narrative genre structure	Does not tell a story	May be missing an orientation, complication or resolution	Has an orientation, complication and resolution	Has an orientation, complication, resolution and coda	Orientation, complication, resolution and coda are engaging
Appropriate use of the narrative genre language features	Words in the story do not connect. Characters or places in the story are not described; no indication of sequence; no indication of what characters are saying, thinking or feeling	Uses simple noun and verb groups; time or causal connectives may be missing	Uses word chains, action verbs, past tense and noun groups to describe the character or setting; time connectiveness to sequence of events; indicates what characters are saying and thinking or feeling	Uses word chains, complex verb groups effectively; uses adjectives and adverbs to add interest to noun and verb groups; beginning to experiment with the genre (for example, organising the time sequence differently) and complex sentences	Successfully manipulates the standard features of the genre narrative to introduce interest (for example, use of present tense to indicate the events are in a dream)

INTERPRETING ASSESSMENT INFORMATION

How should assessment information be interpreted? Traditionally, test results have been interpreted by comparing them with the average performance of other students on the same test, with results reported in the form of a grade (such as 'A', 'B' and 'C'). This procedure 'places' each student in relation to other students ('norm-referenced' assessment). However, the shift from using traditional summative forms of assessment to using formative and diagnostic assessment procedures has given rise to alternative approaches to test-result interpretation. For example, comparison with a predetermined standard or criterion (referred to as 'criterion-referenced' assessment) is used, as is comparison with a curriculum (known as 'curriculum-based' assessment). Alternatively, test results are sometimes compared with the student's own previous performance ('ipsative' assessment).

Norm-referenced assessment

If teachers need to collect information about their students' progress in relation to others' in the class, the school or region, they use 'norm-referenced' (or 'normative') assessment procedures. **Norm-referenced assessment** occurs when one student's score on a test is compared with the average score gained on the test by students of similar age and learning background. In this situation, the mean (or average score) of students who have taken the test provides a standard of performance, or **norm**, against which the scores of individual students on the same test can be compared. Teachers use information from norm-referenced tests to find out if a student has done better than other comparable students and is thus above the norm, or if the student has done worse than other students and is thus below the norm. Norms can be based on student scores drawn from a class, a school, a school district or a wider area.

norm-referenced assessment
Used to compare the performance of individuals or groups with the performance of a comparable group on the same task

norm
The mean or average performance of a group of people

Most tests of achievement used in classrooms are prepared by teachers and are norm-referenced, with norms based on the scores of the whole class. However, norm-referenced tests can also be designed for use with larger groups, with norms based on the scores of a large group of students who are similar to those taking the test; for example, Queensland students aged around 14 years who have studied biology for a year. Many of the norm-referenced tests used in schools in Australia and New Zealand were developed by specialist psychometricians (psychology-test designers) and are published by agencies such as the Australian Council for Educational Research (ACER) and the New Zealand Council for Educational Research (NZCER). These tests are sometimes described as **standardised tests** because they have been designed according to strict rules, must be administered under specified, uniform conditions and have standard procedures for scoring and interpreting results and comparing these with the test norms. The main feature of norm-referenced assessment is that it provides information about individual students' level of achievement when compared with students of similar age and educational background in a specific area of learning. Graham et al. (2010) warned that norm-referenced assessments are not appropriate for Māori, Pasifika or many Indigenous Australian students, as they emphasise competitive goals (doing better than the next person) which clashes with collectivist beliefs. Chapter 11 explores individualism, collectivism and education in more detail.

standardised test
A test designed in accordance with set rules, administered under uniform conditions, and scored and interpreted in terms of identified norms

Criterion-referenced assessment

If a teacher's main interest is to pinpoint how well students have mastered a particular skill, the most appropriate form of assessment may be **criterion-referenced assessment**.

criterion-referenced assessment
Where achievement is compared against a specified criterion or standard

The growing democratisation of education in Western societies culminated, in the final decades of the 20th century, in increasing pressure on schools to provide appropriate education programs for all students regardless of their social, religious or ethnic background, and regardless of disability. One outcome of this change was that educators' focus shifted from normative evaluation of student achievement by means of peer comparison to evaluation based on an identified standard or according to prescribed curriculum goals or outcomes. Norm-referenced tests have been gradually supplemented or replaced with *criterion-referenced tests* that compare individual performance on a set of test items with a specified or predetermined level of performance that is typical of students who are competent on these items (Piper, 1997; Ward & Murray-Ward, 1999). Performance levels are usually organised sequentially in terms of a developmental hierarchy, with student progress measured in terms of achieving progressively higher levels in the sequence. Regardless of class or grade level, students are working towards the achievement of outcomes that are located sequentially along a learning progression. This has been described as an **outcomes approach** to assessment, with student achievement measured against a set of standards (NSW Department of Education and Training, 2005).

outcomes approach
Students work towards the achievement of outcomes located sequentially along a learning continuum

The advantage of using criterion-referenced assessment is that the standards used remain constant over time and place. This can be contrasted with norm-referenced assessment, where norms can vary depending on the achievement level of the group of students on which the norms are based.

Curriculum-based assessment

Traditionally, classroom assessment has had the purpose of discovering how well students have learned what they have been taught. In order to do this, assessment will be based on curriculum objectives and content. Masters (2013) (see Box 13.1) identified a shift in thinking about the purpose of assessment, towards assessment for learning, occurring throughout the teaching learning cycle, as an integral part of the curriculum. In this conception, assessment would always be curriculum-centred, seeking to understand where learners are in their long-term learning journey . The Gonski review (2018) has taken up this suggestion, recommending learning progressions be developed for all curriculum areas, to guide assessment and reporting. See Alonzo (2018) for more on learning progressions and assessment. Assessments derived from the curriculum and carried out as part of the teaching process give vital information about what students have learned and how effective teaching has been. They can also combine teaching and assessment, with students learning through working on and receiving feedback on assessment tasks. Such **curriculum-based assessments** can be used to diagnose students' strengths and weaknesses, and to plan future teaching programs. This type of assessment is usually carried out by a classroom teacher for the purposes of:

■ obtaining information about the level of students' entry skills, so as to decide where to place them within the curriculum

■ defining and planning appropriate teaching objectives

■ determining the degree to which these objectives are met by monitoring students' progress through an instructional sequence

■ developing students' skills and knowledge towards the learning objectives

■ evaluating and refining teaching techniques.

curriculum-based assessment
Assessment that compares individual students' performance with curriculum goals

Types of curriculum-based assessment, and profiles

The type of assessment used by teachers in curriculum-based assessment varies widely. It can include a weekly spelling test of 20 words compiled by the class teacher, or a checklist of gross motor skills for kindergarten children (for example, 'Hop in a straight line', 'Ascend and descend stairs using alternate feet', or 'Kick a ball'). It often involves task analysis of a curriculum area and the preparation of a scope-and-sequence chart. The Literacy and Numeracy learning progressions in Australia and New Zealand (see Box 13.3) and Western Australia's First Steps Developmental Continua are examples of this process. Curriculum **profiles** such as these provide teachers with an ordered sequence or continuum of descriptors of learning outcomes that they can use to chart students' progress. Data derived from profiles provide information about what students need to know and the logical order of this material.

profile
An ordered sequence or progression of learning descriptors that can be used to chart progress

The main advantages of curriculum-based assessment are that it provides for:

■ direct monitoring of the content being taught

■ precise feedback about the effectiveness of teaching

■ frequent modification of teaching strategies in response to student performance

■ a sensitive measure of change

■ the possibility of repeated administrations, which can yield more information than could be generalised from a single administration.

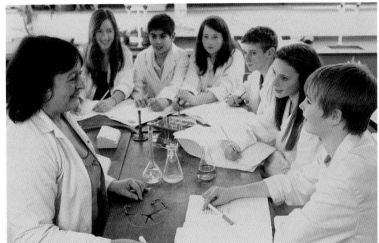

Source: Shutterstock.com/Monkey Business Images

FIGURE 13.6 Curriculum-based assessments can help both students and teachers to focus on students' progress towards curriculum goals. What will be important for these students to know about the task, themselves and the assessment process?

Ipsative assessment

ipsative assessment
Assessment that
compares an
individual's current
achievement with a
previous achievement

If the interest is in how much progress an individual student has made, then 'ipsative assessment' is used. Employed most often to assess performance skills outside a school setting (for example, in sports such as swimming or skiing), **ipsative assessment** can also be used in educational contexts, where it involves an individual's performance in a particular aspect of learning being compared with that person's previous performance. When people talk about their 'personal best' or their 'best performance', they are referring to ipsative assessment. This type of assessment is concerned with an individual's own performance and whether this has improved or deteriorated over time.

The procedures used to collect the information required for ipsative assessment can include formal paper-and-pencil tests, or informal methods such as direct observation, checklists and rating scales, interviews and appraisal of work samples (written, performed or created). Information derived from such sources can be used to compile profiles of student achievement, as part of both ongoing and final assessment.

THINK ABOUT

- How and when will you make use of norm-referenced, criterion-referenced, curriculum-based and ipsative forms of assessment in your work as a teacher?
- What connections do you see between effective assessment and student motivation (see Chapter 8) and self-esteem (see Chapter 4)?

STRENGTHS AND LIMITATIONS OF NORM-REFERENCED, CRITERION-REFERENCED, CURRICULUM-BASED AND IPSATIVE ASSESSMENT PROCEDURES

Traditionally, assessment data has been interpreted by means of norm-referenced assessment, a method that is useful for describing individual or group performance relative to that of other, similar individuals or groups. Norm-referenced assessment is generally understood in the community and is widely used by teachers in classroom practice; however, it has the disadvantage that it does not always provide information about what individuals have learned or what they can and cannot do. The overall level of ability of different groups can also vary widely, meaning that a student's performance on a norm-referenced test may be considered outstanding if comparison is made with a low-ability group, or poor if comparison is made with a high-ability group. Tests that combine norm-referenced and criterion-referenced characteristics, such as NAPLAN, overcome some of these weaknesses.

Interpreting data in criterion-referenced assessment has the advantage of focusing attention on individual students' performance. Those who fail to demonstrate 'mastery' of a specified level of performance can readily be identified and provided with further opportunities for learning. However, a risk with criterion-referenced assessment is that developing a coherently ordered set of tasks to represent the achievement sequence for proficiency in a particular area, or in line with a curriculum, can be a difficult task, requiring skills that may be outside an individual teacher's competency. Widespread implementation of criterion-referenced assessment depends on the availability of such sequenced materials in relevant curriculum areas, and professional development for teachers in their use. See Alonzo (2018) for more on learning progressions and assessment.

direct assessment
Criterion-referenced —
or mastery tests that
assess specific content
from a clearly defined
curriculum

The strength of curriculum-based assessment is its concern with the **direct assessment** of student performance on a set of identified, sequentially ordered objectives that are derived from the curriculum. Assessment occurs frequently and takes place in the classroom as part of daily instruction. Assessment tasks given to each student are derived from the point in the instructional sequence at which the student is currently working, meaning each assessment is tied directly to the student's current learning goals. Information derived from such assessments helps teachers identify exactly what a given student can and cannot do, and teaching can then be tailored to the student's current needs. Curriculum-based assessment is particularly useful for students who are at risk of experiencing problems in some aspect of learning. A limitation of curriculum-based assessment is that it can be time-consuming in terms of collecting assessment data (students can be involved in this task), recording and interpreting the data, and planning specific teaching objectives to ensure student progress.

Ipsative assessment is useful for helping students to become motivated and independent learners. Strategies such as setting personal goals, deciding what needs to be done and monitoring personal progress have been shown to have a positive impact on achievement levels. Students learn to use their own frame of reference in assessment. The process of ipsative assessment is concerned not with common goals shared by other students, but with personal goals and with students 'learning to learn' (Griffin & Nix, 1991, p. 94).

REPORTING THE RESULTS OF ASSESSMENT

Assessment is undertaken for a specific purpose, and that purpose guides decisions about when and how to assess. In the same way, the reporting of assessment results is guided by particular purposes, and by the intended audience.

Who might need information from assessment results? At the most immediate level, such information will be of interest to those involved directly: students and their parents. Tests that provide information for these groups are part of the teaching process. The types of assessments used are usually informal rather than formal, and formative rather than summative in nature. Feedback, particularly for students, is often immediate and given to the student personally. Others who may have an interest – particularly in the results of more formal assessments – include school administrators, potential employers and, in some cases, politicians. These groups require information from tests for administrative purposes such as determining eligibility for a special program, in job selection and in government policy formulation. The reporting of this type of test information tends to be impersonal and by means of official documents and publications, with interested groups often remote from the assessment process. Table 13.2 shows who assessment stakeholders might be and what information they might require.

REPORTING TO STUDENTS

What is the first thing you look at, as a student, when you collect an assignment? For most students it is the mark or grade. This indicates how well you did in the task. After that, what do you look at? If the assignment is a piece of written work, you will look for comments. If the grade is good, you will probably get few comments, but if it is poor, there are likely to be more comments; that is, feedback is usually given on perceived strengths and weaknesses, as seen by the marker, who pays greater attention to weaknesses than to strengths. The marker's aim is to have an impact on the student's next piece of work. This is most likely to occur if the feedback is given to students so that it:

- clearly sets out planned instructional outcomes
- identifies student strengths (what has been done well) and weaknesses (what they need to work on)
- gives full feedback on specific errors and poor strategies, with suggestions for how to improve
- contributes to student motivation (Black & Wiliam, 1998; Linn & Gronlund, 1995, p. 334).

TABLE 13.2 Stakeholders and their information needs

STAKEHOLDERS	INFORMATION NEEDS	ASSESSMENT AND REPORTING METHODS
Students	Feedback on what they did well, what they can improve on, and how.	Informal, personal, immediate, formative, instructional
Parents	Feedback on performance of their child	
Teachers	Feedback on teaching and student performance; diagnosis of student strengths and weaknesses	
Psychologists	Information on student strengths and weaknesses for programming, placement, advising and counselling purposes	
School administrators	Information for screening, eligibility, certification and annual reporting to parents and the community	
Employers	Information about skills and personal characteristics	
Government	Information about standards and for determining funding priorities	
Community	General information on operation of schools	Formal, impersonal, remote, summative, administrative

Source: Adapted from Griffin and Nix (1991, p. 35).

Source: © Jim Wileman/Alamy.

FIGURE 13.7 Compared with other strategies, feedback has one of the strongest effects on student achievement. Effective feedback answers the questions: 'Where am I going?', 'How am I going?' and 'Where to next?'

In a large meta-analysis of thousands of studies of interventions in teaching and learning, Hattie (2005, 2009) found that feedback had one of the strongest effects on student achievement (see Table 13.2). The form of the feedback makes a difference: Black and Wiliam (1998) found that grades were less effective than comments, particularly in terms of student motivation, while Belanger, Allingham and Bechervaise (2004) found that giving grades and comments together was also ineffective – students looked at the grade and either didn't read the comment, or read it as explaining the grade rather than giving them feedback on their learning. Comments alone are shown in this research to be the most effective form of written feedback on a task. While grades may be needed for other reporting purposes (see the section on reporting to parents, below), once again, purpose must be considered: if the intent is to provide feedback to improve learning, the most effective form should be selected. See Table 13.1 for an example of a format (a rubric) that can be used to give feedback about how to improve in terms of the standard of work expected.

Heitink et al. (2015) reported in their review of research on assessment for learning that focused, constructive feedback that makes errors clear and provides suggestions about how to improve can influence student motivation for learning. Gamlem and Smith's study (2013) highlighted the value of feedback that involves dialogue either between teacher and students, or between students. The most effective feedback was provided on the spot, and students were given time to respond to the feedback in working on a task.

Box 13.10 summarises a review of research on effective feedback.

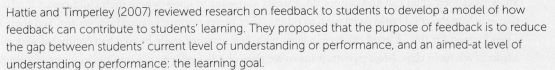

BOX 13.10 RESEARCH LINKS

EFFECTIVE FEEDBACK

Hattie and Timperley (2007) reviewed research on feedback to students to develop a model of how feedback can contribute to students' learning. They proposed that the purpose of feedback is to reduce the gap between students' current level of understanding or performance, and an aimed-at level of understanding or performance: the learning goal.

In this model, effective feedback can operate in terms of three key questions, and at four levels. The questions are:

1 *Where am I going?* (assisting with goal setting, or *feed up*). Feedback at this level is effective when goals are clear and challenging, so that students know what and how well they are to achieve; when students share commitment to the goals, so that they care about and seek the feedback; and when feedback gives information related to the goals, so that, for example, if the goal is 'to write an engaging story', feedback is not just about spelling errors but relates to elements of engaging narratives: vocabulary, structure and ideas.

2 *How am I going?* (or *feedback*). At this level, effective feedback gives information about progress, and about how the student can improve, so that it links to the next question, 'Where to next?' Information can compare students' current level to the goal, which can be done using a specific standard such as an ideal performance, or to their prior performance; it may also relate to success or failure on a particular component.

3 *Where to next?* (or *feed forward*). Hattie and Timperley argue that feedback relating to this question can have some of the greatest impacts on learning. It can lead, for example, to better understanding of the goal, to improved self-regulation, and to deeper understanding.

In answering these questions, teachers can direct feedback at four levels: feedback relating to tasks, processes, self-regulation and the student. Hattie and Timperley argue that the particular focus of feedback determines its effectiveness:

1 *Task feedback* gives information about the task itself and how well it has been achieved. Continuing our example of 'write an engaging story', an example of task feedback is: 'Your story is quite engaging but could include more interesting words to describe the characters.'

2 *Process feedback* is directed at the process of learning or undertaking the task. An example is: 'When editing your work, consider whether your story could be made more interesting or whether the reader's questions are answered, not just whether your spelling and grammar are correct.'

3 *Self-regulation–directed feedback* centres on developing students' confidence to engage more deeply in the task and self-evaluation skills. An example is: 'You have obviously thought carefully about describing the setting of your story in an interesting way. Think about whether you have also done this when describing the characters in your story, and how you could develop their descriptions to make your story even more engaging.'

4 *Self-feedback* focuses on the students themselves. An example is: 'I always love reading your stories. You are an imaginative writer.'

According to Hattie and Timperley's findings, the least effective of these forms is feedback about the self, while feedback about process and self-regulation are most effective for deep processing and mastery of tasks. Task feedback can be effective when that information also contributes to processing and self-regulation knowledge and skills. Its effectiveness is reduced when combined with feedback about the self.

ACTIVITIES

1 Consider feedback you have received (or given) for a range of tasks. What type of feedback was it? How effective was it for your learning?

2 Use the three questions detailed above to give yourself feedback about a recent task.

3 Hattie and Timperley also state that stickers and praise are not effective forms of feedback. Explain why this would be, in terms of their model. What further function might praise serve?

4 Read the full report of the study to consider effective forms of feedback in more detail.

Online Resources
Watch a **video** of a
parent talking about
her ideal report on this
text's website

REPORTING TO PARENTS

What do parents want from the assessment process? Most parents would say 'good marks'! They want to know what their child can and cannot do. Parents also want to know where their child comes in class; that is, where the child ranks in relation to others. They prefer norm-referenced assessment, and there is a good reason for this. A good mark may seem high, but may not really be so when compared with the marks of others in class. Most parents want to see their child's performance not just in terms of a single score or grade, but in the broader context of the class as a whole. They need to have such information reported in a form that is understandable and meaningful. Remember that many parents understand norm-referenced assessment procedures because that is what they remember from their own experiences at school. They often need assistance in understanding information from other types of assessment. Box 13.11 contains a case study of one teacher's reflections on the reporting process.

BOX 13.11 CASE STUDY

ASSESSMENT AND REPORTING

The annual or biannual report card can fill the hearts of teachers (and students) with dread. The thought of having to assign a grade for each student in each strand of each subject can seem overwhelming; however, many teachers are coming to realise that with comprehensive assessment throughout the semester, the formal report card needn't be such an onerous task. One teacher from a small, regional school in NSW finds the task of report writing to be a systematic process rather than an overwhelming burden. She recognises the formal report card as an opportunity to consolidate the assessment data she has gathered and values the opportunity to provide feedback to her students and their parents.

For this teacher, the process of report writing begins by bringing together all the assessment data she has gathered. Work samples are matched with checklists, cross-matched with observations and so on. On a class list, the teacher notes the results for each task so that in reading 'across the list', a general sense of each student's performance can be gained. The teacher then refers to the Board of Studies website and clicks into the Assessment Resource Centre, where work samples for each grade are displayed with explicit criteria. 'I've been reporting using A–E for several years now,' she explains, 'but I always like to refer back to those benchmarks, especially when I begin my report writing. It reminds me of what the standards are for each grade, and it also reminds me that I'm not comparing the students in my class against one another; I'm measuring each student against the syllabus criteria.'

National high-stakes testing can cause teachers to question their credibility as assessors. However, it is important to recognise the value of the teacher as a human instrument: able to assess over time, within varied contexts, monitoring both process and progress. For this teacher, national tests remain just another tool in her toolbox of assessment. Students' test results are acknowledged as she brings together assessment information, but those results are seen in their appropriate context and are not given greater value than other assessments she has conducted: 'National tests are like snapshots of assessment. They tell me what my student could do on that particular day when they were faced with that particular task.'

As the assessment data is brought together and formal grades become evident, this teacher also takes the opportunity to make notes about each student. These notes later form the basis of her report comments and are related to the learning, skills, content, values and attitudes associated with the subject and strand. Comments about each student's demeanour, personality and nature are kept to a minimum and are reserved for the broader general comments box at the end of the report: 'Parents and students want to know what they're doing well, where they can improve and how they can improve. Telling them that their son or daughter has a "sweet nature" and giving them a D in reading doesn't help anyone.'

Source: Gabrielle Stroud.

ACTIVITIES

1   What assessment tools can you identify that this teacher draws on?
2   How has the quality of the assessment data been checked in terms of reliability and validity?
3   How has the teacher considered the needs of parents and students in reporting?

Methods of reporting to parents

Overall, parents get information about their child and the school itself from a variety of sources, including:

- the child and other children and parents
- school newsletters
- regular student–teacher, parent–teacher and three-way (student–parent–teacher) interviews
- report cards
- notes, telephone calls and personal visits to the school
- homework (involving parent confirmation), student diaries and communication sheets
- speech nights, social occasions and formal school meetings (school council and parents' groups)
- school assemblies and public performances
- open days, information days, classroom visits and in- and out-of-school displays and performances
- results from standardised tests, external examinations and tertiary entrance scores (Brady & Kennedy, 2012; Cuttance & Stokes, 2000; Griffin & Nix, 1991).

Principles of good reporting

The New Zealand Ministry of Education (2011a), in its position paper on assessment, sets out the following principles of good reporting:

- *Reporting processes promote student ownership of their learning*, with active participation in all aspects of assessment, including reporting of results. The three-way reporting process described below is one way to do this; children's letters home to parents, as described in Box 13.12, are another.
- *Students should feel ownership of the information that is reported.* This ensures that students understand the basis and content of the report, and how it links to their learning experiences. It enables students to explain, discuss and elaborate on reports to their parents, and builds the three-way partnership between school, family and student.
- *Reporting must meet the needs of parents, family and whānau.* Teachers must ensure the clarity of the information for its audience, catering for diverse families' language and literacy abilities, as well as cultural concerns. They must also consider the desire of parents for feedback, information on their children's progress and about how they can help with their children's learning, and participate in partnership with the school.
- *What is reported is the responsibility of the teacher and school.* While students may be involved in development of the report, it is important that teachers and schools ensure the information reported is dependable.
- *The quality of reporting must be monitored to ensure that it meets these principles.* This involves monitoring of the effectiveness of the communication to families – Did they interpret it correctly? It will also involve monitoring a student's engagement with learning as a result of the report – whether they have achieved great or little success. While areas for improvement should be highlighted, every student should also be given the opportunity to celebrate aspects they can be proud of.

three-way reporting
Reporting that involves student, teacher and parent input

The NSW Department of Education and Training (2005, 2007) identified **three-way reporting** (involving teacher, student and parent input) as a useful strategy for reviewing student achievement. New Zealand's TKI found that the majority of schools using this method reported a rise in parent attendance at conferences, and in parent satisfaction with school. Such reporting may be in the form of students taking home examples of their work that have already been assessed and commented on by the teacher and student. Parents can then respond in turn with their own comments on their child's work. Alternatively, teachers, students and parents can meet and review a portfolio of work. Students can lead these conferences, discussing their work and the activities that were involved, or the discussion can be structured around particular learning goals, with parents, student and teacher contributing to discussion of the child's progress towards their goals. While three-way conferences can be valuable for students' self-evaluation of their learning, as well as parents' engagement in their child's schooling, training for students and teachers in three-way conferencing is essential to facilitate the process.

Common reporting standards have been used across Australia, supported by work samples, to establish a common understanding of each standard across schools, and between teachers within each school. These inform parents of their child's progress in terms of the following scale:

- A – Well above the standard expected at this time of year
- B – Above the standard expected at this time of year
- C – At the standard expected at this time of year
- D – Below the standard expected at this time of year
- E – Well below the standard expected at this time of year.

In 2018, a review of schooling in Australia (Gonski et al., 2018) found that 'reporting against year-level achievement standards hides both progress and attainment for some students and does not amount to a diagnostic assessment of real learning needs which – if met – would lead to growth in learning' (p. 30). It recommended that this approach be replaced by one reporting both current level and learning gains of students, to provide more meaningful information and to highlight growth.

Annual school reports are another component in the process of reporting outcomes and achievements to parents, as well as the wider community. Many parents are interested in information such as individual school results from national literacy and numeracy tests (for example, NAPLAN tests given in years 3, 5, 7 and 9 in Australia) when making decisions about the enrolment of a child.

CourseMateExpress

Online Resources
Go further: Visit some standards sites in Australia and New Zealand via the links on this text's website

CourseMateExpress

Online Resources
Design a user-friendly format for school reports with the **Interactive Activity** on this text's website

THINK ABOUT

- In reporting to parents, should information on student progress be based on grades (that is, norm-referenced tests), standards (that is, criterion-referenced tests), lesson content (that is, curriculum-based tests) or a student's previous results (that is, ipsative assessment)?
- What type of data (norm-referenced, criterion-referenced, curriculum-based or ipsative) would you, as a teacher, prefer to use when reporting to parents on student progress? Would your answer differ if you were teaching in lower or upper primary, or lower or upper secondary grade levels?
- Should reporting focus on academic achievement or on student effort?
- Should assessment results be compared across classes at each grade level in a school, across schools in a community, and/or across States or nationally? Who should have access to this information? Why?
- Watch for ongoing discussion and debate about issues in assessment and reporting in the media, and for any ongoing changes in requirements for reporting at local, State and national levels in response to this debate.

BOX 13.12 CASE STUDY

IMPLEMENTING ACCOUNTABLE ASSESSMENT

It was during the second term when Janet, a Year 1 teacher who had joined the school at the beginning of the year, became aware of staffroom discussions about the type of information given to parents in school reports. At Janet's previous school, student results were reported to parents twice a year. These reports gave an indication of each student's progress relative to the levels identified in the seven essential learning areas of the National Curriculum. At that school, the teachers felt they were responsible for their students' achievement and that the reports they prepared twice a year were a form of accountability to the parents. The teachers made an effort to educate parents about the school's teaching and assessment practices, ensuring that the parents understood what the school was doing and why it was doing it. However, at the new school, teachers seemed to consider that students' results should be reported in terms of what the students could do, rather than how they compared with the standards identified in the National Curriculum levels. The teachers did not see themselves as accountable to the parents and did not want to be judged badly by the results presented in school reports. For example, one teacher put everyone as 'excellent', thinking that to do otherwise would reflect poorly on her own teaching. Most of the teachers believed that the parents were uninformed about what happened at school and accepted the teachers' authority.

Janet's old school was in a predominantly middle-class area of the town, and the students' achievement was around average or above the levels set in the National Curriculum. The new school was in an area that had mainly socially disadvantaged families, with a high proportion of recent immigrants for whom English was a second language. The teachers were not surprised when an assessment of reading achievement carried out the previous year in this school and in neighbouring schools had shown that one year after school entry, the students' average achievement in reading was nine months behind the level achieved by a nationally normed comparison group.

Janet looked at the school policy on reporting to parents to see if teachers were required to report the standards that were being used to assess the progress of each student. She found that, unlike in her previous school, there was no reference to the standard against which student performance should be evaluated. Individual class teachers could decide what was appropriate. Talking to the other teachers, she found that some used terms such as 'average' to describe student achievement, but it was unclear whether this referred to the class average, the grade average or the national average. The top students in some classes were often given an 'excellent' or 'achieved high standard' when the whole class was one or two years behind the national average, while some teachers gave particular students an 'excellent' simply because they felt the students were achieving at their full potential.

Janet asked some of the parents what they understood the rankings of 'excellent' and 'average' on school reports to mean. Some said that they understood it represented their child's achievement in comparison with the rest of the class, while others thought that it referred to all the children of their age, or to a national standard for that grade level. When she quizzed other teachers about the parents' views, one said: 'Do they really think that? They know they live here, and the newspapers make it quite clear when they report negatively about the quality of schooling in this area – so when we say *do well* we mean *doing well for here.*' Janet decided that in this school, teachers were free to decide which standard they would use when reporting student results to parents. She also realised that the parents did not understand which standards were being used. As a result, they were less likely to realise, or blame the teachers, for the gaps that existed between the levels achieved by their children and national standards, though they had high regard for education and wanted their children to enter occupations that required success in national examinations and tertiary study.

Listening to the teachers discussing student reporting in the staffroom, Janet began to understand why the teachers acted as they did in preparing reports for parents. It was partly because of a desire to be positive about the progress of students at that particular school. The deputy principal described the dilemma between honesty and accuracy in this way:

Most of the students arrive at school lacking a whole set of skills that middle-class teachers can just take for granted. These students start a year of so behind and you can't tell parents that. It's a self-esteem thing. I've always taken the children from where they're at and accepted them – now let's get on with it. If the child feels secure, then mum is on his side and learning occurs. We foster the child feeling safe, secure and happy before we start the learning process. We communicate positive messages to the parents and that means not discussing the children's entry levels, so that the confidence of the parents and the self-esteem and security of the child are maintained.

The school's reporting practices were influenced by the social and economic circumstances of the families and their limited educational resources. Teachers were also worried about student safety, recounting how several students had been beaten when they brought home unfavourable reports. School staff were also worried that negative results might affect the image and reputation of the school, leading some parents to enrol their children in other schools in neighbouring suburbs. As the principal described the situation to Janet: 'It's quite unprofessional really – but I would be a fool to report against national standards if neighbouring schools used local ones'.

After thinking about the problems associated with reporting to parents at her new school, Janet decided that she empathised with the teachers and understood their reasons for reporting to parents as they did. However, she felt that some information about national standards should be given to parents so that both teachers and parents had a benchmark for their own assessment standards. Local benchmarks should not be abandoned, for if individual students' results were reported solely against national standards, it was likely that the gap would be seen as the fault of the student or the family. If comparison was made with both a local and a national standard, parents would see that the problem was not just with their child, but with the group as a whole. Then parents could join with other parents and the teachers to decide what was a realistic aspiration and what could be done, individually and collectively, to reduce the gap. She began to float the idea that accountability become a central focus of the school's reporting to parents, and that the parents helped to support their children in achieving their desired goals. Such a proposal would involve considerable effort from teachers at the school, but all agreed that the effort would be worthwhile in terms of the benefits to students and the outcomes of their schooling.

Source: Adapted from Robinson and Timperley (2000).
Reproduced by permission of Taylor & Francis Group LLC. (http://www.tandfonline.com)

ACTIVITIES

1   Read the Gonski (2018) review's judgement on this issue through the link at the end of this chapter (pp. 30–31). Do their conclusions help Janet with her dilemma?

2   Think about your own schooling. What type of information was provided in the reports your parents received? Were they aligned with national or State-based standards? What was the reaction of your parents to the information provided in the reports?

3   If you were a parent of a child who was among 'the 25 per cent of students [who] will always lie in the bottom quartile' (Allum, 2005, p. 15), what type of information would you want to see in your child's school report?

4   Under what conditions might increased accountability in reporting student achievement lead to improvements in academic achievement? What are the disadvantages of this approach to school reporting?

REPORTING FOR TEACHERS

For teachers, one of the main purposes of student assessment is to obtain feedback on their teaching. It is also used to guide the teacher's decisions regarding the next piece of work. On the basis of assessment results, study topics are changed, materials that have been covered but not yet fully understood are revised, or a current topic that has been adequately covered is abandoned in order to begin the next.

Criterion-referenced or curriculum-based assessments carried out as part of the instructional process give teachers vital information about what students have learned and how effective the teaching has been. Such data can be used to diagnose students' strengths and weaknesses, and to plan future teaching programs. It is also helpful to the teacher who will be teaching the students in the following year. This type of assessment begins with the careful analysis of a specific area of teaching in order to identify the skills and subskills that must be mastered by all students who study it. The level of students' entry skills can be measured at the beginning of a new program to decide where to place each student within the curriculum. Assessment data are used to identify appropriate teaching objectives, and ongoing assessment provides a basis for monitoring individual students' progress through a learning sequence. At the end of the learning sequence, student achievement is assessed and the results are used to evaluate and refine teaching methods.

Reporting of results to teachers generally happens in the form of results from standardised or external tests. Teachers can then use that information to evaluate their teaching, and to plan for the future for a particular group of students. But do they? Hattie (2005) argued that 'schools are awash with data', and that teachers are selective in the data they use to evaluate their teaching, concluding that this process should start in the classroom. AsTTle was developed in New Zealand to develop a national assessment program based in classrooms, rather than on external tests. You can read more about it at the Assessment Online website (assessment.tki.org.nz).

REPORTING FOR SCHOOL PSYCHOLOGISTS, COUNSELLORS AND GUIDANCE OFFICERS

Most schools have access to the services of an educational psychologist or school counsellor who is trained to administer and interpret standardised tests of intelligence, aptitude (talent) and personality (see Chapter 9). These tests are often administered to students individually, and the results are used to make decisions about future school placements or to develop classroom management plans. Information derived from such tests is used to advise and support teachers, parents and students in making informed decisions about instructional programs, behaviour management, student placement and other issues related to learning and teaching.

REPORTING TO SCHOOLS AND SCHOOL ADMINISTRATORS

For teachers and parents, the primary focus of assessment is on the individual student. However, at the school level, information from assessment gives important feedback about the curriculum as a whole and about overall progress in learning and teaching within and across grades, and within and across subject areas. At another level, some analyses of school-wide assessment data, particularly at the secondary school level, are used to examine the relative performance of different subject departments to see if one department is more effective than others. Other information of interest to schools is obtained from more formal testing programs such as the NAPLAN tests of reading, writing, spelling, number, space, measurement, and chance and data conducted in years 3, 7 and 9 in Australian schools (MCEETYA, 2008), and the assessment of essential learning areas and skills in a representative sample of 8-year-olds and 12-year-olds each year in New Zealand (NMSSA, 2018). In Australia, these programs provide comparative information about one school's performance in relation to other schools in the district or state. There is a competitive element in such programs, but they provide valuable information for schools about the relative standard of their students. There has been a move to communicate this comparison of school performance to parents as well (Gillard, 2008). It has been widely opposed by educators, who are concerned that publication of school comparison data in the media can be misinterpreted. It can also have negative impacts on school communities and on curriculum when 'teaching to the test' takes up a higher proportion of school time as schools seek to uphold their reputations. School-wide assessment data are also used in the preparation of a school's annual report to parents and the community.

Information from often large-scale assessment programs is used by schools and school systems for such varied purposes as screening, selection, classification, placement, eligibility and certification. Screening, for instance, may involve a quick, simple check of large numbers of students to identify specific characteristics or conditions. This information might then be used to find students who have the potential to become Olympic-standard rowers or champion chess players, those with sensory impairments, or those who are exceptionally gifted in areas such as mathematics, languages, art, music or dance.

REPORTING TO EMPLOYERS

There are two main issues in student assessment that are of interest to prospective employers: What can students do, and are they employable? Employers want to know about fundamental skills such as whether or not recent graduates know the basic number facts, or how well they can spell. Employers also want to know about students' personal characteristics.

REPORTING TO GOVERNMENT

What does the government want out of student assessment? Data from State-based or national assessments provide information about school standards across each of the States and/or across the nation. An example in Australia is the annual national collection of benchmark data in reading and writing literacy and numeracy by ACARA for the federal government. Such information may be used to decide funding priorities, or to identify areas where outstanding progress has been achieved or where special initiatives need to be taken. Alternatively, towards the end of a period in office, a government may want to be able to claim that standards have risen, so voters will continue to support it. International comparisons of schooling are also of interest to governments as measures of the nation's progress against international norms. PISA assesses a sample of 15-year-olds in OECD countries every three years. Many of the changes in testing seen over the last decades of the 20th century were related to the needs and interests of all levels of government.

REPORTING TO THE COMMUNITY

How do you find out what the community wants from student assessment or from other information related to education? Look at the daily newspapers and weekly magazines and monitor the amount and type of information given to the community at large about the operation of their schools. Most Australian city and national daily newspapers have a weekly section that focuses on current educational issues, and community views on current controversies in education can be found, for example, on the Letters to the Editor pages (see Allum, 2005). Education is likely to figure most often during key times in the school year, such as at the start of a school year or during the administration of NAPLAN tests.

CourseMateExpress
Online Resources
Go further: View the latest PISA NAP and NMSSA reports via the links on this text's website.

Other times when education-related issues receive heightened public attention are during the period preceding an election and at times of major change, such as the introduction of a new format for annual school reports by the federal government, or introduction of new curricula, as commenced in Australia from 2014 (ACARA, 2014).

Box 13.13 discusses some implications stakeholders' assessment-information needs may have for educators.

BOX 13.13 IMPLICATIONS FOR EDUCATORS

STAKEHOLDERS' ASSESSMENT NEEDS

In thinking about assessment and the specific needs of different stakeholders, educators need to remember the following:

- For students, assessment feedback is motivating, helps identify strengths and weaknesses, highlights specific errors and indicates areas for improvement.
- Parents want information about student performance that they can understand and that compares individual results with those achieved by other students. They may need help to understand other types of assessment information.
- Teachers want information about instruction outcomes so they can evaluate their own teaching, monitor student learning, identify appropriate teaching objectives and plan further instruction.
- School psychologists, counsellors and guidance officers use assessment information to support teachers, design behaviour-management strategies and make decisions about program placement.
- Schools and school administrators use assessment information to monitor teaching and learning progress within and across grades and curriculum areas. Data from large-scale assessment programs is used for purposes such as screening, selection and certification.
- Employers are interested in assessments that provide information on school leavers' basic competencies and personal characteristics.
- Government bodies are interested in the outcomes of large-scale assessment when this gives comparative information about school standards. Such information helps identify areas where there has been progress and areas where special initiatives are needed.
- The community is interested in assessment results when major changes are introduced or when education becomes a focus of political interest.

RECORDING AND REPORTING ASSESSMENT RESULTS

Having decided what should be assessed and how this information will be collected, the next task is to decide how the results of assessment should be recorded and then reported to students, their parents and other interested stakeholders. Changes in the way that assessment information is collected, together with developments in technology, have resulted in an array of strategies being available for recording assessment data, together with a range of formats for reporting results.

Issues to consider in the collection of information concerning students include privacy and consent. Teachers must be alert to students' and parents' right to privacy in relation to personal information. In addition, parents and students (aged 16 years or older) must be informed in writing of any procedure that involves collecting or disseminating personal information or other information about a student that is not directly relevant or essential to the student's school program. The written consent of parents or older

informed consent
Agreement given by a parent or student for the collection and/or dissemination of information not directly relevant to the student's school program

students indicating that they understand the purpose of the procedure and how it will be carried out (**informed consent**) must be obtained. (See also the discussion of ethical issues in Chapter 1).

A further issue associated with school reporting to parents concerns accountability, either in relation to the teachers' responsibility for the achievement of their students, or the responsibility of both students and parents to contribute to progress in learning at school. Reporting to parents provides an opportunity for teachers to strengthen the partnership between home and school, and to develop a shared understanding of the responsibility and contribution of teachers, students and parents to educational outcomes. An example of the dilemma faced by teachers in relation to accountability and the preparation of school report cards occurs when there is conflict between the need to maintain student confidence and parental trust, while at the same time reporting student progress in terms of State or national standards (see the case study illustrating this dilemma in Box 13.12).

CONCLUDING COMMENTS

Effective assessment and reporting is the key to promoting quality learning and teaching, and involves choices between a wide range of approaches, strategies and tools. Your choice of assessment strategies should be guided by your knowledge and understanding of your students' needs. This chapter should be viewed in light of the development and learning theories presented earlier in this text. For instance, how might an outcome-based approach to instruction or the use of collaborative learning strategies lead to the use of different forms of assessment? Consider also how you might use assessment to improve students' low self-esteem (Chapter 4) or enhance their motivation (Chapter 8). Or think about how you might vary your assessment strategies depending on such factors as the way in which learning experiences are organised (Chapters 6 and 7), gender distribution in the class, students' language backgrounds (Chapter 11) or students' abilities (Chapters 8 and 9). Also reflect on how your style of assessment and reporting might be influenced by your philosophy of teaching and your view of how students learn best (Module II).

STUDY TOOLS

ONLINE STUDY RESOURCES

Visit http://login.cengagebrain.com and use the access code that comes with this book for 12 months' access to the student resources for this text.

The CourseMate Express website contains a range of resources and study tools for this chapter, including:

■ a **self-check quiz**

■ **crosswords**, **flashcards** and a **glossary** to help you revise the key terms from this chapter

■ the **Go further** materials and **interactive activity** mentioned in the chapter.

CourseMateExpress

CHAPTER REVIEW

■ Assessment is the gathering of information about students' learning or achievement. Evaluation is the judgements made about that information.

■ The primary purposes of assessment are:
> improvement of learning: *assessment for learning* or *formative assessment* (providing feedback for students on their progress in learning, and teachers on the effectiveness of their instruction) – this can include assessment as learning (students reflecting on their learning processes as they assess their own and others' work)
> accountability and reporting: *assessment of learning* or *summative assessment* (providing information on learning outcomes).

■ The procedures used in assessment can take many forms depending on the purpose of assessment, including traditional tests and examinations (summative information), direct observation and anecdotal records, portfolios containing examples of student work, the direct assessment of performance and student self-assessment (formative information). Teachers should use a range of tools to gather assessment data.

■ Reporting of assessment results takes different forms depending on the particular audience.

■ Information derived from the assessment process is of immediate interest to teachers and students who want feedback on their teaching and learning, and to parents who want to know how their children are progressing at school.

■ School psychologists use assessment to make decisions about school placements and to assist teachers in developing classroom management plans.

■ School principals and other administrators use this type of information for screening, selection, classification, placement, eligibility and certification.

PUTTING IT TOGETHER

Making links between 'assessment and reporting' and material in other chapters

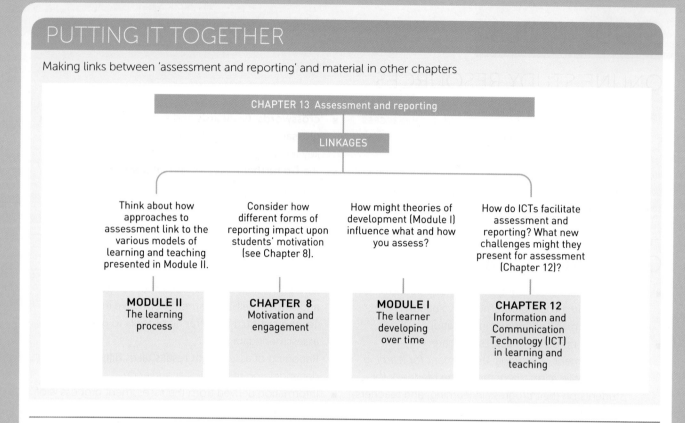

QUESTIONS AND ACTIVITIES FOR SELF-ASSESSMENT AND DISCUSSION

1   List the features of quality assessment. How will you ensure that assessment in your classrooms adheres to these principles?

2   Take an assessment tool such as tests, observations or interviews. List the advantages and disadvantages of your tool, and ways to maximise its effectiveness.

3   Explain why a range of assessment methods is necessary for effective assessment.

4   How would you ensure that assessment is valid and reliable? Think about this in relation to the design, conduct and evaluation of assessments.

5   Identify the key skills and knowledge that you consider to be central to teachers' assessment literacy (skills and knowledge to collect, analyse, interpret and respond to assessment information) that supports student learning. What beliefs accompany these skills and knowledge?

6   What is students' role in assessment? How should teachers involve their students in the assessment process?

7   Collect a resource bank of ideas for reporting assessment information to parents. How might this vary to meet the needs of different cultural groups?

8   Identify the main groups who are interested in the outcomes of assessment in schools. Distinguish between the types of information they are interested in.

FURTHER RESEARCH

SEARCH ME! AND EDUCATION DATABASES

Explore Search Me! education for articles relevant to this chapter. Fast and convenient, Search Me! education is updated daily and provides you with 24-hour access to full-text articles from hundreds of scholarly and popular journals, ebooks and newspapers, including *The Australian* and *The New York Times*. Log in to Search Me! through http://login.cengagebrain.com and use the search terms listed here as a starting point:

- assessment
- assessment for learning
- assessment of learning
- benchmarks
- criterion-references assessment
- diagnostic assessment
- formative assessment
- norm-referenced assessment
- outcomes
- portfolios
- progression grids
- reliability
- school achievement
- school reporting
- standardised test
- summative assessment
- test bias
- validity.

Combining these terms with words such as 'schools', 'students', 'learners' and 'classrooms' (as in 'assessment and schools') will limit your search to material related to schools and young students.

You can also use these terms to explore databases such as ERIC, PsycINFO and the Australian Education Index.

RECOMMENDED WEBSITES

View the National literacy and numeracy learning progressions (K-10) for Australia at: https://www.australiancurriculum.edu.au/resources/national-literacy-and-numeracy-learning-progressions/and for New Zealand at: https://lpf.education.govt.nz Investigate the approach to assessment and reporting at your local department of education.

Australian Council for Educational Research (ACER): www.acer.edu.au

Australian Curriculum Assessment and Reporting Authority (ACARA): www.acara.edu.au/assessment/assessment.html

Queensland Department of Education and Training: http://education.qld.gov.au

New Zealand Council for Educational Research (NZCER): www.nzcer.org.nz

New Zealand Ministry of Education: http://assessment.tki.org.nz. This website has helpful resources, examples and guidance for teachers around multiple aspects of assessment.

NSW Board of Studies: http://arc.boardofstudies.nsw.edu.au/. The Assessment Resource Centre of the NSW Board of Studies, Teaching and Educational Standards supports professional practice in assessment and reporting with exemplars (student work samples, with teacher annotations) linked to the standards from K–12.

NSW Department of Education and Training: www.curriculumsupport.education.nsw.gov.au/timetoteach/assess/index.htm

Assessment for Learning: www.assessmentforlearning.edu.au. This professional development module includes video clips of teachers and students putting strategies into action.

South Australian Department for Education and Child Development: www.decd.sa.gov.au

Tasmanian Department of Education: www.education.tas.gov.au

Victorian Curriculum and Assessment Authority: www.vcaa.vic.edu.au

Western Australian Department of Education and Training: www.eddept.wa.edu.au

RECOMMENDED READING

Brady, L. & Kennedy, K. (2012). *Celebrating student achievement: Assessment and reporting.* Frenchs Forest, NSW: Pearson Education.

Gardner, J. (Ed.). (2012). *Assessment for learning* (2nd ed.). London: Sage Publications.

Glasson, T. (2009). *Improving student achievement: A practical guide to assessment for learning.* Carlton, Vic.: Curriculum Corporation.

Gonski, D., Arcus, T., Boston, K., Gould, V., Johnson, W., O'Brien, L., Perry, L. & Roberts, M. (2018). *Through Growth to Achievement: The Report of The Review to Achieve Educational Excellence in Australian Schools.* Canberra: Commonwealth of Australia. Accessible at https://www.education.gov.au/through-growth-achievement-report-review-achieve-educational-excellence-australian-schools-faqs

Masters, G. N. (2013). *Reforming educational assessment: Imperatives, principles and challenges.* Melbourne: ACER. Retrieved from http://research.acer.edu.au/aer/

New Zealand Ministry of Education (2011). *Ministry of Education position paper: Assessment.* Retrieved from www.minedu.govt.nz/theMinistry/PublicationsAndResources/AssessmentPositionPaper.aspx

REFERENCES

Allum, J. (2005). The dangers of regular school reporting. *Sydney Morning Herald*, 2 November, 15.

Alonzo, A. C. (2018). Exploring the learning progression–formative assessment hypothesis, *Applied Measurement in Education*, *31*(2), 101–103.

Anastasi, A. (1976). *Psychological testing* (4th ed.). New York: Macmillan.

Assessment Reform Group (2006). *The role of teachers in the assessment of learning.* London, University Institute of Education.

Australian Academy of Science. (2008). *Primary connections.* Canberra: Australian Academy of Science.

Australian Curriculum, Assessment and Reporting Authority, (2014). *National report on schooling in Australia 2012.* Sydney: ACARA.

Belanger, J., Allingham, P. & Bechervaise, N. (2004). When will we ever learn? The case for formative assessment supporting writing development. *English in Australia*, *141*, 41–8.

Bennett, R. E. (2011). Formative assessment: A critical review. *Assessment in Education: Principles Policy & Practice*, *18*(1), 5–25.

Biggs, J. B. & Collis, K. F. (1982). *Evaluating the quality of learning: The SOLO taxonomy.* New York: Academic Press.

Black, P. & Wiliam, D. (1998). *Inside the black box: Raising standards through classroom assessment.* London: School of Education, King's College.

Black, P. & Wiliam, D. (1999) *Assessment for learning: Beyond the black box.* University of Cambridge School of Education.

Black, P. & Wiliam, D. (2012a). Assessment for learning in the classroom. In J. Gardner (Ed.), *Assessment for learning in the classroom* (pp. 11–32). London: Sage.

Black, P. & Wiliam, D. (2012b). Developing a theory of formative assessment. In J. Gardner (Ed.), *Assessment for learning in the classroom* (pp. 206–29). London: Sage.

Bloom, B. S. (Ed.). (1956). *Taxonomy of educational objectives: Handbook 1. Cognitive domain.* London: Longmans.

Brady, L. & Kennedy, K. (2012). *Celebrating student achievement: Assessment and reporting.* Frenchs Forest, NSW: Pearson Education.

Brown, G. T. L., Andrade, H. L. & Chen, F. (2015). Accuracy in student self-assessment: directions and cautions for research, *Assessment in Education: Principles, Policy & Practice*, *22*(4), 444–457.

Center, Y. (2005). *Beginning reading: A balanced approach to literacy instruction during the first three years at school.* Sydney: Allen & Unwin.

Cotton, K. (2001). *Classroom Questioning.* Retrieved January 24, 2018, from School improvement research series: https://www.aea267.k12.ia.us/system/assets/uploads/files/1467/classroom questioningresearch.pdf

Cuttance, P. & Stokes, S. A. (2000). *Reporting on student and school achievement.* Canberra: DETYA.

Darling-Hammond, L. & Adamson, F. (2010). Beyond basic skills: *The role of performance assessment in achieving 21st century standards of learning* (SCOPE Student Performance Assessment Series). Stanford, CA: Stanford University, Stanford Center for Opportunity Policy in Education. Retrieved from https://edpolicy.stanford.edu/publications/pubs/111

Earl, L. M. (2003). *Assessment as learning: Using classroom assessment to maximize student learning* (1st ed.). Thousand Oaks, CA: Corwin Press.

Earl, L. M. (2013). *Assessment as learning: Using classroom assessment to maximize student learning* (2nd ed.). Thousand Oaks, CA: Corwin Press.

Feuerstein, R., Rand, Y. & Hoffman, M. (1979). *The dynamic assessment of retarded performers: The learning potential assessment device –Theory, instruments and techniques.* Baltimore, MD: University Park Press.

Forster, M. & Masters, G. (1996). *Performances: Assessment resource kit.* Camberwell, Vic.: ACER.

Gan, M. S. & Hattie, J. (2014). Prompting secondary students' use of criteria, feedback specificity and feedback levels during an investigative task. *Instructional Science*, *42*(6), 861–878.

Gardner, J. (Ed) (2012). *Assessment for learning* (2nd ed.). London: Sage Publications.

Gillard, J. (2008). Speech delivered to ACER Research conference, Brisbane, 11 August. Retrieved from www.acer.edu.au/media/special-address-by-julia-gillard

Glasson, T. (2009). *Improving student achievement.* Carlton, Vic.: Curriculum Corporation.

Gonski, D., Arcus, T., Boston, K., Gould, V., Johnson, W., O'Brien, L., Perry, L. & Roberts, M. (2018). *Through Growth to Achievement: The Report of The Review to Achieve Educational Excellence in Australian Schools.* Canberra: Commonwealth of Australia.

Graham, J., Meyer, L. H., McKenzie, L., McClure, J. & Weir, K. F. (2010). Māori and Pacific secondary student and parent perspectives on achievement, motivation and NCEA. *Assessment Matters*, *2*, 132–57.

Griffin, P. & Nix, P. (1991). *Educational assessment and reporting: A new approach.* Sydney: Harcourt Brace Jovanovich.

Hattie, J. (2005). *What is the nature of evidence that makes a difference to learning?* Paper delivered at ACER conference, August. Retrieved from www.acer.edu.au/documents/RC2005_Hattie.pdf

Hattie, J. (2009). *Visible learning: A synthesis of over 800 meta-analyses relating to achievement.* London: Routledge.

Hattie, J. & Timperley. H. (2007). The power of feedback. *Review of Educational Research*, *77*, 81–112.

Haywood, H. & Lidz, C. (2007). *Dynamic assessment in practice: Clinical and educational applications.* New York: Cambridge University Press.

Heitink, M. C., Van der Kleij, F. M., Veldkamp, B. P., Schildkamp, K. & Kippers, W. B. (2016). A systematic review of prerequisites for implementing assessment for learning in classroom practice. *Educational Research Review 17*, 50–62.

Klenowski, V. & Wyatt-Smith, C. (2011). The impact of high stakes testing: The Australian story. *Assessment in Education: Principles, Policy and Practice*, 1–15.

Klenowski, V. & Wyatt-Smith, C. M. (2014). *Assessment for education: Standards, judgement and moderation.* Los Angeles: Sage.

Lane, S. (2010). *Performance assessment: The state of the art* (SCOPE Student Performance Assessment Series). Stanford, CA: Stanford University, Stanford Center for Opportunity Policy in Education. Retrieved from https://edpolicy.stanford.edu/publications/pubs/116

Lauchlan, F. & Carrigan, D. (2013). *Improving learning through dynamic assessment*. London: Jessica Kingsley Publishers.

Linn, R. L. & Gronlund, N. E. (1995). *Measurement and assessment in teaching* (7th ed.). Englewood Cliffs, NJ: Prentice Hall.

Mahuika, R., Berryman, M. & Bishop, R. (2011). Issues of culture and assessment in New Zealand education pertaining to Māori students. *Assessment Matters, 3,* 183–98.

Marzano, R. J. & Simms, J. A. (2014). *Questioning sequences in the classroom*. Bloomington, IN: Marzano Research Laboratory.

Masters, G. N. (2011). *Assessment and student learning. Australian education review, 57.* Retrieved from http://research.acer.edu.au/aer/12

Masters, G. N. (2013). *Reforming educational assessment: Imperatives, principles and challenges*. Melbourne: ACER.

McDonald, B. (2009). Exploring academic achievement in males trained in self-assessment skills. *Education, 37,* 145–157.

McTighe, J. (2010). *Backward design*. Bloomington, IN: Solution Tree.

Messick, S. (1995). Standards of validity and the validity of standards in performance assessment. *Educational Measurement: Issues and Practice, 14*(4), 5–8.

Ministerial Council on Education, Employment, Training and Youth Affairs. (2008). *Melbourne declaration on educational goals for young Australians*. Canberra: Curriculum Corporation.

New Zealand Ministry of Education. (2011a). *Ministry of Education position paper: Assessment*. Retrieved from www.minedu.govt.nz/theMinistry/PublicationsAndResources/AssessmentPositionPaper.aspx

NMSSA (National Monitoring Study of Student Achievement) (2018). NMSSA brochure. Retrieved from http://nmssa.otago.ac.nz

NSW Department of Education and Training. (2005). *Principles for assessment and reporting in NSW Government schools*. Sydney: NSW Department of Education and Training.

NSW Department of Education and Training. (2007). *Three way assessment strategies and conferences*. Retrieved from www.curriculumsupport.education.nsw.gov.au/timetoteach/report/sbsr/docs2012/3way.doc

Osgood, C. E., Suci, G. J. & Tannenbaum, P. H. (1957). *The measurement of meaning*. Urbana, IL: University of Chicago Press.

Piper, K. (1997). *Riders in the chariot: Curriculum reform and the national interest 1965–1995*. Melbourne: ACER.

Polesel, J., Dulfer, N. & Turnbull, M. (2012). *The experience of education: The impacts of high stakes testing on school students and their families: Literature review*. Sydney: The Whitlam Institute at the University of Western Sydney. Retrieved from www.whitlam.org/the_program/high_stakes_testing

Robinson, V. & Timperley, H. (2000). The link between accountability and improvement: The case of reporting to parents. *Peabody Journal of Education, 75*(4), 66–89.

Rohrer, D. & Pashler, H. (2010). Recent research on human learning challenges conventional instructional strategies. *Educational Researcher, 39,* 406–12.

Rowe, M. B. (1986). Wait time: Slowing down may be a way of speeding up! *Journal of Teacher Education, 37,* 43–50.

Sebba, J., Crick, R. D., Yu, G., Lawson, H., Harlen, W. & Durant, K. (2008). Systematic review of research evidence of the impact on students in secondary schools of self and peer assessment: Technical report. In *Research evidence in education library*. London: EPPI-Centre, Social Science Research Unit, Institute of Education, University of London.

Siegler, R. S. (1976). Three aspects of cognitive development. *Cognitive Psychology, 8,* 481–520.

Sternberg, R. J. (2013). Intelligence, competence and expertise. In A. J. Elliot & C. S. Dweck (Eds), *Handbook of competence and motivation*. New York: The Guilford Press.

Valencia, S. W. & Place, N. (1994). Portfolios: A process for enhancing teaching and learning. *The Reading Teacher, 47*(8), 666–9.

Ward, A. W. & Murray-Ward, M. (1999). *Assessment in the classroom*. Belmont, CA: Wadsworth.

Wyatt-Smith, C. M. & Bridges, S. (2007). Evaluation study report. In *DEEWR & DETA Meeting in the middle: Assessment, pedagogy, learning and educational disadvantage. Literacy and numeracy in the middle years of schooling initiative –Strand A, Project report*. Canberra: Commonwealth of Australia.

Wyn, J., Turnbull, M. & Grimshaw, L. (2014). *The Experience of Education: The Impacts of High Stakes Testing on School Students and Their Families*. University of Western Sydney: The Whitlam Institute.

CREATING A POSITIVE CLASSROOM

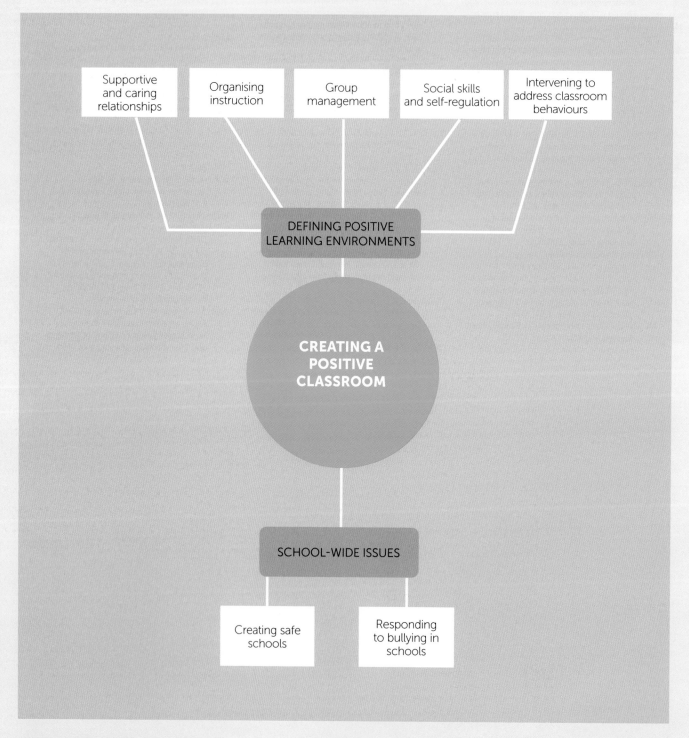

FIGURE 14.1 Chapter 14 concept map

KEY QUESTIONS

After reading this chapter, you should be able to answer the following questions:

- What is a positive learning environment (PLE)?
- What is classroom management?
- What are the different philosophies of classroom management?
- Can you describe your own philosophical approach to creating a positive classroom environment?
- Can you identify the five tasks of a comprehensive approach to creating PLEs and managing classrooms? What is the teacher's role in promoting a safe school?

ONLINE STUDY RESOURCES

Bring your learning to life with **interactive learning**, **study** and **exam preparation tools** that support the printed textbook. CourseMate Express includes **quizzes**, **interactive activities**, **videos**, a tool to help you '**develop your philosophy**' and more.

INTRODUCTION

When you think about a positive classroom environment (PLE) what is it that comes to mind? How about the term 'classroom management'; what is it that comes to mind now? Often we think of managing student behaviour, but how often do we think about creating the most positive learning environment we can? Such PLEs are integral to both effective teaching and your ability to manage that positive learning environment productively (De Nobile, Lyons & Arthur-Kelly, 2017). In this chapter, we consider the teacher's role in creating a positive learning environment and also managing classrooms for ensuring effective work with students. First, we examine these concepts of 'positive learning environments' and 'classroom management' from the perspective of the work of teachers. This includes acknowledgement of the broad and varied approaches applied in schools and classrooms today. Next we consider an integrated and comprehensive approach to the creation of a positive classroom environment and management within that environment, including the relationships developed with students, the pedagogical practices and skills employed, and the strategies used to ensure that classrooms provide a context to support and facilitate learning.

Teaching is also concerned with the welfare of students, usually referred to as a 'duty of care' involving the protection of students from harm. Issues arising from this responsibility, and from the ways in which teachers create 'safe' schools, are important for teachers to consider as we think about classroom environments.

DEFINING POSITIVE LEARNING ENVIRONMENTS

A **positive classroom environment or PLE** is simply explained as a 'place where students are engaged and learning' (De Nobile, Lyons & Arthur-Kelly, 2017, p. 4). In these classrooms the teacher strives to facilitate learning that is engaging and productive, where the teacher acknowledges more positive behaviours in students than corrects or admonishes students. This occurs because the teacher has a good

positive classroom environment (PLE) Defined as a place where students are engaged and learning

relationship with students and knows each student well enough to address their learning needs (see also Chapter 10). As stated by De Nobile et al. (2017), this is not to say that the PLE will never experience inappropriate behaviours, but positive classrooms are generally also preventative spaces.

Defining classroom management

classroom management
The actions of teachers to create a planned and organised classroom environment that supports student learning and socioemotional needs

Did your answer to the question about how you would define 'classroom management' simply refer to controlling students' behaviour? If you compare your answers with those of your peers or other teachers, you may find a wide variety of answers to this question. At a minimum, a definition of **classroom management** must include the planning, management and organisation of learning, and the creation of an environment that facilitates learning and brings out the best in learners; it must be broad enough to consider the positive development of behaviours of the whole individual, including their cognitive and socioemotional needs.

Definitions of classroom management vary widely and reflect many different social, cultural and historical influences. Teachers' individual approaches to classroom management are also influenced by their own beliefs and philosophies about how children develop (Egeberg, McConney & Price, 2016). These beliefs can provide a theoretical lens through which the teachers view their work. Unfortunately, some research has also shown that the beliefs that student teachers bring into teaching are highly resistant to change, reflecting long-held beliefs and attitudes towards teaching and learning (McPherson, 2007). As such, it is important for teachers to recognise their beliefs about classroom management and to start exploring other ways of thinking about and defining this important area of teacher practice.

Philosophies of classroom management

interventionist philosophy
A belief that children's learning and behaviour is an outcome of external factors

interactionalist philosophy
A belief that children's learning and behaviour results from an interaction between internal and external factors

non-interventionist philosophy
A belief that allows for children's learning and behaviour to occur naturally

Wolfgang (2001) identified three different philosophical orientations towards classroom management: the rules and consequences philosophy, the confronting–contracting philosophy, and the relationship–listening philosophy. These philosophies reflect very different views about children and provide a useful framework for thinking about questions of the teacher's role in the PLE and also other beliefs teachers might hold about authority and power. How do we expect children to behave in schools? Why do we believe children should behave in certain ways? Why do we believe the teacher must exert control over student behaviour?

■ *Rules and consequences*. Known as the **interventionist philosophy**. Teachers subscribing to this philosophy believe that learning only occurs as a result of external factors such as rewards and punishments; teachers decide on the desired behaviour and reward or punish accordingly.

■ *Confronting–contracting*. Known as the **interactionalist philosophy**. Teachers who apply this philosophy believe that disruptive behaviour results from conflict between the child's ability to control their needs and the external demands of the classroom. The teacher would 'confront' the child about their behaviour and then allow the child to decide how they would change, making a 'contract' with the child to encourage better behaviour.

■ *Relationship–listening*. Known as the **non-interventionist philosophy**. Teachers who subscribe to this philosophy also view discipline problems as arising from the struggle between the child's individual needs and the needs of the class and curriculum. These teachers view children as inherently good, but in need of supportive adults who listen and provide empathy and understanding. Teachers help children balance their needs in relation to the wider needs of classroom life. (Adapted from Woolfolk Hoy & Weinstein, 2006, p. 194.)

Other researchers have formed similar ways to describe teachers' philosophical beliefs about classroom management, ranging on a continuum from more controlling to least controlling, or more 'autocratic' to 'egalitarian' (Porter, 2007). Interestingly, some research has shown that Australian students report different classroom-management approaches among primary and secondary school teachers, with secondary teachers more likely to use 'traditional' and 'punitive' forms of classroom management associated with 'behaviouristic', 'interventionist' or 'autocratic' philosophies, as we discuss later in this chapter (see Lewis, Romi, Xing & Katz, 2005).

As you can see, approaches to classroom management have certainly been concerned with the management of behaviour, but is it enough to think about behaviour alone? As noted by Jones and Jones (2007), few teachers could ever stick to one program of classroom management because classrooms are far too complex. Instead, it appears that comprehensive approaches to classroom management are essential (Jones & Jones, 2007).

THINK ABOUT

- Which of these classroom-management orientations are you most familiar with from your experience as a student?
- Which approach would you most prefer to adopt as a teacher?
- Can you recognise the influence of behaviourism, humanism, constructivist or social learning theories in each perspective?

Creating a positive classroom

In adopting a broad and comprehensive perspective, we take the approach that the creation of a PLE requires more than simply attending to student behaviours or misbehaviours when they arise. This is also reflected in Evertson and Weinstein (2006, p. 5), who suggest that optimal and positive classroom management comprises five specific tasks. These are:

1 the development of supportive and caring relationships with and among students
2 the organisation and implementation of instruction that optimises students' access to learning
3 the use of group-management techniques that facilitate student engagement with tasks
4 promoting the development of self-regulation and social skills
5 the use of appropriate interventions to respond to classroom behaviours.

Clearly, the creation of a PLE and classroom management is about more than managing behaviour. It is a complex and multifaceted task that includes the teacher's pedagogical work of delivering appropriate instruction, providing an appropriate instructional climate, and ensuring students receive appropriate care and support. In fact, recent research that asked Australian school students about their classrooms confirms the above points. According to students, the most effective classroom managers are those who can manage their classroom and are also teachers who establish warm and caring relationships with their students. They also develop a sense of responsibility in their students and have a high level of student engagement in learning (Egeberg & McConney, 2017). In the remainder of this chapter we explore the five tasks listed above and illustrate linkages with the philosophical orientations we have discussed.

SUPPORTIVE AND CARING RELATIONSHIPS

Teacher John has a Year 4 classroom, with the usual diversity of students whom he fondly describes to his colleagues. There is Skye, 'she is my little star', who is sure to top the class this year, and Caleb, who 'just tries so hard' but still worries him. He describes other students less warmly. 'Amelia? I can't think of anything to say about her on parent–teacher night.' 'And Kyle? I was warned about him. He is a low achiever, he seems to misbehave a lot and constantly annoys me with the silliest questions.'

Do you think that John's beliefs about his students are likely to influence his teaching of those students? What if John's positive hopes for Skye and negative beliefs about Kyle were known to other students? Could these teacher beliefs actually influence the students' achievements or relationships with their peers?

Relationships between teachers and students are at the core of every classroom. If you consider the daily work of John in his Year 4 classroom, he is a teacher of 25 or more students with different support needs and personalities; he, too, has his own beliefs about young people, the type of classroom he would like to create and his own approaches to managing that classroom climate. A wide range of research has closely examined this very sensitive area of classroom life. Questions such as those asked above have been examined in many studies, leading to some clear implications for classroom practice.

Teacher–student relationships

In the earliest studies, many hours of observations of teacher–student interactions in typical classrooms were conducted (Good & Brophy, 1972, 1974; Silberman, 1969). These studies demonstrated that teachers not only developed personal beliefs and attitudes about their students, but that relationships with these students also varied in quality. They described this variation as **differential teacher–student interactions.**

These differential behaviours were described in terms of the attitudes teachers held about different students. They labelled these attitudes:

- attachment
- concern
- indifference
- rejection.

The nature of these differential interactions can be matched to John's descriptions of students in his classroom (see Table 14.1).

differential teacher–student interactions
Qualities of the interaction between teacher and student that lead to different types of relationships

TABLE 14.1 Differential teacher attitudes towards students

TEACHER ATTITUDE	DIFFERENTIAL TEACHER–STUDENT INTERACTIONS
Attachment *Skye*	• These are 'model' students who are compliant and follow teacher requests. • Teachers report the greatest joy in teaching these students. • There is a high level of positive teacher–student interaction. • Teachers exhibit a subtle but not exclusive favouritism.
Concern *Caleb*	• These students are low achievers who ask for and receive high levels of teacher support. • These students experience the highest level of supportive interactions between teacher and student. • Teachers see the high level of support as necessary and appropriate.
Indifference *Amelia*	• These students seem to escape teacher attention. • Interactions with these students are fewer and briefer. • Teachers would be less prepared to talk about these students if their parents dropped into school to discuss their child's progress.
Rejection *Kyle*	• Teachers would be relieved to see these students removed from their classroom. • These students may have conditions that influence their behaviour. • These students are perceived by teachers to be low achievers who also ask for a lot of help. • Teachers do not respond positively, and see requests as inappropriate and overwhelming. • There are high levels of negative interactions, designed to manage and control their behaviours.

As you can see, the interactions between teachers and students can differ according to the teacher's attitude towards the student and some elements of the student's behaviour. Students such as Skye are compliant and obedient, and fit the teacher's idea of the 'model' student. Teachers may expend a lot of teacher time and energy in negative interactions with students like Kyle that are designed to manage their behaviour. Although it may be obvious that teacher–student relationships matter in the classroom, the effects of these relationships can be difficult to tease out and often raise controversy. One area of concern relates to the way teacher interactions with students can influence the climate and morale of the classroom.

Differential interactions in the classroom

An unfortunate consequence of teacher–student interactions is their visibility and impact on other students. Elisha Babad and colleagues have strongly argued that the crux of the problem lies with teachers' differential 'affect' in the classroom, which leads to low morale and student dissatisfaction (Babad, 2005).

Across 25 years of research studies, Babad and colleagues have shown that both young students (Babad, Bernieri & Rosenthal, 1991) and teenage students (Babad, 2005) can accurately detect differential teacher affect and behaviours, after viewing just 10 seconds of video footage of the teacher. These findings are even more remarkable considering that the video footage used in these studies was silent only showing the teacher's non-verbal behaviours such as body language and facial expressions. Moreover, the short video segments did not show the classroom or students to whom the teacher was talking – only the teacher's head and upper body. Students could accurately predict if the teacher was talking to a student whom they favoured or did not favour. They could also tell if the teacher was interacting with a low- or high-achieving student.

High school students who perceive differential teacher behaviour are deeply concerned about this behaviour and teacher fairness in their classrooms (Babad, Avni-Babad & Rosenthal, 2003). Student morale declines when teachers show favouritism towards selected students. This was particularly apparent when students perceived that teachers were giving more emotional and learning support to favoured students and not giving enough support to low achievers (Babad, 2005).

THE TEACHER'S PET PHENOMENON

Babad's study of the 'teacher's pet' phenomenon has generated particular interest among researchers (see Trusz, 2017). This phenomenon arises when a teacher favours a particular student or students and this is visible and obvious to other students in the classroom. In classrooms with teacher pets, students' attitudes towards their teachers are more negative than no-pet classrooms (Trusz, 2017). Early studies (Tal & Badad, 1990) and recent research (Chui et al., 2013) has shown that 'authoritarian' teachers (this could include the more 'interventionist' teacher profile noted earlier) are more likely to form teacher-pet relationships, resulting in awarding higher grades to these students (Tal & Babad, 1990) and increased classroom conflict (Chui et al., 2013). Recently Trusz (2017) replicated these earlier studies with over 2000 students in Poland. Students from junior and senior high school classrooms confirmed that the teacher's pet phenomenon could be found in most classrooms across all levels of high school. As might be predicted, the study also confirmed that students view this teacher behaviour negatively and reported preferential and unfair treatment of 'pets' by their teachers.

THINK ABOUT

1 Do you recall examples of the teacher's pet phenomenon in your school classrooms? Did it cause any problems?
2 Why might authoritarian teachers be more inclined to form 'pet' relationships?

TEACHER BEHAVIOUR AS 'BULLYING'

Other forms of teacher-student relationship have also been investigated. For example, research has described some forms of teacher behaviour as 'bullying' (Twemlow, Fonagy, Sacco & Brethour, 2006). These 'bullying teachers' engaged in acts of humiliating students, hurting students' feelings and being spiteful. Fellow teachers who reported their colleagues as bullies believed that teachers who bully students do so for a range of reasons: they may feel burnt out, may be poorly trained, or even envious of 'smart students'. Some teachers in this study also admitted to bullying their students, being victims of bullying themselves when they were students, and also working with bullying teachers. Unfortunately, schools with bullying teachers also had higher suspension rates of students (Twemlow & Fonagy, 2005).

In a study of more than 56 000 students in grades 7 and 8 in the USA, the researchers classified students into groups who reported not being bullied (87.2 per cent), being bullied by peers (9.3 per cent), bullied by teachers (1.2 per cent) and bullied by both peers and teachers (1.5 per cent) (Datta, Cornell & Huang, 2017). They compared the levels of psychological distress and school adjustment of these students with their peers who reported no bullying. Students bullied by both teachers and peers experienced the highest levels of emotional distress, followed closely by students who reported bullying only by peers. Students who reported being bullied only by their teachers reported the worst school adjustment and lowest grade point averages (GPAs). Specifically, the emotional and cognitive engagement of students who were bullied by teachers was worse than all other students (see Chapter 8 for explanations of student engagement). The researchers considered the important question of why teachers might resort to bullying their students. Some explanations included: teachers are more likely to bully when feeling greater stress, or if they hold a mistaken belief that being 'tough' on students will motivate them to work harder.

In summary, it appears that teacher's beliefs and philosophies might influence their relationships with students and these relationships in turn influence the teacher's ability to create positive classroom environments that engage their students. Can you hypothesise which of the classroom management philosophies might be more associated with teacher bullying behaviours? We know for example that the more authoritarian style was associated with the 'teacher's pet' phenomenon.

Teacher expectations

Another quality of teacher-student relationships that has been closely investigated considers teacher expectations and their influence on student performance and the classroom climate. Teacher expectations are the beliefs teachers hold about students' ability to achieve expected outcomes. There is evidence that perceptions of students are associated with teacher expectations for those students. For example, very early studies demonstrated that 'rejected' students may not, in fact, be low achievers like those in the 'concern' category (Willis & Brophy, 1974). Rather, it appears that teacher perceptions of the student's abilities were tainted by a negative 'halo' around the student; quite simply, the teacher *expected* the student to be a low achiever.

sustaining expectation effect
Expectations that teachers have for their students, which may influence students' achievement or wellbeing in the classroom

Evidence suggests that the expectations teachers hold for students can be reflected in students' achievement. This may be because more favourable treatment meted out to students who are valued more positively may actually enhance their achievement. In contrast, if the teacher expectancy is based on unfavourable bias then this may create a **sustaining expectation effect** (Rubie-Davies, 2008). This means that teacher John, having been forewarned about Kyle, may actually have developed expectations about his learning potential before starting to teach this Year 4 class. He may plan work for Kyle at what he thinks is an appropriate level despite noticing that Kyle is often bored or seems to have finished the work quickly. Thus the sustaining expectation effect means that Kyle's performance or achievement stays the same and the teacher's expectation is sustained because the teacher's planning and pedagogy have thwarted the potential for change (Rubie-Davies, 2008).

There is evidence that teachers do seem to behave differently towards students for whom they hold high or low expectations. They give greater emotional warmth and support to high achievers, as well as more and clearer feedback, and expose them to more challenging materials (see review by Jussim & Harber, 2005). In classrooms where teachers expose students to high expectations, these students tend to achieve more and have higher self-esteem and a greater resistance to problem behaviours (Pianta, 2006). In Table 14.2 we provide a summary of 60 years of research that has documented these differential behaviours (Good, 2014).

TABLE 14.2 Teacher differential behaviours for high and low expectancy students

HIGH EXPECTATIONS	LOW EXPECTATIONS
• Teacher gives more opportunities for responses to the teacher's questions	• Fewer opportunities to respond to the teacher's questions
• Teacher provides more follow-up questions e.g. 'Go on, tell me more.'	• Fewer follow up questions e.g. 'That's not right, anybody else got an idea?'
• Given more time to respond	• Given less time to respond
• More 'stay with' behaviours e.g. teacher prompts and supports with clues	• More 'give up' behaviours e.g. teacher provides the answer or calls on another student.
• More teacher praise	• More teacher criticism and behavioural corrections
• More choice	• Less opportunity to make choices

Source: Adapted from Good, T. (2014). What Do We Know About How Teachers Influence Student Performance on Standardized Tests: And Why Do We Know So Little About Other Student Outcomes? *Teachers College Record, 116*(1).

The potential for such differential behaviours to influence the student's performance, wellbeing and behaviour are demonstrated throughout this text. For example, in Chapter 8 we explored the concepts of student motivation and engagement. There we learned that teacher feedback is a critical motivating factor while opportunities for choice promote a sense of student autonomy and competence. In Chapter 10 we explored the ideas of differentiated instruction and universal design. Students like Kyle may need more time to respond, different ways to make his response and certainly the opportunity to make choices to enrich his learning experiences.

There is disagreement, however, about the effect of differential expectancies on student academic performance or achievement. As summarised by Jussim and Harber (2005), some researchers have claimed that expectancies lead to student achievement because they create a self-fulfilling prophecy in which students come to believe their teacher's expectations and start to behave accordingly. Other researchers claim that expectancies do predict achievement, but only because teacher expectancies are mostly correct (Good & Brophy, 2003). For example, teacher John's concern for Caleb may be well justified and reflect a learning difficulty or other learning support need (see Chapter 10). However, Jussim and Harber (2005) also concluded that self-fulfilling prophecies do indeed exist. The effect of these self-fulfilling prophecies does not, however, affect all students in the same way.

Troublingly, the potential for teacher expectancies to create a self-fulfilling prophecy appears to be stronger for students who are already stigmatised. This includes students from certain racial backgrounds and low socioeconomic class. Although Jussim and Harber (2005) found that teacher expectations for student achievement were more likely to be accurate, students may also feel stigmatised and harshly treated in other ways. For example, studies indicate that students from minority racial backgrounds in the USA are expelled or excluded from schools at much higher rates than other children (see Chapter 10). These children also report that they are disciplined more severely, are given less opportunity to explain themselves, and some had even given up on the hope that they would be treated fairly (Fenning & Rose, 2007; Sheets, 1996, 2002; Sheets & Gay, 1996). In the Australian context, a range of studies have reported that Aboriginal students are similarly over-represented in school suspension data (see Graham, 2012; Zubrick et al., 2005). In New Zealand, similar findings have been reported for Māori students. Rubie-Davies, Hattie and Hamilton (2006) compared teacher expectations for NZ European, Māori, Pacific Islander and Asian students. They found that teacher expectation was high for all students except Māori students. Although Māori students' achievement was actually the same as other groups' at the start of the year, by the end of the school year they had made the least gains in achievement compared with other students (Rubie-Davies, Hattie & Hamilton, 2006). As Jussim and Harber (2005) concluded, much more research is needed to tease out the interactions between teacher expectancies and student outcomes.

CONCLUSIONS ABOUT TEACHER EXPECTANCY

What conclusions should we draw from this research? First, the evidence that teacher expectancy is actually associated with differential treatment of students might cause some alarm. Although it has been difficult to prove the effect on achievement, there is little doubt that the school experience of low-expectancy students who are subject to negative teacher behaviours is probably a miserable one. Indeed, Babad's (1995) research has shown that classroom morale declines when students think differential teacher behaviour is unfair. We also know that bullying, whether at the hands of other students or a teacher, is an extreme form of differential behaviour and has very negative consequences for child development and wellbeing (see Chapter 4). As such, evidence of differential behaviours should cause concern in school communities.

Second, if teacher expectancies are usually accurate predictors of student achievement, shouldn't this mean that teachers could use this information to enhance the school experiences of low-achieving students? For example, if teacher expectancies for indigenous students in Australia or New Zealand are low, shouldn't this mean these teachers react with interventions and support to enhance the achievement of these students? As Good and Brophy (2003) caution, when there are low expectations for a student *and* the teacher does little to assist them, then the student is doubly disadvantaged in the classroom.

Third, the fact that Babad has shown how easily students can see and detect these differential behaviours raises questions about the wider effects on peer relationships and school climate. As we discussed in Chapter 4, a student's social standing with their peers can have an impact on their academic wellbeing and compliance with classroom goals.

Supportive peer relationships

In Chapter 4 we learnt that students who are subject to peer rejection and bullying also suffer a decline in academic performance, and may be too fearful and distracted to focus well in class. As discussed in Chapter 8, student motivation is closely associated with the social goals they set for themselves. However, these goals also have important implications for classroom management. For example, students' prosocial goals for peer relationships are closely linked with prosocial goals for academic work (willingness to work with other students). Social-responsibility goals are also linked to academic-responsibility goals (willingness to follow teacher directions) (Wentzel & Brophy, 2014). As such, positive peer-relationship goals can be associated with positive classroom goals (Wentzel, 2006), and teachers can foster both types of goals to support their classroom management and the development of more positive classroom behaviours. Teachers have an important role to play in determining the social standing of students in their classrooms and how students form relationships with their peers. Research suggests that teacher classroom practices serve as a source of social information for students in the class. Farmer and colleagues went so far as to describe the 'invisible hand' of the teacher's influence on student peer relationships (Farmer, McAuliffe Lines & Hamm, 2011). Students seem to be aware of the way teachers view students. Those perceived to be more troublesome or difficult are more often rejected, and those who are deemed 'smart' more often accepted. Teachers in classrooms with fewer sociometrically accepted students seem to differ in their practices and relationships with students (Ben-Yehuda, Leyser & Last, 2010). Classrooms lower in peer acceptance of students had teachers who made fewer supportive comments to students, were less interested in the students' backgrounds, and had negative views about the inclusion of all students. As discussed in Chapter 4 and later in this chapter, teachers can assist students to develop positive peer relationships, but they must also consider the impact of their own attitudes and behaviours.

A sense of school belonging

There is little question that positive teacher–student relationships and positive peer relationships are associated with a greater sense of school belonging (Juvonen, Espinoza & Knifsend, 2012) and greater compliance with classroom goals (Wentzel & Brophy, 2014). In particular, there is strong evidence that feelings of belonging are associated with academic achievement and students' mental health and wellbeing (Anderman & Leake, 2007). Unfortunately, school belonging and a feeling of 'fitting in' suffers a decline when students make the transition to high school. More than two decades of research has shown that this transition is associated with declines in academic achievement (Chung, Elias & Schneider 1998) and reductions in academic and social self-concept (Bolognini, Plancheral, Bettschari & Halpon, 1996; Wigfield & Eccles, 1994). Eccles et al. (1989; 1993a) have referred to this as a problem of **stage–environment fit**. This term describes the extent to which the school environment matches the student's development stage and the needs of early adolescents.

stage–environment fit
The extent to which the school matches the needs of the developing adolescent

When students enter high school, they find a different set of expectations and a very different classroom climate. Eccles and colleagues cite increased competition between students, an increased level of adult control and reduced quality of the teacher–student relationship as the key sources of student difficulty in the early years of high school (Eccles & Midgley, 1989; Eccles et al., 1993a, 1993b). These years also coincide with a dramatic increase in bullying and peer harassment (Espelage, Holt & Poteat, 2010), which may explain the high rates of suspension and expulsion in the early years of high school. In 2012, 74 per cent of all school suspensions in New South Wales public schools occurred in years 7 to 10. Almost half (48 per cent) of these suspensions were for persistent misbehaviour (not including violence) (NSW Department of Education and Communities, 2013).

One of the clearest conclusions we can reach after reviewing these studies is that teacher–student and student peer relationships are an essential feature to consider in the creation of PLEs; they may become a classroom management concern if not regarded as important by teachers. As shown in Box 14.1, when we listen to the voices of students, they tell us that they value teachers who are warm and supportive, but they also value teachers who are firm and directive. Students also tell us that they appreciate an orderly and well-managed classroom (the importance of good classroom organisation is discussed in the next section).

BOX 14.1 RESEARCH LINKS

WHAT DO GOOD TEACHERS DO?

Students have very clear beliefs about the sort of relationships they want with their teachers. Corbett and Wilson (2002) asked 400 low-income, inner-city high school students about these beliefs. Their responses indicate that 'good teachers' are those who show the following skills and characteristics:

- *They push students to learn.* They do not accept excuses for missed or late work.
- *They maintain an orderly and well-run classroom.* They don't need to shout or yell.
- *They are always available to provide help.* They provide help 'in whatever form the student needs it'.
- *They strive to ensure that students understand materials.* They do not rush through materials, and take time to offer help in a step-by-step fashion.
- *They use a variety of instructional techniques.* This includes group work, lectures, worksheets and hands-on activities.
- *They make an effort to understand student behaviour.* They make an effort to learn about the students' personal and after-school lives.

THINK ABOUT

- Look closely at the students' answers. Are they more concerned with instruction and pedagogy or behaviour management?
- Do any of these student responses surprise you? If so, which answers would you not expect to hear from students?
- Do any of these good teacher skills seem challenging to you? If so, which skills might be hardest to practise and why?

ORGANISING INSTRUCTION FOR ACCESS TO LEARNING

Organising instruction refers to the thoughtful plans and strategies a teacher uses to ensure that lessons run smoothly and learning goals are achieved. Many different perspectives have been adopted to explain how instruction should be organised to manage classroom behaviour. As explained in Chapter 5, behaviourist perspectives focus on corrective strategies, rote learning and careful control of instruction. As we examined in Chapter 6, cognitive views of learning led to the idea that learners are active participants in the learning process, signalling a significant change in the way in which we think about classrooms and the nature of learning. In this chapter, we explore another perspective, one that focuses on the interaction between learners and their classroom environment. Doyle (1986, 2006) adopted an **ecological perspective** from which to consider teaching and learning interactions in the entire classroom environment. From this perspective, classrooms are complex instructional climates with many different features that affect classroom management.

ecological perspective
A view of the classroom as an environment with unique purposes, dimensions, features and processes that have consequences for the behaviour of people in that environment

The study of classrooms as ecological systems has alerted us to the fact that classrooms are busy places. The complex nature of classroom ecologies suggests that special attention must be paid to organising instruction so that students can access learning within this environment. Table 14.3 outlines the six ecological features that Doyle (2006) believes are in place in classrooms before students even arrive. This table also summarises the instructional implications arising from each feature.

Many studies have explored the complexity of the classroom environment and have provided ideas about how the classroom should be organised to provide access to learning for all students. In this sense, access to learning refers to the steps a teacher can take to ensure all students have an opportunity to learn and feel supported in the busy classroom environment.

TABLE 14.3 Features of the classroom environment

FEATURES OF THE CLASSROOM ENVIRONMENT	IMPLICATIONS FOR ORGANISING INSTRUCTION
Multidimensionality – classrooms are crowded places with many different events and tasks, and students of different abilities	• Develop strategies for addressing the wide range of ability levels, preferences and social, emotional, cultural and linguistic backgrounds of students in your classroom.
Simultaneity – many things happen at the same time in a classroom	• Be aware of what is happening at every level; monitor the class and respond to calls for help. • Learn to have 'eyes in the back of your head'. • The challenge of simultaneity may contribute to high levels of stress and burn-out unless you develop coping strategies (see, for example, Brouwers and Tomic, 1999).
Immediacy – the speed at which events in a classroom unfold, with little time to reflect before responding	• Manage time at both micro and macro levels. • Give immediate feedback to students during face-to-face interaction. • Learn to allocate time appropriately for planned learning activities. • Behavioural problems are most likely to arise when students' attention, interest and motivation begin to ebb as a result of poor timing.
Unpredictability – carefully planned classroom activities do not always proceed as planned	• Be flexible – change the lesson plan if the lesson isn't working as expected. • Respond appropriately when the unexpected occurs – if necessary, stop a lesson, re-teach a concept, or check how the students are feeling. • Where possible, turn surprising or unanticipated events into 'teachable moments' or valuable learning opportunities.
Publicness – many people, often students, witness what teachers do, or learn about a teacher's actions from other witnesses	• Be aware that what you do and say is observed and may be discussed outside the classroom. • Be conscious that students can see how their peers are being treated (for example, Babad, 1995). • Use this as an opportunity to model appropriate or desirable behaviour for students.
History – class groups meet regularly and members become familiar over extended periods of time	• Class groups have accumulated and collective memories. • Memories of previous experiences form the building blocks of subsequent activities. • Routines and norms can be established for future classroom activities.

Source: Adapted from Doyle (1986, pp. 394–5; 2006, pp. 98–9).

Good beginnings

One of the most important steps in organising instruction occurs in the very earliest days of the school year, and in the first moments of each class. It is at these times that classrooms establish the routines and norms of classroom life. There is a high level of need for students to feel there is a supportive teacher–student relationship and, as shown in Box 14.1, students actually prefer teachers who set clear directions but who also show warmth and support. Evertson and Emmer (2009) suggest that, like all people, children need a sense of belonging and actually feel safer when they know there is a source of authority in their classroom. They suggest four simple steps you can take to establish such a sense of belonging:

1 *Speak politely and calmly.* Students need to hear teachers using polite language such as 'please' and 'thank you'. A calm voice is reassuring to students and shows that the teacher is in control of their emotions. Teachers act as models for the type of behaviour they expect from their students.

2 *Share information.* Spend time learning each other's names and outside interests. Introduce yourself as a teacher and let students know a few of your outside interests and activities. Take time to get to know your students as individuals.

3 *Use positive statements as often as possible.* Because negative behaviours attract more attention, teachers often make more negative than positive comments. Negative statements may not tell students the correct behaviour and may create a negative atmosphere, affecting other students in the classroom too.

4 *Create a feeling of community.* Teach students how to work cooperatively and create opportunities to work together. Conduct class meetings in which routines and procedures can be established, and social skills such as discussion can be practised (Evertson & Emmer, 2009, p. 63).

Establishing routines and procedures

Effective teachers spend a great deal of time on the careful organisation of instructional tasks by establishing routines and procedures (Evertson, Emmer & Worsham, 2000). In this way, the 'rules' of classroom learning are explained to all students. The most effective teachers do this early in the school year, a period when they spend more time on organisational tasks than they do on instructional tasks (Cameron, McDonald-Conner & Morrison, 2005). Research shows that classrooms where teachers spent more time explaining and orienting students towards tasks actually showed increased literacy outcomes and task engagement (Bohn, Roehrig & Pressley, 2004), and higher levels of cognitive gains in understanding (Helmke, Schneider & Weinert, 1986). In general, the most effective teachers allow plenty of time for organising instruction early in the school year, resulting in less time wasted later in the year (Cameron, McDonald-Conner & Morrison, 2005).

Routines and procedures are particularly important for creating inclusive classrooms in which *all* students can access learning. Careful explanations and clear instructions for tasks are essential for all students, but may be particularly important for students with learning problems. Students with learning difficulties or conditions such as ADHD often have trouble organising themselves and managing time effectively. Students from different cultural backgrounds may also have difficulty recognising procedures and routines that are different from those experienced within their own culture (see Chapter 11). Some differences in social behaviours may surprise teachers who adopt a traditional orientation towards classroom management, but it is important not to assume that students' are deliberately disobeying classroom procedures. Rather, it is more important to carefully explain and even modify some classroom procedures to support some of these cultural differences. See Chapter 11 for further discussion of ways in which to cater for students' cultural backgrounds in the classroom.

Classroom rules

Regardless of which orientation you adopt towards classroom management, there is great commonality among theorists about the most effective classroom rules (De Nobile, Lyons & Arthur-Kelly, 2014). The key goal of all rules should be to prevent problems that would normally interfere with learning. In this respect, it is important that rules be focused on realistic and doable behaviours that can be expected of children at different ages. For rules to have the greatest impact, their numbers should be limited – long lists of rules are not easy to remember and tend to detract from the key behaviours that you really want to focus on. It is very important to remember that rules should be stated in positive language, clearly describing the behaviour you want to see. Rules that are expressed negatively with a series of 'Don't' instructions do not actually describe the correct behaviour to students. Rules should also be reasonable – you should be able to explain (justify) the rule and the consequences to your students and discuss the reasons for rules with students.

Theorists differ in the extent to which they agree about involving students in setting rules. Evertson and Emmer (2009) suggest that although many effective classroom managers do not allow students choice in the rules, they do engage in extensive discussion and explanation of rules with their students, which allows students to discuss the reasoning behind them. Finally, rules must be applied equitably and consistently. As noted by Doyle (1986, 2006), the ecology of classrooms means they are public places – students can see rules being enforced and will recognise when differential enforcement becomes unfair. These key points are summarised in a general checklist for developing rules in Box 14.2.

Evertson and Emmer (2009, pp. 23–4) suggest four key classroom rules that encompass most classroom behaviours. Note that each of these rules is worded positively and states the expected behaviour. These rules are stated in language most children will understand, but terms such as 'respect' may be a little abstract for younger students and will need to be explained using tangible examples of behaviours that define them.

- *Rule 1 Respect and be polite to all people.* This rule covers all aspects of school life, both inside and outside the classroom; the term 'all people' covers adults and other students. This will need to be discussed with students.
- *Rule 2 Be prompt and be prepared.* This rule is relevant to many different parts of the school day, including the start of the day and when students are getting ready for tasks. The rule is particularly relevant for high school students, for whom punctuality becomes a bigger problem for teachers to manage (Little, 2005).
- *Rule 3 Listen quietly while others are speaking.* This rule addresses many of the problems that can disrupt a carefully organised classroom, such as students calling out. In discussing this rule, you could invite students to tell you the types of behaviours that indicate when someone is listening.
- *Rule 4 Obey all school rules.* Although this is quite general, it allows you the chance to talk to students about rules beyond the classroom, such as rules for the playground.

BOX 14.2 CLASSROOM LINKS

RULES CHECKLIST

- Rules should be few in number (six or less)..☐
- Rules should be positively stated, using clear language ....☐
- Reasons should be stated for each rule ....☐
- Consequences should be stated for breaking each rule ....☐
- Rules should be displayed in a public place and often referred to ....☐
- Rules should be taught to students ....☐
- Rules should be enforced with equity ....☐

Source: Adapted from Arthur-Kelly, Lyons, Butterfield and Gordon (2006).

Setting relevant tasks

Organising instruction requires careful attention to the tasks we set for students. The relevance of tasks is associated with the level of interest and meaningfulness of the task to students. When students are not interested and engaged in the task, they can easily become distracted and go 'off task'. Arthur-Kelly, Lyons, Butterfield and Gordon (2006) suggest three elements to consider:

1   *Task relevance*. Consider whether the task has been introduced in a way that lets students know its meaning and importance. Remember that younger students have less 'world knowledge' than older students, so tasks have to be meaningful in a way that considers the student's experience and cognitive development.

2   *Achievable tasks*. Tasks need to be set at appropriate levels to ensure learning occurs. If tasks are too difficult, students can become frustrated, which may lead to behavioural outbursts or even avoidance of tasks. If tasks are too simple, then little learning will occur and behavioural problems can arise from boredom or work completed too quickly. Consider whether you have explained the type of effort and skills needed for the task.

3   *Ensuring success*. Achievable tasks ensure that students experience success. Success builds confidence and self-efficacy. Consider whether the tasks you set can be adapted to the learning needs of students with different ability levels – success for one student may not be the same as success for another student. Students also need feedback about success, as it helps them know if they are on the right track and creates a positive atmosphere in the classroom.

The relevance of tasks is particularly important for teaching in diverse school communities. Students from different cultures may have difficulty relating to tasks that only reflect examples from the teacher's viewpoint, especially if the same cultural background is not shared (Koki, van Broekhuizen & Uehara, 2000). As suggested previously, getting off to a good start with students includes finding out a little about their interests and background – this information can be useful when planning classroom tasks.

Smooth transitions

As we saw in Doyle's analysis of classroom ecology, the typical classroom is made up of many different events. As each classroom activity changes, the classroom is at a point of transition to a new activity. Transitions also occur when students are entering and leaving the classroom. An astonishing amount of time can be taken up by these transitions, with some research suggesting up to 31 transitions per day in a standard primary school classroom, taking up approximately 15 per cent of all classroom time (Rosenshine, 1980). Unfortunately, inappropriate behaviours are more likely to occur at these times.

Smooth transitions are linked to the effectiveness of classroom routines and procedures. Arends (2004) suggests that beginning teachers need to attend to transitions as a series of steps that they want students to follow. In addition, effective teachers use a series of 'cues' and 'signals' to alert students to a change in pace or type of activity. Consider the following steps that a teacher might undertake to transition students from a teacher-directed activity to an individual student activity at their desks.

- Teacher cue: 'We are now going to do a short activity to try out some of these ideas. I will leave these notes on the whiteboard and I'd like you to use these to complete the activity.'
- Step 1: Put your notebooks away and clear your desks.
- Step 2: You will need one pen or pencil and the worksheet that Darren is handing out now.
- Step 3: Begin your work as soon as you get your worksheet.
- Step 4: Raise your hand if you would like some help from me.
- Teacher cue: 'We have five more minutes to complete this worksheet before we will return to the whole group to discuss our ideas' (Arends, 2004, p. 190).

Initially, the teacher might need to write these steps on the whiteboard or have them printed on a worksheet, but these instructions become routines as students gradually learn what teachers expect of them. Younger students may need prompts and reminders more often, while students with learning difficulties or ADHD may need special assistance. Transitions can be harder for these students as they may have trouble refocusing attention after periods of 'down time' (Beattie, Jordan & Algozzine, 2006). Transitions that are carefully teacher-directed, with minimal 'down time', are less likely to result in classroom-management problems.

Organising the physical space

Classrooms are also physical spaces, and you can probably remember several ways of organising tables and chairs from your own classroom experiences – straight rows, small groups, horseshoe shapes, a circle of chairs and so on. Classrooms also have other areas and 'zones' that need to be carefully organised – a large sitting area for floor work is common in primary schools, and secondary schools have laboratories and creative spaces; most classrooms have storage areas and a teacher's desk area.

Jones' (1987) ideas about classroom management include a plan for arranging desks to allow the teacher space to move around the classroom. A teacher's walking path should enable them to supervise students through close proximity (1–3 metres) and eye contact. An example of a classroom arranged to provide a walking path for the teacher is set out in Figure 14.2. If you choose to arrange your desks in different formats, you must still consider the walking path and ensure you can access all students at all points of the classroom.

The study of classroom ecology has shown us that the physical design of settings has clear instructional and group-management implications. If you observe the classroom diagram in Figure 14.2, you will notice that it is set up in a traditional row format. Some of the earliest studies of classroom ecology showed that this type of classroom setting was related to the level of interaction between teacher and students. Adams and Biddle (1970) discovered that the front rows and centre seats were the 'action zone' of the classroom. Students sitting in these seats experienced the highest level of interaction with the teacher. These findings have clear classroom-management implications. Teachers must take care to ensure that interaction with students is spread equitably around the room. We might also consider how the action zone of the classroom could be used to our advantage as teachers. Students who require specialised help or have trouble paying attention might be seated in the action zone, or at least in close proximity to the teacher's walking path.

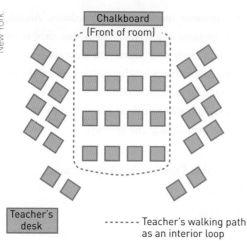

Source: Wolfgang, C.H. (1995). *Solving discipline problems: Methods and models for today's teachers.* (3rd edn). Bostor: Allyn & Bacon, Figure 8.4. Reproduced by permission of John Wiley & Sons, New York.

FIGURE 14.2 The teacher's walking path as an interior loop

Evertson and Emmer's four keys to good classroom layout

Evertson and Emmer (2009) provide four keys to good classroom layout. Each of these keys has clear instructional implications.

1 *Keep high-traffic areas free of congestion.* Just as the teacher needs an easy walking path, students also need clear paths to enter and exit the room or to reach materials. High-traffic areas such as the pencil sharpener or the bin can also be places where students gather, and can become sites of distraction. These high-use areas should be separated from each other so that groups of students do not build up in one area.

2 *Be sure all students can be easily seen from all areas of the classroom.* Effective teachers ensure they can monitor students from all angles of the classroom. Keep a clear line of sight to all work areas and be very careful of the placement of larger pieces of furniture that can block your view of students.

3 *Keep materials and supplies in handy locations.* This is especially relevant in primary school classrooms, where all materials are typically located in one classroom. Time wasting can occur during transitions if students need to walk to different locations to collect commonly used items. Be aware that materials and supplies can also be a source of distraction if they are too handy and visible to students. Use drawers and boxes to keep materials away from distractible students.

4 *Be certain that students can see all presentations and displays from where they are seated.* Fixed pieces of classroom furniture such as the blackboard or whiteboard can limit how you organise your classroom. Try to minimise the number of times students must crane their necks or turn their chairs around to see the main instructional space. Keep this space in an area where the majority of students can easily see the teacher. Presentations and displays can add colour and life to the classroom, but they can also be distracting. Ensure that the main instructional space only includes posters and aides that are the most relevant to that lesson or activity.

In the 'Arranging your own classroom' CourseMate link, you will find an interactive activity that allows you to apply the four keys of good classroom arrangement (Evertson & Emmer, 2009). Your challenge in this activity and in your future classrooms will be to juggle many features of the classroom ecology, as shown in the activity's real classroom example.

CourseMateExpress

Online resources
Try arranging your own classroom with the **Interactive activity** on this text's website

GROUP MANAGEMENT FOR FACILITATING ENGAGEMENT

In the previous section, we introduced the theory of classroom ecology and some important instructional steps that teachers can take to organise lessons in this environment. In this section, we look more closely at the ideas of ecological theorists, who believe that classrooms comprise complex social groups with special management considerations. Doyle (1986, 2006) suggests that classrooms are organised around a set of activities that vary in terms of how students are involved.

■ *Recitation or teacher-led activities.* These frequently involve a whole-class instructional format in which teachers give instruction, ask questions and call on individual students to give answers or recite responses. These types of activities might be used for introducing new materials, reviewing materials covered and checking student understanding.

- *Seatwork activities.* These involve students working independently at their own desks to complete assigned activities. Teachers are free to move around the classroom and monitor activities at this time. These types of activities can be used to give students independent practice and time for individual completion of work.
- *Group activities.* These are associated with students working together in small groups to complete tasks. As discussed in Chapter 6, there is a wide range of cooperative grouping systems, ranging from peer tutoring to reciprocal teaching, and many other cooperative learning strategies.

It is unlikely that teachers would use only one approach to grouping their students. In particular, Brophy (1988) suggests that although most teachers opt for whole-class or teacher-directed strategies, in which they first explain or demonstrate skills, they also use follow-up activities that involve individual seatwork tasks or small cooperative groups. How do teachers manage the groups during these diverse activities?

Strategies of effective teachers

Each of the different classroom activities requires teachers to be particularly aware of group-management implications. Kounin's (1970) study of effective teachers is now a classic piece of research that has shaped our understanding of the strategies used by the most effective classroom teachers (see Table 14.4).

TABLE 14.4 Strategies of effective teachers

STRATEGY	TEACHER BEHAVIOURS
With-it-ness	These teachers have 'eyes in the back of their head'; they constantly scan the classroom for potential disruptions, and they seem to see a disruption almost before it starts. Teachers who are 'with it' have low levels of misbehaviour.
Momentum	Effective teachers maintain the flow of the lesson and do not engage in behaviours that slow down the pace of the lesson. In contrast, 'flip flop' teachers can slow down the pace of the lesson by 'flip flopping' from one instruction to another. Teachers can also 'over-dwell' on instruction by going over the same points again and again. Misbehaviour increases as the momentum decreases.
Smoothness	Effective teachers maintain a smooth flow of activities. 'Flip flop' teachers cause disruption and 'dangle' teachers might start an activity and then leave it 'dangling' to do something else, or might backtrack to explain an instruction they forgot.
Group alerting	Good teachers use a range of cues and signals to keep the group alert and focused, such as waiting a few seconds for quiet, calling on the group for responses, and asking students to use signals to show they can answer a question.
Accountability	Good teachers also keep the group accountable. Strategies such as questioning keep students accountable to the goals of the lesson. Signals that indicate that students should listen to their peers, or wait their turn to speak, also make students accountable to one another.
Overlappingness	Effective teachers can do more than one thing at a time; for example, using signals such as eye contact to bring a student back to attention, while also continuing with the lesson. 'Flip flop' teachers might disrupt the momentum of a lesson by stopping to correct a student, while more effective teachers use good overlapping skills to continue the lesson.
Challenge arousal and variety	Good teachers keep students enthusiastic and involved in seatwork activities by providing varied tasks and assignments that are targeted at the right level of difficulty.

Source: Adapted from Kounin (1970).

MODULE IV EDUCATIONAL PSYCHOLOGY IN CONTEMPORARY CLASSROOMS

- Which of the effective teaching behaviours in **Table 14.4** do you recognise from your experience as a learner?
- Can you recall a teacher who had 'with-it-ness' or was a 'flip-flop' teacher?
- Can you think of a range of cues or signals that an effective teacher might use to manage student behaviour? Remember to include non-verbal cues as well.

Kounin examined the nature of teacher behaviour when students were engaged in typical classroom groupings of teacher-led and seatwork activities. Kounin was trying to understand the most effective use of discipline in classrooms, but he discovered something quite surprising. He found that teachers in both well-managed and poorly managed classrooms used quite similar disciplinary approaches. Therefore, the discipline of individual students did not explain why some classroom teachers were more effective than others were. Rather, he discovered that teachers in the well-managed classrooms had a special talent for managing the *whole* classroom group, preventing misbehaviour from occurring in the first place. Some of the special skills identified in Kounin's research have now become standard descriptions of the most effective teaching strategies. These principles still apply in classrooms today. For example, Kennedy-Lewis (2012) conducted close case studies of teacher practices in specialised community classrooms for students who had been expelled from other schools. Very successful teachers from a range of pedagogical approaches employed consistent use of strategies such as 'with-it-ness' and momentum to build accountability, commitment and rapport with their students. In contrast, teachers who lacked with-it-ness had disciplinary approaches with students that were more harsh and wasted a lot of class time on disciplinary management of students' off-task behaviours. Kounin's observations have stood the test of time and reflect many of the principles of classroom management discussed so far, including the use of effective management strategies to prevent misbehaviour.

Strategies for group management

Kounin's research, along with many other research studies, has given us a number of strategies for managing groups effectively. Student engagement in each of these group settings must be carefully addressed. As explained in Chapter 8, engagement is characterised by students' on-task behaviours, emotional and cognitive responses, and personal participation in the learning process. As you will see in the following summaries, the engagement of students is closely related to group management and the instructional methods examined in the previous section.

- *Recitation or teacher-led activities.* In these activities, the teacher assumes control of instruction and manages the whole group simultaneously. One criticism of teacher-led approaches relates to the idea that such a high level of teacher control calls for a passive level of student engagement (see Box 14.3). This may have significant implications for engagement in the classroom. For example, learners with ADHD have been shown to experience greater problems staying on-task when they are passively engaged in activities such as sitting and watching the teacher (Vile Junod et al., 2006). As such, teachers must have a high level of *with-it-ness* because instruction is often located at the front of the room and not close to where problems may arise. The teacher must also maintain a high level of *momentum* and *smoothness* because all learning is assumed to flow from the teacher to the student. Teachers will need clear *routines* and *group-alerting strategies* to manage question-and-answer strategies used during these activities.

■ *Seatwork activities.* These activities change the nature of group management considerably. During this time, the management exercise is spread across individual students who are usually more actively engaged in the completion of assigned activities. Kounin's research showed that *variety and challenge* was the most important factor related to student engagement during seatwork. This is hardly surprising because the focus has shifted from teacher control of instruction to independent completion of tasks, which requires a high level of self-directed focus from students (see Box 14.3 for a discussion of self-regulatory behaviour during seatwork). Because students are working independently, on-task behaviour cannot be assumed during this type of activity. A high level of *with-it-ness* is essential as the teacher must monitor and scan the classroom for potential problems. Teachers will need to be skilled at *overlappingness* as they attend to individual students while remaining aware of events elsewhere in the classroom.

■ *Group activities.* These involve small groups of students completing assigned tasks or projects. These groups are in themselves complex ecological systems. Kounin's research was conducted at a time when fewer classrooms used small-group or cooperative learning activities. However, later research has shown that the effective group-management skills identified by Kounin are

just as critical in small-group cooperative learning activities in the present day. In a study of 56 cooperative learning lessons, Emmer and Gerwels (2002) found that the most effective teachers were *with-it*, providing high levels of monitoring of group interactions. They made sure that group members were *accountable* for their progress, and they provided hands-on materials and props to be shared by the group, hence providing *challenge arousal and variety*. As discussed in Chapter 7, effective management of small-group work activities requires special attention to social-skill development in the whole group. Specialised social skills involving communication, problem solving and diplomacy can be taught to the whole group as a part of the *routines and procedures* expected during this type of activity.

Source: © Monkey Business Images/Shutterstock

FIGURE 14.3 Some classroom activities may be better suited to group work. This classroom arrangement is allowing students to collaborate on an engaging task.

In summary, there are a variety of approaches to group management in classrooms, and some evidence suggests it may not be wise to stick to a single form of group structure in everyday classrooms. While evidence suggests that primary school teachers are quite adept at using multiple group structures (NICHHD, ECCRN, 2005), some secondary school teachers who adopt traditional orientations might be more reluctant to move away from traditional teacher-led groupings. As shown in Box 14.3, the structure of groups can affect the self-regulation of students, so a mixture of grouping structures might serve to develop a greater range of developmental processes.

BOX 14.3 RESEARCH LINKS

STUDENT SELF-REGULATION IN TEACHER-LED, SEATWORK AND SMALL-GROUP CONTEXTS

Stright and Supplee (2002) conducted a study to explore student self-regulation in teacher-led, seatwork and small-group instructional contexts. They proposed that different instructional contexts might test students' capacity for self-regulation. The study involved 51 Grade 3 children who were observed in their classrooms over the course of one school year. The students were all completing maths or science lessons during the observations. The researchers recorded the children's capacity to self-regulate in five different areas:

1 *Attention to instructions.* The capacity of the child to listen to instructions and wait for instructions, and their capacity to follow the instructions independently
2 *Seeking help when needed.* Asking for assistance, seeking clarification and asking for additional instructions
3 *Monitoring progress.* Checking work, correcting errors, trying new methods or re-reading instructions
4 *Organisation.* The level of organisation shown by a child when approaching tasks
5 *Metacognitive talk.* The child discusses their own thinking strategies with teachers or peers, including sharing problem-solving strategies, explaining why a strategy was used, and verbalising approaches for an academic task.

The results of the study confirmed that instructional groups were related to students' self-regulation. During teacher-directed instruction, students were less likely to attend to instructions, monitor their work or ask for help, but they did show more organisation. During seatwork, students were significantly more likely to monitor their work, attend to instructions and seek help. Small-group activities yielded the highest levels of attentive listening, instructions being carefully read, and metacognitive talk. In contrast, most students did not discuss their thinking strategies during teacher-directed or seatwork activities.

Stright and Supplee concluded that different types of classroom groupings might send different signals to students about expected behaviours. Students may see teacher-directed activities as a passive time in the classroom, and hence self-regulation is reduced. They may wait until seatwork or small-group activities before attending to instructions carefully. Students may feel too intimidated to ask questions and seek help during teacher-directed instruction, or perhaps they receive a signal that this is not the time for asking questions.

ACTIVITIES

1 This study suggests particular advantages of small-group instruction. Draw up three lists and summarise the effects on self-regulation across the three settings.
2 How would you manage your classroom groups to help students develop self-regulation?
3 This study focused on Grade 3 children. Would you expect any difference for older children for whom self-regulatory skills are more developed?

SELF-REGULATION AND SOCIAL SKILLS

The consideration of student self-regulation and social skills is a relatively recent phenomenon. Where once the emphasis was on teacher control of the classroom, these newer concepts emphasise student direction and the capacity to regulate their own behaviour. (Carter & Doyle, 2006). In Chapter 6, we examined self-regulation as a cognitive activity involving the planning, directing and evaluating of one's own thought processes, and in Chapter 8 we explained some theories that link self-regulation with student motivation. As defined in Chapter 4, social skills are specific behaviours that lead to desired relationships and social outcomes for the individual, and these skills may vary across situations and contexts. In combination, self-regulation and social skills are critical tools through which human beings access their world; for students, this includes forming successful social and academic relationships, and controlling the behaviours and impulses that might otherwise undermine these relationships. Many approaches to classroom management now integrate training in self-regulation and social skills, in the belief that these skills can assist students to manage and direct their own behaviour.

Self-regulation approaches

Students learn many self-regulatory skills in the everyday classroom in the first days of school – raising one's hand before speaking, waiting your turn to speak, and learning to be patient while standing in queues. Later in school life, self-regulatory learning continues – managing emotions in playground disagreements stopping and thinking before answering in class, and increased awareness of the reactions of others. Although many of these skills are learned incidentally or emerge because of typical developmental processes, Rogers (2003) maintains that these skills are in fact critical *academic survival skills*, and suggests that many learners will need quite explicit instruction in mastering them. Teachers can play an important role in teaching these skills by reinforcing expected routines and behaviours, and providing clear guidelines for transitions between activities. Students with learning and attention difficulties (see Chapter 10) may require more explicit instruction where the teacher can provide direct explanation of expected behaviours, written or visual cue cards, and verbal and non-verbal signals as a reminder.

In terms of more specific approaches, students are typically taught a range of strategies to assist in monitoring and reflecting upon their own behaviours – particularly those behaviours associated with acting out and reacting inappropriately. Many of these approaches have arisen from cognitive–behavioural therapies which explicitly teach self-regulatory skills, with an emphasis on the student's planning, monitoring or awareness of their own behaviour. For example, in evaluating a strategy to assist students with ADHD, Guderjahn, Gold, Stadler and Gawrilow (2013) found that children who had been specifically trained to consider their goals and make plans for their behaviours fared better than students who merely set goals.

Self-monitoring strategies can also assist some students to recognise and describe their own behaviours by monitoring and recording their own behaviours (Jones & Jones, 2007). For younger students, desired behaviours can be recorded on pictorial charts, while older students may need a discrete card or a diary entry. However, these strategies may not be helpful for students with self-awareness and self-reflection difficulties, who may need more specific scaffolds and supports to enable this behaviour, as described in the intervention for ADHD students above (see Guderjahn, Gold, Stadler & Gawrilow, 2013, for a discussion).

Self-talk strategies can also be used by students who have a reasonable degree of self-awareness. These strategies literally involve students giving themselves verbal cues about how to behave. The main idea with this strategy is to replace negative or absent self-talk with positive and self-reinforcing internal speech. Students can use self-talk to follow instructional steps ('Next, I need to check my answers') or to control negative emotions ('I can finish this if I slow down and relax') (Jones & Jones, 2007). Teachers will need to assist students by providing reinforcement and some strategies to assist in applying self-regulation strategies, and it is important to remember that direct instruction in specific techniques may be essential. As we will see in the following section, many social-skills training programs combine self-regulatory training in a specific instructional model.

self-monitoring strategies
A self-regulatory strategy in which a student pays attention to their own thinking or behaviour and can take steps to change or correct that behaviour

self-talk strategies
A self-regulatory strategy in which students can use internal dialogue in their own mind to send themselves messages about their behaviour or performance

Social skills and problem-solving approaches

In Chapter 4, social skills were explored as a facet of social competence leading to the development and maintenance of healthy peer relationships. In terms of classroom management, social skills are also linked to academic competence and achievement. This is because many of the same social skills that contribute to social competence also contribute to academic competence. Skills such as paying attention to information, following directions, compliance with teacher (or peer) requests, and making appropriate responses, are just as critical in academic contexts as they are in social contexts (Carter & Doyle, 2006). Quite simply, the ability of the child to participate in the classroom in a socially acceptable manner influences their access to academic experiences. If students call out or otherwise act disruptively, or cannot share information with peers, they are likely to be corrected or ignored by teachers and peers (Weinstein, 1991, cited in Carter & Doyle, 2006).

As explained in Chapter 4, most social-skills instruction employs direct instruction, in which specific skills are identified and the child is explicitly trained in those skills. However, many of these programs fail because the training is not effectively reinforced in naturalistic settings such as the classroom and playground. Teachers can play a significant role in developing children's social skills in naturalistic, everyday teaching strategies. One particular focus is on the child's capacity to resolve conflict and solve social problems (Elias & Schwab, 2006). Social problem solving involves the capacity of the student to recognise and interpret the cues of social situations accurately, plan and formulate an appropriate response, and exert self-control over their emotions to enact an appropriate response.

One approach that meets the criteria of being teacher-led and classroom-based was developed in Australia by Linda Peterson (1994). This approach, known as Stop, Think, Do, is a cognitive–behavioural intervention designed to address the needs of children with self-regulation and problem-solving difficulties. These children often have significant problems in interpreting social cues accurately and coming up with appropriate responses (Crick & Dodge, 1994). The Stop, Think, Do approach is widely advocated by Australian educational authorities and used in a large number of schools. Refer to Box 14.4 for an explanation of the approach and strategies.

Research and evaluation of the program has illustrated its effectiveness across age groups ranging from children in the early years of school to children in high school. In one Australian study, primary school children who were judged to have poor social competence showed significant gains in making friends, being accepted by peers, coping with teasing, and controlling aggressive and shy behaviours (Nimmo, 1993). In another study with young adolescents with mild intellectual disabilities, training in Stop, Think, Do resulted in significant gains in verbalising feelings, controlling anger and learning to respond to teasing in non-aggressive ways (Beck & Horne, 1992). Another intervention was conducted among Year 8 students in a high school in Sheffield in the United Kingdom (Day, Murphy & Cooke, 1999). Teachers were trained to use Stop, Think, Do in regular classrooms, resulting in significant improvement in problem solving among the Year 8 participants. Teachers were particularly impressed by the results for students with emotional and behavioural problems, who actually became more engaged and less disruptive over the course of the program.

Social-skills and self-regulation strategies also appear in specific approaches to the management of problem behaviour and student conflict, and will be examined further in the remaining sections of this chapter.

BOX 14.4 CLASSROOM LINKS

STOP, THINK, DO – THE TRAFFIC LIGHT SYSTEM

Stop, Think, Do is a simple intervention based on the three stages of the traffic light signal:

- **STOP** (red) when faced with a problem and think about how you feel before acting.
- **THINK** (orange) about as many alternatives or strategies for solving the problem as you can, remembering that all solutions have consequences.
- **DO** (green) take the most appropriate course of action. If unintended consequences arise, go back to STOP and THINK again.

The instructional strategy

The following steps illustrate the instructional strategy for use as a social-skills training tool with students. In this strategy, students are trained to use the traffic light system as an independent self-management strategy, while teachers stand by as a third-party back-up. The strategy starts with the question 'Who owns the problem?', generating problem ownership by the student.

1 **STOP**: Students are urged not to react but to look and listen to social cues to learn about the problem. Teachers support the student by clarifying the problem and eliciting feeling responses: 'I feel ... because of this problem.'
2 **THINK**: Consider possible solutions with the student; encourage the student to evaluate the various solutions.
3 **DO**: Encourage the student to choose the best solution and act on it. If the solution is not effective, guide them back to the beginning of the process to think again.

Source: Peterson, L. & Adderley, A. (2002). *Stop Think Do Social Skills Training: Primary Years–Ages 8-12.* ACER Press.

INTERVENING TO ADDRESS CLASSROOM BEHAVIOURS

In any discussion of creating a positive learning environment, we must also acknowledge that there are times in classroom life where teachers must respond to disruptive or troublesome behaviours. Consider the following classroom scenario: The teacher asks Suzy to suggest a solution to a problem on the blackboard during a mathematics class, and when Suzy gives a funny reply, all the students laugh. The teacher becomes very angry. After that, whenever the teacher asks Suzy a question, everyone giggles. How could the teacher respond to this behaviour?

As you can see in this example, the teacher's response to student behaviour can set the tone for future interactions with that student and the whole class. As we advocated at the beginning of this chapter, it is very important to consider your philosophy and beliefs about student development and behaviour. Here we will advocate taking a critical approach to many classroom management interventions you may read about or see practised in classrooms. We also point out the sources of evidence about such classroom interventions.

In most classrooms, student behaviour is generally appropriate and does not present a challenge to the teacher. However, there are times when a few children whose behaviour is inappropriate or challenging may cause a disruption to a class. Occasionally, teachers also encounter students whose behaviour is so unusual or difficult to manage that teachers need to seek additional help from experts,

CourseMateExpress

Online resources
Watch a **video** in which
children tell us what
'good' teachers do
to manage student
behaviour

either to develop better strategies for coping with particular students or to find some other solution. It is beyond the scope of this chapter to explain the complexities of emotional and behavioural conditions that affect a small proportion of students. These conditions are complex and best addressed through specialised strategies and remedial programs, and may require the classroom teacher to liaise with other professionals to develop appropriate behaviour support interventions (see more in Chapter 10). As you read this section, it is important to reflect upon the need to balance the preventive strategies outlined in the previous sections and the interventions outlined in this section.

What types of problems do teachers report?

Many of the classroom behavioural concerns reported by teachers involve relatively minor but disruptive behaviours. These behaviours include talking out of turn or hindering other students, behaviours that we might say are relatively trivial in nature (Beaman, Wheldall & Kemp, 2007). Both primary and secondary school teachers report similar types of behavioural concerns, with some variation as children move through the levels of schools (Little, 2005). For example, Little found that talking out of turn was most troublesome in the junior level of high school, while idleness and punctuality became greater concerns in the senior levels of school. There is no doubt that these behaviours might be considered minor, but it is their frequency that can cause disruption and a great deal of stress to teachers (Infantino & Little, 2005). It is important to bear in mind that these types of behaviours are very different from the perceptions presented in common media sources. Behaviours involving aggression and violence attract media attention, yet these are not the typical troublesome behaviours reported by teachers.

What do students think about problem behaviours?

It is interesting that both students and teachers feel that too much time is taken up with managing relatively minor disruptive behaviours (Infantino & Little, 2005). Students themselves report that talking out of turn, talking back to teachers, being out of seat and eating in class are the most troublesome behaviours (Infantino & Little, 2005). Unfortunately, teachers and students (and their parents) differ in their beliefs about the sources of behavioural problems. Although many teachers blame the student's home life or the child's personal characteristics, students and parents cite unfairness and student vulnerability as major factors in causing reactive discipline problems (Porter, 2007). Teacher behaviours perceived to be unfair include rudeness to students, unfairly blaming students and being inappropriately strict or lenient. These behaviours are sources of reactive feelings from students and parents. Parents and students also recognise that some students are more vulnerable than others in classroom life. These are students who are recognised by their peers as suffering emotional or learning difficulties, and may also have family difficulties (Miller, Ferguson & Byrne, 2000). Babad's (1995) research showed that when teachers responded to these students by giving them the extra attention and support they needed, students actually appreciated this type of differential behaviour. Students saw this differential treatment as appropriate, and feelings of warmth and positivity were greater in these classrooms. However, when teachers denied a vulnerable child this support, students reacted with low morale and felt their classrooms were less supportive.

How do teachers respond to behaviours, and is this appropriate?

It may not surprise you to hear that teachers and students sometimes disagree about the teacher's response to behaviour and whether this is appropriate. In part this may be because teachers and students report differing levels of their use of punitive or aggressive responses to student behaviours. Teachers tend to report using fewer aggressive responses than do students (Romi, Lewis, Roache & Riley, 2011). Such responses included escalating punishments, shouting at students, deliberately embarrassing students and using sarcasm towards students. Unfortunately, punitive and aggressive management styles are associated with greater disruption to classroom life and negative reactions from students (Romi, Lewis, Roache & Riley, 2011). Lewis, Romi, Xing and Katz (2005) contend that this could create a climate of 'cyclical' hostilities between teacher and student, causing disruption to other members of the class. Lewis and colleagues argue that while it is understandable that teachers react to provocative student behaviours, it is very important that teachers remember that they are the professionals in the classroom, and that they should not allow themselves to be locked into a 'vicious cycle' (Lewis, Romi, Xing & Katz, 2005, p. 14) of reactivity involving teacher and student.

Types of interventions

As we have seen in the preceding sections, much of the teacher's work in managing classrooms concerns preventive approaches to classroom management. The establishment of warm and supportive relationships, along with clearly organised instructional and group-management strategies, are critical to preventing the emergence of classroom-management problems. In addition to these preventive strategies, teachers must also develop a clear, well-thought-out plan that provides a framework for maintaining and responding to student behaviours. At the beginning of this chapter, we learnt that teachers might hold different beliefs about learning and classroom management. In the next section of this chapter, we will examine these approaches using Wolfgang's (1995) classification of 'interventionist', 'interactionalist' and 'non-interventionist' approaches. Each approach may provide guidelines for coping with some forms of disruptive behaviour, but it is important to remember that very few teachers ever adopt one single approach or orientation, because classroom management is far more complex than that.

Interventionist approaches

Interventionist approaches are guided by a belief that young people *need* adults to exercise control over them. In other words, they are incapable of controlling themselves. These approaches are based on the idea that external forces (such as discipline from teachers and other adults) shape and guide the behaviour of the young person. In this way, many of these approaches are strongly influenced by the principles of behaviourism and applied behaviour analysis (see Chapter 5), and are also consistent with the 'traditionalist' approach adopted by many secondary school teachers.

Lee and Marlene Canter (1992) adopted an interventionist approach known as **assertive discipline**. They strongly believe that firm teacher control is essential for successful classrooms, but they also believe that teachers should be fair and positive in their relationships with students. This control is attained through a **classroom discipline plan**, which should contain the elements of:

- establishment of rules
- supportive feedback – 'catch them being good'
- corrective procedures.

assertive discipline
A high level of teacher control, with firm limit setting and supportive feedback

classroom discipline plan
A planned approach to responding to behaviour, which avoids overly hasty and emotional responses and leads to consistent reactions

ESTABLISHMENT OF RULES
According to the Canters, teachers must set rules by clearly establishing how they want students to behave. These are expressed as observable, doable rules, and should be limited to a maximum of five general rules. They must be observed at all times throughout the day, and the teacher must be consistent in responding to all rule violations in the same manner. Therefore, the consequences of rules also need to be clearly thought through and explained to students.

SUPPORTIVE FEEDBACK
The Canters suggest that teachers must 'catch them being good'. This is based on the assumption that positive behaviours will be reinforced by sincere and meaningful feedback from teachers. Supportive

feedback is based on the concept of praise. Praise in this model is simple, direct and specific about the behaviour that is being praised. The Canters advocate the use of rewards such as certificates, notes sent home and special privileges. The Canters also advocate the use of praise as an incentive to other students who are not behaving appropriately.

CORRECTIVE PROCEDURES

Under the model of assertive discipline, students must be left in no doubt that breaking the rules will be met with negative consequences. However, the Canters are very clear that negative consequences or punishments should not be harmful – they should not embarrass or humiliate the student. Unfortunately, this may conflict with a key idea about tracking student behaviour. When tracking misbehaviour, a number of systems are recommended in which the teacher writes the student's name on a board at the first sign of misbehaviour (Canter & Canter, 1981). For subsequent misbehaviour, a tick is placed next to the name, until a maximum of five ticks is reached. Each tick represents an escalating set of consequences, which become more severe as the number of ticks increases. Clearly, such a public method of naming and punishing students may cause humiliation or even reactive resentment in students; Canter (1996) later recommended that teachers might like to use a clipboard or notebook to keep their tracking private.

Corrective procedures also involve assertive verbal demands in which the teacher repeats the desired behaviour several times, commencing with a hint and escalating to a demand:

- Teacher: It is time to put that phone away now Susan. (hint)
- Susan: I haven't finished this message yet.
- Teacher: Susan, I would like you to switch your phone off and put it in your bag.
- Susan: Just wait a minute!
- Teacher: Put that phone away now. (demand)

When students do not comply with a demand, negative consequences must follow. A range of negative consequences have been suggested, including the well-known strategy of 'time out', in which a student is isolated for a period of time, or the withdrawal of privileges and detentions. The teacher may decide to withdraw a favourite activity from Susan or contact her parents. Parent support is an essential component of the Canters' model. Parents are informed about the disciplinary approach and their support is expected by attending parent–teacher meetings and backing up the teacher by enforcing expectations regarding homework.

Strengths and limitations of interventionist approaches

The Canterian model of assertive discipline is widely applied in Australian schools but is not without its critics. To be fair, the notion of assertive discipline is underpinned by the idea that good discipline shows care and concern for all students. However, it is also underpinned by a strong notion of the teacher's right to control their classroom. As noted by Porter (2007, pp. 42–3), assertive discipline strongly asserts the right of the teacher to 'manage *your* classroom' (Canter & Canter, 2001, p. 33) and set '*your* classroom rules' (Canter & Canter, 2001, p. 66). Such strong methods of teacher control and use of reinforcement raise questions about the long-term effects on children's social and emotional skills, and on their capacity for self-regulation.

Some commentators have raised a concern that there is a lack of empirical evidence about the effectiveness of assertive discipline. As stated by Brophy (2006), the Canters have not published empirical research about their program. Earlier reports presented conflicting and equivocal evidence about the assertive discipline method (Render, Padilla & Krank, 1989), and some reviewers have noted that the assertive discipline approach does not consider other sources or reasons for student misbehaviour, such as poor quality teaching (Crockenberg, 1982; Curwin & Mendler, 1989). Of greater concern are the effects of punishment on students. As outlined by Burden (1995), punishment is largely ineffective in changing students' behaviour because it does not teach behaviours that are more appropriate. Punishment promotes aggression in some students and causes others to withdraw or become less engaged in learning. Finally, assertive discipline is a reactive strategy and, as with any behaviour-management approach, it must be embedded within a wider system of comprehensive classroom management focused on preventing misbehaviour from occurring in the first place. In Chapter 5 we discussed the behaviourist strategy known as 'positive behaviour support' (Simonsen & Sugai, 2009), which contains a specific plan for addressing student behaviour at a school-wide or 'system' level.

Interactionalist approaches

Interactionalist approaches view children's development as a product of interaction between internal and external factors. Rudolf Dreikurs (1968), Thomas Gordon (1974) and Maurice Balson (1992) exemplify the theorists who emphasised the role of the school in preparing students to live in a democratic society through the sharing of power between teachers and students.

Dreikurs' ideas about democratic teaching emerged during the movement towards humanism and reflected a child-centred view of discipline. (See Chapter 7 for more on humanism.) In keeping with Wolfgang's classification of the theory as interactionalist, the approach does retain some elements of teacher control in redirecting the child's misbehaviour.

Dreikurs' ideas of classroom discipline are based on the main assumption that all human beings have a desire to belong and be part of a social group. Therefore, all *mis*behaviour represents a mistaken or misplaced attempt to reach the goal of achieving belonging and control in one's life (Dreikurs, 1968).

As such, the role of the teacher is threefold. First, teachers must *identify the sources of misbehaviour* by understanding the child's goal. Second, they must *break away from their typical reaction* to the child's behaviour, as the motive of misbehaviour may be to seek this reaction. Third, they must *plan a response* that reflects care and concern, and assists the child in identifying their goal and making choices about their behaviour by emphasising the logical consequences of misbehaviour.

THE SOURCES OF MISBEHAVIOUR

According to Dreikurs and other interactionalist theorists, children's misbehaviour is generally motivated by four possible goals (Balson, 1992; Dreikurs, Grunwald & Pepper, 1982, 1998). These goals represent different levels of the child's discouragement with the state of their life – they no longer feel a sense of belonging or significance and believe the only way to regain a sense of belonging is through misbehaviour.

These misplaced goals reflect a hierarchical order, with goals further down the list representing the most discouraged state of the child (Dreikurs, Grunwald & Pepper, 1982). These goals are:

1 *attention* – to gain attention by any means, both active and passive, and constructive and destructive

2 *power* – to overcome feelings of inferiority, real or imagined, by exercising power and control; this could be achieved by becoming the centre of attention or striving to win a perceived battle with a teacher

3 *revenge* – to revenge their loss of status by getting even; this could include lashing out at others, destroying property, or insulting the teacher

4 *inadequacy* – to achieve a sense of care and belonging by displaying helplessness, or to avoid feeling inadequate by avoiding participation and leaving the group.

A teacher's response to misbehaviour should be to observe the student carefully in order to identify the underlying goal motivating the behaviour. Conclusions can be verified by further observation and by questioning the student.

BREAKING THE TYPICAL TEACHER REACTION

Teachers should examine their own reactions to the student's behaviour as well as to the student's responses to correction. For example, when a child seeks attention, teachers may feel annoyance, but they typically respond or react to the child. As such, typical teacher reactions may reinforce the child's misplaced idea that misbehaviour gains attention, and fulfil the child's need to belong. Other examples of typical teacher reactions are outlined in Table 14.5.

TABLE 14.5 Teacher reactions to student misbehaviour

STUDENT'S GOALS	TEACHER'S FEELINGS	STUDENT'S REACTION TO CORRECTION
Seeking attention	Feels minor annoyance but responds with a comment or correction	Temporarily stops behaviour but will likely use the behaviour again to gain attention
Seeking power	Feels upset or personally challenged and fights back or gives in to the child	Behaviour persists, and if teacher overpowers child and 'wins' the battle, then further aggression may occur
Seeking revenge	Feels deeply hurt or threatened and retaliates	Behaviour intensifies or may be modified to a new form of revenge. The teacher's retaliation may be used by the child to justify theirs
Displaying inadequacy	Feels frustrated or gives up on the child	Gives up and does not attempt to change their behaviour

Source: Adapted from Balson (1992, p. 31); Arthur-Kelly, Lyons, Butterfield and Gordon (2006, p. 157).

PLANNING A RESPONSE

Dreikurs believed that encouragement was fundamental to achieving a change in student behaviour. This notion of encouragement is fundamentally different from the concept of praise practised by interventionist teachers. Encouragement focuses on effort rather than achievement and removes a value-based judgement about the student. In contrast, praise often arises after the child has completed a task and makes a direct link to the value of the person because they acted in a praiseworthy way (see Chapter 8 for specific examples of appropriate and inappropriate use of praise).

Teachers can also develop better relationships with their students by discussing important matters with them as soon as possible after they occur (*dealing in the present*). Communication with the student should be conducted respectfully. Teachers can also use **I-messages** to address concerns (Gordon, 1974). These messages focus on the feelings and needs of the speaker rather than the listener. For example, a teacher might offer the following form of encouragement: 'I really enjoyed reading the first draft of your project Kyle; keep it up' is an example of an I-message. The teacher used the personal pronoun 'I' when talking about the feeling the teacher experienced (enjoyment) and the effect of the student's behaviour (project work) on the teacher. These statements can be used in an assertive way to discuss a problem behaviour; for example, 'When I get interrupted during a lesson, I feel frustrated because I have to keep stopping' (De Nobile, Lyons, & Arthur-Kelly, 2017).

I-messages
Using the personal pronoun 'I' to focus on the feelings and needs of the speaker rather than the listener

Teachers' responses to the different motives that underlie student behaviour should include the use of natural or logical consequences that follow the behaviour. **Natural consequences** are outcomes that occur without intervention, while **logical consequences** are contrived to influence behaviour. In each case, the focus is on allowing students to experience the consequences of their actions.

natural consequences
Outcomes that occur without interference

logical consequences
Outcomes contrived to influence behaviour

Balson (1992) gives examples of natural consequences; these are:

- students who do not put their equipment away in the correct place and cannot find it the next time they need it
- students who do not study for a test and then get poor marks on the test.

Examples of logical consequences include:

- students who forget to bring required materials to a class and as a result miss out on an activity
- students who draw on a wall and then have to clean their marks off the wall.

Logical consequences differ from punishment because they do not place the power into the hands of the punisher. Rather, the child is faced with a logical consequence of their behaviour that reveals the cause and effect of their actions. Dreikurs asserts that teachers should make a clear connection between a student's choice over their own actions and facing logical consequences. Democratic discussion in class should be used to establish expected rules and consequences, as this allows the child to understand the connection between actions and logical consequences.

STRENGTHS AND LIMITATIONS OF INTERACTIONALIST APPROACHES

One of the main strengths of the approach described by Dreikurs (1968) and Balson (1992) is its focus on students' understanding of why they behave as they do and the consequences of their behaviour.

The interactionalist approach tends to encourage a high degree of student autonomy, as well as respect between teachers and students (Edwards, 1997). One of the main weaknesses of this approach is that teachers often have difficulty recognising the motives that underlie student behaviour. Moreover, it is probably too simplistic to explain student behaviour in terms of four basic goals, and teachers may have difficulty in identifying logical consequences for inappropriate behaviour. As argued by Kohn (1996), teachers may find it comforting to believe that logical consequences are not a form of punishment, but it probably makes little difference to the child, who may still see the consequence as a punishment. As shown in Figure 14.4, there is always the chance that planned or unplanned consequences may not change behaviour in the intended way.

Source: Martin (1987, p. 159). Used by permission.

FIGURE 14.4 In some situations, natural consequences may not be the best option.

Non-interventionist approaches

Non-interventionist teachers allow the process of learning to occur naturally. The work of William Glasser (1992) and William ('Bill') Rogers (1989, 1998, 2003) represents a model of classroom management in which power is shared more equally between teacher and students than in the interventionist and interactive approaches just discussed, with greater weight on students' roles and responsibilities.

Bill Rogers (1998) sees discipline as arising from the type of learning environment established by the teacher. He views discipline as a teacher-directed activity that seeks to 'lead, guide, direct, manage, or confront a student about behaviour that disrupts the rights of others, be they teachers or students' (Rogers, 1998, p. 11). Here, the focus is on causes of behaviour difficulties and the teacher's responsibility to guide students towards enhanced self-control, self-esteem and personal accountability for their own behaviour.

Glasser and Rogers have both argued that students misbehave because schools fail to fulfil their basic needs. These needs clearly reflect elements of Maslow's hierarchy of needs (see Chapter 7), and include:

- *safety* – feeling safe in the classroom environment
- *belonging* – feeling loved, a sense of comfort and group membership
- *power* – importance, status and being respected
- *freedom* – being free from the control of others, being able to choose, being self-directed and having responsibility for one's own actions
- *fun* – having satisfying and enjoyable experiences.

The key principle of Glasser's choice theory is the idea that *only we can control our own behaviour*. Thus, the teacher's role is to focus on their behaviour, their relationship with children, and their ability to support children in achieving a sense of control in their own lives. In Rogers' approach, teachers can assist students in achieving a sense of control and belonging by helping children to meet these basic needs. They can show care for children by building a feeling of safety in the classroom. They should promote belonging by helping children develop friendships, by giving them tasks that enhance their status in the group, and by allowing choices that encourage self-direction and responsibility. At the same time, learning should be fun (Rogers, 1998). Glasser particularly recommends cooperative learning as a strategy that can assist with many of these tasks. In particular, he asserts that cooperative groups enable students to feel a sense of belonging and a sense of power as they learn to assist less-able group members, and that they provide a means of gaining self-understanding as students evaluate their own actions in groups (Glasser, 1981, as cited in Edwards & Watts, 2008).

BOX 14.5   ABOUT WILLIAM GLASSER

A CASE STUDY OF A CHANGING PHILOSOPHY

The story of William Glasser's ideas about classroom management is an interesting case study of the importance of examining and, if necessary, changing one's personal approach to classroom management.

Glasser (1925–2013) was a psychiatrist who worked in a punitive institution for delinquent teenage girls in California. This experience led him to develop a number of approaches that particularly appealed to many school leaders and teachers around the world. Concepts such as 'time out' and 'levels' for behaviour management can be attributed to Glasser's ideas. His theory of 'reality therapy' adopted a humanist and behaviourist approach, suggesting that teachers should help children become responsible for their own behaviours. The popular take-up of Glasser's ideas led to closer involvement with schools, and in 1996, Glasser travelled to Australia to speak about his approach. However, in talking to teachers, Glasser found a very discomforting use of his methods. He found that teachers were particularly concerned with using his methods for coercive disciplinary approaches, rather than establishing better quality classroom environments. These teachers were overly focused on the behaviourist principles of coercion and manipulative reinforcement techniques. These experiences led Glasser to revise and change his theory of classroom management.

In 1998, Glasser removed ideas of behavioural intervention and replaced these with 'choice theory' (Glasser, 1998). The central belief of choice theory is that only the individual can control their own behaviour. Glasser stated that it is not children who are the problem, but the learning environment itself. In particular, the learning environment must make it possible for children to feel a sense of belonging, power to make decisions, freedom to choose an individual learning pathway, and a sense of fun and engagement during interesting classroom activities. Glasser supported his ideas by conducting interviews with students in different countries, including Australia. He concluded that students become disillusioned by the controlling strategies of teachers, and for students with behaviour problems, this just causes their behaviour to deteriorate (Arthur-Kelly, Lyons, Butterfield & Gordon, 2006).

FIGURE 14.5 Glasser's ideas have significantly influenced ideas about classroom management and discipline in Australia and New Zealand.

Source: William Glasser Institute.

Other research has supported Glasser's choice theory, showing particular effectiveness for individual students with chronic behaviour problems. Most studies have reported reduced absenteeism, lower rates of return to delinquent behaviour, fewer disputes with peers, and more 'on-task' time in classrooms (Porter, 2007).

As such, this case study highlights the importance of revisiting and examining the impact of one's personal theory of classroom management.

TEACHERS AS LEADERS

Glasser (1992) argues that teachers need to become 'lead-managers', not 'boss-managers'. To show this leadership, teachers should facilitate learning by encouraging children to think deeply about the nature of learning, and to help children reach rational decisions to solve conflicts. The way in which curriculum material is presented should emphasise quality school work, with skills developed rather than facts learned, and achievement tests replaced by student self-evaluation. When disruptive behaviour occurs, Glasser proposes that teachers try to stop the misbehaviour through the use of reality therapy (see Box 14.6). Reality therapy is a cognitive–behavioural approach in which the teacher or therapist works with the student to build problem-solving skills. This approach is based on the belief that teachers can help students gain a sense of control in their lives by encouraging self-evaluation, self-regulation and choice. One of the critical points about reality therapy is that the teacher or therapist always focuses on the present behaviour, as this is the context in which change can occur.

BOX 14.6 CLASSROOM LINKS

REALITY THERAPY TECHNIQUES

Edwards and Watts (2008) provide the following steps for conducting a reality therapy interview:

1   Ask: 'What do you want to achieve in this situation?'
2   Ask: 'What are you currently doing or what have you tried to do to achieve this?'
3   Assist the student to evaluate what is working.
4   Assist the student to explore other options that may be available.
5   Plan to act, noting how, when, where and who will act.

Reality therapy is not an overnight behavioural-change technique. Like other social-skills or problem-solving approaches, behavioural change can take a long time to occur. The focus is on moving the child away from negative thoughts and towards more productive strategies for solving problems and gaining control in their own lives.

CourseMateExpress

Online resources
Go further: Read more about Glasser-based school management and discipline on this text's website

RULES, RIGHTS AND RESPONSIBILITIES

A major focus of Rogers' ideas is on the fundamental place of rules, rights and responsibilities in the operation of classroom communities. Although the curriculum is a critical element in classroom management and discipline, a teacher's primary goal is to develop self-control and self-discipline in students through the establishment of fair rules, coupled with an understanding of personal rights and responsibilities within the framework of these rules. Early in a school year, teachers need to discuss with students the fundamental rights that all people in the school should expect:

- the right to feel safe
- the right to be treated with dignity and respect
- the right to learn and teach.

Rules are the other side of rights, and function to safeguard rights. Individual responsibility for actions at school and in the classroom ensures that rules are followed and rights are respected. When misbehaviour occurs, Rogers (1998) suggests that teachers use strategies that move from least to most intrusive, depending on the seriousness of the disruption and the degree to which others' rights are infringed.

STRENGTHS AND LIMITATIONS OF NON-INTERVENTIONIST APPROACHES

The strength of the non-interventionist position presented by Glasser (1992) and Rogers (1998) is in the degree of autonomy and responsibility it gives to students, allowing them to see the consequences of their behaviour and to determine possible solutions (Gordon, Arthur & Butterfield, 1996). Weaknesses concern the difficulties teachers may have in giving students increased autonomy and responsibility without, at the same time, feeling threatened by loss of control. De Nobile, Lyons and Arthur-Kelly (2017) also point out that while more research is needed, existing research reports positive results.

Non-interventionist approaches may also present difficulties for teachers if students do not wish to cooperate in this approach. In a non-interventionist approach, the assumption of choice, autonomy and responsibility is paramount; other approaches may rely on more coercive or punitive techniques to gain student cooperation. Training students through reality therapy may also require particular skills on the part of the teacher, who may not feel equipped to adopt the stance of therapist. It is worth remembering, however, that the techniques of reality therapy are quite similar to those in approaches such as Stop, Think, Do, and teachers have found success in using such approaches in the classroom.

This section has introduced three approaches that reflect the orientations of interventionist, interactionalist and non-interventionist teachers. These approaches are widely used in Australian schools and no doubt across the Pacific region. The critiques contain points that teachers should think about before adopting any single approach to classroom management. Box 14.7 lists some points about each approach that educators need to consider when planning classroom-management strategies.

BOX 14.7 IMPLICATIONS FOR EDUCATORS

MODELS OF CLASSROOM MANAGEMENT IN STRATEGY PLANNING

When planning classroom-management strategies, educators need to be aware of the following:

- In an interventionist model, effective classroom-management strategies include firm teacher control, insistence that rules be followed, and abundant use of praise along with clear punishment strategies. Teachers are responsible for developing and enforcing rules and consequences. Concerns have been raised about the capacity of students to develop personal control and self-regulation strategies.
- In an interactionalist model, students need to understand the consequences of their behaviour and also have a high degree of autonomy and responsibility. Teachers are responsible for understanding the sources of student behaviour and must use abundant encouragement before enforcing logical consequences.
- In a non-interventionist model, students need opportunities to make choices. This model encourages self-direction and responsibility in students, including recognition of class rules and their own rights and responsibilities. Teachers are responsible for guiding students and making them aware of their rights and responsibilities towards themselves and others.

THINK ABOUT

- Towards the start of this chapter, you were asked to consider which of these management styles you would prefer to adopt as a teacher. After studying specific approaches for each of these management styles, have your ideas changed? If so, how?
- In reality, few people ever adopt only one type of approach to classroom management. Which features of these approaches would you most like to adopt?
- Do you think any features of the approaches are incompatible with one another?

SCHOOL-WIDE ISSUES AND APPROACHES

Throughout this chapter, we have largely considered creation of a positive learning environment from the perspective of teachers and students in classrooms. However, the responsibility for creating safe and positive educational experiences also lies with the entire school community.

CREATING SAFE SCHOOLS

In 2013, the Standing Council on School Education and Early Childhood (SCSEEC) produced an updated national framework for ensuring safe and supportive school environments, stating:

> In a safe and supportive school, the risk from all types of harm is minimised, diversity is valued and all members of the school community feel respected and included and can be confident that they will receive support in the face of any threats to their safety or wellbeing.

Source: SCSEEC (2013, p. 2). © Education Services Australia (ESA) (2013).

The principles of the framework outline the right of all members of the school community to safety and support, firmly stating that schools are responsible for developing policies and programs that support and engage all students, foster the skills necessary for developing positive relationships, and protect all children from harm and abuse. The responsibilities of school leaders and teachers are clear – they must make themselves aware of relevant policies and procedures, research and information to help them make the best decisions, and they must engage in training and ongoing education to facilitate this process. Table 14.6 outlines the key elements and strategies of the framework.

TABLE 14.6 Elements and strategies of the *National Safe Schools Framework*

ELEMENT	STRATEGIES AND APPROACHES
Leadership commitment to a safe school	• Being committed to an inclusive school environment with appropriate programs and strategies to foster positive school culture • Engage in evaluation, review and data collection about harassment, violence and bullying
A supportive and connected school culture	• Student connectedness to school; teacher modelling of explicit prosocial values and behaviours, positive and respectful teacher–student–peer relationships • Monitoring and responsiveness to child protection • Cultural sensitivity and recognition of specific needs of different groups in the school community (for example, Indigenous, refugee and immigrant groups)
Policies and procedures	• Develop policies, programs and procedures in collaboration with the whole school community. • Ensure there are relevant policies to address and manage bullying, violence and child protection, and procedures for risk assessment and minimisation
Professional learning	• Ensure all school staff have access to appropriate professional learning that assists in development of understanding and ability to respond to bullying, violence, harassment and child-protection issues
Positive behaviour management	• Selection of an evidence-informed, positive behaviour management approach with clear promotion and recognition of positive behaviour, and consistency in implementation by all staff across the school • Risk-prevention plans for use of technology, for playground activities and off-campus and out-of-school-hours activities
Engagement, skill development and a safe school curriculum	• Enhancing student engagement; extensive use of cooperative learning and relational teaching strategies • Teaching skills to promote cybersafety, social and emotional skills in all subjects, across all year levels
Focus on student wellbeing and ownership	• Enhancing student wellbeing with defined processes and strategies; a strengths-based approach • Multiple opportunities for ownership, decision making, student voice, sense of meaning and purpose
Early intervention and targeted student support	• Effective processes to identify students and families in need of support • Early intervention and follow-up support for skill development
Partnerships with families and community	• Working collaboratively with parents, community organisations and the justice system on all issues of student wellbeing, safety, child maltreatment, aggression, violence and cybersafety

Source: © Education Services Australia (ESA) (2013). ESA is the legal entity for the Standing Council on School Education and Early Childhood (SCSEEC). This extract has been used with permission from ESA. Apart from any uses permitted under the *Copyright Act 1968* (Cth), and use for non-commercial education purposes where the source is acknowledged, this text may not be sold or used for any commercial purpose. Other than as permitted above, no part may be reproduced, stored, published, performed, communicated or adapted by any means without the prior written permission of the copyright owner.

RESPONDING TO BULLYING IN SCHOOLS

The National Safe Schools Framework clearly states that schools have a responsibility to provide a safe environment, free of harassment, violence and bullying. It is now well accepted that bullying is another unacceptable form of violence, and that schools have a responsibility to prevent and respond to this behaviour. However, research consistently shows that teacher responses to bullying are largely ineffective; much bullying is ignored or goes unnoticed, and is underreported by students (Rigby, 2010). If teacher approaches to dealing with bullying are ineffective or if bullying is ignored or neglected in schools, the legal 'duty of care' towards students may be breached.

duty of care
The legal obligation to protect a child of immature age against injury

Supporting students: 'duty of care'

One of the critical responsibilities of teachers, administrators and others involved in the education of children is to be aware of our duty of care. Duty of care is a special responsibility of teachers. It involves

> the need of a child of immature age for protection against the conduct of others, or indeed of himself, which may cause him injury, coupled with the fact that, during school hours the child is beyond the control and protection of his parent and is placed under the control of the schoolmaster who is in a position to exercise authority over him and afford him, in the exercise of reasonable care, protection from injury.

Source: *Warren v Haines* (1986). Australian Torts reports 80-014: *Richards v State of Victoria* (1969) VR 136 (FC), cited by Watson (2003, p. 19).

As stated by Watson (2003), the teacher has a special duty to take reasonable steps to ensure the safety of students and this includes protection from all forms of harm or injury including physical, emotional or psychological harm and injury. While teachers cannot always prevent harm or injury, they should provide adequate supervision inside and outside the classroom. Duty of care also extends to duty on all school premises during school hours, and can extend outside school hours and outside the property (Watson, 2003, p. 19). This is particularly important in any discussion of classroom management and the management of student behaviour.

If schools or teachers have been found to neglect or breach their duty of care, legal consequences can follow. For example, in 2013 the Supreme Court of NSW Court of Appeal upheld a judgment that a school had breached its duty of care toward a student by failing to 'take reasonable steps to bring the bullying of the appellant by other students to an end' (*Oyston v St Patrick's College (No 2)* [2013] NSWCA 310 (23 September 2013)). The judgment noted that the school was obligated in performing its duty of care toward the student to ensure the student was protected from bullying, to take reasonable steps to identify the perpetrators and to take reasonable action to prevent repetition of the bullying by these perpetrators. The school was ordered to provide financial compensation to the former student.

Duty of care requires careful attention to the relevant laws, statutes and school procedures. Teachers should be aware that the States and Territories of Australia have a variety of legislative and mandatory procedures for reporting suspected cases of child abuse. These child-protection and notification guidelines vary from State to State and change from time to time. The National Safe Schools documentation provides a comprehensive breakdown of responsibilities across the States and Territories of Australia (see the reference to this documentation in the websites listed at the end of this chapter).

It is also important for teachers and administrators to be aware that the fact that bullying or aggression may be covert or 'hidden' does not release a school or teacher from their legal obligations or duty of care. Many alleged assaults have occurred in school toilets or other sites that cannot easily be supervised. As such, schools need to develop procedures to ensure adequate supervision, including supervision of all school areas. Similarly, the National Safe Schools Framework clearly states that cybersafety should be a key concern of teachers and schools, and it is important to recognise the risks associated with misuse of social media and other technologies (see more about cybersafety in Chapter 12). Teachers or schools should follow up suspicious use of technologies that affect students, whether occurring in or out of school time. Furthermore, many assaults and incidents of bullying go unreported to teachers. It is especially concerning that students can be unwilling to report assaults and bullying because they perceive that their teachers do not care, will not act, and do not understand bullying, it is particularly important for schools to take a systematic and comprehensive approach to managing bullying and aggression.

A whole-school approach

As described in Chapter 4, bullying and aggression are pervasive behaviours that affect many aspects of school culture and include multiple levels of student involvement. Teachers and schools may also be unaware of or underestimate the extent and prevalence of bullying and harassment. For all of these reasons, the **whole-school approach** to bullying is considered essential in the prevention and management of this behaviour. This is a comprehensive and systems-based strategy for considering the interaction of many features of the individual students, their school community and the wider community outside the school. Whole-school approaches should be supported by clear policies that encourage all members of the school community to take responsibility for the prevention of bullying (see Figure 14.6).

Table 14.7 outlines the components of a whole-school policy (McGrath & Noble, 2006; Rigby, 1996).

whole-school approach An approach that recognises that commitment and cooperation is needed from all members of the school community – teachers, students and parents – to prevent and address bullying

TABLE 14.7 A whole-school policy to address bullying

	POLICY	PROCEDURE FOR IMPLEMENTING POLICY
1	The school's stand in relation to bullying	A clear statement that bullying, harassment and violence is unacceptable. Use unambiguous, strong language and avoid being 'prim and proper' (Rigby, 1996)
2	A succinct definition of bullying ... with examples	A clear statement that bullying is an abuse of power. Defines the different types of bullying, with clear examples, and outlines the roles of the bullying student and the target of bullying. Avoid terms such as 'the victim' as this may suggest weakness; terms such as 'the bully' may also be demoralising (McGrath & Stanley, 2006)
3	Children's rights in respect to bullying	Clearly asserts the rights of all students to a safe environment and the right to be left alone and not harassed
4	The responsibilities of child witnesses to bullying	Defines the steps students can take if they witness bullying; encourages a sense of moral responsibility but provides safe and discreet mechanisms for students to report bullying
5	What the school will do to counter bullying	Defines the roles of teachers and school staff, and describes the actions teachers will take if they become aware of a bullying situation. This would include reference to the specific methods and approaches adopted by the school
6	Undertake to evaluate the effectiveness of the policy	Evaluate and report on the effectiveness of the school policy. Outline the strategies that will be used to evaluate effectiveness and identify the school staff responsible for managing this process

Recent meta-analyses of research evidence have shown that school-based programs only succeed in decreasing bullying by 20–23 per cent, while perceived victimisation only decreases by 17–20 per cent (Ttofi & Farrington, 2011). Other large-scale meta-evaluations have shown that to be effective, school intervention programs must be systemic or whole-school focused (Cantone et al., 2015). They must also be multicomponent: that is, they must address parents, children and teacher responses and beliefs (Vreeman & Carroll, 2007). Collectively, these research evaluations have shown that whole-school, multicomponent programs demonstrate greater effectiveness than stand-alone classroom curricula or social skills training alone.

FIGURE 14.6 A whole-school approach encourages peer support strategies.

THINK ABOUT

- Why are whole school approaches likely to be more effective?
- Why do schools need to evaluate their whole school approach and what might they need to consider in such an evaluation? (see Point 6 of the whole school policy)

A recent international example of a whole school approach can be seen in the KiVa anti-bullying program. KiVa was developed in Finland; the acronym KiVa stands for 'Kiusaamista Vastaan' which means 'against bullying'. The term also means 'nice' in Finnish (Salmivalli, 2010). In this school-wide approach, both prevention and intervention are considered with *universal* prevention strategies for all students, parents and the school community, along with '*indicated*' or *targeted* interventions for identified cases of bullying. This approach is similar to the use of tiered prevention and intervention levels that we saw applied in the school-wide positive behaviour support approach discussed in Chapter 5.

At the universal level in the KiVa program, all students receive training via classroom lessons and online activities, including computer games. Lessons address important social skills such as understanding emotions, group interactions, bystander behaviours and formation of friendships. Parents also receive information and training in a booklet. School-wide strategies include posters displayed around the school and special colourful KiVa vests worn by school staff when they are on playground duty. This reinforces the seriousness of the program and the fact that staff are vigilant in supervising playground behaviours.

At the indicated or targeted level, bullying incidents are carefully screened to see if they meet criteria for treatment within the program. A team of staff form the intervention group. One member of staff interviews the victim to gain an understanding and offer support. Further meetings are then held with the bullies, who are asked to commit to actions and behaviours to help the victimised child. Further follow-up meetings are held with the perpetrators and the victimised child. In a further indication of a school-wide approach, supportive peers with high social status are also recruited to support the victim (Hutchings & Clarkson, 2015).

This is a carefully designed program, with research evaluations in several European countries indicating the effectiveness of this approach. For example, in a large Finnish study, 98 per cent of victims felt their situation had improved (Garandeau, Poskiparta & Salmivalli, 2014).

The philosophy of intervention

Approaches to intervention differ along the philosophical lines described earlier in the discussion of orientations to classroom management. Just as orientations to classroom management vary from punitive, interventionist approaches to humanist, non-interventionist approaches, so too do approaches to bullying.

Punitive or 'traditional' approaches

punitive approaches
Based on the belief that the bully must be punished, and this punishment will stop them from bullying again

Punitive approaches are associated with a traditional 'crime and punishment' philosophy, in which sanctions and consequences are applied to breaking 'no bullying' rules (Rigby, 2010). Punitive approaches are commonly used; international surveys show that teachers resort to punishment for even mild cases of bullying behaviours (Rigby & Griffiths, 2011).

Many people instinctively favour these approaches because bullying is seen as repugnant and we may believe that violence must be punished, but as with other punitive classroom-management strategies, these approaches raise significant concerns. First, schools report that punitive strategies are less effective when bullying is subtle and covert, such as in relational bullying (McGrath & Stanley, 2006). Second, punishment can lead to resentment and hostility, and students who are punished can react with more subtle forms of aggression (Rigby, 2010). There is a valid concern that students might retaliate by bullying in more covert or hidden ways. Researchers from a wide range of countries report only moderate levels of success using punitive approaches (Rigby, 2010). In the case of an extreme form of punishment known as **zero tolerance approaches**, expulsion and suspension are widely regarded as ineffective (Skiba & Rausch, 2006). Strategies such as suspension and expulsion do not lead to improved behaviour for at-risk students and do not improve students' feelings of safety at school (American Psychological Association Zero Tolerance Task Force, 2008); and they can be disproportionately applied to minority students (Skiba, 2014). As illustrated in Box 14.8, researchers also have a duty of care to ensure that no harm is done in their method of intervention.

zero tolerance approaches
A response to bullying or other misbehaviour that reflects extreme intolerance for antisocial behaviours of any kind, allowing no compromise and usually resulting in strict punishment such as school expulsion

BOX 14.8 RESEARCH LINKS

CONSIDERING 'HARM' IN INTERVENTION APPROACHES

In designing the KiVa anti-bullying program, researchers Garandeau, Poskiparta and Salmivalli (2014) explain that they made a choice not to use harsh, punitive discipline or an approach known as restorative justice or mediation in their program. They noted that there is mounting evidence that extreme punitive measures do little to improve students' feelings of safety. They also point out the philosophy behind restorative justice is the idea that the offender or perpetrator must make 'restitution' or make repairs for the harm they have done. To achieve this, the restorative justice or mediation approaches typically require the victim to engage in mediation meetings with the offender. Herein lies the concern of the KiVa researchers. They explain that, if bullying is conceived as an abuse of power between the perpetrator and the vulnerable target of this aggressive behaviour, then any methods or approaches which seek to sustain interactions between the victim and perpetrator could be potentially harmful.

As you can see in the description of the KiVa program above, the researchers decided to intervene in bullying in a non-punitive but quite direct manner, in which perpetrators are asked to take action to improve the situation.

THINK ABOUT

- Why do you think students might feel less safe in schools where severe discipline is used for bullying behaviours?
- Do you think there are other types of conflicts or disagreements that might be suitable for mediation or restorative justice approaches?
- How do you think you would assess or monitor the victim's safety or comfort with the intervention strategy your school might use?

Although adults may want to punish bullies, serious consideration must be given to the legal principles of duty of care and ethical consideration for the wellbeing of children. If punishment and harsh discipline do not stop the bullying, lead to retaliation or do not treat or respond to the behavioural needs of the aggressive child, a school may be considered in breach of its legal duty of care. Similarly, there are serious ethical concerns to be considered if teachers or parents view punishment as 'retribution' against the aggressor, or worse, fail to consider appropriate treatment or help for either the aggressor or the victim. To learn more about approaches such as the restorative justice approach mentioned by the KiVa researchers, go to the CourseMate website shown here.

CourseMateExpress

Online resources
Go further: See more examples of anti-bullying programs on this text's website

Non-punitive approaches

Non-punitive approaches are more similar to the interactionalist approaches to classroom management and have the humanistic qualities of some non-interventionist approaches. However, they are also reactive strategies in which bullying is directly addressed. In these approaches, students involved in bullying are not blamed or punished but are asked to engage in problem solving and discussion of the problem (Rigby, 2010). Examples of non-punitive approaches include the KiVa program discussed above, the Support Group Approach (previously known as the 'no blame approach') (Robinson & Maines, 2008), the Method of Shared Concern (Pikas, 2002), as well as other restorative justice and mediation approaches (Rigby, 2010). Non-punitive approaches differ from punitive approaches in that they are not quick applications of consequences. As shown in Figure 14.7, these methods usually involve a series of interviews or meetings between the adult who is facilitating the method and the perpetrators, the victim or other bystanders.

The Method of Shared Concern illustrates several of the assumptions behind non-punitive approaches. For example, both this method and also the support group approach address bullying as group behaviour. This is supported by considerable evidence that bullying is not simply a dyadic interaction between a bully and a victim (see more about bullying roles and behaviours in Chapter 4). In fact, Swearer, Espelage and Napolitano (2009) argue that bullying is often a group process involving ringleaders and bystanders, who can sometimes encourage the ringleaders to bully but may act to prevent bullying if they are confident enough to defend a victim. Further, these approaches often adopt a treatment or therapeutic stance in the assumption that children who bully can be taught to understand that they have caused harm and can be encouraged to act responsibly.

Source: Shutterstock.com/Image Point Fr

FIGURE 14.7 In non-punitive approaches, teachers engage in serious talks with bullies and victims to elicit empathy and suggestions for resolving the situation.

In the Method of Shared Concern, the emphasis is on group bullying situations and reconstructing the individual's mindset about their involvement in bullying and their capacity to bring about change. These aims are achieved in a series of interviews and meetings with individual children as well as the whole group involved in the bullying interaction. Before taking any action, the situation is carefully investigated and the students involved identified. Interviews are initially held with each individual who has been suspected of being a ringleader or perpetrator. Each interview is conducted in a calm and non-accusative manner. The situation is outlined and the 'plight' or concern about the victimised child is explained. As also seen in the KiVa method, the suspected perpetrators are asked what they could do to improve the situation. The perceived perpetrators are *never* accused or blamed (as this can cause resentment and hostility) but it is made clear that the school is taking the situation seriously and the young person will be required to play a role in helping to remedy the situation. Further, it is also explained that they will be required to attend another interview within a week, to report back on their helpful actions. These interviews are held with each suspected perpetrator *before* the 'victim' is interviewed.

When the victim is interviewed the situation is explained and the victim is invited to tell their story. Reassurance and support is offered. The victim is reassured that the perpetrators or bullies are not 'in trouble' and are not being punished, but have been asked to think about what they could to improve the situation. This reassurance is provided to the victim to allay concerns about retaliation.

Following these initial individual interviews, the situation is carefully monitored. Interviews with each child are held again after one week; each individual is asked to describe what they have done to improve the situation and then positive feedback is given. Monitoring and checking in with the victim continues and the procedure is repeated a few weeks later with the whole group of perpetrators (minus the victim) to discuss and celebrate the progress made towards solving the problem. Eventually, if the victim wishes to participate, a whole-group meeting can occur in which everyone is given positive feedback about improvement in the situation. The emphasis in this final step is not so much to suggest that victims are equally responsible for bringing about change, but the interview is designed to give the victim the chance to speak or perhaps acknowledge their own role in the situation, such as being a provocative victim (Rigby, 2006). The interviewer seeks a commitment from each child that the behaviour has stopped and the situation has improved. It is made clear the school will continue to monitor their behaviour. Because of the higher level of responsibility and perspective-taking assumed of young people in the method, Pikas (1992) recommended the approach generally be used with children nine years and older. This suits the age group in which bullying behaviours peak.

An investigation of the effectiveness of the method of shared concern was conducted in 17 Australian schools (Rigby & Griffiths, 2011). The evidence for specific strategies in the method was closely studied. For example, the investigators assessed whether or not the perpetrators responded positively to the initial explanation of the plight of the victim. In all cases, the perpetrators acknowledged that the situation had caused distress, and most indicated they were concerned about the victim and would help in some way by stopping teasing or restraining their peer group members from acting hurtfully. In the follow-up interviews, the majority of perpetrators had carried out the proposed actions. The target or victim of the bullying reported that bullying or harassment had stopped in all but two of the cases (an 88 per cent success rate). Similarly, most perpetrators reported they felt they had changed and were pleased or proud of their actions. Teachers reported they would use the method again.

SUMMARY OF APPROACHES TO BULLYING

Each of the approaches and interventions described here has received at least some research support and has also been based in evidence or strong application of theory of behavioural change. As stated in relation to classroom-management strategies, it is unlikely that any single approach to bullying will be satisfactory for all cases of bullying, or for all contexts in which bullying, harassment and violence might occur. Although many believe the punitive and non-punitive approaches to bullying are incompatible, Garandeau et al. (2014) report that there is very little research that has compared the two approaches. Rigby (2006) also reports that there are schools that do manage to combine both approaches. In these instances, non-punitive approaches are used with less serious cases, while punitive approaches are used for serious cases and when cases cannot be solved with non-blaming approaches.

The failure of anti-bullying approaches to solve all bullying problems is one of their perceived weaknesses. As such, the large scale meta-evaluations as well as the National Safe Schools Framework advocate a comprehensive approach in which students, teachers and parents are informed and educated, and all members of the school community have rights and responsibilities to prevent bullying, harassment and violence. One aspect of managing a safe school is the creation of appropriate policies, procedures and strategies for dealing with incidents of bullying, harassment or violence. A whole-school policy is advocated, which encompasses preventive and reactive strategies. Teachers have a key responsibility known as a 'duty of care' to protect students from harm, and this relates to the way in which we respond to both bullies and victims.

CONCLUDING COMMENTS

As suggested by ecological theory, classrooms and schools are complex environments. Within this context, the creation of a positive learning environment requires the establishment of quality teacher–student relationships and a supportive classroom climate, and practising pedagogies and organisational strategies that support student learning and engagement. As a teacher, your task is also to find a philosophical approach to classroom management that is congruent with the goals of creating an effective learning environment, is evidence-based and that will support the development and learning of students from different backgrounds and life experiences. The challenge of learning how to manage student behaviour and provide a safe and effective learning environment is one that even experienced teachers can find daunting. When the challenge is met successfully, learning becomes a satisfying and enjoyable experience. Then, the classroom has an atmosphere of cooperation, balance and mutual trust, and teachers are positive and enthusiastic about their teaching.

STUDY TOOLS

ONLINE STUDY RESOURCES

COURSEMATE EXPRESS

Visit http://login.cengagebrain.com and use the access code that comes with this book for 12 months' access to the student resources for this text.

The CourseMate Express website contains a range of resources and study tools for this chapter, including:

- a **self-check quiz**

- **crosswords**, **flashcards** and a **glossary** to help you revise the key terms from this chapter
- the **Go further** materials and **interactive activity** mentioned in the chapter.

CHAPTER REVIEW

- The creation of a PLE through classroom management is best approached with a comprehensive model that includes the development of supportive teacher–student relationships, the careful organisation of instruction, attention to group management, the development of self-regulation and social skills in students, and the use of appropriate interventions to manage behaviour problems.

- Classroom teachers need to identify their own set of beliefs about how children learn and develop, and be aware of how these beliefs can influence their practice.

- Philosophies of classroom management hold very different implications for the creation of a PLE: interventionist, interactionalist and non-interventionist. Each involves a different balance in the relative power of teachers and students over what happens in a classroom.

- Most of the discipline difficulties teachers encounter in their classrooms involve minor disruptions such as talking out of turn, being out of seat or hindering other children. Serious behaviours, such as physical violence, are rarer.

- Procedures for responding to behaviour vary according to different orientations and teacher philosophies, and include traditional approaches in which the teacher exercises strict control through the use of praise and punishment, as well as a focus on developing student control and choice as advocated in more recent theories.

- Teachers have a duty of care for their students that should not be infringed.

- Schools must implement the appropriate strategies to prevent and respond to bullying, harassment and violence.

- Strategies used to combat bullying include punitive and non-punitive approaches such as sanctions and punishments, discussion and counselling, social-skills training, conflict resolution and peer mediation.

PUTTING IT TOGETHER

Making links between 'creating a positive classroom' and material in other chapters

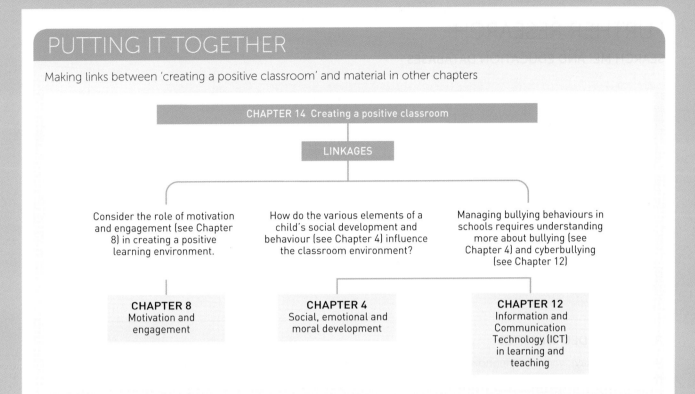

QUESTIONS AND ACTIVITIES FOR SELF-ASSESSMENT AND DISCUSSION

1 Identify some of the characteristics of classroom ecology that influence teaching and learning. What can teachers do to control the effects of these factors on classroom activities?

2 Set up a debate with your tutorial group on the topic: 'Disruptive and inappropriate behaviour at school is the product of a child's home background'.

3 Identify some of the main philosophies of classroom management. What are the key factors that distinguish these different models? In what ways are the models different?

4 Ask some teachers to identify the type of strategies they use to manage their classroom. Can you identify the type of management philosophy each teacher is using? To what extent are these philosophies eclectic?

5 Outline a whole-school approach to preventing and managing bullying, harassment and violence in schools.

FURTHER RESEARCH

SEARCH ME! AND EDUCATION DATABASES

Explore Search Me! education for articles relevant to this chapter. Fast and convenient, Search Me! education is updated daily and provides you with 24-hour access to full-text articles from hundreds of scholarly and popular journals, ebooks and newspapers, including *The Australian* and *The New York Times*. Log in to Search Me! through http://login.cengagebrain.com and use the search terms listed here as a starting point:

- behaviour management
- bullying
- classroom management
- discipline
- disruptive behaviour
- harassment.

Combining these terms with words such as 'schools', 'students', 'learners' and 'classrooms' (as in 'assessment and schools') will limit your search to material related to schools and young students. (Don't forget to search for 'behavior' as well as 'behaviour'.)

You can also use these terms to explore databases such as ERIC, PsycINFO and the Australian Education Index.

Search Me!

RECOMMENDED WEBSITES

Bullying. No Way!: www.bullyingnoway.com.au

Kids Helpline Australia on bullying: www.kidshelp.com.au/kids/information/stories/bullying

National Safe Schools Framework: www.safeschoolshub.edu.au/documents/nationalsafeschoolsframework.pdf

New Zealand Ministry of Education: www.minedu.govt.nz

RECOMMENDED READING

De Nobile, J., Lyons, G. & Arthur-Kelly, M. (2017). *Positive learning environments: Creating and maintaining productive classrooms*. Melbourne: Cengage Learning.

Emmer, E. T. & Sabornie, E. J. (Eds). (2015). *Handbook of classroom management*. Oxford: Routledge.

Evertson, C. M. & Emmer, E. T. (2017). *Classroom management for elementary teachers*. Upper Saddle River, NJ: Pearson.

REFERENCES

Adams, R. & Biddle, B. (1970). *Realities of teaching: Explorations with videotape.* New York: Holt, Rinehart & Winston.

American Psychological Association Zero Tolerance Task Force (Lead Author). (2008). Are zero tolerance policies effective in the schools? An evidentiary review and recommendations. *American Psychologist, 63,* 852–862.

Anderman, L. H. & Leake, V. S. (2007). The interface of school and family in meeting the belonging needs of young adolescents. In S. B. Mertens, V. A. Anfara & M. M. Caskey (Eds). *The young adolescent and the middle school.* (pp. 163–82). Charlotte, NC: Information Age Publishing.

Arends, R. (2004). *Learning to teach.* Toronto: McGraw Hill.

Armstrong, M. & Thorsborne, M. (2006). Restorative responses to bullying. In H. McGrath & T. Noble (Eds), *Bullying solutions: Evidence-based approaches for Australian schools.* Sydney: Pearson Education.

Arthur-Kelly, M., Lyons, G., Butterfield, N. & Gordon, C. (2006). *Classroom management: Creating positive learning environments* (2nd ed.). Melbourne: Thomson Learning. (p. 157)

Babad, E. (1995). The 'teacher's pet' phenomenon, students' perceptions of teachers' differential behavior, and students' morale. *Journal of Educational Psychology, 87*(3), 361–74.

Babad, E. (2005). Guessing teachers' differential treatment of high-and-low-achievers from thin slices of their public lecturing behavior. *Journal of Nonverbal Behavior, 29,* 125–34.

Babad, E., Avni-Babad, D. & Rosenthal, R. (2003). Teachers' brief nonverbal behaviors in defined instructional situations can predict students' evaluations. *Journal of Educational Psychology, 95,* 553–62.

Babad, E., Bernieri, F. & Rosenthal, R. (1991). Students as judges of teachers' verbal and nonverbal behavior. *American Educational Research Journal, 28,* 211–34.

Balson, M. (1992). *Understanding classroom behaviour* (3rd ed.). Melbourne: ACER.

Bauman, S. & Del Rio, A. (2006). Preservice teachers' responses to bullying scenarios: Comparing physical, verbal, and relational bullying. *Journal of Educational Psychology, 98*(1), 219–31.

Beaman, R., Wheldall, K. & Kemp, C. (2007). Recent research on troublesome classroom behaviour: A review. *Australasian Journal of Special Education, 31*(1), 45–60.

Beattie, J., Jordan, L. & Algozzine, B. (2006). *Making inclusion work: Effective practices for ALL teachers.* Corwin Press/Sage Publications. Thousand Oaks, CA.

Beck, J. & Horne, D. (1992). A whole school implementation of the Stop, Think, Do! Social skills training program at Minerva

Special School. In B. Willis & J. Izard (Eds), *Student behavior problems: Directions, perspectives and expectations.* Hawthorn, Vic.: Australian Council for Educational Research.

Ben-Yehuda, S., Leyser, Y. & Last, U. (2010). Teacher educational beliefs and sociometric status of special educational needs (SEN) students in inclusive classrooms. *International Journal of Inclusive Education, 14*(1), 17–34.

Bohn, C. M., Roehrig. A. D. & Pressley, M. (2004). The first days of school in the classrooms of two more effective and four less effective primary-grades teachers. *The Elementary School Journal, 104*(4), 269–85.

Bolognini, M., Plancherel, B., Bettschari, W. & Halpon, O. (1996). Self-esteem and mental health in early adolescence: Development and gender differences. *Journal of Adolescence, 19,* 233–45.

Brophy, J. (1988). Research linking teacher behavior to student achievement: Potential implications for instruction of Chapter I students. *Educational Psychologist, 23,* 235–312.

Brophy, J. (2006). History of research on classroom management. In C. M. Evertson & C. S. Weinstein (Eds), *Handbook of classroom management: Research, practice, and contemporary issues* (pp. 17–43). Mahwah, NJ: Lawrence Erlbaum Associates.

Brouwers, A. & Tomic, W. (1999). Teacher burnout, perceived self efficacy in classroom management and student disruptive behaviour in secondary education. *Curriculum and Teaching, 14,* 7–26.

Burden, P. R. (1995). *Classroom management and discipline.* White Plains, NY: Longman.

Cantone, E., Piras, A. P., Vellante, M., Preti, A., Danielsdóttir, S., D'Aloja, E., Bhugra, D. (2015). Interventions on bullying and cyberbullying in schools: a systematic review. *Clinical Practice and Epidemiology in Mental Health: CP & EMH.* 2015;11(M4) Suppl 1: 58–76.

Cameron, C., McDonald-Connor, C. & Morrison, F. (2005). Effects of variation in teacher organization on classroom functioning. *Journal of School Psychology, 43*(1), 61–86.

Canter, L. (1996). First the rapport – then the rules. *Learning, 24*(5), 12–14.

Canter, L. & Canter, M. (1981). *Assertive discipline follow-up guidebook.* Los Angeles: Canter & Associates.

Canter, L. & Canter, M. (1992). *Lee Canter's assertive discipline: Positive behaviour management for today's classroom.* Santa Monica: Lee Canter & Associates.

Canter, L. & Canter, M. (2001). *Assertive discipline: A take-charge approach for today's educator.* Seal Beach, CA: Canter & Associates.

Carter, K. & Doyle, W. (2006). Classroom management in early childhood and elementary classrooms. In C. M. Evertson & C. S. Weinstein (Eds), *Handbook of classroom management: Research, practice, and contemporary issues* (pp. 373–406). Hillsdale, NJ: Erlbaum.

Chiu, S.-I., Lee, J. & Liang, T. (2013). Does the teacher's pet phenomenon inevitably cause classroom conflict? Comparative viewpoints of three pet-student groups. *School Psychology International, 34*(1), 3–16.

Chung, H., Elias, M. & Schneider, K. (1998). Patterns of individual adjustment changes during the middle school transition. *Journal of School Psychology, 36,* 83–101.

Corbett, D. & Wilson, B. (2002). What urban students say about good teaching. *Educational Leadership, 60*(1), 18–22.

Crick, N. R. & Dodge, K. A. (1994). A review and reformulation of social information-processing mechanisms in children's social adjustment. *Psychological Bulletin, 115,* 74–101.

Crockenberg, V. (1982). Assertive discipline: A dissent. *California Journal of Teacher Education, 9*(4), 59–74.

Curwin, R. L. & Mendler, A. N. (1989). We repeat, let the buyer beware: A response to Canter. *Educational Leadership, 46*(6), 83.

Datta, P., Cornell, D., & Huang, F. (2017). The toxicity of bullying by teachers and other school staff. *School Psychology Review, 46*(4), pp. 335-348. https://doi.org/10.17105/SPR-2017-0001.V46-4

Day, P., Murphy, A. & Cooke, J. (1999). Traffic light lessons: Problem solving skills with adolescents. *Community Practitioner, 72*(10), 322–4.

Donohue, K. M., Perry, K. E. & Weinstein, R. S. (2003). Teachers' classroom practices and children's rejection by their peers. *Journal of Applied Developmental Psychology, 24*(1), 91–118.

Doyle, W. (1986). Classroom organisation and management. In M. C. Wittrock (Ed.), *Handbook of research on teaching* (3rd ed., pp. 392–431). New York: Macmillan.

Doyle, W. (2006). Ecological approaches to classroom management. In C. M. Evertson & C. S. Weinstein (Eds), *Handbook of classroom management: Research, practice, and contemporary issues* (pp. 92–126). Hillsdale, NJ: Lawrence Erlbaum Associates.

Dreikurs, R. (1968). *Psychology in the classroom. A manual for teachers* (2nd ed.). New York: Harper & Row.

Dreikurs, R. & Cassel, P. (1990). *Discipline without tears* (2nd ed.). New York: Dutton.

Dreikurs, R. & Grey, L. (1968). *A new approach to discipline: Logical consequences.* New York: Hawthorne.

Dreikurs, R., Grunwald, B. & Pepper, F. C. (1982). *Maintaining sanity in the classroom: Classroom management techniques* (1st ed.). New York: Harper & Row.

Dreikurs, R., Grunwald, B. & Pepper, F. C. (1998). *Maintaining sanity in the classroom: Classroom management techniques* (2nd ed.). Washington, DC: Taylor and Francis.

Eccles, J. S. & Midgley, C. (1989). Stage/environment fit: Developmentally appropriate classrooms for young adolescents. In R. Ames & C. Ames (Eds), *Research on motivation and education: Goals and cognitions* (Vol. 3, pp. 139–86). New York: Academic Press.

Eccles, J. S., Midgley, C., Wigfield, A., Buchanan, C. M., Reuman, D., Flanagan, C., et al. (1993a). Development during adolescence: The impact of stage-environment fit on adolescents' experiences in schools and families. *American Psychologist, 48*(2), 90–101.

Eccles, J. S., Wigfield, A., Midgley, C., Reuman, D., MacIver, D. & Feldlaufer, H. (1993b). Negative effects of traditional middle schools on students' motivation. *The Elementary School Journal, 93*(5), 553–74.

Edwards, C. H. (1997). *Classroom discipline and management* (2nd ed.). Upper Saddle River, NJ: Prentice Hall.

Edwards, C. H. & Watts, V. (2008). *Classroom discipline and management: Second Australasian edition.* Milton, Qld: Wiley and Sons.

Egeberg, H. M., McConney, A. & Price, A. (2016). Classroom management and national professional standards for teachers: a review of the literature on theory and practice. *Australian Journal of Teacher Education, 41*(7). http://dx.doi.org/10.14221/ajte.2016v41n7.1

Egeberg, H. & McConney, A. (2017). What do students believe about effective classroom management? A mixed-methods investigation in Western Australian high schools. *Australian Educational Researcher 45*(2), 195–216.

Elias, M. J. & Schwab, Y. (2006). From compliance to responsibility: Social and emotional learning and classroom management. In C. M. Evertson & C. S. Weinstein (Eds), *Handbook of classroom management: Research, practice, and contemporary issues* (pp. 309–42). Hillsdale, NJ: Erlbaum.

Emmer, E. T. & Gerwels, M. C. (2002). Cooperative learning in elementary classrooms: Teaching practices and lesson characteristics. *The Elementary School Journal, 103*, 75–92.

Espelage, D., Holt, M. & Poteat, P. (2010). The school context, bullying, and victimization. In J. L. Meece and J. S. Eccles (Eds), *Handbook of research on schools, schooling, and human development* (pp. 146–60). New York: Routledge.

Evertson, C. M. & Emmer, E. T. (2009). *Classroom management for elementary teachers.* Upper Saddle River, NJ: Pearson.

Evertson, C. M., Emmer, E. T. & Worsham, M. E. (2000). *Classroom management for elementary teachers* (5th ed.). Boston: Allyn and Bacon.

Evertson, C. M. & Weinstein, C. S. (Eds). (2006). *Handbook of classroom management: Research, practice, and contemporary issues.* Hillsdale, NJ: Erlbaum.

Farmer, T. W., McAuliffe Lines, M. & Hamm, J. V. (2011). Revealing the invisible hand: the role of teachers in children's peer experiences. *Journal of Applied Developmental Psychology, 32*, 247–256. http://dx.doi.org/10.1016/j.appdev.2011.04.006

Fenning, P. & Rose, J. (2007). Overrepresentation of African American students in exclusionary discipline: The role of school policy. *Urban Education, 42*, 536–59.

Fuller, A. (2006). A resilience-based approach to helping victims and their families. In H. McGrath & T. Noble (Eds), *Bullying solutions: Evidence-based approaches to bullying in Australian schools* (pp. 161–74). Sydney: Pearson Education.

Garandeau, C. F., Poskiparta, E., & Salmivalli, C. (2014). Tackling acute cases of school bullying in the KiVa anti-bullying program: A comparison of two approaches. *Journal of Abnormal Child Psychology, 42*, 981–991.

Glasser, W. (1981). *Stations of the mind: New directions for reality therapy.* New York: Harper & Row.

Glasser, W. (1992). *The quality school: Managing students without coercion* (2nd ed.). New York: Harper-Collins.

Glasser, W. (1998). *Choice theory in the classroom.* New York: HarperPerennial.

Godfrey, J., Partington, G., Harslett, M. & Richer, K. (2001). Attitudes of Aboriginal students to schooling. *Australian Journal of Teacher Education, 26*(1), 33–9.

Good, T. (2014). What do we know about how teachers influence student performance on standardized tests: And why do we know so little about other student outcomes? *Teachers College Record, 116*(1).

Good, T. L. & Brophy, J. E. (1972). Behavioral expression of teacher attitude. *Journal of Educational Psychology, 63*(6), 617–24.

Good, T. L. & Brophy, J. E. (1974). Changing teacher and student behavior: An empirical investigation. *Journal of Educational Psychology, 66*, 390–405.

Good, T. L. & Brophy, J. E. (2003). *Looking in classrooms* (9th ed.). Boston: Allyn and Bacon.

Gordon, T. (1974). *T.E.T.: Teacher Effectiveness Training.* New York: Wyden.

Gordon, C., Arthur, M. & Butterfield, N. (1996). *Promoting positive behaviour: An Australian guide to classroom management.* Melbourne: Nelson.

Graham, L. J. (2012). Disproportionate overrepresentation of Indigenous students in New South Wales government special schools. *Cambridge Journal of Education, 41*(4), 163–76.

Guderjahn, L., Gold, A., Stadler, G. & Gawrilow, C. (2013). Self-regulation strategies support children with ADHD to overcome symptom-related behavior in the classroom. *Attention Deficit Hyperactive Disorder, 5*(4), 397–407.

Helmke, A., Schneider, W. & Weinert, F. E. (1986). Quality of instruction and classroom learning outomes: Results of the German contribution to the classroom environment study of the IEA. *Teaching and Teacher Education, 2*, 1–18.

Hutchings, J. & Clarkson, S. (2015). Introducing and piloting the KiVa bullying prevention programme in the UK. *Educational and Child Psychology 32*(1), 49–61.

Infantino, J. & Little, E. (2005). Students' perceptions of classroom behaviour problems and the effectiveness of different disciplinary methods. *Educational Psychology, 25*, 491–508.

Johnson, D. W. & Johnson, R. T. (1996). Conflict resolution and peer mediation programs in elementary and secondary schools: A review of the research. *Review of Educational Research, 66*, 459–506.

Jones, F. H. (1987). *Positive classroom discipline.* New York: McGraw-Hill.

Jones, V. F. & Jones, L. S. (1998). *Comprehensive classroom management: Creating communities of support and solving problems* (5th ed.). Boston: Allyn and Bacon.

Jones, V. F. & Jones, L. S. (2007). *Comprehensive classroom management: Creating communities of support and solving problems* (8th ed.). Toronto, ON: Pearson.

Jussim, L. & Harber, K. D. (2005). Teacher expectations and self-fulfilling prophecies: Knowns and unknowns, resolved and unresolved controversies. *Personality and Social Psychology Review, 9*(2), 131–55.

Juvonen, J., Espinoza, G. & Knifsend, C. (2012). The role of peer relationships in student academic and extracurricular engagement. In S. L. Christenson, A. L. Reschly & C. Wylie (Eds), *Handbook of research on student engagement* (pp. 387–401). New York: Springer Science+Business Media.

Kagan, S. (1992). *Cooperative learning: Resources for teachers.* San Juan Capistrano, CA: Resources for Teachers.

Kennedy-Lewis, B. L. (2012). What happens after students are expelled? Understanding teachers' successes and failures at one alternative middle school. *Teachers College Record, 114*(12), 1–38.

Kohn, A. (1996). *Beyond discipline: From compliance to community.* Alexandria, VA: Association for Supervision and Curriculum Development.

Koki, S., van Broekhuizen, L. D. & Uehara, D. L. (2000). *Prevention and intervention for effective classroom organization and management in pacific classrooms.* Honolulu: Pacific Resources for Teaching and Learning, Honolulu. Retrieved from www.prel.org/products/Products/Prevention-intervention.pdf

Kounin, J. (1970). *Discipline and group management in classrooms*. New York: Holt, Rinehart & Winston.

Lewis, R., Romi. S., Xing, Q. & Katz, Y. (2005). A comparison of teachers' classroom discipline in Australia, China and Israel. *Teaching and Teacher Education, 21* (2005), 729–41.

Little, E. (2005). Secondary school teachers' perceptions of students' problem behaviors. *Educational Psychology: An International Journal of Experimental Educational Psychology, 25*(4), 369–77.

Maines, B. & Robinson, G. (1992). *Michael's story: The 'no blame' approach*. Bristol: Lame Duck Publishing.

Martin, M. (1987). Managing inappropriate behaviour in the classroom. In J. Ward, S. Bochner, Y. Center, L. Outhred & M. Pieterse (Eds), *Educating children with special needs in regular classrooms: An Australian perspective*. Sydney: Special Education Centre, Macquarie University.

McGrath, H. & Noble, T. (Eds). (2006). *Bullying solutions: Evidence-based approaches to bullying in Australian schools*. Sydney: Pearson Education.

McGrath, H. & Stanley, M. (2006). A safe school (anti-bullying) template for schools. In H. McGrath & T. Noble (Eds), *Bullying solutions: Evidence based approaches to bullying in Australian schools* (pp. 229–78). Sydney: Pearson Education.

McNeely, C. A., Nonnemaker, J. M. & Blum, R. W. (2002). Promoting School connectedness: Evidence from the National Longitudinal Study of Adolescent Health. *Journal of School Health, 72*(4), 138–46.

McPherson, D. (2007). Exploring beliefs in teacher education. Paper presented to Centre for Research in Pedagogy and Practice Conference, Singapore, June.

Miller, A., Ferguson, E. & Byrne, J. (2000). Pupils' causal attributions for difficult classroom behaviour. *British Journal of Educational Psychology, 70*, 85–96.

Morrison, B. (2002). Bullying and victimisation in schools: A restorative justice approach. *Trends & Issues in Crime and Criminal Justice: 219*. Australian Institute of Criminology. Retrieved from www.aic.gov.au/documents/0/B/7/%7B0B70E4C9-D631-40D2-B1FA-622D4E25BA57%7Dti219.pdf

Munns, G. (1998). They just can't hack that: Aboriginal students, their teachers and responses to schools and classrooms. In G. Partington (Ed.), *Perspectives on Aboriginal and Torres Strait Islander Education*, (pp. 171–89). Katoomba, NSW: Social Science Press.

National Institute of Child Health and Human Development, Early Child Care Research Network (NICHHD, ECCRN). (2005). A day in third grade: Classroom quality, teacher, and student behaviors. *Elementary School Journal, 105*(4), 377–94.

Nimmo, J. (1993). Social competence: A pilot study of a cognitive-behavioral social skills program with comparisons of outcomes for inclass and withdrawal groups. Unpublished M.Ed. Thesis, Queensland University.

NSW Department of Education and Communities. (2013). *Suspensions and expulsions 2013*. Retrieved from www.det.nsw.edu.au/media/downloads/about-us/statistics-and-research/key-statistics-andreports/long-suspension-expulsions-2013.pdf

O'Toole, J. & Burton, B. (2005). Acting against conflict and bullying: The Brisbane Dracon Project 1996–2004 – Emergent findings and outcomes. *Research in Drama Education, 10*(3), 269–83.

Olweus, D. (1993). *Bullying in schools: What we know we can do*. Oxford, UK: Blackwell.

Peterson, L. (1994). Stop and think learning: Motivating learning in social groups and individuals. In M. Tainsh & J. Izard (Eds), *Widening horizons: New challenges, directions and achievements. Selected papers from the national conference on behaviour management and behaviour change of children and youth with emotional and behaviour problems* (pp. 70–83). Melbourne: ACER.

Peterson, L. & Adderley, A. (2002). *Stop Think Do Social Skills Training: Primary Years-Ages 8–12*. Melbourne: ACER Press.

Pianta, R. C. (2006). Classroom management and relationships between students and teachers: Implications for research and practice. In C. M. Evertson & C. S. Weinstein (Eds), *Handbook of classroom management: Research, practice, and contemporary issues*. (pp. 685–710). Hillsdale, NJ: Erlbaum.

Pikas, A. (2002). New developments of shared concern method. *School Psychology International, 23*(3), 307–26.

Porter, L. (2007). *Student behaviour: Theory and practice for teachers*. St Leonards, NSW: Allen & Unwin.

Randall, P. (1996). *A community approach to bullying*. Staffordshire: Trentham Books.

Render, G. F., Padilla, J. N. M. & Krank, H. M. (1989). What research really shows about assertive discipline. *Educational Leadership, 46*(6), 72–5.

Resnick, M. D., Bearman, P. S., Blum, R. W., Bauman, K. E., Harris, K. M., Jones, J., Tabor, J., Beuhring, T., Sieving, R. E., Shew, M., Ireland, M., Bearinger, L. H. & Udry, J. R. (1997). Protecting adolescents from harm: Findings from the national longitudinal study on adolescent health. *The Journal of the American Medical Association, 278*(10), 823–32.

Rigby, K. (2006). An overview of approaches to managing bully/victim problems. In H. McGrath & T. Noble (Eds), *Bullying solutions* (pp. 149–60). Sydney: Pearson Education.

Rigby, K. (2010). *Bullying interventions in schools: Six basic approaches*. Camberwell: ACER.

Rigby, K. & Griffiths, C. (2011). Addressing cases of bullying through the Method of Shared Concern. *School Psychology International 32*(3) 345–357, DOI: 10.1177/0143034311402148

Rigby, K. (2007). *Bullying in schools and what to do about it*. Melbourne: ACER.

Rigby, K. & Barrington Thomas, E. (2002). *How Australian schools are responding to the problem of peer victimisation in schools*. Canberra: Criminology Research Council.

Robinson, G., & Maines, B. (2008). *Bullying: A complete guide to the support group method*. London: Sage.

Rogers, B. (2003). *Effective supply teaching: Behaviour management, classroom discipline and colleague support*. London: Paul Chapman.

Rogers, W. A. (1989). *Making a discipline plan: Developing classroom management skills*. Melbourne: Nelson.

Rogers, W. A. (1998). *'You know the fair rule' and much more: Strategies for making the hard job of discipline and behaviour management in school easier*. Melbourne: ACER.

Romi, S., Lewis, R., Roache, J. & Riley, P. (2011) The Impact of Teachers' Aggressive Management Techniques on Students' Attitudes to Schoolwork, *The Journal of Educational Research, 104*(4), 231–240.

Rosenshine, B. (1980). How time is spent in elementary classrooms. In C. Denham & A. Lieberman (Eds), *Time to learn* (pp. 107–26). Washington, DC: National Institute of Education.

Rubie-Davies, C., Hattie, J. & Hamilton, R. (2006). Expecting the best for students: Teacher expectations and academic outcomes. *British Journal of Educational Psychology, 76*(3), 429–44.

Salmivalli, C. (2010). Bullying and the peer group: A review. *Aggression and Violent Behavior, 15*(2), 112–120

Saltmarsh, S. (2005). Disrupting dominant discourses of private schooling. Paper presented at the Australian Association of Research in Education Conference, Parramatta, December. Retrieved from www.aare.edu.au/05pap/sal05126.pdf

Santoro, N., Reid, J., Crawford, L. & Simpson, L. (2011). Teaching Indigenous children: Listening to and learning from Indigenous teachers. *Australian Journal of Teacher Education, 36*(10). Retrieved from http://dx.doi.org/10.14221/ajte.2011v36n10.2

Sheets, R. & Gay, G. (1996). Student perceptions of disciplinary conflict in ethnically diverse classrooms. *NASSP Bulletin, 80*(580), 84–94.

Sheets, R. H. (1996). Urban classroom conflict: Student–teacher perception: Ethnic integrity, solidarity, and resistance. *The Urban Review, 8*, 165–83.

Sheets, R. H. (2002). You're just a kid that's there: Chicano perception of disciplinary events. *Journal of Latinos and Education, 1*(2), 105–22.

Silberman, M. L. (1969). Behavioral expression of teachers' attitudes toward elementary school students. *Journal of Educational Psychology, 60*, 402–7.

Simonsen, B. & Sugai, G. (2009). School-wide positive behavior support. In A. Akin-Little, S. G. Steven, M. A. Bray & T. J. Kehle (Eds), *Behavioral interventions in schools: Evidence-based positive strategies* (pp. 125–40). Washington, DC: American Psychological Association.

Skiba, R. (2014) The failure of zero tolerance, *Reclaiming Children and Youth,* 22 (4), 27-33

Skiba, R. J. & Rausch, M. K. (2006). School disciplinary systems: Alternatives to suspension and expulsion. In G. Bear & K. Minke (Eds), *Children's needs III: Understanding and addressing the developmental needs of children.* Washington, DC: National Association of School Psychologists.

Smith, P. K. (2001). Should we blame the bullies?, *The Psychologist, 14*(2), 61.

Smith, P. K. & Madsen, M. (1997). *A follow-up survey of the DfE anti-bullying pack for schools: Its use, and the development of anti-bullying work in schools.* London: DfEE.

Standing Council on School Education and Early Childhood. (2013). *National safe schools framework.* Retrieved from www.safeschoolshub.edu.au/documents/nationalsafeschoolsframework.pdf

Stright, A. & Supplee, L. (2002). Children's self-regulatory behaviors during teacher-directed, seat-work, and small-group instructional contexts. *The Journal of Educational Research, 95*(4), 235–46.

Theberge, S. K. & Karan, O. C. (2004). Six factors inhibiting the use of peer mediation in a junior high school. *Professional School Counseling, 7*(4), 283–90. Published by American School Counselor Association.

Trusz, S. (2017) The teacher's pet phenomenon 25 years on. *Social Psychology of Education, 20,* 707. https://doi.org/10.1007/s11218-017-9388-8

Ttofi, M. M., & Farrington, D. P. (2011). Effectiveness of school-based programs to reduce bullying: a systematic and meta-analytic review. *Journal of Experimental Criminology, 7,* 27–56

Twemlow, S. W. & Fonagy, P. (2005). The prevalence of teachers who bully students in schools with differing levels of behavioral problems. *American Journal of Psychiatry, 162*(12), 2387–9.

Twemlow, S. W., Fonagy, P., Sacco, F. C. & Brethour, J. R. Jr. (2006). Teachers who bully students: A hidden trauma. *International Journal of Social Psychiatry, 52*(3), 187–98.

Van der Kley, M. & Burn, W. (1993). *The positive playground: How to improve school discipline and enhance school tone.* Christchurch: M. Van der Kley.

Vile Junod, R. E., DuPaul, G. J., Jitendra, A. K., Volpe, R. J. & Cleary, K. S. (2006). Classroom observations of students with and without ADHD: Differences across academic subjects and types of engagement. *Journal of School Psychology, 44,* 87–104.

Vreeman, R., & Carroll, A. (2007). A systematic review of school-based interventions to prevent bullying. *Archives of Pediatrics & Adolescent Medicine, 161*(1), 78–88.

Watson, P. (2003). The supposed safe haven of schools: Bullying and the law. *Plaintiff, 57,* 17–22.

Wentzel, K. R. (2006). A social motivation perspective for classroom management. In. C. M. Evertson & C. S. Weinstein (Eds), *Handbook of classroom management: Research, practice, and contemporary issues* (pp. 619–44). Hillsdale, NJ: Erlbaum.

Wentzel, K. R. & Brophy, J. E. (2014). *Motivating students to learn.* New York: Routledge.

Wigfield, A. & Eccles, J. S. (1994). Children's competence beliefs, achievement values, and general self-esteem: Change across elementary and middle school. *Journal of Early Adolescence, 14*(2), 107–38.

Willis, S. & Brophy, J. (1974). Origins of teachers' attitudes toward young children. *Journal of Educational Psychology, 66,* 520–9.

Wolfgang, C. H. (1995). *Solving discipline problems: Methods and models for today's teachers* (3rd ed.). Boston: Allyn & Bacon.

Wolfgang, C. H. (2001). *Solving discipline and classroom management problems.* New York: John Wiley & Sons.

Woolfolk Hoy, A. & Weinstein, C. S. (2006). Student and teacher perspectives on classroom management. In C. M. Evertson & C. S. Weinstein (Eds), *Handbook of classroom management: Research, practice, and contemporary issues* (pp. 181–219). Hillsdale, NJ: Erlbaum.

Young, S. (1998). The support group approach to bullying in schools. *Education Psychology in Practice, 14,* 32–9.

Zubrick, S. R., Silburn, S. R., Lawrence, D., Mitrou, F. G., Dalby, R., Blair, E., Griffin, J., Milroy, H., De Maio, J. A., Cox, A. & Li, J. (2005). *The Western Australian Aboriginal Child Health Survey: The social and emotional wellbeing of Aboriginal children and young people.* Perth: Curtin University of Technology and Telethon Institute for Child Health Research.

EDUCATIONAL PSYCHOLOGY IN CONTEMPORARY CLASSROOMS

Module IV has identified key issues relating to ICT, assessment and reporting, and positive learning environments in schools, discussing these issues with reference to relevant research in

	ICT IN LEARNING AND TEACHING
Main focus of this chapter	How an understanding of educational psychology can guide the use of ICT in the classroom
Key issues and concepts	Shifts in roles of learners and teachers in classrooms, through technology
	Variation across individuals and groups in access and use of Internet for different purposes, and employing different tools
	Need for digital information skills, ICT literacy skills, and application of critical thinking and metacognitive skills to be taught in order to ensure students' technology use is effective
	Influence of technology use on students' cognitive processing (positively and negatively)
	New ways of learning through technology
	New literacies to be learnt
	Changing modes of assessment
	Changing dynamics of classrooms
	Emergence of cyberbullying and cybersafety
	Potential of technology to address particular learning needs, and provide assistance for learning
Questions to consider as you develop your philosophy	What learning approach underpins the technology I employ, and how does it support students' learning?
	How will I ensure use of technology enhances learning?
	How can I best combine my knowledge of pedagogy and content with my knowledge of ICT?
	How will I manage use of technology to maximise student engagement?
	What responsibilities do I have to keep students safe online? How will I do this?
	How will I employ technology to differentiate learning and teaching?

educational psychology. These topics are ones in which you will be called on to develop your own philosophy and approach. As you review the summary table below, consider the research that underpins various theories and approaches, and how you will make use of it to guide your decisions in these important areas of your learning and teaching practice.

ASSESSMENT AND REPORTING	CREATING A POSITIVE CLASSROOM
The critical role of assessment in the learning and teaching cycle.	The creation of PLEs and effective management of classrooms for optimal learning and teaching outcomes.
The purpose of assessment guides the choice of assessment tools. Movement towards assessment based on determining what students need to learn / where they are going next, rather than judging how much they have learnt of what was taught. All students can progress in their learning; assessment can show where and how. Assessment can also involve learning. A range of sources and types of assessment provides a fuller picture of student learning. Testing can have positive effects on learning, although high-stakes tests can also have negative effects. Quality assessment needs to minimise threats to its reliability and validity. Alignment, moderation and transparency of judgements with reference to an agreed set of standards contribute to quality evaluation. Reporting involves considering the needs of families and students, and can allow them to be partners in the learning process. Reporting may also be done for teachers, school, system and government for purposes of accountability.	A PLE aims to create an environment that supports learners and their learning. The purpose of classroom management is effectively working with students and maximising their learning. Teacher–student relationships are affected by differential teacher attitudes to particular students, and can affect students' social standing with their peers. Teacher expectations can influence the development of student performance; a negative expectation may become a self-fulfilling prophecy and may affect minority learners more severely. Classrooms are complex places with at least the features of multidimensionality, simultaneity, immediacy, unpredictability, publicness and history to be navigated. Managing the whole classroom group well is the key to well-managed classrooms. The 'duty of care' refers to the responsibility of the teacher to ensure a safe place and protect immature children from all forms of harm and injury including psychological harm. The creation of a PLE and managing classrooms and schools effectively includes includes addressing bullying.
What is assessment for? How will I balance assessment for, assessment of, and assessment as learning? What principles of assessment will guide my practice? What combination of tools will provide me with the best information about a student's learning in a particular domain? How will I maximise reliability and validity of assessment to ensure I gather accurate information about my students' learning? What measures will I put in place to guide my evaluation of assessment data? What role will students, their peers and their families have in the assessment process? What will students' progress be measured against (other students / a set of criteria / their own previous progress)? Who will the assessment information be reported to? For what purpose? How will I ensure feedback enhances students' learning? How will my reports to parents involve them and the students in the learning process?	How do my philosophy and beliefs influence my classroom practice? How do I define 'good relationships' with students? What research evidence suggests this relationship is important? How will I support students and their learning through the routines, procedures and rules of my classroom? How will I respond to student behaviour problems? What philosophy will underpin my approach? What can I do in my classroom to prevent negative peer relationships and bullying?

GLOSSARY

Aboriginal English
A dialect distinct from Standard Australian English, and having many variants in different Aboriginal communities

acceleration
Allowing students to move faster through the education system

accommodation
Using fresh information to form a new mental model or schema

achievement motivation
The need to strive for success

action research
Professionals evaluating their own practice with the goal of improving it

active listening
Attending purposefully to the meaning and intention of what another person is saying

adaptation
The process of adjusting to new situations and experiences through the modification of existing schemas (assimilation) or the creation of new schemas (accommodation)

adolescence
The period between childhood and adulthood

affect
A psychological term used to describe emotional states such as feelings and moods

alternative schools
Usually small in size, student-centred and non-traditional, with high staff–student ratio, more individualised instruction, less-structured organisation and a more personal and caring environment

anecdotal record
Objective description of behaviour at a particular time and place, recorded as soon as possible after the behaviour has occurred

animism
The tendency to attribute human characteristics to inanimate objects

antecedent
An event that precedes a behaviour

antecedent–behaviour–consequence (A–B–C)
Behaviour represented as an ongoing chain of activity involving events that immediately precede the behaviour and that follow it

anxiety
Feelings of tension, uneasiness and apprehension

applied behaviour analysis (ABA)
The use of behavioural principles to change behaviour

approach success
A stable motivational tendency to strive for success by tackling moderately difficult tasks with a high expectation of success

approaches to learning
Learner motivational approaches to learning

arousal
Alertness and attentiveness

assertive discipline
A high level of teacher control, with firm limit setting and supportive feedback

assessment
The purposeful gathering and analysis of information about student learning

assessment as learning
Assessment with the goal of helping students to become more conscious of their own thinking and learning processes

assessment for learning
Assessment with the goal of improving learning

assessment literacy
Knowledge and skills for collecting, analysing and interpreting assessment data and evidence of learning, and for applying this information

assessment of learning
Assessment with the goal of judging what students know and can do at a particular point in time

assimilation
Adjusting an existing mental model or schema to fit a new experience

associationism
An explanation of learning as the formation of connections between stimuli and responses

attachment
The strong emotional bond established between infant and caregiver

attention
Allocation of resources to process information

attribution theories
Theories concerned with the way in which an individual's explanations of success and failure influence subsequent motivation and behaviour

authentic assessment
A mode of assessment that uses tasks similar to those performed in the real world

autonomous morality
Moral reasoning that appreciates the perspectives of others and the motives behind their words and actions

autonomy-supportive
Teacher behaviours that foster students' intrinsic motivational resources

aversive
A contingently applied stimulus that the recipient finds undesirable and which reduces the behaviour it follows

avoid failure
A stable motivational tendency to avoid tasks because of a fear of failure and an expectancy for failure on tasks

axon
The long 'arm' of a neuron that carries messages to other cells by means of electrical impulses

baseline
Level of a specific behaviour prior to intervention

basic emotions
The emotions that babies are born with, such as happiness, sadness, anger and fear

basic needs
Lower-level or 'deficit' needs, such as the need for food, safety, love and respect

behaviour
Actions that are observable and measurable

behaviourism
Explanations of learning concerned with the effect of external events on behaviour

being needs (B-needs)
Growth needs that motivate individuals to achieve personal fulfilment and self-actualisation

brain plasticity
The capacity of the brain to change and develop new neural connections throughout the lifespan

bullying
Repeated verbal and/or non-verbal aggression by individuals or groups and directed towards particular victims who find it difficult to defend themselves

CALD
Culturally and linguistically diverse

central executive
In Baddeley's theory of working memory, it controls what working memory attends to, and how it interacts with long-term memory

centration
Concentrating attention on one aspect of a stimulus while ignoring other features

cerebral cortex
The outer layer of the brain, which is responsible for human intelligence

chaining
When one action functions both as a reinforcer for the previous action and as a stimulus for the next

checklist
A set of descriptions of specific behaviours that an observer records as present or not present

child-directed speech
A type of speech directed to young children and characterised by high pitch, short and well-spaced sentences, simple vocabulary and exaggerated intonation

chronosystem
Changes in environments and processes over time that influence development

class inclusion
Understanding that a number of small collections can be combined in different ways to form a larger collection

classical conditioning
The association of an automatic response with a new stimulus

classification
The ability to mentally group objects in terms of similar characteristics; for example, pansies, daffodils and roses are all 'flowers'

classroom discipline plan
A planned approach to responding to behaviour, which avoids overly hasty and emotional responses and leads to consistent reactions

classroom management
The actions of teachers to create a planned and organised classroom environment that supports student learning and socioemotional needs

closeness of the match
The distance between what is already known and new learning

cognition
The mental processes involved in perceiving, attending to, understanding and recalling information

cognitive apprenticeships
Relationships within communities, in which children learn adult ways of thinking, through both explicit teaching and more indirect observation and listening to adult talk

cognitive learning theories
Theories concerned with internal mental processes and how learners manipulate information during learning

cognitive load
The total demands made on working memory at any one time

cognitive style
The way an individual tends to perceive and process information

collaborative learning
Students learning together, drawing on one another's knowledge and skills

collectivistic culture
Typically group-centred, viewing individuals in terms of their relationships, roles and responsibilities in the community

compensation
The ability to see that an increase in one dimension (such as height) is compensated for by a decrease in another dimension (such as width)

computer-assisted instruction (CAI)
A computer and its software are used as a tutor; also known as 'computer-based instruction' (CBI) or 'computer-assisted learning' (CAL)

concrete-operations stage
Piaget's third stage, in which a child is able to mentally manipulate and think logically about objects that are present

conditioned response (CR)
A response evoked by a conditioned stimulus

conditioned stimulus (CS)
A previously neutral stimulus that elicits a conditioned response after pairing with an unconditioned stimulus

conditioning
The establishment of a new association between a stimulus and a response

connectionist model
Views the brain as a complex network of interconnected units of information, with information stored in patterns of connectivity

consequence
An event that follows a behaviour

consequential validity
Intended and unintended consequences of assessment interpretation and use

conservation
The ability to see that certain characteristics (size, height, length, amount) of an object do not change with changes in the object's physical appearance

constructivism
An explanation of learning that views it as a self-regulated process that builds on learners' existing knowledge, and in which learners are active participants

construct validity
A measure of the link between a test and underlying knowledge, attitudes and skills

content validity
A measure of the link between a test and relevant curriculum objectives

contiguity
The association of two events that are always closely paired, or that repeatedly occur at about the same time

contingency
Reinforcement that is only given when the target behaviour is produced

contingency contract
Students sign a contract to indicate that they understand and agree with an intervention plan

conventional morality
Being a good member of society and helping those close to you is a priority

cooperative learning
Students working together to gain rewards for themselves and their group

creativity
The ability to think in novel ways to produce innovative and valuable ideas

criteria
The particular indicators that are being assessed to indicate knowledge or understanding

criterion-referenced assessment
Where achievement is compared against a specified criterion or standard

critical reflection
Analysing what we are thinking and learning by questioning assumptions, perspectives and values related to our thoughts or to new information

crystallised intelligence
Culturally based, fact-oriented knowledge gained through experience

cueing
Using a specific stimulus to elicit a desired response

culture
Systems of knowledge, beliefs, values and behaviour shared by a group of people

culture-sensitive or culture-fair test
A test that does not require culturally based knowledge

curriculum-based assessment
Assessment that compares individual students' performance with curriculum goals

curriculum differentiation
Modification of instruction, materials and assessment procedures to match learner needs

cyberbullying
The use of ICTs and other electronic devices to bully someone

cyberpsychology
The study of psychology and behaviour associated with the use of ICTs and other technologies

deductive reasoning
Using rules or general principles to find general solutions to specific problems

defensive pessimism
A defensive or protective cognitive strategy to lower expectations and hence protect the sense of self when faced with negative outcomes

deferred imitation
Actions copied from models no longer present, the actions having previously been observed and remembered

deficit needs (D-needs)
Basic needs that motivate individuals to action in order to reduce or eliminate the need

dendrites
Branch-like protrusions from a neuron that receive messages from other cells

dependent variable
The variable that is measured in an experiment, to determine whether the independent variable had any effect

developmental cascades
Far-reaching consequences for learning and development that are instigated by a particular developmental achievement

deviation IQ
An IQ score that compares an individual's performance on a test with the expected

average performance of someone in the same age group

diagnostic assessment
Assessment to determine what a student knows and can do, and why a student might be making particular errors

differential teacher–student interactions
Qualities of the interaction between teacher and student that lead to different types of relationships

digital natives
A term used to describe someone who has grown up in the era of digital technologies

direct assessment
Criterion-referenced or mastery tests that assess specific content from a clearly defined curriculum

direct observation
Purposeful and focused looking and listening

discovery learning
The learner actively manipulates materials or ideas in the learning environment and discovers connections between them

discrimination
Learning that it is appropriate to respond to some stimuli but not to others

disequilibrium
Cognitive imbalance resulting from inconsistency between what is known and expected, and something strange and unexpected

distributed cognition
The notion that cognition is shared by individuals who make up communities and who share cultural tools

distributed learning (computer-mediated instruction, or CMI)
Teachers, students and learning resources can be in different locations so that learning and teaching occur independently of time and place

duty of care
The legal obligation to protect a child of immature age against injury

dyadic
Characterised by two elements, or two people, as in the case of friendship

dynamic assessment
A form of interactive assessment that identifies potential for learning and interventions to help achieve this potential

EAL/D
English as an additional language or dialect (replaces ESL or English as a second language); applied to acquisition or learning of English

ecological perspective
A view of the classroom as an environment with unique purposes, dimensions, features and processes that have consequences for the behaviour of people in that environment

educational psychology
A branch of psychology concerned with studying how people learn and the implications for teaching

egocentrism
An individual's belief that everyone sees the world in exactly the same way as that individual

elaboration
Process of linking new information with what is stored in long-term memory

emergent literacy
Understandings about and attitudes towards reading and writing, which are the precursors of acquiring those skills

emotion
A mental or physiological state associated with thoughts, feelings and behaviours

emotional competence
The skills needed to negotiate the demands of the immediate social context

emotional intelligence
The ability to recognise and understand emotions, and to use emotional information to enhance thought

emotional self-regulation
Awareness of and ability to control or alter our emotional state as necessary

encoding
Process of storing information in the long-term memory

engagement
The energy that connects and shows our participation in a context or an activity; it consists of behavioural, cognitive and emotional components

entity theory
A belief that intelligence and ability are fixed traits, and not malleable or easily changed

episodic memory
Memory for life experiences

equilibration
Achieving cognitive balance between what is familiar and known, and what is new or unfamiliar, through the processes of assimilation and accommodation

ethnicity
Membership of a group according to race, nationality or religious background

evaluation
The process of making judgements about the quality of something

executive control
Higher-level functions that help with the control of processes and flow of information

executive functions
These control the processing of information. Key executive functions include inhibitory control, working memory and cognitive flexibility

exosystem
Settings in which the child is not involved, but which nonetheless influence the child's development

expansion
Parents' tendency to respond to young children's utterances by restating them in a more elaborate form

externalising behaviours
Acting out behaviours such as displays of aggressiveness, impulsiveness or non-compliance

extinction
Reduction and cessation of a response following the withdrawal of reinforcement

extrinsic motivation
Motivation arising from the use of external rewards such as food or praise

face validity
The degree to which a test appears to measure what it is intended to measure

fading
The gradual removal of prompts or reinforcers

field dependence
A cognitive style related to perceiving items, events or information as an integral part of a broader context (or 'field')

field independence
The tendency to perceive individual items, events or pieces of information analytically, and as distinct from the broader context (or 'field')

fine motor skills
Movement skills using small muscle groups

fluid intelligence
Non-verbal abilities associated with manipulation of information, seeing complex relationships and solving problems

formal-operations stage
Piaget's fourth stage, in which the individual is now able to think abstractly and logically, to form hypotheses and to solve problems systematically

formative assessment
Information gathered while students are learning, to give information about their progress

frequency distribution
The number of times each score occurs in a range of possible scores

friendship
A close relationship between two people who mutually agree on the importance of this relationship

functionalist perspective
An approach that views emotions as shaping and organising thoughts and behaviours

gender
Those aspects of an individual that relate to the individual's sex; they are biologically and culturally determined

gender schema theory
A theory proposing that children's schemas or understandings about gender influence the way in which they process information and their choices

general mental ability (g)
Basic intellectual capacity

generalisation
Learning to respond to stimuli that are similar to but not the same as those that previously triggered a response

gifted
Significantly superior potential to achieve in one or more domains

goal-directed or intentional action
A sequence of acts produced intentionally to achieve a desired outcome

gross motor skills
Movement skills using large muscle groups

group
An exchange involving several interacting individuals who have formed a relationship and who have some degree of reciprocal influence over one another

growth mindset
A popular term to describe a state of mind that reflects an incremental theory of intelligence and ability

growth needs
Higher-level or 'being' needs, such as the need for self-actualisation

guided participation
Support provided to enable students to participate in expert activities in increasingly expert ways

heteronomous morality
Moral decisions based on the rules of authority figures such as parents

hidden curriculum
Understandings, values and attitudes that are implicit in school structures and in the way material is taught

home schooling
The education of children at home by parents or other adults who take primary responsibility for this education

human agency
The capacity of a person to act on and shape their world

humanism
An orientation or philosophy that recognises the uniqueness of human beings and the qualities of life that contribute to our humanity

hypermedia
A system that links pieces of information such as text, sound, visual images, animation and video in electronic environments

I-messages
Using the personal pronoun 'I' to focus on the feelings and needs of the speaker rather than the listener

ICT literacy
The capacity for purposeful and effective use of ICTs in one's own setting

identity
An internal self-structure in which we organise our beliefs, abilities, needs and self-perceptions

identity achievement
Occurs when adolescents explore several identity roles, but resolve conflicts and feel comfortable with who they are and who they hope to be

identity diffusion
Occurs when young people have little direction, their life and career goals are unclear, and they do not know who they are or who they want to be

identity foreclosure
Describes adolescents who typically form their identity by adopting the occupational and ideological goals of significant others, often their parents

impulsivity
Having a cognitive preference for rapid problem solving

inclusive education
The programs and services provided in most education systems to address the needs of all students in regular schools, regardless of ability or disability

incremental theory
A belief that intelligence and ability are changeable states that are able to grow and develop

independent variable
The variable that is controlled or manipulated in an experiment, to determine its effect

individual education program (IEP)
A planned program of instruction for an individual student, based on assessed needs, strengths and interests

individualistic culture
Focuses on the self as an autonomous individual; successful pursuit of individual goals is valued

inductive reasoning
Inducing general rules or principles from observation of specific examples

information and communication technology (ICT)
Any technology used to access, gather, manipulate and present or communicate information, such as electronic hardware, software and network connectivity

information literacy
The ability to locate, evaluate and use information; it extends beyond technical skills

information-processing model
Likens the human mind to a computer that interprets, stores and retrieves information

informed consent
Agreement given by a parent or student for the collection and/or dissemination of information not directly relevant to the student's school program

inquiry learning
Students learn content and discipline-specific thinking and practical skills by collaboratively investigating and solving a problem

intelligence
A general aptitude and capacity for understanding and learning

intelligence quotient (IQ)
A score on an intelligence test that permits an individual's performance to be compared with the average performance on the test

interaction
A first-order (or superficial) social exchange between two or more individuals, with little emotional commitment

interactionalist philosophy
A belief that children's learning and behaviour results from an interaction between internal and external factors

interest
A cognitive and affective state associated with a heightened state of arousal, leading to increased attention, concentration and persistence

internalisation
The transformation of external processes into internal processes that guide action and thought

internalising behaviours
Inhibited and withdrawn types of behaviours such as loneliness, depression or anxiety

interval schedules
When a reward is given after a set period of time

interventionist philosophy
A belief that children's learning and behaviour is an outcome of external factors

intrinsic motivation
Motivation arising from internal sources, such as an individual's feelings of curiosity, excitement and satisfaction

involuntary minority group
A group of people who have at some point been brought into a society against their will

ipsative assessment
Assessment that compares an individual's current achievement with a previous achievement

jigsaw
A form of cooperative learning in which each group member works individually on components of the one task

joint attention
When carer and child together attend to a stimulus, such as when reading books or playing peekaboo games

lateralisation
The specialisation of functions in the two hemispheres of the cerebral cortex

law of effect
Responses that have a satisfying outcome are likely to be strengthened and repeated

law of exercise
Connections between actions and new consequences are strengthened the more they are repeated

LBOTE
Language background other than English

learning
Permanent or relatively permanent changes in individuals that result from instruction or experience

learning style
Learner preferences for types of learning and teaching activities

least restrictive environment (LRE)
The setting that is as close as possible to that experienced by children who do not have disabilities

levels-of-processing model
A process-oriented approach that attaches most importance to the type and depth of processing taking place

literacy
Engaging with various kinds of texts, and using and modifying language for use in a variety of contexts

locus of control
A tendency to attribute success or failure to internal (controllable) or external (uncontrollable) factors

logical consequences
Outcomes contrived to influence behaviour

loneliness
A cognitive and affective state of feeling disconnected and lacking in supportive relationships

long-term memory
A permanent storage facility for information

macrosystem
Societal and cultural influences on development

mainstreaming
This term refers to the historical movement (approx. 1960s–1980s) that saw the removal of children with disabilities from institutions and segregated schools and the start of educating these children in regular classrooms

maintenance
The continued performance of a learnt action after instruction has ceased

mastery goal
A personal objective to achieve mastery of a task or skill

mental age
The chronological age that typically corresponds with a particular performance level on an intelligence test

mentor
An expert practitioner inducting a novice into their profession

mesosystem
Connections between settings involving the child

metacognition
Higher-order thinking, which involves knowledge of and control over our own cognitive processes

metalinguistic awareness
Awareness of and understandings about language

microsystem
Interactions and activities in the child's immediate environment

mindfulness
A series of practices supporting deliberate focus on current experience, while suspending judgement

mobile learning (mlearning)
Use of mobile devices for learning at any time or place

modelling
A form of prompting that involves demonstrating a desired response for someone to imitate

moderation
The process of teachers comparing and discussing judgements with each other in order to improve consistency of judgement

moral dilemma
A moral problem requiring individual judgements and moral reasoning

morality
The fundamental questions of right and wrong, justice, fairness and basic human rights

moratorium
Refers to the state of adolescents who postpone making a definitive commitment to a single identity or set of values

morphology
The combination of units of meaning in words; for example, listen + ed = past tense of 'listen'

motivation
An internal process that energises, directs and maintains behaviour over time

multiliteracies
The variety of types of language we need to master to be literate in our society

multiple intelligences (MI)
Eight or more domains of intellectual functioning

multistore model
Depicts how information is processed and stored in memory

myelination
The process by which axons are insulated with a sheath of fatty cells, which improves the speed and efficiency of message transmission

natural consequences
Outcomes that occur without interference

nature–nurture debate
Controversy over the relative influence that inherent characteristics and environmental factors have on development

negative reinforcement
Increasing the likelihood of a behaviour being repeated by contingently removing an aversive object or activity

net generation
A term used to describe someone who has grown up in the era of internet connectivity

neuron
A nerve cell

neurotransmitter
A chemical substance that carries messages across the synapse between neurons

neutral stimulus (NS)
An event or happening that has no effect on an organism

new literacies
The skills, strategies and dispositions for using and adapting to rapidly changing ICTs

non-directive teaching
Teaching in which the teacher is a facilitator, guiding students and nurturing their learning

non-interventionist philosophy
A belief that allows for children's learning and behaviour to occur naturally

normal distribution (bell-shaped curve)
A representation of test scores, showing their natural tendency to cluster around the middle (mean) of the distribution and taper off at either side

normalisation
Giving people with disabilities access to the daily experiences and activities available to those in the community who do not have a disability

norm
The mean or average performance of a group of people

norm-referenced assessment
Used to compare the performance of individuals or groups with the performance of a comparable group on the same task

numeracy
The ability to use mathematics effectively and with confidence in a range of contexts

object permanence
Piagetian term used to refer to children's understanding that objects continue to exist even when they are out of sight

operant conditioning
The use of positive and negative consequences to strengthen or weaken voluntary behaviour

operants
Voluntary actions, usually goal-directed

operations
Actions that are governed by rules and logic, and are performed mentally rather than physically

organisation
Process associated with storage and retrieval of information in long-term memory

otitis media
A disease of the middle ear that can affect hearing

outcomes approach
Students work towards the achievement of outcomes located sequentially along a learning continuum

overextension
Inappropriate use of a word for a class of things rather than for one particular thing

overlapping waves model
Siegler's model of strategy use, which states that people have a set of strategies they choose from, and that over time, less efficient strategies are replaced with more efficient ones

over-regularisation
Application of a grammatical rule, ignoring its exceptions

peer acceptance
The likeability and acceptance of a person by their peer group

peer-assisted learning
Encourages social interaction, as peers help each other to learn

peer tutoring
Students are paired in roles of tutor or learner and follow specified learning strategies

perception
Allocation of meaning to an experienced sensation

performance assessment
A mode of assessment that requires a student to engage in a complex task

performance goal
A personal objective to perform well in an area of achievement

performance-approach goal
A personal objective to perform well by demonstrating competence over others and outperforming classmates

performance-avoid goal
A personal objective to complete academic work in order to avoid appearing incompetent

person-first language
The practice of referring to the person or individual before you refer to the label of their condition

perspective taking
The ability to imagine the self in another's position and to understand others' feelings

phonology
The sound system of language

portfolio
A collection of samples of student work used to demonstrate achievement

Positive Behaviour Support (PBS)
A behaviourist intervention designed to improve student behaviour

positive classroom environment (PLE)
Defined as a place where students are engaged and learning

positive education
Applies the principles of positive psychology to education

positive reinforcement
Increasing the likelihood of a behaviour occurring by contingent presentation of a reward immediately following it

postconventional morality
Individuals move beyond the conventional rules of their community to focus more broadly on what is best for society at large, and on ways of promoting justice in society

pragmatics
Rules for the appropriate use of language in social contexts

preconventional morality
Morality is seen as a set of rules handed down by adults

prejudice
A preconceived, uninformed opinion or feeling

Premack principle (Grandma's rule)
Any behaviour that is enjoyed and that occurs often can be used to reinforce behaviours that are not enjoyed and that do not occur often

preoperational stage
Piaget's second stage, in which a child is not yet able to 'operate' or carry out logical physical actions mentally, but is reliant on manipulating real materials

primary reinforcer
An unconditioned (unlearnt) stimulus that is innately rewarding

private speech
Speech used to guide own thinking and actions; it can be both internal (silent) and external (audible)

problem-based learning (PBL)
Students learn content, strategies and learning skills through collaboratively solving problems

procedural memory
Memory about steps or procedures for performing a skill

profile
An ordered sequence or progression of learning descriptors that can be used to chart progress

progressive education
A child-centred approach to education based on a commitment to democratic ideals

prompting
Providing an additional stimulus to elicit a desired response

prosocial behaviour
Positive social behaviours, such as helpfulness, intended to benefit others

psychoanalytic approach
A theoretical stance proposing that personality develops when children move through a series of stages that present conflicts that have to be resolved

psychological constructivism
Focuses on individual learners and how they construct their own knowledge, beliefs and identity

psychosocial crisis
A 'turning point', where individuals experience a temporary state of conflict and disequilibrium

psychosocial development
Psychological development in a social context

puberty
The biological changes associated with sexual maturity

punishment
Weakening or reducing behaviour through contingent use of aversive objects or events

punitive approaches
Based on the belief that the bully must be punished, and this punishment will stop them from bullying again

racism
Discrimination based on race or ethnicity

rating scale
A procedure for recording the degree to which a specific behaviour or characteristic is present

ratio schedules
When a reward is given in a predetermined ratio to the number of responses

readiness
Having the prior experiences and knowledge needed for learning

recasting
Parents' tendency to respond to children's utterances by restating them in the correct grammatical form

reciprocal determinism
The interactive, complementary system formed by people and environments

reciprocal teaching
A teaching approach in which a teacher guides a group of students to ask questions that guide learning

reflectivity
Having a cognitive preference for taking time to solve problems and to analyse oneself and the context

Reggio Emilia
A system of education for the early childhood years, with a particular focus on children expressing their ideas in many different language modes

rehearsal
Repeating items as a memory strategy

reinforcement
Increasing or strengthening the likelihood of a behaviour recurring through use of contingent feedback

reinforcement schedule
The frequency with which reinforcement is delivered

reinforcer
Any event that strengthens the behaviour it follows

relational aggression
A form of harm that intentionally seeks to damage a person's social relationships or reputation

relationship
An exchange between two or more people, resulting from several interactions and taking on emotional significance

reliability
The extent to which a test or measurement device obtains the same result when used on successive occasions

resilience
Positive adjustment despite the experience of significant risk or adversity

respondents
Elicited or reflex reactions to a specific stimulus

response cost
Removal of privileges or something pleasant as a punishment

response (R)
An observable reaction to a known (or unknown) stimulus

retrieval
Process of bringing information stored in long-term memory back to be manipulated in working memory

reversibility
The ability to mentally reverse thought, such as adding back something that has

been taken away or remoulding something to its original shape

risk factor
A factor associated with negative outcomes

rubric
A tool for marking and giving feedback about student work against particular criteria and standards

satiation
The point at which a stimulus that originally functioned as a reinforcer no longer functions as a reinforcer

scaffolding
The support provided to learners to enable a task to be done successfully and more independently by adjusting the assistance to fit the learner's current level of performance

schema
A mental image or cluster of related ideas used to organise existing knowledge and to make sense of new experiences

secondary reinforcer
A conditioned (learnt) stimulus that functions as a reward

self
Who we are, what makes us unique and who we believe ourselves to be

self-actualisation
The achievement of one's full potential

self-concept
A collection of information, ideas, attitudes and beliefs we have about ourselves

self-conscious emotions
Higher-order emotions (such as pride and shame) that require advanced cognitive processes and a capacity to understand how the self might be harmed or enhanced

self-determination theory
People have a basic psychological need for autonomy, a sense of competence and relatedness to other people

self-efficacy
An individual's sense of being able to manage a task effectively and successfully in a particular domain

self-esteem
The level of satisfaction and pride that individuals have in the self

self-handicapping
Actions or choices an individual makes to prevent or hinder performance or achievement

self-monitoring
A metacognitive activity that involves monitoring how well we are understanding and remembering

self-monitoring strategies
A self-regulatory strategy in which a student pays attention to their own thinking or behaviour and can take steps to change or correct that behaviour

self-regulation
A metacognitive activity that involves planning, directing and evaluating one's cognitive processes

self-talk
Private speech uttered aloud

self-talk strategies
A self-regulatory strategy in which students can use internal dialogue in their own mind to send themselves messages about their behaviour or performance

semantic memory
Memory about information and knowledge in the world around us

semantics
The system of meanings associated with language

sensation
Information taken in from the environment through the five senses

sensorimotor stage
The earliest of Piaget's developmental stages, characterised by object permanence, intentional or goal-directed behaviour and deferred imitation

sensory memory
Stores new information, which enters via the sensory register through the five senses, for between one and three seconds

seriation
The ability to mentally arrange objects or elements in terms of a dimension such as length, weight or volume

serious games
Digital games that have been either designed or adapted for specific educational purposes

shaping
Reinforcement of gradual approximations of the target behaviour

simulation
A model of a real system or phenomenon

social cognition
A cognitive capacity to think about and process social information

Social comparison
Evaluation of our self that is based on comparing our abilities to others or social standards

social constructivism
Emphasises the role of social and cultural factors in shaping learning

social constructivist perspective
An approach that emphasises the role of the social context in shaping the development of emotional understanding

social development
The development of skills and understanding necessary for forming relationships and participating in the social context

social interaction (social transmission)
The interactions with others (parents, peers, teachers and so on) that contribute to children's learning experiences

socialisation
The passing of cultural beliefs, knowledge, values and behaviour among members of a group

social referencing
Taking cues from another person's emotional reaction to interpret a situation

sociocognitive conflict
Conflict within the child's thinking resulting from social interaction

sociocultural factors
Factors contributing to individual difference, which have a basis in society and culture

socioeconomic status (SES)
A measure of social and economic position in society; typically a combination of education, occupation and income

sociolinguistic features of language
Cultural conventions directing the use of language

sociometric assessment
The measurement of social networks and connections between people by assessing people's ratings of one another

special education
The system of programs and services provided in most education systems for children who have difficulties in school for a variety of reasons and who need additional support

specific mental abilities (s)
A collection of distinct intellectual abilities

stage–environment fit
The extent to which the school matches the needs of the developing adolescent

Standard Australian English (SAE)
The language of mainstream Australia, and 'standard' in the sense that it does not vary significantly across communities

standard deviation (SD)
A measure of how much test scores vary from the mean of the sample

standardised test
A test designed in accordance with set rules, administered under uniform conditions, and scored and interpreted in terms of identified norms

standards
Detailed descriptions of student achievement used to measure progress within a set of sequentially ordered learning outcomes

state
A temporary condition or feeling

stimulus (S)
An environmental condition or event that activates the senses

summative assessment
Information gathered to give information about students' achievements at a particular time

sustaining expectation effect
Expectations that teachers have for their students, which may influence students' achievement or wellbeing in the classroom

symbolic thought
The ability to represent objects and events mentally

synapse
The gap between the axon and dendrites of two neurons

syntax
The grammatical system that orders the construction of sentences

talent
Significantly superior performance in one or more domains

task analysis
Breaking a task into a series of manageable steps to assist learning

telegraphic speech
Communication using two-word sentences, leaving out smaller words

test anxiety
Fear of performing poorly in tests

test bias
Where particular groups are disadvantaged by factors associated with a test's content and the interpretation of results

three-way reporting
Reporting that involves student, teacher and parent input

token economy
Behavioural system using tokens to reward desirable behaviour

trait
An enduring characteristic

trial-and-error learning
An explanation of learning that states that when an individual is placed in a problem-solving situation, the correct response will be learnt through being reinforced

triarchic model of successful intelligence
Intelligence defined as thinking (analytic), responding to new experiences (creative) and coping with everyday situations (practical)

unconditioned response (UR)
An action triggered spontaneously by a stimulus

unconditioned stimulus (US)
An object, event or happening in the physical environment that causes spontaneous activity in an organism

underextension
Inappropriate use of a word for one thing rather than for a class of things

undermining effect
The idea that some rewards can undermine intrinsic motivation

universal design for learning (UDL)
A set of principles for curriculum planning that allows all students an equal opportunity to learn in that curriculum by planning tasks in which all students can participate

validity
The extent to which a test or measurement device measures what it purports to measure

voluntary minority group
A group of people who have at some point chosen to move to a new society in search of a better life

whole-school approach
An approach that recognises that commitment and cooperation is needed from all members of the school community – teachers, students and parents – to prevent and address bullying

working memory
A working space for short-term storage and manipulation of small amounts of information; contains your conscious thought

zero tolerance approaches
A response to bullying or other misbehaviour that reflects extreme intolerance for antisocial behaviours of any kind, allowing no compromise and usually resulting in strict punishment such as school expulsion

zone of proximal development (ZPD)
The distance between children's current level of competence on a task and the level they can achieve with support or guidance

INDEX

A